The Kingdom of the Cults

Other Books by Walter Martin

Christian Science
Essential Christianity
Herbert W. Armstrong and the Worldwide Church of God
Jehovah of the Watchtower
Jehovah's Witnesses
The Maze of Mormonism
Mormonism
New Age Cults
The New Cults
The Riddle of Reincarnation
Screwtape Writes Again
Walter Martin Speaks Out on the Cults
Walter Martin's Cults Reference Bible

The K·Kingdom of the Cults

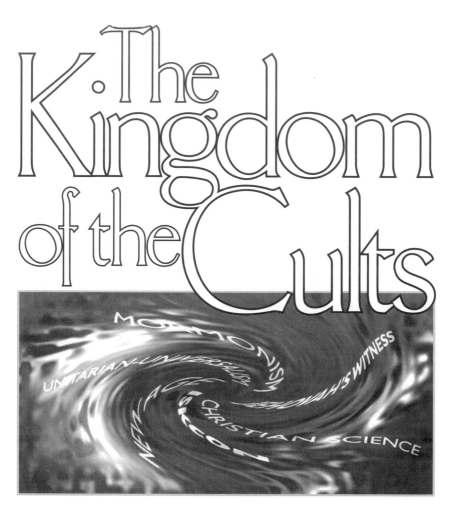

MORMONISM
UNITARIAN-UNIVERSALISM
JEHOVAH'S WITNESS
NEW AGE
CHRISTIAN SCIENCE

Walter Martin

Hank Hanegraaff, *General Editor*

BETHANY HOUSE PUBLISHERS
MINNEAPOLIS, MINNESOTA 55438
A Division of Bethany Fellowship, Inc.

Published by Bethany House Publishers
A Ministry of Bethany Fellowship, Inc.
11300 Hampshire Avenue South
Minneapolis, Minnesota 55438

Printed in the United States of America.

Library of Congress Cataloging-in-Publication Data

Martin, Walter Ralston, 1928–1989
    Kingdom of the cults / by Walter Ralson Martin. — Rev. 30th Anniversary ed.
        p.   .cm.   Includes bibliographical references and index.
    ISBN 1–55661–714–3
    1. Cults—United States—Controversial literature. 2. Sects—United States—Controversial literature. 3. United States—Religion—1960–
4. Apologetics. I. Title.
BL2525.M366   1997
291.9—dc21   97–33773
                                                                      CIP

In Memory of

Peter de Visser

My friend and brother in the common faith.
His help and encouragement made this volume
possible. If you seek his monument, consult the
libraries of the informed.

About the Author

WALTER MARTIN was fondly and respectfully known as "the father of Christian cult apologetics." Many current professional and academic cult apologists credit him with their introduction to the field. He held four earned degrees, having received his Doctorate from California Coast University in the field of Comparative Religions. Author of a dozen books, a half-dozen booklets, and many articles, he was known nationwide as "The Bible Answer Man," host of one of the oldest and most popular nationally syndicated call-in radio programs. He was founder and director of the Christian Research Institute, located in Southern California, which continues to provide cult apologetics information and to sponsor the ever-popular *Bible Answer Man* daily broadcast.

About the General Editor

HANK HANEGRAAFF, author of *Counterfeit Revival*, is president and chairman of the board of Christian Research Institute International, the oldest and largest organization in the world specializing in the study of cults and fringe religious movements, contemporary religious controversies, and related issues. Hanegraaff is heard live daily as host of the nationally syndicated *Bible Answer Man* radio program.

His bestselling book *Christianity in Crisis* was awarded the Gold Medallion by the Evangelical Christian Publishers Association. His other books include *Personal Witness Training: Your Handle on the Great Commission* and *Memory Dynamics: Your Untapped Resource for Spiritual Growth*. He contributes regularly to *Christian Research Journal*. Hanegraaff lives in Southern California with his wife, Kathy, and their eight children.

About the Managing Editor

GRETCHEN PASSANTINO, co-director of Answers in Action, is an award-winning author and investigative journalist who has spent more than two decades in cult apologetics team ministry with her husband, Bob. She helped the late Dr. Walter Martin establish Christian Research Institute in California in 1974, and was his senior research consultant during the ministry's formative California years. She worked with Dr. Martin on various book projects, including *The New Cults* and previous editions of *The Kingdom of the Cults*. She is best-known for *Answers to the Cultist at Your Door*, *When the Devil Dares Your Kids*, and *Satanism*, as well as for her investigative work regarding contemporary Satanism.

About the Research Contributors

Each of the contributors to this updated and expanded edition have years of experience understanding, explaining, and defending the Christian faith, and each is thoroughly competent in the areas for which they provided revising, updating, editing, and/or content for this edition. Richard Abanes, Alan Gomes, Bill McKeever, Richard Mendoza, Bob Passantino, Gretchen Passantino, Cecil Price, and Kurt Van Gorden have remained faithful to the vision of Walter Martin while bringing *The Kingdom of the Cults* to the cutting edge of cult apologetics and scholarship today. Most of the contributors regard the late Dr. Martin as their mentor, and all look to his example as an able defender of the faith "once for all delivered to the saints" (Jude 3).

Acknowledgments to the 1985 Edition

I wish to express my deep gratitude to Pierson Curtis, former senior master of the Stonybrook School, who helped edit and correct the original manuscript; the Rev. Anthony Collarile, Messrs. Herbert Jacobsen, Robert Smith, and John Carter, who offered valuable insights and research data; Mr. Walter Bjorck Jr., of the American Tract Society, who made many helpful manuscript suggestions which were adopted in a number of instances; editor-researcher Gretchen Passantino, who revised the majority of this present edition; researcher Kurt Van Gorden for his invaluable assistance especially on the newer cults; and associate Clark F. Hyman, who also contributed significantly to the revision of this present edition.

Acknowledgments to the Thirtieth-Anniversary Edition

Special thanks are due Dr. Martin's widow, Darlene Martin, for her foresight and faithfulness to her husband's classical text on American cults; researcher-author Richard Abanes for his extra help on technical aspects of this edition; researcher-author Kurt Van Gorden for his careful, groundbreaking work on the Worldwide Church of God and Scientology; author Bob Passantino for his editorial comments and suggestions; the other researchers whose contributions were invaluable to this present edition; and Bethany House editors Kevin Johnson, Steve Laube, and Carol Johnson, whose kind but firm direction followed the project from inception to completion and without whose guidance this new edition would never have been completed.

Publisher's Introduction

While contemporary treatments of multiculturalism evoke images of a tossed salad rather than a melting pot, the proliferation of new religious movements with at least a veneer of Christianity was never greater. From the iconoclastic Branch Davidians of Waco, Texas, to the quiet secrecy of the Soldiers of the Cross, religious pluralism in competition with historic Christianity is at an all-time high. This thirtieth-anniversary edition of *The Kingdom of the Cults* proves the almost prophetic vision of the late Dr. Walter Martin, who warned that the cults were "the great mission field on the Church's doorstep." Today, more than ever, we need the insight of a mature Christian, master apologist, and comprehensive theologian to guide us into cult evangelism at the end of the century.

Dr. Walter Martin died in 1989, after a ministry of almost forty years in cult apologetics. Holding four earned degrees, Dr. Martin was recognized as the leading authority in America on American cults. He was the author of a dozen books, many booklets, and uncounted articles. His *Kingdom of the Cults* is the standard reference work on American cults. He was founder and host of the internationally syndicated, live call-in radio talk program *The Bible Answer Man*, and founder, director, and president of the internationally recognized and acclaimed Christian Research Institute, which continues his vital work today. Dr. Martin taught at various seminaries and Bible colleges through the years and mentored many who have since become leaders in the counter-cult ministry field. He was deservedly called "the Father of cult apologetics."

This edition of *The Kingdom of the Cults* is both old and new. It epitomizes the best in classic cult apologetics pioneered and refined by Dr. Walter Martin. At the same time, it includes the best contemporary information about the onslaught of the cults in America and around the world today. Every effort has been made to maintain the integrity of the original volume. The eternal verities of Scripture are as central to this edition as in Walter Martin's previous editions. The enduring heresies of the traditional cults are reinforced in this edition with contemporary references and documentation. Current statistics, practices, and beliefs are carefully explained and refuted from God's Word. New cults not addressed in previous editions are fully examined and countered in this new edition. This volume reflects the godly spirit and scholastic brilliance of the late Dr. Walter Martin. His clarion call of thirty years ago should ring even louder today as the Christian church faces the new century with evangelistic urgency.

General Editor's Introduction

The revised, updated, and expanded thirtieth anniversary edition of *The Kingdom of the Cults* could not have been released at a more strategic time in church history. More than three decades ago, Walter Martin warned that cultism would have a devastating impact on the culture. Today cultism is having an equally devastating impact on the church. The line of demarcation between the kingdom of the cults and the kingdom of Christ is not only being blurred, it is being obliterated.

Recently, a book entiled *How Wide the Divide?* was released by a major evangelical publisher. This book, coauthored by a professor of a major evangelical seminary, wistfully looks forward to the day "when youth groups or adult Sunday school classes from Mormon and evangelical churches in the same neighborhoods would gather periodically to share their beliefs with each other in love and for the sake of understanding not proselytizing."[1] According to the authors, Mormons and evangelicals agree that "the Father, the Son, and the Holy Spirit are one eternal God."[2] The truth of course is that they do not! As James White, author of *Is the Mormon My Brother?*, aptly points out, "The only way to make such a statement is to so redefine every word used as to make the entire effort meaningless."[3]

In *The Kingdom of the Cults* Walter Martin prophetically warned that the day would come when Christians would be unable and unwilling to "scale the language barrier." Today as never before cultists of all stripes are using Christian terminology while pouring their own meanings into the words, in the process sometimes fooling even conservative evangelical leaders. While the authors of *How Wide the Divide?* suggest that we worship the same God, in reality the God of historical biblical Christianity is vastly different from the God of Mormonism. According to Mormonism, "As man is, God once was; as God is, man may become."[4] Mormon founder Joseph Smith goes so far as to say God was "once a man as we are now."[5] In stark contrast to the God of Mormonism, the God of Christianity is infinite and immutable. The distance between them is the distance of infinity.

In minimizing the "divide" between the kingdom of Christ and the kingdom of the cults one can hope to forge only superficial friendships with cultists. If we genuinely want to influence a cultist for Christ, it is necesssary, as Walter

---

[1]*How Wide the Divide?* (Downer's Grove, Ill.: IVP, 1997), 191.
[2]Ibid., 195.
[3]James White, *Is the Mormon My Brother?* (Minneapolis: Bethany House Publishers, 1997), 213.
[4]Prophet Lorenzo Snow, quoted in Milton R. Hunter, *The Gospel Through the Ages*, 105–106.
[5]*Teachings of the Prophet Joseph Smith*, 345.

Martin did, to tell the truth about the vast chasm that separates us. Walter Martin's witness and writings have been used by the Lord to move multitudes out of cultism into Christianity.

While Walter Martin has gone on to be with his Lord, it is my prayer that *The Kingdom of the Cults,* his *magnum opus,* will equip yet another generation of cult apologists. As you read on, you will be prepared to reach out to the mission field on your own doorstep as well as mission fields in distant lands. More than that you will be inspired to be a tool in the hands of almighty God in the process of changing lives for time and for eternity.

Not only can the lives of individuals be transformed but entire unbiblical movements can be transformed as well. Consider the Worldwide Church of God. In previous editons of *The Kingdom of the Cults,* this movement was listed as a non-Christian cult. This edition, however, notes their journey since then from cultism to the Cross. Joseph Tkach Jr., pastor-general of the Worldwide Church of God, best summarized this transformation when he wrote, "Gone are our obsessions with a legalistic interpretation of the Old Testament, our belief in British Israelism, and our insistence on our fellowship's exclusive relationship with God. Gone are our condemnations of medical science, the use of cosmetics, and traditional Christian celebrations such as Easter and Christmas. Gone is our long-held view of God as a 'family' of multiple 'spirit beings' into which humans may be born, replaced by a biblically accurate view of one God who exists eternally in three Persons: the Father, the Son, and the Holy Spirit. We have embraced and now champion the New Testament's central theme: the life, death, and resurrection of Jesus Christ. Jesus' saving work on behalf of humanity is now the focus of our flagship magazine, *The Plain Truth,* rather than end-time prophectic speculation. We proclaim the sufficiency of our Lord's substitutionary sacrifice to save us from the penalty for sin. We teach salvation by grace, based on faith alone, without resort to works of any kind."[6]

This thirtieth anniversary edition of *The Kingdom of the Cults* not only maintains the integrity of Dr. Martin's profoundly original work but adds current, up-to-date information and in-depth analysis in user friendly fashion. As General Editor, I have preserved Walter Martin's original thoughts while updating and extending them through those who have effectively mastered the spirit of his work. Several completely new chapters, reflecting significant changes in the field of cult apologetics have also been added. These changes are noted in footnotes at the head of chapters.

I would like to express my appreciation to Gretchen Passantino who, as Managing Editor, did the lion's share of the work on this project. I am also deeply grateful for the contributions of the team of contributors she assembled. With the diversity of theological perspectives represented, disagreements on secondary issues are inevitable. Walter Martin and I, for that matter, hold differing views on a variety of issues, such as eschatology. We are all, however, firmly united around the maxim, "In essentials unity, in nonessentials liberty, in all things charity."

Thus with the deepest of gratitude to our Lord Jesus Christ for raising up the ministry of Dr. Walter Martin, we submit to His purposes this new edition of *The Kingdom of the Cults.*

---

[6]*Christian Research Journal* (Rancho Santa Margarita, Calif.: Christian Research Institute, Winter 1996), 53.

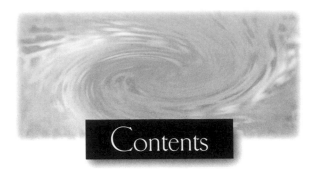

Contents

Chapter I

The Kingdom of the Cults

It has been said of the United States that it is "the great melting pot" for the people of the world. And the contents of that pot would not be complete unless it also included the religions of those masses that now make up the populace of America. This writer has spent over thirty years of his life in research and fieldwork among the religions of America, and this volume, limited as it is by the vastness and complexity of the problem itself, constitutes his evaluation of that vibrant brand of religion that has come to be recognized by many as the "Kingdom of the Cults."

In his study of modern American cults and minority religious movements as found in his text *These Also Believe*, Dr. Charles Braden, emeritus professor at Northwestern University (1954) [and co-author, John C. Schaffer, lecturer (1955) and visiting professor at Scripps College (1954 to 1956)], made a number of observations with which this writer agrees. In regard to the term "cult," for instance, Dr. Braden says the following:

> By the term cult I mean nothing derogatory to any group so classified. A cult, as I define it, is any religious group which differs significantly in one or more respects as to belief or practice from those religious groups which are regarded as the normative expressions of religion in our total culture (Preface, xii).

I may add to this that a cult might also be defined as a group of people gathered about a specific person or person's misinterpretation of the Bible. For example, Jehovah's Witnesses are, for the most part, followers of the interpretations of Charles T. Russell and J. F. Rutherford.

Although founder Russell and his successor Rutherford are long since dead, Jehovah's Witnesses today still look to the Watchtower organization and its Governing Body to understand the Bible. In fact, Jehovah's Witnesses are taught that they *cannot* understand the Bible without the organization explaining it to them.

The Christian Scientist of today is a disciple of Mary Baker Eddy and her

---

This chapter updated and edited by Gretchen Passantino.

interpretations of Scripture. The Mormons, by their own admission, adhere to those interpretations found in the writings of Joseph Smith and Brigham Young and continued by their current president, called the Prophet, Seer, and Revelator. From a theological viewpoint, the cults contain many major deviations from historical Christianity. Yet, paradoxically, they continue to insist that they are entitled to be classified as Christians.

Note, for example, that Jehovah's Witnesses call themselves "Jehovah's *Christian* Witnesses," and the Mormons are officially the Church of *Jesus Christ* of Latter-day Saints," etc.

It is my conviction that the reader is entitled to know the theological position from which this volume is written so that there will be no misconceptions as to the ground for my evaluation. I am a Baptist minister, an evangelical holding to the inerrancy of Scripture, and teach in the fields of Biblical Theology, Comparative Religion, and Apologetics, and am currently Director of the M.A. program at the Simon Greenleaf School of Law (Orange, California).

It is impossible for me to agree with Dr. Braden, "an unrepentant liberal" (p. xi), or to agree that I "hold no brief for any particular cult, nor . . . violently opposed to any" (p. xi). While I am in agreement that "in general the cults represent the earnest attempt of millions of people to find the fulfillment of deep and legitimate needs of the human spirit, which most of them seem not to have found in the established churches" (p. xi), I feel there is still much more to be said. It has been wisely observed by someone that "a man who will not stand for something is quite likely to fall for almost anything." So I have elected to stand on the ramparts of biblical Christianity as taught by the apostles, defended by the church fathers, rediscovered by the Reformers, and embodied in what is sometimes called Reformed theology.

It is the purpose of this book, then, to evaluate the so called cults and isms, which today are found in abundance in America and, in quite a number of cases, on the great mission fields of the world.

Mormonism, Jehovah's Witnesses, and many other cults are growing at alarming rates not only in Third World countries in South America, Asia, and Africa, but also in the former members of the Soviet Union and its satellites. Particularly in those countries where until recently religious faith was criminally punishable, the inheritance of sound doctrine is missing and untold thousands of people are succumbing to the cults.

My approach to the subject is threefold: (1) historical analysis of the salient facts connected with the rise of the cult systems; (2) the theological evaluation of the major teachings of those systems; and (3) an apologetic contrast from the viewpoint of biblical theology, with an emphasis upon exegesis and doctrine.

It is not my desire in any sense to make fun of adherents of cult systems, the large majority of whom are sincere, though I am not adverse to humor when it can underscore a point. A study of the cults is a serious business. They constitute a growing trend in America—a trend that is away from the established Christian churches and the historic teachings of the Bible—an emphasis upon autosoteric efforts, or the desire to save one's self apart from biblical revelation.

It is most significant that those who have written on the cults have only recently stressed the authority of the Scriptures as a criterion for measuring either the truth or falsity of cultic claims. When this book first appeared in 1965, it was

the first to make such a stress on such a large scale. Since then my example has been followed and the Christian is now in a position to readily find the Scripture's verdict on the cults. Dr. Marcus Bach, who has written extensively from a liberal viewpoint on the cults, summed up this attitude of tolerance apart from scriptural authority when he wrote:

> Somehow I felt I must become a representative of the average churchgoer everywhere in America, whose heart was with me in my seeking. If the Jehovah's Witnesses have some heavenly tip-off that the world is coming to an end in 1973,[1] we want to tell our friends about it in plenty of time! If Father Divine is really God, we want to know about it! If Unity is building a new city down in Missouri, we Americans want to get in on the ground floor! If that man in Moscow, Idaho, talked with God, actually and literally, we have a right to know how it's done! Certainly these modern movements suggest that there was a vital, if not always coherent, moving force back of them, giving luster and drive to their beliefs. I decided that I would not concern myself so much with the rivalry among groups as with their realization. I would devote myself more to the *way* than to the *why* of their doctrine. Let others turn ecclesiastical microscopes on them or weigh them in the sensitive scale of final truth; I would content myself with the age-old verdict of Gamaliel: "If this work be of men, it will come to naught; but if it be of God, we cannot overthrow it."
>
> I decided to set forth on my own with no strings attached and no stipend from any university, no commission from any church, no obligation to any individual or group, no bias, no preconceived judgment, no illusions.
>
> "All roads that lead to God are good." As I began my adventure, the fervor of this naïve and youthful conviction rushed over me once more. (*They Have Found a Faith*, 19–21.)

Dr. Bach admits more in this statement than perhaps he intended, for though it is a laudable aim to become "representative of the average churchgoer everywhere in America," his use of the word "if" in the reference to the teachings of the cults indicates that the final truth, grounded in the authority of Scripture and the revelation of Jesus Christ, has not been obtained by the Christian church, and that other sources must be investigated in order to ascertain the whole truth of the Christian message. We are in full agreement that "these modern movements suggest that there was a vital, if not always coherent, moving force back of them, giving luster and drive to their beliefs." But since most if not all the cult systems vigorously oppose the Christian church, particularly in the realm of Christology and soteriology, perhaps it is not at all out of order to suggest that "that force" is the same as that which opposed our Lord and the apostles and has consistently opposed the efforts of the Christian church, the force described by our Lord as "the god of this world."

Liberal scholars, then, have devoted themselves more to "the way" than to "the why" of the doctrines of the cults, and they have adopted the statement of Gamaliel as their creed. It will be remembered that Gamaliel counseled the Jews not to oppose the Christians, for "if this counsel or this work be of men, it will come to naught: But if it be of God, ye cannot overthrow it" (Acts 5:38–39). Let it not be forgotten that Gamaliel's advice is not biblical theology; and if it were followed in the practical realm of experience as steadfastly as it is urged, then

---

[1] They most recently decided on the date of September 1975 as the time of Armageddon, to their later dismay. This new false prophecy cost them thousands of members.

we would have to recognize Islam as "of God," because of its rapid growth and reproductive virility throughout the world. We would have to acknowledge Mormonism (six people in 1830 to over five million in 1982, and around eight million in 1994) in the same category as Islam, something which most liberals are unwilling to do, though some have not hesitated to so declare themselves.

We do not suggest that we "turn ecclesiastical microscopes" on the cults, but rather that they be viewed in the light of what we know to be divine revelation, the Word of God, which itself weighs them, "in the sensitive scale of final truth," for it was our Lord who taught, "If you believe not that I AM, you will die in your sins" (John 8:24). And the final criterion today as always must remain, "What think ye of Christ; whose son is He?"

I must dissent from the view that "all roads that lead to God are good" and believe instead the words of our Lord, "I am the way, the truth, and the life: no man cometh unto the Father, but by me" (John 14:6). It should be carefully noted that Jesus did not say, "I am one of many equally good ways" or "I am a better way than the others, I am an aspect of truth; I am a fragment of the life." Instead, His claim was absolute, and allegiance to Him, as the Savior of the world, was to take precedence over all the claims of men and religions.

I should like to make it clear that in advancing criticism of some of the views of liberal scholars in the field of cults and isms, I do not discount their many valuable contributions. And no singular study, regardless of the time involved and the thoroughness of the investigation, can review all the data and evaluate all the facts necessary to completely understand the origin and development of cultism. My approach is quite honestly theological in its orientation with the aim of contrast and reaffirmation in view. Dr. Van Baalen is correct when he says that "the cults are the unpaid bills of the church" (*Chaos of Cults*, 14). They are this and more, for they are a challenge to the church to affirm once again the great principles and foundations of the Gospel of Christ and to make them meaningful to the present generation. There can be no doubt that the great trend in religion is syncretistic, or a type of homogenization of religions, such as the great historian Arnold Toynbee has more than once suggested.

We are consistently being told in books, articles, council pronouncements, and ecumenical conclaves that we must "play down the things that divide us and emphasize those things which make for unity." This is all well and good if we are speaking about a firm foundation of doctrinal as well as moral and ethical truth, and if we are speaking about true unity within the body of Christ. But if, as some suggest, this be broadened to include those who are not in agreement with the essentials of biblical Christianity, we must resolutely oppose it.

It is most interesting to note that the National Council of Churches and the World Council of Churches, which constitute the spearhead of the ecumenical movement throughout the world, have consistently denied membership to the cults under study in this volume on the ground that they do not recognize or worship Jesus Christ as God and Savior. In 1957, *The Christian Century* printed a series of articles on four prominent cults, which were written by Dr. Marcus Bach. Dr. Bach's presentation was so sympathetic that the then editors of *The Christian Century* were compelled to write an editorial, pointing out the differences between the cults and Christianity. Editor Harold Fey and Managing Editor Theodore Gill wrote that the promises of the cults were empty and could

not satisfy as Christianity could (551). We can sympathize with Fey and Gill's concerns, since any series of articles which present the cults in such a favorable light, though appearing to be objective, does little or nothing for Christianity except to encourage weaker Christians to dabble in what is a dangerous hobby.

As the American Christian church enters the end of this century, ecumenicism has become a deadly cancer, destroying what used to be healthy Christian churches and replacing them with mutant fellowships of "new spirituality" that embrace pantheism, polytheism, goddess worship, new ageism, Hinduism, Buddhism, and agnosticism. The only "faith" not acceptable in our liberal churches today is biblical faith that dares to make exclusive claims about Jesus Christ, the gospel, the Bible, and salvation! The 1993 Parliament of World Religions, held in Chicago, exemplified this quasi-Christianity. "Christian" spokespeople from various liberal churches embraced the faiths of the world as simply alternate ways to experience God, and both liberal Christians and non-Christians united in their condemnation of what they termed narrow-minded, fundamentalist religious bigots. When Christianity denies the biblical faith it ceases to be Christianity at all.

Biblical Perspectives

The age that saw the advent of Jesus Christ was an age rich in religion, stretching from the crass animism and sex worship of the great majority of the world to the Roman pantheon of gods and the Greek mystery religions. One need only peruse Gibbon's *Decline and Fall of the Roman Empire* to become acutely aware of the multiplicity of gods and goddesses, as well as of philosophical and ethical systems that pervaded the religious horizon in that era of history. Judaism had withdrawn itself from any extensive missionary activity, burdened as the Jews were by the iron rule of an unsympathetic Roman paganism. The law of God had been interpreted and reinterpreted through commentaries and rabbinical emendations to the place where our Lord had to say to the religious leaders of His day, "Why do ye also transgress the commandment of God by your tradition? . . . Thus have ye made the commandment of God of none effect by your tradition" (Matthew 15:3, 6).

Into this whirlpool of stagnant human philosophy and perverted revelation came the Son of God who, through His teachings and example, revealed that there was such a thing as divine humanity, and through His miraculous powers, vicarious death, and bodily resurrection, cut across the maze of human doubts and fears and was lifted up, to draw all men unto Him. It has been wisely observed that men are at liberty to reject Jesus Christ and the Bible as the Word of God; they are at liberty to oppose Him and to challenge the Word's authenticity. But they are not at liberty to alter the essential message of the Scriptures, which is the good news that God does care for the lost souls of His children, and so loved us that He sent His only Son to die for us that we might live through Him.

In keeping with this Gospel of God's grace, our Lord not only announced it but He prophesied the trials and tribulations that would encompass His followers, both within the church and without, and He taught that one of the greatest of all these trials would be the challenge of false prophets and false christs

who would come in His name and deceive many (Matthew 24:5). So concerned was Christ in this area that He at one time declared:

> Beware of false prophets, which come to you in sheep's clothing, but inwardly they are ravening wolves. Ye shall know them by their fruits. Do men gather grapes of thorns, or figs of thistles? Even so every good tree bringeth forth good fruit; but a corrupt tree bringeth forth evil fruit. A good tree cannot bring forth evil fruit, neither can a corrupt tree bring forth good fruit. Every tree that bringeth not forth good fruit is hewn down, and cast into the fire. Wherefore by their fruits ye shall know them. Not every one that saith unto me, Lord, Lord, shall enter into the kingdom of heaven; but he that doeth the will of my Father which is in heaven. Many will say to me in that day, Lord, Lord, have we not prophesied in thy name? and in thy name have cast out devils? and in thy name done many wonderful works? And then will I profess unto them, I never knew you: depart from me, ye that work iniquity (Matthew 7:15–23).

Christ pointed out that the false prophets would come. There was not a doubt in the mind of the Son of God that this would take place, and the history of the heresies of the first five centuries of the Christian church bear out the accuracy of His predictions. Christ further taught that the fruits of the false prophets would also be apparent, and that the church would be able to detect them readily. Let us never forget that "fruits" from a corrupt tree can also be doctrinal, as well as ethical and moral. A person may be ethically and morally "good" by human standards, but if he sets his face against Jesus Christ as Lord and Savior and rejects Him, his fruit is corrupt and he is to be rejected as counterfeit. The apostle John understood this when he wrote: "They went out from us, but they were not of us; for if they had been of us, they would no doubt have continued with us: but they went out, that they might be made manifest that they were not all of us" (1 John 2:19).

The Bible, then, does speak of false prophets, false christs, false apostles and "deceitful workers, transforming themselves into the apostles of Christ. And no marvel; for Satan himself is transformed into an angel of light. Therefore it is no great thing if his ministers also be transformed as the ministers of righteousness; whose end shall be according to their works" (2 Corinthians 11:13–15).

We cannot afford to have any concept of the purveyors of erroneous doctrines different from that held by our Lord and the apostles, and agree with the apostle Paul that we must "abhor that which is evil; cleave to that which is good" (Romans 12:9). In the light of Paul's teaching, it is extremely difficult for this writer to understand how it is possible to cleave to that which is good without an abhorrence of that which is evil.

The biblical perspective, where false teachers and false teachings are concerned, is that we are to have compassion and love for those who are enmeshed in the teachings of the false prophets, but we are to vigorously oppose the teachings, with our primary objective the winning of the soul and not so much the argument. It must never be forgotten that cultists are souls for whom Jesus Christ died, for "he is the propitiation for our sins: and not for ours only, but also for the sins of the whole world" (1 John 2:2).

Today, the kingdom of the cults stretches throughout the world, its membership in the millions, with over twenty million cult members in the United

States alone. The church of Jesus Christ has badly neglected both the evangelizing and refuting of the various cult systems, although there is cause for some optimism.

But the problem faces us all the same and continues to grow. The kingdom of the cults is expanding, and when it is remembered that the rate of growth for the Mormon Church in the United States is greater than that of all of the Protestant denominations and the Roman Catholic Church together, the issue comes clearly into focus.

While religious involvement in the United States has become much more individualized, personal, and informal over the last thirty years, making statistical figures dubious at best, religious experimentation is claiming more souls today than ever before. Not only are cult conversion rates astronomical in Third World and former Soviet Union countries, but also Americans thirsty for spiritual reality are consuming cultic doctrine voraciously.[2]

Our purpose in this volume is to further awaken interest to this tremendously important field of Christian missionary effort among the cults, to point out the flaws in the various cult systems, and to provide the information that will enable Christians both to answer cultists and to present effectively to them the claims of the Gospel of Christ, with a deep concern for the redemption of their souls. It is also the aim of this book to so familiarize the reader with the refreshing truths of the Gospel of Christ that he may see the great heritage that is ours in the Christian faith and be challenged more effectively to both live and to witness for the Savior.

The American Banking Association has a training program that exemplifies this aim of the author. Each year it sends hundreds of bank tellers to Washington in order to teach them to detect counterfeit money, which is a great source of a loss of revenue to the Treasury Department. It is most interesting that during the entire two-week training program, no teller touches counterfeit money. Only the original passes through his hands. The reason for this is that the American Banking Association is convinced that if a man is thoroughly familiar with the original, he will not be deceived by the counterfeit bill, no matter how much like the original it appears. It is the contention of this writer that if the average Christian would become familiar once again with the great foundations of his faith, he would be able to detect those counterfeit elements so apparent in the cult systems, which set them apart from biblical Christianity.

Teller training has changed, and most tellers today don't have the intensive training that was once standard. This is because the composition of genuine bills has increased in complexity and unique characterization, making them much more difficult to counterfeit without detection. However, the principle the American Banking Association adopted is still valid: Close familiarity with the genuine is the best protection against the counterfeit. Where once weight and texture were of greatest significance, today laser strips, colored threads, and intricate printing detail signify the genuine. Whether a bill is new or old, however, if it is genuine, it will display the genuine characteristics tellers are taught to recognize. In the same way, Christians who know their faith intimately and use

---

[2]Dr. Martin's clarion call of thirty years ago should ring even louder today as the Christian church faces the new century with evangelistic urgency.

it daily learn to recognize the truth and reject the counterfeit faiths of the cults.

Charles W. Ferguson, in his provocative volume *The New Books of Revelation* (p. 1), describes the advent of modern cult systems as "the modern Babel." He goes on to state that:

> It should be obvious to any man who is not one himself, that the land is overrun with messiahs. I refer not to those political quacks who promise in one election to rid the land of evil, but rather to those inspired fakirs who promise to reduce the diaphragm or orient the soul through the machinery of a cult religion. Each of these has made himself the center of a new theophany, has surrounded himself with a band of zealous apostles, has hired a hall for a shrine and then set about busily to rescue truth from the scaffold and put it on the throne.

Ferguson did the Christian church a great service in the late 1920s by focusing attention upon the rise of the cults. His observations were pithy and to the point, and though they cannot always be endorsed from a biblical standpoint, there can be little doubt that he put his finger upon the cults as a vital emergent force in American Protestantism with which the church of Jesus Christ must reckon. It is with this force that we now come to deal, confident that on the authority of the Scriptures, the Christian church has the answers, and in the Gospel of Christ, a Savior who can provide the cultist with something no cult system has ever been able to originate—peace with God and fellowship with the Father and with His Son, Jesus Christ.

The cults have capitalized on the failure of the Christian church to understand their teachings and to develop a workable methodology both to evangelize and to refute cult adherents. Within the theological structure of the cults there is considerable truth, all of which, it might be added, is drawn from biblical sources, but so diluted with human error as to be more deadly than complete falsehood. The cults have also emphasized the things that the church has forgotten, such as divine healing (Christian Science, Unity, New Thought), prophecy (Jehovah's Witnesses and Mormonism), and a great many other things that in the course of our study we will have opportunity to observe. But let it never be forgotten that where the Gospel of Jesus Christ is proclaimed in power and with what Dr. Frank E. Gaebelein has called "a compelling relevancy," cults have made little or no headway. This has led Dr. Lee Belford, Professor of Comparative Religions at New York University, to state,

> The problem is essentially theological where the cults are concerned. The answer of the church must be theological and doctrinal. No sociological or cultural evaluation will do. Such works may be helpful, but they will not answer the Jehovah's Witness or Mormon who is seeking biblical authority for either the acceptance or rejection of his beliefs.

Sadly, many unbiblical teachings regarding both healing and prophecy are today being promoted in churches and on religious broadcasting, and they are being believed by Christians who have not been equipped from God's Word to recognize and reject such false teachings. Even more than when the first edition of this book was written, the church today has a compelling interest in teaching and equipping its people to recognize error and reject it. Many Christians who are naïvely accepting the false sensationalism of the aberrant churches and tel-

evangelists want to test what they hear with God's Word, but they have not found responsible Bible teachers who can give them the proper tools. Both cultists and misled Christians seek biblical authority for their beliefs. The church must respond to that need with a clear and unwavering focus on the truths of God's Word.

The problem, then, is complex. There is no simple panacea, but it constitutes a real challenge to Christianity that cannot be ignored or neglected any longer. For the challenge is here and the time is now.

Chapter 2

Scaling the Language Barrier

The scientific age in which we live has, in the very real sense of the term, given rise to a new vocabulary, which, unless it is understood, can create enormous problems in the realm of communication. The revolutions in culture that have taken place in the vocabularies of technology, psychology, medicine, and politics have not left untouched the religions of the world in general and the theology of Christianity in particular.

The explosion of microprocessing has enabled us to learn religions via the Internet and argue the existence of God on-line. We can fax the gospel almost instantly anywhere in the world, get a personalized horoscope for $15 per minute by calling 900 "services" such as the Psychic Hotline, and purchase motivational tapes to energize our psyches from television infomercials. Psychotherapy has embraced techniques from astral projection through past-life regression to Zen meditation. "Alternative" medicine abounds even in the prestigious medical research groups such as Southern California's Sharp Health Care, which administers not only one of the top cardiology research facilities at Sharp Memorial Hospital but also the Sharp Center for Mind/Body, which promotes Hindu-based alternative therapies. As well, politics is not immune to religious encroachment, with even a political party dedicated to the principles of Maharishi Mahesh Yogi's Transcendental Meditation. While few evangelical Christians would argue that the United States is ending this century as a *Christian* nation, it is abundantly clear that it is a gloriously inconsistent but exuberant *religious* nation.

Writing in *Eternity* magazine, the noted theologian Dr. Bernard Ramm calls attention to this particular fact when evaluating the theological system of the late Dr. Tillich, leading theological luminary of our day and former Professor of Theology at the University of Chicago's Divinity School. Dr. Ramm charges that Tillich has so radically redefined standard theological terms that the effect upon Christian theology is nothing short of cataclysmic. "Such biblical notions of sin, guilt, damnation, justification, regeneration, etc., all come out retran-

---

This chapter updated and edited by Gretchen Passantino.

slated into a language that is foreign to the meaning of these concepts in the Scriptures themselves."[1]

Dr. Ramm is quite right in his observations, for any student of Paul Tillich's theology and, for that matter, the theology of contemporary neoliberalism and neoorthodoxy will concede immediately that in the theological framework of these two systems of thought the vocabulary of what has been rightly termed by Dr. Edward Carnell as "classical orthodoxy" undergoes what can only be termed radical redefinition. Just how this is effected is worthy of another chapter, but no one informed on the subject seriously questions that this is what has occurred.

It is therefore possible for the modern theologians to use the terminology of the Bible and historical theology, but in an entirely different sense from that intended by the writers of Scripture.

Before attempting to examine the non-Christian cult systems contained in this volume, one must face the fact that the originators and promulgators of cult theology have done exactly the same thing to the semantic structure of Christian theology as did the modern theologians. So it is possible for a Jehovah's Witness, a Christian Scientist, or a Mormon, for example, to utilize the terminology of biblical Christianity with absolute freedom, having already redesigned these terms in a theological framework of his own making and to his own liking, but almost always at direct variance with the historically accepted meanings of the terms.

The student of cultism, then, must be prepared to scale the language barrier of terminology. First, he must recognize that it does exist, and second, he must acknowledge the very real fact that unless terms are defined when one is either speaking or reading cult theology, the semantic jungle that the cults have created will envelop him, making difficult, if not impossible, a proper contrast between the teachings of the cults and those of orthodox Christianity.

On countless occasions, the author has been asked, "Why is it that when I am talking with a cultist he seems to be in full agreement with what I am saying, but when we have finished talking, I am aware of a definite lack of communication, almost as though we were not talking the same language?"

The answer to this question is, of course, that we have not been communicating, because the vocabulary of the cults is not, by definition, the vocabulary of the Bible. Only the Lord knows how many fruitless hours have been spent attempting to confront cultists with the claim of the gospel, when five short minutes of insistence upon definitions of the terms employed in conversation (particularly concerning the nature of God and the person, nature, and work of Jesus Christ) would have stripped the cult theology of one of its most potent tools, that of theological term-switching. Through the manipulation of terminology, it is therefore obvious that the cultist has the Christian at a distinct disadvantage, particularly in the realm of the great fundamental doctrines of biblical theology. The question is, then, how can the interested Christian solve that problem, if indeed it can be solved at all? In short, is there some common denominator that one can use when faced with a cultist of any particular variety, and, if so, how does one put this principle into practice?

---

[1]November 1963, 33.

The cults capitalize on the almost total inability of the average Christian to understand the subtle art of redefinition in the realm of biblical theology. Human nature being what it is, it is only natural that Christian ministers as well as laymen should desire a panacea to the irritating and, at times, frustrating problem of cult terminology. Unfortunately, however, no such panacea exists. But lest we become discouraged with the prospect of facing the ever-multiplying bodies of non-Christian cults unprepared for this conflict (and make no mistake, this is spiritual conflict), proper usage of definitions as a practical tool will rob the cultist of at least two of his advantages: surprise and confusion.

The Riddle of Semantics

The problem of semantics has always played an important part in human affairs, for by its use or abuse, whichever the case may be, entire churches, thrones, and governments have been erected, sustained, or overthrown. The late George Orwell's stirring novel *1984*, in which he points out that the redefinition of common political terms can lead to slavery when it is allowed to pass unchallenged by a lethargic populace, is a classic illustration of the dangers of perverted semantics. It should be of no particular surprise to any student of world history that trick terminology is a powerful propaganda weapon. The communist dictatorship of China, which even the Russian theorists rejected as incalculably brutal and inept, dares to call itself the People's Republic of China. As history testifies, the people have very little, if any, say in the actual operation of communism, and if democracy is to be understood as the rule of the people, the Chinese communists have canonized the greatest misnomer of all time!

Both the Chinese communists and the Russians have paid a terrible price for not defining terminology, and for listening to the siren song of Marxism without carefully studying and analyzing the atheistic collectivism through which the music came.

We must beware of similar language twisting in our own culture, as the current controversies over "politically correct" speech illustrate. In our conscientious concern not to offend or cause emotional turmoil, we talk about "a woman's choice" instead of the willful killing of an unborn child, "revenue enhancement" instead of new taxes, and "fuel conservation" instead of speed limits. The careful Christian will thoughtfully and conscientiously learn the cult's unique vocabularies and properly represent that cult's beliefs in order to carry on a meaningful and significant dialogue with a cultist. Careful attention to actual cult beliefs not only ensures that Christian doctrine is not confused with cultic, but also shows the cultist that the Christian has enough concern about what the cultist believes to make an honest endeavor to understand it and represent it responsibly.

Applying this analogy to the field of cults, it is at once evident that a distinct parallel exists between the two systems. For cultism, like communism, plays a type of hypnotic music upon a semantic harp of terminological deception. And there are many who historically have followed these strains down the broad road to spiritual eternal judgment. There is a common denominator then, and it is inextricably connected with language and the precise definition of terminology. It is what we might call the key to understanding cultism.

Precisely how to utilize the key that will help unlock the jargon of cult semantics is best illustrated by the following facts, drawn from research and practical field work with cultists of every variety.

The average non-Christian cult owes its very existence to the fact that it has
utilized the terminology of Christianity, has borrowed liberally from the Bible
(almost always out of context), and sprinkled its format with evangelical clichés
and terms wherever possible or advantageous. Up to now this has been a highly
successful attempt to represent their respective systems of thought as "Christian."

On encountering a cultist, then, always remember that you are dealing with
a person who is familiar with Christian terminology, and who has carefully redefined it to fit the system of thought he or she now embraces.

A concrete example of a redefinition of terms can be illustrated in the case
of almost any of the Gnostic cult systems that emphasize healing and hold in
common a pantheistic concept of God (Christian Science, New Thought, Unity,
Christ Unity Science, Metaphysics, Religious Science, Divine Science).

In the course of numerous contacts with this type of cultist, the author has
had many opportunities to see the semantic maze in full operation, and it is
awesome to behold. Such a cult adherent will begin talking at length about God
and Christ. He will speak especially about love, tolerance, forgiveness, the Sermon on the Mount, and, as always, the out-of-context perversion of James' "faith
without works is dead."

It should be noted that hardly ever in their discourses will such cultists discuss the essential problem of evil, the existence of personal sin, or the necessity
of the substitutionary atonement of Christ as the sole means of salvation from
sin, through the agency of divine grace and the exercise of faith. In fact, they
conscientiously avoid such distasteful subjects like the proverbial plague and discuss them only with great reluctance. Of course there are exceptions to this rule,
but on the average it is safe to assume that reticence will characterize any exploration of these touchy issues. Both Christian Science and Unity talk of God
as Trinity; but their real concept of God is a pantheistic abstraction (Life, Truth,
and Love constitute the triune divine principles—Christian Science).

The historic doctrine of the Trinity is seldom, if ever, considered without
careful redefinition. If the reader consults the *Metaphysical Bible Dictionary*, published by the Unity School of Christianity, he will see the masterpiece of redefinition for himself. For in this particular volume, Unity has redefined exhaustively many of the cardinal terms of biblical theology, much as Mary Baker Eddy
did in her Glossary of Terms in the book *Science and Health With Key to the Scriptures*. The reader will be positively amazed to find what has happened to biblical
history, the person of Adam, the concept of human sin, spiritual depravity, and
eternal judgment. One thing, however, will emerge very clearly from this study:
Unity may use the terminology of the Bible, but by no stretch of the imagination
can the redefinition be equated with the thing itself.

Another confusing aspect of non-Christian cultists' approach to semantics
is the manner in which they will surprise the Christian with voluminous quotations from no less authority than the Bible, and give the appearance of agree-
ing with nearly every statement the Christian makes in attempting to evangelize
the cultist. Such stock phrases as "We believe that way too; we agree on this

point" or the more familiar, "[Mrs. Eddy, Mr. or Mrs. Fillmore, Mr. Evans, Dr. Buchman, Joseph Smith, or Brigham Young] says exactly the same thing; we are completely in agreement." All such tactics based upon the juggling of terms usually have the effect of frustrating the average Christian, for he is unable to put his finger on what he knows is error, and is repeatedly tantalized by seeming agreement which, as he knows, does not exist. He is therefore often forced into silence because he is unaware of what the cultist is actually doing. Often, even though he may be aware of this in a limited sense, he hesitates to plunge into a discussion for fear of ridicule because of an inadequate background or a lack of biblical information.

The solution to this perplexing problem is far from simple. The Christian must realize that for every biblical or doctrinal term *he* mentions, a redefinition light flashes on in the mind of the cultist, and a lightning-fast redefinition is accomplished. Realizing that the cultist will apparently agree with the doctrine under discussion while firmly disagreeing in reality with the historical and biblical concept, the Christian is on his way to dealing effectively with cult terminology. This amazing operation of terminological redefinition works very much like a word association test in psychology.

It is simple for a cultist to spiritualize and redefine the clear meaning of biblical texts and teachings so as to be in apparent harmony with the historic Christian faith. However, such a harmony is at best a surface agreement, based upon double meanings of words that cannot stand the test of biblical context, grammar, or sound exegesis. Language is, to be sure, a complex subject; all are agreed on this. But one thing is beyond dispute, and that is that in context words mean just what they say. Either we admit this or we must be prepared to surrender all the accomplishments of grammar and scholastic progress and return to writing on cave walls with charcoal sticks in the tradition of our alleged stone-age ancestors. To illustrate this point more sharply, the experience of everyday life points out the absurdity of terminological redefinitions in every way of life.

An attorney who is retained by his client must know the laws that govern trial procedure, cross-examination, and evidence. But above all else he must believe in the innocence of his client. A client who tells his attorney that he is guilty of a misdemeanor but not a felony is using the vocabulary of law. But if his attorney finds out that his client has perverted that vocabulary so that the terms are interchangeable, he will either refuse to defend him or will clarify the terminology before the court, because by definition a misdemeanor is a misdemeanor and a felony is a felony. A man who says he stole only ninety dollars (petty theft), but who really means that it was ninety dollars more or less, and in reality knows that it was in excess of five hundred dollars (grand theft), is playing a game that the law will not tolerate. He will most certainly be punished for such perversions of standard legal terms. In the realm of medicine, a doctor who announces that he will perform an open-heart operation, then proceeds in the presence of his colleagues to remove the gall bladder, and then attempts to defend his action by the claim that open-heart surgery actually means removal of the gall bladder in his vocabulary, could not practice medicine for long! Open-heart surgery is delicate repair of the heart muscle. Removal of the gall bladder is, by definition, surgery of another type. In law and in medicine, therefore, terms are what they are by definition. On the business and professional

level this also holds true. But to the cultists words do not always mean what they have always meant by definition in specific context. And just as the American Bar Association will not tolerate confusion of terminology in the trial of cases, and as the American Medical Association will not tolerate redefinition of terminology in diagnostic and surgical medicine, so also the church of Jesus Christ has every right not to tolerate the gross perversions and redefinitions of historical, biblical terminology simply to accommodate a culture and a society that cannot tolerate an absolute standard or criterion of truth, even if it be revealed by God in His Word and through the true witness of His Spirit.

The major cult systems, then, change the definition of historical terms without a quibble. They answer the objections of Christian theologians with the meaningless phrase, "You interpret it your way and I'll interpret it mine. Let's be broad-minded. After all, one interpretation is as good as another."

A quick survey of how cults redefine Christian terminology illustrates this important observation.

Cult	Term	Cult Definition	Christian Definition
Mormonism	God	Many gods	One God
Jehovah's Witnesses	Jesus Christ	Not god, created by Jehovah	God the Son, Creator of all
Christian Science	Sin	Illusion, error, not real	Disobedience to God
New Age	Salvation	Becoming One with the Universe/God	Reconciliation with God by means of Christ's atonement

Is it any wonder, then, that orthodox Christians feel called upon to openly denounce such perversions of clearly defined and historically accepted biblical terminology, and claim that the cults have no rights—scholastically, biblically, or linguistically—to redefine biblical terms as they do?

We ought never to forget for one moment that things are what they are by definition. Any geometric figure whose circumference is $2\pi r$ is by definition circular. Any two figures whose congruency can be determined by the application of angle-side-angle, side-angle-side, or side-side-side is, by definition, a triangle. To expand this, we might point out that any formula that expresses hydrogen to be in two parts and oxygen to be in one is water, and hydrogen to be in two parts, sulfur in one part, and oxygen in four parts is sulfuric acid. H_2O can never be H_2SO_4. Nor can the Atonement become atonement as the theology of the Gnostic cults (Christian Science, Unity, New Thought) explains it. It simply cannot be, if language means anything.

To spiritualize texts and doctrines or attempt to explain them away on the basis of the nebulous word "interpretation" is scholastic dishonesty, and it is not uncommonly found in leading cult literature. Cultists are destined to find out that the power of Christianity is not in its terminology but in the relationship of the individual to the historical Christ of revelation. The divine-human encounter must take place. One must become a new creation in Christ Jesus, and

the emptying of Christian terminology of all its historical meanings serves only the purpose of confusion and can never vitiate the force of the gospel, which is the person of the Savior performing the historical function of redeeming the sinner by grace.

The Christ of Scripture is an eternal, divine personality who cannot be dismissed by a flip of the cultist's redefinition switch, regardless of how deftly it is done. The average Christian will do well to remember the basic conflict of terminology that he is certain to encounter when dealing with cultists of practically every variety.

Summary

Whenever a Christian encounters a cultist, certain primary thoughts must be paramount in his mind: (1) He must strive to direct the conversation to the problem of terminology and maneuver the cult adherent into a position where he must define his usage of terms and his authority, if any, for drastic, unbiblical redefinitions, which are certain to emerge; (2) the Christian must then compare these "definitions" with the various contexts of the verses upon which the cultist draws support of his doctrinal interpretations; (3) he must define the words "interpretation," "historic orthodoxy," and standard doctrinal phrases such as "the new birth," "the Atonement," "context," "exegesis," "eternal judgment," etc., so that no misunderstanding will exist when these things come under discussion, as they inevitably will; (4) the Christian must attempt to lead the cultist to a review of the importance of properly defining terms for all important doctrines involved, particularly the doctrine of personal redemption from sin, which most cult systems define in a markedly unbiblical manner; (5) it is the responsibility of the Christian to present a clear testimony of his own regenerative experience with Jesus Christ in terminology which has been carefully clarified regarding the necessity of such regeneration on the part of the cultist in the light of the certain reality of God's inevitable justice. It may be necessary also, in the course of discussing terminology and its dishonest recasting by cult systems, to resort to occasional polemic utterances. In such cases, the Christian should be certain that they are tempered with patience and love, so that the cultist appreciates that such tactics are motivated by one's personal concern for his eternal welfare and not simply to "win the argument."

Let it never be forgotten that cultists are experts at lifting texts out of their respective contexts without proper concern for the laws of language or the established principles of biblical interpretation. There are those of whom Peter warns us, who "wrest [the Scriptures] unto their own destruction" (2 Peter 3:16). This is an accurate picture of the kingdom of the cults in the realm of terminology.

Looking back over the picture of cult semantics, the following facts emerge.

1. The average cultist knows his own terminology very thoroughly. He also has a historic knowledge of Christian usage and is therefore prepared to discuss many areas of Christian theology intelligently.

2. The well-trained cultist will carefully avoid definition of terms concerning cardinal doctrines such as the Trinity, the deity of Christ, the Atonement, the bodily resurrection of our Lord, the process of salvation by grace and jus-

tification by faith. If pressed in these areas, he will redefine the terms to fit the semantic framework of orthodoxy unless he is forced to define his terms explicitly.

3. The informed Christian must seek for a point of departure, preferably the authority of the Scriptures, which can become a powerful and useful tool in the hands of the Christian, if properly exercised.

4. The concerned Christian worker must familiarize himself to some extent with the terminology of the major cult systems if he is to enjoy any measure of success in understanding the cultist's mind when bearing a witness for Christ.

We have stressed heavily the issue of terminology and a proper definition of terms throughout this entire chapter. It will not have been wasted effort if the reader has come to realize its importance and will be guided accordingly when approaching the language barrier, which is an extremely formidable obstacle both to evangelizing cultists and to giving a systematic and effective defense of the Christian faith against their perversions.

Chapter 3

The Psychological Structure of Cultism

It is extremely difficult, when approaching the study of the field of non-Christian cults, to appraise accurately such groups without some knowledge of the psychological factors involved in both their formation and growth.

Each cult has what might be called its own "belief system," which follows a distinct pattern and, allowing for obvious differences of personality that exist in any group, can be analyzed and understood in relation to its particular theological structure. Since until recently very little, if anything, has been written on this subject relative to the cults, considerable research was necessary in order to bring this matter under discussion. That it must be discussed and understood as an integral part of the whole complex of the development of American cult systems, no thorough student will deny.

Over the past three decades many professional and lay observers have studied the psychological dynamics of religious conversion and membership. Some of the studies have been extremely thoughtful, scientifically controlled, and useful. Others, unfortunately, have been little more than the promotion of personal biases and preconceptions spruced up with some semiscientific psychological jargon. The initial surge of interest during the decade between 1975–1985 in the psychology of cult involvement coincided with the rise in popularity of therapy, the new emphasis on "victimization" as a precursor to emotional problems, and the increasingly common assumption that religious faith was an emotional state more or less divorced from external, objective reality. As psychotherapy became more and more generally popular, many Christians came to believe that psychology was generally trustworthy and helpful rather than being a secular alternative to spiritual discipleship. These and other factors produced a climate ripe for diagnosing cultic recruitment, conversion, and membership as psychopathological phenomena. While Christians should not reject every psychological discovery or position as wrong, each psychological assumption should be evaluated carefully against the standard of God's Word, the Bible. Psychology can be helpful in observing, understanding, and describing human behavior to

This chapter updated and edited by Gretchen Passantino.

a limited extent. These two principles are foundational to the discussion in this chapter.

In the course of working with cultists it has been the observation of this writer that each cultist, though different as an individual, does share certain psychological traits in common with his fellow members, and a careful study of these similarities has revealed some interesting trends.

It is not possible in one chapter to cover all of the cult systems, so we have limited our observations to Jehovah's Witnesses, Mormons, and Christian Scientists. The Jehovah's Witnesses represent those cult systems that put strong emphasis upon eschatology and prophecy; the Mormons those that emphasize priestly authority, secret rituals, and symbols; and Christian Science, the Gnostic cults, which ground their experience in metaphysical pantheism and physical healing (a fact which contains within itself enough material to merit an entire book on the problem of psychosomatic medicine and healing).

Dr. Milton Rokeach, in his illuminating book *The Open and Closed Mind*, notes that there are three regions or levels that psychologists generally recognize in any belief or disbelief system. The first or central region is that which encompasses the individual's basic primitive outlook on the world in which he lives and asks such questions as, "Is the world a threatening place or is it an accepting place?"

The second or intermediate region is the area of authority. In other words, whose authority is a person willing to accept in matters pertaining to the functions of life?

Finally, there is the peripheral region, which penetrates into the details of the structure of living. The details may vary or change according to the specific content which the authority, once accepted, may invoke.

There is no doubt in my mind that the belief systems of the cults share much in common, and that some of these common factors are worth noting.

First and foremost, the belief systems of the cults are characterized by closed-mindedness. They are not interested in a rational cognitive evaluation of the facts. The organizational structure interprets the facts to the cultist, generally invoking the Bible and/or its respective founder as the ultimate source of its pronouncements. Such belief systems are in isolation; they never shift to logical consistency. They exist in what we might describe as separate compartments in the cultist's mind and are almost incapable of penetration or disruption if the individual cultist is completely committed to the authority pattern of his organization.

Although many people are closed-minded about their religious faith, including many Christians, cultists are usually closed-minded not only because of their own determinations, but also because the cults almost invariably teach their followers not to question, not to interact with outsiders (especially ones critical of the cult's beliefs), and to depend on the cult authority structure to tell them what to believe without any personal reflection at all. So, for example, the Jehovah's Witnesses are told, "If we do not see a point at first, we should keep trying to grasp it, rather than opposing it and rejecting it and presumptuously taking the position that we are more likely to be right than the discreet slave [Watchtower Society]. We should meekly go along with the Lord's theocratic organization and wait for further clarification" (*The Watchtower*, February

1, 1952, 79–80). Jehovah's Witnesses and many other cults severely reprimand any members who question or think for themselves, and some cults even expel members who begin to think independently.

Secondly, cultic belief systems are characterized by genuine antagonism on a personal level since the cultist almost always identifies his dislike of the Christian message with the messenger who holds such opposing beliefs.

The identification of opposing beliefs with the individual in the framework of antagonism leads the cultist almost always to reject the individual as well as the belief, a problem closely linked with closed-mindedness and one that is extremely difficult to deal with in general dialogue with cultists.

Theoretically speaking, if one could drive a wedge between the individual or the personality of the individual (toward whom the cultist is antagonistic) and the theology (which is the real source of the antagonism) it would be possible to deal with the individual cultist by becoming in his or her eyes a neutral objective source of data. The Christian would then become a person who maintains a system of theology opposed to theirs but not necessarily involved on a level of personal antagonism toward the cultist. Experience has shown me that when this is accomplished it is the first step in a systematic undercutting of one of the basic problems all cultists face in interpersonal contact—the problem of hostility toward those who reject their interpretations.

Such a procedure can go a long way toward allaying hostility, for once a cultist, who has been thoroughly "brainwashed" psychologically by his own authority system (The Watchtower Society, Mrs. Eddy's books, the writings of Joseph Smith and Brigham Young), is confronted by a Christian whom he can learn to accept on a personal basis apart from differences of theological opinion, the possibility of communication improves markedly.

In effect, the cultist is faced with a dilemma: "How can this person (the Christian) be such an acceptable personality yet not share my (the cultist's) theology?"

The cultist, then, quite often begins to wonder how it is possible for the Christian to accept him as a person and yet not accept his beliefs. This can be the beginning of rapport in the realm of personal evangelism.

Since almost all systems of authority in cult organizations indoctrinate their disciples to believe that anyone who opposes their beliefs cannot be motivated by anything other than satanic force or blind prejudice and ignorance, a cultist's encounter with Christians who do not fit this pattern can produce startling results. A discerning Christian who gives every indication of being unprejudiced, reasonably learned, and possessed of a genuine love for the welfare of the cultist himself (which is easily detectable in the Christian's concern for his soul and spiritual well-being generally) can have a devastating effect upon the conditioning apparatus of any cult system.

Above all else, Christians must learn that most cults consider that they have freed their adherents from religious exploitation, which they almost always accuse historic Christianity of practicing. In this connection it becomes a vital necessity to demonstrate genuine interest in the cultist as a person for the sake of himself and his personal redemption, rather than as a possible statistic for any given denomination.

The prime task of Christians who would be effective witnesses for Christ in

the midst of the kingdom of the cults is that they be free from all appearance of guile and ulterior motivation, remembering that our main task is to communicate to those who are by their very adherence to cultic systems of belief in virtual isolation from the Christian message.

This isolationism, which can be extreme, must be considered in preparing one's presentation of the gospel to a cultist. It is a very real mental and emotional chain that has a stronghold on the cultist's ability to discern truth from error, light from darkness. If the tragedy of Jonestown on November 18, 1978, when over 900 cult followers of "Rev." Jim Jones committed forced suicide, has taught us anything, it is the despair and isolationism of cultists. The following quote from *People's Temple—People's Tomb* (Phil Kerns with Doug Wead [Plainfield, N.J.: Logos International, 1979], 205) illustrates this graphically:

> A sealed note found on the cult commander's body, apparently written by a follower just prior to the ritual suicide, gave additional credence to this theory. "Dad," the note said, "I see no way out. I agree with your decision—I fear only that without you the world may not make it to communism. For my part I am more than tired of this wretched, merciless planet and the hell it holds for so many masses of beautiful people—thank you for the ONLY life I've known."

More recently, in 1993, the tragic conflagration at the Branch Davidian compound in Waco, Texas, reinforced this sense of utter isolation. Many secular journalists and even law enforcement personnel could not believe that David Koresh's followers would remain faithful to him no matter what. Even the FBI experts who were trained and experienced in hostage situations failed to fully comprehend this mental commitment on the part of the followers. After it became clear that the Branch Davidians would not leave the compound even as it was burning to the ground, and that mothers were willingly sacrificing their own children, outsiders were incredulous. How could a mother refuse to deliver her helpless child out of the fire and into the protective arms of the FBI? What the outsiders failed to understand was that to the Branch Davidians the cleansing fire of God and eternal life after death was preferable to handing their children over to Satan. *They were completely convinced that surrender to the FBI was surrender to Satan.* Seen from this fervently held but tragically wrong position, the Branch Davidians' actions make sense, albeit a macabre and futile sense.

While this volume deals primarily with traditional American cults and therefore will not treat Jim Jones' People's Temple cult in a separate chapter, it does examine the Branch Davidians within the context of the chapter called, "The Apocalyptic Cults." It is important for us to remember that the cultic psychological patterns evidenced in manic proportions at Jonestown and in Waco are present to some degree in each and every cult.

Thirdly, almost without exception, all cultic belief systems manifest a type of institutional dogmatism and a pronounced intolerance for any position but their own. This no doubt stems from the fact that in the case of non-Christian cult systems that wish to be identified with Christianity the ground for their claims is almost always supernatural.

We do not wish to imply that there is no such thing as an authoritative dogmatism that is valid and true (such as the teachings of Jesus Christ), but rather that cult systems tend to invest with the authority of the supernatural whatever

pronouncements are deemed necessary to condition and control the minds of their followers.

Thus it is that when Joseph Smith Jr., the Mormon prophet, and his successor, Brigham Young, wished to implement doctrines or changes of practice in the Mormon Church, they prefaced their remarks with proclamations that God had revealed to them the necessity of such doctrines or practices among the "saints."

An example of this was Charles Taze Russell's bold claim that his writings were indispensable to the study of the Bible for Jehovah's Witnesses, and that to study the Bible apart from his inspired comments was to go into spiritual darkness. Russell also taught that concentration upon his writings even at the expense of studying the Bible would most certainly lead one into deeper spiritual illumination within two years.

Mary Baker Eddy, the founder of Christian Science, also conformed to this pattern by requiring her followers to regard her book *Science and Health With Key to the Scriptures* as a divine revelation, and her religion as a "higher, clearer, and more permanent revelation than before."[1] Mrs. Eddy did not hesitate to state that she would blush to write of *Science and Health With Key to the Scriptures* as she did if she were its author apart from God.[2]

The history of cultism generally begins with an authoritarian pronouncement on the part of the founder or founders. This in turn is institutionalized during their lifetime or after their death into a dogmatic system which requires absolute faith in the supernatural authority of those who received the initial revelation and whose writings and pronouncements are alleged to have transmitted it.

Some interesting studies of institutional dogmatism can be found in such books as George Orwell's *1984*, Eric Hoffer's *The True Believer*, and Crossman's volume *The God That Failed*.

The problem of intolerance is closely linked to institutional dogmatism or authoritarianism, and those systems that embody this line of reasoning are resistant to change and penetration since the cults thrive on conformity, ambiguity, and extremeness of belief.

The fourth and final point in any analysis of the belief system of cults is the factor of isolation.

Within the structure of non-Christian cult systems, one can observe the peaceful coexistence of beliefs that are beyond a shadow of a doubt logically contradictory and which, in terms of psychological analysis, would come under the heading "compartmentalization." In *1984*, George Orwell describes this as "double think." Rokeach commenting on this illustrates the point admirably:

> In everyday life we note many examples of "double think"; expressing an abhorrence of violence and at the same time believing it is justifiable under certain conditions; affirming a faith in the common man and at the same time believing that the masses are stupid; being for democracy but also advocating a government run by an intellectual elite; believing in freedom for all but also

---

[1]From a personal letter of Mrs. Eddy to a student. Quoted in Georgine Milnine, *The Life of Mary Baker G. Eddy and the History of Christian Science* (Grand Rapids: Baker Book House, 1909, 1937).

[2]Mary Baker Eddy, *The First Church of Christ, Scientist, and Miscellany* (Boston: Trustees Under the Will of Mary Baker Eddy, 1941 [first published in 1913]), 1, 15.

believing that certain groups should be restricted; believing that science makes no value judgments, but also knowing a good theory from a bad theory and a good experiment from a bad experiment. Such expressions of clearly contradictory beliefs will be taken as one indication of isolation in the belief system. . . . A final indicator of isolation is the outright denial of contradiction. Contradictory facts can be denied in several ways: on grounds of face absurdity ("it is absurd on the face of it"), "chance," "the exception that proves the rule," and "the true facts are not accessible, and the only available sources of information are biased."[3]

Relating this to the belief system of cults, I do not believe it could be stated with greater clarity. Dr. Rokeach has hit the proverbial nail squarely on the head. Jehovah's Witnesses are well aware of the fact that the Watchtower organization under the leadership of Judge Rutherford maintained that Abraham, Isaac, and Jacob would return to earth before the close of the 1920s, and even bought a home for the patriarchs to dwell in (San Diego, California, Beth Sarim, "the house of princes"). At the same time Jehovah's Witnesses are fully aware of the fact that the patriarchs did not materialize on schedule, yet they cling tenaciously to the same principles of prophetic interpretation that conceived and brought forth the now defunct interpretations of previous Watchtower leaders. How tenaciously they do cling is evident from their latest fiasco, a prediction that the Battle of Armageddon would occur in 1975. It obviously hasn't occurred yet, but faithful Jehovah's Witnesses are still pounding on the doors of America, telling of the "light" they receive through Jehovah's organization.

In fact, the Watchtower lost a significant percentage of its members with the failure of the 1975 date and have refrained from setting a specific date since. However, they have maintained for decades that the generation alive in the second decade of the twentieth century would still have some members living when the Battle of Armageddon took place. As the members of that generation have become fewer and fewer, Jehovah's Witnesses once again began to expect the end at any moment. Finally, in an enormous concession to their lack of prophetic credibility, the Watchtower Society recently changed this teaching as well, even changing the long-standing masthead of one of their premier magazines, which now announces that the end is "soon."

Well-informed Mormon historians and theologians are equally aware that the first edition of *The Book of Mormon* and the present edition of *The Book of Mormon* are quite different in 3,913 separate instances (over 25,000 including punctuation changes), the first edition having been revised and corrected by Joseph Smith and his successors over the last one hundred and fifty years. Yet both the errors and the revisions of *The Book of Mormon* are heralded as divine revelation by Mormons. This is another example of the peaceful coexistence of logical contradiction within the belief system of Mormonism which permits the isolation or compartmentalization of conflicting evidence or concepts.

Still another example of contradiction is the fact that the Christian Science Church has known for many years that though Mary Baker Eddy spoke vigorously against doctors and drugs as well as vigorously affirming the unreality of pain, suffering, and disease, she herself was frequently attended in her declining years by doctors, received injections of morphine for the alleviation of pain,

[3]*The Open and Closed Mind*, 36–37.

wore glasses, and had her teeth removed when they became diseased. However, despite this, the Christian Science Church insists upon the validity of Mrs. Eddy's teachings which deny the very practices Mrs. Eddy herself exemplified. This is a classic example of isolation, which might justly come under the heading of "physician, heal thyself!"

It would be possible to point out many other instances of psychological aberration in the belief systems of the major cults, but it is apparent that we are confronted with those whom the apostle Paul described as victims of the master psychologist and propagandist of the ages, described by our Lord as "the prince of this world" and by the apostle Paul as "the god of this age," the one who by the sheer force of his antagonism to the truth of divine revelation in the person of Jesus Christ has psychologically "blinded the minds" of those who believe not the gospel, "lest the light of the glorious gospel of Christ, who is the image of God, should shine unto them" (2 Corinthians 4:4).

This, of course, is not only a psychological blindness but a spiritual blindness brought about by the isolation of man from God through the rebellion of human nature and the repeated violation of divine law. These are factors that cannot be ignored, for they are a direct reflection of the forces that from "high places" dominate the world in which we live (Ephesians 6:10–12).

The Psychological Conditioning Process

To conclude our observations in this once seldom considered area of cultic analysis, let us consider examples of how the cult systems of Jehovah's Witnesses, Mormonism, and Christian Science condition their adherents to respond to the "outside world" of unbelievers.

In the case of Jehovah's Witnesses, the literature of the Watchtower is replete with examples of a psychological conditioning that elicits a definite pattern of religious reflexes in response to stimuli. As Pavlov's dog salivated at the sound of a bell that represented food, so a true Jehovah's Witness will spiritually and emotionally salivate whenever the Watchtower rings the conditioning bell of Russellite theology. The example that I believe best demonstrates this is taken in context from Watchtower publications and speaks for itself.

The extensive quotes following this paragraph give the historical foundation for the teaching that the Jehovah's Witnesses continue to proclaim consistently today: *All* religious bodies except theirs are corrupt and of the devil. While the historical quotes are much more flowery and pretentious sounding than statements in Watchtower literature today, they express the same sentiment. For example, in a recent publication (*Mankind's Search for God*, 1990), the Watchtower surveys church history and first dismisses Roman Catholicism, then Eastern orthodoxy, and even the Reformation, commenting, "Nearly all the Protestant churches subscribe to the same creeds—the Nicene, Athanasian, and Apostles' creeds—and these profess some of the very doctrines that Catholicism has been teaching for centuries, such as the Trinity, the immortal soul, and hellfire. Such unscriptural teachings gave the people a distorted picture of God and His purpose. Rather than aid them in their search for the true God, the numerous sects and denominations that came into existence as a result of the free spirit of the Protestant Reformation have only steered people in many diverse

directions" (p. 328). In fact, the book concludes, *any* religious body other than the Watchtower Society and its followers is the "great whore of Babylon" condemned by the apostle John and to be destroyed by the coming judgment of God (pp. 370–371). Listen to the venom historically spouted by the Watchtower:

> In Christendom, as surprising as it may seem to some, the false religious teachings create traditions, and commands of men are both directly and indirectly responsible for the physical and spiritual miseries of the poor, notwithstanding Christendom's showy display of charity.[4]
>
> ... Christendom's pretended interest in the poor is sheer hypocrisy ... her priests have done violence to my law and have profaned my holy things ... her princes in the midst thereof are like wolves ravening the prey to shed blood and to destroy souls that they may get dishonest gain ... and her prophets have daubed them with untempered mortar, seeing false visions in divining lies unto them, saying thus says Jehovah when Jehovah hath not spoken ... the people of the land have used oppression and exercised robbery, yea they have vexed the poor and needy and have oppressed the sojourners wrongfully ... oh, wicked Christendom, why have you forsaken God's clean worship? Why have you joined forces and become part of Satan's wicked organization that oppresses the people? Why have you failed to show concern for the poor as Jehovah commands?[5]
>
> The little charitable help the poor get from Christendom is like the crumbs that beggar Lazarus picked up from the rich man's table while the dog licked his ulcerous sores. Neither the crumbs nor the licking remedied the beggarly condition. Only Jehovah can effect a rescue. How comforting then for the dejected, down-trodden people of the earth to learn that there is One higher than the highest of Christendom's moguls ... yes, Jehovah the Almighty hears the cries of the half-dead ones, and in hearing He answers their prayers and sends His good Samaritans to the rescue, even the witnesses who are despised by Christendom.[6]
>
> Haters of God and His people are to be hated, but this does not mean that we will take any opportunity of bringing physical hurt to them in the spirit of malice or spite, for both malice and spite belong to the devil, whereas, pure hatred does not.
>
> We must hate in the truest sense, which is to regard with extreme and active aversion, to consider as loathsome, odious, filthy, to detest. Surely any haters of God are not fit to live on His beautiful earth. The earth will be rid of the wicked, and we shall not need to lift a finger to cause physical harm to come to them, for God will attend to that, but we must have a proper perspective of these enemies. His name signifies recompense to the enemies.
>
> Jehovah's enemies are recognized by their intense dislike for His people and the work these are doing. For they would break it down and have all of Jehovah's Witnesses sentenced to jail or concentration camps if they could. Not because they have anything against the Witnesses personally, but on account of their work. They publish blasphemous lies and reproach the holy name Jehovah. Do we not hate those who hate God? We cannot love those hateful enemies, for they are fit only for destruction. We utter the prayer of the Psalmist, "How long, oh God, shall the adversary reproach, shall the enemy blaspheme thy name forever? Why drawest thou back thy hand, even thy right hand? Pluck it out of thy bosom and consume them" (Psalm 74:10–11).
>
> We pray with intensity and cry out this prayer for Jehovah to delay no longer

---

[4] *The Watchtower* (December 1, 1951): 731.
[5] Ibid., 732–733.
[6] Ibid., 733.

and plead that His anger be made manifest; oh Jehovah, God of hosts . . . be not merciful to any wicked transgressors. . . . consume them in wrath, consume them so that they shall be no more (Psalm 59:4–6, 11–13). These are the true sentiments, desires, and prayers of the righteous ones today. Are they yours . . . how we despise the workers of iniquity and those who would tear down God's organization! . . . "Oh, Jehovah. Let them be put to shame and dismayed forever, yea, let them be confounded and perish that they may know that Thou alone whose name is Jehovah art the most high over all the earth" (Psalm 83:9–18).

. . . The near neighbors of Judah . . . have been the opposers of the Israelites right from the time when refusal was given by them to supply provisions to Israel as they journeyed to the promised land. Moab hired Baalam to curse Israel . . . they had much contempt for Jehovah's people and prided themselves in their own lofty city, her counterpart today being that rich, lofty city, the mighty religious organization standing for the whole of Satan's organization. The modern-day Moabites are the professing Christians whose words and actions are as far removed from Christianity and true worship of Jehovah as Moab was removed from true worship in the covenant of Jehovah. Jehovah had warned Moab of His proposed punishment for her iniquity and opposition.

The modern-day Moabites have opposed Jehovah's Witnesses with a hatred not born of righteousness but from the devil and against all righteousness. Their hatred for God's true people increases as they see upon us the very plain evidence of Jehovah's favor in the obvious disfavor they themselves are in. They put forth every effort to prevent the people of goodwill from entering the new world. They are richer than Jehovah's Witnesses in material things and with it they have much pride and arrogance. . . .

The modern-day Moabites will be brought low, for Jehovah has completely finished with them. Hear just a part of the punishment:

"For in this mountain will the hand of Jehovah rest and Moab shall be trodden down in his place, even as straw is trodden down in the water of the dung hill. He shall spread forth his hands in the midst thereof as he that swimmeth spreadeth forth his hands to win, but Jehovah will lay low his pride together with the craft of his hands."

It is a sure thing that one cannot have much pride left when one is being pressed down into a manure pile, showing the utter contempt Jehovah has for modern-day Moab, keeping her wallowing in the mire of shame.

"For thou has made of a city a heap, of a fortified city a ruin, a palace of strangers to be no city; it shall never be built."

He hath put down them that dwell on high; the lofty city, he layeth it low, he layeth it low even to the ground, he bringeth it even to the dust. The foot shall tread it down, even the feet of the poor and the steps of the needy. . . .

When this happens, what a tremendous change will take place; the tables will be turned! Brought down will be the lofty from dwelling on high as the great, high influential ones of this world to the lowest possible place imaginable, so low and degraded they can only be compared to being trampled under foot by the poor, like straw in a manure heap. Christendom's lofty looks, boastful words, bragging tongue are her superior attitude toward the holy Word of God, her trust in idols, men and riches, such as belong to this world will not provide her with security or any safety from Jehovah's storm and blast. They have no defense nor disgrace. . . .

Christendom's defenses are of no value, but Jehovah's Witnesses have a strong city and this is something to sing about. There are millions who want a safe place and are in need of security; let them know we have a strong city! "Thou shalt call thy walls Salvation, and thy gates Praise" (Isaiah 60:18). Only God's kingdom offers such protection and salvation, for inside the city one is

safe. Those desiring salvation must make for God's organization, and find entrance into it and remain there permanently.

God has been grossly misrepresented by the clergy. If this statement is true, then that alone is proof conclusive that the clergy do not, in fact, represent God and Christ but do represent God's enemy, the devil. . . . If the Bible plainly proves that the doctrines they teach are wrong and their course of action is wrong, then the most that can be said in extenuation of their wrongful teachings and their wrongful course of action is that they have been misled by the evil and seductive influence of Satan, the enemy of God. If the doctrines taught and the course taken by the clergy differ from that which is declared in the Word of God, then the clergy are in no wise safe guides for the people and should no longer be followed by the people.[7]

These doctrines originated with the devil. They have long been taught by his representatives. . . . The clergy have been his instruments freely used to instill these false doctrines into the minds of men. Whether the clergy have willingly done so or not does not alter the fact. If they have now learned that they are wrong they should be eager to get that false thought out of the minds of the people. They do not take such a course.[8]

The clergy have at all times posed as the representatives of God on earth. Satan overreached the minds of these clergymen and injected into their minds doctrines, which doctrines the clergy have taught the people concerning Jesus and His sacrifice. These doctrines have brought great confusion. The apostles taught the truth, but it was not long after their death until the devil found some clergyman wise in his own conceit who thought he could teach more than the inspired apostles.[9]

[The clergy] are willingly or unwillingly the instruments in the hands of the god of this world, Satan, the devil, who has used them to blind the minds of the people, to prevent the people from understanding God's great plan of salvation and reconciliation.[10]

According to the Watchtower, then, the clergy of Christendom are obviously the villains and are the object of "pure hatred." Just how pure hatred differs from good old-fashioned hatred the Watchtower never gets around to explaining, but it is clear that Christendom (all historic denominations and churches) led by the allegedly corrupt clergy has foisted the "satanically conceived" Trinity doctrine and the doctrines of hell and eternal punishment upon the unsuspecting masses of mankind. Clergymen are therefore always suspect and their theology is to be regarded as untrustworthy and inspired by Satan.

Is it any wonder that the usually calm and detached Stanley High, writing in the *Reader's Digest* of June 1940, could state,

> Jehovah's Witnesses hate everybody and try to make it mutual. . . . Jehovah's Witnesses make hate a religion.

The doctrines of hell and eternal punishment that stimulate fear of judgment are "unreasonable" and not in accord with the Watchtower concept of the character of God; therefore, it and the doctrine of the Trinity are satanic in origin and all must be rejected and hated as false.

---

[7]Judge J. F. Rutherford, *Reconciliation* (Brooklyn, N.Y.: Watchtower Bible and Tract Society, 1928), 85.
[8]Ibid., 91.
[9]Ibid., 100.
[10]Ibid., 125.

What the Watchtower does in essence is attach polemic significance to certain common theological terms (Holy Trinity, deity of Christ, hell, eternal punishment, Christendom, immortal soul, etc.). Thus, every time these terms are mentioned by anyone, the reflex action on the part of the Jehovah's Witnesses is instantaneous and hostile.

If we couple this with the Watchtower's heavy emphasis upon the fulfillment of prophecy and a distorted eschatology, the sense of urgency they radiate about Armageddon (which they believe will solve all these problems by annihilating the clergy and all organized religion) begins to make sense and the reason for their actions becomes clear.

When dealing with the average Jehovah's Witness, this entire pattern of preconditioning must be understood so that the Christian can avoid, where possible, direct usage of terms that will almost certainly evoke a theologically conditioned reflex and sever the lines of communication.

Another important point where Jehovah's Witnesses are concerned is the fact that an intricate part of their belief system is the conviction that Christians will always attack Jehovah's Witnesses on a personal as well as a religious level, hence the Witnesses readily assume a martyr or persecution complex the moment any antagonism is manifested toward Russell, Rutherford, their theology, the Watchtower, or themselves. It is apparently a comfortable, somewhat heroic feeling to believe that you are standing alone against the massed forces of "the devil's organization" (a Watchtower synonym for Christendom), and this illusion is made to seem all the more real when unthinking Christians unfortunately accommodate the Witnesses by appearing overly aggressive toward the Watchtower theology or the Witnesses personally.

In the light of Jehovah's Witnesses' insistence upon "pure hatred," one wonders how they live with their own New World Translation of Matthew 5:43–44, which reads,

> You heard that it was said you must love your neighbor and hate your enemy. However, I say to you: continue to love your enemies and pray for those persecuting you; that you may prove yourselves sons of your Father who is in the heavens.

The Watchtower, then, does not hesitate to accuse the clergy and Christendom of provoking all kinds of evil; in fact, they have not hesitated to suggest that Christendom encouraged and did nothing to prevent the two great world wars:

"Had Christendom chosen to do so, she could easily have prevented World Wars I and II."[11]

Some of the basic motivations of the Watchtower are clearly seen in stark contrast with the teachings of Holy Scripture and reveal that there is more than a spiritual disorder involved. Indeed there exist deep psychological overtones, which cannot be considered healthy in any sense of the term.

Whereas Jehovah's Witnesses are preoccupied with Armageddon, the theocracy, the end of the age, and "pure hatred," the Mormons have quite different psychological and theological emphases.

---

[11] *The Watchtower* (December 1, 1951): 731.

At the very core of Mormon theology there is a tremendous emphasis upon authority as it is invested in the priesthood, rituals, and symbols presided over by the hierarchy of the Mormon Church. Mormons are taught from their earliest days that the priesthood has the key to authority, and that one of the marks which identifies the "restoration" of the true church of Jesus Christ on earth is the fact that this priesthood exists and perpetuates that authority.

A devout Mormon will wear symbolic underclothing, which perpetually reminds him of his responsibility and duties as a Mormon. When this is coupled with Mormonism's tremendous emphasis upon baptism for the remission of sins, tithing, and voluntary missionary service, it is seen to bind its followers into a tight, homogeneous circle, escape from which, apart from severe spiritual as well as economic penalties, is virtually impossible.

Every Mormon is indoctrinated with the concept that his is the true Christian religion, or to use their terms, "the restoration of Christianity to earth." The secret rites in the Mormon temples, the rituals connected with baptism for the dead, and the secret handshakes, signs, and symbols bind the average Mormon and his family into what might be called in psychological terms the "in group." Apart from acceptance by this group, the average Mormon can find no peace or, for that matter, community status or prestige.

Instances of discrimination against Mormons who have experienced true Christian conversion are not infrequent in Mormon-dominated areas where a man can lose his business very easily by incurring the disfavor of the Mormon Church.

The social welfare program of the Mormons is another excellent inducement to Mormons to remain faithful, since if the "breadwinner" of the family is injured, loses his job, or dies, the church undertakes the care and support of his family. So effective is this work that during the Great Depression of the 1930s, no Mormon family went hungry and no soup kitchens or bread lines disfigured the domain of Mormondom.

The Mormons also conscientiously invoke the biblical principle of helping each other. They lend to each other, work for each other, and cooperate toward the common goal of bringing "restored Christianity" to the masses of mankind. These and other forces make Mormonism a family-centered religion, which ties the faith of the church to the indissoluble bonds of family unity and loyalty. This forges an incredibly complex system of pressures and intertwining values over which is superimposed the theological structure of the Mormon Church, which stands between the *average* Mormon and the attainment of "exaltation" or progression to godhood. (See chapter on Mormonism for a discussion of this.)

With such great psychological, economic, and religious forces concentrated upon him, it is a courageous person indeed who shakes off these varied yokes and steps into the freedom of a genuine experience with the Son of God. But a growing number are doing just this as the Spirit of God continues to call out the church, which is Christ's body.

Christian Science, unlike the two other cults we have considered, is neither interested in bestowing godhood on its adherents (Mormonism) nor pushing the eschatological panic button of Armageddon (Jehovah's Witnesses).

Christian Science is an ingenious mixture of first-century Gnostic theology, eighteenth-century Hegelian philosophy, and nineteenth-century idealism wo-

ven into a redefined framework of Christian theology with an emphasis upon the healing of the body by the highly questionable practice of denying its objective material reality.

In Christian Science there is a complete separation between the objective world of physical reality (matter) and the spiritual world of supernatural existence (mind). Mrs. Eddy taught that "man as God's idea is already saved with an everlasting salvation."[12]

Hence, it is unnecessary for Christian Scientists to think of themselves as sinners in need of a salvation they believe is already theirs by virtue of the fact that "man is already saved" because he is a reflection of the divine mind. However, in Christian Science there are disturbing psychological aberrations. Mrs. Eddy demanded of her followers that they abstain from any critical contact with the nonspiritual elements of the illusory material world. She forbade the reading of "obnoxious literature," lest Christian Scientists become convinced that the physical body and its diseases, suffering, and inevitable death were real.

There is in Christian Science a subconscious repression, a conscious putting out of one's mind certain things which are disconcerting to the entire configuration of psychological patterns of conditioning. Christian Scientists are conditioned to believe in the nonexistence of the material world even though their senses testify to its objective reality. They continually affirm that matter has no true existence, and thus, in a very real sense, entertain a type of religious schizophrenia. One side of their personality testifies to the reality of the material world and its inexorable decay, while the conditioning process of Christian Science theology hammers relentlessly to suppress this testimony and affirm that the only true reality is spiritual or mental.

In Margaret Mitchell's classic novel *Gone With the Wind*, Scarlet O'Hara, the heroine, when confronted with the harsh realities of life in the wake of the Civil War, repeatedly states, "I'll think about that tomorrow," as if not thinking about it today would eliminate the reality of its claim at that moment.

When working with sensory data, Christian Scientists totally disassociate their religious convictions, for, if they did not, they would not continue to feed, clothe, or house their bodies. But in still another sense, they attempt to master the all-too-obvious frailties of the body by the application of a religion which denies the material reality of that body. A psychologist of the behaviorist school in one sense does the same thing. In the office he may talk about "conditioning" and may associate everything, including his home, with mechanistic psychology; however, at home he still loves his wife and children, and doesn't respond in that same manner. This is one of the chief reasons why Christian Scientists sometimes appear to be almost immune to the conviction of personal guilt as a result of sin. Guilt implies the threat of judgment and a standard which is the basis of that judgment; hence the reality of the concept of sin, which is transgression of the law of God. Christian Scientists desperately want only a "good" world, a pleasant place full of happiness, life, love, and security. This they can have only if they deny the empirical evidence of the opposites of those concepts. In effect, they affirm the reality of "good" at the expense of the antithesis of "good," as

---

[12]Mary Baker Eddy, *Miscellaneous Writings* (Boston: Trustees under the Will of Mary Baker Eddy, 1924 [first published 1896]), 261.

if by denying the existence of evil one had annihilated evil!

There can be no doubt that there is "selective perception" in the mind of the Christian Scientist, which enables him to select those things which are of a metaphysical nature, disassociate them from the sense perception of the physical world, and still maintain his idealistic philosophy and Gnostic theology. This he accomplishes by repressing or suppressing any evidence to the contrary.

By following Mrs. Eddy's advice and avoiding what she would call "obnoxious literature," i.e., evidence that controverts the idealism of Christian Science philosophy, Christian Scientists avoid facing the damaging data of physical reality. It is in effect an act of unconscious suppression, utilized in order to escape the data. Concluding our thoughts in this area we might say that in the kingdom of the cults we are actually seeing a mosaic of abnormal conditioned behavior patterns that express themselves in a theological framework, utilizing Christian terms perverted by redefinition and represented as "new insight," when in truth they are only old errors with new faces. The defense mechanisms on a psychological level are apparent when one considers the background and vocabulary of the cult systems. There exists, beyond a shadow of a doubt, an abnormal behavior syndrome operating in the mentality of most cultists, which causes the cultist (in the case of Christian Scientists) to build his theological system upon a preconditioned and artificially induced criterion of evaluation, i.e., the divine mission and inspiration of Mary Baker Eddy. In the case of other cultists, the names Joseph Smith, "Pastor" Russell, Brigham Young, or any other cult authority figure could be supplied and the conditioned reflex would be virtually the same.

There are many more observations that could be made, but space will not permit. It is my hope that in observing and analyzing the facets of cult behavior patterns already discussed, the reader may obtain a deeper insight and appreciation of the psychological structure of cultism as it continues to influence a growing segment of professing Christendom, which is ill-prepared for the subtleties and dangers of such psychological and theological deviations.

Chapter 4

Critiquing Cult Mind-Control Model

"You've got to get my daughter back!" Margaret pleaded. "She was such a beautiful girl, such a good student! We never had any problems with her until she joined that cult. It's like she's another person, like she's turned off her brain. She used to think for herself; she used to enjoy her friends; she spent time with us. Now her whole life is consumed by the Center. She hardly ever comes home anymore, and when she does it's 'Elijah Enoch this' and 'Elijah Enoch that' and 'The Center teaches . . .' You just have to help me, please. I don't care what it costs or how long it takes!"

The exit counselor, a professional who specialized in interventive counseling with families and their adult children who join objectionable religious movements, patiently explained to Margaret that her daughter was a victim of cult mind control. He explained the four components of mind control: (1) behavior control; (2) thought control; (3) emotional control; and (4) information control.[2] He explained the use of subtle forms of hypnosis and autosuggestion, the social isolationism, the behavior modification techniques, and the autocratic leadership of the cult that all combined to rob her daughter of her freedom to

This chapter written by Bob Passantino and Gretchen Passantino; edited by Gretchen Passantino.[1]

[1]Editor's Note: *Controversy had not settled over the idea of "mind control" operating in cult recruitment by the end of the 1980s. While Dr. Martin did not address this issue exhaustively in print during his lifetime of ministry, he was careful to distinguish the difference between* influence *and* control. *He was well known to exclaim regarding counter-cult evangelism,* "It's not psychology, it's not sociology, it's not anthropology—it's Christology. What you believe about Jesus Christ, that makes the difference for eternity!" *Bob and Gretchen Passantino, the authors of this chapter, were mentored by Dr. Martin, expecially during the formative years of their almost two and one-half decades of cult evangelism work. Their evaluation of the cult mind-control model provides a contemporary survey of a model that is accepted fairly uncritically by many secular and evangelical counter-cult workers. Much of this material appeared in a different form in "Overcoming the Bondage of Victimization" (Cornerstone 22:102–103; 31–42).*

[2]The "exit counselor" in this vignette represents the majority of exit counselors active today. The mind control features mentioned here are recounted in many exit counseling articles and books, most notably in Steven Hassan's *Combatting Cult Mind Control* (Rochester, Vt.: Park Street Press, 1990).

make rational choices. He explained that neither she, her family, nor her daughter were to blame or were especially vulnerable; cult mind control could work on *anyone*.[3]

He explained that cult mind control occurs in three steps: (1) "unfreezing," or upsetting the convert's view of reality; (2) "changing," or imposing a new personal identity on the convert; and (3) "refreezing," or giving the convert a new worldview with new goals, purposes, and activities.[4]

Margaret was told she needed an exit counselor to break through her daughter's bondage to the cult leader and to restore her to mental, emotional, and physical freedom.

The exit counselor assured her that his work was not the same as the deprogrammers popular in the eighties who forcibly kidnapped cult members, held them against their wills, and subjected them to intensely emotional verbal confrontations until they "broke" and left their cults.

The exit counselor explained to her that cult mind control, while appearing much more innocuous and less threatening than prisoner-of-war brainwashing torture, was nevertheless far more powerful, subtle, and effective than anything imagined by any government intelligence agency.[5]

He told her of his own experience leaving a cult, how he had the typical reaction of feeling like he had awakened from a dream, and how he mentally and emotionally "floated" for some time after he left the cult and only felt firm in his renunciation after several months of thinking, studying, and talking with other ex-members.[6]

He encouraged Margaret that if the intervention were successful, her daughter would return to the same emotional and mental stability she had possessed before her cult conversion, and her religious neutrality would give her the best opportunity to make future religious choices free from cult coercion and manipulation.

Finally, the terms of the agreement were discussed. Margaret assured the exit counselor that her daughter had agreed to come home for the weekend specifically to discuss her devotion to Elijah Enoch and the Center. She knew Margaret and her father were going to have a friend who was knowledgeable to talk with her as well, but she didn't as yet suspect that the friend was an exit counselor and that his goal was to induce "cognitive dissonance" in her regarding her involvement in the Center. For the fairly typical sum of $3,000 plus

---

[3]"Anyone, regardless of family background, can be recruited into a cult. The major variable is not the person's family but the cult recruiter's level of skill" (Hassan, 77). "The truth of the matter is, *virtually anyone can get involved in a cult under the right circumstances.* . . . Smart, well-adjusted kids from good Christian homes can and do join cults" (Paul Martin, *Cult-Proofing Your Kids* [Grand Rapids, Mich.: Zondervan Publishing House, 1993], 21).

[4]Hassan, 67.

[5]"Destructive cults today have the added advantage of the thirty years of psychological research and techniques since Mao, making their mind control programs much more effective and dangerous" (Ibid). "The advances in the extreme anxiety and emotional stress production technologies found in coercive persuasion supersede old style coercion that focuses on pain, torture, drugs, or threat, in that these older systems do not change attitudes so that subjects follow orders 'willingly.' Coercive persuasion changes both attitude AND behavior, not ONLY behavior" (Lawrence Wollersheim, *What Is F.A.C.T.'s Purpose and Project Plan?* [Golden, Colo.: F.A.C.T., 1993], App. 1–1).

[6]Martin, *Cult-Proofing*, 182–184.

expenses,[7] the exit counselor and his assistant would devote the next four days to "saving" Margaret's daughter. Of course, there were no guarantees—some newly rescued individuals needed additional expensive in-patient counseling at a special "recovery" center,[8] and one study put failure rates at above 35 percent.[9]

Margaret left her meeting with the exit counselor with confidence and optimism. With a trained professional, a backlog support of sociological and psychological literature, and her own determination to rescue her daughter, Margaret actually looked forward to the coming weekend.

This vignette illustrates the contemporary adversarial approach to cults, new religious movements, and nontraditional churches. Terms, descriptive models, and techniques have been imported from sociology and psychology into interreligious encounters. Cult involvement is no longer described as religious conversion, but as mind control induction. Cult membership is not characterized as misplaced religious zeal, but instead as programming. And the cultist who leaves his group is no longer described as redeemed, but as returned to a neutral religious position. Evangelism of cultists has become intervention counseling; biblical apologetics has become cognitive dissonance techniques. A parent's plea has changed from "How can my adult child be saved?" to "How can my adult child revert to his/her pre-cult personality?" Biblical analysis and evangelism of the cults has virtually disappeared and been replaced by allegedly "value-neutral" social science descriptions and therapy-oriented counseling.

> The cult mind control model must be distinguished from "mere" deception, influence, or persuasion. At the core of the distinctive of mind control is the idea that the individual becomes *unable* to make autonomous personal choices, not simply that his or her choices have been predicated on something false.[10]

British sociologist Eileen Barker points out this difference:

---

[7]Hassan, 143.

[8]Ibid., 185.

[9]The preceding details are found throughout exit counseling literature and are representative of exit counseling expectations and agreements. Similar views and procedures are found in most of the representative literature.

[10]To this, leading exit counselor Steven Hassan adds the importance of what he terms the cults' phenomenally successful practice of hypnosis (Wollersheim and others also consider hypnosis a crucial ingredient, App. 1–3). In fact, Hassan affirms that hypnosis enables mind control perpetrators to increase their success rates impressively above what is possible through other mind control techniques (see p. 34 and others). However, hypnosis expert Dr. Nicholas P. Spanos and others have documented that success rates of hypnosis vary widely because of a number of different factors, and many attempts have extremely low success rates. Even in the ideal setting, (including isolation of the subject, a trust relationship between the subject and hypnotizer, target behavior already acceptable to the subject, and a subject who is clinically highly suggestible) most hypnosis researchers deny that a subject is under "mind control," that is, *unable* to make independent decisions. The *Encyclopedia Britannica* notes, "This experiment is typical of a number of controlled studies that call many earlier extravagant claims about hypnosis into serious question. It now seems quite unlikely that the hypnotized person can transcend his waking potential in physical strength, perceptiveness, learning ability, and productivity. Similarly, it seems most improbable that hypnotized people can be compelled to do what they would be most unwilling to do in the waking state. . . . Altogether then, hypnosis should not be considered as a technique for achieving supernormal performance or control. Rather, it is a collaborative enterprise in which the inner experience of the subject can be dramatically altered ("Hypnosis," 138).

Recruitment that employs deception should, however, be distinguished from "brainwashing" or "mind control." If people are the victims of mind control, they are rendered *incapable* of making the decision themselves of whether or not to join a movement—the decision is made for them. If, on the other hand, it is merely deception that is being practiced, converts will be perfectly capable of *making* a decision—although they might make a different decision were they basing their choice on more accurate information.[11]

Basically, the mind control model assumes *inability to choose*, while deception interferes with the accuracy of the knowledge one uses to *make a choice*.

Twenty years ago, when exit counseling's precursor, deprogramming, first gained popularity, the author and some other evangelical countercult apologists made some important warnings and observations about the inadequacies of the cult mind control/deprogramming approach.

These warnings remain valid even though "brainwashing" has been replaced with "mind control" and "deprogramming" has been changed to "exit counseling."[12]

There is not a *qualitative* difference between the older model and the newer model, but instead a *quantitative* difference. This is important, because most exit counselors respond to criticism of the mind control/exit counseling model by deflecting the criticism, claiming it might have validity in the older model, but certainly not now. While deprogrammers might have once justified illegal kidnapping to rescue a cult member, today's exit counselors tend to be unwilling to talk with a cultist who is not willingly present and also willing to talk. *Fundamentally*, however, both the old model and the new are predicated on the same basic principles:

(1) The cults' ability to control the mind supersedes that of the best military "brainwashers."

(2) Cult recruits become *unable* to think or make decisions for themselves.

(3) Cult recruits *change* personality.

(4) Cultists *cannot* decide to leave their cult.

(5) A successful intervention must break the mind control, find the core personality, and return the individual to his/her pre-cult status.

(6) Psychology and sociology explain cult recruitment, membership, and disaffection.

(7) Religious conversion is termed "mind control" if it meets psychological and sociological criteria, regardless of its doctrinal or theological standards.

(8) These psychological and sociological criteria are not absolute, but fall

[11]Eileen Barker, *New Religious Movements: A Practical Introduction* (London: Her Majesty's Stationery Office, 1989), 17.
[12]Some, such as Wollersheim, describe the development of the mind control process in different stages. Wollersheim talks about "first generation," "second generation," and "third generation" processes of mind control: "Coercive psychological systems can be spoken of in terms of advancing generations, i.e., first, second, third, etc. Each advancing generation has grown more dangerous and powerful than the previous generation" (Wollersheim, App. 2–1).

into a relative continuum from "acceptable" social and/or religious affiliation to "unacceptable."[13]

Where the brainwashing/deprogramming model and the mind control/exit counseling model *differ* are in several nonsubstantive issues, including the following two:

(1) "Brainwashing" is considered primitive and often ineffective; "mind control," including the powerful weapon of hypnosis, is said to be extremely sophisticated, powerful, and compelling.[14]

(2) "Deprogramming" can include coercion, deceit, and physical force or restraint; "exit counseling" avoids those activities[15] but otherwise, like deprogramming, engages in activities such as talking and documenting cultic inconsistencies, deception, and moral lapses.

At the root of both models are the fundamental convictions that cultists are *unable* to make rational decisions, and that psychological/sociological techniques are the most effective ways to free them to make decisions once more. This foundation is the nonnegotiable root of the cult mind control/exit counseling model's fatal flaw. Pioneer coercive deprogrammer Ted Patrick's description of the fundamental aim of deprogramming is *exactly the same* as that of the exit counselors today:

> "When you deprogram people," [Patrick] emphasized, "you force them to think. The only thing I do is shoot them challenging questions. I hit them with things that they haven't been programmed to respond to. I know what the cults do and how they do it, so I shoot them the right question; and they get frustrated when they can't answer. They think they have the answer, they've been given answers to everything. But I keep them off balance and this forces them to begin questioning, to open their minds. When the mind gets to a certain point, they can see through all the lies they've been programmed to believe, and they realize that they've been duped and they come out of it. Their minds start working again."[16]

Evangelical sociologist Ronald Enroth noted early on a similar definition

---

[13]To see the correspondence between deprogramming and mind control, compare, for example, Hassan's references to Chinese and Korean brainwashing (7, 30, 32, and 38) to that promoted during the earlier "deprogramming" phase by Flo Conway and Jim Siegelman, *Snapping: America's Epidemic of Sudden Personality Change* (New York: Dell Publishing Company, Inc., 1979), 102; Hassan's description of exit counseling (121–122) to deprogramming described by Conway and Siegelman (67); Hassan's description of mind control (44, 53–56, and 63) compared to developed brainwashing or "snapping" described by Conway and Siegelman (57).

[14]Hassan (p. 7) says, "Today, many techniques of mind control exist that are far more sophisticated than the brainwashing techniques used in World War II and the Korean War;" and "Mind control involves little or no overt physical abuse. Instead, *hypnotic processes* are combined with *group dynamics* to create a potent indoctrination effect. . . . Destructive cults commonly induce trances in their members through lengthy indoctrination sessions. . . . I have seen many strong-willed people hypnotized and made to do things they would never normally do" (pp. 56–57). Conway and Siegelman (p. 102) say, "Studies of brainwashing, while historically significant, fall far short of explaining the phenomenon we call snapping." Wollersheim compares brainwashing to mind control, saying of mind control systems, "They are distinguished by their complete transcendence of the need to use any physical force or physical constraint. They also are able to alter behavior, ideology, and attitude, not only behavior and ideology . . . by their clandestine, nonconfrontational method of application to groups and in group settings" (App. 2–2).

[15]Hassan, 32, 39.

[16]Conway and Siegelman, 65–66.

of deprogramming, significant because he was one of the first evangelicals to consider the cult mind control model:

> According to University of California psychologist, Dr. Margaret Singer, who has interviewed dozens of ex-cult members, deprogramming is essentially a period of rest and recovery during which young people are given access to information about the cults and encouraged to reestablish relationships with their parents and former friends. In a situation removed from the reinforcing pressures of the cult, the ex-members are encouraged to think for themselves so that they are "once again in charge of their own volition and their own decision-making."[17]

The exit counselors not only echo this fundamental focus, but sometimes even admit that the only significant difference between exit counseling and deprogramming is coercion:

> The noncoercive approach I have developed attempts to accomplish with finesse what deprogramming does with force. Family members and friends have to work together as a team and plan their strategy to influence the cult member. Although the noncoercive approach will not work in every case, it has proved to be the option most families prefer. Forcible intervention can be kept as a last resort if all other attempts fail. The noncoercive approach requires excellent information in order to succeed.[18]

One of the most significant dangers of the cult mind control model is that it abandons objective criteria for determining destructive religious involvement and substitutes a subjectivism that could condemn Christianity as well as the cults.

Approximately two decades ago *Cornerstone* noted the danger of using a subjective or relativistic test for destructive cult involvement and its consequent necessity for strong intervention:

> Recently in Canada Debbie Dudgion, age twenty-three, a Roman Catholic, underwent two weeks of forced deprogramming by Ted Patrick ... at the request of her parents. Luckily, Canada stood up for the rights of the individual and permanently deported Patrick. If our courts refuse the same justice, look at where this could lead us! What about the child who has his hopes set on being a medical missionary in Africa? His parents don't agree, so they grab him home? Or what about the Jew for Jesus? Does he get forcibly dragged back to the synagogue at his parents' wish? You could reverse it and have an even funnier side. What if the parents converted from Judaism to Christianity, but their children remained Jewish? Could these parents then force their children into conforming to Christianity? How absurd! As tough as it may seem, there's a point where you've got to let go. Even if the children are wrong.[19]

In another issue, writer Gary Metz noted,

> "If one follows Jesus' commands, his values and lifestyle must differ radically from the rest of society. This does not qualify one as cultic, rather it means one deeply holds to God's set of values, being compelled by conscience to pay any price to remain consistent with those values. Accordingly, what defines a cult

[17]Ronald Enroth, "Cult/Countercult," *Eternity* (November 1977): 20.
[18]Hassan, 114.
[19]"Deprogramming Deprogrammed," *Cornerstone*, 6:36:9.

must be its theology, not its lifestyle."[20]

Kidnapping and forcible deprogramming have almost disappeared from the scene, replaced by the more legally and ethically defensible exit counseling. However, throughout the history of both deprogramming and exit counseling, converts to evangelical Christianity have been "rescued" and evangelical Christian churches and groups have been accused of practicing mind control. Conway and Siegelman, writing in 1979, set a precedent by accusing evangelical Christians of mind control:

> In recent months we have come upon a number of spurious international blueprints being drawn up or carried out by cultlike organizations so large, so professional in their organization, and so socially acceptable that they appear to have become invulnerable. These groups now permeate the mainstream of American society, and in the current outcry over "the cults," their activities are being largely ignored. . . .
>
> Further down the mainstream, a number of evangelical Christian sects have inaugurated large-scale mass media campaigns of awesome scope and technical sophistication. To cite one example, the Campus Crusade for Christ, among the most visible and enterprising evangelical organizations, has launched a $1 billion crusade aimed at placing inexpensive radio and television sets in more than two million villages around the world. In 1978, the movement announced its new "Here's Life, World" program, complete with a "special task force on technology". . . . Already claiming two million converts in Hong Kong, Mexico, and India, "Here's Life, World" aims to "share the gospel with every person on earth by 1982. . . ."
>
> It is the promotion of this type of delusion and vulnerability to suggestion that we consider most alarming about groups such as these and the techniques they use, along with the possibility that large numbers of people in other countries may soon be laid open to mind control at the direction of self-appointed religious, social, and political leaders.[21]

When we allow the subjectivity of the mind control model to interpret "destructive" cult involvement for us, we threaten the security not only of those who have been tricked by subtle deceit but also those who have made genuine expressions of spiritual commitment.

Doctrinal aberration should distinguish the cults from Christianity, not merely social aberration. The book *Answers to the Cultist at Your Door* outlined steps toward successful cult intervention. None of those steps assume that cultists are unable to think for themselves or that they are emotional or mental prisoners of cults. Instead, it assumes that cultists, just like anyone else, are ultimately responsible for their religious choices:

> Third, in a loving and nonaggressive way, share with your loved one information on the cult and its heretical teachings. Don't shove anti-cult literature down his throat to choke him. Lovingly ask him if he would help you to understand his beliefs and how they relate to the Bible. Share with him your concern that he make his own decisions about what he is being taught. *Express to him your confidence that he is capable of comparing his cult's teachings to the Bible to see if they really measure up.* There are many cultists who really don't know either the im-

---

[20]Gary Metz, "Is Christianity a Cult?" *Cornerstone*, n.d.:26.
[21]Conway and Siegelman, 250–251.

plications of what they have been taught or the true teachings of the Bible. Help get them on the road to a responsible personal choice regarding their beliefs.[22]

Despite such early cautions, the alternative biblical cult apologetics approaches offered, and concerns expressed by nonreligious individuals and groups and by cults, the cult mind control/exit counseling model gained the greatest acceptance among the public, the greatest publicity, and the greatest trust by concerned parents of cult members. Three main factors propelled this viewpoint to the forefront.

First, the infusion into America of many non-Judeo-Christian-based religious movements complicated traditional biblical cult apologetics, since most of the movements' members did not hold the Bible as God's infallible Word. Traditional cults added revelations to the Bible, such as Mormonism's standard works, the Jehovah's Witnesses' "meat in due season" from the Governing Body, or the Christian Scientists' *Science and Health*, but they still regarded the Bible as God's Word, after a fashion. Because of this, Christians could witness to cultists using Scripture and appealing to the authority of Scripture in urging the cultist to test his belief system. However, many of the religious movements that gained popularity during the '70s and the '80s did not hold the Bible to be the rational and accurate revelation of God. A biblical apologetic approach necessarily expanded to include (1) communication of biblical truth in nonbiblical language the cultist could understand; (2) defense of the inspiration and authority of the Bible; and (3) continuing focus on the biblical gospel, including the death, burial, and resurrection of Jesus Christ on our behalf (1 Corinthians 15:1–4).

For many, this seemed too complex and difficult. Couldn't there be a simpler, more "generic" way to reach cultists that didn't depend on a relatively complex understanding and discussion of the Bible?

Second, the eccentricities of the cults became more socially pronounced. In other words, if a college-age young man joined the Mormons at twenty, he would still dress and look about the same, he would still talk about Jesus (albeit a different Jesus), and he would still have a commitment to family values, hard work, and education (even if he took two years off for a "mission"). But if he joined one of the more recently popular religious movements, say, the Hare Krishnas, he would move into a communal living arrangement, trade his sweats and Nikes for a robe and sandals, shave his head, and begin chanting in Sanskrit.

These cults *seemed* more obviously threatening to families than the more traditional cults. Sociologists David Bromley and Anson Shupe have concentrated study on the history of what they term the "anti-cult" industry. They trace the development of the cult mind control/exit counseling model to this strong family aversion to unfamiliar practices, beliefs, and appearances:

> Parents unable to account for the behavioral changes they observed in their offspring, emanating from the role structure of communally organized NRMs [New Religious Movements], concluded that those changes must have been coerced rather than voluntary. The first group of entrepreneurs who acted on behalf of parents to extricate offspring from NRMs, adopted the brainwashing ex-

---

[22]Bob and Gretchen Passantino, *Answers to the Cultist at Your Door* (Eugene, Ore.: Harvest House Publishers, 1981), 189.

planation and conceived of "deprogramming" as the antidote for it. All that remained was to develop the techniques that would yield a reasonable rate of renunciations of membership, which became the standard for a successful deprogramming.[23]

Coupled with eccentric appearances were the sometimes more bizarre and violent actions of some of the groups. Most notable was the 1978 mass murder-suicide of the People's Temple cult in Jonestown, Guyana. Cultism had become deadly—not in isolated, individual, private cases such as a Jehovah's Witness dying by refusing a blood transfusion or a Christian Scientist child dying because his parents didn't believe in using medical aid—but in one massive, unavoidably sensationalistic sacrifice of—in the People's Temple case—913 victims.

Other examples include the Branch Davidian conflagration that claimed close to 100 lives in 1995, and the Heaven's Gate mass suicide of thirty-nine members in 1997. As the perceived threat increased and became more unmistakable, parents and others looked for stronger, more interventive methods to reach cultists.

Third, American society, and many American evangelical churches in particular, adopted a psychological or sociological framework of social interpretation. Instead of judging an individual's behavior according to biblical standards or evaluating a society's actions by biblical ethics, individual and social behavior began to be described, evaluated, and treated from a social science perspective. As the evangelical church finished the 1980s, it was standard for many Christians to have therapists, to attribute their current problems to "dysfunctional" relationships, and to trace their personal inadequacies to emotionally harmful childhoods (everyone became a dysfunctional "adult child" of alcoholism, abuse, isolationism, authoritarianism, etc.). Everyone was a victim. One didn't need to be saved from one's own sins as much as from the sins of others. Psychology and sociology became the accepted means, even within evangelical churches, for understanding human behavior and developing emotionally and spiritually healthy persons.

This new dependency on psychology and sociology not only substituted behavioral theory for biblical theology, it also gave us a relativistic method of determining values. The cult apologist abandoned his value-laden job description and became an "exit counselor," dedicated to liberating his client not only from his objectionable religious affiliation but also from *any* objective, dogmatic religious viewpoint. Any religious values the ex-cultist subsequently acquired would be judged according to how they helped him fulfill his self-image and personal goals (in line with his parents' expectations). These religious beliefs would *not* be judged according to some sort of universal, abstract, invariant standard of religious truth. As exit counselor Steven Hassan notes regarding his own work, "I operate primarily in the realm of psychology and not theology or ideology. My frames of reference for thinking about destructive cults are the influence processes of mind control, hypnosis, and group psychology. I look at *what a group does, not what it believes.*"[24]

---

[23]David G. Bromley and Anson D. Shupe, "Public Reaction Against New Religious Movements," *Cults and New Religious Movements*, Marc Galanter, ed. (Washington D.C.: American Psychiatric Association, 1981), 316–317.

[24]Hassan, 96. Hassan and other exit counselors often *do* judge cultic beliefs as well as practices, despite their *general* focus on behavior.

The mind control model is attractive to many people. First, to the loved ones of the cultist, who can more easily accept the idea that their friend or relative has been mind controlled to separate from them, call them "of the devil," and act oddly than to accept that these were considered choices. Second, to the ex-cultist, who is looking for some way to explain his seemingly irrational behavior as beyond his control. Third, to the exit counselor who enjoys a professional reputation based on helping victims and can command a corresponding professional fee for services.[25] Fourth, to the secularists, who are wary of any religious beliefs and who like a view that attributes dangerous and sinister powers to religious cult leaders.

Sociologist Eileen Barker summarizes, "There are various reasons for the popularity of such an explanation, not the least of which is that it tends to absolve everyone (apart from the new religious movement in question) from any kind of responsibility."[26]

Some people who embrace this new way of evaluating the cults and working with cultists are Christians who believe that the cult mind control model is compatible with a biblical view of the power of evil in the world and a recovery of spiritual health through truth. As attractive as this view is to a variety of people, its fundamental flaws actually don't help loved ones, cultists, counselors, or society.

First, the mind control model fails to support its case that cult recruits are unable to think for themselves and are instead under some sort of mind control.

Second, the cult mind control model fails to give serious weight to the legitimate personal motives of resolution to frustration and inadequacy, fulfillment of dreams, and development of hopes that made the family member vulnerable to the cult in the first place. By its emphasis on the victimization of the cultist, in practice it dismisses any personal value or accomplishment for the cultist. Many people who join cults want to help the needy, forsake materialism, or develop personal independence from their families—not necessarily bad goals, although misguided by false cult teachings. The cult mind control model, however, attributes their cult memberships primarily to mind control and thereby denigrates or discounts such positive activities and goals, disaffiliated to cults as they are.

People who leave cults *without* encountering deprogramming or exit counseling are much more likely to affirm the positive personal aspects of their cult membership than are those who have been taught victimization:

> Wright asked voluntary defectors with no experience of "exit treatment," "When you think about having been a member, how do you feel?" None responded with indifference, 7 percent said "angry," 9 percent felt that they had been duped or brainwashed, and 67 percent declared that they felt "wiser for the experience."[27]

---

[25]While today many exit counselors have graduate degrees, training, and licensing in psychotherapeutic fields, this has become common only in the last decade. At one time, most deprogrammers would agree with Ted Patrick, who boasted that no psychology professional, cleric, or law enforcement person knew anything about mind control or deprogramming compared to his own self-taught expertise.

[26]Barker, 17.

[27]Ibid., 128.

Trudy Solomon's fascinating study of 100 ex-Moonies (sixty-five of whom underwent deprogramming) bears out the relationship between experiencing deprogramming and one's attitudes toward both cult involvement and the exit process:

> The subjects' attitudes toward these interventions varied greatly. While the majority of those who had been deprogrammed felt "very negative" or "somewhat negative" about the process at the time of deprogramming, that negativity, in essence, reversed over time. At the time of sampling, the majority either felt somewhat positive or very positive about their own deprogramming. . . .
>
> Ex-members who viewed the process positively tended to be those who felt they had been brainwashed while in the church, and that they never would have been able to be free of that mind control without the help of deprogrammers. . . .
>
> Those who felt more negatively toward deprogramming tended to discount theories of brainwashing, and they based their own negative reactions largely on what they considered to be the unprofessional conduct of deprogrammers.[28]

Third, the mind control model fails to give proper weight to the role natural suggestibility plays in making one vulnerable to the cults. Highly suggestible people are especially susceptible to religious salesmanship as well as many other "sales pitches."[29]

Finally, if this model is fundamentally flawed, it doesn't provide real help to counselors or cultists and their families and consequently does not "protect" society from the evils of cult movements.[30]

Sociologists Dick Anthony and Thomas Robbins describe the shortcomings of the cult mind control model as threefold: "Its subjective status; a concealed concern with the content of others' beliefs; and an authoritarian denial that unpopular beliefs could be voluntarily chosen."[31]

By contrast, the objectivity and universal standards of the gospel ring clear. As Dr. Walter Martin often said, "It's not psychology, it's not sociology, it's not anthropology, it's *Christology,* what you believe about Jesus Christ, that makes the difference for eternity!"

Sadly, the mind control/exit counseling model epitomizes a "victim" men-

---

[28]Trudy Solomon, "Integrating the 'Moonie' Experience," *In Gods We Trust: New Patterns of Religious Pluralism in America,* Dick Anthony and Thomas Robbins, eds. (New Brunswick: Transaction Books, 1981), 281.

[29]Coercion, persuasion, deception, and emotional appeal are unethical "sales tools" not only among the cults but among unscrupulous promoters in other areas of commitment such as psychics and fortune tellers, some multilevel marketing promoters, some real estate and/or vehicle sales promoters, and on some of the ubiquitous "infomercials" and 900 or 976 "entertainment" phone services. Individuals should exercise good critical thinking and biblical evaluation of *any* promotions, religious or not, especially if one is easily suggestible. Special susceptibility to persuasion is almost totally discounted by most mind control model advocates (see Anthony and Robbins 16).

[30]The apparent success from exit counseling has more to do with natural attrition rates, personal developing maturity, and adopted beliefs regarding its effectiveness than it does with any objectively measurable and attributable effectiveness. Even if exit counseling had the highest rate of success in getting people out of the cults, that success rate would not justify the model. Bombing a door will open it quickly and effectively 100 percent of the time, but it's not the way the door was designed to open. The biblical pattern of evangelism for those caught in false belief is to preach the gospel and challenge personal commitment, not to practice exit counseling to return the individual to a "neutral" religious state.

[31]Anthony and Robbins, 265.

tality. Steven Hassan explains how he describes cult membership to his cult member clients:

> First, I demonstrate to him that *he is in a trap*—a situation where he is psychologically disabled and can't get out. Second, I show him that *he didn't originally choose to enter a trap*. Third, I point out that *other people in other groups are in similar traps*. Fourth, I tell him that *it is possible to get out of the trap*.[32]

This victimization mentality has become the predominant view regarding several other important social issues besides cults: The Bradshaw "model" of adults as "inner children" who never grew up because of their "dysfunctional" families; twelve-step-spawned derivative groups where members seem to focus more on their powerlessness against whatever addictive "illness" they have than on another twelve-step maxim—personal responsibility; and the many "adult children" support groups where members uncover the sources of all their problems—dysfunctional-oppressive parents. The Lorena Bobbitts and the Menendez brothers-types echo, "It's not our fault! We were driven to it! We couldn't help it! We're victims!"[33] One of the most visible applications of the mind control model today is in the area of repressed memories of early childhood abuse (of satanic ritual abuse, simple child abuse, alien or UFO abduction, past lives, etc.).[34] Amazingly, the mind control model is used to describe two contrasting portions of this problem.

First, therapists and clients who believe they have uncovered previously repressed memories of early childhood abuse believe that the original abusers practice mind control on their victims. An extreme example of this is psychologist Corry Hammond, who postulates a sophisticated system of mind control he believes was developed from experimental Nazi systems.[35]

Second, falsely accused parents and other family members often believe that the mind control model, applied to the relationship between the therapist and the accusing client, explains how adult children could sincerely believe and accuse their own fathers, mothers, brothers, uncles, and grandparents of performing unspeakable horrors on them as children, including human sacrifice, rape, incest, mutilation, etc. Many times these adult children have publicly de-

---

[32]Hassan, 121.

[33]Victimization erases one's responsibility for moral actions, sometimes unfairly. Even Robert Lifton, the pioneer thought reform expert exit counselors love to quote, admits that there is at least *legal* responsibility, even for those under ideological totalitarianism: "When Lifton argues that cults sometimes involve commitment to ideologies similar to ideological totalism (1987), he does not appear to intend us to believe that commitments to such perspectives are distinctively involuntary in a legal sense. If those participating in German Nazism and American nuclearism as expressions of ideological totalism are morally and legally responsible for their commitments [and Lifton does argue for this], then one would presume that members of cults are also" (Anthony and Robbins, 24–25). Perhaps this view is why parents lost most of the court conservatorship cases and why those procedures are rarely attempted today. Without a clear-cut, testable criterion, victimization model proponents can expand or contract their paradigm at will, but their paradigm loses all value as well.

[34]See Bob and Gretchen Passantino's "Satanic Ritual Abuse in Popular Literature," *Journal of Psychology and Theology* (1992): 20:3:299–305; Bob and Gretchen Passantino's "Hard Facts about Satanic Ritual Abuse," *Christian Research Journal* (Winter 1992): 21–34; and Robyn M. Dawes, *House of Cards: Psychology and Psychotherapy Built on Myth* (New York: The Free Press, 1994).

[35]Hammond regularly presents his model at training seminars for therapists, including one called "Satanic Cult Programming" at the seventh Ohio Regional Conference on Trauma, Dissociation, and MPD on 4/23/92.

nounced their parents and refused any contact with them for years.

"Recanters" often adopt this view from the family members they once accused to explain how they could have been so gullible. Once adult "survivors" come to the realization that their memories are false[36] (as many of them are doing now), they must deal with the reality that they have accused their loved ones of horrible atrocities. One alleged survivor, struggling to maintain belief in her alleged recovered memories, acknowledged this painful responsibility:

> I wish I could say that I knew [my memories] were 100 percent true. But I can't. If they are all based on falsehoods, I deserve to be damned, and that is really tough. I've made some really important decisions that have affected a lot of people. I still get back to [the feeling that] the essence of the belief has to be true.[37]

Attributing their heinous falsehoods to therapeutic mind control is a more comfortable proposition than coming to terms with their own suggestibility and misplaced trust.

This view fosters a crippling victimization that traps recanters, saying, in effect, "you couldn't do anything to prevent this insidious mind control." This leads many recanters to worry that there is nothing they can do to protect themselves or their loved ones from other mind predators in the future. Speaking about cults, Barker reinforces this point, saying,

> Those who leave by themselves may have concluded that *they* made a mistake and that *they* recognized that fact and, as a result, *they* did something about it: they left. Those who have been deprogrammed, on the other hand, are taught that is was not they who were responsible for joining; they were the victims of mind-control techniques—and these prevented them from leaving. Research has shown that, unlike those who have been deprogrammed (and thereby taught that they had been brainwashed), those who leave voluntarily are extremely *un*likely to believe that they were ever the victims of mind control.[38]

An improper victimization model, whether used to understand cult recruitment, repressed memories, adult emotional distress, or false accusations of abuse does not provide the education, critical thinking apparatus, or coping mechanisms necessary to protect oneself from further victimization. Most importantly, such theories do not focus on the life-transforming gospel as the ultimate solution. Additionally, *true* victims, such as small children, victims of rape, robbery, or murder—those who truly are unable to predict or prevent their victimization—have their predicament cheapened and obscured by those who are misidentified as such.

Sadly, while the mind control model has been predominant in counter-cult counseling, its most vocal critics have not been evangelical, biblically based countercult apologists. Instead, the most prominent critics have been secularists such as civil libertarians, representatives of cults that have been accused of practicing mind control, and those sympathetic to new or aberrant religious move-

---

[36]Hundreds of "victims" now believe their "memories" were therapeutically induced and/or enhanced and that the people they accused are innocent. See especially the False Memory Syndrome Foundation, 3401 Market St., Suite 130, Philadelphia, PA 19104–3318; (215) 387–1865.
[37]Ethan Watters, "Doors of Memory," *Mother Jones* (Jan./Feb. 1993): 76.
[38]Barker, 109.

ments. The public perception has been that if one does not like cult beliefs or cult membership, one must embrace the mind control model. Conversely, if one rejected the mind control model, one was at least a cult compromiser if not a sympathizer or member.[39] Increasingly, however, conservative, evangelical, countercult apologists are rejecting the mind control model as a misdiagnosis of the problem, a misprescription of the solution, and as contrary to a biblical cult evangelism model.[40]

The cult mind control/exit counseling model is more congruent with an *anti-religious* stance than with a Christian one. As Anthony and Robbins note,

> In a sense the project of modern social science, particularly in its Enlightenment origins, has been to liberate man from the domination of retrogressive forces, particularly religion, which has often been seen as a source of involuntariness and a threat to personal autonomy, from which an individual would be liberated by "the science of freedom." (Gay, 1969). This view of religion had been present in the cruder early models of brainwashing such as Sargant (1957), who saw evangelical revivalism as a mode of brainwashing, and who commenced his studies after noting similarities between conversions to Methodism and Pavlovian experiments with dogs, and was also present in the nineteenth-century "counter-subversive" campaigns against Mormons, Catholics, and Freemasons.[41]

In other words, the idea that mind control is the effective weapon of the cults seems to come more from a generally anti-religious bias that sees *all* religion, including Christianity, as opposed to personal autonomy and freedom of mind. Anthony and Robbins' reference to Sargant is crucial, because William Sargant is not only one of the pioneers of mind control research, referred to by many cult mind control model advocates, but also he made strong controversial statements arguing that Christian evangelistic preaching techniques are similar to Communist brainwashing methods:[42]

> Anyone who wishes to investigate the technique of brainwashing and eliciting confessions as practiced behind the Iron Curtain (and on this side of it, too, in certain police stations where the spirit of the law is flouted) would do well to start with a study of eighteenth-century American revivalism from the 1730s onward. The physiological mechanics seem the same, and the beliefs and behavior patterns implanted, especially among the Puritans of New England, have not been surpassed for rigidity and intolerance even in Stalin's times in the U.S.S.R.[43]

This comparison between traditional religious conversions and cult mind control models is a crucial weakness in the cult mind control model. Unless one can show clear, objective, *qualitative* differences between cult recruitment (mind control) and Christian conversion (evangelism), Christians *must* reject the mind

---

[39]See, for example, Ronald Enroth, "Cult/Countercult," 32, where he erroneously assumes countercult advocates must accept the brainwashing model: "Both camps—the cults and their sympathizers and the counter-cult activists and their supporters—can muster the testimony of academicians and clinicians having very impressive credentials."

[40]See Alan Gomes, *Unmasking the Cults* (Grand Rapids, Mich.: Zondervan Publishing House, 1995), 47–80.

[41]Anthony and Robbins, 23.

[42]Sargant, 169.

[43]Ibid., 148.

control model, since it would condemn biblical preaching (Matthew 28:19) with the same weapons as it does cult recruitment. This danger has been noted by secular observers as well as Christians, as Anthony and Robbins note:

> So incapacity, therefore, turns out to be an inability to employ one's prior frame of reference, and, presumably, a brainwashed devotee would be distinguished by his or her not employing his/her old frame of reference. Yet a shift of frame of reference or "universe of discourse" is a frequent meaning of "conversion" itself . . . whether or not it has been "induced." The second approach collapses back into the trivial tautology. A shift of frame of reference is the empirical indicator of lost capacity, but any "convert" is by definition incapable of seeing things as he or she once saw them. Evidence of conversion is automatically evidence of brainwashing, given a sufficiently pejorative view of the conversion outcome. . . .[44]

In fact, William Sargant saw this parallel and in fact advocated using emotionally manipulative techniques for successful Christian recruitment:

> All evidence goes to show that there can be no new Protestant revival while the policy continues of appealing mainly to adult intelligence and reason . . . until church leaders consent to take more advantage of the normal person's emotional mechanism for disrupting old behavior patterns and implanting new.[45]

Sargant believed the subtle emotional techniques used today in political warfare were behind the successes of the early Methodist movement—the same techniques used by John and Charles Wesley to bypass the intellect and entice the emotions:

> With the help of his brother Charles, whose hymns were addressed to the religious emotions rather than the intelligence, [John] hit upon an extremely effective technique of conversion—a technique which is used not only in many other successful religions but in modern political warfare.[46]

Sargant encouraged these practices in the religious arena because he believed that religion was doomed to failure if it competed in the arena of evidence, fact, logic, and history. The psychological benefits of religious belief were important even if the religion itself was based on fiction:

> On the contrary, a better understanding of the means of creating and consolidating faith will enable religious bodies to expand much more rapidly. The preacher can rest assured that the less mysteriously "God works His wonders to perform," the easier it should be to provide people with an essential knowledge and love of God.[47]

The most significant difference mind control model advocates attempt to show, however, is, as noted, tautological (or argued circularly). In brief, this difference could be stated, "It's conversion if you make a choice, and mind control if you are coerced, and the way we distinguish 'choice' from 'coercion' is whether you have been converted or mind controlled."

---

[44]Anthony and Robbins, 14.
[45]Sargant, 95.
[46]Ibid., 96.
[47]Ibid., 237.

In contrast, any *useful* distinction between "mind control" and "conversion," as Anthony and Robbins argue, "must, in order to be admissible, enable analysts (and legal authorities) to clearly distinguish brainwashing as a coercive process that creates involuntariness from other, less incisively coercive processes, that is, to 'draw the line' . . . between groups that thoroughly brainwash from less potent or pernicious groups."[48]

Even Steven Hassan recognizes that the cult mind control/exit counseling model is based on a *continuum* of practice, not a quantifiable standard:

> In this book I will be referring to the *negative* uses of mind control. Not all mind control techniques are inherently bad or unethical; for some, the manner in which they are used is what is important. The focus of control should always remain within the individual. It is fine to use hypnosis to stop smoking, for example, as long as the hypnotist leaves the desire and control to stop with the client and doesn't try to move them toward himself.[49]
>
> Last, what about the philosophical position that "everything is mind control?" Well, it is certainly true that we are influenced throughout our lives. Yet, there is a continuum of influence processes that starts at one end with benign influences (a friend suggested that we see a particular movie) and ends at the other extreme with destructive influences such as indoctrinating a person to kill himself or harm others (Jonestown). Most of the groups I'm concerned with fall near this destructive end of the continuum.[50]

This subjectivity and conveniently expanding-or-contracting definition of coercive persuasion is dangerously imprecise. There is nothing to stop it from slipping wide enough to include legitimate Christian churches, other mainstream religions, highly competitive sports training programs, strongly discipline-centered boarding schools, or any other social or religious institutions that are *perceived* to somehow interfere with one's freedom of choice. The idea of coercive persuasion based on a continuum definition fails:

> Coercive persuasion fails as a theoretical construct for linking potentially questionable acts by unconventional religious movements directly to identifiable harm. Either the issue is narrower, such as physical constraint or preying on the susceptible, or the acts in question do not differ significantly from those by established churches that are never seriously accused of coercive persuasion.[51]

One of the core assumptions of the cult mind control model is that the cult recruit *cannot* make personal moral decisions once he or she has come under the mind control of the cult. This alleged phenomenon initially was called "brainwashing," then "snapping," and now most commonly "mind control" or sometimes "coercive persuasion."[52]

Exit counselor Hassan recognizes the incompatibility of the mind control model with individual personal moral agency:

[48]Anthony and Robbins, 5–6.
[49]Hassan, 7.
[50]Ibid., 44. The continuum description is held by others, including Wollersheim (App. 1–6, footnote 16, 1–7).
[51]John L Young and Ezra E. H. Griffith, "A Critical Evaluation of Coercive Persuasion as Used in the Assessment of Cults," *Behavioral Sciences and the Law* 10:1 (1992), 98–99.
[52]Other terms include "menticide," "thought reform," "thought control," etc. All terms reflect the inability of the recruit to think and/or decide independently from the cult.

First of all, accepting that unethical mind control can affect anybody challenges the age-old philosophical notion (the one on which our current laws are based) that *man is a rational being*, responsible for and in control of his every action. Such a worldview does not allow for any concept of mind control.[53]

If one accepts this involuntariness regarding religious affiliation, then an argument can be made that our Constitution's First Amendment protects *voluntary* converts, but *involuntary* converts are subject to governmental or familial intervention, or, as Anthony and Robbins describe it, "these formulations imply a sort of loophole in the first amendment. The constitutional prohibition against an inquiry into the validity and authenticity of faith arguably does not apply if the faith in question is not voluntarily held or has been coercively imposed."[54]

However, there is no persuasive evidence or way to test scientifically that such involuntariness is common to humankind, and especially there is no quantifiable evidence that involuntariness distinguishes the cults from "legitimate" religion. Instead, we get the idea that cult mind control developed along faulty lines and from a faulty assumption.[55]

Mind control model proponents trace the basis for their "evidence" for involuntariness from studies of the "brainwashing" activities of the Chinese and Koreans on American POWs during the Korean War, from the "thought reform" Marxist "reeducation" plans of China, and from reports of CIA experiments.[56] Although some writers attempt to distinguish brainwashing from mind control,[57] as we have already discussed, there is no *qualitative* difference.

What is the truth about the early brainwashing attempts by the Koreans, Chinese, and Americans? The mind control model proponents are not always candid about this fact:[58] *They were largely unsuccessful.* Even though the Koreans and Chinese used extreme forms of physical coercion as well as persuasive coercion, *very few* individuals subjected to these techniques changed their basic worldviews or commitments.[59] And the CIA experiments (while not using Ko-

---

[53]Hassan, 43; see also Anthony and Robbins (7), which states, "In the influential formulation of Delgado . . . the basic components of voluntariness—*knowledge* and *capacity*—are said to be manipulated in such a manner that the convert never simultaneously possesses both properties."

[54]Anthony and Robbins, 9. Mind control model advocate Wollersheim states, "Any organization using coercive persuasion on its members as a CENTRAL practice that also claims to be a religion is turning the SANCTUARY of the First Amendment into a fortress for psychological assault. It is a contradiction of terms and should be 'disestablished.' Coercive persuasion is a subtle, compelling psychological force that attacks an even more fundamental and important freedom than our 'freedom of religion.' ITS REPREHENSIBILITY AND DANGER IS THAT IT ATTACKS OUR SELF-DETERMINISM AND FREE WILL, OUR MOST FUNDAMENTAL CONSTITUTIONAL FREEDOMS" (Wollersheim, App. 1–9).

[55]See, for example, Anthony and Robbins (271), "Available research is thus not consistent with a model of psychological kidnapping in which an otherwise dutiful and conformist young citizen is hypnotically overwhelmed and imprisoned in a deviant lifestyle which would otherwise be anathema."

[56]See Hassan, 32.

[57]Ibid., 55–56 or Conway and Siegelman, 102.

[58]See Hassan, 38.

[59]For example, "Fewer than 15 percent of the prisoners in Korean detention camps collaborated with the enemy. When the war was over and prisoners were given their freedom, only a few chose to remain in Communist China. Of these, several later rejected the Communist way of life and returned home" (Gary Collins, *Search for Reality* [Santa Ana, Calif.: Vision House Publishers, 1969], 148). Of the 4500 American POWs held in North Korea, only twenty-two elected to stay voluntarily in North Korea after the war (R. Duncan and M. Weston-Smith, compilers, *Lying Truths* [New York: Pergamon Press, 1979], 107–120).

rean or Chinese techniques of torture, beatings, and sometimes death, but substituting experimental drugs and medical therapies)[60] were *so* ineffective that the program was abandoned.[61]

Schein, the pioneering expert in Chinese thought reform "actually thought, as do a number of scholars, that the Chinese program was relatively ineffective."[62] Additionally, Schein and others suggested that changes produced by brainwashing are "more *behavioral* than ideological. He saw genuine ideologist change or *conversion*, as opposed to trivial acts of collaboration, to be quite rare among American POWs."[63] A careful survey of the quantifiable research on the effects of coercive persuasion shows not only that classic brainwashing was largely ineffective, but also that it is inappropriate to draw even a developmental correspondence between classic wartime brainwashing and contemporary American cult conversion.[64]

There seems to be a common assumption underlying cult mind control model advocates who continually link classic brainwashing to cult conversion; that is, their assumption that the new belief (e.g., communism or cult doctrine) is so obviously wrong and repulsive that the only way reasonable people would believe or embrace it is if they were—almost literally—out of their minds. Anthony and Robbins ask, "Why has it been mainly foreign communists and domestic religious minorities who have been popularly believed to use mind control techniques (i.e., not parents, parochial schools, or marine boot camp)?"[65]

Medical doctor J. Thomas Ungerleider and Ph.D. David K. Wellisch focus on this fallacious assumption, that only a mentally incompetent person could join or maintain membership in a cult:

> The issue has been raised whether the techniques are not reprogramming the person back to his or her previous belief system, rather than freeing the individuals to make a rational choice. If the member never does renounce the cult, then he or she is regarded by the deprogrammers as an unsuccessful attempt or failed deprogramming, not as one who now has free will and has still chosen to remain with the cult.[66]

[60]Stephen Budansky, Erica E. Goode, and Ted Gest, "The Cold War Experiments," *U.S. News and World Report* (January 14, 1994): 116:3:32–38.

[61]See Hassan, 189.

[62]Anthony and Robbins, 13.

[63]Ibid., 16.

[64]Wollersheim recognizes that the relative ineffectiveness of classic brainwashing does not argue well for the effectiveness of mind control, and so argues that mind control is almost immeasurably more effective. However, Wollersheim's argument itself uses the continuum explanation, differentiating brainwashing from mind control by degree of skill, intensity, and continuous application rather than by any *qualitative* difference: "It is important to understand that beginning with first-generation programs, scientific methodology was engaged to greater and greater degrees to behaviorally engineer more detailed, effective, and complete SYSTEMS of coercive environmental individual influence" (Wollersheim, App. 2–1,2).

[65]Anthony and Robbins, 265.

[66]Ungerleider and Wellisch, 243. Bromley and Shupe also discuss this in "Witches, Moonies, and Accusations of Evil" (*In Gods We Trust: New Patterns of Religious Pluralism in America*, Dick Anthony and Thomas Robbins, eds. [New Brunswick: Transaction Books, 1981], 253), saying, "Activists in the anti-cult movement do not regard shifts of affiliation to marginal religions as 'true' conversions" and then recite the supposed mind control tactics of the cults. Anthony and Robbins add, "The latent assumption of those who support coercive deprogramming seems to be that no one would ever voluntarily surrender intellectual freedom and flexibility; hence those who submit to regimentation must have been coercively persuaded to do so" (Anthony and Robbins, 267).

With an unfalsifiable test like this, one argues in a circle, never able to test the validity of cult membership.[67] If you leave the cult as a result of deprogramming (or exit counseling), that proves you *were* under mind control. If you return to the cult, that proves you *are* under mind control.[68] The standard for determining mind control is not some objective evaluation of mental health or competency, but merely the *assumed* power of mind control accorded by the critic to the cult.[69]

Nowhere in the generally available literature of the deprogramming or exit counseling advocates is there quantifiable, nonsubjective, uncontaminated, and unambiguous evidence either that cults practice mind control or that, even if they did, it works. Attempts by various therapists, psychologists, and sociologists to link mind control with recognized, testable diagnoses have largely failed, as Brock Kilbourne argues.[70]

When Australian Hare Krishna devotees were given psychological testing by an outside researcher, the results showed that conversion to and attrition from cults are practices done by emotionally stable, normal young people[71]—not mind controlled automatons who can only be returned to psychological life by exit counseling:

> The charge that devotees are incapable of thinking clearly and are in a state of delusion has been analyzed by Dr. Michael Ross, a researcher who gave all forty-two members of the Melbourne, Australia, temple commune a battery of psychological tests. From his study he concluded, among other things, that there is "no evidence for claiming that membership in the movement leads to psychopathology" and that "the argument that joining the Hare Krishna movement is an attempt to stabilize an unstable personality does not appear to have

---

[67]The F.A.C.T. Inc. organization (Fight Against Coercive Tactics, Inc.) commits this unfalsifiability by attributing the same observable characteristics to victims of coercive persuasion as to those who freely choose: "Changing 'attitude' would also include the attitudes and 'appearances' of sincerity and the 'appearances' of enthusiastic commitment. As one can imagine, coercive persuasion applied to building 'sincerity' in a 'religious' context wreaks havoc with and creates many paradoxes surrounding the normal First Amendment Constitutional guidelines for religion and religious beliefs, i.e., the validity of the threshold sincerity test" (Wollersheim, App. 1–2, footnote 2).

[68]If *mind control* were actually the issue with exit counselors, we would expect them to denigrate indoctrination practices only, and never religious beliefs themselves. In fact, however, the beliefs of the groups come under continual attack and are used to buttress charges of mind control. "After all," a concerned parent might say, "only a crazy person would believe the stuff this group propagates." However, as Anthony and Robbins explain, "Parents and deprogrammers claim to be responding not so much to the specific insupportable beliefs, but to a general 'brainwashed state of mind' " manifested by young devotees. If this were so it might be anticipated that deprogramming would not necessarily alter beliefs but would enable devotees to hold their beliefs in a more flexible manner, i.e., a rigid Moonie might become a thinking Moonie. But the assault on specific beliefs is relentless (p. 266).

[69]"When questioned about their abrupt or radical changes by those who know them well, victims of coercive persuasion may aggressively insist their changes were 'for their own good' and were 'freely chosen by themselves.' These two 'beliefs' are standardly infused into the subject in a normal coercive persuasion program. This twist helps minimize legal liability by keeping the victim believing he is doing it to himself and 'voluntarily' changing" (Wollersheim, App. 1–5). If a cultist *did* make a personal moral choice, would he *also* say "It was for my own good" or "I chose this freely for myself"? The distinction cannot be made, other than by assuming cult mind control already.

[70]Brock K. Kilbourne, "Psychotherapeutic Implications of New Religious Affiliation," *Cults and New Religious Movements*, Marc Galanter, ed. (Washington D.C.: American Psychiatric Association, 1989), 138.

[71]Sadly, however, they are without Christ and in desperate need of the gospel, but that is far different than being trapped under mind control.

a strong basis." Indeed, his research indicated that devotees of longer duration "appeared happier and less anxious."[72]

Additionally, there is ample court precedent that those professionals who hold this view of mind control do not meet the Frye legal standard, by which general professional acceptability of a view is necessary before that view becomes admissible in court as expert testimony. In fact, one court found that the mind control model did not even meet a lesser civil standard of a "significant following."[73]

There simply is not enough hard evidence that the social, emotional, mental, and physical factors present during cult recruitment are sufficient to produce the debilitation mind control model advocates allege.[74] It stretches one's credulity to believe that what CIA, Russian, Korean, and Chinese highly trained and technologically supported experts could not accomplish under extremes of mental, emotional, and physical abuse, self-styled modern messiahs like David Koresh (high school dropout), Charles Manson (grade school dropout), and Hare Krishna founder Braphupada (self-educated) accomplished on a daily basis and on a massive scale with control methods measurably inferior to those of POW camp torturers.[75] Do we really believe that what the Soviets couldn't do to Alexander Solzhenitsyn during years of forced labor and torture in the Gulag, Sun Myung Moon could have done by "love bombing" for one week at an idyllic wilderness retreat?

Sociologists Bromley and Shupe point out the absurdity of such a notion:

> Finally, the brainwashing notion implied that somehow these diverse and unconnected movements had simultaneously discovered and implemented highly intrusive behavioral modification techniques. Such serendipity and co-

---

[72]Ruth Tucker, *Another Gospel* (Grand Rapids, Mich.: Zondervan Publishing House, 1989), 279.

[73]The trial court allowed the plaintiff to establish his case [against TM] alleging fraud by presenting expert testimony stating that transcendental meditation was "a system of 'thought reform' that changed its practitioners' worldview" (951). This happened when objections from the defense that the expert testimony was scientifically unsupported theory as well as being irrelevant and inflammatory. The defense drew this standard from the *Frye* case, often applied to expert testimony since it was decided in the 1920s. The Appeals Court pointed out that in its jurisdiction the *Frye* standard had only been applied to criminal cases, and suggested that knowledge of a theory with a "significant following" in the scientific community might be enough to qualify an expert in a civil case. It then concisely noted that the plaintiff had not shown even that lesser standard for his expert's theory that "techniques of thought reform may be effective in the absence of physical threats or coercion" (p. 957), and ordered that this would have to be done at trial (John L. Young and Ezra E. H. Griffith, "A Critical Evaluation of Coercive Persuasion as Used in the Assessment of Cults," *Behavioral Sciences and the Law* 10:1 [1992]:95–96). See also Anthony and Robbins, who note that Margaret Singer and Richard Ofshe's theories of cultic brainwashing, which necessarily assume a hard determinist view of psychology, "run afoul of Frye standard considerations because they do not have general or even substantial acceptance in the relevant scientific communities" (25).

[74]"This theme [debilitation and stress], prominent in the Debility-Dependency-Dread (3D) formulation of Farber *et al.* (1957), and also stressed by Delgado (1977, 1982) is closely related to both defective thinking and hypno-disassociation, as converts are thought to actually become *too debilitated to think straight.* However, in the Communist POW context, physical debilitation was so severe that one-third of the POWs died, yet Schein found that among the survivors the clarity of their thought processes had not been diminished. Singer (1983) testified that serious debilitation and resulting impairment can be produced by a Hindu vegetarian diet and related physical practices" (Anthony and Robbins, 17).

[75]Our sentiments are expressed by others such as Bromley's and Shupe "Witches, Moonies, and Accusations of Evil," Anthony and Robbins, 249.

ordination was implausible given the diverse backgrounds of the groups at issue. Furthermore, the inability of highly trained professionals responsible for implementing a variety of modalities for effecting individual change, ranging from therapy to incarceration, belie claims that such rapid transformation can routinely be accomplished by neophytes against an individual's will.[76]

The abundance of evidence makes it perfectly clear that the first foundation of the cult mind control model, that one becomes a victim of cult recruitment's insidious mind control and hypnosis techniques, is false.

The other foundation of the cult mind control model is that most cult members (who are under mind control) cannot choose to leave of their own free will, but instead must be the focus of a carefully planned and executed professional intervention (exit counseling). The following startling evidence shows that this is also a myth. It is simply not true.

The general public has accepted this myth almost without reservation since the first pronouncements of radical deprogrammers such as Ted Patrick that deprogramming was America's only hope to recover the minds of its youth lost in the morass of the new cults. However, while deprogrammers and later exit counselors promoted their method as the most effective (one deprogramming study fixed recovery rates through deprogramming at 65 percent), a much higher percentage of young people were never inducted into cult membership despite heavy recruitment tactics, and of those who were, converts were leaving their cultic affiliation for a variety of much less compelling reasons than a psychological mind control breakthrough.

In fact, the low rate of recruitment provides ample evidence that even if mind control techniques were used as cult recruiting tools, they didn't work on the vast majority of people, only a few of whom eventually joined the cult.

Steven Hassan even refers to low conversion rates regarding his own involvement with the Unification Church. In his testimony he notes that he was the *first* convert to join at the center in Queens;[77] that during the first three months of his membership he only recruited two more people; [78] and that pressure to recruit new members was only to reach the goal of one new person per member per month,[79] a surprisingly low figure if we are to accept the inevitable success of cult mind control techniques.

Instead, the actual statistics and testimonies are congruent with the idea that cult conversion occurs primarily among young adults who are in an ongoing process of personal exploration and religious experimentation that rarely begins or ends with cult membership, but which might very well involve a relatively short cult association. Researchers who actually interview a large cross-section of potential converts, converts, continuing members, and ex-members agree that cult membership is carefully contemplated and is the result of conscious decision-making:

> Many of these researchers point out that most, if not all, of those who participate in the new religions apparently do so through an exercise of their vo-

[76]Bromley and Shupe, "Public Reaction," 325–326.
[77]Hassan, 20.
[78]Ibid.
[79]Hassan, 24.

lition and that they also usually exercise their volition to leave after a time.[80]

Many have observed that many young people[81] join a cult for a relatively short period of time as part of their growth into adult independence regarding their lifestyles and their religious affiliations, but that once that independence is established to their own satisfaction, they quickly lose their commitment to the cult and gradually return to lifestyles and religious views more like those with which they grew up:

> These several scholars have, explicitly or implicitly, recognized a more ac-tive subject, "working out," or at least actively contributing to, his or her own induction. They have noted that induction into new religions often means a series of affiliative and disaffiliative acts that constitute a conversion career, and that individuals are often only deciding to behave, at least for a time, as a con-vert, playing the convert role as they experiment with ways to affirm their per-sonhood.[82]

The Hare Krishnas provide a good example of the decision-making pro-cesses that actually accompany cult conversion. While ISKCON is exposed by the exit counseling advocates as one of the most successful and powerful mind con-trol cults, careful interviewing of members about their own conversion experi-ences contradicts the mind control view:

> This appraisal [that Hare Krishnas are under mind control] has been chal-lenged by Larry Shinn in his book *The Dark Lord*. Shinn interviewed many Hare Krishnas about their conversion experiences and other aspects of their faith and found that a high percentage claimed they converted to the movement because of the appeal of the philosophical beliefs. His interviews indicated that rather than undergoing sudden conversion experiences, "the far more common pat-tern was for a convert to experience at least a year of occasional and unpres-sured contact with ISKCON, coupled with some significant study of ISKCON's teachings prior to his or her decision to become a devotee and move into a temple." He also discovered that, like the born-again experience of Christians, the enthusiasm of the conversion experience tended to diminish in time.[83]

Not only do cult mind control model proponents grossly overestimate cult conversion rates, they also sadly underestimate the attrition or disaffection rates from cults. The *natural* attrition from cult membership is much higher than the well-publicized 65 percent deprogramming success figure. Statistically, it is much more likely that a new convert *will* leave the cult within the first year of his membership than it is that he will become a hard-core member.

This data, confirming low rates of conversion and high rates of disaffection, is deadly to the cult mind control model. What the data actually shows us is that the bogeyman of cult mind control is nothing but a ghost story, good for in-

[80]James T. Richardson, "The Psychology of Induction: A Review and Interpretation," *Cults and New Religious Movements*, Marc Galanter, ed. (Washington, D.C.: American Psychiatric Association, 1989), 211.
[81]Bromley and Shupe, "Public Reaction" (325–326) point out that cult conversions affect primarily an extremely narrow age band of young adults, something one would not expect if mind control were the devouring power it is claimed to be.
[82]Richardson, 226.
[83]Tucker, 278.

ducing an adrenaline high and maintaining a crusade, but irrelevant to reality.[84] The reality is that people who have very real spiritual, emotional, and social needs are looking for fulfillment and significance for their lives. Ill-equipped to test the false gospels of this world, they make poor decisions about their religious affiliations. Poor decisions, yes, but personally made moral decisions nonetheless.

Eileen Barker documents that the vast majority of people initially interested in cults make no permanent commitment to the cults at all. Out of 1,000 people who attended a resident Moonie program in 1979, 90 percent had no further involvement. Only 8 percent joined for more than one week, and less than 4 percent remained members in 1981, two years later:

> Most people are perfectly capable of rejecting the movements' overtures if they so wish. For example, out of a thousand people who had become sufficiently interested in the Unification Church to attend a residential "Moonie" workshop in the London area in 1979 (when the movement in Britain was at its height and accusations of brainwashing were rife), about 90 percent resisted the members' proselytizing efforts and declined to have any further involvement with the movement. About 8 percent joined as full-time members for more than a week; less than 4 percent were still full-time members two years later—and, with the passage of time, the number of continuing members who joined in 1979 has continued to fall. If the calculation were to start from those who, for one reason or another, had visited one of the movement's centers in 1979, at least 999 out of every 1,000 of those people had, by the mid–1980s, succeeded in resisting the persuasive techniques of the Unification Church.[85]

Another study of new religious movement converts in Montreal replicated Barker's statistics for low conversion rates and high attrition rates. In this survey of more than 1,500 adults, 75 percent dropped out within five years of conversion. Other studies produced even more remarkable figures:

> Bird and Reimer found in their survey of 1,607 adults in Montreal that 75.5 percent of participants in NRMs were no longer participating five years later; the drop-out rate ranged from 55.2 percent for Transcendental Meditation to 100 percent for the Church of Scientology. Rockford found that over half the devotees who had been initiated into ISKCON between 1974 and 1976 had defected within a year, and that there was an even higher attrition rate, starting in 1977, after the death of Prabhupada. In my study of the Unification Church, I found that at least 61 percent of those who joined the movement during a four-month period in 1978 had left within two and a half years. Levine, in his study of over 800 members of NRMs, found that over 90 percent left within two years.[86]

Even exit counselor and ex-Moonie Steven Hassan recognized that he personally was still aware, thinking, and deciding while he was a Moonie:

> In analyzing my own experience, I recognized that what helped me the

---

[84]We are not saying that the cults or new religious movements are harmless. However, the data presented shows that people join, stay in, and leave cults *of their own volition, not because they are mind controlled.* False gospels promote themselves through deceit, persuasion, emotional lures, etc., all of which should be opposed by the clear thinking and biblical argumentation God has given. The spiritual battle against the cults will not be won either by misjudging the nature of the enemy's attack or by using the wrong weapons in our counterattack.

[85]Barker, 18.

[86]Ibid., 105.

most was my own internal voice and my own firsthand experiences, buried beneath all of the thought-stopping rituals of chanting and praying and all the emotional repression. Underneath, the real me wasn't dead.[87]

High attrition rates argue directly against the cult mind control model and each new statistical study confirms that cult members certainly do think for themselves and make radical decisions, even deciding to leave their cults:

> More recently, in the study of new religions an explicit focus on leaving new religions has developed. This area of study has developed as researchers recognized that only a small minority of those who join such groups actually stay for lengthy periods of time. The act of leaving (disaffection, deconversion, or disaffiliation) has, by its very nature, led to greater recognition of the volitional nature of such actions. Thus this area of study contributed its own impetus to the emergence of an alternative paradigm in conversion and recruitment research as more and more research focused on the high turnover rates in newer religions.[88]

Finally, the exit counseling approach is self-refuting. Think about this carefully: If a cultist is under mind control *and cannot think for himself or make his own decisions*, how can the exit counselor's techniques of *rational discourse* and *cognitive challenge* possibly affect the cultist? A cultist who *cannot* think is, in one sense, no different than any other non-thinking thing. *Discussion* cannot motivate *change*. Believing that rational discourse with a non-thinking cultist can be a catalyst for change to a thinking being is as nonsensical as believing that if one conducts the right sort of rational discourse with his computer he will be able to change it into a thinking being. If cultists *don't think*, then *thinking* can't be the key to mental liberation. (In some ways, forcible deprogramming and its concurrent emotional duress makes more *logical* sense within the mind control framework than does the noncoercive exit counseling.)

Exit counseling proponents focus so intently on exit counseling as virtually the only hope for rescuing cult members that observers might reasonably conclude that one can leave a cult only through abrupt, drastic intervention—that is, through exit counseling. The statistical evidence already presented refutes that conclusion, and the evidence should also inspire a search for the true reasons behind continued cult loyalty as well as cult disaffection. The indisputable evidence that the vast majority of people leave NRMs voluntarily suggests that we have to look beyond the movements' evangelizing processes if we want to understand why a particular person does *not* leave.[89]

Statistics bear out that most people who leave cults follow the pattern of any kind of emotional conversion experience. Once the emotional "high" disappears, a great deal of the attraction to the religious movement disappears, and continuing commitment tends to disappear over time. This is true of many "conversions" in Christian churches as well:

> As with the prisoners who are persuaded by brainwashing, the number of people who respond to preaching tends to be relatively small. Even those who report a conversion sometimes turn away from their newfound faith unless they

[87]Hassan, 33.
[88]Richardson, 225–226.
[89]Barker, 138.

are given considerable support and encouragement by other believers.[90]

It is not true that many people leave cults because of serious ongoing emotional troubles that preclude their continued high intensity involvement or that encourage quicker and more direct intervention by family members (such as in exit counseling). Actually, careful interviewing affirms that serious ongoing emotional debilitation *does not* characterize one who leaves a cult:

> Frans Derks carried out a study of thirty-one ex-members of a number of different movements in the Netherlands. Over 80 percent (twenty-five persons) had left voluntarily, three had been deprogrammed, two had been expelled and one had been both expelled and deprogrammed. Derks found that half his sample reported having had no psycho-social problems after leaving. About half the rest of the sample reported having had some such problems only in the period immediately following defection, but these problems had gone by the time of interview (on average, three and a half years after defection). Of the remaining eight, who reported still having had problems at the time of the interview, five also reported having had these problems before they had converted. Although the numbers were too small to make reliable generalizations, the study suggests that around half those who leave an NRM may have some psycho-social problems (they may be "rather emotional") just after they have left the movement, but the chances of their getting over this within a relatively short time are high, unless they have had such problems before they had ever joined the movement.[91]

Researchers and interviewers have discovered that people who deliberately decide to abandon their cult commitment do so as a result of thinking, evaluating, and considering the pros and cons not only of continuing membership but also of reentry into the outside world. These members are not under mind control, but instead are attempting to make wise lifestyle and religious commitment choices:

> Whatever their reasons for leaving, members who departed voluntarily prepared for this task in deliberating over their choice; they felt the decision was essentially their own. In contrast to those abducted and forced out of the group, they thought through their own rationales for leaving and somehow reconciled them with a remaining affection for the group. For those who were deprogrammed, however, the experience was quite different.[92]

This statement hints at how well-intentioned cult mind control/exit counseling advocates may have developed their faulty paradigms: If they inform the cultists they counsel that they have been victims of mind control in need of rescue, it is no surprise that the ex-cultists might then affirm that they were, in fact, under mind control and in need of rescue *simply because they have been told so by "experts" and "professionals."* This is confirmed by Barker, who also notes the lack of any corroborating evidence for this circular "endorsement" of the cult mind control model:

> A small number of movements practice techniques that may adversely affect the reasoning powers of those involved . . . but, even in such movements, people

---

[90]Collins, 149.
[91]Barker, 126.
[92]Marc Galanter, *Cults: Faith, Healing, and Coercion* (New York: Oxford University Press, 1989), 166.

can and do leave of their own accord. There are those, such as deprogrammers with a financial interest in propagating the brainwashing thesis, who continue to ignore or dismiss such statistics, but they do so without providing any contrary evidence beyond the testimonies of a small number of ex-members, several of whom will have been *taught*, while undergoing forcible deprogramming, that they were brainwashed.[93]

The self-endorsing nature of the cult mind control model apart from corroborative evidence is confirmed in the attitudes of ex-members toward their former cults and former cult friends. Ex-cultists who leave on their own retain a much more positive attitude toward their experiences than do those who have been "deprogrammed":

> Differences in perceptions of the church rested in large part on the way members had left the group: those who had been coerced expressed a much more negative view toward the church. . . .
> The deprogrammed former members showed a greater alienation from the church, scoring lower on loyalty toward the members they knew best and on their relative acceptance of church creed. Significantly, all eight respondents who later participated in deprogramming other church members had themselves been deprogrammed. Thus the process did have a lasting effect in sustaining animosity toward the sect.[94]

Frequently exit counselors fail to distinguish between their *therapeutic* roles and their *evidentiary* or *research* roles. The therapeutic role is by nature subjective, emotionally sympathetic, and non-evidentiary. However, for the opinion of the exit counselor to have any validity as an accurate assessment of cult dynamics, the exit counselor must apply rigorous standards of objective scientific testing. This, however, is as sadly lacking among exit counselors as it is among other therapists.[95]

This is borne out time and again by exit counseling advocates who make dogmatic statements about the destructive powers of cult mind control and the healing power of exit counseling without any substantiating evidence, and who continue to promote their model when the contrary statistical evidence is produced. Instead, the exit counseling advocate overlooks his or her own presuppositions and reinterprets any contrary evidence:

> Negative stereotyping and personal biases can cause one to misconstrue contrary evidence as consistent with the cult stereotype as well as to explain how the same cult behavior can be interpreted in diametrically opposed ways.[96]

The remedy for myopic self-delusion is good research technique, something all countercult workers should practice, as Kilbourne encourages,

> In relation to the diagnosis of new religious adherents who come to the attention of the clinician, Kilbourne has specifically recommended the use of objective and standardized testing procedures in conjunction with a case history. Clinicians should make every effort to obtain multiple sources of information (e.g., family, friends, work associates, professional colleagues, and other

---

[93]Barker, 19.
[94]Galanter, 175.
[95]Kilbourne, 138–139.
[96]Ibid., 139.

new religious adherents) in determining a diagnosis of a new religious adherent. They should, moreover, self-consciously seek out evidence at variance with their preconceived ideas and value biases. Seeking consultation from a professional colleague with a different perspective should be actively encouraged.[97]

Those who hold the exit counseling perspective and who attempt to interview ex-cultists usually start with those with whom they are most familiar, e.g., those ex-cultists they have exit counseled out of the cults. However, that group of ex-cultists is an extremely narrow, specialized subgroup of ex-members and it is irresponsible to extrapolate from this narrow group to the entire body of cultists.[98]

One might think that only inexperienced or unprofessional exit counseling proponents would make such an egregious mistake in research, but even the best professionals, such as University of California psychologist Margaret Singer, have extrapolated general observations about cult membership from a very narrow, biased group:

> One prominent therapist [Margaret Singer] who writes on the new religions admits that 75 percent of the clients she interviewed have been the subject of legal conservatorships, and another well-known team of writers [F. Conway and J. Siegelman], in a recent article that claimed to explain effects of life in the groups, admitted that 71 percent had been deprogrammed. Such work is plainly not research on life within new religions, and the limitations of such work should be recognized. This is especially true in light of Solomon's work and Wright's research, which indicates that one major effect of deprogramming is to convince ex-members that they were originally brainwashed by the new religion.[99]

Evangelicals are not immune and even sometimes seem hard pressed to denounce the earlier radical physical intervention of deprogramming because of a passionate belief in the insidious mind control of the cults:

> Those who have approached the procedure [of exit counseling] from a Christian perspective, however, are often more misguided in their efforts than criminal. Ronald Enroth, who himself opposes deprogramming, concedes that sometimes he feels as though he almost has "to come to the defense of the deprogrammers because of the inflammatory rhetoric of anti-anticultists."[100]

Some exit counselors, such as Steven Hassan, may attempt to justify their paradigms even though there is *no* substantive evidence that mind control is either used or effective for cult recruitment. They assume that all people are determined products of their genetics and environment, that personality is the deterministic substance of one's biological composition and life experiences.[101] However, such a determinism actually robs all people, cult leaders as well as cultists, of personal responsibility or morality. After all, as much as the cultist is

---

[97]Kilbourne, 141.
[98]Richardson, 230.
[99]Ibid., 231.
[100]Tucker, 27.
[101]Hassan, 7 and 54. Remember, at issue here is whether or not cult converts *make their own moral choices*, not whether or not these choices are good or bad, well-reasoned or illogical, well-informed or ignorant, from truth or deceit.

"wired" to succumb to cult mind control, cult leaders are "wired" to practice cult mind control. One cannot remove human responsibility without also destroying human morality:

> Some social scientists object to the idea that humans are free to choose. They claim that man is nothing but the result of biological, psychological, and sociological conditions, or the product of heredity and environment. Thus, B. F. Skinner holds that autonomous man is a myth. All of man's so-called "decisions" are actually determined by previous experience. Even some Christians believe that all of men's actions are determined by God, and that they have no free choice.
>
> Such a view of man must be met head-on. If free choice is a myth, so is moral obligation. C. S. Lewis notes that a deterministic view brings about the abolition of man. In an impassioned plea he argues that you cannot strip men of autonomy without denuding them of responsibility: "In a sort of ghastly simplicity we remove the organ and expect of them virtue and enterprise. We laugh at honor and are shocked to find traitors in our midst. We castrate and bid the geldings be fruitful."[102]

The stroke that removes the personal autonomy of the cultist unfortunately also absolves the cult leader. By contrast, those who reject the mind control model affirm the ability and responsibility for personal decision-making regarding cultic involvement:

> One of the main assumptions of this book is that, almost always, people *can* make decisions for themselves. Even when the influence of others may seem well nigh overpowering, individuals can and do continue to resist such influence. Rather than telling members of NRMs that they have been brainwashed and that they must, therefore, submit to a "deprogramming," it is almost certain to be more honest and more constructive to encourage converts actively to examine what they are doing. The underlying *challenge* to be conveyed to the convert is, in other words, that while others care and want to help, it is he or she who must accept the ultimate responsibility for his or her own life.[103]

Psychologist and exit counselor Paul Martin, who is also an evangelical Christian, illustrates in his cult recovery retreat center newsletter how ex-cultists are taught that they have been mind controlled:

> Finally, we offer workshops on the dynamics and techniques of psychological coercion, indoctrination, and persuasion to help the client see that the process whereby he or she was drawn into the cult was a subtle but powerful force over which he or she had little or no control and therefore they need not feel either guilt or shame because of their experience.[104]

Over and over again, exit counseling defenders perpetuate the unsubstantiated myths of cult mind control and exit counseling. Evidence doesn't matter. Logic doesn't matter. Theological presuppositions of individual human moral responsibility don't matter. The paradigm must be preserved at all costs, and anyone who dares to disagree is immediately suspected of (at best) being a dupe of the cults or (at worst) a secret agent of the cults.

---

[102]Em Griffin, *The Mind Changers* (Wheaton, Ill.: Tyndale House, 1976), 29–30.
[103]Barker, 120.
[104]Paul Martin, "Wellspring's Approach to Cult Rehab," *Wellspring Messenger* 4:5 (Nov./Dec. 1993): 1.

Carefully and comprehensively we have defined, examined, and critiqued the cult mind control/exit counseling model. Its origins are in faulty assumptions about the nature and effectiveness of cult conversion tactics, the nature and effectiveness of "mind control," and the nature and effectiveness of exit counseling. We have identified many of the fatal flaws of this approach to the cults.[105]

Many times, in our ministry in cult apologetics, we have been approached by parents who are desperate to recover their adult children who have seemingly abandoned family, reason, and faith for irrational religious fanaticism. While we can encourage the families that the statistics are overwhelmingly encouraging that their sons and daughters' cult affiliation will probably not be permanent, as Christians we cannot stand idly by and wait for natural attrition to set in. We have an obligation before the Lord Jesus Christ to give parents truth from God's Word to help them in sharing the liberating power of the gospel with their children.

People join cults for a variety of reasons, but not because they are under mind control. They join because they are lonely, they want to serve God, they want religious meaning in their lives, they need to be needed, they want to affirm their individual and unique personhood, they want the security of being in God's will, they want to avoid the hypocrisy and sinfulness of the world.

The cults are always ready, holding out answers to those needs. The cults will give recruits friends, set them to work for God, provide them with religious activities, encourage them that their service is a vital part of God's plan, applaud their independence from their parents and the world, assure them of God's control through the organization, and shield them from the enticements of the world.

But every single thing offered by the cults is fake. If members step out of line, their friends abandon them; they can't keep up the grueling work pace, and they're made to feel guilty for letting God down; faith becomes mere ritual; acceptance is conditional; independence is rejected; God's will is as elusive as a dream; and deep inside, behind the happy smiles and busy hands, everyone knows the secret thoughts of fear, rebellion, and shame.

The cults *cannot* meet people's needs because they are missing the only true source of personal redemption and reconciliation: the Lord Jesus Christ.

> Come unto me, all ye that labour and are heavy laden, and I will give you rest. Take my yoke upon you, and learn of me; for I am meek and lowly in heart: and ye shall find rest unto your souls. For my yoke is easy, and my burden is light (Matthew 11:28–30).
>
> I am the door of the sheep. All that ever came before me are thieves and robbers: but the sheep did not hear them. . . . By me if any man enter in, he shall be saved, and shall go in and out, and find pasture. The thief cometh not, but for to steal, and to kill, and to destroy: I am come that they might have life, and that they might have it more abundantly (John 10:7–10).

Cult mind control is a fantasy. Exit counseling seeks to overcome what doesn't exist, and stops short of proclaiming the true freedom and fulfillment available only in Jesus Christ. The cults lie, deceive, and emotionally tantalize,

---

[105]Bromley and Shupe, "Public Reaction," 325–326.

but people can be protected from their lure:

(1) Know God's Word (1 Timothy 2:15).
(2) Become a part of a biblical, supportive, mature church (Philippians 2:1–4).
(3) Learn to ask questions, think logically, and "test all things" (1 Thessalonians 5:21–22).
(4) Combat false belief with biblical truth (2 Timothy 2:4–16).
(5) Protection comes with truth, righteousness, the gospel, faith, and salvation (Ephesians 6:10–18).

Cultists can escape from the false gospels of the cults. Christians who are used by God to reach those in the cults share many things in common:

(1) A sacrificing love for the cultist (1 Corinthians 13:5–7).
(2) A life of commitment and discipleship (Ephesians 5:1–7).
(3) Knowledge concerning not only the cult but, more importantly, the true God (2 Timothy 2:24–26).
(4) Confidence in the all-fulfilling power of the gospel (Romans 1:16).
(5) Commitment to prayer for the cultist's salvation (James 5:13–16; cf. Romans 10:1).

No matter how powerful cult recruitment and discipline may seem, the power of God is immeasurable: "If one of you should wander from the truth and someone should bring him back, remember this: Whoever turns a sinner from the error of his way will save him from death and cover over a multitude of sins" (James 5:19–20).

Chapter 5

Jehovah's Witnesses and the Watchtower Bible and Tract Society

A Brief History

Charles Taze Russell was the founder of what is now known as the Jehovah's Witnesses cult and the energetic administrator that brought about its far-flung organization. The name Jehovah's Witnesses, incidentally, was taken at Columbus, Ohio, in 1931, to differentiate between the Watchtower organization run by Judge Rutherford, Russell's successor, and those who remained as true followers of Russell as represented by The Dawn Bible Students and the Laymen's Home Missionary Movement.

C. T. Russell was born on February 16, 1852, the son of Joseph L. and Anna Eliza Russell, and spent most of his early years in Pittsburgh and Allegheny, Pennsylvania, where at the age of twenty-five he was known to be manager of several men's furnishings stores. At an early age he rejected the doctrine of eternal torment, probably because of the severe indoctrination he had received as a Congregationalist, and as a result of this act entered upon a long and varied career of denunciation aimed at "Organized Religions." In 1870, at the age of eighteen, Russell organized a Bible class in Pittsburgh, which in 1876 elected him "Pastor" of the group. From 1876 to 1878 the "Pastor" was assistant editor of a small Rochester, New York, monthly magazine, but he resigned when a controversy arose over Russell's counterarguments on "the atonement" of Christ.

Shortly after leaving his position, Russell founded *The Herald of the Morning* (1879), which developed into today's *The Watchtower Announcing Jehovah's Kingdom*. From 6,000 initial issues, the publication has grown to 17.8 million copies per month in 106 languages. The other Watchtower periodical, *Awake!*, has a circulation of 15.6 million per month in thirty-four languages. It is true that this magazine has grown until it has surpassed even Russell's fondest dreams. In the year 1884, "Pastor" Russell incorporated "Zion's Watch Tower Tract Society" at Pittsburgh, Pennsylvania, which in 1886 published the first in a series of seven

---

This chapter updated, revised, and edited by Gretchen Passantino.

books (Russell wrote six by himself), now entitled *Studies in the Scriptures* and originally published as *The Millennial Dawn*. The seventh volume was edited from his writings after his death and published in 1917. This seventh volume, *The Finished Mystery*, caused a split in the organization, which culminated in a clean division, the larger group following J. F. Rutherford, the smaller remaining by itself. This smaller group subsequently became "The Dawn Bible Students Association." Meanwhile, under Rutherford's leadership, the "Society" became known by its present common name, "Jehovah's Witnesses," and its corporate name, The Watchtower Bible and Tract Society, with its international office in Brooklyn, New York.

According to Watchtower statistics, in January 1981, the Watchtower Bible and Tract Society (founded 1896), which is the focal point of the organization, had known branches in more than 100 lands and missionary works and Kingdom preaching in over 250. Its literature is distributed in 110 languages, and the Society's volunteers (called "publishers") numbered 563,453. The Society has become a great disseminator of propaganda and a challenge to the zeal of every Christian.

In the year 1908 the headquarters of the movement was transferred to Brooklyn, New York, where property was purchased (17 Hicks Street) and became known as "The Brooklyn Tabernacle." Large tracts of property were purchased by the Society in Columbia Heights as it grew and prospered, until today whole blocks are in their possession. Among the other things the Society owns are a large, up-to-date printing plant, which has produced billions of pieces of literature since its inauguration in 1928 and expansions in 1949 and 1957; a modern apartment building and office quarters; one "Kingdom Farm," which supplies food, wood for furniture, etc.; a Bible school, "Gilead"; and many more enterprises of like character. All employees in the factory are allowed a nominal sum, receive room and board, and work for nothing—no salaries are paid (although workers are given a small amount of spending money each month for incidental personal expenses and purchases—a few years ago that amount was fourteen dollars per month).

Russell continued his teachings until his death on October 31, 1916, aboard a transcontinental train in Texas. The former pastor had a remarkable life, highly colored with legal entanglements, but not without success in his chosen field. In fairness to the reader and in the interest of truth, the full account is quoted from *The Brooklyn Daily Eagle*, November 1, 1916 (Obituary Column), and has been inserted at this point to authenticate beyond doubt the true history of Russell so that even his most devoted followers may realize the character of the man to whose teachings they have entrusted their eternal destiny.

> A year after this publication, *The Watch Tower*, had been established, Russell married Maria Ackley in Pittsburgh. She had become interested in him through his teachings, and she helped him in running the Watchtower.
> Two years later, in 1881, came "The Watch Tower Bible and Tract Society," the agency through which in later years "Pastor" Russell's sermons were published (as advertisements) in newspapers throughout the world. This Society progressed amazingly under the joint administration of husband and wife, but in 1897 Mrs. Russell left her husband. Six years later, in 1903, she sued for separation. The decree was secured in 1906 following sensational testimony and

"Pastor" Russell was scored by the courts.

There was much litigation then that was quite undesirable from the "Pastor's" point of view regarding alimony for his wife, but it was settled in 1909 by the payment of $6,036 to Mrs. Russell. The litigation revealed that "Pastor" Russell's activities in the religious field were carried on through several subsidiary societies and that all of the wealth that flowed into him through these societies was under the control of a holding company in which the "Pastor" held $990 of the $1,000 capital and two of his followers the other $10.

Thus Russell apparently controlled the entire financial power of the Society and was not accountable to anyone.

The *Eagle* column goes on to say:

After the "work" had been well started here, "Pastor" Russell's Watch Tower publication advertised wheat seed for sale at $1.00 a pound. It was styled "Miracle Wheat," and it was asserted that it would grow five times as much as any other brand of wheat. There were other claims made for the wheat seed, and the followers were advised to purchase it, the proceeds to go to the Watch Tower and be used in publishing the "Pastor's" sermons.

The *Eagle* first made public the facts about this new venture of the Russellites and it published a cartoon picturing the "Pastor" and his "Miracle Wheat" in such a way that "Pastor" Russell brought suit for libel, asking $100,000 damages. Government departments investigated the wheat for which $1.00 a pound was asked, and agents of the Government were important witnesses at the trial of the libel suit in January 1913. The "Miracle Wheat" was low in the Government tests, they said. The *Eagle* won the suit.

Prior to entering court the *Eagle* had said,

The *Eagle* goes even further and declares that at the trial it will show that "Pastor" Russell's religious cult is nothing more than a money-making scheme.

The court's decision vindicated the Eagle's statement and proved its reliability.

All during this time the "Pastor's" sermons were being printed in newspapers throughout the world, notably when he made a tour of the world in 1912 and caused accounts to be published in his advertised sermons telling of enthusiastic greetings at the various places he visited. It was shown in many cases that the sermons were never delivered in the places that were claimed.

For the benefit of any Jehovah's Witness who may think that the "Miracle Wheat" fraud is an invention of the "jealous religionists" who are trying to defame the "Pastor's" memory, we document the scandal, trial, and verdict as follows:

From originals (now microfilmed in New York) of *The Brooklyn Daily Eagle*, the following articles with dates and pages: Miracle Wheat Scandal, January 1, 1913, 1–2; Russellite Beliefs, January 22, 1913, 2; Testimony on Wheat, January 23, 1913, 3; Financial statements proving Russell's absolute control, by Secretary-Treasurer Van Amberg, January 25, 1913, 16; Government experts testify on "Miracle Wheat" and ascertain its ordinariness, January 27, 1913, 3; Prosecution and Defense closing arguments, January 28, 1913, 2; Russell loses libel suit, January 29, 1913, 16.

The Watchtower Society has maintained that Russell never made money on

the "Miracle Wheat," and that proceeds from its sale were "contributions" to the organization. They fail to note that Russell controlled the Watchtower Society, owning 990 of the 1,000 shares of its stock. Any contributions to it were also to Russell!

The *Brooklyn Daily Eagle* led the fight to expose the hypocrisy of "Pastor" Russell, and nothing could be more appropriate than their on-the-spot testimony as to his many fraudulent claims. The following documentary evidence is taken from *The Brooklyn Daily Eagle*, February 19, 1912, page 18, and is titled "Pastor Russell's Imaginary Sermons—Printed Reports of Addresses in Foreign Lands That He Never Made—One at Hawaii, a Sample." These excerpts concern the Pastor's "World Tour" and are very enlightening with respect to his reliability and truthfulness.

> "Pastor" Russell, who has found the atmosphere of Brooklyn uncongenial ever since the *Eagle* published the facts concerning his methods and morals, is making some new records in the far parts of the world. He is delivering sermons to imaginary audiences on tropical islands and completing "searching investigations" into the missions of China and Japan by spending a few hours in each country.
>
> Following the *Eagle's* exposure of "Pastor" Russell's "Miracle Wheat" enterprise and its publication of the testimony on the basis of which Mrs. Russell obtained a separation and alimony, the "Pastor" developed the "world tour" idea. He set his printing plant to work to get out advance literature, huge bundles of which were sent to every place where he intended to appear. Then he contracted for advertising space in many American newspapers to print his never-delivered sermons.
>
> His first stop after sailing from the Pacific Coast was Honolulu. And presto!—the newspapers in which advertising space had been engaged printed long cable dispatches that presented the "Pastor's" discourses. In one paper that printed the advertisement the opening sentences read, "Honolulu, Hawaiian Islands: The International Bible Students Committee of Foreign Mission investigation stopped at Honolulu and made observations. Pastor Russell, Chairman of the committee, delivered a public address. He had a large audience and attentive hearing."
>
> Then follows the sermon, full of local color and allusions to the "Paradise of the Pacific": "I can now well understand [the printed report makes the 'pastor' say] why your beautiful island is 'The Paradise of the Pacific.' I note your wonderful climate and everything which contributes to bring about this Paradise likeness."
>
> And so on for two columns.
>
> It has long been known that "Pastor" Russell has a strong imagination, but now it appears that he is even capable of delivering imaginary sermons. *Pastor Russell never spoke in Honolulu during the few hours that his ship stopped there to take on coal.* In the hope of securing an accurate report of his sermon, the *Eagle* wrote to the editor of the *Hawaiian Star*, which is published in Honolulu.
>
> The following reply was shortly thereafter received:
>
> In answer to your inquiry of December 19, concerning Pastor Russell, I would say that he was here for a few hours with a Bible students' committee of foreign mission investigation, but did not make a public address as was anticipated. —Walter G. Smith, Editor, *Star*.

That this was an isolated occurrence is refuted in other documentation. The following evidence is taken from *The Brooklyn Daily Eagle*, January 11, 1913:

Tour of Orient Branded Huge Advertising Scheme

As to the "Pastor's" methods of carrying Russellism to the heathen and the speed with which his searching investigations into the missions of the world are being conducted, the *Japan Weekly Chronicle* of January 11 supplies some interesting information. After explaining how the office of the paper had for weeks been bombarded with Russell literature and advance agents with contracts "just as if the Reverend gentleman were an unregenerated theatrical company," the *Chronicle* says:

"These gentlemen arrived in Japan on Saturday the 30th December. On the following day 'Pastor' Russell delivered a sermon in Tokyo entitled: 'Where Are the Dead?' which, though the title is a little ambiguous, does not seem to have any special connection with the mission work. On Monday it is assumed that the mission work in Japan was begun and finished, for the next day seems to have been devoted to traveling, and on Wednesday 'Pastor' Russell and his coadjutors left Kobe for China in the same vessel in which they had arrived in Yokohama. . . . The truth is that the whole expedition is merely a huge advertising scheme!"

Russell carried on many such advertising stunts, and despite his protestations about earthly governments and laws being organizations of the devil, he was always the first to claim their protection when it was convenient for him to do so.

To mention one instance in addition to the *Eagle* suit, Russell brought suit for "defamatory libel" against the Reverend J. J. Ross, pastor of the James Street Baptist Church of Hamilton, Ontario, when the fearless minister wrote a blistering pamphlet denouncing Russell's theology and personal life. Russell lost this attempt (see *The Brooklyn Daily Eagle*, January 11, 1913), with J. F. Rutherford as his attorney. For the benefit of the interested reader, at this time we recount the facts concerning the libel suit as it actually occurred.

In June, 1912, the Reverend J. J. Ross, pastor of the James Street Baptist Church, Hamilton, Ontario, published a pamphlet entitled "Some Facts About the Self-Styled 'Pastor' Charles T. Russell," which minced no words in its denunciation of Russell, his qualifications as a minister, or his moral example as a "pastor." Russell promptly sued Ross for "defamatory libel" in an effort to silence the courageous minister before the pamphlet could gain wide circulation and expose his true character and the errors of his theology. Rev. Ross, however, was unimpressed by Russell's action and eagerly seized upon the opportunity as a means of exposing Russell for the fraud he was. In his pamphlet, Ross assailed Russell's teachings as revealed in *Studies in the Scriptures* as "the destructive doctrines of one man who is neither a scholar nor a theologian" (7). Rev. Ross scathingly denounced Russell's whole system as "anti-rational, anti-scientific, anti-biblical, anti-Christian, and a deplorable perversion of the gospel of God's dear Son" (7).

Continuing his charges in the pamphlet, Ross exposed Russell as a pseudo-scholar and philosopher who "never attended the higher schools of learning, knows comparatively nothing of philosophy, systematic or historical theology, and is totally ignorant of the dead languages" (3–4). It must be clearly understood at this point by the reader that in a libel suit of the type pursued by Russell, the plaintiff (Russell) had to *prove* that the charges lodged against him by the defendant (Ross) were not true. It is significant to note that Russell lost his suit

against Ross when the High Court of Ontario, in session March, 1913, ruled that there were no grounds for libel; and "the case was thrown out of Court by the evidence furnished by 'Pastor' Russell himself" (15).[1]

"Pastor" Russell refused to give any evidence to substantiate his "case," and the only evidence offered was Russell's own statements, made under oath and during cross-examination by Ross's lawyer, Counselor Staunton. By denying Ross's charges, Russell automatically claimed high scholastic ascendancy, recognized theological training (systematic and historical), working knowledge of the dead languages (Greek, Hebrew, etc.), and valid ordination by a recognized body.[2] To each part of Mr. Ross's pamphlet (and all was read) Russell entered vigorous denials, with the exception of the "Miracle Wheat Scandal," which he affirmed as having "a grain of truth in a sense" to it.[3] "Pastor" Russell had at last made a serious mistake. He had testified under oath before Almighty God, and had sworn to tell "the truth, the whole truth, and nothing but the truth." He was soon to regret his testimony and stand in jeopardy as a perjurer, an unpleasant experience for the "pastor," which more than explains his aversion to the witness chair.

Jehovah's Witnesses cannot deny this documentary evidence; it is too well substantiated. This is no "religionist scheme" to "smear" the "pastor's" memory; I offer it as open proof of their founder's inherent dishonesty and lack of morals, that they may see the type of man to whose doctrines they have committed their eternal souls.

The following reference quotations are taken in part from Mr. Ross's second pamphlet entitled *Some Facts and More Facts About the Self-Styled Pastor—Charles T. Russell:*

> But now what are the facts as they were brought out by the examination on March 17, 1913? As to his scholastic standing he (Russell) had sworn that what was said about it was not true. Under the examination, he admitted that at most he had attended school only seven years of his life at the public school, and that he had left school when he was about fourteen years of age. . . .

The cross-examination of Russell continued for five hours. Here is a sample of how the "pastor" answered. (The following reproduction of the *Russell v. Ross* transcript relative to the perjury charge made against Russell is taken from a copy on file in the headquarters of the cult in Brooklyn and is presented in the interests of thorough investigation.)

> *Question (Attorney Staunton):* "Do you know the Greek alphabet?"
> *Answer (Russell):* "Oh yes."
> *Question (Staunton):* "Can you tell me the correct letters if you see them?"
> *Answer (Russell):* "Some of them; I might make a mistake on some of them."
> *Question (Staunton):* "Would you tell me the names of those on top of the page, page 447, I have got here?"
> *Answer (Russell):* "Well, I don't know that I would be able to."
> *Question (Staunton):* "You can't tell what those letters are? Look at them and see if you know."

[1] *Some Facts and More Facts About the Self-Styled Pastor—Charles T. Russell,* Mr. Ross's second pamphlet.
[2] Ibid., 18.
[3] Ibid., 17.

Answer (Russell): "My way . . ." [he was interrupted at this point and not allowed to explain].
Question (Staunton): "Are you familiar with the Greek language?"
Answer (Russell): "No."

It should be noted from this record of the testimony that Russell frequently contradicted himself, claiming first to know the Greek alphabet, then claiming under pressure that he might make mistakes in identifying the letters, and then finally admitting that he couldn't read the alphabet at all when confronted with a copy of it.

From this it is easy to see that Russell did not "know" the Greek alphabet in any proper sense of the term, since it is assumed that when we say we "know" the English alphabet, for example, we shall be able upon request to name the letters by their correct titles.

"Pastor" Russell, in failing to name the letters of the Greek alphabet, therefore, proved himself a perjurer, for he had previously stated that he "knew" them, thereby implying the ability to recite them, which he could *not* do.

It makes very little difference, therefore, whether the Watchtower wants to admit Russell's guilt or not since their own transcript shows that Russell said he "knew" what was later proved he did not know.

Here is conclusive evidence; the "pastor" under oath perjured himself beyond question. Can one sincerely trust the teachings of a man who thought nothing of such evidence?

This, however, was not all of Russell's testimony, and as Counselor Staunton pressed him further the "pastor" admitted that he knew *nothing* about Latin and Hebrew, and that he had never taken a course in philosophy or systematic theology, much less attended schools of higher learning. Bear in mind now that Russell a short time before had sworn he *did* have such knowledge by denying Mr. Ross's allegations. But there was no way out now; the "pastor" was caught in a bold-faced fabrication and he knew it. However, all was not over yet. It will be remembered that Russell claimed "ordination" and equal if not superior status to ordained and accredited ministers, who at that time were almost all graduates of at least Bible college if not a graduate program in a seminary. Counselor Staunton next smashed this illusion by demanding that Russell answer "Yes" or "No" to the following questions:

Question (Staunton): "Is it true you were never ordained?"
Answer (Russell): "It is not true."

It was necessary at this point for Counselor Staunton to appeal to the magistrate in order to make Russell answer the question directly. The magistrate presiding ruled that Russell must answer the questions put to him. Here is the result of the cross-examination.

Question (Staunton): "Now, you never were ordained by a bishop, clergyman, presbytery, council, or any body of men living?"
Answer (Russell, after a long pause): "I never was."

Once again Russell's "unswerving" honesty received a rude blow; the situation was out of his hands and Russell stood helpless as Counselor Staunton wrung statement after statement from him, which established him beyond doubt

as a premeditated perjurer. Russell further swore that his wife had not divorced him, and that the Court had not granted alimony from him, a statement he soon regretted when Counselor Staunton forced him to admit that the Court did divorce[4] him from his wife, and did award his wife alimony. The evidence was in; the case was clear. Russell was branded a perjurer by the Court's verdict "No Bill." As a result of the Court's action, Ross's charges were proven true and the real character of Russell was revealed, that of a man who had no scruples about lying under oath and whose doctrines were admittedly based on no sound educational knowledge of the subject in question. Much evidence is available concerning Russell's moral life, but I see no reason to inject lewdness into the text. The character of the man is evident for all to see.

Though most Witnesses today have little awareness of their founder or his dubious past, those who are confronted with this evidence generally respond in one of two ways. Either they protest that the organization today should not be judged by any alleged inadequacies of its founder, or they charge the critic with overstating the case and making much more harsh judgments against Russell than the evidence warrants. None, however, is able to dispute the facts as they are reproduced here. Remember, this testimony is presented only as it was preserved *in Watchtower holdings.* The Watchtower is well aware of the facts. A typical Jehovah's Witness response is that Russell was never charged nor convicted of perjury, which is true. However, that Russell *committed* perjury, or lied under oath, whether ever charged, tried, or convicted of it, is obvious to anyone who reads the evidence.

The easily offended "pastor" might have practiced what he preached for once and heeded Christ's injunction concerning the patient enduring of "reviling and persecution" (Matthew 5:11–12), but in Russell's case it is not at all applicable. Russell took every opportunity to make money, and legal clashes were frequent as a result. He maneuvered masterfully just one jump ahead of the law, and had it not been for Rutherford, who was a clever lawyer, the "pastor" might not have been so fortunate. Russell hid, whenever cornered, behind the veil of a martyr for religious toleration, and despite the denunciation of churches and ministers, he somehow succeeded in escaping the effects of damaging publicity. The Christian church fought him openly but without the unified effort needed to squelch his bold approach. Some churches and pastors were united (see *The Brooklyn Daily Eagle,* January 2, 1913, page 18) and called for Russell's silencing as a menace. The "pastor" was also deported from Canada because he hindered mobilization (see *The Daily Standard Union,* November 1, 1916), and in the early stages of World War I he was a prominent conscientious objector, as all of his followers (Jehovah's Witnesses) still are today.

As a speaker, Russell swayed many; as a theologian, he impressed no one competent; as a man, he failed before the true God. Russell traveled extensively, spoke incessantly, and campaigned with much energy for "a great awakening" among the people of the world. In the course of his writings and lectures Russell denied many of the cardinal doctrines of the Bible—the Trinity, the deity of Christ, the physical resurrection and return of Christ, eternal punishment, the reality of hell, the eternal existence of the soul, and the validity of the infinite

---

[4]Neither party, however, obtained an absolute decree.

atonement, to state a few. The honest fact is that Russell had no training or education to justify his interpretation of Scripture. By this it is not meant that great education is a necessary qualification for exegesis, but when a man contradicts practically every major doctrine of the Bible he ought to have the education needed to defend (if that is possible) his arguments. "Pastor" Russell did not have that knowledge, or even the qualifications for ordination by any recognized body. The title "pastor" was assumed—not earned—and to document this fact we quote from the November 1, 1916, edition of *The Brooklyn Daily Eagle:*

> Although he styled himself a "pastor" and was so addressed by thousands of followers all over the world, he had never been ordained and had no ministerial standing in any other religious sect than his own.

Psychologically, the man was an egotist whose imagination knew no bounds and who is classed (by his followers) along with the apostle Paul, Wycliffe, and Luther as a great expositor of the gospel. These are trite words for a man who proffered his writings as necessary for a clear understanding of the Scriptures and who once declared that it would be better to leave the Scriptures unread and read his books, rather than to read the Scriptures and neglect his books.

For the benefit of those so naïve as to believe that the "pastor" did not make such a claim, we document the above assertion from *The Watchtower*, September 15, 1910, page 298, where the "pastor" makes the following statement concerning his *Studies in the Scriptures* and their "indispensable" value when examining the Bible.

> If the six volumes of SCRIPTURE STUDIES are practically the Bible, topically arranged with Bible proof texts given, we might not improperly name the volumes THE BIBLE IN AN ARRANGED FORM. That is to say, they are not mere comments on the Bible, *but they are practically the Bible itself.* . . .
> Furthermore, not only do we find that *people cannot see the divine plan in studying the Bible by itself,* but we see, also, that if anyone lays the SCRIPTURE STUDIES aside, even after he has used them, after he has become familiar with them, after he has read them for ten years—if he then lays them aside and ignores them and goes to the Bible alone, though he has understood his Bible for ten years, our experience shows that within two years *he goes into darkness.* On the other hand, if he had merely read the SCRIPTURE STUDIES with their references, and had *not read a page of the Bible, as such,* he would be in the light at the end of two years, because he would have the light of the Scriptures.[5]

Nowhere is Russell's egotism or boldness better revealed than in that statement. Think of it: According to the "pastor," it is impossible to understand God's plan of salvation independent of Russellite theology. Also, if one's study is of the Bible alone, void of Russell's interpretations, that one will walk in darkness at the end of two years. But there is a ray of hope for all those foolish enough to study God's Word alone. If all will adopt Russellism as a guide in biblical interpretation, mankind will enter into a "new" Kingdom Age; for then, by virtue of the "pastor's" expositions, true understanding of the Bible's basic doctrines will have been arrived at. To quote the Rev. J. J. Ross: "This inspiration has its origin in the pit."

---

[5]Emphasis is ours.

Jehovah's Witnesses pursue this same line of theological interpretation today. Russellism did not die with Charles Taze Russell; it lives under the title *The
Watchtower Announcing Jehovah's Kingdom.* The "pastor's" dream has survived its
author and remains today a living challenge to all Christians everywhere. Let us
recognize it for what it is and unmask the unsound principles upon which it
stands.

Upon Russell's death the helm of leadership was manned by Judge Joseph
Franklin Rutherford, who acquitted himself nobly in the eyes of the Society by
attacking the doctrines of "organized religion" with unparalleled vigor, and
whose radio talks, phonograph recordings, numerous books, and resounding
blasts against Christendom reverberated down the annals of the organization
until his death on January 8, 1942, from cancer, at his palatial mansion, "Beth
Sarim" or "House of Princes," in San Diego, California. He was seventy-two.
Rutherford's career was no less amazing than Russell's, for the judge was an
adversary of no mean proportions, whether in action against "organized religion," which he termed "rackets," or against those who questioned his decisions in the Society.

Throughout the years following Russell's death, Rutherford rose in power
and popularity among the "Russellites," and to oppose him was tantamount to
questioning the authority of Jehovah himself. An example of this one-man sovereignty concerns the friction that occurred in the movement when Rutherford
denounced Russell's pyramid prophecies scheme as an attempt to find God's
will outside the Scriptures (1929). Many followers of Russell's theory left the
Society as a result of this action by Rutherford, only to be witheringly blasted by
the vituperative Judge, who threatened that they would "suffer destruction" if
they did not repent and recognize Jehovah's will as expressed through the Society.

Rutherford also approached at times the inflated egotism of his predecessor Russell, especially when in his pamphlet *Why Serve Jehovah?* he declared in
effect that he was the mouthpiece of Jehovah for this age and that God had
designated his words as the expression of divine mandate. It is indeed profitable
to observe that Rutherford, as do all would-be "incarnations of infallibility,"
manifested unfathomable ignorance of God's express injunctions, especially
against the preaching of "any other gospel" (Galatians 1:8–9). It was under the
leadership of the judge that the Russellites adopted the name "Jehovah's Witnesses" (1931), partly to distinguish Rutherford's group from the splinter
groups that arose after Russell's death.

Fear of retaliation or rebuke was never characteristic of Judge Rutherford,
and quite often he displayed complete contempt for all "religions" and their
leaders. Lashing out against the persecution of the Witnesses in 1933, Judge
Rutherford challenged all of Christendom, especially the Roman Catholic
Church, to answer his charges of religious intolerance. Needless to say, he was
ignored. Rutherford also battled against the Federal Council of the Churches
of Christ in the U.S., and even offered to pay half the time cost for a radio debate
on the subject of persecution. When ignored, Rutherford abated for a time. Few
things, however, were allowed to dampen the judge's vociferous thundering,
and even a term in Atlanta Federal Penitentiary, for violation of the "Espionage
Act" in 1918, failed to silence the judge's attacks. Rutherford was released from

Atlanta in March 1919 and returned to the Witnesses' fold a martyr-hero, a complex readily appropriated by all Witnesses upon the slightest pretext. Indeed they greatly enjoy playing the role of persecuted saints. One only regrets that some of our less prudent administrators have so obligingly accommodated them.

The person of J. F. Rutherford, then, in the light of these facts, cannot be ignored in any true evaluation that seeks valid data concerning the Society's history. The great personal magnetism and the air of mystery that surround the man account most probably for his success as a leader, for he was almost a legendary figure even during his lifetime. The judge shunned photographs, although he was most photogenic and presented both an imposing and impressive figure when attired in his familiar wing collar, bow tie, and black suit. Reading glasses, which hung on a string across His Honor's portly profile, accentuated the illusion of dignified importance, along with the title of Judge, which, contrary to popular opinion, he did hold from the days of his early legal career, when he was a special judge of the Eighth Judicial Circuit Court of Boonville, Missouri. Rutherford also possessed a deep, powerful voice, which was capable of holding large audiences with its crescendo-like effect—but he seldom appeared in public and lived a closely guarded private life. Toward the end of his life, Rutherford's reign was not overly smooth, notably when the deposed head of the Witnesses' legal staff, Mr. Olin Moyle, sued Rutherford and several members of the Watchtower's Board of Directors in 1939 for libel and won his case, a judgment of $25,000, in 1944, two years after Rutherford's demise.

In comparing Russell and Rutherford it must be noted that the former was a literary pygmy compared to his successor. Russell's writings were distributed, some fifteen or twenty million copies of them, over a period of sixty years, but Rutherford's in half that time were many times that amount. The prolific judge wrote over one hundred books and pamphlets, and his works as of 1941 had been translated into eighty languages. Thus, he was the Society's second great champion who, regardless of his many failings, was truly an unusual man by any standard. Russell and Rutherford are the two key figures in the Society's history, and without them it is doubtful that the organization would ever have come into existence. But conjecture never eliminated a problem, and Jehovah's Witnesses are now a problem with which every Christian must cope.

The next president of the combined organization was Nathan Homer Knorr, who was elected president immediately after Rutherford's death. Knorr was responsible for the Gilead Missionary Training School in South Lansing, New York. He followed diligently in the footsteps of Russell and Rutherford, and under his tutelage Christianity saw much opposition. Knorr died in June of 1977, and Frederick W. Franz, a longtime leader and then vice-president of the Society, was elected president, and piloted the Watchtower in the pattern of his predecessors. With each succeeding president, the control of the Society grows stronger.

One of the most distressing traits manifested in the literature and teachings of Jehovah's Witnesses is their seemingly complete disregard for historical facts and dependable literary consistency. At the same time, however, they condemn

all religious opponents as "enemies of God"[6] and perpetrators of what they term "a racket."[7]

For some time this author has been considerably disturbed by Jehovah's Witnesses' constant denial of any theological connection whatsoever with "Pastor" Charles T. Russell, their admitted founder and first president of The Watchtower Bible and Tract Society. Since Russell was long ago proven to be a perjurer under oath, a sworn adversary of historical Christianity, and a scholastic fraud, it is obvious why the Witnesses seek to avoid his influence and memory whenever possible. However, some light should be thrown on the repeated self-contradictions that are committed by the Witnesses in their zeal to justify their position and the ever-wavering doctrines to which they hold. It is my contention that they are following the basic teachings of Charles T. Russell in relation to many biblical doctrines that he denied, and from their own publications I shall document this accusation.

In their eagerness to repudiate the charge of "Russellism," the Witnesses dogmatically say: "But who is preaching the teachings of Pastor Russell? *Certainly not* Jehovah's Witnesses! They cannot be accused of following him, for they *neither quote him as an authority nor publish nor distribute his writings.*[8] This is the statement of the Witnesses' magazine. Now let us compare this with history, and the truth will be plainly revealed.

Historically, Jehovah's Witnesses have quoted "Pastor" Russell numerous times since his death in 1916. The following is a token sample of what we can produce as concrete evidence. In 1923, seven years after the "pastor's" demise, Judge J. F. Rutherford, heir to the Russellite throne, wrote a booklet some fifty-odd pages in length, entitled *World Distress: Why and the Remedy.* In this informative treatise, the new president of The Watchtower Bible and Tract Society and the International Bible Students quoted "Pastor" Russell no fewer than *sixteen* separate times; referred to his books *Studies in the Scriptures* at least twelve times; and devoted six pages at the end of the booklet to advertising these same volumes. Further than this, in a fifty-seven page pamphlet published in 1925, entitled *Comfort for the People,* by the same Rutherford, "His Honor," in true Russellite character, defines clergymen as "dumb dogs (D.D.)," proceeds to quote "Pastor" Russell's prophetical chronology (A.D. 1914),[9] and then sums up his tirade against Christendom universal by recommending Russell's writing in four pages of advertisements at the back of the book.

The dark specter of historical facts thus begins to creep across the previously happy picture of a "Russell-free" movement. As a matter of fact, the Watchtower, its followers, and its publications have *never* been "Russell-free." Jehovah's Witnesses have been forced openly to acknowledge Russell, owing to the effect of my book *Jehovah of the Watchtower,* which gave the true history of Russell's infamous doings, thus necessitating an answer from the Witnesses, even if their response was unreliable in many respects and highly colored. The historical series was run in *The Watchtower* for some months and was entitled "A

---

[6]J. F. Rutherford, *Deliverance* (Brooklyn: Watchtower Bible and Tract Society, 1926), 91.
[7]J. F. Rutherford, *Religion* (Brooklyn: Watchtower Bible and Tract Society, 1927), 88, 104, 133, 137, 140–141, etc.
[8]*Awake!* (May 8, 1951): 26.
[9]Jehovah's Witnesses still hold to it today and teach it as dogma.

Modern History of Jehovah's Witnesses." It was a very weak apologetic. Another history, *Jehovah's Witnesses in the Divine Purpose*, was published still later and gave high praise to Russell as well. The Society's debt to Russell as founder and to his teachings as foundational is still acknowledged in Watchtower publications such as *Jehovah's Witnesses in the Twentieth Century.*[10]

But let us further consult history. In the year 1927, The Watchtower Bible and Tract Society published Judge Rutherford's "great" literary effort entitled *Creation*, which was circulated into the millions of copies, and in which this statement appeared concerning "Pastor" Russell:

> The second presence of Christ dates from about 1874.
> From that time forward many of the truths long obscured by the enemy began to be restored to the honest Christian.
> As William Tyndale was used to bring the Bible to the attention of the people, so the Lord used Charles T. Russell to bring to the attention of the people an understanding of the Bible, particularly of those truths that had been taken away by the machinations of the devil and his agencies. Because it was the Lord's due time to restore these truths, he used Charles T. Russell to write and publish books known as *Studies in the Scriptures*, by which the great fundamental truths of the divine plan are clarified. Satan has done his best to destroy these books because they *explain* the Scriptures. Even as Tyndale's Version of the Bible was destroyed by the clergy, so the clergy in various parts of the earth have gathered together thousands of volumes of *Studies in the Scriptures* and burned them publicly. But such wickedness has only served to advertise the truth of the divine plan.

Concluding this brief historical synopsis of the Watchtower Society's past, we quote the grand finale of J. F. Rutherford's funeral oration over the prostrate remains of "dear brother Russell" who, according to the floral sign by his casket, remained "faithful unto death." Said the judge: "Our brother sleeps not in death, but was instantly changed from the human to the divine nature, and is now forever with the Lord." This episode in Jehovah's Witnesses' history is cited for its uniqueness to show the adoration in which Russell was once held by the theological ancestors of those who deny his influence today.

Leaving the past history of the Witnesses, I shall now answer those who say, "The Society may have quoted him in the past, but that was before Judge Rutherford's death. We do not do it now, and after all, didn't we say 'neither quote . . . publish . . . nor distribute his writings'? This is in the *present* tense, not the past." This would, we agree, be a splendid refutation of our claims if it were true, but as we shall now conclusively prove, it is not! Not only did Jehovah's Witnesses quote the "pastor" as an authority in the past, before Rutherford's death in 1942, but they have done it many times up through the present.

In the July 15, 1950, edition of *The Watchtower* (216), the Witnesses quoted "Pastor" Russell as an authority regarding his chronology on the 2,520-year reign of the Gentiles, which reign allegedly ended, according to his calculations (and Jehovah's Witnesses), in A.D. 1914. To make it an even more hopeless contradiction, they listed as their source *The Watchtower* of 1880, of which "Pastor" Russell was editor-in-chief. Now, if they "do not consider his writings authoritative and do not circulate them," why (1) publish his chronology; (2) quote

his publication as evidence; and (3) admit his teachings on this vital point in their theology?

To shatter any misconception as to their literary shortcomings, I refer the interested reader to a pamphlet published by the Watchtower entitled *Jehovah's Witnesses, Communists or Christians?* (1953). Throughout the major content of this propaganda, Jehovah's Witnesses defend the thesis that they are not communists (which they are not), but, in their zeal to prove "their skirts clean," they quote "Pastor" Russell's writings no fewer than *five times*, refer to them with apparent pride twice (4–5), and even mention *two* of his best-known works, *The Plan of the Ages* (1886) and *The Battle of Armageddon* (1897). Further than this, *The Watchtower* of October 1, 1953, quoted "Pastor" Russell's *Studies in the Scriptures* (4:554) (and Judge Rutherford's *Vindication* [2:311])—convincing evidence indeed that the Watchtower still follows the Russellite theology of its much denied founder. All this despite the fact that they say, in their own words, "Jehovah's Witnesses . . . neither quote him [Russell] as an authority nor publish or distribute his writings." *Jehovah's Witnesses in the Divine Purpose*, a Society history published in 1959, devoted almost fifty pages to Russell and his invaluable contributions to the Society and its doctrines. More recently, the 1973 Watchtower publication *God's Kingdom of a Thousand Years Has Approached* based its assertion of the end of the "Gentile Times" on the studies and declarations of Russell (188).

Through a careful perusal of these facts, it is a simple matter to determine that Jehovah's Witnesses have never stopped being "Russellites," no matter how loudly some have proclaimed the opposite. To those who are enmeshed in the Watchtower's web, we can only say that you are *not* following a "new" theocratic organization; you are following the old teachings of Charles Taze Russell, a bitter antagonist of historical Christianity, who has bequeathed to you a gospel of spiritual confusion. Those who are contemplating becoming members of the Watchtower Society, we ask you to weigh the evidence found here and elsewhere.[11] Judge for yourselves whether it is wiser to trust the plain teachings of the Scriptures and the guidance of the Holy Spirit and the Christian church or to cast your lot with a group of zealous but misled people who are blindly leading the blind down the broad way that leads to destruction. These persons, it should be remembered, have abandoned practically every cardinal doctrine of biblical Christianity for the dogmatic doctrinal deviations of Charles Taze Russell and J. F. Rutherford. In the light of Holy Scriptures, however, Russellism is shown to be a snare from whose grip only Jesus Christ can deliver.

This is the history of Jehovah's Witnesses, the product of Charles Taze Russell, who, because he would not seek instruction in the Word of God, dedicated his unschooled talents to a lone, vain search without the guidance of the Holy Spirit. This attempt has produced a cult of determined people who are persuaded in their own minds and who boldly attempt to persuade all others that the kingdom of God is "present," and that they are Jehovah's Witnesses, the only *true* servants of the living God.

A look at the Watchtower Bible and Tract Society at the end of the century shows that it is a mixture of tradition, innovation, and contradiction. In some

---

[11]See Walter Martin, *Jehovah of the Watchtower* (Minneapolis: Bethany House Publishers, 1975), chap. 1.

respects, especially doctrinally, the Society is clearly the legacy of Charles Taze Russell and Judge Joseph F. Rutherford. In other respects, such as its far-flung missionary and publishing reach, it is clearly a religion poised to invade the twenty-first century. As to its continually waffling position on its role as God's "prophet" for today, it is inconsistent and self-contradictory.

Recent history

On the death of President Frederick Franz in 1992, Society Vice-President Milton G. Henschel was elevated to the position of president. Henschel is even more "team-oriented" than was Franz regarding the highest authority in the Watchtower, the Governing Body. Under the corporate leadership of the Governing Body, the Watchtower publications and meetings have exhibited fewer antagonistic denouncements of the less popular Jehovah's Witness distinctives, such as the rejection of birthday celebrations and higher education. The Governing Body has also encouraged a strong evangelistic outreach overseas, the source of the vast majority of the converts. The Governing Body had continued the unbroken autocracy of the Society, consistently condemning any dissension, any criticism, and any doubt on the part of rank-and-file members. Some observers speculate that whoever succeeds Henschel will complete the transition from the sole domination leadership of Russell to the anonymous string-pulling of the Governing Body. Perhaps by that time the office of president will be no more significant than the chair of a closed meeting.

Total membership in the Watchtower Bible and Tract Society as of the end of 1996 was 5,413,769. Of that number, 975,829 are members in the United States. During 1996, United States Witnesses baptized only 43,663 converts, while worldwide the convert baptisms numbered 366,579. Since door-to-door "preaching" is an essential part of the works necessary for Witnesses to be saved, it is not surprising that Witnesses in the United States spent 178,325,740 hours "preaching," with the worldwide total in 1996 of more than 1.4 *billion* hours. "Bible" studies, which are actually *book* studies for Witnesses and potential converts to learn distinctive Watchtower doctrines and practices, are also essential for spiritual progress in this system. In 1996 American Jehovah's Witnesses reported conducting 530,200 "Bible" studies, while Jehovah's Witnesses worldwide accumulated more than 4.8 *million* "Bible" studies. The annual "Memorial" service of Jehovah's Witnesses is their own unbiblical version of the "Lord's Supper," and although only a minute fraction of the members, the "spiritual class," or "anointed," partake, *all* Jehovah's Witnesses and as many friends, relatives, and prospective members as possible are encouraged to attend. In 1996, almost *13 million* people attended the Memorial service. This is a prime recruiting tool, exemplifying the "unity" of the Watchtower Society to a watching world.[12]

---

[12]Statistics derived from the *1996 Report of Jehovah's Witnesses Worldwide*, published in the first *Watchtower* issue of 1996 and posted on the official Watchtower Society Internet Web site (www.watchtower.org/statistics/1996worldwide report.htm, 1997).

Publications

Contemporary Watchtower publications are truly impressive regarding their distribution and their carefully targeted objectives of recruiting and then training followers who dare not have any independent questions, doubts, or ideas regarding Jehovah's "theocratic" organization. With magazine publications of about 832 million combined issue copies per year, and new book titles each year enjoying publication runs of 3 to 5 million copies each, the power of the written word is well exploited by the Society.

The Watchtower publishes a variety of Bible translations in various languages, as well as its own translation (carefully changed from the originals to support peculiar Watchtower doctrine) in English, the *New World Translation of the Holy Scriptures. The New World Translation* was completed in portions between 1950 and 1960, the complete volume being published in 1961. There have been four revisions, the last in 1984. Greek interlinear New Testament publications include *The Emphatic Diaglott* and *The Kingdom Interlinear Translation of the Greek Scriptures* (1969, revised in 1985). These interlinears use the Westcott and Hort Greek text, their own interlinear translations, and, in the case of *The Kingdom Interlinear*, the *New World Translation* as a parallel. One of their most important booklets is *Reasoning From the Scriptures* (1985, revised in 1989), which answers the most commonly challenged Watchtower interpretations and teachings from Scripture.

Since Rutherford's death, all Society publications are issued without any author credit or anonymously. The Society position is that this preserves the humility of the contributors and focuses attention on God's Word and will rather than on the human agency used to communicate that divine truth. Detractors point out that concealing the identity of the authors makes it impossible for anyone to evaluate the authors' qualifications, expertise, or authority in the areas in which they write.

"Bible Study Aids" include *My Book of Bible Stories* for children, *Revelation—It's Grand Climax at Hand!, Mankind's Search for God, Questions Young People Ask—Answers That Work, The Greatest Man Who Ever Lived,*[13] *Life—How Did It Get Here? By Evolution or By Creation?*, among many others.

Smaller hardcover books include *Knowledge That Leads to Everlasting Life, The Bible—God's Word or Man's?, Let Your Kingdom Come, Happiness—How to Find It, The Secret of Family Happiness, True Peace and Security—How Can You Find It?, Listening to the Great Teacher*, and others. Small pamphlets are distributed by the millions and are used to introduce the teachings of the Watchtower to prospective members and for conducting "Bible" studies with interested parties and newly baptized members.

Current pamphlets include *What Does God Require of Us?, Look! I Am Making All Things New, Jehovah's Witnesses and Education, How Can Blood Save Your Life?, The Divine Name That Will Endure Forever, Should You Believe in the Trinity?*, and *Jehovah's Witnesses in the Twentieth Century.*

Two of the many "Bible Reference Aids" Witnesses use to answer objectors'

---

[13]Remember, for the Watchtower Society Jesus was *only* a man. He was not the incarnation of the eternal Son of God, Second Person of the Trinity.

questions are *All Scripture Is Inspired of God and Beneficial* and *Insight on the Scriptures.*[14]

The two signature magazines of the Society, *The Watchtower*, published in 125 languages, and *Awake!*, published in eighty-one languages, are published semi-monthly. Figures available for each of the January 1996 issues of *The Watchtower* (18.9 million copies) and *Awake!* (15.7 million copies) indicate the widespread influence of the Society.

Activities

The followers of the Watchtower Bible and Tract Society are managed in a closely-controlled, tightly knit organizational structure that is dictated from the Governing Body in Brooklyn, New York, and is not open to any adaptation or revision from any other authority. This is made perfectly clear to all members. The publication *Jehovah's Witnesses in the Twentieth Century* states, "The overall direction comes from the Governing Body at the world headquarters in Brooklyn, New York." The Governing Body is a group of "heavenly class" or "anointed" men (currently numbering twelve) presided over by President Henschel. (There are signs that upon Henschel's death, the Governing Body will be expanded to include some non-heavenly class members as full participants, and that the role of president will be further de-emphasized.)

Prospective members are encouraged to commit themselves to the Society as quickly as possible and become members through baptism by immersion at the local congregational level. New members must immediately begin training for fieldwork by spending time with older members as they conduct their own fieldwork. *Publishers* are Witnesses who commit an average of 1,200 hours per year in "fieldwork," including door-to-door recruitment, sidewalk soliciting, and "book" studies with prospective and new members. Those who dedicate a significantly greater amount of time than 1,200 hours earn the title *Pioneer*, to distinguish them from mere publishers.

Groups meeting together are called *congregations*, but the places where they meet are called *Kingdom Halls*, not churches. Members appointed from higher-up for leadership are called *Overseers* or *Elders*. The person who leads the elder meetings is called the *Presiding Overseer* of the congregation. The *Service Overseer* handles service business within the congregation. *Ministerial Servants* are delegated administrative responsibilities as assistants to the elders.

Circuits are associations of around twenty congregations, supervised by a *Circuit Overseer*. Circuits organize twice-a-year conventions for their member congregations. *Districts* are geographical collections of circuits (twenty-two are in the United States). The *District Overseer* organizes the annual district convention, at which all new teachings and rules from the Governing Body are announced to the members, and at which new publications are presented. Collections of districts are called *Branches*, collections of branches are *Zones*, and the Brooklyn Society office is called the *Headquarters*.

Jehovah's Witnesses have only one day of ceremony each year, the *Memorial*

---

[14]*Insight* (1988) replaces the earlier Society Bible encyclopedia, *Aid to Bible Understanding* (1971), after doctrinal changes and the disfellowshipping of some of its contributors made *Aid* unacceptable.

of Christ's Death at Passover. At this ceremony, held in large auditoriums, all members are expected to be present along with family, friends, and prospective members. The elements of the Lord's Supper are passed through the audience, but only those of the anointed or heavenly class are allowed to partake. (That number is now fewer than 9,000 worldwide since no one born after 1914 is considered eligible for the class.) Jehovah's Witnesses reject celebration of any other religious, national, or cultural holidays (Christmas, Easter, birthdays, Sabbath or Sunday ceremonies, etc.) as pagan and idolatrous. Those members who are caught participating in such holidays can be disfellowshipped.

Each Kingdom Hall has five meetings per week, which all congregation members are expected to attend. The *Public Talk* is usually held each Sunday, and the *Watchtower Study* normally follows, while the *Theocratic Ministry School* is usually a weekday evening meeting, followed by the *Service Meeting*. Each Witness is also required to attend a weekly *Book Study* in addition to his or her own fieldwork, and these book studies may be conducted by the Witness. The fieldwork cannot be neglected, since "every one of the Witnesses, whether serving at the world headquarters, in branches, or in congregations, does this fieldwork of personally telling others about God's Kingdom."[15]

Society Assets

All Kingdom Halls are considered the property of the Society headquartered in Brooklyn and are not under the control or ownership of the local congregations.[16] The Society owns an eight-story factory building in Brooklyn, seven additional factory buildings, a large office complex, nearby Society-owned housing for the 3,000 resident volunteer workers, a farm (which produces food for the volunteers), and a factory (with 1,000 workers) near Wallkill, New York.

The billions of copies of publications are distributed worldwide for a specific "donation" price or, in countries where that practice is not to their tax advantage (such as the United States), on a voluntary donation basis with suggested donation amounts that are far above the negligible cost of printing. Additionally, members and congregations are strongly pressured to ensure that the donations they send to headquarters are at least as much as the suggested amounts, even if some of the materials were distributed on the local level free or at reduced donations. None of the Watchtower workers, even full-time workers, receive any salary for their "Kingdom work," and only a small monthly allowance is given to full-time volunteers for incidental expenses. Extra donations are encouraged by the placement of collection boxes in each Kingdom Hall and by periodic reminders in various publications.

Structural Authority

At first glance, Jehovah's Witnesses seem to be the model of religious democracy. In their informational booklet *What Does God Require of Us?*[17] congre-

---

[15] *Jehovah's Witnesses in the Twentieth Century.*
[16] The Watchtower Society, which has consistently opposed and denounced the Roman Catholic Church, actually compared itself to the Roman Catholic Church in a civil court case over a property dispute.
[17] *What Does God Require of Us?* (Brooklyn: Watchtower Bible and Tract Society, 1997 electronic edition): 2.

gational leaders are described: "These men are not elevated above the rest of the congregation. (Matthew 23:8–10) They are not given special titles. (2 Corinthians 1:24) They do not dress differently from others. Neither are they paid for their work."

However, in reality the Watchtower Society is an absolute autocracy. All authority is vested in the Governing Body, including the authority to understand and teach the Bible.

> So Jehovah's visible organization under Christ is a channel for bringing the divine interpretation of his word to his devoted people.[18]
>
> We acknowledge as the visible organization of Jehovah on earth the Watchtower Bible and Tract Society, and recognize the Society as the channel or instrument through which Jehovah and Christ Jesus give instruction and meat in due season to the household of faith.[19]
>
> If we are to walk in the light of truth we must recognize not only Jehovah God as our father but his organization as our "mother."[20]
>
> Make haste to identify the visible theocratic organization of God that represents his king, Jesus Christ. It is essential for life. Doing so, be complete in accepting its every aspect.[21]
>
> They [Witnesses] must adhere absolutely to the decisions and scriptural understanding of the Society because God has given it this authority over his people.[22]
>
> Avoid independent thinking . . . questioning the counsel that is provided by God's visible organization. . . . Fight against independent thinking.[23]
>
> To receive everlasting life in the earthly Paradise we must identify that organization and serve God as part of it.[24]

Dissent is not permitted and, if discovered, is punished swiftly and completely. Jehovah's Witnesses are excluded from membership or disfellowshipped not merely for gross, unrepentant immorality or heresy but also for *questioning* the teachings and authority of the Society. Should a Witness be disfellowshipped, he learns firsthand what it means to be shunned by the very people he once considered his friends, family, and brothers and sisters in Christ. Witnesses are taught,

> A disfellowshipped person is cut off from the congregation, and the congregation has nothing to do with him. Those in the congregation will not extend the hand of fellowship to this one, nor will they so much as say "hello" or "goodbye" to him. . . . [The congregation members] will not converse with such a one or show him recognition in any way. If the disfellowshipped person attempts to talk to others in the congregation, they should walk away from him. In this way he will feel the full power of his sin. . . . The disfellowshipped person who wants to do what is right should inform any approaching him that he is disfellowshipped and they should not be conversing with him.[25]
>
> What if a person cut off from God's congregation unexpectedly visits ded-

[18]*The Watchtower* (June 1, 1938): 169.
[19]Ibid. (April 15, 1939): 125.
[20]Ibid. (May 1957): 274.
[21]Ibid. (October 1, 1967): 591.
[22]Ibid. (May 1, 1972): 272.
[23]Ibid. (January 15, 1983): 22, 27.
[24]Ibid. (February 15, 1983): 12.
[25]Ibid. (July 1, 1963): 411–413.

icated [Witness] relatives? What should the [Jehovah's Witness] Christian do then? If this is the first occurrence of such a visit, the dedicated Christian can, if his conscience permits, carry on family courtesies on that particular occasion. However, if his conscience does not permit, he is under no obligation to do so. If courtesies are extended, though, the Christian should make it clear that this will not be made a regular practice. . . . The excommunicated relative should be made to realize that his visits are not now welcomed as they were previously when he was walking correctly with Jehovah.[26]

Witnesses are not only to isolate themselves from those who were once Witnesses and have been disfellowshipped or disassociated but also from anyone who is not a Witness and who attempts to present a view contrary to the Watchtower. No Witness is allowed to read dissenting material, whether it is written by a disgruntled Jehovah's Witness, a disfellowshipped or disassociated Witness, or someone who has never been a Witness:

> Have no dealings with apostates. . . . For example, what will you do if you receive a letter or some literature, open it, and see right away that it is from an apostate? Will curiosity cause you to read it, just to see what he has to say? You may even reason: "It won't affect me; I'm too strong in the truth. And besides, if we have the truth, we have nothing to fear. The truth will stand the test." In thinking this way, some have fed their minds upon apostate reasoning and have fallen prey to serious questioning and doubt.[27]

Surprisingly, prospective Jehovah's Witnesses are told that it is right to question what one believes and to search out God's will for ourselves. In what used to be their standard introductory study for new prospective members, *The Truth That Leads to Eternal Life,* they taught,

> We need to examine not only what we personally believe but also what is taught by any religious organization with which we may be associated. Are its teachings in full harmony with God's Word, or are they based on the traditions of men? If we are lovers of the truth, there is nothing to fear from such an examination. It should be the sincere desire of every one of us to learn what God's will is for us, and then to do it.[28]

However, the Society means by this exhortation that one is supposed to test his own *non-Witness* religion, not the teachings of the Watchtower Society. Jehovah's Witnesses are not allowed to study the Bible on their own, to interpret what they read in the Bible for themselves, or to teach directly from the Bible. Rather, they must teach from approved Watchtower publications *about* the Bible. Concerning the Bible the Society says,

> Rather we should seek for dependent Bible study, rather than for independent Bible study.[29]
> He does not impart his holy spirit and understanding and appreciation of his Word apart from his visible organization.[30]
> The Bible is an organizational book and belongs to the Christian congre-

[26] *The Watchtower* (July 15, 1963): 443–444.
[27] Ibid. (March 15, 1986): 12.
[28] *The Truth That Leads to Eternal Life* (Brooklyn: Watchtower Bible and Tract Society, 1968), 13.
[29] *The Watchtower* (September 15, 1911): 4885.
[30] Ibid. (July 1, 1965): 391.

gation as a whole, not to individuals, regardless of how sincerely they may believe
that they can interpret the Bible. For this reason the Bible cannot be properly
understood without Jehovah's visible organization in mind.[31]

We all need help to understand the Bible, and we cannot find the scriptural
guidance we need outside the "faithful and discreet slave" organization.[32]

They [questioners] say that it is sufficient to read the Bible exclusively, either alone or in small groups at home. But, strangely, through such "Bible reading," they have reverted right back to the apostate doctrines that commentaries
by Christendom's clergy were teaching 100 years ago.[33]

The Watchtower Bible and Tract Society has weathered the storms of its
inconsistent and turbulent history by enforcing absolute control over its members and by excluding anyone who dares to question anything. It should not
surprise us, therefore, that most Witnesses have memorized the basic doctrinal
teachings of the Society and will defend them adamantly, even when their defense is irrational, unbiblical, and nonhistorical. We turn now to the doctrines
of Jehovah's Witnesses.

Some of the Doctrines of Jehovah's Witnesses

Below is a comparison of Jehovah's Witnesses' beliefs "then" (during the
1960s) and "now" (in 1997), from the their own publications. Note that although some of the wording has changed, the Witness teachings about the core
doctrines of the faith have remained remarkably unchanged over three decades,
with a few notable exceptions.

THEN (1960s)

I. There is one solitary being from all eternity, Jehovah God, the Creator and Preserver of the Universe and of all things visible and invisible.

II. The Word or Logos is "a god," a mighty god, the "beginning of the Creation" of Jehovah and His active agent in the creation of all things. The Logos was made human as the man Jesus and suffered death to produce the ransom or redemptive price for obedient men.

III. The Bible is the inerrant, infallible, inspired Word of God as it was originally given, and has been preserved by Him as the revealer of His purposes.

NOW (1997)

1. People worship many things. But the Bible tells us that there is only one TRUE God. He created everything in heaven and on earth. . . . God has many titles but has only one name. That name is JEHOVAH.

2. Jesus lived in heaven as a spirit person before he came to earth. He was God's first creation, and so he is called the "firstborn" Son of God. (Col. 1:15; Rev. 3:14) Jesus is the only Son that God created by himself. Jehovah used the pre-human Jesus as his "master worker" in creating all other things in heaven and on earth (Prov. 8:22–31; Col. 1:16–17).

3. Another mark of true religion is that its members have a *deep respect for the Bible.* They accept it as the Word of God and believe what it says.

[31] *The Watchtower* (October 1, 1967): 587.
[32] Ibid. (February 15, 1981): 19.
[33] Ibid. (August 15, 1981): 29.

IV. Satan was a great angel who rebelled against Jehovah and challenged His Sovereignty. Through Satan, sin and death came upon man. His destiny is annihilation with all his followers.

V. Man was created in the image of Jehovah but willfully sinned, hence all men are born sinners and are "of the earth." Those who follow Jesus Christ faithful to the death will inherit the heavenly Kingdom with Him. Men of good will who accept Jehovah and His Theocratic Rule will enjoy the "new earth"; all others who reject Jehovah will be annihilated.

VI. The atonement is a ransom paid to Jehovah God by Christ Jesus and is applicable to all who accept it in righteousness. In brief, the death of Jesus removed the effects of Adam's sin on his offspring and laid the foundation of the New World of righteousness including the Millennium of Christ's reign.

VII. The man Christ Jesus was resurrected a divine spirit creature after offering the ransom for obedient man.

VIII. The soul of man is not eternal but mortal, and it can die. Animals likewise have souls, though man has the preeminence by special creation.

IX. Hell, meaning a place of "fiery torment" where sinners remain after death until the resurrection, does not exist. This is a doctrine of "Organized Religion," not the Bible. Hell is the common grave of mankind, literally *sheol* (Hebrew), "a place of rest in hope" where the departed sleep until the resurrection by Jehovah God.

4. At first, he was a perfect angel in heaven with God. However, he later thought too much of himself and wanted the worship that rightly belongs to God.

5. By disobeying God's command, the first man, Adam, committed what the Bible calls "sin." So God sentenced him to death (Gen. 3:17–19). . . . Adam passed on sin to all his children. . . . Soon Jesus will judge people, separating them as a shepherd separates sheep from goats. The "sheep" are those who will have proved themselves his loyal subjects. They will receive everlasting life on earth. . . . Jehovah has also selected some faithful men and women from the earth to go to heaven. They will rule with Jesus as kings, judges, and priests over mankind. . . . The "goats" are those who will have rejected God's Kingdom. . . . In the near future, Jesus will destroy all goatlike ones.

6. Unlike Adam . . . Jesus was perfectly obedient to God under even the greatest test. He could therefore sacrifice his perfect human life to pay for Adam's sin. This is what the Bible refers to as the "ransom." Adam's children could thus be released from condemnation to death. All who put their faith in Jesus can have their sins forgiven and receive everlasting life.

7. Jesus died and was resurrected by God as a spirit creature, and he returned to heaven (1 Pet. 3:18–22).

8. The dead cannot do anything or feel anything. . . . The soul dies, it does not live on after death.

9. Would a *loving God* really torment people forever? . . . The wicked, of course, are not literally tormented because, as we have seen, when a person is dead he is completely out of existence. . . . And it is also a lie, which the Devil spread, that the souls of the wicked are tormented.[34]

---

[34]*You Can Live Forever in Paradise on Earth* (Brooklyn: Watchtower Bible and Tract Society, 1982), 81–89.

X. Eternal Punishment is a punishment or penalty of which there is no end. It does not mean "eternal torment" of living souls. Annihilation, the second death, is the lot of all those who reject Jehovah God, and it is eternal.

10. Millions of dead ones will be resurrected to human life on the earth (Acts 24:15). If they do what God requires of them, they will continue to live on earth forever. If not, they will be destroyed forever (John 5:28–29; Rev. 20:11–15).

XI. Jesus Christ has returned to earth A.D. 1914, has expelled Satan from Heaven, and is proceeding to overthrow Satan's organization, establish the Theocratic Millennial Kingdom, and vindicate the name of Jehovah God. He did not return in a physical form and is invisible as the Logos.

11. In 1914, Jehovah gave Jesus the authority He had promised him. Since then, Jesus has ruled in heaven as Jehovah's appointed King (Dan. 7:13–14). . . . As soon as Jesus became King, he threw Satan and his wicked angels out of heaven and down to the locality of the earth. That is why things have become so bad here on earth since 1914.

XII. The Kingdom of Jehovah is Supreme, and as such cannot be compatible with present Human Government ("Devil's Visible Organization"), and any allegiance to them in any way which violates the allegiance owed to Him is a violation of the Scripture.

12. God's Kingdom is a special government. It is set up in heaven and will rule over this earth. . . . Jesus' disciples must be *no part of this wicked world* (John 17:16). They do not get involved in the world's political affairs and social controversies.[35]

The Holy Trinity

1. "The doctrine, in brief, is that there are three gods in one: 'God the Father, God the Son, and God the Holy Ghost,' all three equal in power, substance, and eternity" (*Let God Be True*, Brooklyn: Watchtower Bible and Tract Society, 1946 ed., 100).

2. "The obvious conclusion is, therefore, that Satan is the originator of the Trinity doctrine" (*LGBT*, 101).

3. "Sincere persons who want to know the true God and serve Him find it a bit difficult to love and worship a complicated, freakish-looking, three-headed God" (*LGBT*, 102).

4. "The Trinity doctrine was not conceived by Jesus or the early Christians" (*LGBT*, 111).

5. "The plain truth is that this is another of Satan's attempts to keep God-fearing persons from learning the truth of Jehovah and his Son, Christ Jesus. No, there is no Trinity" (*LGBT*, 111).

6. "Any trying to reason out the Trinity teaching leads to confusion of mind. So the Trinity teaching confuses the meaning of John 1:1–2; it does not simplify it or make it clear or easily understandable" (*"The Word," Who Is He? According to John*, 7).

7. Is Jehovah a Trinity—three persons in one God? No! Jehovah, the Father, is "the only true God" (John 17:3; Mark 12:29). Jesus is His firstborn Son, and he is subject to God (1 Cor. 11:3). The Father is greater than the Son (John

---

[35]All statements above except for #9 are taken from *What Does God Require of Us?* (Brooklyn: Watchtower Bible and Tract Society, 1997), electronic version.

14:28). The holy spirit is not a person; it is God's active force (Gen. 1:2; Acts 2:18) (*What Does God Require of Us?*, Brooklyn: Watchtower Bible and Tract Society, 1997, electronic version).

8. "Thus, neither the thirty-nine books of the Hebrew Scriptures nor the canon of twenty-seven inspired books of the Christian Greek Scriptures provide any clear teaching of the Trinity. . . . Thus, the testimony of the Bible and of history makes clear that the Trinity was unknown throughout biblical times and for several centuries thereafter" (*Should You Believe in the Trinity?*, Brooklyn: Watchtower Bible and Tract Society, 1997, electronic version).

Deity of Christ

1. "The true Scriptures speak of God's Son, the Word, as 'a god.' He is a 'mighty god,' but not the Almighty God, who is Jehovah" (*The Truth Shall Make You Free*, Brooklyn: Watchtower Bible and Tract Society, 1943, 47).

2. "In other words, he was the first and direct creation of Jehovah God" (*The Kingdom Is at Hand*, Brooklyn: Watchtower Bible and Tract Society, 1944, 46–47, 49).

3. "The Bible shows that there is only one God . . . greater than His Son . . . and that the Son, as the Firstborn, Only-begotten, and 'the creation by God,' had a beginning. That the Father is greater and older than the Son is reasonable, easy to understand, and is what the Bible teaches" (*From Paradise Lost to Paradise Regained*, Brooklyn: Watchtower Bible and Tract Society, 1958, 164).

4. "Jesus was 'the Son of God.' Not God himself!" (*"The Word," Who Is He?*, 20).

5. "The very fact that he was sent proves he was not equal with God but was less than God his Father" (*TWWIH*, 11).

6. "Certainly the apostle John was not so unreasonable as to say that someone (the Word) was with some other individual ('God') and at the same time was that other individual ('God')" (*TWWIH*, 53).

7. "Thus, Jesus had an existence in heaven before coming to the earth. But was it as one of the persons in an almighty, eternal triune Godhead? No, for the Bible plainly states that in his prehuman existence, Jesus was a created spirit being, just as angels were spirit beings created by God. Neither the angels nor Jesus had existed before their creation" (*Should You Believe in the Trinity?*).

The Holy Spirit

1. "The holy spirit is the invisible active force of Almighty God that moves his servants to do his will" (*Let God Be True*, 108).

2. "As for the 'Holy Spirit,' the so-called 'third Person of the Trinity,' we have already seen that it is not a person, but God's active force" (*The Truth That Leads to Eternal Life*, Brooklyn: Watchtower Bible and Tract Society, 1968, 24).

3. "The Scriptures themselves unite to show that God's holy spirit is not a person but is God's active force by which he accomplishes his purpose and executes his will" (*Aid to Bible Understanding*, Brooklyn: Watchtower Bible and Tract Society, 1969, 1971, 1543).

4. "The Bible's use of 'holy spirit' indicates that it is a controlled force that

Jehovah God uses to accomplish a variety of his purposes. To a certain extent, it can be likened to electricity, a force that can be adapted to perform a great variety of operations" (*Should You Believe in the Trinity?*).

5. "No, the holy spirit is not a person and it is not part of a Trinity. The holy spirit is God's active force that he uses to accomplish his will. It is not equal to God but is always at his disposition and subordinate to him" (*SYBITT?*).

The Virgin Birth

1. "Mary was a virgin. . . . When Joseph learned that Mary was going to have a child, he did not want to take her as his wife. But God's angel . . . said: 'That which has been begotten in her is by holy spirit'. . . . He took Mary his wife home. 'But he had no relations with her until she gave birth to a son' " (Matt. 1:20–25) (*From Paradise Lost to Paradise Regained*, 122–123).

2. "Jesus was conceived by a sinless, perfect Father, Jehovah God. . . . The perfect child Jesus did not get human life from the sinner Adam, but received only a human body through Adam's descendant Mary. Jesus' life came from Jehovah God, the Holy One. . . . Jehovah took the perfect life of his only-begotten Son and transferred it from heaven to . . . the womb of the unmarried girl Mary. . . . Thus God's Son was conceived or given a start as a human creature. It was a miracle. Under Jehovah's holy power the child Jesus, conceived in this way, grew in Mary's womb to the point of birth" (*FPLTPR*, 126–127).

3. "Jesus' birth on earth was not an incarnation. . . . He emptied himself of all things heavenly and spiritual, and God's almighty spirit transferred his Son's life down to the womb of the Jewish virgin of David's descent. By this miracle he was born a man. . . . He was not a spirit-human hybrid, a man and at the same time a spirit person. . . . He *was* flesh" (*What Has Religion Done for Mankind?*, 231).

4. "While on earth, Jesus was a human, although a perfect one because it was God who transferred the life-force of Jesus to the womb of Mary" (*Should You Believe in the Trinity?*).

The Atonement

1. "That which is redeemed or bought back is what was lost, namely, perfect human life, with its rights and earthly prospects" (*Let God Be True*, 114).

2. "Jesus as the glorified High Priest, by presenting in heaven this redemptive price, is in position to relieve the believing ones of Adam's descendants from the inherited disability under which all are born" (*LGBT*, 118–119).

3. "The human life that Jesus Christ laid down in sacrifice must be exactly equal to that life which Adam forfeited for all his offspring: it must be a perfect human life, no more, no less. . . . This is just what Jesus gave . . . for men of all kinds" (*You May Survive Armageddon Into God's New World*, Brooklyn: Watchtower Bible and Tract Society, 1955, 39).

4. "Jesus, no more and no less than a perfect human, became a ransom that compensated exactly for what Adam lost—the right to perfect human life on earth. . . . The perfect human life of Jesus was the 'corresponding ransom' required by divine justice—no more, no less. A basic principle even of human

justice is that the price paid should fit the wrong committed. . . . So the ransom, to be truly in line with God's justice, had to be strictly an equivalent—a perfect human, 'the last Adam.' Thus, when God sent Jesus to earth as the ransom, he made Jesus to be what would satisfy justice, not an incarnation, not a god-man, but a perfect man, 'lower than angels' " (*Should You Believe?*).

Salvation by Grace

1. "Immortality is a reward for faithfulness. It does not come automatically to a human at birth" (*Let God Be True*, 74).
2. "Those people of good will today who avail themselves of the provision and who steadfastly abide in this confidence will find Christ Jesus to be their 'everlasting Father' " (Isaiah 9:6) (*LGBT*, 121).
3. "We have learned that a person could fall away and be judged unfavorably either now or at Armageddon or during the thousand years of Christ's reign or at the end of the final test . . . into everlasting destruction" (*From Paradise Lost to Paradise Regained*, 241).
4. "Make haste to identify the visible theocratic organization of God that represents his king, Jesus Christ. It is essential for life. Doing so, be complete in accepting its every aspect" (*The Watchtower*, October 1, 1967: 591).
5. "To receive everlasting life in the earthly Paradise we must identify that organization and serve God as part of it" (*The Watchtower*, February 15, 1983: 12).

The Resurrection of Christ

1. "This firstborn from the dead was raised from the grave, not a human creature, but a spirit" (*Let God Be True*, 276).
2. "Jehovah God raised him from the dead, not as a human Son, but as a mighty immortal spirit Son. . . . For forty days after that he materialized, as angels before him had done, to show himself alive to his disciples" (*LGBT*, 40).
3. "Jesus did not take his human body to heaven to be forever a man in heaven. Had he done so, that would have left him even lower than the angels. . . . God did not purpose for Jesus to be humiliated thus forever by being a fleshly man forever. No, but after he had sacrificed his perfect manhood, God raised him to deathless life as a glorious spirit creature" (*LGBT*, 41).
4. "Usually they could not at first tell it was Jesus, for he appeared in different bodies. He appeared and disappeared just as angels had done, because he was resurrected as a spirit creature. Only because Thomas would not believe did Jesus appear in a body like that in which he had died" (*From Paradise Lost to Paradise Regained*, 144).
5. "Having given up his flesh for the life of the world, Christ could never take it again and become a man once more. For this basic reason his return could never be in the human body that he sacrificed once for all time" (*You Can Live Forever in Paradise on Earth*, Brooklyn: Watchtower Bible and Tract Society, 1982, 143).

The Return of Christ and Human Government

1. "Christ Jesus returns, not again as a human, but as a glorious spirit person" (*Let God Be True*, 196).

2. "Some wrongfully expect a literal fulfillment of the symbolic statements of the Bible. Such hope to see the glorified Jesus coming seated on a white cloud where every human eye will see him. . . . Since no earthly men have ever seen the Father . . . neither will they see the glorified Son" (*LGBT*, 186).

3. "It does not mean that he [Christ] is on the way or has promised to come, but that he has already arrived and is here" (*LGBT*, 198).

4. "Any national flag is a symbol or image of the sovereign power of its nation" (*LGBT*, 242).

5. "All such likenesses [symbols of a national power, eagle, sun, lion, etc.] are forbidden by Exodus 20:2–6 [the commandment against idolatry]" (*LGBT*, 242).

6. "Hence no witness of Jehovah, who ascribes salvation only to Him, may salute any national emblem without violating Jehovah's commandment against idolatry as stated in His Word" (*LGBT*, 243).

The Existence of Hell and Eternal Punishment

1. "Those who have been taught by Christendom believe the God-dishonoring doctrine of a fiery hell for tormenting conscious human souls eternally" (*Let God Be True*, 88).

2. "It is so plain that the Bible hell is mankind's common grave that even an honest little child can understand it, but not the religious theologians" (*LGBT*, 92).

3. "Who is responsible for this God-defaming doctrine of a hell of torment? The promulgator of it is Satan himself. His purpose in introducing it has been to frighten the people away from studying the Bible and to make them hate God" (*LGBT*, 98).

4. "Imperfect man does not torture even a mad dog, but kills it. And yet the clergymen attribute to God, who is love, the wicked crime of torturing human creatures merely because they had the misfortune to be born sinners" (*LGBT*, 99).

5. "The doctrine of a burning hell where the wicked are tortured eternally after death cannot be true, mainly for four reasons: (1) Because it is wholly unscriptural; (2) it is unreasonable; (3) it is contrary to God's love; and (4) it is repugnant to justice" (*LGBT*, 99).

6. "It is . . . a lie, which the Devil has had spread, that the souls of the wicked are tormented in a hell or a purgatory" (*You Can Live*, 89).

Man the Soul, His Nature and Destiny

1. "Man is a combination of two things, namely, the 'dust of the ground' and 'the breath of life.' The combining of these two things (or factors) produced a living soul or creature called man" (*Let God Be True*, 68).

2. "So we see that the claim of religionists that man has an immortal soul

and therefore differs from the beast is not scriptural" (*LGBT*, 68).

3. "The fact that the human soul is mortal can be amply proved by a careful study of the Holy Scriptures. An immortal soul cannot die, but God's Word, at Ezekiel 18:4, says concerning humans: 'Behold all souls are mine. . . . The soul that sinneth it shall die' " (*LGBT*, 69–70).

4. "It is clearly seen that even the man Christ Jesus was mortal. He did not have an immortal soul: Jesus, the human soul, died" (*LGBT*, 71).

5. "Thus it is seen that the serpent (the Devil) is the one that originated the doctrine of the inherent immortality of human souls" (*LGBT*, 74–75).

6. "The Scriptures show that the destiny of the sinful man is death" (*LGBT*, 75).

7. "The Holy Scriptures alone offer real hope for those who do seek Jehovah God and strive to follow his ways" (*LGBT*, 75).

8. "At death man's spirit, his life-force, which is sustained by breathing, 'goes out.' *It no longer exists.* . . . When they are dead, both humans and animals are in this same state of complete unconsciousness. . . . That the soul lives on after death is a lie started by the Devil" (*You Can Live*, 77).

9. "The human soul ceases to exist at death. . . . Hell is mankind's common grave" (*Jehovah's Witnesses in the Twentieth Century*, electronic version).

The Kingdom of Heaven (a Heavenly One)

1. "Who and how many are able to enter it [the Kingdom]? The Revelation limits to 144,000 the number that become a part of the Kingdom and stand on heavenly Mount Zion" (*Let God Be True*, 136).

2. "In the capacity of priests and kings of God they reign a thousand years with Christ Jesus" (*LGBT*, 137).

3. "He [Christ] went to prepare a heavenly place for his associate heirs, 'Christ's body,' for they too will be invisible spirit creatures" (*LGBT*, 138).

4. "If it is to be a heavenly kingdom, who will be the subject of its rule? In the invisible realm angelic hosts, myriads of them, will serve as faithful messengers of the King. And on earth the faithful children of the King Christ Jesus, including faithful forefathers of his then resurrected, will be 'princes in all the earth'. . . . Then, too, the 'great crowd' of his 'other sheep' . . . will continue to 'serve him day and night,' and many of them will also be 'princes'. . . . They will 'multiply and fill the earth' in righteousness and their children will become obedient subjects of the King Christ Jesus. And finally the 'unrighteous' ones that are to be resurrected then, to prove their integrity, must joyfully submit themselves to theocratic rule. . . . Those who prove rebellious or who turn unfaithful during the loosing of Satan at the end of Christ's thousand-year reign will be annihilated with Satan, the Devil" (*LGBT*, 318–319).

5. "The Creator loved the new world so much that he gave his only begotten Son to be its King" (*LGBT*, 143).

6. "The undefeatable purpose of Jehovah God to establish a righteous kingdom in these last days was fulfilled in A.D. 1914" (*LGBT*, 143).

7. "Obey the King Christ Jesus and flee, while there is still time, to the Kingdom heights. . . . Time left is short, for 'the kingdom of the heavens has drawn near' " (*LGBT*, 144).

8. "Only a little flock of 144,000 go to heaven and rule with Christ. . . . The 144,000 are born again as spiritual sons of God" (*Jehovah's Witnesses in the Twentieth Century*, electronic version).

Jehovah's Witnesses become intensely disturbed whenever they are referred to as "Russellites" or their theology as "Russellism." After a thorough examination of the doctrines of the Society and a lengthy comparison with the teachings of "Pastor" Russell, its founder, the author is convinced that the two systems are basically the same, and whatever differences do exist are minute and affect in no major way the cardinal beliefs of the organization. I believe, however, that in any research project substantiating evidence should be produced for verification whenever possible. I have attempted to do this and as a result have listed below five of the major doctrines of the Jehovah's Witnesses paralleled with the teachings of Charles Taze Russell, their late great "pastor." I am sure that the interested reader will recognize the obvious relationship between the two systems, for it is inescapably evident that Russell is the author of both.

The Teachings of Charles Taze Russell or "Russellism"	The Doctrines of the Jehovah's Witnesses

The Triune Godhead

"This view [the Trinity] suited well 'the dark ages' it helped to produce" (*Studies in the Scriptures*, 5:166).	"Does this [John 1:1] mean that Jehovah God (Elohim) and the . . . Son are two persons but at the same time one God and members of a so-called 'trinity' or 'triune god'? When religion so teaches it violates the Word of God, wrests the Scriptures to the destruction of those who are misled, and insults God-given intelligence and reason" (*The Truth Shall Make You Free*, 45).
"This theory . . . is as unscriptural as it is unreasonable" (*Studies*, 5:166).	"The confusion is caused by the improper translation of John 1:1–3 . . . such translation being made by religionists who tried to manufacture proof for their teaching of a 'trinity' " (*The Truth*, 45–46).
"If it were not for the fact that this trinitarian nonsense was drilled into us from earliest infancy, and the fact that it is so soberly taught in Theological Seminaries by gray-haired professors . . . nobody would give it a moment's serious consideration" (*Studies*, 5:166).	"The obvious conclusion is, therefore, that Satan is the originator of the 'trinity doctrine' " (*Let God Be True*, 101).
"How the great Adversary [Satan] ever succeeded in foisting [the Triune Godhead] upon the Lord's people to bewilder and mystify them, and render much of the Word of God of none effect, is the real mystery" (*Studies*, 5:166).	"The testimony of history is clear: The Trinity teaching is a deviation from the truth, an apostatizing from it" (*Should You Believe?*, electronic version).

The Deity of Jesus Christ

"Our Lord Jesus Christ is *a* God . . . still the united voice of the Scriptures most emphatically asserts that there is but one Almighty God, the Father of all" (*Studies*, 5:55).

"The true Scriptures speak of God's Son, the Word, as 'a god.' He is a 'mighty god,' but not the Almighty God, who is Jehovah—Isaiah 9:6" (*The Truth*, 47).

"Our Redeemer existed as a spirit being before he was made flesh and dwelt amongst men. At that time, as well as subsequently, he was properly known as 'a god'—a mighty one" (*Studies*, 5:84).

"At the time of his beginning of life he was created by the everlasting God, Jehovah, without the aid or instrumentality of any mother. In other words, he was the first and direct creation of Jehovah God. . . . He was the start of God's creative work. . . . He was not an incarnation in flesh but was flesh, a human Son of God, a perfect man, no longer a spirit, although having a spiritual or heavenly past or background" (*The Kingdom Is at Hand*, 46–47, 49).

"The Logos [Christ] himself was 'the beginning of the creation of God' " (*Studies*, 5:86).

"This One was not Jehovah God, but was 'existing in God's form. . . .' He was a spirit person . . . he was a mighty one, although not Almighty as Jehovah God is . . . he was a God, but not the Almighty God, who is Jehovah" (*Let God Be True*, 32–33).

"As chief of the angels and next to the Father, he [Christ] was known as the Archangel (highest angel or messenger), whose name, Michael, signifies 'Who as God' or 'God's Representative' " (*Studies*, 5:84).

"Being the only begotten Son of God . . . the Word would be a prince among all other creatures. In this office he [Christ] bore another name in heaven, which name is 'Michael'. . . . Other names were given to the Son in course of time" (*The Truth*, 49).

The Resurrection of Christ

"Our Lord was put to death in the *flesh*, but was made alive in the *spirit*; he was put to death as a *man*, but was raised from the dead *a spirit being* of the highest order of the divine nature" (*Studies*, 5:453).

"In his resurrection he was no more human. He was raised as a spirit creature" (*TKIAH*, 258).

"It could not be that the man Jesus is the Second Adam, the *new* father of the race instead of Adam; for the *man* Jesus is dead, forever dead" (*Studies*, 5:454).

"Having given up his flesh for the life of the world, Christ could never take it again and become a man once more. For that basic reason his return could never be in the human body that he sacrificed once for all time" (*You Can Live Forever in Paradise on Earth*, 143).

"[Christ] instantly created and assumed such a body of flesh and such clothing as he saw fit for the purpose intended" (*Studies*, 2:127).

"Therefore the bodies in which Jesus manifested himself to his disciples after his return to life were not the body in which he was nailed to the tree. They were merely materialized for the occasion, resembling on one or two occasions the body in which he died" (*TKIAH*, 259).

"Our Lord's human body . . . did not decay or corrupt. . . . Whether it was dissolved into gases or whether it is still preserved somewhere . . . no one knows" (*Studies*, 2:129).

"This firstborn from the dead was raised from the grave not a human creature, but a spirit" (*Let God Be True*, 276).

The Physical Return of Christ

"And in *like manner* as he went away (quietly, secretly, so far as the world was concerned, and unknown except to his followers), *so*, in this manner, he comes again" (*Studies*, 2:154).

"Christ Jesus returns, not as a human, but as a glorious spirit person" (*Let God Be True*, 196).

[Russell's idea of what Christ is saying, and his teaching on the matter.] "He comes to us in the early dawn of the Millennial Day. [Jesus] seems to say . . . 'Learn that I am a spirit being no longer visible to human sight' " (*Studies*, 2:191).

"Since no earthly men have ever seen or can see the Father, they will not be able to see the glorified Son" (*LGBT*, 197).

[Christ] "does not come in the body of his humiliation, a human body, which he took for the suffering of death . . . but in his glorious spiritual body" (*Studies*, 2:108).

"It is a settled scriptural truth, therefore, that human eyes will not see him at his second coming, neither will he come in a fleshy body" (*The Truth*, 295).

The Existence of Hell or a Place of Conscious Torment After Death

"Many have imbibed the erroneous idea that God placed our race on trial for life with the alternative of *eternal torture*, whereas nothing of the kind is even hinted at in the penalty" (*Studies*, 1:127).

"The Bible hell is mankind's 'common grave' " (*Let God Be True*, 92).

"Eternal torture is nowhere suggested in the Old Testament Scriptures, and only a few statements in the New Testament can be so misconstrued as to appear to teach it" (*Studies*, 1:128).

"Hell could not be a place of torment because such an idea never came into the mind or heart of God. Additionally, to torment a person *eternally* because he did wrong on earth *for a few years* is contrary to justice. How good it is to know the truth about the dead! It can truly set one free from fear and superstition" (*You Can Live Forever in Pardise on Earth*, 89).

In concluding this comparison, it is worthwhile to note that as far as the facts are concerned, "Jehovah's Witnesses" is simply a pseudonym for "Russellism" or "Millennial Dawnism." The similarity of the two systems is more than coincidental or accidental, regardless of the Witnesses' loud shouts to the contrary. The facts speak for themselves. Inquisitive persons may ask at this point why the organization assumed the name of "Jehovah's Witnesses." The answer is more than understandable.

After Russell's death, Judge Rutherford, the newly elected president of the Society, saw the danger of remaining "Russellites" and over a period of fifteen years labored to cover up the "pastor's" unpleasant past, which did much to

hinder the organization's progress. In 1931 Rutherford managed to appropriate the name "Jehovah's Witnesses" from Isaiah 43:10, thus escaping the damaging title "Russellites." Rutherford thus managed to hide the unsavory background of Russellistic theology and delude millions of people into believing that Jehovah's Witnesses was a "different" organization. Rutherford's strategy has worked well for the Russellites and, as a result, today those trusting souls and millions like them everywhere sincerely believe that they are members of a "New Kingdom Order" under Jehovah God, when in reality they are deluded believers in the theology of *one* man, Charles Taze Russell, who was proven to be neither a Christian nor a qualified Bible student. Jehovah's Witnesses who have not been in the movement any great period of time deny publicly and privately that they are Russellites; and since few, if any, of the old-time members of "Pastor" Russell's personal flock are still alive, the Society in safety vehemently denounces any accusations that tend to prove that Russell's theology is the basis of the entire Watchtower system. Proof of this is found in a personal letter from the Society to the author dated February 9, 1951, wherein, in answer to my question concerning Russell's influence, they stated: "We are not 'Russellites' for we are not following Charles T. Russell or any other imperfect man. Honest examination of our literature today would quickly reveal that it differs widely from that of Russell's, even though he was the first President of our Society."

Further than this, in another letter dated November 6, 1950, and signed by Nathan H. Knorr, the Society's then legal president, the Society declared that "the latest publications of The Watchtower Bible and Tract Society set out the doctrinal views of this organization, and I think any information you want in that regard you can find yourself without an interview." It is therefore evident from these two official letters that we must judge the faith of the Jehovah's Witnesses by their literature.

A Refutation of Watchtower Theology in Regard to the Triune Deity[36]

One of the greatest doctrines of the Scriptures is that of the Triune Godhead or the nature of God himself. To say that this doctrine is a "mystery" is indeed inconclusive, and no informed minister would explain the implications of the doctrine in such abstract terms. Jehovah's Witnesses accuse "the clergy" of doing just that, however, and it is unfortunate to note that they are, as usual, guilty of misstatement in the presentation of the facts and even in their definition of what Christian clergymen believe the Deity to be.

First of all, Christian ministers and Christian laypersons do not believe that there are "three gods in one" (*Let God Be True*, 100), but *do* believe that there are three Persons all of the same Substance—coequal, coexistent, and coeternal. There is ample ground for this belief in the Scriptures, where plurality in the

---

[36]Jehovah's Witnesses take great delight in pointing out that the word "Trinity" does not appear as such in the Bible. They further state that since it is not a part of Scripture, it must be of pagan origin and should be discounted entirely. What the Witnesses fail to understand is that the very word "Jehovah," which they maintain is the only true name for God, also does not appear as such in the Bible, but is an interpolation of the Hebrew consonants YHWH or JHVH, any vowels added being arbitrary. Thus it is seen that the very name by which they call themselves is just as unbiblical as they suppose the Trinity to be.

Godhead is very strongly intimated if not expressly declared. Let us consider just a few of these references.

In Genesis 1:26 Jehovah is speaking of Creation, and He speaks in the plural: "Let *us* make man in *our* image, after *our* likeness." Now it is obvious that God would not create man in His image and the angels' images if He were talking to them, so He must have been addressing someone else—and who but His Son and the Holy Spirit who are equal in Substance could He address in such familiar terms? Since there is no other god but Jehovah (Isaiah 43:10–11), not even "a lesser mighty god" as Jehovah's Witnesses affirm Christ to be, there must be a unity in plurality and Substance or the passage is not meaningful. The same is true of Genesis 11:7, when God said at the Tower of Babel, "Let *us* go down," and also of Isaiah 6:8, "Who will go for *us*? . . ." These instances of plurality indicate something deeper than an interpersonal relationship; they strongly suggest what the New Testament fully develops, namely, a Tri-Unity in the One God. The claim of Jehovah's Witnesses that the early church Fathers, including Tertullian and Theophilus, propagated and introduced the threefold unity of God into Christianity is ridiculous to the point of being hardly worth refuting. Any unbiased study of the facts will convince the impartial student that before Tertullian or Theophilus lived, the doctrine was under study and considered sound. No one doubts that among the heathen (Babylonians and Egyptians, for example) demon gods were worshiped, but to call the Triune Godhead a doctrine of the devil (*Let God Be True*, 101), as Jehovah's Witnesses do, is blasphemy and the product of untutored and darkened souls.

In the entire chapter titled "Is there a Trinity?" (*Let God Be True*, 100–101), the whole problem as to why the Trinity doctrine is "confusing" to Jehovah's Witnesses lies in their interpretation of "death" as it is used in the Bible. To Jehovah's Witnesses, death is the cessation of consciousness, or *destruction*. However, no single or collective rendering of Greek or Hebrew words in any reputable lexicon or dictionary will substantiate their view. Death in the Scriptures is "separation" from the body as in the case of the first death (physical), and separation from God for eternity as in the second death (the lake of fire, Revelation 20). Death never means annihilation, and Jehovah's Witnesses cannot bring in one word in context in the original languages to prove it does. A wealth of evidence has been amassed to prove it does not. I welcome comparisons on this point.

The rest of the chapter is taken up with childish questions—some of which are painful to record. "Who ran the universe the three days Jesus was dead and in the grave?" (death again portrayed as extinction of consciousness) is a sample of the nonsense perpetrated on gullible people. "Religionists" is the label placed on all who disagree with the organization's views regardless of the validity of the criticism. Christians do not believe that the Trinity was incarnate in Christ and that they were "three in one" as such during Christ's ministry. Christ voluntarily limited himself in His earthly body, but heaven was always open to Him and He never ceased being God, Second Person of the Trinity. At His baptism the Holy Spirit descended like a dove, the Father spoke, and the Son was baptized. What further proof is needed to show a threefold unity? Compare the baptism of Christ (Matthew 3:16–17) with the commission to preach in the threefold Name of God (Matthew 28:19) and the evidence is clear and unde-

niable. Even in the Incarnation itself (Luke 1:35) the Trinity appears (see also John 14:16 and 15:26). Of course it is not possible to fathom this great revelation completely, but this we do know: There is a unity of Substance, not three gods, and that unity is One in every essential sense, which no reasonable person can doubt after surveying the evidence. When Jesus said, "My Father is greater than I," He spoke the truth, for in the form of a servant (Philippians 2:7) and as a man, the Son was subject to the Father willingly; but upon His resurrection and in the radiance of His glory taken again from whence He veiled it (vv. 7–8). He showed forth His deity when He declared, "All authority is surrendered to me in heaven and earth" (Matthew 28:18); proof positive of His intrinsic nature and unity of Substance. It is evident that the Lord Jesus Christ was never inferior—speaking of His nature—to His Father during His sojourn on earth.

Jehovah's Witnesses vs. the Scriptures, Reason, and the Trinity

Every major cult and non-Christian religion that seeks to deride orthodox theology continually attacks the doctrine of the Trinity. Jehovah's Witnesses (the Russellites of today) are the most vehement in this endeavor, and because they couch their clever misuse of terminology in scriptural contexts, they are also the most dangerous. Throughout the whole length and breadth of the Watchtower's turbulent history, one "criterion" has been used in every era to measure the credibility of any biblical doctrine. This "criterion" is *reason*. During the era of "Pastor" Russell, and right through until today, reason has always been "the great god" before whom all followers of the Millennial Dawn[37] movement allegedly bow with unmatched reverence. In fact, the "great paraphraser," as Russell was once dubbed, even went so far as to claim that reason—or the ability to think and draw conclusions—opened up to the intellect of man the very character of God himself! Think of it—according to the "pastor," God's nature is actually openly accessible to our feeble and erring reasoning powers. In the first volume of the *Millennial Dawn* series (later titled *Studies in the Scriptures*), "Pastor" Russell makes God subject to our powers of reasoning. Wrote the "pastor": "Let us examine the character of the writings claimed as inspired (The Bible), to see whether their teachings correspond with the character we have *reasonably* imputed to God" (p. 41). Here it is plain to see that for Russell man's understanding of God's character lies not in God's revelation of himself to be taken by faith, but in our ability to reason out that character subject to the laws of our reasoning processes. Russell obviously never considered Jehovah's Word as recorded in the fifty-fifth chapter of Isaiah the prophet, which discourse clearly negates man's powers of reasoning in relation to the divine character and nature of his Creator.

> For my thoughts are not your thoughts, neither are your ways my ways, saith the Lord. For as the heavens are higher than the earth, so are my ways higher than your ways, and my thoughts than your thoughts (Isaiah 55:8–9).

By this statement God certainly did not say reason and thought should be abandoned in the process of inquiry, but merely that no one can know the mind,

---

[37]Name originally given to the movement by Russell in 1886.

nature, or thoughts of God in all their fullness, seeing that man is finite and He is infinite. The term "reason" and derivatives of it (reasonable, reasoning, reasoned, etc.) are used eighty-eight times in the English Bible, and only *once* in all these usages (Isaiah 1:18) does God address man. Jehovah's Witnesses maintain that since God said, "Come now and let us reason together," He therefore gave reason a high place, even using it himself to commune with His creatures. While this is true, it is only so in a limited sense at best. God never said, "Reason out the construction of my spiritual substance and nature" or "limit my character to your reasoning powers." Nevertheless, Jehovah's Witnesses, by making Christ (the Logos, John 1:1) "a god" or "a mighty god," but not "Jehovah God," have done these very things. In the reference quoted above (Isaiah 1:18), Jehovah showed man the way of salvation and invited him to be redeemed from sin. God never invited him to explore His deity or probe into His mind. The apostle Paul says, "For who hath known the mind of the Lord? or who hath been his counselor? or who hath first given to him, and it shall be recompensed unto him again? For of him, and through him, and to him, are all things: to whom be glory for ever" (Romans 11:34–36).

The biblical, historical Christian faith is reasonable, and reason is given to humans by God as a tool for discerning truth, but one cannot fully comprehend the infinite God with reason alone; and the "reason" demonstrated by the Watchtower is not reason at all, but a complex collection of irrational, contradictory, and false statements masquerading as reason.

But now let us examine this typical propaganda from the Watchtower's arsenal and see if they follow "Pastor" Russell and his theory of reason any better than Russell himself, who talked a great deal about "reason," but who violated every basic law of logic—often more than one at a time. In this article,[38] "The Scriptures, Reason, and the Trinity," the Witnesses constantly appeal to *reason* as the standard for determining what God thinks. The following are quotations that we believe illustrate this point beyond doubt. In addition, we will compare the statements of this article at strategic points with a much more recent publication, *Should You Believe in the Trinity?*[39] to show that the teaching has remained consistent over time.

1. "To hold that Jehovah God the Father and Christ Jesus His Son are co-eternal is to fly in the face of reason" (*Watchtower*). Notice that reason is used as the "yardstick" to determine the validity of a scriptural doctrine. The more recent publication remarks concerning the Trinity: "Is such reasoning hard to follow? Many sincere believers have found it to be confusing, contrary to normal reason, unlike anything in their experience" (*Believe*, electronic version, 1).

2. "Jehovah God says, 'Come now, and let us reason together' (Isaiah 1:18). The advocates of the Trinity admit that it is not subject to reason or logic, and so they resort to terming it a 'mystery.' But the Bible contains no divine mysteries. It contains 'sacred secrets.' Every use of the word 'mystery' and 'mysteries' in the *King James Version* comes from the same Greek root word meaning 'to shut the mouth,' that is to keep secret. There is a vast difference between a secret and a mystery. A secret is merely that which has not been made known, but a

[38] *The Watchtower* (January 1, 1973).
[39] *Should You Believe in the Trinity?* (Brooklyn: Watchtower Bible and Tract Society, 1989), 15–26.

mystery is that which cannot be understood.

"However, contending that since the Trinity is such a confusing mystery it must have come from divine revelation creates another major problem. Why? Because divine revelation itself does not allow for such a view of God: 'God is not a God of confusion. . . .' In view of that statement, would God be responsible for a doctrine about himself that is so confusing that even Hebrew, Greek, and Latin scholars cannot really explain it?" (*Believe*, electronic version, 3).

Once again the interested reader must pay close attention to the Witnesses' favorite game of term-switching. *The Watchtower* makes a clever distinction between the term "mystery" and the term "secret" and declares that "the Bible contains no divine mysteries." In view of the seriousness of this Watchtower exercise in semantics, we feel obliged to destroy their manufactured distinction between "secret" and "mystery," by the simple process of consulting the dictionary.

"Mystery" is defined as (1) "Secret, something that is hidden or unknown"; "Secret" is defined as (1) "Something secret or hidden; mystery." Surely this is proof conclusive that the Bible contains "divine mysteries" as far as the meaning of the term is understood. It must also be equally apparent that Jehovah's Witnesses obviously have no ground for rejecting the word "mystery" where either the Bible or the dictionary are concerned. We fail to note any "vast difference" between the two words, and so does the dictionary. The truth is that the Watchtower rejects the Trinity doctrine and other cardinal doctrines of historical Christianity not because they are mysterious, but because Jehovah's Witnesses are determined to reduce Jesus, the Son of God, to a creature or "a second god," all biblical evidence notwithstanding. They still follow in "Pastor" Russell's footsteps, and one needs no dictionary to substantiate that.

9. "Jehovah God by His Word furnishes us with ample *reasons* and logical bases for all regarding which he expects us to exercise faith. . . . We can make sure of what is right only by a process of reasoning on God's Word."

Here indeed is a prime example of what Jehovah's Witnesses continually represent as sound thinking. They cannot produce even one shred of evidence to bolster up their unscriptural claim that God always gives us reason for those things in which He wants us to "exercise faith." Biblical students (even "International" ones)[40] really grasp at theological straws in the wind when they attempt to prove so dogmatic and inconclusive a statement. A moment of reflection on the Scriptures will show, we believe, that this attempt to overemphasize reason is a false one.

First, does God give us a reason for creating Lucifer and allowing him to rebel against the Almighty? Is such a reason found in the Scripture? It is not, and yet we must believe that he exists, that he opposes God, and that all references in the Scripture to Satan are authoritative. God demands that we exercise faith in their objective truth, yet He *never* gives us a reason for them.

Second, does God anywhere give to man a "reasonable" explanation of how it is possible that He exists in Trinity—as three persons while at the same time retaining oneness of nature and essence? No. Never in Scripture is this explained. Here we see a gross inconsistency of Watchtower reliance upon reason

---

[40]International Bible Students is one of the other names for Russellism.

in their rejection of the Trinity. When compared to their acceptance of the miracles of Jesus, one wonders what they consider "reasonable." If they can believe that Jesus raised Lazarus from the dead, changed the water into wine, and fed five thousand with only two fishes and five loaves, *without* a "reasonable" explanation as to "how" He did this, should the "how" of the Trinity be of more difficulty in "reasonableness"? Surely the former is every much as mysterious as the latter!

Third, does God anywhere give the grieving parent who has lost a child a "reasonable" explanation as to the "why"? That certain physical catastrophes can be traced to the results of sin upon mankind, no one will argue. But is God under any obligation to furnish the parent with a "reason" as to why his child *in particular* was taken? No. Never do the Scriptures address the issue. Yet, through it all, God asks us to believe that these seemingly indescribable evils will ultimately work out His divine plan, and He asks us at times to believe in Him without full explanation or reason (but not irrationally) and with the eyes of faith.

Much, much more could be said along the same lines, but enough has been shown to refute adequately the contention of Jehovah's Witnesses that God *always* gives us "reasons and logical bases" for all regarding which He expects us to exercise faith.

Let us also remember the falsity of their other claim in the same paragraph: "We can make sure of what is right only by a process of reasoning on God's Word." But Jesus said: "The Comforter, which is the Holy Ghost, whom the Father will send in my name, he shall teach you all things, and bring all things to your remembrance, whatsoever I have said unto you" (John 14:26). Now if only by a process of reasoning on God's Word we can make sure of what is right, as Jehovah's Witnesses contend, then Jesus and they are at direct variance, for they do not have the guidance of the Holy Spirit, since they deny His person and deity. In a controversy of this nature we prefer to choose God and His Word as opposed to the Watchtower's jumbled Russellism.

Many people, including cultists, skeptics, and even Christians, erroneously believe that religious faith, and Christian faith in particular, is actually *irrational* or *contrary to reason*. However, God is not irrational and never reports what is irrational. We may not have enough information to make a rational determination about an issue, especially about the "how" or "why" of a situation in which God is involved, but that *lack* should never be confused with a "truth" *contrary* to reason. The doctrine of the Trinity is not "illogical," but, as some have described it, "a-logical," or without comprehensive explanation or analogy. A philosophical approach to the issue of the doctrine of the Trinity clearly demonstrates that it is not illogical or irrational at all. It *would* be illogical to say, "One God is three gods" or "one Person is three persons." It is *not* illogical to say, "One God is three persons." Three outstanding philosophers recently presented a compelling proof of this in "Logic and the Trinity," an article in the scholarly journal *Faith and Philosophy*. They quite correctly state,

> Now if the doctrine of the Trinity really were inconsistent, then it could not express the central truth of the Christian religion, and at least some of the claims made in stating the doctrine would be false. It is useless in this context

to appeal to mystery. Only reality can be a mystery; inconsistency rules out reality.[41]

4. "God, through His Word, appeals to our reason. The Trinity doctrine is a negation of both the Scriptures and reason.

"We also need to keep in mind that not even so much as one 'proof text' says that God, Jesus, and the holy spirit are one in some mysterious Godhead. Not one scripture anywhere in the bible says that all three are the same in substance, power, and eternity. The bible is consistent in revealing Almighty God, Jehovah, as alone Supreme, Jesus as his created Son, and the holy spirit as God's active force" (*Believe*, electronic version, 12).

Like so many other of the Watchtower's clever examples of phraseology, the statement from *The Watchtower* contains a mixture of truth and error, with just enough of the former to make good sense and just enough of the latter to confuse the gullible reader. It is unquestionably true that God through His Word appeals to our reason; were it not so we could not understand His desires. But by the same token, God does not invite our inquiry into His nature or character. Jehovah's Witnesses, however, if their views are rightly understood, assume that human reason is capable of doing precisely that.

The Watchtower has never failed to echo the old Arian heresy. This was a theory popularized by Arius of Alexandria (in Egypt) in the fourth century A.D., which taught that Jesus was the first creature, a second and created god, inferior to Jehovah, the Father. It is upon this theological myth, banished from the church in A.D. 325 (along with Arius), that Jehovah's Witnesses unsteadily base their whole system.

Arius was the most popular proponent of the view that Jesus Christ was created, and it was not until the early church Fathers understood exactly what he was saying that he was uniformly condemned, both at the Council of Nicea in A.D. 325 and in subsequent church rulings. He was condemned because he believed and taught that Jesus Christ was not God, but was created. At the council of Nicea he declared that the Son of God was a created being, created out of nothing. Accordingly, there was a time when He "was not."[42]

Arius was a presbyter, or pastoral assistant, to Bishop Alexander of Alexandria. His popular definitions were given to the public in colorful, easy-to-understand form much like the evangelism techniques of the Jehovah's Witnesses today. Arius took the popular folk tunes of his day and composed new lyrics regarding the creation of the Son. A loose paraphrase of one of his songs clearly expresses his heretical view, although the translation loses the meter and rhyme of the original:

> We praise him as without beginning,
> Because of him who has a beginning.
> And adore him as everlasting,
> Because of him who in time has come to be.
> He that is without beginning

---

[41]John Macnamara, Marie La Palme Reyes, and Gonzalo E. Reyes, "Logic and the Trinity," *Faith and Philosophy*, 11:1 (January 1994): 3–18.

[42]For further information on this important issue in church history, see Bruce L. Shelley, *Church History in Plain Language* (Dallas: Word Publishing, 1995).

Made the Son a beginning of things originated;
And advanced him as a Son to himself by adoption.
He has nothing proper to God in proper subsistence.
For he is not equal, no,
Nor one in essence with him.
Wise is God, for he is the teacher of wisdom.[43]

Jehovah's Witnesses know beyond doubt that if Jesus is Jehovah God, every one of them is going to a flaming hereafter; and hell they fear above all else. This no doubt explains a great deal of their antagonism toward the doctrines of the Trinity and hell. The Witnesses, it must be remembered, consistently berate the Trinity doctrine as of the devil and never tire of proclaiming that the hell of the Bible is the grave. The thought of being punished in unquenchable fire for their disobedience to God is probably the strongest bond holding the Watchtower's flimsy covers together.

Let us further pursue the Watchtower's logic. In *The Watchtower's* article, two other terms are repeated constantly by Jehovah's Witnesses. These terms are "equal" and "coeternal." The terms are used some six times in this particular article and each time it is denied that Jesus Christ is either equal to or coeternal with God His Father. Says *The Watchtower:*

> We see God in heaven as the Superior One. . . . We see his Son on earth expressing delight to do his Father's will; clearly two separate and distinct personalities and not at all equal. Nothing here (Matthew 28:18–20) to indicate that it (The Holy Spirit) is a person, let alone that it is equal with Jehovah God. The very fact that the Son received his life from the Father proves that *he could not be coeternal with him.* (John 1:18; 6:57). . . . Nor can it be argued that God was superior to Jesus only because of Jesus then being a human, for *Paul makes clear that Christ Jesus in his prehuman form was not equal with his father.* In Philippians 2:1–11 (NWT)[44] he counsels Christians not to be motivated by egotism but to have lowliness of mind, even as Christ Jesus had, who, although existing in God's form before coming to earth was not *ambitious* to become equal with his Father. . . . Jesus did not claim to be *The God,* but *only* God's Son. That Jesus is inferior to his Father, is also apparent. . . . The 'Holy Ghost' or Holy Spirit is God's active force. . . . There is no basis for concluding that the Holy Spirit is a person. . . . Yes, the Trinity finds its origin in the pagan concept of a multiplicity, plurality, or pantheon of Gods. The law Jehovah God gave to the Jews stated diametrically the opposite. 'Jehovah our God is *one* Jehovah' (Deuteronomy 6:4).

In the more recent *Should You Believe in the Trinity?* booklet, the same sentiment is echoed:

> The Bible is clear and consistent about the relationship of God to Jesus. Jehovah God alone is Almighty. He created the prehuman Jesus directly. Thus, Jesus had a beginning and could never be coequal with God in power or eternity. . . . Jesus never claimed to be God. Everything he said about himself indicates that he did not consider himself equal to God in any way—not in power, not in knowledge, not in age. In every period of his existence, whether in

---

[43]F. Forrester Church and Terrence J. Mulry, eds., *The Macmillan Book of Earliest Christian Hymns* (New York: Macmillan Publishing Company, 1988), 181.

[44]NWT stands for the *New World Translation of the Holy Scriptures* (Brooklyn: Watchtower Bible and Tract Society, 1961, revised edition 1984).

heaven or on earth, his speech and conduct reflect subordination to God. God
is always the superior, Jesus the lesser one who was created by God. . . . The followers of Jesus always viewed him as a submissive servant of God, not as God's
equal. . . . In his prehuman existence, and also when he was on earth, Jesus was
subordinate to God. After his resurrection, he continues to be in a subordinate,
secondary position. . . . Various sources acknowledge that the Bible does not
support the idea that the holy spirit is the third person of a Trinity. . . . No, the
holy spirit is not a person and it is not part of a Trinity. The holy spirit is God's
active force that he uses to accomplish his will. It is not equal to God but is always
at his disposition and subordinate to him.[45]

Let us briefly examine these statements of the Jehovah's Witnesses and see
if they have any rational content where the Bible is concerned. The Watchtower
maintains that Christ and His Father are "not at all equal," which has been their
boldest insult to Christianity since Russell and Rutherford concocted and promoted the whole Watchtower nightmare. This type of unbelief where Christ's
true deity is concerned has gladdened the hearts of non-intellectuals the country over who find it easier to mock the Trinity than to trust God's Word and His
Son. Concerning His relationship with the Father, the apostle John in the fifth
chapter of his gospel, the eighteenth verse, when speaking of Jesus and the Jews
said, "Therefore the Jews sought the more to kill him, because he not only had
broken the sabbath, but said also God was his Father, making himself *equal* with
God." The Greek word for equal is *ison*, which according to *Thayer's Greek Lexicon*
(p. 307), an acknowledged authority, means "equal in quality as in quantity, to
claim for one's self the nature, rank, authority, which belong to God."

Dr. Thayer, Jehovah's Witnesses might take notice, was a Unitarian who denied Christ's deity even as they do; yet, being honest, he gave the true meaning
of the biblical terms even though they contradicted his views. Thus God's Word
directly contradicts Jehovah's Witnesses, and this they cannot deny.

The Watchtower further contends that since Christ received life from His
Father: "I live by the Father" (John 6:57), He could not be coeternal with Him.
At first glance this seems plausible, especially when coupled with John 5:26: "As
the Father hath life in himself; so hath he given to the Son to have life in
himself." However, taking this text in its context we readily see that it cannot
mean that Christ derived "eternal existence" from the Father. John 1:1 bears
witness that "the Word *was* God"; therefore, eternity was inherent in His
makeup by nature. The logical conclusion must be that the indwelling "life" of
"God the Word" entered time in the form of "the Son of Man," and by this
operation the Father, through the agency of the Holy Spirit, gave the "Son of
Man" to have "life in himself," the same life that was eternally His as the eternal
Word. But it takes more than a glance to support this garbled Watchtower polytheism, as we shall soon see.

Unwittingly, Jehovah's Witnesses answer their own scriptural double-talk
when they quote Philippians 2:5–11. In this passage of Scripture, Paul claims
full deity for Christ and maintains that in His preincarnate life He existed "in
the form of God" and "thought it not something to be grasped" at to be *equal*
with God, but took upon himself the "*form* of a servant, being born in the like-

---

[45] *Should You Believe in the Trinity?* (Brooklyn: Watchtower Bible and Tract Society, 1989), electronic
version.

ness of men" (RSV). The term *equal* here is another form of *ison*, namely *isa*, which again denotes *absolute sameness of nature*, thus confirming Christ's true deity. Further, this context reveals beyond reasonable doubt that *all* references to Christ's being subject to His Father (e.g., John 5:26; 6:57) pertain to His earthly existence, during which "he emptied himself" to become as one of us. This in no way affected His true deity or unity with the Father, for Jesus claimed Jehovahistic identity (John 8:58) when He announced himself to the unbelieving Jews as the "I AM" of Exodus 3:14.

Twice, in the same terms, Jehovah's Witnesses deny what the Scriptures specifically testify, that Christ *is equal* with the Father in essence, character, and nature, which truths the Watchtower's term-switching campaigns can never change.

I should also like to call attention to an extremely bold example of misquoting so commonly found in Watchtower propaganda. On page twenty-two, the Russellite oracle declares, "Paul makes clear that Christ Jesus in his prehuman form was not equal to his Father. In Philippians 2:1–11 (NWT), he counsels Christians not to be motivated by egotism but to have lowliness of mind even as Christ Jesus had, who, although existing in God's form before coming to earth, *was not ambitious to become equal with his Father.*"

Now, as far as the original Greek text of Philippians 2:1–11 is concerned, this is an absurd and plainly dishonest statement. Paul never even mentions Christ being ambitious to attain anything at all or even his lack of ambition, since no Greek term there can be translated "ambition." Jehovah's Witnesses themselves do not use the word "ambition" in their own *New World Translation*, nor does any other translator that we know of. Despite this, however, they introduce the word that clouds the real meaning of the Greek terms. Further than this, and worse, the Watchtower plainly attempts to use Paul's declaration of Christ's deity as a means of confusing the issue. They maintain that Paul here taught that Jesus was inferior in nature to His Father, when in reality Paul's entire system of theology says the opposite. If we are to believe the Greek text, Paul declares that Jesus did *not* consider equality with God something "to be grasped after," or "robbery" (Greek *arpazo*), since He previously existed as the eternal Word of God (John 1:1) prior to His incarnation (John 1:14) and as such fully shared all the Father's prerogatives and attributes. Hence, He had no desire to strive for what was His by nature and inheritance. Paul elsewhere calls Christ "all the fullness of the Deity . . . in bodily form" (Colossians 2:9, NIV), "our great God and Savior" (Titus 2:13, RSV), and "God" (Hebrews 1:8). These are just a few of the references; there are at least twenty-five more that could be cited from Paul's writings and over seventy-five from the balance of the New Testament. Contrary to the Watchtower, then, Paul never wrote their Russellite interpretational paraphrase as recorded on page twenty-two, since even the Greek text bears witness against them.

Jehovah's Witnesses sum up another blast at the Trinity doctrine by informing us that John 1:1 should be rendered, "In the beginning was the Word, and the Word was with God, and the Word was *a god.*" This is another example of the depths to which the Watchtower will descend to make Jesus "a second god" and thus introduce polytheism into Christianity. Needless to say, no recognized translators in the history of Greek exegesis have ever sanctioned such a gram-

matical travesty as the Watchtower translation, and the Watchtower translators know it. Such a rendition is an indication of markedly inferior scholarship and finds no basis whatsoever in New Testament Greek grammar. Both James Moffatt and Edgar Goodspeed, liberal translators, render John 1:1: "The Word was Divine," while most acknowledged authorities read it as "The Word was Deity." Moffatt and Goodspeed, however, admit that Scripture teaches the full and equal deity of Jesus Christ, something Jehovah's Witnesses vehemently deny. Beyond doubt the Watchtower of Jehovah's Witnesses presents a strange dilemma, "ever learning, and never able to come to the knowledge of the truth" (2 Timothy 3:7). The Russellite movements (there are other small branches) all cry loudly the old Jewish Shema, "Hear, O Israel: the LORD our God *is* one LORD" (or, "The LORD is One," Deuteronomy 6:4), and attempt to use it against the doctrine of the Trinity. But once again language betrays the shallowness of their resources. The term *echod*, "one" in Hebrew, *does not* denote *absolute unity* in many places throughout the Old Testament, and often it definitely denotes *composite unity*, which argues for the Trinity of the Deity (Jehovah).

For example, in the second chapter, twenty-fourth verse of Genesis, the Lord tells us that "a man leave[s] his father and his mother, and shall cleave unto his wife: and they shall be one flesh" (in Hebrew, *bosor echod*). Certainly this does not mean that in marriage a man and his wife become one *person*, but that they become one in the unity of their *substance* and are considered as *one* in the eyes of God. Please note, this is true unity; yet *not solitary*, but *composite unity*.

Let us further consider composite unity. Moses sent twelve spies into Canaan (Numbers 13), and when they returned they brought with them a great cluster of grapes (in Hebrew *eschol echod*). Now since there were hundreds of grapes on this one stem, it could hardly be absolute or solitary unity, yet again *echod* (one) is used to describe the cluster. This shows conclusively that the grapes were considered "one" in the sense of their being of the same origin; hence, *composite unity* is again demonstrated. When we use "composite unity" in describing the Trinity, we must be careful to understand the limitations of our analogies. For example, the "one" cluster of grapes is composed of many grapes, but when we speak of the "one" God in an analogous sense, we do not mean that there are three ("many") *gods* in one God. We mean that there are three *persons*, yet one *God*. The distinction is both biblical and theologically accurate.

Jehovah's Witnesses continually ask, "If Jesus, when on the cross, was truly an incarnation of Jehovah, then who was in heaven?" This is a logical question to which the eighteenth chapter of Genesis gives fourteen answers, each reaffirming the other. As recorded in Genesis eighteen, Abraham had three visitors. Two of them were angels (Genesis 19:1), but the third he addressed as *Jehovah God—fourteen times!* Abraham's third visitor stayed and conversed with him and then departed, saying concerning Sodom, "I will go down now, and see whether they have done altogether according to the cry of it, which is come unto me; and if not, I will know" (18:21). And so, "The LORD went his way, as soon as he had left communing with Abraham: and Abraham returned unto his place" (verse 33).

Now if the apostle John is to be believed without question, and Jehovah's

Witnesses agree that he must be, then "No man hath seen God [the Father] at any time; the only begotten Son [Jesus Christ], which is in the bosom of the Father, he hath declared him" (John 1:18). To further confuse the Witnesses' peculiar view of God as a *solitary unit,* Jesus himself said concerning His Father, "You have neither heard his voice at any time, nor seen his shape . . . for God is a Spirit: and they that worship him must worship him in Spirit and in truth" (John 4:24; 5:37).

Now, then, here is the evidence. Moses declares that God spoke face to face with Abraham (Genesis 17:1), and Jesus and John say, "No man hath seen God at any time." But Jesus makes it clear that He is referring to *the Father,* and so does John. The nineteenth chapter of Genesis, the twenty-fourth verse, solves this problem for us once and for all, as even Jehovah's Witnesses will eventually be forced to admit. Moses here reveals a glimpse of the *composite unity* in the Triune God. "Then the Lord rained upon Sodom and upon Gomorrah brimstone and fire *from the Lord* out of heaven." This unquestionably is the only solution to this dilemma. God the Father rained fire on Sodom and Gomorrah, and God the Son spoke and ate with Abraham and Sarah.

Two persons (the third Person of the Trinity is revealed more fully in the New Testament: John 14:26; 16:7–14; etc.) are both called Jehovah [translated LORD in the KJV] (Genesis 18:20; 19:24; cf. Isaiah 9:6; Micah 5:2), and both are *one (echod)* with the Holy Spirit in *composite unity* (Deuteronomy 6:4). God the Father was in heaven, God the Son died on the cross, and God the Holy Spirit comforts the church till Jesus shall come again.

God said in Genesis 1:26, "Let us make man in *our* image, after *our* likeness," not in *my* image, after *my* likeness. Here plurality is seen, obviously, God speaking to His coeternal Son (Christ) and addressing *Him* as an *equal.* Genesis 11:7, with reference to the Tower of Babel, also lends strong support to the Triune God doctrine. Here God, speaking as an *equal* to His Son, declares, "Let *us* go down and there confound their language"—again, plurality and *equal* discourse. In the face of all these texts, the Watchtower is strangely silent. They, however, rally afresh to the attack on page twenty-three of their article and declare that "there is no basis for concluding that the Holy Spirit is a person."

The fact that the Holy Spirit is described as possessing an active *will* ("If I go not away, the Comforter will not come unto you," John 16:7), which is the most concrete trait of a distinct personality, and that He is said to exercise the characteristics of a *teacher* (John 16:8), apparently all falls on deaf ears where the Watchtower is concerned. The literature of Jehovah's Witnesses is also consistently filled with nonsensical questions such as, "How could the one hundred and twenty persons at Pentecost be baptized with a person?" (Acts 1:5, 2:1–4). In answer to this, it evidently escapes the ever-zealous Russellites that the fulfillment of Jesus' prophecy as recorded in Acts 1:5 was explained in chapter two, verse four. Luke here says, "And they were all filled (Greek *eplesthesan*) with the Holy Ghost." Jesus all too obviously did not mean that the apostles would be "immersed" in a person, but filled with and immersed in the power of His presence as symbolized in the tongues like unto fire. If Jehovah's Witnesses ever studied the Scriptures in the open with good scholars and stopped masquerading as biblical authorities, which they are not, it might be interesting to see the results. Of course, great scholarship is not necessary to obtain a saving

knowledge of Jesus Christ from God's Word; even so, when people deny the historical Christian faith and berate those who profess it, they ought to have some scholastic support, and Jehovah's Witnesses have none.

The Watchtower widely cries that they will meet all persons with an open Bible, but to this date not one of their alleged authorities has materialized despite our numerous invitations. We of orthodox Christianity do not desire to maliciously attack anyone's faith merely for the "joy" of doing it; but we must be faithful to our Lord's command to "preach the word and contend for the faith." As long as the Watchtower continues to masquerade as a Christian movement and attack, without biblical provocation or cause, orthodox Christian theology with such articles as "The Scripture, Reason, and the Trinity," etc., so long will our voice be raised in answer to their consistent misrepresentations. God granting us the grace, we can do no other but be faithful to Him "who is the faithful and true witness, the *source* through whom God's creation came" (Revelation 3:14, Knox Version)—His eternal Word and beloved Son, Jesus Christ, our Lord.

Jehovah's Witnesses and the Holy Spirit

Though it is rudimentary to any true student of the Bible, the personality and deity of the Holy Spirit must constantly be defended against the attacks of the Watchtower.

The Watchtower, as has been seen, denies the Holy Spirit's personality and deity, but the following references, only a few of many in Scripture, refute their stand completely:

(1) *Acts 5:3–4.* In verse three, Peter accuses Ananias of lying *to* the Holy Spirit, and in verse four he declares the Holy Spirit to be God, an equation hard for the Watchtower to explain, much less deny. Who else but a person can be lied to?

(2) *Acts 13:2, 4.* In this context the Holy Spirit *speaks* and *sends*, as He does in 21:10–11, where He *prophesies* Paul's imprisonment. Only a personality can do these things, *not* "an invisible active force," as the Jehovah's Witnesses describe Him.

(3) *John 14:16–17, 26; 16:7–14.* These need no comment. *He* is a divine person and He is God (Genesis 1:2).

The New World Translation of the Bible

In any dealings one may have with the Watchtower or its numerous representatives, it is a virtual certainty that sooner or later in the course of events the Watchtower's "translation" of the Bible will confront the average prospective convert. This translation of the entire Bible is called the *New World Translation of the Holy Scriptures.* It is usually abbreviated as NWT.

First published in part in 1950 and later revised in 1951, 1961, and 1984, the New Testament version of this "translation" sold over 480,000 copies before its initial revision, and the entire Bible has now sold tens of millions of copies. This version lies behind a thin veneer of scholarship, which proclaims the Society's daring and boldness in a field into which all informed scholars know Je-

hovah's Witnesses are almost totally unprepared to venture.

The "translation" has had wide distribution on all six continents. Jehovah's Witnesses boast that their "translation" is "the work of competent scholars" and further that it gives a clarity to the Scriptures that other translations have somehow failed to supply. The refutation of such stupendous claims by the Watchtower involve the necessity of a careful examination of their "translation" so that it may be weighed by the standards of sound biblical scholarship. An exhaustive analysis of this work is impossible in this limited space, but we have selected some of the outstanding examples of fraud and deceit from the *New World Translation*. These examples should discourage any fair-minded individual from placing much value upon the Jehovah's Witnesses' Bible.

In their foreword to the *New World Translation of the Christian Greek Scriptures* (NWTCGS—published before the whole Bible appeared in 1950), the translation committee of the Watchtower cleverly claims for itself and its "translation" a peculiar freedom from what they define as "the misleading influence of religious traditions, which have their roots in paganism" (p. 7). This "influence," the Watchtower insists, has colored the inspired Word of God, so it is necessary for them, Jehovah's chosen theocratic representatives, to set aright the numerous alleged examples of "human traditionalism" (p. 6) evidenced in all translations from John Wycliffe's to the present. Should anyone question that this arrogant attitude is the true Watchtower position regarding other translations, the following quote from the foreword to the NWTCGS will dismiss all doubt:

> But honesty compels us to remark that, while each of them has its points of merit, they have fallen victim to the power of human traditionalism in varying degrees. Consequently, religious traditions, hoary with age, have been taken for granted and gone unchallenged and uninvestigated. These have been interwoven into the translations to color the thought. In support of a preferred religious view, an inconsistency and unreasonableness have been insinuated into the teachings of the inspired writings.
>
> The Son of God taught that the traditions of creed-bound men made the commandments and teachings of God of no power and effect. The endeavor of the New World Bible Translation committee has been to avoid this snare of religious traditionalism (p. 6).

From this pompous pronouncement it is only too evident that the Watchtower considers its "scholars" the superiors of such great scholars as Wycliffe and Tyndale, not to mention the hundreds of brilliant, consecrated Christian scholars who produced the subsequent orthodox translations. Such a pretext is of course too absurd to merit refutation, but let it be remembered that the New World Bible translation committee had no known translators with recognized degrees in Greek or Hebrew exegesis or translation. While the members of the committee have never been identified officially by the Watchtower, many Witnesses who worked at the headquarters during the translation period were fully aware of who the members were. They included Nathan H. Knorr (president of the Society at that time), Frederick W. Franz (who later succeeded Knorr as president), Albert D. Schroeder, George Gangas, and Milton G. Henschel (currently the president). None of these men had any university education except Franz, who left school after two years, never completing even an undergraduate degree. In fact, Frederick W. Franz, then representing the translation committee

and later serving as the Watchtower Society's fourth president, admitted under oath that he could not translate Genesis 2:4 from the Hebrew.

From the Pursur's Proof of the cross-examination held on Wednesday, November 24, 1954 (p. 7, paragraphs A-B), examining Frederick W. Franz, vice-president of the Watchtower Bible and Tract Society and sent as representative of the Society and the Translation Communications:

Q: Have you also made yourself familiar with Hebrew?
A: (Franz) Yes.
Q: So that you have a substantial linguistic apparatus at your command?
A: Yes, for use in my biblical work.
Q: I think you are able to read and follow the Bible in Hebrew, Greek, Latin, Spanish, Portuguese, German, and French?
A: Yes.

Later, during the same cross-examination:

Q: You, yourself, read and speak Hebrew, do you?
A: I do not speak Hebrew.
Q: You do not?
A: No.
Q: Can you, yourself, translate that into Hebrew?
A: Which?
Q: That fourth verse of the second chapter of Genesis?
A: You mean here?
Q: Yes.
A: No.

We asked a Hebrew teacher at Biola University/Talbot Theological Seminary if the fourth verse of the second chapter of Genesis was a particularly difficult verse to translate. After all, the pursur's question would hardly have been fair if it were the hardest verse in the Old Testament to translate. The professor said that he would never pass a first-year Hebrew student who could not translate that verse. This is an example of the "scholarship" backing the NWT.

However, the Watchtower "translation" speaks for itself and shows more clearly than pen can, the scholastic dishonesty and lack of scholarship so rampant within its covers. In order to point out these glaring inconsistencies, the author has listed five prime examples of the Watchtower's inaccuracies in translating the New Testament.

The Watchtower's Scriptural Distortions

(1) The first major perversion that Jehovah's Witnesses attempt to foist upon the minds of the average reader is that it has remained for them as "God's true Witnesses" to restore the divine Old Testament name *Jehovah* to the text of the Greek New Testament. But let us observe this pretext as they stated it in their own words.

> The evidence is, therefore, that the original text of the Christian Greek Scriptures has been tampered with, the same as the text of the LXX [the Septuagint—a Greek translation of the Old Testament] has been. And, at least from the third century A.D. onward, the divine name in tetragrammaton [the Hebrew

consonants YHWH, usually rendered "Jehovah"] form has been eliminated from the text by copyists. . . . In place of it they substituted the words *kyrios* (usually translated "the Lord") and *theos*, meaning "God" (p. 18).

The "evidence" that the Witnesses refer to is a papyrus roll of the LXX, which contains the second half of the book of Deuteronomy and which does have the tetragrammaton throughout. Further than this, the Witnesses refer to Aquila (A.D. 128) and Origen (ca. A.D. 250), who both utilized the tetragrammaton in their respective *Version* and *Hexapla*. Jerome, in the fourth century, also mentioned the tetragrammaton as appearing in certain Greek volumes even in his day. On the basis of this small collection of fragmentary "evidence," Jehovah's Witnesses conclude their argument:

> It proves that the original LXX did contain the divine name wherever it occurred in the Hebrew original. Considering it a sacrilege to use some substitute such as *kyrios* or *theos*, the scribes inserted the tetragrammaton at its proper place in the Greek version text (p. 12).

The whole case the Witnesses try to prove is that the original LXX and the New Testament autographs all used the tetragrammaton (p. 18), but owing to "tampering" all these were changed; hence, their responsibility to restore the divine name. Such is the argument, and a seemingly plausible one to those not familiar with the history of manuscripts and the Witnesses' subtle use of terms.

To explode this latest Watchtower pretension of scholarship completely is an elementary task. It can be shown from literally thousands of copies of the Greek New Testament that not *once* does the tetragrammaton appear, not even in Matthew, which was possibly written in Hebrew or Aramaic originally, therefore making it more prone than all the rest to have traces of the divine name in it—yet it does not! Beyond this, the roll of papyrus (LXX) that contains the latter part of Deuteronomy and the divine name only proves that one copy did have the divine name (*YHWH*), whereas all other existing copies use *kyrios* and *theos*, which the Witnesses claim are "substitutes." The testimonies of Aquila, Origen, and Jerome, in turn, only show that *sometimes* the divine name was used, but the general truth upheld by all scholars is that the Septuagint, with minor exceptions, always uses *kyrios* and *theos* in place of the tetragrammaton, and the New Testament never uses it at all. Relative to the nineteen "sources" the Watchtower uses (pp. 30–33) for restoring the tetragrammaton to the New Testament, it should be noted that they are all translations from Greek (which uses *kyrios* and *theos*, not the tetragrammaton) back into Hebrew, the earliest of which is A.D. 1385, and therefore they are of no value as evidence.

These cold logical facts unmask once and for all the shallow scholarship of Jehovah's Witnesses, whose arrogant pretension that they have a sound basis for restoring the divine name (Jehovah) to the Scriptures while inferring that orthodoxy suppressed it centuries ago is revealed to be a hollow scholastic fraud. The Watchtower itself admits, "But apart from [the use of "Jah" in "Hallelujah" in the book of Revelation], no ancient Greek manuscript that we possess today of the books from Matthew to Revelation contains God's name [the tetragrammaton] in full."[46]

---

[46] *The Divine Name That Will Endure* (Brooklyn: Watchtower Bible and Tract Society, 1997), electronic version.

No reasonable scholar, of course, objects to the use of the term Jehovah in the Bible. But since only the Hebrew consonants *YHWH* appear without vowels, pronunciation is at best uncertain, and dogmatically to settle on *Jehovah* is straining at the bounds of good linguistics. When the Witnesses arrogantly claim then to have "restored" the divine name (Jehovah), it is almost pathetic. All students of Hebrew know that any vowel can be inserted between the consonants (*YHWH* or *JHVH*), so that theoretically the divine name could be any combination from JoHeVaH to JiHiViH without doing violence to the grammar of the language in the slightest degree.

(2) *Colossians 1:16*. "By means of him all [other][47] things were created in the heavens and upon the earth, the things visible and the things invisible, no matter whether they are thrones or lordships or governments or authorities" (NWT).

In this particular rendering, Jehovah's Witnesses attempt one of the most clever perversions of the New Testament texts that the author has ever seen. Knowing full well that the word *other* does not occur in this text, or for that matter in any of the three verses (16, 17, 19) where it has been added, albeit in brackets, the Witnesses deliberately insert it into the translation in a vain attempt to make Christ a creature and one of the "things" He is spoken of as having created.

Attempting to justify this unheard-of travesty upon the Greek language and also upon simple honesty, the New World Bible translation committee enclosed each added "other" in brackets, which are said by them to "enclose words inserted to complete or clarify the sense in the English text."[48] Far from *clarifying* God's Word here, these unwarranted additions serve only to further the erroneous presupposition of the Watchtower that our Lord Jesus Christ is a creature rather than the Eternal Creator.

The entire context of Colossians 1:15–22 is filled with superlatives in its description of the Lord Jesus as the "image of the invisible God, the first begetter [or 'original bringer forth'—Erasmus] of every creature." The apostle Paul lauds the Son of God as *Creator* of all things (v. 16) and describes Him as existing "before all things" and as the one by whom "all things consist" (v. 17). This is in perfect harmony with the entire picture Scripture paints of the eternal Word of God (John 1:1) who was made flesh (John 1:14) and of whom it was written: "All things were made by him; and without him was not any thing made that was made" (John 1:3). The writer of the book of Hebrews also pointed out that God's Son "[upholds] all things by the word of his power" (Hebrews 1:3) and that He is Deity in all its fullness, even as Paul wrote to the Colossians: "For . . . in him should all fulness [of God] dwell" (Colossians 1:19).

The Scriptures, therefore, bear unmistakable testimony to the creative activity of God's Son, distinguishing Him from among the "things" created, as *the* Creator and Sustainer of "all things."

Jehovah's Witnesses, therefore, have no conceivable ground for this dishonest rendering of Colossians 1:16–17 and 19 by the insertion of the word "other," since they are supported by no grammatical authorities, nor do they

---

[47]Brackets are part of the NWT text itself.
[48]*New World Translation*, Foreword, 6.

dare to dispute their perversions with competent scholars lest they further parade their obvious ignorance of Greek exegesis.

(3) *Matthew 27:50.* "Again Jesus cried out with a loud voice, and yielded up his breath" (NWT).

Luke 23:46. "And Jesus called with a loud voice and said: Father, into your hands I entrust my spirit" (NWT).

For many years the Watchtower has been fighting a vain battle to redefine biblical terms to suit their own peculiar theological interpretations. They have had some measure of success in this attempt in that they have taught the rank and file a new meaning for tried and true biblical terms, and it is this trait of their deceptive system that we analyze now in connection with the above quoted verses.

The interested student of Scripture will note from Matthew 27:50 and Luke 23:46 that they are parallel passages describing the same event, namely, the crucifixion of Jesus Christ. In Matthew's account, the Witnesses had no difficulty substituting the word "breath" for the Greek "spirit" (*pneuma*), for in their vocabulary this word has many meanings, none of them having any hearing upon the general usage of the term, i.e., that of an immaterial, cognizant nature, inherent in man by definition and descriptive of angels through Creation. Jehovah's Witnesses reject this immaterial nature in man and call it "breath," "life," "mental disposition," or "something windlike." In fact, they will call it anything but what God's Word says it is, an invisible nature, eternal by Creation, a spirit, made in the image of God (Genesis 1:27). Sometimes, and in various contexts, spirit (*pneuma*) can mean some of the things the Witnesses hold, but context determines translation, along with grammar, and their translations quite often do not remain true to either.

Having forced the word "breath" into Matthew's account of the crucifixion to make it appear that Jesus only stopped breathing and did not yield up His invisible nature upon dying, the Witnesses plod on to Luke's account, only to be caught in their own trap. Luke, learned scholar and master of Greek that he was, forces the Witnesses to render his account of Christ's words using the correct term "spirit" (*pneuma*), instead of "breath" as in Matthew 27:50. Thus in one fell swoop the entire Watchtower fabric of manufactured terminology collapses, because Jesus would hardly have said: "Father, into thy hands I commit my *breath*"—yet if the Witnesses are consistent, which they seldom are, why did they not render the identical Greek term (*pneuma*) as "breath" both times, for it is a parallel account of the same scene!

The solution to this question is quite elementary, as all can clearly see. The Witnesses could not render it "breath" in Luke and get away with it, so they used it where they could and hoped nobody would notice either it or the different rendering in Matthew. The very fact that Christ dismissed His spirit proves the survival of the human spirit beyond the grave, or as Solomon so wisely put it: "Then shall the dust return to the earth as it was: and the spirit shall return unto God who gave it" (Ecclesiastes 12:7).

(4) *Philippians 1:21-23.* "For in my case to live is Christ, and to die, gain. Now if it be to live on in the flesh, this is a fruitage of my work—and yet which thing to select I do not know. I am under pressure from these two things; but

what I do desire is the releasing and the being with Christ, for this, to be sure, is far better" (NWT).

In common with other cults that teach soul-sleep after the death of the body, Jehovah's Witnesses translate texts contradicting this view to suit their own ends, a prime example of which is their rendering of Philippians 1:21–23. To anyone possessing even a cursory knowledge of Greek grammar the translation "but what I do desire is the releasing" (v. 23) signifies either a woeful ignorance of the rudiments of the language or a deliberate, calculated perversion of terminology for a purpose or purposes most questionable.

It is no coincidence that this text is a great "proof" passage for the expectation of every true Christian who after death goes to be with the Lord (2 Corinthians 5:8). Jehovah's Witnesses realize that if this text goes unchanged or unchallenged it utterly destroys their Russellite teaching that the soul becomes extinct at the death of the body. This being the case, and since they could not challenge the text without exploding the myth of their acceptance of the Bible as the final authority, the Watchtower committee chose to alter the passage in question, give it a new interpretation, and remove this threat to their theology.

The rendering, "but what I do desire is the releasing," particularly the last word, is an imposition on the principles of sound Greek exegesis. The NWT renders the infinitive form of the verb *analuo* (*analusoi*) as a substantive. In the context of this particular passage, to translate it "the releasing" would require the use of the participle construction (*analusas*), which when used with the word "wish" or "desire" denotes "a great longing" or "purpose" and must be rendered "to depart" or "to unloose." (See Thayer; Liddell and Scott; Strong, Young, and A. T. Robertson.)

Quite frankly, it may appear that I have gone to a great deal of trouble simply to refute the wrong usage of a Greek form, but in truth this "simple" switching of terms is used by the Witnesses in an attempt to teach that Paul meant something entirely different than what he wrote to the Philippians. To see how the Watchtower manages this, I quote from their own appendix to the *New World Translation of the Christian Greek Scriptures* (780–781):

> The verb *a-na-ly'sai* is used as a verbal noun here. It occurs only once more in the *Christian Greek Scriptures*, and that is at Luke 12:36, where it refers to Christ's return. The related noun (*a-na'-ly-sis*) occurs but once, at 2 Timothy 4:6, where the apostle says: "The due time for my releasing is imminent." ... But here at Philippians 1:23 we have not rendered the verb as "returning" or "departing," but as "releasing." The reason is, that the word may convey two thoughts, the apostle's own releasing to be with Christ at his return and also the Lord's releasing himself from the heavenly restraints and returning as he promised.
>
> In no way is the apostle here saying that immediately at his death he would be changed into spirit and would be with Christ forever. ... It is to this return of Christ and the apostle's releasing to be always with the Lord that Paul refers at Philippians 1:23. He says there that two things are immediately possible for him, namely, (1) to live on in the flesh and (2) to die. Because of the circumstances to be considered, he expressed himself as being under pressure from these two things, not knowing which thing to choose as proper. Then he suggests a third thing, and this thing he really desires. There is no question about his desire for this thing as preferable, namely, the releasing, for it means his being with Christ.

The expression *tou a-na-ly'-sai*, or *the releasing* cannot therefore be applied to the apostle's death as a human creature and his departing thus from this life. It must refer to the events at the time of Christ's return and second presence, that is to say, his second coming and the rising of all those dead in Christ to be with him forevermore.

Here, after much grammatical intrigue, we have the key as to why the Witnesses went to so much trouble to render "depart" as "releasing." By slipping in this grammatical error, the Watchtower hoped to "prove" that Paul wasn't really discussing his impending death and subsequent reunion with Christ at all (a fact every major biblical scholar and translator in history has affirmed), but a *third* thing, namely, "the events at the time of Christ's return and second presence." With breathtaking dogmatism, the Witnesses claim that "*the releasing* cannot therefore be applied to the apostle's death. . . . It must refer to the events at the time of Christ's return."

Words fail when confronted with this classic example of unparalleled deceit, which finds no support in any Greek text or exegetical grammatical authority. Contrary to the Watchtower's statement that "the word may convey two thoughts, the apostle's own releasing to be with Christ at his return and also the Lord's releasing himself from the heavenly restraints and returning as he promised," as a matter of plain exegetical fact, Christ's return is not even the subject of discussion—rather it is the apostle's death and his concern for the Philippians that are here portrayed. That Paul never expected to "sleep" in his grave until the resurrection as Jehovah's Witnesses maintain is evident by the twenty-first verse of the chapter, literally: "For me to live is Christ, and to die is gain." There would be no gain in dying if men slept till the resurrection, for "[God] is not the God of the dead, but the God of the living" (Mark 12:27). Clearly, Paul was speaking of but two things: his possible death and subsequent presence with the Lord (2 Corinthians 5:8), and also the possibility of his continuing on in the body, the latter being "more needful" for the Philippian Christians. His choice, in his own words, was between these two (1:23), and Jehovah's Witnesses have gone to great trouble for nothing; the Greek text still records faithfully what the inspired apostle said—not what the Watchtower maintains he said, all their deliberate trickery to the contrary.

Concluding our comments upon these verses in Philippians, we feel constrained to point out a final example of Watchtower dishonesty relative to Greek translation.

On page 781 of the *New World Translation of the Christian Greek Scriptures*, it will be recalled that the committee wrote: "The expression *tou a-na-ly'-sai*, or *the releasing* cannot therefore be applied to the apostle's death as a human creature and his departing thus from this life."

If the interested reader will turn to page 626 of the same Watchtower translation, he will observe that in 2 Timothy 4:6 the Witnesses once more use the term "releasing" (*analuseos*), where all translators are agreed that it refers to Paul's impending death. The *Revised Standard Version*, often appealed to by Jehovah's Witnesses, puts it this way: "For I am already on the point of being sacrificed; the time of my departure has come." (See also *An American Translation* [Goodspeed]; *Authorized Version*; J. N. Darby's *Version*; James Moffatt's *Version*; J. B. Rotherham's *Version*; *Douay Version* [Roman Catholic]; etc.)

Jehovah's Witnesses themselves render the text: "For I am already being poured out like a drink offering, and the due time for my *releasing* is imminent" (2 Timothy 4:6, NWT).

Now, since it is admitted by the Witnesses, under the pressure of every translator's rendering of his text, that this verse refers to Paul's death, and further, since the noun form of the Greek word (*analuseos*) is here used and translated "releasing," why is it that they claim on page 781 that this expression "*the releasing*" (*analusai*—Philippians 1:23) "cannot therefore be applied to the apostle's death as a human creature and his departing thus from this life"? The question becomes more embarrassing when it is realized that Jehovah's Witnesses themselves admit that these two forms (*analusai* and *analuseos*) are "related" (p. 781). Hence they have no excuse for maintaining in one place (Philippians 1:23) that "the releasing" cannot refer to the apostle's death, and in another place (2 Timothy 4:6) using a form of the same word and allowing that it does refer to his death. This one illustration alone should serve to warn all honest people of the blatant deception employed in the Watchtower's "translations," a term not worthy of application in many, many places.

(5) *Matthew 24:3.* "While he was sitting upon the mount of Olives, the disciples approached him privately, saying: 'Tell us, When will these things be, and what will be the sign of your presence and of the conclusion of the system of things?' "(NWT).

Since the days of "Pastor" Russell and Judge Rutherford, one of the favorite dogmas of the Watchtower has been that of the *parousia*, the second coming or "presence" of the Lord Jesus Christ. Jehovah's Witnesses, loyal Russellites that they are, have tenaciously clung to the "pastor's" theology in this respect and maintain that in the year A.D. 1914, when the "times of the Gentiles" ended (according to Russell), the "second presence" of Christ began. (See *Make Sure of All Things*, 319.)

From the year 1914 onward, the Witnesses maintain,

> Christ has turned his attention toward earth's affairs and is dividing the peoples and educating the true Christians in preparation for their survival during the great storm of Armageddon, when all unfaithful mankind will be destroyed from the face of the earth (p. 319).

For Jehovah's Witnesses, it appears, Christ is not coming; He is here! (A.D. 1914)—only invisibly—and He is directing His activities through His theocratic organization in Brooklyn, New York. In view of this claim, it might be well to hearken unto the voice of Matthew who wrote:

> Then if any man shall say unto you, Lo, here is Christ, or there; believe it not. For there shall arise false Christs, and false prophets, and shall shew great signs and wonders; insomuch that, if it were possible, they shall deceive the very elect. Behold, I have told you before. Wherefore if they shall say unto you, Behold, he is in the desert; go not forth: behold, he is in the secret chambers; believe it not. For as the lightning cometh out of the east, and shineth even unto the west; so shall also the coming of the Son of man be (Matthew 24:23–27).

Jehovah's Witnesses, on page 780 of their *New World Translation of the Christian Greek Scriptures*, list the twenty-four occurrences of the Greek word *parousia*,

which they translate each time as "presence." They give the following defense found on page 779:

> The tendency of many translators is to render it here "coming" or "arrival." But throughout the 24 occurrences of the Greek word *parousia* . . . we have consistently rendered it "presence." From the comparison of the *parousia* of the Son of man with the days of Noah at Matthew 24:37–39, it is very evident that the meaning of the word is as we have rendered it. And from the contrast that is made between the presence and the absence of the apostle both at 2 Corinthians 10:10–11 and at Philippians 2:12, the meaning of *parousia* is so plain that it is beyond dispute by other translators.

Following this gigantic claim, namely, that their translation of the word *parousia* is "beyond dispute by other translators," the "theocratic authorities" proceed to list the verses in question.

Now, the main issue is not the translation of *parousia* as "presence," because in some contexts it is certainly allowable (see 1 Corinthians 16:17; 2 Corinthians 7:6–7; 10:10; and Philippians 1:26; 2:12). But there are other contexts where it cannot be allowed in the way Jehovah's Witnesses use it, because it not only violates the contextual meaning of the word but the entire meaning of the passages as always held by the Christian church.

Jehovah's Witnesses claim scholarship for this blanket translation of *parousia*, yet not one great scholar in the history of Greek exegesis and translation has ever held this view. Since 1871, when "Pastor" Russell produced this concept, it has been denounced by every competent scholar upon examination.

The reason this Russellite rendering is so dangerous is that it attempts to prove that *parousia* in regard to Christ's second advent really means that His return or "presence" was to be invisible and unknown to all but "the faithful" (Russellites, of course). (See *Make Sure of All Things*, 319–323.)

The *New World* translators, therefore, on the basis of those texts where it is acceptable to render *parousia* "presence," conclude that it must be acceptable in all texts. But while it appears to be acceptable grammatically, no one but Jehovah's Witnesses or their sympathizers accept the *New World Translation's* blanket use of "presence," be the translators Christian or not. It simply is not good grammar, and it will not stand up under comparative exegesis as will be shown. To conclude that "presence" necessarily implies invisibility is also another flaw in the Watchtower's argument, for in numerous places where they render *parousia* "presence" the persons spoken of were hardly invisible. (See again 1 Corinthians 16:17; 2 Corinthians 7:6–7 and 10:10; Philippians 1:26 and 2:12.)

If the Watchtower were to admit for one moment that *parousia* can be translated "coming" or "arrival" in the passages that speak of Christ's return the way all scholarly translators render it, then "Pastor" Russell's "invisible presence" of Christ would explode in their faces. Hence, their determination to deny what all recognized Greek authorities have established.

The late Dr. Joseph H. Thayer, a Unitarian scholar, translator/editor of one of the best lexicons of the Greek New Testament (and who, incidentally, denied the visible second coming of Christ), said on page 490 of that work, when speaking of *parousia*: "a return (Philippians 1:26). . . . In the New Testament, especially of the Advent, i.e., the future visible return from heaven of Jesus, the Messiah, to raise the dead, hold the last judgment, and set up formally and gloriously

the Kingdom of God." (For further references, see Liddell and Scott, Strong, and any other reputable authority.)

Dr. Thayer, it might be mentioned, was honest enough to say what the New Testament Greek taught, even though he didn't believe it. One could wish that Jehovah's Witnesses were at least that honest, but they are not.

In concluding this discussion of the misuse of *parousia*, we shall discuss the verses Jehovah's Witnesses use to "prove" that Christ's return was to be an invisible "presence" instead of a visible, glorious, verifiable event.

The following references and their headings were taken from the book *Make Sure of All Things*, published by the Watchtower as an official guide to their doctrine.

(1) "Angels Testified at Jesus' Ascension as a Spirit that Christ Would Return in Like Manner, Quiet, Unobserved by the Public" (p. 320).

> And after he had said these things while they [only the disciples] were looking on, he was lifted up and a cloud caught him up from their vision. . . . "Men of Galilee, why do you stand looking into the sky? This Jesus who was received up from you into the sky will come thus in the same manner as you have beheld him going into the sky" (Acts 1:9, 11, NWT).

It is quite unnecessary to refute in detail this open perversion of a clear biblical teaching because, as John 20:27 clearly shows, Christ was not a spirit and did not ascend as one. The very text they quote shows that the disciples were "looking on" and saw him "lifted up and a cloud caught him up from their vision" (v. 9). They could hardly have been looking at a spirit, which by definition is incorporeal,[49] not with human eyes at least, and Christ had told them once before, "Behold my hands and my feet, that it is I myself: handle me, and see; for a spirit hath not flesh and bones, as ye see me have" (Luke 24:39).

So it remains for Christ himself to denounce the Russellite error that He "ascended as a spirit." Moreover, since He left the earth visibly from the Mount of Olives it is certain that He will return visibly even as the Scriptures teach (see Matthew 26:63–64; Daniel 7:13–14; Revelation 1:7–8; Matthew 24:7–8, 30).

Recently the Jehovah's Witnesses "reinterpreted" their prophetic scheme to downplay the significance of 1914. As the Watchtower Society approaches the new millennium, it must somehow account for the fact that the Battle of Armageddon has not yet occurred, even though, according to the Society's interpretation, it was supposed to occur at least within the lifetime of those born by 1914.

For decades the *Awake!* masthead contained the statement, "Most important, this magazine builds confidence in the Creator's promise of a peaceful and secure new world *before the generation that saw the events of 1914 passes away*." However, the November 8, 1995 issue (as well as all subsequent issues) states, "Most important, this magazine builds confidence in the Creator's promise of a peaceful and secure new world *that is about to replace the present wicked lawless system of things*." This is but the latest in a multitude of reinterpretations by the Watchtower to extend their erroneous end times scenario into successive decades as their "prophetic" prowess fails. Following is a chart that shows the successive replacement teachings of the Watchtower over the years.

---

[49]Even angels have to take a human form in order to be seen (Genesis 19:1–2).

Teaching	Statement	Source
"Beginning of the End" in 1799 (later changed to 1914).	"1799 definitely marks the beginning of 'the time of the end.' . . . 'The time of the end' embraces a period from A.D. 1799, as above indicated, to the time of the complete overthrow of Satan's empire. . . . We have been in 'the time of the end' since 1799."	*The Harp of God* (1928 ed.): 235–236, 239.
Christ's "Invisible Presence" begins in 1874 (later changed to 1914).	"The time of the Lord's second presence dates from 1874. . . . From 1874 forward is the latter part of the period of 'the time of the end.' From 1874 is the time of the Lord's second presence."	*The Harp of God*, 236, 239–240.
The Battle of Armageddon ends in 1914 (later changed to "still future").	"The 'battle of the great day of God Almighty' (Rev. 16:14), which will end in A.D. 1914 with the complete overthrow of earth's present rulership, is already commenced."	Charles Taze Russell, *The Time Is at Hand*, 101.
The Battle of Armageddon will end shortly after 1914.	"In the year 1918, when God destroys the churches wholesale and the church members by millions, it shall be that any that escape shall come to the works of Pastor Russell to learn the meaning of the downfall of 'Christianity.' "	Charles Taze Russell, *The Finished Mystery* (1917 ed.), 485.
The Battle of Armageddon will come around 1925.	"The date 1925 is even more distinctly indicated by the Scriptures because it is fixed by the law God gave to Israel. Viewing the present situation in Europe, one wonders how it will be possible to hold back the explosion much longer; and that even before 1925 the great crisis will be reached and probably passed."	*The Watch Tower* (July 15, 1924): 211.
1914 is the starting date for the last generation before the Battle of Armageddon.	"The thirty-six intervening years since 1914, instead of postponing Armageddon, have only made it nearer than most people think. Do not forget: 'This generation shall not pass, till all these things be fulfilled' " (Matt. 24:34).	*The Watchtower* (November 1, 1950): 419.

(*continued on next page*)

People who were present and understood the events of 1914 will live to see the Battle of Armageddon.	"Jesus said, 'This generation will by no means pass away until all these things occur.' Which generation is this, and how long is it? . . . The 'generation' logically would not apply to babies born during World War I. It applies to Christ's followers and others who were able to observe that war and the other things that have occurred in fulfillment of Jesus' composite 'sign.' Some of such persons 'will by no means pass away until' all of what Christ prophesied occurs, including the end of the present wicked system."	*The Watchtower* (October 1, 1978): 31.
Anyone *born* by 1914 will live to see Armageddon.	"If Jesus used 'generation' in that sense and we apply it to 1914, then the babies of that generation are now seventy years old or older. And others alive in 1914 are in their eighties or nineties, a few even having reached one hundred. There are still many millions of that generation alive. Some of them 'will by no means pass away until all things occur' " (Luke 21:32).	*The Watchtower* (May 14, 1984): 5.
Anyone who sees the events signaling the End, regardless of any relationship to 1914, will see the Battle of Armageddon.	"Eager to see the end of this evil system, Jehovah's People have at times speculated about the time when the 'great tribulation' would break out, even tying this to calculations of what is the lifetime of a generation since 1914. However we 'bring a heart of wisdom in' not by speculating about how many years or days make up a generation. . . . 'This generation' apparently refers to the peoples of earth who see the sign of Christ's presence but fail to mend their ways."	*The Watchtower* (November 1, 1995): 17–20.

The Watchtower Bible and Tract Society still has not learned to refrain from prophesying falsely. In the January 1, 1997 *Watchtower* (p. 11), it once again raises expectations among its followers that the Battle of Armageddon is just around the corner:

> In the early 1920s, a featured public talk presented by Jehovah's Witnesses was entitled "Millions Now Living Will Never Die." This may have reflected over-optimism at that time. But today that statement can be made with full confidence. Both the increasing light on Bible prophecy and the anarchy of this dying world cry out that the end of Satan's system is very, very near!

(2) "Christ's Return Invisible, as He Testified That Man Would Not See Him Again in Human Form" (p. 321).

> A little longer and the world will behold me no more (John 14:19, NWT). For I say to you, You will by no means see me from henceforth until you say, "Blessed is he that comes in Jehovah's name!" (Matthew 23:39, NWT).

These two passages in their respective contexts give no support to the Russellite doctrine of an invisible "presence" of Christ for two very excellent reasons:

(a) John 14:19 refers to Christ's anticipated death and resurrection—the "yet a little while" He made reference to could only have referred to His resurrection and subsequent ascension (Acts 1:9–11), before which time and during the period following His resurrection He appeared only to believers, not the world (or unbelievers), hence the clear meaning of His words. Jesus never said that *no one* would ever "see Him again in human form" as the Watchtower likes to make out. Rather, in the same chapter (John 14) He promised to "*come again*, and receive you unto myself; that where I am, there ye may be also" (v. 3). The Bible also is quite clear in telling us that one day by His grace alone "we shall be like him; for we shall *see* him as he is" (1 John 3:2). So the Watchtower once more is forced into silence by the voice of the Holy Spirit.

(b) This second text, Matthew 23:39, really proves nothing at all for the Watchtower's faltering arguments except that Jerusalem will never see Christ again until it blesses Him in repentance as the Anointed of God. Actually the text hurts the Russellite position, for it teaches that Christ will be visible at His coming, else they could not see Him to bless Him in the name of the Lord. Christ also qualified the statement with the word "until," a definite reference to His *visible* second advent (Matthew 24:30).

(3) "Early Christians Expected Christ's Return to Be Invisible. Paul Argued There Was Insufficient Evidence in Their Day" (p. 321).

> However, brothers, respecting the presence of our Lord Jesus Christ and our being gathered together to him, we request of you not to be quickly shaken from your reason nor to be excited either through an inspired expression or through a verbal message or through a letter as though from us, to the effect that the day of Jehovah is here. Let no one seduce you in any manner, because it will not come unless the apostasy comes first and the man of lawlessness gets revealed, the son of destruction (2 Thessalonians 2:1–3, NWT).

This final example from Second Thessalonians most vividly portrays the Witnesses at their crafty best, as they desperately attempt to make Paul teach what in all his writings he most emphatically denied, namely, that Christ would come *invisibly* for His saints.

In his epistle to Titus, Paul stressed the importance of "looking for that blessed hope, and the glorious appearing of the great God and our Savior Jesus Christ" (2:13), something he would not have been looking for if it was to be a secret, invisible *parousia* or "presence."

Paul, contrary to the claims of Jehovah's Witnesses, never believed in an invisible return, nor did any bona fide member of the Christian church up until the fantasies of Charles Taze Russell and his *parousia* nightmare, as a careful

look at Paul's first epistle to the Thessalonians plainly reveals. Said the inspired apostle:

> For this we say unto you by the word of the Lord, that we which are alive and remain unto the *coming* of the Lord shall not prevent them which are asleep.
> For the Lord himself shall *descend* from heaven [visible] with a shout [audible], with the voice of the archangel, and with the trump of God: and the dead in Christ shall rise first (4:15–16, bracketed mine).

Here we see that in perfect accord with Matthew 26 and Revelation 1, Christ is pictured as *coming* visibly, and in this context no reputable Greek scholar alive will allow the use of "presence"; it must be "coming." (See also 2 Thessalonians 2:8.)

For further information relative to this subject, consult any standard concordance or Greek lexicon available, and trace Paul's use of the word "coming." This will convince any fair-minded person that Paul never entertained the Watchtower's fantastic view of Christ's return.

These things being clearly understood, the interested reader should give careful attention to those verses in the New Testament which do not use the word *parousia* but are instead forms of the verb *elthon* and those related to the word *erchomai* (see Thayer, 250ff) and which refer to the Lord's coming as a visible manifestation. These various texts cannot be twisted to fit the Russellite pattern of "presence," since *erchomai* means "to come," "to appear," "to arrive," etc., in the most definite sense of the term. (For reference, check Matthew 24:30 in conjunction with Matthew 26:64—*erchomenon*; also John 14:3—*echomai*; and Revelation 1:7—*erchetai*.)

Once it is perceived that Jehovah's Witnesses are only interested in what they can make the Scriptures say, and not in what the Holy Spirit has already perfectly revealed, then the careful student will reject entirely Jehovah's Witnesses and their Watchtower "translation." These are as "blind leaders of the blind" (Matthew 15:14), "turning the grace of God into lasciviousness, and denying the only Lord God, and our Lord Jesus Christ" (Jude 4). Further, that they wrest the Scriptures unto their own destruction (2 Peter 3:16), the foregoing evidence has thoroughly revealed for all to judge.

The Deity of Jesus Christ

Throughout the entire content of inspired Scripture the fact of Christ's identity is clearly taught. He is revealed as Jehovah God in human form (Isaiah 9:6; Micah 5:2; Isaiah 7:14; John 1:14; 8:58; 17:5 [cf. Exodus 3:14]; Hebrews 1:3; Philippians 2:11; Colossians 2:9; and Revelation 1:8, 17–18; etc.). The deity of Jesus Christ is one of the cornerstones of Christianity, and as such has been attacked more vigorously throughout the ages than any other single doctrine of the Christian faith. Adhering to the old Arian heresy of the fourth century A.D., which Athanasius the great church Father refuted in his famous essay "On the Incarnation of the Word," many individuals and all cults steadfastly deny the equality of Jesus Christ with God the Father, and, consequently, the Triune deity. Jehovah's Witnesses, as has been observed, are no exception to this infamous rule. However, the testimony of the Scriptures stands sure, and the above men-

tioned references alone put to silence forever this blasphemous heresy, which in the power of Satan himself deceives many with its "deceitful handling of the Word of God."

The deity of Christ, then, is a prime answer to Jehovah's Witnesses, for if the Trinity is a reality, which it is, if Jesus and Jehovah are "One" and the same, then the whole framework of the cult collapses into a heap of shattered, disconnected doctrines incapable of even a semblance of congruity. We will now consider the verses in question, and their bearing on the matter.

1. (a) *Isaiah 7:14.* "Therefore the Lord [Jehovah] himself shall give you a sign; Behold, a virgin shall conceive, and bear a son, and shall call his name Immanuel" (literally, "God" or "Jehovah with us," since Jehovah is the only God).

   (b) *Isaiah 9:6.* "For unto us a child is born, unto us a son is given: and the government shall be upon his shoulder: and his name shall be called Wonderful, Counsellor, The mighty God, The everlasting Father, The Prince of Peace."

   (c) *Micah 5:2.* "But thou, Bethlehem Ephratah, though thou be little among the thousands of Judah, yet out of thee shall he come forth unto me that is to be ruler in Israel; whose goings forth have been from of old, from everlasting."

Within the realm of Old Testament Scripture, Jehovah, the Lord of Hosts, has revealed His plan to appear in human form and has fulfilled the several prophecies concerning this miracle in the person of Jesus Christ. Examination of the above listed texts will more than convince the unbiased student of Scripture that Jehovah has kept His promises and did become man, literally "God with us" (Matthew 1:23; Luke 1:32–33; John 1:14).

The key to Isaiah 7:14 is the divine name "Immanuel," which can only be rightly rendered "God with us"; and since there is no other God but Jehovah by His own declaration (Isaiah 43:10–11), therefore Jesus Christ and Jehovah God are of the same Substance in power and eternity, hence equal. This prophecy was fulfilled in Matthew 1:22–23; thus there can be no doubt that Jesus Christ is the son of the virgin so distinctly portrayed in Isaiah 7:14. Jehovah's Witnesses can present no argument to refute this plain declaration of Scripture, namely that Jehovah and Christ are "One" and the same, since the very term "Immanuel" ("God" or "Jehovah with us") belies any other interpretation.

Isaiah 9:6 in the Hebrew Bible is one of the most powerful verses in the Old Testament in proving the deity of Christ, for it incontestably declares that Jehovah himself planned to appear in human form. The verse clearly states that all government will rest upon the "child born" and the "son given" whose identity is revealed in the very terms used to describe His attributes. Isaiah, under the inspiration of the Holy Spirit, describes Christ as "Wonderful, Counsellor, The mighty God, The everlasting Father, The Prince of Peace"—all attributes of God alone. The term "mighty God" is in itself indicative of Jehovah since not only is He the only God (Isaiah 43:10–11), but the term "mighty" is applied to Him alone in relation to His deity. Jehovah's Witnesses dodge this verse by claiming that Christ is *a* mighty god, but not *the* Almighty God (Jehovah). This argument is ridiculous on the face of the matter. However, Jehovah's Witnesses insist that since there is no article in the Hebrew text, "mighty," therefore, does

not mean Jehovah. The question arises: Are there two "mighty Gods"? This we know is absurd; yet Jehovah's Witnesses persist in the fallacy, despite Isaiah 10:21, where Isaiah (*without* the article) declares that "Jacob shall return" unto the "mighty God," and we know that Jehovah is by His own word to Moses "the God of Jacob" (Exodus 3:6). In Jeremiah 32:18 (*with* the article) the prophet declares that He (Jehovah) is "the Great, the Mighty God" (two forms of saying the same thing; cf. Isaiah 9:6; 10:21; Jeremiah 32:18). If we are to accept Jehovah's Witnesses' view, there must be two mighty Gods; and that is impossible, for there is only one true and mighty God (Isaiah 45:22).

The prophet Micah, writing in Micah 5:2, recording Jehovah's words, gives not only the birthplace of Christ (which the Jews affirmed as being the City of David, Bethlehem), but he gives a clue as to His identity—namely, God in human form. The term "goings forth" can be rendered "origin,"[50] and we know that the only one who fits this description, whose origin is "from everlasting" must be God himself, since He alone is the eternally existing one (Isaiah 44:6, 8). The overwhelming testimony of these verses alone ascertains beyond reasonable doubt the deity of the Lord Jesus Christ, who became man, identified himself with us in His incarnation, and offered himself "once for all" a ransom for many, the eternal sacrifice who is able to save to the uttermost whoever will appropriate His cleansing power.

2. *John 1:1.* "In the beginning [or "origin," Greek, *arche*] was the Word, [*Logos*] and the Word was with God, [*ton theon*] and the Word was God [*theos*]."

Contrary to the translations of *The Emphatic Diaglott* and the *New World Translation of the Holy Scriptures*, the Greek grammatical construction leaves no doubt whatsoever that this is the only possible rendering of the text. The subject of the sentence is *Word* (*Logos*), the verb *was.* There can be no direct object following "was" since according to grammatical usage intransitive verbs take no objects but take instead predicate nominatives, which refer back to the subject—in this case, *Word* (*Logos*). In fact, the late New Testament Greek scholar Dr. E. C. Colwell formulated a rule that clearly states that a definite predicate nominative (in this case, *theos*—God) never takes an article when it precedes the verb (was), as we find in John 1:1. It is therefore easy to see that no article is needed for *theos* (God), and to translate it "a god" is both incorrect grammar and poor Greek since *theos* is the predicate nominative of *was* in the third sentence-clause of the verse and must refer back to the subject, *Word* (*Logos*). Christ, if He is the Word "made flesh" (John 1:14), can be no one else except God unless the Greek text and consequently God's Word be denied.

Jehovah's Witnesses, in an appendix in their *New World Translation* (pp. 773–777), attempt to discredit the proper translation on this point, for they realize that if Jesus and Jehovah are "One" in nature, their theology cannot stand since they deny that unity of nature. The refutation of their arguments on this point is conclusive.

The claim is that since the definite article is used with *theon* in John 1:1b and not with *theos* in John 1:1c, therefore the omission is designed to show a difference; the alleged difference being that in the first case the one true God (Jehovah) is meant, while in the second "a god," other than and inferior to the

---

[50]Brown, Driver, and Briggs, *Hebrew Lexicon of the Old Testament,* 426 [a] Item [2].

first, is meant, this latter "god" being Jesus Christ.

On page 776 the claim is made that the rendering "a god" is correct because "all the doctrine of sacred Scriptures bears out the correctness of this rendering." This remark focuses attention on the fact that the whole problem involved goes far beyond this text. Scripture does in fact teach the full and equal *deity* of Christ. Why then is so much made of this one verse? It is probably because of the surprise effect derived from the show of pseudo-scholarship in the use of a familiar text. Omission of the definite article with *theos* does not mean that "a god" other than the one true God is meant. Let one examine these passages where the definite article is not used with *theos* and see if the rendering "a god" makes sense: Matthew 3:9; 6:24; Luke 1:35, 78; 2:40; John 1:6, 12–13, 18; 3:2, 21; 9:16, 33; Romans 1:7, 17–18; 1 Corinthians 1:30; 15:10; Philippians 2:11–13; Titus 1:1, and many, many more. The "a god" contention proves too weak and is inconsistent. To be consistent in this rendering of "a god," Jehovah's Witnesses would have to translate every instance where the article is absent as "a god" (nominative), "of a god" (genitive), "to" or "for a god" (dative), etc. This they do not do in Matthew 3:9; 6:24; Luke 1:35, 78; John 1:6, 12–13, 18; Romans 1:7, 17, etc.

You cannot honestly render *theos* "a god" in John 1:1, and then render *theou* "of God" (Jehovah) in Matthew 3:9, Luke 1:35, 78; John 1:6, etc., when *theou* is the genitive case of the *same* noun (second declension), *without* an article and *must* be rendered (following Jehovah's Witnesses' argument) "of *a* god" not "of God" as both *The Emphatic Diaglott* and *New World Translation* put it. We could list at great length, but suggest consultation of the Greek New Testament by either D. Erwin Nestle or Westcott and Hort, in conjunction with *The Elements of Greek* by Francis Kingsley Ball[51] on noun endings, etc. Then if Jehovah's Witnesses must persist in this fallacious "a god" rendition, they can at least be consistent, *which they are not*, and render every instance where the article is absent in the same manner. The truth of the matter is that Jehovah's Witnesses use and remove the articular emphasis *whenever* and *wherever* it suits their fancy, regardless of grammatical laws to the contrary. In a translation as important as God's Word, every law must be observed. Jehovah's Witnesses have not been consistent in their observances of those laws.

The writers of the claim have exhibited another trait common to Jehovah's Witnesses—that of half-quoting or misquoting a recognized authority to bolster their ungrammatical renditions. On page 776 in an appendix to the *New World Translation of the Christian Greek Scriptures*, when quoting Dr. A. T. Robertson's words, "Among the ancient writers *ho theos* was used of the god of absolute religion in distinction from the mythological gods," they fail to note that in the second sentence following, Dr. Robertson says, "In the New Testament, however, while we have *pros ton theon* (John 1:1–2) it is far more common to find simply *theos*, especially in the Epistles."

In other words, the writers of the New Testament frequently do not use the article with *theos*, and yet the meaning is perfectly clear in the context, namely that the one true God is intended. Let one examine the following references where in successive verses (and even in the same sentence) the article is used

---

[51]New York: Macmillan, 1948, 7, 14.

with *one* occurrence of *theos* and *not* with another form, and it will be absolutely clear that no such drastic inferences can be drawn from John's usage in John 1:1–2 (Matthew 4:3–4; 12:28; Luke 20:37–38; John 3:2; 13:3; Acts 5:29–30; Romans 1:7–8, 17–19; 2:16–17; 3:5; 4:2–3, etc.).

The doctrine of the article is important in Greek; it is *not* used indiscriminately. But we are *not* qualified to be sure in *all* cases what is intended. Dr. Robertson is careful to note that "it is only of recent years that a really scientific study of the article has been made."[52] The facts are not all known, and no such drastic conclusion, as the writers of the appendix note, should be dogmatically affirmed.

It is nonsense to say that a simple noun can be rendered "divine," and yet, at the same time, that same noun *without* the article conveys merely the idea of quality.[53] The authors of this note later render the same noun *theos* as "a god," not as "a quality." This is a self-contradiction in the context.

In conclusion, the position of the writers of this note is made clear in an appendix to the *New World Translation of the Christian Greek Scriptures* (p. 774); according to them it is "unreasonable" that the Word (Christ) should be the God with whom He was (John 1:1). Their own manifestly erring reason is made the criterion for determining scriptural truth. One need only note the obvious misuse in their quotation from Dana and Mantey (pp. 774–775). Mantey clearly means that the "Word was deity" in accord with the overwhelming testimony of Scripture, but the writers have dragged in the interpretation "a god" to suit their own purpose, which purpose is the denial of Christ's deity, and as a result a denial of the Word of God. The late Dr. Mantey publicly stated that he was quoted out of context, and he personally wrote the Watchtower, declaring, "There is no statement in our grammar that was ever meant to imply that 'a god' was a permissible translation in John 1:1" and "It is neither scholarly nor reasonable to translate John 1:1 'The Word was a god.' "[54]

Over the decades the Watchtower and independently minded Jehovah's Witnesses have struggled without success to refute the above presentation regarding the Greek of John 1:1. Their convoluted argumentation is nowhere more evident than in their *Should You Believe in the Trinity?* booklet. Contemporary Witnesses use the contentions from this booklet to argue that John 1:1 should be translated as the New World Translation does: "The word was a god." However, none of these polemics have any more scholarly merit than the earlier arguments we refuted.

For example, the booklet claims, "Someone who is 'with' another person cannot be the same as that other person" (p. 27). This is a complete misunderstanding of the doctrine of the Trinity, which is, simply stated, that within the *nature* of the one true God there are three eternal, *distinct persons*—the Father, the Son, and the Holy Spirit. When we say that Jesus is God, we do not mean that the Son is the same *person* as the Father. That would be in accord with another ancient church heresy known as *modalism.* John 1:1 commits no logical

---

[52]A. T. Robertson, *A Grammar of the Greek New Testament in the Light of Historical Research* (Nashville: Broadman Press, 1934), 755.

[53]Appendix to the *New World Translation of the Christian Greek Scriptures,* 773–774.

[54]Michael Van Buskirk, *The Scholastic Dishonesty of the Watchtower,* P.O. Box 2067, Costa Mesa, CA 92628 (CARIS, 1976): 11.

blunders when it states that the Word (the second person) is with God (the first person) and is himself God.

The sources referred to and quoted in *Should You Believe in the Trinity?* can be summarized in three categories: liberals who do not believe that the Bible is God's Word or that Jesus Christ was anything more than an inspired human; out-dated materials that fail to engage with up-to-date, comprehensive scholarship; and sources used out of context or misinterpreted. A number of valuable critiques of the Watchtower arguments concerning John 1:1 are currently in print[55]

3. *John 8:58.* "Jesus said unto them . . . Before Abraham was [born], *I am*" (bracketed mine).

In comparing this with the Septuagint translations of Exodus 3:14 and Isaiah 43:10–13, we find that the translation is identical. In Exodus 3:14, Jehovah, speaking to Moses, said "I AM," which any intelligent scholar recognizes as synonymous with God. Jesus literally said to the Jews, "I AM Jehovah," and it is clear that they understood Him to mean just that, for they attempted, as the next verse reveals, to stone Him.

Hebrew law on this point states five cases in which stoning was legal—and bear in mind that the Jews were legalists. Those cases were: (1) Familiar spirits, Leviticus 20:27; (2) Cursing (blasphemy), Leviticus 24:10–23; (3) False prophets who lead to idolatry, Deuteronomy 13:5–10; (4) Stubborn and rebellious adult son, Deuteronomy 21:18–21; and (5) Adultery and rape, Deuteronomy 22:21–24 and Leviticus 20:10. Now any honest biblical student must admit that the only legal ground the Jews had for stoning Christ (*actually* they had none at all) was the second violation—namely, blasphemy. Many zealous Jehovah's Witnesses maintain that the Jews were going to stone Him because He called them children of the devil (John 8:44). But if this were true, why did they not try to stone Him on other occasions (Matthew 23:33, etc.) when He called them sons of vipers? The answer is very simple. They could not stone Christ on that ground because they were bound by the law, which gives only five cases, and would have condemned them on their own grounds had they used "insult" as a basis for stoning. This is not all, however, for in John 10:33, the Jews again attempted to stone Christ and accused Him of making himself God (not *a god*, which subject has already been treated at length).[56] Let us be logical: If the Jews observed the laws of stoning on other occasions when they might have been insulted, why would they violate the law as they would have had to do if Jehovah's Witnesses are right about their interpretation of John 8:58? Little more need be said. The argument is ridiculous in its context; there is only *one* "I AM" in the Scriptures (Isaiah 44:6; 48:12; Revelation 1:8, 17–18), and Jesus laid claim to that identity

---

[55]Robert Bowman, *Why You Should Believe in the Trinity* (Grand Rapids: Baker, 1989) and *Jehovah's Witnesses, Jesus Christ, and the Gospel of John* (Baker, 1989); Angel Arellano, *Exposing Should You Believe in the Trinity?*, P.O. Box 4567, West Covina, CA 91791 (Make Sure of All Things, 1990); E. Calvin Beisner, *God in Three Persons* (Wheaton, Ill.: Tyndale House Publishers, 1984); and David Reed, *Jehovah's Witnesses Answered Verse by Verse* (Baker, 1986) and *Answering Jehovah's Witnesses Subject by Subject* (Baker, 1996).

[56]Jehovah's Witnesses point to the *New English Bible*'s rendering of this as "a god" as proof of the validity of their "translation." The fact is, however, that the *NEB* mistranslated this passage, and no reputable translation would support the Watchtower idea that this passage could mean that Jesus Christ was only claiming to be "a god."

for which the Jews, misinterpreting the law, set about to stone Him.

Jehovah's Witnesses declare that the Greek rendering of *ego eimi* (I AM) in John 8:58[57] is "properly rendered in the 'perfect indefinite tense'" ("I have been," not "I AM"). To unmask this bold perversion of the Greek text, we shall now examine it grammatically to see if it has any valid grounds for being so translated.

It is difficult to know what the translator means since he *does not* use standard grammatical terminology, nor is his argument documented from standard grammars. The aorist infinitive as such *does not* form a clause. It is the adverb *prin* that is significant here, so that the construction should be called a *prin* clause. The term "perfect indefinite" is not a standard grammatical term and its use here has been invented by the authors of the note, so it is impossible to know what is meant.

The real problem in the verse is the verb *"ego eimi."* Dr. Robertson, who is quoted as authoritative by the NWT translators, states (p. 880) that *eimi* is "absolute." This usage occurs four times (in John 8:24; 8:58; 13:19; 18:5). In these places the term is the same used by the Septuagint in Deuteronomy 32:39; Isaiah 43:10; 46:4; etc., to render the Hebrew phrase "I (AM) He." The phrase occurs *only* where Jehovah's Lordship is reiterated. The phrase, then, is a claim to full and equal Deity. The incorrect and rude rendering of the NWT only serves to illustrate the difficulty of evading the meaning of the phrase and the context.

This meaning in the sense of full Deity is especially clear in John 13:19, where Jesus says that He has told them things before they came to pass, that when they do come to pass the disciples may believe that *ego eimi* (I AM). Jehovah is the only One who knows the future as a present fact. Jesus is telling them beforehand that when it does come to pass in the future, they may know that "I AM" (*ego eimi*), i.e., that *He is Jehovah!*

In conclusion, the facts are self-evident and undeniably clear—the Greek allows no such impositions as "I have been." The Watchtower's contention on this point is that the phrase in question is a "historical present" used in reference to Abraham, hence permissible. This is a classic example of Watchtower double-talk. The passage is not a narrative, but a direct quote of Jesus' argument. Standard grammars reserve the use of "historical present" to narratives alone. The term is translated here correctly only as "I AM," and since Jehovah is the only *"I AM"* (Exodus 3:14; Isaiah 44:6), He and Christ are "One" in nature, truly the fullness of the Deity in the flesh.

The Septuagint translation of Exodus 3:14 from the Hebrew *ehyeh* utilizes *ego eimi* as the equivalent of "I AM" (Jehovah), and Jesus quoted the Septuagint to the Jews frequently, hence their known familiarity with it and their fury at His claim (John 8:59). Additional Old Testament references to Jehovah as *"I AM"* include Deuteronomy 32:39; Isaiah 43:10; Isaiah 48:12.

4. *Hebrews 1:3.* "He is the reflection of [his] glory and the exact representation of his very being, and he sustains all things by the word of his power" (NWT).

This passage of Scripture, I believe, clarifies beyond doubt the deity of Jesus Christ. It would be illogical and unreasonable to suppose that Christ, who is the

---

[57] *The New World Translation of the Christian Greek Scriptures*, 312, footnote C.

image imprinted by Jehovah's *substance*, is *not* of the substance of Jehovah and hence God, or the second person of the triune Deity. No creation is ever declared to be of God's very "substance" or "essence" (Greek, *hupostaseos*); therefore, the eternal Word, who is "the fulness of the Godhead [Deity] bodily" (Colossians 2:9), cannot be a creation or a created being. The writer of the book of Hebrews clearly intended to portray Christ as Jehovah, or he never would have used such explicit language as "the image imprinted by His substance" (Greek interpretation), and as Isaiah 7:14 clearly states, the Messiah was to be Immanuel, literally "God with us." Jehovah's Witnesses attempt the articular fallacy of "a god" instead of God, in reference to Immanuel; but if there has been "before me . . . no God formed, neither shall there be after me" (Jehovah speaking in Isaiah 43:10), then it is impossible on that ground alone, namely, God's declaration, for any other god ("a god" included) to exist. Their argument, based on a grammatical abstraction, fails to stand here, and the deity of the Lord Jesus, as always, remains unscathed.

   5. *Philippians 2:11*. "And that every tongue should confess that Jesus Christ is Lord, to the glory of God the Father."

   If we compare this verse of Scripture with Colossians 2:9 and Isaiah 45:23, we cannot help but see the full deity of the Lord Jesus in its true light.

   Jehovah spoke in Isaiah 45:23: "I have sworn by myself, the word is gone out of my mouth in righteousness, and shall not return, that unto me every knee shall bow, every tongue shall swear." In Colossians 2:9 the apostle Paul, writing under the inspiration of the Holy Spirit, declares, "For in Him [Christ] dwelleth all the fulness of the Godhead bodily." The literal translation of the Greek word *theotetos* (Godhead) is *Deity*, so in Christ all the fullness (*pleroma*) of the Deity resides in the flesh (*somatikos*).

   In Thayer's *Greek-English Lexicon of the New Testament*, which is referred to as being "comprehensive" by the Watchtower, a complete analysis of *theotetos* (Godhead, Deity) is given, especially its interpretation in the context of Colossians 2:9. Jehovah's Witnesses will do well to remember that Thayer was a Unitarian (one who denies the deity of Christ), and therefore more prone to accept their interpretations than those of evangelical Christianity. But despite his theological views, Thayer was a Greek scholar whose integrity in the presentation of honest facts, despite their disagreement with his beliefs, is the trait exemplified in all legitimate critics and honest scholars. Thayer states that *theotetos* [Godhead, Deity] is a form of *theos* (Deity), or in his own words: "i.e., the state of Being God, *Godhead*" (p. 288, 1886 ed.). In other words, Christ was the fullness of "the Deity" (Jehovah) in the flesh! *The Emphatic Diaglott* correctly translates *theotetos* "Deity"; but the NWT erroneously renders it "the divine quality," which robs Christ of His true deity. The only way to substantiate this inaccurate translation would be to substitute the word *theiotes* (Divinity) and thus escape the condemning evidence of "the Deity," *tes theotetos*. However, documentary evidence reveals that they cannot rightfully do this, for in Thayer's own words, "*theot* (Deity) *differs* from *theiot* (Divinity) as essence differs from quality or attribute." This fact again exposes the deception employed by Jehovah's Witnesses to lead the unwary Bible student astray into the paths of blasphemy against the Lord Jesus. It *cannot* be so translated, for the substitution of one word for another in translation is pure scholastic dishonesty, and Jehovah's Witnesses can produce no

authority for this bold mistranslation of the Greek text. Jesus Christ, according to the words themselves, is the same *essence* and *substance* as Jehovah, and as the *essence* (Deity) differs from the *quality* (Divinity), so He is God—*tes theotetos* (The Deity)—Jehovah manifest in the flesh.

That Jesus and Jehovah are "One" in nature dare not be questioned from these verses, which so clearly reveal the plan and purpose of God. Paul sustains this argument in his epistle to the Philippians (2:10–11) when he ascribes to the Lord Jesus the identity of Jehovah as revealed in Isaiah 45:23. Paul proclaims boldly, "That at the name of *Jesus* every knee should bow . . . and that every tongue should confess that Jesus Christ is Lord, to the glory of God the Father." It is a well-known biblical fact that the highest glory one can give to God is to acknowledge and worship Him in the person of His Son, and as Jesus himself said, "No man cometh unto the Father, but by me" (John 14:6) and "All men should honour the Son, even as they honour the Father" (John 5:23).

It is therefore clear from the context that the wonder of the Godhead is specifically revealed in Jesus Christ to the fullest extent, and it is expedient for all men to realize the consequences to be met if any refuse the injunctions of God's Word and openly deny the deity of His Son, who is "the true God, and eternal life" (1 John 5:20).

6. *Revelation 1:8.* " 'I am the Alpha and the Omega,' says Jehovah God, 'the One who is and who was and who is coming, the Almighty' " (NWT; cf. Revelation 1:7–8, 17–18; 2:8; 22:13; Matthew 24:30; Isaiah 44:6).

In the seventh, eighth, seventeenth, and eighteenth verses of the first chapter of Revelation a unique and wonderful truth is again affirmed—namely, that Jesus Christ and Jehovah God are of the same *substance*, hence coequal, coexistent, and coeternal. In short, *one nature* (but three persons) in its fullest sense. We shall pursue that line of thought at length in substantiating this doctrine of Scripture.

Comparing Matthew 24:30 with Revelation 1:7, it is inescapably evident that Jesus Christ is the one coming with clouds in both the references mentioned.

> And then shall appear the sign of the Son of man in heaven: and then shall all the tribes of the earth mourn, and they shall *see* the Son of man coming *in the clouds of heaven with power* and great glory (Matthew 24:30, emphasis added).
>
> Behold, *he cometh with clouds;* and every eye shall see him, and they also which pierced him: and all kindreds of the earth shall wail because of him. Even so, Amen (Revelation 1:7, emphasis added).

Following this train of thought, we find that Jehovah declares in Isaiah 44:6 that He alone is the first and the last and the *only* God, which eliminates forever any confusion as to their being *two* "firsts and lasts." Since Jehovah is the only God, then how can the *Logos* be "a god," a lesser god than Jehovah, as Jehovah's Witnesses declare in John 1:1? (*The Emphatic Diaglott* and *New World Translation*). Many times Jehovah declares His existence as the "only" God and Savior (Isaiah 41:4; 43:10–13; 44:6; 45:5; 48:12; etc.). This is indeed irrefutable proof, since Christ could not be our Savior and Redeemer if He were not Jehovah, for Jehovah is the only Savior of men's souls (Isaiah 43:11). However, despite the testimony of Scripture that "before me there was no God formed, neither shall there be after me" (Isaiah 43:10), the "a god" fallacy is pursued and taught by

Jehovah's Witnesses in direct contradiction to God's Word. In 1 Corinthians 8:4–6 Paul points out that an idol or false god is nothing and, even though men may worship many things as gods, there is only one true and living God (cf. Acts 5:3–4 and John 1:1 for the other persons of the Trinity).

Revelation 1:17–18 and 2:8 add further weight to the deity of Christ, for they reveal Him as the first and the last, who became dead and lives forever. Now, since Jehovah is the only first and last (cf. Isaiah references), either He and Christ are "One," or to claim otherwise Jehovah's Witnesses must deny the authority of Scripture.

In order to be consistent we must answer the arguments advanced by Jehovah's Witnesses concerning the use of "first" (Greek, *protos*) and "last" (Greek, *eschatos*) in Revelation 1:17 and 2:8.

By suggesting the original use and translation of *prototokos* (firstborn) and implying that "firstborn" necessarily means "first created," instead of *protos* (first) in these passages (see the footnotes to the passages in the *New World Translation of the Christian Greek Scriptures* and *The Emphatic Diaglott*), Jehovah's Witnesses attempt to rob Christ of His deity and make Him a created being with "a beginning" (*Let God Be True*, 107). When approached on this point they quickly refer you to Colossians 1:15 and Revelation 3:14, "proving" that the Logos had "a beginning" (see John 1:1 in both translations). To any informed Bible student, this conclusion is fallacious. *A Greek Lexicon of the New Testament*, translated and edited by J. H. Thayer (1886), states that the only correct rendering of *protos* is "first," and in Thayer's own words, "*The Eternal One*" [Jehovah] (Revelation 1:17). Here again the deity of Christ is vindicated.

Jesus said, "I am Alpha and Omega, the beginning and the end, the first and the last" (Revelation 22:13), and not only this but it is He who is revealing the mysteries to John (Revelation 1:1 and 22:16) and declaring himself to be the "faithful witness" (Revelation 1:5) who testifies "I come quickly" (Revelation 22:20). It is evident that Jesus is the one testifying and the one coming (Revelation 1:2, 7) throughout the book of Revelation since it is by His command (Revelation 22:16) that John records everything. So in honesty we must acknowledge His sovereignty as the "first" and "last" (Isaiah 48:12, Revelation 1:17 and 22:13), the Lord of all, and the eternal Word of God incarnate (John 1:1).

Revelation 3:14 asserts that Christ is the "beginning of the creation of God," and Colossians 1:15 states that Christ is "the firstborn of every creature." These verses in no sense indicate that Christ was a created being. The Greek word *arche* (Revelation 3:14) can be correctly rendered "origin" and is so translated in John 1:1 of the Jehovah's Witnesses' own 1951 edition of the *New World Translation of the Christian Greek Scriptures*. Revelation 3:14 declares that Christ is the faithful and true witness, the "origin" or "source" of the creation of God. This corroborates Hebrews 1:2 and Colossians 1:16–17 in establishing Christ as the Creator of all things and, therefore, God (Genesis 1:1).

Christ is the firstborn of all creation since He is the new Creation, conceived without sin (Luke 1:35), the second Adam (1 Corinthians 15:45 and 47), the fulfillment of the divine promise of the God-man (Isaiah 7:14; 9:6; Micah 5:2), and the Redeemer of the world (Colossians 1:14). John 3:13 states that no one has ascended into heaven but Christ who came down; Philippians 2:11 declares

that He is Lord (Greek, *kurios*), and as such is "the Lord from heaven" of 1 Corinthians 15:47—God—and not a created being or "a god."

The word "firstborn" (*prototokos*) refers not to the first one created or born, but to the one who has the *preeminence* or the right to rule as an heir has the right to rule over his predecessor's estate. The same term is used in the Greek translation of the Old Testament (LXX) in Genesis 25:33, where Esau actually sells his "right of the firstborn" to Jacob because he is hungry. It is also used in Exodus 4:22 by Jehovah regarding Israel as His "firstborn" nation, the nation that receives the blessings of His kingdom. (See also Psalm 89:27; Genesis 49:3; and Jeremiah 31:9, cf. Genesis 41:51–52.) This is the same meaning that "firstborn" carries in Colossians 1:15, 18 regarding Jesus Christ, and in Hebrews 11:17 regarding Isaac, who was Abraham's "son of promise," or "firstborn," but, having been born after Ishmael, not literally his first son born.

The Lord Jesus is also the "firstborn" from the dead (Revelation 1:5)—that is, the one who conquered death by rising in a glorified body (*not* a spirit form— see Luke 24:39–40), which type of body Christians will someday possess as in the words of the apostle John: "It doth not yet appear what we shall be: but we know that, when he shall appear, we shall be like [similar to] him; for we shall see him as he is" (1 John 3:2, bracketed mine). We know that these promises are sure, "for he is faithful that promised" (Hebrews 10:23), and all who deny the deity of Christ might well take cognizance of His warning and injunction when He said,

> For I testify unto every man that heareth the words of the prophecy of this book, If any man shall add unto these things, God shall add unto him the plagues that are written in this book: And if any man shall take away from the words of the book of this prophecy, God shall take away his part out of the book of life, and out of the holy city, and from the things which are written in this book (Revelation 22:18–19).

7. *John 17:5.* "And now, O Father, glorify thou me with thine own self with the glory which I had with thee before the world was" (Jesus Christ).

This passage of Scripture, in cross-reference with Isaiah 42:8 and 48:11, proves conclusively the identity of the Lord Jesus and is a fitting testimony to the deity of Christ.

In Isaiah 42:8 Jehovah himself is speaking and He emphatically declares, "I am the LORD: that is my name: and my glory will I not give to another, neither my praise to graven images." Again in Isaiah 48:11 Jehovah is speaking and He declares, "For mine own sake, even for mine own sake, will I do it: for how should my name be polluted? and I will not give my glory unto another."

It is plain to see from these references in Isaiah that Jehovah has irrevocably declared that His divinely inherent glory, which is of His own nature, cannot and will not be given to anyone other than himself. There is *no* argument Jehovah's Witnesses can erect to combat the truth of God as revealed in these passages of Scripture. The inherent glory of God belongs to God alone, and by His own mouth He has so ordained it to be. God, however, bestowed upon the incarnate Word a certain glory manifested in the presence of the Holy Spirit, through whose power and agency Christ worked while in the flesh, and Jesus in turn bestowed this upon his followers (John 17:22). But it was *not* the glory of

God's nature; rather, it was (and is) the abiding presence of His Spirit. The two quite different types of glory should not be confused. Jesus prayed to receive *back* again the glory He had with the Father "before the world was" (John 17:5). Also, it was *not* the glory given to Him as the Messiah, which glory Christ promised to share with His disciples (v. 22). Nowhere in Scripture are the types of glory equated.

The Lord Jesus Christ, when He prayed in John 17:5, likewise irrevocably revealed that He would be glorified with *the glory of the Father* and that the glory of the Father (Jehovah) was not new to Him, since He affirmed that He possessed it *with* (Greek, *para*) the Father ("the glory which I *had with* thee") even before the world came into existence. Jehovah's Witnesses attempt to answer this by asking that if He were God, where was His glory while He walked the earth?

In answer to this question, the Scriptures list at least four separate instances where Christ manifested His glory and revealed His power and deity. On the Mount of Transfiguration (Matthew 17:2) Christ shone with the inherent glory of God, which glory continued undiminished when in John 18:6 the Lord applied to himself the "I AM" of Jehovahistic identity that radiated glory enough to render His captors powerless at His will. The seventeenth chapter of John, the twenty-second verse, also confirms the manifestation of Jehovah's glory when Jesus, looking forward to the cross, prays for His disciples and affirms the origin of His glory as being the substance of God. The resurrection glory of Christ also serves to illustrate His deity and reveal it as of God himself.

So it is plain to see that the argument Jehovah's Witnesses advance to the effect that Christ did not manifest the glory of himself is invalid and finds no basis in the Scriptures. The truth of the whole matter is that the Lord Jesus did reveal the true glory of His nature in the very works He performed, and as John says (1:14), "And the Word was made flesh, and dwelt among us, (and we beheld his glory, the glory as of the only begotten of the Father,) full of grace and truth."

Paul, in the second chapter of Philippians, removes all doubt on this question when he writes, guided by the Holy Spirit, that Christ never ceased to be Jehovah even during His earthly incarnation. It is interesting to note that the Greek term *huparchon*, translated "being" in Philippians 2:6, literally means "remaining" or "not ceasing to be"; consequently, in the context Christ never ceased to be God, and "remained" in His basic substance; He was truly "God manifest in the flesh."

An average Jehovah's Witness interviewed recently, in attempting to escape the obvious declaration of Christ's deity as revealed in this text, reverted to the old Greek term-switching routine of the Society and asserted that the word "with" (Greek, *para*) in John 17:5 really means "through," and therefore the glory that is spoken of is not proof of Christ's deity since the glory is Jehovah's and is merely shining "through" the Son; it is not His own but a manifestation of Jehovah's glory.

Once again we are confronted with the problem of illogical exegesis, the answer to which must be found in the Greek text itself. We must believe that the grammar of the Bible is inspired by God if we believe that God inspired the writers, or how else could He have conveyed His thoughts without error? Would

God commit His inspired words to the failing grammatical powers of man to record? No! He could not do this without risking corruption of His message; therefore, as the wise and prudent Lord that He is, He most certainly inspired the grammar of His servants that their words might transmit His thoughts without error, immutable and wholly dependable. With this thought in mind, let us consider the wording and construction of the verse.

The Greek word *para* (with) is used in the dative case in John 17:5 and is not translated "through" (Greek *dia*) but is correctly rendered according to Thayer's *Lexicon* as "with," and Thayer quotes John 17:5, the very verse in question, as his example of how *para* (with) should be translated.

Never let it be said that *para* in this context indicates anything less than possessive equality—"the glory which I had with thee before the world was." The Lord Jesus Christ clearly meant that He as God the Son was the possessor of divine glory along with the Father and the Holy Spirit before the world was even formed. Christ also declared that He intended to appropriate that glory in all its divine power once again, pending the resurrection of His earthly temple, which, by necessity, since it was finite, veiled as a voluntary act His eternal power and deity (Philippians 2:5–8). The glory He spoke of did not only shine through the Father; it was eternally inherent in the Son, and since John, led by the Holy Spirit, deliberately chose *para* (literally, "with") in preference to *dia* (through), the argument that Jehovah's Witnesses propose cannot stand up. The Lord Jesus claimed the same glory of the Father as His own, and since Jehovah has said that He will not give His inherent glory to another (Isaiah 42:8), the unity of nature between Him and Christ is undeniable; they are one in all its wonderful and mysterious implications, which, though we cannot understand them fully, we gladly accept, and in so doing remain faithful to God's Word.

8. *John 20:28.* "Thomas answered and said unto him, My Lord and my God."

No treatment of the deity of Christ would be complete without mentioning the greatest single testimony recorded in the Scriptures. John 20:28 presents that testimony.

Beginning at verse 24, the disciple Thomas is portrayed as being a resolute skeptic in that he refused to believe that Christ had risen and appeared physically in the *same* form that had been crucified on the cross. In verse 25 Thomas stubbornly declares that "Except I shall see in his hands the print of the nails, and put my finger into the print of the nails, and thrust my hand into his side, I will not believe." Following through the sequence of events in verses 26 and 27, we learn that the Lord appeared to Thomas together with the other disciples and presented His body bearing the wounds of Calvary to Thomas for his inspection. This was no spirit or phantom, no "form" assumed for the occasion, as Jehovah's Witnesses maintain. This was the very body of Christ that bore the horrible imprints of excruciating torture and the pangs of an ignominious death. Here displayed before the eyes of the unbelieving disciple was the evidence that compelled him by the sheer power of its existence to adore the One who manifested the essence of Deity. "Thomas answered and said unto him, My Lord and my God." This was the only answer Thomas could honestly give; Christ had proved His identity; He was truly "the Lord God." Let us substantiate this beyond doubt.

Jehovah's Witnesses have vainly striven to elude this text in the Greek (*The*

Emphatic Diaglott and the *New World Translation*), but they have unknowingly cor-roborated its authority beyond refutation, as a brief survey of their sources will reveal.

In *The Emphatic Diaglott* (John 20:28, p. 396) *ho theos mou*, literally "the God of me," or "my God," signifies Jehovahistic identity, and since it is in possession of *the definite article*, to use Jehovah's Witnesses' own argument, it must therefore mean "the only true God" (Jehovah), not "a god." On page 776 in an appendix to the *New World Translation of the Christian Greek Scriptures*, the note states, "So, too, John 1:1–2 uses *ho theos* to distinguish Jehovah God from the Word (Logos) as a god, the only begotten god as John 1:18 calls him." Now let us reflect as sober individuals. If Thomas called the risen Christ Jehovah (definite article *ho kurios mou kai ho theos mou*), and Christ did not deny it but confirmed it by saying (verse 29), "Because thou hast seen me, thou hast believed: blessed are they that have not seen, and yet have believed," then no juggling of the text in con-text can offset the basic thought—namely, that Jesus Christ is Jehovah God!

The *New World Translation of the Christian Greek Scriptures* carefully evades any explanation of the Greek text on the aforementioned point, but just as carefully it inserts in the margin (p. 350) six references to Christ as "a god," which they attempt to slip by the unwary Bible student. These references, as usual, are used abstractly, and four of them (Isaiah 9:6; John 1:1, 18; and 10:35) have been men-tioned already in previous points. The question, then, is this: Is there any other god beside Jehovah which Jehovah's Witnesses affirm to be true by their refer-ence to Christ as "a god" (John 1:1; Isaiah 9:6)? The Scriptures give but one answer: an emphatic *NO!* There is no god but Jehovah. (See Isaiah 37:16, 20; 44:6, 8; 45:21–23; etc.)

To be sure, there are many so-called gods in the Scriptures, but they are not gods by identity and self-existence; rather, they are gods by human accla-mation and adoration. Satan also falls into this category since he is the "god of this world," who holds that position only because unregenerate and ungodly men have accorded to him service and worship belonging to God.

The apostle Paul seals this truth with his clear-cut analysis of idolatry and false gods in 1 Corinthians 8:4–6, where he declares that an idol is nothing in itself and that there is no god but Jehovah in heaven or earth, regardless of the inventions of man.

The picture is clear. Thomas adored Christ as the risen incarnation of the Deity (Jehovah); John declared that Deity was His from all eternity (John 1:1); and Christ affirmed it irrefutably: "If ye believe not that I am he [Jehovah], ye shall die in your sins" (John 8:24, cf. Exodus 3:14, bracketed mine). All of the pseudo-scholastic and elusive tactics ever utilized can never change the plain declarations of God's Word. Jesus Christ is Lord of all; and like it or not, Jeho-vah's Witnesses will never destroy or remove that truth. Regardless of what is done to God's Word on earth, it remains eternal in the glory, as it is written, "For ever, O LORD, thy word is settled in heaven" (Psalm 119:89).

9. *John 5:18.* "[He] said also that God was his Father, making himself equal with God."

To conclude this vital topic, this verse is self-explanatory. The Greek term "equal" (*ison*) cannot be debated; nor is it contextually or grammatically allow-able that John is here recording *what the Jews said about Jesus*, as Jehovah's Wit-

nesses lamely argue. The sentence structure clearly shows that *John said it* under the inspiration of the Holy Spirit, and *not* the Jews! Anyone so inclined can diagram the sentence and see this for himself. No serious scholar or commentator has ever questioned it. In the Jewish mind, for Jesus to claim to be God's Son was a claim to equality with God, a fact Jehovah's Witnesses might profitably consider!

We see, then, that our Lord was equal with God the Father and the Holy Spirit in His divine nature, though inferior (as a man), by choice, in His human nature as the last Adam (John 14:28; 1 Corinthians 15:45–47). This text alone is of enormous value and argues powerfully for our Lord's deity.

The Resurrection of Christ

Jehovah's Witnesses, as has been observed, deny the bodily resurrection of the Lord Jesus Christ and claim instead that He was raised a "divine spirit being" or as an "invisible spirit creature." They answer the objection that He appeared in human form by asserting that He simply took human forms as He needed them, which enabled Him to be seen, for as the Logos He would have been invisible to the human eye. In short, Jesus did not appear in the *same* form that hung upon the cross since that body either "dissolved into gases or . . . is preserved somewhere as the grand memorial of God's love"[58]. This, in spite of Paul's direct refutation in 1 Timothy 2:5, where he calls "the *man* Christ Jesus" our only mediator—some thirty years after the resurrection!

The Scriptures, however, tell a completely different story, as will be evident when their testimony is considered. Christ himself prophesied His own bodily resurrection, and John tells us "He spake of the temple of His body" (John 2:21).

In John 20:24–26, the disciple Thomas doubted the literal, physical resurrection of Christ, only to repent of his doubt (v. 28) after Jesus offered His body (v. 27), the same one that was crucified and still bore the nail prints and spear wound, to Thomas for his examination. No reasonable person will say that the body the Lord Jesus displayed was not His crucifixion body, unless he either ignorantly or willfully denies the Word of God. It was no other body "assumed" for the time by a spiritual Christ; it was the identical form that hung on the tree—the Lord himself; He was alive and undeniably tangible, not a "divine spirit being." The Lord foresaw the unbelief of men in His bodily resurrection and made an explicit point of saying that He was not a spirit but flesh and bones (Luke 24:39–44), and He even went so far as to eat human food to prove that He was identified with humanity as well as Deity. Christ rebuked the disciples for their unbelief in His physical resurrection (Luke 24:25), and it was the physical resurrection that confirmed His deity, since only God could voluntarily lay down and take up life at will (John 10:18). We must not forget that Christ prophesied not only His resurrection but also the nature of that resurrection, which He said would be bodily (John 2:19–21). He said He would raise up "this temple" in three days (v. 19), and John tells us "He spake of the temple of his *body*" (v. 21).

---

[58]Charles T. Russell, *Studies in the Scriptures*, 454.

Jehovah's Witnesses utilize, among other unconnected verses, 1 Peter 3:18 as a defense for their spiritual resurrection doctrine. Peter declares that Christ was "put to death in the flesh, but quickened by the Spirit." Obviously He was made alive in the Spirit and by the Spirit of God, for the Spirit of God, who shares the nature of God himself, raised up Jesus from the dead, as it is written, "But if the Spirit of him that raised up Jesus from the dead dwell in you . . ." (Romans 8:11). The meaning of the verse then is quite clear. God did not raise Jesus as merely a spirit but raised Him by His Spirit, which follows perfectly John 20:27 and Luke 24:39–44 in establishing the physical resurrection of the Lord.

The Watchtower quotes Mark 16:12 and John 20:14–16 as proof that Jesus has "other bodies" after His resurrection. Unfortunately for them, the reference in Mark is a questionable source, and a doctrine should not be built around one questionable verse. Neither verse has anything to do with the material reality of Christ's resurrection. The reason that Mary (in Mark 16) and also the Emmaus disciples (Luke 24) did not recognize Him is explained in Luke 24:16 (RSV): "Their eyes were kept from recognizing him" (RSV), but it was "Jesus himself" (v. 15).

Jehovah's Witnesses also try to undermine our Lord's bodily resurrection by pointing out that the doors were shut (John 20:26) when Jesus appeared in the Upper Room. However, Christ had a "spiritual body" (1 Corinthians 15:50, 53) in His glorified state; identical in form to His earthly body, but immortal; consequently, He was capable of entering either the dimension of earth or of heaven with no violation to the laws of either one.

Paul states in Romans 4:24; 6:4; 1 Corinthians 15:15; etc., that Christ is raised from the dead, and Paul preached the physical resurrection and return of the God-man, not a "divine spirit being" without a tangible form. Paul also warned that if Christ is not risen, then our faith is in vain (1 Corinthians 15:14); to us who believe God's Word there is a Man in the Glory who showed His wounds as a token of His reality and whose question we ask Jehovah's Witnesses: "Has a spirit flesh and bones as you see me have?" (Luke 24:39).

The Atonement of Christ

The infinite atonement of the Lord Jesus Christ is one of the most important doctrines of the Bible since it is the guarantee of eternal life through the complete forgiveness of sins to whoever appropriates its cleansing power. The Old Testament clearly teaches that, "it is the *blood* that maketh an atonement for the soul" (Leviticus 17:11, emphasis mine). Hebrews 9:22 corroborates this beyond doubt, for in truth "without shedding of blood is no remission." The Lord Jesus Christ became the one blood sacrifice for sin that insures everlasting life, as John said upon seeing Jesus: "Behold the Lamb of God, which taketh away the sin of the world" (John 1:29). The apostle John writing in Revelation 13:8 declares that the Lamb (Christ) slain from the foundation of the world is God's own eternal sacrifice that cleanses from all sin and provides redemption for lost souls who trust in its efficacy. The writer of the epistle to the Hebrews goes to great length to show that the sacrifices of the Old Testament were types designed to show forth the coming sacrifices of Christ on Calvary (Hebrews 9 and 10). The Hebrew term *kaphar* (covering) and the Greek term *katallage*,

which literally means reconciliation, are used in reference to payment of an obligation or exchange. The picture then portrays Christ as bearing our sins in His own body on the tree (1 Peter 2:24) and giving us peace with God through the *blood* of His cross (Colossians 1:20), which blood is the everlasting covenant that is able to make us perfect, in that God through it empowers us to do His will (Hebrews 13:20–21). The Scriptures give vast testimony to the redeeming power of the Lamb's blood (Romans 3:25; 5:9; Colossians 1:14; Hebrews 9:22; 1 Peter 1:19; 1 John 1:7; Revelation 5:9; 12:11) which *alone* can save and cleanse (Hebrews 9:22).

Charles Taze Russell resigned from a position he once held as assistant editor of a Rochester, New York, newspaper because he disagreed with the editor's view of the Atonement. Whether Russell was right in that disputation or wrong we do not know, but his doctrine of the Atonement and that of the Jehovah's Witnesses we do have knowledge of and know it to be completely unscriptural. Jehovah's Witnesses argue that the Atonement is not wholly of God, despite 2 Corinthians 5:15, 19, but rather half of God and half of man. Jesus, according to their argument, removed the effects of Adam's sin by His sacrifice on Calvary, but the work will not be fully completed until the survivors of Armageddon return to God through free will and become subject to the Theocratic rule of Jehovah. For Jehovah's Witnesses, the full realization of the Atonement is reconciliation with God, which will be completed in relation to the millennial kingdom. This utterly unreasonable and illogical interpretation of Scripture does away with the validity of the "infinite atonement" unconditionally administered by God and through God for man. Russell and Jehovah's Witnesses have detracted from the blood of Christ by allowing it only partial cleansing power, but the truth still stands; it is either all-sufficient or insufficient; and if the latter be the case, man is hopelessly lost in an unconnected maze of irrelevant doctrines which postulate a finite sacrifice and, by necessity, a finite god.

The Physical Return of Christ

Jehovah's Witnesses declare that Christ returned to the temple in 1914 and cleansed it by 1918 for judgment upon sinful men and Satan's organizations. They affirm that since He did not rise physically, neither will He return physically.[59]

The first claim is that Jesus said, "The world seeth me no more" (John 14:19); therefore, no mortal eye shall see Him. The second claim is the intimation that *parousia* (Greek for presence, coming, advent, etc.) in Matthew 24:26–28 can only be rendered "exactly" as *presence;* therefore, Christ is now present, not coming.

These arguments are another example of the half-truths used by Jehovah's Witnesses to lead people astray. To begin with, Thayer, who is esteemed reliable in the field of scholarship, clearly states on page 490 of his *Greek-English Lexicon of the New Testament* that *parousia,* especially in the New Testament, refers to the second coming of Christ in *visible* form to raise the dead, hold the last judgment, and set up the kingdom of God. Christ *is* present; His "presence" is always near

---

[59] *The Truth Shall Make You Free,* 295.

("I will never leave thee," Hebrews 13:5; "I am with you alway, even unto the end of the world," Matthew 28:20), for as God He is omnipresent—everywhere. But that does not mean He is here physically as the Scriptures attest He will be at the Second Advent. The physical return of Christ is the "blessed hope" of Christendom (Titus 2:13), and the language used to portray its visible certainty is most explicit. In Titus 2:13 the Greek word *epiphaneia* ("appearing") is more correctly translated "manifestation" or "visible" from *phanero*, "to make manifest, or visible, or known"[60] The language is self-explanatory. When the Lord returns with His saints, "every eye shall see Him" (Matthew 24:30, cf. Revelation 1:7). How then can Jehovah's Witnesses claim that He has already returned but is invisible? The answer is they cannot and still remain honest scripturally. To further establish these great truths, the apostle Paul writing to Timothy in 1 Timothy 6:14 clearly states that the Lord Jesus will appear physically by using *epiphaneia*, another form of *phanero*, which also denotes visibility or manifestations. In 1 Thessalonians 4:16–17 the Lord's return is revealed as being visible and audible, not invisible as Jehovah's Witnesses affirm.

The Old Testament bears out the physical return of the Messiah, also a wonderful testimony to the consistency of God's Word. Comparing Zechariah 12:10; 14:4 with Revelation 1:7; Matthew 24:30; and Acts 1:9–12, it is obvious that the Lord's ascension was visible, for the disciples *saw* Him rise, and in like fashion (Greek, *tropos*) the angels declared He would return. Zechariah 12:10 quotes Jehovah (further proof of Christ's deity), "And they shall look upon *me* whom they have pierced" (emphasis mine). Revelation 1:7 states that Christ is the one pierced and *visible* to human eyes. Zechariah 14:4 reveals Christ as touching the Mount of Olives at His visible return, and the Scriptures teach that this literally corroborates the angelic proclamation of Acts 1:9–12 even to the Lord's return to the exact location of His ascension, the Mount of Olives (v. 12). The doctrine of the physical return of Christ cannot be denied unless a denial of God's Word also be entered.

Jehovah's Witnesses and Human Government

Jehovah's Witnesses refuse to pay homage in any way to the flag of any nation or even to defend their own individual nation from assault by an enemy. Patriotism as displayed in bearing arms is not one of their beliefs since they claim to be ambassadors of Jehovah and as such deem themselves independent of allegiance to any government other than His. In this age of uncertainty, sincerity is a priceless gem and no doubt Jehovah's Witnesses believe themselves sincere, but all their arguments avail nothing because in Romans 13:1–7 Paul clearly outlines the case for human government as instituted by God. Paul goes to great lengths to stress that the "higher powers" (human governmental rules) are allowed and sanctioned by God. As supposed followers of His Word, the Witnesses ought to heed both Christ and Paul and "render therefore to all their dues: tribute to whom tribute is due; custom to whom custom," which in the context of Romans 13:1–7 clearly means subjugation to governmental rule. Paul settles the question decisively, and in conclusion we quote his teaching:

---

[60]Thayer's *Greek-English Lexicon of the New Testament*, 648.

Let every soul be subject unto the higher powers. For there is no power but of God: the powers that be are ordained of God. Whosoever therefore resisteth the power, resisteth the ordinance of God: and they that resist shall receive to themselves damnation. For rulers are not a terror to good works, but to the evil. Wilt thou then not be afraid of the power? do that which is good, and thou shalt have praise of the same: For he is the minister of God to thee for good. But if thou do that which is evil, be afraid; for he beareth not the sword in vain: for he is the minister of God, a revenger to execute wrath upon him that doeth evil. Wherefore ye must needs be subject, not only for wrath, but also for conscience sake. For this cause pay ye tribute also: for they are God's ministers, attending continually upon this very thing. Render therefore to all their dues: tribute to whom tribute is due; custom to whom custom; fear to whom fear; honour to whom honour (Romans 13:1–7).

The Existence of Hell and Eternal Punishment

The question of the existence of hell and eternal punishment presents no problem to any biblical student who is willing to practice honest exegesis unhindered by the teachings of any organizations of man. Jehovah's Witnesses use emotionally loaded words such as "hellfire screechers" and "religionists," etc., to describe the theological views of anyone who disagrees with their ideology. In order to understand their views, it must first be established that their beliefs are based upon no sound or valid knowledge of the original languages, and it should be remembered that this one factor influences practically every major phase of semantic study. However, we will now consider this problem in its context and contrast it with Jehovah's Witnesses' interpretation, which professes to have solved the problem, though on what grounds it is difficult to ascertain.

1. To begin with, Jehovah's Witnesses use poor reasoning in their construction of grammar. I document to prove the point and reveal this shortcoming. On pages 69 and 70 of *Let God Be True* (1946 ed.) the following statement appears:

> If you were to translate a book from a foreign language into English and there you found the foreign word for bread 65 times, would you translate it 31 times bread, 31 times fish, and three times meat? Of course not. Why? Because if you did your translation would not be correct. For what is bread cannot at the same time be fish or meat and vice versa. The same holds true with the word "sheol." If sheol is the grave, it is impossible at the same time to be a place of fiery torture and at the same time a pit.

It is most interesting to note in passing that in the Watchtower revision of *Let God Be True* (1951), this paragraph was carefully omitted.

To the average Jehovah's Witness then, hell (sheol) is literally "the grave," the place where mortals await the resurrection. Their chief argument is that a Greek or Hebrew word always means one thing and has no contextual connotation. This is a typical Jehovah's Witness approach and again reveals the linguistic failings of the organization. For instance, the very example the author of the chapter uses concerning bread, fish, and meat, etc., is a reality in the text of the Bible, and unless one recognizes the varieties of meanings of words in different contexts, he is unable to understand the plain meaning of Scripture. A little research would have revealed this truth. In the Hebrew text, the word

lechem is translated "bread" 238 times, one time as "feast," twenty-one times as "food," one time as "fruit," five times as "loaf," eighteen times as "meat," one time as "provision," twice as "victuals," and once as "eat." It is clear that "sheol" has differences of meaning which must be decided from the context, not by conjectures of misinformed authors.

2. In the second place, Jehovah's Witnesses have conceived of death as being unconsciousness or extinction, which definition cannot be found in the Bible. Death in the biblical sense never means extinction or annihilation, and not one word, Greek or Hebrew, in either Testament will be found to say that it does. Death in the Bible is portrayed as *separation*. "The soul that sinneth . . . it shall be separated" (Ezekiel 18:4) is a better rendition in the sense that the word conveys. When Adam sinned, his soul became *separated* from God in the sense of fellowship—and consequently, as a result of sin, all men die or are separated from God by Adam's as well as their own sins. But God has provided a reconciliation for us in the person of His Son, and we are "born again," regenerated and reconciled to God by the sacrifice of His Son "in whom we have redemption through his blood, even the forgiveness of sins" (Colossians 1:14, cf. John 3:3–7, 15–16; 2 Corinthians 5:17–21). So then we see that death in reality is not extinction but conscious existence, as is demonstrated in Matthew 17:1–3, when Moses and Elijah talked with Christ. Moses' body was dead—this no one will deny; his soul was also dead according to Jehovah's Witnesses. Then what or who was talking to Christ? The answer is simple. Moses as a living soul spoke to Christ, and he was alive and conscious! Substantiating all this is Christ's own declaration, "I am the resurrection, and the life; he that believeth in me, though he were dead, yet shall he live: And whosoever liveth and believeth in me shall never die" (John 11:25–26). Therefore, death is only the separation between, not the extinction of, personalities (Isaiah 59:1–2; see also 2 Corinthians 5:8 and Philippians 1:21–23).

3. Jehovah's Witnesses claim in *Let God Be True* (p. 96) that "in all places where hell is translated from the Greek word *gehenna* it means everlasting destruction."

This is indeed a bold-faced misrepresentation of the Greek language and certainly ranks next to the "a god" fallacy of John 1:1 as an outstanding example of complete falsehood. There is no evidence that *gehenna* ever means "annihilation" in the New Testament, but, rather, abundant evidence to the contrary. In Matthew 5:22 *gehenna* is portrayed as literally "the hell of fire," and in 10:28 coupled with *apolesai*, "to be delivered up to eternal misery" (see Thayer, 64). It indicates everlasting misery, and in Matthew 18:9 the same words corroborate 5:22, "the hell of fire." If we are to follow through with Jehovah's Witnesses' argument, *gehenna* simply means the smoldering furnaces of Hinnon. But is that fire everlasting? No! For today the valley of Hinnon is not burning, so unless Jesus meant the example for only those living at that time (and this not even Jehovah's Witnesses will affirm), *gehenna* must be what it is, the symbol of eternal separation in conscious torment by a flame that is unquenchable (Isaiah 66:24).

4. It is fruitless to pursue this analysis of the Greek any further, for it must be clear from the contexts that more than the grave or extinction is portrayed in sheol, hades, and gehenna. Without benefit of any complicated textual exegesis, we shall let God's Word speak its own message and commit to the honest

reader the decision as to whether or not eternal punishment, rather than annihilation, is scriptural doctrine. The following verses collectively refer to a
place of everlasting conscious torment where Satan and his followers must remain in future eternal wounding or misery, separated from God's presence and
"the glory of his power" (2 Thessalonians 1:9; cf. Thayer, 443 on *olethros* and
the Latin *vulnus—to wound*).

1. *Matthew 8:11–12*. "And I say unto you, That many shall come from the
east and west, and shall sit down with Abraham, and Isaac, and Jacob, in the
kingdom of heaven. But the children of the kingdom shall be cast out into outer
darkness: there shall be weeping and gnashing of teeth."

2. *Matthew 13:42, 50*. "And shall cast them into the furnace of fire: there
shall be wailing and gnashing of teeth."

3. *Matthew 22:13*. "Then said the king to the servants, Bind him hand and
foot, and take him away, and cast him into outer darkness; there shall be weeping and gnashing of teeth."

4. *Luke 13:24–28*. "Strive to enter in at the strait gate: for many, I say unto
you, will seek to enter in, and shall not be able. When once the master of the
house is risen up, and hath shut to the door, and ye begin to stand without, and
to knock at the door, saying, Lord, Lord, open unto us; and he shall answer and
say unto you, I know you not whence ye are: Then shall ye begin to say, We have
eaten and drunk in thy presence, and thou hast taught in our streets. But he
shall say, I tell you, I know you not whence ye are; depart from me, all ye workers
of iniquity. There shall be weeping and gnashing of teeth, when ye shall see
Abraham, and Isaac, and Jacob, and all the prophets, in the kingdom of God,
and you yourselves thrust out."

5. *2 Peter 2:17*. "These are wells without water, clouds that are carried with
a tempest; to whom the mist of darkness is reserved for ever."

6. *Jude 13*. "Raging waves of the sea, foaming out their own shame; wandering stars, to whom is reserved the blackness of darkness for ever."

7. *Revelation 14:9–11*. "And the third angel followed them, saying with a
loud voice, If any man worship the beast and his image, and receive his mark
in his forehead, or in his hand, the same shall drink of the wine of the wrath of
God, which is poured out without mixture into the cup of his indignation; and
he shall be tormented with fire and brimstone in the presence of the holy angels, and in the presence of the Lamb: And the smoke of their torment ascendeth up for ever and ever: and they have no rest day nor night, who worship the
beast and his image, and whosoever receiveth the mark of his name."

8. *Revelation 19:20*. "And the beast was taken, and with him the false prophet
that wrought miracles before him, with which he deceived them that had received the mark of the beast, and them that worshiped his image. These both
were cast alive into a lake of fire burning with brimstone."

These verses are conclusive proof that everlasting conscious separation
from God and real torment exist, and no possible confusion of terminology can
change their meaning in context. Revelation 20:10 is perhaps the most descriptive of all the verses in the Greek. John positively states that "the devil that deceived them was cast into the lake of fire and brimstone, where the beast and
the false prophet are, and shall be tormented (*basanisthesontai*) day and night
for ever (*aionas*) and ever." The Greek word *basanizo* literally means "to torment," "to be harassed," "to torture," or "to vex with grievous pains" (Thayer,
96), and is used throughout the New Testament to denote great pain and conscious misery, not annihilation, cessation of consciousness, or extinction. Fur

ther proof of the reality of conscious torment, not annihilation, is found in the following verses where *basanizo* is utilized to exhibit the truth of God's eternal justice.

> 1. *Matthew 8:6.* The one *tormented* (suffering) with palsy (*basanizomenos*).
> 2. *Matthew 8:29.* The demons addressing Jesus admit the certainty of future torment (*basanisai*). "Art thou come hither to *torment* us before the time?"
> 3. *Mark 5:7.* Again the demon cries out, "*Torment* (*basanisas*) me not." He obviously feared conscious pain, not extinction.
> 4. *Luke 8:28.* A demon once more reveals his knowledge of coming *torment* (*basanisas*): "*torment* me not" is his supplication to Christ.
> 5. *Revelation 14:10–11.* "He (the believer in the beast) shall be *tormented* (*basanistheasetai*) with fire and brimstone in the presence of the holy angels, and in the presence of the Lamb. And the smoke of their torment ascendeth up for ever and ever: and they have no rest (*anapausis*, Thayer, 40, also Liddell and Scott) day nor night, who worship the beast and his image, and whosoever receiveth the mark of his name."

The Scriptures, then, clearly teach eternal conscious punishment and torment for those who reject Christ as Lord, and the language of the texts leaves no room for doubt that the apostles intended that confirmation. Jehovah's Witnesses think God a "fiend" because He executes eternal righteous judgment. They make much to-do about God being Love but forget that because He is Love, He is also Justice and must require infinite vengeance upon anyone who treads underfoot the precious blood of Christ, who is the Lamb slain for lost sinners from the foundation of the world. Death is not extinction, and hell is not an illusion—everlasting conscious punishment is a terrifying reality of God's infinite justice upon the souls of unbelieving men.

The apostle Paul summed up this certainty in Romans 2:8–9, when he declared that God's indignation (*thumos*) and wrath (*orges*) are upon all who work unrighteousness. These two words have identical usage in Revelation 14:10, where John speaks of the eternal torment of those who serve the Beast, "the wine of the wrath (*orges*) of God, which is poured out without mixture into the cup of his indignation (*thumou*)." So the picture is clear. God is both Love and Justice, and it is not He who condemns man, but man who condemns himself. As it is written: "For by thy words thou shalt be justified, and by thy words thou shalt be condemned" (Matthew 12:37).

5. In *Let God Be True* (p. 93), Jehovah's Witnesses exhibit their lack of knowledge as to what fundamental Christians believe, where, when speaking of the "religious theologians," they declare: "But are not Satan the devil and his demons down in hell keeping the fires and making it hard for those who are in it? This is what is taught by Christendom's clergy." It is nonsense to suppose that the devil and his demons "are in hell keeping up the fires," and no responsible clergyman or Christian would make so childish a statement. Jehovah's Witnesses attribute to Christianity the same caliber of reasoning that appeals to their untutored minds, and to claim that "religionists" teach such doctrines is to reveal ignorance of the facts, a symptom not at all healthy in the processes of logical analysis. Further comment is not justified. Further examination is superfluous.

6. Luke 16:19–31 is claimed by Jehovah's Witnesses to be a parable in the text, but nowhere is this substantiated in Luke's account. It is pure conjecture.

Jehovah's Witnesses claim that this "parable" portrays a coming event, which was fulfilled in A.D. 1918. The rich man represents the clergy and Lazarus the "faithful body of Christ." The clergy is constantly tormented by the truth proclaimed through the faithful remnant (*Let God Be True*, p. 98). Comment on this interpretational travesty is senseless since Jehovah's Witnesses twist the Scriptures to suit their own ends, regardless of the textual background. The Lord Jesus in this account portrayed the condition of a lost soul (the rich man) who rejected God, and a beggar who partook of the Lord's mercy. The rich man went into conscious torment after physical death (Greek, *basanois*), verse 24, and even proclaimed his spiritual conscious anguish (Greek, *odunomai*), "I am being tormented" (see Thayer, 438). There can be no doubt—he was suffering and knew it. Jehovah's Witnesses believe that in order to suffer you must exist physically, but this is naïve to say the least since souls suffer, as is demonstrated in this account. It must also be remembered that Christ, in parables, never used personal names, such as "Lazarus." The language, although literal, is forceful in depicting spiritual suffering.

We must conclude, then, that Luke's account is a record of an actual case, a historical fact in which a soul suffered after death and was conscious of that torment. Regardless of what conjectures are injected at this point, the conclusion is sure: there is conscious punishment after death; and whether it is accepted or not by Jehovah's Witnesses, it still remains a scriptural doctrine substantiated by God's Word.

Satan—the Devil

In Ezekiel 28:16–19, quoted in *Let God Be True* (p. 65), Jehovah's Witnesses maintain Satan's annihilation, but in the light of the Scriptures previously discussed, the area of meanings of the Hebrew words must be considered. The word for "destroy" (*'abad*) does not convey the meaning of annihilation or extinction. The term here used may be rendered validly "to reckon as lost, given up as lost, or cast away" (cf. Ecclesiastes 3:6, and also Gesenius' *Hebrew-English Lexicon*). If Ezekiel 28:19 is as translated in *Let God Be True* (p. 65), "never shalt thou be any more," then the Hebrew word *'ayin* may properly be rendered "to fail" or "to be gone," *not* "to cease to exist" (cf. Isaiah 44:12; 1 Kings 20:40). The use of *'ayin* in Hebrew sentence structure is the standard means employed when negating noun clauses. In 1 Kings 20:40, for example, where the man is spoken of as "gone," the term *'ayin* is utilized to show the man's absence or escape, *not* his extinction. If Jehovah's Witnesses persist in their annihilation doctrine where Satan is concerned, they must also believe that this man was annihilated, and the context rules out that interpretation as absurd. The picture, then, is clear in the light of language interpretation. Satan *must* and *will* endure everlasting torment with his followers, and to this truth God's Word bears irrefutable testimony.

Man the Soul, His Nature and Destiny

Any critical thinker in examining this problem cannot escape the confusion of terms utilized by Jehovah's Witnesses to substantiate their argument that the

soul is not an eternal entity. To carry this argument to any great length is foolish, for the Hebrew word (*nephesh*) and the Greek (*psyche*) possess great areas of meaning impossible to fathom without exhaustive exegesis of the original sources. The root of the problem lies in Jehovah's Witnesses' misconception of the soul as merely a principle of life, not an entity. The Bible clearly teaches in numerous places (Genesis 35:18; 1 Kings 17:21–22; Revelation 6:9–11, to state a few) that the soul departs at the death of the body, that it is not destroyed by physical death, and that it can be restored by God at His discretion.

In an exegetical study it is impossible overemphasize the importance of defining terms, and in regard to the problem at hand it is of the utmost significance. Therefore, before we can decide who or what has immortality, we must know what the term "immortality" itself means. Due to the evolution of any language, we must realize that the area of meanings of words changes as time goes on. The English word "immortal" has, among others, a peculiar meaning of "not mortal." However, in most circles and also in theology, the word generally carries the meaning of "exemption from death." The question that will arise, then, is "When the Scriptures use the term 'immortal,' is this definition all that is meant?" Contrary to the belief of some, there is *no reference* in Scripture that can be given to show that man, or his soul, is immortal.

To go even one step further, there is nothing in Scripture that states anything or anyone is immortal but God himself. Let us analyze this problem. There are two words in the Greek text that are translated "immortality." The first is *athanasia*—it appears three times and is translated "immortality" each time. The other term is *aphthartos*—it is translated "immortality" twice and "incorruption" four times.

Now let us examine the use of these words. The former word, *athanasian*, is used in 1 Timothy 6:16 and is speaking of God, "Who *only* hath immortality (*athanasian*), dwelling in the light which *no man* can approach unto." In 1 Corinthians 15:53–54, we again have *athanasia* used twice, but in the same verse we have *aphthartos* used twice also. Paul here is speaking of the second coming of Christ, and declares (v. 53), "For this corruptible must put on incorruption (*aphtharsian*) and this mortal must put on immortality (*athanasian*)." And (v. 54), "So when this corruptible *shall have put on* (aorist middle subjunctive of the verb *enduo*) incorruption (*aphtharian*), and this mortal *shall have put on* immortality (*athanasian*), then shall be brought to pass the saying that is written, *Death* is swallowed up in victory." We see here that in the two places where *athanasian* is used in reference to man, it is clear that it is an immortality to be given in the future, not one possessed at the present time.

Similarly, when an *aphtharsian* is used here and in Romans 2:7, "seek for," and 1 Peter 1:4, "reserved in heaven for you," it is speaking of the incorruption of man to be given at some future date, not possessed at the present time. Only when immortality or incorruption is used with God, is it in the present tense (1 Timothy 1:17, 6:16; Romans 1:23). Therefore, to say that the saints are immortal (if by immortality we mean *athanasian* or *aphtharsian*), we are not scriptural. We must say the saints *will* be immortal. It is also plain to see in 1 Corinthians 15:53–54 that this immortality (*athanasian*) and this incorruption (*aphtharsian*) will be put on (*endusetai*) as one puts on a garment. Just as Paul exhorts us to put on (*endusasthe*) Christ (Romans 13:14; Galatians 3:27), the armor of light (Romans

13:12), the new man (Ephesians 4:24), and the armor or panoply of God (Ephesians 6:11), we must conclude then that *athanasian* or *aphtharsian* have a larger and broader meaning than to be "everlasting." It must be seen, therefore, that immortality and incorruption, *when given*, will mean a change, not simply the giving and receiving of the attribute—"exemption from death." Jehovah's Witnesses have badly misconstrued the usage of immortality, and that error, coupled with their famous practice of term-switching, has resulted in confusion and poor exegesis.

Now, as to the eternity of the human soul, we must consult the existing language sources. When we use the term "eternal" in association with the soul of man, we mean that the human soul *after* its creating by God will (future) exist somewhere into the eternal, into the everlasting. Since there is only one place where the honest seeker can find pure information on the eternal existence of the soul, and that place is in the revelation that God, who created the soul, has given to man, namely, His Word, let us turn to it and consider therein His revealed will.

First, Revelation does show that God can be known, and second, that man's soul is eternal. In Hebrews 1:1–2 we read, "God, who at sundry times and in divers manners spake in time past unto the fathers by the prophets, hath in these last days spoken unto us by his Son, whom he hath appointed heir of all things, by whom also he made the worlds." All throughout history God has manifested himself to man in different ways, and at no time in history has man been left without a witness of God. In the Old Testament, God manifested himself and His will to man by the prophets, visions, and direct oral contact. However, when the fullness of time was come, God sent forth His Son in the likeness of sinful flesh and completed His progressive revelation. Man, since the time of his creation upon the earth, has always been able to know God and His will, if he so desired, and consequently since the day of Adam, men who know not God are without excuse.

God's revelation is not only a manifestation of God to man, but it is also the answer to the questions, "Where did man come from?" "Is he a spiritual as well as natural being?" "What is his worth?" and "Where is he going?"

God's revelation shows that man is a creation of God, created in God's spiritual image (Genesis 1:26; 5:1; 1 Corinthians 11:7). He was created to have preeminence over other creatures (Genesis 1:28; Psalms 8:6; 82:6; Matthew 6:26; 12:12). He is definitely a spiritual being (Job 32:8; Psalm 51:10; Ecclesiastes 12:7; Acts 7:59; 2 Corinthians 4:13). He is an object of God's love (John 3:16; Revelation 1:5). He sinned and lost God's favor (Genesis 3:1–19). The consequences of Adam's sin passed upon all mankind (Romans 5:12). God sent His Son to redeem man (John 3:16). This redemption is by the vicarious death of Christ (Matthew 26:28; Acts 20:28; Romans 5:9; Colossians 1:20; Hebrews 9:14; 1 Peter 1:18–19; 1 John 1:7; Revelation 1:5; 7:14). This salvation is obtained by a new birth through faith in Jesus Christ (John 3:3–16).

We must conclude that since "God is Spirit" (John 4:24) and as such is incorporeal, He must have imparted to man a spiritual nature created in His own image, or else Genesis 1:26 is not meaningful.

Now the question arises, "If Jesus redeemed those who accept His salvation, what is the difference between those who are redeemed and those who are not?"

It is clear that redemption is not simply favor with God here upon earth. This brings us to the scriptural teaching of the eternal existence of the soul. First of all, there is much evidence that the soul does exist as a conscious entity after it departs from the body, and there is no scriptural evidence to the contrary. In Luke 20:37–38 the Lord Jesus, there speaking of the revelation God gave to Moses, makes it clear that when God said, I AM "the God of Abraham, Isaac, and Jacob," He *was* not the God of the dead, but *is* the God of the living, for Abraham, Isaac, and Jacob had long since been physically dead. The only reasonable conclusion, then, is that these great Old Testament saints of God possessed spiritual natures that transcended physical death.

In Matthew 17 we see Moses and Elijah on the Mount of Transfiguration communing with Christ, yet we know that Moses had been physically dead for centuries, and no record of his resurrection exists in Scripture. Jehovah's Witnesses claim that this was a vision, not a "real" evidence of the soul's existence beyond the grave, and they point to Matthew 17:9, where the English rendition of the Greek (*horama*) is *vision*. However, this Greek term is translated literally in this context as "that which is seen—a spectacle" (see Thayer, 451), not a mere vision.

In Luke 16:19–31 Jesus (remember, this is not a parable) shows the difference between the state of the soul of the redeemed and the state of the soul of the wicked after death. In Revelation 6:9 we see the souls of those who had been martyred for Christ crying out for vengeance. In 2 Corinthians 5:1–9 Paul makes it clear that to be absent from the body is to be consciously "present" or "at home" with the Lord. But the Scriptures go even further, for they speak of a resurrection of the body (Job 19:25; 1 Corinthians 15:35–57; 1 Thessalonians 4:16–17). In 1 Corinthians 15:35–49 is found the answer to this question which the Jehovah Witnesses are laboring under, that is (v. 35), "How are the dead raised up? and with what body do they come?" We notice that in verse 36 Paul addresses one who labors under this question as a "fool."

Now that we have considered the issues of the soul's existence after death and the resurrection of the body, we find Scripture is clear in its teaching that those who reject God's salvation will suffer throughout eternity in outer darkness (Matthew 8:11–12; 13:42–50; 22:13; 2 Peter 2:17; Jude 13; Revelation 14:9–11; 19:20), and those who accept God's salvation will dwell with Christ throughout eternity in joy and peace (John 14:1–3; 17:24; Luke 20:36; 1 Thessalonians 4:17; Revelation 22:5). Here is revealed what we believe is the true meaning of the scriptural terms "immortality" and "incorruption" (*athanasian, aphtharsian*). We must also realize that these words do not apply to God the Father in the same sense that they apply to God the Son. When we come "with" Him from heaven (1 Thessalonians 4:14), we shall be made like Him in the sense that we shall have a soul and body *incapable* of sin, not earthly but heavenly. We shall put on *athanasian* and *aphtharsian* and abide with Christ throughout eternity.

As I stated at the beginning of this point, it would be futile to refute all the errors of thought in the Jehovah's Witnesses' theology. Therefore, I have presented what I feel is sufficient evidence to show that man has an eternal soul and will abide somewhere, either in conscious joy or sorrow eternally, and that those who believe and trust in Christ as their personal Savior will "put on" that immortality when Jesus returns.

Regarding the Jehovah's Witnesses, we can only say as Paul said to the Corinthians in 2 Corinthians 4:3–4: "But if our gospel be hid, it is hid to them that are lost: in whom the God of this world hath blinded the minds of them which believe not, lest the light of the glorious gospel of Christ, who is the image of God, should shine unto them," and as he again states in 2 Thessalonians 2:10–11, "because they received not the love of the truth, that they might be saved. And for this cause God shall send them strong delusion, that they should believe a lie."

Honest study of this problem will reveal to any interested Bible student that man does possess an eternal immaterial nature, which was fashioned to occupy an everlasting habitation either in conscious bliss or torment. This is the nature and certain destiny of the soul of man.

Author's Note

The following partial list of references to the soul and spirit of man as drawn from the Old and New Testaments will, we believe, furnish the interested reader with ample evidence that man is not merely a combination of body and breath forming a living soul, as the Jehovah's Witnesses teach, but rather a soul, or spirit, possessing a corporeal form.

The Hebrew equivalent for soul as used in the Old Testament is *nephesh*, and for spirit *ruach*. The Greek equivalent for soul is *psyche* and for spirit *pneuma*.

1. It is an entity possessing the attributes of life (Isaiah 55:3). It is also separate from the body (Matthew 10:28; Luke 8:55; 1 Thessalonians 5:23; Hebrews 4:12; Revelation 16:3), i.e., it exists independent of material form.

2. The soul departs at the death of the form (Genesis 35:18).

3. The soul is conscious after death (Matthew 17:3; Revelation 6:9–11)

4. The soul of Samuel was conscious after death (1 Samuel 28:18–19).

5. Stephen had a spirit, which he committed to Christ at his death (Acts 7:59).

6. There is definitely a spirit and soul of man (Isaiah 57:16).

7. The spirit is independent of the body (Zechariah 12:1).

8. The spirit, the soul of man, does that which only a personality can do; it "wills" (*prothumon*) (Matthew 26:41).

9. We are instructed to worship in the spirit (John 4:23; Philippians 3:3) because God is a spirit.

10. The spirit of man has the attribute of personality, the ability to testify (Romans 8:16, 26), and also the faculty of "knowing" (1 Corinthians 2:11).

11. The spirit can be either saved or lost (1 Corinthians 5:5). It belongs to God, and we are instructed to glorify Him in it (1 Corinthians 6:20).

12. The spirit or soul goes into eternity and is a conscious entity (Galatians 6:8).

13. Christ is with our spirit (2 Timothy 4:22), for the spirit is the life of the body (James 2:26).

14. We are born of God's Spirit, and as such are spirits ourselves (John 3:5–6).

These references will suffice to show that the immaterial nature of man is far from the combination of breath and flesh that Jehovah's Witnesses maintain.

The Kingdom of Heaven

The human soul, marred and stained as it is by the burden of personal sin, seeks constant escape from the reality of that sin and the sure penalty due because of it. Once the reality of eternal punishment is clouded by idealistic concepts of everlasting bliss without the fear of personal reckoning, the soul can relax, so to speak, and the sinner, unconscious of the impending doom, which is God's justice, rests secure in the persuasion that "God is Love." Laboring under this delusion, it is no wonder that Jehovah's Witnesses can so calmly construct "The kingdom of heaven," for to them God's infinite justice does not exist, and eternal retribution is only an invention of "hellfire screechers."

The biblical kingdom of heaven has many aspects, none of which includes the invented hierarchical construction so vividly outlined in *Let God Be True*. In Luke 17:20–21 the Lord reveals the kingdom of heaven as within the believer in one aspect, but clearly states that the heavenly aspect will be visible and observable at His return (verses 23–26). In Matthew 13 the Lord Jesus portrays the kingdom of heaven symbolically in parables, yet always it is pictured as reality, not as an invisible phantom government. Jehovah's Witnesses arrive at the year A.D. 1914 as the end of the Gentile times and the beginning of the reign of the invisible heavenly King Christ Jesus. How they arrived at this arbitrary date no one can reasonably or chronologically ascertain, but valuable evidence to the effect that "Pastor" Russell formulated the whole hoax is obtainable from the July 15, 1950, copy of *The Watchtower*, where, on page 216, the following statements are found:

> Away back in 1880 the columns of *The Watchtower* had called notice to Bible chronology marking A.D. 1914 as the year for the 2,520-year period to end and referred to by Jesus as "the times of the Gentiles" in his prophecy on the world's end (Luke 21:24). In harmony with this it was expected that in 1914 the kingdom of God by Christ Jesus in the heavens would be fully established, while this world would be involved in an unprecedented "time of trouble." The religious leaders and the systems of Christendom were all set to laugh at Brother Russell and his fellow witnesses of Jehovah over failure of his announced predictions concerning A.D. 1914. But it was no laughing matter when, at the end of July, World War I broke out and by October it had become global in its scope. Christendom's religious mouths were silenced at this frightening turn of events, but not Brother Russell's. October 1, 1914, on taking his place at the breakfast table in the Brooklyn Bethel dining room, he in a strong voice denoting conviction announced: "The Gentile times have ended!"
>
> Knowing that the world had now reached the time for its dissolution, he refused to heed the plea of U.S. President Wilson for all clergymen and preachers to join in nationwide prayer for peace.

To follow through Jehovah's Witnesses' interpretation of the kingdom it is necessary to understand that only 144,000 faithful servants will rule with King Jesus in the heavenly sphere. They quote Revelation 7:4 and 14:1, 3, but neglect to notice that the 144,000 are of the tribes of Israel (Jews), 12,000 of each tribe, and are in no sense to be construed as anything else. This is not figurative; this is actual, because the tribes are listed by name. To follow out their own argument, Jehovah's Witnesses must believe that only 144,000 Jewish members of their organization will be privileged to reign with Christ Jesus. The argument

that they are spiritual Jews is invalid, because even if they were, which they aren't, they would be "children of Abraham," not Israel, and there is a vast difference in interpretation at this point (Galatians 3:29). Ishmael, the father of the Arab race, the ancestor of Muhammad, the founder of Islam, was a son of Abraham (Genesis 16) after the flesh even as Isaac was the father of Jacob, so it can be seen that Abraham's seed differs from the selection of Israel's stock, as it is written, "For in Isaac shall thy seed be called" (Genesis 21:12). The texts are clear that Israel after the flesh is mentioned and not spiritual symbolism; therefore, the 144,000 conjecture pertaining to kingdom rule as advanced by Jehovah's Witnesses crumbles under the light of scriptural truth.

In concluding this point it is imperative to remember that there can be no kingdom without the King, and the Scripture is clear when it states that the true kingdom will be instituted at Christ's visible return.

The Old and New Testaments corroborate each other in establishing the certainty of the visible return and reign of Christ (cf. Zechariah 14:4; Amos 9:8–15; Isaiah 11 and 12; Ezekiel 37:20–28; Luke 17:22ff, and Matthew 24:26–31, to mention only a few). Jehovah's Witnesses unknowingly fulfill the prophecy of Christ in Matthew 24:23ff., where the Lord warns of false Christs and prophets who shall say Christ is here, Christ is there (in the desert, in the secret places, etc.), and shall deceive many with their deceit. Jehovah's Witnesses say He is here now, but the Lord said He would be visible at His return, and that every eye should see Him (Revelation 1:7, cf. Matthew 24:27–30). How then can we doubt His testimony when He himself has said:

> And then shall appear the sign of the Son of man in heaven: and then shall all the tribes of the earth mourn, and they shall see the Son of man coming in the clouds of heaven with power and great glory (Matthew 24:30).

To this we can only say with John: "Even so come, Lord Jesus" (Revelation 22:20).

In drawing this portion of our study of Jehovah's Witnesses to a close it is expedient and vitally necessary that a clear picture of what this cult means to all Christians be presented. This organization has mushroomed from a meager beginning in 1881 until now, when it extends to every part of the globe. Because the cult does away with the doctrine of eternal retribution for sin, it appeals greatly to those who believe they have in it an escape from the penalty of personal transgression. Jehovah's Witnesses offer an illusionary "kingdom" to the personalities who desire importance, and most of all an outlet to vent their wrath upon religious leaders and organizations whose doctrines they assail as "of the devil." We do not believe for one moment that the greater body of these people know the true implications of Charles T. Russell's doctrines; however, let no Jehovah's Witness ever disclaim Russellistic origin. Charles Taze Russell founded, operated, propagated, and gave his life to furthering this cult, and his teachings permeate every major phase of its doctrines, despite the intense aloofness its leaders manifest when his past is mentioned. But now the question arises: "How can so many people be deceived by a so obviously fraudulent religion?" To understand this, the teachings and methods of propagation of the cult must be analyzed.

To begin with, no member of the Society is ever allowed to think independently for himself.

All religious leaders and organizations are pictured as false and anything they say is to be discounted as the "vain philosophies of men." The Scriptures are always made to conform to the Watchtower's beliefs, never Jehovah's Witnesses' beliefs to the Scriptures. Judge Rutherford's legal mind made most of this conjecture and linguistic chicanery reasonable to the minds of the people to whom he addressed it, and his books are masterpieces of illogical and invalid premises and conclusions.

To trace the logic and reasoning processes of Rutherford is the task of a logician, since for Russell or Rutherford contradictory statements can be premises which, regardless of the steps, always have a valid conclusion in their system of thinking. Jehovah's Witnesses' doctrine is a mass of half-truths and pseudo-scholastic material, which to the untutored mind can appear to be "wonderful revelation."

Recently, when I was speaking to an ardent Jehovah's Witness, the following statement fell unashamedly from his lips: "I have never met anyone who knows more about Greek than the Society." In all probability he was right, for had he met someone who did know Greek he would never have become a member of the cult. The Society, to our knowledge, does not have any Greek scholars of any repute in their ranks, and if they do I would welcome any opportunity for them to come out from behind their lexicons and explain their renditions of John 1:1, 8:58, and Colossians 2:9, to mention only a few. (Hebrew scholars are also included in this invitation.) In recent years there have been a few Jehovah's Witnesses who have taken courses in Greek, and even others who teach Greek. However, their renditions of the Greek New Testament into English, and their *theological interpretations* of those renditions, have no academic or scholastic support.

Another trait of the Society is its aversion to attributing individual authorship to its publications since the death of Rutherford. All publications now appear anonymously, copyrighted and published by the Society. By not committing persons to their signatures the Society escapes the unpleasant task of having to answer for their numerous blunders. Their standard answer is, "Many persons worked on the books, not only one particular person," etc. In their predicament, having no recognized scholarship behind them, they have chosen the wisest possible course—silence. The plain truth of the matter is that the "new" books are simply rephrases of Russell's and Rutherford's works and contain no originality other than up-to-date information on world conditions and new approaches to old material.

One of the distinguishing characteristics of an ardent Jehovah's Witness is his or her ability to handle the Scriptures. *The Emphatic Diaglott* and *The Kingdom Interlinear Translation of the Greek Scriptures* with their interlinear readings of the Greek facilitate their progress in this project. Any good Jehovah's Witness, sad to say, can cause the average Christian untold trouble in the Scriptures, though the trouble in most cases has an elementary solution. The Christian is bewildered by the glib manner in which they repeat Scripture verses (usually entirely out of context) and sprinkle their discourses with Greek or Hebrew grammatical terms of which they have no knowledge beyond their *Diaglott* and *Kingdom In-*

terlinear. The boldness with which they collar the unwary pedestrian, intrude on the quiet of a restful evening, attend their conventions, and propagate their literature is a danger signal that evangelical Christianity would do well to heed and take definite steps to combat. As has been observed, the answer to Jehovah's Witnesses, or "Russellism" if you will, is the deity of Jesus Christ, and in teaching that one cardinal doctrine of the Christian faith all energy ought to be expended to the uttermost. All ministers, Sunday school supervisors, Bible and Tract Societies, and teachers should drill their charges in biblical memorization and doctrinal truths, that a united Christian front may be thrown up against this ever-growing menace to sound reasoning in biblical exposition and study. The plan is not difficult, and only procrastination hinders its adoption.

This problem is also the task of Christian colleges, seminaries, and Bible schools, who too long have neglected the institution of strong cult courses in their curricula. The fruit of their neglect is before us today. Must we stand by in silence while the Word of God is defamed, the Lordship of Christ blasphemed, and the faith of generations still unborn is threatened by a group of people who will not listen to honest biblical truths, and dare not contest them in scholastic discussion? It is frustrating and exasperating to carry on a discussion with a person or persons who argue in circles and dodge artfully from one refutation to another. These tactics characterize the preaching and argumentation of Jehovah's Witnesses, which must be met by calm dispositions and truthful scriptural exegesis on the part of well-grounded Christians. Information in the form of documentary evidence and cold facts has met and can meet their perversions and emerge triumphant over them. We as Christians must perform this task without delay; we can ill afford to wait any longer.

The end product of this whole cult is the denial of the Lord Jesus Christ as "very God," and despite their protests that they honor Christ, they do indeed dishonor and "crucify Him afresh" since they deny His deity and lordship. Regardless of their biblical names and proficiency in the Scriptures, they constantly reveal their true character in their actions, which are the diametric opposite of scriptural teachings. The following old adage is most appropriate in describing the doctrines of Jehovah's Witnesses: "No matter how you label it or what color bottle you put it in, poison is still poison." "He that has ears, let him hear." On the cover of *The Watchtower*, Isaiah 35:5 and 43:12 were quoted, and throughout all of their publications they boast themselves as "Jehovah's Witnesses."

There can be no kingdom without the King, however, and His return is visible, with power and glory (Matthew 24:30). Their kingdom has come (A.D. 1914–1918), but with no visible king, power, or glory. Jehovah of the Watchtower is a conjectural myth, a creation of the reactionary theology of Charles Taze Russell, and is conformed to the pattern of Russell's mind and education, which continued through Rutherford, Knorr, Franz, and now Henschel and the Governing Body to the ever-increasing blindness of those misguided souls foolish enough to trust in the Russellite delusion. In comparison to the Scriptures this picture is infinite darkness, for its author is the "Prince of Darkness," and the Word of God clearly and incontestably reveals that "Jehovah of the Watchtower" is not the Jehovah of the Bible, for Jehovah of the Bible is Lord of all—"The great God and our Saviour Jesus Christ" (Titus 2:13).

Selected Terms and Texts Misapplied by Jehovah's Witnesses

To review all the terms and texts that Jehovah's Witnesses have misinterpreted and misapplied to bolster up their fractured system of theology would be impossible in the space here available. Therefore, I have chosen to survey six of their worst perversions of common biblical terms, and various texts that the Watchtower has mauled and mangled almost beyond recognition with little or no regard for hermeneutical principles, contexts, or the laws of sound exegesis.

These examples of Watchtower deceptions are found all neatly cataloged in their handbook of doctrinal subjects, entitled *Make Sure of All Things*, upon which this study is principally based, should any care to check further their authenticity, etc.

Misapplied Terms

1. "Only begotten." (Greek, *monogenes*). Jehovah's Witnesses in their zeal to establish the Christology of Arius of Alexandria have seized upon this Greek term, translated "only begotten" in the New Testament, and unfortunately they have been most successful in hoodwinking many uninformed persons into believing that "only begotten" really means "only generated." From this erroneous view they therefore suggest that since the term is applied to Jesus Christ five times in the New Testament, Christ is but a creature, or as they love to quote Codex Alexandrinus, "The only begotten God" (John 1:18).

It should be noted in this connection, therefore, that the most authoritative lexicons and grammar books, not to mention numerous scholarly works, all render "*monogenes*" as "only or unique: 'the only member of a kin or kind, hence generally only,'" (Liddell and Scott's *Greek-English Lexicon*, 2:1144). Moulton and Milligan, in their *Vocabulary of the Greek New Testament* (416–417), render "*monogenes*" as "one of a kind, only, unique," facts that establish beyond scholarly doubt the truth of the contention that in both classical and Koine Greek the term "*monogenes*" carries the meaning of "only," "unique," or "the only member of a particular kind." The Septuagint translation of the Old Testament (LXX) also utilizes the term "*monogenes*" as the equivalent in translation of the Hebrew adjective "*yachid*," translated "*solitary*" (Psalm 68:6, etc.). This interesting fact reveals that the translators understood "*monogenes*" to have the meaning of uniqueness attached to it, emphasis obviously being placed on "only" and decidedly not on "genus" or "kind."

In other places in the New Testament, such as Luke 7:11–18; 8:42; 9:38; Hebrews 11:17, etc., the rendering "only begotten" in the sense that Jehovah's Witnesses attempt to employ it in their translations and propaganda is an exegetical impossibility; especially in the instance of Hebrews 11:17, where Isaac is called the "only begotten" son of Abraham. Certainly he was not the eldest child, but rather he was the *sole* or *only* precious son in the sense that Abraham loved him in a unique way.

Dr. Thayer in his *Greek-English Lexicon of the New Testament* (417), referring to "*monogenes*," states, "single of its kind, only . . . used of Christ, denotes the only Son of God." Unfortunately, in ancient literature "*monogenes*" became con-

nected with the Latin term *"unigenitus."* However, such a translation is basically incorrect, as any lexicographical study will quickly reveal.

The early church Fathers were in essential agreement that Jesus Christ preexisted from all eternity in a unique relationship to God the Father. In the year 325 at the Council of Nicea it was officially proclaimed that Jesus Christ was of the same substance or nature as the Father, and those who differed from this pronouncement, which the church had always held, were excommunicated. Among them was Arius of Alexandria, a learned presbyter and the Christological father of Jehovah's Witnesses. Arius held that Jesus Christ was a created being, the first and greatest creation of God the Father, that He did not preexist from all eternity and that His only claim to Godhood was the fact that He had been created first and then elevated to the rank of a Deity.

Arius derived many of his ideas from his teacher, Lucian of Antioch, who in turn borrowed them from Origen, who himself had introduced the term "eternal generation," or the concept that God from all eternity generates a second person like himself, ergo the "eternal Son." Arius rejected this as illogical and unreasonable, which it is, and taking the other horn of the dilemma squarely between his teeth, reduced the eternal Word of God to the rank of a creation! It is a significant fact, however, that in the earliest writings of the church Fathers, dating from the first century to the year 230, the term "eternal generation" was never used, but it has been a common misperception of this dogma, later adopted by Roman Catholic theology, which has fed the Arian heresy through the centuries and today continues to feed the Christology of Jehovah's Witnesses.

In the year A.D. 328, in his private creed, Arius interestingly enough applies the term *"gegennemenon"* in reference to Christ, not the terms *"monogenes"* or *"ginomai." "Gegennemenon"* is a derivative of the word *"gennao,"* which is translated "begotten," and rightly so. Further than this, Eusebius of Caesarea, a follower of Arius (ca. 325), also utilized the term *"gegennemenon,"* not *"monogenes,"* a fact which throws a grammatical monkey wrench into the semantic machinations of the Watchtower.

We may see, therefore, that a study of this term *"monogenes"* reveals that in itself it is understood in both the classical and Koine vocabulary to be a term emphasizing uniqueness, i.e., the only one, the beloved, etc.; and there is no good grammatical ground for insisting, as Jehovah's Witnesses do, that it *must* mean "only generated," i.e., "only created."

Regarding the five times in the New Testament where the term *"monogenes"* is applied to Jesus Christ (John 1:14, 18; 3:16, 18; 1 John 4:9), it can be easily seen by the interested reader that the proper rendering "only" or "unique," in keeping with the historical usage of the term, in no way disturbs the context but, in fact, makes it clearer Christologically, eliminating the concept fostered by the Arians and carried on by Jehovah's Witnesses that "only begotten" must infer creation, which it most certainly does not!

As we mentioned before, common misunderstandings regarding the doctrine of eternal generation relative to the preexistence of the Lord Jesus Christ is one of the great stumbling blocks in any intelligent approach to the Christological problems of the New Testament. This fact being true, the author feels it is wiser to return to the original language of Scripture in its description of the

Lord Jesus and His preincarnate existence, where He is referred to prophetically in the Bible as the "eternal Son," but without ambiguity as the eternal Word of God (John 1:1) who "was" from all eternity and who "became" flesh (John 1:14), taking upon himself the nature of man, and as such was "begotten" of the Virgin Mary by the power of the Holy Spirit. The "unique," "only" Son of God, then, whether as a description of his eternal, intimate relationship with the Father and the Holy Spirit or as the incarnate One, was obedient in life and death, whose uniqueness stems from the fact that of all men He was the most precious in the Father's sight. He is beloved above all His brethren, so much that the Father could say of Him when He sent Him into the world, "Thou art my Son, this day have I begotten thee" (Hebrews 1:5), and he is not a creature or a demi-god but "God over all, blessed forever. Amen" (Romans 9:5, RSV footnote).

The Bible clearly teaches that Jesus Christ before His incarnation was the eternal Word, Wisdom, or Logos, of God, preexistent from all eternity, coequal, coexistent, coeternal with the Father, whose intrinsic nature of Deity He shared, and even though clothed in human form He never ceased to be Deity, "God . . . manifest in the flesh" (1 Timothy 3:16), or as Paul put it so directly, "In him dwelleth all the fulness of the Godhead bodily" (Colossians 2:9).

By insisting upon the unambiguous title of the preexistent Christ, orthodox Christianity can successfully undercut the emphasis Jehovah's Witnesses place upon "*monogenes*," showing in contrast that "only begotten" is a term best exemplified by His incarnational example; and further, that Jesus Christ is not called by Scripture the "eternal Son," the error of ambiguity first arising from Origen under the title "eternal generation," but rather He is the living Word of God (Hebrews 4:12), Creator of the Universe (2 Peter 3:5), Sustainer of all things (2 Peter 3:7), First Begotten from the dead (Acts 13:33), and our "Great High Priest, who has passed into the heavens, Jesus the Son of God . . . who can be touched with the feelings of our infirmities and who was in all points tempted like as we are, yet without sin" (Hebrews 4:15). Let us fix these things in our minds, then:

(a) the doctrine of "eternal generation" or the eternal Sonship of Christ, which springs from the Roman Catholic doctrine first conceived by Origen in A.D. 230, is a theory that opened the door theologically to misinterpretation by the Arian and Sabellian heresies, which today still plague the Christian church in the realms of Christology.

(b) Scripture nowhere calls Jesus Christ the eternal Son of God, and the term Son is much more familiar applied to Him in His incarnation.

(c) The term "Son" itself is a functional term, as is the term "Father," and has meaning only by analogy to the fathers and sons we see in the created world. The term "Father," incidentally, never carries the descriptive adjective "eternal" in Scripture; as a matter of fact, only the Spirit is called eternal[61] ("The eternal Spirit"—Hebrews 9:14), emphasizing the fact that the words Father and Son are purely functional, as previously stated.

(d) Many heresies have seized upon the confusion created by the illogical "eternal Sonship" or "eternal generation" misunderstandings of the theory as

---

[61]The Trinity as such is, however, spoken of as "the everlasting God" (Romans 16:26).

it is accepted in Roman Catholicism and Eastern Orthodoxy.

(e) Finally, there cannot be any such thing as eternal Sonship, if by eternal Sonship is meant that the second person of the Trinity is both created and eternal in the same way and the same manner. This would be a logical contradiction of terminology due to the fact that the word "Son" in such a sense predicates time and the involvement of creativity. Christ, the Scripture tells us, as the Logos, is timeless—the *Word was* in the beginning, *not* the *Son!*

The Lord Jesus Christ, true God and true man, is now and for all eternity Son of God and Son of Man; therefore, in this sense there is no contradiction in calling him the eternal Son. But to be biblical in the true sense of the term we must be willing to admit that He was known prior to His incarnation as the eternal Word, and knowledge of this fact cuts across the very basic groundwork and foundation of the Arian system of theology espoused by Jehovah's Witnesses. For if "only begotten" means "unique" or "only one of its kind," there cannot be any ground for rendering it "only generated" as Jehovah's Witnesses often attempt to do in a vain attempt to rob Christ of His deity.

If then we understand the terms "Father" and "Son" as having primary significance in the incarnation, and analogous significance for the conveyance of the mysterious relationship that existed from all eternity between God and His Word, we will be probing deeper into the truth of the Scripture, which teaches us that God calls Christ His eternal Word, lest we should ever forget that He is intrinsic deity (for never was there a moment when God had a thought apart from His Logos or Reason). Further than this, God calls Christ His "Son," lest we should think of the Word as being an impersonal force or attribute instead of a substantive entity existing in a subject-object relationship, the eternal God "who is the Savior of all men, especially of those who believe" (1 Timothy 4:10, RSV).

In summary, since the word "Son" in a temporal sense definitely suggests inferiority and derivation, it is absolutely essential that Christ as the Eternal Word be pointed up as an antidote to the Arian heresy of Jehovah's Witnesses, and in this light we can understand quite plainly the usages of the term "*monogenes*," not in the Jehovah's Witnesses' sense of creatureliness, but in the true biblical sense of "uniqueness," i.e., "the unique or only Son of God," generated in the womb of a woman by the direct agency of the Holy Spirit, "God manifest in the flesh." "The great God and our Saviour, Jesus Christ" (Titus 2:13).

2. "Greater." (Greek: *meizon.*) Another principal term utilized by Jehovah's Witnesses is the term "greater," translated from the Greek *meizon,* as it appears in the gospel of John, chapter 14, verse 28: "Ye have heard how I said unto you, I go away, and come again unto you. If ye loved me, ye would rejoice, because I said, I go unto the Father: for my Father is greater [*meizon*] than I." From this particular text, lifted conveniently out of its context by the ever zealous Russellites, the Watchtower attempts to "prove" that since Jesus in His own words while He was on earth stated that His Father was "greater" than He was, therefore Christ could not be equal with God or one of the members of the Trinity, which Jehovah's Witnesses deny so vehemently.

On the face of the matter this appears to be a good argument from Christ's usage of the word "greater," but a closer examination of the context and of the hermeneutical principles that govern any sound exegetical study of the New Tes-

tament quickly reveals that theirs is a shallow case indeed, and, one that rests rather unsteadily upon one Greek word in a most restricted context.

The refutation of this bit of Watchtower semantic double-talk is found in a comparison with Hebrews, the first chapter, verse 4: "Being made so much *better* than the angels, as he hath by inheritance obtained a more excellent name than they."

The careful student of Scripture will recognize immediately that in the first chapter of Hebrews, the verse previously cited, an entirely different word is utilized when comparing Christ and the angels. This word is *kreitton* and is translated "better" in the *King James Version*. Paralleling these two comparisons, that of Jesus with His Father in John 14:28 and Jesus with the angels in Hebrews 1:4, one startling fact immediately attracts attention. In the fourteenth chapter of John, as the Son of Man who had emptied himself of His prerogatives of Deity (Philippians 2:8–11) and taken upon himself the form of a slave, the Lord Jesus Christ could truthfully say, "My Father is greater than I," greater being a *quantitative* term descriptive of *position*. Certainly in no sense of the context could it be construed as a comparison of *nature* or *quality*.

In the first chapter of Hebrews, however, the comparison made there between the Lord Jesus Christ and angels is clearly one of *nature*. The Greek *kreitton* being a term descriptive of quality, *ergo*, Christ was *qualitatively* better than the angels because He was their Creator (Colossians 1:16–17) and as such He existed before all things and by Him all things consist (vv. 17–19). Since His intrinsic nature is that of Deity (John 8:58, cf. Colossians 2:9), therefore, *qualitatively* He was God manifest in the flesh, while *quantitatively* He was limited as a man and could in all truthfulness state, "My Father is greater than I." When this comparison of *position* in John 14:28 and the comparison of *nature* in Hebrews 1 are clearly understood, the argument Jehovah's Witnesses attempt to raise in order to rob Christ of His deity is reduced to rubble before one of the greatest of all truths revealed in Scripture, i.e., that "God who made the world and all things therein" so loved us as to appear in our form (John 1:1, 14) that the sons of men might through His measureless grace at length become the sons of God.

We should be quick to recognize, however, that had the Lord Jesus said in John 14:28 that His Father was *better* than He was and had used the proper Greek word denoting this type of comparison, another issue would be involved, but in actuality the comparison between Christ and His Father in that context and verse clearly indicates that Jesus was speaking as a man and not as the second person of the Trinity (John 1:1). Therefore, it is perfectly understandable that He should humble himself before His Father and declare that in the present form in which He found himself, His Father most certainly was "greater," *positionally*, than He. One might be willing to admit that the President of the United States is a *greater* man by virtue of his present *position*, authority, and recognition, etc., but it would be a far different matter to assent to the proposition that the President of the United States is a *better* man than his fellow Americans in the sense of *quality*, because such a comparison then involves a discussion of fundamental natures, attributes, etc. In like manner, Jesus, as the incarnate Son of God who had by His own voluntary act of will divested himself of His prerogatives of intrinsic Deity, could speak of His Father as being *positionally* greater

than He was without in any sense violating His true deity and humanity.

Hebrews 1:4 clearly teaches that Christ is better than the angels *qualitatively* from all eternity and that even while He walked the earth, though He was made lower than the angels *positionally* for the suffering of death in the form of a man, never for an instant did He cease to be the Lord of glory who could say with confident assurance, "Before Abraham was I AM" (John 8:58).

Let us constantly be aware of these facts when discussing the nature of Christ with Jehovah's Witnesses, for once the distinction is made between "greater" and "better," their entire argument based upon John 14:28 melts into nothingness, and the deity of our Lord is completely vindicated by the whole testimony of Scripture.

3. "Born again." Many times in their contacts with Christians, Jehovah's Witnesses utilize the evangelical terminology of the gospel of John, chapter 3, where Christ speaking to Nicodemus said, "Except a man be born again he cannot see the kingdom of God" (v. 3). The Witnesses utilize such terminology because they realize that contemporary evangelical efforts, especially those of Dr. Billy Graham, have popularized this term, and the Watchtower is quick to capitalize on any popularization of a biblical term, especially if it can be twisted to serve its own end. The definition that Jehovah's Witnesses give to the new birth or the act of being "born again" is found in *Make Sure of All Things* (48) and is as follows: "Born again means a birth-like realization of prospects and hopes for spirit life by resurrection to heaven. Such a realization is brought about through the water of God's truth in the Bible and God's holy spirit, his active force."

The interested student can see from this definition that the Witnesses reject flatly the concept of the new birth as taught in the New Testament. The Bible teaches us that when we are born again it is through repentance, the washing of water by the Word, and the direct agency of the third person of the Trinity, God the Holy Spirit (John 3, Ephesians 5:26, 1 Peter 1:23, etc.). There is not one verse that may be cited in either the Old or New Testaments to prove that the new birth means "a birth-like realization of prospects and hopes for spirit life by resurrection to heaven," as Jehovah's Witnesses so brazenly misrepresent it. On the contrary, the new birth guarantees eternal life to *all* believers, entrance into the kingdom of heaven, and a resurrection to immortality in a deathless, incorruptible form similar to that of the Lord Jesus Christ's form when He rose from among the dead.

The theology of Jehovah's Witnesses relevant to the new birth is that there will be only 144,000 "spiritual brothers" who will reign with Christ in heaven for a thousand years; and, further, that only these 144,000 will have a resurrection to heaven and a "spirit life" such as that now allegedly enjoyed by "Pastor" Charles Taze Russell and Judge J. F. Rutherford, who are carrying on the work of the Society "within the veil," according to Watchtower teaching.

In direct contrast to this, the Lord Jesus Christ made a universal statement when He said, "Except a man be born again he cannot see the kingdom of God," and we find no record of either Christ, the disciples, or the apostles ever promulgating the 144,000 "spirit brothers" idea espoused so zealously by the Watchtower. A doctrine of such momentous importance, the author feels, would certainly have been carefully defined in the New Testament; yet it is not, and

the only support Jehovah's Witnesses can garner for this weird Russellite interpretation is from the book of Revelation and the mystical number "144,000,"
which, incidentally, the Bible teaches refers to the twelve tribes of Israel, twelve
thousand out of each tribe, and therefore certainly not to members of the
Watchtower's "theocracy."

Christians, therefore, should be continually on guard against the Watchtower's perversion of common biblical terms drawn from evangelical sources,
for in 90 percent of the cases the author has analyzed, the Witnesses *mean* just
the opposite of what they *appear* to say. The new birth, Peter tells us, is a *past*
event in the lives of those who have experienced the regenerating power of
God's Spirit (from the Greek, "having been born again," 1 Peter 1:23); it is not
something to be constantly experienced or to be looking forward to in a type
of ethereal spiritual resurrection as the Witnesses would have us believe. Rather,
it is a fact to be rejoiced in that we "have been born again" and are new creations in Christ Jesus (2 Corinthians 5:17), joint heirs in the glory of the kingdom
that is yet to be revealed.

The Watchtower Bible and Tract Society most decidedly has its "new birth,"
but it is not the new birth of Scripture, nor is their theory taught anywhere
within the pages of the Bible. It is instead the theological brain-child of Charles
Taze Russell, to which the Witnesses cling so tenaciously, and which in the end
will be found to have originated with "the god of this world," who has blinded
their eyes "lest the glorious light of the Gospel of Christ, who is the image of
God should shine unto them" (2 Corinthians 4:4).

4. "Death." In common with other deviant systems of theology, Jehovah's
Witnesses espouse a peculiar and definitely unbiblical concept of death, both
in regard to the physical body and the soul and spirit of man.

According to *Make Sure of All Things* (86), death is defined in the following
manner: "Death: loss of life; termination of existence; utter cessation of conscious intellectual or physical activity, celestial, human, or otherwise."

Reverting to their basic trait of text-lifting and term-switching, Jehovah's
Witnesses garner a handful of texts from the Old and New Testaments that speak
of death as "sleep" or "unconsciousness," and from these out-of-context quotations attempt to prove that at the death of the physical form, man ceases to
exist until the resurrection.

Seizing upon such texts as Ecclesiastes 9:5–6, 10; Psalm 13:3; Daniel 12:2,
etc., the Witnesses loudly contend that until the resurrection, the dead remain
unconscious and inactive in the grave, thus doing away in one fell swoop with
the doctrine of hell and the true biblical teaching regarding the soul of man.

It is impossible in the space allotted here to place all the verses Jehovah's
Witnesses lift out of their contexts back into their proper contextual-
hermeneutical position, and by so doing to show that their theory is an exegetical nightmare, but the following observation can be made.

Despite the fact that in the Old Testament the term "sleep" is used to denote death, never once is such a term used to describe the immaterial nature
of man, which the Scriptures teach was created in the image of God (Genesis
1:26–27). This fact also holds true in the New Testament, as any cursory study
of either Strong's or Young's concordances will reveal. The term "sleep" is always applied to the body, since in death the body takes on the appearance of

one who is asleep, but the term "soul-sleep" or "the sleep of the soul" is never found in Scripture, and nowhere does it state that the soul ever sleeps or passes into a state of unconsciousness. The only way that Jehovah's Witnesses can infer such a doctrine is by assuming beforehand that death *means* sleep or unconsciousness; hence, every time they are confronted with the term "death" they assign the meaning of the temporary extinction of consciousness to it, and by so doing remove from Scripture the doctrine that they fear and hate the most— that of conscious punishment after death for unregenerate souls, continuing on into the everlasting ages of eternity (Jude 10–13; 2 Peter 2:17).

Since we have already covered the doctrine of hell in a previous section, the simplest refutation of Jehovah's Witnesses' perverted terms such as "death" can be found in the Scriptures themselves, where it easily can be shown that death does not mean "termination of existence" and "utter cessation of conscious intellectual . . . activity" as the Watchtower desperately attempts to establish.

The interested reader is referred to the following references: Ephesians 2:1–5; John 11:26; Philippians 1:21, 23; and Romans 8:10. The usage of "death" in these passages clearly indicates a state of existence solely in opposition to the definition that the Watchtower assigns to the word "death," and the reader need only substitute the Watchtower's definition in each one of these previously enumerated passages to see how utterly absurd it is to believe that the body has experienced "the loss of life" or "termination of existence" in such a context where Paul writes, "If Christ be in you, the body is dead because of sin" (Romans 8:10). The inspired apostle here obviously refers to a spiritual condition of separation—certainly not to "termination of existence," as the Watchtower's definition states.

We see, therefore, that death is a separation of the soul and spirit *from* the body, resulting in physical inactivity and a general *appearance* of sleep; however, in the spiritual sense death is the separation of soul and spirit from God as the result of sin, and in no sense of the term can it ever be honestly translated "unconsciousness" or "termination of existence" as Jehovah's Witnesses would like to have it.

In his first epistle to the Thessalonians, the fourth chapter, the apostle Paul spoke of the return of the Lord Jesus Christ and most pointedly made use of the term "sleep" as a metaphor for death (1 Thessalonians 4:13–18), and it is interesting to note his concept:

> But I would not have ye to be ignorant, brethren, concerning them which are asleep, that ye sorrow not, even as others which have no hope. For if we believe that Jesus died and rose again, even so them also which sleep in Jesus will God bring *with* him. For this we say unto you by the word of the Lord, that we which are alive and remain unto the coming of the Lord shall not prevent them which are asleep. For the Lord himself shall descend from heaven with a shout, with the voice of the archangel, and with the trump of God: and the dead in Christ shall rise first: Then we which are alive and remain shall be caught up together with them in the clouds, to meet the Lord in the air: and so shall we ever be with the Lord. Wherefore comfort one another with these words.

Verse 14 indicates that Paul, while using the metaphor "sleep" to describe physical death, clearly understood that when Jesus comes again He will bring

with (in the Greek, *sun*) Him those whose bodies are sleeping. To be more explicit, the souls and spirits of those who are with Christ now in glory (2 Corinthians 5:8; Philippians 1:22–23) will be reunited with their resurrection bodies (1 Corinthians 15); that is, they will be clothed with immortality, incorruptibility, exemption from physical decay, and they will be coming *with* Jesus. The Greek *sun* indicates in a "side-by-side" position, and the bodies that are sleeping will in that instant be quickened, raised to immortality, and reunited with the perfected spirits of the returning saints.

This passage alone would be enough to convince any exegetical scholar that those "sleeping in Jesus" must refer to their *bodies*, since they are in the same verse spoken of as coming *with* Jesus, and by no possible stretch of the imagination could one honestly exegete the passage so as to teach anything to the contrary.

Jehovah's Witnesses are justly afraid of the "everlasting fire" prepared for the devil and his followers (Matthew 25:41), and their entire system of theology is dedicated to a contradiction of this important biblical teaching of God's eternal wrath upon those who perpetrate the infinite transgression of denying His beloved Son. Rightly does the Bible say that "the wrath of God continues to abide upon them" (John 3:36—literal translation) (Revelation 20:10; Mark 9:43, 48; Daniel 12:2).

For the Christian, physical death involves only the sleep of the body, pending the resurrection to immortality, when our resurrection bodies will be joined to our perfected souls and spirits; but in the intermediate state, should we die before the Lord comes, we have the assurance that we shall be *with Him* and that we shall return *with Him*, or as the apostle Paul stated it, "To be absent from the body" is "to be at home (or present) with the Lord" (2 Corinthians 5:8).

5. "Firstborn" (Greek: *prototokos*). The author feels it necessary to include a brief résumé of Jehovah's Witnesses' misuse of the Greek term "*prototokos*" (Colossians 1:15), which the Watchtower lays much emphasis upon. It is used descriptively of the Lord Jesus Christ, and so in their Arian theology it is construed to teach that Christ is the first creature since the word "firstborn" implies that of the *first* child.

In Colossians 1, the apostle Paul speaks of the Lord Jesus Christ as the firstborn of every creature or of all creation. And the Witnesses, always eager to reduce Christ to the rank of an angel, have seized upon these passages of Scripture as indicative of His creaturehood. The Watchtower teaches that since Christ is called the "firstborn of all creation," therefore He must be the first one created, and they cross-reference this with Revelation 3:14, which states that the faithful and true witness (Christ) is "the beginning of the creation of God."

On the surface the argument the Watchtower erects appears to be fairly sound, but underneath it is found to be both shallow and fraudulent. The term firstborn (*prototokos*) may also rightfully be rendered "first begetter" or "original bringer forth" (Erasmus), a term of preeminence, and in Colossians 1 it is a term of comparison between Christ and created *things*. In the first chapter of Colossians, Paul points out that Christ is "before all things" and clearly establishes the fact that the eternal Word of God (John 1:1) existed before all creation (Hebrews 1) and that He is preeminent over all creation, by virtue of the fact that He is Deity; and beyond this, that He is the Creator of all "things," which

to any rational person indicates that if He is Creator of all things, He himself is not one of the "things" created! In the eighth chapter of Romans, verse 29, the word "firstborn" is applied to Christ, clearly denoting His preeminence—not the concept that He is "the first creature made by Jehovah God," as the Witnesses would like us to believe—and in Colossians 1:18 we learn that Christ is "firstborn" from the dead, that is, the one with the preeminence, or right to rule, over death. Again the meaning is that of preeminence, not of creation.

Revelation 3:14, "the beginning of the creation of God," is easily harmonized with the rest of Scripture, which teaches the absolute deity of the Lord Jesus Christ when we realize that the Greek word *arche*, which is translated "beginning," is translated by the Witnesses themselves as "originally" in John 1:1 of their own *New World Translation of the Christian Greek Scriptures*—and this is a good translation at this point—so applying it to Revelation 3:14, Christ becomes the "origin" or the "source" of the creation of God (Knox), and not the very beginning of it himself in the sense that He is the first creation, a fact that Scripture most pointedly contradicts.

Christ is therefore "firstborn," or preeminent, by virtue of the fact that He is Deity, and by virtue of the fact that as the first one to rise in a *glorified* body, he is preeminent over death, or has the right to rule over death. He is therefore preeminent over all creation, and through His power all things consist or hold together. He is not one of the "things" (Colossians 1:16–17), but He is the Creator of *all things*, the eternal Word who possesses the very nature of God (Hebrews 1:5).

6. "Soul and spirit" (Greek: *psyche, pneuma*). Jehovah's Witnesses delight in the assertion that man does not possess an immaterial, deathless nature, and they never tire of proclaiming such teaching to be "a lie of the devil" and a dogma derived from pagan religions (Egyptian, Babylonian, Greek, etc.) The literature of Jehovah's Witnesses is filled with condemnations of the doctrine of the immaterial nature of man. According to the Watchtower, the soul is "a living, breathing, sentient creature, animal or human," and Jehovah's Witnesses also define a spirit as "a life force, or something windlike" (*Make Sure of All Things*, 357).

By so defining these two common biblical terms, the Watchtower seeks to avoid the embarrassing scriptural truth that since man is created in the image of God, and God is Spirit, man must possess a cognizant spiritual entity formed in the image of his Creator (Genesis 1:26–27). To explode this Watchtower mythology is an elementary task when we realize that when the Lord Jesus Christ died upon the cross He said, "Father, into thy hands I commend my spirit" (Luke 23:46), a fact Jehovah's Witnesses are hard put to explain, since if the spirit is nothing but breath or wind, and certainly not a conscious entity as the Bible teaches it is, then it would be fruitless for Christ to commit His breath to the Father—yet He did precisely that! The truth of the matter is that the Lord Jesus Christ committed to His Father His immaterial nature as a man, proving conclusively that the spirit and soul of man goes into eternity as a conscious entity (Galatians 6:8).

It will also be remembered that when Stephen was stoned, he fell asleep in death, but not before he said, "Lord Jesus, receive my spirit" (Acts 7:59), and in that particular context it is rather obvious that he was not referring to the

exhalation of carbon dioxide from his lungs! However, we may safely say that the meanings Jehovah's Witnesses give to soul and spirit will not stand the test of systematic exegesis in either the Old or New Testaments, and no competent Hebrew or Greek scholar today has ever espoused their cause in open scholastic discussion.

Conclusion

Concluding this synopsis of the misapplications and misinterpretations of Jehovah's Witnesses where biblical terms and texts are concerned, the author feels constrained to state that by no means has he thoroughly covered this vast subject.

Jehovah's Witnesses thrive on the confusion they are able to create, and in their door-to-door canvassing they accentuate this trait by demonstrating extreme reluctance to identify themselves as emissaries of the Watchtower until they have established a favorable contact with the prospective convert. To put it in the terms of the vernacular, until they have "made their pitch" they are careful to conceal their identity. To illustrate this particular point more fully, the *New Yorker Magazine*, June 16, 1956, carried a lengthy article by one of its feature writers, Richard Harris, in which Harris recounts his experiences with Jehovah's Witnesses.

In this article, Harris relates that the Witnesses never identified themselves, at first, to prospective converts as Jehovah's Witnesses when Harris accompanied a team of Witnesses on one of their daily canvassing routes in Brooklyn. Harris also pointed out in the article that the Witnesses openly admitted to him that it was necessary for them first to make a successful contact before they fully identified themselves.

In short, Jehovah's Witnesses may be proud to be the only people standing for "Jehovah God," but they are not above neglecting to tell prospective converts their real affiliation if it will help their cause. If evangelical Christianity continues to virtually ignore the activities of Jehovah's Witnesses, it does so at the peril of countless souls. Therefore, let us awaken to their perversions of Scripture and stand fast in the defense of the faith "once delivered unto the saints" (Jude 1).

Author's Note

Nowhere is this point more forcefully demonstrated than in a book written by a former member of the Watchtower Society, W. J. Schnell: *Thirty Years a Watchtower Slave*.[62] In this particular reference, Schnell succinctly stated the Watchtower methodology in the following words:

> The Watchtower leadership sensed that within the midst of Christendom were millions of professing Christians who were not well grounded in "the truths once delivered to the saints," and who would rather easily be pried loose from the churches and led into a new and revitalized Watchtower organization. The Society calculated, and that rightly, that this lack of proper knowledge of

---

[62] *Thirty Years a Watchtower Slave* (Grand Rapids: Baker Book House, 1956), 19.

God and the widespread acceptance of half-truths in Christendom would yield vast masses of men and women, if the whole matter were wisely attacked, the attack sustained and the results contained, and then reused in an ever-widening circle.

Chapter 6

Church of Jesus Christ of Latter-day Saints
(the Mormons)

Historical Perspective

The Church of Jesus Christ of Latter-day Saints is distinctive among all the religious cults and sects active in the United States in that it has by far the most fascinating history, and one worthy of consideration by all students of religions originating on the American continent.

The Latter-day Saints, as they are commonly called, are divided into two major groups, The Church of Jesus Christ of Latter-day Saints (the Mormons), with headquarters in Salt Lake City, Utah, and The Reorganized Church of Jesus Christ of Latter Day Saints with headquarters in Independence, Missouri. Today, over 167 years after the movement's founding, the Mormons own considerable stock in the agricultural and industrial wealth of America and circle the earth in missionary activities, energetically rivaling evangelical Christianity. The former group, which is the main concern of this chapter, claims a membership in excess of nine million (*Ensign* Magazine, May 1995, 22). The Reorganized Church has just over 240,000 members worldwide and has won acceptance in some quarters as a "sect of fundamentalism." The Reorganized Church, which rejects the name "Mormon," is briefly reviewed in this chapter, but there can be little doubt that it is composed of a zealous group of dedicated people. They irritate the Utah Mormon Church consistently by pointing out that court decisions have established their claim that they are the true church and Utah the schismatic. From its founding, the Mormon Church has been characterized by thriftiness, zeal, and an admirable missionary spirit, as even before the advent of World War II, it had more than 2,000 missionaries active on all the mission fields of the world. Since the close of World War II, however, and in keeping with the acceleration of cult propaganda everywhere, the Mormons have around 50,000 "missionaries" active today.

This chapter revised and updated by Bill McKeever and Kurt Van Gorden, and edited by Gretchen Passantino.

The missionary effort of the Mormon Church is seldom matched by any other religious endeavor. The young Mormon children are taught from primary age onward that it is their duty to the church to serve a mission following high school. The entire missionary force is broken down into the following percentages: 75 percent single males, 19 percent single females, and 6 percent married couples.

One interesting fact, however, accounts for this large missionary force, and that is the practice of the Mormon Church to encourage its most promising young people, boys aged nineteen and older and girls aged twenty-one and older, to perform missionary work. Only in recent years did the Mormon Church begin to subsidize the expenses of their American and Canadian missionaries.

Membership in the Mormon Church now increases each year at an average rate of 300,000 conversions and 75,000 children's baptisms. The Mormons have a birthrate of 28.1 per thousand, in contrast to the average 15.9 birthrate of the United States.[1] According to the teaching of the Mormon Church, Mormons are to preserve their bodies always in the best of health and are cautioned against the use of tobacco and alcohol, and even the drinking of tea, coffee, and other caffeine-bearing drinks, such as Coca-Cola. Strongly insistent upon the Old Testament principle of tithing, the Mormon Church requires all temple Mormons and requests members to meet the biblical one-tenth of their gross income.

The facts and figures for the wealth of the Mormon Church have been carefully guarded for years. However, in 1991 the *Arizona Republic* newspaper ran a series entitled "Mormon Inc. Finances & Faith," which estimated that the Mormon Church conservatively "collects about $4.3 billion from its members a year plus $400 million from its many enterprises." Stating that "only a few church officials know how the money is spent," the articles maintained that the church's investment portfolio "easily exceeds $5 billion, including $1 billion in stocks and bonds and another $1 billion in real estate. The reader should bear in mind that the Mormons put this money to good use in the expansion of their church, a truth borne out by the fact that the church is rapidly expanding its real estate holdings, both for commercial and ecclesiastical purposes. The "Saints" now have around fifty temples in operation, with many more either in design or under construction on every continent on the globe. The Mormon university in Utah, Brigham Young University, boasts more than 37,000 students on two campuses.

Promulgated as it is by determined, zealous, missionary-minded people who have a practical religion of "good works" and clean living, the Mormons each year spend millions of dollars in the circulation of the writings and teachings of their prophets and apostles, while proselytizing any and all listeners regardless of church affiliation.[2] In addition to their regular tithing fund, the Mormon Church also encourages what it terms "fast offerings." This unusual

---

[1]The growth of the Mormons since 1900 is an outstanding story: 1900–283,765; 1910–398,478; 1920–525,987; 1930–670,017; 1940–862,664; 1950–1,111,314; 1960–1,693,180; 1970–2,930,810; 1980–4,639,822; and 1990–7,761,112, *1995–1996 Church Almanac.*

[2]As an example, in April 1978, *Reader's Digest* published an eight-page removable advertisement about church programs, the first of a $12 million series aimed at nearly fifty million *Digest* readers.

practice involves the giving up of two meals on the first Sunday of each month, the price of which is turned over to the church as a voluntary contribution to support and feed the poor.

Since education ranks high in Mormon circles, the existence of their "seminary" and "institute" programs for high school and college students with an enrollment of over half a million is what could be expected of such systematic growth. The church also has more than fifty schools outside of the United States, most of which are in Mexico and the South Pacific.

Mormonism, then, is not one of the cults tending to appeal merely to the uneducated, as for the most part Jehovah's Witnesses do, but instead it exalts education, which results in huge amounts of printed propaganda flowing from its presses in the millions of copies annually. The Mormons are also great chapel and temple builders, temples being reserved for the solemnization of "celestial" marriages, sealings, plus proxy baptisms and other ordinances for the dead (nearly 5.5 million sacred endowment rituals performed in 1993 alone). Such temples are forbidden to "Gentiles" (a Mormon term for all non-Mormons) and are truly beautiful buildings, usually extremely costly both in construction and furnishings. Along with their strong emphasis on education, the Mormons believe in sports, hobbies, dramatics, music, homemaking courses for prospective brides, dances, and dramatic festivals. The Mormon organization that sponsors a good deal of this is known as the Mutual Improvement Association, and has sponsored literally thousands and thousands of dances and other programs designed to attract and entertain young people. Each Mormon dance is begun with prayer and closed with the singing of a hymn. Mormonism does all that is humanly possible to make its church organization a home away from home for Mormon children and young people, and its low level of juvenile delinquency is in a marked proportion among Mormons, testifying to the success of the church-centered program.[3]

Emphasizing as they do the importance of missions, the Mormon Tabernacle Choir has become famous and is well known to all radio listeners. The choir contains 350 singers and has a repertoire of hundreds of anthems. The Mormon Tabernacle Choir began network broadcasting in 1929. Those who would tend to write off the Mormons as an influential force in the United States would do well to remember that Mormons have more adherents listed in *Who's Who in America* than any other one religion, and this also holds true for the scientific honor societies of our nation. Mormon leaders have become powerful in almost all branches of American government, headed by former Secretary of Agriculture Ezra Taft Benson, the late thirteenth prophet of the Mormon Church; former Treasury Secretary David M. Kennedy; former Treasurers Angela (Bay) Buchanan and the late Ivy Baker Priest; former Education Secretary Terrel H. Bell; former Michigan governor George Romney; Marriner S. Eccles; numerous U.S. ambassadors; and dozens of U.S. senators and representatives, to name but a few. Far from being an organization of minor influence, the Mormons are indeed a potent political and social force to be reckoned with, a fact that few informed persons would doubt.

---

[3] However, a review of social statistics in the state of Utah, which is at least 76 percent Mormon, shows that rates of divorce, child abuse, teenage pregnancy, and suicide are above the national average and climbing.

Church Organization

The organization and general administration of the Mormon Church is directed by its "General Authorities." At the top is the First Presidency (presently composed of eighty-five-year-old "prophet" Gordon B. Hinckley and two "counselors"), assisted by a "Council of Twelve" apostles, the "First Quorum of the Seventy," the "Second Quorum of the Seventy," and its Presidency, a "Presiding Bishopric," and the Patriarch of the church. All authority resides in the Mormon "priesthood," established under the titles "Aaronic" (lesser) and "Melchizedek" (higher). To the Aaronic priesthood belongs nearly every active male Mormon twelve years of age or over, and if "worthy" these are ordained to the Melchizedek priesthood at age eighteen. The Mormon Church administration is divided into territories made up of "wards" and "stakes," the former consisting of from five hundred to a thousand people. Each ward is presided over by a bishop and his two counselors. The wards are all consolidated into stakes, each of which is supervised by a stake president and two counselors, aided in turn by twelve high priests known as the "stake high council." At the beginning of 1995, there were approximately 21,774 wards and branches, 2,008 stakes, and 303 missions functioning in the Mormon Church. The various auxiliary groups form a powerful coalition for mutual assistance among Mormons, and it is noteworthy that during the Depression in 1929, the Mormon "Bishop's storehouse" saw to it faithfully that few worthy members were in want of the necessities of life.

In their missionary program the Mormons continue to manifest great zeal and quote the Bible profusely. Thus it is that many true Christians have often been literally quoted into silence by the clever disciples of Joseph Smith and Brigham Young, who flourish a pseudo-mastery of Scripture before the uninformed Christian's dazzled eyes and confuse him, sometimes beyond description.

In common with most cults, Mormonism has had its siege of persecutions and slander, but unlike many of the other cults who prefer to "let sleeping dogs lie," the Mormons have attempted at times to defend their "prophets." This has led them into more than one precarious historical dilemma.[4]

The young and boastful Joseph Smith went on record with outlandish statements that later proved to be a trouble source for the Mormon Church. Examination of three examples will suffice. Joseph Smith once said, "No man knows my history," which statement caused endless suspicion by Mormon historians and non-Mormons who began researching Joseph Smith's background and found dozens of improprieties ranging from occult peep-stone seeking, treasure digging, adultery before the polygamy prophecy, and financial schemes. In another instance, Joseph Smith proclaimed "the Book of Mormon is the most correct of any book on the earth," which has been amply refuted by both Mormon scholars and Christian apologists. Another regrettable statement made by Smith was, "I have more to boast of than ever any man had. I am the only man that has ever been able to keep a whole church together since the days of Adam. A large majority of the whole have stood by me. Neither Paul, Peter, nor Jesus ever did it. I boast that no man ever did such a work as I. The followers

---

[4]See Hugh Nibley, *The Myth Makers* (Salt Lake City, Utah: Bookcraft, Inc.), 1958.

of Jesus ran away from Him; but the Latter-day Saints never ran away from me yet" (*History of the Church*, 6:408–409).

The average active Mormon is usually marked by many sound moral traits. He is generally amiable, almost always hospitable, and extremely devoted to his family and to the teachings of his church. Sad to say, however, the great majority of Mormons are in almost total ignorance of the shady historical and theological sources of their religion. They are openly shocked at times when the unglamorous and definitely unchristian background of the Mormon Church is revealed to them. This little known facet of Mormonism is "a side of the coin" that innumerable Mormon historians have for years either hidden from their people or glossed over in an attempt to suppress certain verifiable and damaging historical evidences. Such evidence the author has elected to review in the interest of obtaining a full picture of Joseph Smith's religion.

Early Mormon History

The seeds of what was later to become the Mormon religion were incubated in the mind of one Joseph Smith Jr., "The Prophet," better known to residents of Palmyra, New York, as just plain "Joe Smith."

Born in Sharon, Vermont, December 23, 1805, fourth child of Lucy and Joseph Smith, the future Mormon prophet entered the world with the proverbial "two strikes" against him in the person of his father and his environment.

Joseph Smith Sr. was a mystic, a man who spent much of his time digging for imaginary buried treasure. This fact is, of course, well known to any informed student of Mormonism. Former Mormon historian Dr. D. Michael Quinn has thoroughly documented the fact that both Joseph Smith Sr. and Joseph Smith Jr. were avid treasure-seekers. In his book entitled *Early Mormonism and the Magic World View* (1987), Quinn writes, "Joseph Smith, the founding prophet and president of the new church organized on 6 April 1830, had unquestionably participated in treasure-seeking and seer-stone divination and had apparently also used divining rods, talismans, and implements of ritual magic. His father, one of the Eight Witnesses to the divinity of the Book of Mormon and later the church patriarch, had also participated in divining and the quest for treasure." Quinn states on page 207 that Smith was interested in treasure-seeking even after he became president of the LDS Church and that "occult dimensions of treasure digging was prominent among the first members of the Quorum of the Twelve Apostles, organized in 1835." In the past, Mormon historians have avoided every indication that Joseph Smith owned a peep stone or seer stone. Dr. Quinn's aforementioned book includes photographs of actual seer stones owned by Joseph Smith. It should be noted that D. Michael Quinn was excommunicated from the LDS Church, in 1993, after refusing to keep silent about his unflattering research. This newer honesty among Mormon historians is appearing in other books, like the revision of *The Story of the Latter-day Saints* by J. B. Allen and G. M. Leonard, where they discuss Smith's "youthful experiments with treasure-seeking"[5]

---

[5]J. B. Allen and G. M. Leonard, *The Story of the Latter-day Saints* (Salt Lake City: Deseret Book Company, 1992), 41.

The mother of the future prophet was as much as her husband the product of the era and her environment, given as she was to extreme religious views and belief in the most trivial of superstitions. Lucy Smith later in her life "authored" a book entitled *Biographical Sketches of Joseph Smith and His Progenitors for Many Generations.* When published by the Mormon Church in Liverpool, England, however, it incurred the enduring wrath of Brigham Young, the first successor to Smith, who brought about the suppression of the book on the grounds that it contained "many mistakes" and that "should it ever be deemed best to publish these sketches, it will not be done until after they are carefully corrected" (*Millennial Star,* 17:297–298, personal letter dated January 31, 1885).[6]

Mrs. Smith, of course, was totally incapable of writing such a work, the "ghost writing" being done by a Mrs. Martha Jane Knowlton Coray, who faithfully recorded what came to be known as "Mother Smith's History." We will quote from this work as we progress, as we also will the personal history of Joseph Smith Jr. It is merely mentioned now to indicate the contradictory views held by the Mormon Church and by Smith's mother concerning the prophet's homelife, background, and religious habits.

We return now to the central character of our survey, Joseph Smith Jr. The year 1820 proved to be the real beginning of the prophet's call, for in that year he was allegedly the recipient of a marvelous vision in which God the Father and God the Son materialized and spoke to young Smith as he piously prayed in a neighboring wood. The prophet records the incident in great detail in his book *The Pearl of Great Price* (Joseph Smith—History 1:1–25), wherein he reveals that the two "personages" took a rather dim view of the Christian church, and for that matter of the world at large, and announced that a restoration of true Christianity was needed, and that he, Joseph Smith Jr., had been chosen to launch the new dispensation.

The Mormon Church has always held the position that they alone represent true Christianity. Mormon leaders have consistently taught that after the death of the apostles, true Christianity fell into complete apostasy, making it necessary for a "restoration." Mormon Apostle Bruce R. McConkie, on page 513 of his book *Mormon Doctrine,* writes, "Mormonism is Christianity; Christianity is Mormonism . . . Mormons are true Christians." In 1995 Mormon Apostle Dallin Oaks stated that the differences between "other Christian churches" and the LDS Church "explain why we send missionaries to other Christians" (*Ensign,* May 1995, 84).

It is interesting to observe that Smith could not have been too much moved by the heavenly vision, for he shortly took up once again the habit of digging for treasure along with his father and brother, who were determined to unearth treasure by means of "peep stones," "divining rods," or just plain digging.[7]

History informs us that the Smith clan never succeeded at these multitudinous attempts at treasure hunting, but innumerable craters in the Vermont and New York countryside testify to their apparent zeal without knowledge.

In later years, the "prophet" greatly regretted these superstitious expedi-

---

[6]*Millennial Star,* 27:42 (October 21, 1885).

[7]Peep Stones, Peek Stones, or Seer Stones: supposedly magical rocks, which, when placed in a hat and partially darkened, allegedly reveal lost items and buried treasure. Divining rods were sticks that were supposed to lead to treasure or water, etc.

tions of his youth and even went on record as denying that he had ever been a money-digger. Said prophet Smith on one such occasion, "In the month of October, 1825, I hired with an old gentleman by the name of Josiah Stoal, who lived in Chenango County, State of New York. He had heard something of a silver mine having been opened by the Spaniards in Harmony, Susquehanna County, State of Pennsylvania; and had, previous to my hiring to him, been digging in order, if possible, to discover the mine. After I went to live with him, he took me, with the rest of his hands, to dig for the silver mine, at which I continued to work for nearly a month, without success in our undertaking, and finally I prevailed with the old gentleman to cease digging after it. Hence arose the very prevalent story of my having been a money-digger."[8]

This explanation may suffice to explain the prophet's treasure-hunting fiascoes to the faithful and to the historically inept; but to those who have access to the facts, it is at once evident that Smith played recklessly, if not fast and loose, with the truth. In fact, it often appeared to be a perfect stranger to him. The main source for promoting skepticism where the veracity of the prophet's explanation is concerned, however, is from no less an authority than Lucy Smith, his own mother, who, in her account of the very same incident, wrote that Stoal "came for Joseph on account of having heard that he possessed certain means by which he could discern things invisible to the natural eye" (*History of Joseph Smith by His Mother*, 91–92).

Further evidence, in addition to Mrs. Smith's statement (and *prima facie* evidence, at that), proves beyond a reasonable doubt that the prophet was a confirmed "peep-stone" addict, that he took part in and personally supervised numerous treasure-digging expeditions, and further that he claimed supernatural powers that allegedly aided him in these searches. To remove all doubt the reader may have as to Smith's early treasure-hunting and peep-stone practices, we shall quote two of the best authenticated sources, which we feel will sustain our contention that Smith was regarded as a fraud by those who knew him best. It should also be remembered that Joseph Smith Sr., in an interview later published in *Historical Magazine*, May 1870, clearly stated that the prophet had been a peep-stone enthusiast and treasure-digger in his youth, and, further, that he had also told fortunes and located lost objects by means of a peep stone and alleged supernatural powers therein. Substantiating Joseph's father's account of his rather odd activities is the testimony of the Reverend Dr. John A. Clark after "exhaustive research" in the Smith family's own neighborhood.

> Long before the idea of a Golden Bible entered their minds, in their excursions for money digging . . . Joe used to be usually their guide, putting into a hat a peculiar stone he had through which he looked to decide where they should begin to dig (*Gleanings by the Way*, by J. A. Clark, [Philadelphia: W. J. and J. K. Simon, 1842], 225).

The proceedings of a court hearing dated March 20, 1826—*New York* vs. *Joseph Smith*—revealed that Joseph Smith "had a certain stone which he had occasionally looked at to determine where hidden treasures in bowels of the earth

---

[8]Joseph Smith, *History*, 1:55.

were . . . and had looked for Mr. Stoal several times."[9] The hearing ruled the defendant guilty of money-digging.

Peep-stone gazing was one of several occult practices deemed illegal in the 1820s. That Joseph Smith's peep-stone gazing episodes met their challenge with the law is irrefutably documented. The original court bill of 1826, charging Smith with "glass looking," was discovered by Rev. Wesley P. Walters, in 1971, at the Chenango County Jail, Norwich, New York. The trial for the misdemeanor crime cost two dollars and sixty-eight cents, which Smith apparently paid. A copy of the original court bill is reproduced in Walter Martin's *The Maze of Mormonism* (Santa Ana: Vision House, 1978), 37.

In 1820, Joseph Smith Jr. claimed a heavenly vision that he said singled him out as the Lord's anointed prophet for this dispensation, though it was not until 1823, with the appearance of the angel Moroni at the quaking Smith's bedside, that Joe began his relationship to the fabulous "golden plates," or what was to become the *Book of Mormon.*

According to Smith's account of this extraordinary revelation, which is recorded in the *Pearl of Great Price* (Joseph Smith—History, 1:29–54), the angel Moroni, the glorified son of one Mormon, the man for whom the famous book of the same name is entitled, appeared beside Joseph's bedside and thrice repeated his commission to the allegedly awestruck treasure-hunter. Smith did not write this account down until some years later, but even that fails to excuse the blunder he made in transmitting the angelic proclamation. This confusion appears in the 1851 edition of the *Pearl of Great Price,* wherein Joseph Smith identifies the messenger as Nephi, an entirely different character found in the *Book of Mormon.* This unfortunate crossing up of the divine communication system was later remedied by thoughtful Mormon scribes who have exercised great care to ferret out all the historical and factual blunders not readily explainable in the writings of Smith, Young, and other early Mormon writers. In current editions Moroni is identified as the nighttime visitor. However, whether Nephi or Moroni carried the message to Smith apparently makes little difference to the faithful.

The nightmarish blunder of crediting the revelation of the *Book of Mormon* to Nephi instead of Moroni has never ceased to be a proverbial thorn in the side of Mormon historians. Try as they will, it is impossible to erase it from the handwritten manuscripts of the Mormon Church history, which was supervised by Joseph Smith during his life. A reproduction of the manuscript may be found in Jerald and Sandra Tanner's *Mormonism—Shadow or Reality* (Salt Lake City: Utah Lighthouse Ministry, 1987, fifth edition), 136. Later, in 1842, these manuscripts formed the basis of the published history of Mormonism, again, overseen by Smith before his death, where Nephi appears as the revelatory angel, cf. *Times and Seasons,* vol. 3 (Nauvoo, Ill.: Times and Seasons), 753. The first edition of the *Pearl of Great Price* (1851), with the subtitle "Choice selections of revelations, translations, and narrations of Joseph Smith," contained the name Nephi because the unchallenged history of Mormonism had set such a foundation.

In 1827 Smith claimed to receive the golden plates upon which the *Book of*

---

[9]*Frazers Magazine* (New Series, February 1873): 7:229.

Mormon is alleged to have been written. Shortly after this historic find, unearthed in the hill Cumorah, near Palmyra, New York, Smith began to "translate" the "reformed Egyptian"[10] hieroglyphics, inscribed thereupon by means of the "Urim and Thummim," a type of miraculous spectacles, which the angel Moroni had the foresight to provide for the budding seer. The account of how Smith went about "translating" the plates and of the attendant difficulties with one Martin Harris, his wife, and Professor Charles Anthon, a noted scholar, will be dealt with more fully later in this chapter. However, the plot is obvious to anyone who is even basically informed concerning the real character of Joseph Smith; so we will continue with the prophet's history.

During the period when Joseph was translating the plates (1827–1829), one Oliver Cowdery, an itinerant schoolteacher, visited Smith at the home of his father-in-law (who after some months, for the sake of his daughter, had received Joseph into his home), where he was duly "converted" to the prophet's religion and soon after became one of several "scribes" who faithfully wrote down what Joseph said the plates read, in spite of the fact that he and Smith were separated by a curtain during the "translation." In the course of time, Smith and Cowdery became fast friends, and the progression of the "translation" and spiritual zeal allegedly attained such heights that on May 15, 1829, John the Baptist, in person, was speedily dispatched by Peter, James, and John to the humble state of Pennsylvania with orders to confer the "Aaronic Priesthood" on Joe and Oliver.

This amazing event is recorded in the *Pearl of Great Price* (Joseph Smith—History, 1:68–73), following which Oliver baptized Joe and vice versa; and they spent time blessing one another and prophesying future events "which should shortly come to pass." Smith was careful not to be too specific in recording these prophecies, because of the fact that more often than not Mormon prophecies did not come in on schedule, which no doubt accounted for Smith's hesitancy in alluding to details.

From the now hallowed state of Pennsylvania, immortalized by Smith's initiation into the priesthood of Aaron by John the Baptist, Joseph returned shortly to the home of Peter Whitmer in Fayette, New York, where he remained until the "translation" from the plates was completed and the *Book of Mormon* published and copyrighted in the year 1830. On April 6 of the same year, the prophet, in company with his brothers Hyrum and Samuel, Oliver Cowdery, and David and Peter Whitmer Jr., officially founded a "new religious society" entitled "The Church of Christ" (later to be named the Church of the Latter-day Saints [1834], and finally as the Church of Jesus Christ of Latter-day Saints in 1838). Thus it was that one of the more virulent strains of American cults came into existence—Mormonism had begun in earnest.

Following this "momentous" occasion, a conference consisting of thirty men was called by the "prophet" on June 9, 1830. A few months later missionary efforts were decided upon and some of the newly ordained elders were set aside to become missionaries to the Indians. In September 1830, a zealous preacher, Parley P. Pratt, was "converted" to Mormonism, and allegedly in November, Sidney Rigdon, a powerful Campbellite preacher from Ohio, "saw the light" and

[10]Reformed Egyptian is an undocumented language never seen by any leading Egyptologist or philologist who has ever been consulted on the problem. However, the Mormons still maintain their claim with the full knowledge that these are the facts.

"converted" more than 100 of his congregation to Smith's religion, which had begun to take root outside of New York State and Pennsylvania.

Sidney Rigdon and Parley P. Pratt, it should be noted, were almost from the day of their "conversions" slated for greatness in the Mormon hierarchy, as was Orson Pratt; and it is their writings, along with those of Young, Charles Penrose, and James Talmage, which best argue in favor of the Mormon cause, even to this very day. The role Sidney Rigdon played in the Mormon saga will be discussed later, but it must be remembered that Rigdon would eventually be accused of apostasy and excommunicated from the Mormon Church in 1844. Rigdon soared to the heights of inflammatory rhetoric against the citizens of Jackson County, Missouri, when, on Independence Day, 1838, he virtually challenged the whole state to do pitched battle with the "Saints," who were subsequently terribly persecuted and expelled in November 1838.

Shortly after the original conference meeting in Fayette on April 6, 1830, the nucleus of the Mormon Church moved to Kirtland, Ohio, where in a period of six years they increased to over 16,000 souls. It was from Kirtland that Smith and Rigdon made their initial thrust into Jackson County, Missouri. Joseph and Sidney were no strangers to persecution and suffered the indignity of an old-fashioned "tar-and-feathering," accompanied by a trip out of town on the proverbial rail. While in Missouri, Smith purchased sixty-three acres, which he deemed "holy ground," and there marked the exact spot on which he declared that the temple of Zion, the earthly headquarters of the kingdom of Jesus Christ, was eventually to be built. It is an interesting fact of history that one small branch of Mormonism (The Church of Christ, Temple Lot) today owns that temple site and claims that it once refused five million dollars from the Utah church for the "hallowed ground."

Some of the more prominent divisions of the work of Joseph Smith have survived, though barely, to this day. In the 1990 edition of his book, *Divergent Paths of the Restoration*, author Steven L. Shields lists well over 100 "restoration" churches that claim Joseph Smith, his first vision, and the *Book of Mormon* as their foundation. Most of their differences concern his work and revelations following the *Book of Mormon*. To the far left are those who reject all or nearly all revelations since the early 1830s. These are the Reorganized Church of Jesus Christ of Latter Day Saints (Independence, Missouri), The Church of Christ, Temple Lot (Independence, Missouri), The Church of Christ (Bickerton, Pennsylvania), and other factions. To the far right are the fundamentalist Mormon groups that sustain every revelation of Smith and subsequent prophets through 1890. These often practice polygamy and are mostly located in the Western United States, Canada, and Mexico. Some prominent groups are The Church of the Firstborn, The Order of Enoch, and the communal clans of Johnson, Allred, Barlow, and Musser.

In Kirtland, also, the First Stake of Zion was established and a quorum of twelve apostles was chosen, presided over by a First Presidency of three, supervised by the president, Joseph Smith, the Seer. It appears that the chief reason for the Mormons moving to Kirtland, Ohio, however, was the extreme unpopularity of Smith and his revelations among the people who knew him best and who regarded his new religion as a sham and a hoax, thus hardly recommending them as prospective converts. Smith, of course, had a revelation from God as

authorization for the move. In fact, between the years 1831 to 1844, the "prophet" allegedly received well over 135 direct revelations from God, revelations which helped build Kirtland and, later, the Mormon metropolis of Nauvoo, Illinois. Smith's infamous practice of polygamy was instituted at Kirtland and later confirmed by "divine revelation." Some misinformed persons have declared that Smith was not a polygamist, but one needs only to search the famous Berrian collection in the New York Public Library for volumes of primary information to the contrary, written by Mormon men and women who lived through many of these experiences and testified to the outright immorality of Smith and the leaders of the Mormon Church. Gradually, of course, polygamy filtered down through the Mormon Church, so that it was necessary for the United States government to threaten complete dissolution as well as to confiscate all Mormon property in order to stamp out the accepted practice.

The "fundamentalist" or polygamist Mormon groups claim no revelation was ever given from God for the disbanding of polygamy. They wholeheartedly reject the 1890 "Manifesto" of Wilford Woodruff, claiming this fourth Mormon prophet apostatized from the revelations of Smith, Young, and Taylor. Fundamentalist Mormons delight in publishing revelations of John Taylor (third prophet) and Mormon apostles of that period who despised the United States government for the sake of polygamy. Most fundamentalist Mormons adhere to obscure teachings abandoned by the Mormon Church, such as the Adam-god and the restoration of Zion in Jackson County, Missouri. It is a matter of historical record that leaders of the Mormon Church were tried and convicted of unlawful cohabitation with plural wives after the 1890 Manifesto. For instance, Heber J. Grant, who would later become Mormonism's seventh prophet, was fined $100 after pleading guilty to unlawful cohabitation in September 1899. In 1906, sixth LDS President Joseph F. Smith was found guilty of the same and fined $300. Following his plea Smith stated, "When I accepted the manifesto issued by President Wilford Woodruff, I did not understand that I would be expected to abandon and discard my wives" (*Deseret Evening News*, November 28, 1906).

In 1890, President Wilford Woodruff officially abolished polygamy as a practice of the Mormon Church, one concrete instance, at least, of the fact that the religious convictions of the Mormons were sacrificed for their political and economic survival. The facts still remain that in Kirtland, Nauvoo, Jackson County, etc., the Mormons had a chance to win converts to Smith's religion because they were strangers and the character of the prophet was unknown in those areas. But in New York, Smith was known by the most uncomplimentary terms, some of which have a direct bearing upon a proper understanding of his character. Pomeroy Tucker, in his classic work *The Origin, Rise, and Progress of Mormonism* (New York, 1861), collected a number of duly sworn statements by neighbors of the Smith family and by acquaintances of Joseph Smith Jr., particularly. According to the unanimous consensus of those who testified at the time, Joseph Smith Jr. was known for "his habits of exaggeration and untruthfulness . . . by reason of his extravagances of statement, his word was received with the least confidence by those who knew him best. He could utter the most palpable exaggeration or marvelous absurdity with the utmost apparent gravity" (p. 16).

One of the most interesting statements concerning the early life of the Smith family and of Joseph Jr. was obtained by E. D. Howe, a contemporary of

Smith's, who did tremendous research during Joseph's lifetime. Smith himself never dared to answer Howe's charges, though they were well known to him, so great was the weight of contemporary evidence.

Mr. Howe obtained a statement signed by sixty-two residents of Palmyra, New York, one that cannot be ignored by any serious student of Mormonism:

> We, the undersigned, have been acquainted with the Smith family for a number of years while they resided near this place, and we have no hesitation in saying that we consider them destitute of that moral character which ought to entitle them to the confidence of any community. They were particularly famous for visionary projects, spent much of their time in diggings for money, which they pretended was hid in the earth; and to this day, large excavations may be seen in the earth, not far from their residence, where they used to spend their time in digging for hidden treasures. Joseph Smith Sr., and his son Joseph, were in particular considered entirely destitute of *moral character* and *addicted to vicious habits* (*Mormonism Unveiled* [Painsville, Ohio, 1834], 261).

Mormons attempt to dissuade members from Howe's research by pretending that his publication resulted from the revengeful vendetta of one Dr. Philastus Hurlbut (sometimes spelled Harlburt), a Mormon excommunicated in 1833. The fact that Howe published stories that were publicly circulated previous to Hurlbut's excommunication is incontestable, despite Hurlbut's assistance in research.

Some persons reading this may feel that it is unfair to quote only one side of the story; what about those who are favorable to the Mormons, they will ask. In answer to this, the amazing fact is that *there exists no contemporary pro-Mormon statements from reliable and informed sources who knew the Smith family and Joseph intimately.* It has only been the over-wise Mormon historians, utilizing hindsight over a hundred-year period, who have been able to even seriously challenge the evidence of the neighbors, Joseph's father-in-law, and many ex-Mormons who knew what was going on and went on record with the evidence that not even Mormon historians have bothered to dispute.

As the Mormons grew and prospered in Nauvoo, Illinois, and as the practice of polygamy began to be known by the wider Mormon community and outsiders as well, increasing distrust of prophet Smith multiplied, especially after one of his former assistants, John C. Bennett, boldly exposed the practice of polygamy in Nauvoo. When the prophet (or "general," as he liked to be known in this phase of his career) could tolerate this mounting criticism no more and ordered the destruction of its most threatening mouthpiece, an anti-Mormon publication entitled *The Nauvoo Expositor*, the State of Illinois intervened. The "prophet" and his brother, Hyrum, were placed in a jail in Carthage, Illinois, to await trial for their part in the wrecking of the *Expositor*. However, on June 27, 1844, a mob comprised of some two hundred persons[11] stormed the Carthage jail and brutally murdered Smith and his brother, Hyrum, thus forcing

---

[11]Dr. Martin's numbering the mob at about 200 seems to be a fairly good average in light of the many conflicting sources available. For instance, Willard Richards, who was in the jail cell when the mob attacked, estimated the mob at around 100 to 200 men (*History of the Church*, 7:110). *The Encyclopedia of Mormonism* claims the mob consisted of about 150 men. D. Michael Quinn quotes the Chicago Historical Society and estimates the mob was "about 250 strong" (*The Mormon Hierarchy—Origins of Power*, 1994), 374.

upon the vigorously unwilling prophet's head the unwanted crown of early martyrdom, insuring his perpetual enshrinement in Mormon history as a "true seer."

With the assassination of Joseph Smith, the large majority of Mormons accepted the leadership of Brigham Young, then forty-three years of age and the man who had previously led the Mormons to safety from the wrath of the Missouri citizenry.

In 1846, Young announced that the Saints would abandon Nauvoo. In 1847, after a brutal trek through the wilderness of the Great Plains and the Rocky Mountains, Young brought the first band of Mormons to the valley of the Great Salt Lake and is credited with the exclamation, "This is the place!" The destiny of the Saints was sealed—they were in what was to become the state of Utah.

For thirty years, Brigham Young ruled the Mormon Church and, as is still the case, he inherited the divinely appointed prophetic mantle of the first prophet. So it is that each succeeding president of the Mormon Church claims the same authority as Joseph Smith and Brigham Young—an infallible prophetic succession.

The "spiritual deed" that the Mormons felt entitled them to possession of the valley of the Great Salt Lake was "granted" in June 1848, when the first Mormon crops were largely saved from a plague of locusts by a vast armada of sea gulls; thus, according to Mormon teaching, God gave visible evidence of His blessing upon the Latter-day Saints Church.

We cannot, of course, discuss the history of the Mormons under Brigham Young in great detail because that would easily necessitate a full volume by itself, but suffice it to say that Smith gave the movement its initial thrust and Brigham Young supplied the momentum necessary to establish it as a bona fide religion. Young himself was a character of many facets, and one cannot understand the theology of Mormonism without understanding the tremendous influence exercised upon it by the person of "prophet" Young and his teachings. Smith and Young, in company with the pronouncements of the succeeding presidents, have made Mormon theology what it is, and apart from Brigham Young, Mormonism cannot be thoroughly understood.

Young was a man of indomitable courage, possessed of a canny nature, but given to fits of ruthlessness now conveniently forgotten by Mormon historians. One such evidence of his determination to control Utah was the order that he gave to those involved in the massacre of around 100 non-Mormon immigrants to remain quiet about what has now become known as the infamous Mountain Meadows Massacre. In September 1857, John D. Lee and a group of LDS cohorts devised a plan to mercilessly annihilate a wagon train of virtually helpless immigrants. Twenty years later he was imprisoned, tried, convicted, and executed by the government of the United States for this vicious action.

The Mountain Meadows Massacre has definitely become a lamentable part of Mormon history. Whereas Mormons often like to point to persecutions brought on them from outside sources, this is one area of history where there is no doubt that the Mormons were guilty of the most heinous of crimes. According to *The Comprehensive History of the Church* (4:177), when Brigham Young was told of the deed, he said, "As soon as we can get a court of justice we will ferret this thing out, but till then, don't say anything about it." In her book

entitled *The Mountain Meadows Massacre*, the late LDS historian Juanita Brooks admits that the secrecy surrounding the tragedy has prevented the whole truth from ever being known. It would take nearly two decades before John D. Lee would be made the lone scapecoat. On March 23, 1877, he was executed by firing squad while sitting on the edge of his coffin. Brooks writes on pages 219–220, "The Church leaders decided to sacrifice Lee only when they could see that it would be impossible to acquit him without assuming a part of the responsibility themselves." She also states on page 219 that while Brigham Young and other church authorities "did not specifically order the massacre, they did preach sermons and set up social conditions that made it possible." Before Lee would be executed, he would face excommunication from the LDS Church. This decision, however, was overturned, when on April 20, 1961, The First Presidency and Council of the Twelve reinstated John D. Lee's membership and former blessings.

In his memorable book *The Confessions of John D. Lee*, a consistent sore spot in the Mormon scheme of historical "reconstruction," Lee confessed to his part in the infamous doings, but he swore that he believed he acted upon the approval of Brigham Young. As we further study Mormon theology, it will become apparent that this was not at all beyond the limits of Young's character. He *was* the law in Utah, and as it has been so wisely observed, "Power corrupts and absolute power corrupts absolutely."

Mormonism today, then, is a far cry from quite a number of the principles and practices of its early founders. To be sure, it remains faithful to their basic tenets, but, as in the case of polygamy, when those tenets come in conflict with government statutes or political influence, the Latter-day Saints have wisely chosen to ignore (the word commonly used is "reinterpret") the counsels of their two chief prophets. The history of the Mormons is a vast and complex subject; it is a veritable labyrinth of books, testimonies, affidavits, photographs, hearsay, and opinions, and it is only after the most careful analysis of the contemporary evidence that a picture emerges consistent with verifiable facts. For the average faithful Mormon, one can but have sympathy and regard. He is, by and large, honest, industrious, thrifty, and zealous in both the proclamation and promulgation of his beliefs. One only regrets that he has accepted at face value a carefully edited "history" of the origin and doctrinal development of his religion instead of examining the excellent sources which not only contradict but irrefutably prove the falsity of what is most certainly a magnificent reconstructed history. It is to be hoped that as we further study the unfolding drama of Mormon doctrine and the basis of such doctrine, the reader will come to appreciate the evolution of Mormonism and the pitfalls which most certainly exist in taking at face value the gospel according to Joseph Smith and Brigham Young. The verdict of history, then, is overwhelmingly against the Mormon version, particularly where Smith and Young are concerned. There is a vast amount of documentation all but a few Mormons seem content to ignore, but the facts themselves remain too well verified to be ignored.

A New Revelation—the "Mormon Bible"

Aside from the King James Version of the Bible, which the Mormons accept as part of the Word of God "insofar as it is translated correctly" (*Eighth Article*

of Faith), they have added the *Doctrine and Covenants*, the *Pearl of Great Price*, and the initial volume, the *Book of Mormon*, to the canon of what they would call authorized Scripture—the "Four Standard Works." The last mentioned is a subject of this chapter since it occupies a pivotal place in Mormon theology and history and therefore must be carefully examined. A great deal of research on the part of a number of able scholars and organizations has already been published concerning the *Book of Mormon*, and we have drawn heavily upon whatever documented and verifiable information was available. The task of validating the material was enormous, and so we have selected that information which has been verified beyond refutation and is available today in some of our leading institutions of learning (Stanford University, Union Theological Seminary, the Research Departments of the Library of Congress, the New York Public Library, and others).

It is a difficult task to evaluate the complex structure of the *Book of Mormon*, and the reader is urged to consider the bibliography at the end of this volume if he should desire further and more exhaustive studies.

The Story of the Ancient People

The *Book of Mormon* purports to be a history of two ancient civilizations, which were located on the American continent. According to the Mormon version, the first of these great civilizations, named the Jaredites, left the tower of Babel (about 2,250 B.C., by Mormon reckoning), and emigrated to the Western hemisphere. The Jaredites were destroyed as a result of "corruption" and were punished for their apostasy, their civilization undergoing total destruction.

The second group allegedly left Jerusalem somewhere in the neighborhood of 600 B.C., before the destruction of the city and the Babylonian captivity of Israel. According to traditional Mormon thinking, that group crossed the Pacific Ocean, landing on the west coast of South America. The *Book of Mormon* is supposedly a condensation of the high points of these civilizations. The author of the abridged book was a prophet named Mormon. The book is "the translation of the abridgment of the record of these civilizations" and "includes a brief outline of the history of the earlier Jaredite people, an abridgment made by Moroni, son of Mormon, taken from the Jaredite record found during the period of the second civilization."

The second group, who came to America about 600 B.C., were righteous Jews, led by Lehi and later his son Nephi. This group eventually met a fate similar to the Jaredites and were divided into two warring camps, the Nephites and the Lamanites (Indians). The Lamanites received a curse because of their evil deeds, and the curse took the form of dark skin.

Racism is a charge that has been leveled at the Mormon Church throughout their history by a number of civil rights groups. Naturally, Mormons reject such claims by pointing to a small number of African-American and Native-American members. The fact remains, however, that the god of Mormonism elevates "white" races as supreme and has demeaned African-Americans and Native Americans as "unrighteous." The *Book of Mormon* describes the Native-American curse as, "they were white, and exceeding fair and delightsome; that they might not be enticing unto my people the Lord God did cause a skin of blackness to

come upon them" (2 Nephi 5:21). Post-1981 editions of the *Book of Mormon* have deleted the strength of the racist overtones by changing the word "white," in the original *Book of Mormon,* to "pure," (cf. 2 Nephi 30:6).[12] The racism concerning African-Americans surfaces in the *Pearl of Great Price, Book of Moses* (7:8–12) and *Book of Abraham* (1:24), but is amplified much by Brigham Young's degrading comments found in the *Journal of Discourses* (7:290; 10:110). The *Journal of Discourses* is a twenty-six volume collection of sermons of early Mormon authorities. Even though it is said that today's Mormon Church places little value in them, they are still published by the Church's Deseret Publishing Company. In any case, the past General Authorities took a different view, as is seen in the preface to various volumes written by Brigham Young (1:v), Orson Pratt (3:iii), George Q. Cannon (8:iii), Brigham Young Jr. (11:iii), and Joseph F. Smith (18:iii).

The Mormon's record claims that Christ visited the American continent, revealed himself to the Nephites, preached to them the gospel, and instituted both baptism and Communion, or "the sacrament" as Latter-day Saints call it.

The Nephites, unfortunately, proved to be no match for the Lamanites, and they were defeated by them and annihilated in a great battle near the hill Cumorah, approximately A.D. 421. The traditional view held by the LDS Church is that the hill called Cumorah in the *Book of Mormon* is the same hill where Joseph Smith dug up the gold plates. This would place the final battle between the Nephites and Lamanites near Palmyra, New York, or near the Smith farm. This view has been vehemently challenged by various Mormon scholars who hold to the view that the hill Cumorah of *Book of Mormon* fame was located rather in central America. Both theories have serious flaws and because of this, it is doubtful that a general consensus is forthcoming.

Some fourteen hundred years later, the Mormons claim, Joseph Smith Jr. unearthed Mormon's abridgment, which was written in reformed Egyptian hieroglyphics upon plates of gold, and with the aid of Urim and Thummim (supernatural spectacles) translated the reformed Egyptian into English. It thus became the *Book of Mormon,* which was published in 1830, bearing the name of Joseph Smith Jr. as "Author and Proprietor."

Lest there be any confusion, there are four classes of record plates, which were allegedly revealed to Smith: (1) the plates of Nephi; (2) the plates of Mor-

---

[12]"Instead of 'white and delightsome,' as in most earlier editions, the 1981 edition uses 'pure and delightsome,' in reference to future Lamanite generations. The printer's copy says 'white.' Unfortunately, the remaining portion of the original dictated manuscript does not include this scripture. The 1830 and 1837 editions of the *Book of Mormon,* based on the printer's copy, also say 'white.' However, the 1840 edition, which was 'carefully' revised by the Prophet Joseph Smith, uses 'pure' in place of 'white.' All subsequent editions have reverted to 'white,' probably because the 1852 edition (the next after the 1840) was based on the 1837 edition rather than on the 1840. In the process of arranging the 1981 edition, the committee presented all of the textual corrections along with the reason for each proposed correction to the First Presidency and the Twelve for approval. The decision to use 'pure' in this passage was made not on the basis of the original manuscripts (as were most other cases), but on the 1840 revision by the Prophet Joseph Smith and the judgment of living prophets. This correction does not negate the concept that future generations of Lamanites will become white, but it removes the concept that one has to be white to be delightsome to the Lord." (Robert J. Matthew, *BYU Studies,* vol. 22, no. 4, 398). From CD-ROM *Brigham Young University Studies,* edited by Clinton F. Larson, et al., 33 vols. (Provo, Utah: Brigham Young University Press, 1959–1996. [51 issues added, vols. 21–33]).

mon; (3) the plates of Ether; and (4) a set of plates mentioned throughout the *Book of Mormon* known as the "plates of brass" or brass plates of Laban.

The plates of Nephi recorded mostly the secular history, although the smaller plates of Nephi allegedly recorded sacred events. The second group is an abridgment from the plates of Nephi, which was made by Mormon and which included his commentaries and additional historical notes by his son, Moroni. The third set of plates recorded the history of the Jaredites, also abridged by Moroni, who added his own comments. It is now known as the *Book of Ether.*

The fourth set of plates are alleged to have come from Jerusalem and appear in the form of extracts in Nephite records. They are given over to quotations from the Hebrew Scriptures and genealogies. Joseph Smith is alleged to have received the plates from the hand of Moroni, "a resurrected personage," in the year 1827.

The conflicting methods Smith used for translating the *Book of Mormon* leaves little doubt that the story changed often through its progressive history. Mormon missionaries will only discuss the official version of the church: that Joseph Smith received the golden plates with the Urim and Thummim and viewed the plates through the clear stones to translate the reformed Egyptian hieroglyphics into Elizabethan English. The other version, offered by those who saw Smith conducting his work, purports that he often didn't even look at the golden plates. Instead, he placed a seer stone into a hat and covered his face with the hat to see wonderful visions in the stone concerning the hieroglyphics and English translation (cf. David Whitmer, *An Address to All Believers in Christ* [Richmond, Mo.: 1887], 12; *Deseret News Church Section,* [Salt Lake City: September 20, 1969], 32; Emma Smith, *The Saint's Herald* [Independence, Mo.: May 19, 1888], 310).

Purpose of the *Book of Mormon*

The purpose of the *Book of Mormon* and its mission generally eludes Christian theologians, archaeologists, and students of anthropology because of the many difficulties that the book introduces in the light of already established facts. But the following explanation of the purpose of the book ought to be considered.

> It is a principle of divine and civil law that, "In the mouth of two or three witnesses every word shall be established" (2 Corinthians 13:1). The Bible, its history of the dealings and providences of God with man upon the Eastern continent, is one witness for the truth. The *Book of Mormon* is another witness to the same effect. It recites the providences of God in the basic and vastly important matter of redemption, as also in general in the laws of nature, and indicates that such provisions were not limited, not confined to the Eastern world, "God so loved the *world*" (John 3:16), not a mere portion of it, that he likewise ministered in behalf of the race in the great Western continent. Being the seat of mighty civilizations, it was entitled to and partook of the ministrations of the Father of the race.
> The stated purpose of the *Book of Mormon* (in its introduction) is universal: to witness to the world the truth and divinity of Jesus Christ, and his mission of salvation through the gospel He taught. Its witness is for Jew and Gentile. The house of Israel rejected its Messiah, and in consequence was rejected, scattered,

and the government overthrown. The gospel refused by them was then
preached to the Gentiles. Israel has ever since remained in unbelief in Christ
and without the ministration of inspired men. Bible prophecy frequently declares its restoration in the latter days to divine favor, the gathering of Israel,
and their permanent establishment in their ancient homeland of Israel. The
sealed book, the *Book of Mormon*, is predicted by Bible prophecy and by its own
declarations to be a confirming, additional revelation from God of the Messiahship of Jesus Christ and of the covenants made with their fathers. It repeatedly
predicts regathering, restoration, and other manifold blessings to Israel. The
God of Israel is to make a "new covenant" with that people—not the old Mosaic
covenant, but another and later one, by which they are to be reinstated as a
nation in their holy land. (See also Jeremiah 31:34; Ezekiel 20:33–38, etc., Bible
predictions to the same effect.) The *Book of Mormon* interprets Old Testament
prophecy to that effect, as it recites predictions of its inspired men. It claims to
be part of the new covenant to Israel.

It claims to be the sealed book of Isaiah, chapter 29, which it quotes and
interprets. It recites that as a result of its revealment, Israel would come to an
understanding of the *Christ* message of salvation; that they would no longer fear
but be secured and greatly blessed by divine favor; that the coming forth of its
record would be followed by physical blessing upon Israel to its redemption
from sterility to fertility, and thus made capable of maintaining that nation as
in ancient times. It is a fact that since the appearance of the book that land has
been favored. It produces abundantly. The Jews are now permitted to return
and establish cities and industrial and agricultural units. Many Jews, according
to predictions of the book, are beginning to believe in Christ. Proponents of
the book state that with such predictions fulfilled it is now too late for any similar
fulfillment by another record.

The book declares also that the remnants of the former inhabitants of ancient America, scattered throughout North, Central, and South America—the
Indian populations—will by means of the coming to light of the record of their
fathers be converted to the faith and share in the covenants made with their
progenitors. It indicates their emergence from primitive conditions to enlightenment. It declares that the Gentile nations occupying their lands would favor
their emancipation from degenerate conditions. This is part of the purpose of
the book.

The Gospel of John 10:16 contains a statement of Jesus Christ quoted by
believers in the divinity of the *Book of Mormon*. It reads, "And other sheep I have,
which are not of this fold: them also I must bring, and they shall hear my voice;
and there shall be one fold, and one shepherd." Citing also that Christ declared
these words: "I am not sent but unto the lost sheep of the house of Israel" (Matthew 15:24), they believe that since Jesus Christ, according to the record, never
appeared to the Gentiles, and "salvation is of the Jews," or Israel (John 4:22),
the promise concerning "other sheep" was realized by the appearance of Christ
to the Nephites.[13]

For the Mormons, then, the Bible predicts the *Book of Mormon*; the *Book of
Mormon* interprets Old Testament prophecy and it claims to be part of the new
covenant to Israel. It is also supposed to be "another witness" to the truth of
the Christian gospel. It is unfortunate for the Mormons that this witness is so
often found in conflict with the biblical revelation, as we shall see. It is at the
very least a gross assumption, unjustified by any of the internal evidence of the

[13]R. K. Salyards, Sr., *The Book of Mormon* (Independence, Mo.: Herald House n.d.), 13–16.

book or the testimony of science and history, that the *Book of Mormon* should be considered "part of the new covenant" in any sense.

Scientific Evidence Against the *Book of Mormon*

In an attempt to validate and justify the claims of the *Book of Mormon*, the highest authority in Mormonism, Joseph Smith Jr., the Mormon prophet, related an event which, if true, would add significant weight to some of the Mormon claims for their sacred book. Fortunately, it is a fact on which a good deal of evidence can be brought to bear.

Smith put forth his claim in the book *Pearl of Great Price* (Joseph Smith—History, 1:62–64, 1982 edition), and it is worthwhile to examine it:

> I commenced copying the characters off the plates. I copied a considerable number of them, and by means of the Urim and Thummim I translated some of them. . . . Mr. Martin Harris came to our place, got the characters which I had drawn off the plates, and started with them to the city of New York. For what took place relative to him and the characters, I refer to his own account of the circumstances, as he related them to me after his return, which was as follows: "I went to the city of New York, and presented the characters that had been translated, with the translation thereof, to Professor Charles Anthon, a gentleman celebrated for his literary attainments. Professor Anthon stated that the translation was correct, more so than any he had before seen translated from the Egyptian. I then showed him those which were not yet translated, and he said that they were Egyptian, Chaldaic, Assyriac, and Arabic; and he said they were true characters."

According to Joseph Smith, then, Martin Harris, his colleague, obtained from the learned Professor Charles Anthon of Columbia University a validation of Smith's translation of the reformed Egyptian hieroglyphic characters found on the plates that Moroni made available to him. The difficulty with Smith's statement is that Professor Anthon never said any such thing, and fortunately he went on record in a lengthy letter to Mr. E. D. Howe, a contemporary of Joseph Smith who did one of the most thorough jobs of research on the Mormon prophet and the origins of Mormonism extant.

Upon learning of Smith's claim concerning Professor Anthon, Mr. Howe wrote him at Columbia. Professor Anthon's letter reproduced here from Howe's own collection is a classic piece of evidence the Mormons would like very much to see forgotten.

> New York, N.Y.
> Feb. 17, 1834
> Mr. E. D. Howe
> Painsville, Ohio
>
> Dear Sir:
> I received this morning your favor of the 9th instant, and lose no time in making a reply. The whole story about my having pronounced the Mormonite inscription to be "reformed Egyptian hieroglyphics" *is perfectly false*.[14] Some years ago, a plain and apparently simplehearted farmer called upon me with a note from Dr. Mitchell of our city, now deceased, requesting me to decipher, if

---

[14]Italics are the author's for emphasis.

possible, a paper, which the farmer would hand me, and which Dr. Mitchell confessed he had been unable to understand. Upon examining the paper in question, I soon came to the conclusion that *it was all a trick, perhaps a hoax.* When I asked the person who brought it how he obtained the writing he gave me, as far as I can now recollect, [he gave] the following account: A "gold book," consisting of a number of plates of gold, fastened together in the shape of a book by wires of the same metal, had been dug up in the northern part of the state of New York, and along with the book an enormous pair of "gold spectacles"! These spectacles were so large that if a person attempted to look through them, his two eyes would have to be turned toward one of the glasses merely, the spectacles in question being altogether too large for the breadth of the human face. Whoever examined the plates through the spectacles, was enabled not only to read them, but fully to understand their meaning. All this knowledge, however, was confined at the time to a young man, who had the trunk containing the book and spectacles in his sole possession. This young man was placed behind a curtain, in the garret of a farm house, and, being thus concealed from view, put on the spectacles occasionally, or rather, looked through one of the glasses, deciphered the characters in the book, and, having committed some of them to paper, handed copies from behind the curtain to those who stood on the outside. Not a word, however, was said about the plates having been deciphered "by the gift of God." Everything, in this way, was effected by the large pair of spectacles. The farmer added that he had been requested to contribute a sum of money toward the publication of the "golden book," the contents of which would, as he had been assured, produce an entire change in the world and save it from ruin. So urgent had been these solicitations, that he intended selling his farm and handing over the amount received to those who wished to publish the plates. As a last precautionary step, however, he had resolved to come to New York and obtain the opinion of the learned about the meaning of the paper which he brought with him, and which had been given him as a part of the contents of the book, although no translation had been furnished at the time by the young man with the spectacles. *On hearing this odd story, I changed my opinion about the paper, and, instead of viewing it any longer as a hoax upon the learned, I began to regard it as a part of a scheme to cheat the farmer of his money, and I communicated my suspicions to him, warning him to beware of rogues.* He requested an opinion from me in writing, which of course I declined giving, and he then took his leave carrying the paper with him. *This paper was in fact a singular scrawl. It consisted of all kinds of crooked characters disposed in columns, and had evidently been prepared by some person who had before him at the time a book containing various alphabets. Greek and Hebrew letters, crosses and nourishes, Roman letters inverted or placed sideways, were arranged in perpendicular columns, and the whole ended in a rude delineation of a circle, divided into various compartments, decked with various strange marks, and evidently copied after the Mexican Calendar given by Humboldt, but copied in such a way as not to betray the source whence it was derived.* I am thus particular as to the contents of the paper, inasmuch as I have frequently conversed with my friends on the subject, since the Mormonite excitement began, and well remember that *the paper contained anything else but "Egyptian Hieroglyphics."* Some time after, the same farmer paid me a second visit. He brought with him the golden book in print, and offered it to me for sale. I declined purchasing. He then asked permission to leave the book with me for examination. I declined receiving it, although his manner was strangely urgent. I adverted once more to the roguery which had been in my opinion practiced upon him, and asked him what had become of the gold plates. He informed me that they were in a trunk with the large pair of spectacles. I advised him to go to a magistrate and have the trunk examined. He said the "curse of God" would come upon him should he do this. On my pressing him, however, to pursue the course which I had recommended,

he told me that he would open the trunk, if I would take the "curse of God" upon myself. I replied that I would do so with the greatest willingness, and would incur every risk of that nature, provided I could only extricate him from the grasp of the rogues. He then left me.

I have thus given you a full statement of all that I know respecting the origin of Mormonism, and must beg you, as a personal favor, to publish this letter immediately, should you find my name mentioned again by these wretched fanatics.

Yours respectfully,
Charles Anthon, LL.D.
Columbia University

Professor Anthon's letter is both revealing and devastating where Smith's and Harris' veracity are concerned. We might also raise the question as to how Professor Anthon could say that the characters shown to him by Martin Harris and authorized by Joseph Smith as part of the material copied from the revelation of the *Book of Mormon* were "Egyptian, Chaldaic, Assyriac, and Arabic" when the *Book of Mormon* itself declares that the characters were "reformed Egyptian," the language of the Nephites. Since the language of the *Book of Mormon* was known to "none other people," how would it be conceivably possible for Professor Anthon to have testified as to the accuracy of Smith's translation? To this date, no one has ever been able to find even the slightest trace of the language known as "reformed Egyptian"; and all reputable linguists who have examined the evidence put forth by the Mormons have rejected them as mythical.

Archaeological Evidence

The *Book of Mormon* purports to portray the rise and development of two great civilizations. As to just how great these civilizations were, some excerpts from the book itself adequately illustrate.

"The whole face of the land had become covered with buildings, and the people were as numerous almost, as it were the sand of the sea" (Mormon 1:7).

". . . fine workmanship of wood, in buildings, and in machinery, and also in iron and copper, and brass and steel, making all manners of tools . . ." (Jarom 1:8; 2 Nephi 5:15).

". . . grain . . . silks . . . cattle . . . oxen . . . cows . . . sheep . . . swine . . . goats . . . horses . . . asses . . . elephants . . ." (See Ether 9:17–19).

". . . did multiply and spread . . . began to cover the face of the whole earth, from the sea south to the sea north, from the sea west to the sea east" (Helaman 3:8).

". . . had been slain . . . nearly two million" [Jaredites] (See Ether 15:2).

". . . their shipping and their building of ships, and their building of temples, and of synagogues and their sanctuaries . . ." (Helaman 3:14. See also 2 Nephi 5:15–16; Alma 16:13).

". . . there were ten more who did fall . . . with their ten thousand each . . ." (See Mormon 6:10–15).

". . . swords . . . cimeters . . . breastplates . . . arm-shields . . . shields . . . head-plates . . . armor" (See Alma 43:18–19; 3:5; Ether 15:15).

". . . multiplied exceedingly, and spread upon the face of the land, and became exceeding rich . . ." (Jarom 1:8).

See 3 Nephi 8:9–10, 14; 9:4–6, 8: where cities and inhabitants were sunk in the depths of the sea and earth.

In addition to the foregoing statements from the *Book of Mormon*, which indicate the tremendous spread of the cultures of these races, there are numerous cities catalogued in the *Book of Mormon*, evidence that these were indeed mighty civilizations, which should, by all the laws of archaeological research into the culture of antiquity, have left vast amounts of "finds" to be evaluated. But such is not the case as we shall show. The Mormons have yet to explain the fact that leading archaeological researchers not only have repudiated the claims of the *Book of Mormon* as to the existence of these civilizations, but have adduced considerable evidence to show the impossibility of the accounts given in the Mormon Bible.

The following letter was addressed to the Rev. R. Odell Brown, pastor of the Hillcrest Methodist Church, Fredericksburg, Virginia, an ardent student of Mormonism and its claims. Dr. Brown, in the course of his research, wrote to the Department of Anthropology at Columbia University in New York City. The answer he received is of great importance in establishing the fact that the *Book of Mormon* is neither accurate nor truthful where the sciences of archaeology and anthropology are concerned.

> Dear Sir:
> Pardon my delay in answering your letter of January 14, 1957. The question which you ask concerning the *Book of Mormon* is one that comes up quite frequently. . . . However, . . . I may say that I do not believe that there is a single thing of value concerning the prehistory of the American Indian in the *Book of Mormon* and I believe that the great majority of American archaeologists would agree with me. The book is untrue biblically, historically, and scientifically.
> Concerning Dr. Charles Anthon of Columbia University, I do not know who he is and would certainly differ with his viewpoint, as the Latter Day Saints (Mormons) tell it. What possible bearing Egyptian hieroglyphics would have on either the *Book of Mormon* or the prehistory of the American Indian I do not know. . . . I am,
>
> > Very sincerely yours,
> > Wm. Duncan Strong (Signed)

The Smithsonian Institution in Washington has also added its voice against the archaeological claims of the *Book of Mormon*. Such a highly regarded scientific source the Mormons can ill afford to ignore.

> 1. The Smithsonian Institution has never used the *Book of Mormon* in any way as a scientific guide. Smithsonian archaeologists see no direct connection between the archaeology of the New World and the subject matter of the book.
> 2. The physical type of the Native American is basically Mongoloid, being most closely related to that of the peoples of eastern, central, and northeastern Asia. Archaeological evidence indicates that the ancestors of the present Native Americans came into the New World—probably over a land bridge known to have existed in the Bering Strait region during the last Ice Age—in a continuing series of small migrations beginning from about 25,000 to 30,000 years ago.
> 3. Present evidence indicates that the first people to reach this continent from the East were the Norsemen who briefly visited the northeastern part of North America around A.D. 1000 and then settled in Greenland. There is nothing to show that they reached Mexico or Central America.
> 4. One of the main lines of evidence supporting the scientific finding that

contacts with Old World civilizations, if indeed they occurred at all, were of very little significance for the development of Native American civilizations is the fact that none of the principal Old World domesticated food plants or animals (except the dog) occurred in the New World in Pre-Columbian times. Native Americans had no wheat, barley, oats, millet, rice, cattle, pigs, chickens, horses, donkeys, or camels before 1492. (Camels and horses were in the Americas, along with the bison, mammoth, and mastodon, but all these animals became extinct around 10,000 B.C. at the time the early big game hunters spread across the Americas.)

5. Iron, steel, glass, and silk were not used in the New World before 1492 (except for occasional use of unsmelted meteoric iron). Native copper was used in various locations in pre-Columbian times, but true metallurgy was limited to southern Mexico and the Andean region, where its occurrence in late prehistoric times involved gold, silver, copper, and their alloys, but not iron.

6. There is a possibility that the spread of cultural traits across the Pacific to Mesoamerica and the northwestern coast of South America began several hundred years before the Christian era. However, any such inter-hemispheric contacts appear to have been the result of accidental voyages originating in eastern and southern Asia. It is by no means certain that such contacts occurred; certainly there were no contacts with the ancient Egyptians, Hebrews, or other peoples of Western Asia and the Near East.

7. No reputable Egyptologist or other specialist on Old World archaeology and no expert on New World prehistory has discovered or confirmed any relationship between archaeological remains in Mexico and archaeological remains in Egypt.

8. Reports of findings of ancient Egyptian, Hebrew, and other Old World writings in the New World in pre-Columbian contexts have frequently appeared in newspapers, magazines, and sensational books. None of these claims has stood up to examination by reputable scholars. No inscriptions using Old World forms of writing have been shown to have occurred in any part of the Americas before 1492, except for a few Norse rune stones which have been found in Greenland. (Revised, May 1980.)

From this evidence, it is clear that the cities mentioned in the *Book of Mormon* are imaginary, that elephants never existed on this continent, and that the metals described in the *Book of Mormon* have never been found in any of the areas of contemporary civilizations of the New World. This is not a theologian attempting to discredit the Mormons on the basis of their theology, but recognized archaeological experts challenging the *Book of Mormon* on the basis of the fact that its accounts are not in keeping with the findings of science. Mormon missionaries are generally reluctant to discuss these areas when the evidence is well known, but it *is* evidence, and from the most authoritative sources.

One of the most damaging claims against the archaeology of the *Book of Mormon* was the publication of former Brigham Young University professor Thomas Stuart Ferguson's paper written in 1975. Ferguson founded the Department of Archaeology (later renamed Anthropology) at BYU for the sole purpose of discovering proofs of the *Book of Mormon*. After twenty-five years of dedicated archaeological research, the department had nothing at all to back up the flora, fauna, topography, geography, peoples, coins, or settlements of the book and, in fact, he called the geography of the *Book of Mormon* "fictional." In *Ferguson's Manuscript Unveiled* (Salt Lake City: Utah Lighthouse Ministry, 1988)

the reader is treated to a wealth of insights into the sheer nonexistence of *Book of Mormon* antiquities.

The Mongoloid Factor

It is one of the main contentions of Mormon theology that Native Americans are the descendants of the Lamanites and that they were of the Semitic race; in fact, of Jewish origin. As we have seen, this claim is extensive in Mormon literature, and if evidence could be adduced to show that the Native American could not possibly be of Semitic extraction, the entire story of Nephi and his trip to America in 600 B.C. would be proven false.

It is, therefore, of considerable value to learn that in the findings compiled both by anthropologists and those who specialize in genetics that the various physical factors of the Mediterranean races from which the Jewish or Semitic race spring bear little or no resemblance to those of the Native American. Genotypically, there is therefore little if any correlation, and phenotypically speaking, Native Americans are considered to be *Mongoloid* in extraction, not Mediterranean Caucasoids.

Now, if the Lamanites, as the *Book of Mormon* claims, were the descendants of Nephi, who was a Jew of the Mediterranean Caucasoid type, then their descendants, Native Americans, would by necessity have the same blood factor genotypically, and phenotypic or apparent characteristics would be the same. But this is not at all the case. Instead, the Native American, so say anthropologists, is not of Semitic extraction and has the definite phenotypical characteristic of a Mongoloid. A thorough study of anthropology and such writers as W. C. Boyd (*The Contributions of Genetics to Anthropology*) and Bentley Glass, the gifted geneticist of Johns Hopkins University, reveals that Mormon findings based upon the *Book of Mormon* are out of harmony with the findings of geneticists and anthropologists. There simply is no foundation for the postulation that the Native American (Lamanites, according to the Mormons) is in any way related to the race to which Nephi (a Semite) allegedly belonged.

Corrections, Contradictions, and Errors

There is a great wealth of information concerning the material contained in the *Book of Mormon* and the various plagiarisms, anachronisms, false prophecies, and other unfortunate practices connected with it. At best we can give but a condensation of that which has been most thoroughly documented.

Since the publication of the *Book of Mormon* in 1830, the first edition has undergone extensive "correction" in order to present it in its current form. Some of these "corrections" should be noted.

The former major revision of the *Book of Mormon* was in 1920. That standard edition is still found in many public libraries and in millions of homes. In the latest revision, 1981, a subtitle was added to the cover: "Another Testament of Jesus Christ," and no less than 100 verses were changed without consulting the missing golden plates. A note closing the introduction to the 1981 edition says, "Some minor errors in the text have been perpetuated in past editions of the *Book of Mormon.* This edition contains corrections that seem appropriate to bring

the material into conformity with prepublication manuscripts and early editions edited by the prophet Joseph Smith." Without blushing, the Mormon Church boldly asserts the unfounded claim that the prepublication manuscripts agree with their most recent changes. Our access to the handwritten copies of the original *Book of Mormon* deny such a claim and proves once again that the Mormon Church will sacrifice truth for the sake of public relations.

1. In Mosiah 21:28, it is declared that "King Mosiah had a gift from God"; but in the original edition of the book, the name of the king was Benjamin—an oversight that thoughtful Mormon scribes corrected. This is not, of course, a typographical error, as there is little resemblance between the names Benjamin and Mosiah; rather, it appears that either God made a mistake when He inspired the record or Joseph made a mistake when he translated it. But the Mormons will admit to neither, so they are stuck, so to speak, with the contradiction.

2. When compared with the 1830 edition, 1 Nephi 19:16–20 reveals more than twenty changes in the "inspired *Book of Mormon*," words having been dropped, spelling corrected, and words and phraseology added and turned about. This is a strange way to treat an inspired revelation from God.

3. In Alma 28:14–29:11, more than eighteen changes may be counted from the original edition. On page 303, the phrase, "Yea, decree unto them that decrees which are unalterable," was dropped in later editions, but strangely reappeared in 1981. (See Alma 29:4.)

4. On page 25 of the 1830 edition, the *Book of Mormon* declares:

"And the angel said unto me, behold the Lamb of God, yea, even the Eternal Father."

Yet in 1 Nephi 11:21, the later editions of the book read:

"And the angel said unto me: Behold the Lamb of God, yea even the son of the eternal Father."

5. The Roman Catholic Church should be delighted with page 25 of the original edition of the *Book of Mormon*, which confirms one of their dogmas, namely, that Mary is the mother of God.

"Behold, the virgin which thou seest, is the mother of God."

Noting this unfortunate lapse into Romanistic theology, Joseph Smith and his considerate editors changed 1 Nephi 11:18 (as well as 1 Nephi 11:21, 32; 13:40), so that it now reads:

"Behold, the virgin whom thou seest, is the mother of the Son of God."

From the above, which are only a handful of examples from the approximately 4,000 word changes to be found in the *Book of Mormon*, the reader can readily see that it in no sense can be accepted as the Word of God. The Scripture says, "The word of the Lord endureth for ever" (1 Peter 1:25); and our Savior declared, "Sanctify them through thy truth: thy word is truth" (John 17:17).

The record of the Scriptures rings true. The *Book of Mormon*, on the other hand, is patently false in far too many instances to be considered coincidence.

Added to the evidence of various revisions, the *Book of Mormon* also contains plagiarisms from the King James Bible, anachronisms, false prophecies, and errors of fact that cannot be dismissed. Some of these bear repetition, though they are well known to students of Mormonism.

The testimony of the three witnesses, which appear at the front of the *Book*

of Mormon (Oliver Cowdery, David Whitmer, and Martin Harris) declares that "An angel of God came down from heaven, and he brought and laid before our eyes, that we beheld and saw the plates, and the engraving thereon. . . ."

It is quite noteworthy that Martin Harris denied that he had actually seen the plates with his "naked eyes." In fact, when pressed, he stated, "No, I saw them with a spiritual eye" (Recollections of John H. Gilbert, 1892, Typescript, BYU, 5–6).

The Mormons are loath to admit that all three of these witnesses later apostatized from the Mormon faith and were described in most unflattering terms ("counterfeiters, thieves, [and] liars") by their Mormon contemporaries (cf. *Senate Document 189*, February 15, 1841, 6–9).

A careful check of early Mormon literature also reveals that Joseph Smith wrote prophecies and articles against the character of the witnesses of the *Book of Mormon*, which in itself renders their testimony suspect (cf. *Doctrine and Covenants*, 3:12; 10:7; *History of the Church*; 3:228, 3:232).

Mormons try to cover this historical predicament by saying that two of the three witnesses, Oliver Cowdery and Martin Harris, were rebaptized into Mormonism. What they fail to reveal is more significant: The *Times and Seasons* (2:482) published that Oliver Cowdery denied his *Book of Mormon* testimony. He spent several years as a baptized Methodist before his rebaptism into Mormonism. Martin Harris, likewise, has suspicious circumstances surrounding his rebaptism. He denied the teachings of Brigham Young after rebaptism and was banned from preaching by Young because of their differences. David Whitmer changed the details of his testimony concerning the angel with the golden plates to say that it was a vision and not an actual visitation by an angelic person (*An Address to All Believers in Christ*, p. 32). Certainly testimony from such unstable personalities is dubious at best.

Plagiarisms—The King James Version

A careful examination of the *Book of Mormon* reveals that it contains thousands of words from the King James Bible. In fact, verbatim quotations, some of considerable length, have caused the Mormons no end of embarrassment for many years.

The comparisons of Moroni 10 with 1 Corinthians 12:1–11; 2 Nephi 14 with Isaiah 4; and 2 Nephi 12 with Isaiah 2 reveal that Joseph Smith made free use of his Bible to supplement the alleged revelation of the golden plates. The book of Mosiah, chapter 14, in the *Book of Mormon*, is a reproduction of the fifty-third chapter of Isaiah the prophet, and 3 Nephi 13 copies Matthew 6 almost word-for-word.

There are other instances of plagiarisms from the King James Bible including paraphrases of certain verses. One of these verses (1 John 5:7) is reproduced in 3 Nephi 11:27. The only difficulty with the paraphrase here is that the text is considered by scholars to be an interpolation missing from all the major manuscripts of the New Testament, but present in the King James Bible, from which Smith paraphrased it not knowing the difference.

Another example of this type of error is found in 3 Nephi 11:33–34, and is almost a direct quotation from Mark 16:16, a passage regarded by many New

Testament Greek scholars as one of three possible endings to that gospel. But Joseph Smith was not aware of this, so he even copied in translational variations, another proof that neither he nor the alleged golden plates were inspired of God.

Two further instances of plagiarisms from the King James Bible that have backfired on the Mormons are worth noting.

In the third chapter of the book of Acts, Peter's classic sermon at Pentecost paraphrases Deuteronomy 18:15–19. While in the process of writing 3 Nephi, Joseph Smith puts Peter's paraphrase in the mouth of Christ when the Savior was allegedly preaching to the Nephites. The prophet overlooked the fact that at the time that Christ was allegedly preaching His sermon, the sermon itself had not yet been preached by Peter.

In addition to this, 3 Nephi makes Christ out to be a liar, when in 20:23 Christ attributes Peter's words to Moses as a direct quotation, when, as we have pointed out, Peter paraphrased the quotation from Moses (Acts 3:22–23); and the wording is quite different. But Joseph did not check far enough, hence this glaring error.

Secondly, the *Book of Mormon* follows the error of the King James translation that renders Isaiah 4:5, "For upon all the glory shall be a defense" (see 2 Nephi 14:5).

Modern translations of Isaiah point out that it should read "For over all the glory there will be a canopy," not a defense. The Hebrew word *chuppah* does not mean defense but a protective curtain or canopy. Smith, of course, did not know this, nor did the King James translators from whose work he copied.

There are quite a number of other places where such errors appear, including Smith's insistence in Abraham 1:20 that "Pharaoh signifies king by royal blood," when in reality the dictionary defines the meaning of the term Pharaoh as "a great house or palace."

The *Revised Standard Version* of the Bible renders Isaiah 5:25, "And their corpses were as refuse in the midst of the streets," correctly rendering the Hebrew *suchah* as "refuse," not as "torn." The King James Bible renders the passage "And their carcasses were torn in the midst of the streets." The *Book of Mormon* (2 Nephi 15:25) repeats the King James' text word-for-word, including the error of mistranslating *suchah*, removing any claim that the *Book of Mormon* is to be taken seriously as reliable material.

Anachronisms and Contradictions

Not only does the *Book of Mormon* plagiarize heavily from the King James Bible, but it betrays a great lack of information and background on the subject of world history and the history of the Jewish people. The Jaredites apparently enjoyed glass windows in the miraculous barges in which they crossed the ocean; and "steel" and a "compass" were known to Nephi despite the fact that neither had been invented, demonstrating once again that Joseph Smith was a poor student of history and of Hebrew customs.

Laban, mentioned in one of the characters of the *Book of Mormon* (1 Nephi 4:9), makes use of a steel sword; and Nephi himself claims to have had a steel bow. The ancient Jaredites also had steel swords (Ether 7:9). The Mormons jus-

tify this by quoting Psalm 18:34 as a footnote to 1 Nephi 16:18 in the *Book of Mormon*, but modern translations of the Scriptures indicate that the word translated steel in the Old Testament (since steel was nonexistent) is more properly rendered bronze. Nahum 6:2, NASB, uses "steel" but it is taken from the Hebrew word *paladah*, probably meaning iron.

William Hamblin, in his preliminary report entitled *Handheld Weapons in the Book of Mormon* (1985), published by the Foundation for Ancient Research and Mormon Studies (F.A.R.M.S.) uses the bronze argument as a possible justification for the rendering of steel in the *Book of Mormon*. He writes, "Another possibility is to equate this Jaredite steel with the 'steel' of the King James translation of the Old Testament, which actually refers to the Hebrew word for bronze." The problem with using this explanation to protect the *Book of Mormon* is that it defies Mormon history. Remember, numerous contemporaries of Joseph Smith have claimed that Smith could not continue "translating" the gold plates unless the scribe read each word back to him *correctly*. If the word steel in the *Book of Mormon* should really have been bronze, it undermines the LDS claim that the book was translated by the gift and power of God, since it shows that errors did creep into Joseph Smith's translation.

Mormons sometimes attempt to defend Nephi's possession of a *not yet invented* compass (known in the *Book of Mormon* as a Liahona) by the fact that Acts 28:13 states: "And from thence we fetched a compass." Modern translations of the Scripture, however, refute this subterfuge by correctly rendering the passage: "And from there we made a circle."

Added to the preceding anachronisms is the fact that the *Book of Mormon* not only contradicts the Bible, but contradicts other revelations purporting to come from the same God who inspired the *Book of Mormon*. The Bible declares that the Messiah of Israel was to be born in Bethlehem (Micah 5:2), and the gospel of Matthew (chap. 2, v. 1) records the fulfillment of this prophecy. But the *Book of Mormon* (Alma 7:9, 10) states:

". . . the son of God cometh upon the face of the earth. And behold, he shall be born of Mary, at Jerusalem, which is the land of our forefathers. . . ."

The *Book of Mormon* describes Jerusalem as a city (1 Nephi 1:4) as was Bethlehem described as a separate town in the Bible. The contradiction is irreconcilable.

Another area of contradiction between the Bible and the *Book of Mormon* concerns sin and Mormon baptism at eight years of age. Moroni 8:8 states the doctrine that "little children are whole, for they are not capable of committing sin; wherefore the curse of Adam is taken from them in me." Anyone who thinks that children under age eight cannot sin has not visited the classrooms of today's schools. The Mormon concept directly contradicts Psalm 51:5, which places sin at the point of conception. The book of Romans leaves no exemption to the sin and guilt that Adam passed on to all; no exceptions are made (Romans 5:12–15). Furthermore, it clearly states that "there is none righteous, no, not one" (Romans 3:10–12).

There are also a number of instances where God did not agree with himself, if indeed it is supposed that He had anything to do with the inspiration of the *Book of Mormon*, the *Pearl of Great Price*, the *Doctrine and Covenants*, or the other recorded utterances of Joseph Smith.

In the *Book of Mormon*, for instance, (3 Nephi 12:2; Moroni 8:11) the remission of sins is the accomplishment of baptism:

"Yea, blessed are they who shall . . . be baptized, for they shall . . . receive a remission of their sin. . . . Behold baptism is unto repentance to the fulfilling the commandments unto the remission of sin."

But in the *Doctrine and Covenants* (20:37), the direct opposite is stated:

"All those who humble themselves . . . and truly manifest by their works that they have received of the Spirit of Christ unto the remission of their sins, shall be received by baptism into his church."

Mormon theologians conspicuously omit any serious discussion of the contradiction.

Joseph Smith did not limit his contradictions to baptism; indeed, polygamy is a classic example of some of his maneuvering.

"Go ye, therefore, and do the works of Abraham; enter ye into my law and ye shall be saved. God commanded Abraham, and Sarah gave Hagar to Abraham to wife. And why did she do it? Because this was the law; and from Hagar sprang many people. . . ." (*Doctrine and Covenants*, 132:34, 32).

The *Book of Mormon*, on the other hand, categorically states:

"Wherefore, I the Lord God will not suffer that this people shall do like unto them of old . . . for there shall not any man among you have save it be one wife; and concubines he shall have none; for I, the Lord God, delight in the chastity of woman" (Jacob 2:26–28).

It appears that Smith could manufacture revelations at will, depending upon his desires. In the last instance, his reputation and subsequent actions indicate that sex was the motivating factor.

A final example of the confusion generated between the *Book of Mormon* and other "inspired" revelations is found in this conflict between two works in the *Pearl of Great Price:* the *Book of Moses* and the *Book of Abraham.*

"I am the Beginning and the End, the Almighty God; by mine Only Begotten I created these things; yea, in the beginning I created the heaven, and the earth upon which thou standest" (Moses 2:1).

The *Book of Abraham*, on the other hand, repudiates this monotheistic view and states:

"And then the Lord said: Let us go down. And they went down at the beginning, and they, that is the Gods, organized and formed the heavens and the earth" (Abraham 4:1).

Just how it is possible to reconcile these two allegedly equal pronouncements from Mormon revelation escapes this author, and the Mormons themselves appear reluctant to furnish any concrete explanation.

The question of false prophecies in Mormonism has been handled adequately in a number of excellent volumes, but it should be pointed out that Joseph Smith drew heavily upon published articles both in newspapers and magazines. In fact, one of his famous prophecies concerning the Civil War is drawn chiefly from material already published at the time.

In the *History of the Church*, Volume 1, page 301, Joseph Smith states, "Appearances of troubles among the nations became more visible this season than they had previously been since the Church began her journey out of the wilderness. . . . The people of South Carolina, in convention assembled (in Novem-

ber), passed ordinances, declaring their state a free and independent nation." From this we know that Smith could have been aware of South Carolina's succession as early as November 1832. If not in November, he could have known about this from an article in the *Boston Daily Advertiser & Patriot*, December 10, 1832. This was a full fifteen days before Smith's prophecy, and the Mormon Apostle Orson Hyde was in Boston that day.

Smith declared in *Doctrine and Covenants*, Section 87:

"At the rebellion of South Carolina . . . the Southern States will call on other nations, even the nation of Great Britain . . . and then war shall be poured out upon all nations. . . . And . . . slaves shall rise up against their masters . . . and that the remnants . . . shall vex the Gentiles with a sore vexation."

Though the Civil War did break out some years after Smith's death in 1844, England did not become involved in any war against the United States. "All nations" were not involved in war as was prophesied. The slaves did not rise up against "their masters," and the "remnants" who were Native Americans were themselves vexed by the Gentiles, being defeated in war and confined to reservations.

Prophet Smith was an extremely ineffective prophet here, as well as in *Doctrine and Covenants* 124:22-23, 59, when he prophesied that he would possess the house he built at Nauvoo "for ever and ever."

The fact of the matter is that neither Joseph nor his seed "after him" lived from "generation to generation" in the Nauvoo house. According to *The Comprehensive History of the Church* 1:160, "The Nauvoo House was never completed; and after its unfinished walls had stood unprotected for a number of years and were crumbling to decay, they were taken down; the foundations were torn up and the excellent building stone of which they were constructed sold for use in other buildings in and about Nauvoo." However, the LDS church has rebuilt the house in "Nauvoo" and offers it as a tourist attraction.

These and other instances indicate that Smith was not only a poor scribe but a false prophet, and his prophecy concerning the restoration of Israel to Palestine clearly reveals that he anticipated the millennium in his own lifetime, whereas in reality the prophecy of Ezekiel 37 began to be fulfilled in 1948, more than a hundred years after Smith's death.

The question quite naturally arises in summing up the background of the *Book of Mormon*: Where did the book come from, since it obviously did not come from God? The answer to this has been propounded at great length by numerous students of Mormonism, particularly E. D. Howe, Pomeroy Tucker, and William A. Linn.

All the aforementioned concur that the *Book of Mormon* is probably an expansion upon the writings of Solomon Spaulding, a retired minister who was known to have written a number of "romances" with biblical backgrounds similar to those of the *Book of Mormon*. The Mormons delight to point out that one of Spaulding's manuscripts, entitled "Manuscript Story," was discovered in Hawaii more than 100 years ago, and it differed in many respects from the *Book of Mormon*.

But in his excellent volume *The Book of Mormon*, Dr. James D. Bales makes the following observation, which is of great importance and agrees in every detail with my research:

It has long been contended that there is a connection between the *Book of Mormon* and one of Solomon Spaulding's historical romances. The Latter-day Saints, of course, deny such a connection.

What if the Latter-day Saints are right and there is no relationship between the *Book of Mormon* and Spaulding's writings? It simply means that those who so contend are wrong, but it proves nothing with reference to the question as to whether or not the *Book of Mormon* is of divine origin.

One could be wrong as to what man, or men, wrote the *Book of Mormon*, and still know that it was not written by men inspired of God. One can easily prove that the *Book of Mormon* is of human origin. And, after all, this is the main issue. The fundamental issue is not *what* man or men wrote it, but whether it was written by men who were guided by God. We know that men wrote it, and that these men, whoever they were, did not have God's guidance.

This may be illustrated by *Science and Health With Key to the Scriptures*—the textbook of Christian Science churches. Mrs. Eddy claims to have been its author, under God's direction. There are others who claim she reworked and enlarged a manuscript of Mr. Quimby and the evidence seems to prove that such is the case. But what if those who so maintained failed to prove their case? Would that prove that it was inspired of God? Not at all. It would prove only that Quimby's manuscript had nothing to do with it. But it would not prove that some other uninspired being did not write it. Regardless of what human being or beings wrote *Science and Health*, it is of human, not divine origin. Just so the *Book of Mormon* is of human origin and uninspired, even though it were impossible to prove what particular man wrote it.

It has not been maintained that all the *Book of Mormon* was written by Spaulding. Thus, it has not been claimed that the theological portions were put in by him. Those portions bear the imprint of Smith, Cowdery, and Sidney Rigdon (see the proof offered in Shook's *The True Origin of the Book of Mormon*, pages 126ff.). It is maintained, however, that some things, including a great deal of Scripture, were added to one of Spaulding's manuscripts and that his work was thus transferred into the *Book of Mormon* (see the testimony of John Spaulding, Solomon's brother; Martha Spaulding, John's wife): They maintained that the historical portion was Spaulding's. (E. D. Howe, *Mormonism Unveiled*, 1834, 278ff; Shook, *The True Origin of the Book of Mormon*, 94ff).

The Mormons contend that the discovery of one of Spaulding's manuscripts demonstrates that it was not the basis of the Book of Mormon.

"I will here state that the Spaulding manuscript was discovered in 1884, and is at present in the library of Oberlin College, Ohio. On examination it was found to bear no resemblance whatever to the *Book of Mormon*. The theory that Solomon Spaulding was the author of the *Book of Mormon* should never be mentioned again—outside a museum." (William A. Morton, *op. cit.*, 6.)

There are three errors in the above paragraph: viz., that Spaulding wrote but one manuscript; that the manuscript discovered in 1884 is the one that non-Mormons have claimed constituted the basis of the *Book of Mormon*; that the manuscript in Oberlin bears no resemblance whatever to the *Book of Mormon*.

(a) *Spaulding wrote more than one manuscript.* This was maintained by D. P. Harlburt [Hurlbut] and Clark Braden before the Honolulu manuscript was found (Charles A. Shook, *op. cit.*, 77). Spaulding's daughter also testified that her father had written "other romances." (Elder George Reynolds, *The Myth of the "Manuscript Found,"* Utah, 1833, 104). The present manuscript story looks like a rough, unfinished, first draft.

(b) *The manuscript found in Honolulu was called a "Manuscript Story" and not the "Manuscript Found."* This Honolulu manuscript, *The Manuscript Story*, was in the hands of anti-Mormons in 1854. However, they did not claim that it was the manuscript which was the basis of the *Book of Mormon*. It was claimed that an-

other manuscript of Spaulding was the basis of the *Book of Mormon*, (Charles A. Shook, *op. cit.*, 77, 15, 185. The *"Manuscript Found or Manuscript Stop"* of the late Rev. Solomon Spaulding, Lamoni, Iowa: Printed and Published by the Reorganized Church of Jesus Christ of Latter Day Saints, 1885, 10).

(c) Although the *Manuscript Story* has not been regarded as the *Manuscript Found*, which constituted the basis of the *Book of Mormon*, there is a great deal of resemblance between the *Manuscript* and the *Book of Mormon*. These points of similarity can be accounted for on the basis that the *Manuscript Story* was the first, and rough draft of one of Spaulding's works, which he reworked into the *Manuscript Found*.

"Howe, in 1854, published a fair synopsis of the Oberlin manuscript now at Oberlin (Howe's *Mormonism Unveiled*, 288) and submitted the original to the witnesses who testified to the many points of identity between Spaulding's *Manuscript Found* and the *Book of Mormon*. These witnesses then (in 1834) recognized the manuscript secured by Harlburt and now at Oberlin as being one of Spaulding's, but not the one that they asserted was similar to the *Book of Mormon*. They further said that Spaulding had told them that he had altered his original plan of writing by going farther back with his dates and writing in the old scripture style, in order that his story might appear more ancient" (Howe's *Mormonism Unveiled*, 288; Theodore Schroeder, *The Origin of the Book of Mormon, Re-Examined in Its Relation to Spaulding's "Manuscript Found,"* 5).

This testimony is borne out by the fact that there are many points of similarity between the manuscript in Oberlin College and the *Book of Mormon*.[15]

It is fairly well established historically, then, that the Mormons have attempted to use a manuscript that is admittedly *not* the one from which Smith later copied and amplified the text of what is now known as the *Book of Mormon* as the basis for denying what eye witnesses have affirmed: that it was another Spaulding manuscript (*Manuscript Found*) that Smith drew upon to fabricate the *Book of Mormon*.

Dr. Bales is right when he states:

There are too many points of similarity for them to be without significance. Thus, the internal evidence, combined with the testimony of witnesses, as presented in Howe's book and reproduced in Shook's, shows that Spaulding revised the *Manuscript Story*. The revision was known as the *Manuscript Found*, and it became the basis of the *Book of Mormon* in at least its historical parts. Also its religious references furnished in part the germs of the religious portions of the *Book of Mormon*.

However, in ordinary conversation, and in public debate on the *Book of Mormon*, it is unnecessary to go into the question of who wrote the *Book of Mormon*. The really important issue is whether or not the *Book of Mormon* is of divine origin. There are some Mormons who seem to think that if they can prove that Spaulding's manuscript had nothing to do with the *Book of Mormon*, they have made great progress toward proving its divine origin. Such, however, is not the case. And one should show, from an appeal to the Bible and to the *Book of Mormon* itself, that the *Book of Mormon* is not of divine origin.[16]

Let us not forget that the *Manuscript Story* itself contains at least seventy-five similarities to what is now the *Book of Mormon* and this is not to be easily explained away.

---

[15]James D. Bales, Ph.D., *The Book of Mormon?* (Fort Worth: The Manney Company), 138–142.
[16]Ibid., 146–147.

Finally, students of Mormonism must, in the last analysis, measure its content by that of Scripture, and when this is done it will be found that it does not "speak according to the law and the testimony" (Isaiah 8:20) and it is to be rejected as a counterfeit revelation doubly condemned by God himself (Galatians 1:8–9).

Joseph Smith, the author of this "revelation," was perfectly described (as was his reward) in the Word of God almost thirty-three hundred years before he appeared. It would pay the Mormons to remember this message:

> If there arise among you a prophet, or a dreamer of dreams, and giveth thee a sign or a wonder, and the sign or the wonder come to pass, whereof he spake unto thee, saying, "Let us go after other gods," which thou hast not known, "and let us serve them;" thou shalt not hearken unto the words of that prophet, or that dreamer of dreams: for the Lord your God proveth you, to know whether ye love the Lord your God with all your heart and with all your soul.
>
> Ye shall walk after the Lord your God, and fear him, and keep his commandments, and obey his voice, and ye shall serve him, and cleave unto him.
>
> And that prophet, or that dreamer of dreams, shall be put to death; because he hath spoken to turn you away from the Lord your God, which brought you out of the land of Egypt, and redeemed you out of the house of bondage, to thrust thee out of the way which the Lord thy God commanded thee to walk in. So shalt thou put the evil away from the midst of thee.
>
> If thy brother, the son of thy mother, or thy son, or thy daughter, or the wife of thy bosom, or thy friend, which is as thine own soul, entice thee secretly, saying, "Let us go and serve other gods," which thou has not known, thou, nor thy fathers; namely, of the gods of the people which are round about you, nigh unto thee, or far off from thee, from the one end of the earth even unto the other end of the earth:
>
> Thou shalt not consent unto him, nor hearken unto him; neither shall thine eye pity him, neither shalt thou spare, neither shalt thou conceal him:
>
> But thou shalt surely kill him; thine hand shall be first upon him to put him to death, and afterwards the hand of all the people.
>
> And thou shalt stone him with stones, that he die; because he hath sought to thrust thee away from the Lord thy God, which brought thee out of the land of Egypt, from the house of bondage (Deuteronomy 13:1–10).

The *Book of Mormon* stands as a challenge to the Bible because it adds to the Word of God and to His one revelation, and the penalty for such action is as sobering as it is awesome:

> For I testify unto every man that heareth the words of the prophecy of this book, If any man shall add unto these things, God shall add unto him the plagues that are written in this book:
>
> And if any man shall take away from the words of the book of this prophecy, God shall take away his part out of the book of life, and out of the holy city, and from the things which are written in this book.
>
> He which testifieth these things saith, Surely I come quickly. Amen. Even so, come, Lord Jesus (Revelation 22:18–20).

It does no good for the Mormon to argue that Revelation 22:18–20 only pertains to the book of Revelation, since this serves only to prove our point. In the 1981 edition of the King James Version of the Bible, published by the Mormon Church, they have no less than forty-five verses footnoted in the book of

Revelation where Joseph Smith added and took away from the "words of the book." These footnotes are conveniently noted as JST (Joseph Smith Translation), beginning at Revelation 1:1 and ending at 19:21. He truly did what the apostle John warned against. Smith both added to and took away from the book of Revelation.

We need not make this a personal issue with the Mormons, but a historical and theological issue, which, for all the politeness and tact demonstrably possible, cannot conceal the depth of our disagreement. Even the famous "witnesses" to the veracity of the *Book of Mormon* are impugned by their own history. This does not speak well for the characters of those concerned or for their reliability as witnesses.

It was Joseph Smith who declared theological war on Christianity when he ascribed to God the statement that branded all Christian sects as "all wrong," their creeds as "abominations," and all Christians as "corrupt . . . having a form of godliness, but they deny the power thereof" (Joseph Smith—History 1:19).

The onus of hostility rests upon the Mormons, and their history of persecution (largely the result of their mouthing of Smith's abusive accusations and their practice of polygamy) may be properly laid at their own doorstep. They were the initial antagonists, *not* the Christian church. We do not excuse those who persecuted the early Mormons, but in a great many instances those who were involved were provoked to action by Mormon excesses. (Note: An example of this would be the Mormon expulsion from Jackson County, Missouri.)

We may safely leave the *Book of Mormon* to the judgment of history and Mormon theology to the pronouncements of God's immutable Word. But we must speak the truth about these things and keep foremost in our minds the fact that the sincerity of the Mormons in their faith is no justification for withholding just criticism of that faith or of its refuted source, the *Book of Mormon* and the "revelations" of Joseph Smith. The truth must be spoken in love, but it must be spoken.

The Theology of Mormonism

The Mormon church almost from its inception has claimed what no other church today claims to possess: the priesthoods of Aaron and Melchizedek.

The Mormons maintain that Joseph Smith and Oliver Cowdery received the Aaronic priesthood from the hand of John the Baptist on May 15, 1829, and that "the Melchizedek Priesthood was conferred upon Joseph Smith and Oliver Cowdery through the ministration of Peter, James, and John, shortly after the conferring of the Aaronic order."[17]

In the theology of Mormonism, both the Melchizedek and Aaronic orders are considered to be but one priesthood "without beginning of days or end of years" (*Doctrine and Covenants*, 84:17), and through the authority of this priesthood alone, they maintain, men speak and act in the name of the Lord for the salvation of humanity. In order that this may be clearly understood, the following quotation from the leading Mormon volume on the subject of the priesthood must be considered:

---

[17]John A. Widtsoe, *The Priesthood and Church Government* (Salt Lake City: Deseret Book Company, 1939), 107.

This authoritative Priesthood is designed to assist men in all of life's endeavors, both temporal and spiritual. Consequently, there are divisions or offices of the Priesthood, each charged with a definite duty, fitting a special human need.

The prophet Joseph Smith once said that all Priesthood is Melchizedek. That is to say that the Melchizedek Priesthood embraces all offices and authorities in the Priesthood. This is clearly stated in the *Doctrine and Covenants*, Section 107, Verse 5: "All other authorities or offices in the church are appendages to this (i.c., Melchizedek) Priesthood."

There are two Priesthoods spoken of in the Scriptures, viz., the Melchizedek and the Aaronic or Levitical. Although there are two Priesthoods, yet the Melchizedek Priesthood comprehends the Aaronic or Levitical Priesthood; and is the grand head, and holds the highest authority that pertains to the Priesthood, and the keys of the kingdom of God in all ages of the world to the latest posterity on the earth; and is the channel through which all knowledge, doctrine, the plan of salvation, and every important matter is revealed from heaven.[18]

The Mormon concept of the priesthood holds that God has placed in that church presidents, apostles, high priests, seventies, elders; and that the various offices all share specific authorities.

The president of the church, they maintain, "may hold and dispense the powers of the administrative responsibilities of that office, the power of the Priesthood is decentralized: first, according to offices and the jurisdictions of those respective offices; second, according to individual Priesthood-bearers. This means that while the church as a whole is delicately responsive to central authority for church-wide purposes, the central-local relationships in the organization do not restrict the full initiative and free development of either territorial divisions of the Church, individual quorums, groups of quorums, or the member as an individual. . . . The Priesthood provides a "functional" instrumentality for church government that is at once efficient and responsible in centralization, but flexible and decentralized in actual administration."[19]

It is therefore apparent that in Mormon theology the priesthood occupies a position of great importance and comprehends nearly every male member of the church above the age of twelve in one capacity or another; and therefore by necessity the refutation of the Mormon claims to its possession undercuts the very foundations of Mormonism.[20]

With the foregoing in mind, let us examine the Scriptures that most thoroughly refute the Mormon contentions. The Scripture indeed provides a wealth of information.

In the seventh chapter of the epistle to the Hebrews, Melchizedek, who was the king of Salem and priest of the Most High God, is mentioned briefly in connection with Abraham. The author of Hebrews points out that the priesthood of Melchizedek is superior to the Aaronic priesthood and the administrations of the Levites because Abraham, who was the father of the sons of Levi, paid tithe to Melchizedek. This establishes the fact that Melchizedek was superior to

---

[18]Widtsoe, 102–103.

[19]Ibid., 103.

[20]Until June 1978, men of African descent were denied the priesthood because of a teaching that they were under a curse for their lack of valiance in their premortal existence. Under this ban they were unable to attain the status of "exaltation" (godhood).

Abraham. The writer of Hebrews puts it this way: "And without all contradiction the less is blessed of the better. And here men that die receive tithes; but there he receiveth them, of whom it is witnessed that he liveth. And as I may so say, Levi also, who receiveth tithes, paid tithes in Abraham. For he was yet in the loins of his father, when Melchizedek met him" (7:7–10).

The establishment of the fact that the Melchizedek priesthood is superior to the Aaronic would be virtually meaningless if the writer of Hebrews had not gone on to say:

"If therefore perfection were by the Levitical priesthood (for under it the people received the law), what further need was there that another priest should rise after the order of Melchizedek, and not be called after the order of Aaron? For the priesthood being *changed*, there is made of necessity a change also of the law" (vv. 11–12, emphasis added).

The whole point of the seventh chapter of Hebrews, as any careful exegesis will reveal, is the fact that Jesus Christ who is "a priest forever after the order of Melchizedek" (verse 17) has, by virtue of His sacrifice upon the cross, changed the priesthood of Aaron (verse 12), instituting in its place His own priesthood of the Melchizedek order.

Christ was not of the tribe of Levi and not of the priesthood of Aaron; He was of the tribe of Judah, yet His priesthood is infinitely superior to that of Aaron. It is quite evident that the Levitical priesthood could not evolve into the Melchizedek priesthood, but that it passed away as symbolized by the tearing of the veil leading to the Holy of Holies at the crucifixion (Matthew 27:51).

The writer of Hebrews further states that Christ is our great High Priest and that He has "passed through the heavenlies" to "appear in the presence of God for us." In addition to this, it is declared that "Christ is not entered into the holy places made with hands, which are the figures of the true; but into heaven itself. . . . Nor yet that he should offer himself often, as the high priest entereth into the holy place every year with blood of others; for then must he often have suffered since the foundation of the world: but now once in the end of the world hath he appeared to put away sin by the sacrifice of himself" (Hebrews 9:24–26).

The previous reference is clearly to the truth that the old priesthood, which enabled the priests to enter into the temple apartment once every year on the Day of Atonement, had come to a close because Christ has once offered an eternal atonement for the sins of the whole world (1 John 2:2).

How significant indeed are these facts when placed beside the Mormon claim to possession of the Aaronic priesthood, which God's Word says has been "changed" and completely consummated in the Priest whose order is after Melchizedek, Jesus Christ himself.

Our Lord's priesthood is not dependent upon its continuation from father to son as the Aaronic was through the Levitical order, something necessitated by virtue of the fact that all men die; hence its transference. But the writer of Hebrews tells us that the Lord Jesus Christ "arose after the similitude of Melchizedek." He is "another priest, Who is made, not after the law of carnal commandment [which is temporary by nature], but after the power of an endless life" (Hebrews 7:15–16). The Greek word *akatalutos* is rightly translated "imperishable, indestructible, and indissoluble"; and in this context it refers to His

life. He was not consecrated a priest as were the Levites from father to son, but His priesthood is after the order of endless Being. His is an infinite priesthood because He is eternal.

All this background is of vital importance in refuting the Mormon claims to the perpetuity of the Aaronic priesthood, but even more so in refuting their concept of the Melchizedek priesthood, which they also claim to have received.

In the same chapter of Hebrews, a second Mormon claim is tersely dispensed with by the Holy Spirit in an emphatic and irrevocable manner.

> By so much was Jesus made a surety of a better testament. And they truly were many priests, because they were not suffered to continue by reason of death: But this man, because he continueth ever, hath an unchangeable priesthood. Wherefore he is able to save them to the uttermost that come unto God by him, seeing he ever liveth to make intercession for them. For such an high priest became us, who is holy, harmless, undefiled, separate from sinners, and made higher than the heavens; who needeth not daily, as those high priests, to offer up sacrifice, first for his own sins, and then for the people's: for this he did once, when he offered up himself. For the law maketh men high priests which have infirmity; but the word of the oath, which was since the law, maketh the Son, who is consecrated for evermore (vv. 22–28).

Particular attention should be paid to verse 24, which, in the Greek, is devastating to the Mormon claim. Verse 24, in Greek, literally reads,

"But he continues forever, so his priesthood is untransferable"[21] (Goodspeed).

The Greek word *aparabatos*, literally rendered as *untransferable*, carries the note of finality. Thayer's *Greek-English Lexicon* puts it this way:

"Priesthood unchangeable and therefore not liable to pass to a successor," Hebrews 7:24 (page 54).

Since the word appears but once in New Testament Greek, there is not even the appeal to possible contextual renderings. Here is one instance where no amount of semantic juggling can escape the force of the context and grammar.

The writer of Hebrews, under the inspiration of the Holy Spirit, declares that the priesthood of Melchizedek is the peculiar possession of Jesus Christ, not only by virtue of the fact that He is God and possessed of imperishable life, but because it cannot be transferred to another. It consummated the Aaronic priesthood; it terminated the Levitical order; it resides in the Son of God; and by the will of His Father, it cannot be transferred. There is no escape from the force of these revelations of Scripture, and no exegetical theologian or commentator has ever held otherwise. It is all well and good for the Mormons to claim the priesthoods of Aaron and Melchizedek, but it should be pointed out that they do so by contradicting the expressed teaching of the Word of God that they claim to respect.

In his interesting and informative booklet *Gods, Sex, and the Saints*, Dr. George Arbaugh makes the following observation. "The Mormons are advised that the harvest is ripe and that the sickle should be thrust into the Christian

---

[21]The Mormon claim that Melchizedek conferred his priesthood on Abraham when the latter paid tithe to him (Genesis 18) finds no support in Scripture (*Priesthood and Church Government*, John A. Widtsoe, 109). Mormons should be pressed at this juncture for the biblical evidence, the absence of which affords further opportunity to undercut their already weakened position.

churches. The bold proselytizing usually includes certain stereotyped challenges, questions, and arguments" (p. 39).

Dr. Arbaugh then goes on to point out that the priesthood is one of the
areas the Mormons emphasize. They never tire of stating to any and all who will
listen, particularly to those who are likely proselytes, "You do not have the priesthood!"

To answer this, the alert Christian should point out that the Mormons themselves do not have any priesthood, but that the church of Jesus Christ has always
had a priesthood, a priesthood very clearly taught in the New Testament. This
priesthood was emphasized by the great Reformation theologian Martin Luther,
who described it as "the priesthood of all believers."

Dr. Arbaugh rightly observes,

> There are many millions more priests in the Lutheran Church than in the
> Latter-day Saint organization, for this reason: that every believer is a priest.
> There is a universal priesthood of believers. This means that each believer can
> come to God in prayer, in his own right, and that he can speak about his Lord
> to his fellowmen. He need not wait for some priest to do the essential Christian
> things for him. For that matter, how could any priest do the essential Christian
> thing for you, namely, to love God and your fellowman also?
>
> In the original Mormon Church the only officers were elders, but subse-
> quently many additional offices were established. For this reason *Doctrine and
> Covenants*, Section 20, verses 65 through 67, was "corrected" from the original
> form in the *Book of Commandments*. Mormonism even stoops to falsifying its scrip-
> tures in order to pretend that there have been the same priestly offices in all
> ages (p. 44).

The True Priesthood

In the opening sentences of the book of the Revelation, John the apostle
makes an astounding statement when he declares:

"Blessing and peace to you from him who is, and was, and is coming, and
from the seven spirits before his throne and from Jesus Christ, the trustworthy
witness, the first born of the dead, the sovereign of the kings of the earth. To
him who loves us and has released us from our sins by his own blood—he has
made us a kingdom of priests for his God and Father—to him be glory and
power forever" (1:4–6, Goodspeed).

How incisive is this plain declaration by apostolic authority. Jesus Christ who
is the sovereign of the kings of the earth, the One who continues to love us and
who has released us from our sins through His own blood, has also made us "a
kingdom of priests for His God and Father." Here is the true priesthood indeed.

The Christian does not need temples, secret services, rituals, and mysteries.
His priesthood knows no special offices or power to communicate with the
dead—things that the Mormon priesthood most definitely claims. The Christian
priesthood embraces all those who have been loosed from their sins by the blood
of Jesus Christ, and who enjoy the perpetual love of the Lamb of God who takes
away the sins of the world.

Communication with the dead is a possibility that many Mormons look forward to. In 1877 Wilford Woodruff expounded on the importance of temple
work on behalf of those who are deceased and said, "The dead will be after you,

they will seek after you as they have after us in St. George." (*Journal of Discourses,* 19:229). In his book *Temple Manifestations* (Magazine Printing and Publishing, 1979), Mormon author Joseph Heinerman gives numerous examples of visitations from the dead in Mormon temples.

This concept is further developed in the writings of Peter, who affirms that "You are the chosen race, the *royal priesthood,* the consecrated nation, his own people, so that you may declare the virtues of him who has called you out of darkness into his wonderful light; you who were once no people, but are now God's people; once unpitied, but now pitied indeed" (1 Peter 2:9–10, Goodspeed).

In this context, the words of the apostle establish that long before there were any mythological Mormon priesthoods, there was a priesthood embracing all the redeemed, a "royal priesthood," neither of Aaron nor of Melchizedek. This priesthood is composed of all consecrated "ambassadors for Christ," to quote the apostle Paul, whose task it is to exhort men to "be reconciled to God . . . knowing the terror of the Lord" (see 2 Corinthians 5:20, 11).

As has been observed, Mormonism places great stress upon the priesthood. But as we have also seen, it is not the priesthood described in the Scriptures. Instead, they have substituted the revelation of "prophet" Smith concerning a priesthood, which has been changed (Hebrews 7:12), and a priesthood which by its nature is "untransferable" (7:24). The resulting dilemma is that they have no priesthood at all since their denial of the true deity of Jesus Christ and the nature of God rules out the possibility that they could share in the priesthood of all believers. In order for one to be one of the "kingdom of priests to God His Father" (Revelation 1:4–6) and a member of the "royal priesthood" (1 Peter 2:9–10), one must first have undergone personal regeneration in a saving encounter or experience with the God-Man of Scripture—Jesus Christ. Mormon theology with its pantheon of gods, its perverted view of the Virgin Birth, and its outright condemnation of all churches as an "abomination" (Joseph Smith—History 1:19), removes itself from serious consideration as a form of Christianity. There is more to Christianity than the application of the Christian ethic. There is a great deal more to the gospel than the similarity of terms, albeit redefined. Christianity is not merely a system of doctrinal pronouncements (though they are of vast importance). It is a living, vital experience with the God of the Bible as He was incarnate in the man from Nazareth. Mormonism, with its many doctrinal vagaries and outright denials of historic Christian teachings, disqualifies itself. And its priesthood, on which it places so much emphasis, is shown to be the antithesis of the divine revelation.

It is to be earnestly hoped that more Christians will acquaint themselves with the biblical evidence concerning the true priesthood in which we all participate. It is only when a thorough understanding of the fundamentals of Christian theology is obtained that it is possible to successfully encounter and refute the Mormon doctrine of the priesthood.

The Mormon Doctrine of God

It will be conceded by most informed students of Christianity that one cannot deny the existence of the one true God of Scripture and at the same

time lay claim to being a Christian. The New Testament writers, as well as our Lord himself, taught that there was but one God, and all church theologians from the earliest days of church history have affirmed that Christianity is monotheistic in the strictest sense of the term. Indeed it was this fact that so radically differentiated it and the parental Judaism from the pagan, polytheistic societies of Rome and Greece. The Bible is particularly adamant in its declaration that God recognizes the existence of no other "deities." In fact, on a number of occasions the Lord summed up His uniqueness in the following revelation:

> Ye are my witnesses, saith the Lord, and my servant whom I have chosen: that ye may know and believe me, and understand that I am he: before me there was no God formed, neither shall there be after me. I, even I, am the Lord; and beside me there is no saviour. . . . Thus saith the Lord the King of Israel, and his redeemer the Lord of hosts; I am the first, and I am the last; and *beside me there is no God*. . . . Ye are even my witnesses. Is there a God beside me? *yea, there is no God; I know not any*. . . . *I* am the Lord, and there is none else, *there is no God beside me:* I girded thee, though thou hast not known me. . . . *There is no God else beside me;* a just God and a Saviour; *there is none beside me.* Look unto me, and be ye saved, all the ends of the earth: *for I am God, and there is none else* (Isaiah 43:10–11; 44:6, 8; 45:5, 21–22, emphasis added).

Throughout the Old Testament, God is known by many titles. He is Elohim, Jehovah, Adonai, El Gebor, and He is also spoken of by combinations of names, such as Jehovah-Elohim, Jehovah-Sabaoth, etc. If the Hebrew Old Testament tells us anything, it is the fact that there is but one God: "Hear, O Israel: The Lord our God is one Lord" (Deuteronomy 6:4). And Jewish monotheism, as all know, at length gave birth to Christian monotheism, the one developing from the other by progressive revelation from God the Holy Spirit. It is not necessary to belabor the point; it is common knowledge that the facts as they have been stated are true. But as we approach our study of the Mormon concept of God, a subtle yet radical change takes place in the usage of the vocabulary of Scripture as we shall see.

It must also be admitted at the outset that the Bible does designate certain individuals as "gods," such as Satan who is described by Christ as "the prince of this world" and elsewhere in Scripture as "the god of this world." It must be clearly understood, however, that whenever this term is assigned to individuals, to spirit personalities, and the like, metaphorical and contextual usage must be carefully analyzed so that a clear picture emerges. For instance, the Lord declared to Moses: "See, I have made thee a god to Pharaoh: and Aaron thy brother shall be thy prophet" (Exodus 7: 1). The Hebrew indicates here, when cross-referenced with Exodus 4:16 ("And he shall be thy spokesman unto the people: and he shall be, even he shall be to thee instead of a mouth, and thou shalt be to him instead of God."), that a definite relationship was involved. The context also reveals that Moses, by virtue of the power invested in him by God, became in the eyes of Pharaoh "a god." Aaron in turn became a prophet of the "god" (Moses) that Pharaoh beheld because he was the spokesman for Moses. So metaphorical usage is obviously intended, from the very usage of the language and its contextual analysis. On this point all Old Testament scholars are agreed. But this should never cloud the issue that there is only one true and living God as the previous quotations readily attest.

Another instance of similar usage is the application of the term "Elohim," the plural usage of the term often translated *God* in the Old Testament. In some contexts the judges of Israel are referred to as "gods," not that they themselves possessed the intrinsic nature of Deity but that they became in the eyes of the people as gods, or more literally, "mighty ones" (Psalm 82, cf. John 10:34), representing as they did the Lord of Hosts. In the New Testament usage, the apostle Paul is quite explicit when he declares that in the world, i.e., as far as the world is concerned, "(. . . there be gods many, and lords many,) but to us there is but one God, the Father, . . . and one Lord Jesus Christ" (1 Corinthians 8:5–6), a statement emphasized by our Lord when He stated, "I am the first and the last: I am He that liveth, and was dead; and, behold, I am alive for evermore" (Revelation 1:17–18). We conclude, then, that polytheism is totally foreign to the Judeo-Christian tradition of theology. In fact, it is the antithesis of the extreme monotheism portrayed in Judaism and Christianity. The God of the Old Testament and the God and Father of our Lord Jesus Christ are one and the same Person; this the Christian church has always held. In addition to this, God's nature has always been declared to be that of pure spirit. Our Lord declared that "God is spirit, and they that worship Him must worship Him in spirit and in truth" (John 4:24—as correctly translated from the original Greek text). In numerous other places within the pages of the inspired Word of God, the Holy Spirit has been pleased to reveal God's spiritual nature and "oneness." The apostle Paul reminds us that "a mediator is not a mediator of one, but God is one" (Galatians 3:20). The psalmist reminds us of His unchangeable nature, "From everlasting to everlasting, thou art God" (Psalm 90:2); and Moses records in the initial act of creation that "the spirit of God moved upon the face of the waters" (Genesis 1:2). The "gods" mentioned in Scripture, then, are never gods by either identity or nature; they are "gods" by human creation or acclamation as we have seen. This, then, is a far cry from comparison with the one true and living God described by the writer of the epistle to the Hebrews as "the Father of spirits" (Hebrews 12:9; see also Galatians 4:8–9).

The Mormons misuse John 10:34, "Ye are gods," falsely implying that Jesus endorsed godhood for man. This cannot be true for several reasons. It does not fit the context of John 10:24–36, where Jesus shows his equality with the Father and deservedly is called God. In contrast, the judges (so-called gods) in Psalm 82:6 were so called because of their lofty position over the people, but God rebuked them for their sins, and they were proven to be not gods after all but fallen, sinful men.

How this passage is to support the Mormon position is baffling, because Mormons say they are gods in embryo and they have not yet reached godhood. Whatever they wish John 10:34 to say, it does not support their position. The Mormon can only say he hopes to become a god. Psalm 82 and John 10:34 are in the present tense, a distinction apart from their position.

In fact, upon a reading of Psalm 82, it is a wonder that Mormons would want to identify with the Psalm at all. It says nothing good about these men. But if that is the position they desire, only the judgment of God follows.

➤ Furthermore, the Mormon should be made aware that LDS Apostle James Talmage correctly identified the "gods" of Psalm 82 and John 10:34 when he wrote, "Divinely Appointed Judges Called 'gods.' In Psalm 82:6, judges invested

by divine appointment are called 'gods.' To this Scripture the Savior referred in His reply to the Jews in Solomon's Porch. Judges so authorized officiated as the representatives of God and are honored by the exalted title 'gods.' " (*Jesus the Christ,* 501).

The Truth About the God of the Mormons

In sharp contrast to the revelations of Scripture are the "revelations" of Joseph Smith, Brigham Young, and the succeeding Mormon "prophets." So that the reader will have no difficulty understanding what the true Mormon position is concerning the nature of God, the following quotations derived from popular Mormon sources will convey what the Mormons mean when they speak of "God."

1. "In the beginning, the head of the Gods called a council of the Gods; and they came together and concocted a plan to create the world and people it" (*Teachings of the Prophet Joseph Smith,* 349).

2. "God himself was once as we are now, and is an exalted man . . ." (*Teachings of the Prophet Joseph Smith,* 345).

3. "The Father has a body of flesh and bones as tangible as man's: the Son also; but the Holy Ghost has not a body of flesh and bones, *but is* a personage of Spirit . . ." (*Doctrine and Covenants,* 130:22).

4. "Gods exist, and we had better strive to be prepared to be one with them" (Brigham Young, *Journal of Discourses,* 7:238).

5. "As man is, God once was: as God is, man may become" (Prophet Lorenzo Snow, quoted in Milton R. Hunter, *The Gospel Through the Ages,* 105–106).

6. "Each of these Gods, including Jesus Christ and His Father, being in possession of not merely an organized spirit, but a glorious immortal body of flesh and bones . . ." (Parley P. Pratt, *Key to the Science of Theology,* ed. 1978, 23).

7. "And then the Lord said: Let us go down. And they went down at the beginning, and they, that is the Gods, organized and formed the heavens and the earth" (Abraham 4:1).

8. "Remember that God, our heavenly Father, was perhaps once a child, and mortal like we ourselves, and rose step by step in the scale of progress, in the school of advancement; has moved forward and overcome, until He has arrived at the point where He now is" (Apostle Orson Hyde, *Journal of Discourses,* 1:123).

9. "Mormon prophets have continuously taught the sublime truth that God the Eternal Father was once a mortal man who passed through a school of earth life similar to that through which we are now passing. He became God—an exalted being—through obedience to the same eternal Gospel truths that we are given opportunity today to obey" (Hunter, *op. cit.,* 104).

10. "Christ was the God, the Father of all things. . . . Behold, I am Jesus Christ. I am the Father and the Son" (Mosiah 7:27 and Ether 3:14, *Book of Mormon*).

11. "When our father Adam came into the garden of Eden, he came into it with a celestial body, and brought Eve, one of his wives, with him. He helped to make and organized this world. He is MICHAEL, the Archangel, the ANCIENT OF DAYS! about whom holy men have written and spoken—HE is our

FATHER and our GOD, and the only God with whom we have to do"[22] (Brigham Young, in the *Journal of Discourses*, 1:50).

12. Historically this doctrine of Adam-God was hard for even faithful Mormons to believe. As a result, on June 8, 1873, Brigham Young stated: "How much unbelief exists in the minds of the Latter-day Saints in regard to one particular doctrine which I revealed to them, and which God revealed to me—namely that Adam is our father and God. . . .

" 'Well,' says one, 'Why was Adam called Adam?' He was the first man on the earth, and its framer and maker. He with the help of his brethren brought it into existence. Then he said, 'I want my children who are in the spirit world to come and live here. I once dwelt upon an earth something like this, in a mortal state. I was faithful, I received my crown and exaltation' "*(Deseret News,* June 18, 1873, 308).

It would be quite possible to continue quoting sources from many volumes and other official Mormon publications, but the fact is well established.

The Reorganized Church of Jesus Christ of Latter Day Saints, which disagrees with the Utah church on the subject of polytheism, steadfastly maintains that Joseph Smith Jr. never taught or practiced either polygamy or polytheism, but the following direct quotation from Smith, relative to the plurality of gods and the doctrine that Mormon males may attain to godhood, vexes the Reorganized Church no end. But, it is fact, nonetheless.

The following quotations are excerpted from a sermon published in the Mormon newspaper *Times and Seasons* (August 15, 1844, 5:613–614) four months after Smith delivered it at the funeral of Elder King Follett, and only two months after Smith's assassination in Carthage, Illinois.

Tenth LDS President Joseph Fielding Smith notes that the King Follett sermon was given at the April conference of the Church in 1844 and was heard by around 20,000 people. The argument that Smith was misquoted is discounted by the fact that it was recorded by four scribes, Willard Richards, Wilford Woodruff, William Clayton, and Thomas Bullock. *The Encyclopedia of Mormonism* states that Smith's two-hour-and-fifteen-minute message "may be one of the Prophet's greatest sermons because of its doctrinal teachings."

It is significant that the split in Mormonism did not take place for more than three and a half years. Apparently their ancestors did not disagree with Smith's theology, as they themselves do today. Nor did they deny that Smith preached the sermon and taught polytheism, as does the Reorganized Church today. But the facts must speak for themselves. Here are the above mentioned quotes:

> I want you all to know God, to be familiar with him. . . . What sort of a being was God in the beginning?
>
> First, God himself, who sits enthroned in yonder heavens, is a man like unto one of yourselves . . . if you were to see him today, you would see him in all the person, image and very form as a man. . . .
>
> I am going to tell you how God came to be God. We have imagined that God was God from all eternity. These are incomprehensible ideas to some, but

---

[22]It is important to note that Brigham Young taught that he had "never yet preached a sermon and sent it out to the children of men, that they may not call Scripture" (*Journal of Discourses*, 13:95). That includes the Adam-God Doctrine.

they are the simple and first principles of the gospel, to know for a certainty the character of God, that we may converse with him as one man with another, and that God himself; the Father of us all dwelt on an earth the same as Jesus Christ himself did . . . what did Jesus say? (mark it elder Rigdon) Jesus said, as the Father hath power in himself, even so hath the Son power; to do what? Why what the Father did, that answer is obvious. . . . Here then is eternal life, to know the only wise and true God. You have got to learn how to be Gods yourselves; to be kings and priests to God, the same as all Gods have done before you—namely, by going from a small degree to another, from grace to grace, from exaltation to exaltation, until you are able to sit in glory as doth those who sit enthroned in everlasting power. . . .

Mormon theology is polytheistic, teaching in effect that the universe is inhabited by different gods who procreate spirit children, which are in turn clothed with bodies on different planets, "Elohim" being the god of this planet (Brigham's teaching that Adam is our heavenly Father is now officially denied by Mormon authorities, but they hold firm to the belief that their God is a resurrected, glorified man). In addition to this, the "inspired" utterances of Joseph Smith reveal that he began as a Unitarian, progressed to tritheism, and graduated into full-fledged polytheism, in direct contradiction to the revelations of the Old and New Testaments as we have observed. The Mormon doctrine of the trinity is a gross misrepresentation of the biblical position, though they attempt to veil their evil doctrine in semi-orthodox terminology. We have already dealt with this problem, but it bears constant repetition lest the Mormon terminology go unchallenged.

On the surface, they appear to be orthodox, but in the light of unimpeachable Mormon sources, Mormons are clearly evading the issue. The truth of the matter is that Mormonism has never historically accepted the Christian doctrine of the Trinity; in fact, they deny it by completely perverting the meaning of the term. The Mormon doctrine that God the Father is a mere man is the root of their polytheism, and forces Mormons to deny not only the Trinity of God as revealed in Scripture, but the immaterial nature of God as pure spirit. Mormons have gone on record and stated that they accept the doctrine of the Trinity, but, as we have seen, it is *not* the Christian Trinity. God the Father does not have a body of flesh and bones, a fact clearly taught by our Lord (John 4:24, cf. Luke 24:39). Mormon Apostle James Talmage describes the church's teaching, as follows, in his book *The Articles of Faith*:

> The Church of Jesus Christ of Latter-day Saints proclaims against the incomprehensible God, devoid of "body, parts, or passions," as a thing impossible of existence, and asserts its belief in and allegiance to the true and living God of scripture and revelation. . . . Jesus Christ is the Son of Elohim both as spiritual and bodily offspring; that is to say, Elohim is literally the Father of the spirit of Jesus Christ and also of the body in which Jesus Christ performed His mission in the flesh. . . . Jehovah, who is Jesus Christ the Son of Elohim, is called "the Father" . . . that Jesus Christ, whom we also know as Jehovah, was the executive of the Father, Elohim, in the work of creation as set forth in the book *Jesus the Christ*, chapter IV (48, 466–467).

In these revealing statements, Talmage lapses into the error of making Elohim and Jehovah two separate gods, apparently in complete ignorance of the fact that Elohim "the greater god" and Jehovah—Jesus the lesser god, begotten

by Elohim—are compounded in the Hebrew as "Jehovah the Mighty One," or simply "Jehovah God" as any concordance of Hebrew usage in the Old Testament readily reveals (LORD—Yahweh; God—Elohim). This error is akin to that of Mary Baker Eddy who, in her glossary to *Science and Health With Key to the Scriptures* made exactly the same error, she too being in complete ignorance of the Hebrew language. In this grammatical error, Christian Science and the Mormons are in unique agreement.

Talmage's argument that "to deny the materiality of God's person is to deny God; for a thing without parts has no whole and an immaterial body cannot exist" is both logically and theologically an absurdity. To illustrate this, one needs only to point to the angels whom the Scriptures describe as "ministering spirits" (Hebrews 1:7), beings who have immaterial "bodies" of spiritual substances and yet exist. The Mormons involve themselves further in a hopeless contradiction when, in their doctrine of the preexistence of the soul, they are forced to redefine the meaning of soul as used in both the Old and the New Testaments to teach that the soul is not immaterial, while the Bible clearly teaches that it is. Our Lord, upon the cross, spoke the words, "Father, into thy hands I commend my spirit" (Luke 23:46). Certainly this was immaterial. And Paul, preparing to depart from this world for the celestial realms, indicated that his real spiritual self (certainly immaterial, since his body died) was yearning to depart and to be with Christ, which is far better (Philippians 1:21–23). The martyr Stephen also committed his spirit (or immaterial nature) into the hands of the Father, crying, "Lord Jesus, receive my spirit" (Acts 7:59). And there are numerous passages in both the Old and New Testaments that indicate an "immaterial nature" can exist, provided that form is of a spiritual substance as is God the Father and the Holy Spirit, and as was Jesus Christ as the preincarnate Logos (John 1:1, cf. John 1:14). Far from asserting their "belief and allegiance to the true and living God of Scripture and revelation," as Talmage represents Mormonism, Mormons indeed have sworn allegiance to a polytheistic pantheon of gods, which they are striving to join, there to enjoy a polygamous eternity of progression toward godhood.

One can search the corridors of pagan mythology and never equal the complex structure that the Mormons have erected and masked under the terminology and misnomer of orthodox Christianity. That the Mormons reject the historic Christian doctrine of the Trinity no student of the movement can deny, for after quoting the Nicene Creed and early church theology on the trinity, Talmage, in *The Articles of Faith*, declares: "It would be difficult to conceive of a greater number of inconsistencies and contradictions expressed in words as here. . . . The immateriality of God as asserted in these declarations of sectarian faith is entirely at variance with the scriptures, and absolutely contradicted by the revelations of God's person and attributes . . ." (p. 48).

After carefully perusing hundreds of volumes on Mormon theology and scores of pamphlets dealing with this subject, the author can quite candidly state that never has he seen such misappropriation of terminology, disregard of context, and utter abandon of scholastic principles demonstrated on the part of non-Christian cultists than is evidenced in the attempts of Mormon theologians to appear orthodox and at the same time undermine the foundations of historic Christianity. The intricacies of their complex system of polytheism causes the

careful researcher to ponder again and again the ethical standard that these Mormon writers practice and the blatant attempts to rewrite history, biblical theology, and the laws of scriptural interpretation that they might support the theologies of Joseph Smith and Brigham Young. Without fear of contradiction, I am certain that Mormonism cannot stand investigation and wants no part of it unless the results can be controlled under the guise of "broad-mindedness" and "tolerance."

On one occasion, when the Mormon doctrine of God was under discussion with a young woman leaning in the direction of Mormon conversion, I offered in the presence of witnesses to retract this chapter and one previous effort (*Mormonism*, Zondervan Publishing House, 1958) if the Mormon elders advising this young lady would put in writing that they and their church rejected polytheism for monotheism in the tradition of the Judeo-Christian religion. It was a bona fide offer; the same offer has been made from hundreds of platforms to tens of thousands of people over a twenty-year period. The Church of Jesus Christ of Latter-day Saints is well aware of the offer. To the unwary, however, they imply that they are monotheists, to the informed they defend their polytheism, and like the veritable chameleon they change color to accommodate the surface upon which they find themselves.

G. B. Arbaugh, in his classic volume *Revelation in Mormonism* (1932), has documented in exhaustive detail the progress of Mormon theology from Unitarianism to polytheism. His research has been invaluable and available to interested scholars for over sixty years, with the full knowledge of the Mormon Church. In fact, the Mormons are significantly on the defensive where the peculiar origins of the "sacred writings" are involved or when verifiable evidence exists that reveals their polytheistic perversions of the Gospel of Jesus Christ. It is extremely difficult to write kindly of Mormon theology when they are so obviously deceptive in their presentation of data, so adamant in their condemnation of all religions in favor of the "restored gospel" allegedly vouchsafed to the prophet Joseph Smith. We must not, however, confuse the theology with the person as is too often the case, for while hostility toward the former is scriptural, it is never so with the latter.

Continuing with our study, Apostle Orson Pratt, writing in *The Seer*, declared: "In the Heaven where our spirits were born, there are many Gods, each one of whom has his own wife or wives, which were given to him previous to his redemption, while yet in his mortal state" (p. 37). In this terse sentence, Pratt summed up the whole hierarchy of Mormon polytheism, and quotations previously adduced from a reputable Mormon source support Pratt's summation beyond reasonable doubt. The Mormon teaching that God was seen "face to face" in the Old Testament (Exodus 33:9, 11, 23; Exodus 24:9–11; Isaiah 6:1, 5; Genesis 5:24, etc.) is refuted on two counts, that of language and the science of comparative textual analysis (hermeneutics).

From the standpoint of linguistics, all the references cited by the Mormons to prove "that God has a physical body that could be observed" melt away in the light of God's expressed declaration, "Thou canst not see my face: for there shall no man see me, and live" (Exodus 33:20).

Exodus 33:11 (face to face) in the Hebrew is rendered "intimate," and in no sense is it opposed to verse 20. Similar expressions are utilized in Deuter-

onomy 5:4, while in Genesis 32:30 it is the Angel of the Lord who speaks, *not* Jehovah himself. The Old Testament is filled with theophanies (literally, God-appearances), instances where God spoke or revealed himself in angelic manifestations, and it is accepted by all Old Testament scholars almost without qualification that anthropomorphisms (ascribing human characteristics to God) are the logical explanation of many of the encounters of God with man. To argue, as the Mormons do, that such occurrences indicate that God has a body of flesh and bone, as "prophet" Smith taught, is on the face of the matter untenable and another strenuous attempt to force polytheism on a rigidly monotheistic religion. Progressing beyond this, another cardinal Mormon point of argument is the fact that because expressions such as "the arm of the Lord," "the eye of the Lord," "the hand of the Lord," "nostrils," "mouth," etc., are used, all tend to show that God possesses a physical form. However, they have overlooked one important factor. This factor is that of literary metaphor, extremely common in Old Testament usage. If the Mormons are to be consistent in their interpretation, they should find great difficulty in the Psalm where God is spoken of as "covering with his feathers," and man "trusting under his wings." If God has eyes, ears, arms, hands, nostrils, mouth, etc., why then does He not have feathers and wings? The Mormons have never given a satisfactory answer to this, because it is obvious that the anthropomorphic and metaphorical usage of terms relative to God are literary devices to convey His concern for and association with man. In like manner, metaphors such as feathers and wings indicate His tender concern for the protection of those who "dwell in the secret place of the Most High and abide under the shadow of the Almighty." The Mormons would do well to comb the Old Testament and the New Testament for the numerous metaphorical usages readily available for observation. In doing so, they would have to admit, if they are at all logically consistent, that Jesus was not a door (John 10:9), a shepherd (John 10:11), a vine (John 15:1), a roadway (John 14:6), a loaf of bread (John 6:51), and other metaphorical expressions any more than "our God is a consuming fire" means that Jehovah should be construed as a blast furnace or a volcanic cone.

The Mormons themselves are apparently unsure of the intricacies of their own polytheistic structure, as revealed in the previously cited references from Joseph Smith, who made Christ both the Father and the Son in one instance, and further on indicated that there was a mystery connected with it and that only the Son could reveal how He was both the Father and the Son. Later, to compound the difficulty, Smith separated them completely into "separate personages," eventually populating the entire universe with his polytheistic and polygamous deities. If one peruses carefully the books of Abraham and Moses as contained in the *Pearl of Great Price* (allegedly "translated" by Smith), as well as sections of Ether in the *Book of Mormon, Doctrine and Covenants,* and *Discourses of Brigham Young,* the entire Mormon dogma of the preexistence of the soul, the polygamous nature of the gods, the brotherhood of Jesus and Lucifer, and the hierarchy of heaven (telestial, terrestrial, and celestial—corresponding to the basement, fiftieth floor, and observation tower of the Empire State Building, respectively), and the doctrines of universal salvation, millennium, resurrection, judgment, and final punishment, will unfold in a panorama climaxing in a polygamous paradise of eternal duration. Such is the Mormon doctrine of

God, or, more properly, of the gods, which rivals anything pagan mythology ever produced.

The Holy Spirit in Mormonism

Having discussed the nature and attributes of God in contrast to Mormon mythology and its pantheon of polygamous deities, it remains for us to understand what the Mormon teaching concerning the third person of the Christian Trinity is, since they deign to describe Him as "a personage of spirit."

It is interesting to observe that in their desire to emulate orthodoxy where possible, the Mormons describe the Holy Ghost in the following terms:

"The term Holy Ghost and its common synonyms, Spirit of God, Spirit of the Lord, or simply Spirit, Comforter, and Spirit of Truth occur in the Scriptures with plainly different meanings, referring in some cases to the person of God the Holy Ghost, and in other instances to the power and authority of this great personage, or to the agency through which He ministers. . . . The Holy Ghost undoubtedly possesses personal powers and affections; these attributes exist in Him in perfection. Thus, He teaches and guides, testifies of the Father and the Son, reproves for sin, speaks, commands, and commissions. . . . These are not figurative expressions but plain statements of the attributes and characteristics of the Holy Ghost" (*The Articles of Faith*, 115).

It is interesting to recall that according to Talmage, writer of *The Articles of Faith*, "It has been said, therefore, that God is everywhere present; but this does not mean that the actual person of any one member of the Godhead can be *physically* present in more than one place at one time. . . . Admitting the personality of God, we are compelled to accept the fact of His materiality; indeed, an 'immaterial' being, under which meaningless name some have sought to designate the condition of God, cannot exist, for the very expression is a contradiction in terms. If God possesses a form, that form is of necessity of definite proportions and therefore of limited extension in space. It is impossible for Him to occupy at one time more than one space of such limits . . ." (42–43).

Here exists a contradiction in Mormon theology if ever there was one. Talmage declares that the Holy Spirit is a personage of spirit, obviously "an immaterial being" and obviously God (cf. *Doctrine and Covenants*, 20:28), and yet not possessing a form of material nature; hence, not limited to extension and space, and therefore rendering it possible for Him to occupy at one time more than one space of such limits, in direct contradiction to Talmage's earlier statements in the same volume. For the Mormon, "a thing without parts has no whole and an immaterial body cannot exist" (*Articles of Faith*, 48), and yet the Holy Spirit is a "personage of Spirit," one of the Mormon gods, according to *Doctrine and Covenants*. To cap it all, "He is an immaterial being possessed of a spiritual form and definite proportions!" Mormon theology here appears to have really become confused at the roots, so to speak; but Talmage does not agree with Talmage, nor does *Doctrine and Covenants;* they are forced into the illogical position of affirming the materiality of God in one instance, and denying that materiality in the next instance where the Holy Spirit is concerned.

Parley P. Pratt, the eminent Mormon theologian, further complicated the doctrine of the Holy Spirit in Mormon theology when he wrote: "This leads to

the investigation of that substance called the Holy Spirit or Light of Christ. . . . There is a divine substance, fluid or essence, called Spirit, widely diffused among these eternal elements. . . . This divine element, or Spirit, is immediate, active or controlling agent in all holy miraculous powers. . . . The purest, most refined and subtle of all these substances and the one least understood or even recognized by the less informed among mankind is that substance called the Holy Spirit" (*Key to the Science of Theology*, ed. 1978, 24–25, 64).[23]

In the thinking of Pratt, then, the Holy Spirit is a substance, a fluid, and a person, but this is not the teaching of Scripture, which consistently portrays God the Holy Spirit, third person of the Trinity, as an eternal, omnipotent, omnipresent, omniscient Being, sharing all the attributes of Deity, and one with the Father and the Son in unity of substance. Mormons are, to say the least, divided in their theology on the issue, although Talmage bravely attempts to synthesize the mass of conflicting information and "revelations" found within the writings of Smith and Young and the other early Mormon writers. Try as he will, however, Talmage cannot explain the Mormon confusion on the subject, as evidenced by the following facts.

In *Doctrine and Covenants* 20:37 the following statement appears:

"All those who humble themselves . . . and truly manifest by their works that they have received of the Spirit of Christ unto the remission of their sins, shall be received by baptism into his church."

Joseph Smith the prophet was the recipient of this alleged revelation and he is to be believed at all costs; yet the same Joseph Smith translated the *Book of Mormon*, which unreservedly declared:

"Yea, blessed are they who shall . . . be baptized, for they shall . . . receive a remission of their sins. . . . Behold, baptism is unto repentance to the fulfilling of the commandments unto the remission of sins" (3 Nephi 12:2; Moroni 8:11).

In one instance, Smith taught that baptism follows the initial act—remission of sins—and in the second instance, the initial act—remission of sins—reverses its position and follows baptism. According to Talmage, "God grants the gift of the Holy Ghost unto the obedient; and the bestowal of this gift follows faith, repentance, and baptism by water. . . . The apostles of old promised the ministration of the Holy Ghost unto those only who had received baptism by water for the remission of sins" (*The Articles of Faith*, 163).

The question naturally arises: When, then, is the Holy Spirit bestowed? Or indeed, can He be bestowed in Mormon theology when it is not determined whether the remission of sins precedes baptism or follows it? Here again, confusion on the doctrine of the Holy Spirit is evidenced in Mormon thinking.

It would be possible to explore further the Mormon doctrine of the Holy Spirit, especially the interesting chapter in President Charles Penrose's book *Mormon Doctrine* (Salt Lake City, 1888), in which he refers to the Holy Spirit as "it" more than twenty times—devoid of personality, although, in the usual polytheistic Mormon scheme, endowed with Deity. Penrose closes his comment by stating, "As baptism is the birth of water, so confirmation is the birth or baptism

---

[23]Some Mormons, quoting early Mormon writers, have attempted to differentiate between the Holy Spirit and the Holy Ghost! (See Widtsoe, *Evidences and Reconciliations* [Bookcraft, 1987 edition], 76). This is linguistically impossible in New Testament Greek, as any Greek lexicon reveals. Both Spirit and Ghost are translated from the same Greek word, *pneuma.*

of the Spirit. Both are necessary to entrance into the Kingdom of God. . . . The possessor of the Holy Ghost is infinitely rich; those who receive it can lose it, and are of all men the poorest. But there are various degrees of its possession. Many who obtain it walk but measurably in its light. But there are few who live by its whisperings, and approach by its mediumship into close communion with heavenly beings of the highest order. To them its light grows brighter every day" (pp. 18–19).

Mormonism, then, for all its complexities and want of conformity to the revelation of God's Word, indeed contradicts the Word of God repeatedly, teaching in place of the God of pure spiritual substance (John 4:24) a flesh-and-bone Deity and a pantheon of gods in infinite stages of progression. For Mormons, God is restricted to a narrow, rationalistic, and materialistic mold. He cannot be incomprehensible, though Scripture indicates that in many ways He most certainly is. "My thoughts are not your thoughts, neither are your ways my ways, saith the Lord. For as the heavens are higher than the earth, so are my ways higher than your ways, and my thoughts than your thoughts" (Isaiah 55:8–9). Mormon theology complicates and confounds the simple declarations of Scripture in order to support the polytheistic pantheon of Joseph Smith and Brigham Young. It is obvious, therefore, that the God of the Bible and the "god" of the Mormons, the "Adam-god" of Brigham Young and the flesh-and-bone deity of Joseph Smith are not one and the same; by their nature all monotheistic and theistic religions stand in opposition to Mormon polytheism. Christianity in particular repudiates as false and deceptive the multiplicity of Mormon efforts to masquerade as "ministers of righteousness" (2 Corinthians 11:15).

The Virgin Birth of Christ

One of the great doctrines of the Bible, which is uniquely related to the supreme earthly manifestation of the Eternal God, is the doctrine of the Virgin Birth of Jesus Christ. In one very real sense, this doctrine is indissolubly linked with that of the Incarnation, being, so to speak, the agency or instrument whereby God chose to manifest himself. Time and again the Bible reminds us that Deity was clothed with humanity in the manger of Bethlehem, and Christians of all generations have revered the mystery prefigured by the cryptic words of Isaiah the prophet:

> Behold, a virgin shall conceive, and bear a son, and shall call his name Immanuel. . . . For unto us a child is born, unto us a son is given: and the government shall be upon his shoulder: and his name shall be called Wonderful, Counselor, The mighty God, The everlasting Father, The Prince of Peace (Isaiah 7:14; 9:6).

The apostle Paul refers numerous times to the deity of our Lord, declaring that "In Him dwelleth all the fullness of the Godhead bodily" (Colossians 2:9).

Attempts to minimize the Virgin Birth of Christ or to do away with it altogether, as some liberal theologians have energetically tried to do, have consistently met with disaster. This is true because the simple narratives of this momentous event recorded in Matthew and Luke refuse to surrender to the hindsight reconstruction theories of second-guessing critics.

Some persons have, on the other hand, decided upon a middle course where this doctrine is concerned. They affirm its biological necessity. In a word, Matthew and Luke, who had access to eyewitness testimonies (Mary, Joseph, Elizabeth, etc.), never really believed the teaching as recorded; rather it was a pious attempt to endow Christ with a supernatural conception in order to add glory to His personality. Regardless of how distasteful the unbiblical concepts of liberal and so-called neoorthodox theologians may be concerning the Virgin Birth of our Savior, no group has framed a concept of the Virgin Birth doctrine in the terms employed by the Mormon prophet Brigham Young. Mormon doctrine concerning the Virgin Birth of Christ was first delivered in the pronouncements of Brigham Young and has been consistently found in the teachings of all General Authorities throughout their history. It has never been contradicted and consequently represents the doctrine of the Mormon Church.

Relative to the doctrine of the Virgin Birth of Christ, Brigham Young has unequivocally stated, "When the Virgin Mary conceived the child Jesus, the Father had begotten him in his own likeness. He was *not* begotten by the Holy Ghost. And who was the Father? He is the first of the human family; and when he took a tabernacle [body], it was begotten by his Father in heaven, after the same manner as the tabernacles of Cain, Abel, and the rest of the sons and daughters of Adam and Eve; from the fruits of the earth, the first earthly tabernacles were originated by the Father, and so on in succession. . . . Jesus, our elder brother, was begotten in the flesh by the same character that was in the garden of Eden, and who is our Father in Heaven" (*Journal of Discourses,* 1:50–51).

Now, in order to understand what "prophet" Young was saying, another of his pronouncements found in the same context should be considered:

> When our father Adam came into the garden of Eden, he came into it with a celestial body, and brought Eve, *one of his wives,* with him. . . . He *is our* FATHER *and our* GOD, *and the only God with whom* WE *have to do.*

As we have seen in the Mormon doctrine of "God," Mormon theology teaches that polytheism is the divine order. Belief in many gods is the cornerstone of their theology, and polygamous gods they are. Parley P. Pratt, a leading Mormon writer whose books are recommended by Mormon publishing houses as representing their theological views, also writes concerning this doctrine:

> Each of these Gods, including Jesus Christ and his Father, being in possession of not merely an organized spirit but also a glorious immortal body of flesh and bones . . . (*Key to the Science of Theology,* ed. 1978, 23).

Added to this polytheistic picture are other official Mormon sources, many of whom confirm the sexual conception of Jesus enunciated by Young and many others. Wrote Apostle James Talmage in *The Articles of Faith:*

> His [Christ's] unique status in the flesh as the offspring of a mortal mother [Mary] and of an immortal, or resurrected and glorified, Father [Elohim] (ed. 1974, 473).

Brigham Young, therefore, taught this unbiblical doctrine of which he spoke openly more than once as the following shows:

> When the time came that His first-born, the Saviour, should come into the world and take a tabernacle (body), the Father came Himself and favoured that spirit with a tabernacle instead of letting any other man do it (*Journal of Discourses*, 4:218).

> The birth of the Saviour was as natural as are the births of our children; it was the result of natural action. He partook of flesh and blood—was begotten of his Father, as we are of our fathers (*Journal of Discourses*, 8:115).

The crass polytheism of Mormonism was never more clearly dissembled than in the foregoing statements, and Young's classification of the Father as a glorified, resurrected "man" cannot be misunderstood. The phrase "any *other* man" rules out the efforts of Mormon apologists to defend Young and unmasks the entire anti-Christian teaching.

We see, then, the Mormon teaching concerning our Lord's birth is a revolting distortion of the biblical revelation and one that is in keeping with the Mormon dogma of a flesh-and-bone god. In Mormon thinking, as reflected in the authoritative declarations of one of their prophets, our Savior was produced, not by a direct act of the Holy Spirit, but by actual sexual relations between "an immortal or resurrected and glorified Father" and Mary—a blasphemous view, which takes its place beside the infamous mythology of Greece, wherein the gods fathered human sons through physical union with certain chosen women.

Brigham Young further declared: "He (Christ) was *not* begotten by the Holy Ghost. . . . Jesus, our elder brother, was begotten in the flesh by the same character that was in the garden of Eden, and who is our Father in Heaven" (*Journal of Discourses*, 1:50–51). There can be no mistaking the fact that the Adam-God doctrine is meant here, no matter how vehemently the Mormon apologists of today may deny that it was ever taught. The language is too clear, the cross-reference easily demonstrable, and the denial of His conception by the Holy Spirit evident for all to see.

Mormon leaders, however, while accepting the doctrine as Young declared it, are extremely careful not to allow "the Gentiles" (all non-Mormons) to understand the full impact of the teaching until they have come under extremely favorable Mormon influences. This is understood by the fact that in Leo Rosten's *A Guide to the Religions of America* (1963, 131–141), the Mormons employed the subterfuge of semantics to escape declaring this position to the general public.

In Rosten's book, the question was asked, "Do Mormons believe in the Virgin Birth?" (134). To which the Mormon spokesman, a high-ranking member of the Mormon hierarchy, replied, "Yes. The Latter-day Saint accepts the miraculous conception of Jesus the Christ."

Now, it is obvious that if LDS Apostle Richard L. Evans, the Mormon spokesman, had set forth the doctrine of Brigham Young, a doctrine that has been taught by his church and which appears in authoritative publications, even nominal Christians would have been shocked and goaded to some comments, and the one thing the Mormon Church does not desire is adverse publicity. Indeed they maintain a public relations staff in order to avoid such embarrassments. Mr. Evans resorted to semantic vagaries in an attempt to make his religion appear "orthodox," which it is not.

According to the revelation of the Virgin Birth as recorded within the Scrip-

ture, our Lord was conceived by a direct act of God the Holy Spirit, wholly apart from human agency. The Scripture is explicit in declaring that this conception took place while Mary was "espoused to Joseph, *before* they came together." Matthew, therefore, flatly contradicts Brigham Young in no uncertain terms, declaring: "She was found with child by the Holy Spirit" (Matthew 1:18). And the angel Gabriel, who appeared to Joseph to reassure him concerning the divine origin of Christ's conception, reiterated this fact by declaring, "That which is conceived in her is *of* the Holy Spirit" (verse 20).

Luke, the beloved physician, in his narrative of the Virgin Birth, describes the revelation of our Lord's conception in unmistakable terms: "The Holy Ghost shall come upon thee, and the power of the Highest shall overshadow thee: therefore also that holy thing which shall be born of thee shall be called the Son of God" (Luke 1:35).

Some Mormon apologists have attempted to prove from this verse, however, that the phrase "the power of the Highest shall overshadow thee" in fact refers to the Mormon god's impregnation of Mary, thus proving "the truthfulness" of Brigham Young's assertion. But as we shall see from Matthew's account, this is an impossible contention and is unworthy of further refutation.

It is true that many debates have been instigated over the nature of the Virgin Birth of Christ, but the Christian position has always been based upon a literal acceptance of the event as recorded in the first chapters of Matthew and Luke. It might be noted that even liberal and neoorthodox scholars have repudiated the grossly polytheistic and pagan concept enunciated by Brigham Young and handed down through Mormon theology.

We would do well to remember "prophet" Young's denials, "He (Jesus) was not begotten by the Holy Ghost. . . . Jesus, our elder brother, was begotten in the flesh by the same character that was in the garden of Eden, and who is our Father in Heaven," and contrast them with the reliable testimony of the Word of God:

> "When as his mother Mary was espoused to Joseph, before they came together, she was found with child of the Holy Ghost. . . . The angel of the Lord appeared unto him in a dream, saying, Joseph, thou son of David, fear not to take unto thee Mary thy wife: for that which is conceived in her is of the Holy Ghost" (Matthew 1:18–20).

The Mormon Church today finds itself, no doubt, in a very difficult position where this heinous teaching concerning our Lord's conception is concerned. Some Mormons with whom the author has spoken repudiate vehemently Brigham Young's doctrine of the Virgin Birth, maintaining that he never really taught such a thing; but upon being faced with statements from Young's *Journal of Discourses* and quotations from Mormon periodicals and magazines between the years 1854 and 1878, particularly, they are forced to admit that such was the teaching of their church under Brigham Young. Then, not wanting to appear as though they lack loyalty to President Young, they lapse into silence or reluctantly affirm it.

One Mormon writer and historian, B. H. Roberts, writing in the *Deseret News* (July 23, 1921, Section 4:7) went so far as to deny that the Mormon church taught the Adam-God doctrine or the doctrine of the Virgin Birth as pro-

nounced by Young. Mr. Roberts wrote in answer to the charge of the Presbyterian Church that "the Mormon church teaches that Adam is God . . . and that Jesus is his son by natural generation":

> As a matter of fact, the "Mormon" church does not teach that doctrine. A few men in the "Mormon" church have held such views: and several of them quite prominent in the councils of the church. . . . Brigham Young and others *may* have taught that doctrine but *it has never been accepted by the church as her doctrine.*

The unfortunate thing about Mr. Roberts' statement is that (1) he was not empowered to speak for the church, and (2) he is in direct conflict with the teachings of his church on the subject of prophetic authority, not to mention Talmage's *Articles of Faith* previously cited. He also used a carefully qualified term when he said that "Brigham Young and others *may* have taught that doctrine." As we have seen, Brigham Young *did* teach that doctrine; and according to the Mormon faith, Brigham Young was a prophet of God as was Joseph Smith, in the same category as Jeremiah, Ezekiel, or Daniel. So the fact that Brigham taught it—and no General Authority has ever contradicted it—demonstrates that it is the doctrine of the Mormon Church, despite any claims to the contrary. That the Mormon Church accepts as her doctrine the teachings of Joseph Smith and Brigham Young must, we feel, be documented beyond reasonable doubt so that the reader will become familiar with the unfortunate Mormon habit of redefining terms and qualifying statements to elude detection of their true teachings.

The following quotation is taken from *The Latter-Day Saints Biographical Encyclopedia,* an official publication of the Mormon Church, and clearly reveals the authority of Brigham Young and his high position in the church. In the light of this statement and numerous others, it is hard to see how his doctrines can be denied by the Mormons.

> In a revelation given through the prophet Joseph Smith, Jan. 19, 1841, the Lord says: "I give unto you my servant, Brigham Young, to be a President over the Twelve traveling council, which Twelve hold the keys to open up the authority of my kingdom upon the four corners of the earth, and after that to send my word to every creature."
>
> The Quorum of the Twelve stands next in authority to the Presidency of the Church, and in the case of the decease of the Prophet, the Twelve preside over the church with their president at the head, and thus was brought to the front Brigham Young, the man whom God designed should succeed the prophet Joseph Smith. . . . When the Twelve were sustained as the presiding authority of the Church, Brigham Young arose to speak, and in the presence of the multitude was transfigured by the spirit and power of God, so that his form, size, countenance and voice appeared as those of the martyred Prophet. Even nonmembers were struck with amazement and expected to see and hear the departed Seer.
>
> From that moment doubt and uncertainty were banished from the hearts of the faithful and they were fully assured that the mantle of Joseph Smith had fallen upon Brigham Young. After the martyrdom of Joseph and Hyrum, persecution did not cease; the Prophets were slain but truth did not die. The man who stood at the earthly head was taken away, but the authority which he held had been conferred upon others. . . . During his administration of thirty years as President of the church, he made frequent tours, accompanied by his asso-

ciates in the Priesthood. . . . Though he did not utter so many distinct prophecies, he builded faithfully upon the foundation laid through the Prophet
Joseph Smith, and all his movements and counsels were prophetic, as fully demonstrated by subsequent events. He was a Prophet, statesman, pioneer, and col-
onizer (1:8).

Supplementing this detailed account of Brigham Young's authority and position as a source of doctrinal reliability, the reader will find innumerable statements concerning the government of the Mormon Church in their circulated
literature, all of which indicate that every succeeding first president of the
church wears the "prophetic mantle" of Joseph Smith and Brigham Young; they,
too, are considered prophets of God as were Joseph and Brigham.

When all the facts are considered, two things emerge from the mass of evidence available, which no Mormon writer has yet attempted to explain away—
that is, the fact that the Mormon Church teaches the absolute authority of its
prophetic office and that Brigham Young is regarded as *second* greatest in lineage. When one reads, therefore, Young's statements concerning the nature of
God and the Virgin Birth of our Lord in particular, and duly notes the circuitous
tactics of the Mormons and their pointed lack of official denial where the teachings of Young and other prominent Mormons are involved, there is very little
left to the imagination as to their true teachings. The Christian, who reverences
the revelation God has given concerning the nature of His Son's birth, cannot
find fellowship with the Mormons who subscribe to the teachings of their
prophet. Henceforth, when Mormons speak of "the miraculous conception of
Jesus the Christ," let it be well remembered what they mean by these terms, for
in no way can they be equated with the teaching of the New Testament wherein
God has so effectively spoken: "That which is conceived in her is *of* the Holy
Spirit" (Matthew 1:20).

The blasphemous Mormon concept of Jesus' entrance into this world
through a sexual union between Father God (an exalted man) and the Virgin
Mary is reduced to sireship like that of the lower animal kingdom. Apostle James
Talmage referred to the act as "celestial sireship" (*Jesus the Christ*, 81), and
prophet Ezra Taft Benson said, "The Church of Jesus Christ of Latter-day Saints
proclaims that Jesus Christ is the Son of God in the most literal sense. The body
in which He performed His mission in the flesh was sired by that same Holy
Being we worship as God, our Eternal Father" (*Teachings of Ezra Taft Benson*, 7).

Salvation and Judgment in Mormonism

Personal salvation in Mormonism is one of the doctrines most heavily emphasized, and since Christianity is the Gospel or "Good News" of God's redemption in Christ, it is inevitable that the two should come into conflict.

The Mormon doctrine of salvation involves not only faith in Christ, but baptism by immersion, obedience to the teaching of the Mormon Church, good
works, and "keeping the commandments of God (which) will cleanse away the
stain of sin" (*Journal of Discourses*, 2:4). Apparently Brigham was ignorant of the
biblical pronouncement that "without the shedding of blood there is no remission [of sin]" (Hebrews 9:22).

The Mormon teaching concerning salvation is, therefore, quite the oppo-

site of the New Testament revelation of justification by faith and redemption solely by grace through faith in Christ (Ephesians 2:8–10).

Brigham Young, an authoritative Mormon source by any standard, was quite opposed to the Christian doctrine of salvation, which teaches that a person may at any time sincerely repent of his sins, even at the eleventh hour, and receive forgiveness and eternal life. Wrote Brigham:

"Some of our old traditions teach us that a man guilty of atrocious and murderous acts may savingly repent on the scaffold; and upon his execution will hear the expression 'Bless God! he has gone to heaven, to be crowned in glory, through the all-redeeming merits of Christ the Lord!' This is all nonsense. Such a character will never see heaven" (*Journal of Discourses*, 8:61).

However, Jesus addressed the thief on the cross who had repented of his sins at the last moment, so to speak, crying: "Lord, remember me when thou comest into thy kingdom" (Luke 23:42). The answer of our Savior was unequivocal: "Today shalt thou be with me in paradise" (Luke 23:43).

Mormon teaching skirts these verses by claiming that "paradise" is the spirit prison where the dead go to hear the Mormon "gospel" preached. On page 309 of *Teachings of the Prophet Joseph Smith*, Joseph Smith claimed Luke 23:43 should read, "This day thou shalt be with me in the world of spirits." It should be noted, however, that Smith does not give this rendering in his *Joseph Smith Translation* of the Bible. In the JST it reads the same as the King James Version (in the JST it is verse 44, not 43).

The parable of the laborer (Matthew 20:1–16) presents Christ's teaching that God agrees to give to all who will serve Him the same inheritance, i.e., eternal life. Brigham Young would most likely have been numbered among the voices that "murmured against the good man of the house, saying, These last have wrought but one hour, and thou hast made them equal unto us, which have borne the burden and the heat of the day" (vv. 11–12).

The answer of the Lord is, however, crystal clear: "Friend, I do thee no wrong: did not thou agree with me for a penny? Take what is thine, and go thy way: I will give unto the last workers, even as unto thee. Is it not lawful for me to do what I will with mine own? Is thine eye evil, because I am good?" (vv. 13–15).

Our Lord was obviously teaching, to use a modern illustration, that the "base pay" given to all laborers in the kingdom is the same; namely, eternal redemption. But the rewards are different for length and content of the services rendered, so whoever comes to Christ for salvation receives it, whether at the first hour or the eleventh hour. The "gift of God," the Scripture tells us, is "eternal life," and although rewards for services may be earned as the believer surrenders himself to the power of the Holy Spirit and bears fruit for the Lord, God is no respecter of persons. His salvation is equally dispensed without favor to all who will come.

According to the Mormon scheme of salvation, the gods who created this earth actually planned that Adam, who was to become ruler of this domain, and his wife, Eve, were foreordained to sin so that the race of man who now inhabit this earth might come into being and eventually reach godhood. The fall in the Garden of Eden was necessary for procreation to take place. According to

2 Nephi 2:25 in the *Book of Mormon,* "Adam fell that men might be; and men are, that they might have joy."

Since Mormons believe in the preexistence of the human soul, it is part of their theology that these preexistent souls must take human forms since it is necessary, in order to enjoy both power and joy, that bodies be provided. This was the early Mormon justification for polygamy, which accelerated the creation of bodies for these preexistent offspring of Joseph Smith's galaxy of gods. A careful reading of the *Book of Abraham* will reveal that life on this earth was designed by the gods to discipline their spirit children and at the same time provide them with the opportunities to reproduce and eventually inherit godhood and individual kingdoms of their personal possessions.

According to Mormon revelation, the site for the conception of these plans was near the great star Kolob, and it will come as no surprise to students of Mormonism to learn that Lucifer, who was a spirit brother of Jesus prior to His incarnation, fell from heaven because of his jealousy of Christ. Christ was appointed by the gods to become the Redeemer of the race that would fall as a result of Adam's sin, and it was this office to which Lucifer aspired, hence his antipathy (*Journal of Discourse,* 13:282).

Lucifer is even quoted as saying, "Behold, here am I, send me, I will be thy son, and I will redeem all mankind, that one soul shall not be lost, and surely I will do it; wherefore give me thine honor" (chapter 4 of the *Book of Moses,* found in the *Pearl of Great Price,* catalogs all of these events, including the fall of Satan and the establishment of the Garden of Eden, chapter 6, which Joseph Smith elsewhere "revealed" was really located in Missouri and not the Mesopotamian area).

The *Book of Moses* also records the fact that Cain, the first murderer, was the progenitor of the Negro race, his black skin being the result of a curse by God. On this basis the Mormons avoided and ignored blacks for years in their missionary work, believing that preexistent souls which were considered less than valiant in the "war in heaven" between Christ and Satan were punished by being assigned to black bodies during their mortality. Until 1978, they were denied all of the "blessings" and "privileges" of the priesthood, but a revelation of convenience gave them full access to these glories and neatly removed the last major obstacle to the Mormon "evangelization" of Africa and the rest of the free world.

The Indians, who are supposedly the descendants of the *Book of Mormon's* wicked Lamanites, have allegedly been cursed by the Mormon deity with dark skins as a punishment for the misdeeds of their forefathers. Mormonism, then, is clearly a religion with a shameful history of white supremacist doctrines and practices.

These and many other interesting factors comprise the background of the Mormon doctrine of salvation, but it is also important to understand the Mormons' teaching concerning their redeemer, one of the main areas of their controversy with historic Christianity.

The Mormon Savior

The record of the Bible concerning the Savior of the world, the Lord Jesus Christ, is well known to students of the Scriptures. In Christian theology, there

is but one God (Deuteronomy 6:4; 1 Corinthians 8:4–6), and Jesus Christ is His eternal Word made flesh (John 1:1; 1:14). It was the function of the second person of the Trinity, upon His reception by the sons of men, to empower them to be the sons of God (John 1:12); and this the Scripture teaches came about as a result of God's unmerited favor and His great love toward a lost race.

The Lord Jesus offered one eternal sacrifice for all sins, and His salvation comes not by the works of the law or any human works whatever (Galatians 2:16; Ephesians 2:9), but solely by grace through faith (Ephesians 2:8). The Savior of the New Testament revelation existed eternally as God; lived a holy, harmless, and undefiled life, separate from sinners; and "knew no sin." He was "a man of sorrows, and acquainted with grief" (Isaiah 53:3), "the Lamb of God which taketh away the sin of the world" (John 1:29).

The Savior of Mormonism, however, is an entirely different person, as their official publications clearly reveal. The Mormon "Savior" is not the second person of the Christian Trinity, since, as we have previously seen, Mormons reject the Christian doctrine of the Trinity, and he is not even a careful replica of the New Testament Redeemer. In Mormon theology, Christ as a preexistent spirit was not only the spirit brother of the devil (as alluded to in the *Pearl of Great Price*, Moses 4:1–4 and later reaffirmed by Brigham Young in the *Journal of Discourses*, 13:282), but celebrated his own marriage to "Mary and Martha, and the other Mary," at Cana of Galilee, "whereby he could see his seed, before he was crucified" (Apostle Orson Hyde, *Journal of Discourses*, 4:259; 2:82). As we have seen previously, the Mormon concept of the Virgin Birth, alone, distinguishes their "Christ" from the Christ of the Bible.

In addition to this revolting concept, Brigham Young categorically stated that the sacrifice made upon the cross by Jesus Christ in the form of His own blood was ineffective for the cleansing of *some* sins. Brigham went on to teach the now suppressed but never officially repudiated doctrine of "blood atonement."

To better understand Young's limitation of the cleansing power of Christ's blood, we shall refer to his own words:

> Suppose you found your brother in bed with your wife, and you put a javelin through both of them, you would be justified, and they would atone for their sins, and be received into the kingdom of God. I would at once do so in such a case; and under such circumstances, I have no wife whom I love so well that I would not put a javelin through her heart, and I would do it with clean hands. . . .
>
> There is not a man or woman, who violates the covenants made with their God, that will not be required to pay the debt. The blood of Christ will never wipe that out, your own blood must atone for it; and the judgments of the Almighty will come, sooner or later, and every man and woman will have to atone for breaking their covenants. . . . All mankind love themselves, and let these principles be known by an individual, and he would be glad to have his blood shed. . . . I could refer you to plenty of instances where men have been righteously slain, in order to atone for their sins. . . . This is loving our neighbor as ourselves; if he needs help, help him; and if he wants salvation and it is necessary to spill his blood on the earth in order that he may be saved, spill it" (*Journal of Discourses*, 3:247; 4:219–220).

So clear-cut was Brigham's denial of the all-sufficiency and efficiency of the

atoning sacrifice of Christ in the foregoing quotation that Mormons have had to develop an argument "to explain" what the prophet really meant. It is their contention that a criminal is "executed to atone for his crimes and this is all Brigham Young meant."

However, they completely omit any discussion of the fact that Young's statement is not dealing with this subject at all. Young's statement declared that what Christ's blood could *not* cleanse, a man's own blood atonement could. This teaches that in some instances human sacrifice, which Brigham states took place and which he sanctioned, were efficacious where Christ's blood was not.

The Mormons want no part of the biblical doctrine of the all-sufficiency of Christ's Atonement, in the words of John: "The blood of Jesus Christ his Son cleanses us from *all* unrighteousness" (1 John 1:7, emphasis added). This both contradicts Young and reveals the true biblical teaching.

There can be no doubt from the biblical record that it is in Jesus Christ that we have redemption and that His blood is the means of the cleansing of the conscience (Hebrews 9:14) and of the loosening from sin (Revelation 1:5). It is the very basis of our justification (Romans 5:9).

The Christ of the Mormons cannot save, for He is as the apostle Paul describes him, "another Jesus," the subject of "another gospel," and the originator of a "different spirit," whose forerunner (the angelic messenger, Moroni) was anticipated by the apostle (Galatians 1:8–9), and who along with the entire revelation is to be considered "anathema" or more literally from the Greek, "cursed" by God.

It may be difficult for some to grasp what is in fact an incredible concept, but Mormonism fits perfectly into the descriptions given by the Word of God. The greatest of the apostles, in his second letter to the Corinthian church, after mentioning a counterfeit Jesus, gospel, and spirit, goes on to state that such occurrences should not come as a surprise to the Christian church.

"For such are false apostles, deceitful workmen, transforming themselves into apostles of Christ, and it is not surprising, for Satan himself transforms himself into an angel of light. It is therefore no great marvel if his servants also transform themselves as servants of righteousness whose end will be according to their works" (2 Corinthians 11:13–15, from the Greek).

This is harsh language indeed, but it is the language of God's choosing and it cannot be ignored by anyone who takes seriously the revelations of Scripture and apostolic authority.

Mormonism, with its apostles, priesthood, temples, secret signs, symbols, handshakes, and mysteries, quite literally masquerades as "the church of the restoration"; but at its heart, in its doctrine of the Messiah, it is found to be contrary to every major biblical pronouncement.

Salvation by Grace?

It is common to find in Mormon literature the statement that "all men are saved by grace alone without any act on their part." Although this appears to be perfectly orthodox, it is necessary to study *all* the Mormon statements relative to this doctrine in order to know precisely what they mean.

In one such official Mormon publication (*What the Mormons Think of Christ,*

B. R. McConkie, 1973), the Mormons give their own interpretation:

> Grace is simply the mercy, the love and the condescension God has for his children, as a result of which he has ordained the plan of salvation so that they may have power to progress and become like him. . . . All men are saved by grace alone without any act on their part, meaning that they are resurrected and become immortal because of the atoning sacrifice of Christ. . . . In addition to this redemption from death, all men, by the grace of God, have the power to gain eternal life. This is called salvation by grace coupled with obedience to the laws and ordinances of the gospel. Hence Nephi was led to write: "We labor diligently to write, to persuade our children, and also our brethren, to believe in Christ, and to be reconciled to God; for we know that it is by grace that we are saved *after all we can do.*"
>
> Christians speak often of the blood of Christ and its cleansing power. Much that is believed and taught on this subject, however, is such utter nonsense and so palpably false that to believe it is to lose one's salvation. Many go so far, for instance, as to pretend and, at least, to believe that if we confess Christ with our lips and avow that we accept Him as our personal Saviour, we are thereby saved. His blood, without other act than mere belief, they say, makes us clean. . . . Finally in our day, he has said plainly: "My blood shall not cleanse them if they hear me not." Salvation in the kingdom of God is available because of the atoning blood of Christ. But it is received only on condition of faith, repentance, baptism, and *enduring to the end in keeping the commandments of God* (pp. 27–33, emphasis added).

The above quote is a typical example of what might be termed theological double-talk, which in one breath affirms grace as a saving principle and in the next declares that it is "coupled with obedience to the law and ordinances of the gospel," and ends by declaring that confession of Christ and acceptance of Him as "personal Savior" is "utter nonsense" and "palpably false." McConkie decries the fact that Christ's blood "without other act than mere belief . . . makes us clean" (p. 31).

The biblical position is, however, quite clear in this area; we are saved by grace alone, as previously mentioned, but it in no way enables us to "have power to progress and become like Him." As we have seen, in the Mormon sense such a progression refers to becoming a god, not to the Christian doctrine of sanctification, or of the life of the believer being brought into conformity to the Holy Spirit as clearly enunciated in the epistle to the Romans (chapters 8 and 12).

Mr. McConkie's assertion—that "salvation by grace" must be "coupled with obedience with the laws and ordinances of the gospel" in order for a person to be saved—introduces immediately the whole Mormon collection of legalistic observances and requirements. In the end, salvation is not by grace at all, but it is in reality connected with human efforts: ". . . baptism, and enduring to the end in keeping the commandments of God" (p. 33).

This is not the Christian doctrine of redemption that the apostle Peter described graphically when he wrote:

> Forasmuch as ye know that ye were not redeemed with corruptible things, as silver and gold, from your vain conversation received by tradition from your fathers; but with the precious blood of Christ, as of a lamb without blemish and without spot. . . . Being born again, not of corruptible seed, but of incorruptible, by the word of God, which liveth and abideth for ever (1 Peter 1:18–19, 23).

In diametric opposition to the Mormon concept, the confession of Christ with the lips and the acceptance of Him as "our personal Savior" is indeed the very means of personal salvation. It is the biblical record which states that "with the heart man believeth unto righteousness; and with the mouth confession is made unto salvation" (Romans 10:10). The gospel's command is "believe on the Lord Jesus Christ, and thou shalt be saved" (Acts 16:31). This is, of course, totally foreign to what the Mormons would have us believe. Jesus Christ did not die merely to insure our resurrection, as Mr. McConkie declares (p. 27), but He died to reconcile us to God, to save us by grace, to redeem us by blood, and to sanctify us by His Spirit. But such biblical doctrines the Mormons most decidedly reject. It appears that they cannot conceive of a God who could save apart from human effort, and Nephi's statement betrays this: "For we know it is by grace that we are saved *after all we can do*" (p. 28).

In Mormonism, it is they who must strive for perfection, sanctification, and godhood. Grace is merely incidental.

It was no less an authority than Brigham Young who taught concerning salvation:

"But as many as received Him, to them gave he power to *continue* to be the sons of God" (*Journal of Discourses*, 12:100–101).

In Brigham's theology, "instead of receiving the gospel to become the sons of God, my language would be—to receive the gospel that we may continue to be the sons of God. Are we not all sons of God when we are born into this world? Old Pharaoh, King of Egypt, was just as much a son of God as Moses and Aaron were His sons, with this difference—he rejected the word of the Lord, the true light, and they received it."

In agreement with their doctrine of the preexistence of souls, the Mormons believe that they are already the sons of God and that the acceptance of God merely enables them to "continue to be the sons of God," a direct contradiction of the biblical record which states:

"But as many as received him, to them gave he power to become the sons of God, even to them that believe on his name" (John 1:12).

The apostle Paul points out, with devastating force, the fact that "they which are the children of the flesh, these are *not* the children of God: but the children of the promise are counted for the seed" (Romans 9:8, emphasis added).

The apostle, with equal certainty, affirms that only those who are led by God's Spirit can be called the sons of God (Romans 8:14). It is difficult to see how in any sense of the term, "Old Pharaoh, King of Egypt, was just as much a son of God as Moses and Aaron were His sons," as Brigham Young declared.

The biblical teaching is that "ye are all the children of God *by faith* in Christ Jesus" (Galatians 3:26, emphasis added), a fact Brigham obviously overlooked.

It is one of the great truths of the Word of God that salvation is not of him that wills or of him that strives, but of God who shows mercy (Romans 9:16), and that Jesus Christ has redeemed us from the curse of the law, having become a curse for us (Galatians 3:13).

It was the teaching of our Lord that "all that the Father giveth me shall come to me; and him that cometh to me I will in no wise cast out" (John 6:37), and the salvation which He still offers to lost men is "not by any works of righ-

teousness which we have done, but according to his mercy he saved us" (Titus 3:5).

In the Mormon religion, they boldly teach universal salvation, for as Mr. Evans, the Mormon apostle and spokesman, put it: "Mormons believe in universal salvation that all men will be saved, but each one in his own order" (*Rosten*, p. 136).

It is the teaching of the Scriptures, however, that not all men will be saved, and that at the end of the ages some shall "go away into everlasting punishment: but the righteous into life eternal" (Matthew 25:46).

The somber warnings of the apostle John stand arrayed against the Mormon doctrine of universal salvation:

> And I saw the beast, and the kings of the earth, and their armies, gathered together to make war against him that sat on the horse, and against his army. And the beast was taken, and with him the false prophet that wrought miracles before him, with which he deceived them that had received the mark of the beast, and them that worshipped his image. These both were cast alive into a lake of fire burning with brimstone. . . . And the devil that deceived them was cast into the lake of fire and brimstone, where the beast and the false prophet are, and shall be tormented day and night for ever and ever. . . . And whosoever was not found written in the book of life was cast into the lake of fire. . . . But the fearful, and unbelieving, and the abominable, and murderers, and whoremongers, and sorcerers, and idolaters, and all liars, shall have their part in the lake which burneth with fire and brimstone: which is the second death. . . . The same shall drink of the wine of the wrath of God, which is poured out without mixture into the cup of his indignation; and he shall be tormented with fire and brimstone in the presence of the holy angels, and in the presence of the Lamb: And the smoke of their torment ascendeth up for ever and ever: and they have no rest day nor night, who worship the beast and his image, and whosoever receiveth the mark of his name (Revelation 19:19–20; 20:10, 15; 21:8; 14:10–11).

By no conceivable stretch of the imagination is universal salvation to be found in these passages where the Greek words in their strongest form indicate torment, judgment, and eternal fire that defies human chemical analysis.

The Mormon doctrine of "celestial marriage" derived from their original concept of polygamy and substituted for it in 1890, when they were forced to abandon this immoral conduct lest Utah not be given statehood, is tied to their doctrine of salvation. The Mormons believe that the family unit will endure unto the eternal ages, hence their insistence upon the sealing of Mormon men to many women, and the sealing of their families. It was for this reason that there are many special rites and ceremonies instituted in behalf of the dead (particularly relatives); hence, their practice of baptism for the dead and laying on of hands (for the bestowing of the gift of the Holy Ghost), all by proxy.

Mormon Eschatology

Believing as they do in the literal second advent of Christ, the Mormons teach that at His return the Jews will have been gathered to Palestine, the Mormons will be miraculously gathered together in Missouri, and the judgment of the Lord will be poured out upon the earth everywhere except on old and new Jerusalem. (See *Doctrine and Covenants*, 29:9–11.)

The Mormons also have something in common with the cult of Anglo-Israel, believing as well in the restoration of the ten lost tribes. The difference is that the Anglo-Israelites believe that the ten lost tribes are the English people, whereas the Mormons believe the ten lost tribes are somewhere in what Mormons call the "north country." In the words of Mormon Apostle Bruce McConkie, "In due course the one who holds the keys shall direct the return of the ten tribes from the land of the north. With 'their rich treasures' they shall come to their American Zion to 'be crowned with glory' by 'the children of Ephraim,' who already have assembled at the Lord's house in the tops of the mountain" (*Doctrinal New Testament Commentary*, 2:26). The *Doctrine and Covenants*, 110:11, states that Joseph Smith and Oliver Cowdery were given those keys by which to lead them.

Mormons also believe in the bodily resurrection of all men and in salvation in a three-fold heaven. In Mormon theology, there are three heavens: the telestial, the terrestrial, and the celestial. McConkie states that "most adults" will go to the telestial kingdom and that it is composed of "the endless hosts of people of all ages who have lived after the manner of the world; who have been carnal, sensual, and devilish; who have chosen the vain philosophies of the world rather than accept the testimony of Jesus; who have been liars and thieves, sorcerers and adulterers, blasphemers and murders" (*Mormon Doctrine*, 1966, 778). The second kingdom (the terrestrial) will be inhabited by Christians who did not accept the Mormon message, Mormons who did not live up to their church's requirements, and men of good will of other religions who rejected the revelations of the Latter-day Saints (*Mormon Doctrine*, 1966, 784). The highest or celestial heaven is itself divided into three levels. Only in this highest level is godhood or the possession of a kingdom for one's self and one's family to be gained. This particular estate has as its prerequisite the candidate's having been sealed by celestial marriage in a Mormon temple while upon the earth. Even in the celestial kingdom, godhood is by slow progression, and in the end each who becomes a god will, with his family, rule and populate a separate planet of his own.

It is almost superfluous to comment that this entire scheme of the consummation of Mormon salvation is the antithesis of the biblical revelation, which knows nothing of godhood, either constituted or progressive, and which teaches instead that in heaven the destiny of the redeemed will be the special providence of God himself, which "eye hath not seen, nor ear heard," and which has "never entered into the mind of men" for these are "the things which God hath prepared for them that love Him" (I Corinthians 2:9). God has revealed many of these things to us by His Spirit; but as Paul so eloquently puts it, we "see through a glass, darkly; but *then* face to face" (1 Corinthians 13:12, emphasis added).

Let us understand clearly, then, that salvation in the biblical sense comes as the free gift of God by grace alone through faith in the vicarious sacrifice of Christ upon the cross. The Lord Jesus Christ said, "He that hears my word and believes Him that sent me *has* eternal life, and shall never come into judgment; but has passed out of death into life" (John 5:24, emphasis mine, from the Greek).

The command of the Gospel to all men everywhere is to repent. "Because

[God] hath appointed a day, in which he will judge the world in righteousness by that man whom he hath ordained; whereof he has given assurance unto all men, in that he hath raised him from the dead" (Acts 17:31).

The Scriptures disagree with the Mormons in their insistence upon good works as a *means* of salvation. The book of James clearly teaches (chapter 2) that good works are the *outgrowth* of salvation and justify us before men, proving that we have the faith that justifies us before God (Romans 4 and 5).

No Mormon can today claim that he *has* eternal life in Christ. This is the very power of the gospel, which is entrusted to Christ's church (Romans 1:16–17). Let us therefore use it in an attempt to bring them to redemptive knowledge of the true Christ of Scripture and the costly salvation He purchased for us with His own blood.

John, the beloved apostle, has summed it up:

> If we receive the witness of men, the witness of God is greater: for this is the witness of God which he hath testified of his Son. He that believeth on the Son of God hath the witness in himself: he that believeth not God hath made him a liar; because he believeth not the record that God gave of his Son. And this is the record, that God hath given to us eternal life, and this life is in his Son. He that hath the Son hath life; and he that hath not the Son of God hath not life. These things have I written unto you that believe on the name of the Son of God; that ye may know that ye have eternal life, and that ye may believe on the name of the Son of God. And this is the confidence that we have in him, that, if we ask any thing according to his will, he heareth us: And if we know that he hear us, whatsoever we ask, we know that we have the petitions that we desired of him. . . . And we know that we are of God, and the whole world lieth in wickedness. And we know that the Son of God is come, and hath given us an understanding, that we may know him that is true, and we are in him that is true, even in his Son Jesus Christ. This is the true God, and eternal life (1 John 5:9–15, 19–20).

Let us follow in his train, "for the hour is coming in which no one can work," and the Mormons, too, are souls for whom Christ died.

We have seen in the preceding pages how the Mormon religion utilizes biblical terms and phrases and even adopts Christian doctrines in order to claim allegiance to the Christian faith. Mormons have also come to lay much stress upon public relations and take pains to make certain that they do not use language that might reveal the true nature of their theological deviations. We have also seen that the Mormon Church considers itself alone the true church of Christ in our age, and further that they consider all other groups to be Gentiles and apostates from the true Christian religion.

We further read the words of Joseph Smith himself, whom all Mormons are bound to recognize as the prophet of God, equal if not superior to any of the Old Testament prophets.

Wrote "prophet" Smith concerning an alleged interview with the deity:

> My object in going to inquire of the Lord which of all the sects was right, that I might know which to join. No sooner, therefore, did I get possession of myself, so as to be able to speak, than I asked the Personages who stood above me in the light, which of all the sects was right and which I should join.
>
> I was answered that I must join none of them, for they were all wrong, and the Personage who addressed me said that all their creeds were an abomination

in His sight; that those professors were all corrupt; that: "they draw near to me with their lips, but their hearts are far from me, they teach for doctrines the commandments of men, having a form of godliness, but they deny the power thereof."

He again forbade me to join any of them; and many other things did he say unto me, which I cannot write at this time."[24]

In addition to this statement of Smith's, Twelfth Mormon Prophet Spencer W. Kimball gave the following comment:

Latter-day Saints are true Christians. We cannot understand how anyone could question our being Christians. . . . We are the true followers of Jesus Christ; and we hope the world will finally come to the conclusion that we are Christians, if there are any in the world" (*Teachings of Spencer W. Kimball* [Book-craft, 1982], 434).

From these facts it is evident for all to see that Mormonism strives with great effort to masquerade as the Christian church complete with an exclusive message, infallible prophets, and higher revelations for a new dispensation that the Mormons would have us believe began with Joseph Smith Jr.

But it is the verdict of both history and biblical theology that Joseph Smith's religion is a polytheistic nightmare of garbled doctrines draped with the garment of Christian terminology. This fact, if nothing else, brands it as a non-Christian cult system.

Those who would consider Mormonism would be greatly profited by a thoughtful consideration of the facts and evidence previously discussed, lest they be misled into the spiritual maze that is Mormonism.

---

[24]Joseph Smith, *History*, 1:18–20.

Chapter 7

Christian Science

The Christian Science Church is headquartered on the fourteen-acre complex of the First Church of Christ, Scientist in the Back Bay section of Boston, Massachusetts. According to their official Internet homepage, the group has 2,300 branch churches in over sixty countries throughout the world. Approximately 1,600 of these branch churches are in the United States and about sixty are in Canada. While the church's by-laws forbid releasing membership statistics, outside estimates put the total number of followers at around 150,000. The body is governed by a five-member Board of Directors.

The current president of the Christian Science Church is J. Thomas Black, from Birmingham, Michigan. The organization is run by Black and his Board of Trustees of Boston's First Church of Christ, Scientist, the "Mother" Church. Unlike many cults in which the founder's successors retain the same status as the founder, in Christian Science all spiritual authority is vested in Mary Baker Eddy, not any other presidents, including Black. Christian Scientists call Eddy their "Leader," explaining, "Christian Scientists refer to Eddy as the Discoverer, Founder, and Leader of Christian Science."[1] It is to her writings and teachings that Christian Scientists refer for guidance: "The truth is in the Bible and *Science and Health*. And the proof is in nearly 125 years of consistent healing based on these books. You have come home. . . . This age is awake with discovery. . . . *Science and Health*, the Church that publishes it, and all of those united with this dynamic movement of thought are at the epicenter of this mental awakening."[2]

For decades Christian Science was the matriarch of the Mind Science family. With a large and growing membership, secular and religious respect, and great wealth, the Mother Church predominated the Mind Science movement and was

This chapter updated, revised, and edited by Gretchen Passantino and Cecil Price.

[1]"Questions and Answers: Why Do You Call Her Your Leader?" on the First Church of Christ, Scientist web site (http://www.tfccs.com), 1997.
[2]"Annual Meeting, 1997" on the First Church of Christ, Scientist web site (http://www.tfccs.com), 1997.

more important in almost all respects than Unity School of Christianity, Mind Science, Religious Science, Divine Science, and their other siblings.

However, during the 1960s a trend became apparent. Christian Science was losing members and income at a steady and significant rate. By the mid-'70s Christian Science members and even the public media were aware that the decline was long term and steady. Scandal rocked the Mother Church in 1976 with charges of financial, moral, and spiritual corruption among the top leaders.

In the early '80s the Christian Science cult regrouped its forces and began to present a calm face to the world, and since the middle of the decade has solidified its public image as a benign Christian denomination of thoughtful, spiritually mature people who enjoy a rather intellectual, quiet faith that gives them peace with God without any of the unappealing aspects of traditional Christianity, such as the existence of hell, the doctrine of the Trinity, or the incarnation, resurrection, and atonement of Jesus Christ.

But in the late '80s and early '90s the church again experienced stormy turmoil due to negative media coverage of lawsuits, financial difficulties, and internal upheaval. Several court battles produced international headlines as members were charged with manslaughter, murder, and child abuse for choosing prayer over medical treatment for illness. In Minnesota, one four-week trial in 1994 levied a $14 million punitive damage award against the Mother Church, which a judge later reduced to $10.4 million.[3] In 1995, the Minnesota Court of Appeals overturned this judgment.[4] This court left intact $1.5 million in compensatory damages against the parents and two Christian Science practitioners.[5] The United States Supreme Court refused to hear the appeal of this case.[6] Now the Mother Church, contrary to it's founder's philosophy, has revised its strong prohibition against medical treatment.

Though highly regarded by many, the Christian Science Publishing Society's media operations have struggled for years. According to *Forbes* magazine, the influential newspaper *The Christian Science Monitor* won respect not for proselytizing but for its sober and thoughtful international coverage.[7] Yet it has not turned a profit since 1961 with losses in excess of $250 million.[8] A television venture that began in 1986 was abandoned in mid-1992 after losing $235 million.[9] To obtain cash with these setbacks, in 1992 more than $40 million was borrowed from the employee pension fund to keep the church solvent.[10]

In 1991 a book rejected by the church over forty years ago, *The Destiny of the Mother Church*, which deified church founder Mary Baker Eddy, was published so that the Mother Church might receive a $97 million bequest from a

[3]Thomas Johnson, "Healing and Conscience in Christian Science," *The Christian Century* (June 29-July 6, 1994): 640.
[4][No author listed], "Court Nixes Wrongful Death Award," *Christianity Today* (May 15, 1995): 53.
[5][No author listed], "Christian Science Penalty Overturned," *The Christian Century* (May 3, 1995): 477.
[6][No author listed], "Christian Science Hearing Refused," *The Christian Century* (February 28, 1996): 223.
[7]Norm Alster, "Netty Douglass' Impossible Task," *Forbes* (September 17, 1990): 188.
[8]Ibid.
[9][No author listed], "Monitor Television Fades to Black," *Time* (April 27, 1992): 21.
[10][No author listed], "Television Retreat," *Time* (March 23, 1992): 48.

California church family.[11] According to the April 1, 1992 issue of *The Christian Century*, eight respected church publications editors resigned in protest, as the book violated Eddy's own beliefs.[12] Two other rival beneficiaries, Stanford University and the Los Angeles County Museum of Art, filed suit arguing that the church had not fulfilled the terms of the will.[13] A 1993 settlement gave the church $53 million, with the remainder split between the other two parties.[14] Also, the church was under investigation by the U.S. Postal Service for violation of nonprofit mailing rates.[15]

It is interesting to note that while groups such as the Mormons, Jehovah's Witnesses, and others are enjoying unprecedented growth in Third World and formerly communist countries, Christian Science continues to maintain the bulk of its membership among North Americans, Northern Europeans, and the better educated, more Westernized people of other countries. In terms of American-based cults, Christian Science ranks financially weak compared to the much larger cults of the Mormons and Jehovah's Witnesses, but is still in competition with other Mind Science-based cults individually, such as Science of Mind and the Church of Religious Science.

In 1997, as this book is being revised, the church faces an aging membership. It remains to be seen whether Christian Science will continue to be noteworthy or fade into insignificance in the twenty-first century. For the present, however, the Christian Science cult is a powerful force with which evangelical Christians everywhere must deal. While *The Christian Science Monitor*'s circulation was only 73,000 in 1997, an electronic version is available to millions on the Internet. An abundance of other Christian Science theology web sites exist that espouse the organization's doctrine. Most major university campuses have chapters of Christian Science Organizations (CSOs) consisting of faculty and students who put a mainstream face on current issues with Christian Science philosophy. Furthermore, each branch church maintains a Christian Science Reading Room in a prominent neighborhood location or on church property. These rooms contain Christian Science books, newspapers, journals, and Bible lessons that are available for public use, introducing seekers to Christian Science theology by a veneer of scholarship and a hefty coating of compassion. Newcomers are urged to attend a midweek "testimony" meeting, where more experienced Christian Scientists share their testimonies of "spiritual" healing through Christian Science meditation and prayer.[16]

---

[11]Carolyn Frida, "A Church That Needs Healing," *Newsweek* (March 23, 1992): 60.

[12][No author listed], "Christian Science Turmoil," *The Christian Century* (April 1, 1992): 330.

[13]James L. Franklin, "What Ails Christian Science?" *Christianity Today* (April 26, 1993): 54.

[14][No author listed], "Accord Reached in Book Lawsuit," *Christianity Today* (November 22, 1993): 42.

[15]James L. Franklin, "What Ails Christian Science?" *Christianity Today* (April 26, 1993): 54.

[16]See Robert Peel, *Spiritual Healing in a Scientific Age* (San Francisco: Harper & Row, 1987) for further information. While most of the claims of healing are associated with psychosomatic illnesses such as lower back pain, severe headaches, and other illnesses without physiological foundation, a few testimonies concern the supposed "healing" of more traditionally physiological diseases. However, the conclusive evidence of genuine healing is generally missing. Even the Christian Scientists' best witness, Robert Peel, admits that most healings are nonspecific, temporary, and/or of diseases with a strong psychophysical orientation. When contemporary Christian Scientists say that their healings are "documented," they mean that they have produced enough evidence of the sincerity of their patients that many health maintenance organizations (HMOs) cover prayer treatment by a Christian Science practitioner as they would the care of a chiropractor or other nontraditional medical "healer."

In the rest of this chapter, we shall examine its roots, founder, growth, and controversies, and contrast its teachings with the clear word of Scripture.

Of all the persons destined for religious prominence and success in the nineteenth century, none has eclipsed Mary Ann Morse Baker—better known among the band of faithful Christian Scientists as Mary Baker Eddy, "Mother" and Leader, the "Discoverer and Founder" of Christian Science.

Mary Baker was born in 1821 in Bow, New Hampshire, in the humble surroundings of a farm house and was reared a strict Congregationalist by her parents, Mark and Abigail Baker. The life of young Mary Baker until her twenty-second year was marked with frequent illnesses of both an emotional and physical nature,[17] and the then infant science of mesmerism was not infrequently applied to her case with some success.

In December of 1843, at the age of twenty-two, the future Eddy was married to George W. Glover, a neighboring businessman, whose untimely death of yellow fever in Wilmington, South Carolina, some seven months later reduced his pregnant wife to an emotional and highly unstable invalid, who, throughout the remaining years of her life, relied from time to time upon the drug morphine as a medication.[18]

Supporters of Christian Science have continued to deny Eddy's morphine use, but the evidence is incontrovertible. Her biographer, Robert Peel, noted, "In order to lessen the pain of the move the doctor gave her one-eighth of a grain of morphine."[19] Additional documentation of her morphine use, which increased during the last years of her life, are in the works of James Dittemore, Calvin Frye, and unpublished, handwritten material of Eddy's own. Dittemore was the former director of the Mother Church; Frye was Eddy's assistant until her death. To be sure, no informed person believes that Eddy was a "dope addict," but much evidence from reliable sources is available to show beyond doubt that throughout her life Eddy made repeated use of this drug.[20]

A decade passed in the life of Mary Glover during which she had many trying experiences, and then on June 21, 1853, she married Dr. Daniel M. Patterson, a dentist, who, contrary to the advice of Mary's own father, took the emotionally unstable widow Mary Glover for his bride.

The advice of Mark Baker was indeed ominously accurate, for some years later Mary Baker Glover Patterson divorced Dr. Patterson, who she claimed had abandoned her, and thus her second attempt at matrimony met with crushing disaster.

The third and last marriage of Mary Baker was to one Asa G. Eddy when Mary was fifty-six years of age. Asa Eddy's death of coronary thrombosis prompted Eddy to risk a nearly fatal mistake where Christian Science was concerned. She contested the autopsy report, and the physician she chose confirmed her conviction that Asa died of "arsenic poisoning mentally adminis-

---

[17]Georgine Milmine, *The Life of Mary Baker G. Eddy and the History of Christian Science* (Grand Rapids, Mich.: Baker Book House, 1937), 3–25.

[18]*New York World*, October 30, 1906.

[19]*Mary Baker Eddy: Years of Discovery*, 195.

[20]Ernest Sutherland Bates and John V. Dittemore, *Mary Baker Eddy: The Truth and the Tradition* (New York: Knopf, 1932), 41–42, 151, 445.

tered."[21] Such a radical report prompted an inquiry into the credentials of Eddy's physician, Dr. C. J. Eastman, Dean of the Bellvue Medical College, outside Boston. It was found that "Doctor" Eastman was running a virtual abortion mill, and had no medical credentials whatever to justify his title. He was sentenced to ten years in prison upon his conviction, and the Bellvue Medical College closed. Eddy had contradicted her own advice concerning autopsies.[22] And she would have been far better off to have practiced in this instance what she preached and to have abandoned Asa's remains to the scrap heap of mental malpractice, but the error was virtually unavoidable since Eddy was not to be outdone by any medical doctor. She was an expert healer by her own admission; the "mentally administered poison" report from the autopsy was therefore inevitable. Eddy's letter to the *Boston Post* dated June 5, 1882, in which she accused some of her former students of mentally poisoning Asa Eddy with malicious mesmerism in the form of arsenic is one of the most pathetic examples of Eddy's mental state ever recorded and one which the Christian Science church would like to forget she ever wrote.

The real history of Christian Science, however, cannot be told unless one P. P. Quimby of Portland, Maine, be considered, for history tells us that as Eddy was the mother of Christian Science, so Phineas Parkhurst Quimby was undoubtedly its father. "Dr." Quimby in the late 1850s entitled his system of mental healing "The Science of Man," and had used the terms "The Science of Christ" and "Christian Science" for some time before Eddy gratuitously appropriated the terminology as her own, something she dared not do while the old gentleman was alive and her relationship to him known to all.

Eddy's relationship to Dr. Quimby began when she arrived in Portland, Maine, in 1862 and committed herself to his care for treatment of "spinal inflammation." In November of that same year Eddy noised abroad to all men that P. P. Quimby had healed her of her infirmity. Said the then adoring disciple of Quimby, "I visited P. P. Quimby and in less than one week from that time I ascended by a stairway of 182 steps to the dome of the City Hall and am improving *ad infinitum.*"[23]

In later years Eddy's recollection of Quimby was somewhat different from her earlier echoes of praise, and she did not hesitate to describe him as a very "unlearned man," etc. Dr. Quimby termed his ideas "Science of Health." Eddy entitled her book *Science and Health With Key to the Scriptures* and filled it with numerous plagiarisms from the manuscripts of P. P. Quimby. In fact, Eddy plagiarized a great part of her work from Quimby and other sources and then had it all copiously edited by the Rev. J. H. Wiggin, a retired Unitarian minister. Wiggin revealed his part in her deceptive plan via the posthumous publication of an interview he gave to one Livingstone Wright, later published as a pamphlet entitled *How Reverend Wiggin Rewrote Eddy's Book.*

Our authority for exposing this plagiarism on the part of "Mother" Eddy is none other than Eddy herself, who wrote,

---

[21] *The Boston Post,* June 5, 1882.
[22] See *Science and Health With Key to the Scriptures* by *Mary Baker Eddy* (Boston: Trustees under the Will of Mary Baker G. Eddy, 1934), 196, and the 1881 edition, 1:269.
[23] *Portland Evening Courier,* November 7, 1862.

The best sermon ever preached is Truth practiced. . . . We cannot build safely on false foundations. Truth makes a new creature, in whom old things pass away and "all things are become new." . . . The way to extract error from the mortal mind is to pour in truth through floodtides of Love. Christian perfection is won on no other basis (*Science and Health*, 201).

In addition, Eddy made the following statement on the subject of plagiarism in her book *Retrospection and Introspection*: "There is no warrant in common law and no permission in the gospel for plagiarizing an author's ideas and words" (p. 76). So it appears that out of her own mouth Eddy condemned plagiarism, a practice from which she seemed to have extreme difficulty abstaining.

Eddy's plagiarism of Quimby's writings was well illustrated by *The New York Times* (July 10, 1904), which published parallel columns of Eddy's and Quimby's writings, proving Quimby to have been at least a partial source of her "revelation" of *Science and Health*.

From Quimby's *Science of Man*, expounded by Eddy in 1868, 1869, and 1870.

From Eddy's *Science and Health*, the textbook of the "Christian Science" she claimed to discover in 1866.

If I understand how disease originates in the mind and fully believe it, why cannot I cure myself?

Disease being made by our belief or by our parents' belief or by public opinion there is no formula of argument to be adopted, but every one must fit in their particular case. There it requires great shrewdness or wisdom to get the better of the error. . . .

I know of no better counsel than Jesus gave to his disciples when he sent them forth to cast out devils and heal the sick, and thus in practice to preach the Truth, "Be ye wise as serpents and harmless as doves." Never get into a passion, but in patience possess ye your soul, and at length you weary out the discord and produce harmony by your Truth destroying error. Then you get the case. Now if you are not afraid to face the error and argue it down, then you can heal the sick.

The patient's disease is in his belief.

Error is sickness. Truth is health.

In this science the names are given; thus God is Wisdom. This Wisdom, not an Individuality but a principle, every idea—form, of which the idea, man, is the highest—hence the image of God, or the Principle.

Understanding is God.

All sciences are part of God.

Truth is God.

There is no other Truth but God.

Disease being a belief, a latent delusion of mortal mind, the sensation would not appear if this error was met and destroyed (ed. 1898, 61).

Science not only reveals the origin of all disease as wholly mental, but it also declares that all disease is cured by mind (62).

When we come to have more faith in the Truth of Being than we have in error, more faith in spirit than in matter, then no material conditions can prevent us from healing the sick, and destroying error through Truth (367).

We classify disease as error which nothing but Truth or Mind can heal (427).

Discord is the nothingness of error. Harmony is the somethingness of Truth (172).

Sickness is part of the error which Truth casts out (478).

God is the principle of man; and the principle of man remaining perfect, its idea or reflection—man remains perfect (466).

Man was and is God's idea (231).

Man is the idea of Divine Principle (471).

What is God? Jehovah is not a person. God is Principle (1881 edition, 169).

Another instance of Eddy's plagiarisms is worth documenting. There is no doubt that she copied almost an entire selection from a book by Lindley Murray entitled *The English Reader* (4th ed., Pittsburgh, 1823). This plagiarized material is to be found in Eddy's *Miscellaneous Writings*, and is dated in that book September 30, 1895.

The English Reader, p. 98	*Miscellaneous Writings*, pp. 147–148
The man of integrity . . . is one who makes it his constant rule to follow the road of duty, according as the word of God and the voice of his conscience point it out to him. He is not guided merely by affections, which may sometimes give the color of virtue to a loose and unstable character.	The man of integrity is one who makes it his constant rule to follow the road of duty, according as Truth and the voice of his conscience point it out to him. He is not guided merely by affections which may sometime give the color of virtue to a loose and unstable character.
The upright man is guided by a fixed principle of mind, which determines him to esteem nothing by what is honorable; and to abhor whatever is base or unworthy in moral conduct. Hence we find him ever the same; at all times, the trusty friend, the affectionate relation, the conscientious man of business, the pious worshiper, the public-spirited citizen.	The upright man is guided by a fixed Principle, which destines him to do nothing but what is honorable, and to abhor whatever is base or unworthy; hence we find him ever the same—at all times the trusty friend, the affectionate relative, the conscientious man of business, the pious worker, the public-spirited citizen.
He assumes no borrowed appearance. He seeks no mask to cover him, for he acts no studied part; but he is indeed what he appears to be, full of truth, candor, and humanity. In all his pursuits he knows no path but the fair and direct one, and would much rather fail of success than attain it by reproachful means.	He assumes no borrowed appearance. He seeks no mask to cover him, for he acts no studied part; but he is indeed what he appears to be—full of truth, candor, and humanity. In all his pursuits he knows no path but the fair, open, and direct one, and would much rather fail of success than attain it by reproachable means. He never shows us a smiling countenance while he meditates evil against us in his heart. We shall never find one part of his character at variance with another.
He never shows us a smiling countenance while he mediates evil against us in his heart. . . . We shall never find one part of his character at variance with another.	Lovingly yours, Mary Baker Eddy Sept. 30, 1895

Finally, it should be mentioned that Eddy may have plagiarized from a third source, a portion of a manuscript written by Francis Lieber. Lieber was a distinguished German-American publisher and scholar. In 1936, a minister named Walter Haushalter published a book entitled *Eddy Purloins From Hegel*, in which he made public the contents of a portion of a manuscript reportedly written by Lieber on "The Metaphysical Religion of Hegel." This twelve-page document portion appears to have been plagiarized extensively by Eddy in *Science and Health*.

There is, however, some uncertainty as to the authenticity of the Lieber document. On the one hand, five top scholars examined the manuscript and in 1940 reported that, without a doubt, it was genuinely Lieber's, dated in 1866, and that it had been reproduced in portion without credit by Eddy. These experts included John Calvin French, Ph.D., Johns Hopkins University Librarian;

W. Stull Holt, Ph.D., also of Johns Hopkins; Johannes Mattern, Ph.D.; and a top handwriting and document authority, Arthur P. Myers. Another scholar, Arthur E. Overbury, examined the document personally and declared it authentic. No handwriting experts who have examined the original manuscript have ever declared it to be fraudulent (the study done by experts Osborn and Stein was based on a copy). These would appear to be strong reasons for accepting the Lieber document as genuine.

On the other hand, a great deal of evidence has also been brought to light that raises serious doubts as to its authenticity. A leading expert on Lieber, Frank Friedel, in his 1948 biography of Lieber gave several reasons why he did not accept the manuscript as genuine, and no recognized authority on Lieber has yet come out in support of the document. According to Friedel, the attitude toward Hegel in "The Metaphysical Religion of Hegel" is the exact opposite of that held by the historical Francis Lieber. Although Lieber was a German scholar, the manuscript contains a citation of the title of one of Immanuel Kant's books in German, containing the sort of errors in German that one might expect of an English-speaking person whose German was poor. Furthermore, the manuscript appears to have been plagiarized from a book written in the late 1880s by Otto Pfleiderer, which of course it could not have been if it was written in 1866.

In this light, the question of the authenticity of the Lieber document must be considered unsettled. There would appear to be strong reasons both for and against its genuineness. However, it is, at the very least, an example of the contemporary consensus of opinion in Eddy's day that her writings were not original. On the counts of plagiarism from Murray's *Reader* and from Quimby, the impartial observer must find Eddy guilty. Segments illustrating the parallels between Eddy's work and the "Lieber" document are presented below.

The Metaphysical Religion of Hegel by Francis Lieber

For Hegel and his true disciples there is no truth, substance, life, or intelligence in matter; all is Infinite Mind. Thus matter has no reality; it is only the manifestation of spiri. . . . Therefore science is spiritual, for God is Spirit (85).

Hegel science brings to light truth and its supremacy, universal harmony, God's entirety, and matter's nothingness. For him there are but two realities, God and the ideas of God, in other words spirit and what it shadows forth. Properly, there is no physical science. The Principle of science is God, intelligence, and not matter. Therefore science is spiritual, for God is Spirit and the Principle of the universe is (man). We learn from Hegel that Mind is universal, the first and only cause of all that reality is. Embryology affords no instance of one species

Science and Health with Key to the Scriptures by Mary Baker Eddy

There is no life, truth, intelligence, or substance in matter. All is Infinite Mind and its infinite manifestation, for God is all in all. . . . Spirit is God, and man is His image and likeness. Therefore man is not material; he is spiritual (468).

Christian Science brings to light Truth and its supremacy, universal mind, the entireness of God, good, and the nothingness of evil (293).

There is no physical science, the principle of science is God, intelligence and not matter; therefore, science is spiritual for God is Spirit and the Principle of the universe and man. We learn from science mind is universal, the first and only cause of all that really is.

Embryology affords no instance of one species producing another; of a serpent

producing another, the serpent germinating a bird, or a lion a lamb. The difference is not as great between the opposite species as between matter and spirit, so utterly unlike in substance and intelligence [are they]. That spirit propagates matter or matter spirit, is morally impossible. Hegel repudiates the thought (85–86).

To conclude that Life, Love, and Truth are attributes of personal deity implies there is something in Person superior to Principle. What, then, is the Person of God? Hegel makes clear that He has no personality as we now know personality, for this would imply intelligence and matter.

The body of God is the Idea given of Him, harmonious order of the universe and in man (male and female) formed by Him (82).

germinating a bird, or a lion a lamb. . . . The difference is not as great between opposite species as between matter and spirit, so utterly unlike in substance and intelligence [are they]. That spirit propagates matter, or matter spirit, is morally impossible; science repudiates the thought (10, 264).

To conclude Life, Love, and Truth are attributes of personal deity implies there is something in Person superior to Principle.

What is the Person of God? He has no personality, for this would imply Intelligence in matter; the body of God is the idea given of Him in the harmonious universe, and the male and female formed.

Wrote Eddy in *The First Church of Christ, Scientist, and Miscellany* (Boston: Trustees, 1941, 115) regarding her teachings:

> I should blush to write of *Science and Health with Key to the Scriptures* as I have, were it of human origin, and I, apart from God, were its author. But, as I was only a scribe echoing the harmonies of heaven in divine metaphysics, I cannot be super-modest in my estimate of the Christian Science textbook.

In a letter to a personal friend dated in 1877, Eddy stated concerning Christian Science, "The idea given of God this time is higher, clearer, and more permanent than before" (*Life of Mary Baker G. Eddy*, 73).

Let it not be thought by anyone that Eddy did not personally aspire to equality with Christ as some of her eager followers contend, for in the *Christian Science Journal* of April 1889, Eddy allowed the claim made in her behalf to the effect that she was equal, as chosen successor, to Christ.

In a book entitled *Christ and Christmas* (published in 1884) appear pictures and captions of both Eddy and Jesus Christ. That the two are considered at least on the same spiritual level, if Eddy is not to be regarded higher, is plain to see.

The evidence of the Murray *Reader* and the Quimby manuscripts (and possibly the Lieber document, as well) demonstrates Eddy's total lack of ethics in borrowing what was not hers and indicates that Deity had no part in the authorship of *Science and Health* or other of her writings. One would be foolish indeed to accept her claim at face value in light of such incontrovertible evidence.

The Figment of Divine Authorship

Let us return, however, to Eddy's explanation of how she "discovered" Christian Science.

According to an authorized statement published by the Christian Science Publishing Society of Boston, Eddy, after a fall on a slippery sidewalk February

1, 1866, was pronounced "incurable" and given three days to live by the attending physician (Dr. Alvin M. Cushing). The third day, allegedly her last on earth, Eddy (the statement makes out) cried for a Bible, read Matthew 9:2, and rose completely healed. Thus the statement claims "she discovered" Christian Science.

Corroborating this new story, Eddy in her book *Retrospection and Introspection* (38) declares that in February of 1886 (one month after Quimby's death), she was mortally injured in a sidewalk fall and was not expected to live. She, however, vanquished the angel of death in this skirmish, and on the third day emerged triumphant over her bodily infirmity.

This is the story maintained by the organization today, as a comment on the First Church of Christ, Scientist web site states:

> In 1866 [Eddy] was severely injured in a fall, and turned to the Bible as she had been accustomed to doing. All she had pondered in the past came strongly and clearly to her as she read an account of one of Jesus' healings. She was immediately healed. Convinced that God had healed her, she spent the next several years searching the Scriptures to understand the principle behind her healing. She named her discovery Christian Science and explained it in 1875 when she first wrote *Science and Health*.[24]

Eddy's two statements, the interested reader will note, substantiate each other in every detail; it is therefore most unfortunate that they should both be falsehoods. Eddy never discovered Christian Science in the manner claimed, never was in danger of losing her life in the manner described, and never "rose the third day healed and free," as she maintained.

Two incontrovertible facts establish these truths. They are as follows: (1) Dr. Alvin M. Cushing, the attending physician at Eddy's "illness," denied under oath in a 1,000-word statement that he ever believed or said that she was in a precarious physical condition.[25] Moreover, Dr. Cushing stated (contrary to the claims of Christian Scientists that Eddy always enjoyed robust health) that he further attended her in August of the same year four separate times and administered medicine to her for bodily ailments. (2) Julius Dresser (pupil of the late "Dr." Quimby) received a letter from Eddy dated February 15, 1866, two weeks *after* her alleged "recovery" from the fall on an icy sidewalk. In this letter Eddy alludes to the fall and claims Dr. Cushing resigned her to the life of a cripple. Eddy wrote:

> Two weeks ago I fell on the sidewalk and struck my back on the ice, and was taken for dead, came to consciousness amid a storm of vapors from cologne, chloroform, ether, camphor, etc., but to find myself the helpless cripple I was before I saw Dr. Quimby. The physician attending said I had taken the last step I ever should, but in two days I got out of my bed alone and will walk; but yet I confess I am frightened? . . . Now can't you help me? . . . I think I could help another in my condition . . . that yet I am slowly failing.[26]

Barring the obvious medical error of a doctor administering chloroform

[24]"How Did She Discover Christian Science?" on the First Church of Christ, Scientist web site (http://www.tfccs.com), 1997.
[25]The entire statement is reproduced in Milmine, 84–86.
[26]F. W. Peabody, *The Religio-Medical Masquerade*, 80–81.

and ether to an unconscious person, Eddy's account once again demonstrates her ability to think in paradoxes and contradict all reason and logical expression. The accounts are therefore spurious and complete fabrications.

Horace T. Wentworth, with whose mother Eddy lived in Stoughton while she was teaching from the *Quimby Manuscripts* (1867–1870), has made the following statement, and no Christian Scientist has ever refuted it:

> As I have seen the amazing spread of this delusion and the way in which men and women are offering up money and the lives of their children to it, I have felt that it is a duty I owe to the public to make it known. I have no hard feelings against Eddy, no ax to grind, no interest to serve; I simply feel that it is due the thousands of good people who have made Christian Science the anchorage of their souls and its founder the infallible guide of their daily life, to keep this no longer to myself. I desire only that people who take themselves and their helpless children into Christian Science shall do so with the full knowledge that this is not divine revelation but simply the idea of an old-time Maine healer.

Further than this statement, Wentworth has also recorded as incontestable evidence the very copy of P. P. Quimby's *Manuscripts* from which Eddy taught during the years of 1867 through 1870, a copy which also contains corrections in Eddy's own handwriting. Note, please, all this is undeniable fact—yet Eddy maintains that she *alone* "discovered and founded" the Christian Science religion. What a historical perversion the prophetess of Christian Science has attempted to perpetrate. Let it also be remembered that Eddy claimed for Quimby's theories, which she expanded, Divine import, owning that she only copied what God Almighty spoke.[27]

Let us return now to the personal history of the central figure of this analysis, Mary Baker Eddy—the still-reigning sovereign of Christian Science.

From the home of the Wentworths in Stoughton, Massachusetts, where, as we said, she taught from the Quimby manuscripts, Eddy went on to Lynn, Massachusetts, where she completed her "writing" of *Science and Health*, which she published in 1875. After leaving Lynn, largely because of the revolt of most of her students, Eddy came to Boston and opened what later became "The Massachusetts Metaphysical College" (571 Columbus Avenue), where she allegedly taught some 4,000 students at $300.00 per student over a period of eight years (1881–1889). One cannot help but wonder what would induce a reasonably intelligent person to spend that amount of money for a course that never lasted the length of a college half-semester and which was taught by a staff hardly qualified intellectually to instruct the ninth grade. Eddy herself knew nothing of biblical history, theology, philosophy, or ancient languages. Christian Science sources have attempted for years to prove that Eddy was a scholar in these fields, but the Rev. J. H. Wiggin, her literary adviser for some years, and himself an excellent scholar, has gone on record saying that she was grossly ignorant of the subjects in question.

When Eddy left the thankless community of Lynn, Massachusetts, she was then sixty-one years old and had less than fifty persons she could call "followers." As the calendar neared 1896, however, the indomitable will and perseverance of Mary Baker Eddy began to pay sizable dividends. Her churches and so-

---

[27] *Christian Science Journal* (January 1901).

cieties numbered well over 400 and the membership in them eventually increased from 800 to 900 percent. Considering what she had to work with, Eddy accomplished a financial miracle and a propaganda goal unrivaled for its efficiency and ruthlessness. From her ceaseless efforts for deification and wealth, there flowed continual revisions of *Science and Health*, which the "faithful" were commanded to purchase and sell, or stand in danger of excommunication from the Eddy autocracy. Should the skeptical reader wish proof on this point of history and on Eddy's insatiable greed for the comforts of financial security and power, we quote her announcement to that effect in its entirety:

> Christian Scientists in the United States and Canada are hereby enjoined not to teach a student of Christian Science for one year, commencing on March 14, 1897.
>
> *Miscellaneous Writings* is calculated to prepare the minds of all true thinkers to understand the Christian Science textbook more correctly than a student can.
>
> The Bible, *Science and Health With Key to the Scriptures*, and my other published works are the only proper instructors for this hour. It shall be the *duty* of all Christian Scientists to *circulate* and to *sell* as many of these books as they can.
>
> If a member of the First Church of Christ, Scientist shall fail to *obey* this *injunction* it will render him liable to *lose* his *membership* in this church.—Mary Baker G. Eddy.[28]

Please pay close heed to what Eddy said in the above quote. She did not ask, she commanded all Scientists as their duty to her church to "circulate" and "sell" her works and "obey" her "injunction" under penalty of loss of membership. If, perchance, a method of blackmail is ever rendered legal, it could not be stated in more compelling terminology than this encyclical from the Eddy throne.

But let it be observed that her religious pandering was not limited to one edition of *Science and Health*—no, Eddy extended her tactics to other fields, as well. For example, in February of 1908 she "requested" all Christian Scientists to read the "new" edition of *Science and Health*, which contained on page 442, beginning at line 30, information she affirmed to be of "great importance." Said Eddy:

Take Notice

> I request Christian Scientists universally to read the paragraph beginning at line 30 on page 442 in the edition of *Science and Health*, which will be issued February 29. I consider the information there given to be of *great importance* at this state of the workings of Animal Magnetism, and it will *greatly aid* the students in their individual experiences.—Mary Baker G. Eddy.[29]

One would assume from the tone of the language she used that here was a new revelation imperative to the defense against "Animal Magnetism" (the fiend all Christian Scientists continually ward off mentally), but such was not the case; instead, Eddy merely wrote what she had written a hundred times previously in different language. Said the material of "great importance":

---

[28] *Christian Science Journal* (March 1897).
[29] Ibid. (February 1908).

Christian Scientists, be a law to yourselves, that mental malpractice can harm you neither when asleep nor when awake.

Imagine paying $3.00, a healthy sum for a new book at that time, for these two sentences—the same old volume, excepting this "new" sage advice. And countless loyal Scientists obliged her wish by dutifully pouring their money into the Eddy treasury. It is no wonder that at her death Eddy's personal fortune exceeded three million dollars. None of this, unfortunately, was left to charity.

Current Christian Science esteem for *Science and Health* is still as great. Today Christian Scientists call the Bible and *Science and Health* their only "pastor," noting, "With the Bible and *Science and Health* as our pastor, Christian Scientists turn to prayer and these two books for counsel and healing."[30] Christian Scientists are promised, "Your dual and impersonal pastor, the Bible and *Science and Health With Key to the Scriptures*, is with you; and the Life these give, the Truth they illustrate, the Love they demonstrate, is the great Shepherd that feedeth my flock, and leadeth them 'beside the still waters.' "[31] Christian Scientists have no problem adding Eddy's book to the Bible as having equal divine authority:

> Humanity had the Bible for close to two millenniums without fully understanding how to use its truths in a scientifically provable way to heal and regenerate people like Christ Jesus did. To arrive at that kind of understanding, humanity needed to comprehend the Bible on a deeper level. They needed to "unlock" the Bible, so to speak. It was the specific mission of *Science and Health* to give the world this "key" to the Scriptures—to open up their treasures and enable everyone to use them.[32]

Eddy's reign had very little internal opposition and hence went unchallenged during her lifetime, but after her decease a definite scramble for control of her empire ensued. All but the most exacting students of Christian Science history have overlooked this battle for the vacated throne of Christian Science, but it is an important historical conflict and one that deserves consideration. Upon the death of Eddy, the Christian Science Board of Directors, in good business fashion, assumed control of her thriving empire and consolidated this coup by obtaining from the Massachusetts Supreme Court authority for their self-perpetuating directorate. It was over this issue that a schism appeared in the ranks of Christian Science, and after assuming the title "The Christian Science Parent Church," under the leadership of Annie C. Bill of London, the struggle commenced hot and heavy. John V. Dittemore, a member of the Christian Science Board of Directors, left the Boston camp and joined Bill in editing the *Christian Science Watchman* and acclaimed her as Eddy's successor. It was the contention of "The Parent Church" that Eddy intended to have a successor within a half century of her demise and never intended a self-perpetuating board of directors. The directors, no doubt for good financial reasons, stoutly rejected this view and defended their newfound gold mine. On February 6, 1924, Eddy's name was taken off *The Manual's* list of active officers and thus *The Watchman*

[30]"Questions and Answers: "Why Don't You Have Ministers?" on the First Church of Christ, Scientist web site (http://www.tfccs.com), 1997.
[31]Mary Baker Eddy, *Miscellaneous Writings*, 322.
[32]"The Pastor of the Church of Christ, Scientist" on the First Church of Christ, Scientist web site (http://www.tfccs.com), 1997.

claimed the board had proven its original intentions by fully occupying the most
powerful position in the Christian Science Church, forever eliminating the danger of a successor to Eddy.[33] The claim by Bill and Dittemore that the directors
had usurped the authority of Eddy and acted contrary to her expressed wishes
went unchallenged for the most part by the Christian Science Board of Directors, for Dittemore had strong evidence from *The Memoirs of Adam Dickey*, which
the board suppressed, and excerpts from the unpublished writings of Eddy's
secretary, Calvin A. Frye, that she expected a personal successor within fifty
years. Wrote Eddy:

> In answer to oncoming questions I will say: I calculate that about one-half
> century more will bring to the front the man that God has equipped to lift aloft
> His standard of Christian Science.[34]

But Eddy never picked her successor, and with the advancing years the
Christian Science Parent Church and *The Watchman* faded into obscurity, and
the controversy has long since been forgotten.

Continuing further into the Eddy legend, we are once again confronted
with the cold, impartial testimony of history where Eddy's boundless "gener-
osity" and "selflessness" are concerned. Shortly after the famous "Woodbury
Suit," wherein Eddy was accused of slandering a former disciple, the Christian
Science treasury showed a marked decrease in volume, the result of large legal
fees due in consideration of services rendered during the case. As a result of
this, Eddy perpetrated on the faithful the infamous "Tea Jacket Swindle," calculated to draw from her gullible followers the revenue with which to further
strengthen her treasury. In line with this scheme she drafted the following solicitation to her church universal, which appeared in the *Christian Science Journal*,
December 21, 1899:

> Beloved, I ask this favor of all Christian Scientists. Do not give me on, be-
> fore, or after the forthcoming holiday aught material except three tea jackets.
> *All may contribute to these.* One learns to value material things only as one needs
> them, and the costliest things are the ones that one needs most. Among my
> present needs material are these—three jackets, two of darkish heavy silk, the
> shade appropriate to white hair; the third of heavy satin, lighter shade, but suf-
> ficiently sombre. Nos. 1 and 2 to be common-sense jackets for Mother to work
> in, and not overtrimmed by any means. No. 3 for best, such as she can afford
> for her dressing room.—Mary Baker Eddy

The key to this whole financial angle is to be found in five short words, "*All
may contribute to these.*" Notice Eddy does not request two hundred thousand tea
jackets,[35] merely "contributions" toward them. No one was to send them—only
send the money to buy them. "Mother" Eddy must have enjoyed this neat trick
of replenishing her gold reserve, and none can deny that it was carried off with
a finesse that rivals any confidence game ever conceived. All this, mind you, in
the name of Jesus Christ and under the banner of Christian Science, allegedly
the true religion. Judge Rutherford of Jehovah's Witnesses could not have had

---

[33]*The Christian Science Watchman*, 4:7 (March 1928): 153–154.
[34]Ibid., 4:5 (January 1928).
[35]Estimated Christian Science Church membership in 1899.

Christian Science too far out of mind when he said, "Religion is a racket." Compared to Eddy, "Pastor" Russell and Judge Rutherford of The Watchtower Society were rank amateurs at collecting money. She played for the highest stakes at all times, and with Mary Baker Eddy it was always "winner take all," and she did!

Theological Structure of Christian Science

In outlining the theology of Christian Science, a series of primary quotations taken directly from official Christian Science books will prove far more useful to the average reader than any number of statements made by a non-Christian Scientist. Therefore, to enable the reader to have this valuable source material at his fingertips, I have listed sixteen of the major doctrines of historical orthodox Christianity and under each of their respective headings placed contradictory quotations derived from Eddy's writings, which will, I believe, provide more than sufficient documentation should any dispute ever arise concerning the proper classification of Christian Science as an non-Christian cult.

I. The Inspiration of the Bible
   Referring to Genesis 2:7:

   1. Is this addition to His creation real or unreal? Is it the truth, or is it a lie concerning man and God? It must be a lie (*Science and Health*, 524).
   2. The manifest mistakes in the ancient versions; the thirty thousand different readings in the Old Testament, and the three hundred thousand in the New—these facts show how a mortal and material sense stole into the divine record, with its own hue darkening, to some extent, the inspired pages (*S & H*, 139).

II. The Doctrine of the Trinity and the Deity of Christ

   1. The theory of three persons in one God (that is, a personal Trinity or Triunity) suggests polytheism, rather than the one ever-present I AM (*S & H*, 256).
   2. The Christian who believes in the First Commandment is a monotheist. Thus he virtually unites with the Jew's belief in one God and recognizes that Jesus Christ is not God, as Jesus himself declared, but is the Son of God (*S & H*, 361).
   3. The spiritual Christ was infallible; Jesus, as material manhood, was not Christ (*Miscellaneous Writings*, 84).

III. The Doctrine of God and the Holy Spirit

   1. The Jewish tribal Jehovah was a man-projected God, liable to wrath, repentance, and human changeableness (*S & H*, 140).
   2. God. The great I AM; the all-knowing, all-seeing, all-acting, all-wise, all-loving, and eternal; Principle; Mind; Soul; Spirit; Life; Truth; Love; all substance; intelligence (*S & H*, 587).
   3. (1) God is All-in-all. (2) God is good. Good is Mind. (3) God, Spirit, being all, nothing is matter. . . . GOD: Divine Principle, Life, Truth, Love, Soul, Spirit, Mind (*S & H*, 113, 115).

IV. The Virgin Birth of Christ

1. A portion of God could not enter man; neither could God's fullness be reflected by a single man, else God would be manifestly finite, lose the deific character, and become less than God (*S & H*, 336).
2. Jesus, the Galilean Prophet, was born of the Virgin Mary's spiritual thoughts of Life and its manifestation (*The First Church of Christ Scientist and Miscellany*, 1913, 1941, 261).

V. The Doctrine of Miracles

1. The sick are not healed merely by declaring there is no sickness, but by knowing that there is none (*S & H*, 447).
2. Sickness is part of the error that Truth casts out. Error will not expel error. Christian Science is the law of Truth, which heals the sick on the basis of the one Mind, or God. It can heal in no other way, since the human, mortal mind so-called is not a healer, but causes the belief in disease (*S & H*, 482).
3. The so-called miracles contained in Holy Writ are neither supernatural nor preternatural. . . . Jesus regarded good as the normal state of man, and evil as the abnormal. . . . The so-called pains and pleasures of matter were alike unreal to Jesus; for he regarded matter as only a vagary of mortal belief and subdued it with this understanding (*Miscellaneous Writings*, 199–200).

VI. The Atonement of Jesus Christ

1. The material blood of Jesus was no more efficacious to cleanse from sin when it was shed upon "the accursed tree" than when it was flowing in His veins as he went daily about his Father's business (*S & H*, 25).
2. The real atonement—so infinitely beyond the heathen conception that God requires human blood to propitiate His justice and bring His mercy—needs to be understood (*No and Yes*, 54).

VII. The Death and Resurrection of Christ

1. Jesus' students, not sufficiently advanced to understand fully their Master's triumph, did not perform many wonderful works until they saw him after his crucifixion and learned that he *had not died* (*S & H*, 45–46).
2. His disciples believed Jesus to be dead while he was hidden in the sepulchre, whereas he was alive, demonstrating within the narrow tomb the power of Spirit to overrule mortal, material sense (*S & H*, 44).

VIII. The Ascension and Second Coming of Christ

1. Until he himself ascended—or, in other words, rose even higher in the understanding of Spirit, God. . . . Jesus' unchanged physical condition after what seemed to be death was followed by his exaltation above all material conditions; and this exaltation explained his ascension. . . . In his final demonstration, called the ascension, which closed the earthly record of Jesus, he rose above the physical knowledge of his disciples, and the material senses saw him no more (*S & H*, 46).

IX. Satan and the Existence of Evil

1. Hence, evil is but an illusion, and it has no real basis. Evil is a false belief. God is not its author. The supposititious parent of evil is a lie (*S & H*, 480).

2. All these vagaries are at variance with my system of metaphysics, which rests on God as One and All, and denies the actual existence of both matter and evil. . . . There was never a moment in which evil was real (*No and Yes*, 24).

3. Sin, disease, and death do not originate in God, good. They are not ultimate realities of God's creation and are to be overcome as Jesus taught and illustrated. These evils result from the belief that man is separated from God and that life and substance are in matter, therefore limited and temporal. Instead, life and substance are seen as Spirit, God, therefore unlimited and eternal ("Questions and Answers: What is the Christian Science View of Sin, Disease, and Death?" on the First Church of Christ, Scientist Web site [http://www.tfccs.com], 1997).

X. The Nature and Existence of Hell

1. The sinner makes his own hell by doing evil, and the saint his own heaven by doing right (*S & H*, 266).

2. The olden opinion that hell is fire and brimstone has yielded somewhat to the metaphysical fact that suffering is a thing of mortal mind instead of body: so, in place of material flames and odor, mental anguish is generally accepted as the penalty for sin (*Miscellaneous Writings*, 237).

3. Heaven and hell are not regarded as specific destinations one reaches after death, but as states of thought, experienced in varying degrees here and now, as well as after death ("Questions and Answers" on the First Church of Christ, Scientist Web site [http://www.tfccs.com], 1997).

XI. The Kingdom of Heaven—Its Reality and Significance

1. Definition: HEAVEN. Harmony; the reign of Spirit; government by Principle; spirituality; bliss; the atmosphere of Soul (*S & H*, 587).

2. Heaven is harmony—infinite, boundless bliss. . . . Heaven is the reign of Divine Science (*First Church of Christ, Scientist and Miscellany*, 267).

XII. The Doctrine of Eternal Salvation

1. Man as God's idea is already saved with an everlasting salvation (*Miscellaneous Writings*, 261).

2. One sacrifice, however great, is insufficient to pay the debt of sin (*S & H*, 25).

XIII. The Doctrine of Prayer

1. Prayer can neither change God, nor bring his designs into mortal modes—I have no objection to audible prayer of the right kind; but inaudible is more effectual (*No and Yes*, 39–40).

2. If prayer nourishes the belief that sin is canceled, and that man is made better by merely praying, prayer is an evil. He grows worse who continues in sin because he fancies himself forgiven (*S & H*, 4).

XIV. The Creation of Matter and Its Reality

1. There is . . . no intelligent sin, evil mind, or matter: and this is the only true philosophy and realism (*No and Yes*, 38).

2. There is no life, truth, intelligence nor substance in matter. All is infinite Mind and its infinite manifestation, for God is All-in-all (*S & H*, 468).

XV. Man, the Soul, His True Nature and Destiny

1. Man originated not from dust, materially, but from Spirit, spiritually (*Miscellaneous Writings*, 57).
2. Man is God's image and likeness; whatever is possible to God, is possible to man as God's reflection (*MW*, 183).

XVI. The Existence of Sin, Sickness, and Death

1. DEVIL. Evil; a lie; error; neither corporeality nor mind; the opposite of Truth; a belief in sin, sickness, and death; animal magnetism or hypnotism; the lust of the flesh (*S & H*, 584).
2. DEATH. An illusion, the lie of life in matter; the unreal and untrue; the opposite of Life.

Matter has no life, hence it has no real existence. Mind is immortal. The flesh, warring against the Spirit; that which frets itself free from one belief only to be fettered by another, until every belief of life where Life is not yields to eternal Life. Any material evidence of death is false, for it contradicts the spiritual facts of being (*S & H*, 584).

As the preceding quotations indicate, the teachings of Christian Science are vastly different than those generally understood to comprise the fundamental teaching of historical Christianity. And it would be a foolish student indeed who did not take cognizance of these severe deviations from biblical theology and mark them well as evidence of another gospel, the product of plagiarism, the amalgamation of sources suitably doctored by a professional literary adviser, and made palatable to the average mind by the semantic manipulations of Mary Baker Eddy.

The philosophy of Christian Science is basically unsound syllogism, embodying all the logical mazes that the confused and untrained mind of Eddy wandered through. Theoretically, Eddy was an absolute idealist who denied outright the existence of matter from the tiniest insect to the most gigantic star in the celestial galaxies. But practically speaking, Eddy was a calculating materialist, an individual who thoroughly enjoyed all the material comforts derived from denying their existence. Hundreds of thousands of faithful Christian Scientists supplied their "leader" with all that money could buy and every material benefit available, yet Eddy continually affirmed the nonexistence of these material blessings by teaching in effect that they really did not exist to be enjoyed— they were "illusions of mortal mind," she said. In Eddy's philosophy all that exists is "Mind" (God) and "It" is "Good"; matter has no "real" existence at all. It should be mentioned here that Eddy never defined matter to the satisfaction of any qualified logician, so it must be assumed that she meant those elements that were recognizable to the five senses.

However, Eddy's vaunted metaphysical allegiance to this alleged rule crumbles weakly under the relentless hammering of sound logical principles. Let us see if the rule of inversion is always valid by applying it to similar constructions.

All rabbits are quadrupeds—(inverted) all quadrupeds are rabbits. Now, of course, any intelligent person can easily see that this inversion leads to a false conclusion, since dogs, cats, horses, and elephants are all quadrupeds and it is obvious they have no relation to the rabbit family. No rational person could therefore long entertain such logical absurdity, but it is exactly this kind of

reasoning that forms the basis of Eddy's philosophy and the entire foundation of Christian Science practice. Sin, sickness, and death are equally relegated to these peculiar logical dungeons of Christian Science reasoning processes and then represented as "illusions of Mortal Mind." Regarding this phantom "Mortal Mind," Eddy wrote:

> At best, matter is only a phenomenon of mortal mind, of which evil is the highest degree; but really there is no such thing as *mortal mind*—though we are compelled to use the phrase in the endeavor to express the underlying thought (*Unity of Good*, 50).

These are strange words indeed, are they not—giving a name to an illusion that does not exist, representing it as evil, which is equally nonexistent, and then blaming it for all physical woes, which cannot exist, since there is no reality or existence apart from Mind, or God? This type of reasoning is considered sound thinking by Christian Scientists the world over; however, the reader is urged to form his own conclusions dictated by the obvious facts that matter is demonstrably "real" and its decay and death are an ever-present problem.

These syllogisms—(1) God is all, God is Mind, therefore Mind is all, and (2) Mind is all, matter is not Mind, therefore matter has no existence—are only escape mechanisms from the objective world of material reality to the subjective world of idealism, which can never answer the problems of evil, sin, sickness, or material death since they are negated by the assumption that only Mind exists and it is immaterial, therefore not included in material categories. By denying even that portion of the mind which recognizes these physical realities, and calling it "Mortal Mind," Eddy has forever isolated herself and Christian Science from the realm of objective reality, since the mind that truly rejects the existence of matter must never allow for the limitations of matter, which constitute physical existence. But in practice, no Christian Scientist holds these tenets as an absolute—they all clothe, feed, and house the "illusion of Mortal Mind" called their bodies, and many go to dentists and surgeons for the filling of imaginary cavities and the setting of nonexistent bones.

If these facts are not proof positive that the entire philosophy of Christian Science in principle and practice is a huge philosophical hoax, then the author despairs of man's ability to analyze available evidence and arrive at logical conclusions. Even in its basic propositions, the Eddy philosophy is a sorry foundation for faith by all standards and an almost unbelievable imposition upon the principles of sound logic.

Inspiration and Authority of the Bible

Christian Science, as a theology, and all Christian Scientists, for that matter, both affirm that the Bible is God's Word and quote Eddy to "prove" that their whole religion is based upon the teachings of Scripture. Eddy said:

> The Bible has been my only authority. I have had no other guide in "the straight and narrow way" of Truth (*Science and Health*, 126).

However, Eddy and Christian Science have repudiated and contradicted this affirmation numerous times (see *Miscellaneous Writings*, 169–170, and *Science*

and Health, 517, 537, etc.), and in reality have perverted the clear teachings of the Bible to serve their own ends.

In Psalm 119 we read: "For ever, O Lord, thy word is settled in heaven . . . thy word is very pure . . . thy word is true from the beginning." The prophet Isaiah reminds us: "The word of our God shall stand for ever" (Isaiah 40:8), and Christ himself confirmed these great truths when he said: "The scripture cannot be broken. . . . Heaven and earth shall pass away, but my words shall never pass away" (John 10:35; Matthew 24:35). It will be remembered also that the apostle Paul stamped with divine authority the testimony of the Scriptures when he wrote: "All scripture is given by inspiration of God, and is profitable for doctrine, for reproof, for correction, for instruction in righteousness" (2 Timothy 3:16).

Coupled with these unassailable voices of testimony as to the Bible's authority, it is evident from the words of Jesus himself and the writings of His disciples and apostles that He believed in the authority of the Old Testament most emphatically, and even alluded to Old Testament characters and events as being within a historical context, thus establishing the authenticity and trustworthiness of the Old Testament.

The Bible declares that *it*, not Eddy and Christian Science, is the supreme authority on the activities of God and His relationship to man. Christian Science employs every art and method of paradoxical reasoning to escape the dilemma with which it is faced. It switches terminology around until the terms in question lose all logical meaning, and it spiritualizes texts until they are milked dry of any divine revelation whatsoever. To the average Christian Scientist, the Bible is a compilation of ancient writings "full of hundreds of thousands of textual errors. . Its divinity is . . . uncertain, its inspiration . . . questionable. . . . It is made up of metaphors, allegories, myths, and fables. . . . It cannot be read and interpreted literally"[36] Consequently, Christian Scientists believe, owing to the utter and hopeless confusion that the Bible allegedly engenders without a qualified interpreter, that it is necessary to have someone interpret the Bible for them. Eddy is the divinely appointed person to fulfill this task. Through *Science and Health*, she, they affirm, "rediscovered the healing principle of Jesus and His disciples, lost since the early Christian era," and has *blessed the world* with Christian Science—the "Divine Comforter." To all Christian Scientists, then, since they swear allegiance to Eddy, "the material record of the Bible . . . is no more important to our well-being than the history of Europe and America" (*Miscellaneous Writings*, 170).

The reader is asked to compare this supposedly "Christian" view with the foregoing scriptural references and the words of Christ and the apostle Paul, who said and wrote respectively:

> Sanctify them through thy truth: thy *word* is truth (John 17:17).
> But continue thou in the things which thou hast learned and hast been assured of, knowing of whom thou hast learned them; and that from a child thou hast known the *holy scriptures*, which are able to make thee wise unto salvation through faith which is in Christ Jesus (2 Timothy 3:14–15).

We are told in the words of Peter:

---

[36]I. M. Haldeman, *Christian Science in the Light of Holy Scripture*, 377.

> Knowing this first, that no prophecy of the scripture is of any private inter-
> pretation. For the prophecy came not in old time by the will of man: but holy
> men of God spake as they were moved by the Holy Ghost (2 Peter 1:20–21).

By these things, of course, we do not mean that God dictated or mechani-
cally reproduced the Bible, or even that He wrote tangibly, using the hands of
men as an adult guides the hand of a child, but that God spoke and caused to
be recorded truly and without error those things necessary for our salvation and
an understanding of His sovereign purposes and love. The Bible is the inspired
Word of God, and is wholly dependable in whatever fields it speaks. This, of
course, holds true only for the original manuscripts of the Bible of which we
have excellent reproductions. No scholar to our knowledge, however, holds to
the infallibility of copies or translations, which sometimes suggest textual difficulties. The Bible, therefore, stands paramount as God's revelation to man, the
simple presentation of infinite values and truths clothed in the figures of time
and space. Christian Science, by denying many of these truths and the veracity
of the Bible itself in favor of Eddy's "interpretations," disobeys directly the injunction of God to "study" and "believe" His Word, which alone is able to make
us "wise unto salvation through faith in Christ Jesus."

The Doctrine of the Trinity and the Deity of Christ

One prominent trait of all non-Christian religions and cults is their pointed
denial of the scriptural doctrine of the Trinity and the deity of Jesus Christ.
Christian Science ranges high in this category on the basis that it unequivocally
denies the true deity of our Lord and the triunity of the Godhead (Colossians
2:9). Eddy said, and most decisively so, that "the theory of three persons in one
God (that is, a personal Trinity or Triunity) suggests polytheism, rather than the
one ever-present I AM" (*Science and Health*, 256). Going beyond this declaration
Eddy also wrote: "Jesus Christ is not God, as Jesus himself declared, but is the
Son of God" (*S & H*, 361), and she crowned this travesty with the astounding
"revelation" that "Life, Truth, and Love constitute the triune Person called
God" (*S & H*, 331). Thus it was that with one sweep of an unblushing pen, a
vindictive, ignorant, untrained, and egocentric old woman banished the God of
the Bible from her religion forever. It is hardly necessary to examine at length
the doctrine of the Trinity and the deity of Christ to refute Eddy's vague ramblings, but it is profitable, we believe, to review those passages of Scripture that
so thoroughly unmask the pronounced shallowness of the Christian Science
contentions.

"Let *us* make man in *our* image, after *our* likeness" (Genesis 1:26).

"Let *us* go down, and there confound their language" (Genesis 11:7).

"Who will go for *us*?" (Isaiah 6:8).

Then we could mention Genesis 18 where Abraham addresses God personally as Lord (Jehovah) over ten times; the obvious plurality of the Godhead is
strongly implied if not expressly declared by the use of three angels to represent
God. The fact that God intended to beget a Son after the flesh and of the line
of David by virgin birth (Isaiah 7:14; 9:6; Micah 5:2; Matthew 1:23; Luke 1:35;
cf. Psalm 2:7; Hebrews 1:5; 5:5; Acts 13:33), that this Son in the likeness of flesh
was His eternal Word (John 1:1, 14, 18), and that He is true deity (Colossians

2:9; Philippians 2:8–11; Revelation 1:8, 17–18; Hebrews 1:1–4, etc.) and a separate person from God the Father is all indicative of the truth that Jesus Christ was truly the God-man of prophecy and the personal Messiah of Israel. It is fruitful to note also that Eddy recognizes the "true" God not as Jehovah but as "I AM" (*S & H*, 256), apparently oblivious of the fact that the word "Jehovah" is itself taken from the Hebrew verb form "to be" (Exodus 3:14), literally "I was, I am, I continue to be" or as the Jews render it "the Eternal"—(*YHWH*, the tetragrammaton). Keeping with this vein of thought it will be easily recognized that Jesus identified himself with the same "I AM" or Jehovah—and, in fact, claimed in no uncertain terms that He was that "I AM," (John 8:58) for which the Jews were ready to stone Him to death on the grounds of blasphemy (John 8:59 and 10:30–33).

As to Eddy's argument that Jesus was God's Son, not God, the answer is painfully simple when thoroughly analyzed. The solution is briefly this: Christ was God's Son by nature, not creation, as we are; hence, His intrinsic character was that of Deity—His attributes were Divine—He possessed "all power," etc. (Matthew 28:18). He therefore could not be a true Son unless He were truly divine; therefore, He could not be the Son of God at all without at once being "God the Son," i.e., of the very nature of His Father. The Scriptures declare God's Son is Deity—"The Mighty God . . . the Everlasting Father (Isaiah 9:6), or the Image of God (Colossians 1:15) . . . Impress of His Substance . . . Radiance of His glory" (Hebrews 1:1–3), etc. Innumerable testimonies as to His divinity are given, far too exhaustive to record here, but evidence nonetheless and beyond disputation. To reduce the Trinity so evident at Christ's baptism and the Great Commission ("In the name of the Father and of the Son and of the Holy Spirit," Matthew 28:19) to three of Eddy's choice terms, "Life, Truth, and Love," and declare all else "suggestive of heathen gods" (*Science and Health*, 256) is a prime demonstration of crass indifference to biblical terminology and historical theology—an emphatic Christian Science attitude instituted by Eddy.

John tells us that Christ was by His own admission *equal* in deity to God the Father (John 5:18; cf. Philippians 2:8–11; Colossians 2:9; Hebrews 1:3), yet inferior in position and form during His earthly ministry (John 14:28) as a man. The Eternal Word voluntarily humbled himself, became human and subject to our limitations, even to the death of the cross, the Bible tells us, but never for a moment did He cease to be what by nature and inheritance He always was and will be, God the Son, second person of the Trinity, eternal Creator and Savior of the sons of men.

Therefore, let us remember most clearly that Christian Science offers a dual Christ, a great man inspired by the "Christ idea" as Eddy would have it, one who never really "died" at all for our sins.

The Scriptures hold forth as a ray of inextinguishable light the deity of our Lord and the Trinity of God. We must therefore be ever vigilant in our defense of the personal Jesus who is our personal Savior, lest the impersonal Christ of Christian Science be allowed further opportunity to counterfeit the Christ of the Bible. This counterfeit, so widely taught in Christian Science, is merely another false theory that masquerades under the banner of the Christian religion and attempts to subvert the true Christian faith.

The Personality of God the Father and the Holy Spirit

In Christian Science theology, if it be properly understood, the term "God" is merely a relative one and bears no resemblance whatsoever to the Deity so clearly revealed in the Bible. As has been amply shown, Eddy interchanges the terms "Life," "Truth," "Love," "Principle," "Mind," "Substance," "Intelligence," "Spirit," "Mother," etc. with that of "God"; thus, Christian Science contends that God is impersonal, devoid of any personality at all. Biblically speaking, of course, this is a theological and historical absurdity since the core of Jehovah's uniqueness was His personal nature—I AM—indicative of a reflective and constructive Mind. Jesus repeatedly addressed His Father as a direct object, "I" and "Thou," postulating a logical subject/object relation in communion, and at least twice the Father answered Him (see Matthew 3:17 and 17:5), establishing His independence of person. This would have been impossible if God were circumscribed by Eddy's theology, for only a personality or cognizant ego can think reflectively, carry on conversation, and use the personal pronouns "I" or "He," etc.

The God of the Old Testament and the New is a personal, transcendent Being, not an impersonal spirit or force, and man is created in His image, that of a personal, though finite, being. The higher animals, to whatever degree they "think," are incapable of rationality and, also unlike man, of the faculty of "knowing," as Descartes once put it: "Cogito ergo sum" ("I think, therefore I am").

But far surpassing this elementary distinction between the God of Christianity and that of Christian Science is the inescapable fact that the God of the Bible does what only a personality can do, and these traits forever separate Him from the pantheistic god of Christian Science, which is incapable by definition of performing these things. Briefly, God is described as capable of doing the following things:

1. *God remembers.* "I, even I, am he that blotteth out thy transgressions for mine own sake, and will not remember thy sins" (Isaiah 43:25; also compare Psalm 79:8; Jeremiah 31:20; Hosea 8:13).

2. *God speaks.* "I am the Lord: that is my name: and my glory will I not give to another, neither my praise to graven images" (Isaiah 42:8; see also, Genesis 1:26; Isaiah 43:10–13; 44:6; Matthew 17:5; Hebrews 1:1).

3. *God hears, sees, and creates.* "And God saw that the wickedness of man was great in the earth" (Genesis 6:5); "God heard their groaning" (Exodus 2:24); "and when the people complained . . . and . . . the Lord heard it" (Numbers 11:1); "In the beginning God created the heaven and the earth" (Genesis 1:1).

4. *God "knows,"* i.e., *He has a mind.* "The Lord knoweth them that are his" (2 Timothy 2:19); "God is greater than our heart, and knoweth all things" (1 John 3:20); "For I know the thoughts that I think toward you, saith the Lord" (Jeremiah 29:11).

5. *God will judge the world.* "Therefore I will judge you . . . saith the Lord God" (Ezekiel 18:30); "Therefore thus saith the Lord God unto them; Behold, I, even I, will judge" (Ezekiel 34:20); "For we must all appear before the judgment seat of Christ" (2 Corinthians 5:10).

6. *God is a personal Spirit.* "God is a Spirit: and they that worship him must

worship him in spirit and in truth" (John 4:24); "I am the Almighty God; walk before me, and be thou perfect" (Genesis 17:1); God's Son is declared to be the "express image of his person" (Hebrews 1:3), therefore God is a person.

7. *God has a will.* "Thy will be done in earth, as it is in heaven" (Matthew 6:10); "Prove what is that good, and acceptable, and perfect, will of God" (Romans 12:2); "He that doeth the will of God abideth for ever" (1 John 2:17); "Lo, I come to do thy will, O God" (Hebrews 10:7, 9).

From this brief résumé of some of God's attributes, the interested reader can doubtless see the vast difference between the God and Father of our Lord Jesus Christ and the "Divine Principle" of Eddy's Christian Science. Psychologically speaking, a principle cannot remember; "Life, Truth, and Love" cannot speak audibly; nor can "Substance, Mind, or Intelligence" hear, see, create, know, judge, or will. The God of the Bible does these things; the god of Christian Science cannot. Christian Science may admit that a mind or an intelligence can do these things, but Eddy does not recognize the existence of personality in the Deity, and only a personality has a mind or an intelligence. Eddy's god (Principle) cannot create nor can it exert a will because Principle or even a principle, if you desire, does not possess a will by any logical definition. The god of Christian Science is an *it*, neuter in gender—merely a name—incapable of metaphysical definition or understanding outside of the maze that is Christian Science theology. The apostle Paul triumphantly reminds us, "I know whom I have believed, and am persuaded that he is able to keep that which I have committed unto him against that day" (2 Timothy 1:12). The true Christian has a personal relationship with his Lord; he prays through Christ and the power of the Holy Spirit; he asks that it might be given; indeed, personal contact is the very source of the Christian's life and spiritual peace. Christian Scientists have no such contact and consequently no real spiritual life or peace, only the riddles and incoherencies of Eddy and a basic uncertainty about good health.

Concerning the doctrine of the Holy Spirit and the attitude of Christian Science toward it, little need be said since Eddy's attitude was so obvious, but at the risk of repetition a short review may be profitable. As a matter of course, Eddy denied both the personality and office of the Holy Spirit and for His exalted ministry substituted "Divine Science" (*Science and Health*, 55).

To refute such a decided perversion of Scripture and historical theology one need only recall who the writers of the Bible, and Christ himself, considered the Holy Spirit to be in respect to personality and power. In the sixteenth chapter of John's gospel, Jesus instructed His disciples about their new ministry and duties and promised them a "Comforter" who would strengthen and guide them after His ascension. To quiet their fears Jesus told them that it was essential to the coming of the Comforter, who issued forth from the Father, that He (Jesus) go away. The Lord said:

> If I go not away, the Comforter will not come unto you; but if I depart, I will send him unto you. And when he is come, he will reprove the world of sin, and of righteousness, and of judgment (vv. 7–8).

It is useful to observe that the Greek text uses the masculine pronoun "He" and also "Him" for the Holy Spirit and ascribes to Him a will (v. 7) and the power to "reprove" the world of "sin, righteousness, and judgment" (v. 8).

"Divine Science" has not, will not, and cannot do any of these things because it denies the reality of sin, hence, excluding the need for righteousness, and teaches in place of judgment the pernicious unbiblical doctrine of man's inherent goodness. The Holy Spirit, therefore, is a person with a will and divine power to regenerate the soul of man (John 3) and glorify Jesus Christ. It should also be remembered that He does what only a person can do—He teaches us (Luke 12:12), He speaks to us (Acts 13:2), He thinks and makes decisions (Acts 15:28), and He moves us to do the will of God as He has moved holy men of God to serve in the past (2 Peter 1:21). Further than this the Holy Spirit can be lied to (Acts 5:5), He can be grieved (Ephesians 4:30), and He is often resisted (Acts 7:51). All these things denote dealings with a personality, not an impersonal force, and certainly not "Divine Science." Beyond these things the Holy Spirit sanctifies and separates us from sin and prays to the Father for us that we might be freed from great temptations (Romans 8:26).

Certainly these points of evidence disprove the meager attempts of Christian Science to reduce the third person of the Trinity to a metaphysical catchword ("Divine Science"), and reveal clearly for all to see the semantic deception Eddy has utilized in attempting to undermine this great scriptural truth.

The Miracles of Christ

The doctrine of the virgin birth of Jesus Christ is indissolubly joined with that of the validity of Old Testament prophecy concerning the Messiah of Israel. Isaiah the prophet tells us that "a virgin shall conceive, and bear a son, and shall call his name Immanuel" (7:14), and that this child was to be miraculous in every sense of the word. Indeed, so unique was this child to be that to Him alone of all the sons of men is the name God applied, the "mighty God" to be specific, the "everlasting Father," the "Prince of peace" (9:6). We are told that He shall reign forever (v. 7), and that the zeal of God himself will bring this to pass. Unfolding further the panorama of Old Testament prophecy, we are told that the child in question will be the Son of David (9:7), of royal lineage, and that He will be born in Bethlehem of Judea (Micah 5:2). Even more remarkable than these rays of light from God, the Scriptures further tell us that He was to be crucified for the sins of Israel and the world (Isaiah 53; cf. Daniel 9:26), and that He would rise again to life and come in power to sift the sons of men with eternal judgment (Psalm 22; cf. Zechariah 12:10).

But these facts are all a matter of history, which Jesus of Nazareth fulfilled to the letter, and which only remain to be consummated at His triumphant return as Judge of the world. Both Matthew and Luke declare the human fulfillment of God's plan in Mary's conception of the Christ child (Matthew 1:18–25; cf. Luke 1:30–38). Thus the physical existence of Jesus Christ is a biologically established fact. Christian Science vehemently denies this fact and teaches instead that Mary conceived the spiritual idea of God and named it Jesus (*Science and Health*, 29, 50). Denying as she did the reality of the physical universe, this was a strangely logical step for Eddy as opposed to her usual contempt for all logical form whatsoever. But be that as it may, all the wanderings of Eddy's mind, be they from Dan to Beersheba, can never change the testimony of Old and New Testament Scripture that a demonstrably "real" child was born to Mary, not an

"idea," that this child existed as a concrete physical being apart from His divine nature and is now forever, for our sake, both God and man in Jesus Christ. The Virgin Birth, therefore, is a well-supported biblical doctrine, which contradicts most forcibly the false concept Eddy has incorporated into the Christian Science religion.

Respecting the miracles performed by Christ during His earthly ministry, Christian Scientists, whether they admit it or not, must logically deny that they were miracles in the first place and discount them as merely "illusions of the mortal mind." Eddy states that disease, sin, sickness, and death are all illusions; they are not "real" because only Mind (God) is real and Mind is spiritual, not material. Therefore, following Christian Science theology to its "logical" conclusions, since the "illusion of disease" can exist only in "the illusion called matter," which is itself existent only in the illusion called "mortal mind"—which Eddy denies exists anyway—there were no miracles at all because there was no corporeal body to be diseased, hence no need for a cure. Eddy wrote:

> The sick are not healed merely by declaring there is no sickness, but by knowing there is none (*Science and Health*, 447).

This reasoning on the part of Christian Science theology presupposes the assumption that there is no evil, since God—Good—is all that really exists. Unfortunately it places them in the untenable position of having to account for the origin of the *idea* of evil, for even an illusion must have some basis in experience. In other words, the *idea* of evil is, in itself, an "evil," being contrary to reality; and consequently, if the *idea* of evil exists, then it must either exist within the nature of God ("All is God"), or there must be some real existence outside the nature of God. If "All is God," and evil thoughts exist, then God must have evil thoughts. Or, if "All is God," and God is wholly good, with no evil, then evil thoughts cannot exist. However, everyone who disagrees with Eddy has thoughts that are, in that sense, "evil." Either alternative makes Christian Science theology self-contradictory. Notwithstanding the circularity of this Christian Science argument, the Scriptures send a fresh breath of intellectual honesty into their account of Christ's true attitude toward disease, its reality and cure. The Lord Jesus never told the disintegrating leper, as Eddy's practitioners would, "You have no disease; it cannot exist; only God is good and He is all." Rather, He recognized the physical decay in the leper and by an act of sovereign grace restored the damaged tissue with one short phrase: "I will, be thou clean." It will be recalled that the leper in question said, "Lord, if thou wilt, thou canst make me clean" (Matthew 8:2–3). Christ's answer included none of Eddy's "Divine Science" or treatments by paid "quacktitioners" as they are sometimes called. He merely restored the form His power had originally created (Colossians 1:16) and destroyed the bacteria or root cause responsible for the disease. Jesus never healed by denying the reality of the disease He intended to cure. Rather, He affirmed its reality and glorified God for its cure.

You will remember that at the raising of Lazarus (John 11) Christ waited until his friend was physically dead beyond question (four days) and then restored to the function of life every cell of his decaying body and glorified God for the victory over man's second oldest enemy.[37] We should note in this

---

[37]Satan holds the dubious honor of being the first.

connection that Jesus did not deny the reality of death, as do Christian Scientists. He did not consider it "an illusion"; rather, He verbally confirmed it: "Lazarus is dead" (John 11:14).

Christian Science can find no support for its denial of the physical miracles of Christ; the facts are established. Should the reader desire further proof, however, he or she is urged to consult the following biblical references which prove, we believe, that the miracles of Christ were physical realities, the result of supernatural intervention on the part of God in behalf of His erring creatures:

1. *Matthew 8:14–15*. The healing of Peter's mother-in-law.
2. *Matthew 8:26–27*. Christ stills the tempest.
3. *Matthew 9:2, 6–7*. Jesus heals the palsied man.
4. *Matthew 9:27–30*. Christ restores the sight of two blind men.
5. *Mark 1:32–34*. Jesus heals the sick and casts out devils.
6. *John 2:1–11; John 6:10–14*. The miracles of changing water to wine and the feeding of 5,000 people.

Concluding this discussion, it should be noted in reference to John 2:1–11 and 6:10–14 that Christ would hardly have created wine from water or multiplied loaves and fishes to quench the thirst and satisfy the hunger of nonexistent bodies or "illusions of mortal mind," to quote Eddy. The nature of all Christ's miracles was that of a divine/human encounter, comprising empirically verified physical events to meet human needs—whether hunger, thirst, or suffering—not "illusions," as the theology of Christian Science attempts to make the unwary believe.

The Vicarious Atonement of Christ

There is no doctrine found within the pages of the Bible that is better supported or substantiated than that of the substitutionary death of Christ for the sins of the world. As far back in the biblical record as Exodus, Moses wrote of God's symbolic use of blood for purification and sacrifice. It will be recalled that Jehovah delivered the Israelites from Egypt by causing all the firstborn of the nation, including Pharaoh's own son, to fall under the shadow of sudden death (Exodus 12). The Jews were instructed in this instance to sprinkle the blood of the young lamb on the doorposts and lintels of their homes, and God promised, "When I see the blood, I will pass over" (Exodus 12:13). The Lord also instituted the animal sacrifices of the Levitical era and expressly stated: "It is the blood that maketh an atonement [covering] for the soul" (Leviticus 17:11). Following this typology through into the New Testament, we find that Jesus was called "the Lamb of God, which taketh away the sin of the world" (John 1:29), and further, that His blood shed upon the cross is our atonement or "covering" for sin, even for the sins of all mankind (Matthew 26:28; Romans 5:6–8; Ephesians 1:7; Colossians 1:20; etc.).

The believer in Christ, therefore, is saved by grace alone, through faith in His blood and its efficacy for the cleansing of all sin (Romans 3:25). John, the beloved disciple, reminds us in his powerful epistle, "The blood of Jesus Christ his Son cleanseth us from all sin" (1 John 1:7), and Peter no less resoundingly declares, "Ye were not redeemed with corruptible things, as silver and gold . . . but with the precious blood of Christ, as of a lamb without blemish and without

spot" (1 Peter 1:18–19). Indeed, like a crimson cord binding all the Bible into one compact testimony, the trail of blood courses from Genesis to Revelation, testifying from the mouths of unimpeachable witnesses the wondrous story of God's redemptive love. Listen for a moment to the record of Scripture, and the picture comes clearly into focus: God loved us and sent His Son to be our Savior.

"Christ died for the ungodly," Paul triumphantly cries, and "without shedding of blood there is no remission of sins" (Romans 5:6; Hebrews 9:22); He purchased the church with His own blood (Acts 20:28), Luke informs us, and John adds to the witness by declaring that Christ "washed us from our sins in His own blood" (Revelation 1:5). This was not a pagan sacrifice to placate the wrath of a heathen god's justice, as Eddy wrote, but a sacrifice offered "through the eternal Spirit" to free the sons of men from the curse of sin and open the path of salvation by which we may have "boldness to enter into the holiest by the blood of Jesus . . . a new and living way" to the very throne room of God our Father (Hebrews 10:19–20).

Contrasting this picture of concrete biblical theology with the views of Christian Science, no better illustration of Eddy's repudiation of this doctrine can be shown than that which comes from her own pen. As we have already noted, Eddy, in speaking of the Atonement, said this:

> The material blood of Jesus was no more efficacious to cleanse from sin when it was shed upon "the accursed tree," than when it was flowing in his veins (*Science and Health*, 25).

According to Eddy, Jesus, the disciples and apostles, and the early Christian theologians did not understand the meaning of the vicarious Atonement, but she did! She wrote:

> He atoned for the terrible unreality of a supposed existence apart from God (*No and Yes*, 55).
> The efficacy of the crucifixion lies in the practical affection and goodness it demonstrated for mankind (*Science and Health*, 24).

This is the opposite of anything the Bible teaches. When Jesus said, "This is my flesh which I shall give for the life of the world," and "This is my blood shed for many for the remission of sin," Eddy would have us believe that He anticipated no sacrifice for man's sin at all, but merely martyrdom for "the terrible unreality of a supposed existence apart from God." Further comment on this problem is not deemed necessary in the light of the obvious denial by Christian Science of this historically accepted biblical doctrine, so strongly supported by the Scriptures of both Testaments.

The Death, Resurrection, and Ascension of Christ

In our age of advanced medicine, we read of many miracles ascribed to the labors of medical science; but all these advancements, marvelous though they may be, have only delayed the inevitable decay and death of the body and have yet to guarantee us physical immortality. The Scriptures clearly teach us that "it is appointed unto men once to die, but after this the judgment" (Hebrews 9:27), even as they teach us that our Lord himself physically died at Calvary (Philip-

pians 2:8). In fact, the death of Jesus upon the cross is more thoroughly sub-stantiated from biblical and secular history than is His birth, which makes it even more difficult to believe that rational persons would deny it. Nonetheless, Eddy and Christian Science do deny it, and herein lies the necessity of refuting their illogical contentions.

Joseph of Arimathaea, it will be remembered, requested the dead body of Jesus from Pontius Pilate (Matthew 27:58) and properly prepared it for burial (vv. 59–60), as was the custom of the Jews. One thing that Joseph knew above anything else in the gathering shadows of the Sabbath that marked the solemn hour rent by bitterness, sorrow, and fear, was that the body of the Galilean prophet he buried was physically incapable of life; Jesus of Nazareth was dead. The absolute terror and doubt that gripped the immediate followers of Jesus could have come only from the personal knowledge that He had perished under the unbelieving Judeo-Roman conspiracy and that their cause was without a vis-ible leader and apparently doomed to failure. The apostle Paul tells us repeat-edly, "Christ died" (Romans 5:6); Peter recounts that He "bare our sins in his own body on the tree" (1 Peter 2:24), and John testifies that the soldiers "saw" when they came to Jesus "that he was dead already" (John 19:33). Certainly such intimate accounts cannot be lightly dismissed, yet Eddy and Christian Science boldly assert "His disciples believed Jesus to be dead while he was hidden in the sepulchre, whereas he was alive" (*Science and Health*, 44), and once again Eddy states:

> Jesus' students . . . did not perform many wonderful works until they saw him after his crucifixion and learned that he had not died (*Science and Health*, 45–46).

The issue is a clean-cut one. The Bible says Christ died upon the cross; Eddy and Christian Science say He did not. For those who call themselves Christians, the choice is not a difficult one to make. We hope those who are not Christians will accept the words of the Scripture in preference to Eddy, if only on general principles and the testimony of history.

The resurrection of Christ is treated on a similar basis by the Christian Sci-ence religion, which affirms that He never rose from the dead physically any more than He died physically, Eddy deliberately perverting numerous texts of Scripture to glean support for her unsteady propositions.

So it is that we learn how Christian Science often attempts to change the obvious meaning of texts. In the twentieth chapter of John's gospel, the resur-rected Jesus, to prove to the doubting Thomas that He was not a spirit but gen-uine "flesh and bones," presented His body bearing the imprint of the nails and spear for the disciple's examination. To His disciples at another time Jesus also said, "Handle me . . . for a spirit hath not flesh and bones, as ye see me have" (Luke 24:39). The resurrection of Christ and its startling revelation—namely, that He was who He claimed to be, the Son of God—is the one factor that most probably accounts for the rapid rise of Christianity's power over the lives of men. Here was a genuine opportunity to believe in a Savior who proved His divinity by vanquishing death, and who promised the same victory to those who believe and preach His Gospel. It is no wonder Satan has so vigorously op-posed this doctrine of Scripture, for upon it hangs the verity of our salvation.

As Paul puts it, "If Christ be not raised, your faith is vain; ye are yet in your sins" (1 Corinthians 15:17). Eddy and Christian Science may oppose this truth vigorously—as indeed they do—but the Gospel of Christ will not be hindered by mere denials, and their unbelief does not in any sense nullify the truth of God as the Scriptures so powerfully declare it:

> But now is Christ risen from the dead, and become the firstfruits of them that slept. For since by man came death, by man came also the resurrection of the dead. For as in Adam all die, even so in Christ shall all be made alive[38] (1 Corinthians 15:20–22).

As to the doctrine of the physical ascension of Christ into heaven, another denial is vouchsafed from the pen of Eddy. By the same method she uses to spiritualize the resurrection of Christ, Eddy also spiritualizes His ascension. She describes it this way:

> [The disciples'] dear Master would rise again in the spiritual realm of reality, and ascend far above their apprehension. As the reward for his faithfulness, he would disappear to material sense in that change which has since been called the ascension (*Science and Health*, 34).

Now, to any alert Bible student the ascension of Christ was a physical one; the disciples saw Him carried into the heavenlies visibly; it was not merely an upward stroke on the "spiritual scale" of existence, as Eddy put it, but a change of position from one sphere to another, visible in part to the human eye. In connection with this, one need only remember the testimony of the angels who escorted their Lord to His throne:

> Ye men of Galilee, why stand ye gazing up into heaven? this same Jesus, which is taken up from you into heaven, shall so come in like manner as ye have seen him go into heaven (Acts 1:11).

Beside these great declarations of Scripture, the confused writing of Eddy is conspicuously immature and inadequate because, as always, the Bible, which is the supreme Christian authority, confirms the truth as it really happened, not as Christian Science has imagined it happened.

The Existence of Satan, Evil, and Sin

Probably one of the most obvious doctrines of biblical theology is that of the origin, existence, and final disposition of evil. From Genesis to Revelation one can distinguish the powers set in array against God and His people, powers whose ultimate end is spiritual judgment of the most terrible order. We are told in the Scriptures that Satan or Lucifer, the "god of this world," was once a mighty and perfect angelic son of God whose dazzling and wondrous countenance earned for him the titles "Son of the Morning" and "Covering Cherub" (Isaiah 14:12; Ezekiel 28:14). The Scriptures also tell us that this powerful angel secretly cherished the desire to usurp the throne of his Maker (Isaiah 14:13–14), and upon gathering numerous supporters he rebelled against the sover-

---

[38]Or to more properly grasp the sense of the Greek, "As in Adam all die, so then through Christ shall all be resurrected."

eignty of Jehovah. The outcome of this wicked rebellion was the driving from heaven of Satan and the fallen angels that followed him, and he was subsequently allowed dominion over the celestial universe for reasons best known to God and himself, hence his title "prince of the power of the air" (Ephesians 2:2).

With this rebellion commenced the beginning of all evil or sin, i.e., that which is opposed to the will of God. After his rout in the heavenly encounter, Satan extended his kingdom over the heavenlies and earth, determined to disrupt, if possible, the plans of God. In the Garden of Eden Satan's desires reached fruition, and he succeeded in spiritually corrupting the future parents of the human race, Adam and Eve (Genesis 3). As punishment for this sin against the Lord, Satan was sentenced to a humiliating defeat by the "Seed" of the very creatures he had so willfully wronged (Genesis 3:15). This promised Seed who would bruise the head of Satan was to be the Messiah of Israel, who we have already seen is the Lord Jesus Christ. The final judgment of Satan will come after his complete and utter defeat at Armageddon, when he and all his followers from the ancient days of his heavenly citizenship will then be cast into the lake of fire, there to suffer eternally the righteous judgment of God (Revelation 20:10).

Despite this graphic biblical portrayal of Satan available for all to see, Eddy and Christian Science energetically deny his existence. Further establishing her contention that evil is nonexistent, Eddy flatly states:

> Hence, evil is but an illusion, and it has no real basis. Evil is a false belief. God is not its author. The supposititious parent of evil is a lie (*Science and Health*, 48).
> There never was a moment in which evil was real (*No and Yes*, 24).

Since Christian Science denies the origin of evil or Satan, it is only logical that it should deny evil, and sin as the result of evil. Concerning sin Eddy wrote:

> The only reality of sin, sickness, or death is the awful fact that unrealities seem real to human, erring belief, until God strips off their disguise. They are not true, because they are not of God (*S & H*, 472).
> Sin, sickness, and death are to be classified as effects of error. Christ came to destroy the belief of sin (*S & H*, 473).

Placing this declaration on a level plane with the biblical definition and development of the doctrine of sin, it is seen to be at complete odds with the biblical record. John reminds us that sin, far from being an "illusion" or a nonexistent force, is in reality a very potent enemy of man. "Sin," writes John, "is the transgression of the law," and further, "All unrighteousness is sin" (1 John 3:4; 1 John 5:17). Paul also admonishes, "For the wages of sin is death" (Romans 6:23). One can hardly be expected to believe that the Christian Science teaching about sin is truthful when both John and Paul, inspired spokesmen of God, so clearly contradict it. The Bible innumerable times declares: "All have sinned, and come short of the glory of God" (Romans 3:23), and, "If we say we have not sinned, we make him [God] a liar, and his word is not in us" (1 John 1:10). As to the personality and power of a personal force of evil (Satan), the Bible equally establishes his existence as opposed to Eddy's denials. Jesus, it will be remembered, spoke with Satan, who tempted Him (Luke 4:5–6). This could

hardly have been an illusion, even of the Christian Science variety, and the Lord also announced that He had come "to destroy the works of the devil," whom He described as a liar and a "murderer from the beginning" who "abode not in the truth," . . . "a liar and the father of it" (John 8:44). Eddy's devil, as her literary advisor, the Rev. J. H. Wiggin, so aptly put it, was Malicious Animal Magnetism, which she invented to explain away the rather obvious fact that evil and sin existed despite her affirmations to the contrary. This doctrine eventually became a mania with Eddy and drove her to irrational behavior and fantastically absurd demonstrations of temper, illness, and rapid excursions to different communities "when she felt the fiend closing in."

The Scriptures, therefore, give more than convincing proof "that God will judge sin" and that it is not an illusion but an ever-present enemy, of which all men, including Christian Scientists, must reap the wages in the end. It is comforting to know from a biblical standpoint that though "the wages of sin is death . . . the gift of God is eternal life through Jesus Christ our Lord" (Romans 6:23).

The Doctrines of Prayer and Eternal Salvation

The doctrines of prayer and salvation are inseparably joined in the Scripture with the decree and plan of God to redeem the fallen race of men. The Bible, in places too numerous to recount, encourages, instructs, and even commands us to "pray without ceasing" (1 Thessalonians 5:17) that God may reward our faith in His righteous judgments. The Lord Jesus often prayed to His Father for strength to meet the physical and spiritual rigors of daily life and finally the cross itself (Matthew 26:36). We remember also at the raising of Lazarus, pictured so vividly in the eleventh chapter of John's gospel, Jesus prayed: "Father, I thank thee that thou hast heard me. And I know that thou hearest me always" (vv. 41–42), and that He further instructed us to pray to the Father that seeth in secret; and the Father that seeth in secret will reward us openly (see Matthew 6:6). Above and beyond these elementary examples of Christ's attitude toward prayer, it is a well-established biblical fact that prayer by definition is a direct personal request to God for His intervention, whether it be for the purpose of healing the sick, raising the dead, or simply asking for grace and strength to live our separate lives (Philippians 4:6–7). The entire context of John's seventeenth chapter, for example, is devoted to recording the prayer of Christ for all His disciples, present and future, that they might be protected from Satan and the powers of darkness during their ministry of gospel truth. Jesus understood only too well the need for personal prayer to God in order to maintain close fellowship with our Father, and it is of this that He reminds us when He said: "Men ought always to pray, and not to faint" (Luke 18:1). Prayer to Christian Scientists, however, carries none of the meaning that the Bible so clearly portrays because, as Eddy taught, "prayer to a personal God hinders spiritual growth"[39]

We have seen, of course, that the God of the Bible is a personal Being, not a mere "Principle," as Christian Science contends; therefore, it is easy to see why the meaning of prayer to a Christian and to a Christian Scientist differs markedly. Eddy also wrote concerning prayer:

---

[39]Summarized by I. M. Haldeman, *Christian Science in the Light of Holy Scripture*, 268.

> Audible prayer can never do the works of spiritual understanding, which regenerates . . . (*Science and Health*, 4).
>
> The danger from prayer is that it may lead us into temptation (7).
>
> The mere habit of pleading with the divine Mind, as one pleads with a human being, perpetuates the belief in God as humanly circumscribed—an error which impedes spiritual growth (2).

It is singularly peculiar, in view of these contradictory claims of Eddy, that Jesus addressed His Father as a personal Being and commanded us to pray a personal prayer, "Our Father which art in heaven, Hallowed be thy name. Thy kingdom come. Thy will be done in earth, as it is in heaven" (Matthew 6:9–10).

If "Give us this day our daily bread. And forgive us our debts, as we forgive our debtors" is not a plea to God, then, perhaps Eddy's followers can tell us what in the name of reason it is. Eddy says, further:

> Prayer cannot change the Science of being, but it tends to bring us into harmony with it (*Science and Health*, 2).

What is more evident from this bold negation of Scripture than the fact that Christian Scientists cannot logically claim that they pray in the biblical sense at all, disbelieving as they do the clear definition the Bible gives of what prayer and communication with God really mean? It was written of the Lord Jesus that prayer was His constant habit, His unceasing attitude, and unwearied occupation; it is difficult, therefore, to believe that He would urge us to pray in the sure knowledge that it "might lead us into temptation," as Eddy implied it did. Moreover, the Lord Jesus prayed audibly and commanded His disciples to emulate Him: "Lead us not into temptation." But Eddy says audible prayer itself may lead us into temptation (*Science and Health*, 7). One need look no further for the source of her inspiration. It was obviously the great Counterfeiter (see Genesis 3:4–5). Paul, that noble apostle of personal prayer, instructs us to "let your requests be made known unto God" and to pursue "every thing by prayer and supplication with thanksgiving" (Philippians 4:6). Once again, the inspired apostle flatly contradicts Eddy's unscriptural teachings and those of Christian Science, a fact hardly necessitating further comment upon the subject.

Prayer is the lifeblood of the Christian's spiritual existence, and personal communion with the personal God our ever-present help in trouble, a relationship no Christian Scientist will ever enjoy as long as he or she does not know the God of the Bible or Jesus Christ; both of whom, biblically speaking, Christian Scientists unreservedly deny.

The doctrine of eternal salvation is so well-documented in Scripture that I feel sure no major comment at this stage of study is necessary; however, to clarify the doctrine as it is opposed to the Christian Science perversion of it, I shall here briefly summarize.

Eternal life, the Bible reveals to us, is to be found only in the cross of Christ, that supreme symbol of God's immeasurable love toward a lost and dying world. This life, the Scripture tells us, resides in the person of His Son, Jesus, "the true God" and "eternal life" (John 3:16; 5:24; 6:47; 10:28; 14:6; 17:3; 1 John 5:20, etc.). The Scriptures further testify that God sent His Son to be the "Savior of all men, specially of those that believe" (1 Timothy 4:10). The Lord Jesus Christ by His sacrifice on Calvary has purchased "eternal redemption" for us, prom-

ising that if we trust Him fully we shall at length be with Him where He is (John 17:24). God's Word assures us that our Savior is now at the "right hand of the Majesty on high" (Hebrews 1:3), and that someday, by His matchless grace, we, too, shall leave this vale of tears, forever free of earthly shackles, to "dwell in the house of the Lord for ever" (Psalm 23:6).

> For by grace are ye saved through faith; and that not of yourselves: it is the gift of God: Not of works, lest any man should boast (Ephesians 2:8–9).

This, then, is the true, the Christian meaning of salvation, not only freedom from fear, judgment, and the uncertainties of this earthly life but the knowledge of peace with God "through the blood of His cross" and justification before God by "the power of His resurrection." All these things, according to both John and Peter, are the result of the operation of God's Holy Spirit in the hearts of men, regenerating, renewing, recreating, until eventually, in His redeemed own, the perfect reflection of Christ, God's "express image" (Hebrews 1:3), shall shine forth triumphant over Satan, the flesh, and death itself.

"Ye must be born again," said our Lord to Nicodemus (John 3:3); "being born again . . . of incorruptible seed," writes Peter (1 Peter 1:23); and Paul adds, "Therefore if any man be in Christ, he is a new creature: old things are passed away; behold, all things are become new" (2 Corinthians 5:17). Thus it is seen that God's salvation is not a reformation of man, but a regeneration; not merely a reorganization of his social habits, but a literal saving of his spiritual life—a complete deliverance of the completely lost.

Christian Science, unfortunately, does not hold this view. It teaches instead, as Eddy put it, that salvation is not a personal deliverance from real sin and wickedness, but "boundless freedom and sinless sense," or, as she further stated, "Man as God's idea is already saved with an everlasting salvation" (*Miscellaneous Writings*, 261).

Christian Science does away altogether with the necessity of Christ's death on the cross for sin:

> According to divine law, sin and suffering are not canceled by repentance or pardon (*MW*, 261).

These are strange words in contrast to what Christ said, "I am not come to call the righteous, but sinners to repentance" (Matthew 9:13), and to Peter's immortal sentence, "Christ hath also once suffered for sins, the just for the unjust, that he might bring us to God" (1 Peter 3:18). Christian Science offers no eternal life and no salvation for the soul, denying as it does, sin, and hence the necessity of redemption from it. But God's Word stands sure, in powerful opposition to the falsehoods of Eddy and Christian Science: "All have sinned, and come short of the glory of God," and "There is none righteous, no, not one" (Romans 3:23; 3:10); however, "Believe on the Lord Jesus Christ, and thou shalt be saved" (Acts 16:31). This is God's salvation; this is the central message of the Bible; this is eternal life.

Man, His Spiritual and Material Natures

Without fear of contradiction, all rational persons will admit the reality of their physical existence. There are three principal reasons for this admission, which, briefly stated, are these:

1. Man is capable of perceiving his corporeal form.

2. The demands of the body—such as food, clothing, etc., prove that it has a material existence.

3. The human mind is capable of discerning the difference between concrete and abstract ideas, the body being easily discerned as a concrete proposition.

In view of these three facts, it is worthwhile to note that Christian Science denies without reservation all physical existence, as Eddy wrote:

> Man is not matter; he is not made up of brain, blood, bones, and other material elements. . . . Man is spiritual and perfect; and because he is spiritual and perfect, he must be so understood in Christian Science. Man is idea, the image of Love; he is not physique (*Science and Health*, 475).

Not only did Eddy deny the materially verifiable fact that the body exists, but she even went so far as to correct God in His creative office by asserting that "Man is the offspring and idea of the Supreme Being whose law is perfect and infinite. In obedience to the law, man is forever unfolding the endless beatitudes of Being; for he is the image and likeness of infinite Life, Truth, and Love" (*Miscellaneous Writings*, 82). At this point in her incoherent ramblings and deplorable mental condition, Eddy did the one thing that, by itself, devoid of any theological speculation whatsoever, characterizes her system of reasoning as that of a grossly philosophical perversion. To deny the reality of matter, philosophically speaking, is to predicate the worst type of absurdity, and Eddy was not above such a perpetration.

Genesis 2:7 plainly states that "God formed man of the dust of the ground, and breathed into his nostrils the breath of life; and man became a living soul." Moses further tells us that God created the material Eve, using a part of the material Adam, and David said, "It is he that hath made us, and not we ourselves" (Psalm 100:3). The Scriptures irrefutably declare that God created matter (Genesis 1:1), all forms of living organisms, and finally man himself in the spiritual image and likeness of his immaterial Father. There is, therefore, no conceivable ground, logically speaking, for denying that man exists physically as well as spiritually, and Eddy's repeated attempts to do away with the human body, and for that matter the material universe itself, is only more evidence of her unsound reasoning processes.

In regard to the spiritual nature of man, Christian Science takes a peculiar attitude, but for once an attitude that is logically consistent when followed through. Since man is totally spiritual ("the reflection of God," as Christian Science would have it), and God is perfect and incapable of sin; therefore, man must also be perfect as His reflection and hence incapable of sin. This is exactly what Eddy taught. Witness her own words:

> Man is the ultimate of perfection and by no means the medium of imperfection. . . . If God is upright and eternal, man as His likeness is erect in goodness and perpetual in Life, Truth, and Love. . . . The spiritual man is that perfect and unfallen likeness, coexistent and coeternal with God (*Miscellaneous Writings*, 79).

The logical mind can only deduce from these statements that the biblical account of man's fall from perfection (Genesis 3:6–7) and his definition as a

finite being (Psalm 89:48; 1 Corinthians 15:47) are totally in error and that man is God, because if he coexists with an eternal being (*MW*, 79), he himself is eternal. The weakness of this position can easily be demonstrated by the fact that all material things, including the human body, eventually return to the basic elements of existence, and God is said to have created all that exists, both material and spiritual (John 1:3); therefore, man in both his physical and spiritual forms is a creature, a creation not of a coexistent or inherently eternal character.

In conclusion, it is obvious that the identification of man and God by Christian Science on the basis of a spiritual nature is completely erroneous if the Judeo-Christian viewpoint is to be accepted as to the identity of the true God. Christian Science, it should be noted, claims that it holds the Christian position, and Christian Scientists adamantly repudiate any attempts to show that their teachings are the opposite of what Jesus taught; yet in every possible sense of the biblical record, all things having been considered, there is not the slightest resemblance of the theology of Christian Science to the revelation of the Bible concerning the teachings of Jesus Christ. The soul of man, it is true, is immaterial and was created in the image of God, but the body of man is purely physical in every sense of the word. To deny its reality, as does Christian Science, and attempt to prove that man is totally spiritual, and spiritually perfect at that, is, to say the least, a flagrant perversion of what biblical theology plainly portrays. The soul of man willfully sinned against God in the person of Adam (Isaiah 43:27; Romans 5); the souls of all men have forever been in rebellion against Almighty God from that day forward. It is only through the Gospel of Jesus Christ that this rebellion is brought into submission and that the sins of man's evil soul are cleansed and the soul regenerated to eternal life. To deny these facts on a biblical basis is dangerous, the facts being far too obvious. To explain them away, as does Christian Science, is fruitless; for the "word of the Lord endureth forever," and "it is this Word which through the gospel we preach unto you" (1 Peter 1:25).

Christian Science and Healing

The central claim of Eddy and Christian Science is that she has "restored" to Christendom the power of healing "lost" since the days of the early church. It is continually reiterated in the literature of the cult that their "leader" healed as Jesus did and demonstrated, through Divine Science. Not only this, but Eddy herself boldly asserted that she healed all types of diseases including cancer, tuberculosis, and diphtheria. Eddy wrote to the *New York Sun*, December 19, 1898:

> I challenge the world to disprove what I hereby declare. After my discovery of Christian Science, I healed consumption in the last stages that the M.D.s by verdict of a stethoscope and the schools declared incurable, the lungs being mostly consumed. I healed malignant tubercular diphtheria and carious bones that could be dented by the finger, saving them when the surgeon's instruments were lying on the table ready for their amputation. I have healed at one visit a cancer that had so eaten the flesh of the neck as to expose the jugular vein so that it stood out like a cord.

Notice that Eddy gives no particulars, names of patients, localities, dates, or

witnesses. Indeed, the only persons who ever witnessed her "miraculous" cures were either lackeys of Eddy's without medical training to justify their diagnosis of disease, or Christian Scientists of another era who unfortunately believed as God-breathed truth any claim that either Eddy or her contemporary worshipers conjured up. Eddy's claim of the power to heal presents us with a challenge. Since she denied all of the cardinal doctrines of the Christian faith, we know that her so-called power to heal did not come from God. We are left, then, with two alternatives. Either the so-called healings were not supernatural at all (being actually fraudulent, spontaneous, psychosomatic, etc.) and Eddy stands condemned as a fraud; or they were accomplished by the power of Satan, in the pattern of the magicians of Pharaoh's court in Moses' day (Exodus 7:11, 22). Briefly, let us consider this phase of "Mother" Eddy's long career.

To begin with, it should be known that in the process of investigating Eddy's healing claims, it was discovered that she outrightly refused to treat identical cases of diseases she claimed to have already cured. Even when a prominent Cincinnati physician offered her every such opportunity, Eddy remained strangely silent; indeed, she never mentioned the issue again.[40] This is hardly the attitude one would expect from the alleged successor to Jesus Christ. The foregoing is only one fact of a large number that proves beyond doubt that Eddy did not heal as she claimed. During her long life Eddy allowed her own little granddaughter, her beloved brother Samuel's wife, and her close friend Joseph Armstrong all to die painful deaths of cancer, pneumonia, and pleurisy, and never, to any known evidence of the contrary, did she ever lift her "healing" hand to save them.[41] Instead, she recommended "absent treatment" in all three cases, which consisted of reading her book *Science and Health* and concentrating upon mentally repulsing the organic deterioration. Eddy could have at least paid a call on them, and if her claims were true, healed them "at one visit," but she did not because she could not, and no one knew it better than Mary Baker Eddy. There is an overwhelming mass of evidence from unchallengeable sources that this fact is absolute truth, and no better authority can be quoted than the sworn testimony of Alfred Farlow, then chairman of the Publications Committee of the Christian Science Church and President of the Mother Church in Boston. Farlow's testimony, that of a Christian Scientist in excellent standing with his church and certainly in a position to know the facts about Eddy, clearly stated that he did not know of any healing produced by Eddy in her entire life of any organic disease but that of a stiff leg—hardly a major illness by any reasonable diagnosis (*The Religio-Medical Masquerade*, F. W. Peabody, n.d., 113).

Much more material could be introduced to further verify this contention of history against the Eddy healing legend, but suffice it to say that the issue needs no further support. She who professed to succeed Jesus Christ as the great healer of our age could not heal her closest emotional contacts; and to conceal this great threat to her system, which was based squarely on her alleged failure to heal, Eddy and her contemporaries have masqueraded to the world and to her faithful followers the legend of her miraculous curative power. This power,

---

[40]*New York Sun*, January 1, 1899, by Dr. Charles A. L. Reed.
[41]She did send a personal check to defray the cost of her sister-in-law's operation, but by the time the surgeon operated, the time taken in useless Christian Science treatments had taken a fatal toll and she died.

so widely trumpeted by Christian Science propaganda, history tells us was never exercised or demonstrated openly, for the obvious reason that it was a complete illusion, a phantom of Christian Science publicity and the delusions of Mary Baker Eddy.

Eddy, however, was not above attaching a price tag to the miraculous healings she claimed for her religion, and so she wrote:

> When teaching imparts the ability to gain and maintain health, to heal and elevate man in every line of life—as this teaching certainly does—is it unreasonable to expect in return something to support one's self and a cause? If so, our whole system of education, secular and religious, is at fault, and the instructors and philanthropists in our land should expect no compensation. "If we have sown unto you spiritual things, is it a great thing if we shall reap your carnal things?" (*Miscellaneous Writings*, 38).

But that was Eddy, clever to the last and beyond the comprehension and understanding of even her most intimate friends.

It must never be forgotten that Eddy once wrote:

> A patient hears the doctor's verdict as the criminal hears the death-sentence (*Science and Health*, 198).

Yet she made very rare but real use of doctors for her spasmodic attacks of hysteria, and toward the end of her life she even allowed Christian Scientists the right to use anesthetics, surgery, and the services of orthopedists for breaks and fractures, etc., even though she stoutly opposed such practices at the outset of her career.

No one can ever accuse Eddy of being foolish, because she seemingly made allowance for some situations. But while she provided in a measure for the bodies of her followers, she left their souls poverty stricken, barren, and destitute, robbed of the true Christ and His Gospel of life.

The chief attraction of Christian Science lies in its seeming power over disease and mental conflict, but to quote psychologist David S. Davis:

> What has been induced by suggestion can be cured by suggestion.[42]

Most illnesses "cured" by Christian Scientists are imagined illnesses that lack medical documentation and are seldom thoroughly verified by anyone other than the Scientists or their sympathizers. The physical world to most Christian Scientists is an "illusion of mortal mind," but they are quick to seize every opportunity to avail themselves of all the comforts this same "mortal mind" conjures up.[43]

With this philosophy it is easy to see how even sin with all its hideousness is reduced to a state of mind, and death to a flighty "illusion."

Because the central doctrine of almost all cults is the denial of both the deity and saving work of the Lord Jesus, we must exert renewed effort in preaching and teaching these major doctrines of our Christian heritage. We must be quick to expose error and quicker still to extend to all cultists the love of God

---

[42]Prof. David S. Davis, "A Psychologist Views the Cults," *The Examiner*, I (January/February) 1:11.

[43]Scripture, however, does cite evidence that Satan can counterfeit the miracles of God (Exodus 7:22ff.), and whatever "cures" Christian Science can present are not the work of our Christ.

and the assurance of forgiveness through His Eternal Son, if they will but come to the Christ of Calvary.

Let us not forget that Christian Science can temporarily induce peace of mind, and this cannot be doubted; but, that it is able to cure "diagnosed diseases," give peace of soul, or most of all, peace with God, is a question to which the Bible emphatically says no! The Bible clearly teaches that salvation is effected solely through the grace of God as revealed in Jesus Christ and His substitutionary atonement on the cross. The Christ of Christianity is a personality— God Incarnate (John 1:1–14)—not the "Divine Idea" of a pantheistic nonentity, as Eddy portrayed Him to be.

It is therefore important to remember that Eddy never believed in a personal God nor does any true Christian Scientist today. Eddy's last words, which she scrawled with a trembling hand on a scrap of paper shortly before her death, "God is my life," might just as well have read, "Principle, Love, Spirit, or Intelligence is my life." To her utterly confused mind the God of the Bible did not exist; for her, God was not personal in any sense, since her limited theology only permitted an "it," which was "all in all." Aside from adoring this pantheistic, impersonal deity, Eddy, and consequently all Christian Scientist practitioners today, expound this principle as the master key to the resolution of all human misery. Paradoxically, they deny misery exists, but never tire of trying to convince anyone who will listen, for a handsome fee, that Christian Science can remove this "error of mortal mind" through "prayer." The great byword of Christian Science, incidentally, is "prayer," and they never cease reminding their audience that they always pray to "God" for healing. But is it really prayer? The Scriptures teach that prayer is one's petition to a personal God who sees our needs and answers them (Philippians 4:6–7). Not so in Christian Science. Eddy many times reaffirmed her conviction that prayer to a personal God is a hindrance, not a help. To her and Christian Science the only true prayer is the affirmation of Principle Allness and the identification of one's self with this pantheistic Principle. From this basic misconception stems the illusion of man's inherent goodness and the denial of the "erroneous" ideas that evil or, for that matter, sin, suffering, disease, or even death is real. With this view of life it is easy to see how Christian Scientists can be so apparently happy and so oblivious to everyday worries. Whenever they encounter evil they deny its reality; whenever they behold misery, they affirm its nonexistence; and even when death comes to a loved one, they simply assert that it is an "illusion" since Principle (God) is All, and "It" is good.

It would be possible to go on indefinitely with the many strange interpretations that Eddy gave to the Scriptures. Suffice it to say, she never believed in them as God's Word or worshiped the Savior spoken of therein. The Christian's most holy and sacred doctrine of love—Christ crucified for us and His sacrificial blood our atonement with God—Eddy abruptly dismissed as unnecessary. She equally ignored the existence of hell, Satan, or a literal heaven. (For her, it was a "state of mind.") Nowhere in the annals of cultism is there to be found a person who camouflaged so expertly the "broad way of destruction" under a canopy of apparent serenity as did Mary Baker Eddy. Nevertheless, beneath this "serenity" lies a denial of almost all of orthodox Christianity.

In concluding this survey of Eddy's religion, it is extremely important that

the implications of Christian Science be thoroughly understood by Christians and non-Christians alike. It is important for Christians because ignorance of Christian Science has been one of the main contributing factors to the success of its previous rapid development. For non-Christians it is important because it is an imitation of the true Gospel, which bears no resemblance whatsoever to the historical Christian faith.

Christian Science must be understood and its teachings refuted from the Scriptures that it perverts and wrests to the destruction of many misled souls. But Christian Scientists must be loved and evangelized for the cause of the Gospel and because this is God's command to His church. By far, herein lies the greater challenge.

Biblical Texts Helpful in Refuting Christian Science Theology

1. *The Authority of the Bible.* Psalm 119:140; Isaiah 40:8; Matthew 24:35; John 10:35; 17:17; 2 Timothy 3:16.
2. *The Trinity and the Deity of Christ.* Genesis 1:26; 11:7; 18:1–33; Exodus 3:14; Isaiah 6:8; 9:6; John 1:1, 14; 8:58; Colossians 1:15; 2:9; Hebrews 1:3; Revelation 1:7–8, 16.
3. *The Personality of the Holy Spirit.* Luke 12:12; John 16:7–8; Acts 13:2.
4. *The Virgin Birth and Miracles of Jesus.* Isaiah 7:14; 9:6; Micah 5:2; Matthew 1:18–25; Luke 1:30–38; Matthew 8:14–15, 26–27; 9:2, 6–7, 27–30; Mark 1:32–34; John 2:1–11; 6:10–14.
5. *The Atonement, Death, and Resurrection of Christ.* Exodus 12:13; Leviticus 17:11; Psalm 22; Isaiah 53; Daniel 9:26; Matthew 26:28; 28:5–7; Luke 24:39; John 1:29; 19:33; Romans 5:6–8; Ephesians 1:7; Colossians 1:20.
6. *The Doctrine of Eternal Retribution.* Matthew 13:12, 50; 22:13; Mark 9:44, 46, 48; Luke 3:17; Revelation 20:10.
7. *The Doctrine of Christian Prayer.* Matthew 6:5–15; 7:7–11; Luke 18:1; Philippians 4:6; 1 Thessalonians 5:17; James 5:16.
8. *The Doctrine of Sin.* Romans 3:23; 6:23; 1 John 1:10; 3:4; 5:17.

Chapter 8

The Theosophical Society

Theosophy as a cult system derives its name from the Greek term *theosophia*, meaning literally, divine wisdom. "Its philosophy is a contemporary presentation of a perennial wisdom underlying the world's religions, sciences, and philosophies."[1] And, in the words of J. H. Russell, its teachings are

> At the same time religious, philosophic, and scientific . . . [postulating] one eternal, immutable, all-pervading principle, the root of all manifestation. From that one existence comes forth periodically the whole universe, manifesting the two aspects of spirit and matter, life and form, positive and negative, "the two poles of nature between which the universe is woven." Those two aspects are inseparably united; therefore all matter is ensouled by life while all life seeks expression through forms. All life being fundamentally one with the life of the Supreme Existence, it contains in germ all the characteristics of its source, and evolution is only the unfolding of those divine potentialities brought about by the conditions afforded in the various kingdoms of nature. The visible universe is only a small part of this field of evolution.[2]

Theosophy may be recognized at the outset as a pantheistic form of ancient Gnosticism, which attempts to embrace religious, philosophical, and scientific truth as it is found in all religio-philosophical sources. The Pasadena, California, office explains.

> A primary idea is the *essential oneness* of all beings. Life is everywhere throughout the cosmos because all originates from the same unknowable divine source. Consequently, everything from the subatomic to plants, animals, humans, planets, stars, and galaxies is alive and evolving. Each is divine at its root and expresses itself through spiritual, intellectual, psychological, ethereal,

This chapter updated and edited by Gretchen Passantino.

[1]"Welcome." http://user.aol.com/tstec/hmpage/tsintro.htm:The Theosophical Society (Pasadena, California) Internet World Wide Web page, 1997.
[2]J. H. Russell, "Theosophy," *The New Shaff-Herzog Encyclopedia of Religious Knowledge* (Grand Rapids, Mich.: Baker Book House, 1977), repr., 11:407.

and material ranges of consciousness and substance.[3]

According to the views of theosophists, their Society "is a growing system of thought, the result of careful study and research," and further "it is nothing less than the bedrock upon which all phases of the world's thought and activity are founded."[4] The "Three Declared Objects" of the Theosophical Society include:

>   1. To form a nucleus of the universal brotherhood of humanity without distinction of race, creed, sex, caste, or color.
>   2. To encourage the comparative study of religion, philosophy, and science.
>   3. To investigate unexplained laws of nature and the powers latent in humanity.[5]

This noble ideal dreams of a brotherhood of all faiths, or, if we may use the term, a type of homogenized religion, in which all men will agree to the cardinal tenets of Theosophy in one degree or another. In this respect, it is related to spiritism, Rosicrucianism, Baha'ism, and the Great I AM cults.

In theory, of course, and quite apart from the Christian Scriptures, this idea is most appealing. But even a cursory perusal of man's demonstrably depraved nature as revealed in history and in the Bible renders this Utopian concept an absurd theological farce.

Theosophy as a religion is opposed to virtually every cardinal doctrine of the Christian faith, and finds no support from Judaism, little from Islam, and certainly none from the majority of world religions, with the exceptions of Buddhism and Hinduism. Christianity, Judaism, and Islam all confess a personal God and all believe in a resurrection of the body and in the authority of the Old Testament. Theosophy, on the other hand, rejects *all* these doctrines. Yet it continues to claim qualification for the role as a "unifier and peacemaker in religion."

In fact, Theosophy claims that it is wrong to make any objective religious truth claim: We must only experience religious truth for ourselves in a subjective way.

>   As beings rooted in divinity, we each have the ability to discover reality for ourselves. To do this we must learn to judge what is true and false, real and illusory; not blindly follow the dictates of authority, however high. . . . By following our own spiritual instincts and intuitions, we awaken our latent potentials. Trying to force others to adopt what we believe to be the "proper" avenue of thought may be harmful. Everyone follows his or her own unique path of unfoldment.[6]

It is an interesting fact that Theosophy speaks in glowing terms of the ancient cult of Gnosticism, which thrived in the first three centuries of the Christian era, and which almost succeeded in doing irreparable damage to historic Christian faith. Paul's epistle to the Colossians and the epistle of 1 John are

---

[3] "Some Basic Concepts of Theosophy," Pasadena, California, Web site, 1997, 1.
[4] Irving S. Cooper, *Theosophy Simplified* (Wheaton, Ill.: The Theosophical Press, 1964), 7th ed., 22–23.
[5] "What Is the Theosophical Society?" http://www.theosophical.org: Theosophical Society Internet Web site, 1997.
[6] "Some Basic Concepts," 2.

recognized by all biblical scholars to be direct apologetic thrusts against the teachings that spawned this cult: spiritualizing the Old Testament, redefining contemporary Christian terminology, substituting an impersonal god for the God of revelation, and reducing Jesus Christ to a demigod, or a pantheistic emanation from the unknowable divine essence. The well-known theosophical writer L. W. Rogers, however, disdains the counsel of the Holy Spirit, not to mention the warnings of the apostles Paul and John when he states,

> The antagonism between scientific and religious thought was the cause of great controversy that occurred in the intellectual world in the late nineteenth century. If the early teaching of the Christian Church had not been lost, the conflict could not have arisen. The Gnostic philosophers who were the intellect and heart of the Church had a knowledge of nature so true that it could not possibly come into collision with any fact of science; but unfortunately, they were enormously outnumbered by the ignorant, and the authority passed wholly into the hands of the latter. It was inevitable that misunderstanding followed.[7]

Theosophists are great admirers of the Gnostics, and this is not at all surprising, since they have adopted much of the terminology and vocabulary of ancient Gnosticism, which looked with disdain upon the material properties of both the world and man, depersonalized God, and created various planes of spiritual progression, culminating in universal salvation and reconciliation through reincarnation and the wheel concept of progression borrowed unblushingly from Buddhism.

Theosophy does not hesitate to declare that

> God and man are the two phases of the one eternal life and consciousness that constitutes our universe! The idea of the immanence of God is that He is the universe; although he is also more than it is; that the solar system is an emanation of the Supreme Being as clouds are an emanation of the sea. This conception makes man a part of God, having potentially within him all the attributes and powers of the Supreme Being. It is the idea that nothing exists except God, and that humanity is one portion of him—one phase of his Being.[8]

In the theology of Theosophy there are seven distinct planes in the universe. The Physical is the most dense of these planes; that which is next in the order is called the Astral Plane, and above it, the Mental. There are four higher spiritual planes, but to all except initiates and adepts they are as yet "mere names." Man, of course, has a physical body, a mental body, and an astral body. But at this particular stage of cosmic evolution, with but few exceptions, the so-called higher spiritual bodies are still awaiting organization.[9]

A little further on in the chapter, we shall see what relationship this has to the basic doctrines of Christianity. But there can be little doubt that such hypothetical fancies, saturated with Gnostic terminology and concepts, cannot help but generate conflict where biblical theology is concerned.

Historical Sources

Theosophy is only one of the cults popular in America started by women. Heresy evidently has no gender barrier, although some cults are certainly sexist

---

[7]L. W. Rogers, *Elementary Theosophy* (Wheaton, Ill.: The Theosophical Press, 1956), 22.
[8]Ibid., 23.
[9]H. P. Blavatsky, *Theosophical Glossary* (Los Angeles: The Theosophy Company, 1892, 1973).

in their treatment of women. Other religious movements started by women include Christian Science, Mary Baker Eddy; the Unity School of Christianity, Myrtle Fillmore with her husband, Charles; and the Shakers, Ann Lee. Madam Helena Blavatsky and her successor, Annie Besant, were the founders of Theosophy. Regardless of the gender of a cult leader, male or female, God judges all people by the Gospel of Jesus Christ (Romans 1:16–18), and Joseph Smith, founder of the Mormons, is no more exempt from eternal death for his heresies than is Madam Blavatsky for hers (Matthew 25:46).

The term "theosophy" was introduced, to the best knowledge of reputable scholars, in the third century by a noted philosopher, Ammonius Saccas, the teacher of Plotinus, the great Roman philosopher. Theosophy, however, has a long history traceable directly to the Orient, particularly India, where the Upanishads and Vedas, or Hindu Scriptures, form the basis for no small part of the doctrines. The writings of Gautama Buddha and the early Christian Gnostics also heavily influenced the formulation of theosophical doctrines.

Theosophy claims to be a universal world religion of a distinct nature. But any careful study of its eclectic background readily reveals that much of its "original theology" is borrowed from easily recognizable sources. The modern American history of Theosophy began with the activities of the young and mystically inclined Russian Madam Helena Blavatsky, in the year 1875, in New York City. Helena Petrovna was born in Ekaterinoslav, Russia, in 1831, the daughter of Peter Hahn, the son of the noble Von Hahn family of Germany. At the age of seventeen, Helena married the Czarist general Blavatsky, a cultured gentleman many years her senior, whom she promptly left after only three months of marriage. It is a known fact that Madam was notoriously short of patience and had a violent temper. It is asserted by at least one of her biographers that she married General Blavatsky merely to spite her acid-tongued governess, who, in a moment of sarcasm, declared that even the noble old gentleman would not marry a shrew like Helena. To her credit, Madam Blavatsky repented quite hastily of her revenge upon the governess, but she had already beguiled the General and was forced into a position of compliance with matrimony.[10]

Shortly after her separation from General Blavatsky, Helena embarked upon a long career of travel that eventually led her into the field of mystical religion, which she studied from Tibet, India, and Egypt to Texas, Louisiana, Cuba, and Canada, settling eventually in New York long enough to found, in the year 1875, The Theosophical Society, in conjunction with Colonel H. S. Olcott and W. Q. Judge, two ardent devotees.

In 1879, Madam Blavatsky left the United States for India, and later died in London, England, in 1891. W. Q. Judge split the Society in 1895, and then saw his organization also divided into the "Universal Brotherhood and Theosophical Society" and "The Theosophical Society in America."

Madam Blavatsky held Judge in the highest esteem, and Judge wore her mantle of leadership to all intents and purposes as head of the Aryan Theosophical Society of which he was president until 1896, when he died. Madam Blavatsky also founded the Esoteric School of Theosophy in London in 1888, and during her travels in India and England, influenced profoundly Annie

---

[10]Baseden G. Butt, *Madam Blavatsky* (London: Marchand Bros., 1926), 13.

Wood Besant, who took over leadership of the school after the deaths of Madam Blavatsky, Judge, and his successor, Catherine Tingley.

When Catherine Tingley died in 1929, G. D. Purucker assumed the presidency of the British Society, taking charge of the administrative and policy-making aspects of the Theosophists. Additionally, he developed and explained the more esoteric of Blavatsky's teachings for his students. He died in 1942. The Society was governed by its Cabinet until Colonel Arthur L. Conger was recognized as president in 1945. James A. Long succeeded Conger after the latter's death in 1951. According to the Pasadena office of the Theosophical Society, Long "emphasized the importance of making Theosophy a living force in daily life, and of seeking to read the natural karma of each moment."[11] The present leader, Grace F. Knoche, assumed office as president of the American Society at the time of Long's death in 1971.

Helena Blavatsky was a woman of tremendous physical proportions with piercing, almost hypnotic eyes, and she ruled the Theosophists during her life and in many areas, even after her death, through her literary works—principally *The Secret Doctrine*, which is still regarded as divinely inspired interpretations or oracular instructions by most loyal Theosophists.

Annie Besant (1847–1933) was the most prominent of all the British Theosophical luminaries, and one destined to become a bright star in the political fortunes of India. Among her many accomplishments, Besant founded the Central Hindu College at Benares, India, in 1898, and also the Indian Home Rule League in 1916. In the year 1917, she was elected president of the Indian National Congress and was almost always regarded as a powerful figure in Indian politics.

In 1889, Mrs. Besant, a native of London, became enthralled by the personality and teachings of Madam Blavatsky and forthwith became a devout pupil and disciple. Mrs. Besant believed firmly in the teachings of Madam Blavatsky, and her writings best represent the true doctrines of the cult and are always laudatory of the departed Russian seer.

Mrs. Besant herself had not a few idiosyncrasies, and she was highly mystical in her approach to both life and religion, as evidenced in 1925, when she claimed for her adopted son Krishnamurti, an Indian mystic, the title of "Messianic Leader and Reincarnation of the World Teacher."

Such grandeur, however, was renounced by the new Messiah on November 20, 1931, at Krotana, California, then headquarters of the American branch of Theosophy. Mrs. Besant died in 1933, after which time George Arundale and C. Jinara Jodosa succeeded to the presidency of the American Society.[12]

Theosophy and Christian Theology

According to the literature of the theosophical cult as represented chiefly by Helena Blavatsky, Annie Besant, I. C. Cooper, A. P. Sinnett, L. W. Rogers, and

[11]"History of the Theosophical Society," Pasadena Office Web site, 1997, 2.
[12]See Horton Davies, *The Challenge of the Sects* (Philadelphia, Pa.: Westminster Press, 1961); Charles Ferguson, *Nehru Books of Revelation* (Garden City, N.Y.: Doubleday, 1929); and J. K. Van Baalen, *The Chaos of the Cults* (Grand Rapids, Mich.: William B. Eerdmans Publishing Company, 1962).

C. W. Leadbeater, there is a great fraternity of "Mahatmas" or "Masters," who are highly evolved examples of advanced reincarnations whose dwelling place is somewhere in the far reaches of remote Tibet.[13] These divine beings possessed Madam Blavatsky and utilized her services to reach the generations now living upon the earth with the restored truths of the great religions of the world, which have been perverted by mankind. In this highly imaginative picture, the Theosophists add seven planes of progression, previously noted, through which the souls of men must progress on their way to the Theosophists' "heaven" or Devachan.

In keeping with the Theosophists' concept of heaven, in the final analysis is the *nirvana* of Buddhism, where the absorption of the personality or the soul into a type of world soul eventually extinguishes personal cognizance—the Theosophists also have their "hell," which, oddly enough, resembles the Roman Catholic purgatory, with indescribable tortures and degrees of degradation. The name for this intermediate state of existence where the departed souls suffer for their past sins while awaiting reincarnation, or the chance to start living in a new body, is Kamaloka, where the atmosphere is "gloomy, heavy, dreary, depressing to an inconceivable extent . . . the man who is full of evil passions *looks* the whole of them; bestial appetites shape the astral body into bestial forms, and repulsively human animal shapes are the appropriate clothing of brutalized human souls. No man can be a hypocrite in the astral world and cloak foul thoughts with a veil of virtuous seeming; whatever a man is that he appears to be in outward form and semblance, radiant in beauty if his mind be noble, repulsive in hideousness if his nature be foul."[14]

Contrary to the Christian doctrines of redemption and punishment, Theosophy offers no forgiveness for sin except through myriads of reincarnations ever progressing toward Devachan, and no eternal retribution for man's rebellion or sin, only the evolutionary terrors of Kamaloka. The Theosophical Society maintains that it has three primary objectives, which are "(1) to form a nucleus of the brotherhood of humanity, without distinction of race, creed, sex, caste, or color; (2) to encourage the study of comparative religion, philosophy, and science; (3) to investigate the unexplained laws of nature and the powers latent in man. Assent to the first of these objects is required for membership, the remaining two being optional. 'The Society has no dogmas or creed, is entirely nonsectarian, and includes in its membership adherents of all faiths and of none, exacting only from each member their tolerance for the beliefs of others that he would wish them to exhibit toward his own.' "[15]

Theosophy makes no demands of absolute allegiance to any religion or religious leader, and it is resolutely opposed to any form of dogmatism, particularly that type manifested by the Son of God, who said, "I am the way, the truth, and the life: no man cometh unto the Father, but by me" (John 14:6).

---

[13]See Blavatsky's *Glossary*.
[14]Annie Besant, *The Ancient Wisdom: An Outline of Theosophical Teachings* (London: Theosophical Publishing Society, 1897), 92- 93.
[15]Russell, *Schaff-Herzog*, 408–409.

God and Man in Theosophy

In common with Christian Science, Unity, and other pantheistic theologies, Theosophy conceives of God in strictly impersonal terms, while asserting that man is, in a spiritual sense, part of God. L. W. Rogers put it this way, when he wrote,

> In divine essence, latent power and potential spirituality, man is an image of God, because he is part of Him. The same idea is more directly put in the Psalms, with the assertion "ye are gods." If the idea of the immanence of God is sound, then man is a literal fragment of the consciousness of the Supreme Being, is an embryo-god, being destined to ultimately evolve his latent powers into perfect expression. The oneness of life was explicitly asserted by Jesus. . . . It is an unqualified assertion that humanity is a part of God as leaves are part of the tree, not something a tree has created, in the sense that a man creates a machine, but something that is an emanation of the tree and is a living part of it. Thus only has God made man. Humanity is a growth, a development, an emanation, an evolutionary expression of the Supreme Being. . . . It is simplicity itself when we think of the solar system as simply an emanation of the Supreme Being, as something generated from a central life, an expression of that life which gives rise to the poles within it that we know as consciousness and matter. The human soul is an individualized fragment of that divine life . . . is literally a spark of the divine fire, and latent within it are the characteristics of that central light from which it originated. The theosophical conception of the soul is that it is literally an emanation from God, and since it is therefore of its own essence, it becomes clear why Theosophists assert that man is a god in the making.[16]

In keeping with this position, Mrs. Besant once declared, "man is spiritual intelligence, a fragment of divinity clothed in matter."[17] Mrs. Besant's adopted son, Krishnamurti, once declared that all of us are a part of God and must dig down within ourselves to find the God within us.

These pantheistic views of the Deity are drawn from the deadly trinity of Hinduism, Buddhism, and Gnosticism. And one wonders why Theosophy even attempts to use Christian terms at all, except when it is realized that it is easier to reach the Western mind in terms of the Christian religion than in the language of Hinduism, Buddhism, and Gnosticism. So this is the obvious reason for the utilization of redefined Christian terminology by Theosophists.

Concerning the deity of Jesus Christ and His unique place as *the* Savior of the world, Theosophy declares that all men are innately divine, "so that in time all men become Christs."[18]

The clearest position on this subject, however, is declared by Rogers, who summed up the views of Theosophy where our Lord and His mission are concerned when he wrote,

> Most readers will probably agree that a world teacher known as the Christ did come, and that he founded a religion nearly 2,000 years ago. Why do they think so? They reply that God so loved the world that he sent his son the Christ to bring it light and life. If that is true, how can we avoid the conclusion that

---

[16]Rogers, *Elementary*, 22–25; 19–20.
[17]Annie Besant, *Man's Life in Three Worlds* (London: Theosophical Publishing Society, 1899), 3.
[18]Annie Besant, *Is Theosophy Anti-Christian?* (London: Theosophical Publishing Society, 1901), 16.

he or his predecessors, must have come many times before. The belief that he came but once is consistent only with the erroneous notion that Genesis is history, instead of allegory . . . when a new era in human evolution begins, a world teacher comes in a voluntary incarnation and founds a religion that is suited to the requirements of the new age. Humanity is never left to grope along alone. All that it can comprehend and utilize is taught in the various religions. World teachers, the christs and saviours of the age, have been appearing at propitious times since humanity began existence. . . . In the face of such facts, what becomes of the assertion that God so loved the world that he sent his son to help ignorant humanity about 2,000 years ago—but never before? What about the hundreds of millions of human beings who lived and died before that time? Did he care nothing for them? Did he give his attention to humanity for a period of only 2,000 years and neglect it for millions of years? Has anybody believed that God in his great compassion sent just *one* world teacher for that brief period. . . . If God so loved the world that he sent his son 2,000 years ago, he sent him, or some predecessor very many times before.

Supermen are not myths or figments of the imagination. They are as natural and comprehensive as human beings. In the regular order of evolution, we shall ourselves reach their level and join their ranks, while younger humanity shall attain our present state. As they rose, we too shall rise. Our past has been evolution's night. Our present is its dawn. Our future shall be its perfect day. . . . That is the magnificent future the Theosophist sees for the human race.[19]

The refutation of these non-Christian concepts concerning God and the Lord Jesus Christ are clearly found in various places in the Bible. The personality of God and the deity of Christ are forcefully set forth along with many of the other things that Theosophists deny. The God of the Bible created man and is separate and distinct from him (Genesis 1:27). He is a cognizant ego or personality (Exodus 3:14; Isaiah 48:12; John 8:58), and He is triune—three separate persons—Father, Son, and Holy Spirit, yet one in essence or nature (Deuteronomy 6:4; Galatians 3:20). The God of the Bible cannot be equated with the God of Theosophy, nor can Jesus Christ be redefined so that Christ becomes innately divine, "so that in time all men become Christs."[20] Neither the laws of language, logic, nor biblical theology can permit such extravagances as the Theosophists must insist upon to arrive at such inconceivable equations.

The Theosophist, in his depersonalization of God, however, fails to recognize that man is a cognizant, reflective ego, and that he is a creation of God, in the divine spiritual image, debased though he may be by sin. How is it possible to claim for the creation what is not possessed by the Creator, namely, personality? Are we to assume that the creation, even though part of the divine, is greater in that part, i.e., the possession of ego and personality, than the divine itself? To use the analogy of Rogers, is the spark greater than the flame, the ray greater than the source from which it emanated? Of course not! So, then, neither is man greater than God. If man possesses personality and ego, and the Theosophists grant this, then God, by definition, must be personality and ego— a disconcerting fact, but a fact nonetheless!

The Bible gives much evidence to this effect by underscoring the personality of God in terms of attributes that only a personality can manifest. These traits forever separate Him from the pantheistic God of Theosophy, which is

[19]Besant, *Anti-Christian?*, 260–263.
[20]Ibid., 16.

incapable, by definition, of performing these things.

1. *God remembers.* "I, even I, am he that blotteth out thy transgressions for mine own sake, and will not remember thy sins" (Isaiah 43:25).

2. *God creates.* "In the beginning God created the heavens and the earth" (Genesis 1:1).

3. *God knows, i.e., He has a mind.* "The Lord knoweth them that are his" (2 Timothy 2:19). "For I know the thoughts that I think toward you, saith the Lord" (Jeremiah 29:11).

4. *God is a personal Spirit.* "I am the Almighty God; walk before me, and be thou perfect" (Genesis 17:1).

5. *God has will.* "Lo, I come to do thy will, O God" (Hebrews 10:9).

From this brief résumé of some of God's attributes, the interested reader can doubtless see the vast difference between the God and Father of our Lord Jesus Christ and the impersonal God of Theosophy. Theosophy's God is not a personal being. He cannot remember, He cannot create, He cannot will, He cannot know, because He is not a personality, but an impersonal "it," an abstract, pantheistic principle, not the God of divine revelation.

Theosophy makes the grave error of all Gnostic cults: it divides Jesus and Christ, making Jesus only the outer man and Christ a divine consciousness immanent within Him and within all men, to a greater or lesser degree. For Theosophists, Jesus is not *the* Christ of divine revelation, as distinct from the Christ who is immanent within all men. They do not understand that the word *Christ* (*Christos* in the Greek) is a title corresponding to the Hebrew *Messiah*. It is not a force, essence, or divine spark, as any careful reading of a good Greek lexicon will speedily reveal. In the sixteenth chapter of Matthew's gospel, the apostle Peter affirmed this truth by pointing out in his confession of faith, "Thou art the Christ, the Son of the living God" (Matthew 16:16). And John reminds us that, "Who is a liar but he that denieth that Jesus is the Christ? He is antichrist, that denieth the Father and the Son" (1 John 2:22).

It is unnecessary to pursue this point any further since Christian theology has always maintained that Jesus of Nazareth was the Christ, the anointed Redeemer of God, very God himself (Isaiah 9:6; Micah 5:2; John 1:1, 14, 18; Colossians 2:9; Revelation 1:16–17; Isaiah 44:6; etc.). He is the second person of the Trinity, not the theosophical emanation from the impersonal essence they acknowledge as God. And this is why Theosophy is not Christian and is indeed the very antithesis of historic Christian theology.

In regard to the lengthy statement previously quoted from Rogers, the argument that God must have sent other "world teachers" to meet the requirements for humanity's redemption prior to Christ is the purest speculation and directly contradicts the statement of our Lord who affirmed,

> Verily, verily, I say unto you, He that entereth not by the door into the sheepfold, but climbeth up some other way, the same is a thief and a robber. But he that entereth in by the door is the shepherd of the sheep. To him the porter openeth; and the sheep hear his voice: and he calleth his own sheep by name, and leadeth them out. . . . All that ever came before me are thieves and robbers: but the sheep did not hear them. . . . The thief cometh not, but for to steal, and to kill, and to destroy: I am come that they might have life, and that they might have it more abundantly (John 10:1–3, 8, 10).

The epistle to the Romans points out that God has revealed himself to the hundreds of millions of human beings about whom Rogers is concerned, and that in the face of His revelation, "professing themselves to be wise, they became fools, and changed the glory of the incorruptible God into an image made like to corruptible man, and to birds, and four-footed beasts, and creeping things. Wherefore God also gave them up to uncleanness through the lusts of their own hearts, to dishonor their own bodies between themselves: who changed the truth of God into a lie, and worshipped and served the creature more than the Creator, who is blessed for ever" (Romans 1:22–25). And as a direct result of this, the apostle Paul informs us, God abandoned them to themselves so that "when they knew God, they glorified him not as God . . . but became vain in their imaginations, and their foolish heart was darkened" (Romans 1:21).

So it is apparent that mankind has never been without a witness of God's grace and love, but that every time it has been manifested in His law, His prophets, and finally, in His Son, men have responded with violence, evil, and sin of every proportionate degree, so that they are without excuse and *deserving* of eternal condemnation.

Quite to the contrary, the idea is not preposterous, as Rogers suggests, but consistent with the character of God and His judgment upon depraved human nature (Romans 3:23). It is a fact that Theosophists refuse to face despite the atrocities frequent in even modern society, the horrible Nazi concentration camps, the selective incarceration, torture, and even murder by modern communistic regimes, and the other testimonies to the fallen nature of mankind. They apparently think that when Adam sinned (an allegory) the race fell spiritually upward, a condition controverted by all the facts of history!

It is true that God so loved the world that He gave His only begotten Son, but it is not true that He has many sons, that they came many times, and that Christ was only one among them. This He himself denied, and on far better authority than any Rogers or Theosophy can muster (John 12:44–50).

The Vicarious Atonement

Theosophy is opposed to not only the true biblical teaching of God's personality and nature, as well as the deity of His Son, but it also vigorously denies Christ's substitutionary sacrifice for all sin (1 John 2:2).

One of the most concise statements concerning the views of Theosophy in this area comes from the pen of L. W. Rogers, who wrote,

> Back of the ancient doctrine of the vicarious atonement is a profound and beautiful truth, but it has been degraded into a teaching that is as selfish as it is false. That natural truth is the sacrifice of the Solar Logos, the Deity of our system. Sacrifice consists of limiting himself in the manner of manifested worlds, and it is reflected in the sacrifice of the Christ and other great teachers. Not the sacrifice of life, but a voluntary returning to live in the confinement of material body. Nobody more than the Theosophist pays to the Christ the tribute of the most reverent gratitude; we also hold with St. Paul that each must work out his own salvation. Were it not for such sacrifice, the race would be very, very far below its present evolutionary level. The help that such great spiritual beings have given mankind is incalculable, and is undoubtedly altogether beyond what we were able to comprehend. But to assume that such sacrifice has relieved man

from the necessity of developing his spiritual nature, or in any degree nullify his personal responsibility for any evil he has done, is false and dangerous doctrine. . . . And true, too, we know that any belief that is not in harmony with the facts of life is a wrong belief . . . the vital point against this plan of salvation is that it ignores the soul's personal responsibility, and teaches that whatever the offenses against God and man have been, they may be canceled by the simple process of believing that another suffered and died in order that those sins might be forgiven. It is the pernicious doctrine that wrongdoing by one can be set right by the sacrifice of another. It is simply astounding that such a belief could have survived the middle ages and should continue to find millions who accept it in these days of clearer thinking.

The man who is willing to purchase bliss by the agony of another is unfit for heaven, and could not recognize it if he were there.

A heaven that is populated with those who see in the vicarious atonement the happy arrangement letting them in pleasantly and easily, would not be worth having. It would be a realm of selfishness, and that would be no heaven at all. . . . The hypothesis of reincarnation shows our inherent divinity, and the method by which the latent becomes the actual. Instead of the ignoble belief that we can fling our sins upon another, it makes personal responsibility the keynote of life. It is the ethics of self-help. It is the moral code of self-reliance. It is the religion of self-respect.[21]

The inconsistency of Theosophists is eclipsed only by their apparent lack of concern for the validity of established terms in both philosophy and theology. Here is a classic example of what we mean. Rogers wants Christians to believe that "nobody more than the Theosophist pays to the Christ the tribute of the most reverent gratitude." But he denies categorically the expressions of that very Christ and the prophecies concerning Him, which state that He came for the express purpose of paying the penalty for all sin.

The Theosophist wants no part of the vicarious sacrifice of Jesus; in fact, it is personally repugnant to him. By his own admission, he considers it "an ignoble belief" that we can fling our sins upon another. But this is exactly what we are called upon to do in the New Testament.

The Scriptures bear incontrovertible witness to the truth that "Christ died for the ungodly" (Romans 5:6), and that "The blood of Jesus Christ . . . cleanseth us from all sin" (1 John 1:7). There is no doctrine found within the pages of the Bible that is better supported or substantiated than that of the substitutionary death of Christ for the sins of the world. As far back in the biblical record as Exodus, Moses wrote of God's symbolic use of blood for purification and sacrifice. It will be recalled that Jehovah delivered the Israelites from Egypt by causing all the firstborn of the nation, including Pharaoh's own son, to fall under the shadow of sudden death (Exodus 12). The Jews were instructed in this instance to sprinkle the blood of the young lamb on the doorpost and lintels of their homes, and God promised, "When I see the blood, I will pass over you" (Exodus 12:13). The Lord also instituted the animal sacrifices of the Levitical era and expressly stated, "It is the blood that maketh an atonement for the soul" (Leviticus 17:11).

Following this typology through into the New Testament, we find that Jesus was called the Lamb of God, who takes away the sin of the world (John 1:29),

[21]Besant, *Anti-Christian?*, 201–206.

and further, that His blood, shed upon the cross, is our atonement or covering for sin, even for the sins of all mankind (Matthew 26:28; Romans 5:6–8; Ephesians 1:7; Colossians 1:20).

The believer in Christ therefore is saved by grace alone through faith in His blood, and its efficacy for the cleansing of all sin (Romans 3:25). John, the beloved disciple, reminds us in his powerful epistle of this fact (1 John 1:7), and Peter declares, "[We] were not redeemed with corruptible things, as silver and gold . . . but with the precious blood of Christ, as a lamb without blemish and without spot" (1 Peter 1:18–19).

The pages of the New Testament bear incontrovertible testimony that Jesus Christ on Calvary purchased the church with his own blood (Acts 20:28), and in the great message of Christ to John recorded in the book of Revelation, we are told that He "washed us from our sins in his own blood" (Revelation 1:5). This was not a pagan sacrifice to placate the wrath of a heathen god's justice. The sacrifice was offered through the Eternal Spirit, to free the sons of men from the curse of sin and to open the path to salvation, through which we now can have boldness to enter into the holiest by the blood of Jesus—a new and living way to the very throne of God our Father (Hebrews 10:19–20).

Contrasting this picture of concrete biblical theology with the views of Theosophy, the facts speak for themselves, and they cannot honestly be ignored.

Theosophy, on the other hand, refuses to accept the vicarious atonement of Jesus Christ for the forgiveness of all sin. Instead, Theosophy teaches the inexorable law of Karma (the accumulated weight of one's bad actions that can only be "atoned for" through personal and individual good actions during a succession of lives [reincarnation] and which is sometimes called "the Law of Cause and Effect"). Annie Besant described it as the "law of causation . . . bidding man . . . surrender all the fallacious ideas of forgiveness, vicarious atonement, divine mercy and the rest of the opiates that superstition offers to the sinner."[22]

Consequently, through the application of the law of Karma, the biblical doctrine of the Atonement is neatly supplanted and the authority of Scripture circumvented or negated. Mrs. Besant once wrote that "The atonement wrought by Christ lies not in the substitution of one individual for another. . . ."[23]

As the daughter of an Anglican clergyman and the former wife of another, Mrs. Besant must have known better, but despite this, she never satisfactorily explained what the biblical doctrine of the Atonement *does* mean, if it does not mean what the Christian church has always maintained.

For Theosophists the redemptive love of a personal God as revealed in the substitutionary sacrifice of His most precious possession, His Son, Jesus Christ, is totally unnecessary and is not the way of salvation. This fact alone would remove Theosophy from any serious consideration of compatibility with Christianity, and we can be grateful that the cult today (1984) is so insignificant in number that it does not even appear in the *Yearbook of American and Canadian Churches 1975* (Constant H. Jacquet Jr., ed., New York: Abingdon Press, 1975), although its "chapters" or centers can be found in many major cities of the

---

[22]Annie Besant, *Karma* (London: The Theosophical Publishing Society, 1904), 23.
[23]Besant, *Anti-Christian?*, 11.

United States and throughout the world. Its rate of growth seems considerably slower than it was in the 1920s, and we can hope that the very fact of its complexity and the involved vocabulary utilized to describe its mazelike theology may yet render it more ineffective in an age in which precision of definition is at last coming into its own.

What at first appeared to be a decline has changed to a rise in popularity at the close of the twentieth century (1997), largely through attracting many followers who were first introduced to Eastern religious ideas through the New Age movement. The American "section" headquarters for the Theosophical Society is in Wheaton, Illinois, on a beautiful estate named the Olcott Estate, after the first Theosophical president, Colonel Henry Steel Olcott. The international headquarters is in Adyar, Madras, India. The educational program of the society is in Illinois, engaged in publications, seminars, lectures, correspondence, and classes (both at the Olcott center and in satellite locations).

In order to be Christian, one must conform to the Scriptures. Theosophy fails to meet this requirement and must be considered anti-Christian.

Sin, Salvation, and Prayer

The Christian concepts of sin, salvation, and prayer need but passing mention relative to the reinterpretation they receive at the hands of theosophical writers. The teaching of Theosophy on these principal Christian doctrines is very definite and important and should be understood.

The Bible plainly states that all men have come under the divine indictment of sin (Romans 3:23). The divine remedy for sin, as we have seen, is the redemptive work of Jesus Christ who "died, the just for the unjust to bring us to God" (1 Peter 3:18). So hideous and degrading was human sin in the eyes of a Holy God that it required the God-man's death to satisfy the righteous judgment of His Father. Salvation from sin is full and complete by faith in Jesus Christ "once for all" (Hebrews 10:10). "For the wages of sin is death" (Romans 6:23). Since the Theosophist wants no part of the redeeming sacrifice of the Cross, and since he denies that personal sin must be atoned for by a power outside himself, like Petra of old, he is deceived by the pride of his heart (Obadiah 3). There can be little doubt that Theosophists, like Unitarians, consider salvation gained by character and progression. Theirs must be a God of love who allows the penalty of sin to be worked out on the wheel of reincarnation and by infinite progression. He does not judge; He cannot, for the spectacle of an impersonal principle judging the actions of a personal being is too much for any serious student of the philosophy of religion, and Theosophists are no exception.

The biblical doctrine of prayer also suffers at the hand of Theosophy. In the biblical vocabulary, prayer is personal communion with a personal God, not an abstract force or a cosmic consciousness. Jesus Christ himself encouraged us to pray many times (see Matthew 5:44; 6:6–7, 9; 9:38). He repeatedly emphasized its virtues and benefits. For the Christian, then, prayer is the link with the Eternal by which man can come to "the throne of grace" in the power of the Holy Spirit and find "grace to help in time of need" (Hebrews 4:16).

Salvation for the Christian is by grace and true faith in God's only method for making men holy and through the only "name under heaven given among

men, whereby we must be saved" (Acts 4:12). Human sin makes it necessary for this grand redemption, and since Theosophy denies it, it follows of a necessity that redemption would also be negated. Since Theosophy rejects the God of the Bible or any concept of a personal God, prayer in the biblical sense becomes impossible, and the sinner's most desperate need, which is to "call upon the name of the Lord" that he might be saved, not from a wheel of incarnations, but from eternal, spiritual, and conscious separation from the life and fellowship of God himself, is ignored or denied.

Contrasted to this biblical picture of sin, salvation, and prayer, Theosophy equates God the Father with the pagan gods Buddha and Vishnu,[24] and defines prayer, not as personal supplication for divine mercy and grace (Philippians 4:6–7), but as "concentrated thought."[25] Theosophists also believe that personal sin is removed only by suffering in Kamaloka, "the semi-material plane, to us subjective and invisible, where the disembodied 'personalities,' the astral forms . . . remain. . . . It is the Hades of the ancient Greeks and the Amenti of the Egyptians, the land of Silent Shadows."[26] Personal salvation is obtained through various reincarnations, ending in absorption of the individual ego. These cannot be viewed as pleasant alternatives to biblical revelation, but they are all that Theosophy offers.

Resurrection Versus Reincarnation

In bringing to a conclusion this chapter on Theosophy, it is necessary for the Christian to understand the one great doctrine that forever removes any possibility of realizing fellowship with Theosophists.

The apostle Paul, in his great and grand chapter on the resurrection of the body (1 Corinthians 15), cites the resurrection of Christ and its subsequent effect upon the bodies of all mankind as *the* proof that God exists, that Christ is His Son, and that the redemption of all believers is assured by His personal triumph over the grave.

Paul goes to great lengths in this chapter to show that "if Christ be not raised, your faith is vain; ye are yet in your sins" (v. 17). For the great apostle, our hope for physical immortality lies alone in the triumphant physical resurrection of Christ (v. 14), who visibly and tangibly presented himself alive "by many infallible proofs" (Acts 1:3) to over 500 persons who knew that it was indeed Jesus who had conquered the grave on their behalf.

Our risen Lord also promised that one day we should be physically and morally as He is, and that God the Father, through Him, would raise the believing dead and clothe them with immortality at His second advent (1 Thessalonians 4).

The condition of the Christian in death, however, is not one of suffering or repeated reincarnations while atoning for sin, as Theosophy would have it, but one of cognizant personal joy, literally the state of being "at home with the Lord" (2 Corinthians 5:8).

---

[24]Annie Besant, *The Seven Principles of Man,* (London: The Theosophical Publishing Society, 1902), 58.

[25]Annie Besant, *The Changing World* (London: The Theosophical Publishing Society, 1901), 68.

[26]Blavatsky, *Glossary,* 171–172.

The resurrection of Jesus Christ and, for that matter, the resurrection of all mankind, leaves no room for the Theosophical dogma of concurrent reincarnations. We indeed concur with the apostle Paul that, "If in this life only we have hope in Christ, we are of all men most miserable" (1 Corinthians 15:19). The souls of the dead do not pass through various reincarnations as Theosophy contends; rather, these souls are either experiencing happiness in Christ's presence (Philippians 1:21), in which case, to die is gain; or they are suffering conscious separation from His presence (Luke 16:19–31). In any case, Scripture clearly shows that reincarnation is not man's destiny, nor is it God's revealed plan for perfecting the souls of men. The Bible tells us that Christ died to fully redeem (Romans 5:6; Hebrews 9:26; 10:12).

Out of the Labyrinth, Into the Light

To wend our way completely out of the mazelike labyrinth of Theosophy and its anti-Christian doctrines into the light of biblical reality would probably take many volumes of exacting systematic analysis of this cult. But suffice it to note that Theosophy offers to the sinner no hope of full redemption from sin, only seemingly endless reincarnations; it guarantees no relationship with a loving, personal heavenly Father, and it ignores completely the true nature, person, and work of the Lord Jesus Christ.

The entire system is Eastern in its origin; it is Hinduistic and Buddhistic in its theology, Gnostic in its vocabulary, and Christian only in its key terminology, which is specifically designed to imitate the true content of the gospel.

The Theosophist proudly rejects the Atonement on the cross, preferring to trust in his own righteousness (and the working out of the law of Karma), and is willing to brave the terrors of Kamaloka itself rather than to bow the knee to Jesus Christ (Philippians 2:10–11).

Let us not then be deceived by the veneer of the intellectual and metaphysical jargon the Theosophist has mastered, nor retreat before his attempt to belittle the preaching of the Cross as "foolishness." We need not defer to his alleged "deeper revelation," to his claims that Theosophy is a higher form of revelation for our age. We are informed in Scripture repeatedly that "the preaching of the cross is to them that perish foolishness; but unto us which are saved it is the power of God" (1 Corinthians 1:18). Theosophy is just another attempt to supplant the authority of Christ and Scripture with "the philosophy and empty deceit" of the world (Colossians 2:8).

Theosophy, in common with the other non-Christian religions of the world, offers no living redeemer, no freedom from the power of sin, and in the end no hope for the world to come. Jesus Christ, on the other hand, offers promises by the mouths of prophets and the God who cannot lie that those who trust in and serve Him shall "receive [for their faith] an hundredfold, and shall inherit everlasting life" (Matthew 19:29).

We must seek to win Theosophists to a saving knowledge of the gospel, but we must not forget that their theology has many labyrinths, for "there is a way which seemeth right unto a man," in the words of Solomon, "but the end thereof are the ways of death" (Proverbs 14:12).

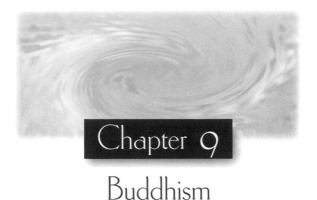

Chapter 9

Buddhism

Editor's Note:
Although Buddhism is a world religion, and thus not technically a "cult" as defined in this book, it is included in this volume because of its strong presence in the United States and its importance as a foundation from which come some contemporary American religious movements that more closely fit this book's definition of a "cult."

When thousands of Chinese laborers flocked to San Francisco in the 1820s, they brought with them new customs, new foods, and a new religion: Buddhism. By 1875 "there were 400 'joss houses' in California—usually incense-soaked, top-story dens, crowded with ancestral relics, little lacquered Buddhas, and dusty *sutra* scrolls [basic teaching texts]."[1]

At the same time the East Coast was getting its own dose of Asian philosophy. Several prominent Westerners had been captivated by Oriental wisdom and were injecting it skillfully into the American academic psyche. Transcendentalist Henry David Thoreau, for example, "fell in love with the *Lotus Sutra*," an A.D. third century Buddhist text. He subsequently translated and published much of it.[2]

Buddhist thought trickled into the religiously inclined of mainstream America for more than one hundred years. Not until the 1960s, however, did Buddhism gain a true foothold in this country. Buddhist authors D. T. Suzuki and Alan Watts (a former Episcopalian priest) had made *Zen* (a form of Buddhism) a household word by that decade. Their many books, which spanned the previous thirty years, "opened the door for Westerners to *become* Buddhists, not just study its message."[3]

Another major wave of Asian immigrants hit American shores in 1978. They

---

This chapter written by Richard Abanes and edited by Gretchen Passantino.

---

[1]"Is Buddha Awakening the U.S.?" *Hinduism Today* 16:7 (July 1994): 1.
[2]Ibid., 16.
[3]Ibid.

came from war-torn Indochinese countries such as Vietnam, Cambodia, Laos, Thailand, and Burma. Within ten years more than a million Buddhists had relocated to the United States. Hundreds of small temples sprang up across America, and two types of Buddhist groups emerged—ethnic Asian Buddhists and ethnic American Buddhists.[4]

Asian Buddhists were bound together not only by religious beliefs, but also by culture, language, ritual, and tradition. American Buddhists, on the other hand, were drawn to the philosophical aspects of Buddhism, which they largely divorced from the more ethnic elements of the religion.

It is undeniable that Buddhism—once a religion of the East—is now a popular faith in the West. American converts to Buddhism number in the hundreds of thousands and include many notable celebrities, among them: Joan Baez, Tina Turner, Richard Gere, Larry Hagman, and Harrison Ford.

In 1993 there were approximately 1,000 Buddhist temples, monasteries, and centers throughout the United States.[5] Some are multimillion-dollar "learning complexes." Consider the 488-acre City of 10,000 Buddhas, located just north of San Francisco, the thirty million dollar Hsi Lai Temple near Los Angeles, and the 125-acre Chuang Yen Monastery in New York. These mega-repositories of Buddhist teachings promote Buddhism "on an unprecedented scale."[6] However, most temples, especially the Asian ones, are very austere, often located in private homes in residential areas or in small industrial parks, and are supported on a marginal level by members and community fund-raising efforts such as weekly Bingo games.

There are literally hundreds of forms of Buddhism, and all of them may be traced back to the essential teachings of a man named Siddhartha Gautama— the Buddha. ("The Buddha" is a Sanskrit title meaning "enlightened." It can be applied to others, but "is particularly applied to Gautama, the founder of Buddhism.")[7] It is with Gautama that any study of Buddhism must begin.

The Enlightened One

Buddhist scholars agree that a historically accurate picture of the Buddha's life is impossible to reconstruct. When narratives about him were finally written down some four hundred years after his death, devotees greatly embellished the accounts of his life, actions, and words. Take, for instance, the following story of the Buddha's birth:

> The child comes forth from his mother while she is standing up and holding on to the branch of a sacred sal tree. He is completely free of any afterbirth and is immediately able to walk and talk. He takes seven steps in each of the cardinal directions and proclaims himself ruler of the universe.[8]

Despite exaggerations about the Buddha, a rough outline of his life can be

---

[4]"Is Buddha Awakening the U.S.?" 16.
[5]James C. Stephens, "Looking at Buddhist America: A Key to World Evangelization," *International Journal of Frontier Missions*, 10:3 (July 1993): 110.
[6]"Is Buddha Awakening the U.S.?" 16.
[7]Geoffrey Parrinder, *A Dictionary of Non-Christian Religions.* (Philadelphia: The Westminster Press, 1971), 53.
[8]C. George Fry, James R. King, Eugene R. Swanger, and Herbert C. Wolf, *Great Asian Religions*, 65.

made. One must continually bear in mind, however, that beyond archaeological evidence proving his historical existence, "we know very little about the circumstances of his life."[9] What we do know is that the India into which he was born had been shaped religiously by Brahmanism, an ancient religion established there more than three thousand years ago by the Aryan conquerors of the indigenous people of the subcontinent. The Aryans were "a powerful group of Indo-European-speaking people"[10] who unified the myriad religions and people groups under an umbrella of religious philosophy that became Hinduism.

These invading conquerors of the Indus Valley forced their vanquished foes to adopt Brahmanism (which later developed into part of Hinduism) for two reasons: (1) to maintain Aryan ethnic purity; and (2) to subjugate the native Indians both spiritually and socially. Brahmanism was able to accomplish these goals because of its caste system, a rigid set of distinctions that divided all persons into the following social/religious classes:

(1) *brahmins* (Aryan priests);

(2) *kshatriyas* (warrior-nobility);

(3) *vaishyas* (the bourgeois, or middle class [businessmen/farmers], viewed as low class by those above them);

(4) *sudras* (servants, not allowed to recite or listen to the Vedas [Hindu scriptures]); and

(5) *outcasts* (the illegitimate, criminals, and those in unclean jobs [e.g., leather workers, barbers, etc.]).[11]

Into this culture was born Siddhartha Gautama, the son of King Suddhodana Gautama, a chieftain (*raja*) of the Shakya clan, a family within the *kshatriya* caste. It is believed that Siddhartha ("he who has accomplished his objectives") was born around 563 B.C.[12] His father apparently reigned over Kapilavastu, "a small district on the Indian slope of the Himalayas in a region that borders between India and Nepal [Northeastern India]."[13]

Shortly after Siddhartha's birth, a hermit named Asita allegedly had a vision of "the rejoicing of the gods at the birth of the man supreme, who was born for the welfare and bliss of all the world."[14] Asita subsequently traveled to Suddhodana's royal court where he was shown the child. The hermit allegedly prophesied the following:

> This Prince, if he remains in the palace, when grown up, will become a great King and subjugate the whole world. But if he forsakes the court life to embrace a religious life, he will become a Buddha, the Savior of the world.[15]

King Suddhodana—believing that contact with human misery would

[9]Alexandra David-Neel, *Buddhism: Its Doctrines and Its Methods* (New York: Avon Books, ed. 1977), 15.

[10]J. Isamu Yamamoto, "The Buddha," *Christian Research Journal* (Spring/Summer 1994): 11.

[11]Fry, et al., *Great Asian Religions*, 42–43.

[12]In *Gautama the Buddha*, author Richard H. Drummond notes that in China and Japan the birthdate for Siddhartha of 1067 B.C. has been traditionally held. Modern Buddhists in Burma, Ceylon, and India, and those of the Theravada school of Buddhism believe 623 B.C. was the year in which the Buddha was born. Buddhists in Thailand, Cambodia, and Laos maintain that he was born in 624 B.C.

[13]Yamamoto, "The Buddha," 12.

[14]*Sutta-Nipata*, 679–698; *Woven Cadences of Early Buddhists*, 102–104, both as quoted in Drummond, *Gautama*, 30.

[15]Buddhist Promoting Foundation (Bukkyo Denod Kyokai), *The Teachings of Buddha*, 3.

prompt Siddhartha to leave home in search of spiritual truth—immediately ordered his servants to forever shield the prince from all contact with evil and suffering. Siddhartha would be a prisoner of luxury. It is said that in order to distract Siddhartha from the cares of this world, King Suddhodana gave his son many possessions, including three palaces and 40,000 dancing girls.

Legend has it that when Siddhartha reached the age of sixteen, five hundred women were sent to him as prospective brides. Eventually he chose as his bride his cousin Yasodhara.[16] According to one account, he won her hand by performing "twelve marvelous feats in the art of archery."[17]

Siddhartha's life was unfolding as his father had planned until the young prince, out of either curiosity or inner discontent, eluded his royal attendants and ventured into the outside world. Over a succession of several days he visited nearby Lumbini Park, where he made some disturbing observations.[18]

He first beheld an old man, broken and bent by age. On the next day, Siddhartha saw a diseased person, possibly a leper. During his third excursion, the prince viewed a corpse. When he took another trip on day four, he met an ascetic (a monk who practices self-denial).

Siddhartha was never the same. He concluded that life is nothing but an experience plagued by sorrow. Why is there so much suffering? How can men escape what seems to be an inescapable round of torment? Is there no end to pain and sorrow? To answer these and other questions, Siddhartha left home and began a spiritual quest for truth. Some say he departed on the very night Yasodhara gave birth to their son, Rahula ("hindrance").[19]

For about six years, young Gautama wandered about as a poor beggar, studying meditation and philosophy. His pilgrimage led him to two yogis (spiritual teachers). He attempted to follow their path of spirituality by eating nothing but seeds and grass, gradually reducing his diet to only a single grain of rice each day.[20] In one experiment, "he ate only dung."[21]

Then he met and joined a company of five monks with whom he practiced various methods of asceticism. He lay on thorns, wore rough-textured clothing, and refused to sit, choosing instead to always crouch on his heels. He "gave up cleansing his body until the dirt was so thick that it would fall from his body of its own weight."[22] He would hold his breath "until it felt as though someone were forcing a heated sword through his skull."[23] He even "slept in a yard where rotting human corpses were laid out to be eaten by vultures and scavengers."[24]

Siddhartha hoped to attain an understanding of life through his self-denial,

---

[16]Drummond, *Gautama*, 31. Other accounts give Yasodhara's name as Yashodhara, Yasohara, Bhaddakacca, and Bimba. Some stories also put Siddhartha's age at marriage as nineteen (cf. The Buddhist Promoting Foundation's *Teachings*, 4).

[17]Yamamoto, "The Buddha," 12.

[18]Drummond, *Gautama*, 32. Other versions of the story say he drove his chariot through the city four times. A few accounts say that he simply envisioned four different states of humanity.

[19]Some accounts say Rahula was born seven days before Siddhartha's departure. Other stories maintain that Siddhartha left on the night of Rahula's conception.

[20]St. Elmo Nauman, *Dictionary of Asian Philosophies* (Secaucus, N.J.: Citadel Press, 1978), 23. Other accounts state his diet consisted of a single bean each day.

[21]Ibid.

[22]Fry, et al., *Great Asian Religions*, 67.

[23]Ibid.

[24]Nauman, *Dictionary*, 23.

but failed. He did, however, gain a realization—neither asceticism (what he was then enduring) nor extravagant living (as he had experienced in the royal court) brought "truth" any nearer. There existed a better path—the Middle Way. A good illustration of this path can be drawn from a stringed musical instrument: "If the strings are strung too loose, they will not play. On the other hand, if they are strung too tight, they will break."[25]

When Siddhartha demonstrated this realization by eating a normal meal in front of his fellow monks, they deserted him. Undaunted, Gautama headed for Gaya (a major city in the northeast of India). There, beneath a full moon in May, he spread a mat under a fig tree on the banks of the Meranjana River and assumed the "lotus" position (sitting in a modified cross-legged position). He vowed to remain there until he understood life's mysteries. It was his thirty-fifth birthday.

After stilling his mind "like a hummingbird poised in mid-air,"[26] Siddhartha began meditating. Within several hours he allegedly saw an "infinite succession of deaths and births in an ever-flowing stream of life."[27] In other words, he had a vision that supported the doctrine of reincarnation, a foundational teaching of the Brahman religion in which he had been raised:

> Thus, with mind concentrated, purified, cleansed . . . I directed my mind to the passing away and rebirth of beings. With divine, purified, superhuman vision I saw beings passing away and being reborn, low and high, of good and bad color, in happy or miserable existences, according to their *karma* (in other words, according to that universal law by which every act of good or evil will be rewarded or punished either in this life or in some later incarnation).[28]

Siddhartha continued meditating until he reached complete enlightenment: "I realized that rebirth has been destroyed, the holy life has been lived, the job has been done, there is nothing after this."[29] Along with his vision came an internal perception of how to obtain liberation from *samsara*, or the cycle of rebirths. The young prince had lost his ignorance about the nature of this world. He understood everything. He had become the "awakened one," the "enlightened one"—the Buddha.

According to Buddhist scriptures, Siddhartha remained under that tree in a state of bliss for seven weeks, after which he faced his first dilemma: Should he share what he had learned with others or keep his knowledge to himself? This may seem like an odd predicament to the Western reader, but in the Eastern world, especially in the Buddha's day, it was common for monks who had obtained wisdom to retreat from society with their knowledge. Gautama chose to remain in the public and impart what he had learned.

Two months later and nearly one hundred miles from where he had achieved enlightenment, the Buddha gave his first sermon. Near the holy city of Benares (modern Veranasi) at Isipatana in the Deer Park, he presented an

---

[25]Adapted from "Little Buddha," Miramax Films, 1994.
[26]"Is Buddha Awakening the U.S.?" 1.
[27]Nauman, *Dictionary*, 24.
[28]Ibid., 24–25.
[29]Henry Warren, *Buddhism in Translations*, 380–381, as quoted in Fry, et al., *Great Asian Religions*, 67–68.

address called the "Wheel of the Doctrine."[30] It contained the Four Noble Truths, which would serve as the foundational teachings of Buddhism.

For more than forty years the Buddha continued instructing all who would listen. Then, tragedy struck at Kusinara in the district of Gorakhpur. Chunda the blacksmith fed the Buddha either spoiled pig's flesh or poisoned mushrooms (truffles).[31] The Buddha quickly fell ill with dysentery and died at the age of eighty.

Buddhism Basics

All of the Buddha's teachings, collectively called the *dharma*, deal with one basic goal—how to escape *samsara*. *Samsara* is the cycle of rebirths that is known more commonly in the West as reincarnation. Freedom from *samsara* leads to *nirvana*, which is commonly thought of as a state of complete deliverance from pain and sorrow, a state of bliss—the Eastern equivalent of heaven.

The *dharma*'s entire purpose is to teach Buddhists how to progress along the path toward *nirvana*. This journey is a progression that can be achieved only by following what the Buddha termed his Four Noble Truths, also called *Pativedhanana*, which translated means "the wisdom of realization." These "truths" center around: (1) the universality of suffering; (2) the origin of suffering; (3) the overcoming of suffering; and (4) the way leading to the suppression of suffering."[32]

The First Noble Truth

Life is full of sorrow and pain, says the Buddha. To believe that life without suffering is possible is to believe an illusion. Here, then, is the First Noble Truth, or *dukkha* (literally, "a bone twisted out of its joint")—every dimension of life is saturated with pain."[33]

According to the Buddha, people do not accept this truth, but instead choose to cope with pain by deceiving themselves into thinking that life is also filled with happiness. This is an illusion because happiness is fleeting and can never compensate for all the suffering that one experiences.

The intolerable anguish of such a concept is understandable when one considers the doctrine of reincarnation that the Buddha was taught throughout his upbringing. Being born again and again into a life filled with pain and sorrow was truly an unbearable thought to him. Siddhartha found that the first step toward being released from this cycle of rebirths is simple acceptance of the fact that life is indeed only one long experience of suffering and that all happiness is but an illusion.

The Second Noble Truth

The Second Noble Truth, *tanha* ("attachment"), teaches that the suffering we encounter is all due to the "false desires of the senses that have been de-

---

[30]E. A. Burtt, *The Teachings of the Compassionate Buddha*, 29, 31.
[31]Geoffrey Parrinder, *Avatar and Incarnation* (New York: Oxford University Press, 1982), 139–140.
[32]Yamamoto, "The Buddha," 15, 33.
[33]Fry, et al., *Great Asian Religions*, 68.

ceived into clinging to the impermanent world.''[34] This is the core of the Buddha's revelation—"the cause of suffering is desire, craving due to ignorance.''[35]

Tanha is closely related to the Buddha's contention that all things in life are meaningless and insignificant because they are temporary. Ignorance (*avidya*) of this truth is a major obstacle that must be overcome if one is to gain freedom from reincarnation. Exactly how *avidya* (ignorance of life's impermanence) and *tanha* (attachment to impermanent things) interact is a rather complicated concept. When simplified it breaks down into the following basic steps:

- Everything in life is temporal, fleeting, and passing. Nothing lasts forever. Possessions, institutions, nations, languages, ideas, and feelings come and go like the wind. They are here today and gone tomorrow.
- All things (e.g., family, friends, desires, etc.) are subject to time and are in the process of passing away. The Buddha interpreted this to mean that nothing has any real meaning or significance.
- According to the Buddha, everything in life is ultimately unreal because it is fleeting. But we ignorantly attribute reality to such things. By doing so, we give them a degree of ongoing significance and permanence and subsequently attach ourselves to them, which in turn causes suffering.

In Buddhist thought, we are somewhat like people watching a movie. If, for example, we are watching the classic film *Romeo and Juliet*, we see the young couple fall in love and watch them as their hope for a life together is destroyed because of feuding families. Tears stream down our cheeks as we behold the star-crossed lovers lying dead. We have attributed reality to what we see on the screen and have become emotionally caught up in something that does not really exist.

Similarly, a modern murder mystery may show a darkened home with a woman inside who is oblivious to the presence of a psychopathic killer lurking upstairs. "We begin gripping more tightly the arms of our seats. Our breathing becomes shorter. . . . We are attaching (*tanha*) ourselves to the insubstantial images, as we do so, we become anxious (*dukkha*).''[36]

Such clinging to unreality is caused not only by our unfortunate attribution of reality and significance to the things around us, but even more so through our belief that we ourselves are significant and lasting. The Buddha taught that the "self" is nothing but a temporary creation that suffers until *nirvana* is reached.

To the Buddha, the "self" is merely a false image comprised of energy, memories, thoughts, hopes, and fears. Mistakenly viewing ourselves as anything more "is the underlying cause of all greed, anger, hatred, alienation, and aversion, as well as the destructive social behaviors that arise from them.''[37]

The Third Noble Truth

Nirodha ("cessation") is the Third Noble Truth. It teaches that the way out of suffering lies in the ability to disengage oneself completely from the false desires

---

[34]Yamamoto, "The Buddha," 33.
[35]Nauman, *Dictionary*, 38.
[36]Fry, et al., *Great Asian Religions*, 70–71.
[37]Ibid., 71.

of the temporary self. It admonishes one to give up all mental, emotional, or physical cravings, because those desires are merely the manifestation of a person's delusion that the "self" is a permanent entity. Hence, all desires are the ultimate cause of all suffering.

Abandoning our earthly desires helps remove our deluded state and bring about the realization that the "self" is but a brief arrangement of impersonal elements. Once this is realized, continued rejection of all desires nullifies their effects. This, when coupled with meritorious positive actions in life, leads to the complete end of suffering—*nirvana.*

The Buddha's teachings on rejection of desire and suppression of emotional attachment is seen perhaps best in the story of a monk named Sangamaji. Like Siddhartha, Sangamaji had left his wife and family to search for truth as a homeless wanderer. While sitting in meditation beneath a tree, his wife approached him and lay their child before him. She asked her husband to nourish her and their child. Sangamaji remained silent until finally the woman took the child and left.

Siddhartha, after observing the incident, reportedly commented, "He [Sangamaji] feels no pleasure when she comes, no sorrow when she goes: a true Brahman released from passion."[38]

The Fourth Noble Truth

The Fourth Noble Truth is the Buddhist life ethic, and it provides practical steps that can be taken to speed one along his journey to *nirvana.* The Buddha taught that this sacred path has eight branches, which comprise various dimensions of an overall lifestyle that must be adopted by someone who desires to be delivered from suffering. It is called the sacred Noble Eightfold Path (*Marga*):

(1) *Right Views (understanding).* Belief that the Four Noble Truths are true, accurate, and reliable.

(2) *Right Aspirations (ambition):* A "total commitment of body, mind, and will to the training and discipline required to extricate oneself from the human predicament."[39] One must resolve to maintain thoughts "free from lust, ill will, cruelty, or untruthfulness"[40] and "renounce the selfish self and sensual pleasures."[41]

(3) *Right Speech (communication):* One's words "must be not only charitable but also free from egocentricity."[42] One must abstain from "gossiping, lying, tattling . . . harsh language, vain talk, or reveling" and speak "kindly, open, and truthful."[43]

(4) *Right Conduct (action):* A "beneficent behavior extended universally to all living things coupled with an abstinence from alcohol and drugs, for a person must have complete control over his mind to accomplish the difficult task of redemption."[44] One should abstain "from killing, stealing, and sexual miscon-

---

[38]*Udana 1:8—The Minor Anthologies of the Pali Canon 2:7* as quoted in Drummond, *Gautama,* 110.
[39]Fry, et al., *Great Asian Religions,* 72.
[40]Nauman, *Dictionary,* 27.
[41]Drummond, *Gautama,* 89.
[42]Fry, et al., *Great Asian Religions,* 72.
[43]Nauman, *Dictionary,* 27.
[44]Fry, et al., *Great Asian Religions,* 72.

duct" and practice actions that are "peaceful, honest, and pure."[45]

(5) *Right Livelihood (vocation)*: A "proper means of support . . . in which a person does not inflict pain on other people or creatures."[46] A butcher, soldier, fisherman, or exterminator would not fit this path.

(6) *Right Effort (endeavor)*: A willingness to reach "deep inside oneself to draw upon all the energy a person possesses."[47] Showing such effort involves "self-training and self-control, self-discipline."[48] The disciple "puts forth will, he makes effort, he stirs up energy, he grips and forces his mind."[49]

(7) *Right Mindfulness (mind control)*: Involves paying "close attention to one's mood, emotions, and feelings," because "all we are is the result of what we have thought."[50] Right mindfulness also means examining "every state of feeling in body or mind."[51]

(8) *Right Concentration (deep meditation)*: A special practice of meditation in which "thought itself . . . [is] annihilated and the mind rests."[52] This trance-like state of consciousness is induced through practicing intense concentration on one single object. It progresses through four stages, the end result being "rapture of utter purity of mindfulness . . . wherein neither ease is felt or any ill."[53]

By following this Fourth Noble Truth, a person supposedly will be able to eliminate all selfish and false desires, the key to obtaining *nirvana.* Those who reach complete "purity of thought and life" become an *arahat,* or someone who is "freed from the necessity of rebirth, ready for the peace of *nirvana.*"[54] This state can be attained only by those who, in this life, distance themselves from all desire:

> This is to know *nirvana,* to have achieved detachment and thereby libera-
> tion. Herein is "Nothingness" experienced, awareness that true Reality is empty
> of grasping, separative selfhood. The religious life has been lived, the way out
> of the human dilemma [reincarnation] has been found and followed, from this
> point onward human life on earth is presumed to be lived in a new dimension
> of Reality.[55]

Those who reach *nirvana* are freed forever from all the anxieties, fears, and desires that possess ordinary people; they are freed "from the eternal round of decay, suffering, and death."[56] They will never again be reborn. It is a state of mind marked in this life by "a sense of liberation, inward peace and strength, insight into truth, the joy of complete oneness with reality, and love toward all creatures in the universe."[57] After death, there is total annihilation.

Such a concept of *nirvana* is slightly different than the one embraced by

---

45Nauman, *Dictionary,* 27.
46Fry, et al., *Great Asian Religions,* 72.
47Ibid.
48Nauman, *Dictionary,* 27.
49Drummond, *Gautama,* 91.
50Fry, et al., *Great Asian Religions,* 72.
51Nauman, *Dictionary,* 27.
52Fry, et al., *Great Asian Religions,* 72.
53Drummond, *Gautama,* 92.
54Nauman, *Dictionary,* 27.
55Drummond, *Gautama,* 92.
56Burtt, *Teachings,* 29.
57Ibid.

the Brahmans of Siddhartha's day and by modern Hindus. Brahmanism/Hinduism teaches that *nirvana* is reached when an individual soul is united with the Universal Soul. This might be comparable to a raindrop (individual soul) falling into the ocean (Universal Soul). The Buddha, on the other hand, believed that *nirvana* is reached when, like a candle flame being blown out, a soul's elements, along with all individual identity, are extinguished.

A doctrinal corollary to reincarnation—*karma*—seeks to explain what factors determine the life into which a person will be reborn. This, too, is slightly reinterpreted by the Buddha. According to the Brahman/Hindu concept of *karma*, one's actions in this life determine the kind of life into which the self or "soul" is reborn.

The Buddha agreed that our good deeds and bad deeds accumulate either merit or debt, and that the ratio of merit to debt determines the state of our next life. But rather than teaching that an individual soul or "self" is reborn, the Buddha maintained that only "karmic matter," or the elements that comprise a person's identity (the "self"), is reborn. Even then, these elements are totally rearranged at rebirth, "much as a 'chariot' is a name for a certain grouping of parts that can be rearranged to be something else while still comprising the same parts."[58]

In other words, the Buddha taught that when someone is reborn, that "person" is not really reborn at all. There is no personal "soul" that continues to exist after someone dies. What is reborn is nothing but rearranged karmic matter that was once a particular individual. The person, or the original "self" that once lived, no longer truly exists. Eventually, through successive rearrangements of *karma*, even those elements that comprised the various persons will be extinguished forever. This is the Buddhist idea of *nirvana*.

Unfortunately, becoming a Buddhist monk is the only way to reach *nirvana* from this present life. One must "abandon ordinary social living and join the monastic community, which Buddha established for those sincere in their quest for liberation."[59] A person can reach *nirvana* only by leaving behind family, friends, and occupation, and joining a *sangha* (an alms-dependent order of Buddhist monks).

This does not mean that the average person cannot follow the Buddha's teachings. They can. But according to the Buddha, they will not be able to attain *nirvana* in this lifetime. Nor will they benefit from "the higher fruits of the *dharma* (such as inner tranquility)."[60] The best they can hope for is to be reborn as an individual who, in that next lifetime, will become a monk. According to the oldest Buddhist tradition, a woman will *never* reach *nirvana* from this life, even if she becomes a Buddhist nun. She must be reborn as a man who becomes a monk.

Buddhist Branches

There are many different Buddhist schools, sects, and branches. Each one interprets the Buddha's core teachings a little differently and holds to a number

---

[58]Yamamoto, "The Buddha," 15.
[59]David L. Johnson, *A Reasoned Look at Asian Religions* (Minneapolis: Bethany House Publishers, 1985), 121.
[60]Yamamoto, "The Buddha," 33.

of distinctive views. Various Buddhist sects sometimes even rely on their own holy writings that are unrecognized as authoritative by other Buddhists.

Attempting to explore all forms of Buddhism would be unmanageable in one chapter. The three main schools of Buddhist doctrine, however, represent the majority of Buddhist movements' essential features. These three schools, which have developed over the centuries following the Buddha, include Theravada ("more monastic and conservative"), Mahayana ("more liberal and lay-oriented"), and Vajrayana, or Tibetan ("the most esoteric").[61]

Theravada Versus Mahayana

Immediately after the Buddha's death, members of his original *sangha* sought to organize their master's teachings into a system of doctrines on which they could agree. They successfully did this and began sharing their beliefs with others. But disagreements soon arose regarding the Buddha's exact words and what he meant by those words. This occurred because his disciples, in accordance with the Indian tradition of oral preservation of spiritual teachings, had not written down any of the Buddha's discourses during his lifetime. Such writings were not compiled until four hundred years after the Buddha's lifetime.

The Buddha's *sangha* eventually split into a number of small groups holding to different interpretations of the *dharma*. Conflict over the meaning of the *dharma* arose not only between individual monks, but also between various monasteries. A severe fragmentation of Buddhism ensued, which by the third century B.C. had produced approximately eighteen different sects. The first major rift between schools occurred from about 200 B.C. to A.D. 200 and led to the formation of two traditions still in existence today—Theravada and Mahayana.

Within the Theravada tradition are Buddhist schools holding to a strict interpretation of the Buddha's teachings. This tradition is often termed the "fundamentalist branch" of Buddhism because it has preserved what is probably the original form of Buddhism.[62]

Mahayana Buddhism includes individuals and schools who subscribe to teachings that are "modifications and amplifications of themes already present in the Theravadin heritage."[63]

When this division took place, followers of the newer way called their belief system Mahayana, which means the "greater vehicle" of salvation, or the "expansive way." They disdainfully labeled the older schools Hinayana, which means the "lesser vehicle" of salvation, or the "exclusive way."[64]

---

[61]"Is Buddha Awakening the U.S.?" 1 (cf. Yamamoto, "The Buddha," 34).

[62]Yamamoto, "The Arrival of Theravada," *Christian Research Journal* (Fall 1994): 17.

[63]Fry, et al., *Great Asian Religions*, 74.

[64]Clark B. Offner, *The World's Religions*, 181, as quoted in Josh McDowell and Don Stewart, *Handbook of Today's Religions* (San Bernardino, Calif.: Here's Life Publishers, 1981), 310.

Theravada	Mahayana
Buddha—Although Siddhartha was a superior man of extraordinary intellect and exceptional talent, he was nonetheless only a human being. He is not worshiped.	*Buddha*—Siddhartha was a sacred manifestation of the Absolute, or *Brahman*. His body and physical actions were merely an illusion. He is often worshiped as a god.
Deliverance—Escaping the cycle of rebirth is dependent upon entrance into a monastery. Only there, through great self-effort, can one attain disengagement from the world and its false desires. Eventually, perhaps through several lifetimes, *nirvana* will be obtained.	*Deliverance*—Escaping the cycle of rebirth may be obtained through self-effort, but such effort is not mandatory, nor is joining a monastery. According to some sects, one may pray to the Buddha for deliverance. His compassion and grace can save everyone, even evil persons.
Ideal—One's life goal is simply to reach *nirvana* and exit this life. Becoming an enlightened one (*arahat*) without regard for others is the accepted attitude.	*Ideal*—The most important goal is to help others reach *nirvana*. One who is enlightened (a *buddha*) will postpone his own "salvation" in order to assist others.

Buddhists of both traditions look to the Buddha as their primary source of truth. But Mahayanists, unlike Theravadins, recognize numerous other Buddhas and *bodhisattvas* (those who help others toward enlightenment and *nirvana*). These personalities are said to be manifestations of the Absolute and, along with the Buddha, are regularly prayed to for assistance. Some are worshiped as gods.

The Theravada and Mahayana scriptures are different as well. The former tradition looks to the Pali Canon (written about 80 B.C.). This text—written in the Pali language and divided into a number of *suttas*—is called the *Tripitaka*, which means literally "three baskets." It is about eleven times as large as the Bible and is arranged in three main divisions: (1) the *Sutta Pitaka* (discourses of Siddhartha); (2) the *Vinaya Pitaka* (precepts and rules for the *Sangha*); and (3) the *Abidhamma Pitaka* (esoteric and philosophical interpretations of the *dharma.*

The Mahayana tradition accepts as authoritative an extensive list of texts called *sutras* (composed primarily between the sixth and first centuries B.C.). The Chinese canon alone encompasses more than 5,000 volumes.[65] Unlike the Theravadin *suttas*, which average only about twenty pages each, the Mahayana *sutras* are very long. They cannot be found in original form in only one language, but instead are written in Chinese, Tibetan, and Sanskrit. Furthermore, since there is no clear limit to the Mahayana canon, recent writings are constantly being added to Mahayana scriptures. This has forced most Mahayana sects to choose favorite texts for common use:

> The fact is that some such selection is necessary, for this extreme bulk of and breadth of the scriptures make it impossible for believers to be acquainted with, let alone understand and practice, the often contradictory teachings found in them.[66]

Followers of Mahayana also take a different view of their scriptures than do

---

[65]Offner, as quoted in McDowell and Stewart, *Handbook*, 310.
[66]Ibid.

followers of Theravada. The latter ascribe value to the Pali Canon because of its literal message. Mahayana Buddhists, however, attribute value to their holy writings not only because of the message contained therein, but also because they believe that the texts themselves possess magical powers which may be drawn upon for protection and material success.

Another difference exists between the Mahayana and Theravada traditions when it comes to *nirvana.* To Theravadins, escape from *samsara*—or the cycle of rebirth—is *nirvana.* It is a state marked by complete deliverance from all pain and sorrow. But in the Mahayana tradition, the whole purpose of becoming a *bodhisattva* is not to escape life, but to remain in life in order to help others reach enlightenment.

If the Theravada explanation of *nirvana* is coupled with the Mahayana concept of what it means to reach enlightenment, then hypothetically the most spiritually advanced persons would never reach *nirvana* because they always forsake escape from *samsara* in order to help others. Consequently, those in the Mahayana tradition have had to change the definition of *nirvana* to "the true state of spiritual perfection" rather than escape from rebirth:

> Thus the perfected Bodhisattva becomes aware that just by being a Bodhisattva he is already in *nirvana.* . . . For him *nirvana* and *Samsara* are not two different realms. . . . Paradoxically put . . . to renounce *nirvana* for oneself, in love for others, is to find oneself in *nirvana,* in its real meaning.[67]
>
> Despite their many differences, Theravada and Mahayana Buddhists share many beliefs in common: (1) reincarnation; (2) karma; (3) the world is constantly changing and is impermanent; (4) the world's changing nature brings suffering; (5) liberation from suffering is possible; (6) deliverance from rebirth and suffering takes place through a change in consciousness; (7) a liberating change in consciousness can be obtained only through following the teachings of the Buddha and/or reliance upon the Buddha's love and mercy.[68]

Vajrayana: Wisdom of Tibet

Vajrayana Buddhism—also known as Tibetan Buddhism, Tantric Buddhism, and Lamaism—is called the "diamond way," which by implication means it is the precious, changeless, pure, and clear way. It developed during the fifth to sixth centuries A.D. as Buddhism spread through northern India, Nepal, and finally Tibet.

At that time, the prevailing belief of Tibet was the Bon religion, "a mixture of shamanism [a form of witchcraft], magic, and primitive nature worship."[69] Vajrayana was born when these practices, along with magical formulae designed to obtain magical powers, were incorporated into Buddhism (A.D. 600–1200).[70] Included in the Vajrayana tradition are a number of advanced meditative techniques: yoga, special hand gestures (*mudras*), spells, and chants. It also derives many of its doctrines from Vedantic and Tantric influences.[71]

---

[67]Burtt, *Teachings,* 162.
[68]Fry, et al., *Great Asian Religions,* 85.
[69]J. Isamu Yamamoto, "Tibetan Buddhists," *Christian Research Journal* (Spring 1995): 9.
[70]Gard, *Great Religions,* 328.
[71]Ibid., 25.

Vedanta is an Indian school of philosophy, which teaches that god (*Brahman*) and the soul (*Atman*) are one. In other words, there is only one ultimate reality—*Brahman*—and the individuality we see is nothing but an illusion. The maker (*maya*) of illusion is ignorance (*avidya*). Enlightenment occurs when one realizes that "the world is not real: only the Absolute, Brahman, is real."[72]

The Tantras are a series of A.D. sixth century scriptures associated with the worship of Shakti, Mother of the Universe. They are made available only to initiates of various Tantric religions (Tibetan Buddhism is only one of many Tantric belief systems). Study of these texts "is said to reveal clairvoyance, clairaudience, telepathy, psychometry, the power of sound, vocal expression, and the composition of music."[73]

The word *tantra* basically means "loom" and refers more specifically to the threads of a loom. This expresses the foundational teaching of Tantraism—all things are interwoven into one ultimate reality. Tantraism is also based on a variety of sex rituals that involve "breathing exercises, meditation, and the prolonged sexual contact known as *maithuna*."[74]

The sexual philosophy within Tantric Buddhism is linked to a number of ideas. There is the belief that erotic love is a profound experience that "opens the mind to a sense of awe and wonder akin to religious experience."[75] Also present is the idea that during the act of sexual intercourse, a transcending of boundaries between participants occurs, leading to an experience of oneness with each other. There exists the additional notion that the best way to escape blinding passion—in this case sexual lust—is to "go into the act that is desired rather than to retreat from it."[76]

Perhaps the most important part of Tantric religions, including Tibetan Buddhism, is the belief that male and female energies reside in everyone. The male energy is said to be the dynamic, powerful, and moving force. The female energy is thought of as static and docile.

These two energies correspond to aspects of one's spirituality. The female side is connected to inward properties such as "wisdom and realization" and is linked to "the more symbolic or intuitive aspects of understanding."[77] The dynamic (male) side "relates to outgoing aspects such as compassion and strength," as well as to cognitive knowledge.[78] The goal of Tantric sex practices is to unite the two spiritual forces through physical union.

Some followers of Tantric religions, however, believe that sexual intercourse is not necessary. They maintain that the sex acts depicted in Tantric art and literature are only symbolic representations of a spiritual unification of both energies that can, through meditation and other practices, lead to a uniting of the male and female energies.

Many of the occult aspects of Tibetan Buddhism also come from Tantraism. The Tantric tradition maintains a close relationship to magic and includes

---

[72]Nauman, *Dictionary*, 343.
[73]Ibid., 328.
[74]Walt Anderson, *Open Secrets: A Western Guide to Tibetan Buddhism.* (New York: Viking Press, 1979), 62.
[75]Ibid.
[76]Ibid.
[77]Ibid., 63.
[78]Ibid.

"secret teachings, scriptures in code, the practice of drawing symbols on the ground, and uttering spells to call up deities, supernatural powers that can be used for good or evil."[79]

According to Walt Anderson, author of *Open Secrets: A Western Guide to Tibetan Buddhism*, the Tantric Buddhist ideal is to yield: "Go ahead and do it, whatever it is, if you think you must and it doesn't harm somebody else. But pay attention; be fully aware of what goes on in your mind and body, of how it really feels."[80]

Buddhism and Christianity

Before examining where Buddhism differs from biblical Christianity, it is only fair to point out some of the areas where Buddhism agrees, to a limited degree and for other reasons, with the Bible. Acknowledging such areas can facilitate open communication between Christians and Buddhists.

First, most Buddhists are taught to live according to several precepts that are in total harmony with Scripture. Such precepts include refraining from stealing, not committing adultery, and not lying. God's Word reflects each of these values (see Exodus 20:14–16).

Second, all Buddhists recognize that this life is temporal. Nothing here has any eternality. All things are finite, limited, and unable to sustain their own existence. So fleeting is this life that to grow attached to anything here is but a manifestation of one's ignorance of reality. This sentiment is reflected in several portions of Solomon's words in the biblical book of Ecclesiastes:

> Vanity of vanities . . . all is vanity. . . . I have seen all the works that are done under the sun; and, behold, all is vanity and vexation of spirit. . . . I gave my heart to know wisdom, and to know madness and folly: I perceived that this also is vexation of spirit. . . . Then I looked at all the works that my hands had wrought. . . . and behold all was vanity and vexation of spirit, and there was no profit under the sun (Ecclesiastes 1:2, 14, 17; 2:11).

Third, Buddhism teaches that all people are subject to suffering. The Bible again supports this belief. Pain, affliction, and human misery are spoken of often in Scripture (Genesis 3:16–19; Job 2:13; Hebrews 11:36–38). God's Word additionally teaches us that although suffering is never a pleasant experience, it can be used to our benefit. Honorable character traits such as patience, humility, compassion, strength, faith, and repentance are all forged in the furnace of adversity (Psalm 119:67, 71; Lamentations 3:19–20; 2 Corinthians 1:4; 12:7; 1 Peter 1:7; 5:10).

Buddhism and Christianity part company, however, concerning a crucial perspective on suffering. Buddhists find no redeeming value whatsoever in suffering. Suffering is only something to escape. One does not grow *through* suffering, but *in spite of* suffering. Additionally, in Buddhism suffering does not intermittently intrude into human life, life *is* suffering:

> Old age is suffering, illness is suffering, death is suffering, being in contact

---

[79]Anderson, *Open Secrets*, 64.
[80]Ibid., 71.

with that which one dislikes is suffering, being separated from that which one likes is suffering, failure to realize one's desire is suffering.[81]

Christians, on the other hand, view suffering—whether it be through injury, illness, disappointment, etc.—as allowed by God and used by Him to shape and refine us for eternal life. The lessons we learn through suffering accumulate for us an eternal weight of glory (2 Corinthians 4:17). We are told to understand the good that can come out of trials and tribulations (James 1:2).

The most decisive point at which Buddhism departs from Christianity involves that mode of deliverance from the suffering and sin of this impermanent world. According to the Buddha, everyone must escape reincarnation through accumulation of good *karma* via good works, plus mental disengagement from the false desires of the world. Self-effort is the key to obtaining *nirvana*, a state most often defined as bliss marked by annihilation of the karmic elements that once comprised a temporary personality. To Buddhists, there is not even a "self" to enjoy the deliverance that will supposedly be obtained through their mental striving.

The foundational doctrine of Buddhism—reincarnation—is clearly contradicted by the Bible. Hebrews 9:27 teaches us that we live only one lifetime, after which comes the judgment of our souls. Scripture further points out that those who have come to faith in Christ will be in God's presence immediately after death, not reincarnated (Philippians 1:21–23; 2 Corinthians 5:8). Those who do not know Christ likewise will not be reincarnated, but go to a place of punishment (Job 21:30–34; Matthew 26:41; 2 Peter 2:9).

Ultimately, believer and unbeliever alike will be resurrected bodily from the grave. Each person's soul will be reunited with their body in a glorified state (1 Corinthians 15:51–52; 1 Thessalonians 4:14–18). God will then judge who is worthy to dwell with Him for eternity. Followers of Christ will be found worthy based on Christ's willing suffering and sacrifice on the cross as the atonement for their sins (Hebrews 2:9). Through His sacrifice we may come to God (1 Peter 3:18). Our faith in Christ (Romans 5:2; 10:9; Ephesians 2:1–10) appropriates for us His work on the cross, and we receive the gift God offers—eternal life in His presence (John 3:16; Romans 6:23; Revelation 22:5).

Unbelievers—because they rejected God either directly (through rejection of the gospel), or indirectly (through rejection of the light of truth given to them regarding God's nature)—will be told to depart from God's presence (Matthew 7:23; Revelation 20:10–14). This concept of positive or negative judgment is foresight to Buddhists because they do not recognize a personal God. The Buddha rejected subservience to a supreme God and, although he did not deny the existence of many equal gods, he felt that worship of such beings was simply another obstruction on the path to *nirvana*.

To the Buddha, gods were inhabiters of the cosmos who, like all other living things, were impermanent. They, too, must eventually escape the cycle of rebirths. According to the Bible, however, there is only one personal, infinite, eternal, unchanging, transcendent God (Psalm 90:2; Isaiah 43:10; Malachi 3:6; Mark 12:29; James 1:17). Scripture further reveals that God is a being to whom we are indeed accountable (Romans 2:16; 14:10; Hebrews 13:4; James 4:12).

---

[81]David-Neel, *Buddhism,* 30.

Sharing the Gospel with Buddhists

A number of difficulties arise when a Christian attempts to share the Gospel of Christ with Asian Buddhists. Asian Buddhists often link cultural, ethnic, and family loyalties to their religious beliefs. Consequently, asking them to jettison their faith in favor of Christianity is like asking them to deny their family, friends, culture, and heritage.

Abandoning Buddhism is especially problematic for Asian Buddhists who have come to America because of intolerable conditions in their homelands. Buddhist teachings provide the worldview framework from which they understand the calamities that have befallen them. Buddhist philosophy colors how they think about their personal identity in relationship to the rest of the world. Buddhist practices may be the only remaining tangible reminders of their native environment.

Frequently Asian immigrants have difficulties with the English language, especially with its cultural, historical, and linguistic assumptions, and consequently do not understand the gospel message communicated by a native Westerner who speaks only English. Asian Buddhists usually have little or no familiarity with Western rationalism, Christian concepts (such as sin, atonement, repentance, resurrection, sanctification, etc.), Christian practices, Christian ethics, and the Bible. In fact, Christians who fail to account for these problems can think they are communicating one idea when the Buddhist understands something completely different. Tissa Weerasingha, a Christian scholar and pastor in Sri Lanka, illustrates,

> If a Buddhist were to be asked, "Do you want to be born again?," he might likely reply, "Please, no! I do NOT want to be born again. I want to reach nirvana." The Buddhist quest is for deliverance from the cycle of rebirths. If a Buddhist confuses "new birth" with "rebirth," the Christian message will be completely distorted.[82]

Non-Asian Christians can communicate much more effectively by defining terms carefully, avoiding "Christian" vocabulary, and focusing on personal stories of righteous living, complete forgiveness, and God's compassion.[83]

Reaching out to American Buddhists presents an equally difficult task. Westerners tend to be "far more interested in what they can experience mystically than what they can understand theologically."[84] Furthermore, American converts often do not embrace Buddhism as a whole, but instead choose to follow those bits and pieces of the religion that are most appealing to them. Many have no clue as to the meaning behind the words they read and chant. Nevertheless, simply the idea of being a Buddhist is exhilarating, especially for those who have become disillusioned with cultural Christianity. For some, there no doubt is a tinge of rebellion resident in the words, "I am a Buddhist."

In order to evangelize Asian Buddhists and American Buddhists effectively, a Christian must be able to answer some basic Buddhist questions: What is the

---

[82]Tissa Weerasingha, "Karma and Christ: Opening Our Eyes to the Buddhist World," *International Journal of Frontier Missions* 10:3 (July 1993): 103.
[83]J. Isamu Yamamoto, "The Arrival of Theravada," *Christian Research Journal* (Fall 1994): 39–40.
[84]Yamamoto, "The Buddha," 34.

318 THE KINGDOM OF THE CULTS

difference between Buddha and Christ? How is Jesus different from a *bodhi-sattva*? Why is Christianity superior to Buddhism?

It has been noted correctly by Timothy Kung, Professor of Oriental Religious Studies at Christ International Theological Seminary in California, that if a Christian "can only point to the strengths of Christianity while dismissing Buddhism as mere superstition, the Buddhist will reject you as too subjective and refuse to talk to you."[85]

Kung suggests several steps for successfully communicating the gospel to Buddhists. First, a Christian must discover how deeply involved in Buddhism the prospective convert is. Some Buddhists have little understanding of Buddhism. Others may be quite familiar with the doctrines of the faith. Second, a good interpersonal relationship with the Buddhist must be established.

The next step involves actual evangelism and may be accomplished not only by pointing out the philosophical errors and shortcomings of Buddhism but also by explaining the superiority of Christianity. One method is to explore the Buddhist's concept of his or her ultimate destination—*nirvana*.

This final state of existence presents innumerable problems for Buddhists who cannot even agree on what the nature of the state is. Many believe it to be extinction. Others suggest it is indescribable in nature. Some hold that it actually occurs in this life as one is liberated from all cares. Still others say it is a paradisaical land akin to the idea of Utopia or even to the Christian idea of heaven.[86]

Christian missionary James Stephens, a former Buddhist and Founder/Director of the Sonrise Center for Buddhist Studies in California, suggests that Christians ask Buddhists to explain *nirvana*. Most followers of the Buddha will have no clear explanation. This opens a door for the following analogy.

Subscribing to a religious system that gives no tangible idea of one's future destiny is like someone going into an airport and simply asking for a ticket. When asked for a destination, the same person responds by saying, "I don't know, just give me a ticket. When I get there, I'll know where it is." Eventually, the person will go *somewhere*. But where? No one in his or her right mind would do such a thing when it comes to a destination in this life. How much more sure should we be of our destination after death? A description of the Christian concept of eternal life can then be shared with less preconceived rejection on the part of the Buddhist listener.

Another way to evangelize Buddhists is through sharing with them the Messianic prophecies fulfilled in Jesus' life, death, and resurrection. The Bible is not merely a collection of wise sayings, ancient beliefs, or spiritually transforming concepts. It also contains history that is fully capable of being verified evidentially. The Old Testament contains hundreds of prophecies concerning the identity of Israel's "Messiah," or "Anointed One." The sheer number of these prophecies would make it virtually impossible for them to occur accidentally in someone's life.[87]

---

[85]Timothy Kung, "Evangelizing Buddhists," *International Journal of Frontier Missions* 10:3 (July 1993): 121.

[86]Norman L. Geisler and Ytaka Amano, *The Reincarnation Sensation* (Wheaton, Ill.: Tyndale House Publishers, 1987), 32–33.

[87]James Stephens, personal interview, July 10, 1995.

Some of these prophecies include Jesus' Virgin Birth (Isaiah 7:14), birth in Bethlehem (Micah 5:2), sacrificial death (Isaiah 53:5), crucifixion (Psalm 22:14–18), and bodily resurrection (Psalm 16:10).

Dr. Henry M. Morris, in his book *The Bible Has the Answer*, details a particularly striking prophecy that, when coupled with the many other prophecies fulfilled in Christ, clearly shows that there was divine omniscience at work in the life of Jesus:

> An even more striking prophecy is given in Daniel 9:24–27. There Daniel was told explicitly that Messiah would come 69 "Sabbaths" (that is, 69 sabbatical years—a total of 483 years) after the decree was given to rebuild Jerusalem, which at that time lay in ruins after Nebuchadnezzar, king of Babylon, had destroyed it. Such a decree was given later by the Persian emperor. Although the exact date of the decree is somewhat uncertain, the termination date of the prophecy must have been some time in A.D. the first century. In fact, it must have been before the destruction of the city and the temple by the Romans in A.D. 70, because the prophecy said quite explicitly, "After [the 483 years] shall Messiah be cut off, but not for himself: and the people of the prince that shall come shall destroy the city and the sanctuary" (Daniel 9:26). Not only must Messiah come before this destruction, but He was also to be "cut off," rejected, and killed, before it came. It is obvious that no one but Jesus could have fulfilled these prophecies. The prophecies absolutely preclude any still future Messiah, except that even that hope also will find its fulfillment in the second coming of Christ.[88]

One might also want to point out to Buddhists that their faith is built on a man about whom very little is known historically. In fact, there is a great deal of evidence that suggests many of the writings about Siddhartha are legends that sprang up over the course of many centuries. It is significant that four hundred years passed before anything about the Buddha was written.

Christianity, however, is built on the claims and actions of a historical person—Jesus of Nazareth—whose followers began transcribing accounts of his life within the lifetimes of his contemporaries and eyewitnesses. This means that the New Testament, which is authoritative for Christians, is much more reliable than Buddhist scriptures.

A series of probing questions may be helpful to reveal the more philosophical problems inherent in Buddhism. *Nirvana* again serves as a good starting point. Reaching *nirvana* is the ultimate goal for a Buddhist, and it can only be reached by removing desires from oneself. This poses an obvious problem: How can *nirvana* ever be reached when wanting to obtain *nirvana* is itself a desire that must be abandoned? It seems that wanting *nirvana* is the very thing that will always prevent someone from ever reaching it.

An essential component of successful evangelism of Asian Buddhists is recognizing the continuing legitimacy of cultural, historic, ethnic, and familial factors that are not contrary to Christian faith. For example, respect for ancestors, honor of elders, loyalty to family, etc. are personal and social values that are important to Christianity as well. The Asian Buddhist can be assured that abandoning Buddhism does not necessitate abandoning one's Asian heritage.

---

[88]Henry M. Morris, *The Bible Has the Answer* (San Diego: Creation-Life Publishers, 1976), 29, cf. Henry M. Morris, *The Bible and Modern Science* (Chicago: Moody Press, 1968), 120.

Additionally, bringing Asian Buddhists in contact with Asian Christians can assure them that even if they are rejected by some Asians for leaving Buddhism for Christianity, Asian Christians will remain faithful.

The most effective precursor to evangelism of Buddhists is prayer. The Bible tells us that we do not struggle against flesh and blood, but against spiritual forces of darkness that blind men's minds (Ephesians 6:12; 2 Corinthians 4:4). This holds especially true when speaking to Tibetan Buddhists, who, through their involvement with occult practices, are vulnerable to demonic influence as well.

In the eighth century a Tibetan Buddhist master named Padmasambhava allegedly prophesied, "When the horses go on wheels, when the iron bird flies, my people shall scatter all over the world and my teachings shall come to the land of the red face."[89]

Buddhist teachings have spread throughout America and continue to do so in this technologically advanced age. But a seemingly fulfilled prophecy by a Buddhist does not mean we should embrace Buddhism. Scripture says that if someone makes a prophecy that comes to pass, they and their doctrines must still be rejected if their teachings lead people away from the true God (Deuteronomy 13:1–5).

The doctrines of Buddhism, like those found in all other world religions, promote beliefs that guide people into a Christless eternity. Christians must share the grace and peace of Jesus Christ, lovingly and gently: "In meekness instructing those that oppose themselves; if God peradventure will give them repentance to the acknowledging of the truth; and that they may recover themselves out of the snare of the devil, who are taken captive by him at his will" (2 Timothy 2:25–26).

---

[89]"Is Buddha Awakening the U.S.?" 16.

Chapter 10

The Baha'i Faith

The Baha'i Faith is a non-Christian cult of distinctly foreign origin that began in Iran in the nineteenth century with a young religious Iranian businessman known as Mirza' Ali Muhammad, who came to believe himself to be a divine manifestation projected into the world of time and space as a "Bab" (Gate) leading to a new era for mankind.

As Christianity, almost since its inception, has had heretics and heresies within its fold, so Islam was destined to experience the same fragmenting forces. Mirza' Ali Muhammad, alias the "Bab," thus became one of the sorest thorns in the flesh of Islamic orthodoxy; so much so that he was murdered by Islamic fanatics in 1850 at the age of thirty-one. He had derived much of his early encouragement and support from a small Islamic sect in Iran, and he was a prominent teacher among them for six years prior to his death. Though Christians have not been known historically for putting to death those who disagreed with them (notable exceptions are the Reformation and Counter-Reformation, the Inquisition, and certain phases of the Crusades), violence may generally be said to follow in the wake of "new" revelations in most other religions, and unfortunately, in the case of Mirza' the pattern held true.

So then, the history of the Baha'i Faith began with the stupendous claims of a young Iranian to the effect that "the religious leaders of the world had forgotten their common origin. . . . Moses, Jesus, and Muhammad were equal prophets, mirroring God's glory, messengers bearing the imprint of the Great Creator."[1]

Today, this still remains the basic tenet of the Baha'i Faith, albeit with the addition of Zoroaster, Buddha, Confucius, Krishna, Lao, and Baha'u'llah, the last great manifestation of the Divine Being, whose name literally means, "the glory of God." The focus of Baha'ism is often popularized as "The Oneness of God, The Oneness of Religion, and the Oneness of Humanity."

This chapter updated and edited by Gretchen Passantino.

[1]Richard Mathison, *Faith, Cults, and Sects in America* (New York: Scribners, 1952), 105.

As Baha'i history records it, the Bab was sentenced to death and was executed July 8, 1850, at Tabriz. In the view of thousands, as the Baha'is tell it, 750 Armenian soldiers raised their rifles and fired at the figure of the prophet. When the smoke cleared, the Bab had not only emerged unscathed from the fusillade of bullets, but the bullets had burned through the ropes that held him, and he stood unfettered.

The story goes on to relate that he then disappeared from their vision, but upon returning to his cell, the guards found him lecturing his disciples. After he had finished speaking with them, he is reported to have said, "I have finished my conversation. Now you may fulfill your intention."

He was then led out before the same firing squad and this time they did not miss.

All of these events were accompanied by the cries of "Miracle! Miracle!" from the assembled populace, who, though they outnumbered the luckless Armenian soldiers, failed to rescue the Bab from his appointment with the Dark Angel.

The Baha'i history of the event also records that a fierce black whirlwind swept the city immediately after the execution of the Bab, somewhat reminiscent of the earthquake and darkness that fell over the earth upon the death of Jesus Christ on Golgotha, eighteen centuries before.

The death of the Bab, however, did not dim the rising star of the new faith. Instead, he had, according to his followers, prophesied that "The oneness of all mankind" was an inevitability, and that in time there would come "a Promised One" who would unify all the followers and would himself be a manifestation of the only true and living God.

Modern Baha'ism considers that the Bab's great prophecy has been fulfilled by Mirza Husayn' Ali, better known to the initiated as "Baha'u'llah," who succeeded the messianic throne of Baha'ism upon the death of his unfortunate predecessor, the Bab.

In the year 1863, this same Baha'u'llah declared himself as that one prophesied by the Bab thirteen years previously, the One who was "chosen of God, and the promised one of all the prophets."[2]

Apparently Baha'u'llah's conviction that he was to play Christ to the Bab's John the Baptist convinced the majority of "Babis," as they were then known. However, his brother, Mirza Yahya, apparently did not receive the message clearly, for he forthwith renounced Baha'u'llah and allied himself with the enemies of the newfound religion, the Ski-ihs.

His nefarious plot, however, miserably failed, and the Baha'i movement gradually evolved into what is known today as the Baha'i Faith, a worldwide religious organization that continues to teach in the tradition of Baha'u'llah, who, despite his claims to immortality, was rather unceremoniously deprived of his earthly existence by the Angel of Death who overtook him in 1892 in Bahji in Palestine. He was seventy-five at the time.

The Baha'is have had their share of persecution, and more than nine thousand were killed between 1850 and 1860. But in their emigration to America in the person of 'Abdu'l Baha, son of Baha'u'llah, who arrived in the United States

---

[2]J. E. Esslemont, *Baha'u'llah and the New Era* (Wilmette, Ill.: Baha'i Publishing Committee, 1951), 38.

in 1912, Baha'ism truly received "a new birth of freedom." Today they carry on their work in more than 235 countries and territories worldwide, representing more than 2,500 ethnic, racial, and tribal groups, and with more than 5 million practitioners.[3]

They have gained some notable converts in the past, and no less a figure than Count Leo Tolstoy spoke warmly of their "spirit of brotherhood," and Woodrow Wilson's daughter became one of the first converts to Baha'ism through the work of Baha'u'llah in the United States. Some members of the rock music group, Crosby, Stills, Nash, and Young, shared their new faith in Baha'ism during public concerts and network television talk shows.

The world headquarters of the Baha'i Faith is in Haifa, Israel, from whence are circulated the writings of Baha'u'llah and 'Abdu'l Baha. Baha'u'llah reputedly left behind him 200 books and tablets, which, along with the writings of his son, constitute the final authority for religious faith and conduct where members of the cult are concerned.

This author had the opportunity to visit the famous nonagon (nine-sided) structure or Temple, as it is known, in Wilmette, Illinois; a building that utilizes the symbolic number nine, sacred to Baha'is. Its architecture is a combination of synagogue, mosque, and cathedral, in which there are nine concrete piers, nine pillars representing the nine living world religions, and nine arches. The building is beautifully centered in a park having nine sides, nine avenues, and nine gateways, and containing nine fountains. The worship service consists of readings from Baha'u'llah, 'Abdu'l Baha, and whatever sources from the major religions are thought to be meaningful for the worshipers that day. Around the central dome of the building are various quotations both inside and out, all of which emphasize the unity of all the great religions of the world.

The Baha'i Faith utilizes the calendar for observances designed by the Bab, which consists of nineteen months, each having nineteen days. New Year's Day falls on March 21. There are no ministers, and no ecclesiastical machinery or organization. The Baha'is employ only teachers who conduct discussion groups in homes or Baha'i Centers, and who are willing to discuss with anyone the unity of all religion under Baha'u'llah.

The Baha'i cult also maintains schools for study in Colorado Springs, Colorado; Geyserville, California; Eliot, Maine; and Davison, Michigan.

The Baha'i Faith today is not directed by an individual representative of God, such as the Bab or The Guardian Shoghi Effendi, but by a council. A British Baha'i center explains,

> The Universal House of Justice is the supreme governing body of the Baha'i Faith to which all Baha'is may turn. Its nine members are elected by National Spiritual Assemblies from all over the world.
>
> The Universal House of Justice consults on all issues and guides the entire Baha'i world within the light and framework of the teachings of Baha'u'llah.
>
> To continue the work of the Hands of the Cause, the Universal House of Justice appointed an International Teaching Centre.
>
> The National Spiritual Assembly in each country is elected every year by delegates at a National Convention. The nine members consult and decide about the affairs of the Faith in that country.

---

[3] "Introduction." http://www.bahai.org: Baha'i Faith Internet Web site, 1997, 1.

Every city, town, and village that has enough adult believers elects a Local Spiritual Assembly to consult on the affairs of the Faith within their community.

All Baha'i Assemblies work within the same framework based on Baha'u'llah's teachings and their decisions should be obeyed by Baha'is. In Baha'i consultation all parties are considered equal.

Individuals are also appointed at various levels to aid in the spread of the Faith and to protect the spiritual health of the Baha'is. They are called Counselors, Auxiliary Board Members, or Assistants to the Auxiliary Board and work closely with the Local and National Spiritual Assembles.[4]

Baha'ism is an Iranian transplant to the United States, a syncretistic religion that aims at the unity of all faiths into a common world brotherhood, in effect giving men a right to agree to disagree on what the Baha'is consider peripheral issues, but unifying all on the great central truths of the world religions, with Baha'u'llah as the messiah for our age. 'Abdu'l Baha did his work well, and when he died at the age of seventy-seven in Palestine (in 1921), he bequeathed a budding missionary arm of his father's faith to Shoghi Effendi (Guardian of the Faith), whose influence continues in and through the teaching hierarchy of the contemporary Baha'i movement in America.

Basic Baha'i Beliefs

Baha'i teaching is often difficult to identify and evaluate because it usually expresses itself in the terminology and images of various religions. However, it does have a set of basic principles, laws, and other teachings to which Baha'is worldwide subscribe, no matter what terminology they might use to express these ideas.

The basic principles of the Baha'i Faith include the oneness of the world of humanity; the foundation of all religions as one; religion must be the cause of unity; religion must be in accord with science and reason; one must pursue independent investigation of truth; equality between men and women; the abolition of all forms of prejudice; universal peace; universal education; a universal language; the spiritual solution of economic problems; and an international tribunal.

The laws and obligations of the Baha'i Faith include to pray and read the Holy Writings (from various religions) daily; to observe the Baha'i Fast from sunrise to sunset on the Baha'i "New Year," March 20–21; to teach the cause of God; to contribute to the Baha'i financial fund; to observe Baha'i Holy Days, including the Nineteen Day Feast (every nineteen days from New Year's Day, or March 20–21); to consider work as worship; to avoid alcohol and other drug abuse; to observe sexual chastity; to obey the government of the land; and to avoid gossip.

The qualifications for becoming a Baha'i differ from country to country, and it is primarily a matter of individual, private faith. However, when one "catches the spark of Faith," understands the identities of Baha'u'llah, the Bab, and 'Abdu'l Baha, respects the Baha'i leadership, and learns and adopts the

[4]"Baha'i Administration." http://www.miracles.win-uk.net/Bahai/BasicFacts/basic6.html: Bahai Faith U.K., 1997, 1–2.

teachings and laws of Baha'ism, then one generally makes a public declaration of faith and is welcomed into his or her local Baha'i community.[5]

An Interview With a Baha'i Teacher

In the course of researching the history and theology of Baha'ism, I conducted numerous interviews with authoritative spokespersons for the Baha'i movement. The following is a transcription of relevant portions of an interview I conducted with one well-prepared and candid Baha'i teacher.

Question: Do you in Baha'ism believe in the Holy Trinity?

Answer: If by the Trinity you mean the Christian concept that the three persons—Father, Son, and Holy Spirit—are all the one God, the answer is no.

We believe that God is one person in agreement with Judaism and Islam. We cannot accept the idea that God is both three and one and find this foreign to the Bible, which Christianity claims as its source. Not a few Jewish scholars are in complete agreement with us on this point, as is the Koran.

Question: Is Jesus Christ the only manifestation of Deity, that is, is He to be believed when He said, "I am the way, the truth, and the life, no man cometh unto the Father, but by me" (John 14:6)?

Answer: No, we believe that Jesus was only one of nine manifestations of the divine being and appeared in His era of time to illumine those who lived at that time. Today, Baha'u'llah is the source of revelation.

Jesus was the way, the truth, and the life for His time but certainly not for all time.

'Abdu'l Baha points out that we are to honor all the major prophetic voices, not just one of them. He said:

> Christ was the prophet of the Christians, Moses of the Jews—why should not the followers of each prophet recognize and honor the other prophets?[6]

'Abdu'l Baha also occupied an exalted place in the thinking of Baha'is. It was he who said:

> The revelation of Jesus was for His own dispensation, that of the Son, and now it is no longer the point of guidance to the world. Baha'is must be severed from all and everything that is past—things both good and bad—everything. . . . Now all is changed. All the teachings of the past are past.[7]

Question: Since you believe that Jesus spoke to His own dispensation, how do you account for the fact that in numerous places in the New Testament both He and His apostles and disciples asserted that He was the same "yesterday, and to day, and for ever" (Hebrews 13:8), and that His words were binding and "would never pass away"?

Answer: You must realize that many of the things written in the New Testament were written long after Jesus died, hence it is impossible to have absolute accuracy in everything. It would be natural for His followers to assert such

---

[5]The material from this section is summarized in "The Baha'i Faith: Basic Facts." http://www.miracles.win-uk.net/Bahai/BasicFacts/basic8.html: The Baha'i Faith, U.K., 1997, 1–2.

[6]*The Wisdom of Baha'u'llah* (Willamette, Ill.: Baha'i Publishing Committee, n.d.), 43.

[7]*Star of the West* (Willamette, Ill.: Baha'i Publishing Committee, December 31, 1913), brochure.

things, but the revelation of Baha'u'llah supersedes such claims.

Question: The resurrection of Jesus Christ from the dead is the true foundation of Christian experience. Does Baha'ism accept His bodily resurrection and ascension into heaven, and do you believe that He is indeed a high priest after Melchizedic's order as intercessor before the throne of God for all men?

Answer: The alleged resurrection of Jesus and His ascension into heaven may or may not be true depending upon your point of view. As I said before, we are concerned with Baha'u'llah and the new era or age, and while we reverence Jesus as we do the great prophets of other religions, we do not believe that it is necessarily important that the Baha'i Faith recognize every tenet of a specific religion. We believe that Jesus conquered death, that He triumphed over the grave, but these are things that are in the realm of the spirit and must receive spiritual interpretation.

Question: Then you do not actually believe in the bodily resurrection of Christ?

Answer: Personally, no. But we do believe that resurrection is the destiny of all flesh.

Question: In Jewish theology and Christian theology, much stress is laid upon sacrificial atonement for sin. The theology of Christianity in particular emphasizes that Jesus Christ is the Lamb of God who takes away the sin of the world. It was John the Baptist who so identified Him, and the New Testament gives ample testimony to His substitutionary atonement for the sins of the world. If, as Christianity maintains, "He is the propitiation for our sins: and not for ours only, but also for the sins of the whole world" (1 John 2:2), why, then, is 'Abdu'l Baha, or, for that matter, Baha'u'llah, important? If God has revealed himself finally and fully as the New Testament teaches in Jesus Christ (Colossians 2:9), why should further manifestation be necessary?

Answer: But, you see, that is precisely our position. God has not finally and fully revealed himself in any of the great manifestations, but through all of them, culminating in Baha'u'llah. A Christian may find spiritual peace in believing in a substitutionary atonement. In Baha'ism this is unnecessary. That age is past. The new age of spiritual maturity has dawned through Baha'u'llah, and we are to listen to his words.

Question: If, as you say, Moses, Buddha, Zoroaster, Confucius, Christ, Muhammad, Krishna, Lowe, and Baha'u'llah are all equal manifestations of the divine mind, how do you account for the fact that they contradict each other, for we know that God is not the author of confusion, or is He?

Answer: While it is true that there are discrepancies between the teachings of the great prophets, all held to basic moral and spiritual values. So we would expect unity here, and in the light of man's perverse nature, variety of expression in the writings and teachings of their disciples.

Question: Do you accept all of the sacred books of the world religions, that is, do you consider them all to be of equal authority with the writings of Baha'u'llah?

Answer: The writings of Baha'u'llah, since they are the last manifestation, are to be considered the final authority in matters of religion so far as the Baha'i faith is concerned.

Question: Jesus Christ taught that salvation from sin could be effected only

by acceptance of Him as the sin-bearer mentioned so prominently in the fifty-third chapter of the prophet Isaiah. Just how in Baha'ism do you deal with the problem of your own personal sin?

Answer: We accept the fact that no one is perfect, but by the practice of principles laid down by Baha'u'llah and by making every effort through prayer and personal sacrifice to live in accord with the character of the divine being revealed in him, we can arrive at eventual salvation as you like to term it.

Question: What you mean, then, is that you, yourself, are cooperating with God in working for your salvation?

Answer: Yes, in a sense I suppose you could say this is true, though God in the end must be merciful to us or no one would be fit to escape the divine judgment.

Question: Then, you do believe in final judgment and the existence of paradise and hell?

Answer: Yes, the Baha'i Faith recognizes divine judgment, though not in the graphic terms that Christians portray it. We know nothing of eternal flames where sinners will be confined forever without respite. We do believe in the paradise of God, which will be the abode of the righteous and in the resurrection and the final righting of all things.

Question: Putting this on a personal basis, without meaning to be offensive, might I ask you if you personally this moment believe that you are a good practicing disciple of Baha'u'llah; and, this being true, do you at this moment know with certainty that your sins have all been forgiven you, and that if you were to be called tonight before the throne of God, you would be judged fit and worthy to enter His kingdom?

Answer: I don't believe any person can make that statement, for no one is perfect or holy enough to merit the paradise of God, and those who so claim to have attained this exalted position are in the eyes of the Baha'i faith presumptuous, to say the very least. I could not at the moment say this for myself, but I hope that this will be the case when I die.

Question: Does the Baha'i Faith recognize the personality and deity of the Holy Spirit of God as revealed in the New Testament?

Answer: I believe it is in your gospel of John that Jesus promised another Comforter who would abide always. We understand this to be the coming of Baha'u'llah, a direct fulfillment of the words of Jesus.

Question: Is it not true that a great deal of your theology is borrowed from Islam and that Muslims have made the same claim for Mohammed where Christ's prophecy in John 14 is recorded as you have for Baha'u'llah?

Answer: There is no doubt that we reverence the Koran as one of the divine manifestations of illumination and Mohammed as one of the nine revelators, but Islam historically has persecuted us; in fact, it was followers of Islam who killed the Bab and persecuted Baha'u'llah.

With reference to the Islamic claim in John 14, I believe it is true they also make this claim.

The above excerpt has much more impact than my analysis alone would have. From an authoritative Baha'i spokesperson, it most clearly expresses what separates Baha'ism from historic Christianity. No true follower of Baha'u'llah, by his own admission, can claim this moment peace with God and the joy of sins

forgiven, an experience that belongs only to those who have put their faith and trust in the grace and sacrifice of the Son of God (John 5:26; 6:47; Ephesians 2:8–10).

The fact that the major prophets of Baha'ism contradict each other is paradoxically overlooked by Baha'ism, which in its quest for an ecumenical syncretism prefers to avoid rather than explain the great contradictions between the major faiths.

As do most cults, the Baha'i faith will pick and choose out of the Bible that which will best benefit the advancement of their own theology, irrespective of context or theological authority. The author was impressed during this interview with the fact that the Baha'i teacher who granted it had been a disciple for more than fifty years and was certainly in a position to understand the historic views of Baha'ism. Throughout the course of the interview, which was held at a Baha'i meeting in her home, we had the opportunity time and time again to present the claims of Jesus Christ, and it became apparent that her "god" was Baha'u'llah. The Baha'i plan of salvation is faith in him plus their own good works. Their concept of hell is largely remedial, not punitive. Their eschatology, a combination of Islam, Judaism, and Christianity; and their authority, the writings of Baha'u'llah and 'Abdu'l Baha.

All of the some thirty persons present took extreme pride in the fact that they had arrived at a faith that they felt was progressively superior to all other religions, and each was magnanimously willing to embrace the truth that was in every one of them to bring about the new era of which their leader had prophesied.

There was no virgin-born Son, there was only an Iranian student; there was no miraculous ministry, there was only the loneliness of exile; there was no power over demons, there were only demons of Islam; there was no redeeming Savior, there was only a dying old man; there was no risen Savior, there was only 'Abdu'l Baha; there was no Holy Spirit, there was only the memory of the prophet; there was no ascended High Priest, there were only the works of the flesh; and there was no coming King, there was only the promise of a new era. In that room the words of the Lord of hosts were fulfilled with frightening accuracy:

> These people honor me with their lips, but their hearts are far from me. They worship me in vain; their teachings are but rules taught by men (Matthew 15:8–9, NIV).

All the Baha'i temples in the world and all the quotations from sacred books cannot alter the fact that the heart of man is deceitful above everything and desperately wicked. Who can understand it? Baha'u'llah could not, but could his disciples today? Penned in the words of our Lord:

> If ye were blind, ye should have no sin: but now ye say, We see; therefore, your sin remaineth. . . . Ye are from beneath; I am from above: ye are of this world; I am not of this world. I said therefore unto you, that ye shall die in your sins: for if ye believe not that I am he, ye will die in your sins. . . . When ye have lifted up the Son of man, then shall ye know that I am he, and that I do nothing of myself; but as my Father hath taught me, I speak these things. . . . He that believeth on me, believeth not on me, but on him that sent me. . . . And if any

man hear my words, and believe not, I judge him not: for I came not to judge the world, but to save the world. He that rejecteth me, and receiveth not my words, hath one that judgeth him: the word that I have spoken, the same shall judge him in the last day. For I have not spoken of myself; but the Father which sent me, he gave me a commandment, what I should say, and what I should speak. And I know that his commandment is life everlasting: whatsoever I speak therefore, even as the Father said unto me, so I speak (John 9:41; 8:23–24, 28; 12:44, 47–50).

A Response to the Interview

After the appearance of the above dialogue in an earlier edition of *Kingdom of the Cults*, Baha'i apologist Udo Schaefer responded to this devastating exposé in a book, *The Light Shineth in Darkness*.[8] None of Schaefer's defenses adequately answered the criticisms. A few of his disclaimers are presented here as examples of the lengths to which Baha'is will go to convince people that they can embrace all religions, including Christianity, at the same time. To the detriment of their status, such statements only serve to verify Walter Martin's original astute biblical analysis and refutation.

Udo Schaefer declares that all Christian critics of Baha'i are biased and unable to be objective or truthful because they fear changing their beliefs:

> The Baha'i Faith gives a particular challenge to orthodox Christians who cannot see its existence as other than a threat to their long-held and cherished beliefs. Many, unable to examine the claim of Baha'u'llah objectively because they are not sufficiently unbiased and detached from their old-fashioned traditional doctrines, nevertheless pass judgment on the Cause of God (55:2).

He goes further, declaring that anyone who attempts to defend an objective, unchanging doctrinal standard in Christianity is spiritually blind and incapable of reformation:

> Someone who is accustomed to think only in the hidebound categories of a dogmatic system that demands exclusiveness, someone who throughout his life has inveighed even against other Christian denominations, directly they deviate from his creedal dogmas, can certainly be expected to give a rigid "no" when challenged from outside. Churchmen just cannot see the rival great religions as other than "lies" or at best issues of truth, half-truth, error, superstition, illusion and charlatanry. . . . This blindness is a fact which has to be accepted (56:1).

As Walter Martin's interview subject asserted, Schaefer agrees that the centrality of the Cross in Christian theology is considered heresy by the "enlightened" Baha'i:

> [The theologian] accused the Baha'is of "helplessness in face of the message of the Cross." In this charge the proverbial 'usperbia theologorum'—the pride of the theologians—is manifested: anyone who deviates from Protestant dogma, who contradicts the central teachings of Christian theology, is "helpless," i.e. intellectually inadequate, or—to put it quite clearly—just too stupid

---

to understand these teachings. This favorite trick of Christian apologists, protecting themselves from undesirable criticism by charging the critic with not knowing what Christian faith is and fighting against a caricature, shows an infuriating arrogance: because the critic is not taken seriously, he is made out to be incapable of passing judgment (76:3).

Regarding the development of Christianity and the subsequent Reformation, Schaefer asserts that the apostle Paul changed Christianity from what Jesus had taught, and the Reformation therefore embraced a heretical imitation of Christianity:

> First then, there was the work of a usurper [Paul] and the split he caused at the time of Christianity's origin; second, Luther's fatal mistake (and the mistake of his Christian successors) in finding the truth where in reality there was error (80:3).

Schaefer quite clearly rejects the central biblical teaching of salvation by grace alone through faith by repeating his false assertion that Paul had corrupted and changed the simple teachings of Jesus himself:

> The most essential and effective alteration of Jesus' message carried out by Paul was in his denying the Law's power of salvation and replacing the idea of the Covenant . . . with faith in Christ and in the atoning power of his sacrificial death; [replacing] the concrete Mosaic law with a mystical doctrine of salvation (82:1).
> The "message of Jesus" with which conservative theologians confront the Baha'is is not the teaching of Jesus but the message of Paul, "the preaching of the Cross," as he called his Gospel (1 Corinthians 1:18; 2:2). And if they say that the basic questions of our existence are only grasped in their true depth in "the preaching of the Cross," I reply with Steinheim who said, "It may be a good philosophical idea, a thoughtful myth, a comfortable emotional religion—that I can accept. Only don't let it be called the teaching and revelation of Christ, but a decline from it" (85:3).

In one bold statement Schaefer dismisses all of Christian orthodoxy regarding justification, original sin, the Trinity, and salvation as a mere invention, foreign to the teachings of Jesus. The teachings of Jesus, he asserts without any evidence, harmonize with the teachings of Baha'ism:

> Measured by the standard of Baha'u'llah's revelation, the Pauline doctrine of Justification, the doctrine of Original Sin, the doctrine of the Holy Trinity, the sacramentalization of the Christian religion, the whole Church plan of salvation . . . these are a deformation of Jesus' teaching (87:1).

Today, the Baha'i Faith still stands diametrically opposed to the Christian faith. There can be no harmony of all world religions, not the least any harmony between Baha'ism and Christianity.

Conclusion

Looking back over our survey of Baha'ism, we can learn a number of things about this strange cult. First, we can discern that, although it is Islamic in its origin, Baha'ism has carefully cloaked itself in Western terminology and has imitated Christianity in forms and ceremonies wherever possible in order to

become appealing to the Western mind.

Second, Baha'ism is eager not to come into conflict with the basic principles of the gospel, and so, Baha'is are perfectly willing that the Christians should maintain their faith in a nominal sense, just so long as they acknowledge Baha'u'llah and the general principles of the Baha'i Faith.

Third, Baha'ism deliberately undercuts the foundational doctrines of the Christian faith by either denying them outright or by carefully manipulating terminology so as to "tone down" the doctrinal dogmatism that characterizes orthodox Christianity.

Baha'ism has few of the credentials necessary to authenticate its claims to religious supremacy. An honest Baha'i will freely admit that in not a few respects their system was patterned after many of the practices of Islam and Christianity.

Baha'is will quickly draw upon the scriptures of any religion of their sacred nine to defend the teachings of Baha'u'llah and 'Abdu'l Baha. In this they have a distinct advantage because not a few of them are well informed concerning the scriptures of the religions of the world, particularly the Old and New Testaments and the Koran.

Thus, it is possible for a well trained Baha'i cultist literally to run the gamut of the theological quotations in an eclectic mosaic design to establish his basic thesis, i.e., that all men are part of a great brotherhood revealed in this new era by the manifestation of Baha'u'llah.

The cardinal doctrines of the Christian faith, including the absolute authority of the Bible, the doctrines of the Trinity, the deity of Jesus Christ, His Virgin Birth, vicarious atonement, bodily resurrection, and Second Coming are all categorically rejected by Baha'ism. They maintain that Christ was *a* manifestation of God, but not the *only* manifestation of the Divine Being.

There is very little indeed that a true Christian can have in common with the faith of Baha'i. There is simply no common ground on which to meet or to talk once the affirmations have been made on both sides of Jesus Christ, as opposed to Baha'u'llah. Of course, there is the common ground of Scripture upon which we can meet all men to proclaim to them the indescribable gift of God in the person of Christ, but there can be no ground for fellowship with the Baha'i Faith, which is, at its very core, anti-Christian theology.

Finally, as is always the case with non-Christian cults, the refutation of Baha'ism must come from a sound knowledge of doctrinal theology as it appears in the Scriptures. No Christian can refute the perversions of the Baha'i Faith unless he is first aware of their existence and of their conflict with the doctrines of the Bible. We must therefore be prepared to understand the scope of the teachings of the Baha'is, their basic conflict with the gospel, and the means by which we may refute them as we witness for Christ.

Chapter II

The New Age Cults

Editor's Note:
Although the New Age movement has features that distinguish it from more traditional cults, most noteworthy is the fact that it is not a monolithic, autocratic organization but, instead, a loose coalition of individuals and organizations united in core beliefs and practices. That is why we have titled this chapter "The New Age Cults." The New Age movement is included in this book because (1) it is religious in character; (2) its forerunner included more traditional cults such as Theosophy, Unity, Christian Science, and Bahaism; so for the most part it claims at least compatibility with Christianity, and includes many people who consider themselves New Agers and Christians; (3) its doctrines and practices are decidedly not Christian, not biblical; and (4) nevertheless, many liberal Protestant and Roman Catholic congregations embrace one or more New Age beliefs and/or practices.[1]

The New Age movement is not easily defined. It has no specific founder, primary leader, central headquarters, organizational structure, or definitive statement of beliefs. Nor does it meet in any one place or at any one particular time. It is not even limited to a single group. As a result, the New Age movement is described in a variety of different ways.

Elliot Miller, a New Age expert, calls it "an extremely large, *loosely* structured network of organizations and individuals bound together by common values (based in mysticism and monism—the worldview that 'all is one') and a common vision (a coming 'new age' of peace and mass enlightenment, the 'Age of Aquarius')."[2]

This chapter written by Richard Abanes and edited by Gretchen Passantino.

---

[1]Shortly before his death, Dr. Walter Martin noted that despite its lip service to tolerance and compatibility with Christianity, the New Age movement is "pointedly anti-Christian and particularly hostile to the unique claim of deity by the Lord Jesus Christ and confirmed by apostolic witness," Walter Martin, *The New Age Cult* (Minneapolis: Bethany House Publishers, 1989), 18.

[2]Elliot Miller, *A Crash Course on the New Age Movement* (Grand Rapids, Mich.: Baker Book House, 1989), 15.

Award-winning journalist and religion writer Russell Chandler character-izes it as "a hybrid mix of spiritual, social, and political forces, and it encom-passes sociology, theology, the physical sciences, medicine, anthropology, history, the human potential movement, sports, and science fiction."[3]

J. Gordon Melton, a nationally recognized chronicler of religions in Amer-ica, has gone so far as to call the New Age movement an international social and religious movement, which has "showed itself to be an important new force in the development of the ever-changing Western culture."[4]

The New Age movement is much more than just an isolated system of re-ligious beliefs and practices. The New Age movement is literally a *movement* of spirituality, health, politics, education, and business that encompasses countless groups seeking to direct the path of society. These groups, while sharing many beliefs in common, often hold numerous distinctive doctrines and at times even disagree with each other on significant issues. Consequently, the New Age move-ment does not fit the standard theological definition of a cult. It is, to be more precise, a *collection* of cults.

The term "New Age" is applied to this "collection of cults" because those involved in it (commonly called New Agers) believe that humanity is currently on the brink of something very significant—an evolutionary leap of man's spir-itual nature—which eventually will bring about the "emergence of a new cycle of human consciousness and experience. . . ."[5]

Unlike previous ages, the coming *new* age will be marked by global peace, mass enlightenment, and unparalleled spiritual advancement. Even now the earth allegedly is being made ready for a final "transformation from outmoded habits, negative energies, and thought forms. . . ."[6] David Spangler, a major New Age spokesperson, explains:

> The New Age is a concept that proclaims a new opportunity, a new level of growth attained, a new power released and at work in human affairs, a new manifestation of that evolutionary tide of events which, taken at the flood, does indeed lead on to greater things, in this case to a new heaven, a new earth, and a new humanity.[7]

New Age author Marilyn Ferguson also sees the New Age movement as a road to positive change:

> Humankind has come upon the control panel of change—an understand-ing of how transformation occurs. We are living in *the change of change*, the time in which we can intentionally align ourselves with nature for rapid remaking of ourselves and our collapsing institutions. . . . We are *not* victims, not pawns, not limited by conditions or conditioning. . . . We are capable of imagination, invention, and experiences we have only glimpsed.[8]

[3]Russell Chandler, *Understanding the New Age* (Dallas: Word Books, 1988), 17.
[4]J. Gordon Melton, *New Age Encyclopedia* (Detroit: Gale Research Inc., 1990), xiii.
[5]David Spangler, *Revelation: The Birth of a New Age* (San Francisco: Rainbow Bridge, 1976), 19.
[6]Marcia Gervase Ingenito, *National New Age Yellow Pages*, 1987 edition, "Colors and New Age Trans-formation," by Elizabeth Long, 61.
[7]Spangler, *Revelation*, 105.
[8]Marilyn Ferguson, *The Aquarian Conspiracy* (Los Angeles: J. B. Tarcher, 1980), 29.

Old Lies in a New Age

Although some New Agers are content to wait passively for the dawning of this harmonious era, the majority of them are activists who feel that its arrival is dependent upon the dissemination and mass acceptance of New Age doctrines. Through organized rallies, huge conventions, free literature, and high profile personalities such as actress Shirley MacLaine, New Age revolutionaries have injected their philosophies into nearly all aspects of our culture. Their beliefs have penetrated the entertainment industry, the food industry, public school curriculums, health care services, the political arena, the business world, and even the United States military.

To understand the New Age movement, Christians must first realize that much of it is not really very "new" at all. Even *Time* magazine has called the New Age "a combination of spirituality and superstition, fad and farce, about which the only thing certain is that it is not new."[9] Behind all of its twentieth-century packaging, terminology, and socio-political agendas, the nuts and bolts of the New Age movement's worldview is ancient occultism. Every technique New Agers use to gain "spiritual truth" can be traced either directly or indirectly back to the pagan mystery religions of Egypt, Babylon, and other cultures. It provides a perfect illustration of Ecclesiastes 1:9–10: "What has been will be again, what has been done will be done again; there is nothing new under the sun. Is there anything of which one can say, 'Look! This is something new'? It was here already, long ago; it was here before our time" (NIV).

The word *occult* (derived from the Latin *occultus*) basically means "hidden/ secret" things. The term is used to describe practices such as astrology, numerology, witchcraft, crystal gazing, necromancy (communication with the dead), magic, and palm reading, which according to the Bible are forbidden to man and cursed by God (Leviticus 20:6; Deuteronomy 18:9–11; Acts 19:19).

These satanically energized methods of obtaining otherwise unobtainable knowledge comprise the very heart and soul of the New Age movement because they are the primary means through which New Age teachings are proclaimed. They may have modern sounding names (e.g., astral projection, psychometry, radiance therapy, channeling), but they are the same practices the church of Jesus Christ has been standing against for more than nineteen centuries.

Besides knowing the role occultism plays in the New Age movement, Christians must also understand that the New Age movement is little more than Hinduism. It is the religion of India disguised in Western terminology and presented as a new brand of spirituality that will prove to be mankind's long-awaited key to Utopia.

The only substantive difference between Hinduism and the New Age movement is that Hinduism is world *denying* while the New Age movement is world *affirming*. No "yuppie" is going to adopt the Hindu tradition of abandoning all worldly possessions to go meditate under a cliff, on a mountain, or in a cave. Out of necessity, Hinduism's asceticism has been replaced by something much more palatable to American tastebuds—materialism. At its doctrinal core, however, the New Age movement is still Hinduism.

Today we see a choice being made between what C. S. Lewis considered to

---

[9]*Time* (December 7, 1987): 62.

be the two most advanced religious systems: Hinduism and Christianity.[10] The conflict between them is unavoidable. Why? Because Hinduism absorbs all religions while Christianity excludes all religions. As a general principle, in fact, the New Age movement accepts all religions. All religions, that is, except ortho-dox Christianity.

This is the danger of the New Age movement. Everything in it has been designed by Satan to do one thing and one thing only—destroy people's faith in the God of the Bible. This we shall now see as we examine the history, doctrines, and practices of the New Age movement.

A Quick Look at How It All Began

In the nineteenth century there emerged several religious groups that would contribute greatly to the development of the New Age movement. One group was The Theosophical Society (see chapter 7), which was founded in 1875 by Helena Petrovna Blavatsky. From Theosophy came (1) Anthroposophy, founded in 1912 by Rudolf Steiner; (2) the Arcane School, founded in 1923 by Alice Bailey; and (3) the "I AM" sects, which began to appear in the 1930s. These related branches of spirituality eventually spawned even more groups, which in turn created countless others.

As Theosophy and its offspring were producing one strain of spiritual be-liefs, the views of psychic healer Phineas P. Quimby were developing another. He taught that all disease is a product of the mind and that many problems are caused simply by "wrong thinking." Quimby's teachings, termed New Thought, gave rise to the numerous Mind Science cults.[11]

All of the above groups, along with the thousands of factions they created, were eventually influenced to varying degrees by spiritism, psychology, science, quantum physics, and the contemporary concerns of society. The resulting blend is what we now call the New Age movement.

God

The god of the New Age movement is not the God of the Bible. Marilyn Ferguson admits that in "the emergent spiritual tradition [the New Age move-ment] God is not the personage of our Sunday school mentality."[12]

New Agers usually define "God" as an impersonal force pervading all cre-ation. This view naturally flows from the New Age movement's most founda-tional belief—monism. Monism, which literally means "one-ism," teaches that all is one and one is all. It asserts that "all reality may be reduced to a single, unifying principle partaking of the same essence and reality."[13]

Every New Ager believes there is ultimately only one substance and that the diversity we perceive is actually unreal. It is all an illusion. "Oneness is the only reality and diversity is its apparent manifestation."[14]

---

[10]C. S. Lewis, *Surprised by Joy* (New York: Harcourt, Brace, Jovanovich, 1955), 239.
[11]Such as Christian Science. See chapter 7.
[12]Ferguson, *Aquarian*, 382.
[13]Chandler, *Understanding*, 341.
[14]Spangler, *Revelation*, 194.

In other words, people only *think* that a rock lying in a field is something entirely separate from the field in which it is lying. Reality is that the rock *is* the field, and the field *is* the rock. Similarly, people only *think* that they are individual entities. Reality is that there is no "you"/"me" distinction. There is only one big "I."

This "I" includes not only every *person*, but also every *thing* (e.g., soil, wooden boards, raindrops). Everyone is everything, and everything is everyone. All are part of the one substance that is usually referred to by New Agers as the Reality, Power, All, Mind, Force, Absolute, Principle, One, or Universal Energy. The ultimate state of consciousness is one in which "all individuality dissolves into universal, undifferentiated oneness."[15]

Often accompanying monism is pantheism, which asserts that everything is God. This concept, too, is embraced by every New Ager. After all, if everything that exists is one, then "God" must also be one with everything. Everything is ultimately God. As New Age personality Benjamin Creme puts it:

> In a sense there is no such thing as God, God does not exist. And in another sense, there is nothing else but God—only God exists. . . . This microphone is God. This table is God. All is God. And because all is God, there is no God. . . . God is everything that you have ever known or could ever know—and everything beyond your level of knowing."[16]

This "all is God/God is all" doctrine coupled with monism's "all is one" concept forms the substructure of not only the New Age movement but also Hinduism. Hindu literature is literally saturated with both pantheism and monism. The concluding portion of the *Vedas*, or the Upanishads, read:

> This whole world is Brahma. Tranquil, let one worship. It as that from which he came forth, as that into which he will be dissolved, as that in which he breathes.[17]

Contrary to the Hinduistic philosophy of the New Age movement, God is not all and all is not God. Genesis 1:1 clearly establishes that God is separate and distinct from the universe. The entire first chapter of Genesis systematically shows that God, rather than being a *part* of all that exists, is the *Creator* of all that exists. Other passages supporting this are Psalm 33:13–14; Isaiah 42:5; 44:24; Acts 17:24–25.

Paul the apostle further demonstrates that God and creation are not one when he mentions those who exchange the truth of God for a lie so they can worship and serve the creature rather than the Creator (Romans 1:18–25). Eldon Winker points out in *The New Age Is Lying to You* that worship of the creature is possible only if the creature is distinct and separate from the Creator.[18]

Also, God is not an impersonal substance or a cosmic force. In Exodus 3:14–15, the Lord applies to himself the divine name "I [first person singular] AM [the verb *to be*]." Only a reflective cognizant ego (mind) can say "I AM." Consequently, God must be a person.

---

[15]Fritjof Capra, *Turning Point: Science, Society, and the Rising Culture*, 37.
[16]Benjamin Creme, *The Reappearance of the Christ and the Masters of Wisdom* (London: Tara Press, 1980), 110–111.
[17]Ibid., 209.
[18]Eldon K. Winker, *The New Age Is Lying to You* (St. Louis: Concordia, 1994), 191.

Additionally, God performs acts that are only possible for a personal being. In Jeremiah 29:11, for example, He declares that He *knows* the *thoughts* He *thinks* toward His people. How can an impersonal force know or think? God hears (Exodus 2:24), sees (Hebrews 4:13), speaks (Leviticus 19:1), knows everything (1 John 3:20), judges (Psalm 50:6), loves (Proverbs 3:12; Jeremiah 31:3) and has a will (1 John 2:17).

In sharp contrast to the impersonal God of the New Age movement, the God of Christianity is an intelligent, compassionate, and personal being. He is the *living* God (Daniel 6:26; 1 Timothy 3:15; 4:10; Hebrews 10:31), and He is the *true* God (2 Chronicles 15:3; Jeremiah 10:10; 1 Thessalonians 1:9). As such, He is also the quintessential enemy of New Agers whose most cherished belief is that *they* are God.

Man

The monistic/pantheistic worldview held by New Agers is what leads them to believe that they are God. This relationship between monism, pantheism, and the divinity of man is evident in *Revelation: The Birth of a New Age:*

> This is the being/embodiment relationship, as exemplified primarily in the Eastern religions and philosophies. . . . This relationship simply affirms that all life is one, that I am one with God and can embody Divinity. . . . God and I do not just communicate; we commune and are one. There is no separation except failure to recognize that there is no separation.[19]

An even clearer picture of this thought is contained in "Teddy," J. D. Salinger's short story about a spiritually precocious boy who at ten years old became "enlightened" while watching his little sister drink milk:

> I was six when I saw that everything was God. . . . My sister was only a very tiny child then, and she was drinking her milk, and all of a sudden I saw that *she* was God and the *milk* was God. I mean, all she was doing was pouring God into God.[20]

Shirley MacLaine (dancer, actress, film star), who "became a major voice in the New Age community following the publication of her book *Out on a Limb*, and the television dramatization of the book,"[21] has made some of the most explicit and widely heard New Age proclamations of self-realized godhood. During one scene in her five-hour television adaptation of *Out on a Limb*, MacLaine unabashedly proclaimed "I AM GOD! I AM GOD!"

In a book produced after *Out on a Limb*, MacLaine attempted to give her "fans" a deeper understanding of the reasoning behind her belief:

> I *know* that I exist, therefore I AM. I *know* that the God-source exists. Therefore IT IS. Since I am part of that force, then I AM that I AM.[22]

The New Age movement's divinity of man doctrine reminds us of the temp-

---

[19]Spangler, *Revelation*, 233.
[20]J. D. Salinger, *Nine Stories*, 288.
[21]Melton, *Encyclopedia*, 270.
[22]Shirley MacLaine, *Dancing in the Light* (New York: Bantam Books, 1985), 420.

tation to divine autonomy entertained by Adam and Eve in the Garden of Eden (Genesis 3:5). It, therefore, produces the same results—physical and spiritual death. Psalm 82 reveals that all men, regardless of whether or not they are called gods, will die as men.

Scripture is filled with passages that contrast God and humankind (Psalm 100:3; Ecclesiastes 5:2; Isaiah 43:7; Jeremiah 27:5; Malachi 2:10; 1 Timothy 2:5). God himself has declared that He alone is God (Isaiah 43:10; 45:21–22). Even the demons recognize that there is only one God (James 2:19).

Some New Agers feel that the concept of a transcendent God is what has actually caused nearly all of the world's problems:

> Two-thirds of evil (for humanity) comes from false God concepts, promoted by clever minds to enslave humanity. There is no God, no one intelligent entity outside His creation.[23]

The root of the world's problems is not the Christian God. It is sin and Satan, two realities the New Age movement has conveniently labeled as nonexistent.

Sin and Satan

According to Scripture, "There is a way that seems right to a man, but in the end it leads to death" (Proverbs 14:12, NIV). This is the path being tread by New Agers. They appeal to no moral standard, are not governed by the God of the Bible or His eternal law, and want nothing to do with an objective code of righteousness. New Agers decide for themselves what is right because they are God:

> God is everything—He is every *thing.* So *any* thing you do, you have an inner action in divinity. Remember that, and do what you want to do.[24]
>
> Contemplate the love of God; how great this Entity-Self is, that is all-encompassing, that will allow you to be and do anything you wish and hold you judgeless. God has never judged you or anyone. If He has then He has judged himself, for who be *you* but He.[25]
>
> We can take all the scriptures and all the teachings, and all the tablets, and all the laws, and all the marshmallows and have a jolly good bonfire . . . because that's all they are worth. Once you are the law, once you are the truth, you do not need it externally represented for you.[26]

Anything is permissible for New Agers because sin and evil are not real. They are only illusions. Evil is "basically the manifestation of a force that is out of place or out of timing, inappropriate to the needs and realities of the situation."[27]

In other words, evil is just a misdirected thought, a glitch in perspective, or a deceptive image originating in the mind of the person perceiving something

---

[23]Two Disciples, *The Rainbow Bridge,* 13.
[24]Douglas James Mahr, *Voyage to a New World* (Lopez, Wash.: Masterworks, Inc., Publishers, 1985), 36.
[25]Ibid., 61.
[26]David Spangler, *Emergence: Rebirth of the Sacred* (New York: Delta, 1984), 144.
[27]Spangler, *Revelation,* 123.

as evil/sin. This belief works out to mean that people actually create the tragic events that take place in their lives:

> It is difficult for someone living in some kind of intolerable situation, experiencing the throes of terrible physical illness or financial ruin, to think of it all as a game, but that is what it is, nonetheless. Not only are they playing a game, but they are playing their own game. The game that they created for themselves to play.[28]
>
> "YOU are the only thing that is real. Everything else is your imagination, movie stuff you've brought into your screenplay to help you see who you really are. . . . There are no victims in this life or any other. No mistakes. No wrong paths. No winners. No losers. Accept that and then take responsibility for making your life what you want it to be."[29]

New Agers are characteristically inconsistent. For instance, they will say there is no evil, and yet contend that some things are inherently "good" (e.g., ecology, natural health, brotherhood). Such positions are irreconcilable because there is supposedly only the one great Absolute, the single Substance that constitutes all reality. Consequently, there cannot be any right and wrong or good and evil.

The few New Agers who see this inconsistency pursue their monism to its logical end by holding that the forces of "evil" are actually "part of God. They are not separate from God. Everything is God. There is nothing else, in fact, but God."[30] To a consistent New Ager, then, sin and evil are only aspects of the same Force permeating all "that is" (a concept clearly advocated in the blockbuster movie *Star Wars*).

Although New Agers may vary somewhat in consistency on the concepts of good and evil, all New Agers view a personal devil as nothing but an illusion:

> The devil was a masterful ploy by a conquering institution to put the fear of God, most literally, into the hearts of little ones—that God had created a monster that would *get them* unless they be good to him. The devil was used to control the world most effectively and even today it is still feared and believed. Someone conjured it up—a God—and thus it became, but only to those who believed.[31]

The Word of God says that the devil, evil, and sin are all very real. Jesus, who is revered even by New Agers as a great teacher, often mentioned Satan (Matthew 13:37–39; Luke 10:18; 13:16). He never said Satan was merely an illusory product of the mind. Instead, Jesus called the devil a "murderer" and "a liar" in whom there was no truth whatsoever (John 8:44).

Jesus' temptation in the desert (Matthew 4:1–11) would have been a perfect opportunity to destroy the illusion of Satan by simply showing that the Adversary was unreal. Instead, Jesus spoke with the devil, was tempted by him, and overcame him.

Regarding sin, the prophet Jeremiah observed that the heart of man is *desperately* wicked (Jeremiah 17:9). All have sinned and fallen short of the glory of

[28]Miller, *Crash Course*, 239 (quoting New Ager Iris Bellhayes).
[29]Chandler, *Understanding*, 28 (quoting Jack Underhill).
[30]Creme, *Reappearance*, 103.
[31]Mahr, *Voyage*, 246.

God (Romans 3:9–12, 23). Everyone stands justly condemned as sinners before the righteous God of the universe (Romans 5:18–19) who judges according to His eternal law (Romans 7:7; James 2:10–11; 1 John 3:4), which is itself holy, just, and good (Romans 7:12).

Such a concept is especially distasteful to New Agers who believe that human nature "is neither good nor bad but open to continuous transformation and transcendence."[32] To New Agers, historic orthodox Christianity is the epitome of all that belongs to the unenlightened, discardable, and patently offensive "old" age, which must soon pass away:

> For two thousand years, we have been called *sinful creatures*. That stigma automatically takes away our ability to remind ourselves that we are great, or that we are equal with God or Christ or Buddha, or whoever.[33]
>
> The Christian religion is replete with guilt and negativity and needs to be changed.[34]
>
> The mystics went some way toward liberating Christianity from its unfortunate servitude to historic fact. (Or, to be more accurate, to those various mixtures of contemporary record with subsequent inference and fantasy, which have, at different epochs, been accepted as historic fact) . . . unfortunately, the influence of the mystics was never powerful enough. . . . Christianity has remained a religion in which the pure Perennial Philosophy [all is one, all is God, we are God] has been overlaid . . . by an idolatrous preoccupation with events and things in time—events and things regarded not merely as useful means, but as ends, intrinsically sacred and indeed divine.[35]
>
> The classroom must and will become an arena of conflict between the old and the new—the rotting corpse of Christianity, together with all its adjacent evils and misery, and the new faith of humanism.[36]

Salvation

New Agers have also rejected the Christian doctrine of humankind's need for salvation. In the New Age movement, people are not fallen creatures and will not be judged because they are divine. We do, however, need to be rescued from ignorance of our godhood.

Freedom from ignorance of one's godhood is, in effect, the New Age movement's brand of "salvation." It is called "god-realization," "enlightenment," "attunement," or "at-one-ment [with God]," and it comes only through what is termed "personal transformation."

Douglas Groothuis writes, "To gain this type of transformation, the three ideas that all is one, all is god, and we are god, must be more than intellectual propositions; they must be awakened at the core of our being."[37]

This transformation is achieved by first looking "within," where all reality and truth exists. Salvation, or "god-realization," comes from the self.

[32]Ferguson, *Conspiracy*, 29.
[33]Mahr, *Voyage*, 176.
[34]Virginia Essene, *New Teachings for an Awakening Humanity* (Santa Clara, Calif.: Spiritual Education Endeavors Publishing, 1986), 81.
[35]Aldus Huxley, *The Perennial Philosophy*, 52.
[36]John Dunphy, "A Religion for a New Age," *The Humanist* (Jan/Feb 1983): 26.
[37]Douglas Groothuis, *Unmasking the New Age* (Downers Grove, Ill.: InterVarsity Press, 1986), 24.

New Agers basically save themselves:

> We already know everything. The knowingness of our divinity is the highest intelligence. And to *be* what we already know is the free will. Free will is simply the enactment of the realization that you are God, a realization that you are divine.[38]

> The aim of *A Course in Miracles* is to lead us from duality to oneness—to the realization of our At-one-ment with God, our Self, and all people—our brothers. In this healing is our Salvation—we are *saved* from our misperceptions of ourselves as separated individuals. When our perception is corrected we remember our true or higher Self. . . . Salvation is really enlightenment.[39]

In order to achieve "enlightenment" and subsequent salvation (oneness with God), New Agers have employed what Russell Chandler calls "a plethora of consciousness-changing techniques, or 'psychotechnologies,' to body, mind, and spirit."[40] These techniques include, but are by no means limited to, meditation, yoga, chanting, guided imagery, "energy" alignment, and hypnosis. New Agers recognize, however, that they will probably not achieve *complete* oneness with the universal Reality through this present life (another inconsistency since New Agers maintain that they are already one with all).

Here is where the doctrines of reincarnation and karma gain particular significance. Reincarnation refers to "the cyclical evolution of a person's soul as it repeatedly passes from one body to another at death. This process continues until the soul reaches a state of perfection."[41] Karma refers to "the 'debt' accumulated against a soul as a result of [perceived] good or bad actions committed during one's life (or lives)."[42]

Douglas Groothuis, who has closely studied New Age teachings, explains how these very complex and sometimes confusing doctrines work together:

> According to most Eastern thought, many lives are required to reach oneness with the One; salvation is a multi-lifetime process of progression or digression. If one accumulates good karma, positive benefits accrue in later lives. Bad karma produces future punishments. Eventually one may leave the cycle of birth and rebirth entirely through the experience of enlightenment. Redemption, if it could be called that, is a process of realizing the true self throughout many lifetimes.[43]

According to New Agers, the moment you recognize your godhood, you can pick up the threads of your karma, find out where you were in your past incarnations, correct the mistakes you made there, and go on to live a perfect life here. Eventually, you will be reabsorbed into the great All from which you originally emanated. This will happen for everyone. As David Spangler asserts, "None are saved. None are lost."[44] Everyone will be saved by their own works coupled with reincarnation.

[38]William Goldstein, "Life on the Astral Plane," *Publishers Weekly* (March 18, 1983): 46 (quoting Shirley MacLaine).
[39]Julius J. Finegold and William M. Thetford, eds., *Choose Once Again: Selections From A Course in Miracles*, 2–3.
[40]Chandler, *Understanding*, 31.
[41]Martin, *New Age Cult*, 133.
[42]Ibid., 129.
[43]Groothuis, *Unmasking*, 150.
[44]Spangler, *Revelation*, 75.

Such beliefs clearly contradict Scripture. There will indeed be some who are saved and some who are lost (Matthew 7:21–23; 25:31–41). Jesus himself prophesied that on the day of judgment many false followers will be told to depart from His presence (Matthew 7:23). Revelation 21:8 reveals that they will not be reincarnated: "but the fearful, and unbelieving, and the abominable, and murderers, and whoremongers and sorcerers, and idolaters, and all liars, shall have their part in the lake which burneth with fire and brimstone: which is the second death."

There are no second, third, fourth, or fifth chances for those who in this life do not accept Jesus Christ as their Lord and Savior (Romans 10:9). Hebrews 9:27 says that "it is appointed unto men once to die, but after this the judgment."

No amount of meditation, yoga, chanting, or astral projecting is going to produce salvation. Salvation is "not of works, lest any man should boast (Ephesians 2:9). Jesus took care of everything at the cross. He bore in his own body our sins (1 Peter 2:24) and no one is going to improve on the Lord Jesus. No one is going to pay for their own sins. "Jesus paid it all," says the old hymn, "All to him I owe. Sin had left a crimson stain. He washed it white as snow" ("Jesus Paid It All," Elvina M. Hall).

Jesus Christ

New Agers contend that the "Christian Church's concept of a vicarious atonement is a misunderstanding of the Christ's function."[45] This is not surprising because the Jesus Christ of the New Age movement is very different than the Jesus Christ of the Bible.

John 1:18 tells us that Jesus Christ came to declare God to us. He was also sent to accomplish that which no one else could do—die for the sins of the ungodly (Romans 5:6, 8). New Agers reject these doctrines because they reject God's personality and transcendence. They only know about an unknowable "thing," a great big "It," which is one with all that exists.

In order to know this "It," New Agers must turn to a host of avatars (or teachers) who, as saviors in their own right, were "way-show-ers." They say that Jesus, rather than being the unique Son of God, was only one avatar (or *Son* of God) among many. All of them, including Jesus, had been prepared for their station as avatars by living and working through countless reincarnations:

> Jesus differed but little from other children, only that in past lives he had overcome carnal propensities. . . . Jesus was a remarkable child, for by ages of strenuous preparation he was qualified to be an avatar, a savior of the world.[46]
>
> In every age Teachers have come forth from this spiritual centre to enable mankind to take its next evolutionary step; we know them, among others, as Hercules, Hermes, Rama, Mithra, Vyasa, Sankaracharya, Krishna, Buddha, and the Christ. All perfect men in their time, all sons of men who became Sons of God, for having revealed their innate Divinity.[47]

---

[45]Benjamin Creme, *Maitreya's Mission* (Amsterdam: Share International Foundation, 1986), 68.

[46]Levi Downing, *The Aquarian Gospel of Jesus the Christ* (Marina del Rey, Calif.: DeVorss and Company, 1981), 13.

[47]Creme, *Reappearance*, 28.

Jesus was unique among these avatars only in that he had an incredible grasp of his deity. As New Agers put it, "Jesus' unique place in history is based upon his unprecedented realization of the higher intelligence, the divinity, the Ground of Being incarnated in him."[48] Jesus was divine "in exactly the sense that we are divine; only we have it in potential, while He has manifested it, perfected himself and *achieved* that divinity."[49]

The idea of multiple avatars is but another Hindu lie that has been adopted by the New Age movement. The New Testament explicitly declares in John 1:18 that Jesus Christ is the "one of a kind" (*monogenes*) Son of God who, in the fullness of time, came to reconcile mankind back to the Lord of the universe (Galatians 4:4–5; Colossians 1:19–20).

New Agers also divide Jesus "the man" from the term "the Christ." Although Jesus may occasionally be referred to as "the Christ," New Agers actually believe that "the Christ" is not a personal entity. It is an expressive form of the great One comprising all things. "The Christ," which came upon Jesus at some point during his life, may come upon *anyone*. (A minority of New Agers maintain that "the Christ" is an *office* now being held by another great avatar.)

The Aquarian Gospel of Jesus the Christ states: "Christ is not man. The Christ is universal love. . . . This Jesus is but man who has been fitted by temptations overcome, by trials multiform, to be the temple through which Christ can manifest to men. . . . Look to the Christ within, who shall be formed in every one of you, as he is formed in me."[50]

Peter the apostle thought differently. He exclaimed to Jesus, "Thou *art* the Christ, the Son of the living God" (Matthew 16:15–16). He did not say, "Thou art a great avatar upon whom rests the Christ."

The apostle Luke also identified Jesus as the Christ: "For unto you is born this day in the city of David a Saviour, which is Christ the Lord" (Luke 2:11).

Passages identifying Jesus as the Christ fill the New Testament from Matthew to Revelation (Matthew 1:16; Luke 24:46; Acts 9:22; 18:28; Ephesians 5:23; Hebrews 3:6; 1 John 5:1; Revelation 11:15). In fact, the entire New Testament was expressly written so that those reading it would realize that Jesus was "the Christ" (John 20:31).

Why would New Agers believe that Jesus is not "the Christ"? The answer is found in 1 John 2:22: "Who is a liar but he that denieth that Jesus is the Christ? He is an antichrist."

We have seen that Hinduism is the basic foundation of the New Age movement. Now we must look at how Hinduism is developed into New Ageism through occultism, one of the devil's oldest means of deception.

New Age Occultism

Occult practices are infused with satanic power and are designed to gather hidden, secret, or mysterious truths. The world of the occult covers everything

---

[48]Douglas Groothuis, *Revealing the New Age Jesus* (Downers Grove, Ill.: InterVarsity Press, 1990), 15 (quoting John White in "Jesus and the Idea of a New Age," *The Quest* (Summer 1989): 14.

[49]Creme, *Reappearance*, 119–120.

[50]Downing, *Aquarian*, 110.

from seances to astrology to witchcraft to Satanism. For New Agers, occult techniques and tools (e.g., Ouiji boards, crystals, tarot cards, etc.) are used to penetrate into a dimension of spiritual reality where they hope to gain knowledge that will help them reunite with the great One. God, however, forbids man to enter such a realm because it is the realm of Satan.

Because there is a great amount of power within this world of the occult, Christians must be careful as well as prayerful when confronting those in its clutches. At the same time, believers in the biblical Jesus must never forget that there is nothing to fear. God, who is in us, is greater than he who is in the world (1 John 4:4). Furthermore, our Lord gave us power over spirits of evil. This promise points out that a Christian's power is in the authority of the risen Jesus Christ.

Having established our authority for confronting the forces of darkness, let us now focus our attention on the New Age Movement's occult practices.

Channeling

Mediumship, or spiritism, is the ancient practice of attempting communication with either departed human spirits or other spiritual entities. Today, this practice has been revived under the banner of "channeling," a practice wherein Ascended Masters (persons who have allegedly died and progressed to higher levels of knowledge) and other departed individuals transmit "truths" to help those searching for enlightenment. It is the "process of receiving information from either the 'higher self' [one's most spiritual part lying beyond the conscious mind] or a metaphysical entity."[51]

The practice has been further defined as the "alleged phenomena in which a nonphysical entity communicates through a human medium, through a channel who links the spiritual and physical worlds. . . . Channeling is the communication of information to or through a physically embodied human being from a source that is said to exist on some level or dimension of reality other than the physical."[52]

Although the entities channeled claim widely different identities, their teachings are essentially the same: (1) God is all; (2) man is God; (3) man creates his own reality; (4) death is unreal; and (5) the self is where all truth resides.

A woman named J. Z. Knight, for example, channels Ramtha, a 35,000-year-old warrior-king and former inhabitant of the mythical civilization of Atlantis. According to Ramtha, "You be unequivocally God. . . ! Do not reckon yourself less, for if you do you will become the lessness of your reckoning."[53]

Lazaris, a multidimensional being who claims to have never incarnated, is channeled by Jach Pursel. Lazaris says that the human condition is "to be saving itself."[54]

There are literally thousands of people channeling. The list of channels and their entities reads like the *TV Guide*. Elliot Miller gives an excellent rundown

---

[51]Kerry D. McRoberts, *New Age or Old Lie?*, 134.
[52]Ted Peters, *The Cosmic Self*, 28.
[53]Mahr, *Voyage*, 24.
[54]Miller, *Crash Course*, 171 (quoting Lazaris, "Do Not Ignore Your Responsibility to Be Free, to Be Limitless, to Found a New World," *Psychic Guide* (Sept/Oct 1987).

of some "channels" that New Agers can tune in to:

> Psychic and parapsychologist Alan Vaughan channels "Li Sung," a small-town philosopher from eighth-century northern China. Nutritionist and psychic healer Iris Belhayes channels "Enid," an "earthy" Irish woman from the nineteenth century. Psychic healer Azena Ramanda is among the many who claim to channel "Saint Germaine," an Ascended Master from the "Seventh Ray." Psychic Virginia Essene is one of an unfathomable number who claim to channel "Jesus." Former country and western singer Jamie Sams channels "Leah from Venus." Former legal secretary Taryn Krive channels "Bell Bell," a giggly six-year-old from the legendary lost civilization of Atlantis . . . full-time medium David Sweetland channels "Matea," a 35,000-year-old spirit who once stalked the Earth as a six-foot-eight-inch black female spice trader. . . . One of the latest New Age crazes in Southern California is channeling dolphins.[55]

Although some "channels" may be nothing more than charlatans trying to make a dishonest dollar, a very real possibility exists that many are participating in voluntary demon possession, an activity the Bible prohibits. God explicitly told the Israelites not to practice divination of any kind (Leviticus 19:26) and forbade them to consult mediums and spiritists (Leviticus 19:31; 20:6; Deuteronomy 18:9–12). God even commanded that sorcerers, mediums, and spiritists be put to death (Exodus 22:18; Leviticus 20:27).

Isaiah 8:19 asks, "Should not a people inquire of their God? Why consult the dead on behalf of the living?" (NIV) The answer to the former question is obviously yes. The answer to the latter is undeniably no. The realm of the dead is not where individuals will find the answers they seek. Nor will they find there the eternal life they desperately want and need. Jesus, in whom resides life itself, came that that He might give life to others (John 10:10). God is not the God of the dead, but of the living (Matthew 22:31–32).

UFOs

Very closely linked to channeling is the New Age Movement's obsession with UFOs and extraterrestrial life. "New Agers have borrowed the term *channeling* from the early flying-saucer movement of the 1950s when a number of people started going into trances and letting the so-called space brothers talk through them."[56]

Numerous "aliens" currently being channeled give messages very similar to the ones coming from Ascended Masters and other departed spirits. UFO contactee Ken Carey recorded that "Christ is the single unified being whose consciousness all share."[57] Gabriel Green, founder of the Yucca Valley, California-based Amalgamated Flying Saucer Club (one of the largest UFO groups in America), says that the UFO mission is to raise our consciousness so we can "recognize our own individual Godhood."[58]

The stated purpose of UFO contact is also strikingly similar to the New Age vision. New Age-UFO writer Brad Stieger assures us that "the Space Beings

---

[55]Miller, *Crash Course*, 156–157.
[56]William Alnor, *UFOs in the New Age* (Grand Rapids, Mich.: Baker Book House, 1992), 87.
[57]As quoted in Ibid., 47.
[58]Ibid., 51.

hope to guide Earth to a period of great unification, when all races will shun discriminatory separations and all of humankind will recognize its responsibility to every other life form."[59]

As peaceful as this account sounds, there is often a very distinct air of malevolence associated with UFOs. Whitley Strieber, in recounting his abduction by a UFO, wrote, "People who face the visitors report fierce little figures with eyes that seem to stare into the deepest core of being. And those eyes are asking for something, perhaps even demanding it. Whatever it is, it is more than simple information. . . . It seems to me that it seeks the very depth of the soul; it seeks communion."[60]

Whatever UFOs are, they are real. Individuals from all walks of life have reported seeing them. A 1987 Gallup Poll showed that 50 percent of Americans believe in UFOs and that one in eleven had seen something they thought was a UFO.[61] Signifying the "reality" of UFOs, however, does not mean identifying UFOs. The question, as Dr. Martin put it, is not "Are they real?" but "What are they?" While the vast majority of them can be reasonably explained as natural or man-made phenomena misidentified, misrepresented, and/or used as hoaxes, those UFO incidents that involve what appear to be direct, communicative contact with humans are invariably associated with what the Bible condemns as demonic or occultic. In *Encounters with UFOs*, a very interesting observation is made:

> Contact with the UFOs often seems to be by occult means. Our visitors have rarely responded to any standard approach, whether it is by aerial pursuit or a ground confrontation. *By contrast, the standard tools of the occult have reportedly established contact in innumerable cases.*[62]

Recent studies indicate that most UFO encounters are either hallucinations or the result of a person's misidentification of secret military aircraft. However, the occultic/New Age aspect of many sightings suggest that some UFO encounters *may be* a combination of psychological hallucination and demonic deception.

Astrology

Astrology, one of the most ancient of all occult practices, teaches that the positions and movements of the stars and planets directly influence human events. One's personality as well as one's character weaknesses and strengths are also affected by such movements. The goal of astrologers is to "read" the cosmos for information that can be used to guide one's life.

According to professional astrological societies, there are approximately 10,000 professional astrologers serving some 20 million clients. In 1987, former White House Chief of Staff Donald Regan revealed that even the President and Nancy Reagan (once a follower of occultist Jeanne Dixon) scheduled activities

---

[59]Brad Stieger, *The Fellowship* (New York: Dolphin/Doubleday, 1988), 67.
[60]Whitley Strieber, *Communion* (New York: William Morrow, 1987), 15.
[61]Bill Lawren, "UFO Report," *OMNI* (October 1987): 144.
[62]John Weldon and Zola Levitt, *Encounters with UFOs* (Irvine, Calif.: Harvest House Publishers, 1975), 102.

based on astrologer Joan Quigley's forecasts:

> Virtually every major move and decision the Reagans made during my time as White House Chief of Staff was cleared in advance with a woman in San Francisco who drew up horoscopes to make certain that the planets were in a favorable alignment for the enterprise. . . . Mrs. Reagan insisted on being consulted on the timing of every presidential appearance and action so that she could consult her friend in San Francisco about the astrological factor. . . . The frustration of dealing with a situation in which the schedule of the President of the United States was determined by occult prognostications was very great.[63]

The Bible explicitly condemns involvement with astrologers, and "those who prophesy by the stars, and those who predict by new moons" (Isaiah 47:12–15). The prophet Jeremiah instructed God's people to "learn not the way of the heathen, and be not dismayed at the signs of heaven; for the heathen are dismayed at them" (Jeremiah 10:2). Scripture gives a further reason why astrology should be avoided: "Take ye therefore good heed . . . lest thou lift up thine eyes unto heaven, and when thou seest the sun, and the moon, and the stars, even all the host of heaven, shouldest be driven to worship them, and serve them" (Deuteronomy 4:15, 19).

On a practical level, there is another reason to avoid astrology. In 1988, the Committee for the Scientific Investigation of the Claims of the Paranormal stated that dozens of rigorous tests by scientists had determined that horoscopes "fail completely in predicting future events." In one test, scientists examined more than 3000 predictions by astrologers and found them accurate less than 10 percent of the time.[64]

From A to Z

New Agers employ a mixed bag of an almost infinite number of occult practices; far too many to identity and fully explore in this chapter. There are, however, words and phrases that may serve as warning signs that a particular belief, practice, or group is involved with the New Age movement and incompatible with the Christian faith. These include: Monism, Pantheism, Reincarnation, Karma, Evolution, Personal Transformation, Unlimited Human Potential, Reality Creating, Energy Alignment, Energy Healing, Energy Focusing, Attunement, At-one-ment, Enlightenment, Inner Power, Goddess Within, Mother Earth, Sensory Deprivation, Intuitive Abilities, Near-Death Experiences, Chakras, Gurus, Tarot, Kabbalah, Pyramids, Crystal, Power, Auras, Color Balancing, Psychic Centering, UFOs, Extraterrestrials, Brotherhood of Light, Higher Consciousness, Cosmic Consciousness, The Christ, Ascended Masters, Spirit Guides, Meditation, Yoga, Guided Imagery, Visualization, Astral Projection, Silver Cord, Inner Light, Out-of-Body Experiences, Mystics, Metaphysical, Holistic Healing, Therapeutic Touch, Biofeedback, Transpersonal Psychology, Hypnotherapy, Paranormal, Parapsychology, Higher Self, Personal Transformation, Values Clarification.

---

[63]Donald T. Regan, *For the Record*, 3, 300, 359.
[64]Chandler, *Understanding*, 221.

Conclusion

Here is the essence of the New Age movement—every religion is perfectly acceptable because each one teaches essentially the same thing. Since all is one and one is all, "God" can be reached by many ways. There is no personal Savior, incarnate Redeemer, or atonement for sins. All religious leaders are equal, be it Buddha, Mohammed, Zoroaster, Confucius, Krishna, or Jesus.

But Scripture declares that Jesus alone is the way, the truth, and the life (John 14:6), and "neither is there salvation in any other: for there is none other name under heaven given among men, whereby we must be saved" (Acts 4:12).

In the New Age movement there also exists no heaven to desire and no hell to fear. There is only a universalism that in the end saves everybody through works and reincarnation. Everybody will be reabsorbed back into the ultimate One. New Ager author Benjamin Creme writes, "The path to God is broad enough to take in all men."[65]

Jesus, however, said that the way to God is narrow. The broad way "is the road that leads to destruction, and many enter through it" (Matthew 7:13, NIV). New Agers desperately need help seeing the narrow way that has been hidden from them by the god of this world (2 Corinthians 4:3–4).

The New Age movement can deceive anybody. It is very subtle and attractive. It talks about a new world, a new religious emphasis, one planet, and one people. It promises peace, disarmament, abolishment of nuclear weapons, prosperity, success, and preservation of the earth. Hedda Lark, spokesperson for a New Age publishing company, says: "I think people are searching for a sense of security in a world that's gone pretty mad, and they have the feeling that there must be more to life than this craziness."[66]

There *is* something more to life than the "craziness" surrounding us, and Christians *must* let New Agers know that it is the biblical Jesus of orthodox Christianity.

---

[65]Creme, *Reappearance*, 120.
[66]Martin E. Marty, "An Old New Age in Publishing," *Christian Century* (November 18, 1987): 1019.

Chapter 12

The Unification Church

Editor's Note:

The Unification Church is one of the best cults at disguising its unusual, nontraditional beliefs from the unsuspecting secular world. This was not always the case, as history testifies regarding the "brainwashing" scare that seemed to follow Unification proselytizing efforts everywhere during the late 1970s and early 1980s. Much like the Mormons in the century before them, however, the Unification leadership rose above the turmoil and began to project a public persona that intrigued many secularists as well as unsuspecting religious leaders—even evangelical Christian leaders. Today, just as the Mormons are more well known for their social welfare programs, family values, and wholesome lifestyles than for their belief in many gods and that you can become a god of your own planet; so the Unification members ("Moonies") are better known for their support of conservative values and right-wing politics than for their belief that Moon is the new Messiah sent to propagate the perfect family on earth. The reputation of the Unification-owned Washington Times *is reaching the caliber of the* Christian Science Monitor *as a publication of pivotal value in the public square. The Unification Church is a fascinating study of how a religious movement can move from everybody's bogeyman to a respected public voice of conservatism in two short decades. Underneath the public veneer, however, Unificationism is no more biblical or Christian than Mormonism or Christian Science.*

The Unification Church, founded and led by the self-proclaimed messiah, Sun Myung Moon, demonstrates the growing trend toward New Age beliefs worldwide.[1] The distinctive features of this kind of cult include (1) its habit of conducting business, especially recruiting, under multiple pseudonyms or anonymously; (2) its Westernization of Eastern religious ideas; and (3) its misinterpretations of Scripture to persuade outsiders that its Eastern religious orientation is compatible with and, indeed, is the fulfillment of biblical Christianity. Groups such as the Unification Church are further characterized

---

This chapter written by Kurt Van Gorden and edited by Gretchen Passantino.

---

[1]See chapter entitled "The New Age Cults" for further information on the New Age movement.

by what appears to be obvious, widespread, and forceful psychological pressure on members to conform and remain loyal to the group at all costs. This psychological pressure is present in all the cults, as we have noted earlier. It is perhaps more obvious with groups newly arrived in America whose converts are mainly young people from families who have had little or no previous exposure to the group.

The Hare Krishnas, Transcendental Meditation, the Church Universal and Triumphant, and other similar groups share many of the same features, but each in their own unique expression. In this chapter on Unification theology and practice, we will touch on some of the teachings that cause the Unification Church to be classified as a non-Christian cult, and moreover, one of the many-faceted New Age cults.

History

On January 6, 1920, Yong Myung Moon (Shining Dragon Moon) was born of Confucian parents, humble farmers, in the town of Dok A, Jung-Juin, the providence of Pyongyang Buk-do, in North Korea. The family converted to the Presbyterian Church in 1930, but the youthful Yong Myung Moon retained ancestral veneration common to Confucianism. According to Unification writer Kwang-Yol Yoo, Moon experimented in contacting ancestors in the spirit world during his early teen years, and his spiritual quest was likened to that of Buddha.[2]

The climax of Moon's spiritual search was a vision he reportedly received of Jesus Christ on April 17, 1936, at age sixteen. The year of Moon's vision varies, with some Unification authorities placing him at age seventeen (eighteen by Korean reckoning).[3] Yoo places Moon at age fifteen (sixteen by Korean reckoning), but the majority of writers place him at age sixteen (seventeen by Korean reckoning). The dubious year and age for which Mr. Moon claimed his vision is reminiscent of the first vision of Joseph Smith, the American Mormon prophet, who also had difficulty giving consistent details about his vision of Jesus Christ. What really devastates Mr. Moon's supposed vision is that every Unification writing gives the date as "April 17, 1936, Easter morning." The most grave error in Unification history occurs here, for our calculations prove beyond a doubt that Moon's vision could not have occurred on Easter morning because April 17, 1936 was a Friday, not a Sunday. Anyone with access to past calendars or computerized calendars can prove the same.

Just how this vision of Jesus unfolded is also questionable. One of the most astounding confessions by Moon himself was under oath in 1982, during a Unification suit against a deprogrammer. Moon, in a New York Federal Court testimony, on May 27 and 28, stated that he had met Jesus, whom he had recognized from "holy cards." He also testified that he had met Moses and Buddha.[4]

[2]Kwang-Yol Yoo (in a five-part series), "Unification Church History From the Early Days," *New Hope News*, Washington, D.C.: The Unification Church, 1:9–10, 12–13; 2:1.

[3]Dr. Young Oon Kim, *Divine Principle* (San Francisco: The Holy Spirit Association for the Unification of World Christianity, 1960, 3rd ed. 1963), ix. Kim was the first Unification missionary to the U.S. She was also a well-read theologian for the Unification Church.

[4]Richard A. Blake, "The Attraction of the Moonies," *America Magazine* (June 12, 1982): 452.

To imagine that the test for identifying Jesus Christ is to match his image with "holy cards" is the height of absurdity. In Yoo's history, Moon was told to complete Jesus' unfinished mission. Strangely, though, Moon claims he already knew that he was to complete Jesus' mission before he had the vision announcing the same.[5]

It is stated in their history that Moon struggled for nine years (the original *The Divine Principles* say seven) to discover the truth of the *Divine Principle*. The *Divine Principle* is authoritative scripture in the Unification Church and is considered superior to the Bible. The varied accounts of its coming forth shade its history equally with that of his vision. It seems that some Unification writers believe the *Divine Principle* came by revelation, while others say it was "discovered."

Astute investigators point to Moon's former teacher, Elder Baik Moon Kim, of Sup Lee, Kyung Gi, North Korea—who founded a church called the Monastery of Israel—at least as its inspiration. Elder Kim had taught similar "principles" to Moon in 1946. Moon's *Divine Principle* was not written until six years later, in 1952. It was also in 1946, while being taught by Elder Kim, that he changed his name to Sun Myung Moon (Shining Sun and Moon). Although he goes by the title "Reverend," there is no history of his ordination by any bona fide denomination in Korea or America. In fact, many of the earliest Unification writings from the 1960s consistently call him "Mr. Moon." It was not until his reemergence in America in the early 1970s that he was quite suddenly known as "Reverend" Sun Myung Moon. The Unification Church ordains no ministers, so Rev. Sun Myung Moon is in a class by himself. One becomes a church member upon completion of a twenty-one-day training course. Members affectionately call Sun Myung Moon their Father.

Shortly following the Second World War, Moon drifted from one "Pentecostal" group to another. From Yoo's history, it is no hidden fact that most of these groups had blended seances, spiritism, ancestral spirit guidance, and a host of occult practices with their untrained "Pentecostal Christian" faith. What one ends up with is spiritism practiced in the name of Christianity, something exercised by many cults and abhorred by all genuine Christians.

It was through these spiritistic endeavors that Moon claimed to discover the nine levels of the spirit world, each of which he subjugated by questioning the spirits he faced. His supposed proof of authenticity is that Jesus, Confucius, Muhammad, and Buddha all appeared and agreed with his conclusions. Finally, Moon faced off with Satan himself and questioned Satan about the fall of Adam and Eve until he found the real cause of the Fall. He claims to have conquered Satan and accomplished what no other man before him has done, including Jesus. According to Moon, the fall of Adam and Eve, which we will discuss in detail later, was first Eve's sexual intercourse with Satan, and second her passing on sin through sexual intercourse with Adam before he had matured to perfection.[6] Like many other cult leaders before him, Moon has brought sexuality to center stage, cloaked in religiosity.

Moon may have been too preoccupied with the subject of sex during the

[5]Yoo, *Early Days*, 5.
[6]Ibid., 7.

formation of his church. There are several reports bearing examination concerning Moon's marriages, bigamy, and promiscuous sexual affairs, called "blood cleansing," with the female members of his church. Even the noted philosopher Dr. Frederick Sontag, who wrote favorably of Moon and had the very rare occasion of interviewing him, could not avoid the rumored escapades of Moon. "There are unconfirmed reports of other marriages," he wrote, "but at least it is clear that his first wife could not accept the religious role thrust on her."[7]

According to a well documented report by Dr. Shin Sa Han, Dean of Religion at Seoul University, Seoul, Korea, Moon's first wife, Choi Sun Kil, married him in 1945 and immediately bore him a son. Dr. Shin reports that Sun Myung Moon was arrested for irresponsible sexual activity at Bo An Police Department, Dae Village, North Korea, on August 10, 1948. He was excommunicated from the Presbyterian Church that same year. Adding more trouble to his history, Moon evidently married Kim X, February 22, 1949, without divorcing his first wife. He was reportedly sentenced to five years in Hung Nan prison, North Korea, for bigamy. Kim X was convicted with him and was sentenced to ten months. During the Korean War, the United Nations Forces bombed Hung Nam and freed the prisoners on October 14, 1950, of whom Moon was one. He made his way southward along a torturous 600-mile journey with two friends and established himself in Pusan, South Korea.

Moon wrote *Divine Principle* in 1951–1952 under postwar hardships in Pusan, but, strong-willed, he trekked onward and established the Unification Church on May 1, 1954, in Seoul, South Korea. Again, he was arrested on July 4, 1955, for irresponsible sexual activity that caused a scandal at Ewha Women's (Methodist) University in Seoul. Several Korean newspapers covered the story. Moon was released October 4, 1955, because the eighty women involved in the incident exercised their right of silence in court. It was also reported by the Church of the Nazarene Korea Mission that Moon's church was involved in an unusual sexual "blood cleansing" rite where a woman was to have sexual intercourse with Sun Myung Moon to cleanse her blood from Satan's lineage. The "cleansed" woman could then cleanse her husband through sexual union with him. This ritual was based upon the Unification doctrine that Eve fell by having intercourse with Satan; therefore, a woman having intercourse with Moon, who is Lord of the Second Advent, would be cleansed. Just as Eve passed Satan's tainted blood lineage on to Adam, likewise the cleansed Unification member passes purification of blood on to her spouse.[8]

Obviously, as Moon's church grew larger, it complicated the doctrine, and his haunting arrest records required abandonment of the rite. There is no evidence it is practiced today.

Sun Myung Moon married his current wife, Hak Ja Han, in March 1960, when he was forty and she was seventeen. She has since borne him thirteen "sin-

[7]Frederick Sontag, *Sun Myung Moon and the Unification Church* (Nashville: Abingdon, 1977), 80. See also, J. Isamu Yamamoto, *The Puppet Master* (Downers Grove, Ill.: InterVarsity Press, 1977), 21. Yamamoto points out that there may have been four marriages.

[8]The major points of this ritual were confirmed by a Korean government cable, February 1963, and sent to the United States Central Intelligence Agency. See James Coates, "Moon Church Traced from Sex Cult, *Chicago Tribune* (March 27, 1978).

less" children, and is referred to as Mother by Unification members. Together, Rev. and Mrs. Moon, Father and Mother, are known as True Parents. Their wedding is viewed as a fulfillment of the "marriage of the Lamb" in Revelation 21:9. To Unification members, this monumental event ushers in the "New Age, the Cosmic Era."[9] Moon and his wife are the first True Parents and have the power to bless other marriages with pureness and "sinless" offspring. Incidentally, this is why the Unification Church conducts massive weddings, with up to 300,000 couples at a time. These blessed couples supposedly are sinless families on earth.

Rev. Moon, steeped in reliance upon spirit guides, sought the spiritist-medium Arthur Ford on May 13, 1964, for insight on his mission. "Mr. Fletcher," the disincarnate spirit that spoke through Ford, evidently discussed pleasing confirmations to Moon, for the Unification Church widely published the seance sitting.[10] Upon realizing that evangelical Christians disdain such practices as abominable before God, the Ford seance, and the often used terms New Age, medium, clairvoyant, and clair-audient are suppressed in current Unification writings. Nevertheless, the true foundation for Moon's revelations, from age sixteen to the present, is rooted in contact with disincarnate spirits in the spirit world.

Moon claimed God appeared to him: "I came to America primarily to declare the New Age and new truth. . . . This is why God appeared to me and told me to go to America to speak the truth."[11] In obedience to his vision, in 1972, he began touring major cities in the United States for his "Day of Hope" crusade. When the infamous Watergate scandal broke out in the White House years of President Nixon, Rev. Moon wasted no time in pouring thousands of dollars into a self-promoting "God loves Nixon" crusade. Moon's opportunism succeeded with instant notoriety throughout the United States. Then came the opposition from parents' groups who claimed that Moon stole their children's minds and future. Moon has fought an uphill battle since then to gain acceptance, even though most critics claim that his celebrity-status supporters are mere dupes, often rewarded in monetary benefits.

Moon divided his twenty-one-year campaign for the restoration of Christianity into three seven-year segments, beginning with his marriage in 1960. The year 1976 was pivotal in Moon's third segment. He poured millions of dollars into two rallies, one at New York's Yankee Stadium and the other at the Washington Monument. His predicted success was dampened at the Yankee Stadium event when it rained relentlessly for three hours. With the stadium less than half full, Moon went on with the show. Moon, who incessantly compares himself with Jesus, spiritualized the Yankee Stadium event, claiming that he and the church had endured their crucifixion, death, and resurrection.

The Washington Monument rally brought better success, drawing some 200,000 to 300,000 people. Moon then claimed that his work had broken down

---

[9]Dr. Young Oon Kim, *Divine Principle* (San Francisco: The Holy Spirit Association for the Unification of World Christianity, 1960, third edition, 1963), iii. The original title of this work was *Divine Principles*. However, since it is much more widely known by its later title, *Divine Principle*, this text uniformly refers to it as such. If the original edition is referred to, that is indicated in the text or footnote.

[10]*Sun Myung Moon* (Washington, D.C.: The Holy Spirit Association for the Unification of World Christianity [HSAUWC], 1969), ii, iii.

[11]Sontag, *Moon and Unification*, 133.

all the walls of the spirit world, and spirits were descending rapidly upon the earth.[12] He predicted the next rally would be held in Moscow.

Rev. Moon's work was to be accomplished by 1981, but to his dismay, he found himself under the scrutiny of a House subcommittee and the Internal Revenue Service in the late 1970s. The latter investigation ended up in charges, and Moon went to trial in 1983, later being convicted of tax evasion. Moon spent thirteen months of an eighteen-month sentence at the federal prison in Danbury, Connecticut. The remaining five months of his sentence was served at a halfway house.

The Unification Church spent 4.5 million dollars to clear Moon's name with a mass-mailing campaign to 300,000 pastors in the United States. The unsolicited mailing contained three video tapes, two books, and introductory letters from Dr. Mose Durst, president of the Unification Church in America. Their main message was couched in fear and hysteria—if Rev. Moon could be sent to prison, then every American pastor faces the same future. In addition, the Unification Church campaigned in the media declaring Moon's innocence and changed the ordeal into governmental racial and religious persecution. Upon entering prison, Moon stated, "I am here today only because my skin is yellow and my religion is Unification Church."[13] Apparently, some Christian leaders took the bait and brushed aside Moon's tax evasion in lieu of ecumenical brotherhood, because "friends of the court" briefs were filed on Moon's behalf by the National Council of Churches, the National Association of Evangelicals, the Untied Presbyterian Church, the American Baptist Churches, the American Methodist Episcopal Church, the Unitarian Universalist Association, the National Black Catholic Clergy Caucus, and the American Jewish Congress.[14] Moon's campaign worked well. Upon his release from prison, August 20, 1985, he was celebrated at a banquet by 1,700 clergy with Baptist evangelist Rev. Jerry Falwell as the main speaker, who unsuccessfully called upon President Reagan to pardon Moon.[15]

What these well-meaning, but perhaps misled, clergy seem to confuse as illegal activities is not justified by a First Amendment religious cloak. Clearly Moon was convicted of evading taxes on $112,000 in personal income derived from interest on $1.6 million he had deposited for the church. He also received another $50,000 in unreported stocks for the taxable years 1973–1976.[16] Rev. Moon's accountant, Takeru Kamiyama, was sentenced for conspiracy to file false tax returns, lying before a grand jury, and obstructing justice.[17] In contrast to Moon's claim that it was the church's funds, the testimony showed he personally purchased $1,500 gold watches, stock, and paid tuition for his children's education from the accounts. Rev. Moon was not persecuted by the IRS: he and his

[12]"Buses, Buses, and More Buses," New Hope News (October 21, 1976): 5.
[13]"Moon Pleads Not Guilty in Tax Case, Cites Discrimination," Christianity Today (November 20, 1981): 7.
[14]John McCaughry, "The Uneasy Case Against Reverend Moon," National Review (December 23, 1983): 1612; Kenneth L. Woodward and Patrice Johnson, "Rev. Moon's New Friends," Newsweek (May 3, 1982): 88.
[15]James H. White, "Unification Church's Anti-Communist Drive," Christian Century (August 28–September 4, 1985): 772.
[16]"Of Moon and Mammon," Time (October 26, 1981): 24.
[17]Jane O'Hara, "Taxing Times for the Reverend," McCleans Magazine (April 5, 1982): 32.

accountant evaded personal taxes and lied to the grand jury, which places them under the same laws as any other American citizen. It is noteworthy that Moon could have received a fourteen-year sentence, so his eighteen-month sentence shows the mercy of the jurors, not persecution.

The Unification Church is not much larger today than it was in the mid–1970s. They still claim about 3 million people worldwide. It is probable that they have fewer followers in the United States than before. They once had 37,000 members in America, but sources close to the church project less than 10,000 today.[18] There are over 900 worship centers in Korea and 55 in the United States. The largest following Moon has is in Japan. The followers are usually called Moonies, and Moon apparently takes no great offense at this since he often uses it in his speeches. He went so far as to predict that there will be a day when they will be called Sunnies, and in the spirit world, Kingies.[19]

Two Distinguishing Features

There are two features that distinguish the Moonies from all other cults: their fund-raising tactics and their mass weddings. Much has been written in magazines and newspapers about the deceptive tactics used in fund-raising, called "heavenly deception." This is the practice of justified lying, which is permissible because it is for good. During one of Moon's training sessions, a student asked, "What about white lies?" Rev. Moon answered, "If you tell a lie to make a person better, then that is not a sin." He further adds, "Even God tells lies very often; you can see this throughout history."[20]

Moonies have been found raising funds from wheelchairs while in perfectly good health. They have even been spotted carrying the wheelchair back to their automobile! Most often they give names of false charities to gain sympathy. On one occasion, as former Moonie Chris Elkins relates, they were heavily reprimanded in Atlanta, Georgia, for selling leftover Girl Scout cookies under false pretenses.[21]

Rev. Moon gloats about how he rakes in huge profits from the unsuspecting public on flowers that cost him eighty cents and sell for a $5.00 donation.[22] At one point he told his followers that he would train them to make $30 million monthly, and then he could purchase the Empire State Building.[23] In all, Moon receives annually approximately $100 million from Japan, $35 million from the United States, and $20 million from Europe in charitable donations.[24] The Mobilized Fund-Raising Teams (MFT) often work fourteen or more hours daily with little sleep and sparse food. This has attributed to a number of vehicular accidents in which several MFT workers have been killed. Rev. Moon admitted

[18]John B. Judis, "Rev. Moon's Rising Political Influence," *U.S. News and World Report* (March 27, 1989): 29.
[19]Sun Myung Moon, *Master Speaks* (March 19, 1978): 6.
[20]Ibid. (March 16, 1972): 11.
[21]Chris Elkins, *What Do You Say to a Moonie?* (Wheaton, Ill.: Tyndale House Publishers, 1981), 55. See also Chris Elkins, *Heavenly Deception* (Wheaton: Tyndale House Publishers, 1980).
[22]Sun Myung Moon, *Master Speaks* (February 8, 1975): 14.
[23]Ibid. (September 20, 1974).
[24]T. Harvey Holt, "A View of the Moonrise," *Conservative Digest* (Jan/Feb 1989): 40.

that eighty-two accidents occurred in one month.[25]

The business holdings and spending power of the Unification Church are unparalleled for any other group its size. They have at least 335 businesses worldwide, and another 280 in the United States. Their business conglomeration rivals any international corporation. They produce weapons, soft drinks, ginseng products, computers, automobile parts, heavy machinery, and clothing; they also own convenience stores, real estate, fishing fleets, daily newspapers, magazines, and journals. One estimate is that the Unification Church controls ten billion dollars worth of businesses.[26]

Moon is known to sink hundreds of millions of nonreturnable dollars into floating the Unification-owned *Washington Times* newspaper and another ten million dollars annually on an intellectual journal. He spent forty-eight million dollars to produce a film, *Inchon*, that flopped at the box office. Over thirty million dollars was allocated to lure scholars and clergy from around the world to conferences in exotic resorts. Foreign students are offered Unification Church scholarships at his universities. And he pledged to build a one-billion-dollar automobile plant in China, called Panda Motors. However, after sinking hundreds of millions into the plant, the Unification Church abruptly closed it in 1991. This vacant building shell stands as a monument to the whimsical decisions Moon makes concerning his shifting financial empire.

The massive weddings that have drawn international attention to Rev. and Mrs. Moon result from their concept of the fall of man. Everything in Unification theology is interpreted through the Taoist philosophy of dualism, Yang and Yin (positive and negative, male and female). When Adam and Eve fell from perfection, they fell two ways, physically and spiritually. Through the Fall, mankind's blood became tainted through Eve's union with Satan.

When Jesus came to earth, His mission was to save man physically and spiritually by getting married. The Jews, John the Baptist, and His disciples failed to form a family unit with Him and find Him a suitable bride. Realizing their failure, He chose to die on the cross and save mankind spiritually. Instead of saving man two ways, corresponding to the fall of man, Jesus saved man spiritually, only halfway.

Therefore, it was necessary for another messiah to come to finish Jesus' incomplete work by finding the perfect bride, marrying, and establishing a God-centered family through which sinless children could be born. In this way sin would be eradicated from the world and man saved both physically and spiritually. Rev. Moon and his wife are these supposed True Parents of mankind. All weddings they bless are cleansed and sinless children are hence born. This is their reasoning for massive wedding ceremonies.

The largest mass wedding was held by satellite television in 160 countries and conducted by Sun Myung Moon. On August 6, 1995, 300,000 couples exchanged their vows. Every couple spends the following forty days in celibacy, and then consummates the marriage for three days, only to practice three additional years of celibacy.

---

[25]Moon, *Master Speaks* (October 3, 1976): 16.
[26]Christopher Byron, "Seems Like Old Times," *New York Magazine* (September 27, 1993): 22.

Lord of the Second Advent

It was not until Moon was released from prison in Danbury that he publicly called himself "Lord of the Second Advent." In his unedited speech, he said, "I am now in the position of Lord of the Second Advent to the world. . . . But with my emergence as the victorious Lord of the Second Advent for the world, a new order has come into being."[27]

In Sun Myung Moon's sermons, he leaves little doubt that he proclaims himself as the new messiah. It is not difficult for any reasonable person to draw the only conclusion he allows. If the messiah is the Lord of the Second Advent, and the Lord of the Second Advent includes the True Parents, then Moon is claiming all titles for himself by claiming to be the True Parent. Under direct questioning, Unification leaders often skirt the issue by claiming that Moon has never called himself the messiah. But decades of official literature, written by top leaders and published at church expense, openly declare Moon's messiahship. One example is Dr. Kim Sudo's *120-Day Training Manual*, which states, "Then they can understand that Rev. Moon is Messiah, Lord of the Second Advent"[28] And, "if only they can understand the fall of man they can understand that Father is the Messiah."[29] Again he writes, "Unless people can understand Father is Messiah, then they cannot move in."[30]

Rev. Moon's oldest son, Heung Jin Nim Moon, died in 1984, at age seventeen, in an automobile accident. Heung was groomed by Rev. Moon for future leadership of his organization, but his sudden death left Moon depressed. His belief in contact with the spirit world became his relief. His son supposedly became king in the spirit world through a proxy marriage ceremony. Then a strange turn of events occurred in 1987. An unnamed Zimbabwean member claimed that Heung began speaking through him as a medium. The Zimbabwean began giving spiritistic utterances from Heung at the Unification Seminary in Barrytown, New York.[31] Moon evidently accepts the utterances as authentic. He has elevated the Zimbabwean to a paid position in the organization. Meanwhile, the theory is that Heung is king in the spirit world, and the twelve remaining children of Rev. and Mrs. Moon represent the twelve tribes of Israel or the twelve disciples of Christ on earth.

Unification Theology Versus the Bible

Unification theology is a homogenization of dualism, using Taoist philosophy and the Bible. The church publishes a number of books to explain this concept, but the most authoritative is *Divine Principle*.

All spiritual and physical entities are described in dualistic terms in Unification theology. Moon believes that God has a "key," called "new truth," which will unlock "all these difficult biblical mysteries."[32] That key is later revealed as

[27]Sun Myung Moon, *CAUSA Seminar Speech* (August 29, 1985): 7–8. Other subsequent published versions have edited these lines out.
[28]Dr. Kim Sudo, *120-Day Training Manual* (HSAWU, n.d.): 160.
[29]Ibid., 222.
[30]Ibid., 400.
[31]Nancy Cooper and Mark Miller, "Rev. Moon's Rising Son," *Newsweek* (April 11, 1988): 39.
[32]Kim, *Principle,* 15.

the Taoist *Book of Changes (I Ching)*, through which Moon interprets the Bible and history.[33] Nothing is exempt in essence or relationship from dualism. "God," Moon revealed, "consists of dual characteristics."[34]

Although the Bible is considered a scripture, it is essentially replaced by Moon's *Divine Principle*. There is no question that Moon distrusts the text of God's Word. He taught, "The Bible, however, is not the truth itself, but contains the truth."[35] To say that the Bible is not truth, but only contains truth, is to cast doubt upon its authority. This argument is quickly laid to rest by the words of Jesus, who said, "Thy Word is truth" (John 17:17). We are also reminded of Psalm 119:151, which says, "Thou art near, O Lord; and all thy commandments are truth."

Moon holds the opinion that the Bible is outdated by our scientific age. He counts it "impossible" in this "modern scientific civilization" to use "the same method of expressing the truth" as found in the New Testament.[36] Therefore, a "new truth must appear."[37] And, like other cult leaders before him, Moon is proclaimed as the sole source for this new truth. The introduction of *Divine Principle* summarizes the matter: "This truth must appear as a revelation from God himself. This new truth has already appeared. . . ! God has sent His messenger. . . . His name is Sun Myung Moon."[38]

We have already seen that Moon's revelations are utterly dependent upon spiritism. Moon indicates that spiritism is a replacement, or substitute, for the Holy Spirit. He taught, "Spirit men pour out spiritual fire. . . . They enable earthly men to see many facts in the spirit world in a state of trance, give them the gift of prophecy, and inspire them spiritually. Through such activities, substituting for the Holy Spirit, they cooperate with earthly men to fulfill the will of God."[39]

It is no wonder, then, that Moon's "new truth" disagrees with the Bible, since he admits that his insight comes from spirits other than the Holy Spirit. The Holy Spirit inspires the true Word of God (2 Peter 1:21). Jesus tells us that the Holy Spirit brings His words to the remembrance of the disciples (John 14:26) as the divine protector from error in Scripture. He also speaks only what is truth (John 16:13), which prevents any distortion in God's message. There cannot be any substitution for the Holy Spirit; such is the warning of Paul (2 Corinthians 11:4).

Contact with departed sprits becomes the test for authenticity in *Divine Principle*. It says, "Any Christian who, in spiritual communication, can see John the Baptist directly in the spirit world will be able to understand the authenticity of all these things."[40] The idea that proof for revelation is grounded in spiritism is in direct violation of God's Word. Anyone who reads Deuteronomy 18:10–12 or Isaiah 8:19–20 will quickly see that God counts all such activity as abominable.

Revelation for Moon carries an unusual dispensational motif. He believes

[33]Kim, *Principle*, 26.
[34]Ibid., 26.
[35]Ibid., 9.
[36]Ibid., 131.
[37]Ibid.
[38]Ibid., 16.
[39]Ibid., 182.
[40]Ibid., 163.

in three "testaments:" the Old Testament, the New Testament, and the Complete Testament. The Complete Testament is *Divine Principle*. Even though the Complete Testament was given by Moon, he indicates that further revelation is yet to come. The "Complete" Testament evidently lacks completeness. A quarter of a century ago Moon promised an additional revelation called "Book Two,"[41] which is yet to surface. Its content, according to Moon, will irresistibly turn the heart of the most stubborn toward him. A book with such powerful influence seemingly should have been released by Moon some years ago, since his church is not much larger today than it was at that time.

God in Unification Theology

God is described in dualistic characteristics by Moon. God's internal essence is both male and female, positive and negative (yang and yin). God's external relationship is subject and object, male and female (yang and yin). Our discussion begins with the essence of God—what is His nature in Unification theology?

Much of the normative terminology found in standard Christian theology is adopted by Unification teachers. When the definitions are examined, however, the semantical changes, however slight, alter the true meaning. Such words as trinity, omnipresent, omnipotent, omniscient, and immutable have lost value in Unification thinking. The god presented by Moon is not the Trinity: he changes, and he has needs, without which he would cease to exist.

Beginning with God's essence, Moon teaches that God "exists with His dual characteristics of positivity and negativity."[42] The standard symbol representing Taoism is a circle with an "s" curve through the middle. The left side is white and the right side black. Each side contains its opposite color represented by a small circle. This symbol also underlies the Unification thesis for God. God is white and black simultaneously. He is positive and negative, male and female, subject and object, yang and yin. The god of Unification theology is dualistic.[43]

In expressing his view of God, Moon teaches, "The *Book of Changes (I Ching)* . . . emphasizes that the foundation of the universe is Taeguk (ultimacy) and from this comes Yang and Yin." He adds, "Taeguk . . . represents God, the subject who contains dual essentialities."[44] The original *Divine Principle*, translated by Dr. Young Oon Kim, explains the relationship, "though there are dual characteristics in God's nature, namely, true fatherhood and motherhood, He appears as a masculine character [subject] to His creation [object]."[45] Moon expounds upon this dual nature, "A man can be divided into two identical halves. Because God is like that He made man the same so He could interact with him. God created everything to resemble himself, especially man."[46]

Rev. Moon apparently has no understanding of the eternal, undivided essence of God. As often stated in creedal form, we do not confuse the persons

---

[41]Moon, *Master Speaks*, HSAUWC (March 16, 1972): 4.
[42]Kim, *Principle*, 24.
[43]Anon., *Outline of The Principle: Level 4* (New York: HSA-UWC, 1980): 4–6.
[44]Kim, *Principle*, 25–26.
[45]Ibid., 3.
[46]Moon, *Master Speaks*, HSAUWC (March 19, 1978): 10.

of the Trinity (Father, Son, and Holy Spirit), nor do we divide the substance (one eternal, omnipotent, omniscient God). In the case of the second person of the Trinity, the Son, the creeds additionally summarize the scriptural teaching that he was one divine *person* who, from the incarnation on, possesses two *natures*, his eternal divine nature and his human nature, which came to be at his conception by the power of the Holy Spirit "overshadowing" the virgin Mary. The personal unity of Christ is indisputable throughout Scripture as Christ said, for example, "Before Abraham was, *I* am" (John 8:58); and Paul affirmed, "There is *one* Lord, Jesus Christ" (1 Corinthians 8:6). The apostle John declares "The Word was God" (John 1:1) and "The Word became flesh" (John 1:14), so that we "beheld *his* glory" (John 1:14). Moon's illustration that God is divisible, the same as man, fails. God does not even divide His attributes with another: "I am the Lord: that is my name; and my glory will I not give to another" (Isaiah 42:8). Had the dualism of Moon been true, the Bible would be false, and we would have to deny the clear statement of Scripture: "Thus saith the Lord, the King of Israel . . . I am the first, and I am the last; beside me there is no God" (Isaiah 44:6). Rev. Moon wishes to correct the Holy Spirit here and say that God is dualistic, but the Holy Spirit's record of truthfulness, unlike Moon's, is spotless.

The Unification Church denies the historical Christian doctrine of the Trinity. Although they use the term "trinity" at times, they have redefined it into any group of three beings. The word "Trinity" is used to summarize what we see of God's nature in the Bible. Therein we find one God and no others (Isaiah 43:10). God is personal as the Father (Matthew 6:9). God is personal as the Son (Matthew 3:17). God is personal as the Holy Spirit (Acts 5:3). And together the three persons are uniquely one God in Scripture (Isaiah 48:16; Matthew 28:19; see also, chapter 5, page 101.)

Dr. Kim apparently misunderstood this biblical doctrine, because she erroneously attaches polytheism to its definition. She said, "Many Christians seem to worship three Gods: Father, Son, and Holy Spirit. . . . We believe the doctrine of the Trinity is mistaken, if it means the Father, Son, and Holy Spirit are three personal Gods."[47] Is it any surprise, then, that Moonies reject the Trinity, when one of their best theologians defines it neither correctly nor historically? Moon also redefines the Trinity: "Jesus and the Holy Spirit become one body centered on God; this is called 'Trinity.' "[48] Even more clearly, in the original *Divine Principle*, Moon teaches, "By uniting with the Holy Spirit, Jesus established the Holy Trinity for the first time—but spiritually."[49] Now Rev. Moon informs us that the Trinity had a beginning! Only after Jesus united with the Holy Spirit the first time did the Trinity begin. It is impossible, by any biblical standard, to arrive at Moon's conclusion without forsaking every Scripture that speaks of God's nature. The Bible speaks from cover to cover of the tri-personal nature of God. Beginning in Genesis 1:26–27; 3:22; 11:7–8, to Isaiah 6:8, we find God speaking of himself as "us" and "our." Throughout the Old Testament we find God speaking of another person who shares His nature, showing more than one per-

[47]Young Oon Kim, *Speeches on Unification Teaching* (Barrytown: Unification Theological Seminary, 1986), 4–7.
[48]Kim, *Principle*, 217.
[49]Ibid., 68.

son (Isaiah 48:16; Jeremiah 50:40; Zechariah 2:8–11; 10:12). In the New Testament the relationship and equality of the persons of God is well established (Matthew 28:19; 2 Corinthians 13:14; and John 15:26).

The word "trinity" for Moon was God's ideal family of Adam and Eve, centered (foundationally) upon God. These three were to become the original trinity, but the fall of man truncated this hope. What occurred in Eden was a satanic trinity, which Moon believes was passed on to humans everywhere. He teaches, "Due to the Fall, Adam and Eve . . . centered on Satan, thus resulting in a trinity centered on Satan. Therefore, their descendants have also formed trinities centered on Satan."[50]

All created entities are in a subject/object relationship with God, according to Moon. Creation is actually God's "second self, the visible God."[51] Moon describes God's nature, "We cannot see God because God exists as a spiritual force."[52] God is "the center," the "internal character" of the physical universe.[53] The universe "is the substantial manifestation of the invisible God."[54] The original *Divine Principle* says, "God is energy itself."[55]

Unification theology is immediately recognized as panentheism; that is, God is said to be invisibly "in" everything, but He is distinguished from the material atoms themselves. Panentheism is superbly dealt with and refuted by Dr. Norman L. Geisler in *Christian Apologetics.*[56] Biblically, if God existed before Creation (and Moonies will admit this), then for Creation to become his "visible second self" it requires a change in his nature. This is refuted by any number of verses that demonstrate God is unchangeable, such as Psalm 102:26–27 or Malachi 3:6.

One other interesting aspect of Creation in Unification theology is that apparently Lucifer and angels assisted God in creating all things. Moon says, "The archangel [Lucifer] had worked with God to create all the things in the universe; he knew everything."[57] Moon also explains, "God created the angels as servants who were to assist in the creation of the universe."[58] Yet one can search the Bible in vain to find a single line that tells of Lucifer or angels assisting in Creation. Instead, we find that Jesus Christ is revealed as Creator in his preexistence (John 1:3, 10; 1 Corinthians 8:6; Colossians 1:16–17; and Hebrews 1:2, 10). The biblical fact is that Jesus created all things, not Lucifer.

The god whom Moon portrays is weak, needful, and without all power. Moon speaks of God as one who is destructible. He says, "Since God must live in everything that is created, God himself must have these two separate elements [Sung Sang and Hyung Sang]. God must have the same nature as the rest of His creation, for without having such characteristics, He would eventually be destroyed by trying to exist in such a world."[59] Again, he says, "If man did not exist

[50]Kim, *Principle*, 217.
[51]Sun Myung Moon, *God's Warning to the World* (New York: HSAUWC, 1985), 18.
[52]Moon, *Master Speaks*, HSAUWC (March 16, 1972): 1.
[53]Kim, *Principle*, 25.
[54]Ibid., 40.
[55]Ibid., 4.
[56]Norman L. Geisler, *Christian Apologetics* (Grand Rapids, Mich.: Baker Book House, 1976), 193–213.
[57]Moon, *Master Speaks* HSAUWC, (March 16, 1972): 8.
[58]Kim, *Principle*, 76.
[59]Moon, *Master Speaks* HSAUWC (March 19, 1978): 9.

then God would vanish."[60] Even *Divine Principle* carries this theme, "In order for God to exist externally, God has dual essentialities."[61] It is utterly inconceivable that God is dependent upon creation for His existence. Biblical verses that speak of His eternality, from everlasting to everlasting, show that He exists independent of creation (1 Chronicles 16:36; Job 36:26; Psalm 41:13; 90:1–4; 93:2; 102:24–27; Isaiah 40:28). God speaks in exacting terms, "God is not a man" (Numbers 23:19); "I am God, and not man" (Hosea 11:9), which forever lay to rest the idea of His dependency upon man.

Jesus in Unification Theology

Sun Myung Moon openly states that "[John 8:58] does not signify that Jesus was God himself. Jesus, on earth, was a man no different from us except for the fact that he was without original sin."[62] In further elaboration, Moon insists, "After his crucifixion, Christianity made Jesus into God."[63] Moon makes all men equal in "divinity" to Jesus, thereby striking a blow at the uniqueness of Christ.[64] In hopes of gaining converts, Moon attributes demigod status to Jesus, saying, "Jesus, being one body with God, may be called a second God."[65] But, far from correct, this statement breeds polytheism, which is rejected throughout the Bible.

Unification theology denies the Virgin Birth of Jesus Christ. Dr. Kim wrote, "If Joseph was not the Father, who was? The New Testament is silent on such matters. . . . As the son of Zechariah, Jesus would become a half-brother to John the Baptist, producing in effect another Abel-Cain relationship at the very beginning of God's new dispensation. This explanation of Jesus' paternity would also serve to illustrate the traditional Christian comparison between Mary and Eve."[66]

Matthew 1:18–25 and Luke 1:26–2:20 give such detail of the virginal conception and birth of Jesus that no serious Bible student could miss it. Just how Rev. Moon and Dr. Kim missed the biblical account indicates the depth of their study. In addition, to suggest that Jesus was born of an incestuous and adulterous relationship between Zechariah and Mary (his sister-in-law) is unspeakable. We see here, as often seen in other cults, how new revelation leads people astray from God's Word.

The vicarious atonement, crucifixion, and resurrection of Jesus were all an unplanned mistake, according to Moon. God's real purpose in sending Jesus was to find a bride, marry, and produce sinless children. The original *Divine Principle* said, "The crucifixion of Jesus was a universal tragedy! The suffering of Jesus on the cross was not the Will of God, nor was it an event predestined by God."[67] It adds, "The crucifixion of Jesus was a secondary choice . . . after it

---

[60]Moon, *Master Speaks*, (May 22, 1977): 6.

[61]Kim, *Principle*, 40.

[62]Ibid., 212.

[63]Sun Myung Moon, *Christianity in Crisis* (New Hope, Washington, D.C.: HSAUWC, 1974), 12.

[64]cf. *Principle*, 209.

[65]Kim, *Principle*, 211.

[66]Young Oon Kim, *Unification Theology and Christian Thought* (New York: Golden Gate Publishing Co., 1975), 116. See also, Kim, *Unification Theology* (New York: HSAUWC, 1987), 171–172.

[67]Kim, *Principle*, 52.

became obvious that he would not be able to fulfill his mission."[68] The current *Divine Principle* agrees, saying, "redemption by the cross has been unable to remove our original sin."[69] Furthermore, "We, therefore, must realize that Jesus did not come to die on the cross."[70] Moon explains that Jesus' marriage was God's primary will, for "there had to be a bride, a Mother—another Eve. So God intended for this perfected Adam—Jesus Christ—to restore his bride, the perfected Eve."[71]

The original *Divine Principle* states the reason for Jesus' demise. "Satan used the condition made by John the Baptist, the disbelieving Jews, and Judas Iscariot to cause Jesus' downfall."[72] The best Jesus could provide for man's dual fall (spiritual and physical) is halfway salvation, spiritual only. Moon teaches, "Because Jewish people disbelieved Jesus and delivered him up for crucifixion, his body was invaded by Satan, and he was killed. . . . Therefore, all the saints since the resurrection of Jesus . . . enjoyed the benefit of the providence of spiritual salvation only."[73] At times Moon shows contempt for the blood of Jesus, "Today the Christian gospel preaches salvation by the blood of Jesus. How ridiculous that is in the sight of God!"[74]

What Rev. Moon fails to realize is that the crucifixion of Jesus was, indeed, the foreordained plan of God in redeeming lost sinners. Revelation 13:8 declares Him "the Lamb slain from the foundation of the world." Far from being ridiculous, and quite opposite of Moon, the apostle Peter calls the blood of Jesus "precious" (1 Peter 1:19–20). Jesus, in His Last Supper, spoke unforgettable words, "For this is my blood of the new testament, which is shed for many for the remission of sins" (Matthew 26:28). Paul encapsulates this truth: "In whom we have redemption through his blood, the forgiveness of sins, according to the riches of his grace" (Ephesians 1:7). Many other verses could be cited to refute Moon's denial of Christ's atoning blood, with which every student of God's Word should be familiar.

It is taught in the Unification Church that there are three main categories of the spirit world, subdivided into nine levels. Each world religion has their compartment, and they graduate from one level to another by assisting people on earth. Jesus, according to Moon, was not bodily resurrected, as plainly taught in Scripture. He was stuck for the past two thousand years in a particular level of paradise, awaiting liberation by Moon in the twentieth century.

On Jesus' resurrection, Moon says, "Many Christians today truly misunderstand. They preach resurrection, but resurrection does not mean that dead bodies will rise again."[75] He informs us that "God was not happy at all to see the resurrected Jesus."[76] All Unification denials of Jesus' resurrection are answered in the Bible. Luke 24:39 and John 20:27 leave no doubt that Jesus rose in His

---

[68]Kim, *Principle*, 60–61.
[69]Ibid., Kim, 142.
[70]Ibid., 144.
[71]Sun Myung Moon, *The New Future of Christianity* (Washington, D.C.: The Unification Church, 1974), 124.
[72]Kim, *Principle*, 172.
[73]Ibid., 148.
[74]Moon, *Master Speaks* (April 8, 1978): 12.
[75]Moon, *Warning*, 136.
[76]Moon, *Master Speaks* (April 3, 1973): 2.

physical body. He predicted it in John 2:19–21 and John 10:17–18. Its fulfillment is in every gospel, and Acts 1:3 reminds us that it was with "many infallible proofs." The apostle Paul gives a wonderful serial account of many, up to 500 people at once, who witnessed the physical resurrection (1 Corinthians 15:1–11).

The Holy Spirit in Unification Theology

Even though the Unification Church has as its official name, The Holy Spirit Association for the Unification of World Christianity (HSAUWC), its followers know little of the third person of the Trinity. As quoted earlier, Moon teaches that disincarnate spirits are a valid substitute for the Holy Spirit, which is abominable doctrine and not short of blasphemy. In furtherance of their mystical labyrinth, Moon informs us that the Holy Spirit is the female aspect of God, and became the spiritual bride of Jesus—his spiritual wife! Moon begins, "The Holy Spirit is a female spirit, this is because she came as the True Mother, that is, the second Eve."[77] He elaborates, "In Christianity we have only spiritual parents. The Holy Spirit is the mother spirit; and with Jesus Christ and the Holy Spirit working together we cleanse our sins and are given rebirth on the spiritual level."[78] Green auras, according to Moon, represent the Holy Spirit.[79] And Dr. Kim adds, "Unification Theology portrays the Holy Spirit not as an individual person, but rather as divine energy. . . . Like God himself, the Spirit is invisible and incorporeal—a bright light or a field of magnetic energy, so to speak."[80]

The biblical understanding of the genuine person and deity of the Holy Spirit is evident in many places (2 Samuel 23:2–3; John 14:26; 15:26; 16:5–15; Acts 5:3–4; and 1 Corinthians 6:19–20). From all of the above Unification theology, one need not go much further than 2 Corinthians 11:4 for refutation. It says, "For if he that cometh preacheth another Jesus, whom we have not preached, or if ye receive another spirit, which ye have not received, or another gospel, which ye have not accepted, ye might well bear with him." Failure in any single point disqualifies one from fellowship, but Moon has succeeded in violation of all three.

Salvation in Unification Theology

Finally, let us examine salvation in Unification theology. As in other areas, Rev. Moon utilizes Christian terms such as "grace," but alters the meaning. It is taught that God did ninety-five percent of the work, and left only five percent for man. But even five percent of works still desecrates what God has said concerning grace (Ephesians 2:8–9; Titus 3:5).

Sun Myung Moon believes that as the Lord of the Second Advent, the second messiah, he must set the foundation for physical salvation, which he claims Jesus failed to accomplish. By uniting with the perfect bride, Rev. and Mrs. Moon

[77]Kim, *Principle*, 215.
[78]Moon, *Master Speaks*, HSAUWC (September 22, 1974).
[79]Ibid. (March 16, 1972): 7.
[80]Kim, *Speeches*, 5.

became True Parents, the Third Adam and Third Eve. They also form a new "trinity" of God, Moon, and Mrs. Moon.[81] Rather than closing prayer in the name of Jesus, Moonies close prayer in the name of the True Parents.[82] Moon and his wife appear in spirit form to members in 120 countries of the world.[83] Moonies believe their works will save them, but more so, spirit ancestors descend upon them and work with them, therefore the spirit gains another level in the spirit world by assisting Moonies on earth.[84] Their goal is to become divine, like God, for this is Moon's promise for the highest level of heaven.[85]

Conclusion

As we survey the history of Rev. Moon and his Unification Church, we find that his practices depart from what is commonly accepted in American culture and contrast sharply to traditional Christian values. The presentation of Unification theology above shows that it is as far removed from biblical Christianity as is Unification culture.

Moonies have left the Unification Church and become Christians when loving Christians have shared their faith from God's Word with them. We must remember that Moonies are lost people for whom Christ our Savior died, so we must make every effort to teach them the truth about the crucifixion, blood, death, burial, resurrection, and grace of Jesus. They need the true Gospel of God that alone can liberate the soul searching for salvation.

We cannot leave this chapter without mentioning the controversial subjects of Moonie brainwashing, mind control, persuasion, coercion, deprogramming, and exit counseling. Void from most literature on this subject is the only solution we see for the Moonie, that is, genuine salvation through the grace of our Lord Jesus Christ. Chris Elkins, former Moonie, now a born again Christian, when asked if he recommends deprogramming, responded, "No. It often doesn't work. In cases of deprogramming that I'm familiar with, nearly 50 percent return to the cult." He adds, "I don't think brainwashing is the method of the Unification Church." When asked about freedom to leave the cult, Elkins said, "Many Moonies leave the Unification Church on their own free will. In fact, the turnover is very high. Some estimates have it that one-third of the membership leaves the Unification Church every two years."[86]

Exit counseling is merely another name for so-called "voluntary deprogramming." It is never to be a substitute for preaching the gospel message to Moonies who are in dire need of salvation. Many testimonies can be gathered of Moonies who left the cult after hearing the genuine gospel message. No deprogramming or exit counseling can match the wonderful grace of Christ.

[81] *Outline of The Principle: Level 4*, 146.
[82] Moon, *Master Speaks* (April 1965): 32.
[83] Ibid. (January 1, 1977): 5.
[84] Kim, *Speeches*, 14–15.
[85] Moon, *New Future*, 72; and Kim, *Theology*, 164.
[86] Elkins, *Deception*, 51–52.

Chapter 13

Scientology

Editor's Note:

This is a textbook examining religious belief systems from a biblical, orthodox Christian doctrinal perspective. Inclusion of groups, religions, and movements in this book does not mean that any of the authors, researchers, or editors presume that everyone will agree with the religious opinions and criticisms expressed here. Because we believe that the Bible teaches personal moral responsibility for every individual regarding the gospel claims of Jesus Christ, we believe that anyone may reject those claims and make a commitment to alternative beliefs. While no one should be forced to accept or reject particular beliefs by others, in the same way no one should be forced to refrain from honest differences of opinion and belief simply out of fear of litigation. It would honor the religious pluralism and freedom legally guaranteed in the United States if differing religious organizations and individuals, like the Church of Scientology and those associated with this edition of this book, would express their differences openly and without fear of intimidation or derision of any kind. That is the spirit in which this chapter is presented.

The Church of Scientology[1] is the most litigious religion in the history of churches founded in the United States. They have been the plaintiffs in an enormous number of lawsuits compared with most churches and/or religions. A few of their court battles have benefited others' rights. In that regard, Scientology's legal claims have helped stay the erosion of religious liberty. On the other hand, critics of Scientology claim that they intended many of their lawsuits as malicious vendettas against ex-members and perceived enemies of the church. These actions by Scientology have soured many people toward their church. Every Christian should cherish their religious freedom as a gift from God. In juggling the freedom of speech and freedom of religion, a Christian can allow freedom of religion for every Scientologist while exercising free speech in labeling Scien-

This chapter written by Kurt Van Gorden and edited by Gretchen Passantino.

---

[1]Scientology, Dianetics, Hubbard, and E-Meter are trademarks and service marks of the Religious Technology Center.

tology a false religion according to the biblical teachings embraced by the historical orthodox Christian church over nearly two thousand years.

Too much ink and paper have labored the point over whether Scientology is a religion. It has all the marks of a religion. It has its own set of scripture, it holds a worldview, and it seeks spiritual enlightenment. By biblical standards we justifiably call it a false religion. We define any religion as false whenever and wherever it departs from the biblical God and His plan of salvation as understood and proclaimed by the historical orthodox Christian church. So yes, Scientology is a religion, but a false religion by biblical standards. Jesus sharply rebuked false teachers of His day without denying their freedom of belief. Consider His "woes" to the Pharisees as an example (Matthew 23:13–30). Religions that deny Christ's deity, atonement, resurrection, and grace lead to an eternal hell and separation from God (John 10:1, 8; Matthew 5:29–30; 10:28; 18:9). Like Jesus, we can freely speak against false religion without denying one's rights to hold such. We must categorically separate denial of rights from proper examination by Scripture. We intend to do the latter only.

This chapter focuses on the theological aspects of Scientology. We will also examine its history to see how it came about. If the founder and the Church of Scientology have a questionable background, then that background warrants examination by Scripture. In 1 Thessalonians 5:22 we are warned to abstain from all appearance of evil. Ephesians 5:11 counsels us, "Have no fellowship with the unfruitful works of darkness, but rather reprove them." We do not find any clandestine or questionable background in the person of Jesus Christ. For centuries people everywhere have investigated the life of Jesus Christ by the same standards which we will apply to L. Ron Hubbard and Scientology. Jesus, being sinless and God incarnate, has no equal, nor can He be superseded by any other (John 1:1; 8:46; 18:20).

The Dianetics movement was once seen as a 1950s fad, which some erroneously thought would fade away as many fads do.[2] Others had a different perspective of Dianetics, calling it a cult from the beginning.[3] Within our theological definition of cultism, we describe the Church of Scientology as a non-Christian cult. In particular, Scientology's magazine *Advance!* speaks of its Buddhistic root, that L. Ron Hubbard is a second Buddha, the Meitreya. It says, "In Buddhist lands Mettaya [also spelled, Meitreya] became a great favorite [second Buddha]. Various cults devoted to him arose."[4] Scientologists acknowledge the religious validity of Buddhistic cults centered on Meitreya in past centuries. What they fail to realize is the same Meitreya-cult syndrome exists in their church, with L. Ron Hubbard as a Meitreya figure.

What is this movement called Scientology? It claims to be a "church" and an "applied religious philosophy." How do its teachings compare with the teachings of the Bible? What background and qualifications does founder L. Ron Hubbard have for developing a system that claims to be "the most vital move-

---

[2]See Martin Gardner, *Fads and Fallacies in the Name of Science* (New York: Dover Publishing, 1957), 263, and Paul Sann, *Fads, Fallacies, and Delusions* (New York: Crown Publishing, 1967), 113ff.

[3]*Time* (July 24, 1950): 64; *Newsweek* (October 16, 1950): 59; *American Mercury* (August 1951): 76; and *Time* (September 3, 1951).

[4]*Advance!* (December 1974): 27:5.

ment on Earth today"?[5] In this analysis of a complex religious and philosophical system, we will explore some answers to these questions. We will provide a survey of Scientology and, by contrast, show the major points at which statements in Scientology materials contradict biblical teaching.

L. Ron Hubbard

The founder of Scientology, Lafayette Ronald Hubbard (L. Ron Hubbard, affectionately called "Ron" by Scientologists), was born on March 13, 1911, in Tilden, Nebraska. Hubbard, a popular science fiction writer of the 1930s and 1940s, changed venues midstream by allegedly announcing at a New Jersey science fiction convention, "Writing for a penny a word is ridiculous. If a man really wanted to make a million dollars, the best way would be to start his own religion."[6] The following year, in May 1950, Hubbard released *Dianetics: A Modern Science of Mental Health,*[7] which has become entry-level reading for converts to Scientology. Hubbard's overnight success with *Dianetics* virtually gave him a new career in writing self-help and religious books. His first book on Scientology was published in 1951, and the Church of Scientology in California was incorporated on February 18, 1954.

Building a global religion of six million adherents (perhaps 200,000 active) in a few decades was no small victory for Mr. Hubbard, whose abilities should not be underestimated. His claim to fame as a writer includes fifteen million published words in science fiction, essays, and articles. He supersedes this with twenty-five million published words for Scientology. Mr. Hubbard's publishing achievements are notable, but his background upholds very few biblical Christian values, as we will see.

He was raised on a small ranch near Helena, Montana, with four hometown churches, but his later cynicism of Christianity betrays his virtually faithless upbringing. His father served a career in the U. S. Navy, which allegedly afforded L. Ron Hubbard frequent travel abroad. He was also one of the youngest Eagle scouts in the history of the Boy Scouts of America.

His books often carry a short biographical sketch of his accomplishments, also described in the Scientology *Dictionary*:

> [He traveled] extensively in Asia as a young man. . . . He studied science and mathematics at George Washington University, graduating from Columbian College. He attended Princeton University and Sequoia University. . . . Crippled and blind at the end of the war [World War II], he resumed his studies of philosophy and by his discoveries recovered so fully that he was reclassified in 1949 for full combat duty. It was a matter of medical record that he has been twice pronounced dead and that in 1950 he was given a perfect score on mental and physical fitness reports.[8]

[5]L. Ron Hubbard, "The Aims of Scientology" (Hollywood: The Church of Scientology Celebrity Center, 1974, 1977), one-page flyer.
[6]*Time* (April 5, 1976): 57.
[7]L. Ron Hubbard, *Dianetics: The Modern Science of Mental Health* (Los Angeles: Bridge Publications, Inc.).
[8]L. Ron Hubbard, *Scientology Abridged Dictionary* (Los Angeles: American Saint Hill Organization [ASHO], 1970), 36–37.

Several competent writers have gathered contradictory evidence of Hubbard's exaggerated vita and have challenged his claims. None are so thoroughly damaging to his credentials than Russell Miller's *Bare-Faced Messiah: The True Story of L. Ron Hubbard*[9] and former Scientologist Bent Corydon's *L. Ron Hubbard, Messiah or Madman?*[10] Miller showed that Hubbard attended high school in America while he was claiming to have been traveling Asia. His medical records showed that he was never crippled, blinded, or wounded in World War II, let alone being pronounced dead twice. Bent Corydon, formerly head of one of the most successful Scientology missions (Riverside, California), has countless court transcripts, affidavits, and firsthand testimonies that lay many of L. Ron Hubbard's claims to rest.[11]

Hubbard's academic degrees have come under question since Sequoia University was discovered to be an unrecognized diploma mill located in a two-story house in Los Angeles. It was closed down in 1958 by an act of the California Legislature.

It is true that he attended George Washington University for two years. He was placed on academic probation, as he said, for "some very poor grade sheets."[12] Although there are times he calls himself a "nuclear physicist," he failed his only class on molecular and atomic physics. He also spent three months in a military course at the Princeton School of Military Government. Nothing has yet surfaced to confirm his alleged degree from Columbian College.

The success of Hubbard's writing skills cannot be argued. The manuscript for *Dianetics* (180,000 words) was supposedly completed in three weeks' time. Those who knew him said that he could type ninety words per minute with the old two-finger method. He had an altered typewriter with special keys for often used words, such as "and," "the," and "but."

His personal qualifications as a religious leader were everything but saintly. His first two marriages were disastrous. His second wife, Sara Northrup Hubbard, sued him for divorce on April 23, 1951, in Los Angeles County Superior Court. The microfilm copy of that case mysteriously vanished from the court records. However, an industrious *St. Petersburg Times* newspaper reporter found the original in storage at the courthouse. It was a twenty-eight page complaint to dissolve their Chestertown, Maryland, marriage of August 10, 1946. This was a bigamous marriage for Mr. Hubbard. He pretended to be a bachelor to Miss Northrup, yet he had not divorced his first wife, Margaret Grubb Hubbard. His first marriage was not legally dissolved until over one year after his second marriage.

His second wife's 1951 divorce allegations contained more than bigamy charges. She claimed sleep deprivation, beatings, strangulation, kidnapping of

[9]Russell Miller, *Bare-Faced Messiah: The True Story of L. Ron Hubbard* (London: Michael Joseph/Penguin Books, Ltd., 1987).
[10]Bent Corydon, *L. Ron Hubbard, Messiah or Madman?* (Fort Lee, N.J.: Barricade Books, 1992).
[11]The prudent Christian reader should exercise discretion in reading these two books. Both contain offensive, vulgar, and obscene quotations attributed to Hubbard and others. Even Scientologists have expressed surprise at the filthy language of their leader. One Scientologist asked, "You mean the leader of the church speaks like *that*?" Another Scientologist responded, "Oh yes, he doesn't believe in keeping anything back" (Miller, *Bare-Faced*, 354).
[12]Miller, *Bare-Faced*, 50.

their child and fleeing to Cuba, and Ron counseling her to commit suicide, "if she really loved him."[13]

Sara Northrup had first met Hubbard through a Pasadena-based occult group led by Jack Parsons, a disciple of the late Alister Crowley, whose alias was "The Beast 666." Crowley was a leading Satanist, sorcerer, and black magician. He founded the Ordo Templi Orientis (OTO), which promoted sexual magick.[14] At its New York headquarters, the group's historical records include letters between Parsons and Crowley that mention Hubbard several times. Northrup was Parsons's girlfriend when they both met L. Ron Hubbard. As Parsons's partner, she represented the Babylonian woman in Revelation, chapter 17, in the New Testament. Before she could fulfill Parsons's plan, Hubbard swept her away in an out-of-state bigamous marriage (representing himself as a bachelor the entire time). In Parsons's letters he blamed Hubbard for taking her from him.

Scientology defends Hubbard's connection to the Parsons black magick cult by stating that he went undercover to infiltrate it on orders of the Naval Intelligence. Supposedly, several prominent scientists were visiting Parsons's OTO temple, and Ron's job was to shut it down. Jack (John Whiteside) Parsons was a noted rocket scientist, but the explanation presented by Hubbard seems far-fetched. It lacks rationalization for why an undercover agent would soil the operation with a bigamous marriage. No record has ever been produced to prove that Naval Intelligence hired Hubbard for such an operation.[15]

Hubbard's working knowledge of black magic and the occult satisfied Parsons. In one letter he wrote to Crowley he speaks highly of Ron's knowledge of the rituals.[16] The Bible, however, condemns occult practices as abominable, and God says that He will cut off the participants from His presence (Deuteronomy 18:9–12).

The resources claimed by Hubbard for Dianetics include, "the medicine man of the Goldi people of Manchuria, the shamans of North Borneo, Sioux medicine men, the cults of Los Angeles, and modern psychology. Among the people questioned about its existence were a magician whose ancestors served in the court of Kublai Khan and a Hindu who could hypnotize cats. Dabbles had been made in mysticism, data had been studied from mythology to spiritualism."[17]

Hubbard's third marriage, to Mary Sue Whipp, lasted the rest of his lifetime. She captivated worldwide attention, in 1977, as the mastermind behind a sinister covert operation against various levels of the United States government that could rival a spy novel. Hubbard was living in California at the time, but his impenetrable shield prevented direct connection with the illegal activities.

---

[13]Corydon reproduced nearly the entire document (Corydon, *Madman*, 302ff).

[14]"Magick" instead of "magic" was used by Crowley and other occultists to distinguish their rituals and spells from the sleight of hand entertainment provided by stage magicians.

[15]Scientologists also defend Hubbard by producing a document signed by Sara Northrup Hubbard declaring false everything she had stated in the divorce papers. Corydon made contact with Sara for his book. She reconfirmed her divorce statements and added that she had signed the disclaimer for protection (Corydon, *Madman*, 305).

[16]Ibid., 275.

[17]L. Ron Hubbard, "Dianetics, the Evolution of a Science," *Astounding Science Fiction* (May 1950): 48.

Hubbard spent his final years in seclusion from the public eye. Top Scientologists isolated him from most family and church members until his death in Creston, California (a small town north of San Luis Obispo). According to a copy of his death certificate, he succumbed to a cerebral vascular accident (stroke) on January 24, 1986. In their refusal to believe that such a great "science of the mind" master could die a horrific death, the word "dead" or "died" was never used at his eulogy. Scientologists announced that L. Ron Hubbard decisively "discarded the body" to move onto the next level of research, outside his body.[18] How this new research would become available to planet earth is left unsaid.

Hubbard himself apparently encouraged an examination of his belief system such as that undertaken in this volume. The seventh article of the Creed of Scientology states, "All men have the inalienable rights to think freely, to talk freely, to write freely on their own opinions and to counter or utter or write upon the opinion of others." If they hold faithful to their creed, they should expect counter writings. With this, we counter the opinions of L. Ron Hubbard.

The Dianetics Movement

Hubbard had no difficulty coining new terms as a science fiction writer. This talent became the bedrock for new terminology in Dianetics and Scientology. Church publications often contain glossaries for the new terms. They also publish a technical dictionary with three thousand new terms and definitions. It is interesting, however, that the word "Scientology" was originally used in 1934 by a German social psychologist, Dr. A. Nordenholz.[19] A French physiologist, Richard Semon, coined "engram" in 1904.[20] Engram is one of the most commonly used words in Dianetics and Scientology.

Dianetics means "through thought" or "through the soul." Hubbard promoted Dianetics by publishing three lengthy excerpts of his theory in the periodical *Astounding Science Fiction*, May 1950, October 1950, and January 1951. According to *Publisher's Weekly*, *Dianetics* sold 55,000 copies in the first two months and more than 750 Dianetics groups started nationwide.[21] They advertised its readership a year later as 150,000 people with 2.5 million followers. Dianetics swept college campuses and blazed through middle-class America with a faddish appeal that evolved into a cultic structure.

The glowing benefits of Dianetics seem virtually unlimited as Hubbard promotes his new "science of the mind."[22] Mankind, according to Hubbard, "is basically good."[23] The basic instinct for all people is survival.[24] Man's environmental conditions and painful experiences result in failure. So if a man changes

[18]Corydon, *Madman*, 17.
[19]George Malko, *Scientology: The Now Religion* (New York: Dell Publishing, 1970), 64. Malko parallels Hubbard's and Nordenholz's models, which reveals some scant hypothetical resemblance (116–119).
[20]Daniel L. Schacter, *Stranger Behind the Engram* (Hillsdale, N.J.: Lawrence Erlbaum Associates, Publishers, 1982), 186.
[21]*Publisher's Weekly* (September 16, 1950): 1124.
[22]Hubbard, *Dianetics*, 7.
[23]Ibid., 26.
[24]Ibid., 29.

his circumstances and eliminates pain, then his condition improves. Two important factors for man's survival, then, are avoiding pain and gaining pleasure.[25]

The structure of man's mind is simplified by dividing the mind into three main categories: the analytical mind, reactive mind, and somatic mind.[26] The analytical mind works like a "perfect computer, it never makes a mistake."[27] It is also the "I" of a person.[28] The reactive mind works on a "totally stimulus/response basis."[29] The reactive mind holds mental picture images of past experiences called "engrams," which are apparently the "single source of aberrations and psychosomatic ills."[30] Some liken the reactive mind to the subconscious mind. The analytical and reactive minds direct the somatic mind and "place solutions into effect on the physical level."[31] This mind keeps the body regulated and functioning.

The problem of humanity is that the reactive mind frequently interrupts the analytical mind. The analytical mind, which essentially "*is* the person,"[32] could flawlessly run a person's life (being a perfect computer) except for the interference from the reactive mind.[33]

It appears that this villain of the analytical mind causes it to shut off. Scientology calls this a moment of unconsciousness, though often the body is awake and animated. Hubbard explains, "When the individual is 'unconscious' in full or in part, the reactive mind is cut in, in full or in part. When he is fully conscious, his analytical mind is fully in command of the organism."[34] During these unconscious moments, the reactive mind takes in a detailed recording from the sensory organs. This recording is not a "memory," but an image, like a motion picture, called an "engram."[35] Everything said, seen, touched, or sensed is recorded by the reactive mind as the "engram." The reactive mind stores this engram, which works to stimulate the person to react to the stimulus.

The example is given: "Suppose as an example of an engram and its effects on the Spirit, Mr. A has a tonsillectomy under anesthetic. During the operation, the surgeon, who wears glasses, comments angrily to a clumsy nurse, 'You don't know what you are doing.' Mr. A recovers. A few months later, Mr. A, a bit tired during a hard day at the office, has an argument with his employer (who happens to also wear glasses), who says, 'You don't know what you are doing.' Mr. A suddenly feels dizzy, stupid, and gets a pain in his throat. There is installed a disk of conditioned semantic response which affects the Thetan (a cyclical reincarnated entity "discovered" by L. Ron Hubbard)."[36] These engrams make

---

[25]Hubbard, *Dianetics*, 44.
[26]Ibid., 61.
[27]Ibid., 62.
[28]Ibid., 61.
[29]Ibid., 577.
[30]Ibid.
[31]Ibid., 56.
[32]Ibid., 61.
[33]Ibid., 66.
[34]Ibid., 82.
[35]Ibid., 83.
[36]Staff of Scientology, *Scientology: A World Religion Emerges in the Space Age* (Los Angeles: Church of Scientology Information Service, 1974), 28.

man react insanely in society, in fact, they make man "mad, inefficient, and ill."[37]

The solution to the reactive mind interrupting the analytical mind is to rid the reactive mind of all engrams. Once this is accomplished, the person is called "clear." The clear person has no reaction to the same situation because no engram stimulates it. The goal of Dianetics is to clear the individual of all engrams of his past.[38] At first, Dianetics only dealt with engrams in this lifetime. After more probing, Scientologists claim that they carry engrams from past lives (reincarnation) which also need to be cleared.

The "clear" person is on the evolutionary journey to the next stage of man, a godlike being called *homo novis*. Hubbard informs us that a clear individual

> . . . can be tested for all psychoses, neuroses, compulsions, and repressions (all aberrations) and can be examined for any autogenetic (self-generated) diseases referred to as psychosomatic ills. These tests confirm the clear to be entirely without such ills or aberrations. Additional tests of his intelligence indicate it to be high above the current norm.[39]

Hubbard continues the potential expectation for the clear. It improves eyesight, stops ear-ringing, increases the IQ, cures the common cold, speeds thinking computations 120 times faster than normal, and saves marriages.[40]

The application of Hubbard's hypothesis is to vanquish the engrams through "Dianetic therapy." This is accomplished by an "auditor" who "audits" the engram through a form of counseling. After *Dianetics* was published, Hubbard introduced an electronic galvanometer, the E-meter, to help in auditing. The "pre-clear" (the person not yet clear) holds two tin cans connected by wires to the E-meter, while the auditor sits opposite him watching the needle on the E-meter. As the auditor gives "commands" to the pre-clear, the needle's fluctuation determines if they have detected a possible engram. By tracking the engram through questioning the pre-clear, they can erase the engram. That may only be the beginning of problems for the pre-clear, though. They may detect other engrams in connection with the first, producing a chain of engrams. It may take years of auditing for a person to become finally clear.

Hubbard claims that his results are scientifically valid and are based upon clinical study. Critics, however, renounced it from the start. *Publisher's Weekly*[41] reported that the American Psychological Association initiated the "first concerted action against" Dianetics at their September 1950 meeting. A resolution, adopted unanimously by the organization's 8,000 members, said that Hubbard's claims for Dianetics "are not supported by empirical evidence of the sort required for the establishment of scientific generalizations."

Dr. Morris Fishbeck, former editor of the *Journal of the American Medical Association*, went on record warning people about "mind-healing cults . . . like Dianetics."[42] Psychologist Eric Fromm aimed his comments at Hubbard's tech-

[37]Hubbard, *Dianetics*, 84.
[38]Ibid., 14.
[39]Ibid.
[40]Ibid., 17–18, 122, 125, 228, 411.
[41](September 16, 1950): 1124.
[42]*Newsweek* (October 16, 1950): 59.

niques. "Dianetics," he said, "has no respect for and no understanding of the complexities of personality." Dr. Fromm revealed that Hubbard had saturated Dianetics in "oversimplified truths, half-truths, and plain absurdities."[43]

One other problem that seemed to face Hubbard was that no "clears" could be found until February 1966, when John McMaster was called the world's first clear. It troubled critics that Hubbard never claimed to be clear himself until some years after *Dianetics* was published. Still, a little known story of an earlier clear is found in several newspapers of 1950.

On August 10, 1950, Hubbard rented the Shrine Auditorium in Los Angeles. An estimated crowd of 4,000 came to see the world's first clear, Miss Sonya Bianca, a physics student from Boston. Fitting with the Dianetic theory, Hubbard announced that she had perfect recall and could remember every moment of her life. When members of the audience questioned her, she could not remember basic physics formulas nor the color of Hubbard's necktie, which she had seen moments before. People began leaving the auditorium as they threw more taunting questions at Bianca. Hubbard quickly explained that he had accidentally placed her in the "now" by calling her to "come out now." Therefore, Hubbard reasoned, she could only remember the present "now" and nothing past. No reporters seemed convinced of his explanation, and on that note the Bianca debacle ended.

Although most Scientologists still claim that the world's first clear came in 1966, this is apparently not true according to Hubbard. In *The Journal of Scientology* (January 15, 1954), Hubbard wrote of how he had cleared fifty people. He added that auditors had cleared many times that number.

The Church of Scientology

The first nonprofit organization Hubbard set up was the Hubbard Dianetic Research Foundation. By November 1950, they had developed three courses in Dianetics. In 1954, the Church of Scientology was founded as a nonprofit corporation. The meaning of Scientology, Hubbard says, is "knowing about knowing, or science of knowledge."[44] The Church of Scientology uses a cross similar to the historical cross of Christianity, with the exception that it has four short sunburst points protruding from the center. The *Technical Dictionary* states that Hubbard borrowed the cross from Christianity. It says, "The model of the cross came from a very ancient Spanish mission in Arizona, a sand casting, which was dug up by Ron."[45] Ministers of Scientology often dress in black clergy garments and a white collar with a three-inch cross hanging from the neck. Since they also use the title "Reverend," they could easily be mistaken for Christian ministers, but their theology tells a different story.

Hubbard's discovery of the "Thetan" contributed to the religious nature of Scientology. They liken the Thetan to man's spirit. In Scientology, the Thetan is a timeless entity, which reincarnates in interplanetary life-forms. Once reach-

---

[43]Sann, *Delusions*, 114.
[44]L. Ron Hubbard, *Dianetics and Scientology Technical Dictionary* (Los Angeles: American St. Hill Organization, 1975), 369.
[45]Ibid., 371.

ing earth as man, its goal is freedom from the cycle of birth and rebirth, which is where Scientology enters the scheme.

Most people who join the church do so after reading *Dianetics*. They follow this with advanced levels and the hope of obtaining "clear" in one lifetime. Additional courses are offered for survival through the eight dynamics of life: self, sex, group, mankind, other life forms, MEST, spirits, and a Supreme Being. The cleared Thetan must learn to gain control over his environment and become an "Operating Thetan" (OT). Matter, energy, space, and time (MEST) are the physical universe. Everything but the Thetan is MEST. A Thetan can potentially control MEST by operating independently of his body.[46] Since the OT no longer needs his body, he can leave it at will through the act of "exteriorization," similar to astral projection.[47] OTs climb eight levels, but the highest course, "Truth Revealed," is only obtainable by a few members.

On the practical level, they often remind Scientologists that "Scientology works." However, Scientologists, whose goal is to make the world a better place, were caught deep in criminal activity that seems contrary to their religion and philosophy. More than 5,000 Scientologists were involved in one of the most clandestine covert spying operations ever aimed at the United States government. Evidently, none of those involved felt any religious or moral obligation to expose the crimes. Quite accidentally, two Scientologists working undercover, using a phony IRS badge to gain entrance to the Assistant U. S. Attorney's office, made a grave mistake and the cover was blown. The three-year operation came to a screeching halt.

These illegal activities were publicized when eleven top Scientologists were indicted in 1977. They named Mary Sue Hubbard, wife of the founder and director of the operation, among those charged with crimes. Court evidence, numbering approximately 33,000 documents, connected Scientologists to infiltrating the government, burglarizing, bugging, wiretapping, and stealing classified information. The operation targeted "the Federal Trade and Atomic Energy Commissions; the National Security Defense Intelligence Agencies; the Departments of Labor, Army, and Navy; the U.S. Customs Service; Interpol, and numerous U.S. police departments."[48] All eleven charged Scientologists originally pleaded innocent to the 28-count grand jury indictment. After much plea bargaining and examining mounting evidence against them, they pleaded guilty to one charge instead of a trial and a heavier sentence. Nine Scientologists (two of the eleven were in England) were sentenced on October 26, 1979. L. Ron Hubbard and twenty-four other Scientologists were named coconspirators, although unindicted.[49] Mary Sue Hubbard and four top Scientologists were given five-year prison terms and fined $10,000 each.

The Church of Scientology argues that it has long been oppressed by the American government. If this were true, then criminal activity is not the correct solution. The religious benefits of Scientology waned at this junction, because a "clear" person, especially an OT, should not be committing crimes. In these cases, Scientology did not work. This is a dark shadow for Operating Thetans,

---

[46]Hubbard, *Technical Distionary*, 279.
[47]Hubbard, *Dianetics*, 115.
[48]*People's Weekly* (August 14, 1978): 23. See also *Christianity Today* (December 7, 1979).
[49]*Reader's Digest* (May 1980): 91.

who are supposedly "cleared of all wrong answers or useless answers that keep them from living or thinking."[50]

The world headquarters for the Church of Scientology is in Clearwater, Florida. For several years, L. Ron Hubbard conducted business out of governmental reach aboard a floating headquarters, the *Apollo*, in international waters. Today's leadership may be imitating its founder with a new floating office, the *Freewinds*. Wealthy Scientologists pay up to $15,000 for a week-long Caribbean cruise aboard the *Freewinds*, while it duplicates as a high-level decision-making office for top Scientologists.[51] Another recent development has been the multimillion-dollar construction of a nuclear-proof vault tunneled into Walker Mountain, near Eureka, California, to store L. Ron Hubbard's writings.

The arm of Scientology reaches into several areas of life. People often point to the success stories of Scientology's anti-drug program. It apparently has a successful drug-rehabilitation program, Narcanon. It has a criminal rehabilitation program, Criminon. And it has a "non-religious" moral education program, The Way to Happiness. (Contrary to their claim, we see the "religion" of L. Ron Hubbard sprinkled throughout the text). Scientology's Celebrity Center caters to renowned figures, often using their endorsements for programs. Those lending their notoriety to Scientology programs include actresses Karen Black, Priscilla Presley, and Kirstie Allie; singers Lou Rawls and Isaac Hayes; actors John Travolta and Tom Cruise; and jazz musicians Chick Corea and Stanley Clarke. These programs often become stepping stones to lead the unaware person into the biblically false teachings of the church, although Scientologists will point out many who have been helped without joining. The testimony of rehabilitation is not to be confused with biblical salvation. We can rejoice when anybody leaves an addictive past, but they are destitute of salvation without Jesus Christ. Many non-Christian groups have used rehabilitative skills, but that says nothing about their doctrines. Scientology's false theology will lead people into an eternal hell without Christ. Recovered alcoholics and drug addicts still need to find a genuine and personal relationship with the Lord Jesus Christ, who alone regenerates man through the working of the Holy Spirit (Acts 4:12; Hebrews 1:2; Titus 3:5).

Scientology Scripture

The source of authority in any religion quickly tells the reader his or her worldview. Much of Scientology's literature never mentions God, Jesus Christ, the Holy Spirit, the Bible, salvation, or other theological terms associated with Christianity. All of L. Ron Hubbard's Scientology writings since *Dianetics* are considered "scripture" by the church. If his writings are scripture, then we must compare them with the genuine Scripture of God, the Bible. Jesus reminds us that we do not gather grapes of thorns nor figs of thistle plants (Matthew 7:16). The fruit of Scientology can be measured by its scripture, the writings of L. Ron Hubbard. We will also draw from their 1954 Articles of Incorporation, which have a systematic outline of their tenets not found in other writings.

[50]Hubbard, *Technical Dictionary*, 75.
[51]*The Cult Observer*, 9:4 (1992): 9.

They described their "Holy Book" in their Articles of Incorporation (2.i.14) as "a collection of the works of and about the Great Teachers, including the work, St. Luke." Yet, strangely, references to Luke's gospel in Scientology writings are virtually nonexistent. Hubbard revealed his sources for his church in his *Phoenix Lectures* (1954). He said, "The [Hindu] Veda . . . is best read in a literal translation from the Sanskrit. . . . A great deal of our material in Scientology is discovered right back there. Tao means knowingness," he said. "In other words, it's an ancestor to Scientology, the study of 'knowing how to know.' " Further, he said, "The Veda, the Tao, the Dharma, all mean knowingness. . . . We first find this Buddha called actually *Bodhi*. . . . This probably would be a Dianetic Release. . . . Another level has been mentioned to me—Arhat, with which I am not particularly familiar, said to be more comparable to our idea of Theta Clear." And, "Dhyana . . . could be literally translated as 'Indian for Scientology,' if you wished to do that."[52] From this we see the eclectic nature of Hubbard's theological authorities. He seemed to favor Buddhistic prophetic interpretation and believed it applied to his life. "The truth of the matter is," he wrote, "that you are studying an extension of the work of Gautama Siddhartha, begun about 2,500 years ago. . . . Buddha predicted that in 2,500 years the entire job would be finished in the West. . . . Well, we finished it!"[53]

Scientology claims its church "does not conflict with other religions or religious practices as it clarifies them and brings understanding of the spiritual nature of man."[54] But Hubbard questioned the origin of the Bible, saying, "It is no wonder we look into the Christian Bible and find ourselves reading the Egyptian *Book of the Dead*." And, "The parables that are discovered today in the New Testament were earlier discovered, the same parables, elsewhere in many places. One of these was the Egyptian *Book of the Dead*, which predates the New Testament considerably."[55] Typical of Hubbard's writings, no evidence or source is provided in support of his claim.

There are important contradictions between the Bible and the sources of Scientology. Jesus, as the unique Son of God, gave no credence to other scriptures or distorted views of God. One example of Jesus distinguishing between truth and error is the account of the Samaritan woman (John 4). The Samaritans are closely related to Judaism, yet he told the Samaritan woman, in John 4:22, that Samaritans do not know whom they worship. If Jesus differentiated between the Samaritan god and the Jewish God, then we should also distinguish between Mr. Hubbard's synthesizing of religions and Christianity. Jesus also challenged world teachers in John 10:8, "All that ever came before me are thieves and robbers." Since the Vedas, Confucius, Lao-tzu (Taoism), the Buddha, and the Egyptian *Book of the Dead* all came before Christ, He openly renounces them as "thieves and robbers." Rather than attempting homogenization, as Hubbard did, Jesus isolated His teachings from all others. Jesus singled himself out as man's only hope (Matthew 7:22–23; John 8:24; 14:6).

Truth for the individual in Scientology is often subjective and existential.

[52]L. Ron Hubbard, *The Phoenix Lectures* (Los Angeles: The Church of Scientology of California Publications Organization United States, 1969), 12, 16, 18, 19.
[53]*Advance!* (December 1974): 5.
[54]L. Ron Hubbard, *Volunteer Minister's Handbook* (Los Angeles: Church of Scientology, 1976), xiv.
[55]Hubbard, *Phoenix Lectures*, 9, 27.

To quote Hubbard, "Know thyself . . . and the truth shall set you free." In contrast, Jesus said, "If ye continue in my word, then are ye my disciples indeed; and ye shall know the truth, and the truth shall make you free" (John 8:31–32). Jesus gave an objective standard for truth: himself (John 14:6) and the Word of God (John 17:17). Never is man called "truth" in the Bible, nor is man's inner self. God is called truth (Deuteronomy 32:4; Isaiah 65:16), as are Jesus (John 14:6), the Holy Spirit (1 John 5:6), the Word of God (John 17:17), and the gospel (Galatians 2:5, 14). Never is man or knowledge of "thyself" called truth.

The subjective nature of truth in Scientology allows variation on some items. Hubbard wrote, "What is true for you is what you have observed yourself."[56] What one person perceives as truth may not be what another person perceives. So, what by normative standards would be called a contradiction outside of Scientology can be synthesized within the organization. An example found in Hubbard's book *Axioms and Logics*, Axiom 31, states, "Goodness and badness, beautifulness and ugliness are alike considerations and have no other basis than opinion."[57] We would biblically challenge the first proposition on the basis that goodness and badness are moral terms, not merely synthesized opinions. By biblical standards, the absolutes of God's moral law provide a basis for determining the value of human conduct. In our following study, Hubbard can apparently state two contradictory and opposing propositions without determining which is true. Hubbard at times can speak of one God (monotheism) and at other times of many gods (polytheism), without denial of either and while affirming truth in both statements. Hubbard also taught that "Truth is relative to environments, experience, and truth."[58] If some truths are relative, in Hubbard's thinking, then he can apparently justify holding two opposing propositions without contradiction. Therefore, there can be one God and many gods simultaneously.

Scientology's Theology

Scientology speaks of a Supreme Being, God, and gods, without telling its members in which, if any, to believe. In *The Scientology Catechism*, it says, "What is the Scientology concept of God? We have no dogma in Scientology and each person's concept is different. . . . Each person attains his own certainty as to who God is and exactly what God means to him. The author of the universe exists. How this is symbolized is dictated by your early training and conscience."[59] Pages 197–220 contain the entire printed version of *The Scientology Catechism*.[60] They further teach, "although the existence of the Supreme Being is affirmed in Scientology, His precise nature is not delineated, since the Church holds that each person must seek and know the Divine Nature in and for himself."[61] They

---

[56]L. Ron Hubbard, *Technical Bulletins* (Los Angeles: Scientology Publications, 1976), 4:203.

[57]L. Ron Hubbard, *Axioms and Logics* (Los Angeles: American St. Hill Organization, 1973), 5.

[58]Ibid., 68.

[59]Staff of Scientology, "The Scientology Catechism," *What is Scientology* (Los Angeles: Church of Scientology of California, 1979), 200.

[60]Staff of Scientology, *Scientology: A World Religion Emerges in the Space Age* (Los Angeles: Church of Scientology Information Service, 1974), 17.

[61]L. Ron Hubbard, *Scientology 8–8008* (Los Angeles: ASHO, 1967), 3.

address God in the monotheistic sense in many places, yet Hubbard also speaks of the activity of gods elsewhere. Their Articles of Incorporation (2.h) states, "Believing that Man's best evidence of God is the God he finds within himself . . . the Church of Scientology is formed to espouse such evidence of the Supreme Being and Spirit as may be knowable to Men."

Hubbard, then, finds no contradiction in promulgating polytheism. In his *Phoenix Lectures*, he indiscriminately allowed for monotheism or polytheism: "Let us take up what amounts to probably ten thousand years of study on the part of Man, on the identity of God or gods. . . ."[62] He also exposes false gods commingled with true gods. "There are gods above all other gods," he wrote. "There is not argument here against the existence of a Supreme Being or any devaluation intended. It is that amongst the gods, there are many false gods elected to power and position. . . . There are gods above other gods, and gods beyond the gods of the universes."[63] Furthermore, he wrote a hymn stating, "There can be love for Gods." And, "Behave[,] Obey[,] Be Courteous[,] To gods[,] Lord Buddha[,] And myself[,] And to your leaders . . ."[64]

Their book on world religion leaves little doubt that the Hindu Brahman is closely paralleled with Scientology's understanding of the Supreme Being. God is spoken of in terms of Hinduism. Though Hubbard provides no strict definition of the Supreme Being, his descriptive characteristics are enough for the Christian reader to see its unbiblical nature. Hubbard rejects the Christian doctrine of the Trinity. His *Phoenix Lectures* state, "The Christian god is actually much better characterized in the Vedic Hymns [Hinduism] than in any subsequent publication, including the Old Testament."[65] Again, he said, "The god the Christians worshiped is certainly not the Hebrew god. He looks *much* more like the one talked about in the Veda."[66] What he mistakenly assumed is that the Hindu "triad" is the basis for the Christian "Trinity." This is not historical or biblical. The Trinity is based solely upon the revelation of God's Word, as noted on pages 112–122. Hubbard also wrote, "For a long while, some people have been cross with me for my lack of cooperation in believing in a Christian Heaven, God, and Christ. I have never said I didn't disbelieve in a Big Thetan but there was certainly something very corny about Heaven *et al.*"[67]

Scientologists are taught by Hubbard that man is part God and can attain a "godlike" nature. He wrote, "A pre-clear is a precise thing, part animal, part pictures, and part God."[68] In Hubbard's evolutionary development of Homo sapiens, he teaches that man will evolve into "*homo novis*," described as "very high and godlike."[69]

Scripture denies the possibility of other gods besides the true God. There

[62]Hubbard, *Phoenix Lectures*, 3.
[63]L. Ron Hubbard, *Hymn of Asia* (Los Angeles: Church of Scientology of California Publications Organization, 1974).
[64]Ibid.
[65]Hubbard, *Phoenix Lectures*, 31.
[66]Ibid., 27.
[67]L. Ron Hubbard, "Heaven," *Hubbard Communication Office Bulletin* (hereafter *HCOB*) (May 11, 1963), one page, as quoted by Kevin Anderson, *Report of the Board of Inquiry into Scientology* (Melbourne: Australia Parliament Government Printer, 1965), 150.
[68]L. Ron Hubbard, *Scientology Clear Procedure, Issue One* (Los Angeles: ASHO, 1969), 21.
[69]L. Ron Hubbard, *History of Man* (Los Angeles: ASHO, 1968), 38.

is but one God (Deuteronomy 4:39; 6:4; Isaiah 43:10; 44:8; Mark 12:32; Ephesians 4:6; 1 Timothy 2:5; and James 2:19).

The Bible always presents a sharp distinction between God and man. Scripture reminds us in Numbers 23:19, "God is not a man, that he should lie." Hosea 11:9 says, "I am God, and not man, the Holy One in the midst of thee." A study of God's omnipotence, omnipresence, and omniscience truncates the words of Hubbard (1 Samuel 2:3; 1 Kings 8:27; Job 42:2; Jeremiah 23:24; 32:17; Romans 11:33).

Scientology's Jesus

When L. Ron Hubbard mentions Jesus Christ, it is rarely in reverence and mostly with disparagement. A few lines previously, we saw that Mr. Hubbard refused to believe in the Christian Christ. Implants are false concepts forced upon a Thetan, and Scientology chalks up "Christ" as an implant more than a million years ago. He wrote, "You will find . . . the Christ legend as an implant in pre-clears a million years ago."[70]

Mr. Hubbard casts doubt upon the uniqueness of Jesus as the Messiah. His *Phoenix Lectures* state, "Now the Hebrew definition of Messiah is one Who Brings Wisdom—a Teacher. Messiah is from 'messenger'. . . . Now here we have a great teacher in Moses. We have other Messiahs, and we then arrive with Christ, and the words of Christ were a lesson in compassion and they set a very fine example to the Western world."[71] It does not take a great deal of biblical knowledge to refute Hubbard here, for many young students in Christian churches are aware that the Hebrew definition for Messiah is "anointed." It does not come from "messenger," but from "to rub" or "anoint." Hubbard proves his ignorance of Hebrew and Christian terminology, which may suggest his disdain toward what he never understood.

The Church of Scientology teaches that Jesus Christ may have believed in reincarnation: "There is much speculation on the part of religious historians as to the early education of Jesus of Nazareth. It is believed by many authorities that Jesus was a member of the cult of the Essenes, who believed in reincarnation. . . ."[72] Hubbard attributes Hindu teachings to Jesus. "Christ," he wrote, ". . . was a bringer of information. He never announced his sources. He spoke of them as coming from God. But they might just as well have come from the god talked about in the Hymn to the Dawn Child . . . the Veda."[73] Hubbard looks down upon Jesus from his OT VIII position, claiming, "Neither Lord Buddha nor Jesus Christ were OT, according to the evidence. They were just a shade above clear."[74]

Let us remember that the apostle Peter dealt with Hubbardian theories long ago. Peter, denying any mythology or legend to Christ, said, "We have not followed cunningly devised fables, when we made known unto you the power and coming of our Lord Jesus Christ, but were eyewitnesses of his majesty"

---

[70]L. Ron Hubbard, *Professional Auditor's Bulletin 31*, quoted by Anderson, *Report*, 150.
[71]Hubbard, *Phoenix Lectures*, 27–28.
[72]Staff, *A World Religion*, 15.
[73]Hubbard, *Phoenix Lectures*, 27.
[74]L. Ron Hubbard, *Certainty Magazine*, 5:10, as quoted by Anderson, *Report*, 150.

(2 Peter 1:16). Jesus also denied anyone could be the Messiah other than himself (Matthew 24:3–5, 11). He unashamedly said, "No man cometh unto the Father, but by me" (John 14:6). Luke settles the idea of multiple ways of salvation in Acts 4:12, "For there is none other name under heaven given among men, whereby we must be saved."

Jesus was not a man looking for salvation with the rest of humanity. He was sinless (John 8:46; 1 Peter 2:22) and had no need to be "a shade above clear." He fully announced His sources (Luke 24:44), which have nothing to do with the Essenes nor the Vedas. In the Bible He is seen as an eternal, active person (Micah 5:2) who is one with the Father (John 10:30) and the second person of the Trinity (Matthew 28:19).

Scientology's View of Man

Beginning with *Dianetics*, Hubbard taught, "Man is basically good." Scientology carries this theme throughout Hubbardian writings. In contrast, biblical Christianity observes that man's nature is basically evil: "There is none righteous, no, not one" (Romans 3:10). Hubbard also borrows the Oriental philosophy that "I am not this body." In contrast, again, the Bible observes both parts of man's nature, the body and the spirit. We have one nature, human, with two parts, physical and spiritual. Biblically, then, man is both physical and spiritual (Ecclesiastes 12:7; Genesis 2:7). The separation of the two is death, for the body without the spirit is dead (James 2:26).

The Thetan (spirit) has some amazing characteristics, according to Hubbard. It is more than eighty trillion years old and dwells somewhere within the skull of an individual.[75] When the individual organism dies, the Thetan reports to an implant station (one is on Mars) before being shot down to earth. This is the "between lives area. Here he 'reports in,' is given a strong forgetter implant, and is then shot down to a body just before it is born."[76] Thetans have been known to fight other Thetans over inhabiting a body. They communicate by telepathy, move objects by kinetics, and travel at high rates of speed. Thetans can be packed in ice and frozen, or they may be dumped into the ocean from a flying saucer. This, Hubbard assures us, "is quite authentic."[77]

Hubbard also taught a Darwinian form of evolution for man. Hubbard has laid out various life-forms in his book *Scientology: A History of Man*. Hubbard often roots the problem for today's Scientologist in engrams collected from past lives. Many common activities also result from past lives. The first stage of life is the Photon Converter, which converted light into energy as its main function. The Photon Converter had nothing to do at night, therefore our need for sleep.

Following later came the jelly fish, but the jelly fish got tired of being pressed against stones. It compensated by forming a shell and becoming the clam. The clam had two hinges that would fight over which one would be opened or closed. This caused engrams. Later, in man's evolution, these hinges

---

[75]L. Ron Hubbard, *Scientology: The Fundamentals of Thought* (Los Angeles: Church of Scientology Publications Organization, 1972), 55.
[76]Hubbard, *History of Man*, 53.
[77]Ibid., 20, 43, 64–66.

became man's jaws. Small barnacle-like spores attached to the outer edge of the clam shell later became the pattern for man's teeth.

Another shellfish was the Weeper, sometimes called the Boo Hoo. Its main function was to adapt to the seashore. It had two small tubes for pumping salt water in and out of its shell. These two holes later became man's eyes. The name Boo Hoo, or Weeper, was coined because some Scientologists would cry due to sand being in the pumping tubes while they recalled this stage.

Hubbard suggests that many of our problems may be traced to former lives. Smoking tobacco results from smokers dramatizing volcanoes they saw in previous lives. Psoriasis is an engram received from when an animal ate you; the psoriasis resembles the digestive fluids of the animal that ate you. Vegetarians got tired of being eaten by animals in former lives. Fear of falling can be traced to being a sloth and falling out of trees.

Hubbard taught that the Pilthdown Man was part of the evolutionary chain for man. He called it man's first real manhood. (Hubbard wrote of Pilthdown Man in 1951, not knowing that two years later, in 1953, scientists would declare it a hoax). Eventually he arrives at Homo sapiens. The next step of the evolutionary chain is *homo novis*. Its status is godlike.

The biblical view of man's origin does not include evolution, where great difficulties arise due to the lack of transitional fossils, spontaneous generation, and cross-breeding species. Each life-form has its origin in God's creative works outlined in Genesis, chapter one. Specifically, man and woman were created to reflect God's image and likeness (Genesis 1:26–27), which separates man from beasts. Due to man's fall from his righteous state, in Genesis, chapter three, all humanity has inherited a sinful nature like Adam's (Romans 5:12). This has resulted in the evil of the world around us.

Hubbard disagreed with the Bible at this point. "It is despicable and utterly beneath contempt to tell a man he must repent, that he is evil."[78] Yet Jesus did just that. He told men to repent and said that they were evil (Matthew 4:17; 7:11).

Scientology's Salvation

Scientologists prefer to use the term "rebirth" instead of "reincarnation," although reincarnation is found in their writings. Hubbard emphasized that salvation is to be free from the endless cycle of birth and rebirth. The way to salvation is to erase engrams through auditing. The proof to many Scientologists that they release engrams through auditing is the accompanying sign. "When one releases an engram," Hubbard wrote, "the erasure is accompanied by yawns, tears, sweat, odor, panting, urine, vomiting, and excreta."[79]

Scientology's view of reincarnation includes extraterrestrial life, evolution on other planets, evolution on earth, implant stations, forgetter implants, and engrams that keep people trapped in reincarnation. The OT III, section three, material was entered into court cases, from which we find Hubbard's journey of the Thetan. He claims this discovery was in December 1967:

[78]Hubbard, *Auditor's Bulletin*, 31.
[79]L. Ron Hubbard, *Science of Survival* (Los Angeles: AHOS, 1973), 2:255.

> The head of the Galactic Confederation (76 planets . . . 95,000,000 years ago) solved overpopulation (250 billion or so per planet) by mass implanting. He caused people to be brought to Teegeeack (Earth) and put an H-bomb on the principal volcanoes . . . and then the Pacific area ones were taken in boxes to Hawaii and the Atlantic ones to Las Palmas and there "packaged." His name was Xenu.
>
> [The result of Hubbard's investigation into this formerly undiscovered data was that] one's body is a mass of individual Thetans stuck to oneself or to the body. . . . Thetans believed they were one. This is the primary error . . . by [a] BODY THETAN is meant a Thetan who is stuck to another Thetan or body but is not in control. . . . A CLUSTER is a group of body Thetans crushed or held together by some mutual bad experience.

Scientologists thought they only needed to clear their Thetan, but now Hubbard tells them they have body Thetans and clusters to be rid of. This keeps them bound to the church for longer periods trying to achieve salvation.

Hubbard tells them that some of these body Thetans have been asleep on their Thetan for seventy-five million years. Ridding it makes the body Thetan as sort of a cleared being. Hubbard also believes he went back four quadrillion years ago (give or take a few years).

These incarnations and reincarnations are the supposed dilemma of the Scientologist. Reincarnation is answered in Hebrews 9:27: "It is appointed unto men once to die, but after this the judgment." Biblically, we live and die once. We have no preexistence in other bodies and we did not come from outer space. Jesus denied preexistent souls for people. "Ye are from beneath; I am from above: you are of this world; I am not of this world" (John 8:23). We find that reincarnation does not fit into God's plan of salvation. Jesus' death upon the cross would be unnecessary if reincarnation were true. Nevertheless, we find that Jesus was foreordained as the "Lamb slain from the foundation of the world" (Revelation 13:8). Jesus' sermons on heaven and hell would be a lie if reincarnation were true. But we find that Jesus always spoke the truth (Hebrews 4:15). Jesus' bodily resurrection from the tomb refutes reincarnation, since He resurrected to the same body (John 20:27). "He showed himself alive after his passion by many infallible proofs, being seen of them forty days, and speaking of the things pertaining to the kingdom of God" (Acts 1:3; see also 1 Corinthians 15:1–8). The resurrection of Jesus is proof that His grace will save us who place our trust in Him for our salvation. Every Christian has what every Scientologist is looking for—that is, salvation.

Conclusion

Scientology is undoubtedly a religion, and deserving of the same freedom of belief and expression as any other religion in the United States, including biblical Christianity. It is also open to the same kind of critical evaluation by the Bible that responsible Christians put their own teachings to on a regular basis (Acts 17:11). When the teachings of Scientology are compared to biblical truth, Scientology is illuminated as the empty façade of biblical imitation it truly is.

Chapter 14

Eastern Religions

Rajneeshism, ISKCON, and Transcendental Meditation

This book has undertaken to survey some of the major cults that exist and are active in the United States today. Over the years, hundreds of smaller cults have come and gone. Often, the fads of society are reflected in the fads of cults or cultic belief. Nowhere is this more evident than in the general American culture's strange preoccupation with anything Eastern or Asian. This "fad" traces its roots to the appearance of a Hindu guru at the Chicago World's Fair at the turn of the century, although popular interest in Eastern things did not explode in American society until the 1960s and 1970s. From Nehru jackets in the 1960s to Tao and the new physics in the 1980s, Eastern influence has pervaded Western society.

As America approaches a new century mark, this fascination with Eastern religions shows no signs of abating. As is amply demonstrated in chapter 10, *The New Age Cults*, Eastern philosophy and theology have invaded almost every level of American society and American religious practice. (See also Appendix C, *The Word Faith Movement*, for evidence that similar ideas have even become popular in the Christian church.) The recent centennial celebration of the Chicago Parliament of World Religions gave Americans a plethora of sights, sounds, and experiences of the East. Representatives from hundreds of religious movements, most of them Eastern in origin or at least by adoption, gathered in one place for more than a week of formal meetings, informal sessions, ceremonies, and rituals. While most Eastern religious influences have been incorporated into New Age cults or even embraced by traditional Protestant and Roman Catholic congregations, three more purely Eastern religions still have a strong presence in America and are discussed in this chapter. The founders of two of the groups have died, but their followers continue to exert a strong religious influence on segments of American society. The third, Transcendental Meditation, is still led

This chapter updated and edited by Gretchen Passantino.

by its founder, Maharishi Mahesh Yogi. It, too, is a strong but subtle influence in American religious practice.

The last few decades have seen the explosive growth of New Age (or occultic) religious cults with their roots in classic Hindu thought. Today, there are literally hundreds of large and small cults in America with Eastern ideas and practices. In this short summary, we will survey the Hindu roots of these cults and then present a quick look at three of the most well-known imports: Rajneeshism, the International Society for Krishna Consciousness (ISKCON, or Hare Krishnas), and Transcendental Meditation (TM). What follows is a brief history and description of Hinduism and a brief introduction to and doctrinal summary of Rajneeshism, ISKCON, and TM.

Hinduism

Hinduism today is not the same as Hinduism five thousand years ago. The Hindu religion has evolved over the past five millenia of Indian religious history. Hinduism seeks to be a synthesis of the various religious ideas and influences from throughout the Indian subcontinent, representing hundreds of separate cultural, social, and tribal groups. The term "Hindu" itself is not indigenous to India. It comes from the Persian designation of the Indus River. Yogi Ramacharaka notes,

> The different Hindu sects, while practically appearing as different religions, in reality regard themselves as but different sects and divisions of the One Eternal Religion of India, of which each, of course, considers itself the best and most favored channel of expression and interpretation.[1]

Scripture

The Hindu scriptures were collected over hundreds of years, beginning with the writing of the oral traditions around the last half of the second millennium B.C. These scriptures are known as the *Vedas* ("wisdom" or "knowledge"). The concluding portion of the Vedas are called the *Upanishads*, which are a synthesis of Vedic teachings. The general assumptions of the Upanishads include a belief in pantheism, karmic retribution, and reincarnation. Perhaps the most well-known section of the Vedas is the Hindu epic called the *Bhagavad-Gita*, which tells the story of the warrior-prince Arjuna, and his charioteer, Krishna, who is actually the disguised incarnation of the Hindu god Vishnu. The Gita was written down and subsequently modified between 200 B.C. and A.D. 200.

An illustration of the pluralism or contradictory nature of Hinduism is found by comparing the god of the Gita with the god of earlier Vedic literature. God, as described by the Gita, is personal and often sounds even monotheistic (only one God exists who is personal and not a part of creation). However, when one reads earlier Vedic scripture, God is presented as being definitely pantheistic (all of existence is, in some way, divine) and perhaps even monistic (all of existence is one, whether any divinity exists at all). The monotheistic charac-

---

[1]Yogi Ramacharaka, *The Philosophies and Religions of India* (Chicago, Ill.: The Yogi Publication Society, 1930), 271–272.

teristics of the Gita were appropriated by the founder of ISKCON, and consequently ISKCON teaches a more monotheistic rather than pantheistic idea of God today.

Contemporary Hinduism

There are three basic classifications into which the hundreds of Hindu sects can be divided: (1) the abstract monists, who stress the philosophical oneness of the universe instead of religious or theistic ideas; (2) the Vishnuites, who are devoted to the worship (in many different manners) of the god Vishnu (in many different manifestations) as the supreme form of divinity; and (3) the Shivaites, who are devoted to the worship of the god Shiva as the highest manifestation of divinity. TM, with its philosophical concentration, relates to the monistic classification, while ISKCON believes that Krishna, the supreme God, is also known as Vishnu and so they are identified with the Vishnuites. Rajneesh differed from them both in that he was philosophically agnostic and pragmatically Hindu. He had no inhibitions about subjecting Hinduism to any interpretation that fit his presuppositions, particularly in the realm of morality.

World religion expert Professor Ninan Smart notes the problems of the varieties of contemporary Hindu systems:

> It might be asked, by way of conclusion, What is the essence of Hinduism? A hard question. There are orthodox Hindus who deny the existence of God. There are others who while not denying God, relegate him to a second place, as a secondary or illusory phase of the Absolute. Amid such a variety of theological views, what remains as necessary to Hindu belief? Certainly the doctrines of rebirth and that of an eternal soul. The picture of the world as a place where the immortal spirit within man is virtually endlessly implicated in the round of reincarnation has dominated the Indian imagination for about three millennia. In addition, a complex social system has given shape to the actual religion of the subcontinent over a long period.[2]

Hindu Beliefs

God. There is no single Hindu idea of God. Hindu concepts of deity can include any of the following: monism (all existence is one substance); pantheism (all existence is divine); panentheism (God is in creation as a soul is in a body); animism (God or gods live in nonhuman objects such as trees, rocks, animals, etc.); polytheism (there are many gods); henotheism (there is one god we worship among the many that exist); and monotheism (there is only one God).

Karma and Samsara. Fundamental to Hindu thought is the idea that all souls are eternal and accountable for their own actions throughout time. Karma refers to the debt of one's bad actions which must be atoned for (through various Hindu systems) in order for one to escape the wheel of *samsara*, or reincarnation (the soul inhabits successive human bodies) or transmigration (the soul inhabits successive bodies—human, animal, or even plants or inanimate objects).

---

[2]Ninan H. Smart, *The Religious Experience of Mankind* (New York: Charles Scribner's Sons, 1976), 155–156.

Salvation. The three major paths to Hindu "salvation" include *karma marga* (method), the way of disinterested action; *bhakti marga*, the way of devotion; and *jnana marga*, the path of knowledge or mystical insight. Jnana marga achieves self-realization through intuitive awareness and mystical insight. Bhakti marga achieves self-realization through ritualistic sacrifice and discipline.

Bhagwan Shree Rajneesh (Rajneeshism)

In terms of media attention and exposure, Bhagwan Shree (Sir God) Rajneesh (born 1931) gradually achieved greater notoriety than any recent cult leader—with the possible exception of Sun Myung Moon. He was indisputably the preeminent Eastern guru of the 1980s.

After Rajneesh was expelled from the United States by the Immigration and Naturalization Service (INS) in 1985, he returned to his religious community in India and continued to rule his followers in the United States through his representatives. Shortly before his death (on January 19, 1990), he repudiated the title "Bhagwan," which means "the embodiment of God," saying it was a "joke." And "the joke is over." Instead, he declared, he was the reincarnation of Buddha and should be addressed as "Rajneesh Gautaman the Buddha." Finally he took the title "Osho Rajneesh," to which he is still referred by his followers, and which is a Buddhist term meaning "on whom the heavens shower flowers."[3] After he "left his body" or died (which his followers attributed to poison from the United States government but others attributed to AIDS), his financial empire in the United States and his closely controlled communities of American believers largely disintegrated. However, his books, tapes, videos, and teachings are still immensely popular, and many who explore alternative belief systems and practices are still attracted to the frenzied practices of Rajneeshism.

In an interview in *Forward* magazine,[4] Eckart Flother, a former follower of Rajneesh, gave an excellent thumbnail sketch of the cult leader's background:

> Rajneesh Chandra Mohan was born on the 11th of December, 1931, in a village in central India, the eldest in a family of five sisters and seven brothers. His childhood was overshadowed by the fact that his father, an unsuccessful businessman, was often on the road. The "father figure" in Rajneesh's life was instead occupied by his grandfather, to whom he became very attached. His grandfather died when he was seven years old. This was a very traumatic experience for young Rajneesh. From then on he felt strangely attracted to the subject of death. In his 1979 diary (which is made public), it is reported that he followed after funerals as other children would follow circuses.
>
> Rajneesh pursued his education and in 1957 obtained a Master of Arts in Philosophy. He proceeded to teach philosophy in two universities between 1957 and 1966. In 1966, Rajneesh resigned from his service as a teacher in order to, as he puts it, concentrate on the wish of God. He felt called to work for the spiritual regeneration of humanity, which he feels is necessary in order to survive the holocaust which he is predicting and fearing.
>
> Rajneesh then became a "master" and called himself "Acharya"[5] Rajneesh,

---

[3] The *Star Telegram* (December 29, 1988): 1:3.
[4] Forerunner of the Christian Research Institute's award-winning journal *The Christian Research Journal.*
[5] "Acharya" means teacher.

and he walked and rode a donkey around India in various states in order to teach people that they have to change their lives and turn around in order to survive.

His mission wasn't very successful, and in 1970 he was a tired and poor man who nevertheless recognized that he possessed charisma and power. In Bombay, he decided to gather people around him to whom he could teach his message. As more and more disciples flocked around him, the apartment where he lived was unable to accommodate them. Thus, in 1974 he moved to Poona, 120 miles south of Bombay, rented several houses, and founded his ashram.[6] There he changed his name from Acharya to Bhagwan (which means God), designed orange robes and a wooden bead necklace for his disciples, and started the movement we are dealing with today.

Rajneesh, bald, bearded, and photogenic, first attained major media exposure in the U.S. in early 1978, when *Time* magazine featured an article on the guru entitled " 'God Sir' at Esalen East." *Time* magazine reported that the charismatic guru had come into vogue among certain celebrities and prominent apostles of the Human Potential Movement who were joining thousands of other spiritual seekers in making the pilgrimage to Rajneesh's ashram in Poona, India. Rajneesh's appeal stemmed partly from his use of "tantric yoga" (involving nudity and free sex) and partly from his incorporation of a wide variety of popular "psychospiritual" therapies and techniques.

In the late '70s and early '80s, Rajneesh's acclaim continued to spread within the New Age movement in America, Great Britain, Germany, and nearly every free-world, industrialized nation. With as many as 6,000 Westerners in Poona at a time, the ashram population rose to 10,000 while 500 Rajneesh centers were established in twenty-two nations by orange and red garbed *Sannyasins*[7] (now more commonly called Rajneeshees) returning from Poona to their homelands. As of 1984, Rajneesh had gathered some 550,000 followers, whose average age was thirty-four.

Current membership figures are not available for the Rajneeshees, but some estimate that the worldwide following of full-time ashram residents is substantially less than the 10,000 faithful who congregate once each year at the Poona (India ashram for the "Buddhafield" festival). At its height, there were nearly 600 "Osho" centers worldwide, but by 1997 the number shrunk to only twenty. However, those who buy, read, view, and listen to Rajneesh materials run into the millions. Those who practice some form of the spiritual exercises and beliefs of Rajneesh probably range somewhere around 50,000 people worldwide. His discourses have been published in more than 650 volumes and translated into thirty languages.

Rajneesh's discourses, which were delivered daily, have been transcribed into over 350 books and diaries. Video- and audiotapes of each discourse have also been produced. These are all disseminated by Rajneesh Foundation International, a multimillion-dollar corporation. As a follower stated in the film *Ashram*, a documentary on the Rajneesh cult, "The organization understood long ago what powerful energy money is." Rajneesh, whose infamous personal fleet

---

[6]An ashram is a religious community/monastery.
[7]Initiated disciples. Males take on the title "Swami," and females go by the appellation "Ma."

of Rolls Royces numbered more than seventy at one time,[8] believed that "spirituality is the luxury and privilege of the rich."[9]

Rajneesh was a self-proclaimed spiritual rebel who thrived on the controversy that he created first in India, and then in America. Tal Brooke, a former devotee of the popular Indian guru Sathya Sai Baba, after visiting Poona effectively summed up the scene there:

> An object of media fascination and horror, Rajneesh is known for his bizarre revelations on sex. He has constructed a vision of the New Man that repudiates all prior norms and traditions. Man, by Rajneesh's thinking, is the hedonist-god, fully autonomous (barring the inner voice of Rajneesh), and free to carve out the cosmos in his own image. He is the sovereign pleasure seeker, self-transcender, who owes nobody anything. The family is anathema, children extra trash. And so long as the Neo-sannyasin has the money, the fun ride continues. Afterward, however, he or she is usually a nonfunctional casualty. Homicides, rapes, mysterious disappearances, threats, fires, explosions, abandoned ashram children now begging in Poona's streets, drug busts—all done by those amazing hybrids in red who believe they are pioneering new and daring redefinitions of the word "love." Christians working in a Poona asylum confirm such accounts, adding the breakdown rate is so high the ashram has wielded political power to suppress reports.[10]

Rajneesh often openly expressed hostility toward established religions: "This is a revolution. . . . I am burning scriptures here, uprooting traditions. . . . Unless I am shot, I'll not be proved right."[11]

By early 1981, threats on Rajneesh's life were reported. The ashram was heavily guarded, and no one was allowed to enter without first being searched for weapons. Then an ashram warehouse was set on fire, and an explosion was set off near the cult's health center. According to the cult's own account, when an actual attempt on the guru's life was made in February 1981, ashram officials hastened a process (which had already been initiated) of looking for a new headquarters.

According to the reputable magazine *India Today*, however, ". . . both police and . . . officials in [Poona] are unanimous in their charge that the incidents were rigged by Rajneesh followers."[12] Why? The Indian periodical explains that "Disclosures in [Poona] last fortnight revealed that the Rajneesh Foundation was up to its neck in income tax arrears, defalcation with the charities commissioner, a major insurance fraud, and a string of cases for criminal offenses that were still being investigated when they left."[13]

The U.S. Consulate in Bombay issued Rajneesh a visa, and on June 1, 1981, he secretly flew to New York with seventeen of his closest disciples.

Once Rajneesh left Poona, his followers spread throughout the West. "In

---

[8]Shortly before Rajneesh was deported by the INS in 1985, his Rolls Royces became the center of speculation that he was in violation of Internal Revenue Service (IRS) regulations as well. His fleet of Rolls Royces were subsequently sold, and since his deportation and death, the ostentatiousness of Rajneeshee leaders has been greatly subdued.

[9]Russell Chandler and Tyler Marshall, "Guru Brings His Ashram to Oregon," *Los Angeles Times* (August 19, 1981): 1:14.

[10]"Pied Piper of Poona," *Eternity* (September 1981): 14.

[11]*This Is a Revolution*, Bhagwan Shree Rajneesh, Videocassette 18C236 (December 28, 1980).

[12]Chander Uday Singh, "Sins of Bhagwan," *India Today* (June 15, 1982).

[13]Ibid.

Europe the present strategy is to establish 'Sacred Cities.' The European News-letter, issue 8, 1981, said: 'A Sannyasin city is to be set up in each major European country; Bhagwan has suggested that the cities should be self-supporting, alter-native societies, which will be models of sannyas.' "[14]

In America, efforts were undertaken to create the ultimate "sacred city," one fit for the "master" himself. On July 10, 1981, the Chidvilas Rajneesh Med-itation Center of Montclair, New Jersey, purchased the Big Muddy Ranch (where the John Wayne movie *Big Muddy* was filmed) for $6 million ($1.5 million of it in cash) from an investment company in Amarillo, Texas. The land, near Ma-dras, Oregon, covers more than 100 square miles. The Center also managed to lease 14,889 acres in the same area from the U.S. Bureau of Land Management.

Two hundred Rajneeshees from sixteen Western countries soon flocked to the Big Muddy, and in September they jubilantly welcomed their master to his new home.

Not long after the ranch was purchased, plans were announced to build "America's first enlightened city," which was to be called *Rajneeshpuram* ("ex-pression" or "city of Rajneesh"). On November 4, 1981, the Wasco County Com-mission voted two-to-one to allow an election to be held the following May to determine if the Big Muddy property should be incorporated as a city.

Since the only ones allowed to vote in such an election are those who *live* on the site (in this case, the Rajneeshees), the outcome was predictable: 154 votes in favor of the incorporation of Rajneeshpuram, none opposed. Rajneesh, his followers, and their "enlightened city" have began making headlines.

Working twelve hours a day, seven days a week for no wages (their basic necessities are provided for), the 2,000 members of the Rajneesh Neo-Sannyas International Commune were appropriately tagged the "red ants" because of their impressive industry and accomplishments. "The Rajneeshees have taken 81,000 acres of rocky, steep, dry and useless land . . . and are building a self-sufficient city complete with dam, substation, parks, housing developments, roads, fields, greenhouses, and airport."[15]

From the beginning, the cult's efforts to carve a paradise out of the Oregon desert were heatedly opposed. The legal status of the city was challenged on two grounds: (1) that it violated the constitutional separation of church and state, and (2) that the Wasco County Commission's decision to allow an incorporation election violated state land-use zoning laws.

As a security measure in case Rajneeshpuram was disincorporated (to make sure the cult has access to municipal powers and services), the Rajneeshees po-litically took over a nearby town, changing its name from Antelope to Rajneesh. Almost all of Antelope's original forty residents (mostly elderly), after being sub-jected to constant observation by the Sannyasin-manned police force, having their taxes tripled to support cult interests, and watching the Rajneesh-domi-nated city council designate an area within a local park for nude sunbathing, quit fighting and moved away.

In the meantime, the Immigration and Naturalization Service (INS) began "conducting an ongoing investigation into suspected violations of immigration

[14]Jens Johansen, "The Master Will Not Speak Again," *New Religious Movements Update*, 5:5/4 (Decem-ber 1981): 81.
[15]Bill Dietrich, "Conflict Over Rajneeshpuram," *Seattle Times* (September 9, 1984): A2.

laws and related criminal statutes by the Rajneesh Foundation International and related organizations and/or their members," said Carl Houseman, Portland's INS District Director.[16] Twenty-five to thirty Rajneeshees (including top leaders) were accused of engaging in "marriages of convenience" between U.S. citizens and foreign nationals. The permanent resident status of Rajneesh himself was also in jeopardy as the INS tried to prove that his original travel visa was granted on the basis of an exaggerated illness.

It was the takeover of Antelope, in particular, that fed the surrounding communities' worst fears about the cult's political ambitions. The Rajneesh Humanity Trust's "share a home" experiment in the fall of 1984, which imported 3,500 street people to the ranch, was interpreted by most observers as a bold (though abortive) attempt to establish a large enough voting bloc to gain political mastery over Wasco County.

The Rajneeshees eclipsed even the national elections in the Oregon media that November, and "rumor controls" had to be started to quiet runaway fears, such as a concern that the cult was threatening to take over the entire state.

Visions of a Jonestown-like confrontation between the Rajneeshees and governmental authorities, entertained ever since the cult purchased the Big Muddy, were fueled by Sheela Silverman, Rajneesh's personal secretary and president of Rajneesh Foundation International. This pugnacious Indian disciple, whose word was final in earthly matters, persistently took an inflammatory stance.

> In an interview on KGW-TV, aired June 29 [1984] . . . Sheela . . . told how she would deal with any attempt to dismantle buildings at Rajneeshpuram. "I will be dead," she said. "I will paint the bulldozers with my blood." Then, in a July 5 article in the *San Francisco Chronicle*, quotations from Sheela implied that she would block any attempt to arrest people at Rajneeshpuram for immigration or other legal violations. "I mean business," Silverman said through (according to the *Chronicle* account) lips trembling with anger. "You will find out what will happen to you if you come here to harm me or Bhagwan or any of my people. . . . I'll take things as they come. We are willing to die for human freedom. I have 100 percent support from my people."[17]

Rajneesh used this controversy to begin inculcating a catastrophic mind-set in his followers. In 1983, the guru published his vision of a worldwide crisis:

> The period of this crisis will be between 1984 and 1999. During this period there will be every kind of destruction on earth including natural catastrophes and man-manufactured auto-suicidal efforts. In other words, there will be floods which have never been known since the time of Noah, along with earthquakes, volcanic eruptions, and everything else that is possible through nature. . . .
> There will be wars which are bound to end in nuclear explosions, hence no ordinary Noah's arks are going to save humanity. Rajneeshism is creating a Noah's ark of consciousness, remaining centered exactly in the middle of the cyclone.
> I say to you that except this [i.e., Rajneeshism] there is no other way.
> Tokyo, New York, San Francisco, Los Angeles, Bombay, etc., all these cities are going to disappear and the holocaust is not going to be confined to certain

[16]Win McCormack and Bill Driver, "Rajneeshpuram: Valley of Death?" *Oregon Magazine* (September 1984): 26.
[17]Ibid., 30–31.

places. It is going to be global so no escape will be possible.
You can only escape within and that's what I teach.[18]

In early 1984, Rajneesh further expounded his vision of impending disaster by specifying that in supposed fulfillment of a prediction made by Nostradamus, Acquired Immune Deficiency Syndrome (AIDS) would kill two-thirds of the world's population.

In 1985, Rajneesh was deported by the INS and Disciple Sheela fled to Germany to escape prosecution for theft and attempted murder. The mortgage holder repossessed Rajneeshpuram in 1989. The Rajneesh presence in the United States is much less ostentatious, numerous, and influential now.

Rajneesh perceived himself as a savior comparable (indeed, even superior) to Jesus. The key to understanding his sense of mission is discovered in these anticipated global catastrophes. He hurriedly attempted to build his "Noah's ark of consciousness" in his followers before mankind destroyed itself. He taught that "a revolution in human consciousness is no more a luxury, it has become an absolute need as there are only two alternatives—suicide or a quantum leap in consciousness, which Nietzsche called Superman."[19]

When asked if Rajneeshees would survive the predicted nuclear holocaust, Rajneesh replied:

> Monkeys took a jump and became human beings, but not all monkeys did. The remaining ones are still monkeys. . . .
> I will not say that Rajneeshees will survive the holocaust, but I can say with an absolute guarantee that those who will survive will be the Rajneeshees and the remaining will be monkeys [i.e., humans who did not evolve into "Superman"] or commit suicide. In fact, the remaining don't matter.[20]

Since Rajneesh believed that he is the only "Awakened One" on the face of the earth, he also believed that he is the only one capable of orchestrating this "quantum leap in consciousness" to save the race. Therefore, all of "Bhagwan's work was directed toward creating the circumstances for this change of consciousness to take place."[21]

Rajneeshpuram, then, can be viewed as a colossal human experiment: the "enlightened Master" trying to create the conditions and spiritual energy (Buddhafield, as Rajneesh called it) necessary to give birth to a super race. Those who cannot or will not fit in with this group "don't matter." All that really matters is that the spiritual aspirations of Bhagwan Shree Rajneesh for mankind be fulfilled.

And what is the spirituality upon which these aspirations are based? Even the briefest exposure to Rajneesh's teachings makes it explicitly clear that "Rajneeshism" is in every respect hostile to the Christian faith. Consider the following samplings from his discourses.

You can be a Christ: Why be a Christian?[22]

---

[18]Bhagwan Shree Rajneesh, *Rajneeshism: An Introduction to Bhagwan Shree Rajneesh and His Religion* (Rajneeshpuram, Ore.: Rajneesh Foundation International, 1985), 56–57.
[19]Ibid., 60.
[20]Ibid., 61.
[21]Ibid., 15.
[22]Videocassette 18C144 (September 2, 1980).

Let *me* be your death and resurrection.[23]

Nobody is a sinner. Even while you are in the darkest hole of your life, you are still divine; you cannot lose your divinity. I tell you, there is no need for salvation, it is within you.[24]

Disobedience is not a sin, but a part of growth.[25]

God is neither a he nor a she. . . . If you say he is a she, I will say he is a he and if you say he is a he, I will say he is a she. . . . Whatsoever your belief is, I'm going to destroy it. . . . [26]

If [Jesus] had a little intelligence and rationality he would not have gone [to Jerusalem and the cross]. But then, there was no need [for Him] to declare [that He was] the Messiah and Son of God. . . . Those messiahs are basically insane. He believed totally that crucifixion was going to prove him right, that's why I believe there was a hidden current of suicidal intent. . . . If anyone is responsible for the crucifixion, he himself is responsible. He asked for it. And no Jewish source or contemporary source says there was a resurrection. Only the New Testament. It is fictitious. There was no resurrection.[27]

The argument the devil gave Eve was that God wants you to remain ignorant. . . . He is jealous. And it makes sense, because the Jewish God is very jealous. He doesn't want them to become equal. This is not a loving father. . . . Knowledge is not a sin. . . . I counsel you to eat of the tree of knowledge. . . . [28]

To anyone who takes biblical teaching seriously, the above quotes unmask once and for all the true spirit underlying and driving Rajneesh and his "religion" (1 Timothy 4:1–6; Matthew 24:4–5, 23–24; 7:15).

Every spirit that does not acknowledge Jesus is not from God. This is the spirit of the antichrist, which you have heard is coming and even now is already in the world (1 John 4:3, NIV).

It would seem evident that the same spiritual power that spoke through the serpent in the Garden of Eden freely speaks through the teachings of Rajneesh. He appears to be unreservedly given over to it. The danger that this fact portends for the thousands of sincere seekers of truth who now adoringly sing to Rajneesh "I place my heart, my heart, in your hand"[29] is a matter demanding serious prayer from the concerned Christian.

The ultimate significance that Rajneesh and his followers attached to their experiment at Rajneeshpuram could potentially have led to a violent confrontation if the government had stepped in to dismantle their dream. And, far from being "centered exactly in the middle of the cyclone," Rajneesh's "ark of consciousness" was fated to capsize in the storm of God's judgment against man's idolatry (e.g., Revelation 16:17–21). Those who naïvely fled to him for refuge instead found themselves swept up in the consequences of his own extreme rebellion and blasphemy.

Sannyasins, and especially those more reachable seekers who are considering but have not yet made a commitment to the principles of Rajneesh, need

---

[23]*Discourses on the Sufi Way*, quoted in the *Victor Valley Daily Press* (September 18, 1981): B3.

[24]*Sannyas* (April, 1978): 18.

[25]*Jesus, Buddha: Their Days Are Finished*, Videocassettes 18C321 and 18C322 (March 7, 1981).

[26]*He or She? On Beliefs—The Book of the Books VI*, Videocassette 18S1M (April 22, 1980).

[27]Bhagwan Shree Rajneesh in a discourse given to thirty disciples at Rajneeshpuram, November 12, 1984.

[28]Ibid.

[29]Dietrich, "Conflict," B3.

to be alerted to the true antihuman, antichrist nature of his teachings, and be pointed instead to the biblical Jesus, who is as different from Rajneesh as light is from darkness.

Eckart Flother is the only person known to date who, after his conversion to Christ, confronted Rajneesh. His own words are, to say the least, compelling:

> In July, right as I was getting more deeply involved with the ashram, I had a very extraordinary experience. On one of those hot, humid Indian nights filled with mosquitoes, I was sitting in my hotel room and reading Rabi Maharaj's book, *Death of a Guru*. Suddenly I saw a brilliantly shining being standing in the hotel room, and He said to me with a mighty voice, "I want you to become my disciple." I immediately understood that Jesus had called me, yet I really didn't know what to do with it.
>
> I went to Rajneesh and told him what had happened to me. As I was talking to him about this experience, I could feel a kind of very warm energy or light radiating from me and I saw that Rajneesh was very irritated, and even startled as he looked at me. He was unable to speak. At that moment I could see that he was not a master like Jesus Christ, as he claims. It was at this time I decided to become a disciple of Jesus.

Flother left Rajneeshism and today devotes considerable time to helping people escape from the system that imprisoned him both spiritually and mentally.

How to Reach the Sannyasins for Christ[30]

Editor: In seeking to communicate with sannyasins from the Christian standpoint, there is the obvious difficulty of their not wanting to use their minds, not wanting to think objectively about what they are experiencing. The more they have progressed within the movement, the more difficult this becomes. Are there any means of approaching them in which one can get them to think critically about what they are experiencing and to look objectively at what Rajneesh is doing to them and to others?

Eckart Flother: I found by working with people who wanted to get out that any logical or rational argument does not help at first.

The approach that I have found useful is to create an emotional situation, such as helping them to recall a childhood situation in the family, or a situation where they felt they needed privacy (which they don't have in the ashram), or a situation where they helped others. I have advised parents and friends to recreate a situation where they showed charity to others. Reliving this normally creates an emotional outburst, a flashback of a previous experience, which is called "snapping back."

After this I have found that I can talk to them on a rational level again, and most of them shake their heads as if to say, "I must have been in a long, long dream."

So one has to first create a situation where they can feel something very deeply that they felt before joining the movement in order to help them to go back and become whole again. Then let them ask questions, because normally

---

[30]*Forward* magazine, 5:1 (Spring 1982). Eckart Flother's responses are indicated by his name at the beginning of the relevant sections.

they say, "Where am I? What was happening?" and they have many questions. Then one can come with a message.

The best approach is not to criticize at first what Rajneesh was doing, but to go through the differences between his teaching and that of Jesus Christ point-by-point, and show the ways in which the teachings of both cope with reality. In this way one can help people make up their minds by themselves, and not impose a certain belief system on them.

Editor: *So you find criticizing Rajneesh or coming against his philosophy in a direct manner is not effective?*

Eckart Flother: Not in the first attempt, because one has to realize that Rajneesh was, in effect, the foundation of their lives, and his belief system was their structure of reference. So if one starts stripping his foundation out from under them, it could be considered dangerous, and no sannyasin would be likely to go for it.

To criticize Rajneesh and his system can be left to the man or woman who comes out, because he or she will find out sooner or later what has happened. If this critical attitude is not appearing two or three weeks after the person has left the movement, it will be important to initiate criticism, but not at first.

Editor: *What are the needs of an individual coming out of involvement with this cult?*

Eckart Flother: It is very important that the family and friends create a very strong and loving support system. It is important that somebody who has been with Rajneesh not only feels supported, loved, and wanted by family and friends, but *needed* as well. They need to feel that they have not only been missing something, but that they've been *missed.*

A second important point I've found is that one of the reasons people leave their families and join Rajneesh is because their parents and friends very often pretended that everything was all right, and nobody had a problem. So parents, family members, and friends must share their problems in dealing with life, and their struggles in coping with reality, to show that they are human, too. It is important that somebody who comes out realizes that to be human means to be imperfect. It means to have problems and not always know how to resolve them.

Above all, not only the sannyasins but also their families and friends must realize that our problems can only be ultimately resolved through a personal relationship with Jesus Christ. He has the answers that we so often lack.

ISKCON (Hare Krishnas)

The second major Hindu sect is the International Society for Krishna Consciousness, or ISKCON, a modern school of Vishnu Hinduism that developed from the fifteenth-century teachings of a man named Chaitanya, who instituted worship of Vishnu as God against the prevailing local worship of Shiva. Chaitanya taught that Krishna was the supreme personality of the Godhead.

ISKCON itself began in the 1960s in New York City, founded by the Vishnu yogi His Divine Grace Abhay Charan De Bhaktivedanta Swami Prabhupada, born in Calcutta, India, in 1896. It was officially incorporated in July 1966. Shortly afterward, Prabhupada traveled to San Francisco and found a ready audience of enthusiastic followers among the hippies of Haight-Ashbury. Hare

Krishnas, the followers of ISKCON, are well known today in America for their fund-raising activities through public solicitation, their public *sankirtanas*, or spiritual chanting, their community vegetarian "feasts," and their often public ceremonies honoring their idols. One of the most well known such ceremonies takes place annually on the beach west of Los Angeles and involves elaborate feasting, a parade as the devotees take their idols to the ocean for "spiritual" bathing, and a mini-festival to which thousands of Southern Californians flock as though it were a country carnival.

Prabhupada received his "calling" to preach the gospel of Krishna to English-speaking people, in 1922, from his spiritual master, Srila Bhaktisiddhanta Sarasvati Thakur. However, it was not until 1936 that he finally assumed the responsibility on the death of his master. As his following grew, he was elevated to a higher spiritual position, in 1950 taking the order of *sannyasa*, which includes the full renunciation of material life.

The ISKCON magazine, *Back to Godhead*, began publication in 1944, and continues today as the best-known publication of the ISKCON publishing company, the Bhaktivedanta Book Trust.

Prabhupada died in 1977. At the time of his death, there were 108 ISKCON centers worldwide, fifty-one volumes of literature published in English, and more than 5,000 full-time communal members, or disciples. His most well-known book is *Bhagavad-Gita As It Is*.

After the death of Prabhupada, inner turmoil and public suspicions threatened to dismantle the international organization. ISKCON went through a series of leadership changes, resulting from inner power struggles, competing claims of succession to Prabhupada, the resignation and/or defection of numerous leaders, the indictment and eventual conviction of various leaders for crimes ranging from tax evasion through drug dealing to murder, and charges by family members of false recruitment and deliberate concealment of underage converts from their parents and authorities.

Once the dust settled, the current leadership structure was instituted. ISKCON is led by a Governing Body Commission, which consists of thirty top leaders worldwide. Day to day operations are handled by the various GBC members in their respective areas of authority, and general policy changes are decided upon during the annual GBC meeting in Mayapur.

ISKCON places of worship (called temples), preaching centers, housing complexes, and other operations work independently of one another but under the direction of the area GBC member. A Temple President runs each temple, assisted by a Treasurer, Secretary, and Temple Commander. In areas where there are not sufficient numbers of full-time practicing initiated devotees for a temple, there might be a preaching center or a *nama-hatta* center servicing the interested but not-yet-initiated community. "All temples, preaching centers, *nama-hatta* centers, restaurants, shops, and so on, must be recognized by ISKCON before they may use the trademarked names of ISKCON, such as 'ISKCON,' 'The Hare Krishna Movement,' 'Govinda's,' and so on."[31]

---

[31]Anon., *ISKCON: The Structure*, Worldwide Web address: onet.se/krishna/main/twohk/iskcon/struct.htm: Bhaktivedanta Book Trust, 1996, 2.

ISKCON Beliefs

God. Although the bulk of Hindu scripture is pantheistic (everything is a part of God), portions of the Hindu scripture, notably the Bhagavad-Gita, are basically monotheistic presentations of Hinduism. Hinduism, in seeking to be a synthesis of a variety of Indian thought and belief, contains within its vast scriptural tradition a variety of beliefs about God, even though those beliefs may contradict one another. Since the Bhagavad-Gita, which implies a form of monotheism, is the most sacred scripture to ISKCON, we find that the ISKCON belief in God is essentially monotheistic, and Krishna is said to be the supreme personality of the Godhead. Any incarnation of the one God is an incarnation of Krishna: "ALL the lists of the incarnations of Godhead are either plenary expansions or parts of the plenary expansions of the Lord, but Lord Sri Krsna is the original Personality of Godhead Himself."[32]

Christ. To ISKCON, Jesus Christ is Krishna's Son, but in a position no more unique to God than any other man could strive to attain. To the Hare Krishna, then, Jesus Christ is not the unique Son of God, God manifest in the flesh. He is not an incarnation of Krishna.

Salvation. Salvation in ISKCON is obtained by removing one's karmic debt through devotion to Krishna and right actions through multiple incarnations: "All these performers who know the meaning of sacrifice become cleansed of sinful reactions, and, having tasted the nectar of the remnants of such sacrifices, they go to the supreme eternal atmosphere."[33] ISKCON also says, "From the body of any person who claps and dances before the Deity, showing manifestations of ecstasy, all the birds of sinful activities fly away upwards."[34] ISKCON salvation comes to those initiates who "follow the four regulative principles, chant sixteen rounds of the Hare Krishna *mantra* on beads every day, and follow all the regulated temple programs."[35]

TM (Transcendental Meditation)

TM is a spiritual practice, or yoga, which was first introduced to the Western world by its founder, Maharishi Mahesh Yogi, as a religious exercise or philosophy. Encountering skepticism from nonreligious Westerners, Maharishi revamped his TM program. In the 1970s, he promoted the movement as a scientifically sound, nonreligious psychological exercise designed to relieve stress, to bring peace to the inner man, thereby having a positive effect on society, and to enable the advanced practitioner to participate in astral projection (his soul leaving his body) and levitation.

TM still wears its secular label in its own promotions today, and most Westerners are unaware of its religious presuppositions and nature.

TM leaders persistently neglect to inform the public of TM's religious

[32]"Siddha Swarup Ananda Goswam," *Jesus Loves KRSNA* (Los Angeles: Vedic Christian Committee and Life Force, Krsan Yoga Viewpoint, 1975): 14.

[33]A. C. Bhaktivedanta Swami Prabhupada, *Bhagavad-Gita As It Is* (New York: The Bhaktivedanta Book Trust, 1968), 81.

[34]A. C. Bhaktivedanta Swami Prabhupada, *The Nectar of Devotion* (New York: The Bhaktivedanta Book Trust, 1970), 75.

[35]Anon., *The Structure*, 1.

nature, and also of the fact that the motivational, health, or political program they are promoting at the moment is actually a TM front project. One of their earliest confrontations with evangelical Christians was in the early 1980s, when Christians in the state of New Jersey successfully used the courts to have TM declared religious. This effectively eliminated the previous public support, adoption, and implementation of its programs, which had been deeply entrenched in the New Jersey public school system, prisons, etc.

More recently, world-famous, popular, alternative health practitioner Dr. Deepak Chopra, a leading TM spokesman, promoted his programs as "spiritual" but not in conflict with traditional Western religious convictions. Chopra promotes meditation-oriented health maintenance programs as costing "a lot less than a single day at a hospital or hotel," but "TM health maintenance courses cost $3400. Seven days of cleansing programs cost $2700, and should be repeated three times a year." In addition, one ex-member claimed that "a prescribed ceremony invoking a Hindu deity to treat endometriosis was priced at $11,500, although the simply 'recommended' ceremony for the condition was only $8,500, and one that would 'suffice' was $3,500."[36] TM has gone so far as to claim that a temporary drop in the crime rate in Washington, D.C., was due to the fact that one percent of the population practiced TM!

One of the most popular recent TM projects is a new political party, the Natural Law Party, which "stands for prevention-oriented government, conflict-free politics, and proven solutions to America's problems designed to bring the life of the nation into harmony with natural law"—all through the practice of TM, of course![37] In the November 1996 national elections in the United States, the Natural Law Party ran 400 candidates in forty-eight states, garnering a scant two million votes total for all races in all states combined. The Natural Law Party presidential candidate, Dr. John Hagelin, received 110,000 votes nationally.[38]

TM Beliefs

God. TM concentrates on those Hindu scriptures which present a pantheistic view of God. Therefore, God in TM is pantheistic, and one's goal is to lose his own personality in the oneness of God. This also, of course, takes away from the unique and separate personality of God: "Being is the living presence of God, the reality of life. It is eternal truth. It is the absolute in eternal freedom."[39]

Jesus Christ. TM ignores Jesus Christ almost entirely, although Maharishi teaches that anyone can become as enlightened as Jesus Christ through the application of TM techniques. It is clear from his neglect of Jesus Christ and from his worldview that he does not consider Jesus Christ to be the unique Son of God, God manifest in the flesh.[40]

---

[36]"Maharishi Ayur-Veda: Guru's Marketing Scheme Promises the World Eternal 'Perfect Health,' " *Journal of the American Medical Association (JAMA)* (October 2, 1991): 1749–1750.
[37]"What Is the Natural Law Party?" E-mail address: http://home.natural-law.org/HISTORY.HTML (1996), 1.
[38]Ibid., 1–2.
[39]Maharishi Mahesh Yogi, *The Science of Being and the Art of Living* (New York: The New American Library, 1968), 22.
[40]See, for example, Maharishi Mahesh Yogi, *Meditation of Maharishi Mahesh Yogi* (New York: The New American Library, 1969), 124–125.

Salvation. Salvation in TM is accomplished by realizing that one is in union with the Creative Intelligence: "The answer to every problem is that there is no problem. Let a man perceive this truth and then he is without problems."[41] This realization comes through practicing the meditations of TM: "A huge mountain of sins extending for miles is destroyed by Union brought about through transcendental meditation, without which there is no way out."[42] Salvation is almost a misnomer, since one is not truly a sinner, but rather forgetful of his oneness with the divine.

Conclusion

In conclusion, Hinduism, for all of its diversity and contradictions, is not compatible with Christianity. In all its forms, Hinduism denies the biblical Trinity, the deity of Christ, and the doctrines of the Atonement, sin, and salvation by grace through the sacrifice of Jesus Christ. It replaces resurrection with reincarnation, and both grace and faith with human works. One cannot, then, achieve peace with God through Hinduism or any of its sects. C. S. Lewis wisely observed that at the end of all religious quests one must choose between Hinduism and Christianity; the former absorbs all others and the latter excludes them. Peace with God is not achieved by looking inside oneself but by looking up to Him of whom Moses and the prophets did write—Jesus of Nazareth, the Christ and Son of God.

---

[41]Maharishi Mahesh Yogi, *Maharishi Mahesh Yogi on the Bhagavad-Gita* (New York: Penguin Books, 1967), 257.
[42]Ibid., 299.

Chapter 15

The Apocalyptic Cults

Revelation is one of the most thought-provoking books of the Bible. It is also one of the most difficult to understand. The text is named after the Greek word *apokalypsis*, which appears in the book's first verse: "The Revelation (*apokalypsis*) of Jesus Christ, which God gave unto him, to show unto his servants things which must shortly come to pass; and He sent and signified it by his angel unto his servant John."

According to W. E. Vine's *Expository Dictionary of New Testament Words*,[1] the term simply means an "uncovering." It is used throughout the Greek translation of the Old Testament (the Septuagint) and the Greek New Testament in various ways. In Luke 2:32, *apokalypsis* describes the "drawing away by Christ of the veil of darkness covering the Gentiles." In Romans 16:25, it refers to the disclosure of God's "mystery" of the ages, His redemptive plan for both Jew and Gentile. Ephesians 1:17 tells of the wisdom and revelation imparted to the soul that has knowledge of God.[2]

The most familiar usage of the term, however, is the one found in Revelation, where it relates to the visible manifestation of Jesus Christ at His Second Coming. (See also 1 Corinthians 1:7–8 and 1 Peter 1:7–9.) Christians everywhere at all times look forward with great anticipation to the day when Jesus will return to earth, raise the dead, pronounce final judgment on every soul, establish a "new heaven and a new earth" (Revelation 21), and initiate the eternal perfected state of the believer.

We know Jesus is coming again because He promised that He would return: "In my Father's house are many mansions. . . . I go to prepare a place for you. And if I go and prepare a place for you, I will come again, and receive you unto myself; that where I am, there ye may be also" (John 14:2–3).

This chapter written by Richard Abanes and edited by Gretchen Passantino.

---

[1] W. E. Vine, Merrill F. Unger, and William White, *Vine's Complete Expository Dictionary of Old and New Testament Words* (Nashville, Tenn.: Thomas Nelson Publishers, 1985), 532.
[2] Ibid.

Scripture further reveals that Christ's return will be glorious (Titus 2:13), marked by the bodily resurrection of the dead in Christ as well as the physical transformation of those Christians who are alive on the earth at that time. Every believer will be given a glorified body fit for immortality (1 Corinthians 15:52–54; 1 Thessalonians 4:15–17).

The *apokalypsis* will also bring about the resurrection and transformation of unbelievers. They, however, will not receive God's love and forgiveness. They will face His wrath (John 5:28–29; Ephesians 2:3; Colossians 3:6; Revelation 6:16). In that day, Christian and non-Christian alike will confess that Jesus Christ is Lord (Philippians 2:9–11). Final judgment will then take place. People who rejected Jesus Christ during their lifetimes will be told to depart from God's presence into everlasting torment (Matthew 7:21–23; 25:46; Revelation 14:11). Individuals who accepted God's free gift of eternal life through the person and work of His Son and the grace given by the Holy Spirit will hear the words every Christian desires to hear: "Come, ye blessed of My Father, inherit the kingdom prepared for you from the foundation of the world" (Matthew 25:34).

Obviously, Jesus' Second Coming is going to be a cataclysmic event of unparalleled proportions. In fact, Scripture indicates that His return will cause reality as we know it to disintegrate. The apostle Peter tells us that when Jesus comes again the heavens will pass away "with a roar" and that "the elements will be destroyed by fire, and the earth and everything in it will be laid bare." He goes on to say that the heavens will be destroyed by fire and the elements will melt in the heat (2 Peter 3:10–13, NIV).

Exactly when will all of these things take place? No one knows. Not a single indication is given in the Bible as to the date of the world's end. Scripture only says that the Lord's Second Coming will be like a thief in the night; in other words, when it is least expected (1 Thessalonians 5:1–2, 2 Peter 3:10). The reason we are not given more information about "the end" can be found in the answer Jesus gave to His disciples when they questioned Him about the establishment of God's kingdom. "It is not for you to know the times or dates the Father has set by His own authority" (Acts 1:7, NIV).

Despite a complete lack of biblical timetables relating to Jesus' Second Coming, predictions about the end of the world have plagued the Christian church for nearly two thousand years. The consequences often have been disastrous.

The Ends That Never Came

One of the earliest doomsday date-setters was a self-appointed prophet named Montanus, who lived in the mid-second century. He assured loyal followers that the new Jerusalem (Revelation 21:2) and God's kingdom would soon appear. But the new Jerusalem never came. Instead, Montanism was labeled heretical, and by A.D. 398 adherents to the movement had been deprived of their right to assemble, their clergy had been outlawed, and their books burned.[3]

In the twelfth century, an Italian monk named Joachim announced that the Antichrist was alive and that the last age of history would begin around 1260.

---

[3]Russell Chandler, *Doomsday* (Ann Arbor, Mich.: Servant Books, 1993), 40.

Joachim, like Montanus, was branded a heretic and his writings condemned. Unfortunately, his prophetic system, consisting of three stages of historical progression, survived various forms to influence, if only indirectly, the thinking of several infamous personalities of later history, including Adolf Hitler and Karl Marx.[4]

After Joachim, Thomas Münzer became a prominent figure in the German peasant revolt (1524–1526) by promising that an extermination of the rich and powerful classes would initiate the return of Christ. Before the decisive battle, Münzer assured followers that victory would be theirs. He was wrong. Four thousand peasants were slaughtered, and Münzer, although he escaped from the battlefield, was eventually captured, tortured, and beheaded.[5]

A decade later, another "prophet"—Mechoir Hofmann—announced that the Second Coming would take place in 1533. The movement began peacefully enough, but when a disciple named Jan Matthys succeeded Hofmann, things began to change. Matthys preached the use of force to cleanse the ungodly from the earth in preparation for Jesus' impending return. The full destruction of the world, said Matthys, would occur by Easter of 1534. But Easter came and went, as did Matthys and his followers, who met a bloody end when the city they had captured was in turn besieged by an army of angry Protestants and Catholics, many of whom had been kicked out of the town for refusing to become baptized devotees of Matthys.

The number of end-time prognosticators from centuries past is so high that it is impossible to mention them all in a chapter of this size. However, one can get an idea of just how many "prophets" have risen to popularity from a partial listing of the various years that were supposed to bring "the end": 500, 999, 1100, 1200, 1245, 1260, 1420, 1528, 1656, 1734, 1844, 1874.[6] Most disturbing is the fact that this list of "prophets" and predictions continues to grow.

Nothing New Under the Sun

There is an old saying: "Those who do not learn from the past are doomed to repeat it." The accuracy of this statement perhaps is seen best in humanity's ongoing obsession with the end of the world. Christian prophecy teacher Edgar Whisenant, for example, predicted that in 1988 Jesus would return, probably between September 11 and September 13. When the September prophecy failed, he revised the date to October 3. When *that* date passed uneventfully, Whisenant maintained that Jesus' return would be "in a few weeks."[7] He continues to revise the date at least yearly.

In 1992, Christian radio personality Harold Camping—the founder of Family Radio and Open Forum—began making similar predictions about the year

---

[4]Chandler, *Doomsday* 41.

[5]Ibid., 43.

[6]Gary DeMar, *Last Days Madness* (Atlanta, Ga.: American Vision, 1994); Chandler, *Doomsday*; B. J. Oropeza, *Ninety-Nine Reasons Why No One Knows When Christ Will Return* (Downers Grove, Ill.: InterVarsity Press, 1994).

[7]Dean C. Halverson, "Eighty-Eight Reasons: What Went Wrong?" *Christian Research Journal* (Fall 1988): 11:2:14; cf. "Rapture Seer Hedges on Latest Guess," *Christianity Today* (October 21, 1988): 43.

1994. In his bestselling book entitled *1994?* he wrote, "When September 6, 1994, arrives, no one else can become saved, the end has come."[8] Camping explained the meaning behind his words so no one would have any doubt as to what he was saying: "No book ever written is as audacious or bold as one that claims to predict the timing of the end of the world, and that is precisely what this book presumes to do."[9] After the predictions of the book failed, Camping claimed that it was only God's mercy that resulted in God giving the world a little more time to repent.

John Hinkle, pastor of Christ Church, Los Angeles, appeared on the Trinity Broadcasting Network's *Praise the Lord* program to share an incredible message that God had allegedly given to him: "On Thursday, June 9, I [God] will rip the evil from this earth."[10] At one of his church services, Hinkle proclaimed that on this date in 1994 people would witness "the most cataclysmic event since the resurrection of Christ."[11] When "God's" date passed, Hinkle and his supporters maintained that the prophecy did, indeed, come to pass, but that it did so invisibly, in the spiritual realm.

The persons deceived into believing false teachers such as these men come from a wide cross-section of the Christian community. Sometimes, however, followers of a particular end-time preacher or "prophet" band together to form a tight-knit group that is based primarily on the prophetic scenarios and predictions put forth by their leader. When the leader additionally incorporates heretical doctrine and enforces allegiance to heresy by his followers, an apocalyptic cult comes into being.

A flurry of activity involving such cults has occurred in recent years. The most publicized cases serve as perfect examples of just how dangerous end-time speculations can be. They also illustrate the common themes associated with persons gripped by "last days madness." We can learn a great deal about this phenomenon by examining briefly their stories.

The Hyoo-Go Movement

The full-page ad appearing in the October 20, 1991 issue of *USA Today* caused quite a stir in the religious community:

RAPTURE
OCTOBER 28, 1992
JESUS IS COMING IN THE AIR

It was only one of many warnings distributed by groups associated with the Korean-based *Hyoo-go* (Korean for "rapture") movement. "One fearful sect predicted that beginning on October 28, 1992, '50 million people will die in earthquakes, 50 million from collapsed buildings, 1.4 billion from World War III, and 1.4 billion from a separate Armageddon.' "[12]

The driving force behind the movement apparently was a Korean bestseller

[8]Harold Camping, *1994?* (New York: Vantage Press, 1992), 533.
[9]Ibid., xv.
[10]John Hinkle, *Praise the Lord* (January 25, 1994).
[11]John Hinkle, excerpt from message at Christ Church, Los Angeles, June 5, 1994.
[12]Oropeza, *Ninety-Nine Reasons*, 11.

titled *Getting Close to the End* (published in the late 1980s), by Lee Jang Rim, which promoted the October 28, 1992 date. Churches involved in the movement included "Rim's Dami Church (known in the United States as Mission for the Coming Days), Taberah World Mission, Shalom Church, and Maranatha Mission Church, to name a few. Worldwide membership fluctuated between twenty thousand and one hundred thousand members."[13]

Adherents to the movement appealed to a number of sources in addition to Rim's teachings to support their doomsday deadline. One brochure, produced by Taberah World Missions, borrowed a twisted time calculation made by American prophecy pundit Jack Van Impe.[14] Divine revelations given to a twelve-year-old boy named Bang-ik Ha also confirmed the October deadline.[15] There was no doubt in the minds of the faithful as October 28, 1992 approached.

As "the end" drew near, social disruption mounted in South Korea. Believers "quit their jobs, sold their homes, abandoned their families, and ran up debts in preparation for the end of the world." Several pregnant women reportedly had abortions "so they would not be too heavy to be lifted to heaven" and at least four followers "committed suicide before October 28."[16]

In response, the South Korean government dispatched 1,500 riot police to Mission for the Coming Days, one of Seoul's largest Hyoo-go churches. Police agencies, fire companies, and ambulances were placed on alert in an effort to prevent a Jonestown-style mass murder/suicide.

The date finally arrived and thousands of followers gathered in various churches around the world, especially in Korea, to await their departure into the heavens. But nothing happened. Fifteen minutes after the deadline passed, Rev. Chang Man-Ho, pastor of the Mission for the Coming Days, took the pulpit and simply said, "Nothing has happened. Sorry. Let's go home."[17]

By October 29, once-loyal followers had not overcome their anger and hurt. Many began weeping uncontrollably. Some physically attacked the preachers who had misled them. One distraught member tearfully commented, "God lied to us."[18] As of November 1992, several parents still searched "for children who were kidnapped and taken to mountain hideouts by some of the more radical rapture sects."[19]

The Branch Davidians

On February 28, 1993, nearly one hundred Federal agents from the United States Treasury Department's Bureau of Alcohol, Tobacco, and Firearms (BATF) attempted to serve a search warrant on Mt. Carmel, a religious community located ten miles west of Waco, Texas. Their plan was to surprise members of the Branch Davidian cult whose self-proclaimed "Son of God" leader,

---

[13]Oropeza, *Ninety-Nine Reasons*, 168.

[14]*Rapture!* (Taberah World Missions, 1992): 3–4.

[15]Quoted in Oropeza, *Ninety-Nine Reasons*, 37.

[16]EP News Service (November 6, 1992): 5.

[17]Ibid.

[18]Reuters, "Korean Sect Stunned as 'Rapture' Doesn't Come," *Orange County Register* (October 29, 1992): A21.

[19]News Service, 5.

David Koresh, had for many years prophesied that "the end" was near.

Although Koresh's prophecies did not precipitate the BATF raid, they did have something to do with the government's assault: The Davidians had stockpiled a massive cache of weapons (including many illegal ones) in preparation for Armageddon.[20] Unfortunately, BATF field commanders made a series of blunders that turned the operation into a disaster. National newspaper headlines following the raid described the outcome all too clearly: "AGENTS MET BY BARRAGE OF GUNFIRE"; "UNWARNED, AGENTS RUSH INTO BULLETS"; "U.S. AGENCY RECORDS ITS BLOODIEST DAY."

That day's ninety-minute gun battle between the government and religious zealots left two federal agents dead and twenty-two others injured (two of them with gunshot wounds so severe they died within hours). Six Davidians had also been killed. The ensuing standoff, which was placed under FBI jurisdiction, lasted fifty-one days. Confusion, rather than expertise, plagued government officials as FBI negotiators and their advisors continually clashed with FBI tacticians over how to resolve the siege.

Then, in the early morning hours of April 19, 1993, the FBI mobilized several tank-like vehicles that punched huge holes into the walls of the Davidian's poorly constructed domicile. Subsequently, tear gas was injected through the newly made gaps in order to force the Davidians from their stronghold. But the government had failed to calculate one factor into their decision: religious fervor.

Six hours after the introduction of tear gas, tiny puffs of smoke began to seep through one of the compounds many second-story windows. Minutes later, the entire structure was engulfed in flames and the world watched in horror as the Branch Davidian fortress burst into a city block-sized funeral pyre.

David Koresh and nearly one hundred of his followers, including approximately two dozen children, met a torturous end. Coroner reports indicated that although many Davidians had perished from the flames and smoke inhalation, a significant number of them, including Koresh himself, had died from single gunshot wounds to the head. Among the dead were several well-educated individuals: an attorney, a nurse, an engineer, and a former police officer.

Recorded conversations made with government listening devices hidden by the FBI prior to the fire revealed that the Davidians started the conflagration by spreading and igniting flammable liquid in the building. Why would they do such a thing? The answer is simple: fire played a major role in their understanding of the biblical features of eschatology (doctrine of the end times, or last things).

According to notes scribbled in the margins of a Bible owned by Branch Davidian Robyn Bunds, one of Koresh's wives, Koresh linked Armageddon (which he believed would be a confrontation with the government) to the sixth seal mentioned in Revelation 6:12, 17.[21] He then tied this seal of judgment to passages such as Joel 2:1–5 and Jeremiah 50. Koresh even quoted Jeremiah 50:22 to the FBI in an April 9 letter he sent out from the compound.

Verses 24–25 and 32 of that passage read as follows: "I have laid a snare for

[20]Ken Carter, "Branch Davidian Firearms," *Machine Gun News* (March 1994): 5.

[21]This section's author, Richard Abanes, was able to obtain Robyn Bund's Bible through her brother, David Bunds. Reference pages were copied and are on file.

thee . . . thou hast striven against the Lord. The Lord hath opened his armory. . . . I will kindle a fire in his cities, and it shall devour all round about him." Interestingly, in an April 13 interview with the *Los Angeles Times*, FBI agent Bob Ricks mentioned that Koresh had warned them that they would be "devoured by fire" if they did not listen to him.[22]

Several other verses highlighted in Robyn's Bible are noteworthy, given the events of the siege's last day:

> The day of the Lord is at hand . . . every man's heart shall melt . . . their faces shall be as flames" (Isaiah 13:6–9).
> His throne was like the fiery flame, and his wheels are burning fire. A fiery stream issued and came forth before him" (Daniel 7:9–10).
> The Lord will roar from Zion . . . and the top of Carmel shall wither. . . . I will send fire" (Amos 1:2–7).

Next to Amos 1:7, Robyn had written the words, "The fire that will cleanse." Even more significant was a link that Robyn had made in her Bible from Amos 2 to Isaiah 4:

> When the Lord shall have washed away the filth of the daughters of Zion, and shall have purged the blood of Jerusalem . . . by the spirit of judgment, and by the spirit of burning. And the Lord will create upon every dwelling place of mount Zion . . . a cloud and smoke by day, and a shining of flaming fire by night: for upon all the glory shall be a defense" (Isaiah 4:4–5).

Next to the portion of Isaiah that reads, "washed away the filth of the daughters of Zion," Robyn had written, "CHANGE THE DNA." Beside the phrase, "a cloud and smoke by day, and the shining of a flaming fire by night," she had scribbled, "FACES OF FLAMES."

Additional notes made by Robyn, when compared with information contained in teaching tapes made by Koresh, indicate that the Davidian leader and his followers expected some type of genetic mutation to take place during the sixth seal judgment. Koresh apparently believed and taught that as God's representative on earth, he would loose fire upon the faithful, killing off their old nature and transforming them into flaming beings of divine judgment who would smite the enemy.

This theory is supported strongly by a final note written by Robyn next to Isaiah 34:2, which reads, "For the indignation of the Lord is upon all the nations, and his fury upon all their armies: he hath utterly destroyed them, he hath delivered them to the slaughter." Next to this verse, Koresh's former wife had scrawled a chilling premonition: "Because we're cloven tongues of fire."

Editor's Note: *The following material on the Branch Davidians was written as news stories in* World *magazine as the events unfolded. It provides a unique, timely perspective (with sad predictive features) from a Christian worldview.*

---

[22]Quoted in Kenneth Samples, Erwin de Castro, Richard Abanes, and Robert Lyle, *Prophets of the Apocalypse: David Koresh and Other American Messiahs* (Grand Rapids, Mich.: Baker Book House, 1994), 79.

Long Wake in Waco: Blaspheming Cult Leader Holds Authorities at Bay in Texas[23]

God's anointed met the enemy at Mount Carmel in ancient Israel. From his sanctuary he watched more than 400 of his enemies prepare for the assault. He alone stood for the Lord, the Almighty, the only true God. He was confident that his enemies would fail. And when they did, he would fulfill God's avenging will. When the Lord answered Elijah's prayers and not those of the prophets of Baal, Elijah slaughtered them all.

Self-styled prophet Vernon Howell, also known as David Koresh, last week reenacted Elijah's ancient stand at his own "Mount Carmel," near Waco, Texas.

Howell is no Elijah. He adopted the name David Koresh to symbolize his belief that he is God's anointed for today. David was God's anointed as the king of Israel; Koresh is a designation of the Persian king Cyrus, who was ordained by God in Isaiah 45 to authorize and finance the rebuilding of the Jewish temple after the Babylonian captivity. When outsiders, including those in the media and law enforcement, call him "David Koresh," he says that proves even his enemies know he is God's anointed. He claims alternatively to be a mere prophet and Jesus Christ, the "Lamb" of Revelation 5, and God's avenger against the world.

The shy, reclusive ninth-grade dropout from Texas has evolved into a despotic cult leader, able to command hundreds of followers and hold off 400 federal agents for days outside his Mount Carmel compound.

Vernon Howell's cult traces its origin to 1929, when Bulgarian immigrant Victor Houteff, dissatisfied with his own Seventh-day Adventist Church in Los Angeles, broke away and moved to Texas to start his church, which he called "the Shepherd's Rod." The Seventh-day Adventists have a tradition, started by founder Ellen G. White, of accepting modern-day prophecy and of expecting the imminent return of Jesus Christ in judgment. Ironically, one of Houteff's contentions with the Seventh-day Adventist Church was that it was not pacifistic enough—he disagreed with its practice of approving member participation in the armed forces in noncombat positions.

At the beginning of World War II, Houteff changed the group's name to Davidic Seventh-day Adventists. When he died in 1957, his wife, Florence, assumed control and prophesied that the Second Coming of Christ would occur by April 22, 1959. Florence resigned from leadership of her 1,400-member group when the prophecy failed.

The Davidic Seventh-day Adventists split during 1959, the core of the group remaining near Waco, Texas, and eventually assuming the name "Branch Davidians" under the leadership of the Roden family. In 1981, Vernon Howell joined the group as handyman assistant to then-leader Lois Roden. In 1983, when Lois's son, George, assumed control of the group, Howell unsuccessfully fought him for control. Howell returned to the headquarters in 1987, led a gun battle against George, was acquitted of attempted murder charges, and assumed control of the group in 1988. From 1986 to 1991 he recruited new members in Canada, Hawaii, California, England, and Australia, and then concentrated on rebuilding and fortifying the headquarters compound, "Mount Carmel," during 1992.

---

[23]Gretchen Passantino, "Long Wake in Waco," *World* (March 13, 1993): 6–8.

Distinctive teachings of the Branch Davidians included that the Sabbath be observed from sundown Friday through sundown Sunday, that Howell, destined to be a martyr, was entitled to 140 wives, and that Howell is Jesus Christ, who will lead the Davidians in carrying out God's final judgment.

Vernon Howell was born in 1960, and spent his childhood in Tyler, Texas. He was diagnosed with "learning disabilities." He dropped out of school in the ninth grade, but claims to have memorized the New Testament by the time he was twelve.

At nineteen, Howell was baptized into the Seventh-day Adventist Church, but was asked to leave less than two years later because of behavior and Scripture interpretation problems. That same year, 1981, he joined the Roden's Davidian sect.

Over the next seven years he grew into his later grandiose persona. He built his base of power, took over the sect, accumulated one legal wife (Rachel, then fourteen) and dozens of other women, and began preaching his version of the end of the world and the last judgment. Howell also pursued his lifelong love of hard rock music, associating with rock musicians, playing with different bands, and recruiting players for "God's" band.

The cult leader's dire predictions of coming warfare and his own martyrdom date back to 1983 or 1984, when, according to one ex-member, "He was always teaching that he was going to be killed and going to be a martyr."

Another ex-member recalled Howell's preoccupation with violence, recounting, "The night I met Koresh . . . he asked me, 'Would you die for Christ?' I said, I guess so. He said, 'Would you kill for him?' I said, no. He turned to my friend and said, 'Hey, you just brought me another weak Christian.' "

The defense attorney for Howell and his followers in the trial over the 1987 gunfight with Roden remembered, "Vernon had told them that some day somebody was going to be coming for them, and that they better be ready."

Perhaps the most chilling connection between Howell and violence is his own interpretations of select Bible passages. Howell identifies himself with Elijah, King David, and the Persian King Cyrus, but he also claims he represents the Second Coming of Jesus Christ, especially as Christ is described in Revelation 5, 10, and 18—the avenging Son of God who will destroy all the unrighteous with his heavenly army. One of his favorite self-descriptions is from Isaiah 11:4, "He will strike the earth with the rod of his mouth; with the breath of his lips he will slay the wicked" (NIV). Taking the language of Isaiah 63 and Revelation 18, he believes that "day of vengeance" has come, and he is the executioner.

The stage was set. Howell, now thirty-three, about the same age as Jesus at his death, worked by his own prophetic agenda. He was ready for war. Bureau of Alcohol, Tobacco, and Firearms agents worked a nine-month investigation that involved informants, surveillance, and undercover infiltration. They were convinced Howell was stockpiling illegal weapons and explosives. Local law enforcement believed he was committing illegal activities including child abuse and unlawful intercourse with minors (he is said to take new "wives" when they were between eleven and fourteen years old).

The plights of the women and especially the children gave the investigation more impetus, and the ATF made its move to serve search and arrest warrants around 9:30 A.M. Sunday, February 28.

Within forty-five minutes, four ATF agents were dead, fifteen wounded, and three cult members were later confirmed dead. Howell himself claimed to have been shot in the abdomen. ATF spokespersons tried to explain the debacle, surmising that someone had tipped Howell off minutes before the raid, and noting that they were unaware of the .50-caliber armor-piercing machine gun in the control tower. They also pointed out that, with so many women and children in the compound, agents were unable to return fire through walls at unseen targets, while Howell's followers shot through walls at the agents.

After the initial assault, a cease-fire allowed ATF agents to remove their dead and wounded, and the long standoff began. Nearby residents noted that Howell's followers had stockpiled supplies. FBI spokesmen noted that the compound was largely self-sufficient with its own well and supplies, and the members were used to doing without electricity or indoor plumbing.

Throughout the next five days, Howell and federal officials negotiated the intermittent release of twenty children and two adults. By Friday, March 5, Howell claimed 106 individuals were left inside the compound. At first Howell had telephone access to the media and granted interviews to the Associated Press and CNN as well as other journalists. However, the FBI later cut his direct communication with anyone but them.

Howell resorted to making promises in exchange for having his taped messages, delivered by children as they left, aired on radio. Tuesday, March 2, he promised everyone would surrender peacefully if his fifty-eight-minute audiocassette message was aired "nationally." It was. Federal authorities delivered the tape to a Waco Christian radio station, which phone-patched the tape to a live national talk show on the Christian Broadcasting Network.

The Phoenix-based CBN show played the entire tape, a rambling, disjointed survey of dozens of disconnected Bible verses, but Howell rescinded his promise to give up. He declared that God had told him not to leave, and he would take further action only when God told him what to do. Given his teachings concerning violence and martyrdom, many ex-members and cult experts were concerned that the standoff could end with further bloodshed.

One hundred seemingly normal, rational people followed him to almost certain death. But as one person agreed, it's easy to suspend disbelief, to become caught up in a charismatic leader's vision. As one person put it, "When you first see him . . . you think, 'Who's this guy kidding?' But when he's talking, it's like something comes over you and you get swept up with it.

"A little bit of charm and you get to the point where you believe this, you believe that, and when you've come so far . . . you believe all of it." And the world sits, mesmerized by live television coverage and screaming newspaper headlines, swept up ourselves, unwittingly, into one madman's vision of the end.

Days of Destruction: Lessons From Dealing With Self-Made Prophets[24]

With excruciating deliberation, the FBI executed successive steps toward peacefully ending their armed standoff with Branch Davidian cult members

---

[24]Gretchen Passantino, "Days of Destruction: Lessons from Dealing With Self-Made Prophets," *World* (May 8, 1993): 19.

near Waco, Texas. They called on years of hostage negotiation experience, panels of forensic psychology experts, teams of crisis intervention specialists, numerous religious, biblical, theological, and cult advisors, and the best anti-terrorist authorities. Step-by-step they narrowed the perimeters, restricted outside contacts, disrupted sleep and daily habits, and pressed the hoped-for peaceful resolution.

In the aftermath of the conflagration, as congressional hearings continue and federal officials investigate, the religious aspects of the Waco disaster will be an important part of their deliberations. Were Koresh's religious convictions weighed heavily enough? Were his followers' fanatical loyalty and resultant actions properly gauged? Was there any way religious insight could have saved lives?

Most agreed Koresh's religious convictions were accurately considered. Koresh was convinced that he was the Lamb of God, that God had appointed him the executor of God's judgment, and that he and his followers were destined for fiery, deadly battle. Koresh's last two letters included challenges such as, "I AM your God and you will bow under my feet. . . . I AM your life and your death. . . . Fear Me, for I have you in My snare."

Even given the inevitability of Koresh's self-destruction, there is some indication that the FBI could have anticipated more accurately the final results with more thorough religious analysis. The FBI was confident the Davidian mothers instinctively would send their children out of the way of the tear gas and demolition, and yet their calculations did not expect the mothers' absolute conviction that sending their children out would be to send them to death at the hands of the enemy. A Justice Department official, speaking with the clarity of hindsight, remarked, "This wasn't a normal hostage situation. . . . They were willing to do anything for this person."

The Branch Davidians believed Koresh's prophecies concerning the inevitability of their martyrdom by fire. Koresh's favorite apocalyptic Scriptures speak of destruction (Revelation 11:5), judgment (Revelation 8:5), and cleansing by fire (1 Corinthians 3:13–15). Koresh often compared himself to the prophet Elijah, who challenged the prophets of the false gods in ancient Israel. He told the story of how Elijah dared the enemies to display divine power through their sacrifices. They failed, and the true God Yahweh sent fire from heaven to consume Elijah's sacrifice on Mount Carmel. The false prophets fled, only to be slaughtered by Elijah. Koresh was their Elijah, they were the sacrifice, and the federal forces were the false prophets destined for destruction.

Whether or not the Davidians set the initial fires, they found themselves cast in the divine drama prefigured by Elijah and consummated by Koresh. In the end, whether they welcomed the flames or were forced by Koresh, there was no escape.

Could the FBI have devised some alternative to frustrate fulfillment of Koresh's fire images? Perhaps. Attorney General Janet Reno said, "Based on what we know now, obviously [what we did] was wrong." But the playwright of the drama wrote only one ending: death and destruction.

We will learn from this tragedy. Law enforcement, psychologists, politicians, talk show hosts, and bureaucrats will suggest legislation, policies, and [they will] plan to prevent another Mount Carmel, just as they did after 1978's mass deaths

of 913 Peoples' Temple members in Jonestown, Guyana. But laws and strategies don't use the most powerful weapons we have as members of a free society: individual commitment to rationality and personal religious responsibility.

The TS

On October 4, 1994, a doomsday cult called the Order of the Solar Temple decided that their "end" had also come. A series of gruesome events signaled their demise, beginning with a fire in a remote chalet in Morin Heights, Quebec. Inside were found the bodies of a man and a woman wearing red-and-gold medallions bearing the letters TS, for *Temple Solaire*, or Solar Temple. In an adjacent villa, police uncovered three more corpses: a couple in their thirties and their three-month-old son. The baby had been suffocated.[25]

Less than twelve hours later a similar fire broke out halfway across the globe in Fribourg, Switzerland, where post-midnight alarms sent fire engines racing toward a farmhouse located in the tiny neighboring village of Cheiry. There, Albert Giacobino, the property's owner, was found dead in his bed, "a plastic bag tied around his head concealing a bullet wound."[26] He, too, was a member of the TS Order.

Further exploration of the property by police and firefighters yielded an underground garage leading to a door. It opened into a meeting room containing, among other things, a pool of blood. Inspection of the room's wooden paneling revealed a secret door accessing a small inner sanctuary decorated entirely in red:

> Inside lay eighteen bodies—men, women, and a boy about ten years old— arrayed in a crude circle, feet toward the center. Many wore red and black or white and gold ceremonial robes, some with their hands tied behind their backs. Most had been shot in the head or neck; ten had plastic bags over their heads.[27]

Another corpse was found in an adjacent room and three more bodies were discovered in an adjoining chapel. The cult's body count would rise again just a few hours later. At approximately 3:00 A.M. an explosive device ignited three ski chalets situated one hundred miles to the south in the city of Granges-sur-Salvan. When firefighters began sifting through its rubble they found "twenty-five people—including at least four children—ten charred beyond recognition."[28]

Cassette tapes and documents uncovered near the bodies "linked the deaths to a belief that the end of the world was imminent."[29] The cult's charismatic leader, forty-six-year-old Luc Jouret, had promised his followers that the world's demise lay just ahead and that he, as the "new Christ,"[30] would be the one to lead them to glory. "The present world chaos is not just by chance," he

---

[25]Tom Post, "Mystery of the Solar Temple," *Newsweek* (October 17, 1994): 43.
[26]Ibid., 42.
[27]Ibid.
[28]Ibid.
[29]"Mass Suicide or Mass Murder?" *U.S. News and World Report* (October 17, 1994): 17.
[30]Robert Davis and Juan J. Walte, "Swiss Cult's Bizarre Last Act Leaves 'Wax Museum' of Death," *USA Today* (October 6, 1994): 6A.

told them. "We have arrived at the hour of Apocalypse."[31]

Like Koresh's followers, Jouret's devotees were not spaced-out losers with a far-off look in their eyes. They were well-respected citizens of the European and Canadian communities. In fact, the Canadian victims included "the mayor of Richelieu, Quebec, and an official in the Quebec finance ministry."[32]

One victim was found carrying a letter for her family. It said that she had come to Switzerland to die. Three other letters were sent by cult members to Jean-Francois Mayer, a Swiss authority. One read, "We are leaving this earth to rediscover, lucidly and freely, a dimension of truth and absoluteness."[33]

Aum Shinrikyo

March 20, 1995, saw yet another deadly episode involving an apocalyptic cult. This time, however, the incident intruded upon the lives of innocent citizens as they commuted to work. Members of the Japanese cult Aum Shinrikyo ("Supreme Truth")—under the direction of their leader Shoko Asahara—reportedly released a Nazi-invented nerve gas called sarin into the Japanese subway system. Twelve people died and more than 5,000 were sickened with "nausea, blurred vision, breathing problems, and other symptoms."[34]

In a 1995 book by Asahara titled *Rising Sun Country: Disaster Approaches*, he prophesied that nerve gas would be the weapon of choice during Armageddon. The subway attacks were meant apparently as a precursor to the world's end. The final battle originally was set to begin sometime between 1997 and 2000, but for some reason Asahara, who has called himself "Today's Christ," decided to move the date up to 1995. To help bring about World War III, Asahara planned a number of terrorist attacks, the likes of which few had ever contemplated:

> To triumph in that war, the cult built a series of munitions factories within its complex. . . . Aum researchers were trying to develop germ weapons—including the Ebola virus—and an assembly line was about to produce automatic rifles. Behind one building's walls was a $700,000 lab able to turn out 132 to 176 pounds a month of the nerve gas sarin—enough to kill six million to eight million people.[35]

Fifty-seven days after the subway attack, Asahara finally was tracked down and taken into custody by Japanese police. Evidence obtained by authorities indicated that the threat posed by the multimillion-dollar Aum Shinrikyo cult was very real: "A notebook kept by one leader reportedly contained shopping lists for arms, and a notation: 'How much do nuclear warheads cost?' The last entry [read] 'November 1995. War.' "[36]

---

[31]Post, *Mystery*, 43.
[32]"Mass Suicide," 17.
[33]Richard Lacoya, "In the Reign of Fire," *Time* (October 17, 1994): 60.
[34]Anthony Spaeth, "Engineer of Doom," *Time* (June 12, 1995): 57; cf. "Police Seize Toxic Chemicals in Raid on Japanese Sect" by Teresa Watanabe, *Los Angeles Times* (March 23, 1995): A1. For an excellent and extensive secular analysis of the Aum Shinrikyo cult, read David E. Kaplan and Andrew Marshall, *The Cult at the End of the World: The Terrifying Story of the Aum Doomsday Cult, from the Subways of Tokyo to the Nuclear Arsenals of Russia* (Crown Publishers, Inc., 1996).
[35]Ibid.
[36]Steven Strasser, "Tokyo Grabs the Doomsday Guru," *Newsweek* (May 29, 1995): 48.

One of the most puzzling aspects of the Supreme Truth cult was its membership, which consisted of some of Japan's most promising minds: "Japanese were puzzled that bright young men with impressive university credentials would join the cult, when they could have had fine careers."[37]

Date-Suggesters: America's *Almost* False Prophets

This book is focused primarily on *cults* which, as we defined in chapter 1, are those religious groups that claim to be Christian, but which deviate from and/or deny at least one essential, biblical, and historical doctrine of the Christian church. Chapters 1 through 4 explain some of the reasons cults develop and expand.

Sadly, one of the reasons is because Christians too often neglect sound teaching or indulge personal speculations as doctrinal truth. Nowhere is this more noticeable than where Christian preoccupation with end times speculation, coupled with careless or imprudent statements by well-known Christian leaders about prophetic future, encourage naïve Christians to use end-times convictions as standards by which to judge orthodoxy. It is regrettable when the end-times speculations of a Christian teacher more closely match the end-times heresies of the apocalyptic cults than the biblical parameters of eschatological Scriptures.

Although false prophecies occur even in Christian churches, by Christian leaders, a new method of date-setting is now being employed by persons preoccupied with end-time speculations, especially within evangelical circles. This new method is perhaps best described as date-*suggesting* rather than date-*setting*. By using words and phrases such as "near," "close," "just ahead," and "not long" to describe when the end of the world will be, prophecy teachers erect for themselves an eschatological safety net. In other words, they can still be wrong about times and dates, but they avoid being labeled false prophets.

Some Christian teachers who indulge in unfounded prognostications are quite well known and respected within evangelical, charismatic, and Pentecostal circles. Their books sell millions of copies. Many of them even have their own programs on Christian television. Although none of them has ever actually said God *told* them that the world was going to come to an end on this date or that date, they have come about as close as one can get to crossing over that line separating false prophets from false teachers.

End times sensationalism is not merely a product of the last decades of the twentieth century. From the Montanists of the early church to the Second Adventists of the nineteenth century, susceptible Christians have been tantalized by erroneous speculations concerning the end times. After the fact, such speculations seem ludicrous, but beforehand they attract numerous believers.

For example, in 1940, Christian evangelist John R. Rice speculated, "Is Mussolini the Antichrist? He may be. I know of no reason why he would not fit the description of this terrible Man of Sin. He is an Italian. He is evidently an atheist. He once debated for atheism. He has the ruthless disposition, the ruling genius. He has an obsession to restore the Roman Empire. Furthermore, he is

---

[37]"The Cult's Broad Reach," *Newsweek* (May 8, 1995): 54.

already in power in Rome. If Christ called for His saints today and if every saved person should be taken out to meet Christ, then soon Mussolini might have a mandate over Palestine, make the prophesied treaty with the Jews, and in three and one-half years, forty-two months, over the whole world. Mussolini is somewhat past fifty, neither too young nor too old for the brief but meteoric rule of the horrible Man of Sin. The Man of Sin must be a ruler at Rome, and Mussolini might be the man."[38]

In 1974, Salem Kirban wrote *Kissinger, Man of Peace?* which asked in a roundabout way whether or not Secretary of State Henry A. Kissinger was not indeed the Antichrist. Included in the book was a chart revealing that when certain numerical values are given to Kissinger's last name, they add up to 666.[39]

The book *When Your Money Fails* by Dr. Mary Stewart Relfe, published in 1981, hovered on the Christian bestsellers list for many months. In it Relfe named Egypt's president Anwar El Sadat as the most likely candidate to be the Antichrist. Her prediction was based on various data including that the Antichrist would be a man of peace (Daniel 11:21, KJV). Sadat was the 1978 Nobel Peace Prize recipient. Despite his tragic assassination on October 6, 1981, the book continued to sell well into the next year.[40]

These fellow believers may be sincere, but are they being responsible? Although none of them ever placed a "thus saith the Lord" before their predictions, the effect is often the same for some listeners, given the force with which they state their "personal" opinions, convictions, and biblical interpretations. After all, when a well-respected Bible teacher and pastor reveals that he is predicating all of his plans on a certain date for the Lord's return, his trusting followers will likely do the same thing. They may forego school, postpone marriage, or give all of their money away only to see the "near," "soon," and "any moment" return of Jesus never materialize.

In a 1992 letter written to the Christian Research Institute, a young couple related the following story: "Our friend and several of her friends are now trying to liquidate their assets and buy land in the country, to live on and grow food on, in the event of a crisis (a form of 'Millennial Madness,' if you will)." It was not a cult leader that influenced these individuals, but a teacher promoted within evangelical circles, Jack Van Impe. Van Impe's 1990 video *A.D. 2000: The End?*, which suggests that Jesus will return in the year 2000, had convinced David and Michele's friend that "the end," complete with a number of catastrophes, was near.[41]

Historian Mark Noll gives a timely warning that church leaders should take to heart: "The verdict of history seems clear. Great spiritual gain comes from living under the expectation of Christ's return. But wisdom and restraint are also in order. At the very least, it would be well for those in our age who predict details and dates for the End to remember how many before them have misread the signs of the times."[42]

[38]John R. Rice, *World-Wide War and the Bible* (Wheaton, Ill.: Sword of the Lord Publishers, 1940), 101.
[39]Salem Kirban, *Kissinger, Man of Peace?* (Iowa Falls, Ia.: Riverside Book and Bible House, 1974), 33.
[40]Mary Stewart Relfe, *When Your Money Fails: The "666 System" Is Here* (Montgomery, Ala.: Ministries, Inc., 1981).
[41]Quoted in Oropeza, *Ninety-Nine Reasons*, 32–33.
[42]Quoted in DeMar, *Madness*, 21.

A Common Eschatological Error

Despite the many centuries of failed predictions and suggestions about "the end," a number of individuals continue to dogmatically assert that doomsday is at hand. The error that seems to appear most frequently in the eschatology of apocalyptic cults, false prophets, and date-suggesters is an assumption that the nearness of our Lord's return can be discerned by current events. This mistake is due in part to what is known as a futurist interpretation of several biblical passages, most notably Matthew 24, which identifies "wars and rumors of wars . . . famines and earthquakes" as being the signs that will precede the coming of the Son of Man.

Many people think that today's natural disasters, man-made catastrophes, social/political unrest, and devastating diseases are unique to this era. Hence, we *must* be living "in the last days" (Acts 2:17) before Jesus' return. Nothing could be further from the truth. To assert that "the last days" only recently began and that the present generation is witnessing never-before-seen tragedies is to believe what is historically untrue and biblically unsound.

First, Scripture tells us that "the last days" actually began when Jesus came to this earth (Hebrews 1:1–2; 1 Peter 1:20). The apostle John goes so far as to describe the era in which he was writing as "the last hour" (1 John 2:18, NIV). Furthermore, applying Matthew 24 to the second coming of Jesus is only one way of interpreting the passage. Many respected theologians and Bible teachers see the "coming of the Son of Man" in this chapter as being figurative language used prophetically in reference to the coming of God's judgment on Israel in A.D. 70, the year Jerusalem was destroyed. Old Testament passages that lend support to such an interpretation would be those that speak of God "coming" in judgment (Exodus 9:15–16; 20:20; Job 36:18; Ezekiel 21:15, 28).

Second, natural disasters such as earthquakes are not taking place with more frequency or intensity now than in centuries gone by. For example, history's worst earthquake, which killed more than 830,000 people, took place in China in 1556.[43] Earthquakes have been occurring regularly since the dawn of time. The Roman philosopher Seneca stated the following in A.D. 65:

> How often have cities in Asia, how often in Achaia, have been laid low by a single shock of earthquake! How many in Macedonia, have been swallowed up! How often has this kind of devastation laid Cyprus in ruins! How often has Paphos collapsed! Not infrequently are tidings brought to us of the utter destruction of entire cities.[44]

Plagues and famines have also been around for thousands of years. The worst case of pestilence, known as the Plague of Justinian, occurred in A.D. 500–650. Through recurring epidemics of bubonic plague, known as Black Death, the lives of an estimated 100 million people have been lost, 75 million in Western Europe alone from 1347 to 1351.[45] History's two worst famines took place in China and India from 1876 to 1879. Between 12 and 17 million people died.[46]

---

[43]James Cornell, *The Great International Disaster Book* (New York: Pocket Books, 1979), 131.
[44]Quoted in DeMar, *Madness*, 252.
[45]Cornell, *Disaster*, 183–184.
[46]Ibid., 155.

Last, wars and rumors of wars are no more prevalent today than they were in the past. There have been very few years in recorded history when a war was not taking place somewhere on the earth. Throughout the many centuries there have been more than fourteen thousand wars fought with estimates of approximately 3.6 billion persons killed.[47] The wars that have taken place within the last hundred years represent nothing more than the tail end of a long and bloody history.

Some Prophecy Guidelines

Christian author Gary DeMar, in his book *Last Days Madness*, mentions a well-known children's story that is particularly relevant to the issues of date-setting *and* date-suggesting:

> Day after day, a Shepherd Boy tended a flock of sheep in the hills above his village. One day, just to cause some excitement, the Shepherd Boy ran down from the hills shouting, "Wolf! Wolf!" The townsfolk came running with sticks to chase the Wolf away. All they found was the Shepherd Boy, who laughed at them for their pains. Seeing how well his trick worked, the Shepherd Boy tried it again the next day. Again he ran down from the hills, shouting, "Wolf!" Again the townsfolk ran to his aid in vain. But the day after, it happened that a Wolf really came. The Shepherd Boy, now truly alarmed, shouted, "Help! Come and help me! The Wolf is killing the sheep!" But this time the townsfolk said, "He won't fool us again with that trick!" They paid no attention to his cries, and the Wolf destroyed the entire flock. When the people saw what happened to their sheep, they were very angry. "There is no believing a liar," they said, "even when he speaks the truth!"[48]

DeMar's comments regarding the story and end times speculations are sobering:

> In the end we learn that the sheep are the ones that are harmed by the shouts of "Wolf!" by the Shepherd Boy. In the same way the people of God— the sheep—are harmed by continual shouts of "the end is near!" God is looking for shepherds after His own heart, "who will feed" the flock on "knowledge and understanding" (Jer. 3:15), not on the latest newspaper headlines. . . . Of course, if you cry "last days" long enough, you just might be the one to get it right, but by then there might not be anyone listening. Preaching about the imminent end of the world has long been used by religious groups as a way of pleading with the lost to commit themselves to Jesus Christ. Such a motivating device can backfire on even the most well-intentioned evangelist. What happens if a listener shouts out, "Preachers like you have been telling us for decades that the world is coming to an end. Why should we believe you now?" By crying wolf and being wrong each time, the church is perceived as unreliable and its doctrines capricious. Skeptics of the Christian faith are likely to conclude that since these self-proclaimed prophets were wrong on the timing of Jesus' return when they seemed so certain . . . then maybe they are wrong on other issues that they teach with equal certainty.[49]

---

[47]Carl Olaf Jonsson and Wolfgang Herbst, *The Sign of the Last Days—When?* (Atlanta: Commentary Press, 1987), 147.

[48]De Mar, *Madness*, 21–22.

[49]Ibid., 22.

In order to avoid the emotional pain and embarrassment that is often felt by victims of false prophecies and false suggestions, a believer should follow a few simple principles when studying eschatology:

(1) *The Bible gives no specific date for Jesus' second coming.* Any teaching that goes beyond the clear meaning of Scripture and assigns never-before-known time calculation is suspect. Even current events such as the 1948 return of the Jews to Israel cannot be used to calculate the nearness of Jesus' return. Nowhere does Scripture mention the year 1948 or any other date. Only by guesswork and preconceived notions can *any* date be inserted into the prophetic time line.

(2) *A new revelation cannot contradict something already in God's Word.* In Acts 1:7 Jesus explicitly declares that future events, including significant prophetic times and ages, are not for us to know. Any "revelation" that contradicts this is not a revelation from God.

(3) *This era is not witnessing an increase in natural disasters and man-made catastrophes.* Earthquakes, famines, storms, outbreaks of disease and wars have been an integral part of mankind's history since before the time of Christ.

(4) *Read prophetic passages of Scripture within their historical, linguistic, and cultural setting.* Biblical prophecies often point to a specific time period, place, and people in the Bible. Consequently, many verses that are being applied to today's events have already had their fulfillment through events of the past rather than the future. Be careful about pulling prophecies out of context.

(5) *Prophecies are sometimes meant to be taken figuratively.* Let Scripture interpret Scripture when it comes to identifying which passages should be taken literally and which ones should be understood figuratively.

(6) *No one has all the answers about the end times.* Everyone is entitled to an opinion, but it must be remembered that there are several eschatological views that are biblically tenable and orthodox: postmillennialism, amillennialism, historic premillennialism, and dispensational premillennialism. No one has a corner on eschatological truth.

All of us must remember that the *time* of Jesus' return is not nearly as important as the *fact* of Jesus' return. As Seventh-day Adventist pastor Ross Winkle says, the "hub of the Christian's hope is in a Person—not in a timetable. And our focus should be on Jesus—not on wars, famines, or earthquakes."[50]

In other words, we should be keeping our eyes on Jesus, the author and perfecter of our faith (Hebrews 12:2), not on intangible and ever-changing speculations about Jesus' return. Our Lord will come back to rescue us from this world of suffering when He knows it will give Him the most glory. It may be today, tomorrow, next year, or 10,000 years from now.

How much more effective might we be in this unbelieving world if we spent fewer hours studying prophecy books filled with guesses, and more hours plumbing the depths of biblical passages relating to love, kindness, self-control, and thoughtfulness? Instead of being obsessed with the timing of Jesus' return, should we not be consumed with the desire to tell people of His death, burial, and resurrection?

At the same time, we should not oppose looking forward to the return of our Lord and Savior. The apostles Paul and John both prayed for Jesus to come

---

[50]Chandler, *Doomsday*, 296.

back (1 Corinthians 16:22; Revelation 22:20). In the interim, Christians should remain focused on meeting the spiritual needs of a dying world that may still have a long road ahead of it. No one has ever benefited from the disappointment and embarrassment inseparably linked to failed prophecies, predictions, and suggestions about "the end." But joyful purpose awaits all those who heed the Great Commission given us by Jesus Christ: "Go ye therefore, and teach all the nations, baptizing them in the name of the Father, and of the Son, and of the Holy Ghost: teaching them to observe all things whatsoever I have commanded you: and, lo, I am with you alway, even unto the end of the world" (Matthew 28:19).

Chapter 16

The Cults on the World Mission Field

We have observed in our study of the various cults that they are particularly effective among those in whom the early seeds of Christianity have been planted. It is much easier for cultists to promulgate their doctrines among young Christians, nominal Christians, and those who have only a passing acquaintance with the Scriptures. Throughout the United States, the various non-Christian cults are in evidence everywhere; they boldly advertise themselves and eagerly covet the one great prize that all of them desperately seek—prestige and recognition as "Christians." This, however, is not always the case, especially on the foreign mission field, and it is with this area that we shall now briefly concern ourselves.

In the summer of 1958, it was the privilege of the author to be a part of the Pastor's Conference Team of World Vision Incorporated, then headed by Dr. Bob Pierce. These conferences were specifically designed to meet the needs of pastors, missionaries, and Christian workers on the various foreign mission fields of Asia and Africa. In the course of this tour of some 25,000 miles, I had opportunity to meet and speak to over 5,000 dedicated Christian workers and students on the problem of non-Christian cults on those mission fields. Beginning in Japan, with the largest pastors' conference in Japanese church history (1560 persons), we journeyed through Formosa (now Taiwan), Hong Kong, Singapore, Thailand, Burma, India, and Ghana, Africa. At the conclusion of the African meetings I had the opportunity to travel throughout Europe, meeting and interviewing Christian workers there, so it was possible for me to get a fairly well-rounded picture of what the various cults were doing in these specific locales. I returned to Europe in 1961 to lecture on the cults, and then interviewed missionaries whose work ranged from Scandinavia through Germany, Switzerland, Italy, Belgium, Holland, and France. I traveled in most of these countries and gathered firsthand impressions, which gave me the theological pulse of cultism in Europe.

A few things emerged very clearly from this unprecedented opportunity, which Dr. Pierce made possible, as well as from my subsequent European trip. I say unprecedented because never before in the history of Christian missions

---

This chapter revised, updated, and edited by Gretchen Passantino.

has any researcher in the field of cults been able to visit so many mission fields in so short a time (two and one-half months), delivering lectures and gathering information on a subject about which very little is known. In the course of my travels I learned much about cult methodology on the mission fields, and in contrast to our previous statements concerning their activities in the United States, the cults generally are happy to remain virtually anonymous until they have established a bridgehead. This is important in an area where a work has already begun or has been functioning for many years.

One missionary explained to me how young converts in particular were the prey of such cults as Jehovah's Witnesses' Watchtower organization and the Mormons' Church of Jesus Christ of Latter-day Saints, two of the most virulent strains of non-Christian cults, and both of which are found on practically every major mission area throughout all of the continents of the world. In addition to their evangelical endeavors, the cults specialize in reaching people in their own language and it is here that the printing establishments of Jehovah's Witnesses, the Mormons, and the Unity School of Christianity are revealed at their effective best. The average missionary who encounters a Jehovah's Witness in Japan, for instance, can expect to find copies of *The Watchtower* and *Awake* magazines translated into the language of the people and dutifully mailed from cult headquarters in Brooklyn, New York. There is also the very real problem of literature to combat these movements; literature that itself must, by the very nature of cult propaganda, also be in the language of the country in question, and such literature today is virtually unobtainable. At the Japanese conference many hours were consumed, both in the lecture period and in private counseling sessions with missionaries and native pastors, explaining the vulnerable areas of cult theology and, in turn, gleaning much valuable information on the tactics of cults abroad.

We learned that Jehovah's Witnesses were making an attempt to convince people that their own translation of the Bible (*The New World Translation*) is "the latest American translation" and should be accepted in questionable areas of theology as "the best and most recent rendering of the original languages."

The informed person, of course, knows that the Watchtower's translation is accepted as sound *only* by the Watchtower and those who have not carefully checked its many perverted renderings. But when one is 15,000 miles from home, laboring among people of a foreign tongue, and generally beset by the pressing problems of hostile indigenous religions (Buddhism, Islam, Shintoism, Taoism, Confucianism, Hinduism, etc.), it is difficult to check these things. And the Watchtower eagerly supplies *their* Bible to all interested persons, converts and pagans alike—something the Christian church has found difficult to accomplish, even in the twentieth century.

The startling growth of Jehovah's Witnesses, and the astronomical figures in publishing and distribution that the Watchtower accomplishes yearly, can only be appreciated when one sees a mission field literally inundated by tracts, pamphlets, Bibles, books, and magazines, all stamped Brooklyn, New York, U.S.A.! The world today is hungry to read, and the underdeveloped countries of Asia and Africa will read anything, even Watchtower propaganda, which appears as a torrent in comparison with the trickle of Christian literature currently in circulation.

It also became apparent, while questioning missionaries, that many of them are disturbed by the fact that Watchtower people always seemingly have enough

literature to proselytize Christian converts, but the missionary has little, if any, literature which will answer such cultists, much less evangelize them or their converts.

A chart of growth for Jehovah's Witnesses over four years illustrates the growing danger of the major cults today. This information has been compiled from the Watchtower's own publications, and one cannot but be astounded at their steady growth and the dedication of their members, of whom those who contributed extraordinary amounts of volunteer door-to-door "missionary" time are called "Kingdom Publishers."

Growth Comparisons for Jehovah's Witnesses Publishers and Baptisms

Year	Average number publishers	Change from previous year	Baptisms	Change from previous year
1978	513,673	−3.15%	20,469	−26.9%
1979	521,370	+1.50%	26,958	+31.7%
1980	543,457	+4.24%	27,811	+3.16%
1981	563,453	+3.68%	28,496	+2.46%

From the above chart, Christian format can draw little comfort, and Christian Bible colleges, institutes, and seminaries would do well to consider the ramifications of such rapid growth, since very little, if anything, is being done to prepare missionaries and ministers to meet these problems, either at home or on the field of world missions.

When it is pointed out that in 1997 less than half of the membership of Jehovah's Witnesses reside in the United States, the gravity of the problem that confronts the Christian church is apparent to all but the most adamantly obtuse. Over 50 percent of their membership is outside of the United States and they are aggressively doing their work in the mission field.

The Witnesses in 1975, at their worldwide communion service known as their Memorial, numbered 4,550,459 persons, as over against 1,553,909 persons in 1961, a total increase of almost 3,000,000 people! In 1988 the number who attended doubled to 9,201,071. And in 1996 the number jumped again to 12,921,933. These statistics should be the cause of significant alarm.

During 1988, Jehovah's Witnesses worldwide spent over 785,000,000 hours in door-to-door work. New members baptized in 1988 were 239,268. Hundreds of millions of pieces of literature were distributed. In 1997, the circulation of their feature publication, *The Watchtower* magazine, reached more than 13,000,000 and was published in more than 100 languages.[1]

It is no wonder that many missionaries are discouraged and that in the United States an increasing number of pastors are beginning to share that discouragement. This stems from the fact that a cult so obviously non-Christian as

[1]"Their Worldwide Organization and Work," *The Official Web Site of Jehovah's Witnesses*, web site address: http://www.watchtower.org, 1997.

Jehovah's Witnesses is becoming increasingly successful in its missionary outreach, particularly in the field of literature, when both clergy and missionary representing the historic Gospel of Jesus Christ find little or no support in this vital area of literary mass evangelism.

The Watchtower Society has not restricted itself, however, merely to the publication of literature on the mission field. Their two-by-two doorstep evangelism has become the plague of the British Commonwealth and most of the countries of Europe, Asia, and Africa.

1996 Report of Jehovah's Witnesses Worldwide[2]

Witnesses	5,413,769
Baptisms	366,579
Congregations	81,908
Preaching Hours	1,140,621,714
Bible Studies	4,855,030
Memorial Attendance	12,921,933

Watchtower missionaries also have made it extremely difficult for truly orthodox Christian efforts throughout the various trouble spots of the world (for example, East Germany, Africa, Japan, Indonesia, Vietnam, and Cuba) by emphasizing the organization's rigid anti-government stand, which is based upon their theological presupposition that all governments are under the direct supervision of Satan and are opposed to the theocratic rule of Jehovah. It is unnecessary to observe that since they identify themselves as Christian and utilize the Bible and vocabulary of Christianity, those who are by nature hostile to the Christian message, and who are seeking only the opportunity to persecute it and restrict its activities, seize upon the Watchtower organization's many statements that to them, at least, seem to incite disloyalty to governmental authority as well as a militant pacifism and allegiance to a theocracy in place of the individual nation.

The Watchtower Society seems totally oblivious to the thirteenth chapter of Romans and its demand that "every soul be subject unto the higher powers. For ... the powers that be are ordained of God." And for the average Jehovah's Witness, all governments and all forms of supposed Christianity, except his own, are enemies to be harassed, vilified, and condemned as tools of Satan. This hardly makes for good public relations, and in the fervent spirit of emerging nationalism, particularly in the so-called underdeveloped countries of the world, those in authority have taken a rather dim view of the Watchtower's activities, resulting in their persecution of true disciples of the cross, who suffer

---

[2]"1996 Report of Jehovah's Witnesses Worldwide," *Official Web Site of Jehovah's Witnesses*, web site address: http://www.watchtower.org, 1997. A 1975 report reads as follows:

Books and Bibles placed in homes	28,410,783
Booklets placed in homes	12,163,807
Watchtower and *Awake* placed in homes	293,705,005
Calls back to interested families	155,336,481
Home Bible studies conducted	1,411,256
Hours in America spent in proselytizing efforts	382,296,208

because of the Watchtower's identification, albeit mistaken, with biblical Christianity.

The Jehovah's Witnesses have taken full advantage of the political openness, social and political unrest, and technological advances of the last two decades of the twentieth century. They have focused on intense evangelism campaigns in former Soviet-controlled countries (Albania, Republic of Benin, Bulgaria, Croatia, Czech Republic, Estonia, Hungary, Republic of Moldova, Poland, Romania, Russia, Slovakia, Slovenia, Ukraine, and Yugoslavia); countries with continuing civil unrest (Cameroon, Colombia, Dominican Republic, El Salvador, Ethiopia, Mozambique, Nicaragua, South Africa, and Sri Lanka); and countries emerging into technological sophistication (Central African Republic, Côte D'Ivoire, French Guiana, Ghana, Guatemala, Guyana, Haiti, Jamaica, Kenya, Malawi, Pakistan, Papua New Guinea, Senegal, and Zambia). There are now Watchtower evangelistic efforts in more than 200 countries, and branch offices in 109 countries worldwide.

All in all, Jehovah's Witnesses are a growing concern everywhere and a challenge to evangelical Christianity, which desires to win them to a redemptive knowledge of Jesus Christ and, in the process, to give every man an answer, "a reason of the hope that is in you . . . Christ in you, the hope of glory" (1 Peter 3:15; Colossians 1:27).

Mormon Missionary Efforts

Even surpassing the Jehovah's Witnesses is the rapidly burgeoning missionary effort of the Church of Jesus Christ of Latter-day Saints (Mormon).

Boasting a missionary force approaching 23,000 full-time workers, and bolstered by a church whose gross income in 1984 was well over one billion dollars, the Mormon cult is moving at a rapid pace, particularly in its new mission fields of South America and Africa. Over the dozen years since the previous edition of this book, the Church of Jesus Christ of Latter-day Saints has continued its remarkable growth pattern, particularly in underdeveloped and formerly communist countries. The threat from the growth of this false gospel in the 1980s is only exceeded by the threat at the close of the century.

The following charts demonstrate the growth of Mormon missions over recent years and should suffice to remind us that Jehovah's Witnesses are not the only cult that competes with Christianity on a large scale on most of the large mission fields.

Growth of the Mormon Church

1900	268,331	1950	1,111,314
1910	393,437	1960	1,693,180
1920	526,032	1962	1,965,786
1930	672,488	1975	3,700,000
1940	862,664	1982	5,000,000+

The following statistical information is from the Church of Jesus Christ of Latter-day Saints official Internet Web site, www.lds.org, under "Global Media Guide," March 1997.

Convert Baptisms Since 1983

1983	189,419	1990	330,877
1984	192,983	1991	297,770
1985	197,640	1992	274,477
1986	216,214	1993	304,808
1987	227,284	1994	300,730
1988	256,515	1995	304,330
1989	318,938		

Latter-day Saint 1997 Statistics

World Membership	9,700,000
United States Membership	4,800,000
Non-U.S. Membership	4,900,000
Female	53%
Male	47%
Congregations	23,200
Temples, Worldwide	51 since 1836; 2 no longer operating or owned by LDS; 15 planned and/or under construction
Literature Languages	145
The *Book of Mormon*	78 million since 1830, 4.5 million in 1995, 90 languages
Missions	300
Missionaries	50,000; 75% young males; 18% young females; 7% married couples
Service Missionaries (health services, agriculture, etc.)	5,000
Missionary Training Centers	15

Mormon missionary work far surpasses that of the Jehovah's Witnesses, and together the missionary efforts of the two cults present a real and present danger to the spread of the true gospel throughout the world today.

The methodology of Mormon missionaries is similar in many respects to that of Jehovah's Witnesses. They, too, are door-to-door canvassers and tireless, round-the-clock "back-callers" on contacts previously made either by themselves or by those missionaries who preceded them. Mormon missionaries, unlike those of the Jehovah's Witnesses, come fully equipped with slick multimedia presentations and free copies of the *Book of Mormon, Doctrine and Covenants,* and *Pearl of Great Price,* the sacred books that they believe "properly interpret" the Bible. Whereas the Jehovah's Witnesses will emphasize the absolute authority of the Scriptures as a supreme criterion for truth, the Mormons will hedge at this juncture, maintaining that the Bible is the Word of God insofar as it is "correctly translated." They will insist gently, but firmly, that the *Book of Mormon* and the other two sacred books "throw light upon the Bible, and explain the Bible in

the light of restored Christianity and the ministry of the prophet Joseph Smith." In fact, today they insist that *The Book of Mormon* be called *The Book of Mormon— Another Testament of Jesus Christ.*[3] In England, where the Latter-day Saints once doubled their membership, they are particularly proud to point out that Brigham Young came from an English background and did missionary work in England himself prior to the assassination of Joseph Smith in 1844. Young returned from England to assume the leadership of the Mormon Church, and some of his wives were English girls whom Brigham Young recruited on his missionary journey. It is not unusual to find second-generation Mormons returning to carry on the family tradition in the country where their parents did missionary work.

Another aspect of Mormon missionary activity is their preoccupation with the anthropological background of the *Book of Mormon*, which leads them to declare that the Native American and the Central and South American Indian races have similar origins and are mentioned in the *Book of Mormon*. They do not hesitate to suggest the linkage of the Inca civilization, the Aztec civilization, and other such archaeologically verified Indian groups as giving credence to the teachings of the *Book of Mormon*. The fact that no reputable archaeologist has ever verified their hypothetical and unsupported propositions (in fact, others have gone on record as repudiating them outright [see chapter on Mormonism]) apparently does not hinder the zeal of Mormon missionaries one whit.

Such archaeological and anthropological razzle-dazzle, however, does have quite an effect on the untutored and uninformed mind outside the United States, where verifications or contradictions of the Mormon claims would be difficult, if not impossible, to obtain. Thus we see that in Mexico and South America particularly, Mormon missionaries appealing to the nationalistic pride of both Indians and Latins are telling them that they are the heirs of great civilizations that the *Book of Mormon* reveals are connected with the origins of Christianity and its nineteenth-century "restoration" through the establishment of the Mormon Church. By utilizing the *Book of Mormon* as a prophetic volume and "new light on the Bible," the Mormons have succeeded to an amazing degree in Mexico and in South America, to the great dismay of many mission agencies and a large company of missionaries. As we previously observed, however, the Mormons are careful not to point out their previous discrimination against the black race, for it simply would not do for the "Restored Church of Jesus Christ" to be on the one hand busily engaged in promoting the archaeological myth of the *Book of Mormon* and the races of the Americas, while on the other virtually ignoring the black race purely on the ground of their skin color and imagined curse! Wherever possible, it is good for Christian missionaries to point out this glaring inconsistency, which is well known in Africa where the Mormons in force have been, until recently, conspicuously absent. For almost all of its controversial history, Mormon missionary efforts were confined to those races that qualified in the theology of Joseph Smith and Brigham Young, but one could hardly seriously consider, on the basis of such racial discrimination, the claims of the Mormons to being the restored church of Christ.

The Mormon missionary approach also differs from that of other cults, par-

---

[3]"Media Style Guide," *Global Media Guide*, 1996.

ticularly Jehovah's Witnesses, in that it emphasizes the need for education, preferring to reach a higher strata of intellect, generally speaking, than the Jehovah's Witnesses have been able to attain. From a standpoint of educational background, social graces, and personal habits, which include a quiet, tolerant regard for evangelical Christianity (something lacking most pointedly in the methods of Jehovah's Witnesses), the Mormons make a good impression on prospective converts and many ex-members of Christian denominations are now the disciples of Joseph Smith and Brigham Young because of this distinctive Mormon emphasis.

A typical Mormon missionary approach is oriented around three prime factors:

1. *The Mormon Church alone has the marks of true Christianity.* It is called the Church of Jesus Christ; it has apostles and prophets; it has a priesthood (Melchizedek and Aaronic) as well as elders and other New Testament practices.

The Mormons claim the unique ability to baptize for the dead (1 Corinthians 15:29), and have sacred extrabiblical literature that interprets the Bible.

2. *The Mormons maintain that Christianity is an open apostasy,* as evidenced by the rise of Roman Catholicism during the Dark Ages and the various and multiple divisions in Christendom since the Reformation.

3. *The outward success of the Mormon Church,* its enormous prosperity and growth since 1830 in the face of persecutions and ostracism (due in part to their own immoral practices of polygamy, one should note), proves conclusively, say the Mormon missionaries, that the Church of Jesus Christ of Latter-day Saints is the restoration of true, biblical Christianity, and should be embraced as such.

Since the average person knows very little of church history, and even less of the backgrounds of Joseph Smith, Brigham Young, and the early "Mormon saints," some of these things will go unchallenged. But if even a general knowledge of the massive contradictions and historical myth-making about the origins of Mormonism is known to a prospective convert, not to mention the Mormons' polytheistic theology, which by definition is not Christian, then the "saints" have a difficult time indeed defending the maze that is their history and theology. Usually when this occurs, they will depart and never return.

The Reverend Gordon Fraser, who has spent some fifty years working as a missionary among the Navaho Indians in Arizona and New Mexico, has had numerous encounters with Mormon missionaries and his judgment in this realm is most relevant.

> The Mormons have striven for years to gain recognition as a Christian body. Until within a decade or so, their claim has been denied by even the most liberal groups of professing Christians. Lately, however, with the general lowering of Christian standards of thought and with the remarkable buildup in the public press and on the radio, the Mormons have achieved their goal in the thinking of the general public. But are the Mormons Christians? If the term covers all who use the name of Christ in their titles or in their teaching, we would have to allow the Mormons their claim, but we would have to include with them the Jehovah's Witnesses, Christian Scientists, and most of the other metaphysical cults, as well as Unitarians, Universalists, Baha'is, and a host of so-called liberal adherents to the various Christian denominations, which were originally completely orthodox.
>
> All of these refer freely to Jesus Christ and use quotations from the Bible

to support their views, but these, along with Mormons, deny what we consider to be the indispensable tenets of true . . . Christianity.

The Mormons are well trained in their methods, and nominal Christians are an easy prey to their arguments. We have yet to see, however, an intelligent and regenerate person who knows the Bible and its doctrines, succumb to Mormonism.

The Mormon missionaries who come to your door will be well-mannered, attractive young people. They will introduce themselves as "Christian missionaries," or will use some other innocuous term.

One team, recently returned from Honduras, announced themselves as members of the Central American Mission. Another team encountered recently merely asked, "Could we step in and have a Christian word with you?"

They will avoid identifying themselves as Mormons or Latter-day Saints until they have gained an audience.

These young missionaries are given very careful training, both in the fine points of good sales approach and in the best methods of appealing to the members of the various churches. It is part of their training to attend services of the various churches, so as to be informed on matters of phraseology and doctrine.

We should insist that such visitors identify themselves. . . .

What Mr. Fraser says is, of course, a sound evaluation of Mormon practices, and we are forced to his conclusion when he says,

Many Christians, uninformed as to the true nature of the Mormon teachings, will defend their Mormon neighbors as good, clean-living, pious and honest folks. They will point to the wonderful relief practices of the Mormon Church. They will extol the thrift and industry of the Mormons as a whole. All these things we recognize and appreciate as valuable contributions to society. We cannot criticize these things. These virtues do not make one a Christian. Satan is delighted when his followers put up a good appearance. We insist that these virtues have nothing to do with one's acceptance before God, if one has never yielded to God's claims concerning His Son, Jesus Christ. When Christians fail to demonstrate the above virtues, they are coming short of God's purpose, but these are the by-products of the Christian life.[4]

We must look beyond the appearances of Mormonism and its missionaries; we must consider the fruit of its tree: not only its social benefits and moral reform but its doctrine, which, as has been noted, is as much fruit from the tree of religion as is the practice of that religion.

In the case of the Mormons, their doctrinal fruit is corrupt, denying as they do the Christian doctrine of the Trinity, the deity of our Lord, and salvation by grace through justifying faith in Jesus Christ (Ephesians 2:8–10). The Jehovah's Witnesses and the Mormons share one thing in common—both are dedicated opponents of historical Christianity. Although they utilize the name of Christ and the methods of Christianity where witnessing and evangelism are concerned, the content of Christianity, which by necessity revolves about the person of Jesus Christ, is either ignored or redefined by them. In the end, it is the gospel of "another Jesus, another spirit" and the product of that supreme architect of religious deviltry, who delights in arraying himself and his ministers as angels of light. Of him Jesus Christ said, "He is a liar and a murderer from the beginning"—Satan, the god of this age.

[4]Gordon R. Fraser, *Is Mormonism Christian?* (Chicago, Ill.: Moody Press, 1977), 7–8, 117.

There is scarcely a mission field of the world that has not felt the impact of these two major cult systems, and we would be foolish indeed, in discussing the problem of missionary activities of the cults, to ignore their methodology and their already fantastic accomplishments in a relatively short amount of time.

Much more could be written on this subject, but everything that needs to be said could hardly be included in a chapter of this length. It might be observed, however, that the cults do share some traits in common when it comes to missionary methodology, and the primary ones are worth noting.

1. *The cults do not generally identify themselves by their popular names* (Jehovah's Witnesses, Mormons, etc.). They prefer such titles as Latter-day Saints or The Holy Spirit Association for the Unification of World Christianity, and generally reveal themselves in their historical connections only when the prospect is on the way to indoctrination.

2. *The literature of many cult systems is unmarked,* so that it is difficult to identify them because of the similarity of terminology employed in the setting forth of their teachings.

3. *Most cultists utilize terminology of historical Christianity* and are masters of evangelical clichés, as Fraser has pointed out.

4. *Their public meetings are seldom identified with the official name of the sponsoring group.* But the fact that many are reluctant to identify themselves underscores some of their divisive methods of proselytizing, which though regretted by some quarters of leadership, still continue on many mission fields around the world.

5. *All major cult systems will use the Bible,* quoting profusely from it, mostly out of context. In the case of Jehovah's Witnesses, they will even offer copies of their own translation (the Mormons have an "inspired version" also) to "aid a deeper understanding of the Scriptures."

6. *Missionaries of the cults will also, when pressed, deny the historic doctrines* of the Trinity, the deity of Jesus Christ, and salvation by grace alone.

7. *Cult missionaries will follow up major evangelistic campaigns,* such as Billy Graham, as they did in England and elsewhere. Mormons and Jehovah's Witnesses specialize in this, and have even been found in counseling rooms after altar calls, attempting to proselytize the young converts.

These are some of the marks of the methods and content of some of the major cults on the world mission fields. There can be no doubt that they are effective and that the church must rise to meet this challenge while there is yet time.

Chapter 17

The Jesus of the Cults

Since the earliest days of Christianity, both apostle and disciple alike have been confronted with the perversion of the revelation God has given us in the person of Jesus Christ. Historically, this perversion has extended not only to the teaching of our Lord but, more importantly, to the person of Christ; for it is axiomatic that if the doctrine of Christ himself, i.e., His person, nature, and work are perverted so that the identity of the life-giver is altered, then the life that He came to give is correspondingly negated. And it is at precisely this juncture that in this day and age we come face to face with the phenomenon that the apostle Paul described in Second Corinthians, chapter eleven, as "the other Jesus."

The problem is twofold, in that we must understand the nature of the "other Jesus" and then give the biblical reasons why it is the obligation of Christians to identify him as a counterfeit and refute his other gospel.

There can be little doubt that the Christian of today can expect to encounter the very same or, at least, similar errors and perversions of the gospel message that his ancestors before him did. He should not be discouraged when they appear to have more success in twisting the truth of God than the Christian has in presenting it.

The epistle to the Galatians reminds us that there are those who would "pervert the Gospel of Christ," and who represent "another gospel," which in reality is not another but a counterfeit of the original, designed by the master craftsman of all evils, our adversary, the devil.

It may seem like oversimplification and naïveté to some people to suggest that Satan is the prime mover and architect of the major cult systems, but a careful consideration of the biblical evidence will allow no other conclusion.

In his Second Corinthian epistle, Paul penned one of the most solemn warnings recorded anywhere in the Bible, to which we have made previous reference. He addressed this warning to Christians who were in great danger of having their minds (not their soul's salvation) corrupted from the simplicity

This chapter updated and edited by Gretchen Passantino.

that is in Christ Jesus. He was afraid, he said, that if someone should come to Corinth preaching "another Jesus, another Spirit, and another gospel," the Corinthians might well be swept along with it to the sterilization of their Christian life and witness for Christ. Paul went on to underscore this point by drawing a deadly parallel between true Christianity and pseudo-Christianity that he likened to a carefully designed copy of the original revelation of God in Christ.

After revealing the existence of a counterfeit Jesus, Holy Spirit, and gospel, Paul completed the parallel by showing that there are also counterfeit "apostles" and counterfeit "disciples" (workers) who transform themselves in appearance and demeanor to appear as ministers of Christ, but in reality, Paul states, they are representatives of Satan (2 Corinthians 11:13). He further informs us that this is not to be considered fantastic, unbelievable, and incredible, for Satan himself is often manifested as "an angel of light." So we are not to be surprised when his ministers emulate their master and disguise themselves as ministers of righteousness (2 Corinthians 11:14–15).

Now, of course, Paul was speaking of those who could be readily identified as spiritual wolves in sheep's clothing the moment their teachings were compared with the true gospel (Galatians 1:8–9), not merely anyone with whom we have a disagreement in the realm of theology.

Simply because Christians disagree on certain peripheral issues cannot be taken as a valid reason for asserting that such are dissenters and ministers of Satan, unless that dissent involves the person and work of our Lord, in which case their unbelief would automatically invoke the apostolic judgment.

The Nature of the Other Jesus

The person and work of Christ is indeed the very foundation of Christian faith. And if it is redefined and interpreted out of context and therefore contrary to its biblical content, the whole message of the gospel is radically altered and its value correspondingly diminished. The early apostles clearly saw this, including John and Jude; hence, their repeated emphasis upon maintaining the identity and ministry of the historical Jesus over against the counterfeits of that Person already beginning to arise in their own era.

The "other Jesus" of the false cults of that day (Gnosticism and Galatianism, or Legalism) threatened the churches at Colosse, Ephesus, and Crete, and invoked powerful apostolic condemnation and warning in the epistles of First John, Galatians, and Colossians.

In order that we may better understand precisely how these Scriptures may be applied in our own day, we need only cite some contemporary illustrations of the "other Jesus" the Bible so graphically warns against, and the entire issue will come into clear perspective.

1. The Jesus of Christian Science

In the theological structure of the Christian Science religion, as we have already seen, Gnosticism was revived and Mrs. Eddy became its twentieth-century exponent. Mrs. Eddy declared concerning *her* Jesus:

The Christian who believes in the First Commandment is a monotheist. Thus he virtually unites with the Jew's belief in one God and recognizes that Jesus Christ is not God as Jesus Christ himself declared, but is the Son of God (*Science and Health*, 152).

Mrs. Eddy spelled out her view so that no one could possibly misinterpret her when she wrote:

The spiritual Christ was infallible; Jesus, as material manhood, was not Christ (*Misc. Writings*, 84).

Now, a careful study of Matthew, chapter sixteen, will reveal that Jesus Christ acknowledged the confession of Peter to the effect that He was Jesus the Christ, the Son of the living God. And it would be foolish to maintain that Jesus was not material manhood in the light of the New Testament record that He was born of woman, subject to the limitations of our nature apart from sin, and physically expired upon the cross in our place. The Jesus of Mrs. Eddy is a divine ideal or principle, inherent within every man, and Jesus was its supreme manifestation. Since Mrs. Eddy denied the existence of the physical universe, she also denied the reality of human flesh and blood, maintaining that it was an illusion of mortal mind. Hence, neither Christ, nor any man, for that matter, possesses a real body of flesh and bones and, for her, Jesus Christ has not come in the flesh.

It seems almost unnecessary to refer to the fact that our Lord acknowledged the reality of flesh and blood when He declared to Peter: "Blessed art thou, Simon Bar-jona: for flesh and blood hath not revealed it unto thee, but my Father which is in heaven" (Matthew 16:17).

At this particular juncture, the words of the apostle John take on new meaning when he declares:

Every spirit that confesseth not that Jesus Christ is come in the flesh is not of God: and this is that spirit of antichrist, whereof ye have heard that it should come; and even now already is it in the world (1 John 4:3).

John's previous words apply with great force to the Jesus of Christian Science and its "prophetess," Mrs. Eddy:

Who is a liar but he that denieth that Jesus is the Christ? He is antichrist, that denieth the Father and the Son (1 John 2:22).

We need not emphasize the point, for it is quite evident that the "other" Jesus of Christian Science is a Gnostic Jesus, an idea, a principle—but not God incarnate (John 1:14). Because of this, although Mrs. Eddy, her literature, and Christian Scientists utilize the name of Jesus, theirs is not the Christ of the Scriptures, but an extremely clever counterfeit about whom the Holy Spirit graciously saw fit to warn the church.

2. The Jesus of Jehovah's Witnesses

The next example is quite different from the Jesus of Christian Science, but another Jesus, nonetheless. According to the theology of the Watchtower,

The true Scriptures speak of God's Son, the Word, as "a god." He is a "mighty god," but not the Almighty God who is Jehovah (*The Truth Shall Make You Free*, 47).

> In other words, he was the first and direct creation of Jehovah God (*The Kingdom Is at Hand*, 46–47, 49).

The founder of Jehovah's Witnesses, Charles Taze Russell, described this Jesus as having been Michael the Archangel prior to his divesting himself of his angelic nature and appearing in the world as a perfect man (*Studies in the Scriptures*, 5:84). For Jehovah's Witnesses, their Jesus is an angel who became a man; he is a god, but he is not God the Son, second person of the Holy Trinity.

As the chapter on Jehovah's Witnesses amply demonstrates, the Scriptures refute this and flatly controvert the Watchtower's theology by teaching that Jesus Christ is the Word, God the only begotten one (John 1:18, from the Greek), and no less than the great "I AM" of Exodus 3:14 (compare John 8:58) and the First and the Last of the apocalyptic-Isaiah contrast, well known to any informed student of the Scriptures (compare Revelation 1:16–17 with Isaiah 44:6).

Just as Mrs. Eddy's Christ is an abstract idea, the Christ of Jehovah's Witnesses is a second god with an angelic background. He, too, qualifies as "another Jesus" in the context of the Pauline prophecy.

3. The Jesus of the Mormons

The teachings of the Mormon religion, which differ from both Christian Science and Jehovah's Witnesses, claim that their god is one among many gods, as evidenced by their own literature:

> Each of these gods, including Jesus Christ and his Father, being in possession of not merely an organized spirit, but a glorious body of flesh and bones (Parley P. Pratt, *Key to the Science of Theology* [1973 ed.], 44; see also, *Doctrine and Covenants*, 130:22).

Theologian Pratt held no unique view where Mormonism was concerned; in fact, the Mormons have a full pantheon of gods. Jesus, who before his incarnation was the spirit-brother of Lucifer, was also a polygamist, the husband of the Marys and Martha, who was rewarded for his faithfulness by becoming the ruler of this earth (see chapter 6, on Mormonism).

The apostle Paul reminds us in his epistle to the Galatians that "God is one" (Galatians 3:20). Numerous passages from the Old Testament, previously cited in the chapter on Mormonism, demonstrate the absolute falsity of the idea that there are a multiplicity of gods and an exaltation to godhood to which men can aspire. As for the concept of Jesus as a polygamist and a brother of Lucifer, this need not be dignified by further comment.

The Jesus of the Mormons is quite obviously "another Jesus" with whom truly redeemed men have nothing in common, even though he be arrayed as an angel of light and with all the credentials of the angel Moroni's angelic proclamation to Joseph Smith, the prophet of the restored Christian religion!

It would be possible to go on listing the other cult systems, but it is apparent that further comment would be superfluous; the evidence is overpowering.

The Jesus of the Christian Scientists, the Mormons, the Jehovah's Witnesses, and of all the cult systems is but a subtle caricature of the Christ of divine revelation. In cult theology, He becomes an abstraction (Christian Science, Unity, Metaphysics, New Thought), a second god (Jehovah's Witnesses, Mormonism,

Rosacrucianism, Baha'ism), a pantheistic manifestation of deity (Spiritism, The Great I AM), the Ascended Master of Theosophy, the avatar of Buddhism, the Enlightened One of the New Age cults, the incomplete Messiah of the Unification Church, the wise one of Scientology, the guru disciple and yoga master of the Eastern religions, the militant avenger of the apocalyptic cults, the prophet of Islam, or the coward of the occultists; but he is still incontrovertibly "another Jesus," who represents another gospel and imparts another spirit, which by no conceivable stretch of the imagination could be called holy.

Herein lies the problem that Christians must face and come to grips with, and there are excellent reasons why it is not only our responsibility but our duty.

To Everyone an Answer

In the course of delivering numerous lectures on the subject of non-Christian cults and their relationship to the Christian church, one of the most frequently asked questions has been, "Why should Christians oppose and criticize the beliefs of others whether they be cults or other world religions?"

To answer this question we must first recognize that to oppose and criticize is neither unethical, bigoted, or unchristian; rather, it is the epitome of proper Christian conduct where a very vital part of the Christian witness is concerned. There are some good people who feel that it is beneath their dignity to engage in the criticism of the beliefs of others, and the society in which we live has done much to foster this belief. "Live and let live" is the motto of our civilization; don't buck the tide of uncritical tolerance or, as the saying goes, "bend with the wind or be broken." In addition to this type of reasoning there also has been promulgated a distinctly noncontroversial spirit mirrored in the fact that leading newspapers and periodicals, not to mention the mass media of communication, radio and TV, refuse to carry advertisements for debates on religious issues for fear of being thought un-American, since it is now fashionable to equate criticism of another's religion with an un-American spirit!

Today's "politically correct" atmosphere of tolerance as the highest virtue takes to new heights the trends that began to develop decades ago. There was a time when "tolerance" meant a respect for others, a willingness to listen to what they had to say, and a commitment to careful evaluation of other beliefs. Honest disagreement was applauded as a sure sign that two parties were seriously engaged in a discussion about objective truth. People could "agree to disagree agreeably," as Dr. Martin used to say. However, today "tolerance" seems to mean that one must hold to no absolutes, no truths, and no convictions; instead, we are to accept the validity and authority of any and all statements without regard to reason, evidence, or truth. What is even more amazing is that anyone who holds the opinion that some opinions are right while others are wrong is considered wrong—a clear case of self-contradiction, which reduces all rational thought to irrationality.

When we criticize the teachings of the cults, we do not disparage cultists' sincerity or the honesty of their convictions. We do, however, care enough about truth and enough about the cultists to be willing to evaluate what they have been taught by Scripture and to lovingly share the truth that is in Christ with them. We should adopt as our motto 2 Timothy 2:24–26: "And the servant of the Lord

must not strive; but be gentle to all men, apt to teach, patient, in meekness instructing those that oppose themselves; if God peradventure will give them repentance to the acknowledging of the truth; and that they may recover themselves out of the snare of the devil, who are taken captive by him at his will."

We must remember, however, that controversy in itself has always been a stimulus to thought and in our own great country has provoked many needed reforms in numerous instances. We might also observe that there is the easily verifiable fact that the criticism of another's religious beliefs does not necessarily postulate personal antagonism toward those who entertain such beliefs. Hence it is possible for a Protestant to criticize Roman Catholicism or Judaism, for example, without being in the least antagonistic to members of either faith. Let us not forget that honest criticism, debate, and the exploration of controversial issues involves the basic right of freedom of speech within constitutional limits; and the New Testament itself, the very cradle of Christianity, reflects in a startling way the fact that the faith of Jesus Christ was built and nourished upon the controversy that it provoked. It was said of the early Christians that they "turned the world upside down" (Acts 17:6); indeed the message of the Cross itself is offensive and controversial by nature. Robert Ingersoll, the late great agnostic and renowned antagonist of Christianity, was wise enough to recognize this fact and stated in his famous lectures, "If this religion is true, then there is only one Savior, only one narrow path to life. Christianity cannot live in peace with any other religion."

There are many reasons why books and chapters like this should be written, but we shall turn to the Bible itself for the basic reasons—believing that in God's Word, the source of our faith, will be found the evidence that its defense is very much His will.

Let us begin by noting the historical fact that Jesus Christ and His apostles warned repeatedly of false prophets and teachers.

Throughout His entire ministry, our Lord was constantly on guard against those who attempted to ensnare Him with trick questions and supposed contradictions between what He taught and the teachings of Moses and the prophets. Added to this, these professional interrogators masqueraded as religious, pious, and even tolerant zealots and professed that they were the descendants of Abraham, heirs to the covenant, and the servants of God. To these people our Lord addressed His most scathing denunciations, calling them, among other things, "whited sepulchers," "children of the devil," "dishonorers of God," "liars," "murderers," and "wolves." Since our Lord was both God and man, He alone could gaze through the centuries and see those who would arise following in the train of His contemporary antagonists, and at least two very graphic prophecies of their characters and objectives are to be found in His discourses.

In the seventh chapter of the gospel according to Matthew, Christ enunciated a very definite warning:

> Beware of false prophets, which come to you in sheep's clothing, but inwardly they are ravening wolves. Ye shall know them by their fruits. Do men gather grapes of thorns, or figs of thistles? Even so, every good tree bringeth forth good fruit; but a corrupt tree bringeth forth evil fruit. A good tree cannot bring forth evil fruit, neither can a corrupt tree bring forth good fruit. Every tree that bringeth not forth good fruit is hewn down, and cast into the fire.

Wherefore by their fruits ye shall know them. Not every one that saith unto me, Lord, Lord, shall enter into the kingdom of heaven; but he that doeth the will of my Father which is in heaven. Many will say to me in that day, Lord, Lord, have we not prophesied in thy name? and in thy name have cast out devils? and in thy name done many wonderful works? And then will I profess unto them, I never knew you: depart from me, ye that work iniquity (Matthew 7:15–23).

From this discourse we learn some very important things. We learn that there shall be false prophets, that they shall appear in sheep's clothing, and that their inward or spiritual nature is that of wolves (v. 15). We are further told that we shall be able to recognize them by their fruits. We are informed that they will prophesy in His name; in His name cast out devils, and in His name perform miracles (vv. 16, 22). With the full knowledge that they would do these things, our Lord then adds "I will profess unto them; I never knew you . . . ye that work iniquity" (v. 23). There can be little doubt that He intended this as a warning, for He prefaces His statements with a very strong Greek term "beware," literally, "be wary of or take care, because of" false prophets. The designation "wolves in sheep's clothing" is therefore not that of some misguided and overzealous Christian apologist, but one that finds its authority in the words of God the Son, and this is the reason why Christians are to listen to it.

Our Lord supplemented His discussion of these individuals when in the twenty-fourth chapter of Matthew Christ declared: "For there shall arise false Christs and false prophets, and shall show great signs and wonders; insomuch that, if it were possible, they shall deceive the very elect" (v. 24).

Further comment on this point is not necessary; He designated them "false Christs" and "false prophets"; it was He who prophesied that they would show great signs and wonders, and it was He who warned that if it were possible, the subtlety of their evil would deceive the very elect, or the church. Apparently our Savior thought it important enough to repeat, for in verse twenty-five He says, "Behold, I have told you before."

The apostle Paul, utilizing the identical language of the Lord Jesus Christ, succinctly phrases a divine warning concerning these same people.

For I have not shunned to declare unto you all the counsel of God. Take heed therefore unto yourselves, and to all the flock, over which the Holy Spirit hath made you overseers, to feed the church of God, which he hath purchased with his own blood. For I know this, that after my departing shall grievous wolves enter in among you, not sparing the flock. Also of your own selves shall men arise, speaking perverse things, to draw away disciples after them. Therefore watch, and remember, that by the space of three years I ceased not to warn every one night and day with tears (Acts 20:27–31).

It appears from this very pointed statement that Paul was not afraid "to declare unto you all the counsel of God." Indeed, the greatest of the apostles warns us to "take heed," and this is to involve not only ourselves but all Christians; and though it is addressed principally to pastors, it underlines the existence of "grievous wolves" about whom Paul says, "I ceased not to warn every one night and day with tears." Should not that which was important to him be as important to us for whom he intended it? It is of no small interest and importance that this charge of Paul to the Ephesian elders was taken very seriously by them, for in Revelation, chapter two, Christ commends the church at Ephesus

for heeding Paul, in that he "tried them which say they are apostles, and are not, and hast found them liars" (v. 2).

Paul, of course, made much mention of such persons elsewhere, describing them as "enemies of the cross of Christ" (Philippians 3:18) and "false apostles, deceitful workers, transforming themselves into the apostles of Christ" (2 Corinthians 11:13). He does not even hesitate to describe them as "Satan's ministers" (2 Corinthians 11:14–15). The first and second epistles to Timothy, also of Pauline authorship, reflect the same attitude: "Now the Spirit speaketh expressly, that in the latter times some shall depart from the faith, giving heed to seducing spirits, and doctrines of devils; speaking lies in hypocrisy; having their conscience seared with a hot iron" (1 Timothy 4:1–2).

The express speaking of the Spirit, of course, underscores the importance of the counsel given, and it is significant to observe that it is to take place in the "latter times," when men shall "depart from the faith," listen to "seducing spirits," and become captives of "the doctrines of demons." This is tremendously strong language in the original Greek and is followed by his counsel in the second epistle to "preach the Word" and to "reprove, rebuke, and exhort with all longsuffering and doctrine" those who in the time to come "will not endure sound doctrine; but after their own lusts shall heap to themselves teachers who shall tickle their ears; and the truth shall be turned into fables" (2 Timothy 4:3–4, from the Greek).

It is more than a casual coincidence that the apostle Peter acknowledges the authority of Christ and Paul by utilizing their very language: "But there were false prophets also among the people, even as there shall be false teachers among you, who privily shall bring in damnable heresies, even denying the Lord that bought them, and bring upon themselves swift destruction" (2 Peter 2:1).

For Peter, it appears "false prophets" were a distinct reality, "false teachers" not figments of overwrought fundamentalist imaginations, and "destructive heresies," which "denied the Lord that bought them," vivid dangers to be guarded against. As we approach the end of the New Testament, we find John, always noted for his doctrine of love, balancing that doctrine magnificently with the teaching of divine judgment upon those whom he describes as "false prophets ... gone out into the world" (1 John 4:1) and "deceivers ... entered into the world, who confess not that Jesus Christ is come in the flesh. This is a deceiver and an antichrist" (2 John 7).

The next to the last book in the Bible, the comparatively small epistle of Jude, is likewise in full agreement with the verdict of our Lord and the other apostles:

> Certain men crept in unawares, who were before of old ordained to this condemnation, ungodly men, turning the grace of our God into lasciviousness, and denying the only Lord God, and our Lord Jesus Christ. . . . These are spots in your feasts of charity . . . clouds they are without water, carried about of winds; trees whose fruit withereth, without fruit, twice dead, plucked up by the roots; raging waves of the sea, foaming out their own shame; wandering stars, to whom is reserved the blackness of darkness for ever (vv. 4, 12–13).

As we have noted, all of the quotations are in context, refer to the same individuals, and characterize them in an identical manner. The description is not pleasant, but it is a biblical one originating with God the Holy Spirit, not

with the so-called interpretational fancies or bigoted intolerances of unin-formed extremists. God used these terms for people He describes in His Word; God warns the church of Christ about their existence, their methods, their teachings, their subtleties, and their final judgment. The church neglects, at her peril, such divine counsel.

There are naturally some who will not agree with this position; they will quote the advice of Gamaliel, which he addressed to the Jews in the book of Acts (5:38–39). They, too, will say, "Let them alone: for if this counsel or this work be of men, it will come to nought: But if it be of God, ye cannot overthrow it; lest haply ye be found even to fight against God." The only difficulty, as we have noted earlier, is that the context clearly indicates the advice was given by Gam-aliel to the Jews, and Gamaliel was not an inspired writer, an apostle, or even a Christian. If his advice is to be followed and his criterion to be recognized, then the thriving growth of the various non-Christian cults, all of which deny the fun-damentals of the Christian faith, must be acknowledged as the work of God! No consistent thinker of Christian orientation could long entertain such a warped conclusion without doing violence to a great portion of the New Testament.

There are also others who, in their attempt to excuse themselves from meet-ing the challenge of the Jesus of the cults, will refer to the ninth verse of Jude where Michael the archangel, when contending with the devil, refused to argue with him but rather referred him to the Lord for rebuke. Once again, however, the context reveals that Michael did not keep silence by choice but by necessity because as the Greek so clearly reveals, "He did not dare bring against Satan a blasphemous judgment," for the simple reason that Satan was his superior in authority. The Greek word translated "durst" in our King James Bible carries the meaning of not doing something for fear of retaliation by a superior power (Greek: *etolmese*), so this line of reasoning also fails.

The reasons why we must answer as well as be prepared to evangelize such people are quite clear. The church must do it because Christ and the apostles commanded her to do so, unpopular though it may be, and to this all true Chris-tians should be unequivocally committed, for no other reason than out of re-spect for our Lord. Certainly if our mothers, wives, children, or country were attacked and misrepresented, our love for them would compel us to defend them. How much more should love for our Redeemer so motivate us in the defense of Him and His Gospel.

The Jesus of the cults is a poor substitute for the incarnate God of the New Testament. Along with the equally important imperative of cult evangelism stands the very real need to give to everyone that asks of us "a reason for the hope that is within us" (1 Peter 3:15). That hope is the Jesus of biblical theology and of history, and once we understand the true nature of the Jesus of the cults we can discharge our duty faithfully and by contrast unmask him and his creator for all to see. We may sum this up with the thought-provoking words of our Lord when with absolute finality He declared: "Behold, I have told you before" (Matthew 24:25).

Chapter 18

Cult Evangelism—
Mission Field on Your Doorstep

The last one hundred years of American history have seen the evangelization of large segments of the American populace to a degree never imagined by any evangelist in the history of Christianity.

Beginning with the evangelical emphasis of American frontier preachers and circuit riders, through the massive impact of D. L. Moody, Gypsy Smith, Billy Sunday, culminating in Billy Graham, and now the enormous "Harvest" crusades, American Christianity has enjoyed great spiritual privileges withheld from the world since the days of the Reformation and the Knox, Wesley, and White-field revivals so dear to the memory of church historians.

Yet there are many people today, in both the clergy and the ranks of the laity, who are seriously reevaluating the meaning of evangelism and its importance, if not to the church, at least to themselves. More and more, Christians are beginning to think in terms of *personal* evangelism as opposed to mass evangelism, primarily because all evangelism, since the earliest days of Christianity, that is, all *successful* evangelism of enduring worth, has been of a personal nature. While it is true that great evangelists draw crowds and preach to multitudes of people, they, too, are dependent upon the so-called "personal touch," as evidenced by the fact that Billy Graham has more than once attempted to remove the "tag line" from his *Hour of Decision* radio program, "The Lord bless you real good," only to have such attempts reversed by the constituency that, despite its size, still desires the feeling of a personal relationship.

The follow-up work of every major evangelical crusade must be on a personal basis to be effective. A stamped envelope and a short memory course are no substitute for the personal workers, whose on-the-spot faithfulness, patience, and perseverance builds up and edifies young converts after the first warm glow of the conversion experience has begun to abate.

This, of course, brings us to a consideration of the all-important question: What is evangelism? Is it merely mass rallies where so-called "wholesale" deci-

This chapter updated and edited by Gretchen Passantino.

sions for Christ are made? Is it, on the other hand, simply the task of the local church to shoulder the responsibility of having a week or two of meetings for revival and evangelistic purposes each year? By evangelism, do we mean massive emphasis on the part of radio and television to communicate the good news of redemption? Or, is evangelism somehow or other bound up with *all* of these forms of expression, and yet, in essence, none of them? Is it perhaps possible that evangelism was intended, in its primary purpose, to be personal and individualistic to the degree that each Christian feels the responsibility to evangelize his neighbor, and that this is really the root of the whole matter from which the tree of church evangelism and mass evangelism, both in crusades and the mass media, are to draw their strength and spiritual stamina? To answer these questions, and to place evangelism in its proper perspective where the challenge of non-Christian cults is concerned, we must consider carefully the pattern laid out for us in the New Testament.

Holding Forth the Word of Life

If anything proceeds from the pages of the New Testament, it is the message that the early Christian church labored under the magnificent obsession of the divine paradox. They were separate as individuals in each congregation, whether it was Ephesus, Corinth, Crete, or Philippi. But in some mysterious sense, they were "one body" in Christ (Ephesians 4:4). Through acceptance of the divine Redeemer, God had shattered and broken down the walls of race, color, and social status. They were no longer "Barbarian, Scythian, bond nor free: but Christ is all, and in all" (Colossians 3:11).

Each of these New Testament Christians was admonished by the Holy Spirit to be an ambassador or representative for his Savior (2 Corinthians 5:20). The apostle Paul set the supreme example of this in the New Testament church by declaring that the primary responsibility of the Christian was to preach the gospel (1 Corinthians 15:1–4), and it is precisely at this juncture that, if we are willing, we can understand the meaning of New Testament evangelism.

The Greek word translated *gospel* literally means "good news," as most Christians well know. But what many do not know is that the word translated *preach* comes from the Greek *evangelizomai,* which means "to publish" the gospel or declare it abroad for all the world to hear.

The early Christians considered themselves evangelists in that sense (1 Corinthians 1:17), and in the writings of Paul, Peter, John, and others, this great unalterable truth shines through. Christianity was not something only entrusted to clergymen, pastors, teachers, or professional evangelists, it was a personal message entrusted to those who had experienced the power of its transforming properties in their own lives, and who went literally from house to house and turned the world upside down because they were not ashamed to proclaim it. The early Christians went forth two by two. They went forth in the power of the resurrected Christ. They went forth with a message—a message based upon experience shared by all and an experience that strengthened and comforted all. These were not people who were preoccupied with the things of the world, with contemporary political intrigues or the reigns of the Caesars, with the showplaces of Ephesus and the coliseums of Rome. These were people

who were possessed by a Spirit totally removed from the spirit of the age in which they lived—a Spirit who commanded them to convict the world of sin, because though they had been its victims they were now its conquerors through their Redeemer.

The incredible zeal with which they proclaimed this message of the living Christ, the Gospel of the Resurrection, the certainty of sins forgiven, the present possession of peace with God, exerted an awesome influence and power over the minds of those with whom they came in contact, almost without exception. The Philippian jailer abused Paul and Silas until he experienced the presence of their Master. Then he, too, with his whole house, believed the incredible. Sergius Paulus, beset though he was by a demonic medium who sought to pervert the gospel and turn him away from the faith of Christ, was stunned by the authority of a man filled with the Holy Spirit. Saul, who was also called Paul, persecuted the church with blind zeal, and yet when he encountered the risen Christ, his amazement turned to faith and he embraced life eternal. Even those who resisted the magnificence of New Testament evangelism were frightened by its clarity and power and felt even as Festus, who raved at the apostle Paul, "Paul, thou art beside thyself; much learning doth make thee mad" (Acts 26:24). Agrippa the king could not be dissuaded even by the remarks of Festus, but withdrew from the presence of the Holy Spirit with the trembling admission, "Almost thou persuadest me to be a Christian" (Acts 26:28).

All of these evangelists had three things in common. First, they had experienced the person of the risen Christ and had passed out of death into life. Second, they were dominated by the Holy Spirit, alien to this world because the world does not know Him and cannot receive Him, because the world is evil and He is God. Third, they obeyed the injunction of the apostles and as ambassadors for Christ fearlessly published the Good News that Light had come into the world, and that God had indeed appointed a day in which He would judge the world in righteousness by the man whom He had ordained and given assurance to all men by raising Him from the dead.

It is not difficult to see why the Christians of the first century were able to spread Christianity throughout the earth without the aid of radio, television, traveling caravan, precision crusades, or yearly evangelistic and revival meetings. Every day was an evangelistic campaign for them; every service a revival meeting; every road a path to someone who needed Christ; every house a dwelling place for those for whom He died. These were people who were evangelists in the full meaning of the term as God had intended and commanded it. They rose to the challenge with a supreme confidence and conviction born of experience and faith, which, despite their limitations and human frailties, made them worthy of the name "saints." They could do all this because they had truly found Him "of whom Moses in the law, and in the prophets, did write, Jesus of Nazareth" (John 1:45), and they had believed Him that "where two or three are gathered together in my name, there am I in the midst of them" (Matthew 18:20).

If we want to have evangelism in the true biblical sense of the term, we must return to the content of the evangel and to the methods of the New Testament church. We must utilize every modern method possible, but we must not allow them to overshadow or interfere with the great personal responsibility that rests

upon every Christian. For in that very real and personal sense, it is true of us as it was of the apostle Paul, "For Christ sent me not to baptize, but to preach the gospel" (1 Corinthians 1:17).

The Philippian Christians were admonished by the apostle Paul to "shine as lights in the world; holding forth the word of life" (2:15–16). This they could do only by being willing to shine in contrast to the darkness that surrounded them and by being willing to stand in the defense of the gospel as they held forth the word of life.

We are told in the simplest terms that the gospel is God's power unto salvation (Romans 1:16), but what *is* that gospel?

The apostle Paul states it for us in what might be called a capsule version. When writing to the Corinthians he said:

> For I delivered unto you first of all that which I received, how that Christ died for our sins according to the scriptures; and that he was buried, and that he rose again the third day according to the scriptures (1 Corinthians 15:3–4).

The very usage of the word Christ in the Pauline theology identifies the office of the Anointed One with that of the second person of the Trinity, He who is God "over all, God blessed for ever. Amen" (Romans 9:5, from the Greek).

Paul does not, however, stop at this, but goes on to point out that Christ died for our sins, that is, in our place, even though we deserved to die as a just payment for our sinful natures and our own sins, a clear statement of the substitutionary atonement of the Cross. Then he concludes with "He rose again the third day," which in the context of 1 Corinthians 15 can only refer to a bodily resurrection (Luke 24:39ff.).

We can see then that the content of the gospel is, at its very minimum, the deity of Christ, the substitutionary atonement of the Cross, and His bodily resurrection from the grave. This good news, when enunciated and published fearlessly by believers, has the effect of convicting men of their sins and leading them to true repentance toward God and faith in the Lord Jesus Christ. J. I. Packer, in his stimulating book *Evangelism and the Sovereignty of God*, has put it this way:

> What was this Good News Paul preached? It was the news about Jesus of Nazareth. It was the news of the incarnation, the atonement, the kingdom, the cradle, the cross and the crown of the Son of God. It was the news of how God glorified His Servant, Jesus, by making Him Christ, the world's long-awaited Prince and Savior. It was the news of how God made His Son man, and how as man, God made Him Priest and Prophet and King, and how as Priest, God also made Him a sacrifice for sins, and how as a Prophet, God also made Him a lawgiver to His people, and how as King, God has also made Him Judge of all the world, and given Him prerogatives, which in the Old Testament are exclusively Jehovah's own—namely to reign until every knee bows before Him, and to save all who call on His Name. In short, the good news was just this, that God has executed His eternal intention of glorifying His Son by exalting Him as the great Savior for great sinners. Such was the Gospel which Paul was sent to preach; it was a message of some complexity, needing to be learned before it could be lived by, understood before it could be applied, and needed therefore to be taught. Hence Paul, as a preacher of it, had to become a teacher. He saw this as part of his calling; he speaks of "the Gospel whereunto I am appointed a preacher . . .

and a teacher" (2 Timothy 1:10ff).[1]

The impact of Packer's statement has lost nothing over the years. It has never been more true that the claims of Christ are the defining issues of salvation and eternal life. What *has* changed is that the average person's understanding of religious terms and ideas is even more abysmal than it was more than twenty years ago. Today most Americans have little or no religious upbringing at all. Young adults and teenagers have likely *never* been inside a church, never heard the gospel presented to them simply and clearly, and have no clue as to what terms such as "righteousness," "atonement," "sin," "sacrifice," "repentance," "salvation," or "born again" mean. Those individuals who have grown up outside the church and are still not believers suffer this ignorance almost universally. It is truly tragic that even people who grow up in a Christian environment, or who have become Christians as adults, all too often are almost as ignorant of the vocabulary and meaning of Christian teaching as others.

The average American is spiritually illiterate, and even American Christians are woefully undereducated. Christians must learn the vocabulary and the teachings of biblical faith, and must have a strong commitment to learning how to share that faith simply, clearly, and persuasively—with other non-Christians as well as cultists. It is not self-esteem, support groups, or Christian bicycling clubs that will bring the light of the gospel to those lost in the darkness of cultic heresies. "The *gospel* . . . is the power of God unto salvation" (Romans 1:16, emphasis added).

Evangelism has content as well as zeal, courage, and an attitude of constant prayer-distinct methods of propagation.

Techniques of Cult Evangelism

It is the testimony of the Word of God that He has raised up the Gentile nations and made available to them the gospel of the kingdom and its messianic King, which Israel rejected because of unbelief. The Scriptures declare that the purpose of God in doing this is to "provoke them to jealousy" (Romans 11:11) that they may perceive what they have lost and repent, that the natural olive branch may be grafted in again, whereas now, only the wild branch (Gentiles) shares the blessing of Messiah's covenant and coming kingdom.

In the kingdom of the cults today, however, we are witnessing something akin to this and yet, despite its corrupt purposes, progressing at an alarming rate of speed. We see the various cult systems, specifically Jehovah's Witnesses, Mormonism, Unity, etc. utilizing the methods of Christianity and of New Testament propagation of the Christian message, wooing converts from professing Christian fellowships, Protestant as well as Roman Catholic. This bewildering proselytizing has caused consternation in many Protestant and Roman Catholic parishes across America and abroad and it is accelerating, not slowing down. Is it the judgment of God upon the Christian church because of her lethargy? Forces of darkness are succeeding with the methods of light while denying the true Light. In order that we may offset the ever-widening circle of cultic influ-

---

[1]James I. Packer, *Evangelism and the Sovereignty of God* (Downers Grove, Ill.: InterVarsity Press, 1975), 47.

ence, Christians must first of all face the fact that we have been woefully delin-
quent in the exercise of our responsibility to evangelize.

Many Christians have taken for granted the great doctrines of the Bible that
they learned and accepted at their conversion. They have not studied to show
themselves "approved unto God, a workman that needeth not to be ashamed,
rightly dividing the word of truth" (2 Timothy 2:15).

The average Christian knows *what* he believes, but is unable to articulate
why he believes, insofar as being able to document the *why* of his belief from the
Scriptures, which he frequently finds a frustrating and exasperating task. The
clergy is largely at fault in this respect because they often settle for an evangelistic emphasis, without doctrinal teaching.

A survey was taken in the Department of Biblical Studies at King's College.
Of some three hundred students polled, fewer than ten had heard a sermon in
the last four years in their respective churches on the doctrines of the Trinity,
the deity and humanity of Jesus Christ, or the relationship of grace and faith to
works. Similar surveys have been conducted in colleges, seminaries, and Bible
institutes in many major cities throughout the country. The result has been almost identical. There *must* be something fundamentally wrong when important
areas of doctrine such as these are neglected or glossed over lightly.

The various cult systems, particularly Jehovah's Witnesses and the Mormons, capitalize on these conditions. Many an embarrassed Christian rushes to
the telephone when he has a Jehovah's Witness "minister" or Mormon "elder"
in his living room to get answers from a generally overworked pastor, when a
little consistent study of the Scriptures on his own would have given him the
confidence to speak a word of personal evangelism to the cultist.

Throughout the world today, Christian missionaries proclaim the unsearch-
able riches of the gospel. Perhaps due to the large funds made available for
world missions in the last one hundred years in the United States, a good many
Christians have become lethargic and apathetic as to their own personal responsibility toward proclaiming the gospel of Christ here at home. They have
given to foreign missions. And they don't see evangelism as something needed
in the United States. Additionally, ministers are discovering their congregations
are dwindling at prayer meetings and Sunday evening services. Television and
other extracurricular social activities have often taken their place.

As we have shown in the preceding chapters, the non-Christian cult systems
in America have grown tremendously in the last one hundred years. By a subtle
utilization of a redefined terminology coupled with a surface knowledge of the
Bible, and encouraged by the fact that a great many Christians are unable to
answer their perversions (a fact which serves to confirm them even more definitely in those deviations), the zeal and missionary activities of the cults have
tremendously increased. The only way to offset this is by a return to positive
Christian evangelism on the fiercely personal basis of door-to-door and neigh-
bor-to-neighbor effort whenever the opportunity presents itself. But over and
beyond this, it is time that the church of Jesus Christ begins to consider the cults
themselves as a mission field—a mission field on the doorstep of the church
wherever she exists in the world, both at home and abroad.

The explosion of technology and information systems during the last
decades of this millennium have rendered cult evangelism and recruitment

more prolific than anyone could have imagined. The proliferation of the Internet has made hundreds of thousands of alternative belief systems as accessible as one's desktop computer and telephone. The simplicity of personal computer operation combined with its amazingly sophisticated capabilities has turned the publishing world upside down, including the ability of cults to publish their false gospels. As alarming as this development is, it also brings us a fresh hope for effective, widespread communication of the gospel. The same advances that enable the cults to evangelize so effectively can and should be used by Christians to proclaim the *truth* of the gospel as evidenced by Jesus Christ and His resurrection from the dead (1 Corinthians 15:1-4). There is no excuse for those who bemoan cultic multiplication through technology. Instead of complaining about it, the committed Christian will support biblical evangelism in any of its missionary forms—including electronics.

This is by no means an impossible task. The last thirty plus years of the writer's life was spent largely in this field and confirmed his opinion that cultists too can be reached with the gospel. They are part of the world that God so loved that He sent His only begotten Son to redeem.

Precisely how we may implement the evangelization of cultists is an important and vital subject about which nothing has been written, comparatively speaking, in the last century and which today presents an ever-expanding challenge to the Christian. We, too, must obey, as did the apostle Paul, the command to publish the Good News and to pick up our credentials as ambassadors for Christ and present them to those who would evangelize *us* with a gospel other than that which the New Testament proclaims.

The following techniques and observations would be useful in any genuine Christian effort to evangelize cultists, when they are offered not as a panacea to the problem but as a tested means toward the end of bringing cultists to personal faith in Jesus Christ. This is the object of all true evangelism in any century.

1. The Human Element

One of the first things that confronts a Christian as he attempts to evangelize a cultist is the psychological barrier that exists in the minds of a great many persons, to the effect that cultists must be a special breed of individuals impervious to standard techniques of evangelism and generally well enough versed in the Bible to confuse, if not convince, the average Christian.

While there is an element of truth in both of these statements, it is generally traceable to experiences the Christian has had personally, either directly or indirectly, with cultists, or to those encounters with cultists in which the Christians did not fare so well. In fact, in not a few instances, they have been routed, frustrated, and embarrassed. This generally brings a tendency toward reticence, lest there be a repeat performance.

In the late 1970s and early 1980s a new form of "cult evangelism" became increasingly popular. Called "deprogramming" first and then "exit counseling," this method assumed that cultists were victims of nearly irresistible, invincible "mind control" or "brainwashing" by cult leaders. This approach is especially appealing to secular sociologists and psychologists, since it completely avoids any mention of "truth or falsity," "good or evil," "biblical or heretical."

It makes the cultist not responsible for his cult membership, the gospel extraneous, and the solution a social reorientation rather than salvation by grace alone through faith. This issue is discussed comprehensively in chapter 4, "Critiquing Cult Mind-Control Model."

The second explanation for this phenomenon is the seemingly implanted fear that cultists should not be permitted to enter the Christian's home, in the light of 2 John 10:

> If there come any unto you, and bring not this doctrine, receive him not into your house, neither bid him God speed.

Now, in context, this passage is a sentence in a letter to the elect lady, in whose home a Christian church quite obviously met, as the early church was prone to do, there being no cathedrals or modern churches such as we know them today. In this connection, a very common one (see Philemon 2), John warns her not to allow anyone to preach in church meetings or teach doctrines that do not honor Christ in every aspect of His person, nature, and work. It is clear that he is referring to false teachers being given a voice in the church, not to a cultist sitting in your living room! That the passage cannot be taken literally in that connection is quite evident, because if a twentieth-century Christian's plumbing froze when the weather was twenty degrees below zero and his cellar was rapidly flooding with water, he would not dream of asking the plumber who came over at 2:00 A.M. to fix the pipes whether he "brought the doctrine of Christ" to his home. Rather, such a question would never enter his mind. Yet the plumber might be a Unitarian, Mormon, or a Jehovah's Witness! Doubtless, Christians have had them in their homes, fixing their plumbing, electricity, or oil burners, and never once inquired of their views concerning the doctrine of Christ. Yet some Christians who utilize 2 John 10 as an excuse for not evangelizing cultists would never dream of using it if the cultist were a plumber.

Many pastors have instructed their flocks on the basis of this passage and other out-of-context quotations to close the doors in the faces of cultists rather than to invite them in and, in the tradition of Christian evangelism, confront them with the claims of Christ. There is no authority in the Word of God for neglecting one's responsibility as an ambassador of Christ, and the cults do not constitute a special category of evangelism.

Another reason is that many Christians (and, sadly, many Christian pastors and churches) have swallowed the secular lie that it is wrong to criticize any religious belief. This view is based on the wrong assumption that religious belief or faith is inherently irrational and untestable, hence, any religious belief is just as "good" or "true" as any other belief. There was a time when the word "tolerance" meant an open-mindedness and respect that allowed for rational exploration and evaluation of differing beliefs and ideas. In today's age of "political correctness," tolerance has come to mean a complete *lack* of evaluation and, instead, an irrational embracing of all ideas and all beliefs as equal. Christians must never forget the admonition of 1 Thessalonians 5:21–22: "Prove all things; hold fast that which is good. Abstain from all appearance of evil." Nor should we forget Paul's comparable words to Timothy: "Keep that which is committed to thy trust, avoiding profane and vain babblings, and oppositions of science [*contradictions*] falsely so called" (1 Timothy 6:20). The prophet Isaiah warned,

"Woe unto them that call evil good, and good evil; that put darkness for light, and light for darkness; that put bitter for sweet, and sweet for bitter! Woe unto them who are wise in their own eyes, and prudent in their own sight!" (Isaiah 5:20–21).

The Christian is probably right in assuming that the average cultist does have a working knowledge of the Bible. Most of them are quite diligent in their study, both of their own literature and that of the Scriptures. And it may be true that the well-trained cultist may appear to be impervious to the proclamation of the gospel and its defense (when necessary). But that he is some special species of unbeliever in whose presence the Christian must remain mute and the Holy Spirit impotent is a gross misconception and should be abandoned by all thinking Christians.

We *must* strive to keep foremost in our minds that cultists are precious souls for whom Jesus Christ offered himself, and that they are human beings who have homes, families, friends, emotions, needs, ambitions, fears, and frustrations, which all men have in common. The cultist is special in only one sense, that he is already "deeply religious," and therefore, probably one of the most difficult persons in the world to reach with the gospel of Christ. He has rejected historical Christianity and entertains in most cases hostility, if not active antagonism, toward its message. The cultist, therefore, considers evangelical Christians his greatest potential, if not actual, adversaries. Hence, an attitude of tolerance and love should always be manifested by the Christian to relieve, where possible, this tension and the hostile feelings of the cult adherent.

The technique of "setting the cultist at ease" takes a great deal of patience, for the individual cultist firmly believes that he has found "the truth." He often considers the Christian message to be inferior to his own revelation. This fact is generally reflected in his attitude of superiority and even genuine resentment when the gospel is presented. This resentment may take many forms, but it always conforms to the general thrust that since he has found the truth, how can the Christian dare to attempt to convert *him*? Cultists believe they already have progressed far beyond the evangelical Christian stage or station on the "religious railroad track" through their special revelations and superior experiences with God.

According to one psychologist, cultists transfer their antagonism for the theology of historical Christianity to those who propagate its message, thus identifying the belief with the individual and personalizing the controversy. If the Christian who is interested in evangelizing cultists would realize this fact at the outset, he could seek to make a careful distinction between the theology of Christianity and the personalities of individual Christians, thereby allowing the cultist to see the Christian as a redeemed personality, independent of his theological structure. This could make possible a forum for objective discussion of biblical truth, subject to the categories of analysis, logical consistency, context, and exegesis.

While this may not necessarily undercut any portion of the cultist's theological system, it will break down or assist in breaking down the psychological conditioning of the cultist to the attitude that any person who disagrees with *his* interpretation of Christianity is automatically an object of antagonism.

In approaching the problem of cult evangelism, it must be remembered

that cultists, in their respective systems of theology, are almost always by nature dependent upon either forms, ceremonies, rituals, good works, right living, or self-sacrifice as a means of pleasing God and obtaining justification. Fundamentally, cultism is a form of self-salvation, emphasizing deliverance from sin through human effort or merit in cooperation with their concept of the personality of the Deity.

The Christian must, therefore, in the light of this fact, point out from Scripture (since most cults recognize it as authoritative or at least partially binding), the folly of self-justification, righteousness, or human effort as a means of obtaining redemption. We should always remember that repentance, atonement, regeneration, resurrection, and retribution in the biblical sense is seldom part of the cultist's vocabulary, and *never* of his personal experience. The Christian must *define*, *apply*, and *defend* the historical meanings of these terms, before it is possible to effectively proclaim the gospel. In a word, one must begin at the beginning, repeat, emphasize, and repeat. This is the sowing of seed that one day, by God's grace alone, will bear fruit to eternal life.

Adherents of the cults are constituted, psychologically speaking, so that they are, almost always, victims of what might be termed a mass delusion of grandeur coupled with a dogged sense of personal pride. As the Scripture records that Satan fell from his first estate through measureless pride (Isaiah 14:12–14), so also today he uses the same weaknesses of the human character as a tool in shaping cult adherents to his own ends. This pride is evident in most cultists, and contributes to the delusion that they are the possessors of the true faith that saves, guardians and defenders of that which is alone holy, and administrators of divine revelation to the mass of mankind who are enmeshed in a Christianity that all cultists agree has been perverted by theologians and philosophers, thus necessitating the true restoration of the gospel through their efforts.

It has been the writer's experience that almost all cultists suffer from the concept that his or her group will at last emerge victorious over all its adversaries, inherit an eternal kingdom, and have the pleasure of viewing its being either tormented or destroyed. Such cultists cling to an illusion of impending and imminent majesty or greatness, which, when linked with their intrinsic concepts of human ability and supposed merit before God, leads to mass delusion and spiritual darkness of the most terrible nature imaginable.

The task of the Christian evangelist is to tactfully reveal the true nature of man as Scripture portrays him. And in a spirit of deep concern and practice of earnest prayer, reveal to the cultist God's view of fallen man and the certain destiny of those who follow in the pride-filled footsteps of Lucifer, "the god of this world" (2 Corinthians 4:4).

The nature of cultists is to be on the defensive, for they are acutely aware of the lack of unity and brotherly love clearly evidenced in many reputedly evangelical movements. They know that evangelicals are united, insofar as the cultist is concerned, only in their opposition to *him*. They, therefore, lay much stress upon the various divisions in orthodox circles, not to mention the lack of clarity where the cardinal doctrines of the Christian faith are concerned. They apparently never tire of stating, "At least we are united; you are divided, even in your own groups." It is this type of accusation that cuts the true Christian deeply. He must answer this charge by admitting differences of opinion on minor issues,

but emphasizing solidarity on the fundamentals of the gospel, which all cultists deny in one form or another.

The Christian must never forget that a well-trained cultist can be a powerful opponent, adept at text-lifting, term-switching, and surprise interpretations of "proof texts." He should be on guard constantly lest he be deceived into admitting something that will later be utilized against him and to the detriment of both the gospel and his personal witness.

2. Common Ground

Before attempting to evangelize a cultist, the Christian should, whenever possible, find a common ground of understanding (preferably the inspiration and authority of the Scriptures or the nature and attributes of God), and work from that point onward. Christian workers must, in effect, become all things to all men that we might by all means save some (1 Corinthians 9:22). The Christian cannot afford to have a superiority complex or reflect the idea that he is redeemed and the cultist is lost. Redemption of the soul is a priceless gift from God and should be coveted in all humility, not superiority, as just that—a gift—unearned and unmerited, and solely the result of sovereign grace.

For any sane approach to the problem of cult evangelism, the necessity of a common ground cannot be overemphasized. Unless some place of agreement, some starting point be mutually accepted by both parties, the discussion can only lead to argument, charges, counter-charges, rank bitterness, and, in the end, the loss of opportunity for further witness; and the soul of the cultist could be forfeited! Friendliness, then—open and free manifestation of Christian love and a willingness to talk over the points of diversions—will go a long way toward allaying the suspicion of the average cultist and open further vistas for profitable and effective witnessing.

Throughout all of this, the Christian should be governed by increased activity in his prayer life, praying wherever possible in the presence of, and with, cultists, so that through the prayers that are uttered, the cultist may sense the relationship of the Christian to Him who is the Father of spirits, and our Father by faith in Jesus Christ.

3. Subliminal Seeding

The advertising industry of America has pioneered in motivational research and has taught us that ideas may be implanted in our minds beneath the level of consciousness or conscious awareness, and that they are dutifully recorded and do in no small measure influence our thinking and actions. Jingles sung on the radio and television quite often motivate people to purchase the product about which the jingle chants.

Christians who wish to evangelize cultists can profit from the findings of such motivational research into subliminal suggestion to an amazing degree.

It is our conviction that the Word of God and prayer, addressed to Him through the Holy Spirit, is the most powerful motivating force in the universe, and can be subliminally utilized in cult evangelism by the implantation of seed thoughts about the gospel of Christ.

How this may be done is best illustrated by examples drawn from the writer's own experiences.

Jehovah's Witnesses are probably the most active and zealous of all the missionaries of cultism in America today. When called upon by Jehovah's Witnesses, the writer for many years employed the following approach with great success.

I would invite the Watchtower adherent or adherents into the living room, but before they had opportunity to speak concerning their literature, I would state that I never discussed religion or the Bible unless such a discussion was preceded by prayer, to which all present agreed. I would then quickly bow my head and address the Lord as Jehovah God. One must be particularly careful in dealing with Jehovah's Witnesses, to always address the Deity by the name Jehovah, or else the Witnesses may not pray or bow their heads. Instead, they will admire the bric-a-brac, thumb through their Bibles, reach for their briefcases, and generally keep occupied until you have completed your prayer. Should the reader be interested in knowing how I learned this, I must confess that, on occasion—I peeked!

When the name of Jehovah is being used, the average Watchtower adherent will immediately bow his head, and after you have finished praying and *before* they can pray, begin the conversation by saying, "Now what was it that you wanted to discuss?"

Always keep in mind in dealing with Jehovah's Witnesses, that they come equipped with a portable arsenal in the form of a briefcase, which contains the major publications of the Watchtower Society for their handy reference. At the outset you must insist that they use nothing but the Scripture and that it must be a recognized translation (King James, Revised Standard Version, New International, New American Standard, etc.). You must further insist upon a discussion of cardinal doctrines, particularly concerning the person, nature, and work of Jesus Christ. Thus deprived of his Watchtower material and his Watchtower translations and circumscribed to the person of Christ in discussion, even the best trained Jehovah's Witness is at a distinct disadvantage. On the other hand, the Christian who is indwelt by the Holy Spirit then has a definite advantage.

After the discussion had gone on for some time, and I had listened to as much of "Pastor" Russell's theology as I could tolerate for one evening, I would remind the Witnesses of the lateness of the hour and asked if we couldn't close with a word of prayer. I would then immediately bow my head and begin praying again.

Now what I have mentioned is, by itself, only an outline of how to conduct one's self in the presence of Jehovah's Witnesses, with one important exception. During my opening and closing prayers I would totally preach the gospel, emphasizing the deity of Christ, His death for our sins, the certainty of knowing that we have eternal life *now*, by faith in Him, and that salvation comes by grace alone, independent of human works. I would profusely quote the Scriptures, and in actuality be preaching a three-minute sermonette, subliminally implanting the true Gospel of Jesus Christ and, I might add, blissfully uninterrupted. For no one, not even the most zealous disciple of "Pastor" Russell, Joseph Smith, or Brigham Young, can interrupt a prayer. I have seen such a methodology or technique of evangelism make a tremendous impact upon Jehovah's Witnesses and other cultists, because, for six minutes of the evening at least, the

Christian has the opportunity to present the true Gospel of Christ without interruption.

We must believe that God's Word will not return unto Him void, but will accomplish what He pleases and prosper in the thing whereto He has sent it (Isaiah 55:11).

4. The Vocabulary of Redemption

Non-Christian cultists of all varieties are prone to one psychological and spiritual insecurity. They are all aware of the fact that they do not *now* possess eternal life or peace with God. In fact, it is toward this end that they are vigorously pursuing the theology and practices of their respective systems.

There can never be a substitute, therefore, for an individual Christian's personal witness to what Christ has done for him. A word of caution, however, must be inserted at this juncture. As we know, cultists have their own vocabulary, so it will be necessary for the Christian to define carefully his terms when he speaks of conversion—its means and its effect upon his spirit, mind, and life. The only really unanswerable argument is the argument of a transformed life, properly grounded in the authority of the Scriptures and motivated by love for God and for one's fellow man. Key terms that must be carefully defined are: new birth or "born again"; justification; atonement; deity and resurrection of Christ; resurrection; forgiveness; grace; and faith. It is inevitable that eternal retribution be discussed, because this is the very thing from which Christ died to save us.

The Scriptures admonish us to be "His witnesses," and in order to do this we must be willing to endure all things and be governed by patience, temperance, grace, and love. Then regardless of how the truth of God be assailed, perverted, or distorted, and no matter how much our own characters and motives are attacked, Christ will be honored by our conduct.

The vocabulary of redemption involves personal involvement, testimony to the effect of Christ's power both to redeem the soul and to transform the individual, his morals, his ethics, his life. And, most of all, it involves the power to impart to him the peace of God that passes all understanding, the peace that Christ said would come only to those who made peace with God (Philippians 4:7).

5. The Secret of Perseverance

One of the most important techniques of cult evangelism is that of perseverance with cultists. Anyone who has ever worked extensively in the field of cults will readily testify that this takes a great deal of grace and understanding on the part of the Christian. Many times cultists will deliberately "bait" Christians (particularly Jehovah's Witnesses and the Mormons) in an attempt to provoke the Christian into losing his patience, thus justifying their own teachings. In order to avoid such pitfalls and to be able to endure the many forms of abuse and persecution, which will come about when a Christian penetrates the theology of the cultist with the sword of the Spirit, one must have discovered a secret that, when prayerfully understood and applied, can make the endurance of *anything*, for the sake of Christ, possible.

If one were attacked, severely assaulted, and abused by a frightened blind man who mistook you for an attacker, it would be possible not only to forgive him but even persevere to the end of loving him, despite his actions. For, after all, both reason and logic argue he *is* blind and, in a sense, not responsible for his actions.

We are forever in debt to the apostle Paul, who pointed out in his second letter to the Corinthians that those who are outside of Christ have indeed been spiritually blinded by the god of this age. Satan has caused a cloak of *delusion* to descend over their minds and understandings, so that Christ's gospel, which is the light of the world, cannot penetrate to them. The secret of perseverance is to know and to understand, regardless of what a cultist says or does, that he is doing it out of spiritual blindness. Since our warfare as Christians is not against flesh and blood (the cultist), but against the spiritual forces of darkness that rule this world (Satan and his emissaries), it is possible to love the cultist, endure his abuses, perversions, and recriminations, while at the same time faithfully bearing witness for Christ.

This technique of cult evangelism should never be minimized. And once it is properly appreciated, it can become a great asset to the Christian. The words of Paul to Timothy explain the Christian's mission in this regard: "And the servant of the Lord must not strive; but be gentle unto all men, apt to teach, patient, in meekness instructing those that oppose themselves; if God peradventure will give them repentance to the acknowledging of the truth; and that they may recover themselves out of the snare of the devil, who are taken captive by him at his will" (2 Timothy 2:24–26).

There are doubtless many more things that could be mentioned in connection with cult evangelism. We might also profitably note that in dealing with religions that have had their origin outside the United States (Baha'ism, Theosophy, Zen, etc.), the Christian ought to have a working knowledge of what the doctrines of these cults are in relation to the historical Christian revelation. It is foolish to attempt to discuss Christian doctrines with those who do not accept the authority of the Scriptures, which is most certainly the case in regard to the three cults just mentioned.

Finally, evangelism, particularly cult evangelism, must never fail to emphasize that Christ and the disciples taught certain irrevocable doctrines as well as consistent ethics and morality.

It has been the experience of the author, based upon numerous personal contacts with cultists of all varieties, that there has yet to be found a cultist who can confuse, confound, or in any way refute a Christian who has made doctrinal theology an integral part of his study of the Scriptures. Cults thrive upon ignorance and confusion where the doctrines of the Scriptures are concerned, but are powerless to shake Christians in their faith or effectively proselytize them when the Christian is well grounded in the basic teachings of the Bible and given over to a study of the great doctrinal truths of the Word of God. These mighty buttresses of Christian theology must no longer be taken for granted by Christian believers, nor should pastors and teachers assume that the average Christian has sound knowledge concerning them. The rise of cultism to its present proportions indicates a great dearth of knowledge where doctrine is involved, and is a decided weakness in the battlements of orthodox theology, which the

church ignores at the risk of innumerable souls.

Accepting the fact that the poison of cultism can be effectively combated only by the antidote of sound doctrine, the next problem is the immunization of Christians against the teachings of the cults. The answer to this problem lies within the pages of God's Word; it involves study (2 Timothy 2:15) on the part of Christians, instruction on the part of the pastor and teacher (1 Timothy 4:1–6), coupled with a willingness to start at the beginning where sound doctrine is concerned, even as the risen Christ did with the doubting disciples, and to reexamine the reason *why* Christians believe what they believe. Particularly recommended for intensive study are the doctrines of biblical inspiration, the Trinity, deity of Christ, personality and work of the Holy Spirit, the Atonement, justification by faith, works, the bodily resurrection of Christ, and the resurrection of all mankind.

The great and true Trinitarian doctrine of God and the deity of Jesus Christ should be inculcated ceaselessly in Christian minds so that the Lord's people may never forget that Jesus Christ is the core of God's plan for the ages. The fact that He vicariously died and bodily arose, thus vindicating His claim to deity through obedience to the righteous character of both His Father's will and law, both of which He perfectly fulfilled at Calvary, must be perpetually emphasized.

It is a well-known fact that no antidote for poison is effective unless it is administered in time and in the proper dosage prescribed by a competent physician. In like manner, Christian doctrine should not be taught in a dry, matter-of-fact way, as it so often is, but should be given in small doses over a long period. The treatment should begin at once, from the Sunday school level right through college and seminary where the need is urgent.

Christians must realize while the opportunity is yet ours that the teaching of sound doctrine does not predicate a dead orthodoxy. When properly understood, a living acceptance of and familiarity with doctrine form the giant pillars of truth upon which our faith rests, a familiarity that has always produced great leaders and effective workers for the proclamation of the Gospel of grace.

The evangelization of cultists is the task of the Christian church of which each Christian is a member, a part of the body of Christ. Until this is recognized, and Christians are urged and encouraged by their pastors and leaders to forsake the portals of Hollywood and the domain of the great god, Television, for door-to-door publishing of the Good News of God's love in Jesus Christ for a lost world, the evangelization of cultists will continue to be one of the great tragedies of the Christian church in our day. It is excellent that we support foreign missions and send the light of God's Gospel around the globe, but it is quite another thing for us to begin here, where the demand is personal, challenging, and equally rewarding. This challenge is cult evangelism—the mission field on *your* doorstep.

Chapter 19

The Road to Recovery

Editor's Note:

Walter Martin first proposed the following projects in 1960, upon the founding of the Christian Research Institute, the largest and oldest cult apologetics and evangelism organization in the world. His foresight almost forty years ago gives these recommendations a poignancy and urgency that are remarkable.

Of particular note is Dr. Martin's vision, in project number two, for the use of a computer-based research program. He saw the gigantic, building-sized mainframe computers of major universities as the satellite repositories of apologetics research by which individuals could access needed information by subscription and return mail. At the time of the original announcement of his plans, most people rejected it as a Jules Verne fantasy that would never see fruition.

The primary source of research at that time was by means of old-fashioned legwork, painstaking firsthand interviews of cult leaders, accumulation of cultic literature by on-site visits to cult meetings and headquarters, and careful perusal of dusty records, files, and books in specialized archives. The few Christians who had committed their lives to researching, writing about, and evangelizing the cults worked in relative isolation, not only from each other but from most other full-time Christian workers, pastors, educators, and missionaries. Records were carefully typed with carbon copies and kept in banks of filing cabinets.

Four decades later the entire face of Christian cult apologetics has changed. Nowhere is this more evident than in the almost unimaginable reaches of the worldwide Internet computer information system. The electronic explosion of the 1980s and 1990s has transformed research, evaluation, publication, and evangelism in the field of cult apologetics. Contemporary electronic developments not only have enabled cults to publish their heresies in unprecedented quantity; these developments also have enabled cult apologetics researchers to track and research those same cultic movements.[1]

This chapter updated and edited by Gretchen Passantino.

---

[1] The Internet is an invaluable contemporary tool for amassing statistical information about various heretical movements. Most groups, even small ones with elite membership restrictions, have at least

When the relatively obscure and very small UFO cult Heaven's Gate ended its more than twenty-year existence by the suicide of its leader and thirty-eight members in March 1997, those few researchers who had seen cult apologetics develop over the decades participated in a remarkable fusion of the old methods and the new technology. Within a few short hours of the discovery of the tragedy, the Christian Research Institute and other Christian cult apologetics organizations were able to access voluminous information from the Internet on the Heaven's Gate cult, their commercial computer software business, their theology, their fascination with the Hale-Bopp Comet and extra-terrestrials, the identity and claims of their leader, Marshall Applewhite, and their fatal destiny. At the same time, those who had worked in the field for decades hunted throughout memories and dusty filing cabinets for the yellowed newspaper clippings, faded flyers, and handwritten notes from our earlier research and evangelism encounters with the group in the mid-1970s.

At the end of the century, what had been mocked as delusion is now a reality through the Christian Research Institute Internet World Wide Web site, www.equip.org. Anyone with a personal computer and a telephone can access the resources of CRI with a simple phone call and a few keystrokes. The Bible Answer Man *radio broadcast, heard daily on more than one hundred stations nationwide, and in Canada by satellite, is also available, live, through the Internet to anyone with a computer connection. Through the resources of CRI and other cult apologetics organizations easily contacted via Internet, answers to the cults have never been so easily available to Christians everywhere. Whether a Christian is evangelizing a Mormon, protesting a public school antireligious policy, testing the doctrines of a new church, or researching a world religion, the answers are available through computers as small and almost as light as a notebook, right in one's own home.*

It is sad that the same five projects Dr. Martin outlined so long ago still need further development and implementation. If his admonitions had been taken seriously by American Christian leadership in 1960, the focus of this chapter at the close of the century would have been a review of the overwhelming resurgence of biblical faith and of the devastation of cultic strongholds. Instead, his plea seems even more urgent today. Cultic doctrine has permeated every religious forum in America, Christian as well as non-Christian. While Walter Martin's ministry was focused primarily on cultic heresies outside *the church, no responsible Christian apologist today can have such a narrow focus, because the cults have come* into *the church itself. Liberal denominations welcome paganism,*

some presence of their own on the World Wide Web. A recent quick scan of the most popular search services for the internet illustrates this point. The "search results" statistics for select groups includes the following:

Internet Web Sites With Information on Biblically Aberrational Groups (Includes Both Pro- and Critical Sites)

Type of Group	Number of Sorted Search "Hits"
Jehovah's Witnesses	8,072
Mormons	9,280
The Theosophical Society	2,665
Buddhism	36,654
The Baha'i Faith	11,418
The New Age Cults	863,207
The Unification Church	6,209
Scientology	25,542
Apocalyptic Cults	31,921
The Worldwide Church of God (formerly aberrational)	38,911
Seventh-day Adventism	366
Islam	69,573
Occultism	29,008

shamanism, and Eastern pantheism into their worship services, hymnals, and statements of faith. Charismatic, Pentecostal, and independent churches are spreading the plague of Word Faith heresies, exacting a toll of their members that is not only spiritual injury, but emotional and physical harm sometimes even culminating in physical death.

Christianity in America suffers because Christians have not taken their scriptural responsibility to heart, to "defend the faith" (Jude 3), "give an answer" (1 Peter 3:15), "test all things" (1 Thessalonians 5:21–22), and "search the scriptures" (Acts 17:11). Without biblical commitment to apologetics or defense of the faith, especially against the heresies of the kingdom of the cults, the church becomes an impotent shell of believers who have no confidence in the truthfulness of their Lord.

It is not too late to make a difference. The new millennium can open with a new commitment to the truth of the gospel, the propagation of the true faith, and the evangelization of those lost in false belief and unbelief. With assistance from the Christian Research Institute and other similar organizations, the cooperation of local churches, and the assistance of pastors and Christian educators, cult evangelism will take a firm stand against cult heresies wherever they may be found—inside the church or outside, in the United States or abroad. Capturing and supporting Walter Martin's original vision can make a measurable difference in the strength of the church.

In the preceding chapters of this volume, we have studied and evaluated in the light of the Word of God the major non-Christian cults or sects that have consistently challenged the missionary outreach of the church of Jesus Christ. All the groups discussed are admitted rivals of historical Christianity. The question quite logically arises, "What action can the church take, in both the ecumenical and independent wings of Christendom, to meet the challenge of contemporary American cults?"

It is the purpose of this chapter to outline both a methodology and a plan whereby we may not only bring the inroads of the cults under control but, more important, to actually take positive steps to evangelize cultists, which of course is the primary task of the Christian church. By traveling what might be called "the road to recovery," the church may once again see the day when, by speaking the truth in love and with clarity, much of the ground lost to non-Christian cults in the last century may be regained. It should never be forgotten that whatever a specific cult offers to attract individuals is infinitesimal compared with what Jesus Christ offers to the soul who will cast all his care upon Him. The church has nothing to fear from the cults as long as she is faithful to her mission of both proclaiming and vigorously contending for the faith that was once for all delivered unto the saints (Jude 3).

It is the feeling of the writer that if the following suggestions were put into immediate practice, both in the United States and on the foreign mission fields, a constructive approach to the mounting problem of cults would emerge.

Project One—Research

In order to provide information of any type for the pastor, teacher, missionary, student, or layman, it is vitally important that there be careful research into the background and theology of the major cult systems. There already exists a considerable amount of data that could be utilized, once it has been validated,

codified, and carefully weighed by mission agencies and field representatives of the major denominations and independent Christian groups. The average cultist is willing to listen to facts, particularly if they are at variance with what he has been taught, but only if those facts, once he checks them, are shown to be accurate and reliable. We have seen more than a few Jehovah's Witnesses and Mormons, for instance, carefully reevaluate their religion as a result of careful research on the part of interested Christians.

Secondly, a statistical breakdown of the growth and development of the major cult systems at home and abroad must be worked out so that those areas where they have grown most rapidly may be plotted and the factors contributing to that growth analyzed in contrast to their lack of growth in other areas.

Thirdly, questionnaires must be sent out to key personnel in all Christian movements, seeking their reaction to the challenge of the cults in those areas under their jurisdiction. In this way, a broad perspective of cult methodology will be obtained.

Clipping service notices can also be utilized,[2] as major population centers through the world are generally the targets of the major sects, and it is always helpful to know the coming and going of cult missionaries, as well as their planned area meetings (international conventions, missionary report sessions, special lectures, etc.).

Of course, a research center dealing with cults is not a new proposal. The Christian Research Institute, of which I am the founder and director, was incorporated in 1960 to meet this need. It is our aim to collate and disseminate information to all Christian groups, ecumenical as well as independent, helping them to win those in the cults to Christ.

Through our facilities as a bureau of information on comparative religions, Christian leaders, missionaries, and workers throughout the world have ready access to information that is currently important. Through our newsletter we are able to provide much of the newest information to the general public. But the project is far too involved to be merely an independent effort. There must be cooperation and the free interchange of information between all concerned Christian groups, followed by financial support, in order that any research project of such scope and magnitude succeed in its objective.[3]

---

[2]Editor's Note: *Although major metropolitan and many suburban newspapers and magazines are now available on-line electronically from around the world, the vast volume of material published daily means that many crucial articles with important research information are lost for cult apologetics research organizations. There are simply not enough hours in the day, nor researchers present, to search daily publications in any comprehensive way. Therefore, in a salute to the past, reliance on periodical clippings culled and forwarded by concerned Christian laypeople to cult apologetics organizations are still an invaluable resource. Armed with publication- and date-identified clippings provided by thoughtful ministry supporters, Christian cult apologists can wage a surprisingly well-informed eductional campaign regarding a myriad of doctrinally questionable groups and individuals.*

[3]Editor's Note: *The Christian Research Institute, directed today by President Hank Hanegraaff, is on the lead-ing edge of popularized cult apologetics. Through the* Bible Answer Man *radio call-in program, the monthly* Newsletter, *the quarterly* Christian Research Journal, *the CRI Internet Web site (www.equip.org), and nu-merous books, pamphlets, information sheets, cassettes, videos, and computer software materials, CRI provides information, research, and evangelism materials worldwide to millions of Christians. Other organizations, such as Watchman Fellowship, Witness Inc., Answers in Action, and Personal Freedom Outreach also provide helpful information on alternative religious belief systems.*

Project Two—Computer Retrieval System

One of the newest ways for combating the forces of the cults is through the use of computers. Christian Research Institute is proposing a plan which, if adopted, could revolutionize the field of apologetics. I propose that a computer information retrieval system be developed that can provide answers on the cults to practically anyone with access to a university or college library. This would be called the Christian Research Lending Library (SENT/EAST).

For example, many of the arguments that Jehovah's Witnesses bring forth against orthodoxy are mangled attempts to force the Greek text of the New Testament into their theological framework. What recourse does the average Christian have against such mistranslation if he does not have any knowledge of New Testament Greek? Through our projected computer network, individuals would be able to tap our resources via computer terminals. This person would be able to type his question at a terminal and receive an almost instantaneous reply complete with documentation.

There are around 60 million cultists and another 60 million Americans who dabble in the occult in the United States today, and this is one way that they can be reached with very little struggle. This computer network will hopefully be used even in other countries. We will be able to take all of our research and information that we have been gathering for the last thirty years and make it available to anyone who needs it.

Of course, there are many things that are necessary to a viable program like this. We need the cooperation of all of the other organizations in this field in the United States and abroad. We need to share the information that is available in so many different locations.

A program like this is also very expensive, and although we visualize that participants in the program will contribute a share of the costs, donations and volunteers are needed to offset the enormous expense.

With the prayers and help of dedicated Christian laymen and leaders all over the country, a program such as SENT/EAST will energize the missionary forces as they seek to bring the gospel to those who are involved in the cults.

Project Three—Specialized Literature

Just as the function of Project One would be the collecting, sorting, and condensing of usable facts and information, so Project Three would be its logical outgrowth, the publication and distribution and also the translation of such material on an international scale. The value of tracts, pamphlets, and books printed and disseminated at cost, both in the United States and on those mission fields where specific cults are rapidly growing is incalculable, as any foreign missionary will readily attest.

Through the facilities of such organizations as the Christian Research Institute and numerous other interested groups, practically all missionaries would have information available for distribution to indigenous churches and to Christian workers on their respective fields, so that it would no longer be possible for such organizations as Jehovah's Witnesses and the Mormons to capitalize on the absence of literature accurately describing their faith and refuting their claims.

In South America alone, where the Mormons and the Jehovah's Witnesses, not to mention the indigenous animistic and spiritistic cults, exist in growing numbers and force of influence, preliminary surveys indicate that almost 90 percent of those questioned not only desire but earnestly request literature that will assist them in both refuting and evangelizing cults.

In the United States and Canada—where much headway is being made by cult systems—universities, colleges, seminaries, Bible institutes, and local churches have consistently requested reliable literature from recognized denominational and independent sources. But because funding and support services are unequal to the task, those organizations—including the Christian Research Institute—that are working tirelessly to provide such information are deluged with more requests than can be handled. Special commissions should therefore be appointed similar to that already sponsored by the World Council of Churches, so that Christian individuals, organizations, churches, and denominations may pool their information and erect a systematic defense against cult proselytizing. Though conservatives and liberals may disagree theologically, they suffer from the inroads of the cults individually, and yearly the ranks of American cultism are swelled by former Methodists, Episcopalians, Lutherans, Baptists, Congregationalists, etc., who attended both liberal and conservative churches until they were won over by the cults.

No serious scholar in the field of cults will deny that there is a desperate need for literature and that it must be doctrinally oriented. But that such literature can be made available without the cooperation of interested churchmen, educators, and layreaders is quite dubious if not impossible. The cults have capitalized upon the fact that the Christian church has not made any really significant effort to halt their proselytizing techniques and to answer their propaganda directed against all forms of Christianity. This has been, in no small measure, a contributing factor to their success. It is true that research will produce and has already produced considerable amounts of useful information, but its printing and distribution is a fundamental concern if we are to deal effectively with the issues that face us.

Project Four—Educational Reevaluation

Samuel Johnson, the great educator, once wrote, "The foundation of every state is the education of its youth," and we would do well to paraphrase this in the context of Christianity: "The future of the church is in the education of its leaders."

As a college professor, the writer has been deeply interested in the courses offered in Bible institutes, colleges, universities, and seminaries, as well as pre-theological schools, dealing with the subject of comparative religions and particularly with non-Christian cults or sects. In this area a very real problem exists, and it will do no good to let the matter rest with this observation. Rather, the facts, appalling as they may be, should be aired.

Since the advent of Christian missionary activities on an organized scale some 200 years ago, the proclamation of the gospel message has faced many problems. Obstacles of language, culture, race, militant nationalism, and the competition between missionaries of different doctrinal persuasions have con-

tributed to a stormy atmosphere in world missions.

In addition to these difficulties, major non-Christian religions such as Islam, Buddhism, Hinduism, Taoism, Shintoism, etc. have actively opposed Christian missionaries, so that progress has been slow in many areas and in some instances hardly recognizable.

Beyond this aspect, however, looms, as we have mentioned, the formidable obstacle of non-Christian American cults, many of which are now worldwide. Some of these movements have proselytized new converts on already established fields with startling success. Utilizing the methods reminiscent of early Christianity, the cults cater to the culture patterns of those they proselytize, provide literature in the language of the people, and, one way or another, keep a certain emphasis on the Bible in the forefront of their work. In many instances they preach a militant "separation" from tobacco, alcohol, and other practices classified as worldly and unspiritual. All these activities are bolstered by their so-called revelations (all of nineteenth-century vintage), with an appeal to which they wage unceasing warfare against all religions, but against Christian denominations in particular. It is significant that they first approach known Christians. Seldom do they attempt to reach the unevangelized, which should be the first step in any genuine missionary program.

We are not to suggest that the activities of these movements be curtailed by law or that they should become the target of an evangelical barrage of abuse. Full freedom of worship and the right to promulgate one's convictions are historical planks in the platform of Protestant evangelism. Even such terms as "sect" or "cult" seem more appropriate in lands with a state church than in open religious situations. But Christianity will need to preserve the distinction between truth and heresy if it is to have a future. Some groups, particularly Jehovah's Witnesses, by their demonstrated hostility to governmental authorities, have frequently jeopardized the reputation and efforts of others of genuine Christian persuasion. As a result, there has been great friction between their workers and Christian missionaries. It is difficult indeed for Christian missionaries to compete successfully with such divisive forces in a positive way and to evangelize missionaries of such zealous groups as the Mormons, Jehovah's Witnesses, and other virulent indigenous groups.

Now we might ask at this juncture, "What is being done to train Christian missionaries abroad (and, for that matter, pastors, teachers, and leaders in the United States) to deal with this growing problem? On the educational level, are Christian institutions taking seriously the needs at home and on the mission fields? Are there mandatory courses for future Christian leaders to aid them in both evangelizing and refuting cultists?"

The cults continually emphasize the Bible, but despite the prominence given the Scriptures, without exception they place themselves in the roles of infallible interpreters of the Word of God, their dogmatism rivaled only by Jesuit scholars. Instead of being the infallible rule of faith and practice, the Bible is relegated to a secondary position. This is accomplished almost subliminally, so that the convert is unaware that his primary authority is not really grounded in Scripture, but rather in the interpretation of Scripture put forth by the respective cult.

Though this fact is well known among missionaries and Christian workers,

it apparently has not filtered back to seminaries, Bible colleges, and Bible institutes. It is a fact that at present less than five percent of all such institutions in the United States require as a prerequisite of graduation that a student take a course on comparative religions or non-Christian American cults, a fact which staggers the imagination when one can see the obvious inroads the cults have made both at home and abroad.

In a classic periodical article, Professor Gilbert Peterson, Chairman of the Department of Religious Education at the Philadelphia College of the Bible, made the following observations concerning the educational curricula of American Bible colleges, institutes, and seminaries:

> Preparation is a word that is found to headline some newspapers, on the lips of statesmen, military leaders, and educators as well as church leaders and mission board directors. It has taken on a significant meaning in our times as the threats of world leaders, nations, and the varied ideologies of men vie for prominence in the world around us. Christian educators need to stop from time to time and evaluate the preparation men and women are receiving in the various Christian schools of higher learning. . . .
>
> It is with a sense of great urgency that the graduates of Bible colleges, along with Christian young people from other educational backgrounds, face the task of living and witnessing to the truth of the Gospel in these troubled times. Each spring a new group of young people receives their diplomas or degrees to serve God as missionaries, both at home and on the foreign field.
>
> In a recent survey conducted by the author—of over twenty-three Bible colleges in the United States and Canada, representing a total number of graduates in excess of 15,000—it was found that approximately twelve and one-half percent of this number or about 1900 individuals are presently serving on the foreign mission fields of the world. Our concern at present is not with the percentage of Bible college graduates going to the mission field, but rather, the preparation they receive in the area of formal cult apologetics before going to the mission field.
>
> In the past ten years the outreach of cults and isms through the mediums of radio, the printed page, and missionary endeavors, has reached enormous proportions. The rapidity of their growth is traceable in large measure to the dearth of information among Christians in regard to what is being promulgated by the various cults on the one hand, and a failure to act upon the scriptural command to resist them on the other. In the survey, questionnaires were sent to over fifty Bible colleges. In the twenty-three schools replying, there is great diversity of requirements in the section of the curriculum dealing with apologetics, cults, and unchristian religions. The course most often required of all graduates was "Cults and Isms." The course usually entailed the study of the history and development of several cults, their doctrinal position, and a refutation of their position from the Scriptures. Apologetics was next in order of numbers of requirements. This course covers a systematic presentation of the reasons and evidences of the Christian faith. The course offered most often was Comparative Religions, with nine schools offering it as an elective, three requiring it for all mission majors, and four schools requiring it of all graduates. This course covers a comparative study of the major living religions of the world.
>
> In order to meet the challenge of our day in preparing our young people to face the present religious world situation, we need to realize what is being offered to the students in our Bible colleges, institutes, and seminaries by way of preparing them to serve Christ in the midst of the rise of cultism. The following is offered as a suggestion as to how we might structure this one area of the curriculum. This is, of course, not a final pronouncement, rather, a rec-

ommendation for exploration of this difficult field.

There is no substitute for a thorough knowledge of the Word of God and the truth of God which it reveals. Courses in direct Bible study and doctrine provide one with the necessary foundation. In addition to this, a three-hour course in Apologetics is needed where the needs of men, the Christian answer to these needs, and the reasons for the uniqueness and truth of Christianity are presented.

It is not enough that one know only his own beliefs when faced by the average non-Christian and cultist, and therefore, following Apologetics there should be a three-hour course in Cults and Isms. This course, as previously suggested, would examine the historical and doctrinal development of such non-Christian groups as Jehovah's Witnesses, Christian Science, Mormonism, Unity, and the like. The course would include the Christian answer to these systems and an evaluation of their terminologies, and an accurate, consistent method of approaching them with evangelism as the goal.

A course such as comparative religions could be offered on an elective basis to give the student a broader view of non-Christian religions. When a student goes to the mission field, a far more detailed study of the religion of that particular field must be made by the missionary candidate, and can be made in comparative religions. Therefore, specialized courses should be offered in these fields. Also the training received in apologetics and cults along the lines of definitive terminology and doctrinal evaluation will prove extremely valuable.

At present, of the twenty-three Bible colleges reporting, ten offer a course in Apologetics, with six requiring it of all students; eleven schools offer a course in Cults, with seven requiring it of all students; sixteen schools offer a course in Comparative Religions, with three requiring it of all mission majors and four requiring it of all students.

This means that a little more than one-fourth of the Bible colleges replying already follow the suggested curriculum outlined or one very similar to it, and a little less than one-half of the reporting schools offer all three courses (Apologetics, Cults, and Comparative Religions) in their present curriculums.[4]

Mr. Peterson's remarks are very much to the point, for when it is remembered that only eleven schools out of twenty-three offered courses on Cult Apologetics, and only seven out of those eleven required it for graduation, the situation is seen to be acute.

In the case of seminaries and Bible institutes in the United States, a detailed study now in preparation indicates even at this early date that the problem of non-Christian cults is not taken seriously by the majority.

Such information will not paint an encouraging picture to be sure, especially in the light of accelerated cult growth on our major mission fields.[5]

Mission fields have the added problem of dealing with certain indigenous cults with strong nationalistic overtones, particularly in Africa and Asia. These groups amalgamate some of the teachings of Christianity with the older pagan

---

[4]Gilbert Peterson, *Religious Research Digest* (December 1961): 8–11.

[5]Editor's Note: *Sadly, the picture has not changed appreciably over the past four decades. Christian Bible schools, colleges, universitites, and seminaries are still woefully under-preparing their students to give a biblical response and persuasive evangelism to those who unwittingly embrace heresy and cultic doctrine. This area of Christian responsibility must be addressed and assumed in the coming decades. A Christian educational system that does not value equipping its students for apologetics and evangelism betrays not only the students and those for whom they minister, but the very cultists who so need the truth of God's Word. Christians who have a genuine concern for the external destinies of those who follow heresy must instigate change on our Christian campuses through vocal and financial support, encouragement, and exhortation.*

religions, particularly animism and spiritism, and come equipped complete with their own special revelations and messiahs. The situation is particularly true in the Philippine Islands, Japan, and Africa, where Christianity is caricatured as a "white man's religion," a Western import superimposed on native cultural and religious patterns. Such an approach by the cults has been disastrously successful, particularly in South America, where in Brazil we have seen a resurgence of spiritism on an unprecedented scale. *Time* magazine even devoted its religious section once to comments by a Roman Catholic missionary deploring the inroads of the spiritists into the Roman Catholic Church. Unfortunately, the same can be said also in respect to some Protestant agencies; so the problem is universal. In passing, it might be noted that the Roman Catholic Church has recently begun detailed research in the area of non-Christian cults and sects, so effective have been the methods of both American-based and indigenous cults in proselytizing Roman Catholic converts.

On the basis of past performance, it is safe to prognosticate that within the next decade, all things remaining constant, the cults will intensify their propaganda activities to three or four times their present rate. The question is, will the church of Jesus Christ rise to the occasion while time remains? The church must be prepared to defend the claims of Scripture interpreted by the Holy Spirit that it alone is "given by inspiration of God, and is profitable for doctrine, for reproof, for correction, and for instruction in righteousness" (2 Timothy 3:16).

The Christian church must also be ready to remind indigenous nationalistic sects that Christianity is an Eastern religion, that Christ was born, died, and was resurrected in Asia, and ascended from the Mount of Olives; so it is anything but "a foreign religion." But if the cults are to be effectively dealt with at home and on the foreign mission fields of the world, then missionaries, pastors, and particularly educators, who mold the curricula of Christian institutions, must press for strong curricula in those institutions. Christians must be taught not only what they believe but why they believe it, that they may be able, as the Scripture admonishes us, to "be ready always to give an answer to every man that asketh you a reason of the hope that is in you with meekness and fear" (1 Peter 3:15).

The teachings of the major sects must be codified and indexed and a running commentary provided for all interested parties in the form of the publication of literature and perhaps a semi-annual journal. It will then be possible to understand the methodology of the cults at home and abroad, to note the areas of their doctrinal emphasis and growth, and their use and abuse of Christian terminology. The church of Jesus Christ, as we have noted, has nothing to fear from the zeal and competition of the cults, but she has much to fear from her own apathy and lethargy in this vital area of missionary concern. The means to evangelize and combat adherents of the cults can be made readily available to all interested parties. It remains for Christians of both ecumenical and independent persuasion to agree to cooperate in the dissemination of pertinent literature on this ever-growing field of mutual concern.

On every front the church is faced with unrelenting and mounting pressures from anti-Christian forces. Our Lord has warned us, "The night cometh, when no man can work" (John 9:4), but the publication of literature may yet

give us some time to work in the twilight that precedes the sunset.

It will do us little good, however, to sponsor research and to publish and distribute literature if at the fountainhead of all Christian work, the educational preparation of Christian leadership, we do not revise the curricula of numerous Bible institutes, colleges, universities, and seminaries to meet these needs, both in the United States and on the mission field. So it appears that education, as always, is of vital significance.

Project Five—Conferences on Cults

A final suggestion to help implement support for a unified approach to the challenge of the cults is the sponsoring of specialized conferences or lectures on the local church level, at Bible conferences and in schools and seminaries, by competent students of the major cult systems. I have used such conferences for years, and other cult-watching organizations have followed the same successful pattern. These conferences continually stimulate a great deal of interest, showing as they would by contrast the differences between the teachings of the cults and historical Christianity. If conducted in a dignified, scholarly, and yet popular manner, with question and answer periods following each lecture, such conferences would serve a dual purpose. They would both explain the divergent doctrines of the cults and, at the same time, strengthen the faith of Christians in the great fundamental teachings of Christianity. The author has been engaged in such a ministry for some years with considerable success, but much more remains to be done. For as the Scripture reminds us, "Lift up your eyes and look on the fields; for they are white already to harvest. . . . The harvest truly is plenteous, but the labourers are few. Pray ye therefore the Lord of the harvest, that he will send forth labourers" (John 4:35; Matthew 9:37–38). Speakers are available from the Christian Research Institute in these areas and there are a few other organizations and individuals throughout the country that provide similar services. However, the need is much greater than the supply, and it must be met quickly.

If the preceding suggestions were adopted and put into operation, it is the conviction of this writer that the major cult systems would soon feel the impact and receive the benefit of the unified Christian witness to the veracity of the faith that they have chosen to reject.

Through the use of good research material, properly disseminated and translated where possible into the language of the fields where the cults are most active, and aided by clipping services which would keep the research center informed of major cult efforts around the world, Christians of all denominations, as well as pastors, educators, and missionaries, would be kept abreast of the activities of the larger cult systems.

Concluding our observation, then, the road to recovery will not be an easy one to travel, and will be fraught with problems and conflicts; but if we will begin to travel it, we will find at the end of it and along the way those who have been delivered from the cults, those who have been dissuaded from joining them, and those who have been both evangelized and strengthened by a determined effort of the Christian church not only to proclaim the message of redeeming grace but to defend the claims and the Gospel of her Savior. We can go a long way toward recovering the ground we have lost, but we must begin now.

Appendix A

The Worldwide Church of God: From Cult to Christianity

Doctrinal heresy is a sin against God (Galatians 5:20). An ideal world would be free from doctrinal heresy and the other results of sin. This ideal world we must await in Christ Jesus who will grant such perfect existence in His future kingdom (Revelation 7:17; 21:4). Until that time we must contend with heresies and cults that dot church history, leaving their mark of remembrance. Cults come and go, but rare indeed is the repentance of cult leadership that results in heresy being replaced with biblical Christianity. Such is the story of the Worldwide Church of God. Once known far and wide as the cult of Armstrongism, it now, through repentance, joins hands with conservative Christians in heralding the gospel. Its official organ, *The Plain Truth* magazine, embraces the very doctrines its past issues condemned. It interviews contemporary Christian leaders it once derided. It accepts advertising from various Christian publishers it once shunned.

The Worldwide Church of God, originally founded by Herbert W. Armstrong (1892–1986), was led through this remarkable change by his successor, Joseph W. Tkach (1927–1995). He reversed Armstrong's most damnable doctrines in full acceptance of the Trinity, Christ's divinity and humanity, the person and deity of the Holy Spirit, the bodily resurrection of Jesus, and salvation by grace through faith alone. Gone is Anglo-Israelism. Gone is the bondage of legalism as a test for fellowship. Gone is the God Family of divine humans. Gone is the exclusivism and cultism.

Not all followers of Armstrong, whose teaching we term "Armstrongism," accepted this welcomed change. Joseph W. Tkach and the administrators made earnest attempts to hold the church together during their doctrinal reexamination period. But those dedicated to Armstrong's cultism grew impatient, forming about fifty splinter groups from 1985 to 1995. These groups are disassociated from the Worldwide Church of God and each claims succession from Armstrong.

Preceding them, another fifty splinter groups separated from Herbert W.

This appendix updated and written by Kurt Van Gorden, and edited by Gretchen Passantino. It replaces the 1985 edition's chapter 12, "Herbert W. Armstrong and the Worldwide Church of God—Anglo–Israelism."

Armstrong during his lifetime. Armstrong's teaching bred a hundred factions of which ninety presently remain. The founder's son, Garner Ted Armstrong, leads quite a successful movement with the Church of God, International. Garner Ted Armstrong was once viewed by millions on television as the flamboyant commentator of *The World Tomorrow* program. Amid charges of sexual misconduct, his forced departure from his father's domain landed him in Tyler, Texas, with thousands of television followers. His playboy lifestyle followed him into the 1990s with new charges of sexual misconduct, again forcing a temporary step-down from his new church (*Los Angeles Times*, Nov. 23, 1995). Nevertheless, faithful Church of God, International members reinstated him as their iconic representative on 315 cable stations in North America. His espoused doctrines follow that of his father, namely, denial of the Trinity, denial of the bodily resurrection, and denial of biblical salvation.

Among those that broke away during the reformation of the Worldwide Church of God, the largest is led by another self-proclaimed successor to Armstrong, Gerald Flurry. The Philadelphia Church of God, located in Edmond, Oklahoma, has a television log of sixty stations in five countries. Their program, *The Key of David*, echoes Armstrong's prophetic speculation. *The Philadelphia Trumpet*, their official magazine, is a constant reminder of Herbert W. Armstrong's old doctrines in the face of the reborn Worldwide Church of God. Gerald Flurry minces no words in prodding and jostling the Worldwide Church of God for its baptism into historical Christianity.

Most of the splinter cults of Armstrongism retain the name "Church of God" somewhere in their title. They mix legalism, including strict Sabbatarianism, with a variety of Armstrong's leading doctrines. Two other noteworthy groups among these are the Global Church of God, located in San Diego, California, and the United Church of God in Arcadia, California. The former has a television following on two superstations covering much of the United States, while the latter publishes *The Good News* magazine and covers thirty television stations with programming.

Joseph Tkach Jr., son of Joseph W. Tkach, currently heads the Worldwide Church of God. Leading this church through the exodus of error was costly, which is seen in the loss of many thousands of members. *The Plain Truth* magazine now circulates approximately 130,000, down considerably from their high of eight million. Much better though is the loss of size than the compromise of truth. *The World Tomorrow* television program has ceased and actual church membership has dropped to half of its normative to 40,000 constituents. Their Pasadena, California, campus is shrinking and the church-supported Ambassador College in Big Sandy, Texas, has closed its doors.

On the positive side, the Worldwide Church of God has a remnant of 300 pastors committed to preaching an uncompromised gospel. Their message is that you must be born again by grace through faith in the shed blood of Jesus Christ. *The Plain Truth* magazine is greeted as a refreshing Christian voice. Prominent denominations and Christian leaders have extended the right hand of fellowship to its church leaders. The church now holds membership in the National Association of Evangelicals, while the magazine is a member of the Evangelical Press Association and the Evangelical Christian Publishers Association.

As for the present changes in the Worldwide Church of God, they wrote, in

an interview with this writer, "The Worldwide Church of God has abandoned unbiblical doctrines of Herbert W. Armstrong." This abandonment may be viewed as parallel to one of Armstrong's toughest decisions, which was to excommunicate his son, Garner Ted Armstrong, from his church. He said, "Perhaps another evidence of the Worldwide Church of God being the one original Church of God is that its apostle did remove his son, who was secularizing God's Church and college, besides other sins."[1] Again, he wrote, "Finally, four leaders . . . came to God's apostle, saying, 'We have to report to you that your son has systematically destroyed all that Christ has built through His apostle and is building something for himself. Like a spoiled child, he wants his own way.' God's apostle, to be not guilty of Eli's sin, removed his son from all authority and disfellowshipped him from the church."[2] In a similar way, those in the Worldwide Church of God have abandoned the false teachings of their founder, Herbert W. Armstrong. It was emotionally painful, for many of them had known Armstrong for decades. But to stand for biblical truth and accuracy one must hurtle all barriers.

The changes did not occur overnight. Their progressive change is reflected in their newest statement of beliefs, which says, "This Statement of Beliefs does not constitute a closed creed. The Church constantly renews its commitment to truth and deeper understanding and responds to God's guidance in its beliefs and practices."[3] Since they have left an open book on their creeds, we write this chapter based upon current publications offered to the public. Accordingly, newer information may demand further analysis.

In the remainder of this chapter we will sketch Herbert W. Armstrong's background and examine his teachings with Scripture. We must be careful to distinguish the doctrines of Armstrongism and today's Worldwide Church of God. The cults that follow Mr. Armstrong's teachings are cults indeed, denying the major tenets of the Christian faith. Based upon the published changes, the Worldwide Church of God is not a cult, however, because it has shown repentance and abandonment of Armstrong's false doctrines and demonstrates adherence to biblical truth. Therefore, we will make known the changes in the Worldwide Church of God that separate it from the cults of Armstrongism. The ninety cults of Armstrongism believe that Mr. Armstrong spoke with the authority of "Elijah." We cannot list all ninety groups on every subject, so we will generalize their teachings as that of "Armstrongism," while comparing it to the Worldwide Church of God or the Bible.

The Rise of Herbert W. Armstrong

Herbert Armstrong, born July 31, 1892, in Des Moines, Iowa, was raised in a Christian home in the Midwestern farmlands. He speaks fondly of his Christian background: "Both my father and mother were of solid Quaker stock. My ancestors came to America with William Penn, a hundred years before the United States became a nation. Indeed, I have the genealogy of my ancestors

---

[1] Herbert W. Armstrong, "Seven Proofs of God's True Church," *The Plain Truth* (April 1979): 3:40.
[2] Ibid., 3.
[3] *Statements of Beliefs of the Worldwide Church of God.* (Pasadena: Worldwide Church of God, 1995), 1.

back to Edward I of England, and through British Royal genealogy back to King Herremon of Ireland, who married Queen Tea Tephia, daughter of Zedekiah, King of Judah."[4] Armstrong also claimed to be a descendent of the biblical King David on his mother's side.[5] These credentials, coupled with his appellation of "apostle" and the second "Elijah," produced his unquestioned authority among his followers.

Armstrong temporarily succeeded in the advertising business, which he claims was special training for his future mission. He wrote, "All this advertising instruction was the most valuable possible training for the real mission in life to which I was later to be called—God's worldwide ministry. It was a training such as one could never receive in any university or theological seminary."[6]

Armstrong's spiritual odyssey was launched primarily through his wife's discovery that "obedience to God's spiritual laws summed up in the Ten Commandments is necessary for salvation. Not that our *works*[7] of keeping the Commandments save us—but, rather, that sin *is* the transgression of God's spiritual law (1 John 3:4) and Christ does not save us *in* our sins, but *from* our sins. We must *repent* of sin—*repent* of transgressing God's law, which means *turning from* disobedience, as a prior condition to receiving God's free gift."[8]

Walter Martin summarized Armstrong's journey:

> [His] Sunday school days had taught him that there are no works to salvation. . . . God's law was done away with. To him religion had not been a way of life but a mere belief, an acceptance of the fact of God's existence, Christ's Virgin Birth, the efficacy of Christ's shed blood. Controversy arose between Mr. and Mrs. Armstrong. She refused to give up the truths she had found. He was angered into his first real study of the Bible, undertaken for the avowed purpose of proving to his wife that "all these churches can't be wrong."[9]
>
> Armstrong's long solitary study of the Scriptures led him to the same conclusions he had fought so bitterly against with his wife. Ambassador Press publications indicate that Armstrong's struggle to change from "traditional" Christian belief to this newfound "legalism" caused within him "a furious inner struggle."[10]

After the study of his Bible and much prayer, we are informed, Mr. Armstrong began writing and doing evangelical work. It was in June of 1931 that Armstrong conducted an evangelistic campaign in Eugene, Oregon, and at that time was "ordained as a minister of Jesus Christ."

His tremendous zeal, tireless energy, writing, speaking, and promotional ability stood Armstrong in good stead through the years and culminated in the founding of the Ambassador College, *Plain Truth Magazine*, which was started in February 1934, and The *World Tomorrow Program*, which originated in Eugene, Oregon, January 1934.

---

[4]Herbert W. Armstrong, *The Autobiography of Herbert W. Armstrong* (Pasadena: Ambassador Press, 1967), 1:26.

[5]Herbert W. Armstrong, "How the Seven Mysteries Were Revealed," *The Plain Truth* (September 1985): 16.

[6]Armstrong, *Autobiography*, 75.

[7]Armstrong continuously used typographical symbols to emphasize his writings, including small capitals, exclamation points, italics, bold face, etc. Quotations in this text are always accurate word-for-word, and usually his unique typesetting is followed, unless it detracts from clear communication.

[8]Roderick Meredith, *The Inside Story of the World Tomorrow Broadcast* (Pasadena: Ambassador Press), 47.

[9]Ibid.

[10]Ibid., 48.

Herbert Armstrong has made it a career to become a senior statesman of diplomacy for his church, and visits the various leaders of established and emerging nations, attracting their attention by his expensive gifts and direct aid programs in areas where the individual country may be in need.

An example of Armstrong's diplomacy was his high standing with the Israeli government, for whom he had sponsored archeological digs, not the least of which was his much-publicized excavations around and underneath the site of the second temple in Jerusalem. The Armstrong religion is strong in England, throughout the United Kingdom, and on the European continent, as well as in the United States.[11]

The Eclecticism of Herbert W. Armstrong

Unsuccessful attempts have been made to unite Armstrong with groups of similar views, such as Seventh-Day Adventists, Jehovah's Witnesses, and Mormonism. In rebuttal, Armstrong's biographer, Roderick Meredith, categorically states that "there was *never* any association in any way with Jehovah's Witnesses, Seventh-Day Adventists, Mormons, or any such sects, as some accusers have falsely claimed."[12] In his *Autobiography*, Armstrong denies having attended any Seventh-Day Adventist church services, although he admits becoming familiar with their literature.[13] We will discover, though, that he was a member of a sect produced from the multiple factions of the Adventist movement.

1. Seventh-Day Adventism, the Church of God (Adventist), and Herbert W. Armstrong

Although past writers, such as George Burnside for the *Bulletin of the Ministerial Association of Seventh-Day Adventist Ministers*, have concluded that Armstrong belonged to offshoots of Seventh-Day Adventism, there is no substance to this claim. However, neither can Armstrong's previous denial of connection with "any such sects" go unchallenged. It seems that the Seventh-Day Adventists and Church of God (Adventist) arose simultaneously from the Adventist remnants of the post-1844 great disappointment. That Armstrong was connected with the Church of God Seventh-Day is no question. The fact that this church is a divergent sect of non-Trinitarian Adventism settles many questions as to Armstrong's apparent source for legalistic teaching and Adventist theology.

This Church of God (Adventist) was strengthened in 1884 by consolidating independent congregations into the General Conference of the Church of God (Adventist). In 1923 the name was changed to the Church of God Seventh-Day, which later ordained Armstrong in Oregon. He worshiped with the Oregon congregation and was baptized by a Baptist minister in 1927. The Oregon state conference formed in 1931, and ordained him that same year. According to information from the Worldwide Church of God, the other connection with Seventh-Day Adventism is only incidental. He read Seventh-Day Adventist literature and counseled with one of their ministers.

---

[11]Walter R. Martin, *Kingdom of the Cults* (Minneapolis: Bethany House Publishers, 1985 ed.), 303–304.
[12]Meredith, *Story*, 48–49.
[13]Armstrong, *Autobiography*, 302, 338.

Governmental splits in the conference provided the exit for Armstrong and his Eugene, Oregon, congregation. In 1934 he had begun radio broadcasting and published the first issue of *The Plain Truth*. He continued loose ties with them until 1947.

The Church of God Seventh-Day's view of God was largely Arian. This unitarian theology promoted anti-Trinitarian sentiments, which provided ammunition for Armstrong against Trinitarians without any Jehovah's Witness alliance. Although Mr. Armstrong rejected Arianism in favor of his "Family of God" doctrine, he maintained staunch anti-Trinitarianism and a number of peripheral doctrines in agreement with the Church of God Seventh-Day.

2. Anglo-Israelism

Walter Martin wrote the following on Anglo-Israelism:

> Anglo-Israelism (sometimes called British-Israelism) is, properly speaking, neither a sect nor a cult since it transcends denominational and sectarian lines and because it does not set up an ecclesiastical organization. It has existed for more than a century in the United States, having come to this hemisphere from England. Apparently it originated there shortly after the close of the Elizabethan era, its "first apostle" being Richard Brothers (1757–1824).
>
> The most vocal proponents of the Anglo-Israelite system of biblical interpretation in North America were James Lovell of Fort Worth, Texas, and Howard Rand of Destiny Publishers.
>
> The teachings of these men and their followers are comparatively innocuous and free from serious doctrinal error. The chief harm results from the appeal to nationalism with its accompanying vanity and the twofold way of salvation which some advocates have implied.[14]

Herbert Armstrong and Anglo-Israelism

Few organized religions teach Anglo-Israelism as does Armstrongism. The Worldwide Church of God brought Anglo-Israelism under biblical review in 1990, and concluded that Armstrong was incorrect. Hence they ceased publication and dissemination of Armstrong's major works on Anglo-Israelism. Most of the splinter cults of Armstrongism, however, readily promote it in their publications and broadcasts. One such group claims a divine calling for keeping Armstrong's teachings in print. The Philadelphia Church of God wrote, "We derive our authority to print the works of Mr. Armstrong from God, and from Mr. Armstrong's own wishes."[15] We see, then, that Armstrong's Anglo-Israelism did not cease with the repentance of the Worldwide Church of God, but has multiplied through the splinter groups.

Walter Martin capsulized the essence of Anglo-Israelism:

> To sum up the theories of the Anglo-Israel cult in a concise manner is not difficult, and to refute them from the Scriptures as noted scholars and biblical expositors have done many times is essentially an elementary task. But with the

---

[14]Martin, *Kingdom*, 306.
[15]Gerald Flurry and Dennis Leap, "The Key of David Vision," *The Philadelphia Trumpet* (March 1997): 24.

advent of Herbert Armstrong's version of the old error and his utilization of it as a cloak for his own confusion on biblical theology, the problem is no longer elementary, in fact, it is quite complex and deserves the careful consideration of responsible Christian ministers and laymen. For it is certain that they will be affected, sooner or later, by the plausible propaganda which flows from the Armstrong presses and out over the airwaves.

We shall deal with Anglo-Israelism, then, only as a prelude to dealing with the theology of Herbert Armstrong, with which it has now become identified in the minds of most people—in England, Canada, and the United States.

The basic premise of the Anglo-Israelite theory is that ten tribes were lost (Israelites) when the Jews were captured by the Assyrians under King Sargon and that these so-called "lost" tribes[16] are in reality, the Saxae, or Scythians, who surged westward through Northern Europe and eventually became the ancestors of the Saxons, who later invaded England. The theory maintains that the Anglo-Saxons are the "lost" ten tribes of Israel and are substituted, in Anglo-Israel interpretation and exegesis, for the Israel of the Bible.[17]

In the heyday of the British Empire, when their colonies spanned the globe under Victoria, Anglo-Israelites were in their glory, maintaining that since the British were the lost tribes and, therefore, inheritors of the covenants and blessings of God, it was obvious that God was honoring His promises and exalting His children in the latter days.

In light of recent history, however, and the loss by Britain of virtually all her colonial possessions, Anglo-Israelites are content to transfer the blessings of the Covenant to the United States, maintaining as they do that Ephraim is Great Britain and Manasseh, the United States. The fact that Ephraim is called "the exalted one" in Scripture and that Manasseh is designated as the inferior of the two, creates both historical and exegetical problems for the Anglo-Israelites. This is particularly true because the United States, the inferior (Manasseh), has now far surpassed the allegedly superior Ephraim, a minor problem that will not long forestall the cogitations and prophetic conjectures of the Anglo-Israelites' school of biblical interpretation.

Relative to the relationship of Israel to Judah in Scripture, Anglo-Israelism maintains that Judah represents the Jews who are still under the divine curse and are not to be identified with Israel at all. In this line of reasoning, all the promises recorded in the Scripture are applied not to a nation (Israel), which, as we have seen, is, in their system of thought, to be identified with Great Britain and the United States!

It is further maintained by Anglo-Israelites that in their migration of the Mediterranean area across Europe to the British Isles, the "lost" tribes left behind them landmarks, bearing names of the tribes. Thus the Danube River and Danzig are clear indications to them of the Tribe of Dan.[18] The term Saxon is obviously derived from the Hebrew and means Isaac-son, or "the son of Isaac!"[19]

Another Anglo-Israel exercise in semantics is their insistence that the Hebrew terms for covenant (*berith*), and for man (*ish*) are to be interpreted as meaning "the man of the covenant,"[20] a fact that would be amusing if it were not for the unpleasant truth that the Hebrew and Anglo-Saxon tongues have as much in common as do Chinese and Pig-Latin!

It is sufficient to point out at this stage that the Hebrew words *berith* and *ish*

[16]J. H. Allen, *Judah's Scepter and Joseph's Birthright* (Boston: A. A. Beauchamp, 1918, 6th ed.), 124–145.
[17]Rev. Commander L. G. A. Roberts, *Commentary on the Book of the Prophet Isaiah* (London: The Covenant Publishing Company, 1951), 159.
[18]Adam Rutherford, *Israel-Britain or Anglo-Saxon Israel* (London: Self-published, 3rd ed., 1936), 36.
[19]Anonymous, *The Roadbuilder: God's Commonwealths, British and American* (Toronto: Commonwealth Publishers, Ltd., 1930), 161ff. See also Rutherford, *Israel-Britain*, 9.
[20]Rutherford, *Israel-Britain*, 30.

literally mean "covenant and man," not, "men of the covenant," as Armstrong and Anglo-Israelites maintain. When to this is added the unbiased and impeccably researched conclusions of the venerable *Oxford English Dictionary* and every other major English work on etymology, there is absolutely no evidence or support for the Anglo-Israelite contention that there is a connection between the Anglo-Saxon tongue and the Hebrew language, the paucity of their claims becomes all too apparent.[21]

Herbert Armstrong, in agreement with other Anglo-Israelites, also theorized that the "Stone of Scone," a coronation stone inset beneath the coronation throne at Westminster Abby, is actually the stone Jacob used for a pillow in Genesis 28:18. If so, this would be the most astounding archaeological evidence for the Old Testament to date. But no serious or credentialed archaeologist has staked his reputation on such a claim.

Following other Anglo-Israelites, Mr. Armstrong believed that the biblical throne of David became the throne of England. The 1953 *Plain Truth* writer Herman Hoeh makes this revelation plain, "that Elizabeth II actually sits on the throne of King David of Israel—that she is a direct descendant, continuing David's dynasty—the very throne on the which Christ shall sit after his return."[22] Armstrong also wrote, "Many kings in the history of Ireland, Scotland, and England have been coronated sitting over this stone—including the present queen. The stone rests today in Westminster Abby in London, and the coronation chair is built over and around it. A sign beside it labels it 'Jacob's pillar-stone.' "[23] The disturbing scientific fact is that the Stone of Scone has been examined and analyzed, and found to be "calcareous, a sandstone of reddish or purplish color and (containing) heterogeneous pebbles" and undoubtedly of Scottish origin. This fact has been reconfirmed by many reputable geologists.[24]

The notable feature of Anglo-Israelite writings is their disregard for scholarly support. They often form superficial conclusions on word associations and unfounded parallelism. Armstrong, in line with other writers, falls into these trappings. For example, he stated,

> The house of Israel is the covenant people. The Hebrew word for "covenant"' is *beriyth*, or *berith*. . . . The Hebrew for "man" is *iysh*, or *ish*. . . . In the original Hebrew language vowels were never given in the spelling. So, omitting the vowel "e" from *berith*, but retaining the "I" in its anglicized form to preserve the "y" sound, we have the anglicized Hebrew for covenant, *brith*.
>
> The Hebrews, however, never pronounced their "h's". . . . So the Hebrew word for 'covenant' would be pronounced in its anglicized form as *brit*.
>
> And the word for "covenant man," or "covenant people," would therefore be simply "*Brit-Ish*." And so, is it mere coincidence that the true covenant people *are called* the "*British*"? And they reside in the "British Isles."
>
> They were descended from Isaac, and therefore are Isaac's sons. Drop the "I" from "Isaac" (vowels are not used in Hebrew spelling), and we have the modern name "Saac's Sons," or, as we spell it in shorter manner, "*Saxons*"![25]

[21]Ibid., 306–309.

[22]Herman L. Hoeh, "The Coronation Stone," *The Plain Truth* (June 1953): 64.

[23]Herbert W. Armstrong, *The United States and Britain in Prophesy* (Pasadena: Ambassador College Press, 1980), 100.

[24]Quoted in Harry W. Loe, *Radio Church of God* (Mountain View, Calif.: Pacific Press Publishing Association, 1970): 78.

[25]Armstrong, *United States*, 95–96.

One could belabor the point with an arsenal of Armstrong quotations from his fifty years of writing. Problematic to his thesis are his spelling gymnastics and twisted words. His confidence in espousing his view is found in supposed land-marks of the lost ten tribes. Regarding the tribe of Dan, he tracks their trail through Europe. "Remember," he wrote, "in the Hebrew, vowels were not writ-ten. . . . Thus, the word 'Dan' in its English equivalent could be spelled, simply, 'Dn.' It might be pronounced as 'Dan,' or 'Den,' or 'Din,' or 'Don,' or 'Dun'— and still could be the same original Hebrew name. . . . Then, in either ancient or later geography, we find these waymarks: "*Dan*-au, the *Dan*-nn, the *Dan*-aster, the *Dan*-dari, the *Dan*-ez, the *Don*, the *Dan*, and the U-d*on*; the Eri-*don*, down to the *Danes*. 'Denmark' means 'Dan's Mark.' ' "[26] The old adage that one could prove nearly anything with extrapolated Bible verses has found its home in Armstrong's works.

The Biblical Answer to Anglo-Israelism

As Dr. Walter Martin pointed out:

> There are two principal areas in which the Anglo-Israel theory must either stand or fall. They are, first, the question whether any tribes *were* lost, and there-fore later reappeared as the British and American nations; second, there is the question of whether or not it is possible, in either the Old or New Testaments, to teach that Israel and Judah are not two names for the same nation.[27]

The final blow to Armstrong's teaching on Anglo-Israelism came after his death by those in leadership at the Worldwide Church of God. In their effort to promote only the truly biblical message, they reexamined and rejected much of Armstrong's message. In particular, they aptly point out the historical and sci-entific weaknesses that devastate the theory.

In a published paper, they state:

> When reading Anglo-Israelite literature, one notices that it generally de-pends on folklore, legends, quasi-historical genealogies, and dubious etymolo-gies. None of these sources prove an Israelite origin for the peoples of north-western Europe. Rarely, if ever, are the disciplines of archaeology, sociology, anthropology, linguistics, or historiography applied to Anglo-Israelism. Anglo-Israelism operates outside of the sciences. Even the principles of sound biblical exegesis are seldom used, for . . . whole passages of Scripture that undermine the entire system are generally ignored.
>
> Why this unscientific approach? This approach must be taken because to do otherwise is to destroy Anglo-Israelism's foundation. Those who apply sci-entific disciplines and the principles of sound historiography to this subject eventually come away disbelieving the theory. . . . Even lay students of the Bible can find serious flaws in the idea.
>
> No firsthand account exists that traces the lost ten tribes in northwestern Europe. No eyewitnesses to European tribal migrations ever claimed an Israelite origin for any of them. No medieval or ancient genealogies ever linked the royal families of the British Isles with the Israelites. Not until the nineteenth century (long after the supposed migration) did anyone attempt to prove such an idea.[28]

[26]Armstrong, *United States*, 97–99.
[27]Martin, *Kingdom*, 310.
[28]Anonymous, *United States and Britain in Prophecy: Study Paper* (Pasadena: Worldwide Church of God, November 1995), 3.

There are a number of Old Testament verses that historically account for the lost ten tribes. Apparently the writers of the Old Testament had no difficulty acknowledging the so-called lost tribes as the house of Israel. The book of Ezra (2:70; 6:17; 8:25; and 10:5) irrefutably demonstrates the accountability of the twelve tribes. One could also reference Nehemiah 7:73 and 12:47 to find an accounting of all the house of Israel. Both historically and, most important, scripturally, we find no support for the wanton theories of Anglo-Israelism.

The second barrier Dr. Martin mentions for refutation is the identification of Israel and Judah as separate nations. This matter can be completely dismissed by careful consideration of the following facts written by Dr. Martin:

> First, after the Babylonian captivity, from which the Jews returned, Ezra records that the remnant were called by the name Jews (eight times) and by the name Israel forty times. Nehemiah records eleven times that they were Jews, and proceeds to describe them as Israel twenty-two times. The book of Esther records their partial restoration, calling them Jews forty-five times, but never Israel. Are we to conclude that only Judah (the Jews), and not Israel, was restored under Zerubbabel and Josiah? History, archaeology, and a study of Hebrew refute this possibility completely.
>
> The sixth chapter of Ezra describes the sin offering, mentioning specifically that "twelve male goats, one for each of the tribes of Israel" were offered for all Israel (v. 17), a fact attested to by Ezra 8:35.
>
> While it is true that in the post-exilic period, we no longer have two kingdoms, but one nation, the prophet Zechariah describes them in comprehensive terms as "Judah, Israel, and Jerusalem" (Zechariah 1:19), literally, "the House of Judah, and the House of Joseph" (Zechariah 10:6). Zechariah 8:13 identifies Judah and the House of Israel as one nation, and Malachi called the Jews Israel or Jacob, in contrast to Esau.
>
> The *coup de grace* to Anglo-Israelism's fragmented exegesis is given by the prophet Amos of Judah, a man specifically set apart by God to prophesy to the ten-tribed kingdom of the North. [Amos, dwelling in Bethel, prophesied against Israel's restoration as a separate kingdom (Amos 9:8–10).] We learn from this prophecy that as a kingdom, the ten tribes were to suffer destruction and their restoration would never be realized. How then is it possible for them to be "lost" for almost three millenniums, and then reappear as the British Kingdom when the kingdom was never to be restored?
>
> Second and finally, the New Testament speaks on the subject of the equation of Israel and Judah as one nation, described alternately and interchangeably as "the Jews" and "Israel."
>
> Peter, at Pentecost, proclaims the message of redemption to "all the house of Israel." Paul in Acts 26:6–7 apparently took Zechariah's statement:
>
>> As you have been an object of cursing among the nations, O Judah and Israel, so will I save you, and you will be a blessing. Do not be afraid, but let your hands be strong (Zechariah 8:13).
>
> In this context, Israel shall indeed be scattered among the nations, and so will Judah, and they shall be redeemed again together to bring forth a blessing in the person of the Messiah, whose gospel is to the Jew first, (not just to the house of Israel but as a separate nation), and also to the Gentiles (Romans 1:16).
>
> A cursory reading of the tenth chapter of Matthew indicates that Jesus Christ himself considered "the lost sheep of the house of Israel," to include "the Jews," since the missionary journeys of the twelve were limited to the environs of Palestine.
>
> It should be recalled also that Pauline theology, especially in the Book of

Romans (chapters 9—11), deals specifically with Israel, not as a nation in the sense of geography, but in the sense of spiritual transgression. He refers to them as God's people who have not been cast away.

If Israel and Judah are separate nations, why then does the apostle Paul describe the Jews as "his brethren" and as "kinsmen according to the flesh," and then identify them as "Israelites, heirs to the promise of God," as those promises are provided for in the coming Messiah?

The apostle Paul made this clear by declaring, "I am a Jew. . . . I am an Israelite. . . . Are they Israelites? So am I" (Acts 21:39; 22:3; Romans 11:1; 2 Corinthians 11:22; Philippians 3:5).

Jesus Christ sprang from Judah as "a Jew," in Anglo-Israelite reckoning, and the apostle Paul declares in Romans that it was in Israel that "Christ came, who is God over all, blessed for ever" (9:5, from the Greek).

Let it not be forgotten that Anna the prophetess was "of the tribe of Asher" (Israel), but she is called "a Jewess" of Jerusalem, facts which forever decimate the concept of Armstrong and British-Israelites that England is the throne of David and is Ephraim, while America is Manasseh.

The words of Jeremiah the prophet conclude our observations, where he states:

"The days are coming, declares the Lord, when I will bring my people Israel and Judah back from captivity and restore them to the land I gave their forefathers to possess" (30:3).

This is proof positive that both the house of Israel and the house of Judah would return from the captivity, and that as the New Testament amply demonstrates, it would be considered as one nation, no longer a kingdom in the historical meaning of that term.

Anglo-Israelism stands refuted by the facts of Scripture and history, and it would be unworthy of attention if it were not being utilized as a tool by the Armstrong cult, which opens a Pandora's box of multiple and destructive heresies, some of which we shall consider.[29]

The Theology of the Worldwide Church of God

I. *The Divine Origin of the Worldwide Church of God*

Our greatest concern between the Worldwide Church of God and the cults of Armstrongism is in their theology. The Worldwide Church of God has moved into biblical Christianity through interaction in the 1990s with evangelical theologians and ministers of various Protestant backgrounds. The Worldwide Church of God gives us insight on the thousands who broke away: "They have placed Mr. Armstrong ahead of the Bible in their own minds."[30]

This admirable step for the Worldwide Church of God is the very stumbling block of the factions. Gerald Flurry, of the Philadelphia Church of God, remarks, "The only hope for today's Laodicean is to get back to what Christ revealed to Mr. Armstrong. . . . The Laodiceans will have to admit that Mr. Armstrong was Christ's messenger. And they will have to believe the message in the same manner Mr. Armstrong did."[31]

The Armstrong cults believe that Armstrong was God's sole channel of divine truth. Armstrong believed that biblical truth had been lost from the first

---

[29]Martin, *Kingdom*, 315–316.
[30]Joseph W. Tkach, "Personal from Joseph W. Tkach," *The Worldwide News* (May 21, 1990): 5.
[31]Flurry & Leap, *Key*, 21.

century until rediscovered by him in 1927. He wrote about himself as the "Elijah" who would preach before the second advent of Jesus Christ. He also taught that he was unique in the human race as Christ's new "apostle" and that he had "restored" essential truths to Christianity. He championed his work in gloating terms, as when he introduced the *Mystery of the Ages* in 1985, saying, "I candidly feel it may be the most important book since the Bible!"[32]

Such self-glorifying sentiments are not uncommon to Armstrong. He had previously announced in January 1979 that his book *The Incredible Human Potential* had Jesus Christ as the author and Mr. Armstrong as the stenographer! "Actually," he wrote, "I feel with deep conviction that I myself did not author this book—that the living Jesus Christ is its real author. I was merely like a stenographer writing it down. And with that understanding, I feel I may say that this is the most important—the most tremendously revealing—book since the Bible!"[33]

Two of Armstrong's books mediate between humanity and the Bible. He claimed his writings were more than mere interpretation or commentary by ruling out all others as equal, second only to the Bible. "I am not writing foolishly," he boldly stated, "but very soberly, on *authority* of the *living Christ!*"[34] These stupendous claims either need to be upheld or exposed as fraudulent. Under the spotlight of God's Word, we will discover the indeed fraudulent nature of Armstrong's twisted biblical texts.

Of his mission, Armstrong said,

> I know of no other who has ever become founder of a religion, or a religious leader of any kind, who ever came into the truth in the way God brought me into it. . . . God brought me through a process that erased former misknowledge—and, as it were, gave me a clear start from "scratch." I wonder if you realize that every truth of God, accepted as truth doctrine and belief in the Worldwide Church of God, came from Christ through me, or was finally approved and made official through me. . . . I was appointed by Jesus Christ, the head of the Church.[35]

Others had less of the Holy Spirit than he did, he affirmed:

> The Holy Spirit is given to us by degrees. . . . I firmly believe that God by His grace granted me a much fuller portion of His Spirit at the very beginning than is the average experience.[36]

Uniquely he is Christ's apostle, "His one apostle for this twentieth century."[37] He revealed that he was the "Elijah" type who precedes the return of Jesus Christ.[38] He claims special privileges during the millennial reign of Christ. According to Armstrong, he will also run the "Headquarters Church" himself under Jesus Christ for the entire planet earth.

His parallels for Elijah, John the Baptist, and himself break down because

[32]As quoted by Gerald Flurry, "Personal," *The Philadelphia Trumpet* (February 1997): 1.
[33]Herbert W. Armstrong, "Personal From . . . ," *The Plain Truth* (January 1979): 45.
[34]Herbert W. Armstrong, "End Vietnam War Now!" *The Plain Truth* (February 1967): 47.
[35]Herbert W. Armstrong, "Personal from . . . ," *The Plain Truth* (February 1977): 17.
[36]Herbert W. Armstrong, "The True Facts of My Own Conversion," *The Plain Truth* (June 1977): 9.
[37]*The Plain Truth* (July 1977): 1; and (February 1978): 43.
[38]Herbert W. Armstrong, *Mystery of the Ages* (Pasadena: Worldwide Church of God, 1985), 8:284–286.

the Bible speaks of one messenger like Elijah, not two messengers. Both Isaiah 40:3 and Malachi 3:1–5 speak singularly of one messenger, which ample New Testament evidence reveals to be John the Baptist (Luke 1:17). Armstrong hangs his premise upon Matthew 17:11; that John the Baptist did not "restore all things."[39] However, the verses following this (Matthew 17:12–13) make it clear from the mouth of Jesus Christ that John indeed fulfilled Malachi's prophecy. Simply because Armstrong does not know how John fulfilled the prophecy gives no justification for claiming that he did not do so, nor that there should be another futuristic "Elijah" type. Anyone who believes in Jesus can rest assured that Jesus knew more on the subject than Armstrong. Furthermore, Matthew 17:13 finalizes the subject in saying, "Then the disciples understood that he was talking to them about John the Baptist." Notice the missing element for Armstrong's theory. It is not John the Baptist and some future figure in the twentieth century, but John the Baptist alone.

In 1958 Mr. Armstrong wrote a letter to Robert Sumner, a writer on cults and false religions. "First," he wrote, "let me say—this may sound incredible, but it's true—Jesus Christ foretold this very work—it is, itself the fulfillment of his prophecy (Matthew 24:14 and Mark 13:10). . . . Astounding as it may seem, there is no other work on earth proclaiming to the whole world this very *same gospel* that Jesus taught and proclaimed!"[40]

Throughout the years Armstrong continually maintained that his organization alone truly represented Christianity, while all others were false. Since 1933, he credited himself with restoring "at least eighteen basic essential truths . . . to the true Church."[41] In order to combat the obvious representation of Christianity during the last two millennia, Armstrong referred to the true church as an "underground" remnant called the "little flock." Armstrong's lofty pedestal crashes to the ground in the face of Jesus' words in Matthew 16:18, where he said that the gates of hell shall not prevail against his church. This demonstration of the church of Christ as a perpetually visible entity destroys Armstrong's notion. What went out in the first century was never lost and continuously grew. The undeniable fact is that the church of Jesus Christ has always been visible and remains so until His return, as Paul said, "throughout all generations" (Ephesians 3:21). The church is built upon the foundation of the apostles and prophets with Jesus Christ as the chief cornerstone (Ephesians 2:20).

In specific reference to the "little flock" statement of Jesus in Luke 12:32, it was never intended as a description of the church for two millennia. It was spoken to the twelve before Christ's crucifixion. The conversion of 3,000 souls in Acts, chapter two, began the rapid church expansion and dispels such folly. Armstrong was not the first to appeal to the "little flock" quotation in support of his small following, but to claim this represents the entire story of the church through nineteen centuries makes the commission of Christ (Matthew 28:19 and Mark 16:15) positively absurd. Christ commissioned his followers to go into the entire world not for a "little flock," but that "a great multitude that no one could count, from every nation, tribe, people and language" (Revelation 7:9) could be reached.

---

[39]Armstrong, *Mystery*, 285.
[40]Personal letter to Robert Sumner, November 27, 1958.
[41]Armstrong, *Mystery*, 207.

Herbert W. Armstrong's View of Scripture

The Bible, according to Mr. Armstrong, was not properly understood since the first century because it was a coded jigsaw puzzle. He claimed special anointing to decode it and put the puzzle together. The story went that God purposefully hid the biblical message from the world until the second Elijah (Armstrong) preached in the final days preceding Christ's return.

On the Bible, Armstrong said, "it is like a jigsaw puzzle which must be assembled piece by biblical piece . . . and since before *a.d.* 70, it has been entirely *suppressed.*"[42] Further, he wrote, "The Bible was a coded book, not intended to be understood until our day in this latter half of the twentieth century. . . . I learned that the Bible is like a jigsaw puzzle—thousands of pieces that need putting together."[43]

Imagine that God hid his Word for 1,900 years awaiting the arrival of Armstrong! In blatant contrast, Jesus told us "Thy word is truth" (John 17:17), thus expressing God's intention for all mankind to find plainly stated, uncoded, unsuppressed truth upon examination. It would have been easier for Armstrong if Jesus had said, "Thy word is a coded jigsaw puzzle," but no such thought exists. The most damaging blow to Armstrong's theory is found in 1 John 2:27 where it states, "You do not need anyone to teach you." Here, the apostle John clearly tells the church that the Holy Spirit teaches us beyond dependency upon Armstrong. So much does God expect the common Christian, led by His Spirit, to understand what they read that the Bible is replete with such references (Psalm 119:4, 104; Luke 11:28; Revelation 1:3).

Armstrong's New Revelations

The introduction to *Mystery of the Ages* states, "The final crystal-clear reason that impelled me to write this book did not fully reveal itself to my mind until December of 1984. It was a mind-boggling realization—a pivotal truth."[44] Again, "All these mysteries were . . . a coded message not allowed to be revealed and decoded until our time."[45] At times Armstrong claimed his writings are "a last warning from the *Eternal God*!"[46] New revelation outside of Scripture is a mark of all of the cults.

1. New Revelations That Breed False Predictions

When one stands parallel with biblical prophets, it becomes a short step to predicting future events. Armstrong wrote, "God dealt with me in no uncertain terms, even as he had dealt with Moses, Isaiah, Jeremiah, Jonah, Andrew, Peter and the apostle Paul."[47] The mark of God's prophets is that they never erred (Deuteronomy 13:1–5; 18:20–22; Isaiah 8:19–20). In contrast, even a false

---

[42]Herbert W. Armstrong, "How Far Can You Get from Being 'A Prophet of Doom'?" *The Plain Truth* (Oct./Nov. 1977): 3.

[43]Armstrong, *Mystery,* xii.

[44]Ibid., x.

[45]Ibid., xiii.

[46]Armstrong, *Vietnam,* 47.

[47]Armstrong, *Mystery,* 14.

prophet may have a sign come to pass (Deuteronomy 13:2), but eventually he will miss the mark, which undoubtedly proves he is not from God.

One may quickly protest that Armstrong claimed he was not a prophet.[48] But when one prognosticates and even adds the biblical "Thus saith the Lord" to his predictions, he is acting in all respects as a prophet. Jeremiah speaks clearly about those who prophesy in God's name when he did not give them the word (Jeremiah 23:25–32). Even if one claims that Armstrong only observed the times, we find biblical injunctions against that as well. A person who falsely predicts the "signs" stands equally as condemned as the false prophet who says "Thus saith the Lord." Armstrong did both. The Bible specifically addresses those who are "observers of times" (Leviticus 19:26; Deuteronomy 18:10, 14; 2 Kings 21:6; and 2 Chronicles 33:6), which is not restricted to divination. May the reader keep in mind Armstrong's self-proclamations of inspiration from God and Christ as we chronologically review a number of false predictions.

> **1934**—As nearly as we can calculate from the dates of ancient history, the year 1936 will see the *end* of the Times of the Gentiles. Those "Times" have not been completely fulfilled until that year.
>
> And for Great Pyramid students, a point in this connection will be of interest. The present depression, or tribulation, is there symbolized as occupying the entire low passage continuing from May 29, 1928, when the tribulation struck Europe, until September, 1936.
>
> The present world-chaos Tribulation, [is] to be followed, by or quickly after 1936, but the heavenly signs, which shall be followed by the "Day of the Lord" . . . to the time-sequences fixed by these prophecies, the Revelation story-flow agrees exactly.[49]
>
> **1938**—But then what will Mussolini and these ten dictators do? Notice the prophecy—absolutely *sure* to happen—in Revelation 17:16–17. . . . Thus shall the Catholic Church come to her final *end. Thus saith the Lord!*
>
> Mussolini and the Pope will hatch up an idea between [them] of setting up a world headquarters at *Jerusalem* —and so Mussolini's armies will enter into *Palestine* (Daniel 11:14), and eventually will capture just half of the city of Jerusalem!
>
> Then, at last, Stalin will decide he is ready. . . . Finally, *all* nations shall be gathered for the final great and mighty battle. . . . It will be at the time of the last of the seven plagues of the great *day of the Lord!* And then shall the *Lord* go forth—the *second coming of Christ!*[50]
>
> **1939**—Once world war is resumed it must continue on through the great Tribulation, the heavenly signs, the plagues of the Day of the Lord, and to the Second Coming of Christ, at the last battle, at Armageddon! . . . This you *may know!* This war will be ended by *Christ's Return!* And war may be started within six weeks! We are just *that near* Christ's coming! That should make every reader stop to think![51]
>
> **1941**—*Plain Truth* readers know world events, *before they occur!* . . . Hitler is the *"Beast"* of Revelation. . . . There, Bible prophecy does indicate that Hitler *must be the victor* in his present Russian invasion![52]
>
> **1943**—But Hitler (or his successor, if there is one), and the False Prophet shall *fight* against Christ! They shall fight desperately to retain their foul system.

[48]Herbert W. Armstrong, *Tomorrow's World* (February 1972): 1ff.
[49]Herbert W. Armstrong, *The Plain Truth* (June/July 1934): 5.
[50]Ibid. (March 1938): 8.
[51]Ibid. (August 1939): 6.
[52]Ibid. (October 1941): 7.

And the *battle* that ensues in this struggle to see whether Hitler's New Order or Christ's Kingdom shall rule this earth for the next *Thousand Years*, is the *battle* of the *great day of God Almighty*! . . . Note it! "And I saw the beast (Hitler) and the kings of the earth (his junior partners), and their armies . . ." (Revelation 19:19). . . . It is *Christ* and the Angels that Hitler will fight! . . . That is to be Hitler's end![53]

1956—*1975 in Prophecy*. . . Mysteries of God, never before understood, now become crystal-clear. God's own time for this revealing has come. . . . Yes, millions of lukewarm, inactive professing Christians will suffer *martyrdom*—and that *before* the anticipated push-button leisure-year of 1975 dawns upon us![54]

1957—God prophesies that finally, within the next fifteen years [by 1972], fully one third of our whole population will die of disease and famine![55]

1962—It's time we face the hard, cold, realistic *fact*: humanity has two alternatives: either there is an Almighty, all-powerful God who is about to step in and set up *the kingdom of God* to rule all nations . . . or else there will not be a human being alive on this earth twenty years [by 1982] from now! . . . It's about time you come to know *who* are the false prophets, and *who* is speaking the true Word of God faithfully![56]

1967—The *"Day of the Eternal"*—a time foretold in more than thirty prophecies—is going to strike between five and ten years [by 1977] from now! You will *know*, then, how *real* it is. . . . I am not writing foolishly, but very soberly, *on authority* of the living *Christ*![57]

It appears that by 1972 Mr. Armstrong realized that date-setting for future events was futile. He wrote, "It is utterly unsafe to try to *set dates* in regard to future prophesied events."[58] In looking over this list we find one failed prediction after another. The Lord did not destroy the Catholic Church through Mussolini in 1936. Jesus did not return at the end of World War II. Hitler was not the beast and did not fight Jesus Christ at Armageddon. One third of the world was not wiped out in 1972. Millions of lukewarm Christians went unmartyred in 1975. And the human race was not extinct by 1982. It would do the ninety factions of Armstrongism well to thoroughly examine their founder's false predictions. It is inescapable that some were credited as from the mouth of God, Christ, or the Lord, which makes them false prophecies readily condemned by the Bible.

2. New Revelations Outside of God's Word

A synopsis of Armstrong's cosmology divulges that he goes far beyond interpreting the Bible by adding to God's revelation:

In the very beginning—before this physical universe was created—there existed *only* the two Superbeings—God and the 'Word'. . . . These two Superpersonages in space *first* created angels, composed solely of spirit, *before* any physical matter was ever produced. . . . When the angels rebelled against the

---

[53]Armstrong, *The Plain Truth* (March/April 1943): 6.

[54]Herbert W. Armstrong, *1975 in Prophecy* (Pasadena: Radio Church of God, 1956), 1, 20.

[55]Armstrong, *The Plain Truth* (December 1957): 23.

[56]Herbert W. Armstrong, *Just What Do You Mean . . . Kingdom of God?* (Pasadena: Ambassador College, 1962), 19.

[57]Armstrong, *The Plain Truth* (February 1967): 47.

[58]Armstrong, *Tomorrow's World* (February 1972): 1.

government of God, the preservation of the physical earth and all of its original beauty and glory ceased—and physical destruction to the surface of the earth resulted. . . . The rebellion of Lucifer and his angels brought this extreme cataclysm to the earth. And in all probability *it did more*! . . . It is apparent, therefore, based upon what is revealed in the Bible, that a similar cataclysm of destruction happened to the surface of our moon and the other planets of our solar system—perhaps extending to all of the astral bodies in the universe. And all of this was caused by the rebellion of Lucifer and his angels.

Satan and his angels were then *disqualified* to administer God's government over the earth. But it is a principle of God that a government must never be without a head. Consequently Satan was to be left here on earth until his successor, who has already been qualified to rule, *is inducted into office*.

In the six days of renewing the face of the earth and lavishly decorating it with flora and fauna, God made it beautiful—gloriously beautiful! . . . The only possible assurance of accomplishing His great purpose of finishing the creation—populating and beautifying the entire universe—was for Him to reproduce himself. . . . God needs millions or billions of perfect and righteous beings, governed by His divine government, *to complete* the creation of . . . not only the other planets of our solar system (now in utter waste and decay), but also our galaxy, and countless other galaxies of the limitless, vast universe.[59]

The story continues:

Then, in His greatest Master Plan of all, God undertook the actual reproduction of himself, through *man*. God created man in His image—form and shape—for a special relationship with God. But Satan got to Adam through Eve, his wife. Adam followed Satan in rejecting the government of God. . . . On Adam's fateful decision and rebellion, Adam's world, descended from him, was sentenced to being *cut off* from God for 6,000 years, after which God decreed Christ should come to *restore* the *government of God* on earth, establishing the *Kingdom of God* with worldwide rule.[60]

In summary, Armstrong argues:

God's *PURPOSE* is to reproduce himself through man—reproduce the *God Family* from the human family. . . . The Messiah, Jesus Christ, would restore the government of God to the planet earth. . . . Since God's *purpose* is to reproduce himself—expand the God *Family*—and since it shall be the world-ruling family, then the *kingdom of God* is the born family of God ruling the entire world.[61]

In this scheme of things, man has a spirit and body, but is incomplete; therefore, he needs another spirit, the Holy Spirit from God. This Holy Spirit comes to impregnate man as a "begotten child of God," but not yet "born again" until birth occurs as a spirit-body in the resurrection. Once born at the resurrection, he becomes a God Being and joins the persons of God as part of the God Family.

All of those who died before Christ's first advent will then be revived in mortal flesh to hear the message and accept Jesus as their savior. The ones who accept Jesus will receive the immortal resurrection of a spirit-body. Hence, they become God Beings and finish creating the many planets in the universe.[62]

[59]Herbert W. Armstrong, "Why Humans Were Put on the Earth," *The Plain Truth* (Oct./Nov. 1978): 3, 45.
[60]Herbert W. Armstrong, "Supernatural Forces on a Collision Course!" *The Plain Truth* (January 1979): 4–5.
[61]Herbert W. Armstrong, "A World Held Captive," *The Plain Truth* (June 1984): 6, 39.
[62]Armstrong, *The Plain Truth* (Oct./Nov. 1977): 3ff.

This story spun by Armstrong is everything but biblical. More than filling gaps in his jigsaw puzzle, he invented a soteriology that expels his followers from genuine salvation.

II. *The Trinity of God and the Divinity of Man*

Armstrong was an outspoken anti-Trinitarian, as revealed in these quotations:

> But the theologians and "Higher Critics" have blindly accepted the heretical and false doctrine introduced by *pagan* false prophets who crept in, that the *Holy Spirit* is a *third person*—the heresy of the "*Trinity.*" This limits God to "Three Persons."[63]
>
> The false Trinity teaching does limit God to three persons. But God is not limited. As God repeatedly reveals, his purpose is to reproduce himself into what well may become billions of God persons. It is the false Trinity teaching that limits God, denies God's purpose and has palpably deceived the whole Christian world.[64]

Armstrong's denial of the Trinity was superseded by his "binitarian" (two persons in the Godhead) view. He held to the deity of Jesus, correctly calling Him Jehovah from the Old Testament. His denial of the deity of the Holy Spirit left him with two persons as God (binitarian), instead of three persons (Trinitarian). Within this scope, however, he diverges into "ditheism" (two god Beings). We have seen in a previous quotation his address of "two Superbeings" and "Superpersonages." He speaks elsewhere: "In the very beginning, before all else, there existed two living Beings composed of Spirit. . . . One was named the Word. . . . The other was named God. . . ."[65] When Armstrong calls the Father and Son two beings, then it is difficult to maintain monotheism, since two beings requires ditheism, a form of polytheism.

The nature of God is spirit, according to Armstrong, but His shape, form, and stature is that of a man! In their correspondence course, he asks, "Does the Father therefore appear like a man? Comment: Christ clearly indicated that the Father has the general form and stature of a mortal man!"[66] *The Plain Truth* reveals, "We are made of material flesh, but in the form and shape of God."[67] And, "Now notice once again Genesis 1:26: 'God (*Elohim*) said, Let us make man in our image, after our likeness (form and shape). . . . ' God is described in the Bible as having eyes, ears, nose, mouth, hair, arms, legs, fingers, toes."[68] Still, "Man was made in the form and shape of God. For example, notice the human hand. God has hands (2 Chronicles 6:4)."[69] Finally, in *Mystery of the Ages*, he reveals,

> Perhaps it will make God more real to you when you realize he is in the

[63]Herbert W. Armstrong, *Just What Do You Mean—Born Again!* (Pasadena: Radio Church of God, 1962), 19.

[64]Armstrong, *Mystery*, 37.

[65]Herbert W. Armstrong, "World Peace Just around the Corner," *The Plain Truth* (Nov./Dec. 1984): 4.

[66]Herbert W. Armstrong, ed., *Ambassador College Bible Correspondence Course (Lesson 9)* (Pasadena: Ambassador College, 1966): 8.

[67]Armstrong, "Just What Do You Mean: Born Again?" *The Plain Truth* (February 1977): 28.

[68]Armstrong, *The Plain Truth* (February 1979): 42.

[69]Armstrong, "Never Before Understood," *The Plain Truth* (September 1981): 26.

same form and shape as a human being. . . . God is invisible to human eyes. . . . But even though God is composed of spirit and not visible matter, God nonetheless does have form and shape. . . . In various parts of the Bible, it is revealed that God has a face, eyes, a nose, mouth and ears. He has hair on his head. It is revealed God has arms and legs. And God has hands and fingers. . . . God has feet and toes and a body. . . . If you know what a man looks like, you know what is the form and shape of God, for he made man in his image, after his very likeness.[70]

In this section we cannot sidestep his "God Family" doctrine. He taught that "God" was a family name for two beings, the Father and Son. The God Family will soon become billions of God Beings comprised of those "born again." The quotations are numerous because he equivocated the terms "immortal," "resurrection," "saved," "born again," "Church of God," "God Family," and "Kingdom of God."[71]

His God Family doctrine projects a future divine human race. He expressed the future divinity of mankind: "God's purpose is to make us immortal like God, until we become God as he is God."[72] Elsewhere he wrote, "That is, once born again, one is born not of a human father in mortal physical human flesh, but of god, impregnated by God's Spirit, in immortal *spirit composition*, as a God Being! *Born of God!*. . . But he is *born again* only in the immortal spirit life to come—at the time of the resurrection. When born again, he will be spirit—no longer mortal flesh and blood."[73] Once again, "You and I potentially may *become God*! For *God* is a collective *Family*—the *Divine Family*—into which *the Church* is to be born!"[74] And, "By a resurrection, we become *born* God personages—personages just as are God the Father and Christ the Son! We shall have the entire *universe* put under our feet (Hebrews 2:8)."[75]

In agreement with the current Worldwide Church of God, Christians need to repudiate such blasphemous doctrines. Their current *Statement of Beliefs* nicely describes, in Trinitarian terms, a refutation to the above heresies of Armstrong. They state, "God, by the testimony of Scripture, is one divine Being in three eternal, coessential, yet distinct Persons—Father, Son, and Holy Spirit."[76] We add to this the scriptural support that there can exist but one God (Deuteronomy 4:39; 6:4; Isaiah 44:6–8; 45:21–22; and Mark 12:32). Yet the Bible also shows us the three distinct Persons within God's nature (Father, Romans 1:7; Son, John 20:28; and Holy Spirit, Acts 5:3–4). All three persons are coequal in the nature of God (Matthew 28:19; Isaiah 48:16). For the avid student of God's Word we recommend a more thorough study of the Trinity found in a number of reliable Bible encyclopedias. (See also, chapter 5, page 101.)

Isaiah 43:10 plays an important role in refutation of Armstrong, for God unequivocally states that "Before me no god was formed, nor will there be one

---

[70]Armstrong, "Never Understood," 26.

[71]Armstrong, *Mystery*, 37–39.

[72]Herbert W. Armstrong, "Why Must Man Suffer?" *The Plain Truth* (October 1983): 21.

[73]Herbert W. Armstrong, "This Is the Worldwide Church of God," *The Plain Truth* (January 1979): 3.

[74]Herbert W. Armstrong, "A Voice Cries Out Amid Religious Confusion," *The Plain Truth* (December 1980): 40.

[75]Armstrong, *The Plain Truth* (September 1980): 30.

[76]*Statement*, 2.

after me." The "God Family," "Born Gods," "God personages," and "God Beings" are dealt a deathblow in the face of Isaiah 43:10. None preceded Him, and absolutely none will follow. Armstrong's idea of two God Beings coexisting in eternity is answered well by Isaiah 44:8, where God tells us He knows of no others beside himself. No other beings existed with Him.

Isaiah succinctly deals with Armstrong's concept that God the Father is in the form, stature, and shape of man. Rhetorically, he asks, "To whom then will you liken God? Or what likeness will you compare to Him?" (Isaiah 40:18, NKJV). Here, Isaiah tells us nothing is likened to God, but Armstrong believes God had parts in comparison to man's likeness. Any number of biblical passages on the omnipresence of God destroys this view. When the Bible states that the "heaven and the heaven of heavens cannot contain You" (1 Kings 8:27, NKJV), then how does Armstrong purpose that he is limited to the form, shape, and stature of man? Scripture answers this well (2 Chronicles 2:6; 6:18; Jeremiah 23:24).

III. *The Nature of Christ*

Armstrongism taught that Jesus was Jehovah, but not the Son, before his birth through Mary. We must understand that his view of the incarnate Christ destroys the very foundation of God's eternal nature! For example, God cannot lie (Hebrews 6:18) because it is against the nature of One who is pure holiness and truth. Armstrong made the immutable, eternal, immortal God contradict His essence by giving up His immortality while on earth and converting His spirit-essence into flesh. He made Jehovah divest himself totally of immortal spirit, convert into flesh, then reconvert His mortal flesh back to immortal spirit at His resurrection, making him the first "born again" saved person. He stopped being "very God" and then became "very God" again. While He was dead, the other God Being, the Father, ran the universe, since the immortality of Jesus was temporarily dysfunctional. Then, when Jesus raised from the dead, He raised in a spirit-body, but not the physical body that had died.

Armstrong wrote:

> Jesus did not become the Son of God until about 4 *b.c.*, when born in human flesh of the virgin Mary.[77]
>
> Christ was converted into flesh . . . he who had existed from eternity . . . he who was *God*—he *was made flesh*—converted *into* flesh, until he *became* flesh; and then he *was* flesh! . . . He divested himself of inherent immortality for the time being. He gave up immortality for us—that he might *die* for us . . . that he, even as we, might be resurrected from the *dead*, and given by the Father immortal life—that is, converted back into spiritual immortality so that he by the resurrection once again *became* divine Spirit—or very *God!*
>
> Jesus was also *God*—he was both human and divine. But he was not *God* inside of, yet separate from, the body of flesh—he, God, *was made flesh*, until he, still *God*—God *with us*—became God *in* (*not* inside of) the human flesh—God manifest *in the flesh* (1 Timothy 3:16). . . . Jesus *died!* Jesus *was dead!* . . . If there were no other Person in the Godhead, then the Giver of all life was dead and all hope was at an end! . . . But the Father still reigned in high heaven!
>
> Not Resurrected in Same Body. . . . Now notice carefully, God the Father

---

[77]Armstrong, *The Plain Truth* (February 1979): 41.

did not cause Jesus Christ to get back into the body that had died. . . . And the resurrected body was no longer human—it was the Christ resurrected *immortal*, once again *changed!* As he had been changed, converted *into* mortal human flesh and blood, subject to death, and for the *purpose of dying for our sins*, now by a *resurrection from the dead, he was again changed, converted into immortality.*[78]

Because they knew what Jesus had looked like—and in his born-again, resurrected body he looked the same, except he now was composed of spirit instead of matter! . . . He was born in a spirit body, which was manifested to his apostles in the same apparent size and shape as when he died.[79]

The Worldwide Church of God, in contrast to Armstrong's wayward Christology, states, "When the Word came in the flesh, though he was fully human and fully divine, he voluntarily set aside the prerogatives of divinity."[80] They also state that he was "two natures in one Person" and "raised bodily from the dead."[81] These statements, written in agreement with historic creeds of Christianity, stand in biblical opposition to Armstrong's fallacy. Add to that these supportive verses on Christ's immutability: "Jesus Christ the same yesterday, and to day, and for ever" (Hebrews 13:8). And, "Before Abraham was, I am" (John 8:58). Jesus, the eternal I AM, could not stop being who He is and then regain an unchangeable nature. That would be a contradiction of terms. Philippians 2:6–8 answers the contrived story of Armstrongism. Jesus had two natures, that of eternal God, and that of a servant, man. Neither nature (*morphe* in Greek) was altered during the incarnation. His deity was not altered by His humanity, and His humanity was unaltered by His being God. This shows that His deity was distinct from His humanity. One did not merge or convert into the other.

According to Colossians 2:9, all the fullness of Deity dwells in him bodily, which means nothing was lacking in his deity, it was the fullness. Had he given up immortality then he would not have the fullness of Deity, but Colossians corrects Armstrongism here. See also John 1:1; 1:18; 5:18; 20:28; Acts 20:28; and Revelation 1:8.

Was Jesus referred to as the Son previous to His incarnation? We find an affirmative answer in the Psalms: "Kiss the Son, lest he be angry" (Psalm 2:12). Also, in Proverbs 30:4 (NKJV), the question is asked, "Who has established all the ends of the earth? What is His name, and what is His Son's name?" We must also remember that Jesus was the "sent Son" (John 3:16) into the world, which agrees with these Old Testament passages that He was the Son before his incarnation.

The physical resurrection of the same body that Jesus had died with on the cross is central to Christianity. It cannot be some non-material spirit-body that only looked similar to the one that died. Paul reminds us that if the Resurrection did not happen, our faith is in vain (1 Corinthians 15:14).

When Jesus made His post-resurrection appearances He offered the print of the nails in His hands (John 20:27) as proof that it was the same crucified body. Otherwise, Jesus would have been deceiving His disciples with imitation prints. He offered His hands and feet as evidence (Luke 24:39). Of utmost im-

---

[78]Armstrong, "Why Christ Died and Rose Again," *The Plain Truth*, abbreviated version (April 1982): 20.
[79]Armstrong, "Personal From . . . ," *The Plain Truth* (January 1978): 44.
[80]Anonymous, *God Is. . . .* (Pasadena: Worldwide Church of God, 1992), 30.
[81]*Statement.*

portance, He denied that He was other than "flesh and bones, as ye see me have" (Luke 24:39). He proved His physical body by eating with His disciples (Luke 24:42; John 21:12–13). This is how Luke can assuredly tell us that He showed himself alive with many infallible proofs (Acts 1:3).

IV. *The Personality of the Holy Spirit*

The teaching of Armstrong on the Holy Spirit is twofold. First he believes that the Holy Spirit was not God, nor a person within the nature of God. Second, he believed the Holy Spirit impregnates the believer (begotten) in Jesus as a down payment for salvation. In this his purpose was to name the Holy Spirit a "divine sperm" and "sperm" impregnating the believer. Once the Holy Spirit leads a person through a faithful life, then the "begotten" person is finally "born again" at the resurrection to become a member of the God Family.

Armstrong specifically focused upon the person and deity of the Holy Spirit. He wrote, "He [Simon the sorcerer] taught, and his false church later (*a.d.* 321) made official, the 'Trinity' doctrine, saying the Holy Spirit of God is a *ghost*—a third spirit *person*—thereby doing away with the fact that we can be begotten by God's Spirit."[82] Further, he says, "The theologians . . . have blindly accepted the false doctrine introduced by *pagan* false prophets who crept in, that the Holy Spirit is a third person."[83]

About the Holy Spirit impregnating the repentant person, he said, "The Holy Spirit also is the divine 'spiritual sperm' that impregnates with immortal God-life!"[84] And, "If 'fertilized' by the male divine sperm of God (his Holy Spirit—actually God-life), he would have been begotten, but not yet born as God."[85]

The Christian doctrine of the Holy Spirit is guarded as precious in the sight of believers. Therefore, denial of His person is an assault upon the very nature of God. The Bible shows us that the Holy Spirit acts only as a person can act or respond (John 14—16; Matthew 12:31; Romans 8:26–27; Ephesians 4:30; and Hebrews 10:29). The Holy Spirit has the attributes that belong only to God (Luke 1:35–37; Isaiah 40:13; Hebrews 9:14). The Holy Spirit is also called God (2 Samuel 23:2–3; Acts 5:1–4; 1 Corinthians 6:19–20).

V. *Salvation*

Armstrong summarized his plan of salvation:

> Salvation, then, *is a process!* . . . But how the "god of this world" (2 Corinthians 4:4) would blind your eyes to that! He tries to deceive you into thinking all there is to it is just "accepting Christ"—with "no works,"—and presto chango, you're pronounced saved![86]
>
> People have been taught, falsely, that "Christ *completed* the Plan of Salvation on the Cross"—when actually it was only *begun* there. The popular denominations have taught, "*Just believe*—that's all there is to it; believe the Lord Jesus Christ, and you are that instant *saved!*" . . . The *blood* of Christ does not finally

---

[82]Armstrong, "Foundation, History, Authority, and Doctrine of the Worldwide Church of God," *The Plain Truth* (February 1978): 41.
[83]Armstrong, *Born Again?* 19.
[84]Armstrong, "Confusion," 6.
[85]Armstrong, "Captive," 42.
[86]Armstrong, *Born*, 21.

save any man. The death of Christ did pay the penalty of sin in our stead—it wipes the slate clean of past sins—it saves us merely from the *death penalty*—it removes that which separated us from God and reconciles us to God. . . . It is only those who, during this Christian Spirit-begotten life, have grown in knowledge and grace, have overcome, have developed spiritually, done works of Christ, and endured unto the end, who shall finally be given immortality—finally changed from mortal to immortal at the time of the second coming of Christ."[87]

Salvation, as outlined in *Mystery of the Ages,* needs to be carefully considered because of the redefinition of terms foisted by Armstrong. Begotten, for example, is the state of the believer on earth after accepting Christ's forgiveness and becoming impregnated by the Holy Spirit. Impregnation by the Holy Spirit is when the Holy Spirit commingles with the human spirit giving it a gestation period until "birth" in the resurrection. Even so, it needs to be remembered that the Holy Spirit is not God to him, but only the "power" or emanation of the Father and Son. The resurrection is defined as the birth of the person, becoming "born again" into a spirit-body, but not a human body. The kingdom of God is the destiny of those "born again" in the resurrection. They will receive rewards for their works on earth.

The dead who died from Adam to Christ will revive into mortal human bodies to receive a chance to hear the gospel during the millennium and accept the message. This is where Armstrongism holds the similitude of soul-sleep. Those who are awakened to a mortal resurrection and believe will be changed to spirit-bodies at the final resurrection. He attempts to steer clear of accusations of "second chance" salvation by saying that this only presents each person with a first chance. Those before Christ, he says, had no first chance.

The faithful resurrected persons will become God Beings in the God Family and rule over cities on this planet or finish God's creation on other planets. Those who rejected the message of Christ will suffer hellfire, albeit temporary. Armstrong's niche is that the soul of the unrepentant is mortal, so the suffering by hellfire will last only until the soul is destroyed. That is the second death. Much of this was evidenced from quotations in our earlier section on Armstrong's cosmology. Tucked neatly within his doctrine of the mortality of the soul is his doctrine of soul-sleep. He appealed to all of the standard arguments advanced by the Seventh-Day Adventists and Jehovah's Witnesses. These, however, are quickly refuted by a number of verses in both the Old and New Testaments that show conscious existence after death: Isaiah 14:9–11; Matthew 17:1–9; 22:32; Mark 9:38–48; Luke 16:19–31; Romans 8:38; 2 Corinthians 5:6–8; Philippians 1:23; and Revelation 6:9.

One stands perplexed after reading *Mystery of the Ages,* wondering where to begin unraveling a soteriology that is so far from Scripture it ranks with science fiction. (Small wonder that the Worldwide Church of God abandoned the book!) Let us suffice the subject by presenting the genuine gospel message from Walter Martin's observations:

In his epistle to the Ephesians, the apostle Paul is adamant in his declaration that "by grace you have been saved through faith; and this is not your own

---

[87]Herbert W. Armstrong, *All About Water Baptism* (Pasadena: Ambassador College Press, 1972), 6–8.

doing, it is the gift of God—not because of works, lest any one should boast" (Ephesians 2:8, from the Greek). Here is the usage of the past tense in reference to Christians, an instance that is amply supplemented throughout the New Testament by such passages as John 5:24; 3:36; 6:47; Romans 8:1; 1 Peter 1:18; and 1 John 5:1, 11–13, 20.

It is wholly unnecessary to pursue this thought further since Armstrong has no scholarly precedent for subdividing the new birth and attempting to attach it to the resurrection of the body, something that the Scripture nowhere does. His is a lame attempt to distort the basic meaning of *gennao*, which he admits is listed in the lexicon as "to be born, to bring forth, to be delivered of." It is only one more indication of the limitations of his resources.

When Jesus Christ addressed Nicodemus (John 3) and spoke of the new birth, He connected this birth to the person of the Holy Spirit whom the disciples received in the Upper Room (John 20) and whose power and presence were manifested at Pentecost (Acts 2). This has always been accepted in Christian theology for just what the Bible says it is, an instantaneous experience of spiritual cleansing and re-creation synonymous with the exercise of saving faith in the person of Jesus Christ and through the agency of the grace of God (Acts 16:31; 2:8–10; Colossians 1:13–14; Galatians 2:20; 1 Corinthians 6:11, 19; 2 Corinthians 5:17).

The apostle Paul instructs us that our salvation has been accomplished not by any efforts on our part, but by "the kindness and love of God our Savior" (Titus 3:4–7). It is not something we must wait for until the resurrection; it is our present possession in Christ totally separate from the immortality of the body, which is to be bestowed at the return of Christ and the resurrection of the body (1 Corinthians 15:49–54; 1 John 3:2; Romans 6:5).[88]

In paraphrase of Walter Martin's conclusions on Armstrongism, there are many other errors in Armstrong's theology that could easily fill a small volume. Let it be said, however, that the theology of Armstrongism contains just enough truth to make it attractive to the unaware listener.

Armstrongism is dangerous as it makes profuse use of the Bible and professes to swear allegiance to only "the plain truth of the Scripture," while, in reality, its allegiance is to the interpretations of the Scripture propagated by Herbert W. Armstrong, whom one author has aptly described as "Mr. Confusion."

Since "God is not the author of confusion" (1 Corinthians 14:33), there is one sure remedy to the problem of the spread of Armstrongism. Turn off the television and radio wherever it is promoted and open your Bible, for within its pages God is always broadcasting the eternal message of the Gospel of grace. A study of the essential doctrines necessary for solid growth in the Christian life can be found within its pages. When this is supplemented by attendance in a truly Christian church where that gospel is preached, there is no need to listen to the Herbert Armstrongs of our day, for as the psalmist so beautifully described it, "The entrance of thy Word giveth light."

---

[88]Martin, *Kingdom*, 328.

Appendix B

The Word Faith Movement

A growing number of pastors, teachers, and evangelists within the Charismatic/Pentecostal circles of the Christian church are advancing what has come to be known as the "Word Faith" movement. Its major leaders include such prominent figures as Kenneth Hagin, pastor of RHEMA Bible Church and founder of RHEMA Bible Training Center; Kenneth Copeland, leader of Kenneth Copeland Ministries; Frederick K. C. Price, pastor of the Los Angeles-based Crenshaw Christian Center (with a purported membership of more than 16,000[1]); and David (Paul) Yongii Cho, who pastors one of the largest churches in the world in Seoul, Korea.[2] Other well-known Word Faith personalities include Gloria Copeland, Robert Tilton, John Avanzini, John Osteen, T. L. Osborne, Marilyn Hickey, Jerry Savelle, Morris Cerullo, Casey Treat, Dwight Thompson, and Oral and Richard Roberts.

Although Word Faith doctrines commonly are disseminated through radio broadcasts, tapes, books, and tracts, primarily they are spread through the Trinity Broadcasting Network (TBN), which regularly airs the programs of more than a dozen Word Faith teachers.[3] Paul and Jan Crouch, the directors of TBN, who are themselves deeply involved in the movement, have also featured Word Faith teachers as special guests on their "Praise the Lord" and "Praise-a-thon" (fund-raiser) programs. The Crouchs' worldwide platform has mainstreamed Word Faith theology to the lives of millions of Christians who would not otherwise have encountered Word Faith theology.

Rarely has Christianity felt an unbiblical influence as all-pervasive as the Word Faith movement. It has enjoyed such an increasing acceptance[4] that to the

This appendix researched and written by Richard Abanes, and edited by Gretchen Passantino.

[1]John Dart, "Huge Faith Dome in L.A.," *Los Angeles Times* (September 9, 1989): II:9–10.
[2]Hank Hanegraaff, *Christianity in Crisis* (Eugene, Ore.: Harvest House Publishers, 1993), 352.
[3]TBN Satellite Schedule, May 1993.
[4]D. R. McConnell, *A Different Gospel* (Peabody, Mass.: Hendrickson Publishers, 1995), xviii.

minds of many it is "no longer just a *part* of the charismatic movement: it *is* the charismatic movement."[5]

Some have labeled its doctrines "heresy," "cultic," "Gnostic," and "a work of Satan."[6] One critic has said that the Word Faith gospel is "perhaps the most subtle heretical system to emerge in our own times."[7] Another has referred to it as "a form of transcendentalism or Gnosticism (from which have come such metaphysical cults as Christian Science, Unity School of Christianity, and now the health and wealth cult)."[8]

At this juncture it would be appropriate to quote Hank Hanegraaff, the president of the Christian Research Institute. "While the Faith movement is undeniably cultic—and particular groups within the movement are clearly cults—it should be pointed out that *there are many sincere, born-again believers within the movement.* I cannot overemphasize this crucial point. These believers, for the most part, seem to be wholly unaware of the movement's cultic theology. . . . They represent that segment of the movement which, for whatever reason, has not comprehended or internalized the heretical teaching set forth by the leadership of their respective groups."[9]

If the gospel of the Word Faith movement is unbiblical, why is it so popular among Christians?

First, the movement "uses so much evangelical and Pentecostal terminology and so many biblical proof texts that most believers are lulled into a false sense of security as to its orthodoxy."[10]

Second, its message is "without question the most attractive message being preached today, or for that matter, in the whole history of the church."[11] D. R. McConnell, a Word Faith critic and a graduate of Word Faith College, Oral Roberts University, observes,

> Seldom, if ever, has there been a gospel that has promised so much, and demanded so little. The Faith gospel is a message ideally suited to the twentieth-century American Christian. In an age in America characterized by complexity, the Faith gospel gives simple, if not revelational, answers. In an economy fueled by materialism and fired by the ambitions of the "upwardly mobile," the Faith gospel preaches wealth and prosperity. The Faith gospel promises health and long life to a world in which death can come a myriad of different ways. Finally, in an international environment characterized by anarchy, in which terrorists strike at will and nuclear holocaust can come screaming from the sky at any moment, the Faith gospel confers an authority with which the believer can supposedly exercise complete control over his or her own environment.[12]

The apostle Paul, writing to the Corinthians about false teachers, said, "I fear, lest by any means, as the serpent beguiled Eve through his subtlety, so your

---

[5]McConnell, *A Different Gospel,* xix.

[6]Ibid.

[7]Judith A. Matt, *The Born-Again Jesus of the Word-Faith Teaching* (Fullerton, Calif.: Spirit of Truth Ministries, 1984), 8.

[8]Rev. Curtis I. Crenshaw, *Man As God: The Word of Faith Movement,* 2.

[9]Hanegraaff, *Christianity in Crisis* (Eugene, Ore.: Harvest House Publishers, 1993), 41.

[10]McConnell, *Different,* xviii.

[11]Charles Farah, *A Critical Analysis: The Roots and Fruits of Faith-Formula Theology,* unpublished paper for the Society for Pentecostal Studies, November 1980, 22.

[12]McConnell, *Different,* xviii.

minds should be corrupted from the simplicity that is in Christ. For if he that cometh preacheth another Jesus, whom we have not preached, or if ye receive another spirit, which ye have not received, or another gospel, which ye have not accepted, ye might well bear with him" (2 Corinthians 11:3–4).

This passage perfectly illustrates today's events. Christians everywhere are not merely tolerating but actually embracing what the Word Faith movement is handing out: a false Jesus, another gospel, and a different spirit.

What *exactly* does the Word Faith movement teach? Why are Word Faith doctrines so spiritually and physically dangerous? Can anything be done to correct brothers and sisters in Christ who have succumbed to Word Faith lies?

These questions must be answered if the unity of the Christian faith is going to be preserved. Far too many have already succumbed to Word Faith teachings in fulfillment of 2 Timothy 4:3–4: "For the time will come when they will not endure sound doctrine; but after their own lusts shall they heap to themselves teachers, having itching ears; and they shall turn away their ears from the truth, and shall be turned unto fables."

Teachings of the Word Faith Movement

1. God is a being who stands approximately six feet tall, weighs some two hundred pounds, and looks exactly like a man.[13]

2. Faith is the literal substance "that God used to create the universe, and He transported that faith with His words."[14] "Here, essentially, is what God did. God filled His words with faith. He used His words as containers to hold His faith and contain that spiritual force and transport it out there into the vast darkness by saying, 'Light, be!' That's the way God transported His faith causing creation and transformation."[15] "The way that He created the world was that, first of all, he conceived something on the inside of Him. He conceived, He had an image, He had a picture."[16]

3. All things, including God, are subject to this "force of faith" because it works according to spiritual "laws" of the universe. "There are laws of the world of the spirit. . . . The spiritual world and its laws are more powerful than the physical world. . . . The world and the physical forces governing it were created by the power of faith—a spiritual force. . . . It is this force of faith which makes the laws of the spirit world function."[17] "The force of faith is released by words. Faith-filled words put the law of the Spirit of life into operation."[18]

4. The greatest thing God conceived of and created was an exact duplicate of himself. This duplicate god—named Adam—was God manifested in the flesh.[19]

[13]Kenneth Copeland, "Spirit, Soul, and Body I" (Fort Worth, Tex.: Kenneth Copeland Ministries, 1985), audiotape #01–0601, side 1, quoted in Hanegraaff, *Crisis,* 121

[14]Charles Capps, *Changing the Seen and Shaping the Unseen* (Tulsa: Harrison House, 1980), 14.

[15]Charles Capps, *Dynamics of Faith and Confession* (Tulsa: Harrison House, 1987), 29.

[16]Jerry Savelle, quoted in Hanegraaff, *Crisis,* 68.

[17]Kenneth Copeland, *The Laws of Prosperity* (Ft. Worth: Kenneth Copeland Publications, 1974), 18–19.

[18]Kenneth Copeland, *The Force of Faith* (Ft. Worth: Kenneth Copeland Publications, 1983), 16.

[19]Charles Capps, "God said, *Let us make man in our image after our likeness.* The word *likeness* in the original Hebrew means "an exact duplication in kind." . . . *Adam was an exact duplication of God's kind!*" from *Authority in Three Worlds* (Tulsa: Harrison House, 1987), 28–29, emphasis in original, quoted in Hanegraaff, *Crisis,* 379.

5. God eventually went to Adam, who was anatomically male and female, and separated the female part from the male part to make a "womb-man" (woman). Adam named this "man with a womb" Eve. She, like Adam, was a god.[20]

6. The Fall caused Adam and Eve's divine natures to be replaced with Satan's nature. They also lost their rights of rulership to planet earth. Even God was barred from having full access to earth because Adam and Eve were under His lordship when they "fell." Through their disobedience Satan became the god of this world.

7. God formulated a scheme to take back the earth, but in order to execute His plan He had to find a human who would invite Him (give Him permission) to work within the earthly realm. Finally, God "got to a point where He had His plan ready for operation. And He saw a man named Abraham."[21] In return for *allowing* God to bring the Messiah through his lineage, Abraham received unlimited health and wealth.

8. For centuries God visualized Jesus. Then, when it was finally time for the Messiah to come forth, God spoke him into existence through faith in the same way that He had visualized and spoken into existence everything else. Bringing forth Jesus, however, was also dependent upon whether or not Mary would lend *her* faith to help form the body of the Lord out of the literal "Word" (confession) God spoke to her: "Mary received the Word of God. *She actually conceived God's Word sent by an angel. Zacharias didn't. . . . Mary received it. She spoke it when she conceived it in her spirit.* Then it manifested itself in her physical body. . . . This is the key to understanding the Virgin Birth. . . . God spoke it. God transmitted that image to Mary. She received the image inside her. . . . The embryo that was in Mary's womb was nothing more than the Word of God. . . . Mary conceived the Word in her spirit. It manifested itself in her physical body."[22] "Mary conceived the Word of God in her heart. . . . Mary conceived the Word sent to her by the angel (God's Word) and conceived it in the womb of her spirit. Once it was conceived in her spirit, it manifested itself in her physical body. *She received and conceived the Word of God in her spirit.* . . . The embryo in Mary's womb was nothing but the pure Word of God—and it took flesh upon itself."[23] "The angels spoke the words of the covenant to her [Mary]. She pondered them in her heart, and those words became the seed. And the Spirit of God hovered over her and generated that seed, which was the Word that the angel spoke to her. And there was conceived in her, the Bible says, a holy thing. The Word literally became flesh."[24]

9. While on earth Jesus was wealthy. He lived in a big house, had a great deal of money, and wore the finest clothes.[25]

10. Although Jesus declared that he walked with God and that God was in Him, he never actually claimed to be God.[26] In fact, during his three years of

---

[20]Kenneth Copeland, *Sensitivity of Heart*, 23, quoted in Hanegraff, *Crisis*, 380.
[21]Frederick K. C. Price, quoted in Hanegraaff, *Crisis*, 381.
[22]Capps, *Dynamics*, 84–87.
[23]Charles Capps, *Authority in Three Worlds* (Tulsa: Harrison House, 1980), 81–83.
[24]Kenneth Copeland, quoted in Hanegraaff, *Crisis*, 381.
[25]John Avanzini on two different TBN broadcasts, quoted in Hanegraaff, *Crisis*, 381–382.
[26]Kenneth Copeland, "Take Time to Pray," *Believer's Voice of Victory* (February 1987): 9.

public ministry "Jesus did not stand in a class by himself. . . . *He was ministering on earth as a human being*—a prophet anointed with the Holy Spirit."[27] Jesus remained sinless so He could redeem men from their satanic natures.

11. In order to redeem humanity, Jesus had to die spiritually as well as physically. When He died spiritually, he died in the same way that Adam died. In other words, He lost His divine nature and was given the nature of Satan. Jesus' death on the cross and His shed blood did not atone for our sins.[28] The atonement took place in hell through the devil's torturing of Jesus' spirit for three days and three nights. Unfortunately for Satan, Jesus was taken to hell "illegally" because He had never sinned. This "technicality" enabled God to use His "force of faith" to revive Jesus' spirit, restore Jesus' divine nature, and resurrect Jesus' body. Through the resurrection process Jesus was "born again."

12. When a person is born again they experience *exactly* what happened to Jesus. Their satanic nature is replaced by God's divine nature. The transformation is so identical to Jesus' transformation that Christians become little gods (small "g") and are as much an incarnation of God as was Jesus.

13. Because Christians are "little gods," they now have access to the "God-kind of faith," which can be used to get virtually anything they want. Christians, rather than God, have authority in the earth over Satan and sickness and disease. Consequently, believers should never pray *God's* will be done.[29]

14. To obtain specific desires, Christians must do three things: (1) loose the power of the "force of faith" by speaking or positively confessing whatever is wanted (e.g., "I am healed," "I am not sick," etc.); (2) *believe* that whatever has been confessed will definitely be received; and (3) ignore or look beyond the visible reality (i.e., remaining sickness, low finances, etc.) and continue claiming what has been confessed.

15. Everything bad, including poverty and sickness, comes from Satan. God's people should have a completely blessed life. A Christian not experiencing such a life is either: (1) in sin; or (2) lacking enough faith to bring about what is desired.

16. The power of audible confession is so great that sometimes a person can unknowingly bring tragedy upon themselves by making *negative* confessions. For example, a woman who is mugged may have actually caused that mugging if at any time prior to the experience she made comments like, "I live in such a dangerous part of the city that I'm afraid I'll be mugged." The woman should have been saying, "I will not be mugged." Similarly, someone who jokingly says "I feel like I'm going crazy" may actually become insane.

Accurate Representation of Word Faith Doctrines

Word Faith supporters often contend that critics of their movement either misquote or take out of context Word Faith teachers. When Word Faith supporters are faced with serious challenges to their unique beliefs, they commonly respond with "My pastor never said that," or "That's not what we believe at all."

---

[27]Kenneth Hagin, quoted in Crenshaw, *Man As God*, 320.
[28]Kenneth Copeland, "Jesus Our Lord of Glory," *Believer's Voice of Victory* (April 1982): 3.
[29]Frederick K. C. Price, cited in Hanegraaff, *Crisis*, 384.

Jesus said, "Every careless word that men shall speak, they shall render account for it in the day of judgment. For by your words you shall be justified, and by your words you shall be condemned" (Matthew 12:36–37, NKJV). Our Lord also commented that men are defiled by what "proceeds out of the mouth" (Matthew 15:11). The following contextual quotes from Word Faith teachers, contrasted to the words of Scripture, show beyond a shadow of a doubt that Word Faith teachers have been defiled by what the apostle Paul called "doctrines of demons" (1 Timothy 4:1).

The Word Faith vs. The Word of God

God (Word Faith)

"He's [God is] very much like you and me. A being that stands somewhere around 6'2", 6'3", who weighs somewhere in the neighborhood of a couple of hundred pounds, little better, [and] has a [hand]span of nine inches across."[30]

"God *spoke* Adam into existence in authority with words (Genesis 1:26, 28). These words struck Adam's body in the face. His body and God's were exactly the same size."[31]

"He [God] measured out heaven with a nine-inch span. . . . The distance between my thumb and my finger is not quite nine inches. So, I know He's bigger than me, thank God. Amen? But He's not some great, big, old thing that couldn't come through the door there. . . . I don't serve The Glob. I serve God, and I've been created in His image and in His likeness."[32]

God (Word of God)

"There is none like unto the Lord our God"(Exodus 8:10).

"Rise up early in the morning, and stand before Pharaoh, and say unto him, 'Thus saith the Lord God of the Hebrews, let my people go. . . . I will at this time send all my plagues upon thine heart, and upon thy servants, and upon thy people, that thou mayest know that there is none like me in all the earth' " (Exodus 9:13–14).

"I am God, and there is none else; I am God, and there is none like me" (Isaiah 46:9).

"Thou art great, O Lord God: for there is none like thee, neither is there any God beside thee, according to all that we have heard with our ears" (2 Samuel 7:22).

"Forasmuch as there is none like unto thee, O Lord; thou art great, and thy name is great in might" (Jeremiah 10:6).

"God is not a man, that He should lie, nor a son of man, that He should repent. Has He said, and shall He not do it? Or has He spoken, and will He not make it good?" (Numbers 23:19, NKJV).

"For He [God] is not a man, that He should relent" (1 Samuel 15:29, NKJV).

"For I am God, and not man" (Hosea 11:9, NKJV).

---

[30]Kenneth Copeland, quoted in Hanegraaff, *Crisis*, 121.
[31]Ibid., 379.
[32]Jerry Savelle, quoted in Hanegraaff, *Crisis*, 122.

Adam (Word Faith)

"God created man and woman an exact *duplicate* of himself."[33]

"God duplicated *himself* in kind! . . . Adam was *an exact duplicate of God's kind!*"[34]

"Did you know that from the beginning of time the whole purpose of God was to reproduce himself?"[35]

"Adam was made in the image of God. He was as much female as he was male. He was exactly like God. Then God separated him and removed the female part. Woman means 'man with a womb.' "[36]

"God's reason for creating Adam was His desire to reproduce himself. I mean a reproduction of himself, and in the Garden of Eden He did just that. He [Adam] was not a little like God. He was not almost like God. He was not subordinate to God even. . . . Adam is as much like God as you can get, just the same as Jesus. . . . Adam, in the Garden of Eden, was God manifested in the flesh."[37]

Adam (Word of God)

"Mankind in God's image and likeness. Two Hebrew words are used in OT passages that assert that man was made in the 'image and likeness' of God (Genesis 1:26–27). The word *selem* means 'image,' 'representation'. . . . *D'mût*, translated 'likeness,' is a word of comparison. It is used to attempt to explain something by referring to something else that it is like. . . . The likeness-image is not of physical form. . . . It is the inner nature of human beings that reflects something vital in the nature of God. . . . The likeness is rooted in all that is required to make a human being a person: in our intellectual, emotional, and moral likeness to God."[38]

"Hebrew scholars point out that the word 'likeness' [*D'mût*]. . . 'defines and limits' the other word translated as image [*selem*]. . . in Genesis 1:26–27 '*to avoid the implication that man is a precise copy of God, albeit miniature.*' "[39]

"The Word became flesh and made his dwelling among us. We have seen his glory, the glory of the One and Only [*unique*], who came from the Father, full of grace and truth" (John 1:14, NIV).

Jesus Christ (Word Faith)

"Spiritual death means something more than separation from God. . . . Spiritual death also means having Satan's nature. . . . Jesus tasted death—spiritual death—for every man."[40]

"Jesus died two deaths. He died spiritually and He died physically."[41]

"He accepted the sin nature of Satan in His own spirit."[42]

Jesus Christ (Word of God)

"Forasmuch as ye know that ye were not redeemed with corruptible things . . . but with the precious blood of Christ, as of a lamb without blemish and without spot" (1 Peter 1:18–19).

"How much more shall the blood of Christ, who through the eternal Spirit offered himself without spot to God . . ." (Hebrews 9:14).

---

[33]Casey Treat, quoted in Hanegraaff, *Crisis,* 361.

[34]Charles Capps, *Authority in Three Worlds* (Tulsa: Harrison House, 1980), 16.

[35]Morris Cerullo, quoted in Hanegraaff, *Crisis,* 358.

[36]Copeland, *Sensitivity of Heart* (Fort Worth, Tex.: KCP Publications, 1984), 23.

[37]Copeland, quoted in Hanegraaff, *Crisis,* 379.

[38]Lawrence O. Richards, *Expository Dictionary of Bible Words* (Grand Rapids: Zondervan Publishing House, 1985), 350–351.

[39]R. Laird Harris, Gleason L. Archer, and Bruce K. Waltke, *Theological Wordbook of the Old Testament* (Chicago: Moody Press, 1980), 1:192.

[40]Kenneth E. Hagin, *The Name of Jesus* (Tulsa: Faith Library, 1981), 31.

[41]Kenneth Copeland, "Jesus Our Lord of Glory," *Believer's Voice of Victory* (April 1982): 3.

[42]Copeland, quoted in Hanegraaff, *Crisis,* 157–158.

"Because He was 'made sin,' . . . impregnated with sin, and became the very essence of sin, on the cross He was banished from God's presence as a loathsome thing. . . . While Christ was identified with sin, Satan and the hosts of hell ruled over Him as over any lost sinner."[43]

"He [Jesus] suffered in His own body, and more important, in His spirit. Jesus experienced the same spiritual death that entered Man in the Garden of Eden. . . . After Jesus was made sin, He had to be born-again. . . . Jesus is a born-again man. (This is the same new birth that the good news of the Gospel still offers to any man who will accept). . . . Jesus was changed from being made sin into a new creature."[44]

The Atonement (Word Faith)

"Do you think that the punishment for our sin was to die on a cross? If that were the case, the two thieves could have paid your price. No, the punishment was to go into hell itself and to serve time in hell separated from God."[45]

"Jesus went into hell to free mankind. . . . When His blood poured out it did not atone."[46]

"In Hell, he [Jesus] suffered death for you and me. . . . Satan was holding the Son of God illegally. God could not go into hell as it was not His domain."[47]

"[That] Word of the Living God went down into that pit of destruction and charged the spirit of Jesus with resurrection power! Suddenly His twisted, death-wracked spirit began to fill out and come back to life. . . . He was literally being reborn before the devil's very eyes. He began to flex His spiritual muscles. . . . Jesus was born again."[48]

"For Christ also hath once suffered for sins, the just for the unjust, that he might bring us to God" (1 Peter 3:18).

"Christ also hath loved us, and hath given himself for us an offering and a sacrifice to God for a sweet-smelling savour" (Ephesians 5:2).

"And when Jesus had cried with a loud voice, he said, 'Father, into thy hands [not Satan's hands] I commend my spirit" (Luke 23:46, bracketed added).

"Jesus Christ the same yesterday, and to day, and for ever" (Hebrews 13:8).

The Atonement (Word of God)

"Jesus the author and finisher of our faith; who for the joy that was set before him, endured the cross [not torture in hell], despising the shame" (Hebrews 12:2, bracketed added).

"When Jesus therefore had received the vinegar, he said, It is finished: and he bowed his head, and gave up the ghost" (John 19:30).

"In whom [Jesus] we have redemption through his blood, the forgiveness of sins, according to the riches of his grace" (Ephesians 1:7).

"Unto him that loved us, and washed us from our sins in his own blood" (Revelation 1:5).

"For it pleased the Father that in him should all fulness dwell; and having made peace through the blood of his cross, by him to reconcile all things unto himself" (Colossians 1:19–20).

"Whither shall I go from thy spirit? or whither shall I flee from thy presence? If I ascend up into heaven, thou art there: if I

[43]Paul E. Billheimer, *Destined for the Throne* (Special TBN Edition, Fort Washington, Pa.: Christian Literature Crusade, 1975 [1988 ed.]), 83.

[44]Gloria Copeland, *God's Will for You* (Fort Worth: Kenneth Copeland Publications, 1972), 5.

[45]Frederick K. C. Price, "If Christ Did Not Rise . . . What Then?" *Ever Increasing Faith Messenger* (June 1980): 7.

[46]Kenneth Copeland, quoted in McConnell, *Different Gospel*, 120.

[47]Kenneth Copeland, *Walking in the Realm of the Miraculous* (Fort Worth: Kenneth Copeland Ministries, 1979), 77.

[48]Copeland, quoted in Hanegraaff, *Crisis*, 170.

make my bed in hell, behold, thou art there" (Psalm 139:7–8).

"And you being dead in your sins and the uncircumcision of your flesh, hath he quickened together with him, having forgiven you all trespasses [sins]; blotting out the handwriting of ordinances that was against us, which was contrary to us, and took it out of the way, nailing it to his cross; and having spoiled principalities and powers, he made a shew [public spectacle, not private defeat in hell] of them openly, triumphing over them in it" (Colossians 2:13–15).

"I lay down my life, that I might take it again. No man taketh it from me, but I lay it down of myself. I have power to lay it down, and I have power to take it again" (John 10:17–18).

"For as the Father hath life in himself; so hath he given to the Son to have life in himself" (John 5:26).

God's Sovereignty (Word Faith)

"When Adam disobeyed God . . . all the dominion and authority God had given to him was handed over to Satan."[49]

"God's on the outside looking in. He doesn't have any legal entrée into the earth. The thing don't belong to Him. . . . This is the position that God's been in. . . . Might say, 'Well, if God's running things He's doing a lousy job of it.' He hasn't been running 'em, except when He's just got, you know, a little bit of a chance."[50]

"God cannot do anything for you apart or separate from faith."[51]

"As a believer, you have a right to make commands in the name of Jesus. Each time you stand on the Word, you are commanding God to a certain extent because it is His Word."[52]

"God does not have physical possession of the earth, Satan does."[53]

God's Sovereignty (Word of God)

"Thine, O Lord, is the greatness, and the power, and the glory, and the victory, and the majesty; for all that is in the heaven and in the earth is thine; thine is the kingdom, O Lord, and thou art exalted as head above all" (1 Chronicles 29:11).

"Thy kingdom is an everlasting kingdom, and thy dominion endureth throughout all generations" (Psalm 145:13).

"Behold, the heaven and the heaven of heavens is the Lord's thy God, the earth also, with all that therein is" (Deuteronomy 10:14).

"Whatsoever is under the whole heaven is mine [the Lord's]" (Job. 41:11, bracketed added).

"The earth is the Lord's, and the fulness thereof; the world, and they that dwell therein" (Psalm 24:1).

[49]Kenneth Copeland, *Our Covenant With God* (Fort Worth: Kenneth Copeland Publications, 1987 ed.), 8.
[50]Copeland, quoted in Hanegraaff, *Crisis*, 132.
[51]Kenneth Copeland, *Freedom from Fear* (Ft. Worth: Kenneth Copeland Publications, 1983), 11.
[52]Copeland, *Covenant*, 40–41.
[53]Frederick K. C. Price, quoted in Crenshaw, *Movement*, 274.

"God can't do anything in this earth realm except what we, the body of Christ, allow Him to do."[54]

"God has been given permission to work in this earth realm. . . . Yes! You are in control! So, if man has control, who no longer has it? God. . . . When God gave Adam dominion, that meant God no longer had dominion. So, God cannot do anything in this earth unless we let Him. And the way we let Him or give Him permission is through prayer."[55]

"The heavens are thine, the earth also is thine: as for the world and the fulness thereof, thou hast founded them" (Psalm 89:11).

"And all the inhabitants of the earth are reputed as nothing: and he [God] doeth according to his will in the army of heaven, and among the inhabitants of the earth: and none can stay his hand, or say unto him, What doest thou?" (Daniel 4:35).

"Declaring the end from the beginning, and from ancient times the things that are not yet done, saying, My counsel shall stand, and I will do all my pleasure" (Isaiah 46:10).

"But our God is in the heavens: he hath done whatsoever he hath pleased" (Psalm 115:3).

"Whatsoever the Lord pleased, that did he in heaven, and in earth, in the seas, and all deep places" (Psalm 135:6).

"And what is the exceeding greatness of his power to usward who believe, according to the working of his mighty power, which he wrought in Christ, when he raised him from the dead, and set him at his own right hand in the heavenly places" (Ephesians 1.19–20).

Man's Divinity (Word Faith)

"I am a little God! Critics, be gone!"[56]

"We are a class of Gods!"[57]

"As a believer, you have the same spiritual capacity that Jesus has. . . . Your spirit is just as big as God's because you are born of Him."[58]

"You don't have a god in you, you are one."[59]

"This eternal life He [God] came to give us is the nature of God. . . . It is, in reality, God imparting His very nature, substance, and being to our human spirits. . . . Eternal life

Man's Divinity (Word of God)

"Ye are my witnesses, saith the LORD, and my servant whom I have chosen: that ye may know and believe me, and understand that I am he: before me there was no God formed, neither shall there be after me" (Isaiah 43:10).

"Is there a God beside me? yea, there is no God; I know not any" (Isaiah 44:8).

"How can ye believe, which receive honour one of another, and seek not the honour that cometh from God only?" (John 5:44).

"And this is life eternal, that they might

---

[54]Price, quoted in Hanegraaff, *Crisis*, 380.
[55]Ibid., 85.
[56]Paul Crouch, *Praise the Lord*, Trinity Broadcasting Network, July 7, 1986.
[57]Copeland, quoted in Hanegraaff, *Crisis*, 116.
[58]Copeland, *Realm*, 16.
[59]Copeland, quoted in Hanegraaff, *Crisis*, 110.

is the nature of God. It is the being or substance of God."[60]

"Many in the great body of Full Gospel people do not know that the new birth is a real incarnation. They do not know they are as much sons and daughters of God as Jesus. . . . Jesus was first divine, and then He was human. So He was in the flesh a divine-human being. I was first human, and so were you, but I was born of God, so I became a human-divine being!"[61]

"The believer is as much an incarnation as was Jesus of Nazareth."[62]

"We are the Word made flesh, just as Jesus was."[63]

know thee the only true God, and Jesus Christ, whom thou hast sent" (John 17:3).

"Thou believest that there is one God; thou doest well: the devils also believe, and tremble" (James 2:19).

"For there is one God, and one mediator between God and men, the man Christ Jesus" (1 Timothy 2:5).

"No man hath seen God at any time; the only begotten [unique, one of a kind] Son [many mss., "God"], which is in the bosom of the Father, he hath declared him" (John 1:18, bracketed added).

"In whom [Christ] we have redemption through his blood, even the forgiveness of sins; who is the image of the invisible God, the firstborn of every creature: for by him were all things created, that are in heaven, and that are in earth, visible and invisible, whether they be thrones, or dominions, or principalities, or powers: all things were created by him, and for him: And he is before all things, and by him all things consist" (Colossians 1:14–17).

"Whom [the Son] he hath appointed heir of all things, by whom also he made the worlds; who being the brightness of his glory, and the express image of his person, and upholding all things by the word of his power, when he had by himself purged our sins, sat down on the right hand of the Majesty on high" (Hebrews 1:2–3).

A Faulty Foundation: Faith in Faith

Many of the preceding doctrines are linked directly to the mistaken concept that faith is a literal substance, "a power force . . . a tangible force . . . a conductive force."[64] According to Kenneth E. Hagin, faith in one's own faith is the secret to getting every desire of the heart:

Did you ever stop to think about having faith in your own faith? Evidently God had faith in His faith, because He spoke words of faith and they came to pass. . . . *Having faith in your words is having faith in your faith.* That's what you've got to learn to do to get things from God: *Have faith in your faith.*[65]

---

[60]Kenneth E. Hagin, *ZOE: The God-Kind of Life* (Tulsa: Kenneth Hagin Ministries, 1989 ed.), 1–2, 27.
[61]Ibid., 40.
[62]Kenneth E. Hagin, "The Incarnation," *The Word of Faith* (December 1980): 14.
[63]Gloria Copeland, quoted in Crenshaw, *Man as God*, 202.
[64]Copeland, *Force*, 10.
[65]Kenneth E. Hagin, *Having Faith in Your Faith* (Tulsa: Faith Library, 1980), 4–5.

To deal adequately with the many biblical passages that Word Faith teachers twist to support their view would take several chapters alone. Consequently, we will examine their misrepresentation and misuse of the two verses they appeal to the most—Hebrews 11:1 and Mark 11:22. These passages are important because each one, studied carefully, actually disproves the very position the faith teachers claim they support.

In *Christianity in Crisis*, a 447-page critique of Word Faith doctrine, Hank Hanegraaff contends that the movement's entire theology "rests on the word 'substance' in Hebrews 11:1: 'Now faith is the substance of things hoped for, the evidence of things not seen.' "[66] He goes on to explain and then refute their argument:

> Faith teachers interpret the word "substance" to mean the "basic stuff" out of which the universe is made. . . . Faith cannot be rightly understood to mean "the building block of the universe," since it is never used in that sense in the book of Hebrews, much less the entire Bible. . . . The word translated "substance" in the KJV is more accurately rendered "assurance" (see NASB). . . . Faith is a *channel of living trust*—and *assurance*—which stretches from man to God. . . . True biblical faith is faith in *God* as opposed to faith in *substance* (or "faith in faith," as Hagin puts it). . . . True biblical faith (*pistis* in the Greek) encapsulates three essential elements : . . *knowledge* . . . *agreement* . . . *trust.*[67]

Greek scholars agree with Hanegraaff: "*Hypostatsis* is translated in the NASB as "assurance," in the NIV as "being sure." Faith provides an inner certainty about things that simply are not open to empirical verification but are communicated by God's Word (Hebrews 11:1). . . . *Pistis* ("faith," "belief") and related words deal with relationships established by trust and maintained by trustworthiness."[68]

Regarding Mark 11:22, Word Faith teachers disregard the standard "Have faith *in* God" translation in favor of an erroneous rendering of the text, which reads, "Have the faith *of* God." Charles Capps writes, "A more literal translation [of Mark 11:22] . . . says, 'Have the God kind of faith, or faith of God.' "[69]

Capps is partially correct. The literal word-for-word translation of the Greek used in Mark 11:22 (*echete pistin theou*) is indeed "Have [*echete*] faith [*pistin*] of God [*theou*]." What Capps is missing, however, is that the grammatical construction of Mark 11:22 makes *theou* an "objective genitive."[70] This means that the noun (i.e., *theou*) is the *object* of the action mentioned (i.e., having faith). In other words, God is the *object* of faith, not the *possessor* of faith. Hence, a proper, meaningful translation is to have faith *in* God.

By embracing a faulty view of faith, thousands have plunged themselves into a veritable cesspool of false teachings. One doctrine inseparably linked to the belief that faith is a force is "positive confession," which maintains that words themselves actually contain the power to change reality (positively or negatively,

---

[66]Hanegraaff, *Crisis*, 69.

[67]Ibid., 69–70.

[68]Richards, *Dictionary*, 80, 116.

[69]Charles Capps, *God's Creative Power Will Work for You* (Tulsa: Harrison House, 1976): 2.

[70]A. T. Robertson, *Word Pictures in the New Testament* (Nashville: Broadman Press, 1930), 1:361.

depending on what kind of words are spoken) when coupled with the faith-force. Put bluntly, "What you *say* is what you get."[71]

Confessing It Means Possessing It

Word Faith celebrity Kenneth Copeland says, "What you are saying is exactly what you are getting now. If you are living in poverty and lack and want, change what you are saying. . . . The powerful force of the spiritual world that creates the circumstances around us is controlled by the words of the mouth."[72] Kenneth E. Hagin, who served for many years as Copeland's mentor, echoes his protégé: "Your right confession will become a reality, and then you will get whatever you need from God."[73]

Positively confessing something is the very first step to getting what is wanted (i.e., healing, a new boat, someone to marry, etc.). The "force of faith" coupled with a carefully conceived positive confession is really the only way to produce results because such methods are what release God's ability to bring about the things desired: "God's Word conceived in the heart, then formed with the tongue and spoken out of the mouth becomes a spiritual force releasing the ability of God."[74]

The stress placed on correct "speaking" often leads to some rather interesting instructions on how to "make" God work:

> What do you need? Start creating it. Start speaking about it. Start speaking it into being. Speak to your billfold. Say, "You big, thick billfold full of money." Speak to your checkbook. Say, "You, checkbook, you. You've never been so prosperous since I owned you. You're just jammed full of money." Say to your body, "You're whole, body! Why, you just function so beautifully and so well. Why, body, you never have any problems. You're a strong, healthy body." Or speak to your leg, or speak to your foot, or speak to your neck, or speak to your back. . . . Speak to your wife, speak to your husband, speak to your circumstances; and speak faith to them to create in them and God will create what you are speaking.[75]

This exhortation, as humorous as it sounds, masks a cruelty that comes through whenever someone in the Word Faith movement faces trials. Just as positive words have the power to create positive (good) results, negative words have the power to create negative (bad) results, at least to the Word Faith followers. Consequently, those suffering have only themselves to blame, say the Word Faith teachers. As Frederick K. C. Price says, "If you keep talking death, that is what you are going to have. If you keep talking sickness and disease, that is what you are going to have, because you are going to create the reality of them with your own mouth. That is a divine law."[76]

---

[71]Charles Capps, quoted in Crenshaw, *Man as God*, 177.
[72]Copeland, *Laws*, 98.
[73]Kenneth E. Hagin, *Right and Wrong Thinking for Christians* (Tulsa: Kenneth Hagin Ministries, 1966), 30.
[74]Capps, *Dynamic*, 33.
[75]Marilyn Hickey, quoted in Hanegraaff, *Crisis*, 63.
[76]Price, *Realm*, 29.

The Sin of Suffering

Those in the Word Faith movement feel the spoken word is so powerful that individuals can bring tragedy upon themselves without even realizing it:

> We live in an environment of our own making—one that we have largely created by our own words.[77]
>
> Whether you realize it or not, you frame your world with your words daily.[78]
>
> Somebody says, "You mean the world that I'm living in right now originated by the words of my mouth?" They certainly did, because the Bible says you are snared by the words of your mouth, you are taken by your words.[79]
>
> With words you bind things, or you loose other things. Sometimes you think you are just being honest, and you loose the devil against your finances by saying things like, "Well, we just never can get ahead" [or] "If I ever do get a job, I lose it."[80]
>
> You *prayed* the problem. Your heart received that as being your will and worked day and night to bring you into a position where the things you were saying would come to pass.[81]

Dr. James Kinnebrew, in his 1988 doctoral dissertation for Mid-America Baptist Theological Seminary, rightly stated, "The faith message is, perhaps above all else . . . an attempt to harmonize the loving righteousness of an omnipotent God with the evil and suffering that prevail in a world gone awry."[82]

Unfortunately, Word Faith proponents explain suffering through a convenient appeal to the sovereignty of man. There are no victims, nothing is out of control, and everything can change because those afflicted are calling the shots. As long as someone possesses enough knowledge about what God has promised, says the right words, and has enough faith, all will be taken care of—bills will get paid, family members will be healed, and money will fall like manna from heaven. One's own words control life because words "are the most powerful things in the universe today."[83] "HEALTH, SUCCESS, HAPPINESS and PROSPERITY are God's Will for YOU when you believe His Word enough to ACT ON IT."[84]

In the Word Faith movement, all suffering is caused by man, rather than God. As Frederick K. C. Price says, "You are suffering because you're stupid!"[85] The only alternative is even worse: "If God is running everything, He does have things in a mess."[86]

The stupidity to which Price refers is expressed either through speaking negative confessions or through not realizing that positive confessions will bring about good things. Kenneth Copeland explains:

> *Your tongue is the deciding factor in your life.* . . . You have been trained since

[77]Kenneth E. Hagin, quoted in Crenshaw, *Man as God*, 188.

[78]Charles Capps, quoted in Ibid., 77.

[79]Jerry Savelle, quoted in Hanegraaff, *Crisis*, 68.

[80]Capps, *Dynamics*, 64.

[81]Capps, quoted in Crenshaw, *Man as God*, 182.

[82]James M. Kinnebrew, *The Charismatic Doctrine of Positive Confession: A Historical, Exegetical, and Theological Critique* (University Microfilms Int.) Order #9029719, 233.

[83]Capps, *Creative Power*, 25.

[84]T. L. Osborne, quoted in Hanegraaff, *Crisis*, 361.

[85]Price, quoted in Crenshaw, *Man as God*, 156.

[86]Kenneth E. Hagin, *The Interceding Christian* (Tulsa: Kenneth E. Hagin Ministries, 1978), 14.

birth to speak negative, death-dealing words. Unconsciously in your everyday conversation, you use the words of death, sickness, lack, fear, doubt, and unbelief: *That scared me to death. That tickled me to death. I laughed until I thought I would die. I'm just dying to go. That makes me sick. I'm sick and tired of this mess. I believe I'm taking the flu. We just can't afford it. I doubt it.* . . . You say these things without even realizing it. When you do, you set in motion negative forces in your life.[87]

Satan is painted into the Word Faith's picture of suffering as simply an adversary who afflicts the ignorant. Like Job, *we* are the ones who bring about our own problems by the words we speak. According to Copeland,

God didn't allow the Devil to get on Job. *Job* allowed the Devil to get on Job. . . . All God did was maintain His [God's] confession of faith about that man. He said "that man is upright in the earth." But Job, himself, said he was *not* upright in the earth. He said, "I'm miserable."[88]

Capps also points out that Job's problems were caused by his own words: "Job activated Satan by his fear. . . . 'The thing which I greatly feared is come upon me' " (Job 3:25).[89]

Scripture, however, indicates that God did indeed allow Job to be afflicted: "The Lord said to Satan, 'Behold, all that he has is in your power; only do not lay a hand on this person' " and "the Lord said to Satan, 'Behold, he is in your hand, but spare his life' " (Job. 1:12; 2:6). Furthermore, Job did not acknowledge his misery until *after* he had been afflicted (Job 3:1–26).

Word Faith teachers are forced into misinterpreting Job's story because they hold that there is "no glory in knuckling down and enduring a trial."[90] In other words, no good whatsoever can come from suffering.

Kenneth E. Hagin asserts, "You cannot find anywhere in the Bible where God causes these things [tragedies] to happen to teach His people something."[91]

The Wheel of Fortune

Financial prosperity to those in the Word Faith movement is more than just a blessing. It is an absolute right. New Testament professor Gordon D. Fee, in his booklet titled *The Disease of the Health and Wealth Gospels*, points out that the "bottom line" reaffirmation to which Word Faith believers always return is this:

God *wills* the (financial) prosperity of every one of his children, and therefore for a Christian to be in poverty is to be outside God's intended will; it is to be living a Satan defeated life. And usually tucked away in this affirmation is a second: Because we are God's children . . . we should always go first-class—we should have the biggest and best, a Cadillac instead of a Volkswagen, because this alone brings glory to God.[92]

[87]Kenneth Copeland, *The Power of the Tongue* (Fort Worth: KCP Publications, 1980): 20–23.
[88]Copeland, quoted in Hanegraaff, *Crisis*, 263.
[89]Capps, *Tongue*, 92.
[90]Copeland, *Force*, 25.
[91]Kenneth E. Hagin, *How You Can Be Led by the Spirit of God* (Tulsa: Kenneth Hagin Ministries, 1978), 91.
[92]Gordon D. Fee, *The Disease of the Health and Wealth Gospels* (Beverly, Mass.: Frontline Publishing, 1985), 4.

In Kenneth Copeland's words, "Jesus bore the curse of the law on our behalf. He beat Satan and took away his power. Consequently, there is no reason for you to live under the curse of the law, no reason for you to live in poverty of any kind."[93]

The Bible names countless individuals who, although they were righteous before God, were poor: Paul the apostle (Philippians 4:11–12); his companions (1 Corinthians 4:9–13); the Old Testament faithful (Hebrews 11:37). Even the Lord Jesus lived in poverty (Matthew 8:20).

These facts, however, are vehemently denied by Word Faith teachers, especially John Avanzini, who assures everyone that "Jesus was handling big money."[94] In fact, he claims, "Jesus had a nice house, a big house—big enough to have company stay the night with Him at the house."[95] Frederick K. C. Price agrees:

> The whole point is I'm trying to get you to see—to get you out of this malaise of thinking that Jesus and His disciples were poor and then relating that to you. . . . The Bible says that He has left us an example that we should follow His steps. That's the reason why I drive a Rolls Royce.[96]

Scripture nowhere indicates that Jesus was wealthy. Instead, it clearly portrays Him as being poor: "For ye know the grace of our Lord Jesus Christ, that, though he was rich, yet for your sakes he became poor, that ye through his poverty might be rich" (2 Corinthians 8:9). Even though this is analogous, figurative language, pointing to the fact that the omnipotent God laid aside His divine primacy (riches) and submitted to human evil on the cross (poverty), it still affirms that neither poverty nor riches have any spiritual stigma attached to them. While a misinterpretation of this verse may tempt some to conclude that Jesus became poor materially so that we may become rich materially, that is not the point at all. Spiritual wealth or life comes to us sinners through the death of Christ. Christians are to be rich in spiritual things (James 2:5), including love, joy, peace, patience, kindness, goodness, faithfulness, gentleness, and self-control (Galatians 5:22–23). Revelation 2:9 speaks of believers who, although poor by worldly standards, are still "rich" because of the spiritual wealth they possess.

Temporal riches are of much less value than spiritual riches. According to Paul, "But they that will be rich fall into temptation and a snare, and into many foolish and hurtful lusts, which drown men in destruction and perdition. For the love of money is the root of all evil: which while some coveted after, they have erred from the faith, and pierced themselves through with many sorrows" (1 Timothy 6:9–10).

Jesus himself said, "Lay up not for yourselves treasures upon earth, where moth and rust doth corrupt, and where thieves break through and steal: But lay up for yourselves treasures in heaven, where neither moth nor rust doth corrupt, and where thieves do not break through and steal: for where your treasure is, there will your heart be also" (Matthew 6:19–21).

[93]Copeland, *Laws*, 51.
[94]John Avanzini, *Praise the Lord*, Trinity Broadcasting Network, videotape, September 15, 1988.
[95]John Avanzini, *Believer's Voice of Victory*, Trinity Broadcasting Network, videotape, January 20, 1991.
[96]Frederick K. C. Price, *Ever Increasing Faith*, Trinity Broadcasting Network, videotape, December 9, 1990.

Health and Healing

In Word Faith theology all believers "should thoroughly understand that their healing was consummated in Christ. When they come to know that in their spirits—just as they know it in their heads—that will be the end of sickness and disease in their bodies."[97] Copeland assures his followers that "*God intends for every believer to live completely free from sickness and disease.*"[98] Copeland also maintains that any time a believer has a problem receiving healing, "he usually suffers from ignorance of God's Word."[99]

Isaiah 53:4–6 is the primary verse misinterpreted by the Word Faith teachers to give the foundation upon which this view is built:

> Surely he hath borne our griefs, and carried our sorrows: yet we did esteem him stricken, smitten of God, and afflicted. But he was wounded for our transgressions, he was bruised for our iniquities: the chastisement of our peace was upon him; and with his stripes we are healed. All we like sheep have gone astray; we have turned every one to his own way; and the Lord hath laid on him the iniquity of us all" (Isaiah 53:4–6).

When Word Faith teachers cross-reference this passage with Matthew 8:17 ("That it might be fulfilled which was spoken by Esaias [Isaiah] the prophet, saying, Himself took our infirmities, and bare our sicknesses"), they conclude that Christians are healed through the crucifixion of Christ.

But Matthew tells us that the Isaiah prophecy was fulfilled BEFORE Jesus had been crucified. Furthermore, he only quotes the first two lines of the prophecy. Why? Because only the first portion of Isaiah 53:4 (NIV) (which *does* mention infirmities) was fulfilled at Peter's house—the scenario of Matthew 8:16:

> When the even was come, they brought unto him many that were possessed with devils: and he cast out the spirits with his word, and healed all that were sick.

Matthew does not quote the rest of the Isaiah passage because it deals with what would be taken away, or healed, through Jesus' death—our transgressions and iniquities, our sins. By Jesus' scourging and crucifixion we were healed (Isaiah 53:5), but healed of the moral effects of sin, separation from God, rather than physical disease (Isaiah 53:6). As the psalmist wrote, "Lord, be merciful unto me: heal my soul; for I have sinned against thee" (Psalm 41:4).

The intense aversion that Word Faith leaders have toward sickness is perhaps most obvious in Price's sermons:

> How can you glorify God in your body, when it doesn't function right? How can you glorify God? How can He get glory when your body doesn't even work? . . . What makes you think the Holy Ghost wants to live inside a body where He can't see out through the windows and He can't hear with the ears? What makes you think the Holy Spirit wants to live inside of a physical body where the limbs and the organs and the cells do not function right? . . . And what makes you think He wants to live in a temple where He can't see out of the eyes, and He can't walk with the feet, and He can't move with the hands? . . . The only eyes

---

[97]Kenneth E. Hagin, *Seven Things You Should Know about Divine Healing* (Tulsa: Kenneth Hagin Ministries, 1979), 54.

[98]Kenneth Copeland, *Welcome to the Family* (Fort Worth: Kenneth Copeland Ministries, 1979), 25.

[99]Kenneth Copeland. *Healed: To Be or Not to Be* (Fort Worth: Kenneth Copeland Ministries, 1979), 13.

that He has that are in the earth realm are the eyes that are in the body. If He can't see out of them then God's gonna be limited.[100]

Such a mind-set becomes even harsher when it is coupled with the Word Faith practice of citing a person's personal lack of faith as the primary cause of a sickness:

> Medicine is not God's highest or best. There is a better way when you know how to use your faith. When you have developed your faith to such an extent that you can stand on the promises of God, then you won't need medicine. That's the reason that I don't take medicine. . . . Thank God, that medication is available if you need it. . . . I have made up my mind that I am going to act on God's Word. . . . If they [Price's family] want to go to the doctor, I'll take them. . . . They may not be able or willing to make the kind of commitment that I have made. Everybody is just not going to make the same commitment. . . . Going to the doctor is not opposed to faith, nor is it opposed to divine healing; it is simply getting it on a lower lever. . . . If your faith is not operating at its highest level, one of the best friends you will ever have will be a good doctor. . . . Do not impose your faith on your family . . . just because you want to believe God. . . . I haven't taken any medicine in seven years, and I don't plan to do so. . . . If you need a crutch or something to help you along, then praise God, hobble along until you get your faith moving to the point where you don't need the crutch.[101]

Does God *guarantee* that Christians will *always* be healed as long as they have enough faith and are not in sin? No, He does not. Instead, His Word gives numerous examples of godly individuals who were not healed: Paul (2 Corinthians 12:7–10; Galatians 4:13–15); Timothy (1 Timothy 5:23); Trophimus (2 Timothy 4:20); and Epaphroditus (Philippians 2:25–27).

Those who feel it is God's will that Christians always be healed often ask, "Since Jesus healed everyone who came to Him while He was on earth, why would He not heal everyone who comes to Him today (as long as they have faith), especially since Jesus is the same 'yesterday, to day, and for ever' (Hebrews 13:8)?"

First, Scripture nowhere states that Jesus healed everyone who was ever brought to Him during His lifetime. The apostle John, at the end of his gospel, noted that "many other things" were done by Jesus that were not recorded. Whether those things might have included "non-healings," we do not know, but we do know that what *was* recorded, including the healings, were recorded so that "ye might believe that Jesus is the Christ, the Son of God; and that believing ye might have life through his name" (John 20:31). They were not recorded to convince us that physical healing for all is guaranteed.

Second, nowhere in Scripture is perfect physical healing for all promised *before* the resurrection and glorification, which will occur at the final judgment (see Revelation 20–22). Physical healing in its ultimate sense can only be a result of the transformation of our "death-doomed" bodies into bodies like His glorious resurrected body (Romans 8:11; 1 Peter 1:24).

Third, healing came from Christ at His will, regardless of the individual's faith. He healed those who believed (Matthew 8:13) and those who did not believe (John 9:1–38).

---

[100]Price, quoted in Hanegraaff, *Crisis*, 259–260.
[101]Frederick K. C. Price, *Faith, Foolishness, or Presumption?* (Tulsa: Harrison House, 1979), 87–93.

The Word Faith concept also includes a physical-symptoms-should-be-ignored principle that leads to unnecessary suffering and sometimes even death. Hagin advises that someone seeking healing "should look to God's Word, not to his symptoms."[102] Real faith, according to Hagin, "*believes the Word of God regardless of what the physical evidences may be.*"[103]

Divine health is something we already possess, says Word Faith teacher Jerry Savelle: "When symptoms come, it is nothing more than the thief trying to steal the health which is already ours. In other words, divine health is not something we are trying to get from God; it is something the Devil is trying to take away from us! . . . When the Devil tries to put a symptom of sickness or disease in my body, I absolutely refuse to accept it."[104]

Countless tragedies have resulted from such thinking. One of the most widely publicized cases involved Larry and Lucky Parker, who, rather than giving insulin to their diabetic son Wesley, followed Word Faith teachings and positively confessed his healing. After Wesley died in a diabetic coma on August 23, 1973, Larry and Lucky were tried and convicted of manslaughter.[105] Thousands of equally tragic stories often go unnoticed. For instance:

> Thirty-eight-year-old Christine Klear (a mother of three small children) died of breast cancer after she and her husband Douglas decided, through "the influence of TBN," to positively confess her healing and forego medical treatment.[106]
>
> While she was still in her mid-forties, doctors told F. Elizabeth Scott that she had breast cancer. Instead of undergoing medical treatment, she trusted the teachings of her favorite Bible teachers, Kenneth Hagin, Kenneth Copeland, and Marilyn Hickey. Mrs. Scott refused to acknowledge her physical symptoms and positively confessed a healing. Five years later the cancer-induced pain had become so unbearable that she began radiation therapy and "pleaded" with doctors to do something. She died that same year.[107]
>
> After Mary Turk discovered she had colon/rectal cancer, she made a vow of faith to Word Faith teacher Robert Tilton. In order not to violate her "vow," she refused medical attention and believed that she was healed despite her symptoms. She died an agonizing death as the cancer spread throughout her entire abdominal cavity.[108]

Word Faith leaders have responded to these deadly fruits of their labor by blaming those who died. The deceased simply did not have enough faith to bring about their healing. Price, for example, admits, "I have watched people die, and my heart went out to them, but their faith was not developed, and it couldn't bring the healing to pass, and they died. It wasn't the will of God that they die, but their faith wasn't sufficiently developed."[109] Charles Capps agrees, "*Many people die needlessly* because they said, 'If I believe I'm healed, I'll throw

[102]Kenneth E. Hagin, *The Real Faith* (Tulsa: Kenneth Hagin Ministries, 1970), 13.
[103]Ibid.
[104]Jerry Savelle, *If Satan Can't Steal Your Joy* (Tulsa: Harrison House, 1982), 9.
[105]Larry Parker, *We Let Our Son Die* (Irvine, Calif.: Harvest House Publishers, 1980).
[106]Private letter from Douglas L. Klear to the Christian Research Institute, n.d., 2.
[107]Author Richard Abanes' interview with Doug Scott, son of F. Elizabeth Scott, on June 23, 1994.
[108]Author Richard Abanes' interview with Ole Anthony of the Trinity Foundation, who investigated the case, on June 23, 1994.
[109]Price, *Presumption*, 94.

away all my medicine,' *when their faith was not developed to that level.*"[110]

Such cold-blooded remarks are causing even more deaths as staunch believers in Word Faith theology try to prove to themselves and to those around them that they have enough faith to be healed and that God's "best" belongs to them. According to D. R. McConnell:

> The most consistent reports of abuse caused by the Faith doctrine of healing involve the treatment of those in the movement with chronic and/or terminal illnesses. Because of the belief that listening to a "negative confession" can infect one's faith, not many in the Faith movement are willing even to be around, much less listen to, those who are seriously ill. . . . A believer is shunned, isolated, and ostracized as though he was an unbeliever—which, by definition, is precisely what he is, or else he would not be ill in the first place. . . . The time when a dying believer needs a word of encouragement is when he receives a sermonette on the failure of his faith. . . . When a dying believer needs his faith the most is when he is told that he has it the least. . . . When he needs support of a sensitive, supportive body of believers is when he is ostracized and isolated as though he himself was infectious. Perhaps the most inhumane fact revealed about the Faith movement is this: When its members die, they die alone.[111]

Why, Why, Why?

The Christian church was first introduced to Word Faith teachings through Kenneth E. Hagin, also known as "Dad" Hagin by those who admire him. He got his doctrines from E. W. Kenyon, an individual who was greatly influenced by the metaphysical mind science cults such as Christian Science, Unity School of Christianity, and Church of Religious Science. Kenyon's interest in the metaphysical cults was intense. In fact, "his knowledge of the origins and teachings of these groups was extensive."[112] Some call this link the "Kenyon Connection."[113]

Hagin often refers to Kenyon as a great teacher, but what many Word Faith followers do not know is that "Dad" actually plagiarized much of what Kenyon wrote; in other words, to take someone else's written material and publish it as one's own, either in whole or in substantial part. Hagin copied what Kenyon wrote without giving him proper credit. It is nearly impossible to find one instance where Hagin credits Kenyon for material copied (often verbatim, or word-for-word). This certainly challenges Hagin's integrity and status as a trustworthy man of God.

In the works that contain the following passages, Hagin gives no credit to Kenyon. Instead, he passes off what he has written as his own. Hagin has plagiarized so much of Kenyon's literature that only a small portion of it can be quoted in this chapter.

Kenneth E. Hagin	E. W. Kenyon
The twenty-second Psalm gives a graphic picture of the crucifixion of Jesus—more vivid than that of John, Matthew, or Mark who witnessed it.[114]	The twenty-second Psalm gives a graphic picture of the crucifixion of Jesus. It is more vivid than that of John, Matthew, or Mark who witnessed it.[115]

[110]Capps, *Dynamics*, 155.
[111]McConnell, 166.
[112]Ibid., 44.
[113]Ibid., 30.
[114]Kenneth E. Hagin, quoted in McConnell, 8.
[115]E. W. Kenyon, quoted in McConnell, 9.

Faith is grasping the unrealities of hope, and bringing them into the realm of reality. Faith, we know, grows out of the Word of God.[116]

As you do this your faith will abound. The reason faith is throttled and held in bondage is that you've never dared to confess what God says you are. Remember that faith never grows beyond your confession. Your daily confession of what the Father is to you, of what Jesus is doing for you now at the right hand of the Father, and of what His mighty Holy Spirit is doing in you will build a solid, positive faith life. You will not be afraid of any circumstances.[118]

This gives us the key that unlocks the great teachings of identification. Christ became one with us in sin that we might become one with Him in righteousness. He became as we were to the end that we might become as He is now. He died to make us live. He became weak to make us strong. He suffered shame to give us glory. He went to hell to take us to heaven. He was condemned to justify us. He was made sick that healing might be ours.[120]

It's not a problem of faith, but it's a problem of knowing your legal rights in Christ, and taking the place of son or daughter, and actually playing the game with Him.[122]

Faith is grasping the unrealities of hope and bringing them into the realm of reality. Faith grows out of the Word of God.[117]

As you do this your faith will abound. The reason your faith is throttled and held in bondage is because you have never dared to confess what God says you are. Remember that faith never grows beyond your confession. Your daily confession of what the Father is to you, what Jesus is now doing for you at the right hand of the Father, and what the mighty Holy Spirit is doing in you will build a positive, solid faith life. You will not be afraid of any circumstance.[119]

This gives us the key that unlocks the great teaching of identification. Christ became one with us in sin that we might become one with Him in righteousness. He became as we were to the end that we might become as He is now. . . . He died to make us alive. . . . He became weak to make us strong. He suffered shame to give us glory. He went to hell to take us to heaven. He was condemned to justify us. He was made sick that healing might be ours.[121]

It is not a problem of faith; but a problem of knowing your legal rights in Christ, and then taking your place as a son or daughter and actually playing the game with Him.[123]

Conclusion

God's people always have been, and always will be, plagued by false teachers and false prophets (2 Corinthians 11:13; Galatians 2:4; 2 Peter 2:1–3). Jesus himself said, "Beware of false prophets, which come to you in sheep's clothing, but inwardly they are ravening wolves" (Matthew 7:15).

Paul the apostle, during his farewell address to the Ephesian church, warned of two kinds of "wolves" in sheep's clothing: those who attack the church from the outside; and those who poison it from the inside: "Take heed therefore unto yourselves, and to all the flock over which the Holy Ghost hath made you overseers, to feed the church of God, which he hath purchased with his own blood. For I know

---

[116]Kenneth E. Hagin, "What Faith Is #2," *Faith Study Course*, 20.

[117]E. W. Kenyon, *The Two Kinds of Faith: Faith's Secrets Revealed* (Seattle: Kenyon's Gospel Publishing Society, 1942), 7.

[118]Kenneth E. Hagin, "How to Turn Your Faith Loose #3," *Faith Study Course*, 59.

[119]E. W. Kenyon, *The Two Kinds of Life* (Seattle: Kenyon's Gospel Publishing Society, 1971).

[120]Kenneth E. Hagin, quoted in McConnell, 9.

[121]E. W. Kenyon, quoted in McConnell, 8.

[122]Kenneth E. Hagin, "Seven Steps to the Highest."

[123]E. W. Kenyon, *In His Presence* (Seattle: Kenyon's Gospel Publishing Society, 1969), 218.

this, that after my departing shall grievous wolves enter in among you, not sparing the flock. Also of your own selves shall men arise, speaking perverse things, to draw away disciples after them" (Acts 20:28–30).

Although the Word Faith movement is devouring many with false doctrines, those still faithful to the pure gospel need not fear or be discouraged. The apostle Peter said: "But there were false prophets also among the people, even as there shall be false teachers among you, who privily shall bring in damnable heresies, even denying the Lord that bought them, and bring upon themselves swift destruction. And many shall follow their pernicious ways; by reason of whom the way of truth shall be evil spoken of. And through covetousness shall they with feigned words make merchandise of you: whose judgment now of a long time lingereth not, and their damnation slumbereth not" (2 Peter 2:1–3).

Appendix C

The Puzzle of Seventh-day Adventism

Preface

In a volume such as this dealing with the problem of non-Christian cults, the question might logically be asked, "Why include Seventh-day Adventism, especially since the writer has classified them in a full-length volume as a Christian denomination?"

The answer to this is that for over a century Adventism has borne a stigma of being called a non-Christian cult system. Whether or not this was justified in the early development of Adventism, this has already been discussed at length in an earlier book,[1] but it should be carefully remembered that the Adventism of today is different in not a few places from the Adventism of 1844, and with that change the necessity of new evaluation comes naturally.

Together with the Evangelical Foundation (founded by the late Dr. Donald Grey Barnhouse and publishers of the now-defunct *Eternity* magazine), we conducted a thorough new evaluation of the Seventh-day Adventists several years ago. The results of that new evaluation were presented comprehensively in the book *The Truth About Seventh-day Adventism* and then later in the previous editions of this volume.

It is my conviction that one cannot be a true Jehovah's Witness, Mormon, Christian Scientist, etc., and be a Christian in the biblical sense of the term; but it is perfectly possible to be a Seventh-day Adventist and be a true follower of Jesus Christ despite certain heterodox concepts, which will be discussed.

Such Christian leaders as Louis T. Talbot, M. R. DeHaan, John R. Rice, Anthony A. Hoekema, J. K. Van Baalen, Herbert Bird, and John R. Gerstner have taken the position that Adventism is in fact a cult system; whereas, the late Donald Grey Barnhouse, myself, E. Schuyler English, and quite a few others have concluded the opposite.

This appendix updated, revised, and edited by Gretchen Passantino.

[1]Walter Martin, *The Truth About Seventh-day Adventism* (Grand Rapids: Zondervan Publishing House, 1960).

Since the opposing view has had wide circulation over a long period of time, I felt it was necessary to include here Seventh-day Adventism as a proper counterbalance—presenting the other side of Adventism and representing the theology of Adventism as the Adventists themselves believe it and not as many critics have caricatured it.

This, of course, is not to be construed in any sense of the term as an endorsement of the entire theological structure of Seventh-day Adventism, a portion of which is definitely out of the mainstream of historical Christian theology and which I have taken pains to refute. But I believe it is only fair and ethical to consider both sides of an extremely difficult and provocative controversy, which shows very little sign of abating in our day.

Evangelical ministries to cults continue to hold differing opinions on whether or not Seventh-day Adventism is properly cultic or not. Part of the ambiguity arises from differing definitions of the words "cult" and "cultic." (See chapter 1 for the theological definition governing this volume.) Others come from orthodox theological positions, such as traditional Reformed, that reject Arminian viewpoints as heretical, and thus reject Adventism on that ground. Dr. Ruth Tucker, of Trinity Evangelical Divinity School, observes,

> An overview of Seventh-day Adventism seems to indicate that the determining factors on whether a religious movement is a "cult" or not are not always black and white. There are gray areas, and this movement would fall into such an area as an ambiguous category—its historical roots being more "cultic" than its present-day perspective. . . . Indeed, when the distinctive doctrines of the Seventh-day Adventists are not strongly emphasized, most Protestant evangelicals would probably find themselves far more at home in an Adventist church than in a liberal mainline Protestant one.[2]

Seventh-day Adventism today is much more a "church" than a "cult." How it maintains its status over the coming years will be determined by how it continues to respond to the major tenets of orthodoxy while retaining its distinctives in minor areas. Notes Adventist professor Gary Land,

> If, as seems to be the case, Seventh-day Adventism is a sect that has moved a long way toward becoming a church, its fundamental struggle in the coming years will be, as Donald McAdams has put it, "to retain the spark, commitment and message that gave the sect its original power, while accepting the institutional, structural and cultural changes that are the inevitable concomitant of growth in the real world." Though holding fast to its belief in the imminent Second Coming of Christ, Adventism will have to face resolutely the implications of the command given by the nobleman of Christ's parable, "Occupy till I come."[3]

In fact, during the last thirty years the Seventh-day Adventist denomination has seen turbulence, both administratively and doctrinally, that is more extensive than any turmoil in the organization's history. Administratively, there have been a number of Adventist leaders and pastors who have been removed from

---

[2]Ruth A. Tucker, *Another Gospel: Alternative Religions and the New Age Movement* (Grand Rapids, Mich: Zondervan Publishing House, 1989), 116.
[3]Gary Land, ed., *Adventism in America* (Grand Rapids, Mich.: William B. Eerdmans Publishing Company, 1986), 230.

their positions because of supposed or proven improper financial activities, including misappropriation of funds. On the United States federal government level, the IRS, SEC, FBI, and Justice Department have all initiated investigations, and some Seventh-day Adventist conference administrators may even face trial for fraud. Doctrinally, the church has developed a large rift between those members and leaders who are solidly within the evangelical Christian camp and those members and leaders who, because of their emphasis on works-righteousness, legalism, and the prophetic status accorded to founder Ellen G. White, may well move the denomination over time outside of the evangelical camp and perhaps even into actual cultism.

There is a third growing faction within Seventh-day Adventism that is much more theologically liberal than either the traditionalists or the evangelicals, and the future may even bring *three* Adventist groups, one aligning itself roughly with mainstream, theologically liberal Protestantism, one with sectarian or cultic groups, and one with mainstream evangelicalism. Writing in *Christianity Today* in 1990, author Kenneth Samples provides a conclusion with which we can still agree toward the end of the 1990s:

> In the late 1970s, Seventh-day Adventism was at the crossroads: Would it become thoroughly evangelical? Or would it return to sectarian traditionalism? Denominational discipline in the 1980s against certain evangelical advocates gave a strong indication that there is a powerful traditionalist segment that desires to retain Adventism's 1844 "remnant" identity. As well, the liberal perspective, with its emphasis on pluralism, appeals to many Adventists. While Evangelical Adventism has lost ground in the 1980s, its supporters remain, though they are not nearly as prominent today.[4]

Since I have always stressed the importance of doctrinal integrity in my evaluations of religious movements, the doctrinal upheaval in Adventism is of special concern. Consequently, on February 16, 1983, I wrote the General Conference of Seventh-day Adventists (Washington, D.C.), calling for the Conference's public and official statement reaffirming or denying the authority of the Adventist book *Questions on Doctrine*[5] which was the representative Adventist publication on which I based my earlier evaluation and book. The current standard doctrinal exposition book is called *Seventh-day Adventists Believe: A Biblical Exposition of Seventeen Fundamental Doctrines* and was published by the General Conference in 1988. In almost all cases, this newer volume agrees in substance with *Questions on Doctrine*. On April 29, 1983, W. Richard Lesher, vice-president of the General Conference, responded in a personal letter. His reply read, in part:

> You ask first if Seventh-day Adventists still stand behind the answers given to your questions in *Questions on Doctrine* as they did in 1957. The answer is yes. You have noted in your letter that some opposed the answers given then, and, to some extent, the same situation exists today. But certainly the great majority of Seventh-day Adventists are in harmony with the views expressed in *Questions on Doctrine.*
>
> Secondly, you addressed the question of the interpretation of Scripture in

---

[4]Kenneth R. Samples, "The Recent Truth about Seventh-day Adventism," *Christianity Today* (February 5, 1990): 21.

[5]*Questions on Doctrine* (Washington, D.C.: Review and Herald Publishing Association, 1957).

relation to the writings of Ellen White. As an attested agent of the prophetic gift we believe communication based on Ellen White's revelatory experience to be trustworthy and dependable. However, we do not believe that the writings of Ellen White exhaust the meaning of Scripture. We still hold with the statements on Ellen White included in *Questions on Doctrine.*

On the basis of the above letter, dialogue with several Adventist leaders, and the continuing state of flux within Adventism itself, I must, for the time being, stand behind my original evaluation of Seventh-day Adventism as presented comprehensively in my first book on the subject and later in this volume. Only events not yet unfolded, but within the knowledge of the Lord himself, will determine whether my evaluation will need to be revised in the future. It is my prayer that the aberrational currents within contemporary Adventism will not prevail and that Adventism will continue to be an evangelical, albeit unique, Christian denomination.

It was Dr. Donald Grey Barnhouse who said that simply because a person is a member of a specific denomination there is no reason to suppose that the entire denomination is represented by that person's theology, nor is it proper to assume that because there are heretical Baptists, Presbyterians, Methodists, Episcopalians, etc., that all such denominations are therefore heretical.

To expand upon this we might say that simply because a denomination is Christian in its profession does not guarantee that all members of that denomination are Christian by their confession and experience. Hence, it is our position that Seventh-day Adventism as a denomination is essentially Christian in a sense that all denominations and groups professing Christianity are Christian if they conform to the classical mission of Christianity as given in the Bible and the creeds and counsels of the Christian church. But this does not mean that all Baptists, all Methodists, all Episcopalians, all Lutherans, or all Adventists are necessarily Christians. This is a matter between the individual and God and is to be viewed in the light of the revelation of Scripture and the testimony of the Holy Spirit.

This section on Seventh-day Adventism is an attempt to present for consideration facts that are little known in many areas and often distorted in others. It is an effort to examine, commend, and criticize where necessary the theological structure of the Adventist denomination, and is submitted with a prayerful hope that honest investigation, even if it does not agree with our preconceived notions, is to be encouraged and profited from, under the guidance of the Spirit of God.

The Seventh-day Adventists Today

The Seventh-day Adventist church today claims around nine million members worldwide in more than 200 countries with over 40,000 churches and 12,690 ordained, active ministers. It is growing especially rapidly in Third World countries, "adding more than one new member by baptism every forty-eight seconds of every day and organizing four new congregations daily. . . . From the Church's beginnings in the United States, today, nine out of ten members live elsewhere—in 206 other countries of the world."[6]

---

[6]Seventh-day Adventist official web site, http://www.adventist.org, 1997.

Seventh-day Adventists are headquartered in Silver Spring, Maryland, but also operate twelve international administrative offices and thirteen Agencies of the General Conference in the United States and the Philippines.

> In just a century and a half the Seventh-day Adventist Church has grown from a handful of individuals, who diligently studied the Bible in search for truth, to a worldwide community of over [nine] million members and millions of others who regard the Adventist Church as their spiritual home. Although the name "Seventh-day Adventist" was chosen in 1860, the denomination was not officially organized until May 21, 1863, when the movement included some 125 churches and 3,500 members.[7]

The Historical Background of Seventh-day Adventism

Seventh-day Adventism sprang from the "Great Second Advent Awakening," which shook the religious world just before the middle of the nineteenth century when a reemphasis on the second advent of Jesus Christ was rampant in Britain and on the continent of Europe. Before long, many of the Old World views of prophetic interpretation crossed the Atlantic and penetrated American theological circles.

Based largely upon the apocalyptic books of Daniel and Revelation, the theology of the Advent Movement was discussed in the newspapers as well as in theological journals. New Testament eschatology competed with stock market quotations for front-page space, and the "seventy weeks," "twenty-three hundred days," and "the abomination of desolation" (Daniel 8—9) were common subjects of conversation.

Following the chronology of Archbishop Ussher, and interpreting the 2300 days of Daniel as 2300 years, many Bible students of various denominations concluded that Christ would come back about the year 1843. Of this studious number was one William Miller, a Baptist minister and resident of Lower Hampton, New York. The Great Second Advent Awakening, which swept the United States in the 1840's, stemmed largely from the activities of this William Miller, who confidently taught in the year 1818 that in "about" twenty-five years, i.e., 1843, Jesus Christ would come again. As Miller himself put it, "I was thus brought in 1818 at the close of my two-year study of the Scriptures to the solemn conclusion that in about twenty-five years from that time all the affairs of our present state would be wound up."[8]

Miller further wrote:

> I believe the time can be known by all who desire to understand and to be ready for His coming. And I am fully convinced that some time between March 21, 1843 and March 21, 1844, according to the Jewish method of computation of time, Christ will come and bring all His saints with Him; and that then He will reward every man as His work shall be.[9]

At length his associates set October 22, 1844, as the final date when Jesus Christ would return for His saints, visit judgment upon sin, and establish the kingdom of God upon earth.

---

[7]Seventh-day Adventist official web site.
[8]Francis D. Nichol, *The Midnight Cry* (Washington, D.C.: Review and Herald, 1944), 35.
[9]William Miller, *Signs of the Times* (January 25, 1843).

One need only read the words of the Lord Jesus Christ to realize that Miller was teaching in contradiction to the Word of God. Jesus said, "But of that day and hour knoweth no man, no, not the angels of heaven, but my Father only" (Matthew 24:36; also 24:42, 44; 25:13).

The gospel of Mark also shows that dates cannot be set, for in verse 35 of chapter 13 our Lord stated, "Watch ye therefore: for ye know not when the master of the house cometh." And almost His last words to His disciples are a rebuke to those who set dates: "It is not for you to know the times or the seasons, which the Father hath put in his own power" (Acts 1:7). Certainly this should have been deterrent enough for William Miller and his associates, but, sad to say, it was not.

Compare the two positions, Miller versus the Scriptures: God declared that no man would know the time; Miller stated that he did know the time. God said the times and seasons were within His own power; the Millerites declared that they had the prophetic key given to them. Jesus Christ stated, "No man knows the day or the hour," but the Millerites set the exact day (October 22, 1844). And history bears a bitter record of their terrible disappointment.

Lest anyone reading the various accounts of the rise of "Millerism" in the United States come to the conclusion that Miller and his followers were "crackpots" or "uneducated tools of Satan," the following facts should be known:[10] The Great Advent Awakening movement that spanned the Atlantic from Europe was bolstered by a tremendous wave of contemporary biblical scholarship. Although Miller himself lacked academic theological training, actually scores of prophetic scholars in Europe and the United States had espoused Miller's views before he himself announced them. In reality, his was only one more voice proclaiming the 1843/1844 fulfillment of Daniel 8:14, or the 2300-day period allegedly dating from 457 B.C. and ending in A.D. 1843–1844.

William Miller was born in Pittsfield, Massachusetts, on February 15, 1782, and while he was still a young child his family moved to Lower Hampton, New York, close to the Vermont State border. Miller was raised by a deeply religious mother, but despite her zeal for his conversion, Miller became a deist. Only after a soul-searching experience that culminated in his conversion did he begin his preparation for ministry in the Baptist church. A great many books have been written about William Miller and the Millerite movement, but to this writer's knowledge none of them proved Miller to be dishonest or deceptive in his prophetic interpretation of Scripture. Indeed, he enjoyed the reputation, among all who knew him, of being an honest, forthright Christian. One does not have to endorse the errors of Millerism, therefore, to respect the historical figure of William Miller. Regardless of his shortcomings, Miller was a deeply religious Christian who, had he had a more extensive understanding of the Scriptures, most probably would never have embarked upon his disastrous date-setting career.

Clearly it may be seen that although Miller popularized the 1843/1844 concept of Christ's coming again, he was by no means alone. If we condemn him,

---

[10]The various charges to the effect that the Millerites were fanatics who waited on rooftops attired in white "ascension robes" anticipating the return of Christ; and further, that insanity swept the Millerite ranks in 1843 and 1844 in the wake of the "Great Disappointment" are purely mythological in character and have little basis in verifiable facts (see *The Midnight Cry*, 321–498).

we must also condemn a large number of internationally known scholars who were among the most highly educated men of their day. Yet they, too, had a blind spot in prophetic interpretation and endorsed this fallacious system of date-setting. Regardless of the number of scholars who confirmed his errors, however, the fact remains that Miller and the Millerite movement operated contrary to the express injunctions of Scripture. Both Miller and his followers lived to reap the reward of their foolhardy quest and to suffer crushing humiliation, ridicule, and abject despair.

William Miller set the time for the return of the Lord between March 21, 1843 and March 21, 1844, reckoning according to the Jewish calendar.[11] As the first-named date approached, religious frenzy shook the Millerite world—the Lord was coming back!

Though the followers of Miller were zealous and sincere, stark disappointment awaited them as the Jewish year 1843 faded from time and the Lord did not come. When the dream closest to their hearts failed to materialize, they eagerly sought enlightenment from William Miller, who replied with characteristic honesty. Wrote Miller, in the very shadow of spiritual anguish:

> Were I to live my life over again, with the same evidence that I then had, to be honest with God and man I should have to do as I have done. Although opposers said it would not come, they produced no weighty arguments. It was evidently guess-work with them; and I then thought, and do now, that their denial was based more on an unwillingness for the Lord to come than on any arguments leading to such conclusion. I confess my error, and acknowledge my disappointment; yet I still believe that the Day of the Lord is near, even at the door; and I exhort you, my brethren, to be watchful and not let that day come upon you unawares.[12]

In the wake of this stunning declaration, the Millerites strove vainly to reconcile their interpretations of the prophetic Scriptures with the stark truth that Christ had not returned. With one last gasp, so to speak, Miller reluctantly endorsed "The Seventh-Month Movement," or the belief that Christ would come on October 22, 1844, the tenth day of the seventh month according to the Karaite reckoning of the Jewish Sacred Calendar.[13] Once again the Millerites' hopes were lifted, and October 22, 1844 became the watchword for the return of the Lord Jesus Christ. The outcome can best be summed up in the words of Dr. Josiah Litch, a Millerite leader in Philadelphia who wrote on October 24: "It is a cloudy and dark day here—the sheep are scattered—the Lord has not come yet."[14]

From Litch's statement, it is easy to piece together the psychological framework of the Millerites in the wake of these two disappointments. They were a shattered and disillusioned people—Christ had not come to cleanse the "sanctuary" (the earth), to usher in judgment, and to bring the world into subjugation to the "everlasting gospel." Instead, the sky was cloudy and dark, and the historical horizons were black with the failure of the Millerite movement. There

---

[11] *The Midnight Cry,* 169.
[12] Sylvester Bliss, *Memoirs of William Miller* (Boston, Mass.: n.p., 1855), 256.
[13] *The Midnight Cry,* 243.
[14] Ibid., 256.

was, of course, terrible confusion, of which God, Scripture tells us, is not the author (1 Corinthians 14:33).

The final phase of the movement closed with the "Great Disappointment of 1844," but as the Millerites disbanded, there emerged other groups, such as the First-day Adventists. However, in our study we are concerned primarily with three segments that later fused to produce the Seventh-day Adventist denomination. William Miller, it should be noted, was *never* a Seventh-day Adventist and stated that he had "no confidence" in the "new theories" that emerged from the shambles of the Millerite movement. Dr. LeRoy Froom, professor of prophetic interpretation at the Seventh-day Adventist Theological Seminary, Takoma Park, Washington, D.C., in the fourth volume of his masterful series *The Prophetic Faith of Our Fathers*, succinctly states what Miller's position was:

> Miller was outspokenly opposed to the various new theories that had developed following October 22, 1844, in an endeavor to explain the disappointment. He deplored the call that had been given to come out to the churches, and he never accepted the distinctive positions of the Sabbatarians. The doctrine of the unconscious sleep of the dead and the final destruction of the wicked was not, he maintained, part of the original Millerite position, but was introduced personally by George Storrs and Charles Fitch. He even came to deny the application of the parable in *The Midnight Cry* to the Seventh-month Movement and eventually went so far as to declare unequivocally that the movement was not "a fulfillment of prophecy in any sense."[15]

Aside from chronological speculation, therefore, the theology of William Miller differed from Seventh-day Adventist theology on three distinct points: He denied the Seventh-day Sabbath; the doctrine of the sleep of the soul; and the final, utter destruction of the wicked—all doctrines held by the Seventh-day Adventist denomination. Also, he never embraced the "sanctuary" and "investigative judgment" theories developed by Seventh-day Adventists. For William Miller the era of chronological speculation was over, and he died shortly after the fiasco, a broken and disillusioned man who was, nevertheless, honest and forthright when in error or when repudiating error. I believe he now enjoys the presence of the Lord whose appearing he so anxiously awaited.

In order to understand the background of Seventh-day Adventist history and theology, let us look at the three segments of Millerism, which eventually united to form the Seventh-day Adventist denomination. Each of these groups held a distinctive doctrine. The group headed by Hiram Edson in western New York proclaimed the doctrine of the sanctuary "as embracing a special or final ministry of Christ in the Holy of Holies in the *heavenly* sanctuary," thus giving new meaning to the message "The Hour of God's Judgment Has Come." The second group, headed by Joseph Bates, whose main following was in Massachusetts and New Hampshire, advocated the observance of the Seventh-day Sabbath "as involved in the keeping of the commandments of God." The third group, in Maine, emphasized the "Spirit of prophecy" or "the testimony of Jesus," which they believed was to be made manifest in the "remnant" (Revelation 14:6–12; also Revelation 12:17; 19:10) or "the last segment of God's church of

---

[15] *The Prophetic Faith of Our Fathers* (Takoma Park, Washington, D.C.: Review and Herald Publishing Association, 1950), 828–829.

the centuries." Between the years 1844 and 1847 the thinking of these groups crystallized and was actively declared and promulgated in the writings of their respective leaders: Hiram Edson, O.R.L. Crosier, Joseph Bates, James White, and Ellen G. White.

At this point in our historical analysis of Seventh-day Adventism, we believe it will be profitable to briefly review "The Great Disappointment of 1844" and its relationship to the Seventh-day Adventist doctrines of the heavenly sanctuary and the investigative judgment. The entire superstructure of the Millerites' prophetic interpretation was based upon their view of the book of Daniel, chapters eight and nine, with particular emphasis upon Daniel 8:14 and 9:24–27. The Millerites believed that the prophecy of the seventy weeks of Daniel nine must date from the year 457 B.C., which, as recent archaeological evidence confirms,[16] was the exact date of the decree of King Artaxerxes to rebuild Jerusalem (Daniel 9:25). Tracing the seventy weeks of Daniel on the theory that, as the Hebrew indicated, it should be rendered "seventy weeks of years" or 490 years, the Millerites arrived at the date A.D. 33; that is, from 457 B.C. to A.D. 33. Since this date generally corresponds with Christ's crucifixion, Millerites then linked it to Daniel 8:14—"Unto two thousand and three hundred days; then shall the sanctuary be cleansed"—with the seventy weeks of years prophecy, and the 2300 days became 2300 years. Thus, if you subtract 490 years (adding, of course, A.D. 1 to 33), the figure arrived at is 1843. Many biblical scholars have historically shown that in Scripture a day frequently symbolizes a year; further, that the seventy weeks and 2300 days of Daniel could have begun on the same date. And that date, according to the Millerites, was 457 B.C. In *The Prophetic Faith of Our Fathers*,[17] Dr. LeRoy Froom shows that many expositors had embraced the same method of interpretation, which is no argument for accepting it, but a strong argument for the *right* of the Millerites to do so.

As we have seen, when the Millerite calculations failed, all appeared to be lost; but a singular event took place only three days later in a cornfield near Port Gibson, New York, which changed the face of Adventist history and brought about a reinterpretation of the eighth and ninth chapters of the book of Daniel, an interpretation which is a keystone in the arch of the Seventh-day Adventist view of prophecy.

On October 25, 1844, following the "Great Disappointment," Hiram Edson, a devout Adventist and follower of William Miller, was wending his way homeward with his friend O.R.L. Crosier. In order to avoid the mocking gazes and taunts of their neighbors, they cut across a cornfield.

As they walked through the cornfield in deep silence and meditation, Hiram Edson stopped, became more deeply immersed in meditation, and then with upturned face indicative of a heartfelt prayer for spiritual light, he suddenly received a great spiritual "revelation." In the words of Dr. Froom,

> Suddenly there burst upon his mind the thought that there were two phases to Christ's ministry in the Heaven of Heavens, just as in the earthly sanctuary of old. In his own words, an overwhelming conviction came over him "that

---

[16]Siegfried H. Horn and Lynn H. Wood, *The Chronology of Ezra 7* (Washington, D.C.: Review and Herald Publishing Association, 1959).

[17]*The Prophetic Faith of Our Fathers*, vols. 1–4.

instead of our high priest coming out of the most holy of the heavenly sanctuary to come to this earth on the tenth day of the seventh month at the end of the twenty-three hundred days, He for the first time entered on that day the second apartment of that sanctuary, and that He had a work to perform in the most holy before coming to this earth."[18]

In that instant, according to Seventh-day Adventist history, Hiram Edson found the reason why the Millerites had been disappointed. They had expected Christ to come to earth to cleanse the sanctuary, but the sanctuary was not the earth. It was located in heaven! Instead of coming to earth, therefore, Christ had passed from one "apartment" of the sanctuary into the other "apartment" to perform a closing work now known as the "investigative judgment." In the year 1846, this new interpretation of Daniel was convincingly put forth by O. R. L. Crosier[19] who outlined and defended Hiram Edson's concept in a lengthy article in a special number of *The Day Star*, a Millerite publication in Cincinnati, Ohio. F. D. Nichol in *The Midnight Cry* refers to "a fragment," which Edson wrote about his experience in the cornfield. But as Dr. Froom has pointed out, Edson himself really believed that Christ had passed from the "holy place" to the "most holy" place in the heavenly sanctuary. The Old Testament tabernacle was divided by a veil into two apartments, the holy place and the most holy place. In the most holy place was the Ark of the Covenant. Into this apartment the high priest went once a year to sprinkle blood upon the mercy seat to make atonement for the sins of the people. In Christian theology, this blood symbolized prophetically the death of the Lord Jesus Christ, the Lamb of God, for the sins of all the world.

Transferring this Old Testament ceremonial concept to the New Testament, and making an extremely literalistic interpretation of the book of Hebrews, Edson and Crosier formulated the doctrines of "the heavenly sanctuary" and "investigative judgment." These concepts are now understood to mean that in 1844 Christ entered the "second phase" of His ministry in the heavenly sanctuary, and ever since has been reviewing the cases of believers to determine their worthiness for eternal life. Further, He will come forth from the "second apartment," or finish the "second phase" of His ministry in the sanctuary, to usher in judgment upon the world at His Great Second Advent. This, in essence, was the interpretation that shaped the later concepts of the "heavenly sanctuary" and the "investigative judgment" in Seventh-day Adventist theology. Thus, good Millerite-Adventists were justified in endorsing the work of William Miller. They even maintained that God had allowed Miller to make mistakes for the greater blessing of the "little flock." In her *Early Writings*, Ellen G. White made this assertion:

> I have seen that the 1843 chart was directed by the hand of the Lord, and that it should not be altered; that the figures were as He wanted them, that His

---

[18]*The Prophetic Faith of Our Fathers*, IV:881. An extremely literalistic concept, which is refuted by Hebrews 9:12, 24 and Acts 1, which show that at His ascension Christ entered into the "holy places," not the "second apartment" of the heavenly sanctuary in 1844. Seventh-day Adventists have redefined their teaching in terms of "phases."

[19]Crosier later rejected this concept, though it was endorsed by Ellen G. White and other prominent Adventist leaders. (See D. M. Canright, *Life of Mrs. E. G. White*, 107.)

hand was over and hid a mistake in some of the figures so that none could see it until His hand was removed.[20]

In this context, White was distinctly referring to Fitch's prophetic chart, utilized by the Millerites, which led them to the year 1843 instead of the date that she considered to be correct—October 22, 1844.

F. D. Nichol, in *Ellen G. White and Her Critics*,[21] attempts to explain White's statement in the light of Acts 24, Mark 16, Exodus 8:15, and Exodus 10. Of course, any are at liberty to accept his interpretation of the problem, which I do not. The fact remains, however, that the Millerites erred in their prophetic, chronological interpretation of the book of Daniel, and only the concept of Hiram Edson in the cornfield and the explanatory writings of O. R. L. Crosier, buttressed by the "revelations" of Ellen G. White, saved the day.

Although I do not accept White's explanation or the interpretations of Edson, Crosier, Froom, or Nichol, I would be at a loss to account for the growth and development of Seventh-day Adventism apart from the psychological framework of the "Great Disappointment of 1844." Therefore, I have carefully reviewed the doctrines that evolved from the Edson-Crosier-White pronouncements. The psychological factor is very important in Seventh-day Adventist history.

The second of the three Millerite-Adventist groups mentioned is also of great historical import. In Fairhaven, Massachusetts, following the "Great Disappointment of 1844," one Joseph Bates, a retired sea captain, issued a forty-eight-page pamphlet entitled *The Seventh-day Sabbath, A Perpetual Sign* (self-published, 1846). In it he argued for the Sabbath as a divine institution ordained in Eden, prefigured in Creation, and buttressed at Mt. Sinai. Some three years later Bates wrote a second pamphlet entitled *A Seal of the Living God* (self-published, 1849), based largely upon Revelation 14:9–12. Bates' Sabbatarianism exerted a great influence upon what later became the Seventh-day Adventist denomination.

In Volume 4 of *The Prophetic Faith of Our Fathers* (957–958), Dr. Froom sums it up:

> This became henceforth a characteristic and separating feature of Sabbatarian Adventist preaching. Bates here held that the message of Revelation 14 is the foundation of the full Advent message "Fear God and give glory to Him, for the hour of His judgment is come." This, he maintained, began to be fulfilled in the preaching of the Millerite movement. And the second angel's message on the fall of Babylon, with its climax in the call "Come out of her my people" was likewise initially sounded in 1844–1848. . . . They must not stop with the first two messages. There is a third inseparable in the series to be received and obeyed—namely, full obedience to God's holy commandments, including the observance of the Seventh day as a Sabbath. But that obedience is by faith. The Sabbath was next set forth as the "seal of God" as based on the sealing work of Revelation 7. On January 8, 1849, Bates issued his tract "A Seal of the Living God." From the fact of John's declaration that the number of sealed was 144,000, Bates drew the conclusion that the "remnant" who keeps the com-

[20]*Early Writings* (Washington, D.C.: Review and Herald Publishing Association, n.d.), 74.
[21]*Ellen G. White and Her Critics* (Washington, D.C.: Review and Herald Publishing Association, n.d.), 332–334.

mandments of God and have the testimony of Jesus Christ would number 144,000. So, to the concept of Christ entering the most holy place in the heavenly sanctuary on October 22, 1844, for the final work of judgment and the receiving of His kingdom, was added the Sabbath as involved in the third of this commission series of special "latter-day" messages. This concept of the "seal" was likewise built into the message of the Sabbath, as an added prophetic element. And this thought was similarly attested by Ellen White who wrote: "This seal is the Sabbath," and described the "most holy place" in which was the ark (Revelation 11:19), containing the Ten Commandments with a halo of light surrounding the fourth! Thus the Sabbath and the sanctuary became inseparably tied together.

The third group, which fused with the other two to form the Seventh-day Adventist Church, emphasized "the Spirit of prophecy" (Revelation 19:10). This body of former Millerites accepted the interpretations of one Ellen G. Harmon of Portland, Maine. Ellen Harmon, later Mrs. James White, was recognized by this group as the possessor of the "Spirit of prophecy," a restoration of the spiritual gift of prophecy (1 Corinthians 12:10) or counsel to the Seventh-day Adventist Church. White had numerous visions that confirmed many Adventist doctrines. When the Edson, Crosier, Bates, and White adherents joined forces, the Seventh-day Adventist denomination was launched.

Today the Seventh-day Adventist church seems to downplay White's role as a "prophet," describing her as "a gifted author, speaker, and administrator, who . . . enjoyed God's special guidance."[22] In any case, the church today clearly affirms that any post-biblical prophet's words must be tested by the Bible: "The Scriptures retain authority even over the gifts that come from the Holy Spirit, including guidance through the gift of prophecy or speaking in tongues."[23]

Although the name "Seventh-day Adventist" for the denomination was not officially assumed until 1860 at a conference held in Battle Creek, Michigan, nevertheless, Seventh-day Adventism had been launched. In 1855, Adventist headquarters were established in Battle Creek and remained there until 1905, when they were transferred to Takoma Park, a Maryland suburb of Washington, D.C.

The three distinctive doctrines of Seventh-day Adventism—the Sabbath, the Sanctuary, and the "Spirit of prophecy"—will be discussed later. The Adventists had a definite theological platform, which for many years remained almost constant. In recent years, however, there has been a definite movement toward a more explicit declaration of belief in the principles of the Christian faith and the tenets of Christian theology. In short, "clarification" and "redefinition" have characterized recent Seventh-day Adventist theological activities.

> Seventh-day Adventists are one of the fastest-growing Christian churches in the world today adding more than one new member by baptism every forty-eight seconds of every day and organizing four new congregations daily. Membership in the world Church exceeded nine million in mid–1996, with an average of 1,801 people being added each day—a sign of solid growth. From the Church's beginnings in the United States, today, nine out of ten members live else-

---

[22]Seventh-day Adventist official web site, http//www.adventist.org, 1997.
[23]*Seventh-day Adventists Believe: A Biblical Exposition of Twenty-Seven Fundamental Doctrines* (Washington, D.C.: Ministerial Association, General Conference of Seventh-day Adventists, 1988), 13.

where—in 206 other countries of the world.

Growth in Chinese believers has been phenomenal in a country without a national Church organization. During 1993 one congregation, led by two local elders, held the second largest single baptism in Seventh-day Adventist history, when 4,415 became believers. In 1994, 2,300 were baptized over two days in a province in Northern China. With the fall of Communism in Eastern Europe and the former Soviet Union, new doors of opportunity for mission and educational work have opened. The first-ever Seventh-day Adventist church building in Albania was officially dedicated in the city of Korce, and two Adventist schools have moved to new locations in the Czech Republic and Romania.

Seventh-day Adventists are communicating to their different publics using new communications technologies. A new personal and corporate communication era began for the Church when the Adventists On-line forum on CompuServe Information Service opened in July 1994. More than 5,400 members joined the forum by October of 1996, and 300 are now joining each month. Church members can directly communicate with clergy and church leaders, and users can download news about the Church, information files, inspirational materials, and statistics. Recently Adventists On-line added a second forum with twenty-three message and library areas such as: Children's Ministry, Family Ministry, Youth Ministry, Pathfinders, Church Officers, Net Evangelism, Sabbath School, and Home Study International. In 1994 Adventist News Network (ANN), an official press agency from world headquarters, was launched; and Adventist Communication Network (ACN) began broadcasting via satellite to 500 churches in North America. In the past two years, the Network has grown and now has more than 2,000 churches downlinking four satellite programs regularly. Recently ACN produced Net '96, a live five-week series of meetings with evangelist Mark Finley, to more than 100,000 viewers. Adventist World Radio (AWR) continued its expansion in 1994 by adding new languages and transmitters. Today, AWR broadcasts 1,000 hours per week in more than forty languages from eighteen transmitters in seven international locations. In 1995, the Seventh-day Adventist Church entered the world of Internet with a Web page providing information about the Church.

Seventh-day Adventists have one of the broadest centralized Protestant educational systems in the world (5,530 schools, colleges, and universities) and have one of the most comprehensive networks of health-care providers (635 hospitals, clinics, medical launches and medivac planes, orphanages, and homes for the elderly). Adventists speak in at least 717 languages and another thousand dialects, leading to the establishment of fifty-six Church-owned printing plants and editorial offices including the newest in Russia and Bulgaria.[24]

---

[24]From the homepage of the Seventh-day Adventist Church, http://www.adventist.org. Additional statistics include:

Church membership (world)		**8,812,555**
North America membership		838,898
Baptisms and professions of faith		659,899
Ordained ministers, active		12,690
Total active employees		144,022
Educational Program Enrollment		
Primary schools	4,522	656,143
Secondary schools	930	200,702
Tertiary institutions	81	56,470
Total schools	5,530	913,315
Health Ministry		
Hospitals and sanitariums		157
Clinics and dispensaries		349

We cannot hope to cover the entire scope of Seventh-day Adventism's historical development in this brief résumé; but we see that from meager beginnings in the wake of the "Great Disappointment of 1844" and the collapse of the Millerite movement, the Seventh-day Adventist denomination has pressed forward and expanded until today it constitutes an important, albeit controversial, segment of American Protestantism.

Although this is but a background sketch, the reader can readily see that in Seventh-day Adventism, religious historians have an interesting subject for study, a subject from which many unusual theological speculations have emerged and continue to emerge.

Psychological Factors

One of the principal problems in understanding the Seventh-day Adventist movement is discovering the psychological motivation and basis of this thriving denomination of zealots.

I. *Early Handicaps*

From the beginning, the Adventists were regarded with grave suspicion by the great majority of evangelical Christians, principally because the Seventh-day Adventists were pre-millennial in their theology. That is, they believed that Christ would come before the millennium and saw themselves squarely in opposition to the predominant post-millennial and a-millennial schools of thought of that era. The "Great Disappointment of 1844" and the collapse of the Millerite movement naturally brought pre-millennialism into disrepute. Certain authors of the time considered pre millenarians "peculiar," even to the point of condemning pre-millennialism outright, and dubbed as "Adventist" all who

---

Nursing homes & retirement centers, orphanages & children's homes 99
Physicians, dentists, residents, and interns employed 3,675
Graduate nurses employed 15,439
Outpatient visits 8,880,209
Assets of health-care institutions (1994) $4,823,743,160

Publishing Work
Publishing houses and branches 56
Literature evangelists, credentialed & licensed 7,485
Languages used in publications and oral work 717
Languages used in publications 229

Sabbath Schools
Sabbath schools 85,987
Sabbath school membership 10,360,712

Contributions
Total tithes and offerings (world) $1,332,781,946
North America $804,357,655
Total tithes and offerings per capita (world) $173.56
North America $989.22

Broadcast and Bible School Ministries
Radio stations used each week 924
TV stations used each week 1,229
Bible school enrollments 492,319
Bible school graduates 250,237

held that view of eschatology. This is especially interesting when we consider that pre-millennialism is an accepted school of thought in eschatology today and that those who hold post-millennial and a-millennial views are considered by the pre-millenarians to be peculiar.

Thus the Adventists started out with two great psychological handicaps: They had incurred disapproval of the group or the mainstream of Christianity, and the Millerites from which they sprang had been publicly humiliated by the failure of their chronological calculations. These two factors and the constant jeering by opposing schools of eschatology united the Seventh-day Adventists into a closely knit group, habitually on the defensive and suspicious of the motives and intentions of other Christians.

Moreover, the Adventists were drawn together by the "special truths" of the Advent message. They were convinced that they had a proclamation for the world—a great "last-day message." Later we shall describe how this attitude widened the chasm between Adventists and Christians of other denominations. It is sufficient here to note that the Adventists considered themselves a special "remnant people" ordained by God to revive certain neglected truths of the Christian message. Filled with burning zeal to fulfill this mission, they laid themselves open to serious misunderstanding by Christians of other denominations who did not agree with them about the proper day of worship, the state of the dead, and investigative judgment.

Engaged in open conflict with Christians of virtually all denominations, the Adventists retreated into an "exclusivistic shell," despising what they termed "certain antinomian tendencies in contemporary Christian theology." They laid strong emphasis upon man's responsibility to the moral law of God, which eventually brought upon them the label "Galatianists" or "legalists." Now, as we shall see, there can be little doubt that there was and still is legalism in Adventism, as in some other Christian churches; but when we consider these early psychological factors, certain of which still pertain today, their reactions are understandable, though hardly defensible.

Of course the aforementioned "neglected" truths made few friends for the Adventists with Christians of other denominations, mainly because these truths were frequently presented in such manner as to arouse opposition instead of inviting investigation. Seventh-day Adventism has woefully demonstrated many times the old but true adage, "Not what we say but how we say it makes or breaks a case."

II. *Identity Concealed*

In his book *Answers to Objections,* F. D. Nichol demonstrates how the psychological defense that Adventists erected in their early days has carried over into modern times. Nichol quotes the charge:

> When Seventh-day Adventist ministers go into a community to hold a series of lectures they conceal at first their denominational connection. They thus hope to draw into their audience people who would never have come if they knew Seventh-day Adventists were conducting the meetings. This is a form of deception. There is something the matter with a religious body that is afraid to identify itself as soon as it begins to carry on any activity in a community.[25]

---

[25]*Answers to Objections* (Washington, D.C.: Review and Herald Publishing Association, 1952), 421–422.

Nichol answers:

> Now, it is a fact that during most of the history of the Seventh–day Adventist church, the very word Adventist has conveyed to the minds of most people a picture of a deluded band of fanatics sitting on housetops in ascension robes, awaiting the opening of the heavens. This story of ascension robes has become a part of American folklore and has been embalmed in impressive encyclopedias. And the ascension robe story is only part of the fanciful picture that has come to the minds of many when they have heard the word Adventist.
>
> The ascension robe story is a myth, and 99 percent of related stories are likewise myths—as has now been proved—but that has not prevented people from believing them. The net result has been that many people have seen Seventh-day Adventists only through the distorting mists of slanderous myths. This is nothing new in religious history; witness, for example, the early history of the Quakers and the Baptists.
>
> It should not be difficult, therefore, for any reasonable person to see why Adventist ministers through the past years have sought first to cause people to see them simply as Christian preachers before announcing their Adventist connection. After all, we seek to be first, and before all else, Christian preachers of righteousness. Then we hope to build on the timely messages from Bible prophecy that may be described in the words of the apostle Peter as "present truth" for these last days of earth's history.
>
> It has undoubtedly been true in years past that Adventists could not have gotten a crowd out to hear them, in certain cities at least, if they had revealed their identity at the outset. But we think that proves not the weakness of the Adventist case, but the strength of distorted ideas founded on fanciful myths. The other side of the picture is that many people, after they have attended Adventist meetings for a time, frankly admit that they have changed their ideas about us and are glad that they first came to the meetings not knowing who was conducting them.
>
> In more recent years our activities have become so much better known that in many places the former distorted picture has been largely corrected. Accordingly, we are increasingly following the plan of announcing at the outset the Adventist sponsorship of the public meetings. That is what we like to do, and what we hope ere long to be able to do everywhere. We are not ashamed of our Adventism, far from it. . . . No, we don't want to boast, we simply want to proclaim to the world a message that we earnestly believe should be given at this time. And if, in order to secure an initial hearing, we must at first conceal the name, we do so for a brief period only with a view to a clear-cut announcement of our Adventist connections a little later in the meetings. Then those who have been coming may decline to come further, if they desire. They generally decide to stay!
>
> Unhappily, as the literature of many objectors to Adventism reveals, it is they who have often been most active in spreading the distorting myths regarding us. And then they are wont to add, as though to prove conclusively their case against us, that we sometimes fail to reveal our Adventist connection at the outset of a series of evangelistic lectures! If they will help us to clear away completely the slanderous myths that folklore has often thrown around the name Adventist, we will be most happy to preface every one of our public meetings with the announcement of its Adventist sponsorship! In the meantime we shall, in such instances and areas as the situation necessitates, follow the precedent set by our Lord's instruction to His disciples as regards the time of disclosing our name.

Thus we see that some Adventist leaders, at least, maintain the premise that everyone's prejudice against them is based on myths and folklore, and on the

fact that they deliberately disguise themselves until they can obtain a hearing and demonstrate that they are Christians. These practices have given rise to the charge of proselytizing and it is not without foundation. In general, however, Nichol makes some very good points, though inadvertently he reveals only too clearly that he and many Adventists have been reared in this unhealthy climate of distrust, prejudice, and suspicion.

The only difficulty with Nichol's statement about identifying themselves is that the burden of proof lies not upon the other denominations, but upon the Adventists themselves. By openly saying who they are, they can refute these charges of deception and proselytizing.

On page 420, Nichol makes the mistake of using passages in the gospel of Matthew (8:4; 9:30; 16:20), where Christ enjoined secrecy, to prove that Adventists are only following Him when they conceal their identity, and he unfortunately tries to establish that such a behavior pattern on the part of Adventists is "honorable." Says Nichol:

> We have yet to hear any devout Christian expressing misgivings and doubts about the ministry of Christ or declaring that He was ashamed or afraid because He concealed His identity for a time. Evidently, then, this much at least may be established at the outset as being proved by these texts; concealing one's identity is not an insult or proof that one is either ashamed or afraid. There may be honorable and altogether reasonable grounds for such concealment.

Although Nichol's argument appears plausible, the cases are not parallel, for over and against the incidents that he cites, the Lord Jesus did many miracles in public and taught openly in the Temple as He himself declared before Caiaphas (John 18:20). To compare the motives of Adventists with the motives of the Lord Jesus Christ is just a bit more than I am willing to concede.

True, there is much misinformation about Adventist history and theology, but not infrequently it can be traced to unfortunate statements in their own official publications. Although other denominations are likewise guilty, Adventists have largely been outside the mainstream of Christian fellowship and so are in an unenviable position. They must go the "second mile" in this respect.

It is evident, then, that because of the opposition and abuse suffered in their early days, and also because of the "special truths" of the Advent message and emphasis upon certain areas of theology, the Adventists have been at a distinct psychological disadvantage and so have tended to band together against other churches. Other denominations, of course, have encouraged this recluse-like behavior by endless repetition of some of the Millerite myths. These factors, therefore, must be soberly evaluated if we are to understand Seventh-day Adventism.

Adventist Theology and Classical Orthodoxy

For many years Seventh-day Adventists have been handicapped by the lack of a comprehensive volume that adequately defines their doctrinal position. Many publications clearly set forth certain aspects of Adventism, particularly the writings of F. D. Nichol, LeRoy Froom, and Ellen G. White, whose role is that of inspired commentator and "messenger" to the Adventist denomination.

Except for the brief statement of fundamentals in the Seventh-day Adventist Yearbook, the average Adventist has been somewhat at a loss to explain conflicting theological opinions within his denomination, and even expressions in the writings of Ellen G. White were in certain contexts so ambiguous as to frustrate even the most devout believer. As a result of this, in 1957 the General Conference of Seventh-day Adventists released the first definitive and comprehensive explanation of their faith, an authoritative volume entitled *Questions on Doctrine.*

This book truthfully presents the theology and doctrine that the leaders of Seventh-day Adventism affirm they have always held. Members of other denominations will find it a reliable source to consult when seeking to understand what the Adventists themselves describe as "the position of our denomination in the area of church doctrine and prophetic interpretation."[26]

There can be no doubt of the fact that there are conflicting statements in Adventist publications and diverse opinions about certain areas of Adventist theology and interpretation, some of which is quite the opposite of classical orthodox Christianity; but this situation is not peculiar to the Adventist since all Christian denominations have various "wings," in most instances quite vocal, which are a source of constant embarrassment because they represent their own particular interpretations of the denomination's theology as the viewpoint of the denomination itself.

It is, therefore, unfair to quote any one Adventist writer or a group of writers as representing "the position of our denomination in the area of church doctrine and prophetic interpretation," even though the writings of such persons may in a large area qualify as Adventist theology. One must consult in good faith what the denomination itself represents as its theology and assume that the Seventh-day Adventist theologians know better than non-Adventists the implications and conclusions that they are willing to admit as representative of their church's theology.

This section is divided into several parts, each of which contains statements of the official Adventist position of particular aspects of theology, and is thoroughly documented from the primary source material provided in *Questions on Doctrine.* It is hoped that the reader will weigh carefully the declarations of the Seventh-day Adventist Church as represented by its General Conference, which alone is empowered to speak for the denomination. They have asserted initially, and reaffirmed currently, the authoritative force of *Questions on Doctrine* as accurately representative of Adventist doctrine. Until such time as there is clear, unequivocal, and equally authoritative evidence to the contrary, we must let the doctrine revealed in this book stand as Adventist doctrine. These doctrinal points we shall present and biblically evaluate below.

It is unnecessary to document at great length the fact that Seventh-day Adventism adheres tenaciously to the foundational doctrines of Christian theology as these have been held by the Christian church throughout the centuries. Dr. Anthony Hoekema, who believes that Seventh-day Adventism is a non-Christian cult, makes this interesting admission, and since Dr. Hoekema is no friend of Adventism, his testimony on this point could hardly be called prejudiced:

I am of the conviction that Seventh-day Adventism is a cult and not an evan-

---

[26] *Questions on Doctrine,* 8.

gelical denomination. . . . It is recognized with gratitude that there are certain soundly scriptural emphases in the teaching of Seventh-day Adventism. We are thankful for the Adventists' affirmation of the infallibility of the Bible, of the Trinity, and of the full deity of Jesus Christ. We gratefully acknowledge their teachings on creation and providence, on the incarnation and resurrection of Christ, on the absolute necessity for regeneration, on sanctification by the Holy Spirit, and on Christ's literal return.[27]

It is puzzling to me, as a student of non-Christian cult systems, how any group can hold the above doctrines in their proper biblical context, which Dr. Hoekema admits the Adventists do, and still be a non-Christian cult. However, we shall deal with this aspect of the critics of Adventism at the end of the chapter; therefore, suffice it to say that the Adventists do have a clean bill of health where the major doctrines of Christian theology are involved.

Lest there be any doubt on the subject, the following quotations taken from *Questions on Doctrine* are still upheld by the Seventh-day Adventist hierarchy as authoritative, and forthrightly declare the Seventh-day Adventist position in relation to historical Christianity as well as those areas where Adventism differs from the orthodox Christian position.

I. *Inspiration and Authority of the Scriptures*

1. Seventh-day Adventists believe that all Scripture, both Old and New Testaments, from Genesis to Revelation was "given by inspiration of God" (2 Timothy 3:16), and constitutes the very Word of God—the truth that "liveth and abideth for ever" (1 Peter 1:23). We recognize the Bible as the ultimate and final authority on what is truth (26).

2. Seventh-day Adventists hold the Protestant position that the Bible and the Bible only is the sole rule of faith and practice for Christians. We believe that all theological beliefs must be measured by the living Word, judged by its truth, and whatsoever is unable to pass this test, or is found to be out of harmony with its message, is to be rejected (28).

3. We believe in the authority, veracity, reliability, and truth of the Holy Scriptures. The same union of the divine and the human that is manifested in Christ, exists in the Bible. Its truths, revealed, are "given by inspiration of God" (2 Timothy 3:16), yet are couched in the words of men (27–28).

II. *The Nature of Christ*

1. Jesus Christ is very God, and He has existed with the Father from all eternity (22).

2. Christ, the Word of God, became incarnate through the miraculous conception and the Virgin Birth; and He lived an absolutely sinless life here on earth (22).

3. Christ is called the Second Adam. In purity and holiness, connected with God and beloved by God. He began where the first Adam began. Willingly He passed over the ground where Adam fell, and redeemed Adam's failure (650).

4. In taking upon himself man's nature in its fallen condition, Christ did not in the least participate in its sin. He was subject to the infirmities and weaknesses by which man is encompassed. . . . He was touched with the feeling of our infirmities, and was in all points tempted like as we are. And yet He "knew no sin." He was the Lamb "without blemish and without spot." . . . We should

---

[27]Anthony Hoekema, *The Four Major Cults* (Grand Rapids, Mich.: William B. Eerdmans Publishing Company, 1963), 389, 403.

have no misgivings in regard to the perfect sinlessness of the human nature of Christ (651).

5. In His human nature He maintained the purity of His divine character. . . . He was unsullied by corruption, a stranger to sin. . . . He was a mighty petitioner, not possessing the passions of our human, fallen natures, but compassed with like infirmities, tempted in all points like as we are (658–659).

6. He was perfect, and undefiled by sin. He was without spot or blemish. . . . Jesus, coming to dwell in humanity, received no pollution (660).

III. *The Atonement*

1. Those who teach that a completed atonement was made on the cross view the term in its popular theological sense, but really what is meant by them is that on Calvary the all-sufficient atoning sacrifice of Christ was offered for our salvation. With this concept all true Christians readily and heartily agree. "We are sanctified through the offering of the body of Jesus Christ, once for all" (Hebrews 10:10). Those who view this aspect of the work of Christ as a completed atonement, apply this term only to what Christ accomplished on the cross. They do not include in their definition the application of the benefits of the atonement made on the cross to the individual sinner (342).

2. Seventh-day Adventists do not believe that Christ made but partial or incomplete sacrificial atonement on the cross (349).

3. Most decidedly the all-sufficient atoning sacrifice of Jesus our Lord was offered and completed on the cross of Calvary. This was done for all mankind, for "he is the propitiation . . . for the sins of the whole world" (1 John 2:2). This sacrificial work will actually benefit human hearts only as we surrender our lives to God and experience the miracle of the new birth. In this experience, Jesus our high priest applies to us the benefits of His atoning sacrifice. Our sins are forgiven, we become the children of God by faith in Christ Jesus, and the peace of God dwells in our hearts (350).

4. When, therefore, one hears an Adventist say, or reads in Adventist literature—even in the writings of Ellen G. White—that Christ is making atonement now, it should be understood that we mean simply that Christ is now making application of the benefits of the sacrificial atonement He made on the cross; that He is making it efficacious for us individually, according to our needs and requests. Mrs. White herself, as far back as 1857, clearly explained what she meant when she wrote of Christ's making atonement for us in His ministry:

> The great Sacrifice had been offered and had been accepted, and the Holy Spirit which descended on the day of Pentecost carried the minds of the disciples from the earthly sanctuary to the heavenly, where Jesus had entered by His own blood to shed upon His disciples the benefits of His atonement (354–355).

5. When the Father beheld the sacrifice of His Son, He bowed before it in recognition of its perfection. "It is enough," He said, "the Atonement is complete" (663).

IV. *The Resurrection*

1. Jesus Christ arose literally and bodily from the grave. He ascended literally and bodily into heaven. He now serves as our advocate in priestly ministry and mediation before the Father (22).

2. There shall be a resurrection both of the just and the unjust. The resurrection of the just will take place at the second coming of Christ; the resurrection of the unjust will take place a thousand years later, at the close of the millennium (John 5:28–29; 1 Thessalonians 4:13–18; Revelation 20:5–10) (14).

V. *The Second Coming*

1. [Jesus Christ] will return in a premillennial, personal, imminent second advent (22).

2. As our denominational name indicates, the second coming of Christ is one of the cardinal doctrines of the Adventist faith. We give it such prominence in our beliefs because it occupies a pivotal place in Holy Scripture, not only in the New Testament, but also in the Old (449).

3. Jesus will assuredly come the second time.... [His] second advent will be visible, audible, and personal.... Seventh-day Adventists believe on the evidence of Scripture that there will be one visible, personal, glorious second coming of Christ (451–452, 459).

VI. *The Plan of Salvation*

1. The vicarious, atoning death of Jesus Christ, once for all, is all-sufficient for the redemption of a lost race.... Man was created sinless, but by his subsequent fall entered a state of alienation and depravity.... Salvation through Christ is by grace alone, and through faith in His blood.... Entrance upon the new life in Christ is by regeneration, or the new birth.... Man is justified by faith ... sanctified by the indwelling Christ through the Holy Spirit (22–23).

2. Every person in order to obtain salvation must experience the new birth. This comprises an entire transformation of life and character by the recreative power of God through faith in the Lord Jesus Christ (John 3:16; Matthew 18:3; Acts 2:37–39) (12).

3. The law of the Ten Commandments points out sin, the penalty of which is death. The law cannot save the transgressor from his sin, nor impart power to keep him from sinning. In infinite love and mercy, God provides a way whereby this may be done. He furnishes a substitute, even Christ the Righteous One, to die in man's stead, making "him to be sin for us, who knew no sin; that we might be made the righteousness of God in him" (2 Corinthians 5:21). That one is justified, not by obedience to the law, but by the grace that is in Christ Jesus. By accepting Christ, man is reconciled to God, justified by His blood for the sins of the past, and saved from the power of sin by His indwelling life (13).

4. One who truly understands and accepts the teachings of the Seventh-day Adventist Church can assuredly know that he is born again, and that he is fully accepted by the Lord. He has in his soul the assurance of present salvation, and need be in no uncertainty whatsoever. In fact, he may know this so fully that he can truly "rejoice in the Lord" (Philippians 4:4), and in "the God of his salvation" (Psalm 24:5) (105).

5. Nothing we can ever do will merit the favor of God. Salvation is of grace. It is grace that "bringeth salvation" (Titus 2:11). It is "through the grace of the Lord Jesus Christ we shall be saved" (Acts 15:11). We are not saved by "works" (Romans 4:6; Ephesians 2:8–9; 2 Timothy 1:9), even though they be good works.... Neither can we be saved by "law" (Romans 8:3), nor by the "deeds" or the "works" of the law (Romans 3:20; Galatians 3:2, 5, 10).... The law of God was never designed to save men. It is a looking glass, in which, when we gaze, we see our sinfulness. That is as far as the law of God can go with a sinful man. It can reveal his sin, but is powerless to remove it or to save him from its guilt and penalty and power (108–109).

VII. *The Spiritual Nature of Man*

1. Some have maintained that man was created mortal, so far as his body was concerned, and that he possessed an immortal entity called either a "soul" or a "spirit." Others have felt equally certain that man was not in any sense created immortal. They have been convinced that man was not in possession of an ethereal soul, or spirit, which survived death as a conscious entity, apart from

the body. . . . We as Adventists believe that, in general, the Scriptures teach that the soul of man represents the whole man, and not a particular part independent of the other component parts of man's nature; and further, that the soul cannot exist apart from the body, for a man is a unit (511, 515).

2. We as Adventists have reached the definite conclusion that man rests in the tomb until the resurrection morning. Then, at the first resurrection (Revelation 20:4–5), the resurrection of the just (Acts 24:15), the righteous come forth immortalized, at the call of Christ the Life-giver. And they then enter into life everlasting, in their eternal home in the kingdom of glory. Such is our understanding (520).

VIII. *Punishment of the Wicked*

1. In the expression "eternal punishment," just as in "eternal redemption" and "eternal judgment," the Bible is referring to all eternity—not as of process, but as of result. It is not an endless process of punishment, "but an effectual punishment, which will be final and forever" (540).

2. We reject the doctrine of eternal torment for the following major reasons: (1) Because everlasting life is a gift of God (Romans 6:23). The wicked do not possess this—they "shall not see life" (John 3:36); "no murderer hath eternal life abiding in him" (1 John 3:15). (2) Because eternal torment would perpetuate and immortalize sin, suffering, and woe, and contradict, we believe, divine revelation, which envisions the time when these things shall be no more (Revelation 21:4). (3) Because it seems to us to provide a plague spot in the universe of God throughout eternity, and would seem to indicate that it is impossible for God himself ever to abolish it. (4) Because in our thinking, it would detract from the attribute of love as seen in the character of God, and postulates the concept of a wrath which is never appeased. (5) Because the Scriptures teach that the atoning work of Christ is to "put away sin" (Hebrews 9:26)—first from the individual, and ultimately from the universe. The full fruition of Christ's sacrificial, atoning work will be seen not only in a redeemed people but in a restored heaven and earth (Ephesians 1.13–14) (543).

IX. *The Sanctuary and the Investigative Judgment*

1. *Does your teaching of the sanctuary service mean that the work of Christ on Calvary was not an all-sufficient, complete, once-for-all sacrifice—a sacrifice that obtains for us eternal redemption? Or was something subsequently necessary to make the sacrificial work of Christ effective for the salvation of man?*

To the first part of the question our answer is an unequivocal *No.* The death of Christ on Calvary's cross provides the only sacrifice by which man can be saved. . . . This "one sacrifice" (Hebrews 10:12) or "one offering" of Christ was "forever" (verse 14), and wrought "eternal redemption" (Hebrews 9:12) for man. The sacrifice was completely efficacious. It provided complete atonement for all mankind, and will never be repeated, for it was all-sufficient and covered the needs of every soul (356–357).

2. The expression "once" or "once for all," in connection with the sacrifice of Christ, is deeply significant. . . . "He died to sin once for all" (Romans 6:10); "offering of the body of Jesus Christ once for all" (Hebrews 10:10). He did this not by "the blood of goats and calves" but by "his own blood." He entered once for all into the holy place (or "holiest"), "thus securing an eternal redemption" for us (Hebrews 9:12, RSV).

The Greek word here translated "holy place" is *hagia,* and is in the plural form. A correct translation would be "the holies," or "holy places," as in Hebrews 9:24. This entrance, Scripture teaches, occurred at His ascension to glory (Acts 1), having already finished His sacrificial work on the cross. The word translated "obtained," in the Greek is from *heurisko,* and is rendered "found,"

"procured," "gained," or in the RSV, "secured" (380–381).

3. Jesus our surety entered the "holy places," and appeared in the presence of God for us. But it was not with the hope of obtaining something for us at that time, or at some future time. No! *He had already obtained it for us on the cross.* And now as our high priest He ministers the virtue of His atoning sacrifice to us (381).

4. The time of the cleansing of the sanctuary, synchronizing with the period of the proclamation of the message of Revelation 14, is a time of investigative judgment; first, with reference to the dead, and second, with reference to the living. This investigative judgment determines who of the myriad sleeping in the dust of the earth are worthy of a part in the first resurrection, and who of its living multitudes are worthy of translation (1 Peter 4:17–18; Daniel 7:9–10; Revelation 14:6–7; Luke 20:35) (15).

5. The great judgment scene of heaven will clearly reveal those who have been growing in grace and developing Christ-like characters. Some who have professed to be God's people, but who have disregarded His counsel, will in amazement say to the Lord, "Have we not prophesied in thy name? and in thy name have cast out devils? and in thy name done many wonderful works?" His reply to such will be brief but emphatic: "I never knew you. Depart from me, ye that work iniquity" (Matthew 7:22–23) (417).

6. In view of the principles here set forth, it seems to us abundantly clear that the acceptance of Christ at conversion does not seal a person's destiny. His life record after conversion is also important. A man may go back on his repentance, or by careless inattention let slip the very life he has espoused. Nor can it be said that a man's record is closed when he comes to the end of his days. He is responsible for his influence during life, and is just as surely responsible for his evil influence after he is dead (420).

7. It is our understanding that Christ as high priest concludes His intercessory ministry in heaven in a work of judgment. He begins His great work of judgment in the investigative phase. At the conclusion of the investigation the sentence of judgment is pronounced. Then as judge, Christ descends to execute or carry into effect that sentence. . . . When God's final sentence of judgment is consummated, the redeemed will be singing the song of Moses and the Lamb (422).

8. The blotting of names out of the book of life is, we believe, a work of the investigative judgment. A complete and thorough check of all the candidates for eternal life will need to be completed before Christ comes in the clouds of heaven, for when He appears, the decisions for life and death are already made. The dead in Christ are called to life, and the living followers of Christ are translated (1 Thessalonians 4:15–17)—the entire citizenry of the everlasting kingdom. There's no time subsequent to the second advent for such decisions (438–439).

X. *The Scapegoat Teaching*

1. Two goats were obviously required, and used, on the Day of Atonement, because there is a twofold responsibility for sin—first, my responsibility as the perpetrator, agent, or medium; and second, Satan's responsibility as the instigator, or tempter, in whose heart sin was first conceived.

Now, concerning my sin, Christ died for my sins (Romans 5:8). . . . He assumed my responsibilities, and His blood alone cleanses me from all sin. . . . The atonement for my sin is made solely by the shed blood of Christ.

And concerning Satan's sin and his responsibility as instigator and tempter, no salvation is provided for him. He must be punished for his responsibility. There is no savior, or substitute, to bear his punishment. He must himself "atone" for his sin in causing men to transgress, in the same way that a master

criminal suffers on the gallows or in the electric chair for his responsibility in the crimes that he has caused others to commit. It is in this sense only that we can understand the words of Leviticus 16:10 concerning the scapegoat, "To make an atonement with him."

Under criminal law, the instigator, or mastermind, may be punished more severely than his agents. . . . Satan is the responsible mastermind in the great crime of sin, and his responsibility will return upon his head. The crushing weight of his responsibility in the sins of the whole world—of the wicked as well as the righteous—must be rolled back upon him. Simple justice demands that while Christ suffers for my guilt, Satan must also be punished as the instigator of sin (397, 399).

2. Satan makes no atonement for our sins. But Satan will ultimately have to bear the retributive punishment for his responsibility in the sins of all men, both righteous and wicked. Seventh-day Adventists, therefore, repudiate *en toto* any idea, suggestions, or implication that Satan is in any sense or degree our sin bearer. The thought is abhorrent to us, and appallingly sacrilegious. Such a concept is a dreadful disparagement of the efficacy of Christ and His salvation, and vitiates the whole glorious provision of salvation solely through our Savior.

Satan's death a thousand times over could never make him a savior in any sense whatsoever. He is the archsinner of the universe, the author and instigator of sin. . . . Only Christ, the Creator, the one and only God-man, could make a substitutionary atonement for men's transgressions. And this Christ did completely, perfectly, and once for all, on Golgotha (399–400).

XI. *The Sabbath and the Mark of the Beast*

1. We believe that the Sabbath was instituted in Eden before sin entered, that it was honored of God, set apart by divine appointment, and given to mankind as a perpetual memorial of a finished creation. It was based upon the fact that God himself had rested from His work of creation, had blessed His Sabbath, or rest day, and had sanctified it, or set it apart for man (Genesis 2:1–3; Mark 2.27) (149).

2. We believe that the restoration of the Sabbath is indicated in the Bible prophecy of Revelation 14:9–12. Sincerely believing this, we regard the observance of the Sabbath as a test of our loyalty to Christ as Creator and Redeemer.

Seventh-day Adventists do not rely upon their Sabbath-keeping as a means of salvation or of winning merit before God. We are saved by grace alone. Hence our Sabbath observance, as also our loyalty to every other command of God, is an expression of our love for our Creator and Redeemer.

We are saved through the righteousness of Jesus Christ received as a gift of grace, and grace alone. Our Lord's sacrifice on Calvary is mankind's only hope. But having been saved, we rejoice that the righteous requirements of the law are fulfilled in the experience of the Christian "who walks not after the flesh but after the spirit," and who by the grace of God lives in harmony with the revealed will of God (153, 190).

3. *Do Seventh-day Adventists teach in their authorized literature that those who worship on Sunday and who repudiate in its entirety the Seventh-day Adventist teaching as a consequence have the mark of apostasy, or "the mark of the beast"? Does not Mrs. White teach that those who now keep Sunday already have the mark of the beast?*

Our doctrinal positions are based upon the Bible and not upon Mrs. White's writings. But since her name has been introduced into the question, an explicit statement from her pen should set the record straight. The following was penned by her in 1899: "No one has yet received the mark of the beast. Testing time has not yet come. There are true Christians in every church, not excepting the Roman Catholic communion. None are condemned until they have had the light and seen the obligation of the fourth commandment. But

when the decree shall go forth enforcing the counterfeit Sabbath, and the loud cry of the third angel shall warn men against the worship of the beast and his image, the line will be clearly drawn between the false and the true. Then those who still continue in transgression will receive the mark of the beast" (183).

4. To your inquiry, then, as to whether Mrs. White maintained that all those who do not see and observe the seventh day as the Sabbath now have the "mark of apostasy," the answer is definitely no (184).

5. We hold the firm conviction that millions of devout Christians of all faiths throughout all past centuries, as well as those today who are sincerely trusting in Christ their Savior for salvation and are following Him according to their best light, are unquestionably saved (184).

XII. *The Question of Unclean Foods*

1. It is true we refrain from eating certain articles . . . but not because the law of Moses had any binding claims upon us. Far from it, we stand fast in the liberty with which God has set us free (623).

2. Our health teaching is not a matter of religious taboo; in fact it is much more than careful selection in diet. It is, to us, the following of a well-balanced health program. We feel it to be our Christian duty to preserve our bodies in the best of health for the service and glory of God. We believe that our bodies are the temples of the Holy Spirit (1 Corinthians 3:16; 2 Corinthians 6:16), and that whether therefore we eat, or drink, or whatsoever we do we should "do all to the glory of God" (1 Corinthians 10:31) (634).

XIII. *The "Remnant Church"*

1. *It is alleged that Seventh-day Adventists teach that they alone constitute the finally completed "remnant church" mentioned in the book of Revelation. . . . Do Adventists maintain that they alone are the only true witnesses of the living God in our age?*
The answer to this threefold question will depend quite largely on the definition given to the word "remnant." If, as is implied in the second part, "remnant" is taken to mean the church invisible, our answer to the first part is an unqualified no. Seventh-day Adventists have never sought to equate their church with the church invisible—"Those in every denomination who remain faithful to the Scriptures" (186).

2. It is in a spirit of deep humility that we apply this Scripture to the Advent Movement and its work, for we recognize the tremendous implications of such an interpretation. While we believe that Revelation 12:17 points to us as a people of prophecy, it is in no spirit of pride that we thus apply the Scripture. To us it is the logical conclusion of our system of prophetic interpretation (191).

3. But the fact that we thus apply this Scripture does not imply in any way that we believe we are the only true Christians in the world, or that we are the only ones who will be saved (191–192).

4. Seventh-day Adventists firmly believe that God has a precious remnant, a multitude of earnest, sincere believers, in every church (192).

5. We believe the majority of God's children are still scattered in this way throughout the world. And of course, the majority of these in Christian churches still conscientiously observe Sunday. We ourselves cannot do so, for we believe that God is calling for a reformation in this matter. But we respect and love those of our fellow Christians who do not interpret God's Word just as we do (192–193).

6. We fully recognize the heartening fact that the host of the true followers of Christ are scattered all through the various churches of Christendom, including the Roman Catholic Church. These God clearly recognizes as His own. Such do not form a part of the "Babylon" portrayed in the Apocalypse (197).

Author's Notes

1. *The Concept of Christ's Sinful Human Nature*
  Since almost all critics of Seventh-day Adventism contend that Seventh-day Adventists believe Christ possessed a sinful human nature during the Incarnation, a word should be said to clarify this point. These charges are often based on an article in *Signs of the Times*, March 1927, and a statement in *Bible Readings for the Home Circle*, edition of 1944. Regarding the first reference, a critical article states:

> My . . . quotation is from L. A. Wilcox, for many years an editor of *The Signs of the Times*, which according to the latest figures given by the Adventists has been published by them for eighty-two years. Certainly a statement by an editor of that publication may be considered official. I'm sure that anything that Mr. Wilcox wrote did not just happen to get in. In March 1927 he wrote, "In His [Christ's] veins was the incubus of a tainted heredity like a caged lion ever seeking to break forth and destroy. Temptation attacked Him where by heredity He was weakest, attacked Him in unexpected times and ways. In spite of bad blood and an inherited meanness, He 'conquered.' "
>
> And again, in the December 1928 issue of *Signs of the Times*, this editor Mr. Wilcox stated: "Jesus took humanity with all its liabilities, with all its dreadful risks of yielding to temptation."[28]

First, L. A. Wilcox was never on the editorial staff of *Signs of the Times*. Moreover, Mr. L. A. Wilcox, who wrote the article, in a letter dated April 26, 1957, stated:

> The writer of the *Signs* article was a very young man in 1927, and not by any means always felicitous in his phraseology. I know, for I was the writer. The first sentence quoted is crude and shocking and theologically inaccurate, and I was properly spanked for it by Adventist officials, which proves that this article cannot be truly represented as "official" or "authoritative."
>
> It is no more than fair to point out that no man has taught more earnestly or fervently than I, as an Adventist minister, the deity of the Lord Jesus Christ, the sinlessness of Christ, salvation by grace, righteousness by faith, the finished work of Calvary, a Christ-centered religion, than I—with the "Amen" of Seventh-day Adventist leadership.

Virtually every critic of Seventh-day Adventism, including the author quoted above, also uses a statement quoted from *Bible Readings for the Home Circle* (1944 edition, 174)—even though in 1945 the statement was expunged by Adventists because it was not in line with official Adventist theology.
  A further quotation often seized upon is taken from the book *Desire of the Ages* by Ellen G. White. On page 117, she says, "Our Savior took humanity, with all its liabilities. He took the nature of man, with the possibility of yielding to temptation." White also speaks of "fallen nature." Understandably, not having read all she has written on the subject, these critics conclude that she means that Christ possessed a sinful, carnal, or degenerate human nature. However, White's writings clearly indicate that when she speaks of the fallen nature of Christ, she means the physical properties of the race, which degenerated since

---

[28] *The King's Business*, April 1957.

the time of Adam, who was created perfect without the ravages of sin upon either his physical or spiritual being. Adam did not age before the Fall, but Christ was born into the world a true man and with the curse of sin operative upon the physical properties of the human race. For over thirty years He endured the aging process. He could not have reached this point in life without organic changes taking place in His body, and were He not subject to the physical decline of the race, he would not have been a true man, "made under the law" (Galatians 4:4). White's position has been held by many eminent scholars who have never been accused of being either heretics or non-Christians. Why, then, should she and the Adventists be condemned for holding this view? For centuries Christians have argued about the human nature of Christ. Some have believed that He could have sinned, but did not. Others, including this writer, that He could not have sinned. However, it is a theological issue not likely to be resolved by trite phrases and dogmatic pronouncements.

It is true that various Adventist publications, in the past and present, sometimes have contradicted one another. However, at its release and up through this year (see, for example, the quote presented earlier from the April 29, 1983, Adventist letter to me), *Questions on Doctrine* presents the official position of the Adventist denomination regarding Christ's sinless nature. It is to that position that I can say "Amen."

Dr. Anthony Hoekema, in his volume *The Four Major Cults*, falls into the same error as E. B. Jones, Louis Talbot, and other critics of Seventh-day Adventism and ignores totally the fact that Wilcox publicly and in print (1957) repudiated his position. This fact they all know but seem determined to ignore since Wilcox's statement suits so well their assumption that despite official Adventist statements on doctrine, they, the critics, know more than the Adventists do about their own faith!

2. *The Concept of Incomplete Atonement*

It is also often charged that inherent in Adventist theology is the unbiblical teaching that "the atonement was not finished on the cross of Calvary." Certain Seventh-day Adventist sources are cited to bolster these charges. For instance, Uriah Smith, a prominent Adventist of the past, stated in his book *Looking Unto Jesus*, "Christ did not make the atonement when He shed His blood upon the cross." Other earlier writers such as J. H. Waggoner have expressed the same thought. He said, "There is a clear distinction between the death of Christ and the atonement."[29] Even some later writers like C. H. Watson have been influenced by these early exponents of Adventism.

However, a little investigation of these writings would show that Smith and Waggoner wrote eighty years ago. As demonstrated elsewhere in this book, this concept has been repudiated by the Seventh-day Adventist denomination. The current position of the Seventh-day Adventist denomination—not the opinions of a few scattered writers over a hundred-year period—should be considered in judging this charge of an "incomplete atonement."

Current Adventist writings teach that the atonement was completed on the cross, and no less an Adventist than Ellen G. White, writing in the *Review and*

---

[29] *The Atonement in the Light of Nature and Revelation*, n.p., n.d., 181.

Herald, September 21, 1901, stated: "Christ planted the cross between heaven and earth and when the Father beheld the sacrifice of His Son, He bowed before it in recognition of His perfection. 'It is enough,' He said. 'The atonement is completed.' " In the same periodical, under the date of August 16, 1899, White stated, "No language could convey the rejoicing of heaven or God's expression of satisfaction and delight in His only begotten Son when He saw the completion of the atonement."

Many more quotations could be cited, but critics usually overlook the greater number of statements relative to the completeness of the atonement that are readily available in past and present Seventh-day Adventist literature.

Nothing could be clearer than the Adventist declaration that:

> When . . . one hears an Adventist say or reads in Adventist literature—even in the writings of Ellen G. White—that Christ is making atonement now, it should be understood that we mean simply that Christ is now making application of the benefits of the sacrificial atonement He made on the cross; that He is making it efficacious for us individually, according to our needs and requests. Mrs. White herself, as far back as 1857, clearly explained what she means when she writes of Christ's making atonement for us in His ministry:

> > The great Sacrifice had been offered and had been accepted, and the Holy Spirit which descended on the day of Pentecost carried the minds of the disciples from the earthly sanctuary to the Heavenly, where Jesus entered by His own blood to shed upon His disciples the benefits of His atonement (*Questions on Doctrine*, 354–355).

Is Seventh-day Adventism a Non-Christian Cult?

We earlier mentioned Dr. Anthony Hoekema's book *The Four Major Cults*, in which he classifies Seventh-day Adventism as a non-Christian cult system. It is necessary for me to take exception with Dr. Hoekema in this area because, in my opinion, the reasons which Dr. Hoekema gives cannot be justified by the Word of God, historical theology, or present-day practices in denominational Christianity as a whole. To illustrate this point, Dr. Hoekema stated, "I am of the conviction that Seventh-day Adventism is a cult and not an evangelical denomination. In support of this evaluation I propose to show that the traits that we have found to be distinctive of the cults do apply to this movement" (389).

Dr. Hoekema then proceeds to list his reasons:

1. An extra-scriptural source of authority (Ellen G. White).
2. The denial of justification by grace alone.
   a. The investigative judgment.
   b. The keeping of the Sabbath.
3. The devaluation of Christ.
4. The group as the exclusive community of the saved.

It is Dr. Hoekema's contention that Ellen White is an extrabiblical authority in that her counsels are taken to be manifestations of the gift of prophecy (1 Corinthians 12). But granting that the Adventists are entitled to believe that this gift was manifested in White as evidence of the *charismata* (a fact Dr. Hoekema could hardly honestly challenge since the gifts of the Spirit have been and are still manifested in the Christian church), why does he not take into consid-

eration the repeated emphasis of Adventist writers concerning their official pronouncement, *Questions on Doctrine*, to the effect that they do not consider White to be an extra-biblical authority, but that her writings are only authoritative in those areas where they are in agreement with the Word of God, which is the final standard for judging all the gifts of the Spirit?

If the Adventists put White's writings on a par with Holy Scripture; if they interpreted the Bible in the light of her writings, and not the reverse; if they willingly admitted this and owned it as their position, his criticism would be justified, but they do not do so. Dr. Hoekema has apparently ignored what the Adventists say they believe concerning White in favor of what he thinks they mean as a result of his deduction from certain of their publications. It is far safer to accept at face value the published statements of a denomination representing its theology, particularly if, as in the case of *Questions on Doctrine*, they are answering direct questions bearing on the subject, than it is to rely upon one's own preconceived interpretations, as Dr. Hoekema has apparently done in this instance.

It is a serious charge to maintain that any professing Christian group denies justification by grace alone as the basis of eternal salvation; and, if the Adventists were guilty of this, surely there would be ground for considering them as a cultic system. However, literally scores of times in their book *Questions on Doctrine*, and in various other publications, the Adventists affirm that salvation comes only by the grace of God through faith in Jesus Christ's sacrifice upon the cross.

Why it is necessary again for Dr. Hoekema to question the sincerity of the Adventists in this area and yet accept at face value their other statements concerning their faith in the Scriptures, the Trinity, the full deity of Jesus Christ, Creation, Providence, Incarnation, the resurrection of Jesus Christ, the absolute necessity for regeneration, sanctification by the Holy Spirit, and Christ's literal return, is a puzzling inconsistency in his presentation. (See *The Four Major Cults*, 403.)

Dr. Hoekema insists that the investigative judgment and the keeping of the seventh-day Sabbath are part of the reasons why he classifies Seventh-day Adventists as cultists, but, in doing this, he makes his Calvinistic interpretation of theology the criterion while ignoring the claims of the Arminian school and of semi-Arminian and semi-Calvinistic theologians, many of whom take strong exception to Dr. Hoekema's pronounced Calvinism. On the basis that Dr. Hoekema would call the Adventists a cult, the same charge could be leveled against all devoted Calvinists who consider the *Institutes of the Christian Religion* and Calvin's *Commentaries* every bit as much illumination and guides in the study of the Scriptures as the Adventists do where White's writings are concerned. In addition to this, the Seventh-day Baptists are Arminian in their theology and keep the seventh-day Sabbath. Are they, too, a non-Christian cult? They certainly meet some of Dr. Hoekema's qualifications.

Underscoring his Calvinistic oppositions, Dr. Hoekema writes:

> Adventists further teach that it is possible for a person through subsequent sinful deeds and attitudes to lose the justification he once received. This teaching implies that one can only be sure of retaining his justification if he continues to do the right kind of deeds and to maintain the right attitudes throughout the rest of his life (390).

This point on the investigative judgment is clear evidence of Arminianism in which Dr. Hoekema finds sufficient ground to justify the cult label being applied to Adventists. But why only to Adventists? Why not to Pentecostals, Methodists, Anglicans, Episcopalians, Lutherans, and others who accept the same Arminian premises, though they have not carried them out to the literalism that the Adventists have in the investigative judgment?

Relative to Sabbatarianism, the fourteenth chapter of Romans justifies the keeping of the seventh-day Sabbath or any other day by any Christian who believes he is keeping it unto the Lord. It can become legalistic as Sunday can become legalistic, but merely because the seventh day is honored instead of the first day is no ground for the description of "cult."

Dr. Hoekema, on page 394 of his volume, affirms that:

> Seventh-day Adventists do not . . . deny the full deity of Jesus Christ or the doctrine of the Trinity. . . . Seventh-day Adventists today affirm Christ's complete equality with the Father, and the preexistence of the Son from eternity. . . . Adventists also accept the doctrine of the Trinity, and that of the personality and full deity of the Holy Spirit.
>
> As far as the work of Christ is concerned, Seventh-day Adventists teach the vicarious, substitutionary atonement of Christ. Yet there remains some ambiguity in their teachings on the question of whether the atonement has been finished on the cross, since Mrs. White says on more than one occasion that Christ is making atonement for us today and frequently refers to a "final atonement" after the one completed on the cross.

Dr. Hoekema follows this up by listing five reasons for his feeling that the Adventists "devalue" Christ. Three of these points involve Arminianism, concerning which Dr. Hoekema has an admitted prejudice; the fourth concerns the Sabbath, which is a matter of Christian liberty, unless one presupposes Calvin's interpretation; and the fifth reiterates the old accusation that the Seventh-day Adventists believe that "the sins of all men will be laid on Satan just before Christ returns, and that only in this way will sin finally be 'eradicated' or 'blotted out' of the universe" (395–396).

Once again, Dr. Hoekema defeats his own case by admitting that the Adventists are soundly orthodox in their Christology, hardly a devaluation of Christ!

The implications and deductions that he draws from their Arminianism cannot be considered as evidence against the Adventists, since not only they but the entire Arminian school of theological interpretation could argue vigorously for the principles that the Adventists lay down.

Finally, the Adventists themselves have repeatedly affirmed that Christ alone vicariously bears the sins of the world and that Satan only bears "his responsibility" for tempting the world to sin.

A careful reading of the book *Questions on Doctrine*, which Dr. Hoekema lists in his bibliography in *The Four Major Cults*, would have answered his question regarding White's usage of the terms "making atonement now" and "final atonement."

The Adventists declare forthrightly that whenever terms of this nature are used, they understand them to refer to the benefits of the atonement of Christ being shed abroad through the ministry of the Holy Spirit, and disown com-

pletely any implication or suggestion that the atonement of Christ was not completed on the cross.

Dr. Hoekema, in company with other critics of Adventism, has not hesitated to draw upon repudiated sources to underscore the claim that the Adventists devalue Christ. On page 114 of *The Four Major Cults*, Dr. Hoekema states,

> One of the best known is the statement by L. A. Wilcox, to the effect that Christ conquered sin "in spite of bad blood and an inherited meanness." Though the discussion of this matter in *Questions on Doctrine* implies that the denomination would now repudiate this statement, nowhere in the book are we definitely told that this has been done.

In my book *The Truth About Seventh-day Adventism*, conclusive proof was introduced of the total repudiation of that statement by Wilcox himself. Dr. Hoekema lists the book in his bibliography, but unfortunately omits reference to Wilcox's repudiation in order to utilize Wilcox's statement. This is not a fair representation of what the Adventist denomination has taught or teaches in this area.

These are a few of the problems that face the interested student of the puzzle of Seventh-day Adventism, and they must be fairly considered before hastily classifying Adventism as a non-Christian cult.

Ellen G. White and the Spirit of Prophecy

In most religious movements, one extraordinary and gifted personality dominates the scene, and so it was with Seventh-day Adventism. This dominant personality was and is today, through her writings, Ellen G. White. She was one of the most fascinating and controversial individuals ever to appear upon the horizon of religious history. Her memory and work have been praised by Adventists and damned by many of their enemies since the early years of the movement. Born Ellen Gould Harmon at Gorham, Maine, in 1827, and reared a devout Methodist in the city of Portland, White was early recognized as an unusual person, for she bore witness to certain "revelations," which she believed she had received from heaven.

When Ellen was thirteen, the Harmon family came under the influence of the Millerite movement. William Miller delivered a series of addresses in the Casco Street Christian Church in Portland in 1841 and 1842. At the age of seventeen, Ellen embraced the Adventist faith of the Millerites.[30] Although deeply stirred by Miller's sincerity and his chronological calculations, the Harmon family remained in fellowship with the Chestnut Street Methodist Church of Portland, which in 1845 disfellowshipped them because they believed in the premillennial second advent of Jesus Christ.

Despite her youth, Ellen Harmon passed through trying times, emotionally, physically and spiritually, between 1837 and 1843. In the words of Dr. Froom, "She rebelled against the dismal prospects resulting from an early accident, and its attendant invalidism.[31] In 1840, at a Methodist camp meeting at Buxton,

---

[30]Ellen G. White, *Life Sketches* (Washington, D.C.: Review and Herald Publishing Association, n.d.), 64–68.

[31]*The Prophetic Faith*, 4:978.

Maine, Ellen Harmon found wonderful deliverance and "her burden rolled from her shoulders," for she experienced great joy in learning that she was truly a child of God, which she publicly confessed afterward by requesting baptism by immersion. Many points still perplexed her, among them the doctrine of the eternal punishment of the wicked, which in subsequent years she surrendered to as well as the concept of conditional immortality and the sleep of the soul while awaiting the resurrection. In December 1844, after "The Great Disappointment," while visiting a friend in Portland, Ellen Harmon experienced what she termed her first vision that portrayed the "vindication" of the Adventist faith. In that vision she claimed to see the Adventists triumphant over their critics—pressing upward to heaven in the face of insuperable obstacles.

For many years controversy has raged about White and her "revelations," and there are conflicting opinions within and without Adventism regarding both the extent and nature of her "revelations" and "inspiration." The position of Ellen White in Adventist teaching, then, is most significant and must be understood if we are to get a proper picture of this people. The writings and counsels of Ellen Harmon (later Ellen G. White by her marriage to James White, a prominent Adventist leader) are termed the "Spirit of prophecy," an expression taken from Revelation 19:10. Adventists believe that in the last days special counsels from God are to be revealed, which neither add to nor contradict Scripture, and that these counsels are primarily for the Seventh-day Adventist denomination. And, while following these counsels, they claim they always test them by the Word of God. Finally, they believe that the visions of Mrs. White and her counsels to their denomination are the "Spirit of prophecy" for their church.

There is a circular reasoning involved in defending White. Adventists say that the writers of the Bible did the same thing in quoting (without credit) pagan sources as did White. If they are permitted to do so, then she should be permitted to do so. That only holds, however, if one assumes that White is to be considered as one of the writers of the Bible. That is giving her a rank official Adventist representatives won't give her!

Through the years, some over-zealous Adventist writers have given the impression that everything White said or wrote, even in private letters, was inspired and infallible. This is decidedly not the official position. The Adventist denomination readily admits that not everything White said or wrote was either inspired or infallible, although some individual Adventists still cling to that idea. Until the Adventists officially repudiate the doctrinal statements of *Questions on Doctrine* and officially espouse the errant doctrinal statements of some Adventists and Adventist factions, we can use *Questions on Doctrine* as representative of the denomination's official views. This we have done below.

I. *Seventh-day Adventist Statements—Life and Ministry of Ellen G. White*[32]

> 1. We do not regard the writings of Ellen G. White as an addition to the sacred canon of Scripture. We do not think of them as of universal application as is the Bible, but particularly for the Seventh-day Adventist Church. We do not regard them in the same sense as the Holy Scriptures, which stand alone and unique as the standard by which all other writings must be judged (89).

---

[32]Page numbers are in *Questions on Doctrine,* unless otherwise indicated.

2. Seventh-day Adventists uniformly believe that the canon of Scripture closed with the Book of Revelation. We hold that all other writings and teachings, from whatever source, are to be judged by and are subject to the Bible, which is the spring and norm of the Christian faith (89–90).

3. I recommend to you, dear reader, the Word of God as the rule of your faith and practice. By that Word we are to be judged (90).

4. The Spirit was not given—nor can it ever be bestowed—to supersede the Bible; for the Scriptures explicitly state that the Word of God is the standard by which all teaching and experience must be tested (90).

5. We have never considered Ellen G. White to be in the same category as the writers of the canon of Scripture (90).

6. It is in . . . the category of messengers [other than the biblical writers] that we consider Ellen G. White to be. Among Seventh-day Adventists, she was recognized as one who possessed the gift of the Spirit of prophecy, though she herself never assumed the title of prophetess (91).

7. Seventh-day Adventists regard her writings as containing inspired counsel concerning personal religion and the conduct of our denominational work. . . . That portion of her writings, however, that might be classified as predictions, actually forms but a small segment. And even ▓▓▓▓▓ deals with what is coming on the earth, her statements are only ▓▓▓▓▓▓▓▓ Bible prophecy (92).

8. In His Word, God has committed to me▓ salvation. The Holy Scriptures are to be accepte▓ revelation of His will. They are the standard of▓ trines, and the test of experience (92–93, quoting▓

9. While Adventists hold the writings of Ellen G. White in ▓▓▓▓▓▓▓▓ these are not the source of our expositions. We base our teachings on the Scripture, the only foundation of all true Christian doctrine. However, it is our belief that the Holy Spirit opened to her mind important events and called her to give certain instructions for these last days. And inasmuch as these instructions, in our understanding, are in harmony with the Word of God, which Word alone is able to make us wise unto salvation, we as a denomination accept them as inspired counsels from the Lord. But we have never equated them with Scripture as some falsely charge. Mrs. White herself stated explicitly the relation of her writings to the Bible: "Little heed is given to the Bible, and the Lord has given a lesser light to lead men and women to the greater light" (*Review and Herald*, January 20, 1903; *Questions on Doctrine*, 93).

10. While Seventh-day Adventists recognize the Scripture canon closed nearly two thousand years ago and that there have been no additions to this compilation of sacred books, yet we believe that the Spirit of God, who inspired the Divine Word known to us as the Bible, has pledged to reveal himself to the church and through the various gifts of the Spirit. . . . It is not our understanding that these gifts of the Spirit take the place of the Word of God, nor does their acceptance make unnecessary the Scripture of truth. On the contrary, the acceptance of God's Word will lead God's people to a recognition and a manifestation of the Spirit. Such manifestations will, of course, be in harmony with the Word of God. We know that some earnest Christians have the impression that these gifts ceased with the apostolic church. But Adventists believe that the closing of the Scripture canon did not terminate heaven's communication with men through the gifts of the Spirit, but rather that Christ by the ministry of His Spirit guides His people, edifying and strengthening them, and especially so in these last challenging days of human history (93–95).

11. The Spirit of prophecy is intimately related to the gift of prophecy, the one being the Spirit that indicted the prophecy, the other the evidence of the gift bestowed. They go together, each inseparably connected with the other. The

gift is the manifestation of that which the Spirit of God bestows upon him whom, according to His own good purpose and plan, He selects as the one through whom such spiritual guidance is to come. Briefly then, this is the Adventist understanding of Ellen G. White's writings. They have been for a hundred years, to use her own expression, "a lesser light" leading sincere men and women to "the greater light" (96).

12. Concerning the matter of church fellowship, we would say that while we revere the writings of Ellen G. White . . . we do not make acceptance of her writings as a matter for church discipline. She herself was explicit on this point. Speaking of those who did not fully understand the gift, she said: "Such should not be deprived of the benefits and privileges of the church, if their Christian course is otherwise correct and they have formed a good Christian character" (*Testimonies*, vol. 1, 328; *Questions on Doctrine*, 96–97).

13. We therefore do not test the world in any manner by these gifts. Nor do we in our intercourse with other religious bodies who are striving to walk in the fear of God, in any way make these a test of Christian character (J. N. Andrews in *Review and Herald*, February 15, 1870; *Questions on Doctrine*, 97).

14. [illegible] thrice General Conference president, speaking of the [illegible] pressly declares that Adventists believe that God called [illegible] this time, among this people. They do not, however, [illegible] of Christian fellowship" (*Review and Herald*, June [illegible] 97).

[illegible] church it has not been customary to disfellowship [illegible] ze the doctrine of spiritual gifts. . . . A member [illegible] excluded from membership because of his inability [illegible] doctrine of spiritual gifts and its application to the second advent movement" (98).

It may be seen from these quotations that Seventh-day Adventists hold to the restoration of the "gift of prophecy" in the last days of the Christian church, and that they believe this restoration occurred in the life and ministry of Ellen G. White. The Adventists differ from other churches in that while they hold the Bible to be the unique, complete, infallible, and inerrant Word of God, they maintain that in specific contexts Ellen White's writings are to be accepted by Adventists as "testimonies" from the Spirit of God to guide their denominational activities.

Dr. Wilbur M. Smith has summed up the objections of most evangelicals where Seventh-day Adventism's emphasis upon White and the Spirit of prophecy is involved when he recently observed White's place in the new Seventh-day Adventist Bible Commentary.

> I do not know any other denomination in all of Christendom today that has given such recognition, so slavishly and exclusively, to its founder or principal theologian as has this commentary to the writings of Ellen White. At the conclusion of every chapter in this work is a section headed, "Ellen G. White Comments." For example, on Genesis 28, the blessing conferred upon Jacob, there are less than three pages of comment, but at the end, forty references to the various works of Ellen White. In addition, at the end of the first volume of this commentary is a section again headed, "Ellen G. White Comments," containing eighty columns of material quoted from her writings. There is no section devoted to anyone else—Calvin, Luther, Wesley, or anyone else.
>
> The Preface to this commentary contains the statement: "At the close of each chapter is a cross reference or index to those passages in Ellen G. White's writings that comment on the various texts in that chapter." And the second

sentence following reads: "The Advent movement has grown strong through the study of the Bible; and it can be said with equal truth that the movement has been safely guided in that study by the light shining from the Spirit of prophecy." I would say that the writers of this commentary believe that "the Spirit of prophecy" has rested conclusively upon Ellen G. White, for no one else is so classified in this work.[33]

Dr. Smith is correct in his evaluation of the place of Ellen G. White's writings in the denomination. Seventh-day Adventists are of necessity committed to her visions and counsel because they believe that the Spirit of prophecy rested upon her and upon no other person of their group.

This writer rejects this concept of inspiration but one should carefully note that, for Adventists, "inspiration" in connection with White's writings has a rather different meaning from the inspiration of the Bible. Adventists freely admit that the Bible is objectively the Word of God, the final authority in all matters of faith and morals. But the writings of White cannot be so regarded, and they are the first to say so. Apparently, they have adopted a qualified view of inspiration as related to her writings—"a lesser light to lead men and women to the greater light"—which emphasizes subjective interpretation as the criterion for determining specifically where in White's writings the "Spirit of prophecy" has decisively spoken. There is no doubt in my mind that the Adventists are defending a situation which is at best precarious and at times contradictory. But this position, as a matter of religious liberty, they are entitled to hold so long as they do not make faith in White's writings a test of fellowship between themselves and other denominations, and do not attempt to compel other Christians to accept the "testimonies" of White as indispensable to a deeper, richer experience of Christian consecration and life.

If Seventh-day Adventists did indeed claim for White inspiration in every area of her writings, then we might well be cautious about having fellowship with them. However, this they do not do, as I have amply demonstrated from official denominational sources. Since they do not consider White's teachings the source of their expositions of faith, the claim that one has only to refute Ellen G. White and her writings in order to refute Seventh-day Adventism falls by its own weight.

II. *Mrs. White and Her Critics*

Through the years a great deal of literature has appeared, criticizing the life and works of Ellen G. White. These criticisms have ranged from the mild judgment that White was a sincere but emotionally disturbed mystic to the charge that she was a "false prophetess" who sought material gain and deliberately plagiarized much of her writing. In the interest of honest investigation and truth, and since it is impossible in a book of this size to analyze all the conflicting data, we shall present some highlights of the controversy and let the reader determine the validity of these charges.

The inspiration for 90 percent of the destructive personal criticisms leveled against White is found in the writings of Dudley M. Canright, an ex-Adventist leader of great ability, and a one-time personal friend of Ellen G. White and her

---

[33]In a letter to the author.

husband, James, as well as a great number of prominent Adventist leaders. Canright, one of the most able of the Seventh-day Adventist writers and debaters of his day, left the movement because he lost faith in the inspiration of White and in many doctrines then held by the Adventist Church. While it is true that Canright thrice ceased to preach, his credentials as a minister were never revoked. He finally resigned from the Seventh-day Adventist ministry in 1887 to become a Baptist minister. By Canright's own admission, his personality conflicts with Ellen G. White and her advisers were largely responsible for his turning away from the active ministry at the times mentioned. He, however, apparently maintained close personal relations with James White, Mrs. White's husband, and other prominent Seventh-day Adventist leaders, as is evident from the correspondence quoted below. Canright rebelled violently against Arianism (the denial of the deity of Christ) and extreme legalism, which existed among some of the early Seventh-day Adventists; and his convictions led him later to write two volumes (*Seventh-day Adventism Renounced*, and *Life of Mrs. E. G. White*), which systematically and scathingly denounced Seventh-day Adventism theologically and impugned the personal motives and integrity of White.

In these two volumes, D. M. Canright laid the foundation for all future destructive criticism of Seventh-day Adventism, and careful research has confirmed the impression that nearly all subsequent similar publications are little more than repetitions of the destructive areas of Canright's writing, buttressed by standard theological arguments. This is especially true of the writings of a former Seventh-day Adventist missionary printer, E. B. Jones, editor of a small news sheet, *Guardians of the Faith*, who has issued a number of vitriolic pamphlets against Seventh-day Adventism, all of which are drawn almost exclusively from Canright and other critics, and are for the most part outdated and in some cases both scholastically and ethically unreliable. It can be seen, therefore, that what D. M. Canright has written about Ellen G. White is of prime importance as firsthand evidence, and no Seventh-day Adventist apologist, regardless of the scope of his knowledge of Adventism or the breadth of his scholastic learning, can gainsay all that Canright has written.

In the March 22, 1887 issue of the *Review and Herald*, his former brethren wrote of Elder Canright:

> We have felt exceedingly sad to part in our religious connection with one whom we have long esteemed as a dear brother. . . . In leaving us he has taken a much more manly and commendable course than most of those who have withdrawn from us, coming voluntarily to our leading brethren and frankly stating the condition of mind he was in. He did this before his own church in our presence and so far as we know has taken no unfair underhanded means to injure us in any way. He goes from our midst with no immoral stain upon his character. He chooses associations more pleasant to himself. This is every man's personal privilege if he chooses to take it.

Writing to Canright on May 22, 1881, from Battle Creek, Michigan, James White, Ellen's husband, stated, "It is time there was a change in the offices of the General Conference. I trust that if we are true and faithful, the Lord will be pleased that we should constitute two of that Board." In another letter to Canright, dated July 13, 1881, James White said, "Brother Canright, I feel more interest in you than in any other man because I know your worth when the Lord

is with you as a laborer." It is apparent, therefore, that Canright was in good standing with the Adventists, despite his later renunciation of White's testimonies and the "special truths" of the Adventist message.

In 1951 a carefully documented volume of almost 700 pages was issued by the Review and Herald Publishing Association of Washington, D.C. The author was Francis D. Nichol, leading apologist of the Seventh-day Adventist denomination. This volume, entitled *Ellen G. White and Her Critics*, attempts a point-for-point refutation of many of the charges made by D. M. Canright in his *Life of Mrs. E. G. White*. Nichol has dug deep into early Adventist history—even beyond Canright's day. In addition, after reading both Nichol and Canright, I have concluded that there is much to be said on both sides. But Canright, we believe, has the edge because he can say, "I was there" or "White said. . . ," and contradictory contemporary statements are not to be found where many of Canright's charges are concerned.

My own conclusion is that in some areas (particularly theology) Canright's statements are irrefutable, especially with regard to his personal relationships with White and the leading members of the Adventist denomination. It is also significant to note that many charges that are based on personal experiences and have been well documented have never been refuted.

By this I do not mean that all of Canright's writing is to be trusted, for many of his criticisms of White's activities have been neatly undercut by contemporary evidence unearthed by F. D. Nichol and others. Where Nichol is concerned, "methinks he doth protest too much," and he often goes to extremes to defend White. This, in my judgment, has hurt his case and has proved nothing except that he is a devoted disciple of White and therefore strongly biased. Nonetheless, Nichol is the most able Adventist apologist.

III. *The Verdict of the Evidence*

After considering all the evidence obtainable, of which the foregoing is only a part, this writer is convinced that Ellen G. White was a highly impressionable woman, strongly influenced by her associates. That she sincerely believed the Lord spoke to her, none can fairly question, but the evidence set forth in this book gives good reason, we believe, to doubt the inspiration of her counsels, whether Seventh-day Adventists will concede this or not.

My personal evaluation of the visions of Ellen G. White is best summed up in the following statement from a friendly critic. In 1847, at the outset of her work, one of White's cousins stated,

> I cannot endorse Sister Ellen's visions as of Divine inspiration, as you and she think them to be; yet I do not suspect the least shade of dishonesty in either of you in this matter. I may, perhaps, express to you my belief in the latter without harm—it will, doubtless, result either in your good or mine. At the same time I admit the possibility of my being mistaken. I think that what she and you regard as visions from the Lord are only religious reveries in which her imagination runs without control upon themes in which she is most deeply interested. While so absorbed in these reveries she is lost to everything around her. Reveries are of two kinds: sinful and religious. In either case, the sentiments in the main are obtained from previous teaching or study. I do not by any means think that her visions are from the Devil.[34]

_____
[34]Reproduced in Elder James White, *A Word to the Little Flock* (n.p., 1847), 29.

If Seventh-day Adventists are to defend their claim for White's inspiration, they must explain a number of contradictions in her writings. They would do better to admit, we believe, that she was very human, capable of errors in judgment, and subject to lapses of memory.

It is my considered opinion that Ellen G. White had an extremely complex personality, and that she plagiarized materials because she believed the Lord had shown her that what the sources said was the truth. She simply appropriated material and gave it out. Her actions cannot be excused, but they can be understood as the actions of a Christian who made mistakes. She was both mortal and a sinner like anyone else. I think those around her aided and abetted her in her "cover-up." Also, I think the White estate continued the cover-up for many years after her death. No objective person, in possession of all the facts, can doubt this.

The difference between her and, for example, the Jehovah's Witnesses, is not the crime itself. What she did was wrong. The difference is in the nature of the person we are talking about. Was Jehovah's Witness founder Charles Taze Russell a Christian? Did he hold to the foundations of the gospel? Did he promulgate the things of Christianity and stand in their defense? No. Did Ellen White? Yes. Therefore, although she committed the same crime he did, she cannot be judged on the same basis as Charles Russell. She was a Christian who committed a sin. Christians can and do commit sins.

A biblical false prophet was not a believer. A biblical false prophet was a servant of the devil attempting to lead people away from the truth. White, in my opinion, made false statements. She misused what she claimed was the prophetic gift she had. But one cannot say that she was like a biblical false prophet. Of course, technically, all would agree that the person who prophesies in the name of God and turns out to be wrong has prophesied falsely. But White was not as a biblical false prophet because she was a true Christian, even though what she did was sinful.

White was definitely influenced in some of her writings by time and circumstances, and also by the powerful personalities who surrounded her. Some Adventists maintain that this would in no way prevent her conveying messages from the Lord. However, as I see it, anyone who attempts to prove she was divinely inspired or infallible (no informed Adventist holds the latter) must first dispose of the evidence here presented, as well as other evidence that space does not admit to include. F. D. Nichol, in *Ellen G. White and Her Critics*, makes a masterful attempt to answer some of these problems, but not all of them can be answered with a good conscience or an airtight defense of White and her actions. It does not detract from her stature as a sincere Christian or from the quality of her contribution to insist upon an honest and systematic evaluation of her statements by thinking Adventists, or to ascertain to what degree Adventists may rightfully maintain that the Lord "spoke" through White. Non-Adventists, of course, reject the claims made for White and her writings and hope that Adventists will some day amend their questionable view of "Ellen G. White and the Spirit of prophecy."

After reading the publications of the Seventh-day Adventist denomination and almost all the writings of Ellen G. White, including her *Testimonies*, the writer believes White was truly a regenerate Christian woman who loved the Lord Jesus

Christ and dedicated herself unstintingly to the task of bearing witness for Him as she felt led. It should be clearly understood that some tenets of Christian theology, as historically understood, and White's interpretations of them do not agree; indeed, they are at loggerheads. Nevertheless, Ellen G. White was true to the cardinal doctrines of the Christian faith regarding the salvation of the soul and the believer's life in Christ. We must disagree with White's interpretation of the sanctuary, the investigative judgment, and the scapegoat; we challenge her stress upon the Sabbath, health reform, the unconscious state of the dead, and the final destruction of the wicked, etc. But no one can dispute the fact that her writings conform to the basic principles of the historical gospel, for they most certainly do. However, we must not assume as many Adventists do that White's writings are free from theological and exegetical error, for they are not. Although I believe that the influence of White's counsels on the Adventist denomination parallels the influence of J. N. Darby of the Plymouth Brethren and A. B. Simpson of the Christian and Missionary Alliance, the claim that she possessed a "gift of prophecy" akin to that described in 1 Corinthians 14, as believed by the Seventh-day Adventist Church, I cannot accept.

Contemporary Adventists affirm that White was not infallible, did borrow (unfortunately, usually without attribution) from other sources, and taught from within a nineteenth-century theological context. Adventist professor Gary Land notes, "The research of the 1970s established three points: Ellen White borrowed much material from others; she was a part of late-nineteenth-century culture; and she was not inerrant. From the furor of opposition to Ronald Number's study in the mid–1970s, the denomination—though obviously uncomfortable with public discussion of the issue—had by the end of the decade moved toward accepting the general points that the entire body of research had established."[35]

Many critics of Seventh-day Adventism have assumed, mostly from the writings of professional detractors, that White was a fearsome ogre who devoured all who opposed her, and they have never ceased to make the false claim that Seventh-day Adventists believe that White is infallible, despite the often-published authoritative statement to the contrary. Although Seventh-day Adventists do hold White and her writings in great esteem, they maintain that the Bible is their only "rule of faith and practice." Christians of all denominations may heatedly disagree with the Seventh-day Adventist attitude toward White, but all that she wrote on such subjects as salvation or Christian living characterizes her as a Christian in every sense of the term.

Farther on in this discussion, we shall look at White's relations with the Adventist denomination, particularly in the field of theology. Enough has been presented here, however, to show that she was a most interesting personality, far different from the "Sister White" idealized beyond reality in certain Seventh-day Adventist publications.

Dudley M. Canright, the chief critic of Seventh-day Adventism, has, I feel, rendered good service in this respect. He has presented the human side of White from the standpoint of a firsthand friendship that lasted through the for-

---

[35]Gary Land, ed., *Adventism in America* (Grand Rapids, Mich.: William B. Eerdmans Publishing Company, 1986), 223.

mative years of the Seventh-day Adventist denomination. Despite his criticisms of Seventh-day Adventism and of White, Canright himself never ceased to believe that despite what he believed to be her errors in theology and her mistaken concept of visions, she was a regenerate Christian. With his brother, Canright attended the funeral of White in 1915. His brother describes the occasion thus: "We joined the passing throng, and again stood by the bier. My brother rested his hand upon the side of the casket, and with tears rolling down his cheeks, he said brokenly, 'There is a noble Christian woman gone!' "[36]

The controversy between Seventh-day Adventist historians and the personal recollections of D. M. Canright will probably never be settled this side of heaven, but beyond question, Canright has left an indelible mark upon the history of both the denomination and Ellen G. White, a woman of great moral fortitude and indomitable conviction. Her influence will doubtless affect the religious world through the Seventh-day Adventist denomination for many years to come.

The Sleep of the Soul and the Destruction of the Wicked

The doctrine of conditional immortality, commonly called "soul-sleep" outside Adventist circles, and its necessary corollary, annihilation, have been cardinal teachings from the beginning of the Seventh-day Adventist Church. They must be dealt with from an exegetical standpoint if the theology underlying the basic premise is to be understood. These positions, incidentally, are held today by the Advent Christian Church, an affiliate of the National Association of Evangelicals, and by outstanding Bible scholars in not a few denominations.

The purpose here is essentially to review the historical position of the Christian church from the days of the apostles to the present, and to examine the teaching of the Scriptures on these subjects. Many noted Christians of the past believed in conditional immortality, among them Martin Luther, William Tyndale, and John Wycliffe, all of whom were competent Greek scholars. Luther even stated that he could not support the doctrine of immortality of the soul, which he called one of the "endless monstrosities in the Roman dunghill of decretals."[37] Tyndale declared that:

> In putting them [the souls of the departed dead] in heaven, hell, and purgatory you destroy the arguments wherewith Christ and Paul doth prove the resurrection. . . . And again, if the souls be in heaven, tell me why they be not in as good case as the angels be? And then what cause is there for their resurrection?[38]

However, in his *Commentary on Genesis*, Luther later categorically stated, "In the interim [between death and resurrection], the soul does not sleep but is awake and enjoys the vision of angels and of God, and has converse with them."[39]

In any case, neither preponderance of one opinion nor the opinions of a

---

[36]W. A. Spicer, *Our Day in the Light of Prophecy* (Washington, D.C.: Review and Herald Publishing Association, n.d.), 127.
[37]Weimar edition of Luther's *Works*, VII:131–132.
[38]*An Answer to Sir Thomas More's Dialogue*, Parker's 1850 reprint, book 4, chap. iv, 180–181.
[39]*Works*, 25:321.

few great thinkers can validate theological speculation or interpretation. The Christian church does not base its belief in the conscious bliss of departed saints on the opinions of individuals, no matter how prominent or learned, but upon the historical, biblical foundation of the Christian faith.

I. *Textual Analysis*

The Seventh-day Adventist doctrine of the sleep of the soul is best expressed in their own words: "We as Adventists believe that, in general, the Scriptures teach that the soul of man represents the whole man, and not a particular part independent of the other component parts of man's nature; and further, that the soul cannot exist apart from the body, for man is a unit. . . . We, as Adventists, have reached the definite conclusion that man rests in the tomb until the resurrection morning. Then, at the first resurrection (Revelation 20:4–5), the resurrection of the just (Acts 24:15), the righteous come forth immortalized at the call of Christ, the Lifegiver, and they then enter into life everlasting in their eternal home in the kingdom of glory. Such is our understanding."[40]

In the 1988 explanation of Adventist doctrine, *Seventh-day Adventists Believe,* the grave is described: "The grave is not a place of consciousness. Since death is a sleep, the dead will remain in a state of unconsciousness in the grave until the resurrection, when the grave (*Hades*) gives up its dead."[41]

The key to the preceding statements, of course, is the last phrase of the former quote: "They then enter into life everlasting in their eternal home in the kingdom of glory." Now, the majority of Christians through the centuries have held that this proposition contradicts the teaching of the Word of God contained in the following passages:

1. *1 John 5:11–13:* "And this is the record, that God hath given to us eternal life, and this life is in his Son. He that hath the Son hath life; and he that hath not the Son of God hath not life. These things have I written unto you that believe on the name of the Son of God; that ye may know that ye have eternal life, and that ye may believe on the name of the Son of God." In the grammar and context of this passage eternal life (*eionion zoes*) is the present possession of every believer in the Lord Jesus Christ, and if the term eternal life does not include conscious fellowship then the whole New Testament meaning is destroyed. The Holy Spirit used the present indicative active of the verb *echo*, expressing present, continuous action. Thus we see that the believer, having been regenerated by the Holy Spirit, already possesses never-ending life as a continuing quality of conscious existence.

2. *John 11:25–26:* "Jesus said unto her, I am the resurrection and the life: he that believeth in me, though he were dead, yet shall he live: and whosoever liveth and believeth in me shall never die. Believest thou this?" The context here indicates that the Lord Jesus Christ was consoling Martha upon the death of her brother Lazarus. Therefore, the words "life" and "dead" must refer to that particular occasion. To attempt to wrest the meanings of these terms from their expressed context, and to teach that the end of the age is primarily in view or somehow close, is a violation of the grammar and context.

[40] *Questions on Doctrine,* 515, 520.
[41] *Seventh-day Adventists Believe,* 353.

All thorough students of the Word of God, including the Adventists, recognize that in any study of the doctrines of eternal life and immortality, it is vitally essential to apply the hermeneutic principle (comparing all texts on a given subject) of interpretation, and the application of this principle, we believe, leads to the following facts. The root meanings for the words "death" and "life" in the New Testament usage ("death" *thanatos*, in its verb form *apothnesko*, and "life" *zoe*, or its verb form *zac*) are respectively "separation or to separate" from communion or fellowship. The Scriptures describe two types of death, physical and spiritual, the former being the separation of the body from the soul, and the latter being the separation of the soul from God as the result of sin. Also, two kinds of life are spoken of in the New Testament: physical life (*bios*), which is the union or communion of body and soul; and spiritual life (*zoe*), which is the communion or fellowship of the soul with God. These terms we equate with the Greek of the New Testament, and they are essential to an understanding of Christ's words to Martha.

He was assuring her that despite the physical evidence of death, Jesus, the eternal Word of God made flesh, was himself the source of life. And as such, He was able to give life, even though death had actually occurred. Let us therefore take His words literally.

Christ's primary purpose was to comfort Martha. And what better comfort could He give than the knowledge that her family's limited concept of life as dependent upon the resurrection was depriving her of the joyous knowledge that the Prince of Life gives to the believer eternal life, unaffected by physical death.

Now let us look carefully at this context with no violation to hermeneutics or grammar, and this great truth becomes clear. John 11:20 tells us that as soon as Martha heard that Jesus was coming to Bethany, she went out to meet Him. In verse 21 she greets Him thus: "Lord, if thou hadst been here, my brother had not died." In answer to her obvious affliction and grief, Jesus, with divine compassion, stated, "Thy brother shall rise again." Verse 24 indicates, however, that Martha thought He was referring to the resurrection of the dead which will take place at "the last day."

To dispel her confused and grief-instilling concept of life (spiritual life), Jesus gives comfort beyond measure: "I am the resurrection and the life," He declares; "he that believes in me, even though he were dead, yet shall he live, and the one living and believing in me shall never die."

Now it is apparent from the context of verse 25 that Jesus was referring to Martha's brother Lazarus, one who believed in Him and had physically died. Christ's promise is, "yet shall he live." But going beyond this, Jesus lifts the veil and reveals that, in the realm of the physically alive, whoever believes in Him shall never experience the greatest of all terrors, spiritual death.

The Greek is extremely powerful in verse 26, for our Lord deliberately used the double negative, a construction which intensifies with great emphasis that to which it is applied. Jesus could not grammatically have been more emphatic in stating that the believer, who is alive both physically and spiritually, can never experience loss of communion or fellowship as a spiritual entity, though his body may "become" dead.

We see, further, that Seventh-day Adventists have no warrant for the idea

that death is a state of unconsciousness. The New Testament frequently indicates that the unregenerate man is already "dead," but not even the Adventists would say that he was extinct or unconscious! Some instances of this are: Matthew 8:22, "Let the dead bury their dead"; John 5:25, "The hour is coming, and now is, when the dead shall hear the voice of the Son of God: and they that hear shall live"; and Ephesians 2:1, "You hath he quickened, who were dead in trespasses and sins."

Admittedly, in the New Testament death is compared with sleep, but this is recognized by Bible scholars generally as a grammatical metaphor. One does not develop a doctrine from a figure of speech, as conditional immortalists apparently have done, but upon the sound principles of biblical hermeneutics, contextual analysis, and linguistic exegesis. The application of these principles leads to the one conclusion that the Scripture unreservedly teaches, that eternal life is vastly different from "immortality"; although immortality will be bestowed upon the believer at the resurrection, in this life he already possesses "eternal life," a spiritual quality of existence that will at length be united with the physical quality of incorruptibility, which the Bible speaks of as immortality, and "we shall be like him; for we shall see him as he is" (1 Corinthians 13:12; 1 John 3:2). A study of these words in any Greek lexicon, and of their use in the New Testament, will show that immortality and eternal life are neither identical nor synonymous. For certain Adventist writers therefore to treat these terms as interchangeable is clearly a linguistic impossibility.

3. *2 Timothy 1:10:* The apostle Paul writes that God's eternal purpose "is now made manifest by the appearing of our Saviour Jesus Christ, who hath abolished death, and hath brought life and immortality to light through the gospel." In this verse "life" (*zoe*) and "immortality" (*aphtharsian*) are clearly distinguished. Life has been bestowed upon the believer at the moment of regeneration by faith in Jesus Christ (1 John 5:11–12); immortality is a future gift, to be bestowed upon the believer's body at the second advent of our Lord, or as Paul expressed it, "This corruptible must put on incorruption (*aphtharsian*), and this mortal must put on immortality" (1 Corinthians 15:53, *athanasian*).

Again, in Romans 2:7, the apostle clearly distinguishes between "eternal life" as a conscious quality of spiritual existence bestowed upon the believer as a gift; and "immortality," which, in this connection in the New Testament, refers to the resurrection bodies of the saints or to the nature of God himself. Thus, God's Word clearly indicates the difference between "life" as spiritual existence and "immortality" as incorruptibility in a body like that of our risen Lord.

4. *Philippians 1:21–24:* "For to me to live is Christ, and to die is gain. But if I live in the flesh, this is the fruit of my labour: yet what I shall choose I know not. For I am in a strait betwixt two, having a desire to depart, and to be with Christ; which is far better: nevertheless to abide in the flesh is more needful for you."

Seventh-day Adventists say here:

> Of course it will be better to be with Christ, but why, it must be asked, should we conclude that the apostle expects immediately upon death to go at once into the presence of Christ? The Bible does not say so. It merely states his desire to depart and be with Christ. One might reason that the implication is to the effect that being with Christ would be immediately on his departure. But it must be

admitted that such is not a necessary implication, and it certainly is not a definite statement of the text. In this particular passage, Paul does not tell us when he will be with his Lord. In other places he uses an expression similar to one in this passage. For instance, he says, "The time of my departure is at hand" (2 Timothy 4:6). The Greek word used in these two texts, *analuo*, is not used very often in the Greek New Testament, but the word has the meaning "to be loosened like an anchor." It is a metaphor drawn from the loosened moorings preparatory to setting sail.[42]

Now, of all the texts in the New Testament on the state of the believer after the death of his body, this one alone gives us Paul's mind on the subject, so we need to pay strict attention to what he says. In the main, Seventh-day Adventists support their arguments with Old Testament passages, most of which, I maintain, are taken out of context while ignoring metaphorical usages, implications, or deductions. To treat literally such words as "sleep," "death," and "destroy" is, I feel, unwarranted. However, in the New Testament, when faced with a positive statement like this one by the apostle Paul, it seems that they refuse to be literal and insist upon metaphors, deductions, and implications. They seem unwilling to accept the apostle's statement at face value. The noted Adventist author F. D. Nichol, in his book *Answers to Objections*, states that if Philippians 1:21–24 were the only passage about the condition of man in death, he would be forced to acknowledge the accepted orthodox position. Nichol then attempts to strengthen his argument by taking texts out of context to "prove" that Paul does not mean what he most decidedly says. With this thought in mind, let us examine the context and grammar of the apostle's statement, for it answers the Seventh-day Adventist contention.

In verse 21 Paul states that to continue to live is Christ and to die "is gain." Since Paul was ordained to preach the Word of God to the Gentiles while enjoying fellowship with the living Christ, what would he gain by death or unconsciousness? According to the Adventist idea, fellowship with Christ would end and Paul would merely go to sleep until the resurrection. This argument violates both context and grammar.

Verse 23 is grammatically uncomplicated. It is a series of coordinate statements tied together by the conjunctions *kai* and *de*. The phrase "to depart and be with Christ, which is far better" (*eis to analusai kai sun christo einai*) is grammatically devastating to the Seventh-day Adventist position. The preposition *eis* plus the definite article *to* shows "true purpose or end in view"—the strong desire that causes Paul's dilemma. Both infinitives (*analusai* and *einai*) have one construction—they are used with one definite article—and so are one thought, one grammatical expression: literally, "my desire is to the 'to depart and to be with Christ.' " In simple English, Paul's one desire has a twofold object: departure and being with Christ! If departure did not mean his immediately being with Christ, another construction would have been employed. It therefore seems impossible that soul-sleep was in the mind of the apostle since he desired to depart from his body and to spiritually enjoy the presence of his Lord. The Second Advent could not have been in view in this passage, for the context indicates that Paul expected death—and instantaneous reunion with Christ—*then*, not at the resurrection. There would have been no need of his staying to instruct

---

[42] *Questions on Doctrine*, 527–528.

the Philippians (v. 24) if he were speaking of the Second Advent, for they would all be glorified together and no longer in need of His presence to strengthen them. Most translators and recognized Greek authorities contend that Philippians 1:21–24 teaches the historical position of the Christian church, i.e., the conscious presence of the believer with Christ at the death of the body.

As quoted above, the Adventists, in common with all conditional immortalists, say, "Why . . . should we conclude [from this remark] that the apostle expects immediately upon death to go at once into the presence of Christ? The Bible does not say so. It merely states his desire to depart and [to] be with Christ." We answer that the context of the chapter, the grammatical construction of the verse, and every grammar book on New Testament Greek usage teaches that from the construction utilized the apostle expected to go at once into the presence of his Lord. Nevertheless the Adventists insist, "The Bible does not say so. It merely states his desire to depart and [to] be with Christ." This statement is not accurate, it is not exegetically sound, and it will not stand the test of contextual criticism. It is only an attempt, I believe, to justify a doctrine that is not supported by the Word of God.

In reply to the Adventist statement, "In this particular passage, Paul does not tell us when he will be with his Lord," we point out that the apostle categorically states that his desire is "to depart." If this departure did not mean immediate presence with Christ, he would have used a different grammatical construction, as previously noted; but as it stands, it can have no other meaning. In the face of these facts, Seventh-day Adventists disregard the preponderance of historical scholarship in favor of the doctrine of "soul-sleep."

5. *1 Thessalonians 4:13–18:* "I would not have you to be ignorant, brethren, concerning them which are asleep, that ye sorrow not, even as others which have no hope. For if we believe that Jesus died and rose again, even so them also which sleep in Jesus will God bring with him. For this we say unto you by the word of the Lord, that we which are alive and remain unto the coming of the Lord shall not prevent them which are asleep. For the Lord himself shall descend from heaven with a shout, with the voice of the archangel, and with the trump of God: and the dead in Christ shall rise first: then we which are alive and remain shall be caught up together with them in the clouds, to meet the Lord in the air: and so shall we ever be with the Lord. Wherefore comfort one another with these words."

This final passage, I believe, refutes the Adventist teaching on the intermediate state of the dead. It is marked by explicit emphasis of construction in the Greek and cannot be ignored by any serious student of the language.

The key is the preposition *sun*, which carries the primary meaning of "together with." In verse 14, the Holy Spirit tells us that God intends to bring with Him (*sun auto*), that is, with Jesus at His second advent, believing Christians who have experienced physical death. The physical state of their bodies is described as "sleep," a common metaphor in the New Testament. In every instance where the word "sleep" is used to describe death, it always refers to the body and cannot be applied to the soul, especially since "sleep" is never used with reference to the soul. This fact Seventh-day Adventists seem to overlook.

The second use of *sun* is in verse 17, which tells us that believers who survive to the coming of the Lord will be caught up together with them (*sun autois*),

that is, with the dead in Christ (*oi nekroi en Christo*) to meet the Lord in the air. Here again, *sun* has no meaning other than "together with," a fact most difficult for Seventh-day Adventists to explain.

The last use of the preposition *sun* is also in verse 17: "And so shall we ever be with the Lord" (*sun kurio*). It is quite obvious, therefore, that at the second advent of Christ, those who at death departed to be spiritually with the Lord (Philippians 1:21–24) *return* with Him or "together with" Him to claim their resurrected, immortal bodies. Simultaneously, their corrupting bodies in the graves, spoken of as "asleep," are instantly metamorphosed or changed and re-united with the returning personalities. This fact is consistently emphasized by continual use of the preposition *sun*, "together with." Since the preposition *sun* means "together with" both times in verse 17, grammatically it cannot mean something altogether different in the same context and parallel usage of verse 14. Therefore, if at Christ's advent our bodies are to go with Him physically (verse 16), it is obvious that the saints who preceded us in death have been with Him from the moment of death, since they accompany Him in His return (verse 14).

A final grammatical point is the Holy Spirit's use of *nekroi*, which through-out the New Testament refers primarily to the physical body of man, and only metaphorically to the soul. We see, then, that the corpses (*nekroi*) of the physi-cally dead saints are to be raised and united with their returning souls (verse 14). Not once does the context or grammar indicate that the souls of departed believers are "asleep." Instead, it categorically states that they are "with Jesus" or returning "together with" Jesus.

The great hope of the believer is the joy of personal union with the Lord, and this union, the apostle Paul tells us, takes place at the death of the body. That this has been the position of the large majority of the Christian church since the times of the apostles, the Adventists have never denied. In 1 Thessa-lonians 4, the apostle Paul was giving comfort to people who were mourning for departed loved ones; and his words carry the undeniable conclusion that they are not "dead" in the usual pagan sense. Although physically dead, they are spiritually alive and with Christ, awaiting the day when they will return "together with him" (verse 14) to claim their inheritance of completion, physical immor-tality, or incorruptibility.

II. *"Soul" and "Spirit"*

For a fuller treatment of Adventist teaching on soul-sleep, we must discuss briefly the Bible's use of "soul" and "spirit." In the Old Testament, the words "soul" and "spirit" are the Hebrew *nephesh* and *ruach*. In the New Testament they are the Greek *psuche* and *pneuma*. Although in the Old Testament *nephesh* and *ruach* frequently refer only to the principle of life in both men and animals, in many other places they mean the intellectual and spiritual nature of man. Such verses as Isaiah 57:16, Zechariah 12:1, Isaiah 55:3, and Genesis 35:18[43] belie

---

[43]"For I will not contend for ever, neither will I be always wroth: for the spirit should fail before me, and the souls which I have made" (Isaiah 57:16); "The burden of the word of the Lord for Israel, saith the Lord, which stretcheth forth the heavens, and layeth the foundation of the earth, and formeth the spirit of man within him" (Zechariah 12:1); "Incline your ear, and come unto me: hear, and your soul shall live; and I will make an everlasting covenant with you, even the sure mer-cies of David" (Isaiah 55:3); "And it came to pass, as her soul was in departing, (for she died) that she called his name Benoni: but his father called him Benjamin" (Genesis 35:18).

the Adventists' criterion for determining the spiritual nature of man. On page 522 of *Questions on Doctrine*, the Adventists list eight Scripture passages about death to show that at the death of the body, the intellect, will, and spirit of man (*nephesh* and *ruach*) lapse into unconsciousness pending the resurrection. However, seven of these are from the Old Testament and each refers to the body. Adventists lean strongly on the book of Ecclesiastes, especially 9:5–6, to substantiate their doctrine. But Ecclesiastes 12:7 tells us that upon the death of the body, "the spirit [*ruach*] shall return unto God." Unlike the mere principle of life in the animals, man possesses a cognizant, immaterial nature created in God's image.[44]

It is a basic Christian principle, with which Adventists agree, that the Old Testament must be interpreted by the New Testament, and not the reverse. However, where conditional immortality is involved, Adventists do not follow this principle. The New Testament teaches that the immaterial nature of man (soul and spirit) is separate from the body (Matthew 10:28; Luke 8:55; 1 Thessalonians 5:23; Hebrews 4:12; Revelation 16:3),[45] and also that it is independent of man's material form and departs from that form at death to go either into the presence of the Lord (Philippians 1:23) or into a place of punishment (Luke 16). In Acts 7:59, Stephen committed his spirit (*pneuma*) into the hands of the Lord Jesus Christ. This establishes the fact that the immaterial nature of man is independent of his body. At the same time, the Scripture tells us, "He [Stephen] fell asleep" in death; that is, his physical body took on the appearance of "sleep." But he as a unit did not die; he merely experienced separation of the soul from the body, and he went to be with the Lord, into whose hands he had committed his spiritual nature.

In Luke 23:46, the Lord Jesus Christ said, "Father, into thy hands I commend my spirit." This verse would be meaningless if it applied only to the "breath of Jesus." The classic example of the penitent thief, who in his last moments believed on the Lord Jesus Christ, is proof that eternal life is a quality including conscious existence. It does not terminate with the death of the physical but continues in never-ending personal fellowship with our Lord. "Today shalt thou be with me in paradise" (v. 43) is the guarantee of the Son of God that those who trust Him will never be separated from His presence and fellowship. Seventh-day Adventists, in company with other conditional immortalists, attempt to explain this by reading the text with different punctuation: "Verily, I say unto thee today, shalt thou be with me in paradise." The reason is that Christ's statement calls into serious question their doctrine of soul-sleep. More-

---

[44]It is almost universally agreed among biblical scholars that Ecclesiastes portrays Solomon's apostasy and is therefore questionable for determining doctrine. It sketches man's life "under the sun" and reveals the hopelessness of the soul apart from God.

[45]"And fear not them which kill the body, but are not able to kill the soul: but rather fear him which is able to destroy both soul and body in hell" (Matthew 10:28); "And her spirit came again, and she rose straightway: and he commanded to give her meat" (Luke 8:55); "And the very God of peace sanctify you wholly; and I pray God your whole spirit and soul and body be preserved blameless unto the coming of our Lord Jesus Christ" (1 Thessalonians 5:23); "For the word of God is quick, and powerful, and sharper than any two-edged sword, piercing even to the dividing asunder of soul and spirit, and of the joints and marrow, and is a discerner of the thoughts and intents of the heart" (Hebrews 4:12); "And the second angel poured out his vial upon the sea; and it became as the blood of a dead man: and every living soul died in the sea" (Revelation 16:3).

over, Adventists seem to overlook the important fact that whenever Jesus used the words, "Verily I say unto you," He never qualified them because qualification was unnecessary. It would have been redundant for Jesus to say, "Verily I say unto you, that is, today I am saying unto you. . . ." By this type of interpretation, the Adventists violate the plain sense of one of Christ's common expressions of emphasis.

In Matthew 17:3, we see Moses and Elijah with Christ on the Mount of Transfiguration. We know that Moses died (Deuteronomy 34:5), and Elijah was translated (2 Kings 2:11). However, it *was* Moses who was communing with our Lord. Since the Scripture nowhere states that Moses had been raised from the dead for this occasion (Adventists attempt to teach this from the book of Jude, where such an assertion is not made), it is evident that the soul of Moses appeared to our Lord. Thus, conscious existence is a necessary predicate of the intermediate state.

It is the strong conviction of mine, based upon Scripture, that the doctrine of soul-sleep cannot stand in the light of God's revelation. Perhaps the reader will think that there has been too much space given to the meanings of words and the grammar of the Greek New Testament. However, this is most essential because the crux of Adventist argument, it seems to me, is a denial of the meaning of terms in their context. For example, they say:

> There is nothing in the word *psyche* [soul] itself that even remotely implies a conscious entity that is able to survive the death of the body. And there is nothing in the Bible use of the word indicating that the Bible writers held any such belief. . . . There is nothing inherent in the word *pneuma* [spirit] by which it may be taken to mean some supposed conscious entity of man capable of existing apart from the body, nor does the usage of the word with respect to man in the New Testament in any way imply such a concept. . . . A careful study of all the adjectives used in Scripture to qualify the word "spirit" as applied to man, indicates that not one even remotely approaches the idea of immortality as one of the qualities of the human "spirit."[46]

As demonstrated in Matthew 10:28, Jesus Christ apparently believed and taught that the soul was more than "body and breath," which Seventh-day Adventism teaches, for He said, "Fear not them which kill the body, but are not able to kill the soul."

Seventh-day Adventist writers charge that orthodox theologians have been overly dogmatic about the nature of man, while Adventists have maintained a guarded reserve. But Adventists have been equally dogmatic in denouncing the orthodox position. To be dogmatic one should have a sound, scholarly basis for his dogmatism, and such a basis exegetically speaking is conspicuously absent from the historical position of conditional immortalists. As mentioned above, Adventists generally confuse "immortality" with "eternal life." We quite agree that "a careful study of all the adjectives used in Scripture to qualify the word 'spirit' as applied to man, indicates that not one even remotely approaches the idea of immortality," as our Adventist brethren have stated. But as we have shown, "immortality" refers only to the resurrection body of the saints and to the nature of God himself. Therefore, since the saints are to be clothed with

---
[46]*Questions on Doctrine*, 514, 517–518.

their resurrection bodies at the Second Advent, they do not now possess "immortality." For Adventists to confuse "immortality" with "eternal life" and then to argue that "immortality" means "eternal life" and is never applied to the spirit is logical and theological error.

The question of soul-sleep, however, should cause no serious division between Christians since it does not affect the foundational doctrines of the Christian faith or the salvation of the soul. It is merely an area of theological debate and has no direct bearing upon any of the great doctrines of the Bible. The ground of fellowship is not the condition of man in death but faith in the Lord Jesus Christ and the love He commanded us to have one for another (John 13:34–35). Seventh-day Adventists are welcome to hold this doctrine, but when one is faced with such concrete Old Testament instances as Samuel's appearance to Saul (1 Samuel 28:18–19) and such New Testament accounts as those given by the apostle Paul (2 Corinthians 5:8), "to be absent from the body, and to be present with the Lord," or (Philippians 1:23) "to depart, and to be with Christ; which is far better," it is difficult to see how our Adventist brethren can sufficiently substantiate their claim for the "sleep of the soul."

III. *Hell and Punishment as Taught in New Testament Greek*
The grammar of the Greek New Testament teaches unquestionably the doctrine of hell and eternal punishment. Nowhere is this more pointedly brought out than in the following passages:

1. *Matthew 5:22 and 10:28:* "Whosoever shall say, Thou fool, shall be in danger of hell fire," and "Fear him which is able to destroy both soul and body in hell."

In both passages the Greek word *gehenna* portrays a place of punishment for the unsaved. *Gehenna* originally meant the Valley of Hinnom, a garbage dump that smoldered perpetually outside Jerusalem. The rabbis believed that punishment after death could be likened to *gehenna* and often threatened their people with punishment after death. The Lord Jesus Christ, however, pointed out to the unbelieving Jews that those who rejected Him could look forward to everlasting *gehenna*. In Matthew 10:28, He coupled *gehenna* with *apolesai*, which Thayer's Greek lexicon defines as "to be delivered up to eternal misery." Gehenna, then, symbolizes eternal separation and conscious punishment for the spiritual nature of the unregenerate man. This eternity of punishment is also taught in the Old Testament; e.g., "Their worm shall not die, neither shall their fire be quenched" (Isaiah 66:24).

2. *2 Thessalonians 1:8–9:* "In flaming fire taking vengeance on them that know not God, and that obey not the gospel of our Lord Jesus Christ: who shall be punished with everlasting destruction from the presence of the Lord and from the glory of his power."

From the context, "everlasting destruction" is to be that of "flaming fire," visited upon those who "obey not the gospel of our Lord Jesus Christ." The heart of the problem here is the meaning of the word "destruction," which the Adventists claim is reduction to a state of nonexistence (*Questions on Doctrine*, 14). As a matter of fact, the Greek word *olethros* used here has the clear meaning of "ruining." (For this and the following lexical studies, any standard New Testament Greek lexicon or grammar bears out the meanings presented here.) We

see then, that everlasting destruction or "ruination" is the lot of those who know not God. Many people who are not well versed in Greek try to make "destruction" synonymous with "annihilation." This does violence to New Testament Greek, which supports no such concept. A common illustration will show the fallacy of this idea.

In the course of her work, a housewife may change a light bulb. What happens if it drops to the floor and breaks? It is, of course, "destroyed," but no one would say that it had been annihilated, for there is a difference between the function of an object and its nature. The function of the bulb is to give light. When broken, its function is destroyed, but the glass remains, although in fragments, and so does the metal base. Although the bulb has been "ruined" or "destroyed," it certainly has not been "reduced to nothing."

The Bible teaches that unregenerate mankind will suffer the eternal wrath of God and must undergo destruction and ruin of their original function which was "to glorify God and to enjoy Him forever." But the human spirit, created in the image of God (Genesis 1:26–27), remains intact, a spiritual entity of eternal existence, capable of enduring eternally the righteous and just Judge.

3. *Revelation 20:10:* "The devil who deceived them was cast into the lake of fire and brimstone where the beast and the false prophet are, and they will be tormented day and night into the everlasting of the everlasting" (literal translation).

The root meaning of the Greek word *basanizo* is "to torment, to be harassed, to torture or to vex with grievous pain," and is used throughout the New Testament to denote great conscious pain and misery, never annihilation or cessation of consciousness. The reader who wishes to pursue this point may look up the following verses where this word is used: Matthew 8:6, 29; Mark 5:7; Luke 8:28; Revelation 14.10–11. In each place, *basanizo* means conscious "torment." In Revelation 14:10–11, speaking of the followers of the Beast, unmistakably it means torment or punishment, everlasting or never-ceasing.

In Revelation 20:10, Satan, the beast, and the false prophet are described as tormented (*basanis thesontai*) "day and night into the everlasting of the everlasting." So if language means anything at all, in these contexts alone the theory of annihilation or, as the Adventists say, the final destruction of the wicked, is itself annihilated.

4. *John 3:36:* "He that believeth on the Son hath everlasting life: and he that believeth not the Son shall not see life, but the wrath of God abideth on him."

Our fourth and final grammatical point relative to the doctrine of annihilation is made by coupling Romans 2:8–9 and Revelation 14:10 with John 3:36. Jesus tells us that the one who believes in the Lord Jesus Christ already has everlasting life (present tense); and then, of one who "believes not the Son," he states that he "shall not see life, but the wrath of God abideth on him." The Greek word *menei*, here translated *abide*, appears several times in the New Testament. It carries the idea of continuous action (see John 1:33; 2:12; 8:31; 15:9). Thus, in John 3:36 the Holy Spirit says that the wrath of God continually abides on the one who "believeth not the Son." Comparing this with Romans 2:8–9, we see that those who do not obey the truth but do evil are the objects of God's wrath, which Revelation 14:10–11 describes as eternal. "The same shall drink of the wine of the wrath of God . . . and the smoke of their torment ascendeth

up for ever and ever: and they have no rest day nor night."

Orges, translated "wrath," appears in each of the verses cited, so there can be no doubt that the same subject is being discussed. It is apparent then that, far from the comparatively blissful prospect of total annihilation, those who "have not the Son of God have not life,"[47] and "the wrath of God continues upon them."[48] God's wrath even now hangs like the sword of Damocles over the heads of those who deny Jesus Christ. It will strike when the rebellious soul goes into eternity and appears before the bar of God's eternal justice.

Seventh-day Adventists should not be ostracized because they cling to this doctrine, since they believe that an undetermined period of punishment will elapse before the actual ultimate destruction of the wicked with Satan and his host.

Dr. Francis Pieper, the great Lutheran scholar and author of the monumental *Christian Dogmatics*, states my views in essence when he says:

> Holy Scripture teaches the truth of an eternal damnation so clearly and emphatically that one cannot deny it without, at the same time, rejecting the authority of Scripture. Scripture parallels the eternal salvation of the believers and the eternal damnation of the unbelievers. Whoever therefore denies the one must, to be consistent, deny the other (Matthew 25:46). We find the same juxtaposition and antithesis in other passages of Scripture. This parallelism proves that the term eternity in the sense of limited duration as sometimes used in Holy Writ, is inapplicable here. We must take the predicate eternal in its proper or strict sense, a sense of *sine fine* in all Scripture texts that use it to describe the duration and the penalties of the wicked in yonder life (see 2 Thessalonians 1:9; Matthew 18:8; Mark 3:29). . . . The objections raised in all ages to the endlessness of the infernal punishment are understandable; for the thought of a never-ending agony of rational beings fully realizing their distressing plight is so appalling that it exceeds comprehension. But all objections are based on the false principle that it is proper and reasonable to make our human sentiments and judgments the measure of God's essence and activity.
>
> This is the case in particular with those who contend that an everlasting punishment of a part of mankind does not agree with the unity of God's world plan, or that it is compatible neither with divine love nor with divine justice, who accordingly substitute for eternal damnation eventual salvation by gradual improvement in the next life, or an immediate or later annihilation of the wicked. Against such views we must maintain the general principle that God's essence, attributes, and actions exceed our comprehension, that we can therefore not know *a priori* but only from God's revelation in His Word what agrees or conflicts with God's essence and attributes. The nature of eternal damnation consists in eternal banishment from the sight of God or, in other words, in being forever excluded from communion with God. . . . To illustrate the terrible agony setting in with this banishment from the sight of God, the dogmatician points to the agony of the fish removed from its element. But there is this difference; the fish that is removed from its element soon dies, whereas the man who is banished from communion with God must by God's judgment live on, "is guilty of eternal judgment" (Mark 3:29).[49]

---

[47]i.e., personal communion or fellowship with Christ. Spiritual death is the opposite of eternal life in that the soul is deprived of such communion or fellowship and is conscious of it.

[48]Death (spiritual), far from being unconsciousness, is eternal conscious endurance of God's just wrath.

[49]Francis Pieper, *Christian Dogmatics* (Grand Rapids, Mich.: Zondervan Publishing House, n.d. (reprint), 3:544–555.

Seventh-day Adventists would do well to heed Dr. Pieper's observation as well as the testimony of the Christian church generally for the last two thousand years. But most important, they should heed the teaching of the Word of God that the soul of man, whether regenerate or unregenerate, exists after the death of the body. The justice of God makes everlasting punishment for the unregenerate and everlasting life for the saved to be two sides of one coin—God's justice and God's love. We believe the Bible clearly teaches that there is neither authority nor warrant for the doctrines of conditional immortality and annihilation. God grant in the fullness of His wisdom that none of His children will persist in setting up their standards as the criterion to determine His perfect righteousness. It is my opinion that Seventh-day Adventists have done just this; first by predicating that a God of love would not eternally punish a conscious being, and second by attempting to force the Scriptures into their frame of thought while seeming to ignore context, hermeneutics, and exegesis. Their fellow Christians can only pray that they may soon be led to embrace the historical position of the church, which is the antithesis of the sleep of the soul and the annihilation of the wicked.

The Sabbath, the Lord's Day, and the Mark of the Beast

Certainly the most distinctive doctrine promulgated by the Seventh-day Adventist denomination, and one of the two from which they derive their name, is the Seventh-day Sabbath. How Adventists came to hold the Sabbath as the true day of worship, and why they continue to champion it and jealously urge it upon all who worship on Sunday, provides the key to understanding their psychological and theological motivations.

I. *The Sabbath or the Lord's Day*

Seventh-day Adventists from the beginning have always attempted to equate the Sabbath with the Lord's Day. Their principal method for accomplishing this is to link Mark 2:28 with Revelation 1:10, and thus to undercut one of the strongest arguments against their position, i.e., the Lord's Day as opposed to Sabbath observance.

They reason that since "the Son of Man is Lord also of the Sabbath" (Mark 2:27–28), when John says he "was in the Spirit on the Lord's day" (Revelation 1:10), the Sabbath and the Lord's Day must be the same! The weakness of their position is that they base their argument on an English translation instead of on the Greek original. When one reads the second chapter of Mark and the first chapter of Revelation in Greek, he sees that there is no such interpretation inherent in the grammatical structure. The Greek of Mark 2:28 clearly indicates that Christ did not mean that the Sabbath was His possession (which the Adventists would like to establish); rather, He was saying that as Lord of all He could do as He pleased on the Sabbath. The Greek is most explicit here.

Nothing could be clearer from both the context and the grammar. In Revelation 1:10, the Greek is not the genitive of possession, which it would have to be in order to make *te-kuriake* (the Lord's) agree with *hemera* (day). John did not mean that the Lord's Day was the Lord's possession, but rather that it was the day dedicated to Him by the early church, not in accordance with Mosaic law,

but in obedience to our Lord's commandment of love.

We may certainly assume that if the Sabbath had meant so much to the writers of the New Testament, and if, as Adventists insist, it was so widely observed during the early centuries of the Christian church, John and the other writers of Scripture would have equated it with the Lord's Day, the first day of the week. Scripture and history testify that they did not, and Adventists have, therefore, little scriptural justification for their Sabbatarianism.

A. *Testimony of the Fathers*

The church Fathers provide a mass of evidence that the first day of the week, not the seventh, is the Lord's Day. Some of this evidence is here submitted for the reader's consideration. In company with the overwhelming majority of historians and scholars, we believe that not only the New Testament but the following citations refute Sabbatarianism. We have yet to see any systematic answer to what the Christian church has always believed.

1. *Ignatius, Bishop of Antioch*, in the year A.D. 110, wrote: "If, then, those who walk in the ancient practices attain to newness of hope, no longer observing the Sabbath, but fashioning their lives after the Lord's Day on which our life also arose through Him, that we may be found disciples of Jesus Christ, our only teacher."

2. *Justin Martyr* (100–165): "And on the day called Sunday, all who live in cities or in the country gather together in one place and memoirs of the apostles or the writings of the prophets are read, as long as time permits. . . . Sunday is the day on which we all hold our common assembly because it is the first day on which God, having wrought a change in the darkness in matter, made the world; and Jesus Christ our Saviour on the same day rose from the dead."

3. *The Epistle of Barnabas* (between 120 and 150): " 'Your new moons and your Sabbaths I cannot endure' (Isaiah 1:13). You perceive how He speaks: Your present Sabbaths are not acceptable to me but that which I had made in giving rest to all things, I shall make a beginning of the eighth day, that is a beginning of another world. Wherefore also, we keep the eighth day with joyfulness, a day also in which Jesus rose from the dead."

4. *Irenaeus, Bishop of Lyons* (about 178): "The mystery of the Lord's resurrection may not be celebrated on any other day than the Lord's Day."

5. *Bardaisan* (born 154): "Wherever we be, all of us are called by the one name of the Messiah, namely Christians and upon one day, which is the first day of the week, we assemble ourselves together and on the appointed days we abstain from food."

6. *Cyprian, Bishop of Carthage* (200–258): "The Lord's Day is both the first and the eighth day."

7. *Eusebius* (about 315): "The churches throughout the rest of the world observe the practice that has prevailed from the apostolic tradition until the present time so that it would not be proper to terminate our fast on any other day but the resurrection day of our Saviour. Hence, there were synods and convocations of our bishops on this question and they unanimously drew up an ecclesiastical decree which they communicated to churches in all places—that the mystery of the Lord's resurrection should be celebrated on no other than the Lord's day."

8. *Peter, Bishop of Alexandria* (about 300): "We keep the Lord's Day as a day of joy because of Him who arose thereon."

9. *Didache of the Apostles* (about 70–75): "On the Lord's own day, gather yourselves together and break bread and give thanks."

10. *The Epistle of Pliny* (about 112, addressed to the Emperor Trajan): "They [the Christians] affirmed . . . that the whole of their crime or error was that they had been wont to meet together on a fixed day before daylight and to repeat among themselves in turn a hymn to Christ as to a god and to bind themselves by an oath (*sacramentum*). . . . These things duly done, it had been their custom to disperse and to meet again to take food—of an ordinary and harmless kind. Even this they had ceased to do after my edict, by which, in accordance with your instructions, I had forbidden the existence of societies."

Thus it appears that from apostolic and patristic times, the Christian church observed the Lord's Day or the first day of the week; further, the Jewish Sabbath, in the words of Clement of Alexandria (about 194) was "nothing more than a working day."

In their zeal to establish the authority of the Sabbath, Adventists either reject contrary evidence as unauthentic (and so they conflict with the preponderance of scholastic opinion), or they ignore the testimony of the early church. Although they seem unaffected by the evidence, the fact remains that the Christian church has both apostolic and historical support for observing the Lord's Day in place of the Sabbath.

B. *"Authoritative Quotations"*

Recently the Adventist radio program *Voice of Prophecy* circulated a thirty-one-page pamphlet entitled *Authoritative Quotations on the Sabbath and Sunday*. In it they quoted "leading" Protestant sources to "prove" that Sunday usurped the Sabbath and is a pagan institution imposed by Constantine in A.D. 321.

However, many of the sources quoted actually establish what the Adventists flatly deny; i.e., that the Seventh-day Sabbath is not the Lord's Day or the first day of the week, but is, in fact, the seventh day as its name indicates.

Since the Adventists are willing to quote these authorities to buttress their position in one area, surely they will give consideration to contradictory statements by these same authorities in another:

1. "The Lord's Day did not succeed in the place of the Sabbath. . . . The Lord's Day was merely an ecclesiastical institution. . . . The primitive Christians did all manner of work upon the Lord's Day" (Bishop Jeremy Taylor, *Ductor Dubitantium*, Part 1, Book 2, Chapter 2, Rule 6, Sections 51, 59).

2. "The observance of the Lord's Day [Sunday] is founded not on any command of God, but on the authority of the church" (*Augsburg Confession of Faith*, quoted in *Catholic Sabbath Manual*, Part 2, Chapter 1, Section 10).

3. "But they err in teaching that Sunday has taken the place of the Old Testament Sabbath and therefore must be kept as the seventh day had to be kept by the children of Israel" (J. T. Mueller, *Sabbath or Sunday*, 15–16).

4. "They [the Catholics] allege the Sabbath changed into Sunday, the Lord's Day, contrary to the Decalogue as it appears; neither is there any example more boasted than the changing of the Sabbath Day" (Martin Luther, *Augsburg Confession of Faith*, Article 28, Paragraph 9).

5. "Although it [Sunday] was in primitive times and differently called the Lord's Day or Sunday, yet it was never denominated the Sabbath, a name constantly appropriate to Saturday, or the seventh day both by sacred and ecclesiastical writers" (Charles Buck, *A Theological Dictionary*, 1850, 537).

6. "The notion of a formal substitution by apostolic authority of the Lord's Day [meaning Sunday] for the Jewish Sabbath (or the first for the seventh day). . . . The transference to it, perhaps in a spiritualized form of the Sabbath obligation established by promulgation of the fourth commandment, has no basis whatever either in Holy Scripture or in Christian antiquity" (Sir William Smith and Samuel Cheetham, *A Dictionary of Christian Antiquities*, Volume 2, 182, article on the Sabbath).

7. "The view that the Christian's Lord's Day or Sunday is but the Christian Sabbath deliberately transferred from the seventh to the first day of the week does not indeed find categorical expression till a much later period. . . . The Council of Laodicea (A.D. 364) . . . forbids Christians from Judaizing and resting on the Sabbath Day, preferring the Lord's Day and so far as possible resting as Christians" (*Encyclopedia Britannica*, 1899 ed., Volume 23, 654).

Thus the Adventists have in effect destroyed their argument by appealing to authorities who state unequivocally that the first day of the week is the Lord's Day and that it was observed by the early Christian church from the time of the apostles.

It should also be carefully noted that in their "Authoritative Quotations" the Adventists overlook the fact that nearly all the authorities argue forcefully for the Lord's Day as the first day of the week, and state that legal observance of the Sabbath terminated at the cross (Colossians 2:16–17). The Adventists also, in their compilation of quotations, appeal even to the Church of Jesus Christ of Latter-day Saints (Mormon), and to Fulton Ousler, a Roman Catholic laywriter. The Mormons are a non-Christian cult, a fact which the Adventists admit; and Ousler, a layman, hardly represents the position of Rome.

On page thirteen of this same pamphlet, the Adventists make misleading use of the ellipsis. The following is a direct quotation as it appears:

> Sunday (*dies-solis*, of the Roman calendar, day of the sun, because dedicated to the sun), was adopted by the early Christians as a day of worship. The sun of Latin adoration they interpreted as the "sun of righteousness." . . . No regulations for its observance are laid down in the New Testament, nor, indeed, is its observance even enjoined (Schaff-Herzog, *Encyclopedia of Religious Knowledge*, 1891 ed., Volume 4, Article on Sunday).

Now here is the paragraph as it appears in the *Encyclopedia*:

> Sunday (*dies-solis*, of the Roman Calendar, day of the sun, because dedicated to the sun), was adopted by the early Christians as a day of worship. The sun of Latin adoration they interpreted as "the sun of righteousness." SUNDAY WAS EMPHATICALLY THE WEEKLY FEAST OF THE RESURRECTION OF CHRIST, AS THE JEWISH SABBATH WAS THE FEAST OF THE CREATION. IT WAS CALLED THE "LORD'S DAY," AND UPON IT THE PRIMITIVE CHURCH ASSEMBLED TO BREAK BREAD (Acts 20:7; 1 Corinthians 16:2). No regulations for its observance are laid down in the New Testament, nor, indeed, is its observance even enjoined; YET CHRISTIAN FEELING LED TO THE UNIVERSAL ADOPTION OF THE DAY, IN IMITATION OF APOSTOLIC PRECE-

DENCE. IN THE SECOND CENTURY ITS OBSERVANCE WAS UNIVERSAL. (Sentences in capital letters were omitted by the writer of the Adventist pamphlet on page 22. This mutilation of authoritative sources first occurs in *The Present Truth*, Volume 1, Number 9, published in the 1880s. So our Adventist brethren apparently failed to check the quotation's validity.)

Such use of the ellipsis is not uncommon in certain Seventh-day Adventists' writings in connection with the Sabbath, the Lord's Day, etc., and we regret that they resort to it in order to substantiate their position.

In this pamphlet they quote Martin Luther, despite the well-known fact that Luther violently opposed Sabbatarianism. His refutation of his Sabbatarian colleague, Dr. Carlstadt, is a monument to his apologetic genius. Thus, to quote Luther in order to support the doctrine of the Seventh-day Sabbath suggests that Adventists are not familiar with Luther's theology.

We admire the boldness of our Adventist brethren in their claims for the Sabbath, but their boldness is misplaced and leads to a distorted concept of the value of the law of God, for when a person believes and teaches that "the fourth commandment is the greatest commandment in the Decalogue," it is apparent that he has no understanding of the spirit of the law. Volume 4 of the *International Standard Bible Encyclopedia* represents the reasons why the Christian church observes the Lord's Day in preference to the Sabbath, and also clearly states (2629–2634) the Seventh-day Adventist position.[50] On page 2633 the Adventists contend: "According to church history the seventh-day Sabbath was observed by the early church, and no other day was observed as a Sabbath during the first two or three centuries."

This sentence epitomizes the Adventist propensity for overstating their case; i.e., attempting to read "Sabbath" into "Lord's Day," which all leading authorities confute as we have seen.

II. Primary Anti-Sabbatarian Texts

In more than one place, the New Testament comments unfavorably upon the practice of any type of legalistic day-keeping. In fact, from the ascension of Christ on, the New Testament or early church observed the first day of the week or the Lord's Day (Revelation 1:10), as we have endeavored to show. Besides the passages that contrast the Lord's Day with the Sabbath, the apostle Paul—Hebrew of the Hebrews and Pharisee of the Pharisees, apart from our Lord, the outstanding New Testament authority—on the Law of Moses declared that the Sabbath as "the law" was fulfilled at the cross and was not binding upon the Christian (Colossians 2:16–17). Since the subject is so vast in scope, the reader is referred to the bibliography, especially to Dr. Louis Sperry Chafer's *Grace*, and Norman C. Deck's *The Lord's Day or the Sabbath, Which?* These contain excellent refutations of Sabbatarianism. D. M. Canright in *Seventh-day Adventism Renounced* also dealt exhaustively and ably with the Sabbath subject.

To narrow the issue down to simple analysis, we shall review the major New Testament texts that in context and in the light of syntactical analysis refute the Sabbatarian concept, and substantiate the historical position of the Christian church since the days of the apostles and the Fathers.

---

[50]Bible Question Column in *Signs of the Times* (January 8, 1952).

A. *Colossians 2:13–17*

Of all of the statements in the New Testament, these verses most strongly refute the Sabbatarian claim for observance of the Jewish Sabbath. Let us listen to the inspired counsel of Paul, not only the greatest of the apostles, but once a Pharisee whose passion for fulfilling the law outperformed that of the most zealous Seventh-day Adventist:

> And you, who were dead in trespasses and the uncircumcision of your flesh, God made alive together with him, having forgiven us all our trespasses, having canceled the bond which stood against us with its legal demands; this he set aside, nailing it to the cross. He disarmed the principalities and powers and made a public example of them, triumphing over them in him. Therefore let no one pass judgment on you in questions of food and drink or with regard to a festival or a new moon or a sabbath. These are only a shadow of what is to come; but the substance belongs to Christ (Colossians 2:13–17, RSV).

This translation, one of the best from the Greek text today, contains tremendously important teaching.

First, we who were dead have been made alive in Christ and have been forgiven all trespasses and sins. We are free from the condemnation of the law in all its aspects, because Christ took our condemnation on the cross. As already observed, there are not two laws, moral and ceremonial, but one law containing many commandments, all perfectly fulfilled by the life and death of the Lord Jesus Christ.

"Therefore," the apostle Paul boldly declares, "let no one pass judgment on you in questions of food and drink or with regard to a festival or a new moon or a sabbath. These are only a shadow of what is to come; but the substance belongs to Christ."

In the face of this clear teaching, Sabbatarians revert to their dual-law theory and argue that Paul is referring only to observance of the Jewish ceremonial law, not to the Sabbath which, they insist, is a moral precept because it is one of the Ten Commandments. We have seen, however, that the Ten Commandments are but a fragment of the moral law encompassed by the commandment "Thou shalt love thy neighbor as thyself" (Leviticus 19:18; Romans 13:9).

Sabbatarians overlook the mass of contradictory evidence and appeal to certain commentators who do not analyze the uses of the word "Sabbath," or exegete the New Testament passages where the word occurs. Such commentators are Albert Barnes, *Notes on the New Testament;* Jamieson, Fausset, and Brown, *Critical and Explanatory Commentary;* and Adam Clarke in his *Commentary.* If a commentator's opinion is not in accord with sound exegesis, it is *only an opinion,* and the commentators named above make no grammatical or textual analysis of the second chapter of Colossians!

Many New Testament commentators try to retain the moral force of the Sabbath (although all of these transfer it to the first day of the week) because it is the subject of the fourth commandment. For this serious theological error there is no warrant in the New Testament. Sabbatarians fail to mention that all the commentators whom they cite repudiate the Sabbath, and most of them teach that the true Sabbath was the Lord's Day (Revelation 1:10), carried over by the early church from apostolic tradition as a memorial to redemption or the re-creation of mankind through the regenerative power of the Holy Spirit.

Adventists are therefore without historical or exegetical support when they make the Lord's Day the same as the Sabbath.

With regard to this passage, Adventists maintain that since the word in Colossians 2:16 (*sabbaton*) is in the plural, it means the ceremonial Sabbaths, not the weekly Sabbath, which they contend is still in effect. However, their argument seems to be that Colossians 2:16–17 refers to Sabbaths and feast days that were shadows of things to come, and thus part of ceremonial laws; but that the Seventh-day Sabbath is not a shadow of redemption but a memorial of Creation and part of the moral law. The leading modern translations, following the best New Testament scholars, render Colossians 2:16 as "a Sabbath" or "a Sabbath day," not "Sabbath days" as in the King James Version. Their reason for doing this is well stated by W. E. Vine:

> *Sabbaton* or *sabbata*, the latter the plural form, was transliterated from the Aramaic word, which was mistaken for a plural: hence the singular *sabbaton* was formed from it. . . . In the epistles the only direct mentions are in Colossians 2:16 "a Sabbath day" (RV), which rightly has the singular . . . where it is listed among things that were "a shadow of things to come"; i.e., of the age introduced at Pentecost, and in Hebrews 4:4–11 where the perpetual *sabbatismos* is appointed for believers. . . . For the first three centuries of the Christian era the first day of the week was never confounded with the Sabbath; the confusion of the Jewish and Christian institutions was due to declension from apostolic teaching.[51]

Supplementing Dr. Vine's statement is the comment of M. R. Vincent:

> Sabbath days (*sabbaton*), the weekly festivals revised correctly as day, the plural being used for the singular. See Luke 4:31 and Acts 20:7. The plural is only once used in the New Testament of more than a single day (Acts 17:2). In the Old Testament, the same enumeration of sacred seasons occurs in 1 Chronicles 23:31; 2 Chronicles 2:4; 2 Chronicles 31:3; Ezekiel 45:17; Hosea 2:11.[52]

As Dr. Vincent points out, the revisers' rendering of *sabbaton* in the singular accords with the use of the word throughout the New Testament. It is significant that in fifty-nine of sixty occurrences in the New Testament, Adventists affirm that they refer to the *weekly* Sabbath; but in the sixtieth occurrence they maintain it does not, although all grammatical authorities contradict them.

With regard to Albert Barnes, whom the Adventists delight to quote because he agrees with their interpretation of Colossians 2, his comments are demolished by Dean Henry Alford, a truly great biblical exegete whom the Adventists also frequently quote. Wrote Dean Alford concerning Colossians 2:

> Let no one therefore judge you (pronounce judgment of right or wrong over you, sit in judgment on you) . . . in respect of feasts or new moon, or Sabbaths (i.e., yearly, monthly, or weekly celebrations). (The relative may refer either to the aggregate of the observances mentioned, or to the last mentioned, i.e., the Sabbath. Or it may refer to all.)[53]

---

[51]W. E. Vine, *An Expository Dictionary of New Testament Words* (Old Tappan, N.J.: Fleming H. Revell Company, 1940), 311–313.

[52]M. R. Vincent, *Word Studies in the New Testament* (MacDill AFB, Fl.: MacDonald Publishing Company, n.d.), 2:494.

[53]D. H. Alford, *The New Testament for English Readers* (Grand Rapids, Mich.: William B. Eerdmans Publishing Company, n.d.), 1299–1300.

After making significant comments on the grammar, Dean Alford went even further in his insistence that in verse seventeen, grammatically speaking, the apostle Paul contrasts all the Jewish laws with their fulfillment in Christ, the former being a shadow, pointing forward to the real substance (*soma*), which was Christ.

Alford summed up his comments thus:

> The blessings of the Christian covenant: These are the substance, and the Jewish ordinances the mere type of resemblance, as the shadow is of the living man. . . . We may observe that if the ordinance of the Sabbath had been in any form of lasting obligation on the Christian church, it would have been quite impossible for the apostle to have spoken thus. The fact of an obligatory rest of one day, whether the seventh or the first, would have been directly in the teeth of his assertion here: The holding of such would have been still to retain the shadow, while we possess the substance. And no answer can be given to this by the transparent special-pleading, that he is speaking only of that which was Jewish in such observances: the whole argument being general, and the axiom of verse seventeen universally applicable.[54]

We see that, from a grammatical standpoint, if the Adventists insist that Colossians 2:16 refers only to ceremonial Sabbaths, they run against the use of the word for weekly Sabbaths in the entire New Testament; and, as Alford points out, if "Sabbaths" be allowed, it must include all Sabbaths, weekly, monthly, or yearly. On the other hand, if Adventists admit the correction of the revisers and render Colossians 2:16 "a Sabbath day," its use in the New Testament still refers almost exclusively (see Acts 17:2) to the weekly Sabbath, which Adventists maintain is permanent, although Paul deliberately classes it with the penalty for violating the ordinances that Christ by His death nailed to the cross! (Colossians 2:14).

Dr. J. B. Lightfoot, an acknowledged authority on New Testament Greek, makes this interesting observation:

> The word *sabbata* is derived from the Aramaic *shabbatha* (as distinguished from the Hebrew), and accordingly preserves the Aramaic termination of "a." Hence it was naturally declined as a plural noun, *sabbata, sabbaton*. The New Testament *sabbata* is only once used distinctively as more than a single day, and there the plurality of meaning is brought out by the attached numeral (Acts 17:2).[55]

It is apparent, therefore, that the use of "Sabbath" in the New Testament refutes the Adventist contention that in Colossians 2 it means Sabbaths other than the weekly Sabbath of the Decalogue. Since it is impossible to retain the "shadow" while possessing the "substance" (Colossians 2:17), the Jewish Sabbath and the handwriting of ordinances "which was contrary to us" found their complete fulfillment in the person and work of the Lord Jesus Christ.

Seventh-day Adventists are also deprived of the support of Albert Barnes, because he admits that if Paul had "used the word in the singular number, 'the Sabbath,' it would then of course have been clear that he meant to teach that

---

[54]Alford, 1300.

[55]D. H, Alford, *Commentary on Colossians* (Grand Rapids, Mich.: William B. Eerdmans Publishing Company, n.d.), 225.

that commandment had ceased to be binding and that a Sabbath was no longer to be observed.[56]

Since Barnes makes this admission, and since modern conservative scholarship establishes the singular rendering of "Sabbath" in the New Testament (see RSV, et al.), Adventists find even less support for their position.

We conclude our comments on this passage of Scripture by observing that in Numbers 28 and 29, which list the very "ordinances" referred to in Colossians 2:16–17, the Sabbath is grouped with burnt offerings and new moons (Numbers 28:1–15). Since these offerings and feasts have passed away as the shadow (*skia*), fulfilled in the substance (*soma*) of the cross of Christ, how can the Seventh-day Sabbath be retained? In the light of this Scripture alone, I contend that the argument for Sabbath observance collapses, and the Christian stands under "the perfect law of liberty," which enables him to fulfill "the righteousness of the law" by the imperative of love.

B. *Galatians 4:9–11*

> But now that you have come to know God, or rather to be known by God, how can you turn back again to the weak and beggarly elemental spirits, whose slaves you want to be once more? You observe days, and months, and seasons, and years! I am afraid I have labored over you in vain (RSV).

Paul's epistle to the Galatians was primarily a massive theological effort to bolster the young church against the Judaizers who added to the gospel of grace "another gospel" (1:6), and sought to "pervert the gospel of Christ" (1:7).

Though steeped in Jewish lore and the law of Moses, Paul steadfastly opposed the Judaizers. The entire epistle to the Galatians is an apologetic against those who would seek to bring the Christian "under the law." After mentioning the errors into which the Galatian church had fallen, Paul, evidently with great disgust, remarks, "You observe days, and months, and seasons, and years! I am afraid I have labored over you in vain." In the Greek the expression "days, and months, and seasons, and years," matches both the Septuagint (Greek) translation of the ordinances in Numbers 28 and 29, of which all Sabbaths are a principal part, and the ordinances mentioned in Colossians 2. Paul was familiar with the Septuagint and quoted it, and the law, including the weekly Sabbaths, was so cherished by the Judaizers of his day that its legalistic observance called forth his strong words. Adventists insist that Paul meant ceremonial feasts and yearly Sabbaths, not the weekly Sabbath; but Paul's language and the Septuagint translation of Numbers 28 and 29 refute their objections. It is one thing to interpret your way out of a verse when your interpretation is feasible; it is another to ignore grammar, context, and comparative textual analysis (hermeneutics) as our Adventist friends and others appear to do. To substantiate their interpretation of Paul's statements they do not practice exegesis (taking out of), but eisegesis (reading into) the texts.

After studying Seventh-day Adventist literature, it is my opinion that the overwhelming majority of Seventh-day Adventists do not actually consider themselves "under the law." I believe they fail to realize that by trying to enjoin

---

[56] *The New Testament for English Readers*, 229.

Sabbath observance upon other members of the body of Christ, they are in serious danger of transgressing the gospel of grace. To them Paul says,

> Tell me, you who desire to be under the law, do you not hear the law? . . .
> Now before faith came, we were confined under the law, kept under restraint
> until faith should be revealed. So that the law was our custodian until Christ
> came, that we might be justified by faith. But now that faith has come, we are
> no longer under a custodian; for in Christ Jesus you are all sons of God, through
> faith (Galatians 4:21; 3:23–26, RSV).

Bearing in mind that "the law" in its larger connotation includes the entire Pentateuch, it is apparent from Paul's language that one is "under the law" when he attempts to observe any part of it, because the Christian has been freed from the law. Seventh-day Adventists are doubtless Christians, saved by grace, but we do not find scriptural warrant for their attempt to enjoin the Sabbath upon their fellow believers.

C. Romans 13:8–10

> Owe no one anything, except to love one another; for he who loves his
> neighbor has fulfilled the law. The commandments, "You shall not commit adultery, You shall not kill, You shall not steal, You shall not covet," and any other
> commandment, are summed up in this sentence, "You shall love your neighbor
> as yourself." Love does no wrong to a neighbor; therefore love is the fulfilling
> of the law (RSV).

It is really unnecessary to comment extensively upon the foregoing verses because they speak plainly for themselves.

The Greek word *pleroma*, translated respectively "fulfilled" and "fulfilling" in Romans 13:8–10, RSV, appears ninety times in the New Testament and has the same basic meaning. The apostle Paul surely understood this term; since the Adventists confess the divine inspiration of the Scriptures, they must concede that the Holy Spirit guided his pen. Quoting from the Decalogue upon which the Adventists rely for perpetual Sabbath-keeping, Paul declares, "The commandments . . . are summed up in this sentence, 'You shall love your neighbor as yourself.' Love does no wrong to a neighbor; therefore love is the fulfilling of the law." In verse eight the apostle declares, "He who loves his neighbor has fulfilled the law"; and since he quotes from the Decalogue as part of the law, the fourth commandment is also fulfilled, not by rigid observance of a given day, but by loving one's neighbor as oneself! Since it is impossible in the Christian context to love one's neighbor at all apart from loving God as the prerequisite, the issue is clear. The false teaching that love of one's neighbor does not fulfill all the law of God comes from a failure to realize that our love for God and neighbor stems from God's initiating act of love in Christ. This law of love is first enunciated in Leviticus 19:18, which our Lord coupled with the commandment to "love the Lord thy God" (Deuteronomy 6:4–5), and stated that observance of those two commandments fulfilled "all the law and the prophets."

While our Adventist brethren may seek to escape the implications of Colossians 2:14–17 and to explain away Galatians 4:9–11, in the present passage the Holy Spirit twice declares that love fulfills the law. They cannot exempt the

Sabbath from this context without destroying the unity of the "Eternal Ten," hence their dilemma.

In Galatians Paul also declares, "The whole law is fulfilled in one word. 'You shall love your neighbor as yourself' " (5:14, RSV). So we see that Paul's theology rested upon the imperative of love. Therefore, it is my conviction that the Holy Spirit, not the Christian church, is the authority for the nullification of all Sabbath-keeping. How any student of New Testament Greek could read the unmistakable language of the apostle and then exclude the Sabbath commandment from his argument passes my understanding.

D. *Romans 14:4–6, 10, 12–13*

> Who are you to pass judgment on the servant of another? It is before his own master that he stands or falls. And he will be upheld, for the Master is able to make him stand. One man esteems one day as better than another, while another man esteems all days alike. Let every one be fully convinced in his own mind. He who observes the day, observes it in honor of the Lord. He also who eats, eats in honor of the Lord, since he gives thanks to God; while he who abstains, abstains in honor of the Lord and gives thanks to God. . . . Why do you pass judgment on your brother? Or you, why do you despise your brother? For we shall all stand before the judgment seat of God. . . . So each of us shall give account of himself to God. Then let us no more pass judgment on one another, but rather decide never to put a stumbling-block or hindrance in the way of a brother (RSV).

In this writer's opinion, and according to Romans 14, the Seventh-day Adventist is entitled to observe the Seventh-day Sabbath if he feels that this is what God desires. Further than this, the Holy Spirit adjures us not to "pass judgment" on our fellow Christians regarding such matters as observance of days and diet. I believe that Seventh-day Adventists, Seventh-day Baptists, and Sabbatarians of other religious groups have the right to worship on the seventh day in the liberty wherein Christ has made us free. It is wrong and unchristian to discriminate against Sabbatarians merely because they "esteem" the Sabbath above the first day of the week, or the Lord's Day. I suggest it is no more legalistic for them to observe the seventh day out of conviction than it is for the Christian church to observe the first day. It is a matter of liberty and conscience.

If Seventh-day Adventists, however, would follow the biblical teaching of Romans 14 with regard to those who wish to observe Sunday, we would not have the conflict that has been generated by their dogmatic insistence that all should worship on the Sabbath. The sad fact is, however, that all Sabbatarians transgress the very counsels given by the apostle Paul in the above cited passage.

Of course, Seventh-day Adventists feel that they are called upon to perpetuate or promulgate certain truths that they believe are found in the Word of God, and which they believe are to be emphasized in "these last days." Furthermore, they believe that the counsels of Ellen G. White emphasize the importance of these truths. Granting their basic premise that God has indeed spoken to them concerning Sabbath observance, it is easy to see the source of their zeal. But I feel that there is good evidence that the "Spirit of prophecy" is not what they claim; and their "special truths" have, to say the least, questionable theological origins. Non-Adventists reject the claims that they make for White,

and merely because Adventists accept her counsel is no reason for other Christians to feel bound to do so. We repeat—the faith the Adventists place in "the Spirit of prophecy," which has endorsed their "special truths," sincere though they may be, does not entitle them to contradict the counsel of the Holy Spirit as revealed in the Word of God. This I believe they have done. I could cite scores of references from contemporary Adventist writers who do indeed pass judgment upon their Christian brethren and upon the Christian church at large, because the latter do not observe the Seventh-day Sabbath. It is my opinion in these cases that they neglect the counsel of the Holy Spirit: "One man esteems one day as better than another, while another man esteems all days alike. Let everyone be fully convinced in his own mind. He who observes the day, observes it in honor of the Lord. . . . Happy is he who has no reason to judge himself for what he approves . . . for whatever does not proceed from faith is sin" (Romans 14:5–6, 22–23, RSV).

By contending that other members of the body of Christ should recognize "the Spirit of prophecy," Seventh-day Adventists appear to juxtapose the "Spirit of prophecy" with the Holy Spirit who says, "Then let us no more pass judgment on one another, but rather decide never to put a stumbling-block or hindrance in the way of a brother" (v. 13).

There can be little doubt that the great majority of Christians who worship on Sunday would never have discriminated against the Seventh-day Adventists, had the latter not insisted upon "passing judgment" on first-day observance as opposed to Sabbath-keeping. Although motivated by the best intentions and sincere in faith, Adventists have nevertheless put a stumbling block or hindrance in the way of fellow Christians by their rigid Sabbatarianism. It is indeed unfortunate that such a source of strife exists among Christians.

The fourteenth chapter of Romans is a masterpiece on the subject of Christian liberty, not only in diet but in worship, and in the context of all Paul's writings on the subject it appears that Adventists ignore the plain teaching of Scripture about the observance of days. We ask, should they not be more charitable in the light of 1 Corinthians 13? They would thus avoid opposition from their fellow Christians.

These four passages from the writings of Paul reflect the position of the historical Christian church from the times of the Fathers and the Reformers to the leading exegetical commentators of our day. The reader should remember that Adventist arguments, although buttressed by selected Bible passages (sometimes cited out of context), must be studied in the clear light of these four passages, which contain the comprehensive New Testament teaching on Sabbatarianism. The early Christian church met upon the first day of the week (1 Corinthians 16:2). The disciples received the Holy Spirit on the first day of the week; collections were taken for the saints on the first day of the week; and historical evidence establishes that the first day of the week was the Lord's Day, the memorial of the new creation in Christ Jesus that completely fulfilled the law in Christ.

No amount of argument by Adventists can alter these facts, and if we believe the apostle Paul was inspired by the Holy Spirit, it is apparent that we must reject Sabbatarianism. We do not judge Seventh-day Adventists for their Sabbath observance, and they in turn should extend the same charity to their fellow

Christians. Only in the recognition of the principles of Romans 14 can true unity in the body of Christ be realized. There can be no legislation of moral choice on the basis of "special revelation." This we believe is the case in Seventh-day Adventism, for it was Ellen G. White's "Vision" confirming Joseph Bates' "Seal of the Living God" concept as set forth in his pamphlet on the Sabbath that established Sabbatarianism in Seventh-day Adventism. The Bible must be the supreme court of appeal and authority, and the verdict of this court, it appears to me, invalidates the contentions of our Adventist friends.[57]

III. *Author's Note on "The Mark of the Beast"*

The subjects of the Seventh-day Sabbath and the mark of the beast already have been covered in sufficient detail. However, it is often charged that Adventists teach that salvation depends upon observance of the seventh day as Sabbath, and that the mark of the beast (Revelation 13:16–17) rests upon all Sunday-keepers. For this reason, the record should be examined.

One ex-Adventist layman writes that there are "characteristic false doctrines of the sect . . . [notably] the obligation of seventh-day Sabbath observance on the part of all professing Christians, the 'mark of the beast' for Sunday-keepers." Now if this charge were correct, we too would doubt the possibility of fellowship with Adventists. But such is not the case. Ellen G. White on a number of occasions pointedly denied what is claimed to be the position of the Adventist denomination on this point. Wrote White:

> No one has yet received the mark of the beast. Testing time is not yet come. There are true Christians in every church, not excepting the Roman Catholic communion. None are condemned until they have had the light and have seen the obligation of the fourth commandment. . . . Sunday-keeping is not yet the mark of the beast, and will not be until the decree goes forth causing men to worship this idol Sabbath.[58]

In addition to this quotation, the Adventists have stated,

> When Sunday observance shall be enforced by law, and the world shall be enlightened concerning the obligation of the true Sabbath, then whoever shall transgress the command of God, to obey a precept which has no higher authority than that of Rome, will thereby honor popery above God.[59]

To sum up, the Adventists declare,

> God surely does not hold men accountable for truth that has not yet come to their knowledge and understanding. . . . We hold the firm conviction that millions of devout Christians of all faiths throughout all past centuries, as well as those today who are sincerely trusting in Christ their Saviour for salvation and are following Him according to their best light, are unquestionably saved. Thousands of such went to the stake as martyrs for Christ and for their faith. Moreover, untold numbers of godly Roman Catholics will surely be included. God reads the heart and deals with the intent and understanding. . . . Seventh-day Adventists interpret the prophecies relating to the beast and the reception

---

[57]For further study on the issue see D. A. Carson, General Editor, *From Sabbath Day to Lord's Day* (Grand Rapids, Mich.: Zondervan Publishing House).
[58]*Questions on Doctrine*, 183–184.
[59]Ibid., 178.

of his work as something that will come into sharp focus just before the return of our Lord in glory. It is our understanding that this issue will then become a worldwide test.[60]

The statement, then, that Seventh-day Adventists believe that anyone who is a Sunday-keeper has the mark of the beast or the mark of apostasy is made without regard to the facts. Why do these critics attempt to make it appear that Adventists believe that their fellow Christians are lost? The authoritative statements of this denomination are available for all to read. Doubtless some Seventh-day Adventist writers have gone contrary to the teaching of the denomination, but to indict the entire denomination for the excesses of a few is neither ethical nor Christian.

The Sanctuary, the Investigative Judgment, and the Scapegoat

The foundation of Seventh-day Adventism is its view of prophecy, which is of the historicist school of interpretation, a school that maintains that prophecy is to be understood in the light of consecutive fulfillment in history. The exaggeration of this idea led William Miller and his followers to teach that the 2300 days of Daniel 8:14 were actually 2300 years. Figuring from 457 B.C., the now verified time of the decree to rebuild Jerusalem (Daniel 9:25), the Millerites thought that A.D. 1843 would be the date of the second advent of Jesus Christ. Miller and his followers, among whom were James and Ellen G. White and other prominent Seventh-day Adventists, understood "the sanctuary" of Daniel 8:14 to be the earth that would be cleansed by Christ at the "great and terrible Day of the Lord," which they interpreted as the second advent of Christ. We have seen, however, that the Millerites were bitterly disappointed; and when Christ did not appear, Miller himself renounced the system and all resultant movements, including Seventh-day Adventism. But the early Seventh-day Adventists, relying upon the "vision" of Elder Hiram Edson, transferred the location of the sanctuary from the earth to heaven, and taught that in 1844 Christ went instead into the second apartment of the sanctuary in heaven (which contemporary Seventh-day Adventists term the second phase of His ministry), there to review the cases of those deemed to be worthy of eternal life. This phase of our Lord's ministry the Seventh-day Adventists call the "investigative judgment." This unique theory is intended, I believe, to discipline Christians by the threat of impending judgment and condemnation upon those whose cases are decided upon unfavorably by our Lord. When concluded, the investigative judgment will usher in the second advent of Jesus Christ, according to the Seventh-day Adventist theology, and the devil, prefigured by the second or scapegoat of Leviticus 16 *(Azazel)*, will bear away unto eternal destruction or annihilation his responsibility for causing sin to enter the universe.

James White, a stalwart Seventh-day Adventist leader, when first confronted with the doctrine of the investigative judgment, opposed it *en toto*, giving in substance the very arguments put forth by all subsequent ex-Seventh-day Adventists. And it was only after considerable time that James White finally acceded to the doctrine of the investigative judgment. There are many critics of Seventh-day

---
[60]*Questions on Doctrine,* 178, 184–185.

Adventism who, when approaching the sanctuary, investigative judgment, and scapegoat concepts, deride and mock the early Adventists and their descendants for accepting such unsupported, extrabiblical theories, but derision is not the answer, and it should be remembered that Adventists hold these doctrines in sincerity. Therefore, if they are ever to be persuaded of the mistaken nature of their faith, in these areas at least, only the facts of Scripture and the guidance of the Holy Spirit will bring it about.

The view of Hiram Edson is, so far as this writer is concerned, an attempt to escape the terrible calamity that befell the Millerite movement and the disappointment and embarrassment that must have followed the failure of the Millerite prophecies and their interpretations of the book of Daniel. We shall confine ourselves in this short analysis to the salient points of the theological issues raised by these special teachings or doctrines of the Advent message. In the matter of prophetic interpretation, this writer is convinced that the Holy Spirit has wisely veiled from the prying eyes and intellect of man many great truths that will doubtless be revealed toward the end of the age. It is not for us to judge whether the preterist, historicist, or futurist schools of interpretation are correct, and we ought not to overly concern ourselves with when Christ is coming, whether before, during, or after the Great Tribulation. Rather, we ought to be concerned that He *is* coming, because His coming is indeed "the blessed hope" of the Christian church (Titus 2:13), which hope Adventists and non-Adventists alike who share the Christian message and faith anticipate with joy.

The heavenly sanctuary and investigative judgment teaching is still an integral part of foundational Adventist doctrine. It is described in point twenty-three of the "Fundamental Beliefs of Seventh-day Adventists" in the following words:

> There is a sanctuary in heaven, the true tabernacle, which the Lord set up and not man. In it Christ ministers on our behalf, making available to believers the benefits of His atoning sacrifice offered once for all on the cross. He was inaugurated as our great high priest and began His intercessory ministry at the time of His ascension. In 1844, at the end of the prophetic period of 2300 days, He entered the second and last phase of His atoning ministry. It is a work of investigative judgment, which is part of the ultimate disposition of all sin, typified by the cleansing of the ancient Hebrew sanctuary on the Day of Atonement. In that typical service the sanctuary was cleansed with the blood of animal sacrifices, but the heavenly things are purified with the perfect sacrifice of the blood of Jesus. The investigative judgment reveals to heavenly intelligences who among the dead are asleep in Christ and therefore, in Him, are deemed worthy to have a part in the first resurrection. It also makes manifest who among the living are abiding in Christ, keeping the commandments of God and the faith of Jesus, and in Him, therefore, are ready for translation into His everlasting kingdom. This judgment vindicates the justice of God in saving those who believe in Jesus. It declares that those who have remained loyal to God shall receive the kingdom. The completion of this ministry of Christ will mark the close of human probation before the Second Advent.[61]

---

[61] *Seventh-day Adventists Believe: A Biblical Exposition of Twenty-Seven Fundamental Doctrines* (Washington, D.C.: Ministerial Association, General Conference of Seventh-day Adventists, 1988), 312. (These twenty-seven doctrines were published earlier in a special edition of the *Adventist Review*, 1981.)

I. *The Sanctuary*

Since the Seventh-day Adventists believe that the sanctuary to be cleansed is in heaven (Daniel 8:14), which the Millerites identified as the earth (a regrettable early mistake), we might ask, What is the purpose of the heavenly sanctuary and its cleansing? What are the Adventists really teaching?

The book of Hebrews definitely sets forth a "heavenly sanctuary" of which Christ is the minister (Hebrews 8:1–2), and the writer of the epistle repeatedly contrasts the Lord Jesus Christ, our risen high priest, with the Aaronic priesthood. He shows that as a priest after the order of Melchizedek, Christ derives His authority from the power of "an endless life" (Hebrews 7:16), and that He was both high priest and an offering on Calvary.[62] And this Adventists also emphasize.

It is futile, therefore, to argue that the word "sanctuary" does not apply to heaven or something of a heavenly nature, since the Scriptures teach that it does. But the Adventists' error is that they draw from the Scriptures' interpretations that cannot be substantiated by exegesis, but rest largely upon inference and deduction and are taken from theological applications of their own design.

In their sanctuary teaching, the Adventists do indeed declare, in the words of Ellen G. White:

> As anciently the sins of the people were by faith, placed upon the sin offering and through its blood transferred in figure to the earthly sanctuary, so in the new covenant the sins of the repentant are by faith placed upon Christ and transferred in fact to the heavenly sanctuary. And as the typical cleansing of the earthly was accomplished by the removal of the sins by which it had been polluted, so the actual cleansing of the heavenly is to be accomplished by the removal or blotting out of the sins that are there recorded.[63]

Here we have the very heart of Seventh-day Adventist teaching relative to the expiation of sin, which is that the sins of believers have been transferred, deposited, or recorded in the heavenly sanctuary, and are now being dealt with in the investigative judgment.

Let us again listen to White:

> In the sin offerings presented during the year, a substitute had been accepted in the sinner's stead; but the blood of the victim had not made full atonement for the sin. It had only provided a means by which the sin was transferred to the sanctuary. By the offering of the blood the sinner acknowledged the authority of the law, confessed the guilt of his transgression, and expressed his faith in Him who was to take away the sin of the world; but he was not entirely released from the condemnation of the law. On the day of atonement the high priest having taken an offering for the congregation went into the most holy place with the blood and sprinkled it upon the mercy seat above the table of the law. Thus the claims of the law that demanded the life of the sinner were satisfied. Then in his character of mediator the priest took the sins upon himself and, leaving the sanctuary, he bore with him the burden of Israel's guilt. At the door of the tabernacle he laid his hands upon the head of the scapegoat, confessed over him all the iniquities of the children of Israel and all their transgressions and all their sins, putting them upon the head of the goat. And as the

---

[62]Hebrews 7:2, 4–7, 14, 16, 22, 25–26; 8:1–2, 6–8, 10; 9:2–12, 14, 23–24, 26–28; 10:1–10, 12, 19–21.
[63]*The Great Controversy*, 421–422.

goat bearing these sins was sent away, they were with him regarded as forever separated from the people.[64]

White further stated, "Not until the goat had been thus sent away did the people regard themselves as freed from the burden of their sins.[65]

The Adventist teaching is that Christ as our high priest transferred the sins of believers (i.e., the record of sins, in Adventist thinking) to the heavenly sanctuary, which will be finally cleansed at the conclusion of the great Day of Atonement, the investigative judgment having been concluded. Then the cases of all the righteous having been decided, their sins will be blotted out, followed by the return of the Lord Jesus Christ in glory. White made it clear that the sin transferred to the sanctuary in heaven would remain there until the conclusion of the investigative judgment and the subsequent cleansing of the sanctuary.

> The blood of Christ, while it was to release the repentant sinner from the condemnation of the law, was not to cancel the sin; it would stand on record in the sanctuary until the final atonement; so then the type, the blood of the sin offering removed the sin from the penitent but it rested in the sanctuary until the day of atonement.[66]

To substantiate this particular position, Adventists quote Acts 3:19 in the King James Version: "Repent ye therefore, and be converted, that your sins may be blotted out, when the times of refreshing shall come from the presence of the Lord."

The chief difficulty with the Adventist contention is that the Greek of Acts 3:19 does not substantiate their teaching that the blotting out of sins will take place as a separate event from the forgiveness of sins. According to modern translations (the Revised, the American Standard, the Revised Standard, and the New International Versions), the text should read "Repent therefore and turn again that your sins may be blotted out, that times of refreshing may come from the presence of the Lord." Peter was urging his listeners to repent, to turn from their sins, in order to receive the forgiveness that comes only from the presence of the Lord. This text gives our Adventist brethren no support for their "heavenly sanctuary" and "investigative judgment" teachings.

II. *The Investigative Judgment*

The Bible explicitly declares that when one accepts Christ as Lord, God freely forgives all his sins and ushers him from spiritual death to spiritual life solely on the merits of the perfect life and death of the Lord Jesus Christ. To this Adventists fully agree, and this makes their teaching on investigative judgment inconsistent. In John 5:24 the Greek deals a devastating blow to the Seventh-day Adventist concept of investigative judgment: "He that hears my word and believes him that sent me has everlasting life and shall not come under judgment but is passed from death to life" (literal translation).

Christians, therefore, need not anticipate any investigative judgment for

---

[64] *The Great Controversy*, 421–422.
[65] Ellen G. White, *Patriarchs and Prophets* (Washington, D.C.: Review and Herald Publishing Association, n.d.), 355–356.
[66] Ibid., 357.

their sins. True, we shall all appear before the judgment seat of Christ to receive the deeds done in the body (2 Corinthians 5:10), but this has nothing to do with any investigative judgment. It is a judgment for rewards. Several judgments are mentioned in the Bible, but it is my opinion that not one passage substantiates the "investigative judgment" theory—for theory it truly is, relying upon out-of-context quotations and supported by the "Spirit of prophecy." They are welcome to this dogma, but faithfulness to New Testament teaching forbids the idea that "the blood of Christ, while it was to release the repentant sinner from the condemnation of the law, was not to cancel the sin; it would stand on record in the sanctuary until the final atonement" or "until blotting out of all sins." The Scriptures clearly teach, "If we confess our sins, he is faithful and just to forgive us our sins, and to cleanse us from all unrighteousness" (1 John 1:9). Further evidence of the completeness of the forgiveness of God and the cleansing power of the blood of Christ is found in the first chapter of the book of Hebrews, where the Holy Spirit informs us that Christ as "the image of God" "upholds all things by the word of his power" and that on Calvary He by himself purged our sins (Hebrews 1:3).

For the word translated "purged" or "purification" the Holy Spirit chose the Greek word *katharismon*, from which we derive *cathartic*. Hence it is said of the Lord Jesus and His sacrifice that He alone, "by himself," gave to our sinful spiritual natures the complete catharsis of forgiveness and purification on the cross. Christians may now rejoice that the Lord Jesus Christ is not engaged in weighing our frailties and failures, for "He knoweth our frame; he remembereth that we are dust" (Psalm 103:14). We cannot, therefore, accept the Adventist teaching on the investigative judgment since we are convinced that it has no warrant in Scripture. We must reject what we believe to be their unbiblical concept that the sins of believers remain in the sanctuary until the day of blotting out of sins.

Our Adventist brethren, in teaching this doctrine, are overlooking the fact that "the Lord knoweth them that are his" (2 Timothy 2:19), and it was no less an authority than the Lord Jesus Christ who declared, "I . . . know my sheep" (John 10:14). The apostle Paul declares that "Christ died for the ungodly . . . while we were yet sinners, Christ died for us . . . we were reconciled to God by the death of his Son" (Romans 5:6, 8, 10). This does not balance with the Seventh-day Adventist teachings of the heavenly sanctuary, the transfer of sins and the investigative judgment. In his epistle to the Colossians the apostle Paul further declared, "Having made peace through the blood of his cross . . . you, that were sometime alienated and enemies in your mind by wicked works, yet now hath he reconciled in the body of his flesh through death, to present you holy and unblameable and unreprovable in his sight" (1:20–22). Once again the Holy Spirit declares that we are now reconciled through the death of Christ, having been forgiven all our trespasses through the blood of the cross (Colossians 2:13–14).

Seventh-day Adventists, relying upon Daniel 7:9–10; 8:14; and Revelation 14:7; 11:18, which refer to "judgment" and "books," attempt to "prove" that the investigative judgment is meant, but examination of each of these texts in context reveals the paucity of the claim. None of these texts has anything to do with any judgment going on now. Neither the grammar nor context supports

such a contention. One can only base this interpretation by acknowledging the Adventist premise that the historicist school of prophetic interpretation is the only accurate one, and by accepting the Adventist definition of the sanctuary and judgment. It is significant that non-Adventist biblical scholars have never allowed these so-called "investigative judgment" interpretations, because there is no scriptural warrant for them apart from implication and inference.

As mentioned previously, James White at first categorically denied the teaching of the investigative judgment and gave good reasons for his rejection. Although he later embraced this doctrine, his objections are still valid:

> It is not necessary that the final sentence should be given before the first resurrection as some have taught; for the names of the saints are written in heaven and Jesus and the angels will certainly know who to raise and gather to the New Jerusalem. . . . The event that will introduce the judgment day will be the coming of the Son of Man to raise the sleeping saints and to change those that are alive at that time.[67]

Relative to the time for the beginning of the great judgment, James White quoted, "I charge thee therefore before God, and the Lord Jesus Christ, who shall judge the quick and the dead at [not before] his appearing in his kingdom" (2 Timothy 4:1).[68]

Asked when he expected the judgment of Daniel 7 to take place, James White stated,

> Daniel in the night vision saw that judgment was given to the saints of the most high, but not to mortal saints. Not until the ancient of days comes will the little horn cease prevailing, which will not be until he is destroyed by the brightness of Christ's coming.[69]

We see by this that James White at the beginning rejected the investigative judgment with good reasons. But two more of his statements are quite revealing:

> The advent angel, Revelation 14:6–7, saying with a loud voice, "Fear God, and give glory to him; for the hour of his judgment is come" does not prove that the day of judgment came in 1840 or in 1844, nor that it will come prior to the Second Advent. . . . Some have contended that the day of judgment was prior to the Second Advent. This view is certainly without foundation in the Word of God.[70]

At that time, James White was on good biblical ground, but he later forsook this position for the theories and prophetic speculation promulgated by his wife and other influential Adventist leaders. The Lord Jesus Christ himself placed the judgment after His second advent when He said, "When the Son of man shall come in his glory, and all the holy angels with him, then shall he sit upon the throne of his glory: and before him shall be gathered all nations" (Matthew 25:31–32). One need only read the following passages to see that the judgments of God upon believers and unbelievers are future events. Notice the language employed:

[67]*A Word to the Little Flock* (1847), 24.
[68]James White in the *Advent Review* (August 1850); the brackets are his.
[69]Ibid.
[70]Ibid.

1. "The quick and the dead at his appearing and his kingdom" (Acts 10:42; 1 Peter 4:5; 2 Timothy 4:1).

2. "When the Son of Man shall come in his glory . . . he shall set the sheep on his right hand, but the goats on the left" (Matthew 25:31–33).

3. The wheat and the tares: "The harvest is the end of the world" (Matthew 13:24–30, 36–43).

4. "For we must all appear before the judgment seat of Christ; that every one may receive the things done in his body . . . whether it be good or bad" (2 Corinthians 5:10).

5. "So then every one of us shall give account of himself to God" (Romans 14:10–12).

6. "Every man's work shall be made manifest: for the day shall declare it" (1 Corinthians 3:13).

In addition to these verses, which unmistakably indicate future judgment, the writer to the Hebrews declares, "As it is appointed unto men once to die, but after this the judgment" (Hebrews 9:27). This, to any non-Adventist, is conclusive evidence that there is no investigative judgment now going on for believers to fear.

Hebrews 4:13 also exposes the faulty concept of investigative judgment: "Neither is there any creature that is not manifest in his sight: but all things are naked and opened unto the eyes of him with whom we have to do." Since our Lord knows the disposition of "cases" allegedly being reviewed in heaven, what need is there for "investigative judgment"? We believe the Scriptures decidedly do not warrant such a doctrine.

Concluding our comments on the investigative judgment, note that rewards for believers will be meted out after the second coming of our Lord, or at "the resurrection of the just," for the resurrection of life (John 5:29; Luke 14:14). Even the Adventists concur in believing that the judgment of the wicked will not take place until the end of the millennial age (Revelation 20:11–12; Matthew 25:31–46). Once again the investigative judgment theory conflicts with the biblical teaching on judgment regarding both believer and unbeliever. To this writer's mind, the great error of the sanctuary and investigative judgment teachings is the premise that sins confessed by Christians are not fully dealt with until the conclusion of the investigative judgment, a position Scripture will not allow.

Adventists, in the opinion of conservative biblical scholars, not to mention the liberal wing of Protestantism, are only speculating with their sanctuary and investigative judgment theories. Actually, most are agreed that they have created doctrines to compensate for errors in prophetic interpretation. But the very doctrines intended to solve their theological problems have in turn only increased their dilemma—a dilemma which they have yet to solve! Romans 8:1 declares, "There is therefore now no condemnation [i.e., judgment] to them which are in Christ Jesus" (bracketed added); and here every Christian's case must rest. We can never be indicted again for our sins or convicted for them, because Christ has fully paid the penalty. For those who believe in Jesus Christ, there is no judgment for the penalty of sin, i.e., eternal separation from God. However, as 2 Corinthians 5:10 teaches, we shall be judged for how we live as Christians. Seventh-day Adventists, we believe, needlessly subscribe to a doctrine that neither solves their difficulties nor engenders peace of mind. Holding as

they do to the doctrine of the investigative judgment, it is extremely difficult for us to understand how they can experience the joy of salvation and the knowledge of sins forgiven. Of course, this is true of so-called Arminian theology on the whole, which teaches that eternal life, given by God to the believer, is conditioned by the sustained faith of the believer in the grace of God.

There is, however, clarification and summary of the doctrine of investigative judgment in *Questions on Doctrine.*

> It is our understanding that Christ, a high priest, concludes His intercessory ministry in heaven in a work of judgment. He begins His great work of judgment in the investigative phase. At the conclusion of the investigation, the sentence of judgment is pronounced. Then as judge, Christ descends to execute, or carry into effect, that sentence. For sublime grandeur, nothing in the prophetic word can compare with the description of our Lord as He descends the skies, not as a priest, but as King of kings and Lord of lords. And with Him are all the angels of heaven. He commands the dead, and that great unnumbered host of those that are asleep in Christ spring forth into immortality. At the same time those among the living who are truly God's children are caught up together with the redeemed of all ages to meet their Saviour in the air, and to be forever with the Lord. . . .
>
> As we have suggested, Seventh-day Adventists believe that at the second coming of Christ the eternal destiny of all men will have been irrevocably fixed by the decisions of a court of judgment. Such a judgment obviously would take place while men are still living on the earth. Man might be quite unaware of what is going on in heaven. It is hardly to be supposed that God would fail to warn men of such an impending judgment and its results. Seventh-day Adventists believe prophecy does foretell such a judgment, and indeed point out the very time at which it is to begin. . . .
>
> When the high priest in the typical service had concluded his work in the earthly sanctuary on the Day of Atonement, he came to the door of the sanctuary. Then the final act with the second goat, Azazel, took place. In like manner, when our Lord completes His ministry in the heavenly sanctuary, He, too, will come forth. When He does this, the day of salvation will have closed forever. Every soul will have made his decision for or against the divine Son of God. Then upon Satan, the instigator of sin, is rolled back his responsibility for having initiated and introduced iniquity into the universe. But he [Satan] in no sense vicariously atones for the sins of God's people. All this Christ fully bore, and vicariously atoned for, on Calvary's cross.[71]

It is apparent, then, that for Adventists the investigative judgment is something very real, and they believe that the final blotting out of their sins depends upon the results of that judgment, culminating in the final destruction (annihilation) of the wicked and of Satan, typified by the scapegoat of Leviticus 16.

III. *The Scapegoat*

Perhaps no doctrine of Seventh-day Adventism has been more misunderstood than the teaching concerning the scapegoat (Leviticus 16). Because of certain unfortunate choices of words by a few Adventist writers, the impression has been given that Adventists regard Satan as a partial sin bearer for the people of God. This may be accounted for by the fact that in the early days of Adventism

---

[71] *Questions on Doctrine,* 422–423, 444.

they built much of their theology on the typology of the Mosaic sanctuary, using almost exclusively the phraseology of the King James Version. Hence they got into difficulty when dealing with such involved Old Testament concepts as the scapegoat. Not a few scholars, however, support the Seventh-day Adventist concept that Azazel represents Satan. Be that as it may, the important thing is the place of the scapegoat with regard to the atonement of Christ. Do Seventh-day Adventists believe that Satan eventually becomes their vicarious sin bearer? Not at all! This writer is convinced that the Adventist concept of the scapegoat in connection with the Day of Atonement, the sanctuary, and the investigative judgment is a bizarre combination of prophetic interpretation and typology; but it is by no means the soul-destroying doctrine that many people think it is. Let the Adventists speak for themselves:

> We take our stand without qualification on the gospel platform that the death of Jesus Christ provides the sole propitiation for our sins (1 John 2:2; 4:10); that there is salvation through no other means or medium, and no other name by which we may be saved (Acts 4:12); and that the shed blood of Jesus Christ alone brings remission for our sins (Matthew 26:28). That is foundational.
>
> When Satan tempted our first parents to take and eat of the forbidden fruit, he as well as they had inescapable responsibility in that act—he the instigator, and they the perpetrators. And similarly, through the ages—in all sin, Satan is involved in responsibility, as the originator and instigator, or tempter (John 8:44; Romans 6:16; 1 John 3:8).
>
> Now concerning my sin, Christ died for my sins (Romans 5:8). He was wounded for my transgressions and for my iniquities (Isaiah 53). He assumed my responsibilities, and His blood alone cleanses me from all sin (1 John 1:7). The atonement for my sin is made solely by the shed blood of Christ.
>
> Concerning Satan's sin, and his responsibility as instigator and tempter, no salvation is provided for him. He must be punished for his responsibility. . . . He must himself "atone" for his sin in causing men to transgress, in the same way that a master criminal suffers on the gallows or in the electric chair for his responsibility in the crimes that he has caused others to commit. It is in this sense only that we can understand the words of Leviticus 16:10 concerning the scapegoat, to make atonement with him.
>
> Satan is the responsible mastermind in the great crime of sin, and his responsibility will return upon his own head. The crushing weight of his responsibility in the sins of the whole world—of the wicked as well as of the righteous—must be rolled back upon him. Simple justice demands that while Christ suffers for my guilt, Satan must also be punished as the instigator of sin.
>
> Satan makes no atonement for our sins. But Satan will ultimately have to bear the retributive punishment for his responsibility in the sins of all men, both righteous and wicked.
>
> Seventh-day Adventists therefore repudiate *en toto* any idea, suggestion, or implication that Satan is in any sense or degree our sin bearer. The thought is abhorrent to us, and appallingly sacrilegious.
>
> Only Christ, the Creator, the one and only God-man, could make a substitutionary atonement for men's transgressions. And this Christ did completely, perfectly, and once for all, on Golgotha.[72]

To be sure, the Seventh-day Adventists have a unique concept of the scape-

---

[72] *Questions on Doctrine*, 396, 398–400.

goat, but in the light of their clearly worded explanation, no critic could any longer with honesty indict them for heresy where the atonement of our Lord is concerned. The Adventists have stated unequivocally that Jesus Christ is their sole propitiation for sin and that Satan has no part whatsoever in the expiation of sin. This writer agrees that Satan is the master criminal of the universe and that it is axiomatic, therefore, that he should suffer as the instigator of angelic and human rebellion. There are, of course, many interpretations of Leviticus 16 set forth by learned scholars, the great majority of whom are most certainly not Adventists; so at best the question is quite open. The *Abingdon Bible Commentary* (Methodist) relative to Leviticus 16 and the scapegoats states,

> On the goats lots are to be cast, one for Jehovah and the other for Azazel. The translation "Dismissal" in the Revised Version margin here (cf. removal in ASV margin) is inadmissible being based on a false etymology. What the word meant is unknown but it should be retained as a proper name of a wilderness demon.

To this statement could be added the opinions of Samuel Zwemer, E. W. Hengstenberg, J. B. Rotherham, and J. Russell Howden, the last of whom wrote in the *Sunday School Times* of January 15, 1927:

> The goat for Azazel as it is sometimes misleadingly translated, typifies God's challenge to Satan. Of the two goats, one was for Jehovah signifying God's acceptance of the sin offering; the other was for Azazel. This is probably to be understood as a person being parallel with Jehovah in the preceding clause. So Azazel is probably a synonym for Satan.

Although Seventh-day Adventists have no exegetical support for their sanctuary and investigative judgment theories, one thing is certain: They have more than substantial scholastic support for assigning the title "Satan" to Azazel in Leviticus 16 concerning the scapegoat. Nevertheless, where the Scripture does not speak specifically it is far wiser to withhold comment. Many critics, in their zeal to shred Seventh-day Adventism and classify it as "a dangerous non-Christian cult," lay much stress upon the scapegoat teaching. In the light of current Adventist statements concerning their concept of the scapegoat, the misunderstandings of the past have at last been brought out into the open, clarified, and presented in a plausible manner.

Much, much more could be written concerning the Seventh-day Adventist concepts of the sanctuary, investigative judgment, and the scapegoat, since they are inseparably linked together. But such writers as W. W. Fletcher (*The Reasons for My Faith*) and other ex-Seventh-day Adventists have exhaustively refuted the position of their former affiliation. The reader is urged to consider the bibliography for additional information on this subject. The saving grace of the entire situation is that the Adventists fortunately deny the logical conclusions to which their doctrine must lead them; i.e., a negation of the full validity of the atonement of Christ, the validity of which they absolutely affirm and embrace with considerable fervor—a paradoxical situation at best!

IV. *Author's Note on "The Scapegoat"*

We could wish that some of the earlier nonrepresentative Seventh-day Adventist statements on the scapegoat teaching had not been made or, better

yet, that they were not still circulated in some quarters. However, to ignore their honest current declarations is, I believe, fundamentally unfair. It appears to me to be little more than blind prejudice. One review of the book *Questions on Doctrine* contains an error frequently found in critical writings. Imputing to their account a position the Adventists do not hold, the review then proceeds to destroy it as if, in the final analysis, it had both exposed and refuted a pernicious error. While it is true that the Seventh-day Adventists do believe that Azazel, in Leviticus 16, does represent Satan, their interpretation of it is far removed from this reviewer's straw man. After quoting the Seventh-day Adventist statement: "Seventh-day Adventists repudiate *en toto* any idea . . . that Satan is in any sense our sin bearer," this review states, "but then two entire chapters are devoted to proving that Satan did bear our sin." It goes on to describe the Adventist position as "repulsive blasphemy" and "unholy twisting of the Scripture. If the Seventh-day Adventists were sound in everything but this and still held this one gross error, we would still have to consider them as an unscriptural cult."[73]

Now, with some other portions of this review we are in agreement. But many of the statements show a marked predisposition toward removing various statements from context and placing them together to prove contradiction without respect to their setting. It ignores all the Seventh-day Adventist statements that contradict these out-of-context criticisms. The very chapter alluded to clearly shows that Adventists repudiate the meaning the reviewer has attached to the scapegoat concept. As we have noted, it is regrettable that this teaching has been so stated in some Adventist writings as to give the impression that the scapegoat represents Satan in the vicarious role of sin bearer, but the Adventists have clarified this beyond reasonable doubt in the large majority of their publications.

Questions on Doctrine clarifies the concept of the scapegoat in Seventh-day Adventist theology. For Adventists, when the Lord Jesus Christ returns He will place upon Satan the full responsibility for his role of instigator and tempter to sin. Since Satan caused angels and man to rebel against their Creator, Adventists reason that Azazel, the scapegoat of Leviticus 16, is a type of Satan receiving the punishment due him. However, as we have seen, Adventists repudiate the idea that Satan is their vicarious sin bearer in any sense. They point out, and rightly so, that in Leviticus 16 only the first goat was slain as the vicarious offering. The second goat was not killed but was sent into the wilderness to die. Satan similarly bears the weight of guilt and final punishment culminating in annihilation as the master criminal who has promulgated sin during the period of God's grace toward lost men. To quote the Adventists again:

> Satan's death a thousand times over could never make him a savior in any sense whatsoever. He is the archsinner of the universe, the author and instigator of sin. . . . Only Christ, the Creator, the one and only God-man, could make a substitutionary atonement for men's transgressions. And this Christ did completely, perfectly and once for all on Golgotha.[74]

Law, Grace, and Salvation

In order to understand the Adventist view of law and grace, especially in relation to eternal salvation, we must consider the Adventist antipathy toward antinomianism.

---

[73] *The King's Business* (March 1958): 22–23.
[74] *Questions on Doctrine*, 400.

The very word "antinomian" (*anti*, against, and *nomos*, law) describes the conflict between those who believe that not only were the Ten Commandments abrogated at Calvary but even the principles underlying them were "abolished" so that the Christian is bound neither by them nor by those who believe that the Decalogue is as binding today as when it was given at Sinai.

From the beginning of church history, the great majority of evangelical Christians have been as strongly opposed to antinomianism as are the Adventists. Unfortunately, however, the latter have tended to label antinomian anyone who disagrees with their definition of "the law of God." Consequently, this has created a great problem in semantics, which has disrupted the lines of communication, so to speak, between Adventists and other Christians. Although we believe in obeying the laws of God and in good works as the evidence of saving faith, we strenuously object to "commandment-keeping" to the extent of supposed spiritual superiority. A principal cause of their legalistic tendencies is the Adventists' abhorrence of antinomianism.

By virtue of the fact that they obey the Fourth Commandment as well as the other nine, Adventists maintain that they alone are God's commandment-keeping church. To be sure, theologians have differed over the nature and extent of the moral law of God, and doubtless the controversy will continue until our Lord comes again. Any group, however, that feels they are the only ones that keep God's commands is likely to foment schism in the body of Christ.

From their beginning, Adventists have concentrated upon "the law of God," and in *Questions on Doctrine* they devote thirty-four pages to the exposition of this subject. Although the Adventists repudiate legalism, that is, the doctrine that keeping the law merits salvation, a legalistic spirit does exist in some of their teaching. For example, although denying that the ceremonial law is binding upon Christians, they quote from it to defend their classifying certain foods as "unclean." Although Adventists reject antinomianism, in their desire to avoid the abuses of grace they actually abuse grace by magnifying the letter of the law. How Adventists arrived at this position has been well explained by D. M. Canright (*Seventh-day Adventism Renounced*, chapter 17). In one place, Canright sets forth a series of propositions which, in some areas, are exegetically irrefutable, and with which I am in full agreement.

Now let us examine the Adventist claim that the law is binding upon the Christian, as stated in their Fundamental Beliefs, *Questions on Doctrine*, and wherever their writings touch on this subject.

I. *The Principle of Law*

To begin with, we agree to the proposition that the principle underlying the moral laws of God is indeed eternal and consistent with His character. However, we must distinguish between the principle of the law of God and the expression of that principle in specific statutes such as those in the Pentateuch. Because Adventists do not seem to make this distinction, it appears to this writer that they relate law to grace, which is an unhealthy practice. They claim that "the Law" was in effect in Eden and during all the centuries thence to Sinai. Wherever the Bible speaks of "commandments" or "law," most Adventists apparently assume that it means the Decalogue. We must, however, clearly differentiate between the principle of the law of God and the function of the law of

God as revealed in the Pentateuch. Not only the Adventists but many historical Protestant groups have failed to make this distinction, and therefore have been guilty of carrying over into the New Covenant some of the legalistic Jewish functions of the law.

A. *The Dual-Law Theory*

In *Questions on Doctrine*, the Adventists distinguish between "the moral law of God—the Decalogue—and the ceremonial law," setting forth the distinctions in two columns.[75] In column one is the Decalogue, which was spoken by God, written by Him on tables of stone, given to Moses, and deposited in the Ark. It dealt with moral precepts, revealed sin, and is in effect today. They insist that Christians must "keep the whole law" (James 2:10), and that we shall be judged by this law (James 2:12). They believe that the Decalogue is established in the life of a Christian by faith in Christ (Romans 3:31), and that Christ magnified the law (Isaiah 42:21), which Paul described as "spiritual" (Romans 7:14).

In column two, Adventists analyze the law of ceremonial ordinances, which were abolished at the cross. They contrast this with "the moral law of God—the Decalogue," stating that the latter was not abolished because it was separate from the ceremonial law. Concerning the ceremonial law, Adventists teach that it was spoken and written by Moses and given to the Levites who deposited it by the side of the Ark, and that it governed ceremony and ritual. This law prescribed offerings for sins, but the apostles gave no commandment to keep it, and the Christian is not bound by it nor can he be blessed by it. Indeed, they say, "the Christian who keeps this law loses his liberty"; it "was abolished by Christ," and was "the law of a carnal commandment" containing nothing of a moral nature, the Decalogue being "the moral law of God."

Now although there are both moral and ceremonial aspects of the law in the Pentateuch, as well as civil and judicial, nowhere does the Bible state that there is any such juxtaposition of ceremonial with moral law. In fact, the whole Bible teaches that "the law was given through Moses" (John 1:17) and that it is essentially a unit, a fact that the Adventists have overlooked. We make this observation after comparing the application of the term "law" in the Old and New Testaments.

To illustrate: As noted above, the Adventists claim that the law of Moses and the Decalogue are separate, the one being ceremonial, the other "the moral law of God." Therefore, although the ceremonial law was abolished at the cross, the moral law remains in effect; and so they insist in "commandment-keeping," not to earn salvation, but, as it works out in the practice of many, to retain salvation. If, however, the ceremonial law and the Decalogue are inextricably bound together, and if both are referred to as "the law," the distinction that the Adventists and others make between them is fictitious. To prove this is to nullify their interpretation concerning "the moral law." Let us examine the Scriptures to see whether such a distinction as they propose can be sustained.

The highest authority on this subject is the Lord Jesus Christ. When speaking of "the law," He alluded to both moral and ceremonial precepts; e.g., Mark 10:19 (moral) and Luke 5:12–14 (ceremonial). The Gospels abound with similar

---

[75] *Questions on Doctrine*, 130–131.

references to "the law" without distinguishing between the moral and the ceremonial, and certainly not teaching that they are separate codes.

We do not mean that the law has no moral and ceremonial aspects, for it has, but they are only aspects, not separate codes or units. They are parts of the one law, which "was our schoolmaster to bring us unto Christ, that we might be justified by faith" (Galatians 3:24). The apostle Paul, certainly an authority on "the law," dogmatically affirms that the role of the schoolmaster has ceased and that the Christian is "dead to the law." Note, also, that the word "schoolmaster" is in the singular, which destroys the Adventist notion that there is more than one law. If the moral law were separate from the ceremonial law, instead of both being aspects of one law, Paul would have had to write that the laws were our schoolmasters to bring us to Christ, and that now "we are no longer under schoolmasters." But he knew and taught that the law was a unit and that it was perfectly fulfilled as such in the life of our Lord and on the cross of Calvary.

By His perfect life, the Lord Jesus met all the requirements of the moral aspect of the law. By His death, He fulfilled all the ceremonial ordinances that prefigured His incarnation and sacrifice. He himself said,

> Think not that I am come to destroy the law, or the prophets: I am come not to destroy, but to fulfill. For verily I say unto you, till heaven and earth pass, one jot or one tittle shall in no wise pass from the law, till all be fulfilled (Matthew 5:17–18).

Which law did Christ fulfill? If He fulfilled only the ceremonial law as the dual-law theory states, the moral law is yet to be satisfied. But "Christ is the end of the law for righteousness to every one that believeth" (Romans 10:4); and as we have shown, there are no distinct codes such as moral as contrasted with ceremonial law. The distinction is arbitrary and contradicts the declaration of Scripture that the believer lives by a higher principle: "The law of the Spirit of life in Christ Jesus hath made me free from the law of sin and death" (Romans 8:2).

In order to maintain the dual-law theory against the biblical declaration that the one law has divisions or aspects, Adventists must explain why this is true in relation to at least twenty passages in the New Testament, a dozen of them in the words of Jesus Christ. The Holy Spirit teaches that there are not two laws, but one; that this law is not only in the five books of Moses but in the Prophets and the Psalms as well. Christ looked upon moral, ceremonial, and prophetic precepts as parts of the one law, which pointed to His life, ministry, death, and resurrection. As He said to His disciples that first Easter Day, "These are the words which I spake unto you, while I was yet with you, that all things must be fulfilled, which were written in the law of Moses, and in the prophets, and in the psalms concerning me" (Luke 24:44).

A study of the relevant biblical passages (including John 8:17 cf. Deuteronomy 19:15; John 10:34 cf. Psalm 82:6; John 12:34 cf. Psalm 72:17; John 15:25 cf. Psalm 35:19; and John 19:7 cf. Leviticus 24:16) should convince any objective reader that the law is a single gigantic structure comprised of several aspects: moral, ceremonial, civil, judicial, and prophetic. This whole structure was referred to by Christ and the apostles under the heading of "the law," and which structure was completely fulfilled in the life and death of the Lord Jesus Christ

who instituted the universal principle of divine love as the fulfillment of every aspect and function of the law. Our Lord said:

> Therefore all things whatsoever ye would that men should do to you, do ye even so to them: for this is the law and the prophets. . . . Thou shalt love the Lord thy God with all thy heart, and with all thy soul, and with all thy mind. This is the first and great commandment. And the second is like unto it. Thou shalt love thy neighbor as thyself. On these two commandments hang all the law and the prophets (Matthew 7:12; 22:37–40).

Instead of the Adventist belief that the law must be "kept" as a sign of obedience to God, Christ here teaches that the Christian obeys God when he obeys the supreme commandment of love. This teaching is reiterated by the greatest of the apostles, who wrote to the Galatians, "All the law is fulfilled in one word, even in this; Thou shalt love thy neighbor as thyself" (Galatians 5:14). Obviously, if we love our neighbors as ourselves, we do so because we love God with all our hearts, souls, and minds. If we do not so love God, we cannot love our neighbors as ourselves. Thus on this "great commandment" rests the law in all its aspects.

Note the language of these passages, for they indicate the strong emphasis given by our Lord. In Matthew 22:40 Christ uses the Greek word *holos*, translated sixty-five times in the New Testament as "all," forty-three times as "whole," twice as "every whit," once "altogether," and once "throughout." With these renditions all lexicons agree, so there can be no linguistic doubt that the all-inclusive principle that binds and seals all aspects of the law into a unit to be fulfilled in the life of a believer, because it has been fulfilled by the Savior, is once again declared to be "love."

The apostle Paul uses an entirely different word to sum up the unifying principle of the law and the only principle which the Scriptures say fulfills it. This is the Greek word *pas*.

In the New Testament *pas* is translated 748 times as "all," 170 times as "all things," 117 times as "every," forty-one times as "all men," thirty-one times as "whosoever," twenty-eight times as "everyone," twelve times as "whole," and eleven times as "every man." We see then how the Holy Spirit rendered linguistically impossible any escape from the clear declaration that the principle of love indeed fulfills all the precepts of the law in their entirety since the two terms used most frequently in the New Testament to describe inclusiveness were utilized by both Christ and Paul to enunciate this vital issue.

Finally, notice Paul's powerful admonition to the believers at Rome:

> Owe no man any thing, but to love one another: for he that loveth another hath fulfilled the law. For this, Thou shalt not commit adultery, Thou shalt not kill, Thou shalt not steal, Thou shalt not bear false witness, Thou shalt not covet; and if there be any other commandment, it is briefly comprehended in this saying, namely, Thou shalt love thy neighbor as thyself. Love worketh no ill to his neighbor: therefore love is the fulfilling of the law (Romans 13:8–10).

In this context the greatest authority on the law in the New Testament, next to Jesus Christ, used the very emphatic Greek word *etera*, which is translated forty-two times in the New Testament as "other." Unquestionably the apostle Paul not only considered the law a unit of which the Decalogue is only a part (quoting five of the Ten Commandments) but he indicated the rest of the law—

ceremonial, civil, and judicial—by the word "other." Thus if one is to be a true "commandment-keeper," he has only to obey the divine principle of love, and God looks upon this as fulfillment of "the law." The Holy Spirit does not specify the moral, ceremonial, or civil law. He emphatically states that love is the fulfillment of "the law"—a tremendously important statement, to say the least!

It is significant that in the thirteenth chapter of Romans, after quoting five of the ten commandments that the Adventists steadfastly affirm constitute "the moral law," the apostle conspicuously omits what the Adventists maintain is God's great "seal"—the Sabbath. In fact, the words "any other commandment" must include even the Sabbath in the law of love. Nowhere is this more decidedly emphasized than in the usage of a peculiar term that appears but twice in the New Testament; here in Romans 13:9, and again in Ephesians 1:10. The term in question is the Greek *anakephalaioutai*, which in both instances means "to sum up, to repeat summarily, and so to condense into a summary . . . to bring together."

We see that the apostle Paul, under the inspiration of the Holy Spirit, taught in both Romans 13:9 and Ephesians 1:10 that as God in the fulness of time intended to "gather together," (KJV) or "sum up" (RSV), those whom He had chosen in Christ, in like manner He has forever condensed or summed up, comprehended or gathered together, the law in all its aspects and divisions under the all-embracing principle of love. By not adhering strictly to the established laws of sound biblical interpretations, Seventh-day Adventists seem to have overlooked this fact in the New Testament. In the course of our study of Seventh-day Adventist literature, we have been impressed by the fact that some Adventists will cite texts largely out of their context and grammatical structure in what appears to be an attempt to enforce an arbitrary theory of two laws (moral and ceremonial) upon the believer in the age of grace. In so doing, they violate that principle which the apostle Paul states "sums up" or "condenses" all of the commandments of the entire law, perfectly fulfilling them under the one heading, "the great commandment," upon which, our Lord declared, "hang all the law and the prophets," the imperative of love.

On page 131 of *Questions on Doctrine* it is stated that the ceremonial law is now "abolished" (Ephesians 2:15); and, "the Christian who keeps this law is not blessed," but "loses his liberty" (Galatians 5:1, 3). Nevertheless, Adventists religiously observe some ceremonial laws, especially with regard to "unclean food." Now, although they deny that their rejection of "unclean" food is based on Mosaic prohibitions, all their literature on the subject appeals to the very law that they insist has been "abolished." Under the covenant of law, nowhere but in the Mosaic ceremonial aspects of the law are people forbidden to eat oysters, clams, lobsters, crabs, reptiles, rabbits, and swine's flesh, but the Adventists still claim the validity of such prohibition. We wish that they would be consistent in following their dual-law theory and abandon their "unclean foods" restriction, which binds them to what even they admit is an abolished ceremonial teaching; a teaching which they also declare can cause the Christian to "lose his liberty" and miss the blessings of God. Writing on this subject of unclean foods with apostolic authority and the power of the Holy Spirit, the apostle Paul unequivocally declared, "Therefore let no one pass judgment on you in questions of food and drink" (Colossians 2:16, RSV). And he warns Tim-

othy that in the latter days some persons will "enjoin abstinence from foods that God created to be received with thanksgiving by those who believe and know the truth. For everything created by God is good, and nothing is to be rejected if it is received with thanksgiving, for then it is consecrated by the Word of God and prayer." Finally, he sums it up thus:

> I know, and am persuaded in the Lord Jesus, that nothing is unclean in itself: but to him that esteemeth any thing to be unclean, to him it is unclean. . . . For the kingdom of God is not meat and drink; but righteousness, and peace, and joy in the Holy Ghost. For he that in these things serveth Christ is acceptable to God, and approved of men (Romans 14:14, 17–18).

From these texts it is apparent that Adventists limit their own liberty in Christ by voluntary bondage to ceremonial precepts, and it is the dual-law theory that has largely caused their confusion and the consequent error of law-keeping.

For this teaching, which lapses so easily into legalism, we find no biblical authority since it is demonstrably true that the law of Moses and the Decalogue are a unit described throughout Scripture as "the law." The fact that the Decalogue was written on stones (Exodus 31:18) and the law of Moses written in a book (Exodus 24:4, 7; Deuteronomy 31:24) in no way proves that one is moral and the other ceremonial. As we have seen, the law of Moses, written in a book, and deposited by the Levites by the side of the Ark, deals not only with ceremonial ritual matters, but with those moral precepts contained in the Decalogue itself. One could not be fulfilled, as Christ prophesied and accomplished, and the other left unfulfilled, for then God's sacrificial plan would not have been consummated at Calvary.

B. *"Law" in the New Testament*

When New Testament writers spoke of "the law," they usually meant all five books of Moses, which contain moral, ceremonial and civil ordinances. It was national and applied only to Israel and to anyone who became an Israelite. Nowhere in Scripture is it applied to anyone else. Although the Gentiles, as Paul says, "have not the law," its great moral principle applied to them, so that the Gentiles "do by nature that which is contained in the law," but they did not come under law as given to Israel.

Acts 15:23–32 describes how the leaders of the Christian church at Jerusalem, all Jews, were very careful not to impose the demands of the law upon the Gentiles. For them, the complete "law"—moral, ceremonial, and civil—had been fulfilled, and the one law to observe now was to love God and your neighbor. St. Augustine remarked, "Love God, and do as you please," for if we truly love God with heart, soul, mind, and strength, we do only those things that please Him. This is "the law" of the New Testament, the only guide for the Christian. We are "no longer under the law, but under grace," and the function of the "schoolmaster" (Galatians 3:24) has forever and irrevocably ceased.

Let us see how these first Christian leaders solved the problem of "the law":

> And they wrote letters by them after this manner; the apostles and elders and brethren send greetings unto the brethren which are of the Gentiles in Antioch and Syria and Cilicia. Forasmuch as we have heard, that certain which

went out from us have troubled you with words, subverting your souls, saying, Ye must be circumcised, and keep the law: to whom we gave no such commandment: It seemed good unto us, being assembled with one accord to send chosen men unto you. . . . We have sent therefore, Judas and Silas. . . . For it seemed good to the Holy Ghost, and to us, to lay upon you no greater burden than these necessary things; that ye abstain from meats offered to idols, and from blood, and from things strangled, and from fornication: from which if ye keep yourselves, ye shall do well. Fare ye well (Acts 15:23–25, 27–29).

Since "the law" includes the precepts of the Pentateuch and certain sections of the Psalms and Prophets, this message to the Gentiles contradicts all dual-law teachers who insist that we must for any purpose "keep the law." We know from a comparison of the New Testament with the Old that the Decalogue of itself is not the entire moral law of God, as our Adventist brethren often insist, for there are many other commandments that are neither inferred from, implied, nor contained in the Decalogue, but which are just as moral as anything appearing in Exodus 20. Although nine of the Ten Commandments are enunciated in the New Testament, we have seen that they are "comprehended, summed up, or condensed" in the words of Paul in the great commandment of love (Romans 13:8; Galatians 5:14). So the Adventists have no argument against the total fulfillment of all the law by the life and death of our Savior.

In Acts 15:24, the leaders of the church in Jerusalem reiterate this principle in their letter to the Gentiles in Antioch, Syria and Cilicia: "Certain which went out from us have troubled you with words, subverting your souls, saying, Ye must be circumcised, and keep the law: to whom we gave no such commandment."

Now, although Seventh-day Adventists affirm that law-keeping cannot merit salvation, nevertheless they teach that by breaking the law one forfeits salvation. They invoke a principle that was fulfilled in the life and death of Christ, and in so doing they place themselves in direct opposition to the great law of love enunciated by Christ and the apostles, and are in effect putting "a yoke upon the neck of the disciples, which neither our fathers nor we were able to bear" (Acts 15:10). To those who invoke the law as the criterion of obedience in the Christian life, the Word of God replies, "We gave no such commandment" (Acts 15:24).

Paul's phrase "any other commandment" in Romans 13:9, of course, includes abstinence from meats offered to idols, blood, things strangled, and fornication, for love of God would enjoin discernment and obedience in all these things.

To support their argument that a Christian must obey the commandments, Adventists and other Christian bodies cite such passages as the following:

If ye love me, keep my commandments. He that hath my commandments, and keepeth them, he it is that loveth me (John 14:15, 21). And hereby we do know that we know him, if we keep his commandments. He that saith, I know him, and keepeth not his commandments, is a liar, and the truth is not in him. . . . And whatsoever we ask, we receive of him, because we keep his commandments, and do those things that are pleasing in his sight. . . . He that keepeth his commandments dwelleth in him, and he in him. And hereby we know that he abideth in us, by the Spirit which he hath given us. . . . By this we know that we love the children of God, when we love God, and keep his commandments. For this is the love of God, that we keep his commandments: and his

commandments are not grievous (1 John 2:3–4; 3:22, 24; 5:2–3).

We, too, yield to the authority of those verses; but the fallacy of the position lies in the concept that the word "commandments" always refers to the Ten Commandments, which Adventists maintain are "the moral law of God." This claim cannot be substantiated from Scripture; in fact, it is contradicted by the Bible. Let us see how the Lord Jesus and the apostle John applied the words "commandments" and "law." First, consider the conversation of our Lord with the lawyer in Luke 10:25–28:

> And, behold, a certain lawyer stood up, and tempted him, saying, Master, what shall I do to inherit eternal life?
> He said unto him, What is written in the law? how readest thou?
> And he answering said, Thou shalt love the Lord thy God with all thy heart, and with all thy soul, and with all thy strength, and with all thy mind; and thy neighbor as thyself.
> And he said unto him, Thou hast answered right: this do, and thou shalt live.

Clearly, the Lord Jesus did not subscribe to the Seventh-day Adventist view that "commandment-keeping means keeping all of the Ten Commandments," none of which He mentions in this passage. Christ did not say, "Keep the Ten Commandments, especially the fourth one, and thou shalt live." He said, in effect, "Obey the law of love upon which all the law and the prophets rest, and thou shalt live." This refutes the Adventist claim that when Jesus spoke of commandments He meant only the Decalogue.

Among those who listened to our Lord's discourse in the Upper Room was the apostle John, who records the "new commandment . . . that ye love one another; as I have loved you" (John 13:34). To this commandment John refers in the passages quoted from his first epistle. Nowhere does he mention the Decalogue or any part of the moral law of God. Instead, he writes:

> This is his commandment, That we should believe on the name of his Son Jesus Christ, and love one another, as he gave us commandment. . . . And this commandment have we from him, That he who loveth God love his brother also (1 John 3:23; 4:21).

And in his second epistle he says,

> I beseech thee, lady, not as though I wrote a new commandment unto thee, but that which we had from the beginning, that we love one another. And this is love, that we walk after his commandments. This is the commandment, That, as ye have heard from the beginning, ye should walk in it" (2 John 5–6).

From this it is clear what John means when he speaks of "commandment" or "commandments."

How different from ironclad obedience to what many, including Adventists, sometimes call "The Eternal Ten." By "the righteousness of the law" and fulfillment of the law, Christ and all the New Testament writers mean not the Ten Commandments but the eternal law of love. The motivating power of the universe—love—is to motivate obedience to God. By loving Him and one another we fulfill all moral law. The chief function of the law was to reveal sin and to

"slay" the soul that righteousness might come by faith, and it was given for the unregenerate, not the redeemed: "Knowing this, that the law is not made for a righteous man, but for the lawless and disobedient, for the ungodly and for sinners, for unholy and profane, for murderers of fathers and murderers of mothers, for manslayers" (1 Timothy 1:9).

C. *The Charge of Pharisaism*

By believing they are God's commandment-keeping church, Adventists have exposed themselves to the charge of Pharisaism. Because they monopolize such passages as the following, they give the impression of claiming to be the only people on earth: (1) "That keep the commandments of God;[76] (2) "They that keep the commandments of God, and the faith of Jesus"; and (3) "Blessed are they that do his commandments, that they may have the right to the tree of life, and may enter in through the gates into the city" (Revelation 12:17; 14:12; 22:14).

We admire the desire of our Adventist brethren to obey the commandments of God; but, we ask, what commandments? If they answer, "The Decalogue," we reject their effort to bring us under bondage, for we "are not under the law, but under grace" (Romans 6:14). If some fail to recognize that "the law" of the New Testament is love for God and for one another, and that it fulfills and supersedes all previous embodiments of divine principle, then the issue is clear. Such people speak like "a noisy gong or a clanging cymbal," because they do not give supremacy to the "new" and "great commandment."

Concluding this section on the principle of law, we may sum up our position briefly:

The Adventist insistence that there are two separate codes of laws, the moral and the ceremonial, and that the former is in effect today and the latter was abolished at the cross, finds, we believe, no exegetical or theological basis in Scripture. We have also shown that they select numerous texts out of context and juxtapose them in order to validate their contention. We have seen that the greatest of all commandments is not included in the Decalogue or "moral law." And yet upon this great commandment, love for the Lord and for one's neighbor, "hang all the law and the prophets." The nineteenth chapter of Leviticus alone is sufficient to refute the dual-law theory, for it contains moral, ceremonial, and civil laws sometimes all appearing in the same verse, and yet Leviticus is called by Christ, "the law," as are the other four books of Moses.

The Adventist contention that since the Ten Commandments were spoken by God, inscribed on stone, and placed within the Ark, they are superior to the law written by Moses in a book and placed by the side of the Ark is fallacious. This is true because the book placed by the side of the Ark actually contains more moral law than does the Decalogue itself. It is, therefore, superior to the Decalogue, at least in scope.

The Bible refutes the Adventist contention that the law was in force in Eden and that it was known to Adam, Noah, Abraham, and the patriarchs. Not one

---

[76]All the oldest and best Greek manuscripts of Revelation 22:14 read, "They that wash their robes," so the verse gives no support whatever for "commandment-keeping." This fact well-informed Adventists recognize, but a large segment still attempt to utilize certain faulty and incorrect English translations to "prove" their position.

verse of Scripture can be cited free from inference, deduction, and implication that teaches such a doctrine. The Word of God states,

> The law was given by Moses. . . . Did not Moses give you the law? . . . If therefore perfection were by the Levitical priesthood (for under it the people received the law). . . . The covenant, that was confirmed before of God in Christ, the law, which was four hundred and thirty years after, cannot disannul. . . . The Lord our God made a covenant with us in Horeb. The Lord made not this covenant with our fathers, but with us (John 1:17; 7:19; Hebrews 7:11; Galatians 3:17; Deuteronomy 5:2–3).

The Adventists' contentions, therefore, concerning the eternal nature of the Decalogue and the time of its application to man are mere conjecture. Although we admit that the principle of the law was, in effect, written upon the hearts of men by the Holy Spirit, so that they were judged by it (Romans 2), there is a vast difference between the principle of the law and the embodiment of that principle in a given code (Sinaitic-Mosaic), which the Adventists fail to recognize.

Finally, the Old Testament Scriptures all teach the unity of the law. Christ endorsed it, and the apostles pointed out that its chief purpose was to condemn man and show him his need of redemption that he might come to Christ, the author and fulfiller of all the law. We who are "led of the Spirit . . . are not under the law" (Galatians 5:18), for "love is the fulfilling of the law" (Romans 13:10). This love energizes us to "walk not after the flesh, but after the Spirit" that in us "the righteousness of the law might be fulfilled" (Romans 8:4). In Jeremiah 31:31–34, the prophet states that under the new covenant, God would write His law "in their inward parts, and write it in their hearts." In 2 Corinthians 3:3, the apostle Paul declares that Christians are "the epistle of Christ . . . written not with ink, but with the Spirit of the living God; not in tables of stone, but in fleshy tables of the heart." The motive for obedience to this law is the imperative of love: "We love him, because he first loved us" (1 John 4:19).

The great foundational moral law of the universe is therefore declared to be unchanging love. This is vastly different from the national or Mosaic law given only to Israel. That law was designed to be fulfilled, even though it was based upon the eternal principles of the moral character of God (Colossians 2:14–17). And when its fulfillment did take place and the character of God was imputed to the believer and imparted to his life by the power of the indwelling Spirit, the entire Mosaic system passed away; but the eternal principle, the law's foundation, remained, and is operative today as the law of love, the supreme "commandment" and the only "law" under which the Christian is to live.

The concept of law in Seventh-day Adventism, then, leads them to the unbiblical and at times legalistic position that although they are "under grace," by failing to "keep the commandments" they are in danger of coming "under law" again.

The Word of God, however, describes the Christian under grace as "dead to the law" that he might "live unto God" (Galatians 2:19), and nowhere is it taught that one can "come alive" again so that the function of the law is resumed.

II. *The Relationship of Grace to Salvation*

Although Adventists lay great stress on "commandment-keeping" and "obedience to the moral law of God as contained in the Ten Commandments," they devote a large portion of their writings to the New Testament doctrine of grace. As we saw earlier, Seventh-day Adventists believe in salvation by grace alone, and vehemently deny that "law" plays any part as a basis for redemption. In their own words,

> Salvation is not now, and never has been, by law or by works; salvation is only by the grace of Christ. Moreover, there never was a time in the plan of God when salvation was by human works or effort. Nothing men can do, or have done, can in any way merit salvation.
>
> While works are not a means of salvation, good works are the inevitable result of salvation. However, these good works are possible only for the child of God whose life is inwrought by the Spirit of God. . . . One thing is certain, man cannot be saved by any effort of his own. We profoundly believe that no works of the law, no deeds of the law, no effort however commendable, and no good works—whether they be many or few, sacrificial or not—can in any way justify the sinner (Titus 3:5; Romans 3:20). Salvation is wholly of grace; it is the gift of God (Romans 4:4–5; Ephesians 2:8).[77]

These and many similar clear-cut statements in current authoritative Seventh-day Adventist literature reveal that, despite the "dual-law theory" and the peculiar concept that the law is still operative in the life of the believer, Adventists confess the basis of their salvation to be grace, and grace alone, the only basis upon which God deigns to save the fallen children of Adam.

In chapter 14 of *Questions on Doctrine*, Adventists spell out their allegiance to divine grace as the only channel of salvation: "According to Seventh-day Adventist belief, there is, and can be, no salvation through the law, or by human works of the law, but only through the saving grace of God."[78]

Christians who are familiar with historical theology know that the Adventists' position on law, though tinged with legalism, has its roots in the basic Arminian position that one receives salvation as a free gift of God; but, once he has received this gift, the believer is responsible for its maintenance and duration, and the chief means of accomplishing this is "commandment-keeping" or "obedience to all the laws of God."

Since Adventists are basically Arminian, we may logically deduce that, in a sense, their salvation rests upon legal grounds. But the saving factor in the dilemma is that by life and by worldwide witness, Adventists, like other so-called Arminians, give true evidence that they have experienced the "new.birth," which is by grace alone, through faith in our Lord and His sacrifice upon the cross. One would be callous and uncharitable indeed not to accept their profession of dependence upon Christ alone for redemption, even though there is inconsistency in their theological system.

Some Christians make a great issue of the teaching of "eternal security," and perhaps rightly so because it is an important truth. However, no matter how strongly we may feel about it, our conviction does not entitle us to judge the motives and spiritual condition of other believers in this respect. This is our

---

[77] *Questions on Doctrine*, 141–142.
[78] Ibid., 135.

principal reason for taking the position that Seventh-day Adventists are Christians who believe the historical gospel message. They cannot rightly be called non-Christian cultists or "Judaizers," since they are sound on the great New Testament doctrines including grace and redemption through the vicarious offering of Jesus Christ "once for all" (Hebrews 10:10) and give evidence of "life in Christ."

For many centuries, there has been much controversy over the juxtaposition of the principles of law and grace in the Scriptures. If evangelicals today were asked, "Do you believe that grace and law are in direct opposition?" the answer in most cases would be a strong affirmative. Through the years, confusion has been caused by the abuse of both principles by two groups of equally sincere Christians. One group believes that all law has ceased; the other that the Ten Commandments are still God's standard of righteousness and must be obeyed or salvation is forfeited. What both groups have failed to grasp is that the great conflict is not between law and grace as such; rather, it centers around a proper understanding of their relationship and respective functions.

We have established that love is the ground and source of the doctrine of grace, but the law was necessary to expose the sinfulness of sin and the depth of man's moral depravity. When law becomes the ground of salvation or of restraining the Christian from practicing sin, it intrudes upon the province of grace. When a Christian is not controlled by love, grace is abused and its purpose is nullified. All law is fulfilled by love, as our Savior and the apostles taught, but the Christian can never please God if he obeys for fear of the law. Life under law binds the soul, for the tendency is for man to obey not because he wants to please God but because he fears God's judgment. Under grace, love works upon the regenerate heart, and what was legalistic duty under law becomes gracious obedience under grace. Actually, grace and love demand more than the law, which to the Pharisees required only outward obedience. Grace commands us to "do the will of God from the heart" (Ephesians 6:6). Seventh-day Adventists declare that they obey the law not out of fear but out of love for God. However, it is to be regretted that in a large proportion of their literature on the subject, they declare that the keeping of the law is necessary to maintain salvation, and thus they introduce the motive of fear instead of the biblical imperative of love.

The apostle John defined the issue when he wrote, "The law was given by Moses, but grace and truth came by Jesus Christ" (John 1:17). As a governing principle, a measure of righteousness, a schoolmaster, and an instrument of death, the law was supplanted by grace—the unmerited favor of God. All believers in the Lord Jesus Christ, having passed from death to life through the sacrifice of the Son of God, possess the divine nature and righteousness. Because He first loved us, we are compelled and impelled to love and serve Him. In obedience to the great law of love, the Christian fulfills the righteousness of the law (not the law itself; this Christ alone did); and by the transforming power of the indwelling Holy Spirit he will "walk not after the flesh, but after the Spirit" (Romans 8:4).

Seventh-day Adventists believe, we repeat, that they are saved by grace. However, they are often prone to believe that their remaining saved depends on "commandment-keeping."

More recently, an Adventist professor summed up the church's present un-

derstanding of this issue as a generally unified but still tension-filled affirmation of salvation by grace alone through faith—evidenced by obedience. Dr. Gary Land, Andrews University in Berrien Spring, Michigan, explained,

> The committee issued a statement on "the dynamics of salvation." Because humanity is desperately in need of salvation, it said, God has taken the initiative to provide it. When the individual human being, with the Holy Spirit's help, decides to accept reconciliation with God, he receives a new status in Christ, encompassed by such terms as justification, reconciliation, forgiveness, adoption, and sanctification. This new status involves a new life in Christ characterized by new birth, restoration, growth, grace and faith, assurance, and praise. Consummation is achieved with Christ's Second Coming, which will restore the universe to a "perfect, sinless state."
>
> In essence, the statement addressed the righteousness by faith debate by analyzing the theological terms involved, attempting to bring together all elements of the subject, and placing the whole within an Adventist eschatological context. Although it included an emphasis on sanctification, that concept was now one of several elements. By offering an enlarged understanding of salvation, the statement appeared to provide room for both sides of the debate.
>
> It appears on the surface that the righteousness by faith debate pivoted on the technical issue of a definition. But the fact that so many people could get so disturbed over the question indicates that it hit a raw nerve within Adventism. The justification by grace through faith position seems to have appealed to a large number of Adventists because it offered an assurance of salvation that they felt the traditional emphasis on sanctification had not allowed. On the other hand, many of those who opposed the new teaching feared that it might open the door to an antinomianism that would undermine the Adventist concern with God's law. . . .
>
> In the view of most denominational theologians, Seventh-day Adventists had the unique problem and unique opportunity of understanding the relationship of justification and sanctification, or law and gospel, in a way that did justice to both.[79]

That current Adventist teaching regarding sanctification is based on grace, not works, is clear from the Adventists' doctrinal discussion in *Seventh-day Adventists Believe*, which states,

> True repentance and justification lead to sanctification. Justification and sanctification are closely related, distinct but never separate. They designate two phases of salvation: Justification is what God does *for* us, while sanctification is what God does *in* us.
>
> Neither justification nor sanctification is the result of meritorious works. Both are solely due to Christ's grace and righteousness. . . . The three phases of sanctification the Bible presents are: (1) an accomplished act in the believer's past; (2) a process in the believer's present experience; (3) and the final result that the believer experiences at Christ's return.[80]

III. *The Author of Salvation*

Because He took our sins upon himself, in obedience to His Father's will, the Lord Jesus "became the author of eternal salvation unto all them that obey

---

[79]Gary Land, ed., *Adventism in America* (Grand Rapids, Mich.: William B. Eerdmans Publishing Company, 1986), 218–219.
[80]*Seventh-day Adventists Believe*, 123.

him" (Hebrews 5:8–10). This truth Seventh-day Adventists believe. They strongly assert their belief in the deity of the Lord Jesus Christ, His equality with the Father, and His perfect, sinless human nature, and expound these truths in detail. However, they teach that before His incarnation the Lord Jesus Christ bore the title of Michael the archangel. This interpretation differs greatly from that of Jehovah's Witnesses who believe that Christ was a created being and that "He was a god, but not the Almighty God who is Jehovah."[81] The Adventists make this very clear:

> We emphatically reject the idea . . . and the position held by the Jehovah's Witnesses. We do not believe that Christ is a created being. We as a people have not considered the identification of Michael of sufficient prominence to dwell upon it at length either in our literature or in our preaching. . . . We believe that the term Michael is but one of the many titles applied to the Son of God, the second person of the Godhead. But such a view does not in any way conflict with our belief in His full deity and eternal preexistence, nor does it in the least disparage His person and work.[82]

Although a number of authoritative commentators support the Adventist view, the New Testament, I believe, does not warrant this conclusion. Most of the evidence that the Adventists submit is from the book of Daniel, the rest from the Apocalypse. By comparing such designations as "angel of Jehovah," "angel of the Lord," "Prince," and "Michael," the Adventists conclude that Michael is another title for the Lord Jesus Christ. But Seventh-day Adventists maintain that although he is called "the archangel" (*archangelos* or "first messenger"), he is not a created being since, in the Old Testament, "angel of Jehovah" is a term of Deity. In the light of this, we do not judge them because of their view of Michael, but call the reader's attention to the ninth verse of the book of Jude, which says, "Yet Michael the archangel, when contending with the devil he disputed about the body of Moses, durst not bring against him a railing accusation, but said, The Lord rebuke thee" (v. 9).

The word translated "durst" in the King James Bible is the archaic past tense of "dare"; so Michael "did not dare" bring against Satan a railing or blasphemous (*blasphemos*) judgment. The Greek word for "dare" is *tolmao* and appears sixteen times in the New Testament, and in the negative always means "not daring through fear of retaliation." Thus if Michael was Christ, according to the Seventh-day Adventists, "He did not dare" to rebuke Satan for fear of retaliation.

Adventists agree that fifteen times in the New Testament *tolmao* carries the meaning indicated. But, since its use in Jude 9 refutes their notion that Michael is a title of Christ, they reverse its meaning here! As the Adventists know, none of the commentators to whom they appeal has grammatically analyzed or diagrammed the passage in the Greek or for that matter commented upon exclusive usage of *tolmao* in the Scripture of the New Testament. The agreement of such commentation therefore gives no validity whatever to the Adventists' misuse of *tolmao*. The preincarnate Christ, the *Logos*, having the nature of God (John 1:1), certainly would not refer the creature Satan to God the Father for

[81] *Let God Be True* (Brooklyn, N.Y.: Watchtower Bible and Tract Society, 1952), 100.
[82] *Questions on Doctrine*, 71.

rebuke. While He was on earth, Christ the Creator rebuked Satan many times. Would He then fear him during His preincarnate life? Scripture contradicts this.

The Adventist explanation is:

> The devil, the prince of evil, could rightly be said to deserve a railing accusation, but to such a thing Michael would not stoop. To say that Michael could not, in the sense that He did not have the power or the authority to do so, would not be true. It is not that Michael could not, in the sense of being restricted, but rather that He would not take such an attitude.[83]

This statement appears to be an attempt to escape the fact that the word "dare" (*tolmao*) in the New Testament always connotes fear, including its use in Jude 9. The text teaches that because Michael did not have the authority to rebuke Satan, "he did not dare" to do so through fear of superior retaliation. There is no implication that Michael's position was so high that he "would not stoop." The context, grammar, and root meaning of *tolmao* contradict the Adventists' attempt to make this text support their view of Michael. All authorities on Greek grammar agree that the Adventist interpretation violates the classic and New Testament usage of *tolmao*.

Thus the Adventist statement about Michael is neither linguistically nor scripturally accurate. Although they repudiate the Jehovah's Witnesses' position, they wrest this passage from its true meaning and read into it their own theory concerning Michael as Christ.

In conclusion, I am convinced of the sincerity of the Adventists' claim to regeneration and allegiance to the New Testament principle of saving grace. I appreciate their high regard for the law of God and their desire to obey it. I cannot agree, however, with their insistence upon linking "commandment-keeping" to observance of the ceremonial law, especially with regard to "unclean" foods. I feel, moreover, that they err in saying that Michael is a title of Christ, and I believe that I have shown that they violate the linguistic and scriptural meaning of Jude 9.

Author's Note

One of the chief critics of Seventh-day Adventism is a vocal ex-Adventist printer of Minneapolis, a man who has written much against his former church. Writing in *The Sword of the Lord*, August 2, 1957, he bitterly assailed Seventh-day Adventists as willful deceivers. Since his writings are repeatedly quoted by most of the other critics we shall discuss his charge, but in the interest of brevity we shall confine ourselves to one of his chief areas of criticism—law and salvation in Seventh-day Adventist theology.

This critic quotes the book *Steps to Christ*, by Ellen G. White, in the following manner: "The condition of eternal life is now just what it has always been . . . perfect obedience to the law of God."

He then maintains that Seventh-day Adventism teaches this, and on the surface it appears that he has proved his point; namely that to Adventists, salvation is a combination of grace, faith in Christ, plus the keeping of the law. A closer

---

[83] *Questions on Doctrine*, 80.

look at the statement in the context from which the critic removed it, however, serves to refute this position. Wrote White in the very same context:

> We do not earn salvation by our obedience, for salvation is the free gift of God to receive by faith. But obedience is the fruit of faith . . . here is the true test. If we abide in Christ and the love of God dwells in us, our feelings, our thoughts, our actions will be in harmony with the will of God as expressed in the precepts of His Holy law. . . . Righteousness is defined by the standard of God's holy law as expressed in the ten precepts given on Sinai. That so-called faith in Christ that professes to release men from the obligation of obedience to God is not faith but presumption. "By grace are ye saved through faith." But "faith if it has not works is dead." Jesus said of himself before He came to earth, "I delight to do thy will, O my God. Yea, thy law is within my heart." And just before He ascended again to heaven, He declared, "I have kept my Father's commandments and abide in his love." The Scripture says, "Hereby we do know that we know him, if we keep his commandments. He that saith he abides in him ought also himself to walk even as he walked," because "Christ also suffered for us, leaving us an example, that ye should follow his steps."
>
> The condition of eternal life is now just what it always has been—just what it was in Paradise before the fall of our first parents—perfect obedience to the law of God, perfect righteousness. Since we are sinful, unholy, we cannot perfectly obey a holy law. We have no righteousness of our own with which to meet the claims of the law of God. But Christ has made a way of escape for us. He lived on earth amid trials and temptations such as we have to meet. He lived a sinless life. He died for us and now He offers to take our sins and give us His righteousness. If you give yourself to Him and accept Him as your Saviour, then sinful as your life may have been, for His sake you are counted righteous. Christ's character stands in place of your character and you are accepted before God just as if you had not sinned.
>
> So we have nothing in ourselves of which to boast. We have no ground for self exaltation. Our only ground of hope is in the righteousness of Christ imputed to us by His Spirit working in and through us.[84]

In the light of White's complete statement on this subject, we see that our critic omitted her principal thesis, that we are saved by grace. There are not a few instances of similar carelessness on the part of the writer of this article. The result is that his work is largely discredited and discounted by those who know the proper methods of research.

Seventh-day Adventists are well aware of the law and grace problem and in *Questions on Doctrine* they state,

> There has been regrettable misunderstanding as to our teaching on grace, law, and works, and their interrelationships. According to Seventh-day Adventist belief, there is, and can be, no salvation through the law or by human works of the law, but only through the saving grace of God. This principle, to us, is basic.[85]

Further the Adventists state:

> Salvation is not now, and never has been, by law or works; salvation is only by the grace of Christ. Moreover, there never was a time in the plan of God when salvation was by human works or effort. Nothing men can do, or have done, can in any way merit salvation.

---

[84]Ellen G. White, *Steps to Christ* (Washington, D.C.: Review and Herald Publishing Association, 1945), 36–49.

[85]*Questions on Doctrine*, 135.

While works are not a means of salvation, good works are the inevitable result of salvation. . . . One thing is certain, man cannot be saved by any effort of his own. We profoundly believe that no works of the law, no deeds of the law, no effort however commendable, and no good works—whether they be many or few, sacrificial or not—can in any way justify the sinner (Titus 3:5; Romans 3:20). Salvation is wholly of grace; it is the gift of God (Romans 4:4–5; Ephesians 2:8). (*Questions on Doctrine,* 141–142.)

Ellen G. White, certainly an authoritative voice in Adventism, summarized it thus:

Christ is pleading for the church in the heavenly courts above, pleading for those for whom he paid the redemption price of his own lifeblood. Centuries, ages, can never diminish the efficacy of this atoning sacrifice. The message of the gospel of His grace was to be given to the church in clear and distinct lines, that the world should no longer say that Seventh-day Adventists talk the law, but do not teach or believe Christ.[86]

---

[86]Ellen G. White, *Testimonies to Ministers* (Mountain View, Calif.: Pacific Press, n.d.), 92.

Appendix D

Islam: The Message of Muhammad

Islam is a major world religion distinctly different from Christianity. But it is the world's second largest religion with numbers coming closer to Christianity every day. Mosques are springing up in many "Christian" areas, and anyone in any major metropolitan area probably lives near several Muslims. Unfortunately, most Christians understand very little about Islamic teaching[1] and are afraid to witness to them.

"There is no God but Allah, and Muhammad is the prophet (or messenger) of Allah" is the great *Shahada*, or "confession," which faithful Muslims around the world declare daily. This declaration of faith effectively distinguishes Muslims from every other world religion, including Christianity and Judaism. Almost a billion people worldwide claim Allah as their God and Muhammad as their prophet.[2] Islam is one of the four largest religions in the world, along with Christianity, Judaism, and Hinduism.

In this short survey of Islam, we will define the most important terms of this religion, mention its most prominent sects, and summarize its basic teaching contrasted with biblical Christianity. We will also give practical advice for sharing the gospel with a Muslim.

Millions of people embrace the Islamic faith. Entire countries are ruled and dominated by Islamic teachings, practices, and laws. Much of the Western world is dependent on Islamic nations for a major portion of its petroleum needs.

This appendix revised and updated by Richard Mendoza, and edited by Gretchen Passantino.

---

[1]Editor's Note: *Although Islam is a world religion, and thus not technically a "cult" as defined in this book, it is included in this volume because of its growing presence in the United States and its influence in American religious life.*

[2]The 1994 edition of *The World Almanac and the Book of Facts* (Mahway, N.J.: Funk and Wagnalls, 1993), 726–727, reports that there were 971,328,700 Muslims worldwide as of 1992, and that in the United States there were an estimated six million Muslims. That is larger than the total number of Eastern Orthodox, Episcopalians, Presbyterians, and Seventh-day Adventists. It is even larger than the number of Mormons in the United States. The only Christian denominations with more members than Islam are Baptists, Lutherans, Methodists, Pentecostals, and Roman Catholics.

Western towns, universities, and businesses are seeing a larger influx of Muslims than has ever been seen before. Islam is a religious, social, and political force that every Christian should be aware of.

Western Christians, especially, need to equip themselves to give an active defense of the biblical faith against the claims of Islam and to share the gospel of Jesus Christ in love with the followers of Muhammad. Aware of this challenge, let us begin our survey of Islam.

Definitions

Islam, like many religions, has its own vocabulary to describe its beliefs. A quick look at some of the most important religious terms in Islam will provide a basis for further discussion of Islamic history and belief.

Islam[3] is the name of the religion that came out of the revelations and teachings of Muhammad. Islam is the Arabic term for "submission." Jane I. Smith argues that "in the broadest terms, I believe that . . . while *Islam* originally meant at once the personal relationship between man and God *and* the community of those acknowledging this relationship, it often has come to be used as one *or* the other, with a greatly increased emphasis on the objectified systemization of religious beliefs and practices."[4]

However, according to another scholar, Islam originally meant

> "defiance of death (for the sake of God and his prophet)" or "readiness for defiance of death." The expression is thus semantically related to *gihad* [*jihad*], "warlike effort (for God and his prophet)," which implies also, secondarily, the sacrifice of property (viz. livestock) as a preparation for warlike action (see, e.g., Sura 9, v. 89). The religion of Muhammad, according to the usual definition, derived from the Quran, is based on two principles: *gihad* and *iman* ("faith"), or, by another definition, on *Islam* and *iman* (see, e.g., Sura 49, v. 14).[5]

Muslim[6] is the name given to one who adheres to the religion of Islam. *Muslim* is a cognate of *Islam*, and means "one who submits." The Muslim submits to the will of Allah as revealed by Muhammad.

Allah is the Islamic name for God and cannot be translated easily into English. One Muslim writer defined it thus: "The word means the unique God Who possesses all the attributes of perfection and beauty in their infinitude. Muslims

---

[3]Since there is no standardized method of transliterating Arabic script into Roman script, Islamic terms are often spelled in a variety of ways (e.g., Muhammad, Mohammed; Moslem, Muslim, etc.). We have chosen to use the spelling most popular with Muslims who write in English.

[4]Jane I. Smith, *An Historical and Semitic Study of the Term "Islam" as Seen in a Sequence of Quran Commentaries* [Harvard Dissertations in Religion] (Missoula, Mont.: Scholars Press for Harvard Theological Review, 1975): 2.

[5]M. M. Bravmann, *The Spiritual Background in Early Islam: Studies in Ancient Arab Concepts* (Leiden, The Netherlands: E. J. Brill, 1972), 8. For more studies on the etymology and usage of "Islam" and related words, see Ignaz Goldziher, *Introduction to Islamic Theology and Law*, trans. Andras and Ruth Hamori (Princeton, N.J.: Princeton University Press, 1981), 3–4, footnote b.

[6]It is incorrect to refer to a Muslim as a "Mohammadan." Muslims have a strong aversion to anything resembling idol worship. If a Muslim would accept the appellation "Mohammadan," he would think that he could be accused of worshiping Mohammed.

feel strongly that the English word 'God' does not convey the real meaning of the word 'Allah.' "[7]

Muhammad was an Arab born in the city of Mecca in A.D. 570 (died A.D. 632). He claimed that he was the prophet to restore true religion and the praise of Allah throughout the world, just as Jesus Christ was a prophet in His time for His people. Muhammad means "the one who is praised."

Quran (also spelled Koran or Qur'an) is Arabic for "the recitation," and refers to the collection of revelations supposedly given by Allah through his archangel to Muhammad and preserved as the Islamic scripture. Muslims believe in the Law of Moses, the Psalms of David, and the Injil, or gospel of Jesus Christ. However, they believe that those Scriptures were superseded by the scripture given through Muhammad, and that the Bible used by Christians and Jews is a distorted version of those other scriptures. Wherever the Bible contradicts Islam, the Muslim says the Bible is incorrect. *Sura* refers to the divisions within the Quran, and roughly corresponds to our "chapter." The Quran contains 114 revelations, each composing one sura or chapter. The shortest revelations appear first, the longest ones last. There is no chronological arrangement in the Quran. Also important in Islamic literature is the *Hadith*, Arabic for the "collected traditions." These are the supposed words of Muhammad and are the customs that provide source material for the intricate political and social structure of Islam.

Caliph is Arabic for "deputy" and refers to the main leaders of Islam, especially the immediate successors of Muhammad. *Ayatollah* refers to a spiritual master or leader in Shi'ite Islam.

"Schools" of Islam[8]

Out of the almost one billion Muslims worldwide, by far the greatest number are members of the Sunnite school. They accept the first four caliphs in direct succession from Muhammad and no others. The Sunnis[9] practice a moderate form of Islamic literary interpretation. Ninety percent of the Muslims in the Middle East are Sunnis (e.g., 90 percent of the Egyptian Muslims, 90 percent of the Jordanian Muslims, 90 percent of the Saudi Arabian Muslims, and 98 percent of the Libyan Muslims).

The second largest school of Islam is the Shi'ite school. Although much smaller than the Sunnite school, the Shi'ite school is much more literal in its interpretation and application of the Quran and is much more militant than

[7]Badru D. Kateregga, with David W. Shenk, *Islam and Christianity* (Grand Rapids, Mich.: William B. Eerdmans Publishing Company, 1980), 1.

[8]"School" as used here means "school of thought" and is comparable to denominations in Christianity.

[9]Sunni (from *sunnah*, "custom" or "tradition") Islam is considered to be the orthodox form of Islam and consists of four different rites (Maliki, Shafi'i, Hanafi and Hanbali). It came into existence after a political rival attempted to take the Caliphate away from Ali, who was the cousin, son-in-law, and fourth successor of Muhammad. Ali was elected Caliph in 656, but faced multiple conflicts throughout the Islamic empire. While Ali was winning the battle of Siffin (657) against the powerful governor of Damascus, he agreed to have an arbitrator to resolve the conflict in order to avoid further bloodshed. It was at this point that the first religious split occurred and that Sunni Islam could be seen as the majority faction.

the Sunnite. Ninety-five percent of Iran's Muslims are Shi'ites, and today Iran is a Shi'ite Islamic republic. Azerbaijan, Bahrain, Iraq, and Yemen also have large numbers of Shi'ites. The name Shi'ite is a corruption of *Shi'at Ali* ("partisans of Ali") and refers to the fact that they rejected all subsequent caliphs who were not descendants of Ali. For the Twelver Shi'ites, there followed a line of twelve *Imams*, or spiritual heads (in Sunni Islam "imam" refers only to a leader of a congregation), who claimed Ali as an ancestor. Most of them were killed, and the twelfth and final Imam, Muhammad, disappeared as a child in A.D. 878; it is believed that eventually he will miraculously return to his people (as the *Mahdi*) in a manner not altogether unlike the Judeo-Christian Messiah. He is the hidden Imam who will bring about a golden age before the end of the world, and only he has the right to declare *gihad*. Shi'ites are especially strong in Iran, Iraq, Afghanistan, and Pakistan. The Ishmailites, or Sevener Shi'ites, hold that Ismail was the final Imam. The billionaire Aga Khan is the current leader of the Ishmailites; and the Zaidites or Zaydis of Yemen hold that all war is *gihad*.[10]

Another Muslim school of note is the Ahmdiyan school, which was founded in the 1800s by Mirza Ghulam Ahmad (1839–1908) of Punjab, India. He claimed to be the Messiah and the very image of Muhammad. He taught that Christ fainted and was revived by medication (an ointment called Marham Esau ["Jesus salve"]) and traveled to India, where he died in Kashmir. This small group has produced the bulk of Islamic apologetics against Christianity and Judaism over the last forty years. The Ahmdiyans are highly visible on American campuses and practice strong proselytizing techniques on American students.

The Sufi "school" is the mystical school of Islam.[11] Sufis are rejected by many conservative Muslims. Some Sufi writings seem to reject the strict unitarian monotheism of traditional Islam for a form of "immanent pantheism."

---

[10]Caesar E. Farah, *Islam* (New York: Barron's Educational Services, 1994), 185.

[11]Other schools include Wahhabism (a literal, puritanical form of Sunni Islam held by the Saudi rulers), Ibadites (who believe that the Quran is created and are spiritual descendants of the Kharijite "Seceders," who broke away from the main group after Ali compromised with the Caliphate, and thrive in Oman and a few African countries), Qarmatians (a communal, property- and wife-sharing group found mostly in Yemen), and the Khojas or Mawlas of India, Oman, northern Syria, and Zanzibar, who are derived from the infamous, hashish-smoking Assassins. Islam also has its sects, such as the esoteric Druze who are not considered Muslims by orthodox Sunnis and believe in ten Imams, similar to the Shi'ites. They live primarily in Israel and Lebanon. Like the Druze, the Alawites are esoteric and considered outside of Islam by orthodoxy. They claim to be followers of Ali (hence the name) and they believe in reincarnation, that women do not have souls, and that God presented himself as divine emanations through Salman, Muhammad, and Ali. They have a separate holy book (the *Kitab al-Majmu*) and also have Gnostic and even Masonic religious elements. President Hafez Assad of Syria is an Alawite, and they are most populous in Syria, although still a minority. Another group getting some notoriety is the Muslim Brotherhood, or *Ikhwan*, a xenophobic Egyptian fundamentalist group that strongly believes that Islamic civil law, *sharia*, should be the law of the state. Members of this group are known for their terrorist activities, and a member's offshoot was responsible for the death of Egyptian president Anwar El-Sadat (Thomas W. Lippman, *Understanding Islam: An Introduction to the Muslim World* [New York: Mentor Books, 1990], 157–165). Other contemporary groups include the Hezbollah (Party of God) and Hamas, both devoted to the destruction of Israel. (For more, see Farah, 170–387, and John Esposito, *The Islamic Threat* [New York: Oxford University Press, 1993].)

History

According to Scripture, the ancestors of modern Arabs can be traced back to Shem and are properly known as Semites. Shem's descendant Eber gave rise to two lines: Peleg's line, from which Abraham is descended, and Joktan's line, which contains the names of many Arab groups. However, many Arab tribes trace their ancestry to Ishmael, the firstborn son of Abraham.[12] The word *Arab* refers to nomads or bedouins and may be connected with the word for desert or wilderness.[13] The original meaning expanded to refer to Arabic speakers and those living in Arabia. "Arabness" seems to be inherited through the male since intermarriage with non-Arab women was common and is still permitted by the Quran. The Spanish Umayyad Caliph Abd-er Rahman III (ruled 929–961), who was proud of his ancestry from the former ruling clan of Mecca before Muhammad, was actually only 0.93 percent Arab.[14]

The first recorded extrabiblical mention of Arabs was during the reign of Assyrian king Shalmaneser III (859–824 B.C.). Early Arabian kingdoms include Magan, Dilmun, Sa'ba, Ma'īn, Qatablān, and Hadramaut. Their deities included 'Athtar the male Venus star, Ilmuqah (also known as Hawbas, 'Amm, Anbay, Wadd, Sin, or Mawl) the moon god, and a sun goddess, Dhāt Ba'adān or Dhāt Himyan.[15] Among nomadic groups, the basic ruling unit consisted of an elected leader, or *sheikh*, who had no authoritative powers and was only considered "first among equals," and was usually selected from a powerful "sheikhly" family that was governed by custom or tradition (*sunnah*).[16] Their religion was polytheistic and was related to the paganism of the ancient Semites. The beings it adored were in origin the inhabitants and patrons of single places, living in trees, fountains, and especially in sacred stones. There were some gods in the true sense, transcending in their authority the boundaries of purely tribal cults. The three most important were Manāt, 'Uzza, and Allāt. These three were themselves subordinate to a higher deity, usually called Allah. The religion of the tribes had no real priesthood; the migratory nomads carried their gods with them in a red tent forming a kind of ark of the covenant, which accompanied them to battle. Their religion was not personal but communal. The tribal faith centered around the tribal god, symbolized usually by a stone, sometimes by some other object. It was guarded by the "sheikhly house," which thus gained some religious prestige. God and cult were the badges of tribal identity and the sole ideological expressions of the sense of unity and cohesion of the tribe. Conformity to the tribal cult expressed political loyalty. Apostasy was the equivalent of treason.[17]

The Koran mentions these pagan deities in Sura 53:19–20: "Have ye seen Lat, and 'Uzzā, and another, the third (goddess), Manāt?"[18] This is followed by

---

[12]For more information, see Louis Bahjat Hamada, *Understanding the Arab World* (Nashville: Thomas Nelson, 1990), 40–59.
[13]A. K. Irvine, "The Arabs and Ethiopians," in D. J. Wiseman, ed., *Peoples of Old Testament Times* (Oxford University Press, 1973), 289–290.
[14]Cited in Peter Mansfield, *The Arabs* (New York: Penguin Books, 1978), 46.
[15]Irvine, "The Arabs and Ethiopians," 303.
[16]Bernard Lewis, *The Arabs in History* (New York: Harper & Row, 1966), 29–30.
[17]Ibid., 30. "Cult" in this sense refers to ritualized worship of supernatural beings and includes ancestor worship, nature worship, and worship of gods or God.
[18]From the translation of A. Yusuf Ali, *The Holy Qur'ān: Translation and Commentary* (Brentwood, Md.: Amana Corp., 1983 [1934]), 1445.

an assertion (vss. 21–23) that these goddesses, the daughters of Allah the moon god according to pre-Islamic Arab theology,[19] are mere human creations that divide God into parts. These deities were popular at Mecca at the time of Muhammad's birth. Lat, or al-Lat ("the goddess"), was the sun god; 'Uzza, or al-'Uzzā ("the mighty one"), the planet Venus; and Manāt, the god of good fortune. Other gods mentioned in the Quran include Wadd (another Moon god, mentioned above), Suw'a, Yaghuth, and Nasr (Sura 71:23). Of these gods, al-'Uzza appears to be the supreme deity in Mecca.

It is believed by some scholars that Allah, or al-Ilah ("the god"), can be traced to Ilāh, the South Arabian moon god. Henotheism, or the worship of only one god while not denying the existence of other gods, may have existed in pre-Islamic society. The Quran speaks of *hanifs,* pre-Islamic Arab monotheists who were neither Christian nor Jewish. Extant evidence shows that Allah meant "the (one) God" for the many Christians, Jews, monophysites, and Nestorians who lived throughout the Arabian peninsula.[20]

Muhammad was born in Mecca, near the Middle Western coastal region of Arabia, between 570 and 580, to Abdullah (or Abd Allah), who died two months after he was born, and Aminah, who died when he was six. Mecca was a large commercial city known for the Ka'aba ("cube"), a building famous for its 360 idols containing images of the moon god Hubal, al-Lāt, al-'Uzza and Manāt, and the Black Stone. Muhammad's family was of the relatively poor Hashemite clan of the Quraysh tribe, and it is the patriarch of that tribe, Fihr (known as *qirsh,* or "shark") of the Kinānah tribe, who Muslims claim to be a descendant of Ishmael and an inheritor of God's promise to Hagar in Genesis 21:18.[21] After the death of his mother, he was sent to live with his grandfather, Abd-al-Muttalib, who provided a Bedouin foster mother for him, Halimah, and was raised in the desert. After the death of his grandfather when Muhammad was eight, he re-

[19]See Alfred Guillaume, *Islam* (London: Penguin Books, 1954), 6.

[20]Ibid., 7. *Monophysitism* is the belief that Christ has a single divine nature that inhabits a fleshly body, which has a different nature than other human bodies, or that the human and divine natures were mixed. It may be traced to Apollinaris (c. 310–390) and Eutychius (c. 378–454) and presently continues in some Armenian, Coptic, Ethiopian, and Syrian Jacobite churches. *Nestorianism* is a heresy that was falsely attributed to Nestorius (d. c. 451), Patriarch of Constantinople; namely, that Christ had two persons and two natures. He actually taught that Mary was the *Christotokos* ("Christ-bearer"). Christ possessed a common *prosopōn* (literally "face," but used here metaphorically for "person," especially for one's innermost being). See Peter Toon, "Nestorianism; Nestorius" in J. D. Douglas, ed., *The New Dictionary of the Christian Church* (Grand Rapids, Mich.: Zondervan, 1978), 699–700.

[21]A divine promise is given regarding Ishmael's descendants in verse 16:10 (also 17:20; 21:13, 18): they are to make a great nation. According to 16:11–12, Ishmael will be "a wild ass of a man," which may mean "unrestrained," but can also mean "lawless" since he will be constantly fighting with all men while "he shall dwell in (or preferably *against* [see Derek Kidner, *Genesis: An Interpretation and Commentary,* Tyndale Old Testament Commentaries (Downer's Grove, Ill.: InterVarsity Press, 1967), 127], or *in defiance of,* Victor P. Hamilton, *The Book of Genesis, Chapters 1–17,* The New International Commentary on the New Testament [Grand Rapids, Mich.: Eerdmans, 1990], 454–455) the presence of his brethren" (v. 12). Ishmael and his mother, Hagar the Egyptian (Genesis 16; 21:9), left Abraham after Sarah found Ishmael to be mocking during or after the feast given for the weaning of Isaac (Genesis 21:9–12). They wandered to Beersheba in southern Canaan (v. 14) and later to Paran in the southern Sinai region (v. 21). His twelve children ruled as princes from Havilah (central or northern Arabia) to Shur (northern Sinai) according to Genesis 25:12–18. Muhammad, according to Muslim historians, is descended from either Nebajoth, Ishmael's firstborn, or Kedar, his second son. Many authorities, however, are dubious of an Ishmaelite ancestry for Muhammad, noting that the issue was first brought up only after Meccan Jews refused to convert to Islam.

turned to Mecca to live with his uncle, Abu Talib. All of his early familial background is from traditional sources and may not be accurate.

At twenty-five, Muhammad married a wealthy forty-year-old widow, Khadijah, after she proposed to him. Muhammad remained with Khadijah for twenty-
five years and had two sons, who died in infancy, and four daughters. After Khadijah died in 619 or 620, Muhammad married a widow of a disciple and a seven-
year-old (who moved in with him when she was ten), Ayisha. His seventh wife
was his ex-daughter-in-law; by the time of his death he had twelve wives and two
concubines (including Maryam, an Egyptian Coptic slave).[22] Interestingly, Sura
4:3 limits the number of wives to four, and in Sura 4:31 marriage to one's daugh-
ter-in-law was prohibited. But in Sura 33:36–40, Muhammad was conveniently
given a new revelation from God that ordered Zaid, Muhammad's adopted son,
to divorce his wife so Muhammad could marry her by God's command. This is
called abrogation, to be discussed later.

According to extra-Quranic sources, Muhammad's first mystical experience
was allegedly being attacked by two men who cut his belly open in search of
something. His foster mother thought he was demon-possessed after finding
him standing and not having appeared to be the victim of any violence. He later
claimed his nonexistent attackers to be angels who cleansed his heart. In A.D.
610, he claimed to have received his first of a series of revelations of the Quran
from God through the angel Gabriel. His first disciple was his wife, then his
cousin Ali, then his slave, and then his friend Abu Bakr. His following grew without many problems: first with slaves and the poor and oppressed, and then some
wealthy clans, because, according to some, he used the so-called Satanic verses
(a now-deleted version of Sura 53:19 that advocated the worship of the three
daughters of Allah; later the angel Gabriel chided Muhammad for claiming divine inspiration for this verse and told him he did this on his own while under
Satan's power) in preaching to the unconverted. Muslim apologists claim the
Satanic verses incident never happened and he had always derided the existence
of pagan gods. At any rate, others began to challenge him, although his movement continued to grow. His wife and his uncle, who was his protector, both
died in 619 or 620. The following year he was offered protection from powerful
families in Yathrib. The next significant event was the *hijra*.

The *hijra* ("migration") is the name of the event that marks the beginning
of Islam. After his uncle Abu Talib died, the leaders of the various Meccan tribes
and clans vowed to assassinate him. The angel Gabriel warned him of this, and
he and his friend Abu Bakr fled to Yathrib, 280 miles north of Mecca. Yathrib
was a town dominated by Jewish groups but was at that time without a stable
government, primarily consisting of feuding Arab factions and mediating Jewish
tribes. Muhammad, after arriving on September 20, 622, temporarily remained
as other Muslim followers emigrated and built up troop strength. Soon he established the *umma*, a theocracy (or dictatorship) under his authority, and held
complete control of Yathrib, renamed Medina.

Badr was conquered in 626, and in 627 a Meccan army 10,000 strong arrived
to attack Medina, but Muhammad and his 3000 men had prepared by digging

---

[22]Ali Dashti believes that he had sixteen wives, two concubines, and four "lovers" (see *Twenty-Three
Years: A Study of the Prophetic Career of Mohammed* (London: George Allen & Unwin, 1985), 120–138.

a trench around the city. The Meccans later gave up and turned back. The Medinans retaliated by attacking a Jewish tribe, the Banu Qurayza, for allegedly conspiring with the Meccans, and killed all the 800 male Jews of this tribe while selling all of the women and children into slavery. Two other Medinan Jewish tribes, the Banu Qaynuqa and the Banu Nadr, were driven from their homes and had all of their property confiscated. In 628, they conquered another group of Jews at Khaybar, and paid the *jizya*[23] to be left alone. Finally, in 630, they conquered Mecca. On June 8, 632, Muhammad died. His successors soon wrested Palestine and Syria away from the Byzantines (629–641), conquered Iraq and Persia (633–643), Egypt (639), Tripoli (644), Toledo in Spain and western India (712), Crete (825), and Sicily (899). In West Africa, Muslims under Almoravid rulers pillaged the capital of Ghana (1076). Nubia, in East Africa, survived, as did a few small Christian nations until the 1500s.

Arab domination of conquered lands did not last forever, and soon many Muslim states declared their independence. In the early 1000s, the Seljuk Turks, who had only recently embraced Islam, began taking over territory previously held by Arab Muslims. By 1055 Tughrul Beg, leader of the Seljuk Turks, took control of Baghdad. Eventually under the Ottoman Turks, who supplanted the Seljuks, Muslims went far into Europe, conquering Serbia (1459), Greece (1461), Bosnia (1463), Herzegovina (1483), Montenegro (1499), parts of Hungary (1526–1547) and Poland (1676). Although there were wars with European countries in the interim, many countries did not regain independence until the 1800s. Montenegro did not win independence until 1799, Serbia in 1817, Greece in 1821, and Bulgaria in 1878. Many Middle Eastern areas held by the Turks were lost under Napoleon Bonaparte, and later held by the British and French.

Moreover, many modern Middle Eastern countries did not come into existence as we know them until the early twentieth century. Iraq became independent in 1921, Egypt in 1937, Lebanon in 1945, Syria in 1946, Jordan in 1946, and Kuwait in 1961.

Muslim and Non-Muslim Relations

Apparently when Muhammad started his new movement, he encouraged nonbelievers to freely consider Islam: Sura 2:256 says, "Let there be no compulsion in religion." Later, however, he seemed to have developed a much harsher attitude: Sura 9:5 says, "Fight and slay the idolaters wherever you find them, and seize them, and besiege them, and lie in wait for them." What may be considered crimes against the state and crimes against God are dealt with in Sura 5:33, "The punishment of those who wage war against God and His Apostle, and strive with might and main for mischief through the land is: execution, or crucifixion, or the cutting off of hands and feet from opposite sides, or exile from the land." Jews and Christians are "People of the Book" (Sura 5:5; 5:19), but that does not mean that Muhammad had the highest regard for them; in Sura 5:41 Jews are called people "who will listen to any lie" and Christians are

---

[23]A special poll tax non-Muslim "People of the Book" paid in order to have legal rights and protection. They were also to be excluded from military service.

enemies (Sura 5:14), and Muslims were not to have Christians and Jews as friends (Sura 5:51).

The Pact of Omar, originally written around 637 by Christians under Caliph Omar I, essentially imported most of the religious rights of Christians (and Jews) and gave them to Muslims: They agreed not to repair damaged churches or erect new ones, agreed to provide shelter to any Muslim traveler, agreed not to display crosses on churches, agreed not to preach too loudly when a Muslim happened to be present, agreed not to bear arms, and agreed not to adopt any aspect of Muslim culture, among other conditions, in order to receive Muslim protection. Any failure to follow these provisions meant loss of protection and possible persecution. Despite such restrictions (which were taken over from an earlier version that gave Christians this authority), many Christians and Jews became intellectual leaders in Islamic nations, and many held high political positions. Both monophysites and Nestorians apparently preferred life under Muslim Arab rule, rather than under Byzantine or Roman Catholic rule, due to the much higher frequency of persecution under Eastern Orthodoxy and Catholicism.

However, penalties for not following the strict demands could be quite severe. In 1796 the early American statesman Joel Barlow described conditions in Turkish-controlled Algeria: "The number of mosques . . . is infinite in Algiers. One can look in while passing before the door, but it is forbidden for an Infidel to enter. The penalty for this crime is to become a Muhammadan, to be hanged, or burned alive, depending on whether one is a Christian or a Jew. If it happens to me, through intoxication or some other accident to fall into this death, I shall become a Muhammadan immediately, for I have not enough religion of any kind to make me a martyr."[24]

Christians and Jews under Islamic rule usually fared well, in many cases much better than in Roman Catholic Western Europe. Eastern Christians, such as Theophanes (writing in the early 800s), regarded Islam as a heresy and challenged it as they had challenged Arianism, monophysitism, and monothelitism. The earliest Western Christian contacts with Islam were when the Muslims conquered Spain. Christians paid the *jizya* in exchange for their freedom. By the ninth century, Christians and Jews worked as tax collectors, political ministers, bodyguards, and soldiers. Except for a brief revolt in Toledo in 837 by some Christians and Jews, most Spanish Christians regarded Muslims as fellow monotheists who held the Bible in high regard; one priest complained about the large numbers of Spaniards who preferred to study Arabic literature to Scripture. Things changed in the 850s, when Eulogius (d. 859) denounced Islam as a heresy and called Muhammad "the Antichrist" and a false prophet. In Córdova during this time about fifty Spaniards denounced Islam and were put to death.[25] Except for Francis of Assisi (1181 or 1182–1226) and Raymond Lull (1235–1315),[26] there were no significant evangelistic missions to Muslims until

---

[24]Charles Burr Todd, *Life and Letters of Joel Barlow* (New York: Da Capo Press, 1970), 127 (letter dated March 14, 1796).

[25]Kenneth Baxter Wolf, "The Earliest Spanish Christian Views of Islam," *Church History*, 55:3 (September 1986).

[26]Lull was a Spanish missionary and philosopher who sought to win over Jews and Muslims by rational argumentation. He began his missionary work at age forty, and was stoned to death in North Africa on June 30, 1315, after preaching before a crowd in an open market.

Henry Martyn spread the gospel in Muslim India in the early 1800s.

Although as late as the fourteenth century Islam continued to be seen as a Christian heresy, dialogue and debate was almost nonexistent.[27]

From the example of the Medinan Jews, to the more recent examples of the 50,000 Greeks and Armenians massacred in 1822, the 10,000 Armenians and Nestorians murdered in 1850, 11,000 Maronites and Syrians in 1860, 15,000 Bulgarians in 1876, 10,000 Armenians in 1894, 325,000 Armenians from 1895–1908, 30,000 Armenians in 1909, and 80 percent of the Armenian population (1.5 million) wiped out in 1915–1918, religious persecution has been a frequent occurrence under Islam. Idi Amin Dada murdered at least 300,000 fellow Ugandans in the 1970s. In the '80s and '90s, Muslim Arabs in North Sudan were either starving or selling into slavery Black Christians and animists in the South. Oppression against non-Muslims in general, but Christians in particular, has also occurred in Libya, Mauritania, Nigeria, and Tanzania. In 1990 it was believed that Mauritania had at least 400,000 slaves. In 1994 Iran began a campaign of persecution against Christians, especially the Assemblies of God. Even in the more "moderate" Muslim nations, such as Saudi Arabia, importation of a Bible, Christian evangelism, and conversion from Islam may be considered capital offenses. The nations where such extreme measures exist are those that practice a strong adherence to Islamic law (sharia). According to The State of Religion Atlas, as of 1993 sixteen countries have sharia nationalized into their state legal systems.[28]

Oppression of Muslims by Christians has occurred in Chad and in Ethiopia under Haile Selassie II. The horrible civil war in predominantly Roman Catholic Rwanda, which began in 1994, has resulted in the deaths of hundreds of thousands. Moreover, to argue that a particular belief is false because of its history is to commit a logical fallacy. It does not follow that because of the many errors or even the atrocities on the part of the adherents of a religion that the theology of that particular religion is necessarily in error. The theology of any religion must be judged separately from the behavior of its participants. Furthermore, it must be admitted that many Christians and so-called Christians have committed their share of atrocities: the Crusades, witch burnings, and the Inquisition being prime examples.

Islamic Beliefs

At first glance, Islamic belief appears to be almost compatible with Christianity and/or Judaism. Often people claim that the Muslims believe in the same God as Christians: "They just don't accept Jesus Christ." However, as we shall see, the Muslim God is not like the Christian God. Islam rejects the biblical doctrines of the Trinity and the deity of Christ.

---

[27]Dante in his Divine Comedy, 28:31–36, refers to Muhammad as a heretic and a "sower of scandal and schism."

[28]Joanne O'Brien and Martin Palmer. The State of Religion Atlas (New York: Touchstone Books, 1993), 64–65. For slavery in Mauritania see Watts Star Review (July 14, 1994): A–1; for contemporary slavery see Africa Reports, especially the article by Janet Fleischman, "Ethnic Cleansing" (Jan./Feb. 1994) and follow up letter (71) in the May/June issue.

God

For the Muslim, Allah is the only true God. There is no such blasphemous thing as the "Trinity." The Muslim God is unapproachable by sinful man, and the Muslim's desire is to submit to the point where he can hold back the judging arm of Allah and inherit eternal life in an earthly paradise of gluttony and sexual gratification. Muslims have no concept of God as a loving and compassionate Father.

To the Muslim, God is not only a harsh, wrathful God, even though he is those things too. The Muslim considers his God loving and merciful, as Sura 11:90 says, "Ask forgiveness of your Lord, then repent to Him; surely my Lord is All-compassionate, All-loving" and 85:14 says, "He is the All-forgiving, the All-loving." The Quran is clear that Allah is compassionate and merciful, but aside from the two above passages where God is called the "All-loving," there is not a single passage in the Quran that indicates that God loves any portion of mankind, nor is there a single verse that indicates that people can know God on a personal, relational level (although Muslims believe God to be a person). Unlike the Christian, the Muslim cannot have a *personal* relationship with God. Scripture tells us that those who trust in Christ, do the Father's will, and have been redeemed have been adopted as sons (Romans 8:14–15; Galatians 3:26). We are heirs of God (Galatians 4:7) and the Father deals with us as His children (Matthew 12:47; Mark 3:35; Hebrews 12:5, 7). We can even be called His friends (John 15:13–15; James 2:23). On the other hand, those who deny the Son have the devil for their father (John 8:44). "All-loving" appears to be nothing more than a divine name that describes God's mercy on those who repent and practice Islam, as opposed to being a personal characteristic.

To Muslims God has no likeness (Sura 42:11), is transcendent (Sura 4:171), is unknowable (apart from revelation), and is wholly other and totally different. He is neither physical nor spirit. The Bible, contradicting the Quran, tells us that we have been created in God's image and likeness (Genesis 1:26–27) and that we have knowledge of God in our hearts (Romans 1:19–20). Moreover, Scripture tells us that God is spirit (John 4:24).

Currently, there are two schools of thought within Sunnah that offer varying interpretations of who God is. According to the orthodox school, God is said to have a "face, hand, and soul, but it is not legitimate to inquire how, for these belong to his qualities; God has no body."[29] Guillaume adds that in the *Fiqh Akbar*, a creed compiled around the year 1000 and representative of orthodoxy, "Allah is absolute in his decrees of good and evil. He does not resemble his creatures in any respect. He has existed from eternity with his qualities, those belonging to his essence and those pertaining to his activity."[30] The Quran is the eternal speech of God, the angel Gabriel to Muhammad. The Quran contains terms that attribute qualities to God, and the orthodox Muslim believes that God has attributes, but is not sure what they mean. If God is good, is *good* to be understood univocally (equal meanings) or equivocally (totally different meanings)? Christian missionary and Islamic scholar Kenneth Cragg elaborates:

Classical Muslim theology developed a form of compromise solution, in

---

[29]Guillaume, 135.
[30]Ibid.

effect inclining to the negative answer. There developed the idea of *Al-Mukhal-afah*, "the difference." Terms taken from human meanings—and there are of course no others—were said to be used of God with a difference. They did not convey the human connotation but were used in those senses of God. When the further question was pressed: What, then, do they convey as applied to God? no precise answer could be formulated. Islam here falls back upon a final agnosticism. Terms must be used if there is to be religion at all. But only God knows what they signify.[31]

Nevertheless, the Muslim believes that God is neither physical nor spirit. God is a totally unique being that has no similarity in any sense to any other being. To the Muslim, to believe otherwise would mean that God somehow shares his attributes and by implication leads to the grave sin of *shirk* (Sura 4:116; 5:72; 9:31), assigning partners to God.

The other school consists of "Muslim scholars, many of them thoroughly established in Western centers of learning, who reject the minutiae of traditional Quranic commentary, plead for the 'major themes' of the book, and aim to invoke them by intelligent translation of their meaning in the seventh century A.D. to their relevance today."[32] One example that Cragg has in mind is Fazlur Rahman, who in *Major Themes of the Qur'an* tells us that "the Qur'an is no treatise about God and His nature: His existence, for the Qur'an, is strictly functional."[33] Yet Rahman does find that within the Quran it can be shown that God is an organic unity, transcendent, merciful, purposeful, good, and omnipotent. He also allows for metaphors in the Quran,[34] something orthodox Islam seems to have historically avoided. To do otherwise might lead to contradiction, such as where one day can equal a thousand years (Sura 32:5) or 50,000 years (Sura 70:4). He also argues that the laws of nature, including moral laws, can be created and uncreated at will by Allah.[35] This seems to indicate *voluntarism*, that is, it is from the deeds and acts of God that standards are derived. This is opposed to *essentialism* where standards would be derived from God's nature.

One of the prerogatives of the Quran is *abrogation*, a legal term referring to the "destruction or annulling of a former law by an act of the legislative power, by constitutional authority, or by usage."[36] This is something taught in three separate places in the Quran. Sura 2:100/106 says, "And for whatever verse we abrogate or cast into oblivion, we bring one better or like it"; Sura 13:39 has, "Every term has a Book. God blots out, and He establishes whatsoever He will; and with Him is the Mother of all Books"; and Sura 16:101 (A. J. Arberry's translation) says, "And when we exchange a verse in the place of another verse—and God knows very well what He is sending down—they say, 'The art a mere forger!' Nay, but the most of them have no knowledge. Say: 'The Holy Spirit [in Islam the angel Gabriel is the Holy Spirit] sent it down from the Lord in truth, and to confirm those who believe, and to be a guidance and good tidings to those who surrender."[37] On pages 89 and 90 Rahman argues that abrogation in the

---

[31] *The Call of the Minaret* (Maryknoll, N.Y.: Orbis Books, 1985), 48–49.

[32] Ibid., 22.

[33] *Major Themes of the Qur'an* (Minneapolis: Bibliotheca Islamica, 1980), 1.

[34] Ibid., 66.

[35] Ibid., 13, 78–79.

[36] *Black's Law Dictionary*, abridged 5th ed. (St. Paul, Minn.: West Publishing Co., 1983), 3.

[37] *The Koran Interpreted* (London: George Allen & Unwin, 1955).

Quran does not have the legal meaning, but should be understood as "substitution" necessary for progressive revelation. Since substitution means replacing one thing for another for some purpose, why is it necessary if the Quran is the eternal speech of God? This seems to indicate that God can change his mind, something vastly different from the biblical God who is unchangeable in His character and essence. If God is the All-knowing, on what basis is there a need to substitute? Jesus said He did not come to destroy the Law, but to fulfill it (Matthew 5:17) and that heaven and earth would pass away before even the smallest jot or tittle would pass away (5:18). Scripture is never abrogated, because God does not change (Malachi 3:6). So despite all arguments to the contrary, if the Quran is abrogated, we run into a multitude of theological problems. Here are six:

1. The Quran cannot be trusted because it contains "divinely inspired" contradictions. If God has a history of abrogating his own revelation, the "eternal speech of God," how can one be certain that he will not abrogate it again in the future?

2. It may be argued that it cannot be abrogated again in the future since Muhammad was "the last prophet." But how do we know that God will not abrogate that and send us more prophets?

3. If God can abrogate his eternal speech, how can we trust him with our eternal soul? Shall we depend on his mercy and compassion? How do we know that he will continue to be as merciful in the future as he has been in the past? How do we even know that he has been merciful in the past since the mercy sections of the Quran may themselves actually be substitutions?

4. If God has done any abrogating, as the Quran indicates, it does not indicate progressive revelation, which is additive, but rather contradiction and annulment, which subtracts from revelation since at least some portion of past revelation has been canceled. This would mean that God either did not know how future contingent events would turn out, or that he did but purposefully changed his mind. So the God of Islam is either not All-knowing or is a liar. A third possibility would be that God can have the attribute of omniscience and not have it at the same time (thereby actualizing a contradiction) by not only not having a physical or spiritual nature, but by not having a nature of any kind![38] Obviously this is absurd, but it does seem to follow from the Quranic view of God.

5. If God can abrogate past divine revelation it seems to indicate intellectual weakness at the very least. It not only causes problems for omniscience, since he did not have sufficient foreknowledge to avoid the need for abrogation, but also for omnipotence (because if he did have sufficient foreknowledge he apparently did not have the power to carry out effective preventive measures), as well as other attributes.

6. If the Muslim God is not consistent, then his creatures have no foundation for morality and ethics. Morality and ethics must either be absolute, invariant, and universal or not absolute, invariant, and universal. There is no third option. If God is not invariant, then the moral/ethical system derived from him

---

[38]For more on this concept, see Alvin Plantinga, *Does God Have a Nature?* (Milwaukee, Wis.: Marquette University Press, 1980), especially 91.

would necessarily be inconsistent and we would essentially be on our own. We would be autonomous (a law unto ourselves) because we lacked that divine absolute standard that exists only in Christianity. If each person had their own moral standard, there could be no legal basis for a society of any kind. This would seem to conflict with the Muslim concept of sharia. This would make it not only inherently contradictory but impossible.

Finally, there should be a word about the claim that the Quran misunderstands the Christian doctrine of the Trinity. This is unlikely, as Geoffrey Parrinder convincingly argues.[39] In pre-Islamic Arabia, a heretical Christian sect developed called the Collyridians. They were primarily women, originally from Thrace, who believed the Virgin Mary was a goddess and offered cylindrical cakes (*kollureoes* in Greek, from which their name is derived) to her and then ate them. It is perhaps this group that the Quran is addressing in Sura 5:116 ("O Jesus, son of Maryam! Did you say to mankind: Take me and my mother for two gods beside Allah?"), as the Bishop of Salamis in Greece, Epiphanius (c. 315–403), had rebuked them earlier.[40] He also wrote about another group who believed that Mary had sexual relations with a Roman soldier named "Panther," called the Anticomarionites.[41] This sounds a lot like the Talmudic anti-Christian writings Tosefta, *Hullin*, 2:22ff, and Babylonian Talmud *Abodah Zarah* 27b, and referred to by Origen, *Against Celsius*, book 1, chap. 32. Joseph Klausner[42] and F. F. Bruce believed this could be a corruption of the Greek word for virgin, *parthenos*.[43] Elsewhere the Quran seems to be attacking the heresy of Patrippassianism (that is, the Father became the Son and suffered on the cross), such as in Suras 5:17 and 5:72, where identifying all of God with Jesus was condemned. In other parts of the Quran, however, such as Sura 9:30, Christian beliefs are accurately identified and attacked.

Jesus Christ

To the Muslim, Jesus Christ is merely one of the many prophets of Allah (Sura 4:171; 5:74). According to Islam, the prophet Muhammad supersedes Jesus Christ. Jesus Christ is not the Son of God or a part of any Trinity (Sura 5:17; 5:116; 19:35).[44] We are told that He was nothing but a slave on whom God showed favor (Sura 43:59; yet elsewhere we are told the Messiah is not a slave [Sura 4:172]). Jesus Christ did not atone for anyone's sins, although He was himself sinless (Sura 3:46) and is one of those who are near to God (Sura 3:45). Positively, the Quran says that Jesus Christ performed miracles (Sura 3:49;

---

[39]*Jesus in the Qur'an* (New York: Oxford University Press, 1974), 133–141.

[40]Epiphanius, *Panarion*, in *The Panarion of St. Epiphanius, Bishop of Salamis: Selected Passages*, trans. and ed. Philip R. Amidon, S.J. (New York: Oxford University Press, 1990), 353–354.

[41]Ibid., 348–352.

[42]*Jesus of Nazareth: His Life, Times, and Teaching* (Boston: Beacon Press, 1964 [1925]), 23–24

[43]*Jesus and Christian Origins Outside the New Testament* (Grand Rapids, Mich.: Eerdmans, 1974), 57–58, 62, 175.

[44]It is possible, as Geoffrey Parrinder argues, that Muhammad was not refuting Christianity, but early pseudo-Christian cults. The Islamic "trinity" referred to may be related to the Collyridian heresy previously mentioned. The Nestorians would have agreed that to say "God is Christ" would be misleading since to them it would imply that *all* of God is Christ. This is the reason they objected to the term *theotokos* ("God bearer"), preferring instead *Christotokos*, or if *theotokos* were to be used it would be in combination with *anthrotokos* ("man bearer"). It is known that there were many Nestorian missions to Arabia in Muhammad's day.

5:110) and was the Messiah (Sura 3:45; 4:157, 171). Jesus Christ did not die on the cross. Various Muslim traditions say that He either miraculously substituted Judas Iscariot for himself on the cross, or that God miraculously delivered Him from the hands of the Romans and Jews before He could be crucified. Most Muslims believe that Jesus Christ was taken bodily into heaven without having died (Sura 4:157). However, Sura 199:33 says He died and would be resurrected.

It is interesting to compare Jesus and Muhammad according to the Quran. Jesus did miracles (Sura 3:49; 5:110), but Muhammad did not (Sura 13:8: "thou art a warner [of coming divine judgment] only"; also 6:37; 6:109; 17:59 and 17:90–93); Jesus was sinless (Sura 3:46), but Muhammad sinned and needed forgiveness (Sura 40:55: "ask forgiveness of thy sin"; 42:5: "ask forgiveness for those on the Earth"; 47:19: "ask forgiveness for thy sin"; 48:2: "that Allah may forgive thee of thy sin"). Jesus was called "the Messiah" and was even born of a virgin (3:45–57)! Yet Muhammad is supposed to be the greatest of the prophets.

Sin and Salvation

The Quran teaches that all have sinned: "If God were to take mankind to task for their wrongdoing, he would not leave here one living creature" (Sura 16:61a; see also 42:5), and were created weak (Sura 4:28). We are even told that Muhammad sinned (Sura 40:55; 47:19; 48:2). Every Muslim who hopes to escape the judgment of Allah must fulfill the works of the Five Pillars of the Faith (Sura 10:109):

1. Recitation of the *Shahada* ("There is no God but Allah, and Muhammad is the prophet of Allah");

2. Five daily prescribed prayers (*Salat* or *Namaz*) in Arabic. These prayers include genuflection and prostration in the direction of the holy city, Mecca;

3. Almsgiving (*Zakat*), which is unlike tithing since Muslims are only required to give one-fortieth of their income as charitable contributions;

4. Fasting (*Saum* or *Ruzeh*) during the entire month of Ramadan, when Muslims are supposed to fast from all food and drink from sunrise to sunset in atonement for their own sins over the previous year (however, after sunset many Muslims enjoy a feast and some get up before sunrise to eat some more before the sun rises and the fast begins again);

5. A pilgrimage (*Hajj*) to Mecca, the holy city, at least once in a Muslim's lifetime.

Holy War (*gihad*) used to be a condition of faith, and early Muslims believed it was their sacred duty to murder anyone who would not embrace the one true faith. Contemporary Islam is much more moderate, although some groups talk of restoring *gihad* as one of the essentials of Islamic faith. Literally, *gihad* means "struggle" or "utmost effort" and in most cases signifies prayerful effort, although Muhammad and many of his successors have called for *gihad*, which resulted in the deaths of many "infidels."[45]

---

[45]For more, see Thomas W. Lippman, *Understanding Islam: An Introduction to the Muslim World* (New York: Mentor Books, 1990), 112–120.

Sharing the Gospel with a Muslim

The key topics of discussion between a Christian and a Muslim should be the nature of God, the identity and deity of Jesus Christ, and salvation by grace alone apart from works. Christians can share with Muslims that the Christian God transcends humankind's finitude and sinfulness because He cares about and loves people individually. Divine love is a concept missing from Islam and yet essential to human peace and happiness with God. A powerful witness of Scripture to God's love is John 3:16: "For God so loved the world, that He gave His only begotten Son, that whosoever believeth in him should not perish, but have everlasting life." When told about Jesus, many Muslims will refuse to listen, claiming that our Scriptures are distorted and untrustworthy. The Christian can refer the interested Muslim to the many fine volumes available showing the inerrancy and inspiration of the Bible, both Old and New Testaments. This can provide a foundation for the Christian to present the New Testament teaching that Jesus Christ is truly God and is the only way to salvation (see chapter 5 on Jehovah's Witnesses for a thorough discussion of the deity of Christ).

Another approach would be to show how the Muslim view of a voluntaristic God who can abrogate the scriptures of Judaism, Christianity, and Islam prevents any system of morality and ethics from ever existing. Such a God is self-contradictory and prevents us from ever knowing anything for certain, especially our salvation. The Christian can also share how the Quran holds to a high view of Scripture (Sura 4:47; 4:54) and that believers should check the Quran against the Bible (Sura 5:44–49; 10:95). The Muslim may charge that Jews and Christians have mistranslated the Bible, but the Quran says that they only *misinterpret* and *disbelieve* it (Sura 3:70–71). According to the Quran, only Jews have mistranslated Scripture (Sura 2:75–79; 4:46). Textually, all variations of the Quran were destroyed by Caliph Uthman (ruled 646–656), and his version is the only version in existence.

The Old Testament has several extant versions that were around many years before Muhammad was even born, such as the Septuagint, the Syrian Peshitta, and the Targums. The New Testament has at least 9,000 manuscript copies existing before Muhammad, as well as over 36,000 quotations in the writings of the early church Fathers. The Quran cites its elegance as evidence for its inspiration (Sura 17:88), but many eloquent books have been written throughout history, from the *Iliad* and the *Odyssey* to *Paradise Lost* and *Moby Dick*. Does their eloquence also make them divine revelation? Obviously eloquence, even if true (and it is debatable that the Quran is stylistically elegant), is totally irrelevant.

The evidence clearly shows that the Bible we have is very close to the original and that it has not been tampered with. Moreover, there are multiple discrepancies in the Quran as well as many places where it contradicts Scripture. Sura 11:42–43 contradicts Genesis 6—7 by saying that Noah had a son who died in the Flood and Sura 3:41 contradicts Luke when it says that Zechariah was speechless for three days (Luke 1:18–20). Sura 61:6 claims that Muhammad fulfills prophecy both in the Torah and in the Gospels.

The Quran claims to fulfill prophecies in Deuteronomy 18:15–18 and John 14:16. Deuteronomy 18:15–18 is a portion of a speech given by Moses to the Israelites, beginning at Deuteronomy 5:1, in which Moses prophesied that God

would raise up a prophet like him from their midst. The meaning of this prophecy is partially explained in verse 34:10: "And there arose not a prophet since in Israel like unto Moses, *whom the Lord knew face to face*" (italics added). Yet the Quran was revealed to Muhammad by the angel Gabriel, not directly by God, and Muhammad never claimed to be a descendant of Israel, but of Ishmael. If the Quran is to fulfill the Torah and the Gospels as it claims, the Muslim should read Acts 3:22–23, in which Peter speaks of Jesus as the prophet spoken of by Moses.

John 14:16 reports that Jesus said that the Father will give the Helper to His disciples and that He would abide with them forever. Verse 17 adds that He would dwell with them and be in them. The Greek word for "Helper," or more properly "Advocate," *paracletos*, is claimed by Muslim apologists to be *periclutos*, "renowned." Somehow this word, which is not found anywhere in the New Testament, is understood by Muslims to mean "praised one," since the Sura claims that Jesus prophesied that he was sending the "good tidings of the Messenger who comes after me, whose name shall be Ahmad ["Praised One"]." To add to their claim, Muslim apologists argue that the verse has been tampered with by Christians (contradicting Sura 2:73–79). But there is not a single manuscript copy that has *periclutos*, nor is there any contextual sense where Muhammad could somehow be fitted into the verse. Muhammad, being human, could not abide with Christ's disciples forever, dwell with them over 500 years before he was born, nor live in them. If he could, he would be a much greater prophet than he claimed! On the other hand, there is ample evidence to suggest that Sura 61:6 was interpolated after Muhammad's death. W. Montgomery Watt cogently shows that "*it is impossible to prove that any Muslim child was called Ahmad after the Prophet before about the year 125.*"[46]

At any rate, John 14:26 specifically identifies the *paracletos* with the Holy Spirit.[47] Sometimes the Muslim will argue that the rapid spread of Islam shows the truth of the religion (Sura 41:53), but several empires have spread faster than Islam, such as the empires under Alexander the Great and Genghis Khan. One could also counter that the rapid spread of communism was evidence of its truthfulness. At any rate, their argument is simply an appeal to irrelevancy.

Next, tell the Muslim the good news that salvation and peace with God does not depend on his own insufficient efforts, but on the grace of God displayed through the atonement of Jesus Christ on the cross. No one can work his way to heaven (or Muslim paradise). The Muslim will agree that Allah could justly choose to bar all men from paradise since no man is perfect as Allah is perfect. However, *biblical* salvation does not depend on man's imperfections. Biblical salvation depends on the work and love of God. "For by grace are ye saved through faith; and that not of yourselves; it is the gift of God: not of works, lest any man should boast" (Ephesians 2:8–10).

---

[46]*Early Islam: Collected Articles* (Edinburgh: Edinburgh University Press, 1990), 43–50. Italics his. The year 125 means 125 years after the Hijra according to the Muslim dating system (ca. A.D. 755. For additional evidence that this is a later insertion, see Parrinder, *Jesus*, 96–100.

[47]For more on the meaning of *paracletos*, see Leon Morris, *The Gospel According to John*, The New International Commentary on the New Testament (Grand Rapids, Mich.: Eerdmans, 1971), 662–666. For more contradictions between the Bible and the Quran, see Gleason L. Archer, Jr., *A Survey of Old Testament Introduction* (Chicago: Moody Press, 1964), 498–500, as well as the previously mentioned works by Parrinder and Dashti.

Finally, the Christian should love the Muslim. Muslims have a definite zeal for God. They desire to follow God and express their worship of God through their lives. The Christian should respect Muslims' sincere intentions and share with them the life-changing Gospel of Jesus Christ. The Christian should also share the fact that he believes God is great. When a Christian can demonstrate the power of the Word of God through the Holy Spirit and use his own life as an example of the joy and peace possible to those who love Jesus Christ, he becomes an effective example to the Muslim of the opportunity to know and worship the true God rather than Muhammad's distorted concepts about God.

Supplemental Section: the Nation of Islam

With an estimated 100,000 members in the United States,[48] the Nation of Islam is a force to be reckoned with. Spike Lee's 1992 film *Malcolm X* and the many well-publicized speeches of Rev. Louis Farrakhan and Khallid Abdul Muhammad have helped to keep the Nation of Islam in the national spotlight for years. It is influential among African-Americans of all generations, but especially the young. Rappers and rap groups such as Public Enemy and Ice Cube and numerous African-American college and university student publications actively promote many of the beliefs and ideas held by the Nation of Islam.

The Nation [of Islam] derives from a group called the Moorish-American Science Temple in Newark, New Jersey, established in 1913 by B. Timothy Drew (1866–1929). Drew (who changed his name to Noble Drew Ali), a black North Carolinian, claimed to have received a commission from the king of Morocco to spread Islam in the United States, but his version of Islam avoided African ancestral teachings and instead taught that all non-whites are Asians. Christianity is the white Europeans' religion, and Islam is for the Asian, or more specifically, the Moor (black Asians). After Drew died, he was succeeded by John Givens El in Chicago and Wallace D. Fard (or Farad) in Detroit, each claiming to be the reincarnation of Drew. El's followers are known as Moorish Americans and Fard's as Black Muslims of the Nation.

Fard, who changed his name to Wallace Fard Muhammad, claimed to have been born in Mecca in 1877 and to have been trained as a diplomat for the Arabian Kingdom of Hejaz. However, he seems to have worked as a street vendor and amateur magician before becoming a minister of the Nation who promoted black separatism and himself as a Christ figure. He taught that Asians, blacks in particular, were inherently good and whites were inherently evil. Using the Bible, the Quran, and his own books, he also taught that eventually Asians and whites would fight it out in the battle of Armageddon.[49]

In the late 1950s and early 1960s the FBI had a misinformation campaign, which claimed Fard was actually a Caucasian. His real name was Wallace Dodd Ford and he was born in Hawaii on February 25, 1891. His parents were the British Zared Ford and Maori Beatrice Ford of New Zealand. He also had been

[48]Frank S. Mead and Samuel S. Hill, *Handbook of Denominations in the United States* (Nashville: Abingdon Press, 1990), 61. Others report much lower figures, such as ten to thirty thousand. Members often refuse pollsters' questions and defer to their leaders.

[49]Clifton E. Marsh, *From Black Muslims to Muslims* (Metuchen, N.J., and London: The Scarecrow Press, 1984), 41–50. Other sources for Fard include Jehovah's Witnesses literature.

released from San Quentin on May 27, 1929, for selling heroin before moving to the predominantly black section of Chicago and then to Detroit.[50]

Fard left the Nation after being arrested in 1933, and was succeeded by Elijah Muhammad (Elijah Poole, 1898–1975) in Chicago. Under Fard's leadership the Nation had grown to receive at least 8,000 members, and under Elijah Muhammad's leadership the movement went national. With Malcolm X (Malcolm Little, 1929–1965) as Elijah Muhammad's prized speaker for the Nation, members grew to perhaps 300,000. Membership began to decline after Malcolm left the Nation, altered his beliefs, became El-hajj Malik El Shabazz, and was finally murdered. But Elijah Muhammad remained steadfast in his beliefs. Before and during World War II he fostered political friendship with the Japanese as a means to destroy white America before and during World War II. Later in the 1980s, under his successor, the Nation had an alliance with Libya, another country that was considered a political enemy of the United States.

Elijah Muhammad was followed by his son, Warith (Wallace Deen) Muhammad, who changed the group to a form of Islamic orthodoxy. The Nation became The World Community of Al-Islam in the West (later the American Muslim Mission) and has forsaken the racial separatism, racism, and belief in the divinity of Wallace Fard. Ministers became imams, and temples became mosques. The belief that blacks are descendants of the Asian tribe of Shabazz was converted to a belief that they are Bilalians, that is, they have a spiritual bond with the first Ethiopian who became Muslim (Bilal). Accordingly, the newspaper of the Nation, *Muhammad Speaks*, became the *Bilalian News* and later the *Muslim Journal.* Voting is now encouraged and strict dress codes relaxed.[51] To account for his father's teachings, Warith Muhammad says they need to be understood metaphorically.

In 1977 the Honorable Louis Abdul Farrakhan (born 1933) broke away from the movement to retain the original name and beliefs of the Nation as it was under Elijah Muhammad. Farrakhan is a charismatic speaker who has appeared on television numerous times, is a sought-after speaker by African-American university student groups, and publishes his beliefs and opinions in *The Final Call.* He is also well known for his hatred of whites and Jews, and was accused by Malcolm X's widow of involvement in the assassination of her late husband.[52] In 1984 he denounced Judaism as "a gutter religion" and referred to Adolf Hitler as a "wickedly great man."[53] In 1993 he tried to sell the public a softer image of himself by reaching out to politically mainstream and "progressive" African-Americans and being involved in a national summit of black political leaders, including many from the Black Congressional Caucus. He even had dinner with a rabbi.[54]

Despite his attempts to reach out, he agreed with the "truths" spoken by his then spokesman, Khallid Abdul Muhammad, at Kean College, New Jersey, on

---

[50]Karl Evanzz, *The Judas Factor: The Plot to Kill Malcolm X* (New York: Thunder's Mouth Press, 1992), 131–146. The fact that Fard had a white father is not significant since it is recognized by Black Muslims that most American blacks have at least one white ancestor. Malcolm X, who had a white grandfather, was aware of Fard's white father.

[51]Marsh, *From Black,* 94–95.

[52]"Malcolm X's Widow Accuses Farrakhan," *Orange County Register* (March 13, 1994): News–33.

[53]*Time* (February 28, 1994): 25–26.

[54]*Newsweek* (June 28, 1993): 30.

November 29, 1993. In the speech, Muhammad called the Pope a "cracker" and referred to Jews as "bloodsuckers" who are in a conspiracy to control the finances of the world. They even control the presidency of the United States regardless of who is in office.[55] Farrakhan followed up Muhammad's speech with rhetoric of his own condemning whites and Jews.[56] Despite all this, a 1994 poll showed that 63 percent of African-Americans believe Farrakhan speaks the truth,[57] and a New York Times survey reports that over one-third of African-Americans polled "express a favorable view" of him.[58] The most recent publicity event, the "Million Man March" on Washington D.C., although it did not draw the number of participants anticipated, did demonstrate Farrakhan's ability to convince many Christian leaders (especially African-American leaders) that he is a peace-loving man who is no more prejudiced or intolerant than any Christian.

This kind of rhetoric is consistent with the historical beliefs of the Nation. They believe in a sort of Platonic idealism or quasi-pantheistic dualism that teaches that all members of the Nation are God, but that Allah is incarnate only in Wallace Fard Muhammad, who is also the Mahdi and the Messiah.[59] Not only that, but God was at one time a scientist who wanted to create a single language on the earth, but was unable to do so. After failing in doing this, he decided to destroy the earth, only succeeding in causing the moon to separate from the earth 66 trillion years ago.[60] This is something clearly condemned by the Quran, which in innumerable places teaches that God is One. But like orthodox Islam, they reject the Christian concept of God as a Spirit, or to use their word, a "spook."

However, if "all Black Muslims are Allah, and Allah is incarnate as Wallace Fard Muhammad" is their doctrine, why have Asians—especially blacks (according to them)—made mistakes like anyone else? Is Allah "All-knowing" or not? If Black Muslims are Allah, how could they be deceived by the devil? If Allah can be deceived, why trust him? Why trust the writings of Wallace Fard Muhammad, Elijah Muhammad, Louis Farrakhan, the Quran, or the Bible, when they might be full of errors as well? If I am Allah, how can I trust myself? Ultimately we are left with a radical form of agnosticism and skepticism.

Another historical belief of the Nation is that the earth and the original Black Man were created by Allah, and that all living blacks are descendants of the tribe of Shabazz. Fifty thousand years ago, the members of the tribe suffered the misfortune of having their hair turned kinky by another mad scientist who wanted to make life hard for them.[61]

[55] New York Times (January 16, 1994): A–11.

[56] "Farrakhan attacks Jews and Whites," Orange County Register (February 28, 1994): News–3.

[57] Time (February 28, 1994): 22.

[58] Orange County Register (March 3, 1993): News–27.

[59] C. Eric Lincoln, The Black Muslims in America, 3rd ed. (Grand Rapids, Mich. and Trenton, N.J.: Eerdmans and Africa World Press, 1994), 68–69. See also paragraph 12 of Muhammad Speaks (July 13, 1973), quoted in C. Eric Lincoln, The Black Church Since Frazier (New York: Schocken Books, 1974), 199; and Malcolm X, Alex Haley, and Betty Shabazz, The Autobiography of Malcolm X (New York: Ballantine Books, 1965), 158, 161.

[60] Elijah Muhammad, Message to the Blackman in America (Newport News, Va.: United Brothers Communications, 1992 [1965]), 31.

[61] Ibid., 31.

Many years later, a 600-year-old scientist, Yakub, who was exiled to the island of Patmos, began experimenting with genetics and created the brown man. Two hundred years later, he created the red man, then the yellow in another 200 years, and finally, in another 200 years he created the white man. This was about 6600 years ago, in 4004 B.C.[62] This Yakub is the same Jacob of the book of Genesis, allegedly distorted by the writers of the King James Version of the Bible (which, according to them, included William Shakespeare and Francis Bacon).[63] The white man is the devil and was given 6000 years to rule the earth, a period that ended in 1914.[64] Therefore, it should be no surprise that the white man has invented nuclear weapons, concentration camps, or even the virus causing AIDS. The Quran, however, says that Allah created mankind in different colors as a sign of his glory (Sura 30:22).

Christianity is the white man's religion and only a true Asian can be a Muslim, but it is the Jew who is the "brains" of the white-dominated world. If German Nazis happen to kill Jews, that is simply one group of whites killing another, or one problem among many for the devil. Farrakhan frequently says he is not anti-Semitic because he does not wish the extermination of the Jewish people. Here he equivocates since that is not what "anti-Semitic" means, although it may include that meaning. It means "hostile expressions toward, or negative behavior against, individuals or groups because of their Jewish faith or heritage."[65] In American usage "anti-Semitic" refers specifically to Jews, although Arabs are also Semites. Farrakhan also holds that modern Jews are all descendants of the Khazars, a Turkish tribe that lived in the Caucasus Mountains from about 700–1100. Their book *The Secret Relationship Between Blacks and Jews* claims that modern Jews, as descendants of the Khazars, are the people primarily responsible for African slavery.[66]

---

[62]The version of the Bible apparently used by Fard and Elijah Muhammad was the *King James Version* with marginal notes by Bishop Ussher. On pages 94–95, Elijah Muhammad wrote, "When was the beginning? There in the Genesis the writer tells us that this is [*sic*] was 4004 B.C." James Ussher (1581–1656) was the archbishop of Almagh and was famous for, among other things, his bizarre chronology, in which he came up with a figure for Creation that was totally original: Saturday, October 22, 4004 B.C. This was published in the marginal notes of the 1701 edition of the *King James Version*, and remained popular for over 200 years. Somehow it was concluded by Fard and Elijah Muhammad that this was part of the text.

[63]This is similar to the orthodox Muslim claim of intentional Christian mistranslation. While the translating committee for the *King James Version* did not include the forenamed historical celebrities, even if it did and they *had* intentionally mistranslated the KJV, it would be irrelevant, because the Roman Catholic Spaniards (who must be included in this claim for the "400 years of slavery and oppression" argument to be true) used a Bible based on the *Latin Vulgate*, the Puritans used the *Geneva Bible*, and the many varied versions in existence today are based on older Greek manuscripts and therefore much more accurate than the text behind the KJV. Incidentally, both Bacon and Shakespeare had non-Christian beliefs, Bacon being an empiricist philosopher and Shakespeare an Elizabethan "free-thinker." Neither was known for being a Greek or Hebrew scholar or devoutly Christian in any sense. The KJV was translated and written by a group of fifty-four scholars from Cambridge, Oxford, and Westminster, and we have forty-seven names available to us today (Charles C. Butterworth, *The Literary Lineage of the King James Bible, 1340–1611* (New York: Octagon Books, 1971 [1941]), 208). Neither Bacon nor Shakespeare are on that list, and both were very famous during their lifetimes.

[64]Elijah Muhammad, *Message*, 110–118; and Malcolm X, et al., *Autobiography*, 159–167. This is a distortion of the Watchtower (Jehovah's Witness) teaching that the Christ returned invisibly in 1914.

[65]Leonard Dinnerstein, *Antisemitism in America* (New York: Oxford University Press, 1994), ix.

[66]Published in Chicago by Third World Press, 1992. This conspiratorial theory has been soundly refuted by Harold Brackman, *Farrakhan's Reign of Historical Error: The Truth Behind the Secret Relationship Between Blacks and Jews* (Los Angeles: Simon Wiesenthal Center, 1992).

The Nation is known for promoting pseudo-scholarship in many other areas in order to justify their erroneous beliefs. They are taught that blacks have endured 400 years of slavery under white Christian America, but while acknowledging the horrible record of white Christians who did not follow biblical teachings on oppressing their fellow human beings created in God's image, it must also be acknowledged that orthodox Islam was involved in the African slave trade much earlier than white Europeans, and it continues to be practiced in some Muslim countries today.[67] As David Brion Davis says, "Although black captives had appeared in Egyptian iconography in the third millennium B.C. . . . through Hellenistic and Roman times, the Arabs and their Muslim allies were the first people to develop a specialized, long-distance slave trade from sub-Saharan Africa. They were also the first people to view blacks as suited by nature for the lowest and most degrading forms of bondage."[68]

Theologically, the Nation of Islam is not very sophisticated. It is rejected by all orthodox Muslim religious leaders, and clearly contradicts the unitarian concept of God that Islam holds to. Moreover, it is guilty of *shirk* (Sura 4:116; 5:72; 9:31), or associating things with God. Not all translations of the Quran are accepted by the Nation. Only Muslim translations, such as A. Yusuf Ali's *The Holy Quran: Translation and Commentary*, and the translation by Maulvi Muhammad Ali are accepted; translations by Christians are poisonous.[69] The Nation also holds to the Ahmdiyan Islam belief that Jesus Christ was not actually crucified, but later died in Kashmir. The Quran teaches Jesus was taken into heaven and gives no indication that he died in India (Sura 4:157; 199:33). Moreover, they differ with both Christianity and Islam by denying a physical resurrection and instead affirming a mental resurrection. (One wonders why Allah needs a mental resurrection.)

What are some helpful ways of sharing the gospel with the Black Muslim? First of all, while acknowledging the racism and apartheid in America that existed until the 1960s and 1970s civil rights legislation, it is important to realize that Black Muslims are simply replacing one form of oppression for another, one much worse. It is slavery to an oppressive cult that binds people to a bigoted ideology and a heretical view of God.

Ideally, if Christian churches had stayed true to the Gospel of Jesus Christ while exemplifying a strong sense of community, there would be a much stronger witness for non-Christians than in the past. Many Black Muslims have experienced the lack of love and the hypocrisy and politics that mark many so-called Christian churches.

Another thing that many Black Muslims have not had is an explanation of what Christianity really is—presented in a rational, logical manner. They have heard that Christians believe contradictory things that must be accepted on

---

[67]The enslavement of others was practiced by Muhammad and was extended to Africa shortly after his death. The first West Africans enslaved by Europeans were brought to Portugal in 1441, and African slaves were first brought to the English-speaking portion of what is now the United States in 1619.

[68]*Slavery and Human Progress* (New York: Oxford University Press, 1984), 8. See also, Bernard Lewis, *Race and Slavery in the Middle East: An Historical Inquiry* (New York: Oxford University Press, 1990), and Orlando Patterson, *Slavery and Social Death: A Comparative Study* (Cambridge, Mass.: Harvard University Press, 1982).

[69]Elijah Muhammad, *Message*, 21.

faith alone. The Christian needs to understand and share the fact that his faith is logical and not contrary to logic. Black Muslims have experienced a barrage of false beliefs presented in a systematic manner that seem to fit in with their experiences or the experiences of their ancestors. They can also be shown that, despite the racism that has existed among many professed Christians, the New Testament absolutely condemns it (Acts 8:26–40; Galatians 2:11–21; 3:28).

The Bible tells us that if we hate our brother we are walking in spiritual darkness (1 John 2:11) and that he who does not love does not love God (1 John 4:8).

Finally, the Nation, like Islam, is a works-oriented religion. They have some positive entrepreneurial enterprises, but a large return is expected by the Nation not only for alms, but for Nation-owned businesses as well. Raboteau writes that they demand "the federal government set aside separate land for Afro-Americans in reparation for slavery. Black Muslims refused to vote [this has been lifted under Farrakhan], to participate in armed services, or to salute the flag. The separate identity of members of the Nation of Islam was reinforced by a strict ethical code. Alcohol, drugs, tobacco, sports, movies, and cosmetics were forbidden, along with pork and other foods identified as unclean or unhealthy."[70] They are even encouraged to eat no more than one meal a day. Violation of their codes may result in strong penalties.

Like orthodox Islam, the Nation is an extremely works-oriented group. Therefore, exposure to the Christian doctrines of grace can be a very effective witness. To the Muslim especially, salvation by grace should be "good news."

---

[70]Albert J. Raboteau, "Afro-American Religions: Muslim Movements," Mircea Eliade, ed., *The Encyclopedia of Religion*, vol. 1 (New York: Macmillan Publishing Company, 1987), 101–102.

Appendix E

Unitarian Universalism

Come, return to your place in the pews,
and hear our heretical views:
You were not born in sin so lift up your chin,
you have only your dogmas to lose.

—Leonard Mason, Unitarian Universalist minister[2]

In the past thirty years, Christian apologists have virtually ignored the Unitarian Universalist Association (UUA), leaving it to spend its force in what they perceived to be random doctrinal chaos. Perhaps apologists felt this was a safe course, since the UUA was in steady decline and was therefore seen as less threatening than more virulent groups—such as the Jehovah's Witnesses and the Mormons—who were aggressively proselytizing and reaping a harvest of souls.[3] Though larger than some notorious and well-publicized cults, such as the Worldwide Church of God and The Way, International, the perceived threat was less because the UUA was not evangelistic, keeping largely to itself.

Much has changed, however, and Christian apologists can no longer ignore the UUA. Two factors support this conviction: (1) the UUA has moved further away from even its unorthodox "Christian" roots and into arguably more

This appendix written by Dr. Alan W. Gomes.[1]

[1]Dr. Alan W. Gomes adapted this material from his article "Unitarian Universalists and the Second Law of Theological Thermodynamics: The Rise of Militant Pluralism," *Trinity Journal* 17NS (1996): 147–166. Used by permission.

[2]John Sias, from interviews with Rev. Steve Edington, *One Hundred Questions That Non-Members Ask About Unitarian Universalism* (n.p.: Transition Publishing, 1994), 1.

[3]A review of the classic works on cult apologetics readily bears out the fact that the UUA was at best relegated to a footnote or an appendix. For example, the previous edition of *The Kingdom of the Cults* by Walter Martin devoted a scant six-page appendix to them. Other major works on cults (e.g., Ruth Tucker, *Another Gospel*) ignore them altogether.

serious forms of theological error;[4] and (2) the UUA has shed its passivity and is now spreading its "saving message" with a vengeance—quite literally—in its attempt to blunt the so-called "religious right."[5]

Apologists need to put this latest strain of Unitarianism under the microscope and formulate ways to inoculate against it. To do so, apologists must: (1) gauge accurately the importance and influence of the UUA, from a demographic and statistical standpoint; (2) have a basic understanding of the group's doctrinal roots; (3) assess its present doctrinal trajectories, both in continuity and discontinuity with its historical manifestations; and (4) pay due attention to current UUA efforts at spreading its influence. Only then can evangelical apologists formulate a reasoned course of action. Such are the limited goals of this chapter, which is largely descriptive. A thorough refutation of UU theological views is also needed but lies beyond our present scope. However, such a refutation is provided in the new book *Unitarian Universalism* in the *Zondervan Guide to Cults and Religious Movements*, which is recommended the interested reader consult.[6]

Importance of the Unitarian Universalist Association: Vital Statistics and Demographics

For a religious group so largely ignored, the UUA is surprisingly influential, far beyond what its official membership figures might suggest. Russell Chandler notes that the Unitarian Universalist Association has "exerted influence far greater than its numerical strength."[7]

Yet, according to recent surveys, 60 percent of Americans know "little or nothing" about the UUA,[8] often confusing it with the "Unification Church" or "Unity School of Christianity."[9] According to the official membership rolls, there are presently 205,583 members of the UUA worldwide in 1,036 congregations.[10]

---

[4]In speaking of Unitarianism's "Christian" roots, I do not wish to be misunderstood as implying that this group was ever genuinely Christian. Historical Unitarianism regarded itself as Christian and arose out of a historically Christian context. In most instances I have placed the word "Christian" in quotation marks or have provided other qualifiers to avoid confusion, unless the context makes it plain enough that the attribution is one of self-description.

[5]Neil Chethik, "The Saving Message: The New UU Evangelists," *The World*, 9:3 (May/June 1995): 14–18; Russell Chandler, "Unitarians: Oneness in Diversity," *Los Angeles Times* (May 27, 1986): Part I, 1, 20–21; Diane Winston, "Unitarian 'Boomer' Following Growing," *Denver Post* (May 9, 1991): 2-A; Gayle White, "Tide Turns for Unitarians as Scope Widens, Membership Grows," *Atlanta Journal and Constitution* (January 13, 1990): B–9; David B. Parke, "Theological Directions of Unitarian Universalism for the Next Twenty-Five Years," *Unitarian Universalist Christian*, 44; 3–4 (1989): 5–20; Jack Mendelsohn, *Meet the Unitarian Universalists* (Boston: Unitarian Universalist Association, 1993); Scott W. Alexander, ed., *Salted With Fire: Unitarian Universalist Strategies for Sharing Faith and Growing Congregations* (Boston: Skinner House, 1995); Lawrence X. Peers, *The Congregational Handbook: How to Develop and Sustain Your Unitarian Universalist Congregation* (Boston: Unitarian Universalist Association, 1995).

[6]Alan W. Gomes, *Unitarian Universalism* (Grand Rapids, Mich., Zondervan Publishing Company, 1998).

[7]Chandler, "Unitarians: Oneness in Diversity," 1.

[8]Ibid. See also Winston, "Unitarian 'Boomer' Following Growing," 2-A; Tony A. Larsen, "Evangelizing Our Children," chapter in *Salted With Fire*, 124.

[9]Chethik, "The Saving Message," 16, quoting Rev. Al Boyce.

[10]*Unitarian Universalist Association 1995–96 Directory* (Boston: Unitarian Universalist Association, 1995), 38.

The UUA is almost entirely an American phenomenon: officially, 198,131 Unitarians reside the United States, with 6,420 in Canada. Massachusetts, the Unitarian stronghold, boasts the largest concentration of UUs, with a total of 33,640 registered Unitarians in 145 congregations.[11]

In the mid–1960s, official UUA membership stood at around 250,000, and steadily declined for seventeen years to a low of 166,000 in 1980. Since 1981 the trend has reversed and membership has grown to its present level.[12]

Official figures notwithstanding, the total number of Americans who consider themselves UUs far outstrips the number who have bothered to sign the membership roster. In 1990, Barry A. Kosmin and Seymour P. Lachman, researchers at the City University of New York, surveyed 113,000 people across the continental United States on matters of religious self-identification, correlating these responses with a variety of demographic measures. This computer-generated survey represents "the largest and most comprehensive poll ever on religious loyalties, and the most accurate and detailed as to geographical distribution."[13]

This fascinating and well-crafted study turned up some surprising facts about Unitarian Universalists. According to this survey, there are actually about 502,000 Americans who regard themselves as Unitarian Universalists—over twice the number published by the UUA.[14]

Interestingly, this means that there are nearly as many UUs as Muslims in the United States (527,000) and significantly more than Buddhists (401,000)[15]— groups that arguably generate more attention from missiologists and apologists than the UUA.[16]

Also noteworthy is the social status and prestige of Unitarian Universalists. Kosmin and Lachman's study shows that UUs sit on top of the sociological heap. They calculated an aggregate score of four important social indicators: pattern of employment, extent of home ownership, level of education, and median family income. The Unitarian Universalists hold first place, with second through fifth places going to Disciples of Christ, agnostics, Congregationalists, and Episcopalians respectively. (Jehovah's Witnesses bring up the rear in thirtieth place.)[17]

For example, fully 49.5 percent of UUs are college graduates (higher than

---

[11]*Unitarian Universalist Association 1995–96 Directory*, 39. Note that Unitarians not part of the Unitarian Universalist Association are found in other parts of the world, particularly in Romania (80,000) and in Great Britain (10,000), where historical Unitarianism made significant inroads in the sixteenth and seventeenth centuries. Though organizationally distinct, these foreign groups do maintain some contacts with the UUA.

[12]Chandler, "Unitarians: Oneness in Diversity," 20.

[13]Barry A. Kosmin and Seymour P. Lachman, *One Nation Under God* (New York: Harmony Books, 1993), 2.

[14]Ibid., Table 1–2, p. 16. Interestingly, Kosmin and Lachman (p. 2) point out that Catholics, Baptists, Methodists, Episcopalians, Lutherans, and Presbyterians have similarly underreported membership figures, while the actual number of religious Jews, Muslims, and Eastern Orthodox Christians is actually *less* than shown on the official records. Of particular interest to cult apologists is the fact that Mormons are among the groups with significantly over-reported membership figures (p. 289).

[15]Kosmin and Lachman, *One Nation Under God*, Table 1–2, p. 16.

[16]It is important to note that this study measured religious *self-identification*: respondents were asked simply to state their religious affiliation, and their responses were recorded. No predefined categories were imposed from without; the classifications were determined after the fact.

[17]See note 16.

Jews at 46.7 percent, Roman Catholics at 20 percent, Mormons at 19.2 percent, and Baptists at 10.4 percent);[18] and their median annual household income is $34.8K (second only to Jews, at $36.7K).[19]

Unitarians also have been disproportionately influential in our country's highest institutions. There has been a "marked overrepresentation" of Unitarian U.S. Supreme Court justices appointed since 1790 (i.e., eight),[20] and in more recent times, the UU presence in the 101st Congress (1989–1991) was disproportionately high.[21]

A total of five United States presidents professed Unitarianism.[22]

Thus, Unitarian Universalists have often been the movers and shakers in society, and the majority of people are unaware of that fact.

The Doctrinal Direction of Unitarian Universalism

As noted elsewhere, heterodox religious movements observe a kind of "second law of theological thermodynamics."[23]

Unorthodox theological systems generally slide further away from orthodoxy over time, devolving into a kind of "doctrinal entropy." Few groups illustrate this principle as clearly as the UUA. When compared to its "Christian" roots, the extent of the UUA defection from even the most liberal brand of Christian faith becomes striking.

"Christian" Roots.[24] The UUA traces its roots to the radical wing of the Reformation, which considered itself the true heirs of New Testament Christianity.[25]

Though never viewed as genuinely Christian by its orthodox foes, it has until this century seen itself as such. Earl Morse Wilbur, in his monumental *History of Unitarianism*, points out that the flow of Unitarianism was from Poland and Transylvania through Germany and Holland to England and America.[26]

---

[18]See note 16; "Educational Ranking by Religious Group," Table 7–1A, p. 258.

[19]Ibid., "Income Ranking by Religious Group," Table 7–1C, p. 260. Note that although Jews slightly edged out the Unitarians on this particular measure, the Unitarians still received the top *aggregate* score for social prestige.

[20]Ibid., 252–253.

[21]Ibid., 253.

[22]They are John Adams, John Quincy Adams, Thomas Jefferson, Millard Fillmore, and William Howard Taft. Although some would classify Jefferson as a deist rather than a Unitarian, the categories are by no means mutually exclusive. Also, "In 1825 Thomas Jefferson wrote to Dr. Benjamin Waterhouse, 'The population of my neighborhood is too slender and is too much divided into other sects to maintain any one preacher well. I must therefore be contented to be a Unitarian by myself.' " See William F. Schulz, "About the Church of the Larger Fellowship," in *The Unitarian Universalist Pocket Guide*, second edition (Boston: Beacon, 1993), 97; Chandler, "Unitarians: Oneness in Diversity," 21. Jefferson also stated, "I confidently expect that the present generation will see Unitarianism become the general religion of the United States." (George N. Marshall, *Challenge of a Liberal Faith*, revised, updated, and enlarged [New Canaan, Conn.: Keats Publishing, 1980], 29.)

[23]Alan W. Gomes, "Winds of Change in the Worldwide Church of God: With Special Emphasis on the Doctrine of the Trinity," *Presbyterian* 20:2 (1994): 91.

[24]See note 4 for an explanation of the sense in which I consider Unitarianism's roots to be "Christian."

[25]For a fine, general treatment of the radical reformation, see George H. Williams, *The Radical Reformation* (Philadelphia: Westminster, 1962).

[26]Earl Morse Wilbur, *History of Unitarianism*, 2 vols. (Boston: Beacon Press, 1945), 1:4. See also, Lloyd F. Dean, "The Withering of Unitarianism," *Gordon Review* 5;1 (Spring 1959): 15. Though sometimes the connections are loose, the movements are related nonetheless.

Throughout this migration, the various manifestations of Unitarianism all claimed Christian allegiance.

It is neither possible in the space available nor necessary to give a detailed treatment of Unitarian history. Several fine works are available to be consulted on this subject.[27]

In this context it will be sufficient to consider but three representative luminaries of classic Unitarianism: one each from the Continent, England, and America. This is not to gloss over individual differences between thinkers or to suggest that they were all cut from the same cloth. The point is simply to show the representative attitude toward the Christian faith of Unitarianism that is classically held.

Faustus Socinus (1539–1604): the Beginnings of Unitarianism

The beginnings of Unitarianism as a movement may be traced, in their proximate origins, to the radical anti-Trinitarians of the sixteenth century who were active on the Continent. Servetus, an anti-Trinitarian who was burned at the stake in 1553, is often seen as the direct forerunner or even founder of the movement.[28] However, the anti-Trinitarian party actually grew and was organized under the able leadership of Faustus Socinus (1539–1604), an Italian who migrated to Poland.[29] Socinus became the de facto leader of the so-called "Polish Brethren," known officially as the Minor Reformed Church.[30] He champi-

---

[27]The best work on Socinianism/Unitarianism in Europe and America is Earl Morse Wilbur's two-volume *History of Unitarianism.* See also Henry H. Cheetham, *Unitarianism and Universalism: An Illustrated History* (Boston: Beacon Press, 1962); Sydney E. Ahlstrom and Jonathan S. Carey, *An American Reformation: A Documentary History of Unitarian Christianity* (Middletown, Conn.: Wesleyan University Press, 1985); J. H. Allen, *An Historical Sketch of the Unitarian Movement Since the Reformation* (New York: Christian Literature Co., 1894); Earl Morse Wilbur, *Our Unitarian Heritage* (Boston: Beacon, 1925); and Conrad Wright, *The Beginnings of Unitarianism in America* (Starr King Press; distributed by Beacon Press [Boston], n.d.).

[28]George N. Marshall, *Challenge of a Liberal Faith*, 15.

[29]The best comprehensive, general history of Socinianism, including the lives and backgrounds of both Laelius and Faustus Socinus, is Earl Morse Wilbur's two-volume *History of Unitarianism*, cited earlier. Another thorough but much older work is Otto Fock's classic *Der Sozinianismus nach seiner Stellung in der Gesamtentwicklung des christlichen Geistes, nach seinem historischen Verlauf und nach seinem Lehrbegriff* (Keil: C. Schröder, 1847). For compact treatments of Socinus, see Alexander Gordon, "The Sozzini and Their School," *Theological Review*, 65 (1879): 293–322; Earl Morse Wilbur, "Faustus Socinus, Pioneer," *Hibbert Journal*, 33 (1935): 538–548 (hereafter cited as "Pioneer"); David Cory, *Faustus Socinus* (Boston: Beacon Press, 1932); and H. J. McLachlan, *Socinianism in Seventeenth-Century England* (Oxford: Oxford University Press, 1951), 3–24.

More recent discussions of Socinian history include Delio Cantimori, *Eretici Italiani del Cinquecento* (Florence: G. C. Sansoni, 1967); Zbigniew Ogonowski, "Faustus Socinus," in *Shapers of the Religious Traditions in Germany, Switzerland, and Poland, 1560–1600,* ed. Jill Raitt (New Haven: Yale University Press, 1981), 195–197; George H. Williams, *The Radical Reformation*, 518 ff.; Giampaolo Zucchini, "Unpublished Letters Added to the Letters of Fausto Sozzini, 1561–1568," *Socinianism and its Role in the Culture of the Sixteenth to Eighteenth Centuries* (Warsaw: Polish Academy of Sciences, 1983), 17–24; Ralph Lazzaro, "Four Letters from the Socinus-Calvin Correspondence (1549)," *Italian Reformation Studies in Honor of Laelius Socinus*, ed. John A. Tedeschi (Florence: Felice Le Monnier, 1965), 215–230; and David Willis, "The Influence of Laelius Socinus on Calvin's Doctrines of the Merits of Christ and the Assurance of Faith," *Italian Reformation Studies*, 231–241.

[30]Wilbur, *History of Unitarianism*, 1:328. Note that Poland was the most religiously tolerant country of the day. Indeed, King Sigismund (1540–71), himself a Unitarian, issued the first public decree of religious toleration. See F. Forrester Church, "Deeds Not Creeds," *Our Chosen Faith: An Introduction to Unitarian Universalism*, by John Buehrens and F. Forrester Church (Boston: Beacon, 1989), 58.

oned their cause in writing and in oral debate, entering the lists with the orthodox as he attacked their cardinal doctrines, including the Trinity, the deity of Christ, and the doctrine of satisfaction.[31]

The overtly biblical character of Socinus' theology is especially relevant. The Unitarians saw themselves as true followers of Christ who "showed to us the way of salvation, which we may obtain by imitating him."[32] They believed that their faith embodied the most accurate representation of biblical teaching. One hardly can peruse the works of Socinus without observing that he sought biblical support for his positions at every turn. Speaking of the Unitarianism of this period, Arthur Cushman McGiffert notes, "Christianity became in their hands more completely than ever before a book religion."[33] Indeed, Socinus himself wrote one of the first works of modern biblical apologetics, arguing for the veracity of the biblical miracles and the general reliability of the Bible.[34] Some have called Socinus a "rationalist" because he attacked orthodoxy on rational grounds,[35] but this classification is inaccurate. Socinus made it clear that the Bible, rightly understood, does not contradict sound reason. Any interpretation of Scripture that contradicts right reason cannot be a correct exegesis of the text; Socinus would "seek another interpretation" that would "produce an interpretation of those passages which is both internally consistent and which agrees with the general tenor of Scripture."[36]

---

[31]For example, see his *Explicatio primae partis primi capitis euangelistae; Tractatus de Deo, Christo, & Spiritu Sancto; De Jesu Christi filii Dei natura sive esentia, nec non de peccatorum per ipsum expiatione disputatio, adversus Andream Volanum;* and especially his *De Jesu Christo Servatore, hoc est, cur & qua ratione Jesus Christus noster servator sit, Fausti Socini Senensis disputatio.* The collected works of Socinus represent the first two volumes of the *Bibliotheca Fratrum Polonorum quos Unitarios Vocant,* ed. Andreas Wissowatius (Irenopoli [Amsterdam], 1668) (hereafter cited as *BFP*). Many of the main Socinian writings are in this collection with the noteworthy omission of the *Racovian Catechism,* the main Socinian statement of faith.

For modern treatments of Socinus' Christology and soteriology, see John C. Godbey, "A Study of Faustus Socinus' *De Jesu Christo Servatore*" (Ph.D. diss., University of Chicago, 1968); Godbey, "Fausto Sozzini and Justification," *Continuity and Discontinuity in Church History,* eds. F. F. Church and T. George; *Studies in the History of Christian Thought,* 10 (Leiden: E. J. Brill, 1979); Alan W. Gomes, "*De Jesu Christo Servatore,* Part III: Historical Introduction, Translation, and Critical Notes" (Ph.D. diss., Fuller Theological Seminary, 1990); and Alan W. Gomes, "*De Jesu Christo Servatore:* Faustus Socinus on the Satisfaction of Christ," *Westminster Theological Journal,* 55 (1993): 209–31. On the continent his doctrine was known as "Socinianism" and his followers "Socinians." In Transylvania, England, and eventually America, the movement was commonly called "Unitarianism."

[32]"*De Jesu Christo Servatore,*" 1:1–2.

[33]Arthur Cushman McGiffert, *Protestant Thought Before Kant* (New York: Charles Scribner's Sons, 1924), 115.

[34]"*De Sacrae Scripturae Autoritate,*" *BFP,* Tomus 1.264.

[35]See, for example, *An Encyclopedia of Religions,* 1921 ed., s.v. "Socinians" by Maurice A. Cauney; and Bengt Hägglund, *History of Theology* (St. Louis: Concordia, 1968), 322. For a recent work of the same persuasion, see Martin I. Klauber and Glenn S. Sunshine, "Jean-Alphonse Turrettini on Biblical Accommodation: Calvinist or Socinian?" *Calvin Theological Journal,* 25 (1990): 13. Others have tempered this conclusion by classifying Socinianism as a hybrid of rationalism and supernaturalism. See McLachlan, *Socinianism,* 12; Philip Schaff and J. Herzog, *A Religious Encyclopedia or Dictionary of Biblical, Historical, Doctrinal, and Practical Theology* (New York: Funk and Wagnalls, 1891), s.v. "Socinianism"; Clow, s.v. "Socinianism"; and Adolph Harnack, *History of Dogma,* 7 vols. (New York: Russell and Russell, 1958), 7:159.

[36]"*De Jesu Christo Servatore,*" 3.6.282. Socinus is here speaking in the context of the doctrine of satisfaction. His point is that even if certain passages appear to teach Christ's satisfaction, they cannot really do so, and he would seek an alternative interpretation in order to harmonize such passages with the overall tenor of Scripture.

Don't misunderstand the statement that Socinus based his interpretations on Scripture. Socinus was wrong to reject orthodoxy; his effort was flawed. The point here is simply to highlight the effort as such, which reveals much about early Unitarian attitudes toward the Christian faith in general and toward Scripture in particular.

John Biddle (1615–1662), the Father of English Unitarianism

John Biddle, known as the Father of English Unitarianism, had not read Socinus before he formed his judgments on the Trinity. Biddle arrived at his initial convictions quite apart from Socinus, though he eventually did come into possession of Socinus' writings. Biddle's *Twelve Arguments Drawn Out of Holy Scripture*, which attempted to refute the orthodox doctrine of the Godhead, rested "at every step solely on statements of Scripture."[37] Likewise, his *A Confession of Faith Touching the Holy Trinity According to the Scripture* attempted to prove both from reason and from Scripture that the doctrine of the Trinity is illogical and unbiblical.[38] In 1654, Biddle published his *Twofold Catechism*,[39] in which "the answers are exclusively in the language of Scripture."[40] Wilbur pointed out that in Biddle's preface to the work, he lamented that other catechisms foist human constructs on the biblical text rather than taking Scripture at its literal word.[41]

Again, the point here is not to endorse Biddle's conclusions or to suggest that they are in any sense orthodox or to intimate that they are legitimately biblical. In fact, Biddle's overly literalistic interpretations of Scripture were considered bizarre in his own day and are largely considered so even today.[42]

But even these obviously heterodox views ought not to obscure the point at issue, namely, that Biddle considered Scripture to be the authoritative rule of Christian faith and sought to base his views on it.

William Ellery Channing (1780–1842), the Apostle of American Unitarianism

Dr. William Ellery Channing, arguably the greatest light of American Unitarianism, was the most robust and articulate Unitarian advocate of his day. It was under his influence that the American Unitarian Association was founded in May of 1825.[43] Channing's so-called "Baltimore sermon," preached at the ordination of Jared Sparks in 1819, marked a watershed in the debate. This sermon stands as one of the most pungent apologetics for the Unitarian approach to the Christian faith. As F. Forrester Church observes, "Channing's sermon was published and reprinted seven times, and became the most popular pamphlet

---

[37]Wilbur, *History of Unitarianism*, 2:194.
[38]Ibid., 195.
[39]The full title is *A Twofold Catechism: The One Simply Called a Scripture-Catechism: The Other, a Brief Scripture-Catechism for Children* (1654).
[40]Ibid., 202.
[41]Ibid., 203.
[42]For example, Biddle ascribed bodily parts to God, restricted him to a particular spatial locale, and affirmed God's "openness" by limiting his knowledge. See, Ibid.
[43]Mendelsohn, *Meet the Unitarian Universalists*, 14.

in America since Thomas Paine's *Common Sense*."[44]

In this clarion call to Unitarianism, Channing gathered a chain of biblical citations to prove the exegetical soundness of Unitarian theology and Christology. He made his commitment to Holy Writ explicit: "We regard the Scriptures as the records of God's successive revelation to mankind, and particularly of the last and most perfect revelation of his will by Jesus Christ. Whatever doctrines seem to us to be clearly taught in the Scriptures, we receive without reserve or exception."[45] Further, he declared that there can be no real contradiction in Scripture; seeming contradictions are only apparent, not genuine, for "God never contradicts in one part of Scripture what He teaches in another."[46]

Thus, whether one considers Socinus in the sixteenth century, Biddle in the seventeenth, or Channing in the nineteenth, classic Unitarians affirmed Scripture's authority, whatever one may think of their conclusions.

The Slide Away from Unitarian "Christianity"

Just as space did not permit a detailed examination of Unitarianism in its "biblical" phase, neither is it possible to trace all of the steps in the dissolution of that phase. Only the briefest summary must here suffice.

Nineteenth-Century Transcendentalism

Lloyd F. Dean, in an older but still pertinent article, identified the key steps in Unitarianism's abandonment of theism generally and of Christian theism in particular.[47] Dean considered early nineteenth-century Transcendentalism as pivotal: "At this point," Dean states, "Unitarianism passed from the status of a heresy to that of a clearly non-Christian philosophy."[48] Dean cited Ralph Waldo Emerson in particular. "Following intuition as a guide, Emerson and the Transcendentalists considered nature the Oversoul of which man was a part."[49] Thus, intuition replaced Scripture; "immanent divinity in man himself both makes this possible and guarantees the accuracy of the conclusions reached."[50] Unitarian Duke T. Gray pinpoints in Emerson a philosophical shift from the authority of Jesus Christ to "the sovereignty of the self." That shift having taken place, further developments in Unitarian theology were, in Gray's opinion, "merely footnotes" to this.[51]

Channing was aghast at the seemingly pantheistic doctrines Emerson es-

[44]Church, "Neighborhood," *Our Chosen Faith*, 121.

[45]William Ellery Channing, "Unitarian Christianity," *Three Prophets of Religious Liberalism: Channing, Emerson, Parker*, edited and with an introduction by Conrad Wright (Boston: Beacon, 1961), 48.

[46]Ibid., 52.

[47]L. F. Dean, "The Withering of Unitarianism," 13–29.

[48]Ibid., 16–17.

[49]Ibid., 21.

[50]Ibid., 21–22.

[51]Duke T. Gray, "Letter to the Christians," *The Unitarian Universalist Christian*, 47, nos. 3–4 (Fall/Winter 1992): 43. Gray observes, "In the Emersonian epistemology, each individual person is invited to tailor-make a designer religion out of one's own experience, needs, and taste. As one seminary faculty friend and U.U. Christian colleague expressed it, 'You read Emerson, and then go out and destroy the Church.' "

poused. The situation was so grim for the "conservative" Unitarian wing that in one rather ironic instance, Andrews Norton of Harvard (a prominent Unitarian theologian and ally of Channing) was so desperate to stem the tide that he republished a critique of Emerson appearing in the Calvinistic *Princeton Review*![52]

The Erosion of Christian Uniqueness

Another element leading to the dissolution of Christian consensus among both Unitarians and Universalists was an increasingly global and pluralistic approach toward world religions. Emerson also demonstrates this shift, as his writings were at times a conduit of Hindu and Eastern mystical beliefs. As George N. Marshall observes, "By the 1850s, Emerson had fully launched the emerging Unitarian movement upon the quest for its larger inclusiveness in the family of world religions."[53] This pluralistic impulse would achieve its terminal velocity by mid-twentieth century.

On the Universalist side, the 1948 Massachusetts Universalist Convention radically redefined what it meant by the term "Universalist." Whereas the term historically referred to those who affirmed universal salvation, the label was "refashioned to mean a 'universal world religion,' " a syncretistic blend of various global faith positions.[54] The Unitarians likewise embodied this "global impulse" in their "shift away from explicitly Christian symbols, rites, and thought forms toward other faiths, peoples, and struggles."[55] The activities of minister John Haynes Holmes of New York illustrate this clearly.[56] "In the years following the Armistice [he] reconstituted the Unitarian Church of the Messiah as the Community Church of New York, proclaimed Gandhi the greatest man in the world, and in a bold act of syncretism assimilated the festivals of the world's major religions into the church's liturgical year."[57]

Twentieth-Century Humanism

Humanism stands as another major way station on the road to Unitarian doctrinal diversity. The humanist-theist controversy rocked Unitarianism, particularly between 1918 and 1937.[58] As Edd Doerr of *The Humanist* journal observes, "Half of the signers of the 1933 *Humanist Manifesto I* were Unitarian Universalist ministers, as were the first four presidents of the American Humanist Association, the AHA's first executive director, and this journal's first editor. The two surviving *Manifesto* signers, Lester Mondale and Edwin H. Wilson, are both Unitarian ministers."[59] The humanists affirmed the doctrine of evolution rather

---

[52]Dean, "The Withering of Unitarianism," 21.
[53]Marshall, *Challenge of a Liberal Faith*, 87–88.
[54]Gray, "Letter to the Christians," 44.
[55]Parke, "Theological Directions of Unitarian Universalism for the Next Twenty-Five Years," 10.
[56]Holmes was co-founder of the American Civil Liberties Union and the National Association for the Advancement of Colored People.
[57]Parke, 10.
[58]Mason Olds, "Religious Humanism and Unitarianism," *Religious Humanism*, 12, no. 1 (1978): 15.
[59]Edd Doerr, Book Reviews: "The Quality of Religious Life in Unitarian Universalist Congregations: A Survey by the Commission on Appraisal and Our Chosen Faith: An Introduction to Unitarian Universalism," *The Humanist* (May/June 1990): 45.

than of special creation, gave science and reason the place of supremacy, and sought to found ethical values on a human rather than a divine basis.[60] Thus, "the highest value is the complete realization of human personality and the quest for the good life here and now."[61] Some within the Unitarian movement vigorously opposed this antitheistic philosophy but to no avail; humanism carried the day.[62]

In 1989, a UUA survey of its membership showed that fully three-fourths of all members considered themselves to be some flavor of humanist.[63] (Some options included "humanist-existentialist," "feminist-humanist," and even "Christian-humanist."[64]) However, it appears that the UUA is departing from its rationalistic and humanistic stance toward a more "spiritual" position. This has caused disquiet among some humanists within the movement to the point where even some of the staunchest have left in protest.[65]

The Current State of Unitarian Universalist Pluralism

The Move from Humanism to Alternative Spiritualities

The leaven of tolerance and pluralism has bred new doctrinal ferment in the UUA. It appears that humanism, which once held sway, is loosening its grip. Humanists Paul Kurtz and Vern Bullough observe, "While humanism is influential in the UUA, it is not the dominant voice." They conclude, "There seems to be some basis for the interpretation that, although humanism is a strong strand of the UUA, there are many other strands, and humanism seems to be diminishing in influence as a spiritualistic concern begins to be felt more strongly."[66]

This departure from humanism has not escaped notice both within and without the movement.[67] Past president William F. Schulz conceded that the

---

[60]Paul Kurtz and Vern L. Bullough, "The Unitarian Universalist Association: Humanism or Theism?" *Free Inquiry* 11, no. 2 (Spring 1991): 12–13.

[61]Ibid. Kurtz and Bullough mention the distinction between religious and secular humanists, which is worth observing. They point out that while all humanists "eschew any belief in a supernatural deity or salvation of the soul," there is disagreement as to whether "either the terms *God, religion,* and *religious* should be used in describing humanism. Many humanists felt that these terms could be redefined in a naturalistic sense. Ever since, the humanist movement has been divided in this linguistic debate, with some feeling that use of such language clouds the issue, is inappropriate, and apt to confuse; others hold that religious language is perfectly legitimate and that the strategy to advance the cause of humanism is to enter and influence liberal churches."

[62]A good, concise historical summary of this controversy appears in Olds, "Religious Humanism and Unitarianism."

[63]Doerr, Book Reviews, 45.

[64]In this context the term "Christian-humanism" refers to a syncretistic blend of twentieth-century humanism and radically liberal Christianity, not to the Renaissance humanism of Erasmus and other sixteenth-century literati.

[65]Kurtz and Bullough, "The Unitarian Universalist Association: Humanism or Theism?" 13: "Where does the UUA stand today in regards to humanism? Many feel that it is de-emphasizing its humanistic roots and putting more attention on religious values and spiritual concerns. We should point out that both authors of this article had been members of the UUA for many decades, but resigned because we felt that the UUA was becoming increasingly theistic and Christian in its message."

[66]Ibid., 13–14.

[67]See, for example, Winston, "Unitarian 'Boomer' Following Growing,"; Parke, "Theological Directions of Unitarian Universalism for the Next Twenty-Five Years"; and Alexander, *Salted With Fire* (*passim*).

skeptical stance that has characterized the UUA "has been in transposition for at least the past decade." Schulz affirmed that UUs are now recognizing "that there are some angles from which the Spirit cannot be glimpsed by even the sharpest empirical eye."[68]

Gustav Neibuhr, in his article entitled "With a New Spiritualism, Unitarians Welcome People of All Beliefs," points out that many UU pulpits have abandoned their "cool, cerebral sermons on the greatness of human reason" and now preach a more "spiritual" message instead.[69] Neibuhr correlates earlier declines in membership (e.g., in the '60s and '70s) with the abandonment of God-talk in Unitarian churches. Neibuhr quotes Scott Alexander, minister of the Unitarian Church of the Larger Fellowship, who speaks of the influx of spiritual seekers now making the UUA their homes. "They don't come to church anymore to hear some dry humanist tell about the United Nations and world federalist thinking."[70] David Parke, in charting the theological direction of Unitarianism for the next quarter century, observes that "increasing numbers of men and women have come to our congregations not from orthodoxy but from secularism." These people often seek "a robust, textured, life-giving religious faith."[71]

Many link this renewed spiritual interest with an influx of "baby boomers" who are seeking a spiritual home. Of this group, Arvid Straube notes, "The word 'God' is much less problematic to the boomer seekers in our churches than it may have been to previous generations of potential Unitarian Universalists. . . . They are thirsty for spirit from whatever source."[72]

Where are the popular spiritual watering holes in today's UUA?

The New Age and Unitarian Universalist Spirituality

For some UUs, New Age spirituality seems to fit the bill. Unitarian Ann Fields speaks of "our collective consciousness, which, in every instant of time, grows richer and more vibrant, as the universe becomes aware of itself." This process she calls God, "the spiritual evolution of the cosmos—creation flowing free."[73] Past president Schulz likewise affirms that "Everything is . . . dependent and connected in an elaborate web of creation. A holistic view of creation is becoming more and more central to a sophisticated understanding of what being is all about." He cites approvingly Capra's monistic worldview, embracing a "deep ecology" of "the divine One."[74]

Some connect the New Age emphasis with the UUA's traditional stress on social activism: "We have to realize that these [ministries toward the homeless, the environment, etc.] are all part of a whole. . . . When we can establish harmony of earth, mind, and spirit, we'll have what we need to save ourselves and

[68]William F. Schulz, Foreword, *Our Chosen Faith*, xiv.

[69]Gustav Neibuhr, "With a New Spiritualism, Unitarians Welcome People of All Beliefs," *Washington Post* (July 6, 1993): A–3.

[70]Ibid.

[71]Parke, "Theological Directions of Unitarian Universalism for the Next Twenty-Five Years," 18.

[72]Arvid Straube, "Spirituality and Church Growth," *Salted With Fire*, 173.

[73]Ann Fields, "Continuous Creation," *Unitarian Universalist Views of God*, ed. Doris Hunter (Boston: Unitarian Universalist Association, n.d.), 3.

[74]Chandler, "Unitarians: Oneness in Diversity," 21.

save the world."[75] The UUA's seventh principle in its *Statement of Principles and Purposes* also embodies the New Age thrust when it speaks of the UUA's "respect for the interdependent web of all existence."[76]

Neo-Pagan Spirituality in the Unitarian Universalist Association

Neo-pagans have also made significant inroads in the UUA. In 1985, Neo-pagans formed the Covenant of Unitarian Universalist Pagans at the UUA General Assembly in Atlanta. Among the group's stated goals are "the study and practice of contemporary pagan and Earth and nature-centered spirituality," "networking among pagan UUs," and "working for the healing of the Earth."[77] According to Lattin, as of 1991 the affiliate had grown to sixty chapters nationwide.[78]

Some, though not all, of the interest in Neo-paganism is connected to radical feminism. As Kosmin and Lachman observe, goddess religions, which revere matriarchy and regard the Earth as a goddess, have become increasingly important in some feminist circles. The UUA has warmly embraced the Neo-pagan fringe. "Wicca priestesses have been accepted into Unitarian seminaries and gained academic credibility as a result."[79] Past president William F. Schultz affirms that paganism "fits very neatly with our tradition. . . . For us, a religion grounded in nature is part and parcel of our heritage. . . . We have gone too far on this side of rationalism."[80]

Accordingly, one is not surprised to find a "popular Unitarian course" entitled "Cakes for the Queen of Heaven," which teaches women about worshiping the goddess.[81] One also finds Neo-pagan hymns in the lately revised hymnbook *Singing the Living Tradition.*[82] Included in this eclectic menagerie are feminist and Neo-pagan hymns and readings, such as the song "We are Dancing Sarah's Circle" by feminist theologian Nelle Morton; a reading entitled "The Womb of the Stars" by Joy Atkinson ("written to acknowledge and celebrate the 'interdependent web' of existence, using maternal imagery to speak about the cosmos-source of our being"); a reading entitled "I who am the beauty of the green earth" from Starhawk's *Spiral Dance;* and Starhawk's prayer entitled "Earth mother, star mother."[83]

Evangelism and Church Growth Among Unitarian Universalists

From the foregoing it should now be clear that Unitarian Universalism has continued its slide ever further away from its once Christian framework. Indeed,

---

[75]White, "Tide Turns for Unitarians as Scope Widens, Membership Grows," B–9.

[76]The UUA adopted the "Principles and Purposes" as bylaws at the 1984 and 1985 General Assemblies. They are reproduced in numerous UUA publications. See, for example, the *Unitarian Universalist Association 1995–96 Directory,* 3.

[77]*Unitarian Universalist Association 1995–96 Directory,* 352.

[78]Don Lattin, "Pagans to Light Up the Year's Longest Night," *San Francisco Chronicle* (December 21, 1991): A–19.

[79]Kosmin and Lachman, *One Nation Under God,* 154.

[80]Ibid., citing William F. Schulz.

[81]Christina Robb, "In Goddesses They Trust," *Boston Globe* (July 9, 1990): sec. 32:2. The article also mentions that goddess religion is a "hot" topic at some theology schools, such as Episcopal and Harvard Divinity in Cambridge. This is due to the emphasis in those schools on women's issues.

[82]Unitarian Universalist Association, *Singing the Living Tradition* (Boston: Beacon Press, 1993).

[83]Jacqui James, ed., *Between the Lines: Sources for Singing the Living Tradition* (Boston: Unitarian Universalist Association, 1995), 59, 103, 116–117.

as Gray observes, "The UUA is unique in the annals of Church History—it being perhaps the only branch of the Body of Christ ever to vote itself out of Christendom and declare itself no longer a Christian denomination, but an interfaith Association."[84]

At this juncture, an evangelical might well ask whether these developments are really cause for concern. After all, one might argue as follows: (1) The group never was truly orthodox. Therefore, why should evangelicals regard this "doctrinal slide" with alarm? The Unitarians have just exchanged one flavor of doctrinal error for another. (2) The UUA has always kept to itself anyway. Therefore, whatever its views and however great its doctrinal shift, would not the most prudent course be simply to ignore it rather than call attention to it?

Both questions merit serious consideration but space does not permit a detailed explication of both. As to the first, a Unitarianism that has scuttled even a liberal Christian framework arguably poses a greater *societal* danger than a Unitarianism within the Judeo-Christian orbit. The spread of humanism, Neopaganism, multicultural religious pluralism, and New Age spiritism only speeds the erosion of our country's precipitously weakened "Christian" moral base. Also, from an apologetic standpoint, this lack of common ground makes the task of evangelism that much more difficult, since such "givens" as biblical authority (however watered down) and the importance (if not uniqueness) of Jesus Christ must now be proven and not automatically assumed.

Even granting that Unitarianism's present doctrinal pluralism is no worse than its earlier heterodox "Christian" stance, it is certainly no more salutary; their doctrinal positions are, from an orthodox perspective, as objectionable as ever, even if no worse. Thus, the second question is the one of the greatest concern. From the vantage point of an evangelical Christian apologist, is the best course to ignore the UUA or is there reason to think that its increasingly heterodox views will spread if left unchecked?

Embracing the "E" Word

For years the UUA refrained from any mention of "evangelism" except in a derisive context. By their own admission, the words "evangelism" and "evangelist" were virtual Unitarian expletives, for evangelism by nature was seen as hostile to the twin ideals of tolerance and pluralism. Unitarians were careful to avoid "proselytizing" or seeking "converts" in the traditional sense. [85] However, this "laid-back" approach has given way to systematic efforts at outreach and growth, which have now become fashionable among a newer and more aggressive breed of UUs.[86] "UUA officials have even begun using . . . 'the dreaded e-word.' The association's new training course, *Sharing the Unitarian Universalist Faith*, includes 'evangelism' in its subtitle."[87] And whereas old-guard Unitarians

---

[84]Gray, "Letter to the Christians," 41. This took place at the 1985 UUA General Assembly.

[85]George N. Marshall, "Unitarian Universalism," *Encounters With Eternity: Religious Views of Death and Life After Death*, Christopher Jay Johnson and Marsha G McGee, eds. (New York: The Philosophical Library, 1986), 300. See also Marshall, *Challenge of a Liberal Faith*, 237.

[86]Larsen, "Evangelizing Our Children," *Salted With Fire*, 124.

[87]Chethik, "The Saving Message," 18. On the traditional reluctance of Unitarians even to use the word "evangelism" in polite company, see also Scott W. Alexander, Introduction, *Salted With Fire*, 1.

explicitly disavowed that Unitarianism was a "salvation religion,"[88] the "new UU evangelists" proudly tout their "saving message."[89]

Leading the charge is the Rev. Scott Alexander, senior minister of the 2,000-member Church of the Larger Fellowship in Boston, the largest congregation in the denomination.[90] Alexander recently published *Salted With Fire*, a strategy guide that presents a militant program for expansion through evangelism. Though not all UUs embrace Alexander's approach, it does appear to have high-level support. Alexander's book sports contributions from leading denominational officials, including a foreword by past president William F. Schulz and a chapter by current president John A. Buehrens.[91] Indeed, the spirit of the volume seems well in keeping with Schulz's own preelection campaign promise, in which he vowed to make Unitarian Universalism "a household word."[92] Even if resisted by traditionalists within the movement, the new evangelistic thrust appears to be here to stay, if the demand for Alexander's seminars and printed materials is any indication. Since 1993, Alexander has visited nearly half of the denomination's twenty-three districts and reports that he simply cannot keep up with the clamor for his workshops.[93]

Fueling this new interest in outreach is a desire to counteract the so-called "religious right." Alarmed by an increasingly conservative shift in the political climate, these UU evangelists feel they must blunt the religious right's attack by presenting the Unitarian alternative. Alexander states, "The religious right has shown us how endangered our values are, how high are the stakes. We're realizing that if we don't stand up in the public square and proclaim our beliefs, our message will never be heard."[94] He directly credits the activism of the religious right with instilling "a renewed sense amongst Unitarian Universalists . . . that we have a unique and valuable religious vision to offer others!"[95] Alexander says that the Unitarians have a "saving message," a message that he wants to broadcast as never before.

Just what is the "saving message"—this Unitarian version of the "good news"? According to Harvey M. Joyner Jr., "The 'good news' of Unitarian Universalism is that it gives us a 'safe house' in which to wage our own heresy, whatever tradition we might have come from."[96] In short, the saving Unitarian message is *pluralism*—"a theology centered on tolerance, interdependence, and compassion."[97]

---

[88]Marshall, "Unitarian Universalism," *Encounters With Eternity*, 302.

[89]Chethik, "The Saving Message," 14–18.

[90]For a biographical sketch of Rev. Alexander, see Craig Wilson, "Minister Preaches Gay Acceptance," *USA Today* (August 20, 1991): sec. D, 4:2.

[91]Alexander, in his introductory essay, describes the book as "comprised of twenty-two essays written by a group of unashamedly evangelistic Unitarian Universalist leaders from all over the continent" (p. 5).

[92]Chandler, "Unitarians: Oneness in Diversity," 1, 20.

[93]Chethik, "The Saving Message," 14–15.

[94]Ibid., 14.

[95]Ibid., 15, citing Scott Alexander's book, *Salted With Fire*.

[96]Harvey M. Joyner Jr., "The Bold Witness," *Salted With Fire*, 76. Likewise, the Rev. Al Boyce did a 50,000-piece mailing in the Miami area, outlining the main Unitarian beliefs. In it he assures readers that "heretics are welcome" (Chethik, "The Saving Message," 17).

[97]Scott Alexander, quoted in Chethik, "The Saving Message," 15.

Church Growth, Unitarian Style

Pragmatically, the new UU evangelists are systematically applying well-calculated techniques to grow their churches. One approach is to make greater use of mass media. Always supportive of left-wing social causes, the UUs are seeking greater media coverage for their social agenda. For example, in August 1992 the First Unitarian Church in Portland, Oregon, decided to protest an Oregon ballot initiative designed to keep homosexuals from receiving special rights. They tied a red ribbon around the entire block occupied by the church, declaring it a "hate-free zone."[98] They also put signs up at various anchor points along the ribbon, proclaiming, "Hate is not a family value," "Hate-Free Zone," and other such sentiments. The media came out in force: three TV stations, two radio stations, and a newspaper covered the event. [99] Apparently the publicity paid off: the congregation grew by 41 percent in the year following the coverage.[100]

The UU evangelists are also taking some lessons from the evangelical church growth movement. They are finding that they can apply evangelical church growth techniques with little or no adaptation. The UUs have no difficulty separating form from content: "Religious liberals can learn from and employ these evangelical methods," Alexander states, "without in any way adopting, mimicking, or supporting their orthodox message." Alexander goes on to state that many UUs "have enthusiastically adopted (and adapted) the evangelical techniques of religious conservatives to trumpet and spread our *liberal* 'good news.' "[101] For example, the growth-oriented Unitarians are courting the baby boomers, tailoring services to meet their felt needs. Taking a page from the church growth playbook, the Rev. Suzanne Meyer (minister of the First UU Church of New Orleans) declares that "if the new evangelism is going to succeed, Sunday services must appeal to a new generation of churchgoers looking primarily for spiritual and emotional nourishment. . . . That means, among other things, more inspiring music, richer liturgy, and less intellectualism from the pulpit."[102] In her chapter "Courting the Baby Boomers," she strikes the same chord. She notes that "boomers are seeking spiritual nurture and direction. Their tastes are wide-ranging and eclectic and embrace both traditional religious symbols as well as New Age philosophies."[103] Thus, the new "spiritual" direction of the UUA (cited earlier) is the perfect prescription for growing a boomer church.[104] Likewise, the UUA's "openness to different family forms, deep antiauthoritarianism, [and] egalitarian sex roles" fits the boomer ethos well.[105] Not surprisingly, a recent *Newsweek* article dubbed the UUA the "quintessential boomer church."[106]

These efforts are already paying dividends: the UUA is now growing at a rate of about four percent per year[107]—its best growth in twenty years.

---

[98]Marilyn Sewell, "Slaying Dragons of Hate with Ribbons of Love," *Salted With Fire*, 250.

[99]Ibid., 250–251.

[100]Chethik, "The Saving Message," 17.

[101]Alexander, Introduction, *Salted With Fire*, 2–3 (emphasis in the original).

[102]Chethik, "The Saving Message," 18.

[103]Suzanne P. Meyer, "Courting the Baby Boomers," *Salted With Fire*, 94.

[104]See the discussion of Unitarian spirituality in this essay.

[105]Winston, "Unitarian 'Boomer' Following Growing," 2-A.

[106]See Kenneth L. Woodward, et al., "And the Children Shall Lead Them: Young Americans Return to God," *Newsweek* (December 17, 1990): 50–56.

[107]*Unitarian Universalist Association 1995–96 Directory.*

Some Modest Suggestions

How should Christians respond, especially professional Christian apologists? The first and most important step is informational and educational. Christians must be made aware of today's UUA and what a serious challenge it poses. Most Christians see the UUA (if they've heard of it at all) as a group of dormant, non-proselytizing humanists, declining in membership and talking primarily to themselves. Unfortunately, this perspective appears to be as common among "cult watchers" as it is among the general Christian public. This view is twenty years out of date and has led to a serious and possibly even dangerous disregard of this group. This chapter represents a practical step toward sounding the alarm among thoughtful Christians to take the UUA seriously. A further and more detailed critique is now available in a new book entitled *Unitarian Universalism*.[108] It is the only evangelical critique of the UUA produced in recent memory. Hopefully, it will spur other researchers to devote renewed attention to this group and to develop even more resources for dealing with it.

Second, apologists must map out a strategy for countering and evangelizing the UUA. Doing so will not be simple: Because of the departure from its Christian base, much "pre-evangelism" is required. Apologists need to focus special energy on certain key pressure points of UUA theology. The watershed issues are the reliability and authority of Scripture, the uniqueness of Jesus Christ, and the necessity of faith in Him. However diverse the UUA may be, there is considerable unanimity in their rejection of historical Christian orthodoxy on these foundational doctrinal topics. A robust and relevant apologetic in these areas will be crucial if any progress is to be made. This will not be an easy sell to a group whose trinity is pluralism, tolerance, and freedom.

Finally, given the diverse doctrinal positions within the UUA, evangelism may best be done collaboratively; apologists with specialized expertise may need to pool resources to accomplish the task. For example, one cannot speak of a UU *doctrine* of God but must deal rather with the Unitarian *doctrines* of God. Therefore, apologists particularly versed in countering, say, a pantheistic view of Deity (e.g., an expert on the New Age movement) ought to help craft strategies that would work well against pantheistic forms of UU belief. Viewed from another angle, as apologists work in their specialty areas, they should cast a weather eye for connections between their research interests and the UUA: the UUA remains a safe haven for such groups as Neo-pagans and radical feminist theologians. As apologists work to counteract, for example, Neo-pagans generally, they need to note the linkage with the UUA and adapt their polemic to take this linkage into account.

Concluding Thoughts

"There is a Men's Support Group, a Friday Morning Meditation Group, a Hatha Yoga group, the Wednesday Night Minister's Class, a Parenting Class, a Spiritual Autobiography Class, a New Physics Class, a Neo-Pagan group, and

---

[108]Alan W. Gomes, *Unitarian Universalism* (Grand Rapids, Mich.: Zondervan Publishers, 1998). Part of the fifteen-volume *Zondervan Guide to Cults and Religious Movements* series.

several Women's Spirituality groups. In addition, there are Saturday workshops, such as Living With Awareness and Compassion, Spirituality in the Workplace, and Chinese Medicine."[109]

Yes, the Unitarian Universalists have something for everybody. The denomination is a one-stop spiritual supermarket. Through its adoption of church growth principles, it seeks to maximize its tremendous market potential, tapping into legions of savvy baby boomer consumers. Unfortunately, what the Unitarians cannot provide a generation of hungry seekers is the one food that will satisfy: the Lord Jesus Christ, the Living Bread from heaven. Christians must take this mission field seriously, holding forth the Bread of Life to a group that prides itself on knowledge but which never comes to a knowledge of the truth. May God cause many in the UUA to buy that food without price, which only the Triune God of Scripture can supply.

---

[109]Arvid Straube, "Spirituality and Church Growth," *Salted With Fire,* 169–170.

Bibliography

General References

Adair, James R., and Ted Miller, eds. *Escape From Darkness*. Wheaton, Ill.: Victor Books, 1982.

Alnor, William M., and Ronald Enroth. "Ethical Problems in Exit Counseling," *Christian Research Journal*, 14:3:1992.

Anderson, Susan M., and Philip G. Zimbardo. "Resisting Mind Control," *USA Today*, November 1990.

Anthony, Dick, and Thomas Robbins. "Law, Social Science, and the 'Brainwashing' Exception to the First Amendment," *Behavioral Sciences and the Law*, 10:1:1992.

Atkins, G. *Modern Religious Cults and Movements*. New York: Fleming H. Revell Co., 1923.

Bach, Marcus. *Strange Sects and Curious Cults*. New York: Barnes and Noble Books, 1961.

———. *They Have Found a Faith*. New York: Bobbs-Merrill, 1946.

Barker, Eileen. *New Religious Movements: A Practical Introduction*. London: Her Majesty's Stationery Office, 1989.

Bjornstad, James. *Counterfeits at Your Door*. Ventura, Calif.: Gospel Light Publications, 1979.

———. "Cultic and Christian Conversion: Is There a Difference?" *Update*, 6:1:1982.

Boa, Kenneth. *Cults, World Religions, and You*. Wheaton, Ill.: Victor Books, 1977.

Braden, Charles S. *These Also Believe*. New York: Macmillan, 1951.

Bromley, David G., and Edward F. Breschel. "General Population and Institutional Elite Support for Social Control of New Religious Movements: Evidence From National Survey Data," *Behavioral Sciences and the Law*, 10:1:1992.

Bromley, David G., and Anson D. Shupe. *Strange Gods*. Boston: Beacon Press, 1981.

———. "Public Reaction Against New Religious Movements," *Cults and New Religious Movements*. (Marc Galanter, ed.). Washington, D.C.: American Psychiatric Association, 1989.

Budansky, Stephen, Erica E. Goode, and Ted Gest, "The Cold War Experiments," *Newsweek*, January 24, 1994.

Clark, Elmer T. *The Small Sects in America*. (rev. ed.) Nashville: Abingdon Press, 1949.

Collins, Gary. *Search for Reality*. Santa Ana, Calif.: Vision House Publishers, 1969.

Conway, Flo, and Jim Siegelman. *Snapping: America's Epidemic of Sudden Personality Change*. New York: Dell Publishing Company, Inc., 1979.

———. "Deprogramming Deprogrammed," *Cornerstone* magazine, 6:36.

Dart, John. "Doubt Cast on 'Brainwashing' by Cults," *The Los Angeles Times*, November 19, 1983.

Davies, Horton. *The Challenge of the Sects*. Philadelphia: Westminster Press, 1961.

Davis, Deborah (Linda Berg) with Bill Davis. *The Children of God: The Inside Story.* Grand Rapids, Mich.: Zondervan, 1984.

Davis, Deborah, with Bill Davis. "Cults, Brainwashing, and Personal Responsibility," *Forward,* Summer 1985.

Duncan, R., and M. Weston-Smith, compilers. *Lying Truths.* New York: Pergamon Press, 1979.

Enroth, Ronald. "Cult/Countercult," *Eternity,* November 1977.

Enroth, Ronald, et al. *A Guide to Cults and New Religions.* Downers Grove, Ill.: InterVarsity Press, 1983.

Enroth, Ronald. *Youth, Brainwashing, and the Extremist Cults.* Grand Rapids: Zondervan Publishing House, 1977.

Ferguson, Charles. *New Books of Revelation.* Garden City, N.J.: Doubleday-Doran, 1929; first published as *Confusion of Tongues* in 1928.

Ferm, Vergilius. *Religion in the Twentieth Century.* New York: Philosophical Library, 1948.

Freyd, Pamela, ed. *Newsletter.* Philadelphia: False Memory Syndrome Foundation, various issues.

Galanter, Marc. *Cults: Faith, Healing, and Coercion.* New York: Oxford University Press, 1989.

Galanter, Marc, ed. *Cults and New Religious Movements: A Report of the American Psychiatric Association.* Washington, D.C.: American Psychiatric Association, 1989.

Gerstner, John H. *The Theology of the Major Sects.* Grand Rapids, Mich.: Baker Book House, 1960.

Griffin, Em. *The Mind Changers.* Wheaton: Tyndale House, 1976.

Gruss, Edmond C. *Cults and the Occult.* Grand Rapids, Mich.: Baker Book House, 1982.

Hassan, Steven. *Combatting Cult Mind Control.* Rochester, Vt.: Park Street Press, 1990.

Hesselgrave, David J., ed. *Dynamic Religious Movements.* Grand Rapids, Mich.: Baker Book House, 1978.

Hoekema, Anthony A. *The Four Major Cults.* Grand Rapids, Mich.: Eerdmans Publishing Company, 1963.

Langone, Michael D. "Treatment of Individuals and Families Troubled by Cult Involvement," *Update,* 7·1·1983.

Langone, Michael D., and Paul R. Martin. "Deprogramming, Exit Counseling, and Ethics: Clarifying the Confusion," *Christian Research Journal,* 15:3:1993.

Lewis, Gordon R. *Confronting the Cults.* Grand Rapids, Mich.: Baker Book House, 1966.

MacHovec, Frank. "Cults: Forensic and Therapeutic Aspects," *Behavioral Sciences and the Law,* 10:1:1992.

Martin, Paul R. *Cult Proofing Your Kids.* Grand Rapids, Mich.: Zondervan, 1993.

Martin, Paul R. "Dispelling the Myths: The Psychological Consequences of Cultic Involvement," *Christian Research Journal,* Winter/Spring 1989.

Martin, Walter R. *The Christian and the Cults.* Grand Rapids, Mich.: Zondervan, 1956, republished as *The Rise of the Cults.* Ventura: Gospel Light Publications, 1984.

———. *Walter Martin's Cults Reference Bible.* Santa Ana, Calif.: Vision House Publishers, 1981.

Mathison, Richard R. *Faiths, Cults and Sects of America.* Indianapolis, Ind.: Bobbs-Merrill, 1960.

Mayer, F. E. *Religious Bodies of America.* St. Louis: Concordia, 1954.

Mead, Frank S. *Handbook of Denominations in the United States,* rev. ed. Nashville: Abingdon, 1956.

Melton, J. Gordon. *The Encyclopedia of American Religions.* (2 vols.) Wilmington, N.C.: McGrath Publishing Company, 1978.

Neve, J. L. *Churches and Sects in Christendom.* Minneapolis: Augsburg, 1952.

Ogloff, James R. P., and Jeffrey Pfeiffer. "Cults and the Law: A Discussion of the Legality of Alleged Cult Activities," *Behavioral Sciences and the Law,* 10:1:1992.

Passantino, Robert, and Gretchen Passantino. *Answers to the Cultist at Your Door.* Eugene, Ore.: Harvest House Publishers, 1981.

―――. "The Hard Facts about Satanic Ritual Abuse," *Christian Research Journal*, Winter 1992.

―――. "Satanic Ritual Abuse in Popular Christian Literature: Why Christians Fall for a Lie While Searching for the Truth," *Journal of Psychology and Theology*, 20:3:1992.

Petersen, William J. *Those Curious New Cults*. New Canaan, Conn.: Keats Publishers, Inc., 1973.

Peterson, Gilbert. *Religious Research Digest*, December 1961.

Pfeifer, Jeffrey, and James R. P. Ogloff. "New Religious Movements and the Law: Past Interactions and New Directions," *Behavioral Sciences and the Law*, 10:1:1992.

Robbins, Thomas, and Dick Anthony, eds. *In Gods We Trust: New Patterns of Religious Pluralism in America*. New Brunswick: Transaction Books, 1981.

Rosten, Leo, ed. *Religions in America*. New York: Simon & Schuster, 1962, 1963.

Sanders, J. Oswald, and J. Stafford Wright. *Some Modern Religions*. London: Tyndale Press, 1956.

Sargant, William. *Battle for the Mind*. London: Pan Books, 1957.

Schaff, Philip, and Johann Herzog. *The New Schaff-Herzog Encyclopedia of Religious Knowledge*. 15 vols. Grand Rapids, Mich.: Baker Book House, n.d.

Shupe, Anson, and David G. Bromley. "The Modern American Anti-Cult Movement: A Twenty-Year Retrospective," *Association for the Sociology of Religion*, August 1991.

―――. *The New Vigilantes: Deprogrammers, Anti-Cultists, and the New Religions*. Beverly Hills: Sage Library of Social Research, 1980.

Singer, Margaret Thaler. "Coming Out of the Cults," *Psychology Today*, January 1979.

Sire, James W. *Scripture Twisting*. Downers Grove: InterVarsity Press, 1980.

Sparks, Jack. *The Mind Benders*. Nashville: Thomas Nelson Publishers, 1977.

Spittler, Russell P. *Cults and Isms*. Grand Rapids, Mich.: Baker Book House, 1962.

Strong, James. *Strong's Exhaustive Concordance of the Bible*. New York: Abingdon-Cokesbury Press, n.d.

Tucker, Ruth. *Another Gospel*. Grand Rapids, Mich.: Zondervan, 1989.

Van Baalen, Jan Karel. *Chaos of the Cults*, 4th rev. ed. Grand Rapids, Mich.: Eerdmans Publishing Company, 1962.

Watters, Ethan. "Doors of Memory," *Mother Jones*, January/February, 1993.

Wyrick, Herbert M. *Seven Religious Isms*. Grand Rapids, Mich.: Zondervan, 1940.

Young, John L., and Ezra E. H. Griffith. "A Critical Evaluation of Coercive Persuasion as Used in the Assessment of Cults," *Behavioral Sciences and the Law*, 10:1:1992.

Authority of the Scriptures

Allis, Oswald T. *The Old Testament: Its Claims and Its Critics*. Nutley, N.J.: Presbyterian and Reformed Publishing Company, 1972.

Archer, Gleason L. *Encyclopedia of Bible Difficulties*. Grand Rapids, Mich.: Zondervan, 1982.

Bruce, Frederick Fyvie. *The Books and the Parchments: Some Chapters on the Transmission of the Bible*. Revised Edition. Westwood, N.J.: Fleming H. Revell Company, 1953.

Bruce, F. F. *The New Testament Documents: Are They Reliable?* Grand Rapids, Mich.: Eerdmans Publishing Company, 1953.

Geisler, Norman L. *Christian Apologetics*. Grand Rapids, Mich.: Baker Book House, 1976.

―――. *Decide for Yourself: How History Views the Bible*. Grand Rapids, Mich.: Zondervan, 1982.

Geisler, Norman L. and William E. Nix. *From God to Us*. Chicago: Moody Press, 1974.

―――. *A General Introduction to the Bible*. Chicago: Moody Press, 1968.

Laird, R. *Inspiration and Canonicity of the Bible*. Grand Rapids, Mich.: Zondervan, 1966.

Lewis, C. S. *The Case for Christianity*. New York: Macmillan, 1956.

Lewis, Gordon R. *Testing Christianity's Truth Claims: Approaches to Christian Apologetics*. Chicago: Moody Press, 1976.

McDowell, Josh. *Evidence That Demands a Verdict: Historical Evidence for the Christian Faith*. Arrowhead Springs, Calif.: Campus Crusade for Christ, 1972.

————. *More Evidence That Demands a Verdict: Historical Evidence for the Christian Scriptures.* Arrowhead Springs: Campus Crusade for Christ, 1975.

————. *More Than a Carpenter.* Wheaton: Tyndale House, 1980.

Montgomery, John W. *History and Christianity.* Downers Grove: InterVarsity Press, 1965.

Unger, Merrill Frederick. *Archaeology and the New Testament.* Grand Rapids, Mich.: Zondervan, 1962.

————. *Archaeology and the Old Testament.* Grand Rapids, Mich.: Zondervan, 1966.

Jehovah's Witnesses

Ball, Francis K. *The Elements of Greek.* New York: Macmillan, 1950.

Bergman, Jerry. *Jehovah's Witnesses and Blood Transfusions.* Costa Mesa, Calif.: CARIS, 1979.

————. *Jehovah's Witnesses and Mental Illness.* Costa Mesa: CARIS, 1983.

Bowser, Arthur. *What Every Jehovah's Witness Should Know.* Denver: B/P Publications, 1975.

Breese, Dave. *Know the Marks of the Cults.* Wheaton: Victor Books, n.d.

Bullions, Peter. *Principles of Greek Grammar.* New York: Farmer, Bruce and Company, n.d.

Carnell, E. J. *An Introduction to Christian Apologetics.* Grand Rapids, Mich.: Eerdmans Publishing Company, 1950.

Cline, Ted. *Questions for Jehovah's Witnesses.* Ventura: Gospel Light Publications, 1975.

Cole, Marley. *Jehovah's Witnesses, the New World Society.* New York: Vantage Press, 1955.

Cooper, Lee. "Publish or Perish: Negro Jehovah's Witnesses' Adaptation in the Ghetto," *Religious Movements in Contemporary America.* Irving Zaretsky and Mark P. Leone, eds. Princeton, N.J.: Princeton University Press, 1974.

Countess, Robert H. *The Jehovah's Witnesses New Testament.* Phillipsburg, N.J.: Presbyterian and Reformed Publishing Company, 1982.

Davies, Horton. *Christian Deviations.* New York: Philosophical Library, 1954.

Dencher, Ted. *The Watch Tower Versus the Bible.* Chicago: Moody Press, 1961.

————. *Why I Left Jehovah's Witnesses.* Ft. Washington, Pa.: Christian Literature Crusade, 1966.

Deissmann, Adolf. *Light From the Ancient East.* New York: Harper, 1951.

Finnegan, Jack. *Light from the Ancient Past.* Princeton, N.J.: Princeton Press, 1946.

Gaebelein, Arono C. *The Hope of the Ages.* Our Hope, n.d.

Gerstner, John H. *The Theology of the Major Sects.* Grand Rapids, Mich.: Baker Book House, 1963.

Gruss, Edmond C. *Apostles of Denial.* Nutley: Presbyterian and Reformed Publishing Company, 1970.

————. *The Jehovah's Witnesses and Prophetic Speculation.* Nutley: Presbyterian and Reformed Publishing Company, 1972.

Gruss, Edmond C., ed. *We Left Jehovah's Witnesses: A Non-Prophet Organization.* Nutley: Presbyterian and Reformed Publishing Company, 1972.

Hamilton, Floyd E. *The Basis of Christian Faith.* New York: Harper, 1949.

Hoekema, Anthony A. *The Four Major Cults.* Grand Rapids, Mich.: Eerdmans Publishing Company, 1963.

Hoekema, Anthony A. *Jehovah's Witnesses.* Grand Rapids, Mich.: Eerdmans Publishing Company, 1972.

Irvine, William C. *Heresies Exposed.* Neptune, N.J.: Loizeaux Brothers, 1955.

Kauper, Paul G. *Religion and the Constitution.* Baton Rouge: Louisiana State University Press, 1964.

Knoch, Adolf E. *Concordant Version New Testament.* (Greek Translation) Los Angeles: Concordant Publishing Concern, 1931.

Knox, Ronald. *Translation of the Bible.* 3 vols. New York: Sheed & Ward, 1953.

Lewis, Gordon R. *The Bible, the Christian, and Jehovah's Witnesses.* Philadelphia: Presbyterian and Reformed Publishing Company, 1966.

Machen, J. G. *The Origin of Paul's Religion.* Grand Rapids, Mich.: Eerdmans Publishing Company, 1950.

————. *The Virgin Birth of Christ.* Grand Rapids, Mich.: Eerdmans Publishing Company, 1950.

MacMillan, A. H. *Faith on the March.* Englewood Cliffs, N.J.: Prentice Hall, 1957.

Magnani, Duane, and Arthur Barrett. *Dialogue with Jehovah's Witnesses.* 2 vols. Clayton, Calif.: Witness Inc., 1983.

Martin, Walter and Norman Klann. *Jehovah of the Watchtower.* Minneapolis: Bethany House Publishers, 1981.

Mayer, F. E. *Jehovah's Witnesses.* St. Louis: Concordia Publishing House, 1943.

Metzger, Bruce M. "The Jehovah's Witnesses and Jesus Christ," *Theology Today,* April 1953.

Moulton, J. H. *A Grammar of the New Testament Greek,* 3rd. ed. Edinburgh: Tavil T. Clark, n.d.

Newman, John Henry. *The Arians of the Fourth Century.* London: Longmans Green, 1911.

————. *St. Athanasius.* Vols. 1, 2. London: Longmans Green, 1911.

————. *Basic Writings of St. Augustine.* New York: Random House, 1950.

Pegis. *Basic Writings of St. Thomas Aquinas.* New York: Random House, 1950.

Ross, Rev. J. J. *Some Facts and More Facts about the Self-Styled Pastor, Charles T. Russell.* Self-published, n.d.

Sanders, J. Oswald. *Heresies Ancient and Modern.* Edinburgh: Marshall, Morgan & Scott, 1954.

Schnell, W. J. *Into the Light of Christianity.* Grand Rapids, Mich.: Baker Book House, 1958.

————. *Thirty Years a Watchtower Slave.* Grand Rapids, Mich.: Baker Book House, 1956.

Souter, Alexander. *The New Testament in Greek.* Oxford: Oxford University Press, 1947.

Spittler, Russell P. *Cults and Isms.* Grand Rapids, Mich.: Baker Book House, 1962.

Stroup, Herbert Hewitt. *The Jehovah's Witnesses.* New York: Columbia University Press, 1945.

Thiessen, Henry. *An Introduction to the New Testament.* Grand Rapids, Mich.: Eerdmans Publishing Company, 1948.

Thomas, F. W. *Masters of Deception: An Expose of the Jehovah's Witnesses.* Grand Rapids, Mich.: Baker Book House, 1970.

Van Baalen, Jan Karel. *Chaos of the Cults.* 4th rev. ed. Grand Rapids, Mich.: Eerdmans Publishing Company, 1962.

Van Buskirk, Michael. *The Scholastic Dishonesty of the Watchtower.* Costa Mesa: CARIS, 1976.

Warfield, Benjamin B. *Christological Studies.* Princeton: Princeton University Press, 1950.

Watters, Randall. *Thus Saith. . . . The Governing Body of Jehovah's Witnesses.* Manhattan Beach: Bethel Ministries, 1982.

Westcott, B. F., and F. J. A. Hort. *The New Testament in the Original Greek.* New York: Macmillan, 1885, 1943.

Whalen, William J. *Armageddon Around the Corner.* New York: The John Day Company, 1962.

Wilson, Robert Dick. *A Scientific Investigation of the Old Testament.* Philadelphia: Sunday School Times, n.d.

Wright, J. Stafford. *Some Modern Religions.* Chicago: InterVarsity Press, 1956.

Wulfken, George W. *Let There Be Light.* Self-published, n.d.

Young, C. D. *An English Greek Lexicon.* London, n.p., 1859.

Young, E. J. *An Introduction to the Old Testament.* rev. ed. Grand Rapids, Mich.: Eerdmans Publishing Company, 1958.

Young, G. Douglas. *Grammar of the Hebrew Language.* Grand Rapids, Mich.: Zondervan, 1951.

Young, Robert. *An Analytical Concordance to the Bible.* New York: Funk & Wagnalls Company, 1919.

Magazine and Newspaper Articles

The Brooklyn Daily Eagle, back issues, 1912, 1913, 1916, 1942.

The Brooklyn Daily Times, November 1, 1916, 4.

The Daily Standard Union, back issue, November 1, 1916, 5.

Dawn Bible Students Association. *When "Pastor" Russell Died.* n.d.

Davidson, Bill. "Jehovah's Traveling Salesman," *Reader's Digest,* 50:77–80, January 1947.

The New York Times, back issues, 1916.

Russell, Charles Taze. *Our Most Holy Faith: A Collection of Writings and Sermons of Pastor Charles Taze Russell.* Dawn Bible Students Association, 1948.

Stewart, E. D. "The Life of Charles Taze Russell," *Overland Monthly*, Los Angeles, 1917.

Watchtower Bible and Tract Society Publications

Awake! magazine.

The Emphatic Diaglott. Interlinear Greek-English Translation of the New Testament, n.d.

Let God Be True. rev. ed. 1952.

Make Sure of All Things. 1953.

The New World Translation of the Hebrew Scriptures. rev. ed. 1951.

The New World Translation of the Hebrew Scriptures. vol. 1. 1953.

Russell, Charles Taze. *Studies in the Scriptures.* vols. 1–7, n.d.

Rutherford, J. F. *The Harp of God; Creation; Religion; The Kingdom; Salvation; Deliverance; Children; Enemies; Light; Government; Why Serve Jehovah?; Jehovah's Witnesses—Why Persecuted?; Religious Intolerance—Why?.*

Rutherford, J. F. Pamphlets (out of print). *A Great Battle in the Ecclesiastical Heavens* (1915); *Can the Living Talk With the Dead?* (1920); *Talking With the Dead* (1920); *Prohibition and the League of Nations* (1920); *Millions Now Living Will Never Die* (1920); *Comfort for the Jews* (1925); *Restoration* (1927); *The Last Days* (1928); *The Kingdom: The Hope of This World* (1931); *Liberty* (1932); *What Is Truth?* (1932); *What You Need* (1932); *Where Are the Dead?* (1932); *Who Is God?* (1932); *Health and Life* (1932); *Hereafter* (1932); *Home and Happiness* (1932); *Keys of Heaven* (1932); *The Kingdom* (1932); *Causes of Death* (1932); *Final War* (1932); *Good News* (1932); *The Crisis* (1933); *Dividing the People* (1933); *Escape to the Kingdom* (1933); *Intolerance* (1933); *Angels* (1934); *Beyond the Grave* (1934); *Favored People* (1934); *His Vengeance* (1934); *His Works* (1934); *Righteous Ruler* (1934); *Supremacy* (1934); *World Recovery* (1934); *Who Shall Rule the World?* (1935); *Government* (1935); *Loyalty* (1935); *Universal War Near* (1935); *Choosing Riches or Ruin* (1936); *Protection* (1936); *Armageddon* (1937); *Safety and Comfort* (1937); *Uncovered* (1937); *Face the Facts* (1938); *Warning* (1938); *Fascism or Freedom* (1939); *Government and Peace* (1939); *Judge Rutherford Uncovers the Fifth Column* (1940), *Refugees* (1940); *God and the State* (1941). Published by the International Bible Students Association.

———. Pamphlets (out of print). *Armageddon; Divine Healing; Born of the Spirit; Hope Beyond the Grave; Does God Answer Prayer?; When a Man Dies; What Can a Man Pay?; His Chosen People; Hope for a Fear-Filled World; The Day of Judgment; Spiritualism; Our Lord's Return; The Truth About Hell; Father, Son, and Holy Spirit; God and Reason; Jesus the World Savior; God's Plan, Creation.* The Dawn Bible Student Association.

The Watchtower magazine.

Mormonism

Anderson, Edward H. *A Brief History of the Church of Jesus Christ Latter Day Saints.* Jackson County, Mo.: Zion's Printing and Publishing Company, 1928.

Anderson, Einar. *Mormonism.* Chicago: Moody Press, 1956.

Argaugh, G. B. *Gods, Sex, and the Saints.* Rock Island: Augusta Press, 1957.

Arrington, Leonard J., and Davis Bitton. *The Mormon Experience.* New York: Alfred A. Knopf, Inc., 1979.

Bales, James D. *The Book of Mormon?* Rosemead, Calif.: Old Paths Book Club, 1958.

Baskin, R. N. *Reminiscences of Early Utah.* Self-published, 1914.

Beadle, J. H. *Polygamy or the Mysteries and Crimes of Mormonism.* Philadelphia: The National Publishing Company, 1882.

Bennett, Wallace Foster. *Why I Am a Mormon.* New York: T. Nelson, 1958.

Brewer, David I. *Utah Elites and Utah Racial Norms.* Salt Lake City: Modern Microfilm Company, n.d.

Brodie, Fawn M. *No Man Knows My History—The Life of Joseph Smith, the Mormon Prophet.* New York: Alfred A. Knopf, Inc., 1957, 1971.

Brooks, Juanita, ed. *On the Mormon Frontier: The Diary of Hosea Stout*. Salt Lake City: University of Utah Press, n.d.

Budvarson, Arthur. *The Book of Mormonism—True or False?* Grand Rapids, Mich.: Zondervan, 1941.

Call, Lamoni. *2,000 Changes in the Book of Mormon*. Salt Lake City: Modern Microfilm Company, n.d.

Cannon, Frank J. *Under the Prophet in Utah*. Boston: C. M. Clark, 1911.

———. *Brigham Young and His Mormon Empire*. New York: Fleming H. Revell Company, 1913.

Clark, J. A. *Gleanings by the Way*. n.p., 1842.

Codman, Jr. *The Mormon Country*. U.S. Publishing Company, 1874.

Corrill, John. *A Brief History of the Church of Christ of Latter-day Saints*. No publishing information.

Cowan, Marvin W. *Mormon Claims Answered*. Salt Lake City: Marvin W. Cowan, 1975.

Draper, Maurice I. *Christ's Church Restored*. Independence, Mo.: Herald Publishing House, 1948.

Erickson, Ephraim D. *The Psychological and Ethical Aspects of Mormon Group Life*. Chicago: University of Chicago Press, 1922.

Etenhouser, R., and A. B. Phillips. *Three Bibles Compared*. Independence: Herald Publishing Company, 1954.

Evans, R. H. *One Hundred Years of Mormonism*. Salt Lake City: Deseret News, 1905.

Folk, Edgar E. *The Mormon Monster*. New York: Fleming H. Revell, 1900.

Fraser, Gordon H. *Is Mormonism Christian?* Chicago: Moody Press, 1957.

Gibbs, Josiah F. *The Mountain Meadows Massacre*. Salt Lake City: *Salt Lake Tribune*, 1910.

Goodspeed, Edgar J. *The New Testament—An American Translation*. Chicago: University of Chicago Press, 1923.

Hanson, Klaus. *Quest for Empire*. East Lansing: Michigan State University Press, n.d.

Hickman, William A. *Brigham's Destroying Angel*. New York: G. A. Crofutt, 1872.

Hield, Charles R. *Baptism for the Dead*. Independence: Herald Publishing Company, 1953.

History of the Mormons or Latter-day Saints. New York: Auburn- Derby and Miller, 1852.

Hoekema, Anthony A. *Mormonism*. Grand Rapids, Mich.: Eerdmans Publishing Company, 1974.

Hougey, Hal. *Archaeology and the Book of Mormon*. Los Angeles: Pacific Press, 1973.

———. *Truth About the 'Lehi Tree of Life' Stone*. Los Angeles: Pacific Press, 1973.

Howe, E. D. *Mormonism Unveiled*. 1834.

Hunter, Milton R. *The Gospel Through the Ages*. Salt Lake City: Melchizedik Priesthood Course of Study, 1945–1946.

Ivins, Stanley S. *The Moose Thatcher Case*. Salt Lake City: Modern Microfilm Company, n.d.

Jenson, Andrew. *Latter-day Saint Biographical Encyclopedia*. Salt Lake City: Self-published annual, 1901–1936.

———. *Plural Marriage*. vol. 6. Salt Lake City: The Historical Record of the Church of Jesus Christ of Latter-day Saints. May 1887.

Jonas, Larry. *Mormon Claims Examined*. Salt Lake City: Modern Microfilm Company, n.d.

Kidder, Daniel P. *Mormonism and the Mormons*. New York: G. Lane & P. P. Sanford, 1842.

Lamb, M. T. *The Golden Bible*. New York: Ward and Drummond, 1887.

Lee, John Doyle. *A Mormon Chronicle*. San Marino, Calif.: Huntington Memorial Library, 1955.

Lewis, William. *The Church of Jesus Christ: How Shall I Know It?* Independence: Herald Publishing House, n.d.

Linn, William Alexander. *The Story of the Mormons*. New York: Macmillan, 1902.

Lyford, C. *The Mormon Problem*. New York: Hunt and Eaton, 1866.

Martin, Stuart. *The Mystery of Mormonism*. New York: E. P. Dutton and Company, n.d.

Martin, Walter R. *The Maze of Mormonism*. Santa Ana: Vision House Publishers, 1978.

McConkie, Bruce R. *Mormon Doctrine*. Salt Lake City: Bookcraft, 1958, 1966, 1978.

———. *What the Mormons Think of Christ*. Salt Lake City: Bookcraft, n.d.

McElveen, Floyd C. *The Mormon Illusion.* Ventura: Gospel Light Publications, 1979.

Meyer, Edward. *Ursprung und Geschichte der Mormonen mit Exkursen ueber Anfange des Islams und des Christentums.* n.p., 1912.

Mulder, William. *Among the Mormons.* New York: Alfred A. Knopf, Inc., 1958.

Nutting, J. D. *The Little Encyclopedia of Mormonism.* Cleveland: Utah Gospel Mission, 1927.

O'Dey, Thomas F. *The Mormons.* Chicago: University of Chicago Press, 1957.

Peck, Reed. *Reed Peck Manuscript.* Salt Lake City: Modern Microfilm Company, reprint, n.d.

Penrose, Charles W. *Mormon Doctrine Plain and Simple or Leaves From the Tree.* Salt Lake City: G. Q. Cannon, 1897.

Petersen, LaMar. *Problems in Mormon Text.* Salt Lake City: Modern Microfilm Company, n.d.

Petersen, Mark E. *Race Problems as They Affect the Church.* Salt Lake City: Modern Microfilm Company, n.d.

Pratt, Orson. *Pamphlets by Orson Pratt.* Liverpool: R. James, 1851.

Pratt, Parley P. *Key to the Science of Theology.* Liverpool: F. D. Richards, 1855.

Reiser, A. H., and Marian G. Merkley. *What It Means to Be a Latter-day Saint: Course of Study for the First Intermediates Department.* Salt Lake City: Bookcraft, 1946.

Richards, Le Grand. *A Marvelous Work and a Wonder.* Salt Lake City: Deseret Book Company, 1950.

Rosten, Leo. *A Guide to the Religions of America.* New York: Simon and Schuster, 1963.

Rushton, John W. *The Apostasy and the Restoration.* Independence: Herald Publishing House, n.d.

Sackett, Charles C. *What's Going On In There?* Thousand Oaks, Calif.: Ex-Mormons for Jesus, 1982.

Schindler, Harold. *Orrin Porter Rockwell: Man of God, Son of Thunder.* Salt Lake City: University of Utah Press, n.d.

Shields, Stephen L. *Divergent Paths of the Restoration.* Bountiful, Ut.: Restoration Research, 1982.

Shook, Charles A. *The True Origin of the Book of Mormon.* Cincinnati, Oh.: Self-published, 1914.

Smith, Elbert A. *Differences That Persist Between the Reorganized Church of Christ Latter-Day Saints and the Utah Mormon Church.* Independence: Herald Publishing House, 1943.

Smith, Ethan. *View of the Hebrews.* Poutney, Me.: Smith & Shute, 1823.

Smith, Joseph Jr. *A Book of Commandments for the Government of the Church of Christ.* Reprinted by the *Salt Lake Tribune,* 1884.

———. *The Book of Mormon.* Salt Lake City: The Church of Jesus Christ of Latter-day Saints, various editions and publishers from 1830–1979.

Smith, Joseph Fielding, compiler. *Teachings of the Prophet Joseph Smith.* Salt Lake City: Deseret Book Company, 1976.

Smith, Lucy Mack. *Biographical Sketches of Joseph Smith.* Liverpool: S. W. Richards, 1853.

Snowden, James H. *The Truth About Mormonism.* New York: George H. Durant Company, 1926.

Spalding, F. S. *Why Egyptologists Reject the Book of Abraham.* Salt Lake City: The Arrow Press, n.d.

Spencer, Orson. *Letters Exhibiting the Most Prominent Doctrines of the Church of Jesus Christ of Latter-day Saints.* Liverpool: Self-published, 1848.

Starks, Arthur E. *A Complete Concordance to the Book of Mormon.* Independence: Herald Publishing House, 1950.

Stenhouse, T. B. *The Rocky Mountain Saints.* New York: B. Appleton Company, 1873.

Stewart, George. *Priesthood and Church Welfare.* Salt Lake City: Deseret Book Company, 1939.

Swartzell, William. *Mormonism Exposed.* Self-published, 1840.

Talmage, James E. *The Articles of Faith.* Salt Lake City: The Church of Jesus Christ of Latter-day Saints, 1952.

Tanner, Jerald. *Changes in Joseph Smith's History.* Salt Lake City: Modern Microfilm Company, n.d.

———. *Changes in the Key to Theology.* Salt Lake City: Modern Microfilm Company, n.d.
———. *Changes in The Pearl of Great Price.* Salt Lake City: Modern Microfilm Company, n.d.
———. *The Negro in Mormon Theology.* Salt Lake City: Modern Microfilm Company, n.d.
Tanner, Jerald, and Sandra Tanner. *The Case Against Mormonism.* vol. 1. Salt Lake City: Modern Microfilm Company, n.d.
———. *The Changing World of Mormonism.* Chicago: Moody Press, 1981.
———. *Joseph Smith and Polygamy.* Salt Lake City: Modern Microfilm Company, n.d.
———. *Joseph Smith's Curse Upon the Negro.* Salt Lake City: Modern Microfilm Company, n.d.
———. *Joseph Smith's Strange Account of the First Vision.* Salt Lake City: Modern Microfilm Company, n.d.
———. *Mormonism—Shadow or Reality?* Salt Lake City: Modern Microfilm Company, 1972, 1982.
———. *The Mormon Kingdom.* Salt Lake City: Modern Microfilm Company, n.d.
———. *The Mormon Papyri Question.* Salt Lake City: Modern Microfilm Company, n.d.
———. *Revealing Statements by the Three Witnesses to the Book of Mormon.* Salt Lake City: Modern Microfilm Company, n.d.
———. *3,914 Changes in the Book of Mormon.* Salt Lake City: Modern Microfilm Company, n.d.
Taylor, Samuel W. *Rocky Mountain Empire: The Latter-day Saints Today.* New York: Macmillan, 1978.
Thayer, Joseph Henry. *Greek-English Lexicon.* Grand Rapids, Mich.: Zondervan, 1973.
Tope, Wallace W. *On the Frontlines.* La Canada-Flintridge, Calif.: Frontline Ministries, 1980, 1981.
Tucker, Pomeroy. *Origin, Rise, and Progress of Mormonism.* n.p., 1867.
Tullis, F. La Mond, ed. *Mormonism: A Faith for All Cultures.* Provo, Ut.: Brigham Young University Press, 1978.
Turner, Wallace. *The Mormon Establishment.* Boston: Houghton Mifflin Co., 1966.
Van Wagoner, Richard S., and Steven C. Walker. *A Book of Mormons.* Salt Lake City: Signature Books, 1982.
Walters, Wesley P. *New Light on Mormon Origins from the Palmyra [N.Y.] Revival.* La Mesa, Calif.: Utah Christian Tract Society, 1973.
Wardle, James D. *Selected Changes in the Book of Mormon.* Salt Lake City: Modern Microfilm Company, n.d.
Weldon, Roy. *Other Sheep: Book of Mormon Evidences.* Independence: Herald Publishing House, 1956.
Whitmer, John. *John Whitmer's History.* Salt Lake City: Modern Microfilm Company, reprint, n.d.
Widtsoe, John A. *Priesthood and Church Government.* Salt Lake City: Deseret Book Company, 1939.
Witte, Robert C. *Where Does It Say That?* Safety Harbor, Fla.: Ex-Mormons for Jesus, 1982.
Young, Brigham. *Journal of Discourses.* Salt Lake City: Church of Jesus Christ of Latter-day Saints, 1901.
Young, Eliza. *Wife No. 19: A Life in Bondage.* n.p., 1872.

Christian Science

Writings of Mary Baker Eddy
Christ and Christmas
Christian Science Versus Pantheism
Christian Science Hymnal, with five hymns written by Mary Baker Eddy. Christian Science Publishing House, 1909.
Christian Healing
The First Church of Christ, Scientist, and Miscellany
Manual of the Mother Church

Message to the Mother Church, June 1900
Message to the Mother Church, June 1901
Message to the Mother Church, June 1902
Miscellaneous Writings
No and Yes
The People's Idea of God
Poems
Pulpit and Press
Retrospection and Introspection
Rudimental Divine Science
Science and Health With Key to the Scriptures (various editions)
Unity of Good

General Bibliography

A Complete Concordance to the Writings of Mary Baker Eddy (other than *Science and Health*)
A Complete Concordance to Science and Health With Key to the Scriptures
The Christian Science Journal
The Christian Science Sentinel
The Christian Science Monitor
Armstrong, Joseph. *The Mother Church.* Boston, Mass.: Christian Science Publishing Society (CSPS), 1937.
Bates, Ernest Sutherland, and John V. Dittemore. *Mary Baker Eddy—The Truth and the Tradition.* New York: Alfred A. Knopf, Inc., 1932.
Beasley, Norman. *The Cross and the Crown: The History of Christian Science.* New York: Duell, Sloan & Pearce, 1952, 1963.
The Blight That Failed. New York: Charles Scribner's Sons, 1929.
Boa, Kenneth. *Cults, World Religions, and You.* Wheaton: Victor Books, 1977.
Boltzly, Rev. Oliver D. *The Death Plot in Christian Science.* Minneapolis: The Lutheran Literary Board, 1935.
Braden, Charles S. *Spirits in Rebellion.* Dallas: Southern Methodist University Press, 1963.
Dakin, Edwin Franden. *Mrs. Eddy.* New York: Charles Scribner's Sons, 1929.
Dickey, Adam. *Memoirs of Mary Baker Eddy.* London: Robert G. Carter, 1927.
Douglass, R. C. *Christian Science: A Defense.* n.p., n.d.
Dresser, Horatio W., ed. *The Quimby Manuscripts.* New York: Thomas Y. Crowell Company, 1921.
Gray, James M. *The Antidote to Christian Science.* Chicago: Moody Press, n.d.
Gruss, Edmond C. *Cults and Occult.* Grand Rapids, Mich.: Baker Book House, 1982.
Hadden, Robert A. *Christian Science and the Christian Scriptures Compared and Contrasted.* American Prophetic League, 1952.
Haldeman, Isaac Massey. *Christian Science in Light of Holy Scripture.* New York: Fleming H. Revell Company, 1909.
Hanna, Septimus J. *Christian Science History.* Boston: CSPS, 1899.
Haushalter, Walter M. *Mrs. Eddy Purloins From Hegel.* Boston: A. A. Beauchamp, 1936.
Hawkins, Ann Ballew. *Phineas Parkhurst Quimby.* Self-published, 1951.
Hoekema, Anthony A. *Christian Science.* Grand Rapids, Mich.: Eerdmans Publishing Company, 1974.
Johnston, Julia Michael. *Mary Baker Eddy: Her Mission and Triumph.* CSPS, 1946.
Judah, J. Stillson. *The History and Philosophy of the Metaphysical Movements in America.* Philadelphia: The Westminster Press, 1967.
Martin, Walter R. *Walter Martin Speaks Out on the Cults.* Ventura, Calif.: Vision House Publishers, 1983.
Martin, Walter R., and Norman H. Klann. *The Christian Science Myth.* Grand Rapids, Mich.: Zondervan, 1956.
Meekan, M. *Mrs. Eddy and the Late Suit in Equity.* Self-published, 1908.

Miller, Elliot. "Christian Science" in *Walter Martin's Cults Reference Bible*. Santa Ana: Vision House Publishers, 1981.

Milmine, Georgine. *The Life of Mary Baker G. Eddy and the History of Christian Science*. New York: Doubleday, Page & Company, 1909. Reprinted by Baker Book House, 1971.

Moore, Rev. A. Lincoln. *Christian Science—Its Manifold Attraction*. Theodore E. Schulte Publishing Company, 1906.

Paget, Stephen, M.D. *The Faith and Works of Christian Science*. London: Self-published, 1909.

Peabody, Frederick W. *The Religio-Medical Masquerade*. New York: Fleming H. Revell, 1910.

Peel, Robert. *Spiritual Healing in a Scientific Age*. San Francisco: Harper & Row, 1987.

Phillips, Jane. *Mary Baker Eddy's Early Writings Compared With the Quimby Manuscripts*. Pasadena, Calif.: Toujours Publishing Company, 1931.

Powell, Lyman P. *Mary Baker Eddy*. New York: Macmillan, 1930.

Ramsay, E. Mary. *Christian Science and Its Discoverer*. Boston: CSPS, 1935.

Riddle, T. Wilkinson. *Christian Science in the Light of Holy Scripture*. London: Marshall, Morgan and Scott, 1931.

Riley, Woodbridge, W. Frederick Peabody, and Charles E. Humiston. *The Faith, the Falsity, and the Failure of Christian Science*. Nutley: Fleming H. Revell, 1925.

Sheldon, Henry C. *Christian Science So-Called*. Nashville: Abingdon Press, 1913.

Smith, Clifford P. *Historical Sketches*. Boston: CSPS, 1941.

Snowden, James H. *The Truth About Christian Science*. Philadelphia: Westminster Press, 1920.

Stewart, Herbert. *Christian Science—True or False*. Belfast: Graham L. Healy, Ltd., n.d.

Tenney, Rev. Herbert McIville. *Christian Science: Its Truths and Errors*. The Burrows Brothers Company, 1888.

Tomlinson, Irving C. *Twelve Years With Mary Baker Eddy*. Boston: CSPS, 1945.

Twain, Mark. *Christian Science*. New York: Harper, 1907.

Wilbur, Sybil. *The Life of Mary Baker Eddy*. Boston: CSPS, 1923.

Williamson, Margaret. *The Mother Church Extension*. Boston: CSPS, 1939.

Witmer, George W. *Christian Science in the Light of the Bible*. St. Louis: Concordia Publishing House, 1949.

Woodbury, Josephine C. *War on Heaven*. Boston: S. Usher Printer, 1897.

Christian Science Wartime Activities. Boston: CSPS, 1939–1947.

Legal Aspects of Christian Science. Boston: CSPS, 1899.

Newspaper and Magazine Articles

Arena magazine. Selected copy regarding Mrs. Eddy and Christian Science.

Buckley, Dr. J. M. "Dr. J. M. Buckley on Christian Science," *North American Review*, July 1901.

Cabot, M.D., Richard C. "100 Christian Science Cures," *McClures* magazine, August 1908.

"The Deadly Parallel," *New York Times*, July 10, 1904.

Fishbein, M.D., Morris. "Mary Baker Eddy," *Plain Talk*, 1:2, November 1927:21–26.

McClures magazine. Selected copy regarding Mrs. Eddy and Christian Science.

The New York Herald Tribune. Article and editorial on Christian Science, December 12–13, 1951.

The New York Times. Selected material on Christian Science.

The New York World. Selected material on Christian Science.

Woodbury, Josephine C. "Quimbyism or the Paternity of Christian Science," *Arena*, May 1899.

Wright, Livingston. "How Reverend Wiggin Rewrote Mrs. Eddy's Book," *New York World*, n.d.

The Theosophical Society

Besant, Annie. *The Ancient Wisdom: An Outline of Theosophic Teaching*. London: The Theosophical Society, 1897.

――――. *An Autobiography*. London: The Theosophical Society, 1893.

――――. *The Changing World*. London: The Theosophical Publishing Society, 1901.

――――. *Is Theosophy Anti-Christian?* London: The Theosophical Publishing Society, 1901.

――――. *Karma*. London: The Theosophical Publishing Society, 1904.

――――. *Man's Life in Three Worlds*. London: The Theosophical Publishing Society, 1899.

――――. *The Seven Principles of Man*. London: The Theosophical Publishing Society, 1902.

Blavatsky, Helena Petrovna. *Isis Unveiled*. Wheaton: Theosophical Publishing House, 1972.

――――. *The Key to Theosophy—An Abridgement*. Wheaton: Theosophical Publishing House, 1972.

――――. *The Secret Doctrine*. London: The Theosophical Society, 1893.

――――. *Theosophical Glossary*. Los Angeles: The Theosophical Company, 1892, 1973.

Braden, Charles S. *These Also Believe*. New York: Macmillan, 1960.

Butt, Baseden G. *Madam Blavatsky*. London: The Theosophical Society, 1926.

Cooper, Irving S. *Theosophy Simplified*, 7th ed. Wheaton: The Theosophical Press, 1964.

Davies, Horton. *The Challenge of the Sects*. Philadelphia: Westminster Press, 1961.

Ellwood, Robert S. Jr. *Alternative Altars*. Chicago: University of Chicago Press, 1979.

Ferguson, Charles. *Nehru Books of Revelation*. Garden City, N.J.: Doubleday, 1929.

Judah, J. Stillson. *The History and Philosophy of the Metaphysical Movements in America*. Philadelphia: The Westminster Press, 1967.

Kuhn, Alvin B. *Theosophy: A Modern Revival of Ancient Wisdom*. New York: H. Holt & Company, 1930.

Leadbeater, Charles W. *Textbook of Theosophy*. Chicago: The Theosophical Press, 1925.

McNiele, E. R. *From Theosophy to Christian Faith*. London: Longmans Green & Company, 1919.

Olcott, Henry S. *Old Diary Leaves: An Authentic History of the Theosophical Society*. Madras, India: The Theosophical Publishing Society, 1935.

Rogers, L. W. *Elementary Theosophy*. 6th ed. Wheaton: The Theosophical Press, 1956.

Russell, J. H. "Theosophy," *The New Schaff-Herzog Encyclopedia of Religious Knowledge*. Grand Rapids, Mich.: Baker Book House, 1977 (reprint).

Sheldon, H. C. *Theosophy and New Thought*. New York: Houghton Mifflin Co., 1916.

Sinnett, Alfred Percy. *The Theosophical Movement. 1875–1925. A History and a Survey*. New York: E. P. Dutton, 1925.

Sloan, Ellen M. *Modern Theosophy, Whence, What, Whither?* St. Paul: The Way Press, 1922.

Symonds, John. *Madame Blavatsky: Medium and Magician*. London: Odhams Press, 1959.

Van Baalen, Jan Karel. *The Chaos of the Cults*, 4th rev. ed. Grand Rapids, Mich.: Eerdmans Publishing Company, 1962.

Williams, Gertrude Leavenworth. *Priestess of the Occult, Madam Blavatsky*. New York: Alfred A. Knopf, Inc., 1946.

Wilson, Colin. *The Occult—A History*. New York: Random House, 1971.

Buddhism

Anderson, Walt. *Open Secrets: A Western Guide to Tibetan Buddhism*. New York: Viking Press, 1979.

Arvon, Henri. *Buddhism*. New York: Walker and Company, 1962.

Barrett, William. *Zen Buddhism: Selected Writings of D. T. Suzuki*. New York: Doubleday, 1956.

Chen-Chi-Chang. *The Practice of Zen*. New York: Harper, 1959.

Conze, Edward. *Buddhism: Its Essence and Development*. New York: Harper & Row, 1951.

David-Neel, Alexandra. *Buddhism: Its Doctrines and Its Methods*. New York: Avon Books, 1977.

Eerdmans Handbook to the World's Religions. Grand Rapids, Mich.: Eerdmans Publishing Company, 1982.

Fry, C. George, James R. King, Eugene R. Swanger, and Herbert C. Wolf. *Great Asian Religions*, n.p., n.d.

Geisler, Norman L., and Ytaka Amano. *The Reincarnation Sensation*. Wheaton: Tyndale House, 1987.

Guenther, Herbert V. *Buddhist Philosophy in Theory and Practice.* Middlesex: Penguin Books, 1971.

Humphreys, Christmas. *Zen Buddhism.* London: Allen and Unwin, 1957.

"Is Buddha Awakening the U.S.?" *Hinduism Today,* July 1994.

Johnson, David L. *A Reasoned Look at Asian Religions.* Minneapolis: Bethany House Publishers, 1985.

Kapleau, Philip, ed. *The Three Pillars of Zen.* Boston: Beacon Press, 1965.

Kung, Timothy. "Evangelizing Buddhists," *International Journal of Frontier Missions,* July 1993.

Layman, Emma McCloy. *Buddhism in America.* Chicago: Nelson-Hall, 1976.

Linssen, Robert. *Living Zen.* New York: Grove Press, 1958.

McDowell, Josh, and Don Stewart. *Handbook of Today's Religions.* San Bernardino, Calif.: Here's Life Publishers, 1981.

Melton, J. Gordon. *Encyclopedia of American Religions.* vol. 2. Wilmington, N.C.: McGrath Publishing Company, 1978.

Nauman, St. Elmo. *Dictionary of Asian Philosophies.* Secaucus, N.J.: Citadel Press, 1978.

Ogata, Sohaku. *Zen for the West.* New York: Apollo, Williams, Morrow, 1962.

Parrinder, Geoffrey. *Avatar and Incarnation.* New York: Oxford University Press, 1982.

————. *A Dictionary of Non-Christian Religions.* Philadelphia: The Westminster Press, 1971.

Robinson, Richard H. *The Buddhist Religion.* Belmont, Calif.: Dickenson Publishing, 1970.

Stephens, James C. "Looking at Buddhist America: A Key to World Evangelization," *International Journal of Frontier Missions,* July 1993.

Suzuki, D. T. *Essays in Zen Buddhism.* 3 vols. London: n.p., 1949, 1951.

Suzuki, D. T. *An Introduction to Zen Buddhism.* New York: Philosophical Library, 1949.

Suzuki, D. T. *Manual of Zen Buddhism.* New York: Grove Press, 1960.

Watts, Alan. *The Spirit of Zen.* New York: Grove Press, 1958.

————. *The Way of Zen.* New York: Pantheon Books, 1959.

————. *The Way of Liberation in Zen Buddhism.* San Francisco: American Academy of Asian Studies, 1955.

Weerasingha, Tissa. "Karma and Christ: Opening Our Eyes to the Buddhist World," *International Journal of Frontier Missions,* July 1993.

Yamamoto, J. Isamu. The Arrival of Theravad," *Christian Research Journal,* Fall 1994.

————. *Beyond Buddhism.* Downers Grove: InterVarsity Press, 1982.

————. "The Buddha," *Christian Research Journal,* Spring/Summer 1994.

————. "Tibetan Buddhists," *Christian Research Journal,* Spring 1995.

The Baha'i Faith

Magazine Articles

Bach, Marcus. "Baha'i: A Second Look," *Christian Century,* April 10, 1957.

"We Love All Religions," *Time,* April 26, 1963.

Publications from the Baha'i Publishing Trust, Willmette, Ill..

Abdu'l-Baha. *Some Questions Answered.*

Baha'u'llah. *Gleanings From the Writings of Baha'u'llah,* 1952.

Baha'u'llah and Abdu'l-Baha. *Baha'i World Faith.*

Principles of the Baha'i Faith.

Sears, William. *Release the Sun.*

Shoghi, Effendi. *Promised Day to Come.*

Star of the West. Willmette: Baha'i Publishing Committee, December 31, 1913.

Townsend, George. *The Promise of All Ages.*

Willoughby, John. *All Things Made New.*

The Wisdom of Baha'u'llah. Willmette: Baha'i Publishing Committee, n.d.

Additional Bibliography

Enroth, Ronald, et al. *A Guide to Cults and New Religions.* Downers Grove: InterVarsity Press, 1983.

Esslemont, J. E. *Baha'u'llah and the New Era.* Wilmette, Ill.: Baha'i Publishing Trust, 1970 (reprinted from 1923).

Gruss, Edmond C. *Cults and Occult.* Grand Rapids, Mich.: Baker Book House, 1982.

Martin, Walter R. *Walter Martin Speaks Out on the Cults.* Ventura, Calif.: Vision House Publishers, 1983.

Mathison, Richard. *Faith, Cults, and Sects in America.* New York: Scribners, 1952.

Miller, Elliot. "The Baha'i Faith" in *Walter Martin's Cults Reference Bible.* Santa Ana: Vision House Publishers, 1981.

Miller, William McElwee. *What Is the Baha'i Faith?* Grand Rapids, Mich.: Eerdmans Publishing Company, 1977.

Van Baalen, Jan Karel. *Chaos of the Cults.* 4th ed. revised. Grand Rapids, Mich.: Eerdmans Publishing Company, 1962.

The New Age Cults

Alnor, William. *UFOs in the New Age.* Grand Rapids, Mich.: Baker Book House, 1992.

Chandler, Russell. *Understanding the New Age.* Dallas: Word Books, 1988.

Creme, Benjamin. *Maitreya's Mission.* Amsterdam: Share International Foundation, 1986.

———. *The Reappearance of the Christ and the Masters of Wisdom.* London: Tara Press, 1980.

Downing, Levi. *The Aquarian Gospel of Jesus the Christ.* Marina del Rey, Calif.: DeVorss & Company, 1981.

Dunphy, John. "A Religion for a New Age," *The Humanist,* January/February 1983.

Essene, Virginia. *New Teachings for an Awakening Humanity.* Santa Clara, Calif.: Spiritual Education Endeavors Publishing, 1986.

Ferguson, Marilyn. *The Aquarian Conspiracy.* Los Angeles: J. P. Tarcher, 1980.

Goldstein, William. "Life on the Astral Plane," *Publishers Weekly,* March 8, 1983.

Groothuis, Douglas. *Revealing the New Age Jesus.* Downers Grove: InterVarsity Press, 1990.

———. *Unmasking the New Age.* Downers Grove: InterVarsity Press, 1986.

Lawren, Bill. "UFO Report," *OMNI,* October 1987.

Lewis, C. S. *Surprised by Joy.* New York: Harcourt, Brace, Jovanovich, 1955.

MacLaine, Shirley. *Dancing in the Light.* New York: Bantam Books, 1985.

Mahr, Douglas James. *Voyage to a New World.* Lopez, Wash.: Masterworks, Inc., Publishers, 1985.

Marty, Martin E. "An Old New Age in Publishing," *Christian Century,* November 18, 1987.

Melton, J. Gordon. *New Age Encyclopedia.* Detroit: Gale Research Inc., 1990.

Miller, Elliot. *A Crash Course on the New Age Movement.* Grand Rapids, Mich.: Baker Book House, 1989.

Spangler, David. *Emergence: Rebirth of the Sacred.* New York: Delta, 1984.

———. *Revelation: The Birth of a New Age.* San Francisco: Rainbow Bridge, 1976.

Steiger, Brad. *The Fellowship.* New York: Dolphin/Doubleday, 1988.

Strieber, Whitley. *Communion.* New York: William Morrow, 1987.

Weldon, John, and Zola Levitt. *Encounters with UFOs.* Irvine, Calif.: Harvest House Publishers, 1975.

The Unification Church

Anonymous. *Outline of the Principle.* New York: The Holy Spirit Association for the Unification of World Christianity (HSAUWC), 1980.

Bjornstad, James. *Sun Myung Moon and the Unification Church.* Minneapolis: Bethany House Publishers, 1976.

Blake, Richard A. "The Attraction of the Moonies," *America Magazine,* June 12, 1982.

"Buses, Buses, and More Buses," *New Hope News,* October 21, 1976.

Byron, Christopher. "Seems Like Old Times," *New York Magazine*, n.d.

Coates, James. "Moon Church Traced From Sex Cult," *Chicago Tribune*, March 27, 1978.

Cooper, Nancy, and Mark Miller. "Rev. Moon's Rising Son," *Newsweek*, April 11, 1988.

Durham, Deanna. *Life Among the Moonies: Three Years in the Unification Church*. Plainfield, N.J.: Logos International, 1981.

Edwards, Christopher. *Crazy for God*. Englewood Cliffs, N.J.: Prentice-Hall, Inc., 1979.

Elkins, Chris. *Heavenly Deception*. Wheaton: Tyndale House, 1980.

———. *What Do You Say to a Moonie?* Wheaton: Tyndale House, 1981.

Geisler, Norman L. *Christian Apologetics*. Grand Rapids, Mich.: Baker Book House, 1976.

Holt, T. Harvey. "A View of the Moonrise," *Conservative Digest*, January/February, 1989.

Judis, John B. "Rev. Moon's Rising Political Influence," *U.S. News and World Report*, March 27, 1989.

Kemperman, Steve. *Lord of the Second Advent*. Ventura, Calif.: Gospel Light Publications, 1981.

Kim, Dr. Young Oon, ed. *The Divine Principles*. San Francisco: HSAUWC, 1960, 1963.

Kim, Dr. Young Oon. *Speeches on Unification Teaching*. Barrytown, N.Y.: Unification Theological Seminary, 1986.

———. *Unification Theology*. New York: HSAUWC, 1987.

———. *Unification Theology and Christian Thought*. New York: Golden Gate Publishing Company, 1975.

Martin, Walter R. *The New Cults*. Ventura, Calif.: Vision House Publishers, 1981.

McCaughry, John. "The Uneasy Case Against Reverent Moon," *National Review*, December 23, 1983.

"Moon Pleads Not Guilty in Tax Case, Cites Discrimination," *Christianity Today*, November 20, 1981.

Moon, Sun Myung. *CAUSA Seminar Speech*. Washington, D.C.: HSAUWC, August 29, 1985.

———. *Christianity in Crisis*. Washington, D.C.: HSAUWC, 1974.

———. *God's Warning to the World*. New York: HSAUWC, 1985.

———. *Master Speaks*, various issues.

O'Hara, Jane. "Taxing Times for the Reverend," *McCleans Magazine*, April 5, 1982.

"Of Moon and Mammon," *Time*, October 26, 1981.

Passantino, Robert, and Gretchen Passantino. *Answers to the Cultist at Your Door*. Eugene, Ore.: Harvest House Publishers, 1981.

Sontag, Frederick. *Sun Myung Moon and the Unification Church*. Nashville: Abingdon Press, 1977.

Sudo, Dr. Kim. *120-Day Training Manual*. Washington, D.C.: HSAUWC, n.d.

Sun Myung Moon. Washington, D.C.: HSAUWC, 1969.

White, James H. "Unification Church's Anti-Communist Drive," *Christian Century*, August 28-September 4, 1985.

Woodward, Kenneth L., and Patrice Johnson. "Rev. Moon's New Friends," *Newsweek*, May 3, 1982.

Yamamoto, J. Isamu. *The Puppet Master*. Downers Grove: InterVarsity Press, 1977.

Yoo, Kwang-Yol. "Unification Church History From the Early Days," *New Hope News*, Washington, D.C.: The Unification Church.

Scientology

Alexander, Brooks, and Dean C. Halverson, eds. *Scientology: The Technology of Enlightenment*. Berkeley: Spiritual Counterfeits Project, 1982.

Anderson, Kevin. *Report of the Board of Inquiry Into Scientology*. Melbourne: Australia Parliament Government Printer, 1965.

Cooper, Paulette. *Scandal of Scientology*. New York: Tower Publications, 1971.

Corydon, Bent. *L. Ron Hubbard: Messiah or Madman?* Fort Lee, N.J.: Barricade Books, 1992.

Evans, Chris. *The Cults of Unreason*. New York: Dell Publishing Company, Inc., 1973.

THE KINGDOM OF THE CULTS

"Federal Prosecutors Unveil the Astonishing Intrigues of the Scientology Church," *People* magazine, August 14, 1978.

Foster, Sir John G. *Enquiry Into the Practice and Effects of Scientology*. London: Her Majesty's Stationery Office (report to the British government), n.d.

Gardner, Martin. *Fads and Fallacies in the Name of Science*. New York: Dover Publications, 1957.

Hubbard, L. Ron. *The Aims of Scientology*. Hollywood: The Church of Scientology Celebrity Center, 1974, 1977.

———. *Axioms and Logics*. Los Angeles: American St. Hill Organization, 1973.

———. *Dianetics and Scientology Technical Dictionary*. Los Angeles: American St. Hill Organization, 1975.

———. "Dianetics: The Evolution of a Science," *Astounding Science Fiction*, May 1950.

———. *Dianetics: The Modern Science of Mental Health*. Los Angeles: Bridge Publications, 1950.

———. "Heaven," *Hubbard Communication Office Bulletin*, May 11, 1963.

———. *History of Man*. Los Angeles: American Hill Organization, 1968.

———. *Hymn of Asia*. Los Angeles: The Church of Scientology of California Publications Organization, 1974.

———. *The Phoenix Lectures*. Los Angeles: The Church of Scientology of California Publications Organization, 1969.

———. *Science of Survival*. Los Angeles: American Hill Organization, 1973.

———. *Scientology 8–008*. Los Angeles: American Hill Organization, 1967.

———. *Scientology Abridged Dictionary*. Los Angeles: American Hill Organization, 1970.

———. *Scientology Clear Procedure*. Los Angeles: American Hill Organization, 1969.

———. *Scientology: The Fundamentals of Thought*. Los Angeles: The Church of Scientology Publications Organization, 1972.

———. *Technical Bulletins*. Los Angeles: Scientology Publications, various issues.

———. *Volunteer Minister's Handbook*. Los Angeles: Church of Scientology, 1976.

Kaufman, Robert. *Inside Scientology*. New York: Olympia Publications, 1972.

Malko, George. *Scientology: The Now Religion*. New York: Dell Publishing, 1970.

Martin, Walter R. "Scientology." cassette tape. Ventura, Calif.: Vision House Publishers, 1976.

Methvin, Eugene H. "Scientology: Anatomy of a Frightening Cult," *Readers Digest*, May 1980.

———. "Scientology: The Sickness Spreads," *Readers Digest*, September 1981.

Miller, Russell. *Bare-Faced Messiah: The True Story of L. Ron Hubbard*. London: Michael Joseph/Penguin Books Ltd., 1987.

Sann, Paul. *Fads, Fallacies, and Delusions*. New York: Crown Publications, 1967.

Schacter, Daniel L. *Stranger Behind the Engram*. Hillsdale, N.J.: Lawrence Erlbaum Associate, 1982.

Scientology: An In-Depth Profile of a New Force in Clearwater. Clearwater, Fla.: *St. Petersburg Times*, 1980.

Smith, Ralph Lee. "Scientology: Menace to Mental Health," *Today's Health*, December 1968.

Staff of Scientology. "The Scientology Catechism," *What Is Scientology?* Los Angeles: The Church of Scientology of California, 1979.

———. *Scientology: A World Religion Emerges in the Space Age*. Los Angeles: Church of Scientology Information Service, 1974.

Wallis, Claudia. "Mystery of the Vanished Ruler," *Time* magazine, January 31, 1983.

Eastern Religions

Anderson, Sir Norman, ed. *The World's Religions*. rev. ed. Grand Rapids, Mich.: Eerdmans Publishing Company, 1975.

Anderson, J. N. D. *Christianity and Comparative Religion.* Downers Grove: InterVarsity Press, 1970.

Bjornstad, James. *The Transcendental Mirage.* Minneapolis: Bethany House Publishers, 1976.

Bouquet, A. C. *Hinduism.* rev. ed. London: Hutchinson University Library, 1962.

Chandler, Russell, and Tyler Marshall. "Guru Brings His Ashram to Oregon," *The Los Angeles Times,* August 19, 1981.

Dietrich, Bill. "Conflict Over Rajneeshpuram," *Seattle Times,* September 9, 1984.

Goswam, Siddha Swarup Ananda. *Jesus Loves KRSNA.* Los Angeles: Vedic Christian Committee and Life Force, Krsna Yoga Viewpoint, 1975.

Haddon, David, and Gail Hamilton. *TM Wants You!* Grand Rapids, Mich.: Baker Book House, 1976.

Johansen, Jens. "The Master Will Not Speak Again," *New Religious Movements Update,* 5:5/4, December 1981.

Levine, Faye. *The Strange World of the Hare Krishnas.* New York: Fawcett Publications, 1974.

Lewis, Gordon R. *What Everyone Should Know About Transcendental Meditation.* Ventura, Calif.: Gospel Light Publications, 1975.

"Maharishi Ayur-Veda: Guru's Marketing Scheme Promises the World Eternal Perfect Health," *Journal of the American Medical Association (JAMA),* October 2, 1991.

Mangalwadi, Vishal. *The World of the Gurus.* Chicago: Cornerstone Books, 1977.

McCormack, Win, and Bill Driver, "Rajneeshpuram: Valley of Death?" *Oregon Magazine,* September 1984.

Miller, Elliot. "Inside ISKCON." Part One and Two. *Forward* magazine, 4:1:1; 4:2:3.

"Pied Piper of Poona," *Eternity,* September 1981.

Prabhupada, A. C. Bhaktivedanta Swami. *Bhagavad-Gita as It Is.* New York: The Bhaktivedanta Book Trust, 1968.

———. *The Nectar of Devotion.* New York: The Bhaktivedanta Book Trust, 1970.

Rajneesh, Bhagwan Shree. *Rajneeshism: An Introduction to Bhagwan Shree Rajneesh and His Religion.* Rajneeshpuram, Ore.: Rajneesh Foundation International, 1985.

Ramacharaka, Yogi. *The Philosophies and Religions of India.* Chicago: The Yogi Publication Society, 1930.

Singh, Chander Uday. "Sins of Bhagwan," *India Today,* June 15, 1982.

Smart, Ninan. *The Religious Experience of Mankind.* New York: Charles Scribner's Sons, 1976.

Spiritual Counterfeits Project. *TM in Court.* Berkeley: Spiritual Counterfeits Project, 1978.

Stillson, Judah J. *Hare Krishna and the Counterculture.* New York: John Wiley and Sons, 1974.

Weldon, John, and Zola Levitt. *The Transcendental Explosion.* Irvine, Calif.: Harvest House Publishers, 1976.

Yamamoto, J. Isamu. *Hare Krishna Hare Krishna.* Downers Grove: InterVarsity Press, 1978.

Yogi, Maharishi Mahesh. *Maharishi Mahesh Yogi on the Bhagavad-Gita.* New York: Penguin Books, 1967.

———. *Meditation of Maharishi Mahesh Yogi.* New York: The New American Library, 1969.

———. *The Science of Being and the Art of Living.* New York: The New American Library, 1968.

Zaehner, R. C. *Hinduism.* 2nd ed. Oxford: Oxford University Press, 1966.

The Apocalyptic Cults

Camping, Harold. *1994?* New York: Vantage Press, 1992.

Carter, Ken. "Branch Davidian Firearms," *Machine Gun News,* March 1994.

Chandler, Russell. *Doomsday.* Ann Arbor, Mich.: Servant Books, 1993.

Cornell, James. *The Great International Disaster Book.* New York: Pocket Books, 1979.

"The Cults Broad Reach," *Newsweek,* May 8, 1995.

Davis, Robert, and Juan J. Walte. "Swiss Cult's Bizarre Last Act Leaves 'Wax Museum' of Death," *USA Today,* October 6, 1994.

DeMar, Gary. *Last Days Madness.* Atlanta: American Vision, 1994.

Halverson, Dean. "Eighty-Eight Reasons: What Went Wrong?" *Christian Research Journal,* Fall 1988.

———. "Rapture Seer Hedges on Latest Guess," *Christianity Today,* October 21, 1988.

Hunt, Dave. *How Close Are We? Compelling Evidence for the Soon Return of Christ.* Eugene, Ore.: Harvest House Publishers, 1993.

———. *A Cup of Trembling.* Eugene, Ore.: Harvest House Publishers, 1995.

Jeffrey, Grant. *Armageddon: Appointment With Destiny.* Toronto: Frontier Research, 1988.

Jonsson, Carl Olaf, and Wolfgang Herbst. *The Sign of the Last Days—When?* Atlanta: Commentary Press, 1987.

"Korean Sect Stunned at 'Rapture' Doesn't Come," *Orange County Register,* October 29, 1992.

Lacoya, Richard. "In the Reign of Fire," *Time,* October 17, 1994.

Lindsey, Hal. *The 1980s: Countdown to Armageddon.* King of Prussia, Pa.: Westgate Press, 1980.

"Mass Suicide or Mass Murder?" *U.S. News and World Report,* October 17, 1994.

Missler, Chuck. "Peace and Safety," *Personal Update,* October 1993.

———. "Romanov Eagle Returns," *Personal Update,* January 1994.

Oropeza, B. J. *Ninety-Nine Reasons Why No One Knows When Christ Will Return.* Downers Grove: InterVarsity Press, 1994.

Passantino, Gretchen. "Days of Destruction: Lessons From Dealing with Self-Made Prophets," *World,* May 8, 1993.

———. "Long Wake in Waco," *World,* March 13, 1993.

Post, Tom. "Mystery of the Solar Temple," *Newsweek,* October 17, 1994.

Rice, John R. *Worldwide War and the Bible.* Wheaton: Sword of the Lord Publishers, 1940.

Samples, Kenneth, Erwin de Castro, Richard Abanes, and Robert Lyle. *Prophets of the Apocalypse: David Koresh and Other American Messiahs.* Grand Rapids, Mich.: Baker Book House, 1994.

Smith, Chuck. *Future Survival.* Costa Mesa, Calif.: Calvary Chapel, 1978.

Spaeth, Anthony. "Engineer of Doom," *Time,* June 12, 1995.

Strasser, Steven. "Tokyo Grabs the Doomsday Guru," *Newsweek,* May 29, 1995.

Van Impe, Jack. "Messiah 1975? The Tribulation 1976?" *The Jack Van Impe Crusade Newsletter,* April 1975.

Walvoord, John F. *The Nations in Prophecy.* Grand Rapids, Mich.: Zondervan Publishing Company, 1988.

Watanabe, Teresa. "Police Seize Toxic Chemicals in Raid on Japanese Sect," *The Los Angeles Times,* March 23, 1995.

The Worldwide Church of God

Magazine Articles

Ambassador Report. P.O. Box 4068, Pasadena, Calif., 91106, various issues.

Campbell, Robert. "Herbert W. Armstrong: Does He Really Love the Plain Truth?" *Moody Monthly,* October 1972.

———. "Herbert W. Armstrong: Mr. Confusion," *The King's Business,* February 1962.

Flurry, Gerald. "Personal," *The Philadelphia Trumpet,* February 1997.

Flurry, Gerald, and Dennis Leap. "The Key of David Vision," *The Philadelphia Trumpet,* March 1997.

Hopkins, Joseph Martin, (No Title Cited.) *Christianity Today,* December 17, 1971.

Knuteson, Darby, and Campbell Knuteson. *The Delusions of Herbert W. Armstrong.* A reprint of *The Discerner,* January/March 1962.

"Mr. Jones, Meet Herbert W. Armstrong," *Eternity,* October 1972.

The Plain Truth, various issues.

Tarr, Leslie. "Herbert W. Armstrong: Does He Really Love the 'Plain Truth,' " *Moody Monthly,* September 1972.

The Worldwide News, various issues.

Additional Bibliography

Allen, J. H. *Judah's Scepter and Joseph's Birthright.* 6th ed. Boston: A. A. Beauchamp, Publisher, 1918.

Anderson, Stanley E. *Armstrongism's 300 Errors Exposed by 1300 Bible Verses.* Nashville: Church Growth Publications, 1973.

Anonymous. *God Is . . .* Pasadena: Worldwide Church of God, 1992.

———. *The Roadbuilder: God's Commonwealths, British and American.* Toronto: Commonwealth Publishers, Ltd., 1930.

———. *The United States and Britain in Prophecy: Study Paper.* Pasadena: Worldwide Church of God, November 1995.

Armstrong, Herbert W. *All About Water Baptism.* Pasadena: Ambassador College Press, 1972.

Armstrong, Herbert W., ed. *Ambassador College Bible Correspondence Course.* Pasadena: Ambassador College, 1966.

Armstrong, Herbert W. *The Autobiography of Herbert W. Armstrong.* Pasadena: Ambassador Press, 1967.

———. *Just What Do You Mean—Born Again!* Pasadena: Radio Church of God, 1962.

———. *Just What Do You Mean . . . Kingdom of God?* Pasadena: Ambassador Press, 1962.

———. *Mystery of the Ages.* Pasadena: Worldwide Church of God, 1985.

———. *1975 in Prophecy.* Pasadena: Radio Church of God, 1956.

———. *The United States and Britain in Prophesy.* Pasadena: Ambassador Press, 1980.

Benware, Paul N. *Ambassadors of Armstrongism: An Analysis of the History and Teachings of the Worldwide Church of God.* Philadelphia: Presbyterian and Reformed Publishing Company, 1975.

Buchner, J. L. F. *Armstrongism Bibliography.* Sydney, Australia: Self-published, 1983.

Chambers, Roger R. *The Plain Truth About Armstrongism.* Grand Rapids, Mich.: Baker Book House, 1972.

De Loach, Charles F. *The Armstrong Error.* Plainfield, N.J.: Logos International, 1971.

Grant, Robert G. *The Plain Truth About the Armstrong Cult.* n.p., n.d.

Hopkins, Joseph M. *The Armstrong Empire.* Grand Rapids, Mich.: Eerdmans Publishing Company, 1974.

Kirban, Salem. *The Plain Truth About the Plain Truth.* Huntington Valley, Pa.: Salem Kirban, Inc., 1970.

Larson, Egon. *Strange Cults and Sects.* New York: Hart Publishing Company, 1972.

Leyendecker, Ruth, and Wayne Leyendecker, with Roger F. Campbell, "We Escaped From Armstrongism" in James R. Adair and Ted Miller, eds. *We Found Our Way Out.* Grand Rapids, Mich.: Baker Book House, 1965.

Lowe, Harry W. *Radio Church of God: How Its Teachings Differ From Those of Seventh-day Adventists.* Mountain View, Calif.: Pacific Press Publishing Association, 1970.

Marson, Richard A. *The Marson Report Concerning Herbert W. Armstrong.* Seattle: The Ashley-Calvin Press, 1970.

Meredith, Roderick. *The Inside Story of the World Tomorrow Broadcast.* Pasadena: Ambassador Press, n.d.

Ord, David R. *The Jet-Set Galatians.* Exeter, Devon, UK: The Paternoster Press, 1982.

Piepkorn, Arthur C. *Profiles in Belief.* vol. 4. San Francisco: Harper & Row, 1979.

Petersen, William J. *Those Curious New Cults.* New Canaan, Conn.: Keats Publishing, 1973.

Roberts, Rev. Commander L. G. A. *Commentary on the Book of the Prophet Isaiah.* London: The Covenant Publishing Company, 1951.

Rutherford, Adam. *Israel-Britain or Anglo-Saxon Israel.* 3rd ed. London: Self-published, 1936.

Smith, Noel. *Herbert W. Armstrong and His World of Tomorrow.* Springfield, Mo.: Bible Baptist Tribune, 1964.

Smith, Paul B. *Other Gospels.* Denver: Gospel Advance Press, 1970.

Sumner, Robert L. *Herbert W. Armstrong: False Prophet.* Murfreesboro, Tenn.: Sword of the Lord Foundation, 1961.

Wilson, Paul. *The Armstrong Heresy: A Brief Examination.* Denver: Wilson Foundation, n.d.

Word Faith Movement

Articles and Magazines

Believer's Voice of Victory, various issues.
Dart, John. "Huge Faithdome in L.A.," *The Los Angeles Times,* September 9, 1989.
Ever Increasing Faith Messenger, various issues.

Additional Bibliography

Billheimer, Paul E. *Destined for the Throne.* Special TBN edition. Ft. Washington, Pa.: Christian Literature Crusade, 1975, 1988.
Capps, Charles. *Authority in Three Worlds.* Tulsa: Harrison House, 1980.
———. *Changing the Seen and Shaping the Unseen.* Tulsa: Harrison House, 1980.
———. *Dynamics of Faith and Confession.* Tulsa: Harrison House, 1987.
———. *God's Creative Power Will Work for You.* Tulsa: Harrison House, 1976.
Cho, Paul (David) Yongii. *The Fourth Dimension.* South Plainfield, N.J.: Bridge Publishing, Inc., 1983.
Copeland, Gloria. *God's Will for You.* Ft. Worth: Kenneth Copeland Publications, 1972.
Copeland, Kenneth. *The Force of Faith.* Ft. Worth: Kenneth Copeland Publications, 1983.
———. *Freedom From Fear.* Ft. Worth: Kenneth Copeland Publications, 1983.
———. *Healed: To Be or Not to Be.* Ft. Worth: Kenneth Copeland Ministries, 1979.
———. *The Laws of Prosperity.* Ft. Worth: Kenneth Copeland Publications, 1974.
———. *Our Covenant With God.* Ft. Worth: Kenneth Copeland Publications, 1987.
———. *The Power of the Tongue.* Ft. Worth: Kenneth Copeland Publications, 1980.
———. *Sensitivity of Heart.* Ft. Worth: Kenneth Copeland Publications, 1984.
———. *Walking in the Realm of the Miraculous.* Ft. Worth: Kenneth Copeland Publications, 1979.
———. *Welcome to the Family.* Ft. Worth: Kenneth Copeland Ministries, 1979.
Farah, Charles. *A Critical Analysis: The Roots and Fruits of Faith-Formula Theology.* Unpublished paper for the Society of Pentecostal Studies, November 1980.
Fee, Gordon D. *The Disease of the Health and Wealth Gospels.* Beverly, Mass.: Frontline Publishing, 1985.
Hagin, Kenneth E. *Having Faith in Your Faith.* Tulsa: Faith Library, 1980.
———. *How You Can Be Led by the Spirit of God.* Tulsa: Kenneth Hagin Ministries, 1978.
———. *The Interceding Christian.* Tulsa: Kenneth Hagin Ministries, 1978.
———. *The Name of Jesus.* Tulsa: Faith Library, 1981.
———. *Right and Wrong Thinking for Christians.* Tulsa: Kenneth Hagin Ministries, 1966.
———. *Seven Things You Should Know About Divine Healing.* Tulsa: Kenneth Hagin Ministries, 1979.
Hanegraaff, Hank. *Christianity in Crisis.* Eugene, Ore.: Harvest House Publishers, 1993.
Harris, R. Laird, Gleason L. Archer, and Bruce K. Waltke. *Theological Wordbook of the Old Testament.* Chicago: Moody Press, 1980.
Kenyon, E. W. *In His Presence.* Seattle: Kenyon's Gospel Publishing Society, 1969.
———. *The Two Kinds of Faith: Faith's Secrets Revealed.* Seattle: Kenyon's Gospel Publishing Society, 1942.
———. *The Two Kinds of Life.* Seattle: Kenyon's Gospel Publishing Society, 1971.
Kinnebrew, James M. *The Charismatic Doctrine of Positive Confession: A Historical, Exegetical, and Theological Critique.* University Microfilms, Int., Order #9029719.
Matt, Judith. *The Born-Again Jesus of the Word-Faith Teaching.* Fullerton, Calif.: Spirit of Truth Ministries, 1984.
McConnell, D. R. *A Different Gospel.* Peabody, Mass.: Hendrickson Publishers, 1995.
Parker, Larry. *We Let Our Son Die.* Irvine, Calif.: Harvest House Publishers, 1980.
Price, Frederick K. C. *Faith, Foolishness, or Presumption?* Tulsa: Harrison House, 1979.
Richards, Lawrence O. *Expository Dictionary of Bible Words.* Grand Rapids, Mich.: Zondervan, 1985.

Robertson, Archibald Thomas. *Word Pictures in the New Testament.* Nashville: Broadman Press, 1930.

Savelle, Jerry. *If Satan Can't Steal Your Joy.* Tulsa: Harrison House, 1982.

Seventh-day Adventism

The Adventist Home; Child Guidance; Christ's Object Lessons; Counsels on Diets and Foods; Early Writings; Education; Evangelism; Messages to Young People; The Ministry of Healing; Steps to Christ. Takoma Park, Md.: Review and Herald Publishing Association, n.d.

The Acts of the Apostles; Christian Experience and Teachings; The Desire of the Ages; The Great Controversy; Index to the Writings of Ellen G. White; Patriarchs and Prophets; Prophets and Kings; Testimonies for the Church, vols. 1–9; *Testimonies to Ministers; Thoughts From the Mount of Blessings.* Mountain View, Calif.: Pacific Press Publishing Association, n.d.

Seventh-day Adventist Publications

Anderson, R. A. *The Shepherd Evangelist.* Takoma Park, Md.: Review and Herald Publishing Association, n.d.

———. *Unfolding the Revelation.* Mountain View, Calif.: Pacific Press Publishing Association, n.d.

Andreason, M. L. *The Book of Hebrews.* Takoma Park, Md.: Review and Herald Publishing Association, n.d.

———. *God's Holy Day.* Takoma Park, Md.: Review and Herald Publishing Association, n.d.

———. *The Sabbath.* Takoma Park, Md.: Review and Herald Publishing Association, n.d.

———. *The Sanctuary Service.* Takoma Park, Md.: Review and Herald Publishing Association, n.d.

———. *What Can a Man Believe?* Mountain View, Calif.: Pacific Press Publishing Association, n.d.

The Bible Made Plain: A Series of Short Bible Studies for the Home Circle Upon the Fundamentals of the Christian Faith. Takoma Park, Md.: Review and Herald Publishing Association, n.d.

Bible Readings for the Home. Takoma Park, Md.: Review and Herald Publishing Association, n.d.

Bollman, Calvin P. *Sunday: Origin of Its Observance in the Christian Church.* Takoma Park, Md.: Review and Herald Publishing Association, n.d.

Branson, W. H. *In Defense of the Faith.* Takoma Park, Md.: Review and Herald Publishing Association, n.d.

Bunch, Taylor G. *Behold the Man.* Southern Publishing Association, n.d.

———. *The Ten Commandments.* Takoma Park, Md.: Review and Herald Publishing Association, n.d.

Christian, Lewis Harrison. *The Fruitage of Spiritual Gifts: The Influence and Guidance of Ellen G. White in the Advent Movement.* Washington, D.C.: Review and Herald Publishing Association, 1947.

Church Manual. Takoma Park, Md.: General Conference of Seventh-day Adventists, n.d.

Cottrell, Raymond F. *Perfection in Christ.* Washington, D.C.: Review and Herald Publishing Association, 1965.

———. *The True Sabbath.* Southern Publishing Association, n.d.

Daniels, A. G. *The Abiding Gift of Prophecy.* Mountain View, Calif.: Pacific Press Publishing Association, n.d.

———. *Christ Our Righteousness.* Takoma Park, Md.: The Ministerial Association of Seventh-day Adventists, n.d.

Dixon, Louis J. *Law or Grace?* Southern Publishing Association, n.d.

Everson, Charles T. *The Rich Man and Lazarus.* Southern Publishing Association, n.d.

———. *Who Are the Angels?* Takoma Park, Md.: Review and Herald Publishing Association, n.d.

Froom, Leroy E. *The Coming of the Comforter.* Takoma Park, Md.: Review and Herald Publishing Association, n.d.

———. *Finding the Lost Prophetic Witness.* Takoma Park, Md.: Review and Herald Publishing Association, n.d.

———. *The Prophetic Faith of Our Fathers.* Vols. 1–4. Takoma Park, Md.: Review and Herald Publishing Association, n.d.

General Conference Young People's Department of Missionary Volunteers: Studies in Bible Doctrine. Takoma Park, Md.: Review and Herald Publishing Association, n.d.

Genesis-John. Takoma Park, Md.: Review and Herald Publishing Association, n.d.

Haskell, S. N. *Bible Hand Book.* Takoma Park, Md.: Review and Herald Publishing Association, n.d.

Haynes, Carlyle B. *The Christian Sabbath: Is It Saturday or Sunday?* Southern Publishing Association, n.d.

———. *From Sabbath to Sunday.* Takoma Park,Md.: Review and Herald Publishing Association, n.d.

———. *The Gift of Prophecy.* Southern Publishing Association, n.d.

———. *Life, Death, and Immortality.* Southern Publishing Association, n.d.

———. *Seventh-day Adventists: Their Work and Teachings.* Takoma Park, Md.: Review and Herald Publishing Association, n.d.

Horn, Sigfried H., and Lynn H. Wood. *The Chronology of Ezra Seven.* Takoma Park, Md.: Review and Herald Publishing Association, n.d.

How to Handle Objections. Prepared by the publishing department of the Secretaries of the Southern Union Conference. Southern Publishing Association, n.d.

Jamison, T. Housel. *A Prophet Among You.* Mountain View, Calif.: Pacific Press Publishing Association, n.d.

Johns, Varner J. *The Secret Rapture and the Antichrist.* Mountain View, Calif.: Pacific Press Publishing Association, n.d.

Lickey, Arthur E. *Fundamentals of the Everlasting Gospel.* Takoma Park, Md.: Review and Herald Publishing Association, n.d.

Marsh, F. L. *Evolution, Creation, and Science.* Takoma Park, Md.: Review and Herald Publishing Association, n.d.

Maxwell, Arthur S. *The Coming King.* Mountain View, Calif.: Pacific Press Publishing Association, n.d.

Maxwell, Arthur S. *Your Friends the Adventists.* Mountain View, Calif.: Pacific Press Publishing Association, n.d.

Moseley, Calvin Edwin. *The Lord's Day.* Southern Publishing Association, n.d.

Nichol, Francis D. *Answers to Objections.* Takoma Park, Md.: Review and Herald Publishing Association, n.d.

———. *The Certainty of My Faith.* Takoma Park, Md.: Review and Herald Publishing Association, n.d.

———. *Ellen G. White and Her Critics.* Takoma Park, Md.: Review and Herald Publishing Association, n.d.

———. *The Midnight Cry.* Takoma Park, Md.: Review and Herald Publishing Association.

Odom, Robert L. *The Final Crisis and Deliverance.* Southern Publishing Association, n.d.

———. *How Did Sunday Get Its Name?* Southern Publishing Association, n.d.

———. *Sunday in Roman Paganism.* Takoma Park, Md.: Review and Herald Publishing Association, n.d.

Problems in Bible Translation. Takoma Park, Md.: Review and Herald Publishing Association, n.d.

Reed, W. E. *The Bible, the Spirit of Prophecy, and the Church.* Takoma Park, Md.: Review and Herald Publishing Association, n.d.

Richards, H. M. S. *Hard Nuts Cracked.* Southern Publishing Association, n.d.

Robinson, D. E. *The Story of Our Health Message.* Southern Publishing Association, n.d.

The Seventh-day Adventist Bible Commentary. vols. 1–5. Takoma Park, Md.: Review and Herald Publishing Association, n.d.

Seventh-day Adventist Church Directory: United States and Canada. Takoma Park, Md.: Review and Herald Publishing Association, n.d.

Seventh-day Adventist Year Book, 1957. Takoma Park: Review and Herald Publishing Association.

Seventh-day Adventists Believe . . . A Biblical Exposition of Twenty-Seven Fundamental Doctrines. Washington, D.C.: Ministerial Association, General Conference of Seventh-day Adventists, 1988.

Smith, Uriah. *Daniel and the Revelation.* vols. 1–2. Takoma Park, Md.: Review and Herald Publishing Association, n.d.

Spalding, Arthur W. *Sister White.* Takoma Park, Md.: Review and Herald Publishing Association, n.d.

Spicer, W. A. *Our Day in the Light of Prophecy.* Takoma Park, Md.: Review and Herald Publishing Association, n.d.

Straw, W. E. *Origin of Sunday Observance.* Takoma Park, Md.: Review and Herald Publishing Association, n.d.

Walker, Allen. *The Law and the Sabbath.* Southern Publishing Association, n.d.

Werner, A. J. *Fundamentals of Bible Doctrine.* Takoma Park, Md.: Review and Herald Publishing Association, n.d.

Wheeler, Ruth. *His Messenger.* Takoma Park, Md.: Review and Herald Publishing Association, n.d.

Wilcox, F. M. *The Coming Crisis.* Takoma Park, Md.: Review and Herald Publishing Association, n.d.

———. *The Lord's Day, the Test of the Ages.* Mountain View, Calif.: Pacific Press Publishing Association, n.d.

———. *Questions Answered.* Mountain View, Calif.: Pacific Press Publishing Association, n.d.

Additional Bibliography

Biederwolf, William Edward. *Seventh-day Adventism: the Result of a Predicament.* Grand Rapids, Mich.: Eerdmans Publishing Company, n.d.

Bird, Herbert S. *Theology of Seventh-day Adventism.* Grand Rapids, Mich.: Eerdmans Publishing Company, 1961.

Bliss, Sylvester. *Memoirs of William Miller.* Boston, n.p., 1853.

Booth, A. E. *Seventh-day Adventism: What Is It?* n.p., n.d.

Buswell, J. Oliver Jr. *The Length of Creative Days.* New York: Shelton College, 1950.

Canright, Dudley M. *Hard Nuts for Seventh-day Adventists.* n.p., n.d.

———. *Life of Mrs. E. G. White.* Nashville: B. C. Goodpasture, 1948.

———. *Seventh-day Adventism Renounced.* Grand Rapids, Mich.: Baker Book House, 1961 reprint from 1889.

Chafer, Louis Sperry. *Grace.* Van Kampen Press, 1947.

Davies, Horton. *Christian Deviations.* New York: Philosophical Library, 1954.

Deck, Norman C. *The Lord's Day or the Sabbath, Which?* Sydney, Australia: Bridge Printery, Ltd., n.d.

Dictionary of American Biography. New York: Charles Scribner's Sons, n.d.

Douty, Norman F. *Another Look at Seventh-day Adventism.* Grand Rapids, Mich.: Baker Book House, 1962.

Dugger, A. F. *The Bible Sabbath Defended.* Stanbury, Mo.: The Church of God Publishing House, n.d.

Dungan, D. R. *Sabbath or Lord's Day, Which?* Nashville: Harbinger Book Club, n.d.

Feinberg, Charles L. *The Sabbath and the Lord's Day.* Van Kampen Press, n.d.

Fletcher, W. W. *The Reasons for My Faith.* Sydney: William Brooks & Company, Ltd., n.d.

Hoekema, Anthony. *The Four Major Cults.* Grand Rapids, Mich.: Eerdmans Publishing Company, 1963.

Ironside, H. A. *What Think Ye of Christ?* New York: Loizeaux Brothers, n.d.

Irvine, William C. *Heresies Exposed.* New York: Loizeaux Brothers, n.d.

Jones, E. B. *The Answer and the Reasons: Eye-opening Information Regarding Seventh-day Adventism.* Oak Park: Designed Products, n.d.

———. *Free Indeed: The Author's Testimony Concerning His Deliverance from Seventh-day Ad-*

ventism. Oak Park: Designed Products, n.d.

———. *Forty Bible-Supported Reasons Why You Should Not Be a Seventh-day Adventist.* Oak Park: Designed Products, n.d.

Land, Gary, ed. *Adventism in America.* Grand Rapids, Mich.: Eerdmans Publishing Company, 1986.

Martin, Walter R. *The Truth about Seventh-day Adventism.* Grand Rapids, Mich.: Zondervan, 1960.

Miller, William. *Apology and Defense.* n.p., 1845.

———. *A Few Evidences of the Time of the Second Coming of Christ.* n.p., 1831.

Paxton, Geoffrey J. *The Shaking of Adventism.* Grand Rapids, Mich.: Baker Book House, 1977.

Pieper, Francis. *Christian Dogmatics.* Grand Rapids, Mich.: Zondervan, n.d. (reprint).

Pollock, A. J. *Seventh-day Adventism Briefly Tested by Scripture.* London: The Central Bible Truth Depot, n.d.

Putnam, C. E. *Legalism and the Seventh-day Question: Can Sinai Law and Grace Coexist?* Chicago: Moody Press, n.d.

Rowell, J. B. *Seventh-day Adventism Examined.* Norwalk, Calif.: Challenge Publishing Company, n.d.

Smith, Oswald J. *Who Are the False Prophets?* Toronto: The People's Press, n.d.

———. *Who Are the Seventh-day Adventists and What Do They Teach?* Toronto: Hugh Warren, Wesley Press and Publishing House, n.d.

Talbot, Louis T. *What's Wrong With Seventh-day Adventism?* Grand Rapids, Mich.: Dunham Publishing House, n.d.

Tucker, Ruth. *Another Gospel: Alternative Religions and the New Age Movement.* Grand Rapids, Mich.: Zondervan, 1989.

Vincent, M. R. *Word Studies in the New Testament.* MacDill AFB, Fla.: MacDonald Publishing Company, n.d.

Vine, W. E. *An Expository Dictionary of New Testament Words.* Old Tappan, N.J.: Fleming H. Revell Company, 1940.

Magazine Articles

The Advent Herald magazine, various issues.

The Advent Shield and Review magazine, various issues.

Auchincloss, Douglas. "Peace With the Adventists," *Time* magazine, December 31, 1956.

Baer, James E. "The Seventh-day Adventists," from the series "The Bible and Modern Religions," *Journal of Theology,* January 1956.

Barnhouse, Donald Grey. "Are Seventh-day Adventists Christian?" *Eternity,* September 1956.

Bibliotheca Sacra, April 1956.

Bird, Herbert S. "Another Look at Adventism," *Christianity Today,* April 28, 1958.

Eternity, September 1956; June 1958.

Hulbert, Terry C. "Seventh-day Adventism Weighed in the Balances," *The Discerner Magazine,* October/December 1956.

Jones, E. B. "The Historical Background of Seventh-day Adventism," and "Seventh-day Adventism and the Gospel of Grace," *The Sunday School Times,* 1954.

———. "Seventh-day Adventists' Counterfeit Gospel," *Christian Victory,* February 1952.

King's Business, April 1957; March 1958.

Lindsell, Harold. "What of Seventh-day Adventism?" *Christianity Today,* March 31, 1958; April 14, 1958.

Martin, Walter R. "Are Seventh-day Adventists Evangelical?" *Christian Life,* October 1956.

———. "Seventh-day Adventism Today," *Our Hope,* November 1956.

Pickering, Ernest. "Can We Fellowship With Seventh-day Adventists?" *The Voice* of the Independent Fundamental Churches of America, October 1956.

Review and Herald magazine, various issues.

Sabbath-School Quarterly magazine, various issues.

Samples, Kenneth. "The Recent Truth about Seventh-day Adventism," *Christianity Today*, February 5, 1990.

"Seventh-day Adventists and the Date of Creation," *The Examiner* magazine, March/April 1952.

Signs of the Times magazine, various issues.

Sword of the Lord, various articles, August 2, 1957.

These Times magazine, various issues.

Yost, Frank H. "A Seventh-day Adventist Speaks Back," *Christianity Today*, July 21, 1958.

Islam

Abdul-Haqq, Adijah Akbar. *Sharing Your Faith With a Muslim.* Minneapolis: Bethany House Publishers, 1980.

Accad, F. E. *Theological Principles in the Torah, the Zabur, the Injil, and the Qur'an.* Colorado Springs, Colo.: Navigators, n.d.

Ali, A. Yusuf. *The Holy Qur'an: Translation and Commentary.* Brentwood, Md.: Amana Corporation, 1983 (reprinted from 1934).

Bavinck, J. H. *The Church Between Temple and Mosque.* Grand Rapids, Mich.: Eerdmans Publishing Company, 1981 (reprint).

Black's Law Dictionary, abridged 5th ed. St. Paul: West Publishing Company, 1983.

Brackman, Harold. *Farrakhan's Reign of Historical Error: The Truth Behind the Secret Relationship Between Blacks and Jews.* Los Angeles: Simon Wiesenthal Center, 1992.

Bravmann, M. M. *The Spiritual Background in Early Islam: Studies in Ancient Arab Concepts.* Leiden, The Netherlands: E. J. Brill, 1972.

Bruce, F. F. *Jesus and Christian Origins Outside the New Testament.* Grand Rapids, Mich.: Eerdmans Publishing Company, 1974.

Christian Witness Among Muslims. Ghana, W. Africa: Africa Christian Press, 1971.

Clair-Tisdall, Rev. W. St. *A Manual of the Leading Muhammadan Objections of Christianity.* London: Society for Promoting Christian Knowledge, 1904.

———. *The Sources of Islam.* Edinburgh: T. & T. Clark, n.d.

Cragg, Kenneth. *The Call of the Minaret.* New York: Oxford University Press, 1964.

Dashti, Ali. *Twenty-Three Years: A Study of the Prophetic Career of Mohammad.* London: George Allen & Unwin, 1985.

Davion, Edward, et al. *Unreached Peoples '80.* Elgin, Ill.: David C. Cook Publishing Company, 1980.

Davis, David Brion. *Slavery and Human Progress.* New York: Oxford University Press, 1984.

Dinnerstein, Leonard. *Antisemitism in America.* New York: Oxford University Press, 1994.

Early Islam: Collected Articles. Edinburgh: Edinburgh University Press, 1990.

Elder, John. *The Biblical Approach to the Muslim.* Fort Washington, Pa.: Worldwide Evangelism Crusade, 1974.

Epiphanius. *The Panarion of St. Epiphanius, Bishop of Slamis: Selected Passages.* Philip R. Amidon, trans. and ed. New York: Oxford University Press, 1990.

Esposito, John. *The Islamic Threat.* New York: Oxford University Press, 1993.

Evanzz, Karl. *The Judas Factor: The Plot to Kill Malcolm X.* New York: Thunder's Mouth Press, 1992.

Farah, Caesar E. *Islam.* New York: Barron's Educational Services, 1994.

"Farrakhan Attacks Jews and Whites," *Orange County Register*, March 13, 1994.

Fleischman, Janet. "Ethnic Cleansing," *Africa Reports*, January/February 1994.

Fry, C. George, and James R. King. *Islam: A Survey of the Muslim Faith.* Grand Rapids, Mich.: Baker Book House, 1980.

Gilchrist, John. *Christianity and Islam Series.* Durban, Republic of South Africa: Jesus to the Muslims, 1980.

Glasser, Carol A. *Muslim Awareness Seminar.* Altadena, Calif.: Samuel Zwemer Institute, 1981.

———. *Quran and Bible Series.* Durban: Jesus to the Muslims, 1981.

Goldsack, W. *The Origins of the Qur'an*. London: Christian Literature Society, 1907.

Goldsmith, Martin. *Islam and Christian Witness*. Downers Grove: InterVarsity Press, 1982.

Haley, Alex, and Betty Shabazz. *The Autobiography of Malcolm X*. New York: Ballantine Books, 1965.

Hamada, Louis Bahjat. *Understanding the Arab World*. Nashville: Thomas Nelson Publishers, 1990.

Handbook for Christians Working With Iranians in North America. Altadena, Calif.: Samuel Zwemer Institute, 1980.

Hanna, Mark. *The Truth Path*. Colorado Springs, Colo.: International Doorways Publishers, 1975.

Hirji-Walji, Hass, and Jaryl Strong. *Escape From Islam*. Wheaton: Tyndale House, 1978.

Irvine, A. K. "The Arabs and Ethiopians," J. D. Wiseman, ed. *Peoples of Old Testament Times*. Oxford University Press, 1973.

Jeffery, Arthur, ed. *Material for the History of the Text of the Qur'an: The Old Codices*. New York: AMS, Inc., 1975.

Jones, L. Bevan. *Christianity Explained to Muslims*. Calcutta: Baptist Mission Press, 1937.

———. *The People of the Mosque*. London: Student Christian Movement Press, 1932.

Kateregga, Badru D., and David W. Shenk. *Islam and Christianity*. Grand Rapids, Mich.: Eerdmans Publishing Company, 1980.

Kershaw, R. Max. *How to Share the Good News With Your Muslim Friend*. Colorado Springs, Colo.: Fellowship of Faith for Muslims, 1978.

Lewis, Bernard. *The Arabs in History*. New York: Harper & Row, 1966.

———. *Race and Slavery in the Middle East: An Historical Inquiry*. New York: Oxford University Press, 1990.

Lincoln, C. Eric. *The Black Church Since Frazier*. New York: Schocken Books, 1974.

———. *The Black Muslims in America*. 3rd ed. Grand Rapids, Mich.: Eerdmans Publishing Company, 1994.

Lippman, Thomas W. *Understanding Islam: An Introduction to the Muslim World*. New York: Mentor Books, 1990.

"Malcolm X's Widow Accuses Farrakhan," *Orange County Register*, March 13, 1994.

Mansfield, Peter. *The Arabs*. New York: Penguin Books, 1978.

Marsh, Charles R. *Share Your Faith with a Muslim*. Chicago: Moody Press, 1975.

Marsh, Clifton E. *From Black Muslims to Muslims*. Metuchen, N.J. and London: The Scarecrow Press, 1984.

McCurry, Don M., ed. *Sharing the Gospel With Iranians*. Altadena, Calif.: Samuel Zwemer Institute, 1982.

———. *The Gospel and Islam: A 1978 Compendium*. Monrovia, Calif.: Missions Advanced Research Communications Center, 1978.

Mead, Frank S., and Samuel S. Hill. *Handbook of Denominations in the United States*. Nashville: Abingdon Press, 1990.

Morris, Leon. *The Gospel According to John*. Grand Rapids, Mich.: Eerdmans Publishing Company, 1971.

Muhammad, Elijah. *Message to the Black Man in America*. Newport News, Va.: United Brothers Communications, 1992.

Muslim/Christian Cross-Cultural Dating & Marriage. Altadena, Calif.: Samuel Zwemer Institute, 1981.

O'Brien, Joanne, and Martin Palmer. *The State of Religion Atlas*. New York: Touchstone Books, 1993.

Parrinder, Geoffrey. *Jesus in the Qur'an*. New York: Oxford University Press, 1977.

Parshall, Phil. *New Paths in Muslim Evangelism*. Grand Rapids, Mich.: Baker book House, 1980.

Patterson, Orlando. *Slavery and Social Death: A Comparative Study*. Cambridge, Mass.: Harvard University Press, 1982.

Pfander, C. G. *The Mizanu'l Haqq: Balance of Truth*. London: Religious Tract Society, rev. 1910 (from original by Clair-Tisdall).

Plantinga, Alvin. *Does God Have a Nature?* Milwaukee, Wis.: Marquette University Press, 1980.

Raboteau, Albert J. "Afro-American Religions: Muslim Movements," Mircea Eliade, ed. *The Encyclopedia of Religion.* vol. 1. New York: Macmillan, 1987.

Register, Ray G. *Dialogue and Interfaith with Muslims.* Kingsport: Moody Books, 1979.

Sell, Canon. *Outlines of Islam.* London: Christian Literature Society for India, 1912.

Smith, Jane I. *An Historical and Semitic Study of the Term "Islam" as Seen in a Sequence of Quran Commentaries.* Missoula, Mt.: Scholars Press for Harvard Theological Review, 1975.

Spencer, H. *Islam and the Gospel of God.* Delhi, India: S.T.C.K., 1956.

Todd, Charles Burr. *Life and Letters of Joel Barlow.* New York: Da Capo Press, 1970.

Vander Werff, Lyle L. *Christian Mission to Muslims: The Record. Anglican and Reformed Approaches to India and the Near East, 1860–1938.* South Pasadena: William Carey Library, 1977.

Watts Star Review, July 14, 1994.

Wilson, Christy J. *Today's Tentmakers: Self-support—An Alternative Model for Worldwide Witness.* Wheaton: Tyndale House, 1979.

Wolf, Kenneth Baxter. "The Earliest Spanish Christian Views of Islam," *Church History.* 55:3, September 1986.

Your Muslim Guest: A Practical Guide to Friendship and Witness for Christians Who Meet Muslims in North America. Toronto: Fellowship of Faith for Muslims, 1975.

Zwemer, Samuel. *Islam: A Challenge to Faith.* New York: Student Volunteer Movement for Foreign Missions, 1907.

Unitarian Universalists

Braden, Charles S. *The World's Religions.* New York: Abingdon Press, 1954.

DeWolf, Harold F. *Present Trends in Christian Thought.* New York: Association Press, 1960.

Ferm, Vergilius. *Encyclopedia of Religion.* New York: Philosophical Library, 1945.

Kegley, Charles W., and Robert W. Bretall. *The Theology of Paul Tillich.* New York: Macmillan, 1961.

Kimmel, William, and Geoffrey Clive. *Dimensions of Faith.* New York: Twayne Publishers, 1959.

Machen, John G. *Christianity and Liberalism.* New York: Macmillan, 1923.

———. *What Is Faith?* New York: Macmillan, 1935.

MacKintosh, Hugh Ross. *Types of Modern Theology from Schleiermacher to Barth.* New York: Charles Scribner and Sons, 1937.

Nash, Arnold S. *Protestant Thought in the Twentieth Century.* New York: Macmillan, 1951.

Piepkorn, Arthur C. *Profiles in Belief.* vol. 4. San Francisco: Harper & Row, 1979.

Rosten, Leo. *Religions in America.* New York: Simon & Schuster, 1963.

Scholefield, Harry, ed. *Unitarian Universalist Pocket Guide.* Boston: Beacon Press, 1963.

———. *A Pocket Guide to Unitarianism.* Boston: Beacon Press, 1954.

Spittler, Russell P. *Cults and Isms.* Grand Rapids, Mich.: Baker Book House, 1962.

Wilbur, Earl Morse. *A History of Unitarianism.* Cambridge: Harvard University Press, n.d.

Scripture Index

1 Corinthians

2 Corinthians

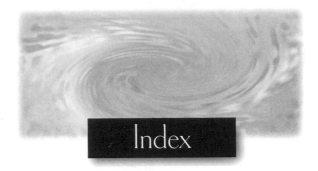

Index

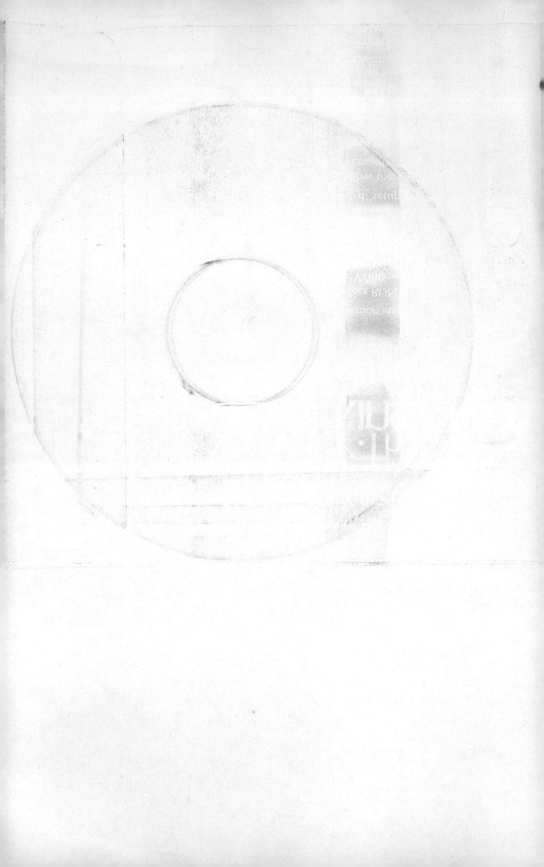